A Superior Body of Men

M.S. James

authorHOUSE®

AuthorHouse™ UK
1663 Liberty Drive
Bloomington, IN 47403 USA
www.authorhouse.co.uk
Phone: 0800.197.4150

Published by AuthorHouse 03/18/2016

ISBN: 978-1-4969-9541-4 (sc)
ISBN: 978-1-4969-9542-1 (hc)
ISBN: 978-1-4969-9543-8 (e)

Print information available on the last page.

This book is printed on acid-free paper.

is book is dedicated to

Ann Denby

INTRODUCTION

When I first started researching Military Pensioners in 1982, this work was intended to be my 'aide memoir' but over the years as I become more knowledgeable about the complexity of Military Pensions and have acquired more information on the subject of Military Pensioners in general and of those in Western Australia in particular my 'aide memoir' slowly evolved into this Biographical Index.

As this Index is designed to work in conjunction with the influential work on the Enrolled Pensioner Guards to Western Australia "The Veterans" by Frank Broomhall, I have designed it so the layout is similar to that publication

ACKNOWLEDGEMENTS

Over the years so many people have helped me and sadly some of those I came to depend upon for assistance are no longer with us, never the less I remember them with gratitude and affection.

Frank Broomhall whom I knew for only a few years and in retrospect this was to be such a short length of time. Without his help and his willingness to explain the complexities inherent with Western Australian Military Pensioners and other discharged military personnel in the Colony, I would not have the understanding of the subject that I have now.

Garth Thomas from the PRO Kew who patiently helped me to locate the information on those of Enrolled Pensioner Guards who perished onboard the '*Emma*' Gay Fielding who was always willing to give help and advise when-ever she could. Vale 'Mess Mate' your prompt unstinting and knowledgeable assistance is sadly missed.

And to those whom I can still ask for help.

In the UK thanks to Ian Baxter of the IOLOC at the British Library. Without his encyclopaedic knowledge and willingness to answer my questions even when I met him in the local supermarket, I would not have depth of understanding of the peculiarities of the Military Establishment based in India nor appreciate the difference between the two Military Pension Systems.

Tim Thomas IOLOC at the British Library, who assisted me especially with the Ecclesiastical Records, Court of Director's and the Judicial Proceeding Records for the Honorable East India Compan. Headley Sutton IOLOC at the British Library who has now inherited my interminable questions The IOLOC Document Distribution and Retrieval Staff, without their patient assistance I would not have been able view the number of documents that I did Mark Dutton and Ann Morrow at The National Archives Kew,The Archival Staff at the National Army Museum. The Librarians at the London Library, East India Club and the Bengal Officers Club – London.

The Staff at the Naval Studies Library and Plymouth Reference Library Plymouth.

Lieut. Colonel Les Wilson Curator of the Queens Regiment.

Museum now retired but who is still willing to answer any of my military questions especially those appertaining to the 31st [Huntingdonshire] Regiment]

M.S. James

David Hawkins for helping me with information on the Convict

Transports, Treasury and Home Office documents and the James Adlam family

For those who have helped me in Western Australia my very special thanks goes to two people, Debbie Beavis whom I consider to be an historical researcher and author par excellence and who has constantly encouraged me to publish this Index.

Phillipa Ward. who has been unstinting in her support over many years and so generous in allowing me to use all her Military Pensioner Land Title research

My thanks also to Lorraine Dearnley; Helen and Bob Pearce; Elizabeth Rummins; Helen Gunnell; Molly Bergh and Jeanette Lee all of whom have helped significantly with my research into our Enrolled Pensioner Guards.

Robyn Hukin who kept alive the interest in our Enrolled Pensioner Guards before the EPG Special Interest Group was formed and was co-speaker with me on a number of occasions.

The Librarians at the Fremantle Library.

The Staff at the Western Australian State Library.

Anne Davis and the members of The Kojonup Family History Society.

The staff of Authorhouse for their patience and professionalism.

INTRODUCTORY NOTES

This Biographical Index includes a number of entries for Military Pensioners and former soldiers who either took their discharge in the Colony or arrived here by their own means The differences between these groups has been briefly described on page B1 paragraphs 2 and 3 of "The Veterans" by F.H Broomhall.

Also there are some 'non' Enrolled Pensioner Guard entries which have been included for no other reason than that I found them interesting to research.

Maintaining accuracy of information has and will always be a problem, especially if that information has come from more than one primary source and from different geographical localities.

The Index entries are as accurate as I have been able to check. Where I've been unable to check and verify my information against primary source documents, I've placed a question mark in front of the particular entry or prefaced the entry with the phrases "the following information may not refer to" or included the word "possibly" and in many cases not included the information.

Not only are there problems maintaining accuracy from having to research between repositories and different countries, there is the problem with knowledge of the people who originally compiled the document for instance the *w*hereabouts of places and lists

The following example shows the difference which can occur between WO Records and the Passenger Lists

DAVEY		William private 50th Foot
	21 Apr 1857	Discharged to pension Pension paid 2nd East London Pension District 8d. per diem
	9 June 1862	Arrived per '*Norwood*'' [1] [Passenger List] according to WO records William Davey arrived per '*Norwood*'' in 1867

Differing spellings of names — due to the differences I've found between the names in the Western Australian records to those in the War Office Records, and between the WO records themselves, included all the different variations I've sighted.

Dates of birth death and marriage are often only approximate. especially if using various sources, therefore calculation of age in particular can be difficult. The dates transcribed for births, death and marriages in this Index are in most cases the registration dates therefore the appropriate Parish Registers or the Civil Registration documents must be checked to show the actual date of the occurrence

A Question Mark "?" along side an entry or name means I have not been able to confirm the information through primary sources however secondary sources may indicate that the information to be correct

Medal Entitlement — these have been included if I have sighted the relevant Discharge to Pension document where the medal entitlement has been annotated, or the Medal Rolls.

A number of entries in the Biographical Index are incomplete due to the lack of documentary information. These omissions are not due to my lack of diligence or dedication in researching. In some cased primary source records which were available to me when I first started researching are nor longer extant. This is due mainly to the general wear and tear on these documents caused in most cases by the number of time they have been handled — especially photocopied. Also I have found that with a number of digitalised images on the Internet go not refer to the discharged soldier in question.

Although the layout of this Index is similar to 'The Veterans' where-ever possible I have sourced my information from different record streams to those used in "The Veterans".

There are about 250 other 'old soldiers' who's names have been included in this Index as they too settled in Western Australia. Some have been included in this Index and the others will be detailed in future publications

This Biographical Index has concentrated on the details of ordinary soldiers thereby excluding those Officers who have emigrated also excluded are former soldiers who have been convicted of various crimes and transported to the Colony.

The utmost care has been taken in transcribing the information for this Index and has been compiled in good faith; it has been researched from sources believed to be accurate and reliable. However, it is recommended that the reader does their own check of primary sources and other relevant documents to verify the information herein, thereby making their own assessment of the statements and information discussed in this index.

MAIN SOURCES

The National Archives Kew

CO18/81	Colonial Office
WO/1-'s	War Office 'In-letters'
WO4/-'s	Secretary at War Out-Letters
WO16/-'s	New Series Muster Books and Pay Lists
WO22/-'s	Royal Hospital Chelsea Pension District Registers
WO22/259	Greenwich Pension Payments for Western Australia
WO25/-'s	Various War Office Registers
WO43/-	Old Series Papers
WO116/40 - 107	Royal Hospital Chelsea Pension Registers
WO117/-	Royal Hospital Chelsea Pension Registers
WO118/20 – 34	Kilmainham Hospital Examination Registers
WO119/-	Kilmainham Hospital Pension Registers
WO97/-'s	Royal Chelsea Hospital Soldiers 'Discharge to Pension Documents'
WO100/-	Medal Rolls
ADM101/252	Convict Ships [some] Surgeon's Logs
ADM157/-	Royal Marine Attestation Records
ADM158/-	Royal Marine Description Books

The British Library — India Office and Oriental Collections

L/AG/23/-	Lord Clive Pension Fund Registers
L/MIL/9/-	Depot Recruitment Lists and Embarkation Lists
L/MIL/10/-	Bengal Army Long Rolls and Casualty Returns
L/MIL/10/-	Register of East India Company European Soldiers Bengal
L/MIL/11/-	Madras Army Long Rolls and Casualty Returns
L/MIL/11/-	Register of East India Company European Soldiers Madras
L/MIL/12/-	Bombay Army Long Rolls and Casualty Registers
L/MIL/12/-	Register of East India Company European Soldiers Bombay
N1/-	Bengal Ecclesiastical Registers
N2/-	Madras Ecclesiastical Registers
N3/-	Bombay Ecclesiastical Registers
L/MIL/5/73 - 105	Indian Mutiny Medal Rolls

National Army Museum
- Hodson's Index
- Army Lists

United Kingdom — other Repositories
- GRO
- The Guildhall London
- Bishopsgate Institute
- The Police Historical Museum

The Central Library — Plymouth

State Library Western Australia

Parish Registers for –
United Kingdom
India
Australia

Newspapers
British Library Newspaper Collections
Central Library Plymouth Newspaper Collections
Microfilm of Indian newspapers held at Reid Library University of Western Australia
The National Library of Australia online collections – 'Trove'
The New Zealand online newspaper collection
Newspaper Collections held by various East India Clubs in London

Web Sites
The National Archives [Kew United Kingdom]
Rootsweb
Familysearch
Dead Person's Society
FIBIS
Ancestry
Findmypast
Historical Newspapers
Various Regimental Web sites

Land Records held at State Library of Western Australia
Item No. 37/5
Item Title Land applications - Adlam-Gallagher
Start Date 1 Jan 1851 End Date 31 Dec 1880
Consignment No. 5000
Record series containing this item 1839 LAND APPLICATIONS BY ENROLLED PENSIONERS 1 Jan 1851 - 31 Dec 1880 Detail

Western Australian 'Memorials'

Western Australian Police Gazettes

ABREVIATIONS

AVRI	Australian Vital Records Index
b.	both for birth and baptism
B.E.	Bengal European
b. reg	Birth registration
c	date approximation for births/baptisms, marriages/'partnerships' deaths/burials
Comp.	Company
HC	Honorable Company [Honorable East India Company]
HEIC	Honorable East India Company
Eur	European
m.	Married and/or 'partnered' or co-habiting
ptve	private
RA	Royal Artillery
RHA	Royal Horse Artillery
RGA	Royal Garrison Artillery
RM	Royal Marines
RM	Resident Magistrate
S.O.	Staff Officer
S.O.P.	Staff Officer Pensions
Sth Aust	South Australia
W.A.	Western Australia
WAGR	Western Australian Government Railways
West Aust	Western Australia
WO	War Office
UK	United Kingdom

TABLE OF CONTENTS

The Biographical Index

ABBOTT	Patrick, private
	18th Foot
2 Oct 1855	Discharged the Service Chatham
1855	Pension paid Manchester
	9d. per diem
1855	Pension paid Athlone
1855	Dublin
	Manchester
1858	Dublin
1858	Athlone
1858	
15 Apr 1864	Arrived per *'Clara'* [2]
Oct 1864	To South Australia per *'Sea Ripple'*
1865	Pension paid Adelaide South Australia
1871	Applied to have pension paid in the UK on arrival from South Australia
1876	Pension paid Dublin
1879	Re admitted as In-Pensioner Kilmainham
1902	Died
Service and Personal Details:	
Place of Birth:	St Marys Athlone Westmeath
Age on Enlistment:	18 years
Period of Service:	1851 — 1855
Age on Discharge:	22 years 2 months
Length of Service:	4 years 27 days
Foreign Service:	Crimea [no time period given]
Medal Entitlement:	Crimea
Reason for Discharge:	Unfit for further service due to wound to right arm received during attack on the Redan
Character:	Good
Trade or Occupation:	Labourer
Can Sign Name:	X his mark on discharge
Height:	5' 6¾"
Hair:	Brown
Eyes:	Hazel
Complexion:	Fresh

ADAMS	Thomas, private
	5th Foot
24 Aug 1852	Discharged the Service Chatham
1852	Pension paid 1st West London Pension District
	6d. per diem for 3 years
30 Apr 1853	Arrived per *'Pyrenees'* [2] as a Convict Guard
1855	Employed as Mounted Constable at Port Gregory
Sept 1855	Pension ceased
Feb 1887	according to a newspaper death notice a Thomas Adams — Pensioner arrived on the *'Pyrenees'* 1853 died at Newcastle in his 80th year
Service and Personal Details:	
Place of Birth:	Ealing [Eling] London Middlesex

Age on Enlistment:	19 years
Period of Service:	1838 — 1852
Age on Discharge:	33 years
Length of Service:	13 years 40 days
Foreign Service:	Mediterranean 3 years 1 month
	Mauritius 4 years 4 months
Reason for Discharge:	Disease of Liver from moving a ladder when off duty [stated he was on duty on the Public Works at Mauritius]
Character:	Good
Trade or Occupation:	Labourer
Can Sign Name:	Yes
Height:	5' 9"
Hair Colour:	Dark Brown
Eyes:	Blue
Complexion:	Sallow
Intends to Reside:	Ealing Middlesex

ADLAM	James, private [981]
	8th Foot
13 June 1854	Discharged the Service Chatham
	Pension paid Trowbridge
	1/- per diem
1857	Men departing District [Trowbridge - WO22/108]
10 July 1857	Arrived per *'Clara'* [1]
1864	Application for Land — Greenough Flats Lot 14 [sic] Free Grant [CONS 5000 37/5]
1865	Subscriber to Greenough Mechanic Institute
1867	Pound keeper at Greenough
May 1874	Pension increased to 1/3d. per diem
1874	Application for Title to Greenough Locs G13 and G14 - Bootenal, Victoria District
1880	In charge of Arms at Greenough District
1881	Recommended for £15 Pensioner's Grant
Nov 1893	Died Greenough aged 73

Service and Personal Details:

Place of Birth:	Consley nr. Warminster Wiltshire
Age on Enlistment:	19 years
Period of Service:	1833 — 1854
Age on Discharge:	40 years 8 months
Length of Service:	20 years 276 days
Foreign Service:	West Indies 3 years 102 days
	North America 2 years 235 days
	India 7 years 94 months
Reason for Discharge:	Hepatic derangement and general disability
Character:	Very Good
Trade or Occupation:	Labourer
Can Sign Name:	Yes
Height:	5' 6½"
Hair Colour:	Brown
Eyes:	Grey
Complexion:	Fresh
Distinguishing Marks:	A mark on the right cheek

AHERN

	John, Serjeant
	68th Foot
Surname Variants	AHERNE; AHEARN
5 Jan 1861	Discharged the Service Fermoy
22 Jan 1861	Admitted to Pension Pension paid 1st Cork Pension District 1/6d. per diem
1862	Pension paid Gloucester
15 Feb 1863	Arrived per *'Merchantman'* [1]
1865	On Nominal List to proceed to Camden Harbour per *'Tien Tsin'* with wife Rosanna and daughter
1881	Pension increased to 2/- per diem for service in the Enrolled Pensioner Force
24 Aug 1881	Assigned North Fremantle Lot P61
24 Dec 1883	Granted Fee Simple North Fremantle Lot P61
28 Jan 1884	According to Heritage Council John Ahern Military Pensioner become proprietor of North Fremantle Lot P52
1889	Died Geraldton

Service and Personal Details:		
Place of Birth:	Somerstown Co. Cork	
Age on Enlistment:	18 years	
Period of Service:	1839 — 1860	
Age on Discharge:	39 years 4 months	
Length of Service:	21 years 134 days	
Foreign Service:	Quebec	3 years
	Malta 7 months	
	Turkey & Crimea	1 year 9 months
	Ionian Isles	1 year 4 months
	East Indies	3 years 5 months
Medal Entitlement:	Long Service & Good Conduct; with gratuity; Crimea with clasps and Turkish Crimean.	
Reason for Discharge:	Own Request having completed 21 years service	
Character:	Very Good	
Trade or Occupation:	Labourer	
Can Sign Name:	Yes	
Height:	5' 5¼"	
Hair Colour:	Dark Brown	
Eyes:	Grey	
Complexion:	Fresh	
Intends to Reside:	Cork	

AHERN

	Michael, Corporal
	8th Foot
Pervious Regiment	17th Foot
Surname Variant	AHERNE
23 July 1861	Discharged the Service Gosport Pension paid 1st Cork Pension District 1/2½d. per diem
31 Dec 1862	Arrived per *'York'*
1864	ptve M Ahern Pensioner Force at Fremantle contributed to the Greenough Fire Relief Fund

1878	Pension increased to 1/8½d. per diem for service in the Enrolled Pensioner Force
5 Aug 1884	Granted Cockburn Sound Lot 231 Willagee Swamp
Dec 1885	For Sale - Cockburn Sound Loc P231 of 20 acres known as "Wilgy [sic] Swamp". The property is 2½ miles from Fremantle Town boundary and in the middle of the Fremantle Commonage
June 1897	Residing Fremantle
1898	Died

Service and Personal Details:

Place of Birth:	Shandon Co. Cork	
Age on Enlistment:	21 years	
Period of Service:	1840 — 1861	
Age on Discharge:	42 years	
Length of Service:	21 years 184 days	
Foreign Service:	East Indies	19 years 315 or 365 days
Medal Entitlement:	Indian Mutiny	
Reason for Discharge:	Length of Service	
Character:	Very Good	
Trade or Occupation:	Labourer	
Can Sign Name:	Yes	
Height:	5' 6½"	
Hair Colour:	Brown	
Eyes:	Hazel	
Complexion:	Fresh	
Intends to Reside:	Cork Ireland	

Marriage Details: Bombay Ecclesiastical Returns [Z/N/3]

Groom: Name:	Michael Ahern
Age:	28 years
Status:	Bachelor
Rank:	private HM 8th Regiment
Place:	Colobah
Father:	Michael Ahern
Bride: Name:	Mary Butler
Age:	15 years
Status:	Spinster
Father:	Edward Butler

AINSWORTH William, gunner and driver

Royal Regiment Artillery – [RA 6th Battalion]

14 Apr 1846	Discharged the Service Woolwich
1846	Pension paid 2nd North London Pension District
1/- per diem	
1848	Pension paid 1st East London Pension District

1848	Pension paid Bolton	
18 Oct 1851	Arrived per *'Minden'*	
1856	Applies for Toodyay Lot P2	
1862	His new house partly destroyed in the floods at Toodyay	
6 Mar 1863	Died aged 51	
Service and Personal Details:		
Place of Birth:	Blackburn Lancaster	
Age on Enlistment:	18 years	
Period of Service:	1825 — 1846	
Age on Discharge:	39 years	
Length of Service:	21 years 68 days	
Foreign Service:	Jamaica	5 years 1 month
	Halifax Nova Scotia	2 years 4 months
Reason for Discharge:	Chronic Rheumatism	
Character:	Good	
Trade or Occupation:	Weaver	
Can Sign Name:	Yes	
Height:	5' 7½"	
Hair Colour:	Dark Brown	
Eyes:	Grey	
Complexion:	Fresh	
Distinguishing Marks:	Scar on fore part of right leg	

AITCHISON	John, Sapper Royal Sappers and Miners	
Surname Variant	ATCHISON	
Dec 1861	Discharged after 13 years service and qualified for remission on grant of £10	
Service and Personal Details:		
Place of Birth:	Canongate Edinburgh	
Age on Discharge:	41 years	
Length of Service:	20 years 3 months	
Foreign Service:	Gibraltar	6 years 4 months
	Australia	10 years 4 months
Reason for Discharge:	Granted a Free Discharge to settle in Colony with gratuity and Right of Registry for a Deferred Pension on him attaining 60 years	
Character:	Bad	
Trade or Occupation:	Plumber and Painter	
Height:	5' 10"	
Hair Colour:	Grey	
Eyes:	Grey	
Complexion:	Tanned	

ALCOCK	Andrew, private 4th Foot
Surname Variant	ALLCOCK
23 Nov 1852	Discharged the Service Chatham Pension paid Worcester 1/- per diem
1852	Pension paid Gloucester
1853	Oxford
1856	Enlisted into the 90th Foot as Robert Radcliffe
1857	"Discovered and replaced back on pension"
19 Aug 1859	Arrived per *'Sultana'*
May 1867	Allegedly "Accidentally shot by his comrade Johnson"
7 May 1867	Died Fremantle
Service and Personal Details:	
Place of Birth:	Bromsgrove Worcestershire
Period of Service:	1831 — 1852
Age on Discharge:	39 years 2 month
Length of Service:	21 years 14 days
Foreign Service:	New South Wales 5 years 4 months East Indies 10 years 5 months
Reason for Discharge:	Unfit for further service subject to lumbago
Character:	Indifferent
Trade or Occupation:	Labourer
Can Sign Name:	Yes
Height:	5' 9"
Hair Colour:	Brown
Eyes:	Grey
Complexion:	Sallow
Distinguishing Marks:	Scar on forehead above right eye

ALLAN	John, Colour Serjeant 42nd Foot
Surname Variant	ALLEN
10 Aug 1847	Discharged the Service Chatham 1/10½d. per diem
1847	Pension paid Inverness
1847	Aberdeen
16 Apr 1850	Pension increased to 2/- per diem
11 Oct 1851	Arrived per *'Minden'*
1851	Sergeant Major commanding the Guard
Jan 1857	Contributed 3/- to the Florence Nightingale Fund
1858	Pension paid Madras
1862	Mauritius "Wife left destitute in India — 8d. a day stopped from pension for wife"
1864	Pension paid Bombay
Service and Personal Details:	
Place of Birth:	Elgin Morayshire
Age on Attestation:	19 years
Length of Service:	1825 — 1847

Age on Discharge:	41 years	
Period of Service:	21 years 327 days	
Foreign Service:	Gibraltar	6 years 1 month
	Malta	6 years 11 months
	Corfu	1 year 10 months
Reason for Discharge:	Found unfit for further service	
Character:	Very Good	
Trade or Occupation:	Labourer	
Can Sign Name:	Yes	
Height:	5' 7"	
Hair Colour:	Sandy	
Eyes:	Grey	
Complexion:	Sallow	
Intends to Reside:	Aberdeen	

ALLEN	Arthur, Serjeant	
	RA Depot Brigade	
Surname Variant	ALLAN	
20 Apr 1869	Discharged the Service Woolwich	
	Pension paid 2nd North London Pension District 1/7d. per diem	
1870	Pension paid Woolwich	
1870	Pension paid 2nd North London Pension District	
19 Feb 1874	Arrived per *'Naval Brigade'*	
2 Oct 1875	Assigned North Fremantle Lot P49	
1881	Pension increased to 1/9½d. per diem for service in the Enrolled Force	
1881	On Enrolled Guard Nominal Roll — Fremantle	
Mar 1881	Applied for grant towards cost of cottage	
7 Sept 1883	Granted Fee Simple North Fremantle Lot P49	
1884	Inspector Naval Artillery, Arthur Allen - Suspension from Duty	
1892	Residing Perth Road North Fremantle	
Nov 1892	Died aged 65	
Service and Personal Details:		
Place of Birth:	Woolwich Kent	
Age on Enlistment:	18 years 4 months	
Period of Service:	1847 — 1869	
Age on Discharge:	40 years 1 month	
Length of Service:	21 years	
Foreign Service:	Corfu	2 years 11 months
	Crimea	1 year 1 month
Medal Entitlement:	Crimea with clasp	
Reason for Discharge:	Having completed 21 years service	
Character:	Good	
Trade or Occupation:	Labourer	
Can Sign Name:	Yes	
Height:	5' 8½"	
Hair Colour:	Brown	
Eyes:	Blue	
Complexion:	Fresh	

Intends to Reside: Leicester Square	Middlesex Artillery Volunteers	
ALLEN	William, private	
	13th Foot	
Surname Variant	ALLAN	
10 July 1860	Discharged the Service Chatham	
	Pension paid Clonmel	
	8d. per diem	
9 June 1862	Arrived per *'Norwood'* [1]	
Feb 1864	ptve W Allan serving in the Pensioner Force Perth contributed to the Greenough Fire Relief Fund	
1864	To South Australia from West Australia per *'Sea Ripple'*	
1873	Correspondence with W.O.	
Service and Personal Details:		
Place of Birth:	St Marys Clonmel Co. Tipperary	
Age on Enlistment:	17 years 11 months	
Period of Service:	1854 — 1859	
Age on Discharge:	23 years 2 months	
Length of Service:	5 years 4 days	
Foreign Service:	Malta	4 months
	Crimea	3 months
	Gibraltar	5 months
	Cape of Good Hope	1 year
	East Indies	2 years 3 months
Medal Entitlement:	Indian Mutiny	
Reason for Discharge:	Wounded left arm	
Character:	Good	
Trade or Occupation:	Servant	
Can Sign Name:	Yes	
Height:	5' 6"	
Hair Colour:	Dark Brown	
Eyes:	Blue	
Complexion:	Fresh	
ALLMOND	Thomas, Staff Serjeant [Military Pensioner]	
	99th foot	
5 Apr 1849	Arrived per *'Radcliffe'*	
1 Feb 1852	Transferred to General Service [Staff] and was appointed Commandant's Clerk	
1854	Member of the Swan Mechanic' Institute [as was Thomas Leonowens husband of Anna]	
26 Jan 1871	Discharged the service Perth West Australia	
	2/- per diem	
Dec 1885	Died Adelaide South Australia	
Service and Personal Details:		

Place of Birth:	Abingdon [sic] Berkshire
Age on Attestation:	24 years
Period of Service:	1842 — 1852 [in the 99th Regiment] 1852 — 1871 [as Commandant's Clerk]
Age on Discharge:	52 years
Length of Service:	28 years 141 days
Foreign Service:	Australian Colonies 27 years
Reason for Discharge:	Unfit for service due to age
Character:	Very Good
Trade or Occupation:	Joiner
Can Sign Name:	Yes
Height:	5'5"
Hair Colour:	Brown
Eye Colour:	Hazel
Complexion:	Fresh
Intended Residence:	London Middlesex England

ALLS John, private
Royal Canadian Rifles

12 Apr 1864	Discharged the Service Chatham Pension paid Londonderry 1/1d. per diem
22 Dec 1865	Arrived per *'Vimiera'*
1870	Pension paid Sydney

Service and Personal Details:

Place of Birth:	Belfast Co. Antrim
Age on Attestation:	18 years
Period of Service:	1839 — 1864
Age on Discharge:	43 years
Length of Service:	24 years 267 days [reckoned]
Foreign Service:	Bermuda 5 years 3 months North America 16 years 5 months
Reason for Discharge:	Having completed 25 [sic] years service
Character:	Good
Trade or Occupation:	Baker
Can Sign Name:	Yes
Height:	5' 6½"
Hair Colour:	Light
Eyes:	Grey
Complexion:	Fair
Intends to Reside:	Londonderry Co Antrim

ANDERSON Francis, private
2nd/18th Foot

Aug 1861	Discharged the Service Bullevant Pension paid Preston 9d. per diem
1862	Pension paid Bermuda
15 Feb 1863	Arrived per *'Merchantman'* [1]

10 May 1867	Died	
Service and Personal Details:		
Place of Birth:	Castlebar Co Mayo	
Age on Attestation:	20 years	
Period of Service:	1840 — 1861	
Age on Discharge:	41 years 4 months	
Length of Service:	21 years 16 days	
Foreign Service:	Bombay	242 days
	China	6 years 216 days
	Bengal	4 years 236 days
	Burmah	1 year 240 days
Medal Entitlement:	China; Burmah [sic]	
Reason for Discharge:	Having completed 21 years service	
Character:	Latterly Good	
Trade or Occupation:	Shoemaker	
Can Sign Name:	Yes	
Height:	5' 5½"	
Hair Colour:	Brown	
Eyes:	Grey	
Complexion:	Sallow	
Intends to Reside:	Preston England	

ANDERSON	Hugh, private	
	30th Foot	
Previous Regiment	73rd	
10 July 1855	Discharged the Service Chatham	
	Pension paid 2nd North London Pension District	
	9d. per diem	
12 Sept 1864	Arrived per *'Merchantman'* [2] with wife Jane	
1866	Stationed Champion Bay	
1868	Dismissed	
1868	Pension paid Auckland New Zealand	
1887	Wellington	
1890	Wellington	
Service and Personal Details:		
Place of Birth:	Aughagallen Co Antrim	
Age on Attestation:	17 years 10 months	
Period of Service:	1847 — 1855	
Age on Discharge:	25 years	
Length of Service:	7 years 343 days	
Foreign Service:	?Crimea	[no time period given]
Medal Entitlement:	?Crimea with clasp	
Reason for Discharge:	Unfit for further service	
Character:	Good	
Trade or Occupation:	Tailor	
Can Sign Name:	Yes	
Height:	5' 5"	
Hair Colour:	Brown	
Eyes:	Brown	
Complexion:	Fresh	

ANDERSON	James, driver RHA
9 Oct 1849	Discharged the Service Woolwich 7d. per diem for 2 years
1851	Pension paid Deptford
1851	Residing High Road Lee
18 Oct 1851	Arrived per *'Minden'*
Oct 1851	Pension expired
Service and Personal Details:	
Place of Birth:	Eltham Lee Kent
Age on Enlistment:	21 years 10 months
Period of Service:	1840 — 1849
Age on Discharge:	30 years 259 days
Length of Service:	9 years 259 days
Reason for Discharge:	Defective Hearing and Impaired Health
Character:	Exemplary
Trade or Occupation:	Farmer's Servant
Can Sign Name:	Yes
Height:	5' 5"
Hair Colour:	Black
Eyes:	Grey
Complexion:	Dark

ANDERSON	Thomas, Corporal 44th Foot
3 June 1856	Discharged the Service Chatham Pension paid Belfast W. O. — Refused increase to pension of 1/1½d. or 1/3d per diem [depending on record]
12 Sept 1864	Arrived per *'Merchantman'* [2] with wife Anna
1871	Employed as Lock-up keeper at Greenough
4 Dec ****	W.O. Correspondence to Under Treasury Perth Western Australia Instructions to have the man medically examined
1907	Instruction from Treasury for pension to be increased to 24d. [2/-] per diem
Service and Personal Details:	
Place of Birth:	Lurgan Armagh
Age on Enlistment:	circa 17 years 5 months
Period of Service:	1846 — 1856
Age on Discharge:	27 years 6 months
Length of Service:	9 years ** days
Foreign Service:	Malta 3 years Gibraltar 2 years 11 months Turkey 4 months Crimea 1 year 2 months
Medal Entitlement:	Crimea with clasp
Reason for Discharge:	Unfit for further service. Deformity of left humerus due to gunshot fracture; also flesh wound on right side of chest from ball afterwards being cut out midway between the ?**** of the ilium and the navel

Character:	Good
Trade or Occupation:	Labourer
Can Sign Name:	Yes
Height:	5' 6"
Hair Colour:	Fair
Eyes:	Blue
Complexion:	Fair

ANGUS

	James, gunner
	RHA
Surname Variants	AGNUS; AGNES
13 July 1852	Discharged the Service Woolwich
	6d. per diem for 18 months
19 Aug 1853	Arrived per *'Robert Small"*
1854	Employed by Commissariat
1906	Died

Service and Personal Details:

Place of Birth:	St Clements Aberdeenshire
Age on Enlistment:	18 years 9 months
Period of Service:	1845 — 1852
Age on Discharge:	25 years 294 days
Length of Service:	7 years 15 days
Reason for Discharge:	Unfit for further service due to enlargement of the veins of the left testicle
Character:	Very good
Trade or Occupation:	Printer
Can Sign Name:	Yes
Height:	5' 8"
Hair Colour:	Red
Eyes:	Light Blue
Complexion:	Fair

ANNEAR

	Samuel, private
	Royal Sappers and Miners
8 Apr 1845	Discharged the Service Woolwich
1845	Pension paid Falmouth
	1/-½d. per diem
31 Mar 1850	To Tilbury Fort
1 June 1850	Arrived per *'Scindian'*
1850	Appointed Cook to Convict Establishment
1851	Employed as an Assistant Warder
1853	Died

Service and Personal Details:

Place of Birth:	Tavistock Devonshire	
Age on Enlistment:	18 years	
Period of Service:	1823 — 1845	
Age on Discharge:	39 years 6 months	
Length of Service:	21 years 190 days	
Foreign Service:	Barbados	4 years 10 months
	Halifax Nova Scotia	7 years 2 months

Reason for Discharge:	Chronic Rheumatism
Character:	Good
Trade or Occupation:	Smith
Can Sign Name:	Yes
Height:	5' 9½"
Hair Colour:	Grey
Eyes:	Grey
Complexion:	Fresh
Distinguishing Marks:	Scar on forehead

APPLEBEE	Thomas, private EIC
	1st Bombay European Fusiliers
	Out Pension No 116
3 Sept 1860	Admitted to Out-Pension
	Pension paid 2nd North London Pension District
	1/- per diem
1860	Pension paid Edinburgh
1863	West London
27 May 1863	Arrived per *'Clyde'*
1865	Pension paid Western Australia
18 Jan 1866	To London per *'Fitzroy'*
1866	Pension paid Jersey
1870	Trowbridge
Service and Personal Details:	
Where Born:	St Martins London Middlesex
Trade or Occupation:	Bookbinder
Age on Enlistment:	20 years
Date Attested:	5th December 1838
Where Enlisted:	London
Embarked India:	1839 per *'Thetis'*
Presidency:	Bombay
Length of Service:	21 years 1½ months
Age on Discharge:	41 years
Reason for Discharge:	To be pensioned — time expired
Character:	Good
Medal Entitlement:	Indian Mutiny
Height:	5' 6½"
Complexion:	Fresh
Eye Colour:	Grey
Hair Colour:	Brown
Intends to Reside:	Oxford Market

ARBUCKLE	John, Corporal EIC
Bengal Horse Artillery	
	Out Pension No 125
7 Nov 1861	Discharged the Service
1 Dec 1861	Admitted to Out-Pension
	Pension paid 2nd Glasgow Pension District
	1/- per diem
1862	Pension paid 1st Glasgow Pension District
27 May 1863	Arrived per *'Clyde'*
1868	Pension paid Perth Western Australia

1867	Employed as Coachman to Governor
1868	Charged with assaulting his wife
Mar 1868	Advertised that he was not answerable for his wife's debts
1868	Departed colony per '*Hougoumont*' in charge of a consignment of horses
May 1869	The case of Mrs. Arbuckle, Pensioner's wife, her husband away and she cannot support herself. Mrs Arbuckle recommended for temporary relief
1870/71	Pension paid 2nd Glasgow Pension District
1874	2nd Glasgow Pension District

Service and Personal Details:

Where Born:	Hamilton Lanarkshire
Trade or Occupation:	Brick maker
Where Enlisted:	Edinburgh
Presidency:	Bengal
Length of Service:	21 years 3 months or 22 years
Age on Discharge:	41 or 45 [depending on record source]
Reason for Discharge:	Time expired
Character:	Good
Height:	5' 7"
Complexion:	Fresh
Eye Colour:	Grey
Hair Colour:	Brown
Intends to Reside:	Glasgow

ARCHDEACON James, Serjeant

Royal Engineers — "B" Battery 4th Brigade

Previous Regiment	4th Light Dragoons
6 June 1865	Discharged the Service Woolwich
1861	Residing Deptford Surrey
1968	Arrived per '*Hougomont*'
1868	Warder Fremantle Prison
1870	Constable Canning River Police
1873	Sergeant Major Drill Instructor
1880	Time Keeper/ Supervisor Jarrahdale Timber Co.
18 June 1882	Aged 50
11 Aug 1883	Deferred Pension forms dispatched from W.O. to Colonial Treasurer Fremantle West. Aust.
1889	1st Class Constable WA Police
Aug 1890	Died

Service and Personal Details:

Place of Birth:	St James Dublin	
Age on Attestation:	18 years 6 months	
Period of Service:	1850 — 1865	
Age on Discharge:	32 years 11 months	
Length of Service:	14 years 300 days [reckoned]	
Foreign Service:	India	1 year 167 day
	Turkey & Crimea	2 years 26 days
	Expedition to China	1 year 18 days
Medal Entitlement:	Crimean with 2 clasp; Turkish Crimean; China with clasp for Taku Forts	

Reason for Discharge:	At Own Request Free, having completed 14 years service, with Right of Registry for Deferred Pension of 4d. per diem on his attaining 50 years of age
Character:	Very Good
Trade or Occupation:	Carpenter
Can Sign Name:	Yes
Height:	5' 11"
Hair Colour:	Light Brown
Eye Colour:	Brown
Complexion:	Fresh
Distinguishing Marks:	Pock pitted on face
Remarks:	Slightly wounded in wrist and cheek at Crimea

ARCHER	John, private EIC Bengal European Infantry Out Pension No 69
25 May 1847	Discharged the Service
May 1847	Embarked for UK per *'Alfred'* Pension paid Dublin Pension District 9d. per diem
30 Apr 1853	Arrived per *'Pyrenees'* [2]
Dec 1855	Departed for South Australia per '*Vivid*"
1856	Pension paid Adelaide
Service and Personal Details:	
Where Born:	Dublin
Trade or Occupation:	Paper Stainer or Labourer
Length of Service:	7 years 2 months
Age on Discharge:	27 years
Character:	Good
Reason for Discharge:	Epilepsy and mania, or Impaired vision - Ophthalmia of long standing [depending on record source]
Height:	5' 5 ¼"
Character:	Good
Complexion:	Fresh
Visage:	Oval
Eye Colour:	Blue
Hair Colour:	Light/Sandy

ARDILL	George, Corporal RM
Surname Variants	ARDILLE; ARDILE
1851	a George Ardile aged 29, born Tipperary Corporal Royal Marines stationed at Chatham
1851	Discharged the Service £9/4/- per annum
1853	Arrived per *'Robert Small'*
1861	Pension paid New South Wales
Service and Personal Details:	
Place of Birth:	Tipperary Ireland

Age on Attestation:	24 years 3 months	
Period of Service:	1846 — 1851	
Length of Service:	5 years	
Reason for Discharge:	Invalided	
Trade or Occupation:	Plasterer	
Can Sign Name:	Yes	
Character:	Good	
Height:	5' 7½"	
Hair Colour:	Brown	
Eyes:	Grey	
Complexion:	Brown	

ARMITAGE William, private

	68th Foot
13 July 1852	Discharged the Service Pension paid 1st Manchester Pension District 1/- per diem
6 Apr 1854	Arrived per *'Sea Park'*
no date	Assigned Perth Military Pensioner Lot 107
1858	Agreed to paid off cost of Cottage in instalments
Jan 1865	Application for Title to Perth Lot 107
1873	Pension increased to 1/3d. per diem for 9 years service in the Enrolled Force
Sept 1870	On Perth District Electoral List
1877	Died

Service and Personal Details:

Place of Birth:	Huddersfield Yorkshire	
Period of Service:	1830 — 1852	
Age on Discharge:	40 years 4 months	
Length of Service:	21 years 147 days	
Foreign Service:	Gibraltar	3 years 4 months
	Jamaica	3 years 6 months
	Canada	2 years 10 months
Reason for Discharge:	Worn out and consequently unfit for further service	
Character:	Good	
Trade or Occupation:	Shoemaker	
Can Sign Name:	blank	
Height:	5' 7¼"	
Hair Colour:	Brown	
Eyes:	Hazel	
Complexion:	Sallow	
Intends to Reside:	Huddersfield Yorkshire	

ARMSTRONG Alexander

	42nd Foot
	Assistant Warder
29 Jan 1862	Arrived per *'Lincelles'* [WA State Archives Accession AN24/6 [SROWA] have an Alexander Armstrong arriving on the *'Lincelles'*]
1901	an Alexander Armstrong died aged 76

Comments:	Served in the Crimea — [Erickson] No military pension — [Baker]

ARMSTRONG	James, gunner [Corporal] RA Depot Brigade
Previous Regiment	Bengal Artillery 2nd Co. 3rd Battalion
6 July 1869	Discharged the Service Netley Pension paid 1st Liverpool Pension District
16 Dec 1869	Residing Manchester 1/3d. per diem
1871	Pension paid Paisley
1873	Greenwich
19 Feb 1874	Arrived per *'Naval Brigade'*
Apr 1875	Wife Bridget remanded for stabbing and wounding Mary O'Brien wife of William Rowe
1881	Pension increased to 1/5½d. per diem for service in the Enrolled Force
3 Feb 1881	Assigned ?Perth Pensioner Allotment 269/Y

Service and Personal Details:		
Place of Birth:	Clogheen Tipperary	
Age on Enlistment:	21 years	
Period of Service:	1850 — 1869	
Age on Discharge:	42 years 3 months	
Length of Service:	21 years 88 days	
Foreign Service:	India	18 years 137 days
Medal Entitlement:	Indian Mutiny	
Reason for Discharge:	Debility from long service and severe contusion of the right shoulder when in active service during the Mutiny	
Character:	Very Good	
Trade or Occupation:	Labourer	
Can Sign Name:	Yes	
Height:	5' 9"	
Hair Colour:	Red	
Eyes:	Grey	
Complexion:	Fresh	
Intends to Reside:	Liverpool then Chic?*** Illinois America	

ARNOLD	Thomas, private 81st Foot
28 Feb 1854	Discharged the Service Chatham Pension paid Coventry 1/- per diem
24 May 1855	Arrived per *'Stag'*
Jan 1857	Contributed 1/- to the Florence Nightingale Fund
1857	To South Australia from Western Australia
*c*1865	Died

Service and Personal Details:	
Place of Birth:	Sutton Colefield [sic] Warwickshire
Age on Enlistment:	18 years 1 month
Period of Service:	1833 — 1854

Age on Discharge:	39 years 1 month	
Length of Service:	21 years 354 days	
Foreign Service:	Gibraltar	3 years 6 months
	West Indies	3 years 5 months
	Canada 4 years	3 months
Reason for Discharge:	Chronic Rheumatism	
Character:	Good	
Trade or Occupation:	Ribbon Weaver	
Can Sign Name:	X his mark on discharge	
Height:	5' 9½"	
Hair Colour:	Brown	
Eye Colour:	Grey	
Complexion:	Fresh	
Intends to Reside:	Nuneaton Warwickshire	

ARNOTT Robert, private
50th Foot

Surname Variant	ARNOLD
28 Aug 1855	Discharged the Service Chatham Pension paid Newcastle-upon-Tyne 1/- per diem
15 Apr 1864	Arrived per *'Clara'* [2]
1865	To South Australia from Fremantle per *'Ann Anderson'* "Pension stoppage of 45 days for leaving colony"
2 Mar 1865	Pension paid South Australia from Fremantle

Service and Personal Details:

Place of Birth:	Jarrow Gateshead Durham	
Age on Attestation:	18 years 8 months	
Period of Service:	1843 — 1855	
Age on Discharge:	31 years [30 years 10 months]	
Length of Service:	11 years 327 days	
Foreign Service:	East Indies [sic]	4 years 168 days
Medal Entitlement:	?Crimea with clasps	
Reason for Discharge:	Unfit for further service. Disabled on the right side from musket ball at Inkerman [sic]	
Character:	Latterly good	
Trade or Occupation:	Pitman	
Can Sign Name:	X his mark on Attestation	
Height:	5' 7½"	
Hair Colour:	Light	
Eyes:	Grey	
Complexion:	Pale	

ARTHURS Joseph, private
99th Foot

Surname Variant	ARTHUR
24 Aug 1840	Discharged the Service Dublin Pension paid Longford 9d. per diem

1847	Pension paid Athlone
19 Aug 1853	Arrived per *'Robert Small'*
Jan 1857	Contributed 2/- to the Florence Nightingale Fund
Dec 1857	York Lot P15 of 4 acres assigned to a Jas [sic] Arthurs – [two room cottage and garden]
1859	On York Census with wife and five children
May 1863	Application for Title to York Lot P15 by a Jas. [sic] Arthurs [two room cottage and garden]
1864	private J Arthurs serving in the Pensioner Force at York contributed to the Greenough Fire Relief Fund
30 Sept 1873	Pension increased to 1/3d. per diem for 16 years service and from the date of ceasing to draw pay in the Enrolled Force
1875	Residents Office York: J. Arthur [sic],Pensioner and his wife require Portwine. They have been ill with Dysentery and are unable to get well so I have therefore sent a bottle as they are very poor.
25 Apr 1875	Died aged 68 at York

Service and Personal Details:

Place of Birth:	St Marys Dublin	
Age on Attestation:	18 years	
Period of Service:	1824 — 1840	
Age on Discharge:	34 years	
Length of Service:	16 years 117 days	
Foreign Service:	Mauritius	11 years 158 days
Reason for Discharge:	Rheumatic Fever, Extensive Varicose Veins and Debility of Constitution	
Character:	Good efficient and trustworthy	
Trade or Occupation:	Cotton Spinner	
Can Sign Name:	X his mark on discharge	
Height:	5' 10"	
Hair Colour:	Brown	
Eye Colour:	Brown	
Complexion:	Sallow	

ASH Abraham, private
64th Foot

7 May 1867	Discharged the Service Pension paid 2nd North London Pension District 1/- per diem
9 Jan 1868	Arrived per *'Hougoumont'*
1868	Employed as Assistant Warder
1877	Died – buried East Perth Pioneer Cemetery

Service and Personal Details:

Place of Birth:	Swimbridge Devon	
Age on Attestation:	18 years	
Period of Service:	1846 — 1867	
Age on Discharge:	39 years	
Length of Service:	21 years 11 days	
Foreign Service:	India	12 years 3 months
Medal Entitlement:	Persia with clasp and Indian Mutiny	

Reason for Discharge:	Own Request after 21 years service
Character:	Good
Trade or Occupation:	Labourer
Can Sign Name:	Yes
Height:	5' 11½"
Hair Colour:	Brown
Eyes:	Hazel
Complexion:	Dark
Distinguishing Marks:	Scar on front of left shin
Intends to Reside:	2 Exchange Court; The Stand; London

ATKINSON	John, private
	2nd Dragoon Guards
2 Nov 1847	Discharged the Service Newbridge
27 Dec 1847	Admitted to Out-Pension
Jan 1848	Pension paid Carlisle
	9d. per diem
1 June 1850	Arrived per *'Scindian'*
16 July 1850	Assigned Freshwater Bay Loc P236
Jan 1857	Contributed 1/- to the Florence Nightingale Fund
Sept 1858	Application for Title to Freshwater Bay Loc P236 & P250
26 Nov 1874	Died – buried East Perth Pioneer Cemetery

Service and Personal Details:

Place of Birth:	Kendal Westmoreland
Age on Attestation:	19 years 3 months
Period of Service:	1830 — 1847
Age on Discharge:	36 years 4 months
Length of Service:	17 years 34 days
Reason for Discharge:	Chronic Rheumatism
Character:	Very Good
Trade or Occupation:	Saddler
Can Sign Name:	Yes
Height:	6' 0½"
Hair Colour:	Sandy
Eyes:	Grey
Complexion:	Fair

ATKINSON	Robert, Serjeant
	87th Foot
22 Aug 1865	Discharged the Service
	Pension paid Carlow
	1/8d. per diem
1865	Pension paid Cavan
1866	Pension paid Chatham
4 July 1866	Arrived per *'Belgravia'*
1867	Pension paid Melbourne
1867	New Zealand
1869	Pension paid 2nd Dublin Pension District

Service and Personal Details:

Place of Birth:	Enniscorthy Wexford
Age on Attestation:	19 years
Period of Service:	1844 — 1865
Age on Discharge:	40 years 3 months
Length of Service:	21 years 5 days
Foreign Service:	East Indies 10 years 9 months
	China 1 year 6 1 month
Reason for Discharge:	Own Request having served 21 years
Character:	Very Good
Trade or Occupation:	Miller
Can Sign Name:	Yes
Height:	5' 9"
Hair Colour:	Grey
Eyes:	Hazel
Complexion:	Sallow
Distinguishing Marks:	Letter "D" on left side
Intends to Reside:	Castle Hill Cavan Ireland

ATKINSON	William, private 94th Foot
6 Jan 1857	Discharged the Service Chatham Pension paid Preston 9d. per diem
1862	Pension paid Bermuda
15 Feb 1863	Arrived per *'Merchantman'* [1]
1864	private W Atkinson serving in the Pensioner Force at Perth contributed to the Greenough Fire Relief Fund
8 Apr 1875	Granted Northam Loc 4
1878	Pension increased to 1/3d. per diem for service in the Enrolled Force
1881	Northam — Pensioner W Atkinson applies for employment
1885	Died

Service and Personal Details:	
Place of Birth:	Kilmore Co. Mayo
Age on Attestation:	18 years
Period of Service:	1839 — 1857
Age on Discharge:	36 years
Length of Service:	17 years 288 days
Foreign Service:	East Indies 12 years 10 months
Reason for Discharge:	Unfit for further service
Character:	Very Good
Trade or Occupation:	Servant
Can Sign Name:	Yes
Height:	5' 6"
Hair Colour:	Brown
Eyes:	Hazel
Complexion:	Fresh
Intends to Reside:	Liverpool Lancaster

ATTWOOD	Edwin, Corporal 66th Foot
25 May 1864	Discharged the Service Netley 1/- per diem Pension paid Bristol
15 Aug 1865	Arrived per *'Racehorse'*
24 Aug 1881	Assigned Perth Railway Block Lot 153/V
1881	Pension increased to 1/6d. per diem for service in the Enrolled Force
15 Dec 1883	Granted Fee Simple Perth Railway Block Lot 153/V
1888	Pensioner Attwood recommended as Night Watchman on dredge by Warder Passmore
June 1897	Residing South Terrace Fremantle
1898	Died buried Fremantle Cemetery

Service and Personal Details:

Place of Birth:	St Cuthbert Wells Somerset	
Age on Attestation:	about 21 years	
Period of Service:	circa 1842 — 1863	
Age on Discharge:	41 years 7 months	
Length of Service:	20 years 306 days	
Foreign Service:	Gibraltar	4 years 1 month
	West Indies	3 years 5 months
	Canada	3 years 4 months
	East Indies	5 years 2 months
Reason for Discharge:	Chronic Rheumatism	
Character:	Very Good	
Trade or Occupation:	Labourer	
Can Sign Name:	Yes	
Height:	5' 8¾"	
Hair Colour:	Light Brown	
Eyes:	Grey	
Complexion:	Fresh	
Distinguishing Marks:	Scar on back of right shoulder	
Intends to Reside:	Bristol	

AUSTIN	James, private RM
Surname Variant	AUSTEN
3 Aug 1848	Admitted to Out-Pension £21/12/- rate per annum
21 May 1851	Arrived per *'Mermaid'*
27 Mar 1852	Appointed Police Force Perth
Jan 1857	Contributed 2/- to the Florence Nightingale Fund
Sept 1870	On Perth District Electoral List
1850s – 1860s	Serving in Police Force
1871	Barrack Serjeant and Pound-keeper Perth
Jan 1873	Died – buried East Perth Pioneer Cemetery

BAGG	George, private RM
1846	Admitted to Out-Pension
Jan 1850	Pension paid Cardiff

	£6/-/- per annum
1 June 1850	Arrived per *'Scindian'*
Nov 1852	Assigned Pensioner Lot P3 at York
Jan 1857	Contributed 2/- to the Florence Nightingale Fund
1859	Application for Title to York Lot P3
Aug/Sept 1861	Applied to purchase York Suburban Lot 2 at £3/-/- per acre
1864	private G Bagg serving in the Pensioner Force at York contributed to the Greenough Fire Relief Fund
1865	Pensioner Bagg's wife died of severe burns caused by her clothing being set alight from attending her oven
Jan 1872	Died Kojonup

Service and Personal Details:

Place of Birth:	Widmore Somerset
Date of Birth:	1818
Marine Division:	Woolwich
Period of Service:	1839 — 1846
Age on Attestation:	21 years
Reason for Discharge:	Invalided for 'fractura' [sic] contracted in the service
Trade or Occupation:	Agricultural labourer
Can Sign Name:	X his mark on discharge
Character:	Good
Remarks:	Discharged due to injury Served in operations on [sic] coast of Syria

BAGLEY Patrick, private

	99th Foot
Surname Variant	BAGLAY
9 July 1861	Discharged the Service Cork
Pension paid Longford	
	1/- per diem
1862	Pension paid Bermuda
15 Feb 1863	Arrived per *'Merchantman'* [1]
1864	private P Bagley serving in the Pensioner Force at Perth contributed to the Greenough Fire Relief Fund
1868	Granted Greenough Loc 33
14 Dec 1873	Died Land Grant to widow Bridget
1876	Geraldton — Bridget Bagley in receipt of outdoor relief money

Service and Personal Details:

Place of Birth:	Tullamore Offaly
Age on Attestation:	18 years
Period of Service:	1839 — 1861
Age on Discharge:	39 years 10 months
Length of Service:	21 years 21 days
Foreign Service:	Australian Colonies 13 years 10 months
Reason for Discharge:	Own Request having completed 21 years
Character:	Good
Trade or Occupation:	Labourer

Can Sign Name:	X his mark on discharge [witnessed]	
Height:	5' 6½"	
Hair Colour:	Dark Brown	
Eyes:	Grey	
Complexion:	Florid	
Intends to Reside:	Longford	
BAILEY	Job, private	
	RM	
Surname Variants	BAILY; BAYLEY	
3 July 1851	Admitted to Out-Pension	
1853	Pension paid Trowbridge	
	£15/4/- per annum	
19 Aug 1853	Arrived per *'Robert Small'*	
Jan 1857	Contributed 2/- to the Florence Nightingale Fund	
Dec 1857	Assigned Pensioner Lot P6 at York	
26 Apr 1860	Purchased York Lot 269	
1864	private Job Bailey serving in the Pensioner Force at York contributed to the Greenough Fire Relief Fund	
May 1863	Application for Title to Lot P6 at York	
1876	Summoned for carting for hire without a license	
1886	Died	
Service and Personal Details:		
Place of Birth:	Wiltshire	
Age on Attestation:	18 years	
Marine Division:	Portsmouth	
Period of Service:	1830 — 1851	
Length of Service:	21 years	
Reason for Discharge:	Length of Service	
Comments:	Documents missing from box	
BAIN	John, gunner and driver	
	RA 11th Battalion	
13 July 1852	Discharged the Service Woolwich	
1853	Pension paid 2nd Edinburgh Pension District	
	1/- per diem	
1854	Pension paid Turkey	
	[possibly serving with Army Ambulance Corps]	
4 Aug 1855	Embarked for England	
1855	Pension paid Edinburgh	
2 Apr 1856	Arrived per *'William Hammond'*	
Jan 1857	Contributed 2/- to the Florence Nightingale Fund	
1861 Pension paid Melbourne		
Service and Personal Details:		
Place of Birth:	Edinburgh Scotland	
Age on Enlistment:	19 years 2 months	
Period of Service:	1831 — 1852	
Age on Discharge:	40 years 5 months	
Length of Service:	21 years 171 days	
Foreign Service:	Corfu	4 years 10 months
	Spain	11 months

	Malta 6 years 3 months
Reason for Discharge:	Chronic Rheumatism
Character:	Exemplary
Trade or Occupation:	Mason
Can Sign Name:	Yes
Height:	5' 9"
Hair Colour:	Dark Brown
Eyes:	Dark
Complexion:	Dark

BAKER	Robert, private
	34th Foot
26 Feb 1849	Discharged the Service Boyle
27 Mar 1849	Admitted to pension
	Pension paid 1st Portsmouth Pension District
	9d. per diem
1 June 1850	Arrived per *'Scindian'*
1851	Appointed Assistant or Night Warder Fremantle
1851	Assigned land North Fremantle Lot14 [Acc 36]
1861	To South Australia from Western Australia
May 1861	To South Australia per *'Kestrel'*
1862	Pension paid South Australia
*c*1871	Died
Service and Personal Details:	
Place of Birth:	Beccles Suffolk
Age on Attestation:	17 years
Period of Service:	1831 — 1849
Age on Discharge:	34 years 11 months
Length of Service:	16 years 341 days
Foreign Service:	North America 5 years 4 months
Reason for Discharge:	Varicose Veins
Conduct:	Good
Trade or Occupation:	Labourer
Can Sign Name:	Yes
Height:	5' 10"
Hair Colour:	Brown
Eye Colour:	Dark
Complexion:	Dark
Intends to Reside:	Portsmouth

BALDWIN	John, private [320]
	59th Foot
11 Aug 1841	Discharged the Service Fort Pitt Chatham
27 Aug 1841	Discharge Approved
	Pension paid Kilkenny
	6d. per diem
1848	Pension paid 2nd Dublin Pension District
28 June 1851	Arrived per *'Pyrenees'* [1]
23 Apr 1854	"Struck off Force"
	"Dismissed from Force due to misconduct"
May 1855	Restored
Jan 1857	Contributed 1/- to the Florence Nightingale Fund

1866	Employed as Assistant Warder
Sept 1867	John Baldwin, Pensioner, unable to support himself and wife and 4 children. He is a shoemaker by trade, but unable to procure work due to the fact that the Master Shoemakers in the town prefer men boarding in their houses. It is also well known that most of the Master Shoemakers of this town have originally been of the Bond class, and prefer workman of their own stamp
1873	Pension increased to 10½d. per diem for service in the Enrolled Force
1874	Died

Service and Personal Details:

Place of Birth:	New Castle Staffordshire	
Age on Attestation:	16 years	
Period of Service:	1825 — 1840	
Age on Discharge:	31 years	
Length of Service:	13 years 310 days [years served after 18]	
Foreign Service:	East Indies	13 years 48 days
	Gibraltar	1 year 229 days
	Malta	3 years 326 days
	Corfu	250 days
Reason for Discharge:	Scrofulous Ulcers on right hip	
Character:	Good	
Trade or Occupation:	Shoemaker	
Can Sign Name:	X his mark on discharge	
Height:	5' 6½"	
Hair Colour:	Brown	
Eyes:	Grey	
Complexion:	Pale	
Intends to Reside:	Kilkenny	

BALL — see — BULL Edward, private
35th Foot

BALL — see — BOLL William, private
8th Foot

BANDY — Thomas, private
98th Foot

9 May 1848	Discharged the Service Chatham 1/- per diem
25 Oct 1850	Arrived per *'Hashemy'*
1851	Allocated ½ acre Lot 16 at Butler's Swamp
Sept 1851	Convicted of robbing Mr Croft's store
1852	"Committed felony, "stealing 4 pairs of boots at Perth Australia — sentenced to 7 years transportation"
1872	Restored to pension
Nov 1881	Assigned Perth Town Block Lot 155/V
Jan 1884	Application for Crown Grant for Perth Town Lot 155/V

May 1884	Granted Fee Simple Perth Town [Railway] Lot 155/V
1896	Died Perth Western Australia

Service and Personal Details:

Place of Birth:	Turneston Buckinghamshire
Age on Enlistment:	16 years
Period of Service:	1825 — 1848
Age on Discharge:	39 years
Length of Service:	20 years 249 days
Reason for Discharge:	Chronic Rheumatism and Hernia
Character:	Good
Trade or Occupation:	Shoemaker
Can Sign Name:	Yes
Height:	5' 5½"
Hair Colour:	Fair
Eyes:	Grey
Complexion:	Sallow
Intends to Reside:	Chatham

BANNON Patrick, Serjeant
50th Foot

Surname Variant	BANNAN
27 Mar 1849	Discharged the Service Chatham Pension paid Liverpool 1/8d. per diem
1849	Pension paid Londonderry
28 June 1851	Arrived per *'Pyrenees'* [1]
1852	Appointed Gaoler York
1853	10/- stopped from pay due to stores not accounted for at York
Jan 1857	Contributed 2/6 to the Florence Nightingale Fund
1857	To South Australia from Western Australia per *'Robert Clyde'* "£4/6/- paid for passage"
1865	Pension paid South Australia

Service and Personal Details:

Place of Birth:	Derravoland Co. Fermanagh	
Age on Attestation:	18 years	
Period of Service:	1832 — 1849	
Age on Discharge:	34 years 8 months or 35 years	
Length of Service:	16 years 263 days	
Foreign Service:	New South Wales	7 years 119 days
	East Indies	3 years 342 days
Medal Entitlement:	Bronze Star Punniar	
Reason for Discharge:	Severe gunshot wound in upper part of right thigh	
Character:	Good	
Trade or Occupation:	Labourer	
Can Sign Name:	Yes	
Hair Colour:	Brown	
Eyes:	Grey	
Complexion:	Fresh	
Intends to Reside:	Liverpool	

BARKER	Joseph, private	
	12th Foot	
Previous Regiment	6th Foot	
Surname Variants	BAKER; BARRETT	
28 June 1864	Discharged Approved	
	Pension paid 1st Liverpool Pension District	
	1/1d. per diem	
9 Jan 1868	Arrived per *'Hougoumont'*	
1880	Pension increased to 1/6½d. per diem from date of ceasing to draw pay in the Enrolled Force of Western Australia	
1880	To Invalid Depot	
3 July 1880	Died – buried East Perth Pioneer Cemetery	
Service and Personal Details:		
Place of Birth:	Colne Lancashire	
Age on Attestation:	17 years	
Period of Service:	1841 — 1863	
Age on Discharge:	39 years 8 months	
Length of Service:	21 years 243 days	
Foreign Service:	Mauritius	8 years 2 months
	Cape of Good Hope	7 years 5 months
Medal Entitlement:	Long Service and Good Conduct with gratuity; Kaffir War	
Reason for Discharge:	Own Request having completed 21 years service	
Character:	Exemplary	
Trade or Occupation:	Weaver	
Can Sign Name:	X his mark on discharge	
Height:	5' 8½"	
Hair Colour:	Dark Brown	
Eyes:	Grey	
Complexion:	Fair	
Intends to Reside:	Liverpool	

BARR	Joseph, private	
	22nd Foot	
24 Nov 1863	Discharged the Service	
Pension paid Paisley		
11d. per diem		
15 Aug 1865	Arrived per *'Racehorse'*	
1867	Died — lost onboard the *'Emma'*	
Service and Personal Details:		
Place of Birth:	Greenock Renfrewshire	
Age on Attestation:	19 years 9 months	
Period of Service:	1842 — 1863	
Age on Discharge:	40 years 11 months	
Length of Service:	21 years 42 days	
Foreign Service:	East Indies	9 years 93 days
	Malta	3 years 101 days
Medal Entitlement:	Good Conduct	
Reason for Discharge:	Own Request having served 21 years	

Character:	Good
Trade or Occupation:	Tinsmith
Can Sign Name:	Yes
Height:	5' 9½"
Hair Colour:	Dark Brown
Eyes:	Grey
Complexion:	Fresh
Intends to Reside:	Greenwich

BARR	Robert, private [2188]
	81st Foot
Previous Regiment	15th Foot
8 June 1852	Discharged the Service Dublin
	Pension paid 2nd Dublin Pension District
	8d. per diem for 2½ years
1852	Pension paid Kilkenny
31 Aug 1853	Arrived per *'Phoebe Dunbar'*
Sept 1882	Died

Service and Personal Details:

Place of Birth:	Hamilton Lanarkshire	
Age on Enlistment:	17 years	
Period of Service:	1831 — 1852	
Age on Discharge:	38 years 1 month	
Length of Service:	10 years 130 days	
Foreign Service:	Canada	2 years 2 months
Reason for Discharge:	Unfit for further service	
Character:	Good	
Trade or Occupation:	Weaver	
Can Sign Name:	X his mark on discharge	
Height:	5' 7½"	
Hair Colour:	Fair	
Eyes:	Grey	
Complexion:	Fresh	
Intends to Reside:	Dublin	

BARR	William, private
	42nd Foot
4 June 1867	Discharged the Service Netley
1867	Pension paid 1st Glasgow Pension District
	1/- per diem
1867	Pension paid Paisley
1869	Glasgow
1872	Paisley
1873	Greenwich
19 Feb 1874	Arrived per *'Naval Brigade'*
1882	Died
14 Sept 1882	Inquest at Fremantle, before J. G. Slade,R.M. and Coroner, on the body of William Barr, pensioner, who died on the 14th inst., from an overdose of opium administered by Frederick Scanlan. Verdict " Manslaughter against Frederick Scanlan."

Service and Personal Details:		
Place of Birth:	Greenock Scotland	
Age on Enlistment:	16 years 11 months	
Period of Service:	1845 — 1867	
Age on Discharge:	39 years 3 months	
Length of Service:	20 years 163 days	
Foreign Service:	West Indies	1 year
	Corfu	1 year 10 months
	Crimea	1 year 4 months
	India	8 years 8 months
Medal Entitlement:	Crimea with clasp; Turkish Crimea; Indian	
Mutiny with clasp		
Reason for Discharge:	Unfit for further duty	
Character:	Very Good	
Trade or Occupation:	Curder [sic]	
Can Sign Name:	Yes	
Height:	5' 9¼"	
Hair Colour:	Fair	
Eyes:	Grey	
Complexion:	Fresh	
Intends to Reside:	Glasgow	

BARRATT	Edward, private	
	1st Foot Guards [Grenadier Guards]	
Surname Variant	BARRETT	
1851	Stationed at St James's Palace Ambassador's Court Barracks	
28 Oct 1856	Discharged the Service London	
	Pension paid Northampton	
	1/- per diem	
28 Dec 1863	Arrived per *'Lord Dalhousie'*	
1864	Pension paid Western Australia	
Oct 1864	To South Australia per *'Europa'*	
1864	Pension paid South Australia	
Service and Personal Details:		
Place of Birth:	Oundle Huntingdonshire	
Age on Attestation:	20 years	
Period of Service:	1843 — 1856	
Age on Discharge:	33 years	
Length of Service:	12 years 353 days	
Foreign Service:	"the Army in the East"	11 months
Medal Entitlement:	Crimean with clasps	
Reason for Discharge:	Wounded in action at Inkerman	
Character:	Very Good	
Trade or Occupation:	Labourer	
Can Sign Name:	Yes	
Height:	5' 8½"	
Hair Colour:	Brown	
Eyes:	Grey	
Complexion:	Fresh	
Intends to Reside:	Huntingdonshire	

BARRETT	John, private [362]
	61st Foot
Surname Variant	BARRATT
22 Jan 1847	Discharged the Service Chatham
	Pension paid 1st London Pension District
	1/- per diem
1 June 1850	Arrived per *'Scindian'*
1850	Assigned Freshwater Bay Locs 10 and 14
Jan 1857	Contributed 1/- to the Florence Nightingale Fund
1857	Pension increased to 1/6d. per diem due to him being totally blind
Apr 1869	Mrs. Barrett, wife of Pensioner J. Barrett, is unable to work for her living
1869	Died
Service and Personal Details:	
Place of Birth:	St Johns Limerick
Age on Attestation:	20 years
Period of Service:	1825 — 1847
Age on Discharge:	41 years
Length of Service:	21 years 220 days
Foreign Service:	Ceylon 11 years ? months
Reason for Discharge:	Chronic Rheumatism and Varicose Veins in both legs
Conduct:	Latterly Good
Trade or Occupation:	Clerk
Can Sign Name:	Yes
Height:	5' 7¼"
Hair Colour:	Light
Eye Colour:	Grey
Complexion:	Fresh
Married:	Alice
Children:	Catherine b. *c*1847 England
	Mary Ann b. *c*1849 England
	m. *c*1871 Henry Albert Fremantle
	Ellen b. *c*1855 Fremantle [murdered *c*1883]
	m. *c*1873 Dominic Pontevivo Perth

BARRETT	see — BARKER Joseph, private
	12th Foot

BARRETT	Richard, private EIC
	2nd Bengal European Infantry
	Out Pension No 501
11 Aug 1858	Admitted to Out-Pension
	Pension paid Sligo
	1/3d. per diem
4 July 1866	Arrived per *'Belgravia'*
1868	Employed as Assistant Warder
9 Nov 1869	Application to purchase Fremantle Town Lot 30
June 1885	Application for Crown Grant for Cockburn Sound Lot P10

3 Mar 1886	Granted Cockburn Sound Lot P10 Coogee
	Employed as messenger for the Fremantle branch of the West Australian Bank
1891	Corporal in the Fremantle Rifle Volunteers
23 Sept 1891	Died aged 51
Service and Personal Details:	
Where Born:	Castlebar Co Mayo
Trade or Occupation:	Shoemaker
Age on Enlistment:	circa 24 years
Presidency:	Bengal
Length of Service:	2 years
Age on Discharge:	26 years
Character & Conduct:	Very Good
Reason for Discharge:	Right shoulder joint useless from wound from a piece of shell — Delhi 14 Sept 1857
Medal Entitlement:	Indian Mutiny with clasp for Delhi
Height:	5' 5¼"
Complexion:	Fresh
Eye Colour:	Hazel
Hair Colour:	Brown
Intends to Reside:	Castlebar Sligo

BARRON	Cornelius, private [1783]	
	Royal Canadian Rifles	
Pervious Regiment	75th Foot	
Surname Variants	[some] BARRAN; BARON; BERREN; BARROW	
9 Aug 1870	Discharged the Service Chichester	
	Pension paid 2nd Plymouth Pension District 7½d. per diem	
1873	Pension paid Greenwich	
19 Feb 1874	Arrived per *'Naval Brigade'*	
29 Nov 1883	Charged with committing aggravated assault on his wife	
31 Jan 1884	Application for Crown Grant North Fremantle Lot P83	
8 Aug 1884	Granted Title North Fremantle Lot P83	
1891	Died	
Service and Personal Details:		
Place of Birth:	Doon Limerick Co. Tipperary	
Age on Attestation:	18 years	
Period of Service:	1853 — 1870	
Age on Discharge:	35 years 3 months	
Length of Service:	18 years 67 days	
Foreign Service:	East Indies	8 years 8 month
	Canada	3 years 8 months
Medal Entitlement:	Indian Mutiny with four clasps	
Reason for Discharge:	18 years service and Disbandment of Corps	
Character:	Good	
Trade or Occupation:	Labourer	
Can Sign Name:	X his mark on discharge	

Height:	5' 10"
Hair Colour:	Light Brown
Eyes:	Hazel
Complexion:	Fresh
Intends to Reside:	Devonport Devon
Description:	in 1883
Age:	50 years
Stature:	Middling stout
Height:	5' 9"
Hair Colour:	Grey
Eye Colour:	Grey
Visage:	Long
Complexion:	Pale
Married:	m. *c*1863 Elizabeth Hill Devonport Devon
	b. *c*1842 Wilcove Torpoint Cornwall [Deaf]
Children:	Mary Ann b. *c*1864 Devonport Devon
	Cornelius b. *c*1866 Portsmouth Hampshire
	John b. *c*1868 Canada
	George b. *c*1870 Canada
	m. *c*1895 Maud Fitzpatrick Fremantle
	Agnes b. *c*1875 Perth
	Elizabeth Ann b. *c*1880 Fremantle

BARRON	John, private
	10th Foot
Previous Regiment	58th Foot
13 July 1852	Discharged the Service Chatham
Aug 1852	Pension paid Londonderry
	1/- per diem
31 Aug 1853	Arrived per *'Phoebe Dunbar'*
Jan 1857	Contributed 1/- to the Florence Nightingale Fund
1875	Pension paid Western Australia
1895	Died

Service and Personal Details:		
Place of Birth:	Raphoe Donegal	
Age on Attestation:	18 years	
Period of Service:	1831 — 1851	
Age on Discharge:	41 years [sic]	
Length of Service:	20 years 224 days	
Foreign Service:	Ceylon	3 years
	India	9 years
Medal Entitlement:	Sutlej; Punjaub with clasps for Moultan and Goojerat	
Reason for Discharge:	Worn out with Intermittent Fever and impaired constitution	
Character:	Good	
Trade or Occupation:	Labourer	
Can Sign Name:	X his mark on discharge	
Height:	5' 6"	
Hair Colour:	Brown	
Eyes:	Hazel	
Complexion:	Sallow	

Intends to Reside: Londonderry

BARRY John, Colour Serjeant
39th Foot

13 June 1854	Discharged the Service Charles Fort
8 Aug 1854	Discharged to pension
	Pension paid Tralee
	2/- per diem
1855	Pension paid Tralee
18 July 1855	Arrived per *'Adelaide'*
Jan 1857	Contributed 2/- to the Florence Nightingale Fund
1857	Pension paid New Zealand
1875	New Zealand

Service and Personal Details:

Place of Birth:	Tralee Co Kerry
Age on Attestation:	21 years 160 days
Period of Service:	1833 — 1854
Length of Service:	21 years 160 days
Age on Discharge:	42 years 5 months
Foreign Service:	East Indies 13 years
Medal Entitlement:	Meritorious and Long Service with gratuity; and Battle Mahrajpore 1843
Reason for Discharge:	Varicose Veins in both legs
Character:	Very Good
Trade or Occupation:	Labourer
Can Sign Name:	Yes
Height:	5' 8½"
Hair Colour:	Fair
Eyes:	Grey
Complexion:	Fair
Intends to Reside:	Tralee

BARRY John, private
91st Foot

12 Oct 1847	Discharged the Service Chatham
	Pension paid 1st Glasgow Pension District
	7d. per diem
30 Apr 1853	Arrived per *'Pyrenees'* [2]
1856	Pension paid 2nd West London Pension District
1856	Pension paid Glasgow
17 Aug 1860	Died

Service and Personal Details:

Place of Birth:	Avondale Lanarkshire
Age on Attestation:	18 years
Period of Service:	1832 — 1847
Age on Discharge:	33 years
Length of Service:	14 years 282 days
Foreign Service:	St Helena 3 years 5 months
	Cape of Good Hope 7 years 8 months
Reason for Discharge:	Paralysis caused by fit of Apoplexy
Character:	Good
Trade or Occupation:	Weaver

Can Sign Name:	Yes
Height:	5' 6½"
Hair Colour:	Light
Eyes:	Blue
Complexion:	Fresh

BARRY	Michael, gunner EIC Madras Artillery Out Pension No 563
17 Oct 1860	Discharged the Service
14 Dec 1860	Admitted to Out-Pension Pension paid 2nd Cork Pension District 1/- per diem
22 Dec 1865	Arrived per *'Vimiera'*
1866/7	Stoppages of half pension
22 Sept 1883	Assigned North Fremantle Lot P77
30 Aug 1884	Granted Fee Simple North Fremantle Lot P77
1886	Mary Barry the wife of a pensioner Michael Barry applied for an arrest warrant against her husband
1887	the daughter of Michael Barry applied to the Court for a doctor to visit her father who suffered from heart disease and was unable to obtain medical aid
1887	Died

Service and Personal Details:

Where Born:	Cork Ireland
Trade or Occupation:	Labourer
Presidency:	Madras
Length of Service:	21 years 6 months
Age on Discharge:	43 years [or 33 years]
Character:	Good
Reason for Discharge:	Unfit for further service or time expired
Height:	5' 5" or 5' 5½
Complexion:	Fresh
Eye Colour:	Grey
Hair Colour:	Brown or Dark Brown
Intends to Reside:	Cork

BARTON	see — BURTON Edwin, private EIC Bombay Infantry

BASKERVILLE	John, Corporal EIC Bombay Artillery
Surname Variant	BUSKERVILLE Out Pension No 263
Feb 1842	Discharged the Service
11 Oct 1843	Admitted to Out-Pension Pension paid Hereford Worcester 1/- per diem
25 Oct 1850	Arrived per *'Hashemy'*
1851	Employed as Night Warder Convict Service
1851	Appointed Assistant Overseer Bunbury
18 Nov 1858	Assigned Pensioner Lot 6 at Bunbury

4 Dec 1858	Application for Title Bunbury Pensioner Lot P6
31 Dec 1858	Granted Fee Simple for Bunbury Lot P6
1867	Died

Service and Personal Details:

Where Born:	Hereford
Trade or Occupation:	Labourer
Presidency:	Bombay
Length of Service:	15 years 4 months
Age on Discharge:	34 years
Reason for Discharge:	Worn out from service and Ruptured
Height:	5' 10½"
Complexion:	Fair
Visage:	Oval
Eye Colour:	Blue
Hair Colour:	Brown or bald
Married:	1.] 28 Jan 1832 Mary Clark Solapoor India
Children:	a Sarah Baskerville b. c1836 baptised 4th
Married:	2.] 27 Nov 1837 Harriet Stringer India
Marriage Details:	Bombay Ecclesiastical Returns N3/31/13 27th Nov 1837 John Baskerville Widower Corporal Honorable [sic] Company Horse Artillery and Harriet Stringer Spinster

BASS see — BARR Robert, private
81st Foot

BATEMAN Edward, private
15th Hussars

Previous Regiment	8th Hussars
24 Aug 1852	Discharged the Service Chatham 8d. per diem for 3 years
19 Aug 1853	Arrived per *'Robert Small'*
17 Mar 1854	Left colony without permission

Service and Personal Details:

Place of Birth:	Toberton Hampshire
Age on Enlistment:	18 years 6 months
Period of Service:	1839 — 1852
Age on Discharge:	31 years
Length of Service:	12 years 82 days
Foreign Service:	East Indies 4 years 246 days
Reason for Discharge:	General Debility and Scrophula attendance with Rheumatic Pains; Suppurating Gland in neck and impaired heath contracted at Bangalore
Character:	Good
Trade or Occupation:	Clerk
Can Sign Name:	Yes
Height:	5' 7¼"
Hair Colour:	Dark Brown

Eyes:	Hazel
Complexion:	Dark
Distinguishing Marks:	Scar on the forehead. Mark of burn on the left temple and left arm and an anchor on left arm

BATES	George, private
	23rd Foot
31 July 1855	Discharged the Service Chatham
	Pension paid Derby
	8d. per diem
1857	Pension paid Birmingham
1857	Wolverhampton
1857	Derby
24 Nov 1858	Arrived per *'Edwin Fox'*
25 July 1859	Found dead with his throat cut

Service and Personal Details:	
Place of Birth:	Liverpool
Age on Attestation:	20 years
Period of Service:	1854 — 1855
Age on Discharge:	21 years or 20 years 11 months
Length of Service:	314 days [reckoned]
Foreign Service:	Crimea [no time period given]
Medal Entitlement:	none give on Discharge Document
Reason for Discharge:	Amputation of middle finger of the left hand caused by gunshot wound
Character:	Appears to have been Good
Trade or Occupation:	Labourer
Can Sign Name:	Yes
Height:	5' 5¾"
Hair Colour:	Dark Brown
Eyes:	Hazel
Complexion:	Sallow
Intends to Reside:	Derby

BATES	John, private EIC
	2nd Bombay European Infantry
	Out Pension No 454
1856	Embarked UK per *'HCS Seringapatam'*
4 June 1856	Admitted to Out-pension
	Pension paid 1st Dublin Pension District
	9d. per diem
24 Nov 1858	Arrived per *'Edwin Fox'*
1864	private J Bates serving in the Pensioner Force at Kojonup contributed to the Greenough Fire Relief Fund
1866/7	Pension paid Perth Western Australia
1873	Residing Kojonup
May 1885	Assigned Kojonup Town Lot 20
1886	Residing Kojonup Town Lot 20
1886	Both his Land Grants [P14 & Lort 20] cancelled
1886	Died
Dec 1886	An old man named Bates was found dead in the bush near Kojonup

1886	Resident magistrate Williams — Inquest on Pensioner J. Bates
Jan 1886	At Kojonup Police Station — Inquest verdict 'Death from natural causes'
28 Dec 1886	Minutes taken at the Inquest on the body of Pensioner J. Bates
Service and Personal Details:	
Where Born:	Banger Co. Down
Trade or Occupation:	Servant
Age on Enlistment:	19 years
Presidency:	Bombay
Length of Service:	16 years 3 months
Age on Discharge:	35 years
Character:	Good
Reason for Discharge:	Rheumatism and disease of the heart
Height:	5' 6½"
Complexion:	Dark
Eye Colour:	Hazel
Hair Colour:	Dark Brown
Intends to Reside:	1st Dublin Division

BATLEY

BATLEY	Richard, private 86th Foot
Previous Regiment	8th Foot
Surname Variants	BATELY; BATTLEY; BRATLEY
10 Aug 1861	Discharged the Service Templemore
20 Aug 1861	Discharge Approved Pension paid Carlow 1/- per diem
27 May 1863	Arrived per *'Clyde'*
1864	private R Batley serving in the Pensioner Force at Fremantle District contributed to the Greenough Fire Relief Fund
1868	Assistant Warder stationed Fremantle
1875	Pension paid Western Australia
1878	Pension increased to 1/5½d. per diem for service in the Enrolled Pensioner Force Employed as a messenger for the Colonial Treasury
Nov 1883	Application for Title Perth Lot 25/H
24 Jan 1884	Warder Richard Batley: his services no longer required at Rottnest
1887	Died shot himself — [second attempt at suicide]
Oct 1887	Inquest held at Perth Police Court before J. C. H. James, Acting P.M. and Coroner on the body of Richard Batley, Pensioner, Verdict — "Suicide." Buried - East Perth Pioneer Cemetery
Service and Personal Details:	
Place of Birth:	Carlow Co. Carlow
Age on Enlistment:	17 years 3 months
Age on Discharge	39 years
Period of Service	1839 — 1861
Length of Service:	21 years 30 days
Foreign Service:	East Indies 16 years 11 months

Medal Entitlement:	Central India with clasp
Reason for Discharge:	Own Request having served 21 years and impaired health from a head wound received at Jhansi 1858. Wounded by musket ball in the back of the head at Jhansi on the 3rd April 1858
Character:	Very Good
Trade or Occupation:	Cordwainer
Can Sign Name:	Yes
Height:	5' 8"
Hair Colour:	Light Brown
Eyes:	Grey
Complexion:	Fresh
Distinguishing Marks:	Mark of bullet wound on hand
Intends to Reside:	Carlow

BATTIE George, private
25th Foot

Surname Variant	BEATTIE
26 Oct 1852	Discharged the Service Chatham Pension paid Ayr 1/- per diem
2 Apr 1856	Arrived per *'William Hammond'*
1859	Pension paid Ayr Scotland
1859	North London
1859	Pension paid Jersey
2 Aug 1866	Died

Service and Personal Details:

Place of Birth:	Glenluce Wigtown	
Age on Attestation:	19 years	
Period of Service:	1832 — 1853	
Age on Discharge:	39 years 6 months	
Length of Service:	20 years 123 days	
Foreign Service:	Cape of Good Hope	2 years 195 days
	East Indies	10 years 4 days
Reason for Discharge:	Worn out and suffering from Hepatic Disease	
Character:	Indifferent	
Trade or Occupation:	Labourer	
Can Sign Name:	Yes	
Height:	6' 0½"	
Hair Colour:	Brown	
Eyes:	Brown	
Complexion:	Fresh	

BEARD Daniel, private
74th Foot

Pervious Regiment	51st Foot
22 Mar 1859	Discharged the Service Aberdeen Pension paid Cambridge 1/- per diem
1859	Pension paid Dorchester
1864	2nd North London Pension District

11 Jan 1864	Embarked per *'Clara'* [2]	
1865	Pension paid South London	
1865	Brighton	
27 June 1872	Died	
Service and Personal Details:		
Place of Birth:	Eversden Cambridgeshire	
Age on Attestation:	19 years	
Period of Service:	1837 — 1859	
Age on Discharge:	39 years 8 months	
Length of Service:	21 years 10 days	
Foreign Service:	New South Wales	7 years 4 months
	East Indies	12 years 4 months
Reason for Discharge:	Own Request having served 21 years	
Character:	Good	
Trade or Occupation:	Labourer	
Can Sign Name:	Yes on discharge	
Height:	5' 7"	
Hair Colour:	Dark	
Eyes:	Dark	
Complexion:	Dark	
Intends to Reside:	Eversdean Cambridgeshire	
Married:	1854 Sarah O'Hare Vepery India	
Children:	Elizabeth b.1855 Madras India	
	William b.1857 Madras India	
	Emma b. *c*1860 Cambridge England	
	Winifred b. *c*1862 Cambridge England	
	Jane b. *c*1864 Cambridge England	
	Daniel b. *c*1865 Surrey	
	George b. *c*1868 Betchworth	
	Alice b. *c*1871 Dorking Surrey	

BEASLY George, Serjeant Major

	77th Foot	
Surname Variant	BEASLEY	
11 Oct 1853	Discharged the Service	
	Pension paid Exeter	
	2/2½d. per diem	
24 May 1855	Arrived per *'Stag'*	
1856	Pension paid Cape of Good Hope	
Service and Personal Details:		
Place of Birth:	Walcott Bath Somerset	
Age on Attestation:	22 years 2 months	
Period of Service:	1832 — 1853	
Age on Discharge:	43 years 3 months	
Length of Service:	21 years 30 days	
Foreign Service:	Mediterranean	5 years 4 months
	Jamaica	3 years
	North America	2 years 2 months
Reason for Discharge:	To serve on the permanent staff of the 1st East Devon Militia	

Character:	Exemplary and Trustworthy
Trade or Occupation:	Tailor
Can Sign Name:	Yes
Height:	5' 10¼"
Hair Colour:	Brown
Eyes:	Hazel
Complexion:	Fresh

BEASLEY

	Stephen, private 40th Foot
Surname Variants	BEAZLEY; BEESLEY
6 May 1850	Discharged the Service Dublin
11 June 1850	Admitted to Out-Pension Pension paid Bristol Pension District 6d. per diem for 2 years
18 Oct 1851	Arrived per *'Minden'*
1852	Pension ceased
4 June 1886	Correspondence with Imperial Pension Office Adelaide

Service and Personal Details:

Place of Birth:	Wivelscombe Somerset	
Age on Attestation:	24 years 3 months	
Period of Service:	1842 — 1850	
Age on Discharge:	32 years 2 months	
Length of Service:	7 years 319 days	
Foreign Service:	East Indies	2 years 8 months
Medal Entitlement:	Bronze Star Battle of Mahrajapore	
Reason for Discharge:	Disease of the Heart and constitutional disability	
Character:	Good	
Trade or Occupation:	Labourer	
Can Sign Name:	X his mark on discharge	
Height:	5' 6"	
Hair Colour:	Brown	
Eyes:	Grey	
Complexion:	Fair	
Intends to Reside:	Taunton	

BEATTIE

see — BATTIE George, private
25th Foot

BEATTY

	John, Sapper Royal Sappers and Miners
Surname Variant	BEATTIE
Dec 1861	Discharged the Service Fremantle West. Aust.
1886	Awarded Deferred Pension of 6d. per deim

Service and Personal Details:

Place of Birth:	Fahan Ballymahone Co Donegal	
Age on Attestation:	19 years	
Period of Service:	1845 — 1861	
Age on Discharge:	35 years	
Length of Service:	16 years 26 days	
Foreign Service:	Western Australia	10 years 4 months

Reason for Discharge:	Granted a Free Discharge to settle in Colony with 12 months pay and Right of Registry for a Deferred Pension on him attaining 60 years
Character:	Very Good
Trade or Occupation:	Miner
Can Sign Name:	Yes
Height:	5' 8¼"
Hair Colour:	Light Brown
Eyes:	Grey
Complexion:	Fair
Intends to Reside:	Fremantle Western Australia

BEAVIS — Martin, private
54th Foot

11 Sept 1849	Discharged the Service Chatham Pension paid Deptford 7d. per diem for 2 years
May 1852	Embarked per *'William Jardine'* Disembarked Plymouth

BEECH — Joseph, private
37th Foot

1861	Stationed Medway Kent
4 June 1861	Discharged the Service Colchester Pension paid Coventry 1/1½d. per diem
31 Dec 1862	Arrived per *'York'*
1864	Pension paid Sydney

Service and Personal Details:

Place of Birth:	Canterbury Kent	
Age on Attestation:	20 years 2 months	
Period of Service:	1839 — 1861	
Age on Discharge:	41 years 3 months	
Length of Service:	21 years 109 days	
Foreign Service:	Halifax	2 years 8 months
	Ceylon	9 years 9 months
	Bengal	3 years 5 months
Medal Entitlement:	Indian Mutiny; Good Conduct with gratuity	
Reason for Discharge:	Own Request on completion of 21 years service	
Character:	Very Good	
Trade or Occupation:	Shoemaker	
Can Sign Name:	Yes	
Height:	5' 7"	
Hair Colour:	Brown	
Eyes:	Hazel	
Complexion:	Pale	

BENNETT — John, gunner
RA Depot Brigade

Previous Regiment	Madras Artillery
18 Nov 1862	Discharged the Service Woolwich

	Pension paid Jersey
	1/- per diem [Indian Rate]
1863	Pension paid 2nd Dublin Pension District
27 May 1863	Arrived per *'Clyde'*
	"His wife absconded before embarkation of the Guard"
1864	Half pension to be paid to wife in Dublin
1864	private J Bennett serving in the Pensioner Force at Perth contributed to the Greenough Fire Relief Fund
1865	Pension paid South Australia

Service and Personal Details:	
Place of Birth:	Yarmouth Norfolk
Age on Attestation:	21 years
Period of Service:	1842 — 1862
Age on Discharge:	40 years 11 months
Length of Service:	21 years 327 days
Foreign Service:	India 17 years 2 months
Reason for Discharge:	On completion of 21 years service
Character:	Very Good
Trade or Occupation:	Labourer
Can Sign Name:	Yes
Height:	5' 9"
Hair Colour:	Light Brown
Eyes:	Hazel
Complexion:	Fresh
Intends to Reside:	Jersey

BENNETT	Standish O'Grady, private [631]
	10th Foot
Surname Variant	BURNETT
13 Aug 1850	Discharged the Service Chatham
	Pension paid 1st Cork Pension District
	1/- per diem
1851	Pension paid Limerick
31 Aug 1853	Arrived per *'Phoebe Dunbar'*
1854	Employed as Night Warder
1854	Deserted from the Enrolled Force
1858	Pension paid Melbourne
1875	Died aged 75 Victoria

Service and Personal Details:	
Place of Birth:	Fermoy Cork
Age on Attestation:	18 years
Period of Service:	1828 — 1850
Age on Discharge:	40 years
Length of Service:	21 years 14 days
Foreign Service:	[none given but as the proceeding of the Regimental Board took place at Ferozepore on the 30th September 1849 he had to be in India at that date]
Medal Entitlement:	Sutlej with clasp Sobraon; Punjaub with clasps for Mooltan and Goojerat

Reason for Discharge:	Chronic ophthalmia and constitution worn out from length of service
Character:	Good
Trade or Occupation:	Labourer
Can Sign Name:	Yes
Height:	5' 10"
Hair Colour:	Fair
Eyes:	Grey
Complexion:	Sallow

BENSON	Michael, private [1496] 34th Foot
13 Nov 1849	Discharged the Service Chatham Pension paid 1st Dublin Pension District 6d. per diem for 2½ years
28 June 1851	Arrived per *'Pyrenees'* [1]
1851	Serving as police constable — Perth
1861	Keeper of Perth Lock-up
1864	a Michael Benson purchased Perth Town Lot E28 for £6/-/- with frontage to Wellington Street
Sept 1870	Entered on Perth District Electoral List
1873	Employed as Gaoler — Perth
1874	Transferred to Fremantle Gaol
1882	Correspondence with W.O. — the 'A44' to S.O. Perth Western Australia
1882	Full amount of Temporary Pension authorized but not entitled to Deferred Pension due to not having held a Good Conduct Badge for six months issued date before discharge
1893	Correspondence with W.O.
1897	Residing Perth
1897	Died buried Anglican section of East Perth Pioneer Cemetery
1897	Grant of Probate

Service and Personal Details:		
Place of Birth:	Lanesborough Longford Co. Tipperary	
Age on Attestation:	21 years 2 months	
Period of Service:	1838 — 1849	
Age on Discharge:	32 years	
Length of Service:	10 years 203 days	
Foreign Service:	Mediterranean	3 years 8 months
Reason for Discharge:	Rheumatism and Periostiles [sic]	
Conduct:	Good	
Trade or Occupation:	Gardener	
Can Sign Name:	Yes	
Height:	6' 1"	
Hair Colour:	Dark Brown	
Eye Colour:	Blue	
Complexion:	Fresh	
Intends to Reside:	Dublin	

BENTLEY	John, private 28th Foot
Surname Variant	BENTLY
24 Apr 1861	Discharged the Service Fermoy
18 June 1861	Admitted to Out-Pension Pension paid 1st Manchester Pension District 8d. per diem
31 Dec 1862	Arrived per *'York'*
1864	private J Bentley [sic] serving in the Pensioner Force at Fremantle District contributed to the Greenough Fire Relief Fund
5 Mar 1871	Died aged 49 buried in Anglican section of the East Perth Pioneer Cemetery
Service and Personal Details:	
Place of Birth:	Tullamore Kings County
Age on Attestation:	18 years
Period of Service:	1843 — 1861
Age on Discharge:	35 years 4 months
Length of Service:	17 years 91 days
Foreign Service:	East Indies 3 years 98 days Malta 42 days Turkey & Crimea 1 year 14 days
Medal Entitlement:	Crimea with clasps; Turkish Crimea
Reason for Discharge:	Chronic ulcer on left leg. Received blow on leg from hand spike in the Crimea
Character:	Good
Trade or Occupation:	Labourer
Can Sign Name:	X his mark on discharge
Height:	5' 7"
Hair Colour:	Light
Eyes:	Blue
Complexion:	Fine
Intends to Reside:	Stratford Essex

BERRY	William Warren, Staff Serjeant [per newspaper] 58th Foot — Northamptonshire
1886	Emigrated to New South Wales
1895	Settled in Western Australia
circa 1898	Purchased catering business of Farley and Stone which he developed into the Alexander Tearooms chain.
1942	Died at his residence in King Street Subiaco aged 87
Place of Birth:	Devon
Date of Birth:	*c*1855
Foreign Service:	South Africa
Campaign Served:	Zululand 1878
1st Boer War	1879 — 1880

BERRIMAN	John, private RM
Surname Variant	BERRYMAN

July 1848	Admitted to Out-Pension
	Assigned Freshwater Bay Loc 1073
Sept 1870	On Perth District Electoral List
20 Apr 1886	Application for Crown Grant Freshwater Bay Loc 1073 at Butlers Swamp
1887	Died – buried East Perth Pioneer Cemetery

Service and Personal Details:

Place of Birth:	Sutton Courtney Whitechurch Southampton
Age on Attestation:	18 years
Marine Division:	Portsmouth
Period of Service:	1830 — 1848
Length of Service:	18 years 2 months 16 days
Reason for Discharge:	Rheumatism contracted in the Service
Trade or Occupation:	Labourer
Can Sign Name:	X his mark on discharge
Remarks:	Served in the operations off the coast of China
Height:	5' 8¾
Hair Colour:	Light Brown
Eyes:	Grey
Complexion:	Fresh

BESWICK Frederick, Serjeant
39th Foot

Surname Variants	BESTNICK; BERSWICK
1865	Appointed to Lancashire Militia
28 July 1868	Discharged the Service Kinsale
	Pension paid Preston
	1/8d. per diem on re-computation [sic] of service
1868	Pension paid Birmingham
1869	Chatham
1869	Birmingham
1871	possibly arrived per *'Strathmore'*
1 April 1871	Pension paid Western. Australia from the Birmingham Pension District
1881	Pension increased to 2/- per diem for service in the Enrolled Force
1884	Granted Cockburn Sound Loc 175 Willagee Swamp
source not verified	Frederick Beswick and Thomas McGovern were charged at Fremantle on 3rd inst by P.C. White., with disorderly conduct, and damaging a fence, being the property of Barry Woods. Fined " 20s. each, or default 14 days hard labor [sic] each."
1891	Died Fremantle District aged 63

Service and Personal Details:

Place of Birth:	Tilbury Fort Essex	
Age on Enlistment:	14 years	
Period of Service:	1842 — 1868	
Age on Discharge:	40 years 2 months	
Length of Service:	7 years 214 days re-computated [sic] to — 21 years 12 days	
Foreign Service:	East Indies	4 years 106 days
	Gibraltar	234 days

	Crimea	1 year 144 days
	Canada	3 years 155 days
	Bermuda	123 days
	Bermuda	3 years 251 days
Medal Entitlement:	Crimean and Turkish Crimean; [Bronze Star]	
Reason for Discharge:	Own Request after 21 years service and serving with the 1st Lancashire Militia	
Character:	Very Good	
Trade or Occupation:	Labourer	
Can Sign Name:	Yes	
Height:	5' 10¼"	
Hair Colour:	Dark Brown	
Eyes:	Dark	
Complexion:	Sallow	
Intends to Reside:	Lancaster	

BETTS

	William, private [800]	
	13th Light Dragoons	
25 Oct 1853	Discharged the Service Chatham	
	Pension paid Coventry	
	1/- per diem	
10 Sept 1856	Arrived per *'Runnymede'*	
1856	"Off Enrolled Guard Force Roll"	
1859	Pension paid Coventry	
	North London	
	Coventry	
1875	Pension paid Coventry	
Service and Personal Details:		
Place of Birth:	Banbury Oxfordshire	
Age on Attestation:	20 years	
Period of Service:	1829 — 1853	
Age on Discharge:	44 years 3 months	
Length of Service:	23 years 151 days	
Foreign Service:	East Indies	10 years
Reason for Discharge:	Unfit for further service due to Chronic Rheumatism	
Character:	Much improved of late	
Trade or Occupation:	Baker	
Can Sign Name:	Yes	
Height:	5' 8"	
Hair Colour:	Dark Brown	
Eyes:	Hazel	
Complexion:	Dark	
Remarks:	Present in the Kurnoul [sic] Campaign of 1839	
Intends to Reside:	Banbury	

BEW

	Abraham, private
	73rd Foot
Surname Variant	BEWS
21 June 1855	Discharged the Service Chatham
1855	Pension paid Jersey
	1/- per diem

1858	Pension paid 2nd Plymouth Pension District	
19 Aug 1859	Arrived per *'Sultana'*	
1869	Had a large tub stolen by Thomas Marshall	
1873	Pension increased to 1/3d. per diem for 7½ years service in the Enrolled Force	
24 Aug 1881	Assigned Perth Railway Block	
15 Dec 1883	Granted Fee Simple Perth Railway Block	
24 Jan 1885	For Outdoor Poor Relief	
June 1885	Abraham Bew — a Pensioner for Relief [SRO]	
1887	Died – buried East Perth Pioneer Cemetery	
Service and Personal Details:		
Place of Birth:	St Andrews Cardiff Glamorganshire	
Age on Attestation:	18 years	
Period of Service:	1832 — 1855	
Age on Discharge:	42 years	
Length of Service:	20 years 348 days	
Foreign Service:	Gibraltar	3 months
	North America	3 years 1 month
	South America	8 months
	Cape of Good Hope	7 years
Reason for Discharge:	Worn out	
Character:	Latterly Good	
Trade or Occupation:	Labourer	
Can Sign Name:	Yes	
Height:	5' 10½"	
Hair Colour:	Brown	
Eyes:	Hazel	
Complexion:	Fresh	
Distinguishing Marks:	Letter 'D' on left hand	
Intends to Reside:	Jersey	

BEWSHER	William, private [1264]	
	20th Foot	
Previous Regiment	57th Foot	
Surname Variant	BREWSHER;	
19 Apr 1859	Discharged the Service Chatham	
	1/1½d. per diem	
	Pension paid 2nd Plymouth Pension District	
1861	Residing 72 Pembroke St. Devonport Devon	
27 May 1863	Arrived per *'Clyde'*	
1864	private W Bewsher serving in the Pensioner Force at Perth contributed to the Greenough Fire Relief Fund	
Aug 1900	Died [late of Bunbury] — buried Picton	
1900	Grant of Probate	
Service and Personal Details:		
Place of Birth:	Lymington Hampshire	
Age on Attestation:	18 years 11 months	
Period of Service:	1837 — 1859	
Age on Discharge:	41 years	
Length of Service:	21 years 74 days	
Foreign Service:	Bermuda	5 years 190 days

	North America	6 years 56 days
	Crimea	1 year 310 days
	East Indies	314 days
Medal Entitlement:	Crimea with clasps; Turkish Crimean; Indian Mutiny	
Reason for Discharge:	Chronic Rheumatism and slightly wounded in the back of the neck by a musket ball at Lucknow	
Character:	Very Good	
Trade or Occupation:	Sawyer	
Can Sign Name:	Yes	
Height:	5' 7½"	
Hair Colour:	Light	
Eye Colour:	Grey	
Complexion:	Fair	
Married:	*c*1849 Eleanor Summers Canada	
Children:	Frederick George b. *c*1850 Canada m. *c*1874 Mary Walker Perth Elizabeth b. *c*1852 Canada m. *c*1867 George Griffin Bunbury William b. *c*1858 Plymouth Devon Edward b. *c*1860 Devonport Devon Harriett Martha b. *c*1862 d. *c*1877 Arthur b. *c*1868 Bunbury	

BIRCH Thomas, private
66th Foot

3 July 1855	Discharged the Service Chatham Pension paid 2nd West London Pension District 6d. per diem for 2 years	
10 July 1857	Arrived per *'Clara'* [1]	
1857	Appointed Assistant Warder	
1863	Died	
Service and Personal Details:		
Place of Birth:	Guildford Surrey	
Age on Attestation:	18 years	
Period of Service:	1841 — 1855	
Age on Discharge:	31 years 10 months	
Length of Service:	13 years 207 days	
Foreign Service:	Gibraltar	2 years 6 months
	West Indies	3 years 4 months
	Canada	3 years 4 months
Reason for Discharge:	Varicose Veins in the left leg	
Character:	Indifferent	
Trade or Occupation:	Labourer	
Can Sign Name:	Yes	
Height:	5' 7½"	
Hair Colour:	Dark Brown	
Eye Colour:	Hazel	
Complexion:	Fresh	
Intends to Reside:	Hollywell St., Westminster	

BIRCH	see — BREE Thomas, private EIC 1st Bombay Fusiliers
BIRD	John, Corporal 83rd Foot
18 Apr 1865	Discharged the Service Aldershot Pension paid Worcester 1/- per diem
1866	Pension paid Nottingham
1866	Worcester
1867	Leicester
9 Jan 1868	Arrived per *'Hougoumont'*
1869	Died — "Effects to brothers and sisters"

Service and Personal Details:

Place of Birth:	Lentwardine Herefordshire
Age on Attestation:	17 years 3 months
Period of Service:	1845 — 1865
Age on Discharge:	36 years 9 months
Length of Service:	18 years 340 days [excluding under age]
Foreign Service:	East Indies 12 years 320 days
Medal Entitlement:	Central India with Clasp
Reason for Discharge:	Unfit for further service
Character:	Very Good
Trade or Occupation:	Labourer
Can Sign Name:	Yes
Height:	5' 6¾"
Hair Colour:	Dark Brown
Eye Colour:	Grey
Complexion:	Fair
Intends to Reside:	Brand Hill Ludlow Shropshire

BISHOP	Charles, private RM £15/4/- per annum
1856	To South Australia from Western Australia
April 1856	To South Australia per *'Guyon'*
BISHOP	Thomas, Serjeant [2006] Royal Canadian Rifles
Previous Regiment	20th Foot
8 July 1862	Discharged the Service Chatham Pension paid Jersey 1/10d. per diem
1862	Pension paid Woolwich
28 Dec 1863	Arrived per *'Lord Dalhousie'*

The following two entries may not necessarily refer to Thomas Bishop EPG

30 June 1870	Fremantle Asylum Thomas Bishop and Carty Mcarthy [sic] at present time both men are of sound mind.
16July 1870	Comptroller General — Re local Pensioner: T. Bishop a Lunatic.

1875	Pension paid Western Australia
4 June 1878	Pension increased to 2/5½d. per diem for service in Enrolled Force
16 July 1885	Joined Enrolled Guard — stationed Perth
no date	Assigned Loc 1064 at Freshwater Bay
?Oct 1886	Application of Pensioner Thomas Bishop for grant of land of approx 9 acres
1887	Pensioner Serjeant Thomas Bishop asking for additional land grant at Butlers Swamp
Oct 1886	Secretary of State — Re. Application of Pensioner Thomas Bishop for Good Conduct Medal and gratuity.
1892	Residing Pensioners Barracks
Nov 1892	Died - buried East Perth Cemetery
	Freshwater Loc 1064 and 1065 to wife Annie

Service and Personal Details:

Place of Birth:	Wiltshire	
Age on Attestation:	18 years	
Period of Service:	1837 — 1862	
Age on Discharge:	43 years 3 months	
Length of Service:	25 years 27 days	
Foreign Service:	Bermuda	5 years 6 months
	North America	15 years 1 month
Reason for Discharge:	Length of Service	
Character:	Very Good	
Trade or Occupation:	Labourer	
Can Sign name:	Yes	
Height:	5' 7½"	
Hair Colour:	Brown	
Eye Colour:	Grey	
Complexion:	Fresh	
Intends to Reside:	Newcastle on Tyne	

BLANEY Thomas, gunner

	Coastal Brigade [6th Battery RA]
6 Nov 1866	Discharged the Service Woolwich
	Pension paid Armagh
	10d. per diem
1867	Pension paid Leeds
1867	Birmingham
9 Jan 1868	Arrived per *'Hougoumont'*
1869	Pension paid Calcutta
1870	Demerara

Service and Personal Details:

Place of Birth:	Dungannon Co. Tyrone	
Age on Attestation:	18 years	
Period of Service:	1845 — 1866	
Age on Discharge:	39 years 5 months	
Length of Service:	21 years 16 days	
Foreign Service:	Bermuda	4 years 8 months
Reason for Discharge:	Having completed 21 years service	

Character:	Very Good
Trade or Occupation:	Labourer
Can Sign Name:	Yes
Height:	5' 10"
Hair Colour:	Brown
Eye Colour:	Light Brown
Complexion:	Fair
Intends to Reside:	Dungannon

BLEWER William, private
24th Foot

13 Aug 1850	Discharged the Service Chatham Pension paid Essex 8d. per diem
24 May 1855	Arrived per *'Stag'*
Jan 1857	Contributed 2/- to the Florence Nightingale Fund
Nov 1857	Charged with appropriating a pocket book and contents for his own use. The Bench concurred with Mr Leake's defense [sic] that there was no case to put to a jury and directed the jury to acquit William Blewer
1858	To South Australia from Western Australia
1875	Pension paid Adelaide South Australia

Service and Personal Details:

Place of Birth:	Grays Tilbury Fort Essex
Age on Attestation:	20 years 5 months
Period of Service:	1845 — 1850
Age on Discharge:	26 years 10 months
Length of Service:	4 years 107 days
Foreign Service:	East Indies 3 years 4 months
Medal Entitlement:	Punjaub Campaign
Reason for Discharge:	Gunshot wound to the right foot in action at Chillianwallah
Character:	Good
Trade or Occupation:	Labourer
Can Sign Name:	blank; X his mark on Attestation
Height:	5' 8"
Hair Colour:	Brown
Eyes:	Hazel
Complexion:	Fresh
Intends to Reside:	Purfleet Essex

BLIGHT William, private
RM

1853	Serving in Royal Marines Plymouth Division
1856	Admitted to Out-Pension Pension paid Plymouth £9/4/- per annum
1858	Residing Exeter District
1861	County Constable residing Shelbear Devon
1863	Pension paid 2nd Plymouth Pension District
22 Dec 1865	Arrived per *'Vimiera'*

circa 1877	To South Australia
1897	Attended Memorial Service Hindmarsh Sth. Aust.
1898	Attended Memorial Day Adelaide
1899	SROWA — William Blight a pensioner — asking return of Land grant
1905	Died South Australia
Service and Personal Details:	
Place of Birth:	St Germans Cornwall
Year of Birth:	1824
Age on Attestation:	18 years
Marine Division:	Plymouth
Period Served:	1842 — 1856
Length of Service:	14 years 2 months 9 days [reckoned]
[15 years 9 months]	
Age on Discharge:	32 years
Reason for Discharge:	Invalided
Can Sign Name:	Yes
Trade or Occupation:	Labourer
Height:	5' 6½"
Complexion:	Freckled
Eye Colour:	Blue
Hair Colour:	Brown
Remarks:	The following information is from William Blight's Police Record of Service [there is no mention of this on his Royal Marine Record of Service]
From 1849 — 1853	he was coachman and groom to Colonel Bury Volunteered to join the medical staff in the Crimea and went out with 'D' Troop Royal Artillery Served at Scutari Hospital Injured when onboard the '*Great Tasmania*' in the Black Sea
Married:	Sept Qtr 1844 Sarah Rowse Stoke Dameral
Children:	Hannah b. *c*1846 Plymouth Devon Jane b. *c*1852 [March Qtr] Plymouth
Married:	Elizabeth
Children:	Thomas b. *c*1853 Devon Lawrence b. *c*1852 Devon Frederick b. *c*1858 Devon Alfred b. *c*1858 Devon John b. *c*1860 Devon Charles John b. *c*1867 Perth [mother Elizabeth Williams]

BLOOMER	Edward, bombardier EIC Bengal Artillery Out Pension No 587
Nov 1860	Discharged the Service
24 June 1861	Admitted to Out-Pension Pension paid 2nd Dublin Pension District 1/- per diem
1865	Pension paid 2nd Dublin Pension District

15 Aug 1865	Arrived per *'Racehorse'*
7 July 1868	Died aged 47
24 Jan 1871	Residents Office Fremantle To the Honorable Colonial Secretary. Report re: Ann Bloomer [wife of deceased Pensioner], Applying for herself and 3 boys viz, Christopher B. aged 8 years, James B. aged 6 and Richard B. aged 3, to be admitted to the Poor House

Service and Personal Details:

Where Born:	Knockbridge Co. Cavan
Trade or Occupation:	Labourer
Date Enlisted:	29 Feb 1844
Where Enlisted:	Edinburgh
Presidency:	Bengal
Length of Service:	18 years 8 months
Age on Discharge:	41 or 42 years [depending on record]
Character:	Very Good
Reason for Discharge:	Unfit for further service. Left leg broken on duty and constitution broken up by exposure in the field.
Medal Entitlement:	Capture of Delhi and Siege of Lucknow and was awarded 'batta' for both campaigns
Height:	5' 8¾"
Complexion:	Fair
Eye Colour:	Blue
Hair Colour:	Fair
Intends to Reside:	Chapel Izod West Dublin
Married:	?3.] Ann, Mary or Mary Ann Brady
Children:	Christopher b. *c*1863 m. *c*1888 Mary Jane Potter Perth James b. *c*1865 Richard b. *c*1868 Perth m. *c*1888 Jane White Perth

BLUNDEN	David, private 15th Foot
Surname Variants	BLUNDON; BLUNDELL; BLUNDREN
22 Feb 1849	Discharged the Service Brecon
13 Mar 1849	Admitted to Out-Pension Pension paid Southampton 7d. per diem for 3 years
18 Oct 1851	Arrived per *'Minden'*
1852	Pension ceased
1852	Appointed Night Warder
1872	Died aged 56

Service and Personal Details:

Place of Birth:	Ellisfield Basingstoke Hampshire
Age on Attestation:	23 years 1 month
Period of Service:	1839 — 1849
Age on Discharge:	32 years 4 months
Length of Service:	9 years 138 days

Reason for Discharge:	Inflammation of the lungs which started 1840, since then as always had cough
Character:	Good
Trade or Occupation:	Labourer
Can Sign Name:	Yes; X his mark on Attestation
Height:	5' 7½"
Hair Colour:	Brown
Eye Colour:	Grey
Complexion:	Fresh

BLYTHE

	James, private
	21st Foot
Surname Variant	BLYTH
Sept 1833	Arrived per *'Jane'*
31 July 1840	Discharged at own request
1841	a James Blythe was paid Constable expenses
1857	a James Blythe died at Bunbury

Service and Personal Details:

Place of Birth:	Forfar Dundee Scotland
Age on Enlistment:	19 years
Period of Service:	1831 — 1840
Date of Enlistment:	1831
Age on Discharge:	29 years
Length of Service:	9 years
Foreign Service:	Australian Colonies
Reason for Discharge:	Own Request
Character:	Good
Trade or Occupation:	Wheelwright
Remarks:	John Blyth has been a good and well conducted soldier

BODON

	Henry, private
	4th Foot
Surname Variant	BODEN
22 Feb 1849	Discharged the Service Winchester
27 Mar 1849	Admitted to Pension
	Pension paid Ballymena
	6d. per diem for 3 years
21 Dec 1852	Pension made permanent
10 Sept 1856	Arrived per *'Runnymede'*
1857	Assistant Warder Convict Establishment
July 1861	Died

Service and Personal Details:

Place of Birth:	Clooghill [sic] Antrim
Age on Attestation:	19 years 6 months
Period of Service:	1836 — 1849
Age on Discharge:	31 years 8 months
Length of Service:	12 years 54 days
Foreign Service:	East Indies 9 years 11 months
Reason for Discharge:	Impaired Constitution and Varicose Veins of the left leg

Character:	Good
Trade or Occupation:	Weaver
Can Sign Name:	Yes
Height:	5' 6"
Hair Colour:	Fair
Eyes:	Grey
Complexion:	Fair
Intends to Reside:	Belfast Co. Antrim

BOGUE	John, private [69]
	96th Foot
Surname Variants	BOAG; BOUGE; BOAGUE
22 Feb 1847	Arrived per *'Java'* with regiment
15 May 1849	Discharged the Service Perth West Australia
1890	Died 88

Service and Personal Details:

Place of Birth:	Hincham	
Age on Attestation:	16 years	
Period of Service:	1824 — 1849	
Age on Discharge:	43 years	
Length of Service:	14 years 9 days [after the age of 18 years and time deduction for Desertion]	
Foreign Service:	North America	9 years
	In Australia	7 years
Reason for Discharge:	Is worn out and unfit for service in India	
Character:	Indifferent but revised to Good	
Trade or Occupation:	Labourer	
Can Sign Name:	X his mark on discharge	
Height:	5' 6½"	
Hair Colour:	Dark Brown	
Eye Colour:	Blue	
Complexion:	Sallow	
Remarks:	Daughter Theresa married	
	m. 1863 Henry Webb Perth	
	m. 1866 William Loughlan Perth	
	m. 1886 William Gaunt Perth	
	m. 1893 George Edmund Leeder Perth	

BOLL	William, private
	8th Foot
Surname Variant	BALL
25 May 1852	Discharged the Service Chatham
	Pension paid Ballymena
	1/- per diem
18 July 1855	Arrived per *'Adelaide'*
Jan 1857	Contributed 2/- to the Florence Nightingale Fund
1857	To South Australia from Western Australia
1875	Pension paid Adelaide

Service and Personal Details:

Place of Birth:	Connor Ballymena Co. Antrim
Age on Enlistment:	18 years

Period of Service:	1831 — 1852	
Age on Discharge:	39 years	
Length of Service:	20 years 277 days	
Foreign Service:	West Indies	6 years 7 days
	North America	2 years 239 days
	East Indies	5 years 92 days
Reason for Discharge:	Hepatic Disease and Chronic Rheumatism	
Character:	Indifferent but latterly good	
Trade or Occupation:	Labourer	
Can Sign Name:	Yes	
Height:	5' 9"	
Hair Colour:	Red	
Eyes:	Hazel	
Complexion:	Fair	
Intends to Reside:	Ballymena Co. Antrim	

BOLTON

	Joseph, private [570]	
	73rd Foot	
25 Sept 1848	Discharged the Service Dublin	
	Pension paid Edinburgh	
	1/- per diem	
18 Oct 1851	Arrived per *'Minden'*	
1851	Serving in Police Force	
13 Feb 1864	Fremantle Residents Office — Recommendation: Catherine Bolton, an aged woman and wife of Joseph Bolton to be admitted to Poor House	
23 Jan 1864	Died	

Service and Personal Details:

Place of Birth:	Edinburgh Midlothian Scotland	
Age on Attestation:	19 years	
Period of Service:	1826 — 1848	
Age on Discharge:	40 years 9 months	
Length of Service:	21 years 81 days	
Foreign Service:	Gibraltar	2 years 8 months
	Malta	4 years 3 months
	Ionian Islands	3 years 10 months
	North America	3 years
Reason for Discharge:	Chronic Rheumatism and Intermittent Fever	
Character:	Bad	
Trade or Occupation:	Bookseller	
Can Sign Name:	Yes	
Height:	5' 8¼"	
Hair Colour:	Brown	
Eye Colour:	Hazel	
Complexion:	Fair	

BOND

	James, private [697]
	17th Foot
25 Sept 1849	Discharged the Service Chatham
	Pension paid Leicester
	1/- per diem
1 June 1850	Arrived per *'Scindian'*

	"Good Conduct gratuity of £5 paid by Commissariat until transferred to Staff Officer Pensions — Capt. Bruce"
1852	Deserted Enrolled Pensioner Force
1852	"Struck off List for desertion from Convict Guard in Western Australia"
1858	"Restored with pay and arrears for 6 years Good Conduct Medal returned"
1860	Pension paid Melbourne
Service and Personal Details:	
Place of Birth:	Hinckley [sic] Leicestershire
Age on Attestation:	18 years
Period of Service:	1828 — 1849
Age on Discharge:	39 years
Length of Service:	21 years 42 days
Foreign Service:	New South Wales 5 years 4 months East Indies 10 years 11 months
Medal Entitlement:	Good Conduct with gratuity; Afghan; Ghuzni and storming of fortress of Kelat;
Reason for Discharge:	Chronic Rheumatism
Conduct:	Very Good
Trade or Occupation:	Framework Knitter
Can Sign Name:	Yes
Height:	5' 11"
Hair Colour:	Sandy
Eye Colour:	Grey
Complexion:	Dark

BONNER	John, private 69th Foot
13 Jan 1852	Discharged the Service Chatham Pension paid 1st Cork Pension District 6d. per diem
18 July 1855	Arrived per *'Adelaide'*
1861	Charged with drunkenness
Apr 1864	"If Bonner is, as he says starving, I should imagine it to be entirely his own fault that he being so, being too lazy to work" [ACC36] Although the man is evidently of bad character he cannot be left to starve, therefore if he persists in his application for relief from the Govt., let Col. Bruce's suggestion be carried out by the Clerk of Works, finding some employment for Bonner either in the public garden or about the garden of the Colonial Hospital. In return for 1/- per day. Signed Hampton
2 Aug 1866	To his Excel. The Gov. Hampton — John Bonner and family plea for help. Letter from Col. Bruce that Bonner has periodically over past ten years applied for relief due to his and his wife's own misconduct
1878	Left Colony
1878	Pension paid Cork

Service and Personal Details:
Place of Birth: Athlone Westmeath
Age on Attestation: 17 years
Period of Service: 1836 — 1852
Age on Discharge: 32 years
Length of Service: 14 years 81 days
Foreign Service: West Indies 1 year 2 months
North America 3 years 6 months
Mediterranean 1 year 3 months
Reason for Discharge: Lumbago and General Debility

Character: Good and well conducted
Trade or Occupation: Tailor
Can Sign Name: Yes

Height: 5' 5¼"
Hair Colour: Light Brown
Eyes: Hazel
Complexion: Fair
Intends to Reside: Cork

BOOTH Samuel [James], private
35th Foot
24 May 1851 Discharged the Service Dublin
15 July 1851 Admitted to Pension
Pension paid Derby
9d or 6d per diem [depending on record]
30 Apr 1853 Arrived per *'Pyrenees'* [2]
Absent from colony with leave
1854 Liable to repay £15 allowance for cottage.
1858 Pension paid Melbourne
1876 Correspondence with W.O. regarding payment of pension

Service and Personal Details:
Place of Birth: St Marys Belper Derbyshire
Age on Attestation: 18 years
Period of Service: 1837 — 1851
Age on Discharge: 32 years 3 months
Length of Service: 14 years 108 days
Foreign Service: Mauritius 9 years 97 days
Reason for Discharge: Chronic Rheumatism and enlarged veins in both legs

Character: Good
Trade or Occupation: Labourer
Can Sign Name: X his mark on discharge

Height: 5' 10¼"
Hair Colour: Light Brown
Eyes: Grey
Complexion: Fair
Distinguishing Marks: Vaccine scar on right arm
Intends to Reside: Cow Hill Belper Derbyshire

BOTT Charles, private

	63rd Foot
27 Feb 1857	Discharged the Service Birr Barracks
24 Mar 1857	Admitted to Out-Pension
	Pension paid Birmingham
	8d. per diem
24 Nov 1858	Arrived per *'Edwin Fox'*
1863	Pension paid Perth Western Australia
24 Apr 1871	Residents Office Fremantle — Pensioner Charles Bott Admission to Colonial Hospital.
12 July 1873	Died - buried East Perth Cemetery

Service and Personal Details:

Place of Birth:	Birmingham Warwickshire	
Age on Attestation:	22 years 5 months	
Period of Service:	1839 — 1857	
Age on Discharge:	39 years 8 months	
Length of Service:	17 years 112 days	
Foreign Service:	East Indies	upwards of 6 years
Reason for Discharge:	Varicose Veins of both legs and Debility	
Character:	Very good	
Trade or Occupation:	Clockmaker	
Can Sign Name:	Yes	
Height:	5' 6¾"	
Hair Colour:	Dark Brown	
Eyes:	Hazel	
Complexion:	Fresh	
Remarks:	Mole spot on the breast	
Intends to Reside:	Birmingham	

BOURKE	Patrick, Corporal
	52nd Foot
Surname Variants	BURKE; BURK; BUCK
10 May 1853	Discharged the Service Dublin
	Pension paid Chatham
	1/4d. per diem
1855	Serving in West Kent Militia
1857	Pension paid Salisbury
31 Dec 1862	Arrived per *'York'*
1865	Pension paid Perth Western Australia
1868	Died

Service and Personal Details:

Place of Birth:	Cashel Tipperary	
Age on Attestation:	19 years	
Period of Service:	1832 — 1853	
Age on Discharge:	40 years	
Length of Service:	21 years 22 days	
Foreign Service:	Gibraltar	2 years 5 months
	West Indies	3 years 5 months
	North America	5 years 4 months
Reason for Discharge:	Appointed to serve on the Militia Staff	
Character:	Good and efficient	
Trade or Occupation:	Labourer	
Can Sign Name:	Yes on Discharge	

Height:	6'
Hair Colour:	Black
Eyes:	Hazel
Complexion:	Fair

BOX	Thomas, private 57th Foot
Previous Regiment	31st Foot
24 July 1855	Discharged the Service Chatham Pension paid 2nd Dublin Pension District 8d. per diem
1857	Pension paid Carlisle Served in Cumberland Militia
29 Jan 1862	Arrived per *'Lincelles'*
Oct 1867	Mrs Box, wife of Pensioner Box from 57th, has applied for relief
1878	Pension increased to 1/-½d. per diem for service in the Enrolled Force
1879	Died

Service and Personal Details:

Place of Birth:	St Nicholas Dublin	
Age on Attestation:	17 years 4 months	
Period of Service:	1846 — 1855	
Age on Discharge:	23 years 1 month	
Length of Service:	7 years 288 days	
Foreign Service:	Corfu & Ionian Isles	1 year 7 months
	"Army in the East"	7 months
Medal Entitlement:	Crimea	
Reason for Discharge:	Wounded in thigh at Inkerman	
Character:	Good	
Trade or Occupation:	Labourer	
Can Sign Name:	X his mark on discharge	
Height:	5' 6"	
Hair Colour:	Brown	
Eyes:	Grey	
Complexion:	Fresh	

BOYLE	Edward, private 86th Foot
26 July 1859	Discharged the Service Chatham Pension paid 2nd Belfast Pension District 9½d. per diem
28 Dec 1863	Arrived per *'Lord Dalhousie'*

1876	Dean of Perth: 'I beg leave to recommend James Boyle, aged 10 years, as a fit case for admission to the Boy's Swan Orphanage on the Government list. He is the son of Enrolled Military Pensioner Edward Boyle who now lies in the last stage of Consumption at the Military Hospital. The boy is homeless and the father without any means. I have received his daughter aged 17 years, as a temporary inmate of the Girls' Orphanage until she can be forwarded to a situation in York.'
Jan 1877	Died – buried East Perth Pioneer Cemetery
Service and Personal Details:	
Place of Birth:	Templemore Co. Tipperary
Age on Attestation:	18 years
Period of Service:	1836 — 1859
Age on Discharge:	40 years 7 months
Length of Service:	21 years 340 days
Foreign Service:	East Indies 15 years 11 months
Medal Entitlement:	Served in the Campaign in the Scind 1842/1843; present at the defence of the Residency near Hyderabad 1843; Present at the battle of Meanee 1843; Present at the Battle of Hyderabad 1843; Served in the campaign under Major DelaMotte in the Maharatta Country in 1844; Present at the taking of the Forts of ?Punalu and Powanghur in 1844
Reason for Discharge:	An old soldier suffering from Chronic Inflammation of the Liver the result of 10 years residence in India and is worn out
Character:	Good
Trade or Occupation:	Shoemaker
Can Sign Name:	X his mark on discharge
Height:	5' 7¾"
Hair Colour:	Brown
Eyes:	Grey
Complexion:	Fresh
Remarks:	Gunshot wound to left hip Hyderabad
Distinguishing Marks:	Pock-pitted
Intends to Reside:	Belfast

BOYNE	Thomas, private 86th Foot
Surname Variant	BYRNE
28 Mar 1854	Discharged the Service Chatham Pension paid 2nd Plymouth Pension District 1/- per diem
18 July 1855	Was to arrive per Convict Ship *'Adelaide'* "Died on voyage out from the effects of an accident"
Service and Personal Details:	
Place of Birth:	Tullow Co. Carlow
Age on Attestation:	18 years
Period of Service:	1832 — 1854

Age on Discharge:	39 years 6 months
Length of Service:	21 years 144 days
Foreign Service:	East Indies 9 years 9 months
Reason for Discharge:	Chronic pains and Dyspnoea caused by climate and military service
Character:	Good
Trade or Occupation:	Labourer
Can Sign Name:	X his mark on discharge
Height:	5' 10¼"
Hair Colour:	Brown
Eyes:	Hazel
Complexion:	Sallow
Distinguishing Marks:	Pock pitted
Intends to Reside:	Chatham

BRADLEY	John Alex, Serjeant [356]
	99th Foot
Previous Regiment	97th Foot
18 July 1865	Discharged the Service Cork
	Pension paid 1st Liverpool Pension District
	1/4½d. per diem
	Pension paid 1st Cork Pension District
22 Dec 1866	Arrived per *'Corona'*
1868	To Melbourne from Fremantle
1868	Pension paid Melbourne
Service and Personal Details:	
Place of Birth:	Leighton Bridge Carlow Ireland
Age on Attestation:	31 years 6 months [on enlistment with 99th Foot]
Period of Service:	1843 — 1865 [total service]
Age on Discharge:	40 years 1 month
Length of Service:	22 years 14 days [total service]
Foreign Service:	Ionian Isles 2 years 2 months
	Malta 1 year 7 months
	North America 4 years 8 months
	Turkey & Crimea no period given
Medal Entitlement:	Good Conduct and Long Service with gratuity; Crimea with clasp; Turkish Crimean
Reason for Discharge:	Own Request having served over 21 years
Character:	Very Good
Trade or Occupation:	Servant
Can Sign Name:	Yes
Height:	5' 7¾"
Hair Colour:	Brown
Eyes:	Brown
Complexion:	Fresh
Intends to Reside:	Liverpool Lancaster

BRAMLEY	John, private
	1st Foot
Surname Variant	BRAMLY
9 June 1853	Discharged the Service Birr
9 Aug 1853	Admitted to Out-Pension

	1/- per diem	
	Pension paid Nottingham	
18 July 1855	Arrived per *'Adelaide'*	
1858	To South Australia from Western Australia	
1875	Pension paid South Australia	
1888	Died	
Service and Personal Details:		
Place of Birth:	Alfreton Derbyshire	
Age on Attestation:	21 years	
Period of Service:	1832 — 1853	
Age on Discharge:	42 years 4 months	
Length of Service:	21 years 129 days	
Foreign Service:	Canada	7 years 2 months
	West Indies	2 years 5 months
Reason for Discharge:	General Debility caused by length of service	
Character:	Very Good	
Trade or Occupation:	Labourer	
Can Sign Name:	Yes	
Height:	5' 7"	
Hair Colour:	Light	
Eyes:	Brown	
Complexion:	Fresh	

BRANAGAN	Charles, private	
	31st Foot	
Previous Regiment	95th Foot	
Surname Variants	[some] BANAGHAN; BRANNAGAN; BRAMAGAN; BRAMNAGAN; BRANIGAN	
12 July 1845	Discharged the Service Chatham	
	Pension paid 1st Belfast Pension District	
	1/- per diem	
6 Apr 1854	Arrived per *'Sea Park'*	
10 Nov 1854	Died	
Service and Personal Details:		
Place of Birth:	St Johns Sligo	
Age on Attestation:	18 years	
Period of Service:	1823 — 1845	
Age on Discharge:	39 years	
Length of Service:	20 years 280 days	
Foreign Service:	East Indies	17 years
Medal Entitlement:	Afghan War	
Reason for Discharge:	Chronic Hepatitis	
Character:	Tolerably Good	
Trade or Occupation:	Sawyer	
Can Sign Name:	X his mark on discharge	
Height:	5' 6½	
Hair Colour:	Dark Brown	
Eyes:	Grey	
Complexion:	Sallow	
Intends to Reside:	Belfast	

BRANNAN	Edward, private 31st Foot
Surname Variants	[some] BRANNON; BRENNAN; BRANNION
31 Oct 1856	Admitted to Out-pension Pension paid 1st Manchester Pension District 8d. per diem
19 Aug 1859	Arrived per *'Sultana'*
1864	Corporal E Brennan serving in the Pensioner Force at Fremantle contributed to the Greenough Fire Relief Fund
1864	To South Australia from Fremantle per *'Europa'*
1865	Pension paid Adelaide
1876	Adelaide
Service and Personal Details:	
Place of Birth:	Salford Manchester
Age on Discharge:	19 years
Length of Service:	1 year 6 months
Foreign Service:	Crimea 7 months
Medal Entitlement:	Crimea with clasps
Reason for Discharge:	Incontinence of urine due to severe wound on the groin and upper part of left thigh
Character:	Good
Trade or Occupation:	Labourer
Height:	5' 6"
Hair Colour:	Brown
Eyes:	Blue
Complexion:	Fair
BREE	Thomas, private EIC 1st Bombay Fusiliers
Surname Variants	BRICE; BIRCH
Out Pension No 582	
6 June 1861	Admitted to Out-pension Pension paid Hull District 9d. per diem
1861	Pension paid Sligo Pension District
1862	Pension paid 2nd Glasgow Pension District
31 Dec 1862	Arrived per *'York'*
1865	Appointed Assistant Warder
1873	"In prison"
1889	Allocated Loc 235 at Cockburn Sound
30 Sept 1889	Ann Bree ?widow of Thomas Bree granted Cockburn Sound Loc 235 at Willagee Swamp
****	Pensioner increased to 1/- for campaign service
Service and Personal Details:	
Where Born:	Dromore Sligo or Skreen Sligo
Trade or Occupation:	Labourer
Age on Enlistment:	19 years
Date Attested:	1847
Where Enlisted:	Glasgow
Embarked India:	1847 per *'Boyne'*
Presidency:	Bombay

Length of Service: 15 years 3 months
Age on Discharge: 33 years 4 months or 34 [depending on record]
Reason for Discharge: Unfit for further service due to disease of the heart

Character: Fair
Medal Entitlement: Jellalabad; Punjaub with clasps for Goojerat; Mooltan; and Indian Mutiny

Height: 5' 6½"
Complexion: Fair
Eye Colour: Grey
Hair Colour: Fair
Intends to Reside: Hull Yorkshire

BRENNAN Eugene, private
95th Foot
3 July 1855 Discharged the Service Chatham
Pension paid Tralee
10d. per diem
1857 Pension paid Salisbury
1858 Dublin
19 Aug 1859 Arrived per *'Sultana'*
1863 To New South Wales from Fremantle
1892 Pension paid New South Wales
1905 W.O. correspondence with Under Secretary Sydney N.S. W. — Pension increased to 1/2d' per diem from 26th Jan 1905

Service and Personal Details:
Place of Birth: Kenmare Kerry
Age on Attestation: 21 years
Period of Service: 1847 — 1855
Age on Discharge: 29 years 4 months
Length of Service: 8 years 117
Foreign Service: Turkey & Crimea 11 months
Medal Entitlement: Crimea with clasp
Reason for Discharge: Wounded at the Battle of Alma — gunshot wound to the groin

Character: Very Good
Trade or Occupation: Labourer
Can Sign Name: Yes

Height: 5' 8¾"
Hair Colour: Sandy
Eyes: Grey
Complexion: Fresh
Remarks: Repatriated from Scutari
Intends to Reside: Kenmare Kerry

BRENNAN Michael, private
40th Foot
Surname Variant BRENNEN
17 Apr 1846 Discharged the Service Chatham
28 Apr 1846 Admitted to Out-Pension
1849 6d. per diem conditional for 3 years

1851	Pension made permanent
1865	Pension paid Kilkenny
15 Aug 1865	Arrived per *'Racehorse'*
1874	Pension increased to 9½d per diem
1875	Died – buried East Perth Pioneer Cemetery

Service and Personal Details:

Place of Birth:	Gowran Kilkenny
Age on Attestation:	18 years
Period of Service:	1835 — 1846
Age on Discharge:	28 years 3 months
Length of Service:	10 years 102 days
Foreign Service:	East Indies 8 years 304 days
Medal Entitlement:	2nd Afghan Campaign medal inscribed with 'Candahar' 'Ghuznee' 'Caboul'
Reason for Discharge:	Extensive ulceration of both legs
Character:	Good
Trade or Occupation:	Labourer
Can Sign Name:	blank
Height:	5' 7¾"
Hair Colour:	Light Brown
Eyes:	Blue
Complexion:	Fresh
Intends to Reside:	Kilkenny

BRENNAN Patrick, private
6th Foot

Previous Regiment	20th Foot
17 Dec 1845	Discharged the Service Mullingar
10 Feb 1846	Admitted to Out-Pension
	Pension paid Kilkenny
	1/- per diem
25 Oct 1850	Arrived per *'Hashemy'*
1851	Assigned land Bunbury
24 Mar 1855	Died

Service and Personal Details:

Place of Birth:	Comer Kilkenny
Age on Attestation:	17 years
Period of Service:	1823 — 1845
Age on Discharge:	40 years
Length of Service:	21 years 192 days
Foreign Service:	East Indies 18 years 8 months
Reason for Discharge:	Chronic Rheumatism, and general debility
Character:	Indifferent
Trade or Occupation:	Labourer
Height:	5' 7"
Hair Colour:	Brown
Eyes:	Grey
Complexion:	Dark

BRINDLEY Henry, private
2nd Foot

24 July 1860	Discharged the Service Chatham
1860	Pension paid Athlone
1861	Birmingham
	1/1d. per diem
31 Dec 1862	Arrived per *'York'*
1868	Died
20 Jan 1899	Victoria Loc 9 Grant awarded to his widow Kate Miller

Service and Personal Details:

Place of Birth:	Macclesfield Chestershire	
Age on Attestation:	21 years	
Period of Service:	1839 — 1860	
Age on Discharge:	42 years 1 month	
Length of Service:	20 years 202 days	
Foreign Service:	East Indies	5 years 11 months
	Cape of Good Hope	8 years 4 months
Medal Entitlement:	Good Conduct with gratuity of £5	
Reason for Discharge:	Worn out from service and climate	
Character:	Very Good	
Trade or Occupation:	Tailor	
Can Sign Name:	Yes	
Height:	5' 7¼"	
Hair Colour:	Light Brown	
Eyes:	Grey	
Complexion:	Fresh	
Intends to Reside:	Athlone	

BRISTER	Henry, Serjeant
	66th Foot
18 July 1856	Discharged the Service Plymouth Citadel
19 July 1856	Pension paid Plymouth
	1/6½d. per diem
10 Sept 1856	Arrived per *'Runnymede'*

Service and Personal Details:

Place of Birth:	Hammersmith London Middlesex	
Age on Attestation:	19 years	
Period of Service:	1835 — 1856	
Age on Discharge:	40 years	
Length of Service:	21 years and 4 days	
Foreign Service:	Canada	2 years 5 months
Reason for Discharge:	About to embark for Australia in charge of Convicts	
Character:	Good	
Trade or Occupation:	Labourer	
Can Sign Name:	Yes	
Height:	5' 8"	
Hair Colour:	Brown turning Grey	
Eyes:	Grey	
Complexion:	Dark	
Intends to Reside:	Australia	

BRITT	Patrick, private	
	90th Foot	
Previous Regiment	87th Foot	
26 Sept 1848	Discharged the Service Chatham	
	Pension paid Kilkenny	
	1/- per diem	
25 Oct 1850	Arrived per *'Hashemy'*	
1851	Employed in Convict Establishment	
1860	Pension paid Adelaide	
1875	South Australia	
Service and Personal Details:		
Place of Birth:	St Patrick Kilkenny	
Age on Attestation:	18 years	
Period of Service:	1827 — 1848	
Age on Discharge:	39 years	
Length of Service:	21 years 9 days	
Foreign Service:	Ceylon	3 years 7 months
	Mauritius	3 months
	Cape of Good Hope	1 year 9 months
Reason for Discharge:	Severe palpitations of the heart	
Character:	Very Good	
Trade or Occupation:	Labourer	
Can Sign Name:	Yes	
Height:	5' 6"	
Hair Colour:	Grey	
Eyes:	Hazel	
Complexion:	Fresh	
Intends to Reside:	Kilkenny	

BRITT	Thomas, gunner and driver	
	RA 3rd Battalion	
1851	Residing Charlton Greenwich	
14 Oct 1851	Discharged the Service Woolwich	
	Pension paid Woolwich	
	1/- per diem	
14 Nov 1854	W.O. correspondence — "Thomas Britt for Western Australia with family"	
Service and Personal Details:		
Place of Birth:	St Margarets Kent	
Age on Attestation:	17 years	
Period of Service:	1829 — 1851	
Age on Discharge:	39 years 10 months	
Length of Service:	21 years 287 days	
Foreign Service:	Ceylon	8 years 3 months
Reason for Discharge:	Chronic Rheumatism	
Character:	Exemplary	
Trade or Occupation:	Labourer	
Can Sign Name:	Yes	
Height:	5' 9"	
Hair Colour:	Brown	
Eyes:	Hazel	

Complexion:	Fair
Married:	Margaret
Children:	Mary Anne b. *c*1839 Ireland
	Sarah b. *c*1842 Colombo East Indies
	Margaret b. *c*1845 Trincomalee East Indies

BRITTON	Robert, private
	83rd Foot
Surname Variants	BRITTAIN; BRITON
30 Dec 1856	Discharged the Service Chatham
	Pension paid 2nd Glasgow Pension District
	6d. per diem
1858	Pension paid Paisley
8 June 1858	Arrived per *'Lord Raglan'*
1859	Appointed Assistant Warder
1859	Warder in charge of the Claisebrook party of prisoners
1870	To Bunbury per *'Wild Wave'*
?1 Feb 1872	Died WO correspondence G84848 — S.O.P. in reply — "Man died"
Feb 1872	Died - Buried East Perth Pioneer Cemetery

Service and Personal Details:	
Place of Birth:	Renfrew Scotland
Age on Attestation:	18 years
Period of Service:	1837 — 1856
Age on Discharge:	37 years 5 months
Length of Service:	17 years 262 days
Foreign Service:	North America 5 years
	East Indies 6 years 9 months
Reason for Discharge:	Disease of the Heart caused by military service
Character:	Latterly good
Trade or Occupation:	Dyer
Can Sign Name:	Yes
Height:	5' 9"
Hair Colour:	Red
Eyes:	Blue
Complexion:	Fair

BROADBROOK	John, Corporal
	69th Foot
Surname Variants	BROADHOOK; BROADHAK
31 Mar 1857	Discharged the Service Chatham
	Pension paid Fermoy
	10d. per diem
1859	Pension paid Waterford
1860	Clonmel
9 June 1862	Arrived per *'Norwood'* [1]
23 Aug 1862	Died

Service and Personal Details:	
Place of Birth:	St Mary Youghal Cork
Age on Attestation:	18 years 6 months

Period of Service:	1838 — 1857	
Age on Discharge:	36 years 8 months	
Length of Service:	16 years 292 days	
Foreign Service:	Mediterranean	3 years 4 months
Reason for Discharge:	Chronic Cough and shortness of breath	
Character:	Generally good	
Trade or Occupation:	Cabinet Maker	
Can Sign Name:	Yes	
Height:	5' 7½"	
Hair Colour:	Sandy	
Eyes:	Grey	
Complexion:	Fresh	
Intends to Reside:	Youghall Cork	

BROADLEY

	James, private [1607]	
	64th Foot	
Surname Variant	BRADLEY	
25 Sept 1860	Discharged the Service Canterbury	
	Pension paid 2nd Glasgow Pension District	
	8d. per diem	
15 Apr 1864	Arrived per *'Clara'* [2]	
1865	"Left colony without leave — pension stopped"	
12 Apr 1865	Pension re-commenced and paid Madras	
1865	Pension paid Madras	
1866	Madras	
Service and Personal Details:		
Place of Birth:	Barony Glasgow Lanarkshire	
Age on Attestation:	19 years	
Period of Service:	1839 — 1860	
Age on Discharge:	40 years	
Length of Service:	21 years 19 days	
Foreign Service:	Jamaica	6 months
	North America	2 years ? months
	East Indies	11 years 4 months
Medal Entitlement:	Persia with clasp	
Reason for Discharge:	His having completed 21 years service	
Character:	Latterly indifferent	
Trade or Occupation:	Labourer	
Can Sign Name:	Yes	
Height:	5' 8"	
Hair Colour:	Black	
Eyes:	Grey	
Complexion:	Dark	
Intends to Reside:	Glasgow	

BROPHY

	James, private
	41st Foot
Previous Regiment	6th Foot
15 May 1854	Discharged the Service Templemore
13 June 1854	Admitted to Out-Pension
	Pension paid Jersey
	7d. per diem for 3 years [to be reviewed]

18 July 1855	Arrived per *'Adelaide'*
Sept 1855	Charged with military offence
1855	Pension paid Adelaide
1860	Manchester
1864	Pension made Permanent

Service and Personal Details:

Place of Birth:	Mount Mellick Co. Queens
Age on Attestation:	22 years
Period of Service:	1839 — 1854
Age on Discharge:	37 years
Length of Service:	15 years 6 days
Foreign Service:	East Indies 3 years 11 months
Medal Entitlement:	Medal for service in Afghanistan
Reason for Discharge:	Chronic Catarrh
Character:	For the last 7 years his character has been good
Trade or Occupation:	Stuff Weaver
Can Sign Name:	Yes
Height:	5' 5¾"
Hair Colour:	Dark Brown
Eyes:	Grey
Complexion:	Dark

BROWN Denis, private
4th Foot

Surname Variant	BROWNE
13 Sept 1853	Discharged the Service Pension paid 1st Cork Pension District 6d. per diem
10 Sept 1856	Arrived per *'Runnymede'*
1858	Stationed Rottnest
1865	a Dennis [sic] Brown Pensioner died aged 38

Service and Personal Details:

Place of Birth:	St Nicholas Cork
Age on Attestation:	20 years
Period of Service:	1839 — 1853
Age on Discharge:	33 years
Length of Service:	13 years 13 days
Foreign Service:	East Indies 7 years 8 months
Reason for Discharge:	Ulceration of the back of the right thigh
Character:	Very Good
Trade or Occupation:	Servant
Can Sign Name:	Yes
Height:	5' 6½"
Hair Colour:	Black
Eyes:	Grey
Complexion:	Sallow
Intends to Reside:	Cork

BROWN James, gunner & driver
RA 6th Battalion

8 July 1851	Discharged the Service Woolwich

	Pension paid 2nd Glasgow Pension District	
	1/- per diem	
1851	Pension paid 1st Glasgow Pension District	
1851	2nd Dublin Pension District	
1853	Jersey	
24 May 1855	Arrived per *'Stag'*	
	Allocated West Guildford Lot P116 of 2 acres	
8 Sept 1863	Died	
Service and Personal Details:		
Place of Birth:	Rathdrum Wicklow	
Age on Attestation:	18 years	
Period of Service:	1830 — 1851	
Age on Discharge:	39 years	
Length of Service:	21 years 21 days	
Foreign Service:	West Indies	5 years 6 months
	Mauritius	8 years 6 months
Reason for Discharge:	Chronic Rheumatism	
Character:	Very Good	
Trade or Occupation:	Labourer	
Can Sign Name:	Yes	
Height:	5' 9¼"	
Hair Colour:	Dark Brown	
Eyes:	Blue	
Complexion:	Swarthy	

BROWN	John, private	
	92nd Foot	
15 May 1848	Discharged the Service Limerick	
11 July 1848	Admitted to pension	
	Pension paid 2nd Edinburgh Pension District	
	1/- per diem	
31 Aug 1853	Arrived per *'Phoebe Dunbar'*	
31 Dec 1857	Assigned Bunbury Lot P2	
27 Apr 1863	Application for Title to Bunbury Lot P2	
3 Feb 1875	Died	
		Service and Personal Details:
Place of Birth:	Dalmeny Linlithgow	
Age on Attestation:	19 years	
Period of Service:	1827 — 1848	
Age on Discharge:	40 years	
Length of Service:	21 years 63 days	
Foreign Service:	Gibraltar	1 year 9 months
	Malta	5 years 4 months
	West Indies	2 years 10 months
Reason for Discharge:	Worn out from length of service	
Character:	Good	
Trade or Occupation:	Labourer	
Can Sign Name:	Yes	
Height:	5' 7"	
Hair Colour:	Dark Brown	
Eyes:	Grey	

Complexion:	Dark
Children:	John — a pensioner's child on board *'Phoebe Dunbar'*
BROWN	John, private
	RM
3 May 1849	Admitted to Out-Pension
	£13/12/- per annum
1852	Pension paid Leicester
Oct 1852	To WA as Convict Guard [WO22/42]
7 Feb 1853	Arrived per *'Dudbrook'*
	Schoolmaster Pensioner Village
1855	Charged with military offence
Jan 1855	Found guilty of feloniously shooting at Ann Buckley at Port Gregory. Sentenced to 2 years imprisonment with hard labour
BROWN	Michael, private
	22nd Foot
27 Mar 1869	Discharged the Service Chatham
11 Apr 1869	Admitted to Out-Pension
	Pension paid Limerick
	1/2½d. per diem
1870	Pension paid Cork
1872	Cardiff
1872	Gloucester
1873	Greenwich
19 Feb 1874	Arrived per *'Naval Brigade'*
11 Nov 1880	Joined Enrolled Guard — stationed Perth
1881	Pension increased to 1/3d. per diem for service in the Enrolled Force
4 July 1881	Assigned Perth Town Lot 120/V
1881	Application for 150 [sic] acres at North Beach for Michael Brown [Pensioner]
17 Nov 1883	Granted Fee Simple for Perth Town Lot 120/V
June 1897	Residing Perth
1900	Died
Service and Personal Details:	
Place of Birth:	Croome [sic] Co. Limerick
Age on Attestation:	18 years
Period of Service:	1846 — 1869
Age on Discharge:	40 years 3 months
Length of Service:	22 years 87 days reckoned
Foreign Service:	East Indies 7 years 2 months
Medal Entitlement:	Long Service with gratuity of £5, according to newspaper dated 24th Feb 1900 he was also awarded a medal for North West Frontier and was wearing it at the time of his horrific and untimely death
Reason for Discharge:	Own Request after 22 years service
Character:	Very Good
Trade or Occupation:	Shoemaker
Can Sign Name:	X his mark on discharge

Height:	5' 9"
Hair Colour:	Fair
Eyes:	Blue
Complexion:	Fresh
Intends to Reside:	Croomer [sic] Limerick

BROWN	Richard, private [573]
	6th Dragoons
18 Nov 1848	Discharged the Service Dublin
9 Jan 1849	Admitted to Out-Pension
	Pension paid 1st Dublin Pension District
	6d. per diem for 2½ years
1849	Pension paid Enniskillen
	Manchester
	Enniskillen
25 Oct 1850	Arrived per *'Hashemy'*
31 July 1851	"Detected having unnatural connection with a mare at Perth. Escaped from prison. and ordered to be struck off the Roll" [War Office Letter N° 131060/1]

Service and Personal Details:	
Place of Birth:	Co. Fermanagh
Age on Attestation:	19 years
Period of Service:	1838 — 1848
Age on Discharge:	28 years 11 months
Length of Service:	9 years 339 days
Reason for Discharge:	Extensive Varicose Veins
Character:	Good
Trade or Occupation:	Labourer
Can Sign Name:	Yes
Height:	5' 9"
Hair Colour:	Brown
Eyes:	Blue
Complexion:	Sallow

BROWN	Samuel, private
	53rd Foot
Previous Regiment	52nd Foot
19 Nov 1861	Discharged the Service Chatham
	Pension paid London
	8d. per diem
27 May 1863	Arrived per *'Clyde'*
1865	Pension paid Perth Western Australia
1866	Appointed Assistant Warder
1868	Pension paid London
1869	Kings Lynn

Service and Personal Details:	
Place of Birth:	Walworth Surrey
Age on Attestation:	18 years
Period of Service:	1852 — 1861
Age on Discharge:	27 years 3 months

Length of Service:	9 years 45 days
Foreign Service:	East Indies 4 years 6 months
Medal Entitlement:	Indian Mutiny
Reason for Discharge:	Wounded by bullet in the back of neck at Cawnpore and sword thrust in back at Lucknow
Character:	Good
Trade or Occupation:	Carpenter
Can Sign Name:	Yes
Height:	5' 8½"
Hair Colour:	Light Brown
Eyes:	Grey
Complexion:	Fair
Intends to Reside:	London Middlesex

BROWN Thomas, Colour Serjeant
17th Foot

Previous Regiment	6th Foot
12 Oct 1847	Discharged the Service Chatham Pension paid Guernsey 1/10d. per diem
May 1850	Pension increased to 2/- per diem
25 Oct 1850	Arrived per *'Hashemy'*
1863	Residing in Perth District
1873	Correspondence with W.O. The request for awarding an increase of pension due to service in the Western Australian Enrolled Force refused because the man is already in receipt of the maximum rate
1875	Ceased to draw pay in the Enrolled Pensioner Force
1880	Died Fremantle aged 77

Service and Personal Details:

Place of Birth:	Warsall [sic] Staffordshire
Age on Attestation:	20 years
Period of Service:	1826 — 1847
Age on Discharge:	43 years 9 months
Length of Service:	21 years 111 days
Foreign Service:	East Indies 20 years 2 months
Reason for Discharge:	Worn out and Chronic Cough
Character:	Exemplary
Trade or Occupation:	Labourer
Can Sign Name:	Yes
Height:	5' 7"
Hair Colour:	Brown
Eyes:	Grey
Complexion:	Sallow
Intends to Reside:	Ipswich

BROWN William, private
64th Foot

Previous Regiments	17th Foot; 78th Foot

27 Aug 1861	Discharged the Service Chatham Pension paid 1st Cork Pension District 9d. per diem
28 Dec 1863	Arrived per *'Lord Dalhousie'*
1872	a William Brown residing at Fremantle
June 1873	Convicted at Fremantle of stealing one pair of lasts and 2 pairs of slippers
9 Jan 1874	Perth Poor House — William Brown, Pensioner charged with deserting his five children now in Poor House
circa March 1874	Transferred from Fremantle to 1st Perth
1874	Charged with neglecting to support his five children
Dec 1874	Convicted Perth Police Court of assaulting his wife and sent to prison for one month
Jan 1875	In prison for 21 days for drunk and incapable Half pension suspended and rest given to children during his imprisonment
Jan 1881	Pension increased to 1/2d. per diem for service in the Enrolled Force
Nov 1881	Pension reduced to 11d. per diem as his service in the Enrolled Force amended from 11 years to 5 years
18 Dec 1883	Granted Perth Town Lot 270/Y
1883	Pensioner William Brown — to be relieved of the cost of maintenance of his children in the Roman Catholic Orphanage
1886	Died
Service and Personal Details:	
Place of Birth:	St Marys Shandon Cork
Age on Attestation:	18 years
Period of Service:	1839 — 1861
Age on Discharge:	39 years 7 months
Length of Service:	20 years 328 days
Foreign Service:	East Indies 20 years 3 months
Medal Entitlement:	Persian Campaign 1856/7; Indian [Bengal] Mutiny with clasp 1857
Reason for Discharge:	Length of service and impaired health
Character:	Latterly good
Trade or Occupation:	Shoemaker
Can Sign Name:	X his mark on discharge
Height:	5' 6"
Hair Colour:	Black
Eyes:	Hazel
Complexion:	Fresh
Intends to Reside:	Cork

BROWNE	William, private [520] 13th Dragoons
Surname Variant	BROWN
10 Oct 1843	Discharged the Service Chatham Pension paid Marlborough 6d. per diem

1845	Pension paid Trowbridge
1849	Falkland Islands
1853	Trowbridge
29 Jan 1862	Arrived per *'Lincelles'*
Aug 1863	Died - buried East Perth Pioneer Cemetery
	"Balance of pension unclaimed"

Service and Personal Details:	
Place of Birth:	Marlborough Wiltshire
Age on Attestation:	24 years
Period of Service:	1828 — 1843
Age on Discharge:	40 years [39 years 2 months]
Length of Service:	15 years 82 days
Foreign Service:	East Indies 11 years 5 days
Reason for Discharge:	Worn out and Hernia
Character:	Good and efficient
Trade or Occupation:	Bricklayer
Can Sign Name:	Yes
Height:	5' 10¾"
Hair Colour:	Brown
Eyes:	Grey
Complexion:	Fresh
Intends to Reside:	Marlborough

BRUCE	Robert John, private [Military Immigrant]
	2nd Dragoons
3 Oct 1846	Discharged the Service Newbridge
10 Nov 1846	Admitted to Out-Pension
1893	Died aged 72

Service and Personal Details:	
Place of Birth:	Leith Edinburgh
Age on Attestation:	19 years
Period of Service:	1841 — 1846
Age on Discharge:	24 years
Length of Service:	4 years 323 days
Reason for Discharge:	Varicose Veins left leg
Character:	Indifferent
Trade or Occupation:	Labourer
Can Sign Name:	Yes
Height:	5' 9¾"
Hair Colour:	Dark Brown
Eyes:	Grey
Complexion:	Fresh

BRYAN	Thomas, Serjeant
96th Foot	
18 Sept 1859	Discharged the Service Manchester
11 Oct 1859	Admitted to Out-Pension
	Pension paid Lough
	1/7d. per diem
	Pension paid while serving in Lough Militia
1860	Pension paid Newry

1861	Preston
27 May 1863	Arrived per *'Clyde'*
circa June 1874	Transferred from 2nd Perth Pension District to 1st Perth Pension District
1878	Pension increased to 2/1d. per diem for service in the Enrolled Force
1879	Pension paid Perth Western Australia
1879	Transferred to Melbourne
1907	W.O. correspondence

Service and Personal Details:

Place of Birth:	St John's Well Kilkenny Co. Kilkenny	
Age on Attestation:	16 years	
Period of Service:	1836 — 1859	
Age on Discharge:	none given	
Length of Service:	21 years 83 days	
Foreign Service:	Australia	7 years 5 months
East Indies	5 years 10 months	
Gibraltar	10 months	
Reason for Discharge:	Own Request having served over 21 years	
Character:	Very Good	
Trade or Occupation:	Labourer	
Can Sign Name:	Yes	
Height:	5' 8"	
Hair Colour:	Light Brown	
Eyes:	Grey	
Complexion:	Fresh	
Married:	*c*1846 Deborah Phillips Tasmania	
Children:	Rebecca b. *c*1846 Tasmania m. *c*1878 William Richard Smith Perth John Joseph [Tom/Thomas] b.1852 Lahore India m. *c*1878 Annie Buggins Fremantle Michael b. *c*1854 m. *c*1877 Ellen McDonnell [sic] Perth Margaret [born at Aldershot] Hampshire Thomas William b. *c*1861 m. *c*1883 Ellen Forbes Tasmania Katherine Alfred b. *c*1866 married Adeline Harriet [according to his obituary — younger brother of Thomas Bryan printer of Perth W.A.]	

BRYCE	James, private 26th Foot
Surname Variant	BRICE
19 Feb 1861	Discharged the Service Dublin
5 Mar 1861	Admitted to Out-Pension Pension paid Paisley 9d. per diem
15 Aug 1865	Arrived per *'Racehorse'*
1866	Stationed Rottnest Island

1878	Pension increased to 11½d. per diem for service in the Enrolled Force
24 Aug 1881	Assigned Perth Railway Block Lot 146/V
15 Dec 1883	Granted Fee Simple Perth Railway Block Lot 146/V
Dec 1885	Superintendent of Poor Houses recommends Pensioner James Bryce, for outdoor relief
1886	In Mt Eliza Invalid Depot
1888	Died aged 69 at Mount Eliza Invalid Depot

Service and Personal Details:

Place of Birth:	Paisley Renfrewshire	
Age on Attestation:	20 years	
Period of Service:	1840 — 1861	
Age on Discharge:	41 years	
Length of Service:	21 years 16 days	
Foreign Service:	East Indies	1 year 3 months
China	1 year 6 months	
Gibraltar	3 years 2 months	
Canada	1 year 6 months	
Bermuda	4 years 11 months	
Reason for Discharge:	Own Request having completed 21 years service	
Character:	Good	
Trade or Occupation:	Weaver	
Can Sign Name:	Yes	
Height:	5' 6¾"	
Hair Colour:	Fair	
Eyes:	Grey	
Complexion:	Fair	
Intends to Reside:	12 Stevenson Street Paisley Scotland	

BRYNE see — BOYNE Thomas, private
86th Foot

BUCK see — BOURKE Patrick, Corporal
52nd Foot

BUCKLEY Jeremiah, gunner EIC
Bombay Artillery 1st Battalion — 2nd Comp.
Out Pension No 273

Dec 1843	Discharged the Service
1844	Embarked UK per '*Thomas Coutts*'
15 May 1844	Admitted to Out-Pension Pension paid Cork Pension District 9d. per diem
1849	Pension paid 1st East London Pension District
1852	2nd East London Pension District
7 Feb 1853	Arrived per '*Dudbrook*'
1873	Settled on Greenough Flats
4 May 1874	Received Title to Greenough Locs G19 and G20
1876	Died aged 67

Service and Personal Details:

Where Born:	Cork

Trade or Occupation:	Labourer
Age on Enlistment:	19 years
Date Enlisted:	15th Sept 1829
Where Enlisted:	Cork
Embarked India:	6th Jan 1829 per '*Herefordshire*'
Presidency:	Bombay
Length of Service:	15 years 3 months
Age on Discharge:	34 years
Character:	Good
Reason for Discharge:	Diseased glands in neck and injury of the head
Height:	5' 7¾"
Complexion:	Fresh [when enlisted]
	Dark [when discharged]
Visage:	Round
Eye Colour:	Blue
Hair Colour:	Sandy Red
Remarks:	Transferred to Horse Brigade January 1832
Married:	Anne [wife aged 24 on 1851 census]
Children:	Ellen b. *c*1850 Lambeth
	Margaret b. *c*1851 Wapping St Georges

BUCKLEY Lawrence [Laurence], private

74th Foot	
Previous Regiment	25th Foot
14 July 1857	Discharged the Service Chatham
	Pension paid Perth Scotland
	1/- per diem
1857	Pension paid 2nd North London Pension District
1860	Pension paid Deptford
31 Dec 1862	Arrived per '*York*'
1864	private J L Buckley serving in the Pensioner Force at Fremantle District contributed to the Greenough Fire Relief Fund
11 Aug 1867	Died

Service and Personal Details:

Place of Birth:	Rathkeal Limerick	
Age on Attestation:	21 years	
Period of Service:	1836 — 1857	
Age on Discharge:	42 years	
Length of Service:	20 years 293 days	
Foreign Service:	Cape of Good Hope	2 years 4 months
	East Indies	14 years 3 months
Reason for Discharge:	Old and inactive from length of service	
Character:	Very Good	
Trade or Occupation:	Labourer	
Can Sign Name:	Yes	
Height:	5' 7"	
Hair Colour:	Brown	
Eyes:	Grey	
Complexion:	Fresh	
Intends to Reside:	No 1 Munday's Yard Leather or Ladder Lane St Andrew's London or Newcastle Limerick	

BUCKLEY	Timothy, private
	61st Foot
20 Nov 1860	Discharged the Service
	Pension paid Bristol East Wales Pension District
	11d. per diem
1861	Pension paid Cavan
15 Apr 1864	Arrived per *'Clara'* [2]
1865	To Sydney from Western Australia
1865	Pension paid Auckland New Zealand
1899	Correspondence with War Office

Service and Personal Details:

Place of Birth:	Mallow Cork
Age on Attestation:	18 years 1 month
Period of Service:	1839 — 1860
Age on Discharge:	39 years 3 months
Length of Service:	21 years 9 days
Foreign Service:	East Indies 13 years 6 months
Medal Entitlement:	Punjaub with clasps; Indian Mutiny with clasp
Reason for Discharge:	At his own request having completed 21 years service and loss of sight of the left eye from ophthalmia. Slightly wounded by a musket ball Delhi 1857
Character:	Good
Trade or Occupation:	Shoemaker
Can Sign Name:	Yes
Distinguishing Marks:	Pock pitted
Intends to Reside:	Swansea
Height:	5' 7½
Hair Colour:	Dark Brown
Eyes:	Grey
Complexion:	Fresh

BULL	Edward[Edwin], private
	35th Foot
Previous Regiments	24th Foot; St Helena Corps
Surname Variant	BALL
May 1859	Discharged the Service Chatham
7 June 1859	Admitted to Out-Pension
	Pension paid South London
	10d. per diem
11 Feb 1861	Arrived per *'Palmeston'*
1865	Pension paid Western Australia
1867	a Corporal Ball [sic] of North Fremantle gave evidence at a trial
May 1868	Died Fremantle

Service and Personal Details:

Place of Birth:	Marylebone Middlesex
Age on Attestation:	18 years
Period of Service:	1838 — 1859
Age on Discharge:	38 years 2 months
Length of Service:	21 years 11 days

Foreign Service:	America	3 years 2 months
	St Helena	6 years 1 month
Reason for Discharge:	Having completed 21 years service	
Character:	Very good	
Trade or Occupation:	Labourer	
Can Sign Name:	Yes	
Height:	5' 7"	
Hair Colour:	Brown	
Eyes:	Hazel	
Complexion:	Fair	
Distinguishing Marks:	Scar on right cheek	
Intends to Reside:	London	

BUNTER Luke, private
RM

1855	Admitted to Out-Pension £21/12/- per annum
1868	Residing Black Flats Geraldton
Nov 1891	Died aged 79 Geraldton

Service and Personal Details:

Place of Birth:	Beadpole [sic] Bridport Dorsetshire
Age on Attestation:	19 years
Marine Division:	Plymouth
Period Served:	1833 — 1855
Length of Service:	21 years 1 month
Reason for Discharge:	Length of Service
Trade or Occupation:	Labourer
Can Sign Name:	Yes
Remarks:	Married — 2 children on discharge
Height:	5' 7¾
Hair Colour:	Light
Eyes:	Hazel
Complexion:	Fresh
Married:	*c*1847 Jane Simmons Dorset
Children:	Sarah Ann b. *c*1849 Devon m. *c*1866 Michael Murphy Greenough Mary b. *c*1851 Dorset m. *c*1870 William Herbert Greenough James b. *c*1856 Dorset m. *c*1877 Sarah Ann More Northampton

BURGESS William, private
Rifle Brigade

12 Oct 1852	Discharged the Service Chatham 1/- per diem
14 Aug 1854	Arrived per *'Ramillies'*
1861	Departed Western Australia for England
1861	Pension paid 2nd West London Pension District
1876	Admitted to Chelsea Workhouse

Service and Personal Details:

Place of Birth:	Bapchild Kent	
Age on Attestation:	23 years 5 months	
Period of Service:	1830 — 1852	
Age on Discharge:	45 years	
Length of Service:	21 years 190 days	
Foreign Service:	North America	5 years
	Malta & Ionian Isles	4 years 7 months
	Cape of Good Hope	3 years 7 months
Medal Entitlement:	Kaffir War of 1846/7	
Reason for Discharge:	Chronic Cough and worn out	
Character:	Good	
Trade or Occupation:	Labourer	
Can Sign Name:	Yes	
Height:	5' 10½"	
Hair Colour:	Grey	
Eyes:	Hazel	
Complexion:	Fresh	
Intends to Reside:	Chatham	

BURK	Richard, private	
	106th Foot	
Previous Regiment	2nd Bombay European Light Infantry	
Surname Variant	BURKE	
2 June 1863	Discharged the Service Netley	
	Pension paid Kilkenny	
	7d. per diem	
12 Sept 1864	Arrived per *'Merchantman'* [2]	
1866	To Adelaide from Western Australia	
1867	Died	
Service and Personal Details:		
Place of Birth:	St Johns Kilkenny	
Age on Attestation:	21 years	
Period of Service:	1849 — 1863	
Age on Discharge:	35 years	
Length of Service:	15 years 98 days	
Foreign Service:	East Indies	13 years 6 months
Medal Entitlement:	Persia 1856 — 1857	
Reason for Discharge:	Scurvy; General ?Cachexia and Syphilitic	
Rheumatism		
Character:	Indifferent	
Trade or Occupation:	Labourer	
Height:	5' 7¼"	
Hair Colour:	Fair	
Eyes:	Grey	
Complexion:	Fresh	
Remarks:	Elected for Indian Pension Rules on volunteering for the British Army	
Intends to Reside:	Kilkenny	

BURKE	see — BOURKE Patrick, Corporal	
	52nd Foot	

BURKE	Patrick, gunner
	RA 2nd Battalion
Surname Variant	BUCK
13 Apr 1847	Discharged the Service Woolwich
	Pension paid Athlone
	1/- per diem
21 May 1851	Arrived per *'Mermaid'*
1851	Assigned and occupied North Fremantle Lot P6
Jan 1857	Contributed 2/- to the Florence Nightingale Fund
1858	Application for Title North Fremantle Lot P6
1858	Granted Fee Simple North Fremantle Lot P6
1861	To South Australia from Western Australia
1868	Died South Australia
Service and Personal Details:	
Place of Birth:	Ballinlaugh Roscommon
Age on Attestation:	17 years
Period of Service:	1825 — 1847
Age on Discharge:	39 years 69 days
Length of Service:	21 years 103 days
Foreign Service:	Corfu 7 years 10 months
Reason for Discharge:	Chronic Rheumatism
Character:	Very Good
Trade or Occupation:	Servant
Can Sign Name:	Yes
Height:	5' 7¼"
Hair Colour:	Brown
Eyes:	Hazel
Complexion:	Fair

BURNETT	see — BENNETT Standish, private
	10th Foot

BURNS	Andrew, private
	63rd Foot
Surname Variants	BURNES; BARNES
17 July 1846	Discharged the Service Chatham
Pension paid Tullamore	
1/- per diem	
21 May 1851	Arrived per *'Mermaid'*
1851	Assigned and occupied North Fremantle Lot P16
Jan 1857	Contributed 2/- to the Florence Nightingale Fund
July 1881	at Fremantle, Andrew Burns, pensioner, charged with the trespass of a horse upon the railway approach. Fined £10 and costs of £1 12s. 6d., or 3 months hard labour
1884	W.O. H86123 — correspondence to O.P.P. Perth Western Australia Inc. [sic] Enrolled Pensioner
1885	Died
1889	Mrs Andrew [Ann] Burns proprietor of Fremantle Lots P16; P18; P19 and 224
Service and Personal Details:	
Place of Birth:	Mullingar Westmeath

Age on Attestation:	18 years	
Period of Service:	1825 — 1846	
Age on Discharge:	41 years	
Length of Service:	20 years 345 days	
Foreign Service:	Van Dieman's Land	5 years 9 months
	East Indies	10 years 9 months
Reason for Discharge:	Chronic Liver Complaint	
Character:	Good	
Trade or Occupation:	Weaver	
Can Sign Name:	X his mark on discharge	
Height:	5' 9"	
Hair Colour:	Black	
Eyes:	Blue	
Complexion:	Sallow	
Intends to Reside:	Mullingar	

BURNS William, gunner EIC

Bengal Artillery	
Surname Variant	BURNES
Out Pension No 620	
16 July 1862	Admitted to Out-Pension Pension paid 2nd Glasgow Pension District 9d. per diem
28 Dec 1863	Arrived per *'Lord Dalhousie'*
1864	To Adelaide from Perth Western Australia
1871	Pension paid New Zealand
1875	Melbourne

Service and Personal Details:

Where Born:	Wigtown Galloway
Trade or Occupation:	Gardener
Where Enlisted:	Glasgow
Presidency:	Bengal
Length of Service:	17 years 6 months
Age on Discharge:	39 years
Character:	Good
Reason for Discharge:	Worn Out
Height:	5' 8¼"
Complexion:	Fresh
Eye Colour:	Brown
Hair Colour:	Brown
Intends to Reside:	Galloway

BURNS see — BYRNE Martin, private
84th Foot

BURTON Edwin, private EIC [L/MIL/9/42]
1st Bombay European Regiment [Infantry]
Out Pension No 443

Jan 1855	Discharged the Service
May 1855	Embarked for UK per *'Ann Michell'*
1855	Admitted to Out-pension Pension paid South London Pension District 9d. per diem

10 Sept 1856	Arrived per *'Runnymede'*
1875	Pension paid Western Australia
30 Apr 1883	Assigned North Fremantle Lot P96
30 Aug 1884	Granted Fee Simple North Fremantle Lot P96
1888	Died aged 70

Service and Personal Details:

Where Born:	St Leonard's Shoreditch London Middlesex
Trade or Occupation:	Cooper or Weaver [depending on record]
Age on Enlistment:	20 years 3 months
Date Attested:	12 May 1838
Where Enlisted:	Tower Hill
Embarked India:	1st June 1838 per *'Aurora'*
Presidency:	Bombay
Length of Service:	16 years 9 months or 16 years 3 months
Age on Discharge:	38 or 40 years [depending on record]
Character:	Good
Reason for Discharge:	Rupture and chronic disease of the liver
Height:	5' 7½"
Complexion:	Fresh
Visage:	Round
Eye Colour:	Grey or Hazel [depending on record]
Hair Colour:	Light Brown or Dark Brown
Intends to Reside:	Walworth Rd South London or Tower Hill

BURTON Henry, Corporal
54th Foot

14 Mar 1844	Discharged the Service Templemore
6 Apr 1844	Admitted to Out-Pension
	Pension paid Taunton
	1/-½d. per diem
1844	Pension paid Bridgewater
1 June 1850	Arrived per *'Scindian'*
Aug 1850	Assigned and occupied South Perth Loc P10
1864	Corporal H Burton serving in the Pensioner Force at York contributed to the Greenough Fire Relief Fund
1873	Pension increased to 1/1½d. per diem for 2½ years service in the Enrolled Force
1874	Pension increased to 1/2d. per diem
1881	Application for free grant of 5 acres at South Perth Number 10 on behalf of Henry Burton [Pensioner]
1883	Assigned Military Pensioner Lot 275/Y
18 Jan 1884	Granted Fee Simple Pensioner Lot 275/Y Wanneroo Road
April 1885	Died - buried East Perth Pioneer Cemetery

Service and Personal Details:

Place of Birth:	Axminster Devonshire	
Age on Attestation:	18 years	
Period of Service:	1822 — 1844	
Age on Discharge:	39 years 7 months	
Length of Service:	21 years 218 days	
Foreign Service:	East Indies	17 years
Reason for Discharge:	Chronic Rheumatism	

Character:	Good
Trade or Occupation:	Shoemaker
Can Sign Name:	Yes
Height:	5' 7½"
Hair Colour:	Dark Brown
Eyes:	Hazel
Complexion:	Fresh

BURTONSHAW	John, private 54th Foot
23 Mar 1842	Discharged to pension Depot Fort Pitt Pension paid Liverpool 7d. per diem
21 May 1851	Arrived per *'Mermaid'*
1852	"Off Roll for misconduct"
1855	Restored to Enrolled Force Roll
1857	To South Australia from Western Australia
1857	Pension paid Melbourne
1858	Pension paid Calcutta
Service and Personal Details:	
Place of Birth:	Liverpool Lancashire
Age on Attestation:	20 years
Period of Service:	1826 — 1842
Age on Discharge:	35 or 38
Length of Service:	15 years 118 days
Foreign Service:	East Indies 13 years
Reason for Discharge:	Palpitations and great shortness of breath
Character:	Rather irregular and intemperate but otherwise good
Trade or Occupation:	Cooper
Can Sign Name:	Yes
Height:	5' 7" on discharge
Hair Colour:	Brown
Eyes:	Grey or Hazel [depending on record]
Complexion:	Sallow or Dark

BUTCHART	John, private 79th Foot
Surname Variants	BUTCHARD; BRITCHARD
10 Aug 1847	Discharged the Service Chatham Pension paid Dundee 1/- per diem
2 Aug 1852	Arrived per *'William Jardine'*
Jan 1857	Contributed 2/- to the Florence Nightingale Fund
1864	private J Butchart serving in the Pensioner Force Fremantle District contributed to the Greenough Fire Relief Fund
1864	a John Butchart purchased Fremantle Town Lot 628, 629 and 634 for £6/-/- per lot
1865	a John Butchart described as a farmer keeping cattle - residing about 2 miles out of Fremantle

1872	a John Butchart residing at Fremantle
1873	Granted Land at the 'Pensioner Colony' at North Fremantle
1889	Son David proprietor of Fremantle Lots P10 and P24
1892	Died [according to the newspaper aged 100 years and had fought at Waterloo and in the Crimea]
1935	Instructions of the Executor of the Will of the late David Butchart to auction a portion of North Fremantle Lot P10

Service and Personal Details:

Place of Birth:	Dundee Forfar	
Age on Attestation:	20 years	
Period of Service:	1825 — 1847	
Age on Discharge:	43 years	
Length of Service:	20 years 321 days [reckoned]	
Foreign Service:	Canada	10 years 1 month
	Gibraltar	5 years 6 months
Reason for Discharge:	Chronic Rheumatism and pains in chest	
Character:	Good	
Trade or Occupation:	Mackler [Hay Dresser]	
Can Sign Name:	Yes	
Height:	5' 9"	
Hair Colour:	Fair	
Eyes:	Blue	
Complexion:	Fair	

BUTLER	Thomas, private
	3rd Foot
Previous Regiment	48th Foot
16 Oct 1855	Discharged the Service Chatham
	1/- per diem
1855	Pension paid Limerick
1855	Serving in Limerick Militia
1857	Pension paid Carlow
1857	Limerick
1859	2nd Plymouth Pension District
1860	Jersey
1861	Limerick
1861	1st East London Pension District
1861	Jersey
1862	Jersey
1864	1st Liverpool Pension District
1864	1st Glasgow Pension District
1864	1st Belfast Pension District
1865	Jersey
22 Dec 1866	Arrived per *'Corona'*
1875	Assigned Cockburn Sound Loc 173 Willagee Swamp
1876	Residing Fremantle District
1878	Pension increased to 1/4d. per diem for service in the Enrolled Force
1881	Granted Fee Simple Cockburn Sound Loc 173

10 Dec 1883	Submitted a claim against the Government for £52/13/8 for improvement affected on his grant of land which was reclaimed by the Crown for a Crown Reserve
1886	Died Fremantle District

Service and Personal Details:

Place of Birth:	Lowcurren Queens County	
Age on Attestation:	18 years	
Period of Service:	1847 — 1855	
Age on Discharge:	27 years	
Length of Service:	8 years 205 days	
Foreign Service:	Greece	5 months
	Malta	1 month
	Crimea	5 months
Medal Entitlement:	Crimea	
Reason for Discharge:	Disabled by cannon shot to right hand at the Redan and other wounds	
Character:	Good	
Trade or Occupation:	Labourer	
Can Sign Name:	Yes	
Height:	5' 7"	
Hair Colour:	Light Brown	
Eyes:	Grey	
Complexion:	Fresh	
Intends to Reside:	Limerick	

BUTLER	Thomas, private
	80th Foot
Previous Regiment	13th Foot
30 Dec 1856	Discharged the Service Chatham
	Pension paid 2nd Dublin Pension District
	8d. per diem
1856	Pension paid Tullamore
28 Dec 1863	Arrived per *'Lord Dalhousie'*
1874	Pension increased to 1/1½d per diem for service in the Enrolled Force
1880	Died

Service and Personal Details:

Place of Birth:	?Tunfield Co. Kildare
Age on Attestation:	19 years
Period of Service:	1839 — 1856
Age on Discharge:	36 years
Length of Service:	16 years 313 days
Foreign Service:	East Indies 13 years 9 months
Medal Entitlement:	Burma 1841/1842 Pegu and Prome 1852/1853 — three medals for service in the field
Reason for Discharge:	Varicose Veins
Character:	Good
Trade or Occupation:	Labourer
Can Sign Name:	Yes

Height:	5' 6½"
Hair Colour:	Fair
Eyes:	Grey
Complexion:	Fresh

BUTLER	William, private	
	9th Foot	
18 May 1852	Discharged the Service Galway	
13 July 1852	Admitted to Out-Pension	
	Pension paid 1st Dublin Pension District	
	1/- per diem	
30 Apr 1853	Arrived per *'Pyrenees'* [2]	
1859	To South Australia from Perth West Australia	
1859	"A letter for him returned unclaimed"	
Service and Personal Details:		
Place of Birth:	St Werburgh Dublin	
Age on Attestation:	20 years	
Period of Service:	1831 — 1852	
Age on Discharge:	41 years 1 month	
Length of Service:	20 years 316 days	
Foreign Service:	Mauritius	2 years 195 days
	East Indies	11 years 124 days
Medal Entitlement:	Afghan Campaign 1842; Sutlej 1845/6 with clasps for Moodkee, Ferozeshar ; Sobroan	
Reason for Discharge:	Chronic Rheumatism and impaired health	
Character:	Latterly very good	
Trade or Occupation:	Cabinet Maker	
Can Sign Name:	Yes	
Height:	6' 0½"	
Hair Colour:	Dark Brown	
Eyes:	Hazel	
Complexion:	Fair	
Intends to Reside:	Dublin	

BUTT	Samuel, private	
	91st Foot	
Previous Regiment	75th Foot	
14 May 1850	Discharged the Service	
	Pension paid 2nd Glasgow Pension District	
	1/- per diem	
1852	Pension paid Ballymena	
19 Aug 1853	Arrived per *'Robert Small'*	
1868	Granted Greenough Locs G17 and G18	
1868	Died	
Service and Personal Details:		
Place of Birth:	Strathnorla Co. Donegal	
Age on Attestation:	18 years	
Period of Service:	1829 — 1850	
Age on Discharge:	39 years 2 months	
Length of Service:	21 years 4 days	
Foreign Service:	Cape of Good Hope	17 years 8 months
Reason for Discharge:	Chronic Rheumatism	

Character:	Good
Trade or Occupation:	Cotton Dresser
Can Sign Name:	Yes
Height:	5' 9½"
Hair Colour:	Brown
Eyes:	Brown
Complexion:	Fair
Intends to Reside:	Glasgow Lanarkshire
Married:	Frances

BUTTERWORTH — Samuel, gunner & driver
Royal Artillery

13 Apr 1847	Discharged the Service Charlemont
3 May 1847	Admitted to Out-Pension
	Pension paid 2nd Manchester Pension District
	1/- per diem
1 June 1850	Arrived per *'Scindian'*
Jan 1857	Contributed 2/6 to the Florence Nightingale Fund
1865	Pension paid Perth Western Australia
1850	Assigned Freshwater Bay Locs 13 and 15
1860	Application for Title Freshwater Bay Loc P227 and P246
18 July 1873	Died - buried East Perth Pioneer Cemetery

Service and Personal Details:

Place of Birth:	Manchester Lancashire	
Age on Attestation:	20 years	
Period of Service:	1825 — 1847	
Age on Discharge:	41 years	
Length of Service:	21 years 195 days	
Foreign Service:	West Indies	6 years 4 months
	Corfu	7 years
Reason for Discharge:	Chronic Rheumatism; Bronchitis and Hernia on left side	
Character:	Very Good	
Trade or Occupation:	Calico Printer	
Can Sign Name:	Yes	
Height:	5' 8½"	
Hair Colour:	Light Brown	
Eyes:	Blue	
Complexion:	Fair	
Intends to Reside:	Manchester	
Married:	*c*1868 Martha Tranailles Perth	

BYRNE — James, private
14th Dragoons

Previous Regiment	4th Light Dragoons
Surname Variant	BRYAN
9 June 1846	Discharged the Service Chatham
	Pension paid Birmingham
	9d. per diem

1846	Pension paid Drogheda
25 Oct 1850	Arrived per *'Hashemy'*
Jan 1857	Contributed 2/6 to the Florence Nightingale Fund
1873	Pension increased to 1/2d. per diem when he ceased to receive payment in Enrolled Force of Western Australia
July 1873	Died - buried East Perth Pioneer Cemetery
1874	Correspondence with W.O.

Service and Personal Details:

Place of Birth:	Newbridge Kildare
Age on Attestation:	22 years
Period of Service:	1827 — 1846
Age on Discharge:	42 years 6 months or 40 years 10 months
Length of Service:	18 years 292 days
Foreign Service:	East Indies 18 years
Reason for Discharge:	Unfit for further service and Rheumatism
Character:	Good
Trade or Occupation:	Labourer
Can Sign Name:	X his mark on discharge
Height:	5' 10¼"
Hair Colour:	Brown
Eyes:	Grey
Complexion:	Fresh
Intends to Reside:	Birmingham

BYRN	John, private Cape Mounted Rifles
Previous Regiment	45th Foot
Surname Variant	BYRNE
18 Aug 1863	Discharged the Service Canterbury Pension paid 2nd Dublin Pension District 9d,. per diem
15 Aug 1865	Arrived per *'Racehorse'*
1867	Lost onboard the *'Emma'*

Service and Personal Details:

Place of Birth:	St Marks Dublin
Age on Attestation:	18 years
Period of Service:	1842 — 1863
Age on Discharge:	39 years
Length of Service:	21 years 11 days
Foreign Service:	Cape of Good Hope 19 years 10 months
Medal Entitlement:	Kaffir War 1853
Reason for Discharge:	Own Request. Free to pension having completed 21 years service
Character:	Good
Trade or Occupation:	Labourer
Can Sign Name:	X his mark on discharge
Height:	5' 7½"
Hair Colour:	Dark Brown
Eyes:	Grey

Complexion:	Fresh
Intends to Reside:	c/o Staff Officer of Pensions Dublin

BYRNE	Laurence [Lawrence], private
	12th Foot
Previous Regiment	87th Foot
Surname Variant	BRYNE
9 July 1861	Discharged the Service Plymouth Citadel Pension paid 1st Plymouth Pension District 11d. per diem
1862	Pension paid Carlow
15 Apr 1864	Arrived per *'Clara'* [2]
June 1878	Pension increased to 1/5d. per diem for service in the Enrolled Force
Nov 1878	Reverted to former pension rate
1881	Pension increased to 1/5d. per diem
1 Jan 1883	Joined Enrolled Force — stationed Perth
30 Mar 1885	Granted Cockburn Sound Loc 174 Willagee Swamp
1897	Residing Perth
9 Mar 1897	Died

Service and Personal Details:		
Place of Birth:	Rathdrum Co. Wicklow	
Age on Attestation:	18 years	
Period of Service:	1840 — 1861	
Age on Discharge:	39 years 2 months	
Length of Service:	21 years 70 days	
Foreign Service:	Mauritius	9 years 11 months
	Cape of Good Hope	7 years 1 month
Medal Entitlement:	Cape and Good Conduct	
Reason for Discharge:	His having completed 21 years service	
Character:	Very Good	
Trade or Occupation:	Labourer	
Can Sign Name:	X his mark on discharge	
Height:	5' 7¾"	
Hair Colour:	Brown	
Eyes:	Grey	
Complexion:	Fresh	
Intends to Reside:	Arklow Co. Wicklow	

BYRNE	Martin [Matthew], private
	84th Foot
Surname Variants	BURNES; BURNS
24 Aug 1852	Discharged the Service Chatham 1/- per diem Pension paid Maryborough
6 Apr 1854	Arrived per *'Sea Park'*
no date	Assigned Perth Military Pensioner Lot 112
1875	Pension paid Western Australia
Jan 1857	Contributed 1/- to the Florence Nightingale Fund
Sept 1877	Application for Title to Perth Lot 112 Employed as a carter for the Commissariat at Fremantle

10 Apr 1880	Died aged 73 at the Invalid Depot	
Service and Personal Details:		
Place of Birth:	Kilmacey Wexford	
Age on Attestation:	22 years	
Period of Service:	1831 — 1852	
Age on Discharge:	43 years	
Length of Service:	20 years 256 days	
Foreign Service:	West Indies	2 years 98 days
	East Indies	9 years 145 days
Reason for Discharge:	Declining health	
Character:	Very Good	
Trade or Occupation:	Servant	
Can Sign Name:	X his mark on discharge	
Height:	5' 7"	
Hair Colour:	Brown	
Eyes:	Grey	
Complexion:	Fair	
Intends to Reside:	Maryborough Co. Queens	

BYRNE	Thomas [John], private	
	50th Foot	
Previous Regiments	40th; 31st	
Surname Variant	BRYNE	
24 July 1855	Discharged the Service Fermoy	
	Pension paid Preston	
	1/- per diem	
1856	Pension paid Bolton	
1862	Bermuda	
15 Feb 1863	Arrived per *'Merchantman'* [1]	
1874	Pension increased to 1/3d. per diem	
1885	Died aged 63	
28 Mar 1889	Title to Victoria Loc 10 granted to son John Thomas	
Service and Personal Details:		
Place of Birth:	Ferns Co. Wexford	
Age on Attestation:	19 years 2 months	
Period of Service:	1840 — 1855	
Age on Discharge:	circa 33 years	
Length of Service:	14 years 153 days	
Foreign Service:	Crimea	[no time period given]
Medal Entitlement:	Crimea with clasps for Alma and Inkerman	
Reason for Discharge:	Gunshot fracture of right tibia received at Inkerman	
Character:	Good	
Trade or Occupation:	Labourer	
Can Sign Name:	Yes	
Height:	5' 6¼"	
Hair Colour:	Brown	
Eyes:	Grey	
Complexion:	Fresh	

Intends to Reside:	Preston
BYRNE	William, private EIC [L/MIL/12/111] 1st Bombay Fusiliers — 1st European Infantry Out Pension No 553
14 Aug 1860	Admitted to Out-Pension Pension paid Kilkenny 1/- per diem
31 Dec 1862	Arrived per *'York'* Pension increased to 1/6d per diem
2 Feb 1870	Residents Office Fremantle — re. Burns [Byrnes], Authorization requested to admit pensioner's wife to Asylum for safe keeping. William Byrnes is EIC with pension rate of 1/6 per diem and is not in the Enrolled Force
1872	Charged with indecent behaviour and being drunk
1873	Died
Service and Personal Details:	
Where Born:	Castle Comer Co. Kilkenny
Trade or Occupation:	Collier
Date Attested:	Nov 1840
Embarked India:	*'Lady East'*
Presidency:	Bombay
Length of Service:	19 years 6 months
Age on Discharge:	39 years
Character:	none given
Reason for Discharge:	Time expired
Medal Entitlement:	Indian Mutiny
Height:	5' 7¾"
Complexion:	Fresh
Eye Colour:	Blue
Hair Colour:	Dark Brown
Intends to Reside:	Kilkenny
CABLE	Joseph, private 1st Foot
19 Oct 1853	Discharged the Service Birr
13 Dec 1853	Admitted to Out-Pension Pension paid Leicester 1/- per diem
2 Apr 1856	Arrived per *'William Hammond'* as a Convict Guard
Jan 1857	Contributed 1/- to the Florence Nightingale Fund
1863	Stationed Perth District
1864	private J Cable Pensioner Force Perth contributed to the Greenough Fire Relief Fund
1873	Pension increased to 1/3d. per diem for 15 years 4 months service in the West. Aust. Enrolled Force
1880	Died aged 66

12 July 1880	at the Fremantle Police Court, before J. G. Slade, R.M. and Coroner, on the body of Joseph Cable, who died suddenly on the 11th inst. Adjourned to 13th inst. The adjourned inquest on the body of Joseph Cable was resumed at Fremantle, on the 13th inst., when a verdict of "death from natural causes" was returned.

Service and Personal Details:		
Place of Birth:	St Margarets Leicestershire	
Age on Attestation:	17 years 9 months	
Period of Service:	1832 — 1853	
Age on Discharge:	39 years	
Length of Service:	21 years 28 days	
Foreign Service:	Canada	7 years 2 months
	West Indies	2 years 5 months
Reason for Discharge:	General Debility	
Character:	Good	
Trade or Occupation:	Woolcomber	
Can Sign Name:	X his mark on discharge	
Height:	5' 9"	
Hair Colour:	Brown	
Eyes:	Grey	
Complexion:	Fresh	
Intends to Reside:	Leicester	

CADDEN	John, Serjeant
	27th Foot
16 Feb 1869	Discharged the Service Chatham
	Pension paid Paisley
	1/5d. [17d.] per diem
1869	Pension paid Glasgow
1873	Greenwich
19 Feb 1874	Arrived per *'Naval Brigade'*
circa June 1874	Transferred from Fremantle to 2nd Perth District
1880	Residing at Fremantle Barracks
1881	Pension increased to 1/7½d. per diem for service in the Enrolled Force
1881	Handling explosives at the Fremantle Magazine
13 Apr 1881	Assigned Cockburn Sound Loc P4
16 June 1884	Granted Cockburn Sound Loc P4 Willagee Swamp
27 May 1889	Died at the Colonial Hospital buried in Anglican section of East Perth Pioneer Cemetery

Service and Personal Details:		
Place of Birth:	Lowthers Town Fermanagh	
Age on Attestation:	17 years 11 months	
Period of Service:	1850 — 1869	
Age on Discharge:	39 years	
Length of Service:	17 years 66 days	
Foreign Service:	East Indies	9 years 364 days
Medal Entitlement:	Indian Mutiny	
Reason for Discharge:	Nearly a cripple with Chronic Rheumatism	

Character:	Very Good	
Trade or Occupation:	Labourer	
Can Sign Name:	Yes	
Height:	5' 8¾"	
Hair Colour:	Brown	
Eyes:	Brown	
Complexion:	Dark	
Intends to Reside:	Paisley Scotland	

CAFFEREY

	Thomas, private 88th Foot	
Surname Variants	[some] CAFFERY; CAFFRAY; CAFFREY	
30 June 1843	Discharged the Service Chatham Pension paid 2nd Dublin Pension District 10d. per diem	
28 June 1851	Arrived per *'Pyrenees'* [1]	
1855	Received £15 grant in respect to Kojonup Lot P6	
Jan 1857	Contributed 2/- to the Florence Nightingale Fund	
27 Sept 1862	Purchased Kojonup Lot P12	
1865	Pension paid Adelaide South Australia	
1868	New South Wales	

Service and Personal Details:

Place of Birth:	St Michaels Dublin	
Age on Attestation:	19 years	
Period of Service:	1825 — 1843	
Age on Discharge:	37 years	
Length of Service:	17 years 336 days	
Foreign Service:	Malta	2 years 3 months
	Ionian Isles	10 years 8 months
Reason for Discharge:	Chronic Liver Complaint	
Character:	Good	
Trade or Occupation:	Butcher	
Can Sign Name:	Yes	
Height:	5' 6½"	
Hair Colour:	Brown	
Eyes:	Dark Hazel	
Complexion:	Swarthy	
Intends to Reside:	Dublin	

CAIRNS

	James, private RA 5th Brigade	
Surname Variant	CAIRNES	
6 June 1865	Discharged the Service Woolwich	
1/- per diem		
9 Jan 1868	Arrived per *'Hougoumont'*	
1870	Pension paid Singapore	
1873	Woolwich	

Service and Personal Details:

Place of Birth:	Omagh Tyrone	
Age on Attestation:	20 years	

Period of Service:	1843 — 1865
Age on Discharge:	41 years 7 months
Length of Service:	21 years 5 days
Foreign Service:	Canada 6 years
	Crimea 1 year 1 month
Medal Entitlement:	Crimean with clasp and Turkish Crimea
Reason for Discharge:	Having completed 21 years service
Character:	Good
Trade or Occupation:	Labourer
Can Sign Name:	Yes
Height:	5' 10¾"
Hair Colour:	Fair
Eyes:	Hazel
Complexion:	Fair
Intends to Reside:	Woolwich

CALLAGHAN	James, private 30th Foot
Surname Variants	CALLIGAN; O'CALLAGHAN
29 Jan 1856	Discharged the Service Chatham Pension paid Kilkenny 8d. per diem
28 Dec 1863	Arrived per *'Lord Dalhousie'*
1867	Appointed Assistant Warder
1875	Pension paid Western Australia
July 1879	Assigned Perth Military Pensioner Lot 147/Y
1879	Payment of £15 [pounds] sanctioned
11 Nov 1880	Joined Enrolled Guard — stationed Perth
1881	Pension increased to 1/2d. per diem for service in the Enrolled Force
Apr 1881	Application for Title to Perth Lot 147/Y the following entry may not necessarily refer to James Callaghan 30th Foot
July 1886	Patrick Murphy asking as to the whereabouts of Pensioner James Callaghan, [SROWA]
June 1897	Stationed at Perth
1908 Died	

Service and Personal Details:	
Place of Birth:	Kilkenny Kilkenny
Age on Attestation:	25 years
Period of Service:	1854 — 1855
Age on Discharge:	26 years 6 months
Length of Service:	1 year 95 days
Foreign Service:	Crimea [no time period given]
Medal Entitlement:	None annotated on his "Discharge to Pension Documents" but in newspaper account of his funeral [Trove] as him having the Crimean medal with clasp and Turkish Crimean
Reason for Discharge:	Weakness in lower extremities and gunshot wound to both hips at the Redan
Character:	Very Bad

Trade or Occupation:	Tailor
Can Sign Name:	Yes
Height:	5' 6"
Hair Colour:	Black
Eyes:	Brown
Complexion:	Sallow
Intends to Reside:	Kilkenny

CALLAGHAN John [James], Serjeant
63rd Foot

Surname Variant	O'CALLAGHAN
8 Mar 1861	Discharged the Service Belfast
2 Apr 1861	Admitted to Out-Pension
	Pension paid 2nd Belfast Pension District
	1/7d. per diem
15 Feb 1863	Arrived per *'Merchantman'* [1]
1875	Pension increased to 1/10d. per diem for 6 years service in the Enrolled Force of West. Aust.
1879	a John O'Callaghan died aged 56

Service and Personal Details:

Place of Birth:	Castleblaney Monaghan
Age on Attestation:	18 years 7 months
Period of Service:	1840 — 1861
Age on Discharge:	38 years 8 months
Length of Service:	21 years 14 days
Foreign Service:	East Indies 7 years
Reason for Discharge:	Completed 21 years service
Character:	Good
Trade or Occupation:	Shoemaker
Can Sign Name:	Yes
Height:	5' 5¾"
Hair Colour:	Dark Brown
Eyes:	Blue
Complexion:	Fresh
Intends to Reside:	Belfast

CALLAGHAN Patrick, private EIC
1st European Fusiliers
Out Pension No 567

17 Oct 1860	Admitted to Out-pension
	Pension paid 2nd Liverpool Pension District
	1/- per diem
1861	Pension paid 1st Dublin Pension District
1862	Pension paid 2nd Glasgow Pension District
31 Dec 1862	Arrived per *'York'*
circa Sept 1874	Transferred from 1st Perth District to Fremantle
circa Dec 1875	Transferred from Fremantle to 1st Perth District
1880	Died aged 59

Service and Personal Details:

Where Born:	Stilorgan Dublin
Trade or Occupation:	Labourer
Length of Service:	21 years 5 months

Age on Discharge:	41 years
Character:	none given
Reason for Discharge:	Time expired
Height:	5' 8 ½" or 5' 6¼"
Complexion:	Dark or Sallow
Visage:	Oval
Eye Colour:	Grey or Hazel
Hair Colour:	Dark Brown or Black
Intends to Reside:	Liverpool

CALLAGHNAN Cornelius, private
2nd Foot

Surname Variants	CALLAGHAN; CALLGHAN; CALLAGHAM
21 Oct 1850	Discharged the Service Newry
	Pension paid 1st Cork Pension District
	6d. per diem for 3 years
19 Aug 1853	Arrived per *'Robert Small'*
1853	Appointed Night Warder
1896	Died aged 75

Service and Personal Details:

Place of Birth:	St Peters Co. Cork	
Age on Attestation:	19 years	
Period of Service:	1839 — 1850	
Age on Discharge:	30 years 5 months	
Length of Service:	11 years 169 days [reckoned]	
Foreign Service:	East Indies	5 years 11 months
Reason for Discharge:	Chronic Rheumatism	
Character:	Indifferent but latterly good	
Trade or Occupation:	Labourer	
Can Sign Name:	Yes	
Height:	5' 8½"	
Hair Colour:	Dark brown	
Eyes:	Brown	
Complexion:	Fresh	
Intends to Reside:	No. 1 Curtis Lane Co. Cork	

CALLANAN John, private
5th Dragoon Guards

Surname Variants	CALLENAN; CALLNAN
29 July 1848	Discharged the Service Birmingham
26 Sept 1848	Admitted to Out-Pension
	Pension paid Birmingham
	1/- per diem
1850	Pension paid Longford
1851	Dublin
1853	Carlow
19 Aug 1853	Arrived per *'Robert Small'*
1854	Pension paid Western Australia
1874	Victoria

Service and Personal Details:

Place of Birth:	Beagh Galway
Age on Attestation:	18 years

Period of Service:	1824 — 1848
Age on Discharge:	42 years
Length of Service:	24 years 199 days
Reason for Discharge:	Unfit for further service Chronic Rheumatism and general debility
Character:	Good Trustworthy and Sober
Trade or Occupation:	Labourer
Can Sign Name:	X his mark on discharge
Height:	6' 0¾"
Hair Colour:	Brown
Eyes:	Grey
Complexion:	Fresh
Intends to Reside:	Birmingham

CALSON	John, private RM
Surname Variants	CAULSON; COLSON; COULSON Admitted to Out-Pension £15/4/- per annum
1848	Pension paid 3rd Plymouth District from 2nd East London Pension District
1851	a John Calson Greenwich Pensioner
Dec 1854	From South London to 3rd Plymouth Pension District
1854	Arrived per *'Ramillies'*
1854	Pension paid Western Australia
1855	Military court appearance
1856	On Rottnest detachment the following entries may not necessarily refer to John Calson Royal Marine
Jan 1857	a private J.W. Coulson contributed 2/- to the Florence Nightingale Fund
Dec 1865	a John Coulson purchased Fremantle Town Lot S17 of 5 acres for £5/0/0
1872	a John Coulson residing at Fremantle
1877	a John Coulsen Charged at Fremantle Police Court for leaving his horse and cart unattended in a public street
1879	a John Coulsen died aged 66

Service and Personal Details:

Place of Birth:	Haslingdon Lancashire
Age on Attestation:	18 years
Marine Division:	Woolwich
Period Served:	1827 — 1848
Length of Service:	21 years 9 days
Reason for Discharge:	Time served
Trade or Occupation:	Weaver the following family information may not necessarily refer to John Calson RM
Married:	Mary Ann or Eliza
Children:	Isabel b. 1850 m. *c*1867 John Litton Fremantle

CALVERT	John, private [2022]

	83rd Foot
1 Dec 1863	Discharged the Service Pension paid 2nd Belfast Pension District 10d. per diem
22 Dec 1866	Arrived per *'Corona'*
20 Sept 1879	Assigned North Fremantle Lot P60
1881	Pension increased to 1/3½d. per diem for service in the Enrolled Force
1881	Handling explosives at the Fremantle Magazine
Aug 1881	Correspondence to War Office from Staff Officer Pensioners Fremantle
Oct 1881	Amendment to pension to 1/4d. per diem from 12 years 9 months service in the Enrolled Force to 13 years 2 months
20 Dec 1883	Granted Fee Simple North Fremantle Lot P60
Oct 1888	The Resident magistrate requests that Pensioner Calvert to be admitted to the Colonial Hospital
Nov 1888	Died - buried East Perth Pioneer Cemetery

Service and Personal Details:

Place of Birth:	Lurgan Armagh
Age on Attestation:	18 years 5 months
Period of Service:	1842 — 1863
Age on Discharge:	39 years 7 months
Length of Service:	21 years 14 days
Foreign Service:	East Indies 11 years 1 month
Medal Entitlement:	Indian Mutiny with clasp for Central India [from Newspaper 'Trove']
Reason for Discharge:	Own Request having served over 21 years
Character:	Good
Trade or Occupation:	Cambric Weaver
Can Sign Name:	Yes
Height:	5' 7"
Hair Colour:	Dark Brown
Eyes:	Hazel
Complexion:	Fresh
Remarks:	Ineligible for Army of Reserve
Intends to Reside:	Lurgan Co. Armagh

CAMERON	Hugh, gunner Royal Artillery
Pervious Regiment	Madras Artillery [1st Battalion]
18 May 1869	Discharged the Service Dover Pension paid Glasgow 1/- per diem
1871	Arrived possibly per *'Strathmore'*
1880	Pension paid Perth Western Australia
1881	Pension increased to 1/3½ per diem for service in the Enrolled Force
1881	Assigned Perth Lot 269/Y
1883	Application for Title to Perth Lot 269/Y
1885	Employed by W Traylen, printer Barrack Street with a pay rate of 18/- per week
1886	Imprisoned for 7 days for habitual drunkenness

1891	Residing Melbourne Rd.,
Jan 1892	Died - ? buried East Perth Pioneer Cemetery

Service and Personal Details:

Place of Birth:	Kilmarnock Ayrshire
Age on Attestation:	20 years
Period of Service:	1849 — 1869
Age on Discharge:	39 years 7 months
Length of Service:	21 years 28 days
Foreign Service:	East Indies 4 years 314 days
Reason for Discharge:	Having completed 21 years service
Character:	Fair
Trade or Occupation:	Groom
Can Sign Name:	Yes
Height:	5' 8"
Hair Colour:	Fair
Eyes:	Grey
Complexion:	Fresh
Intends to Reside:	Glasgow

CAMPBELL Joseph Alexander
79th Foot

1882	Promoted to Serjeant Major
17 June 1884	Arrived per *'Bonnington'*
Feb 1884	Appointed Chief of Instructional Staff in Western Australia
1886	Promoted to Chief Staff Officer
1890/1902	Camp Commander and Chief Instructor at Karrakatta In 1901 appointed Action Commandant of the Commonwealth Military Forces in West. Australia
1902	Retired
1902 — 1924	Hon. General Secretary of the St John's Ambulance Association
1917	Departed England in charge of the troops onboard a troop ship
Apr 1924	died at his home

Service and Personal Details:

Place of Birth:	Ireland
Date of Birth:	1842
Age on Attestation:	15 years
Foreign Service:	India Egypt
Medal Entitlement:	Indian Mutiny
Married:	*c*1871 Roseanna Ilott India
Children:	Henry ?*c*1872 Joseph Robert b. *c*1874 England a Major A Campbell predeceased father a Corporal H A Campbell killed at Gallipoli

CAMPBELL George, private
79th Foot

10 Aug 1847	Discharged the Service Chatham Pension paid Thurso 1/- per diem
25 Oct 1850	Arrived per *'Hashemy'*
1855	Gaoler Fremantle
1863	Stationed Perth District
1864	Pension paid Van Diemans Land [sic]
1864	private G Campbell serving in the Pensioner Force at Perth contributed to the Greenough Fire Relief Fund
1867	Instructed the Albany Volunteer Artillery
1870	Residing Perth
1873	Pension increased to 1/3d. per diem for 12 years 10 months service in the Enrolled Force
Aug 1874	Assigned Pinjarra Sub Lot 78 of approx 5 acres
1875 Pension paid VDL [sic]	
Oct 1877	Notice given that George Campbell pensioner residing at Pinjarrah [sic] is entitled to that parcel of land known as Perth Building Lot N3 in Fee Simple
22 July 1882	Applied for Title to Pinjarra Sub Lot 78
19 Dec 1882	Granted Fee Simple Pinjarra Sub Lot 78 Colonial Surgeon recommends Pensioner George Campbell to be admitted to Mt Eliza Poor House
Jan 1886	Admitted to Poor House
Mar 1886	Died - buried East Perth Pioneer Cemetery

Service and Personal Details:

Place of Birth:	Latheron Wick Caithness	
Age on Attestation:	17 years	
Period of Service:	1825 — 1847	
Age on Discharge:	41 years	
Length of Service:	20 years 64 days	
Foreign Service:	Canada	7 years 3 months
	Gibraltar	5 years 6 months
Reason for Discharge:	Chronic Rheumatism	
Character:	that of a Good Soldier	
Trade or Occupation:	Labourer	
Can Sign Name:	Yes	
Height:	5' 7"	
Hair Colour:	Dark Brown	
Eyes:	Hazel	
Complexion:	Dark	
Intends to Reside:	Wick Caithness	

CAMPBELL	George, gunner
RA 8th Battalion	
8 Apr 1851	Discharged the Service Woolwich Pension paid 2nd Glasgow Pension District 1/- per diem
2 Aug 1852	Arrived per *'William Jardine'*
1854	Pension paid Western Australia

Service and Personal Details:

Place of Birth:	Strumness [sic] Orkney Isles	
Age on Attestation:	17 years	
Period of Service:	1828 — 1851	
Age on Discharge:	39 years 6 months	
Length of Service:	21 years 190 days	
Foreign Service:	Mauritius	10 years 9 months
	Malta	3 years 11 months
Medal Entitlement:	Good Conduct	
Reason for Discharge:	Varicose Veins and Chronic Rheumatism	
Character:	Exemplary	
Trade or Occupation:	Sawyer	
Can Sign Name:	Yes	
Height:	5' 7½"	
Hair Colour:	Brown	
Eyes:	Blue	
Complexion:	Sallow	

CAMPBELL John, private [1048]
Rifle Brigade [2nd Battalion]

Previous Regiment	42nd Foot
8 Sept 1846	Discharged the Service
1846	Pension paid 2nd Glasgow Pension District 1/- per diem
1850	Pension paid 2nd Manchester Pension District
18 Oct 1851	Arrived per *'Minden'*
20 Nov 1852	Assigned of York Pensioner Lot P11
Jan 1857	Contributed 1/- to the Florence Nightingale Fund
May 1859	Application for Title to P11 at York
1860	Departed Western Australia for Ceylon

Service and Personal Details:

Place of Birth:	Barony Lanarkshire	
Age on Attestation:	18 years	
Period of Service:	1825 — 1846	
Age on Discharge:	39 years	
Length of Service:	21 years 21 days	
Foreign Service:	Gibraltar	6 years 2 months
	Malta	2 years 9 months
	Corfu	2 years 6 months
	Bermuda	10 months
	North America	3 years 9 months
Reason for Discharge:	Unfit for further service	
Character:	Up to 1844 very good but latterly bad	
Trade or Occupation:	Carpenter	
Can Sign Name:	Yes	
Height:	6'	
Hair Colour:	Black	
Eyes:	Hazel	
Complexion:	Dark	
Intends to Reside:	Glasgow	

CAMPBELL Kenneth, private [drummer]
72nd Foot

11 Sept 1849	Discharged the Service Pension paid 1st Edinburgh Pension District 8d. per diem
18 Oct 1851	Arrived per *'Minden'*
1853	4th Offence — Charged by wife Ellen for repeatedly ill-treating her
Jan 1857	Contributed 2/- to the Florence Nightingale Fund
Sept 1870	On Perth District Electoral List
1872	"In prison" - pension suspended
1873	Pension increased to 11d for 6½ years service in Enrolled Force of Western Australia
Aug 1874	Applies for £15 Grant for Perth Town Lot 127/Y
Jan 1878	Charged with assaulting his wife Ellen
Jan 1881	Application for Title to Perth Lot 127/Y
Apr 1890	Died - buried East Perth Pioneer Cemetery

Service and Personal Details:

Place of Birth:	Dalkeith Edinburgh Scotland	
Age on Attestation:	14 years	
Period of Service:	1824 — 1849	
Age on Discharge:	39 years	
Length of Service:	24 years 10 months [4 years deducted from service for being under age on enlistment and being in prison]	
Foreign Service:	Cape of Good Hope	11 years 11 months
	Gibraltar	3 years 2 months
	West Indies	1 year 4 months
Reason for Discharge:	Worn out	
Conduct:	Indifferent	
Trade or Occupation:	Tobacconist	
Can Sign Name:	Yes	
Height:	5' 4½"	
Hair Colour:	Light Brown	
Eye Colour:	Blue	
Complexion:	Fair	
Intends to Reside:	Edinburgh	

CAMPBELL	William, private [366] 42nd Foot
24 Aug 1847	Discharged the Service Chatham Pension paid Glasgow 1/- per diem
18 Oct 1851	Arrived per *'Minden'*
1852	Died - ? buried East Perth Pioneer Cemetery
1852	Body of Pensioner Campbell washed ashore at Freshwater Bay

Service and Personal Details:

Place of Birth:	Barony Lanarkshire Scotland	
Age on Attestation:	18 years	
Period of Service:	1825 — 1847	
Age on Discharge:	40 years	
Length of Service:	22 years 2 days	
Foreign Service:	Gibraltar	6 years 1 month

	Malta	6 years 11 months
	Corfu	1 year 10 months
Reason for Discharge:	Weak and worn out	
Character:	Good	
Trade or Occupation:	Weaver	
Can Sign Name:	Yes	
Height:	5' 9½"	
Hair Colour:	Sandy	
Eyes:	Hazel	
Complexion:	Fair	
Intends to Reside:	Glasgow	

CANDLE see — CARROLL Michael
Rifle Brigade 2nd Battalion

CANNON John, trooper [534]
1st Life Guards

14 June 1837	Discharged the Service Pension paid Wales East Pension District 6d. per diem for 1 year
1845	Granted a Permanent Pension of 6d per diem
14 Aug 1854	Arrived per *'Ramillies'*
1854	Pension paid Western Australia
1855	Adelaide South Australia

Service and Personal Details:

Place of Birth:	Shalbourne Hungerford Berkshire
Age on Attestation:	19 years 4 months
Period of Service:	1834 — 1837
Age on Discharge:	22 years
Length of Service:	2 years 209 days
Reason for Discharge:	Ruptured both sides when on duty as a hayman in the stables of the Horse Guards
Character:	that of a Good soldier, trustworthy and sober
Trade or Occupation:	Labourer
Can Sign Name:	Yes
Height:	6'
Hair Colour:	Brown
Eyes:	Blue
Complexion:	Fair
Remarks:	£24/12/11 to be stopped for passage of wife and daughter

CANTWELL Thomas, Corporal [1087]
97th Foot

9 July 1861	Discharged the Service Camp Colchester Pension paid Limerick 1/2d. per diem
27 May 1863	Arrived per *'Clyde'* [according to obit — arrived per *'Merchantman'* in 1863]
1868	Purchased Fremantle Town Lot 836 and 837

1875	Applies for £15 improvement grant
1879	Pension increased to 1/8d. per diem for 15 years service in the Enrolled Force
1880	Died
1883	Application for Transfer of Land by Honora Cantwell of Fremantle
1887	Mrs Honora Cantwell proprietor of land at Beaconsfield

Service and Personal Details:

Place of Birth:	Gillen Firbane Kings County	
Age on Attestation:	18 years 6 months	
Period of Service:	1838 — 1861	
Age on Discharge:	41 years 8 months	
Length of Service:	23 years 83 days [reckoned]	
Foreign Service:	Corfu	5 years 11 months
	Malta	1 year 7 months
	North America	4 years 9 months
Reason for Discharge:	Having completed upwards of 23 years service and at his own request	
Character:	Good	
Trade or Occupation:	Labourer	
Can Sign Name:	Yes	
Height:	5' 9"	
Hair Colour:	Dark Brown	
Eyes:	Hazel	
Complexion:	Fresh	
Intends to Reside:	Little Barrington St., Limerick Ireland	

CAPLE

	William, private 56th Foot
Surname Variant	CAPEL
15 Jan 1847	Discharged the Service Chatham Pension paid Cavan 10d. per diem
25 Oct 1850	Arrived per '*Hashemy*'
no date	Assigned Perth Military Pensioner Lot 110
Jan 1857	Contributed 2/- to the Florence Nightingale Fund
May 1861	Application for Title to Perth Lot 110
Sept 1870	On Perth District Electoral List
1872	Summons to hearing for debt of 11/10d which was withdrawn
Oct 1880	Died - buried East Perth Pioneer Cemetery

Service and Personal Details:

Place of Birth:	Somerset	
Age on Attestation:	17 years	
Period of Service:	1826 — 1847	
Age on Discharge:	42 years or 36 years 10 months	
Length of Service:	18 years 58 days	
Foreign Service:	West Indies	7 years 3 months
Reason for Discharge:	Asthma	
Character:	Good but latterly inefficient soldier	

Trade or Occupation:	Labourer
Can Sign Name:	Yes
Height:	5' 8¾"
Hair Colour:	Dark Brown
Eyes:	Hazel
Complexion:	Sallow
Distinguishing Marks:	Marks of blistering on chest
Intends to Reside:	BallyJamesDuff Co. Cavan

CAREY Lawrence, private
32nd Foot

27 July 1852	Discharged the Service Chatham Pension paid South London 6d. per diem for 2½ years
30 Apr 1853	Arrived per *'Pyrenees'* [2]
Nov 1855	Left colony without leave.
1856	W.O. Correspondence — "Refused further pension" "No further information on him"

Service and Personal Details:

Place of Birth:	St Saviours Surrey
Age on Attestation:	19 years
Period of Service:	1841 — 1852
Age on Discharge:	30 years
Length of Service:	9 years 277 days
Foreign Service:	East Indies 5 years 22 days
Medal Entitlement:	Punjaub with clasps for siege of Mooltan and Battle of Goojerat
Reason for Discharge:	Chronic Hepatitis
Character:	Latterly Good
Trade or Occupation:	Labourer
Can Sign Name:	Yes
Height:	5' 10"
Hair Colour:	Light
Eyes:	Hazel
Complexion:	Fresh

CARMICHAEL Samuel, private
91st Foot

26 July 1859	Discharged the Service Pembroke Dock Pension paid 2nd Glasgow Pension District 9d. per diem
1 July 1864	According to WO records — embarked per *'Merchantman'* [2]
15 Apr 1864	According to shipping lists — arrived per *'Clara'* [2]
July 1869	a D Carmichael was drunk and incapable in Perth
1872	Summons to hearing for claim of £6/9/11d
circa June 1874	Transferred from Fremantle to 1st Perth District
1878	Pension increased to 1/-½d. per diem for service in the Enrolled Force
1879	To South Australia from Perth West Australia

Service and Personal Details:

Place of Birth:	Girvan Ayrshire	
Age on Attestation:	18 years	
Period of Service:	1838 — 1859	
Age on Discharge:	39 years	
Length of Service:	21 years 6 days	
Foreign Service:	St Helena	3 years 4 months
	Cape of Good Hope	12 years 10 months
Reason for Discharge:	Having completed 21 years service	
Character:	Good	
Trade or Occupation:	Labourer	
Can Sign Name:	Yes	
Height:	5' 7¾"	
Hair Colour:	Brown	
Eyes:	Grey	
Complexion:	Fresh	
Intends to Reside:	Glasgow Scotland	

CARR	John, private & drummer
	29th Foot
6 June 1848	Discharged the Service Chatham
1849	Assistant Prison Warder — Portland Prison
	Pension paid Salisbury
	9d. per diem
1 June 1850	Arrived per *'Scindian'*
1850	Employed as Warder Fremantle
1851	Dismissed
2 Apr 1852	Appointed Constable Police Force Perth
4 May 1852	Resigned from Perth Police Force
1852	Pension paid South Australia
1865	South Australia

Service and Personal Details:

Place of Birth:	Clonmel Tipperary
Age on Attestation:	14 years
Period of Service:	1826 — 1848
Age on Discharge:	35 years 6 months
Length of Service:	17 years 55 days
Reason for Discharge:	Chronic Rheumatism and Hernia
Character:	Good
Trade or Occupation:	Gardener
Can Sign Name:	Yes
Height:	5' 6"
Hair Colour:	Brown
Eyes:	Grey
Complexion:	Fresh
Intends to Reside:	Tower Hill London

CARR	William, private
	89th Foot
27 Jan 1857	Discharged the Service Chatham
	9d per diem

11 Feb 1861	Arrived per *'Palmeston'*
1864	private W Carr serving in the Pensioner Force at Perth contributed to the Greenough Fire Relief Fund
1878	Pension increased to 1/3d. per diem for service in the Enrolled Force
5 Apr 1881	Night Warder Perth Goal reported drunk on duty
1881	Assigned Perth Railway Block Lot 151/V
1883	Title Application for Perth Lot 151/V
July 1893	Died — buried East Perth Pioneer Cemetery

Service and Personal Details:

Place of Birth:	Ballycastle Co. Antrim	
Age on Attestation:	18 years	
Period of Service:	1838 — 1857	
Age on Discharge:	36 years 8 months	
Length of Service:	18 years 256 days [reckoned]	
Foreign Service:	North America	10 months
Reason for Discharge:	Bad Varicose Veins	
Character:	Good or Very Good depending on record source	
Trade or Occupation:	Labourer	
Can Sign Name:	Yes	
Height:	5' 6¾"	
Hair Colour:	Red	
Eyes:	Blue	
Complexion:	Fair	

CARROLL Cornelius, private
74th Foot

13 Oct 1863	Discharged the Service Perth Scotland Pension paid 1st East London Pension District 10d. per diem
4 July 1866	Arrived per *'Belgravia'*
1868	Pension paid East London Pension District
5 Jan 1871	Died

Service and Personal Details:

Place of Birth:	Tipperary Co. Tipperary	
Age on Attestation:	18 years 5 months	
Period of Service:	1842 — 1863	
Age on Discharge:	39 years 7 months	
Length of Service:	21 years 68 days	
Foreign Service:	Cape of Good Hope	2 years 9 months
	East Indies	8 years 2 months
Medal Entitlement:	Kaffir War	
Reason for Discharge:	Own Request on completion of 21 years service	
Character:	Good	
Trade or Occupation:	Labourer	
Can Sign Name:	Yes	
Height:	5' 8"	
Hair Colour:	Light Brown	
Eyes:	Blue	
Complexion:	Fresh	

Intends to Reside:	London
CARROLL	John, private 6th Dragoon Guards
26 May 1852	Discharged the Service Pension paid 1st Manchester Pension District 7d. per diem for 3 years
6 Apr 1854	Arrived per *'Sea Park'*
1854	a John Carroll appointed Night Warder
1855	"Left colony without transfer"
Service and Personal Details:	
Place of Birth:	Tullow Carlow
Age on Attestation:	21 years
Period of Service:	1841 — 1852
Age on Discharge:	32 years 2 months
Length of Service:	11 years 27 days
Reason for Discharge:	Varicose Veins of right leg
Character:	Very Good
Trade or Occupation:	Currier
Can Sign Name:	Yes
Height:	5' 9½"
Hair Colour:	Brown
Eyes:	Blue
Complexion:	Fair
Intends to Reside:	Davenport [sic]
CARROLL	John, private [drummer] 25th Foot
Previous Regiment	57th Foot
Surname Variant	CARROL
8 June 1865	Discharged the Service Preston
4 July 1865	Admitted to Out-Pension Pension paid 1st Manchester Pension District 9d. per diem
9 Jan 1868	Arrived per *'Hougoumont'*
1872	a John Carrol serving in the Enrolled Force at Fremantle
1876	Died
Service and Personal Details:	
Place of Birth:	Sydney New South Wales
Age on Attestation:	14 years
Period of Service:	1840 — 1865
Age on Discharge:	39 years
Length of Service:	21 years 4 days [reckoned]
Foreign Service:	India 11 years 4 months Gibraltar 1 year 4 months Malta 2 years Quebec 10 months
Reason for Discharge:	Own Request having served 21 years
Character:	Good
Trade or Occupation:	None
Can Sign Name:	Yes

Height:	5' 7"
Hair Colour:	Dark Brown
Eyes:	Brown
Complexion:	Fair
Intends to Reside:	Manchester

CARROLL Michael, private
Rifle Brigade 2nd Battalion

11 Aug 1846	Discharged the Service Chatham
Sept 1846	Pension paid Guernsey 1/- per diem
May 1848	Pension paid Tullamore
Dec 1849	Pension paid 2nd Dublin Pension District
28 June 1851	Arrived per *'Pyrenees'* [1]
Oct 1851	Appointed Night Warder
Jan 1852	Resigned or dismissed from Convict Service
1852	Assigned North Fremantle Lot ?P21
Jan 1857	Contributed 1/- to the Florence Nightingale Fund
1859	Granted Fee Simple North Fremantle Lot ?P21
1861	Departed Western Australia for Adelaide
Sept 1877	Died North Adelaide South Australia

Service and Personal Details:

Place of Birth:	Roscommon Ireland	
Age on Attestation:	20 years	
Period of Service:	1825 — 1846	
Age on Discharge:	41 years	
Length of Service:	21 years 5 days	
Foreign Service:	Malta	6 years 1 month
	Ionian Isles	5 years 3 months
Reason for Discharge:	Chronic Pulmonic disease	
Character:	Very Good	
Trade or Occupation:	Labourer	
Can Sign Name:	Yes	
Height:	5' 6½"	
Hair Colour:	Fair	
Eyes:	Grey	
Complexion:	Fair	
Intends to Reside:	Edinderry Londonderry	
Married:	Bridget [*c*1860 found enveloped in flames a short distance from the ferry]	
Children:	Mary b. *c*1839 Woolwich m. *c*1853 George Frost Fremantle	

CARROLL Patrick, gunner EIC
Bombay Artillery 1st Battalion 3rd Company
Out Pension No 243

2 Jan 1841	Discharged the Service
1841	Embarked UK per *'Lady Jane Clarke'*
2 July 1841	Admitted to Out-Pension Pension paid Kilkenny 9d. per diem

1849	Pension paid Kilkenny
25 Oct 1850	Arrived per *'Hashemy'*
31 Dec 1857	Assigned Bunbury Pensioner Lot P3
4 Dec 1858	Application for Title Bunbury Pensioner Lot P3
1869	Granted Free Simple Bunbury Town Lot 97
1871	Died aged 57

Service and Personal Details:

Where Born:	Kilmacord Kilkenny or Waterford [depending on record source]
Trade or Occupation:	Labourer
Age on Enlistment:	20 years
Date of Enlistment:	18th June 1827
Date Attested:	6 Aug 1830
Where Enlisted:	Liverpool
Embarked India:	1831 per *'Buckinghamshire'*
Presidency:	Bombay
Length of Service:	10 years 6 months
Age on Discharge:	31 years
Reason for Discharge:	Loss of third and little finger of the left hand
Character:	Very Good
Height:	5' 8½" [on discharge]
Complexion:	Fresh [Dark on discharge]
Visage:	Oval
Eye Colour:	Grey
Hair Colour:	Brown
Remarks:	District deserter — Enlisted on the 18th and deserted 26th June 1827. Re-joined the Depot 6th Aug 1830. Transferred to Horse Artillery 1834

CARROLL	Thomas, private 18th Foot
22 Jan 1856	Discharged the Service Chatham Pension paid Liverpool 1/- per diem
10 Sept 1856	Arrived per *'Runnymede'*
1858	To South Australia from Western Australia

Service and Personal Details:

Place of Birth:	Ennis Co. Clare
Age on Attestation:	18 years
Period of Service:	1834 — 1856
Age on Discharge:	39 years
Length of Service:	20 years 361 days
Foreign Service:	Ceylon; & China & East Indies & Burma 18 years 1 month
Reason for Discharge:	Chronic Catarrh caught Rangoon in 1852 and Dyspnoea
Character:	Very Good
Trade or Occupation:	Labourer
Can Sign Name:	X his mark on discharge

Height:	5' 9½"
Hair Colour:	Brown
Eyes:	Grey
Complexion:	Fresh
Intends to Reside:	Clare Castle Co. Clare

CARSON	James, private 57th Foot
Surname Variant	CARSONS
25 June 1861	Discharged the Service Cork Pension paid 1st Belfast Pension District 1/- per diem
1862	Pension paid Bermuda
15 Feb 1863	Arrived per *'Merchantman'* [1]
1864	private J Carson serving in the Pensioner Force at Fremantle District contributed to the Greenough Fire Relief Fund
1865	Assistant Warder at Champion Bay
22 Oct 1866	Purchased Geraldton Town Lot 230
1868	Granted Greenough Locs G5 and G6
1874	Convicted at Geraldton for assaulting Corporal Patten and sentenced to 14 days imprisonment and on the same date in defaulting on finding sureties to keep the peace towards his wife for 6 months
1875	Reported by S.O.P. to be bordering on insanity. His pension to be paid to his wife during imprisonment
Nov 1877	Staff Officer Pensions; James Carson Request for assistance with employment as cannot sustain his home on Pension which is 1/- per day
June 1878	Application for Title Greenough Loc G5 and G6 at Bootenal Victoria District
1884	Died

Service and Personal Details:

Place of Birth:	Belfast Co. Antrim	
Age on Attestation:	20 years	
Period of Service:	1840 — 1861	
Age on Discharge:	41 years 1 month	
Length of Service:	21 years 35 days	
Foreign Service:	East Indies	5 years 2 months
Reason for Discharge:	Own Request having served 21 years	
Character:	Very Good	
Trade or Occupation:	Butcher	
Can Sign Name:	Yes	
Height:	5' 5¼"	
Hair Colour:	Dark Brown	
Eyes:	Brown	
Complexion:	Fresh	
Intends to Reside:	Belfast	

CARSON	Samuel, private 73rd Foot
Previous Regiment	22nd Foot

13 Sept 1853	Discharged the Service Cape of Good Hope Pension paid Cape Good Hope 1/- per diem
1855	Pension paid Ballymena
1855	Birr
1855	Pension paid 2nd Dublin Pension District
10 July 1857	Arrived per *'Clara'* [1]
1858	Subscribed to Indian Relief Fund
1862	Pension paid Sydney

Service and Personal Details:

Place of Birth:	Dunagan Co. Antrim	
Age on Attestation:	19 years	
Period of Service:	1831 — 1853	
Age on Discharge:	none given	
Length of Service:	21 years 222 days [reckoned]	
Foreign Service:	West Indies	3 years
	Gibraltar	3 months
	North America	3 years 1 month
	South America	8 months
	Cape of Good Hope	6 years 7 months
Medal Entitlement:	Kaffir War	
Reason for Discharge:	Chronic Rheumatism and Scurvy	
Character:	Very Good	
Trade or Occupation:	Weaver	
Can Sign Name:	X his mark on discharge	
Height:	5' 7½"	
Hair Colour:	Dark	
Eyes:	Hazel	
Complexion:	Dark	
Intends to Reside:	Cape of Good Hope	

CARTER	John, private EIC 1st Bombay European Regiment [Infantry] 2nd European Regiment Out Pension No 435
Jan 1855	Discharged the service
22 May 1855	Admitted to Out-Pension Pension paid Falmouth 9d. per diem
8 June 1858	Arrived per *'Lord Raglan'*
1864	Pension paid Western Australia
1865	Pension paid Adelaide District South Aust.
circa 1867	Died

Service and Personal Details:

Where Born:	Helston Cornwall
Trade or Occupation:	Labourer
Age on Enlistment:	20 years 5 months
Where Enlisted:	London
Date Attested:	Feb 1840
Embarked India:	1840 per *'Northumberland'*
Length of Service:	14 years 7 months or 14 years 11 months
Age on Discharge:	37 years
Reason for Discharge:	Hepatitis

Character:	Indifferent
Height:	5' 7"
Complexion:	Fresh
Eye Colour:	Hazel
Hair Colour:	Dark Brown
Intends to Reside:	St Mary's Axe London

CARTER	Matthew, private
	15th Hussars
22 Oct 1850	Discharged the Service Chatham
1850	Pension paid Cambridge
	1/-½d. per diem
18 Oct 1851	Arrived per *'Minden'*
1852	Pension paid Western Australia
1859	Recorded on York census
31 Mar 1863	Transferred from Perth Western Australia
1863	Pension paid Madras
1875	Madras

Service and Personal Details:

Place of Birth:	St Peters Cambridge	
Age on Attestation:	18 years	
Period of Service:	1825 — 1850	
Age on Discharge:	44 years	
Length of Service:	24 years 235 days	
Foreign Service:	East Indies	10 years 104 days
Reason for Discharge:	Worn Out from length of service	
Character:	Good and efficient	
Trade or Occupation:	Shoemaker	
Can Sign Name:	Yes	
Height:	5' 8"	
Hair Colour:	Brown	
Eyes:	Hazel	
Complexion:	Fresh	
Remarks:	Marks of leeches on right side and of bleeding on both arms	
Intends to Reside:	Cambridge	

CARTY	Daniel, private [1830]
	21st Foot [2nd Battalion]
Previous Regiment	63rd Foot
Surname Variants	McCARTY; McCARTHY
13 Dec 1872	Discharged the Service Stirling Castle
7 Jan 1873	Admitted to Out-Pension
	Pension paid 1st East London Pension District
	1/1d. per diem
19 Feb 1874	Arrived per *'Naval Brigade'*
1 June 1881	Assigned Perth Town Lot 134/V
	Pension increased to 1/3½d. per diem for service in the Enrolled Force
11 Nov 1880	Joined Enrolled Guard — Perth
Oct 1883	Granted Fee Simple Perth Town Lot 134/V

1888	Catherine Carty [relic of Hugh O'Hanlon] applied to be registered as the proprietor of Nth Fremantle Lot P87
1897	Stationed at Perth
1909	Attended Veteran's Dinner
1915	Residing 7 Axon Street Subiaco

Service and Personal Details:

Place of Birth:	Bandon Cork	
Age on Attestation:	21 years	
Period of Service:	1851 — 1873	
Age on Discharge:	40 years 3 months	
Length of Service:	21 years 12 days	
Foreign Service:	Turkey	1 month
	Nova Scotia	5 years 11 months
	Crimea	9 months
	East Indies	3 years 10 months
Medal Entitlement:	Good Conduct with gratuity; Crimean with clasps; Turkish Crimean;	
Reason for Discharge:	Having served 21 years	
Character:	Good	
Trade or Occupation:	Labourer – servant on discharge	
Can Sign Name:	X his mark on discharge	
Height:	5' 8¾"	
Hair Colour:	Dark Brown	
Eyes:	Hazel	
Complexion:	Sallow	
Intends to Reside:	London	

CARTY	Michael, private 90th Foot
Surname Variant	McCARTHY
4 Dec 1855	Discharged the Service Chatham Pension paid 2nd West London Pension District 8d. per diem
1856	Pension paid Salisbury
1858	Clonmel Limerick
12 Sept 1864	Arrived per *'Merchantman'* [2]
1876	Convicted of being drunk on parade; sentenced to prison for 56 days; pension suspended
April 1877	Michael CARTY, — pensioner on enrolled force at Perth was charged by L.C. McCaffery and P.C. Payne with stabbing David Marchant with a bayonet, with intent to do grievous bodily harm. Sentenced to 1 month imprisonment; half pension suspended other half paid to wife
1878	Pension increased to 1/2d. per diem for service in the Enrolled Force
Nov 1881	Assigned Perth Lot 272/Y Wanneroo Rd
Sept 1883	Application for Title Perth Lot 272/Y

Service and Personal Details:

Place of Birth:	Annacarthy Co. Tipperary

Age on Attestation:	24 years
Period of Service:	1845 — 1855
Age on Discharge:	33 years
Length of Service:	10 years 184 days
Foreign Service:	Crimea 10 months
Medal Entitlement:	Crimea
Reason for Discharge:	Wounded in left hand in the trenches
Character:	Good
Trade or Occupation:	Labourer
Can Sign Name:	blank; Yes on Attestation
Height:	5' 9¼"
Hair Colour:	Dark Brown
Eyes:	Grey
Complexion:	Fair
Intends to Reside:	Ballingarry Limerick

CASEY	Patrick, private 64th Foot
Surname Variants	CASSY; CASSEY
11 March 1864	Discharged the Service Gosport
22 Mar 1864	Admitted to Out-Pension Pension paid Dorchester 1/1d. per diem
1 July 1864	Pension paid Birr
1 Apr 1865	Kilkenny
1866	2nd Dublin Pension District
22 Dec 1866	Arrived per *'Corona'*
1869	Appointed Assistant Warder
1878	Pension increased to 1/5½d. per diem for service in the Enrolled Force
no date	W.O. correspondence stating that man had re-entered the Enrolled Force, and that the increase granted by Chelsea Commissioners had been suspended
1880	S.O.P. Application for 20 acres that being P1 at Clarence, Cockburn Sound, by Patrick Cassy [sic].
1880	Died - ? buried East Perth Pioneer Cemetery
1881	Widow applies for Fee Simple for land grant at Coojee [sic]

Service and Personal Details:

Place of Birth:	?Toomavara Tipperary
Age on Attestation:	17 years 6 months
Period of Service:	1842 — 1863
Age on Discharge:	39 years
Length of Service:	21 years 47 days
Foreign Service:	India 11 years 8 months
Medal Entitlement:	Good Conduct with gratuity; Persian, Bengal [Indian] Mutiny
Reason for Discharge:	Own Request having served 21 years
Character:	Very Good
Trade or Occupation:	Labourer

Can Sign Name:	X his mark on discharge
Height:	5' 7"
Hair Colour:	Light Brown
Eyes:	Blue
Complexion:	Fresh

CASHEN	James, private 13th Foot
Surname Variants	[some] CASHIN; CASHON; CASSIAN, CASHIAN, CASSION; CASH; CUSON
25 Aug 1846	Discharged the Service Chatham
1856	Pension paid Birr 9d. per diem
27 May 1863	No departure information found
1867	Pension paid Western Australia
1872	Summons to hearing for claim of £6/14/10
1873	Pension increased to 1/- per diem for 6½ years service in the Enrolled Force
26 June 1881	Assigned Perth Town Lot 84/E at Claisebrook
14 Dec 1883	Granted Fee Simple for Perth Town Lot 84/E Claisebrook
April 1885	Died from cancer

Service and Personal Details:		
Place of Birth:	Birr King's Co.	
Age on Attestation:	18 years	
Period of Service:	1825 — 1846	
Age on Discharge:	39 years 6 months	
Length of Service:	20 years 49 days	
Foreign Service:	East Indies	19 years 6 months
Medal Entitlement:	Afghan Kabul Jellalabad	
Reason for Discharge:	Impaired Constitution from service in India	
Character:	Bad	
Trade or Occupation:	Labourer	
Can Sign Name:	X his mark on discharge	
Height:	5' 7¼"	
Hair Colour:	Brown	
Eyes:	Grey	
Complexion:	Fresh	
Distinguishing Marks:	Marks of corporal punishment	
Intends to Reside:	Parsonstown Kings County	

CASHMAN	John, private 74th Foot
Previous Regiment	25th Foot
23 July 1861	Discharged the Service Chatham Pension paid East London Pension District 10d. per diem
15 Aug 1865	Arrived per *'Racehorse'*
1873	"Not Appeared" — Off Pension

Service and Personal Details:	
Place of Birth:	St Marys Cork
Age on Attestation:	19 years 7 months

Period of Service:	1839 — 1861	
Age on Discharge:	41 years 3 months	
Length of Service:	21 years 24 days	
Foreign Service:	Cape of Good Hope	2 years 9 months
	East Indies	18 years
Medal Entitlement:	Medal and prize money for siege and capture of ?Shorapore	
Reason for Discharge:	Worn out from long service	
Character:	Good	
Trade or Occupation:	Labourer	
Can Sign Name:	Yes	
Height:	5' 9"	
Hair Colour:	Dark Brown	
Eyes:	Blue	
Complexion:	Sallow	
Distinguishing Marks:	Leech bites all over abdomen and right side	
Intends to Reside:	Chatham	

CAVAN Edward, private
86th Foot

4 Mar 1862	Discharged the Service Dublin	
1865	Pension paid 1st East London Pension District 10d. per diem	
9 Jan 1868	Arrived per *'Hougoumont'*	
1872	an Edward Cavan died	

Service and Personal Details:

Place of Birth:	Bagnelstown Carlow	
Age on Attestation:	18 years	
Period of Service:	1841 — 1862	
Age on Discharge:	39 years 11 months	
Length of Service:	21 years 13 days	
Foreign Service:	East Indies	17 years
Medal Entitlement	Central India with clasp	
Reason for Discharge:	Own Request having served 21 years	
Character:	Good	
Trade or Occupation:	Labourer	
Can Sign Name:	X his mark on discharge	
Height:	5' 7¾"	
Hair Colour:	Fair	
Eyes:	Blue	
Complexion:	Fresh	
Intends to Reside:	Portsmouth	

CEELEY Thomas, private
54th Foot

Surname Variants	[some] CREELY; CEELY; CEILEY; SEALEY
23 Jan 1849	Discharged the Service Chatham
	Pension paid 1st East London Pension District 1/- per diem
18 Oct 1851	Arrived per *'Minden'*
1861	Died Albany

Service and Personal Details:		
Place of Birth:	Cripplegate London Middlesex	
Age on Attestation:	20 years	
Discharge Medical:	Tuesday January 1849	
Period of Service:	1826 — 1848	
Age on Discharge:	42 years 11 months	
Length of Service:	21 years 340 days	
Foreign Service:	India	11 years 214 days
Reason for Discharge:	Chronic Hepatitis	
Character:	Good	
Trade or Occupation:	File cutter	
Can Sign Name:	Yes	
Height:	5' 11"	
Hair Colour:	Brown	
Eye Colour:	Hazel	
Complexion:	Swarthy	
Intends to Reside:	Mile End Town London	

CHAMBERS	Henry, private 68th Foot
18 Nov 1856	Discharged the Service Fermoy Pension paid Armagh 7d. per diem for 4 years
1865	Pension paid 2nd Liverpool Pension District
1866	Pension made permanent
22 Dec 1866	Arrived per *'Corona'*
1868	Purchased Fremantle Town Lot 630
1872	a Henry Chambers residing at Fremantle
1878	Pension increased to 1/- per diem for service in the Enrolled Force
1878	Granted Cockburn Sound Loc 219 Willagee Swamp
1880	Died
1881	Title of Cockburn Sound Loc 219 transferred to widow Sarah Ann

Service and Personal Details:		
Place of Birth:	Lifford Co. Donegal	
Age on Attestation:	17 years	
Period of Service:	1842 — 1856	
Age on Discharge:	33 years 1 month	
Length of Service:	12 years 357 days	
Foreign Service:	Malta	3 years 1 month
	Crimea	10 months
Medal Entitlement:	Crimea clasps for Alma; Inkerman; Balaclava	
Reason for Discharge:	Varicose Veins in both legs	
Character:	Good	
Trade or Occupation:	Carpenter	
Can Sign Name:	Yes	
Height:	5' 11"	
Hair Colour:	Brown	
Eyes:	Brown	
Complexion:	Sallow	

Intends to Reside:	Moy Co. Tyrone
CHAMBERS	John, private 7th Dragoon Guards
Previous Regiment	6th Dragoon Guards
28 Mar 1865	Discharged the Service Canterbury Pension paid Nottingham
1866	Sheffield 10d. per diem
9 Jan 1868	Arrived per *'Hougoumont'*
20 Aug 1885	John Chambers — Asks for Grant of Land being a Pensioner.
23 Oct 1885	Correspondence from S.O. Perth West. Australia
Feb 1888	Died aged 68 at the Mount Eliza Invalid Depot
Service and Personal Details:	
Place of Birth:	Reasby Lincolnshire
Age on Attestation:	17 years 2 months
Period of Service:	1839 — 1865
Age on Discharge:	42 years 10 months
Length of Service:	24 years 8 days
Foreign Service:	Cape of Good Hope 5 years 2 months East Indies 6 years 5 months Crimea & Turkey 10 months
Medal Entitlement:	Kaffir War; Crimean with clasp; Turkish Crimean; Indian Mutiny
Reason for Discharge:	Own Request after 24 years service
Character:	Very Good
Trade or Occupation:	Barber
Can Sign Name:	Yes
Height:	5' 9"
Hair Colour:	Brown
Eyes:	Grey
Complexion:	Sallow
Intends to Reside:	?Smitherbey nr. Kirton Lindsay Lincolnshire
CHAPMAN	William private RM
25 Jan 1857	Admitted to Out-Pension Pension paid 1st Plymouth District ? £21/12/-
30 Sept 1858	Departed Plymouth for Western Australia
1879	Geraldton — Report on death of pensioner William Chapman
19 Jan 1880	Inquest held before George Eliot — the Geraldton Government Resident and Coroner on the body of William Chapman [pensioner], who died suddenly on 19th inst. Verdict — "Death from Natural Causes."
Service and Personal Details:	
Place of Birth:	Devon
Date of Birth:	1816
Age on Attestation:	18 years

Marine Division:	Plymouth
Period of Service:	1834 — 1857
Age on Discharge:	41 years
Length of Service:	22 years
Reason for Discharge:	Length of Service

CHARTRES	Henry, Corporal EIC
	Bombay Horse Artillery
	Out Pension No 279
13 Dec 1843	To be Pensioned in Europe [L/MIL/12/109]
1844	Embarked UK per *'Falcon'*
12 June 1844	Admitted to Out-Pension
	Pension paid 1st East London Pension District
	1/- per diem
1851	Residing Whitechapel
7 Feb 1853	Arrived per *'Dudbrook'*
19 Nov 1865	Application for Title to Guildford Loc 115
1872	Relinquished Guildford Loc 115 — 'believed to have been sold'
1873	Pension paid 2nd East London Pension District
1874	Birmingham Pension District

Service and Personal Details:	
Where Born:	Marlow Buckinghamshire
Trade or Occupation:	Gardener
Date Enlisted:	1823
Where Enlisted:	London
Embarked India:	per *'Farquaharson'*
Presidency:	Bombay
Length of Service:	21 years 1 month
Age on Discharge:	40 years
Reason for Discharge:	Length of Service and Own Request
Character:	Good
Height:	6'
Complexion:	Sallow
Visage:	Oval
Eye Colour:	Hazel
Hair Colour:	Dark Brown

CHILDERHOUSE	John [James], Colour Serjeant
	40th Foot [Depot]
26 Apr 1853	Discharged the Service Plymouth
	Pension paid 2nd Plymouth Pension District
	2/- per diem
1855	Serving in Devon Militia
1855	Pension paid Limerick
1856	Barrack Serjeant Monaghan
11 Feb 1861	Arrived per *'Palmeston'*
	[acted as Serjeant-Major of the Guard onboard]

July 1861	John Childerhouse, Catherine Childerhouse, and their daughter Agnes Childerhouse were charged with receiving, harbouring and maintaining Edward James Salter also known as Edward Holmes an escaped prisoner of the Crown under sentence of 18 years penal servitude. The Jury returned a verdict of "Not Guilty"
1868	To Melbourne from Perth West Australia
1869	Pension paid Melbourne
1876	a John Childerhouse died Melbourne Victoria

Service and Personal Details:

Place of Birth:	Bandon Cork	
Age on Attestation:	12 years	
Period of Service:	1826 — 1853	
Age on Discharge:	39 years	
Length of Service:	21 years 5 days	
Foreign Service:	East Indies	10 years 10 months
Medal Entitlement:	Afghan with clasps for Candahar Ghuznee Cabool; Bronze Star Maharajpoor	
Reason for Discharge:	To serve in the South Devon Militia	
Character:	Good	
Trade or Occupation:	Labourer	
Can Sign Name:	Yes	
Height:	5' 6"	
Hair Colour:	Brown	
Eyes:	Hazel	
Complexion:	Fresh	
Intends to Reside:	Plymouth — serving with the South Devon Militia	
Married:	Catherine Foley b. *c*1818 England [died at the age of 105 and said to have had 18 children in total]	
Children:	Agnes Claire b. 1844 Meerut India	

CHURCH Frederick, gunner & driver RA 11th Battalion

11 Oct 1853	Discharged the Service Woolwich Pension paid South London 7d. per diem
1855	Served in Turkish Contingent
1859	Pension paid Brighton
1859	South London
29 Jan 1862	Arrived per *'Lincelles'*
1878	Pension increased to 1/3d. per diem for service in the Enrolled Force
1880	Increase suspended
1881	Pension increase of 1/3d. to be re-instated
Nov 1883	Died - buried East Perth Pioneer Cemetery

Service and Personal Details:

Place of Birth:	Croydon Surrey

Age on Attestation:	21 years 5 months
Period of Service:	1837 — 1853
Age on Discharge:	37 years 1 month
Length of Service:	15 years 69 days
Foreign Service:	West Indies 3 years 1 month
Reason for Discharge:	Rupture right groin caused by saving a cadet from drowning
Character:	For the last 6½ years very good but previously Very Bad
Trade or Occupation:	Carpenter
Can Sign Name:	Yes
Height:	5' 9"
Hair Colour:	Dark Brown
Eyes:	Blue
Complexion:	Sallow

CHURCH

	William, gunner & driver RA 8th Battalion
24 Feb 1857	Discharged the Service Woolwich Pension paid Bristol 8d. per diem
1857	Pension paid Wales East
1857	Bristol
24 Nov 1858	Arrived per *'Edwin Fox'*
1861	Convicted of breach of contract
1865	New South Wales from Fremantle
1866	Pension paid New South Wales

Service and Personal Details:

Place of Birth:	Wells Somerset	
Age on Attestation:	21 years 5 months	
Period of Service:	1835—1857	
Age on Discharge:	43 years 1 month	
Length of Service:	21 years 46 days	
Foreign Service:	Canada	3 years 3 months
	Gibraltar	7 years 7 months
Reason for Discharge:	Chronic Rheumatism	
Character:	Indifferent	
Trade or Occupation:	Labourer	
Can Sign Name:	Yes	
Height:	5' 10"	
Hair Colour:	Dark Brown	
Eyes:	Grey	
Complexion:	Sallow	
Distinguishing Marks:	Cut under left eye	

CLAFFEY

	Patrick, private 65th Foot
26 Mar 1850	Discharged the Service Chatham Pension paid Tullamore 1/- per diem
2 Aug 1852	Arrived per *'William Jardine'*

1853	To be employed as Assistant Warder without sanction from Staff Officer Pensions
1855	Employed as Night Warder
1863	Residing Fremantle area
1873	Pension increased to 1/2½d. per diem for 4 years service in the Enrolled Force
1881	Assigned Lot 274/Y Wanneroo Rd
1882	Died buried East Perth Pioneer Cemetery
1883	Title Application to Perth Lot 274/Y

Service and Personal Details:		
Place of Birth:	Kilbeggan Westmeath	
Age on Attestation:	18 years	
Period of Service:	1827 — 1850	
Age on Discharge:	41 years	
Length of Service:	23 years 4 days [reckoned]	
Foreign Service:	North America	3 years 122 days
	New Zealand	2 years 272 days
Reason for Discharge:	Chronic Rheumatism and Dyspnoea	
Character:	Good	
Trade or Occupation:	Labourer	
Can Sign Name:	X his mark on discharge	
Height:	5' 8"	
Hair Colour:	Light Brown	
Eyes:	Hazel	
Complexion:	Sallow	
Intends to Reside:	Kilbeggan West Meath	
Married:	Mary Jane ?McGiff	
Children:	Ann	
June 1873	an Ann Claffey took David Marchant to Court for Breach of Promise	
	Reuben Patrick b. *c*1872 Perth	
Jan 1915	Was missing — Description of him given by Criminal Investigation Department Perth Reuben Claffey, native of Western Australia, aged about 32 years, station hand and ex-policeman. Height about 5 feet 9 or 10 inches, medium build, fair hair, high forehead, blue eyes, oval face, fair complexion, small fair moustache; very quietly spoken. Last heard of in 1914 at Port Headland on board the ss Paroo	

CLANCY	Patrick, private
	44th Foot
Previous Regiments	61st Foot; 57th Foot
6 Nov 1855	Discharged the Service Chatham
	Pension paid Kilkenny
	9d. per diem
8 June 1858	Arrived per *'Lord Raglan'*
1864	private P Clancy serving in the Pensioner Force at Fremantle District contributed to the Greenough Fire Relief Fund
1868	Pension paid Melbourne Victoria

1876	"No information found about this man"	
Service and Personal Details:		
Place of Birth:	Callan Kilkenny	
Age on Attestation:	18 years	
Period of Service:	1853 — 1855	
Age on Discharge:	20 years	
Length of Service:	2 years 280 days	
Foreign Service:	Malta	2 months [approx]
	Crimea	4 months [approx]
Medal Entitlement:	Crimea	
Reason for Discharge:	Crippling of the right hand from gunshot wound during attack on the Redan	
Character:	Good	
Trade or Occupation:	Carpenter	
Can Sign Name:	Yes	
Height:	5' 6"	
Hair Colour:	Brown	
Eyes:	Hazel	
Complexion:	Fresh	
Intends to Reside:	Callan Kilkenny	

CLANCEY

	Peter, private 6th Foot	
Previous Regiment	89th Foot	
Surname Variant	CLANCY	
8 Nov 1847	Discharged the Service Fermoy	
8 Feb 1848	Admitted to Out-Pension Pension paid Drogheda 1/- per diem	
1850	Pension paid Fort Garry	
1854	Chatham	
10 July 1857	Arrived per *'Clara'* [1]	
19 Nov 1862	Died aged 53 Fremantle	
Service and Personal Details:		
Place of Birth:	Balruddery Dublin	
Age on Enlistment:	18 years	
Period of Service:	1825 — 1848	
Age on Discharge:	39 years 10 months	
Length of Service:	21 years 313 days	
Foreign Service:	East Indies	12 years 6 months
Reason for Discharge:	Chronic Rheumatism	
Character:	Good	
Trade or Occupation:	Labourer	
Can Sign Name:	Yes	
Height:	5' 6¾"	
Hair Colour:	Brown	
Eyes:	Brown	
Complexion:	Fair	

CLARK

Charles, private
40th Foot

Surname Variant	CLARKE
12 Aug 1845	Discharged the Service Chatham Pension paid South London 9d. per diem
1848	Pension paid Oxford
1848	Plymouth
1849	Woolwich
1 June 1850	Arrived per *'Scindian'* "Wife did not proceed with husband in consequence of her disgusting conduct at Tilbury so no part of his pension is to be paid for her support"
1850	Assigned and occupies Freshwater Bay Loc P258
Nov 1851	Employed as Assistant Overseer Convict Service
Dec 1852	Resigned from Convict Service
Jan 1857	Contributed 2/- to the Florence Nightingale Fund
1858	Application for Title Freshwater Bay Loc P258
17 Aug 1875	Pension increased to 1/3d. per diem from date of ceasing to draw pay in the Enrolled Force having served 21 years 8 months
24 May 1882	Died - buried East Perth Pioneer Cemetery [Band master according to daughter's obituary]

Service and Personal Details:

Place of Birth:	St Margarets London	
Age on Attestation:	22 years	
Period of Service:	1827 — 1845	
Age on Discharge:	40 years	
Length of Service:	17 years 281 days	
Foreign Service:	East Indies	14 years 119 days
Reason for Discharge:	Chronic Rheumatism	
Character:	Good	
Trade or Occupation:	Servant	
Can Sign Name:	Yes	
Height:	5' 8"	
Hair Colour:	Dark	
Eyes:	Hazel	
Complexion:	Dark	
Intends to Reside:	London	

CLARK	Thomas, private 26th Foot
Surname Variant	CLARKE
13 Mar 1849	Discharged the Service Cork
24 Apr 1849	Admitted to Out-Pension 7d. per diem for 2 years to 14th May 1851
25 Oct 1850	Arrived per *'Hashemy'* the following information may not necessarily refer to Thomas Clark 26th Foot
1885	a Thomas Clarke Military Pensioner — made application for a position of Night Warder at Perth Gaol

Service and Personal Details:

Place of Birth:	Killard Co. Cavan

Age on Attestation: 18 years
Period of Service: 1841 — 1849
Age on Discharge: 25 years 4 months
Length of Service: 7 years 122 days
Foreign Service: East Indies 7 months
Reason for Discharge: Chronic Ophthalmia

Character: Very Good
Trade or Occupation: Labourer
Can Sign Name: Yes

Height: 5' 5"
Hair Colour: Brown
Eyes: Blue
Complexion: Fresh
Intends to Reside: Edinburgh Scotland

CLARK William, gunner and driver
RA
Surname Variant CLARKE
17 Nov 1857 Discharged the Service Woolwich
Pension paid Ayr
6d. per diem Conditional pension for 1 year
1862 Pension paid Paisley
1863 Pension paid 2nd Glasgow Pension District
1866 Pension made permanent
9 Jan 1868 Arrived per *'Hougoumont'*
1868 Pension paid Melbourne
1900 W.O. correspondence with Under Treasurer Melbourne
1901 W.O. recommendation made for special pension increase to 15d. per day '[1/3d]

Service and Personal Details:
Place of Birth: Kilmarnock Ayrshire
Age on Attestation: 21 years
Period of Service: 1854 — 1857
Age on Discharge: 24 years 7 months
Length of Service: 3 years 257 days
Foreign Service: Crimea 1 year 2 months
Medal Entitlement: Crimea with clasp
Reason for Discharge: Fell from horse and fractured left wrist

Character: Good
Trade or Occupation: Labourer
Can Sign Name: X his mark on discharge

Height: 5' 8¼"
Hair Colour: Dark
Eyes: Blue
Complexion: Ruddy
Remarks: Fractured wrist in Sept 1855 incurred while on duty carrying stores from Balaclava to Camp Sebastopol

CLARKE George, private [drummer]

	9th Foot
Surname Variant	CLARK
23 June 1846	Discharged the Service Chatham Pension paid 1st Manchester Pension District 1/- per diem
1 June 1850	Arrived per *'Scindian'*
Aug 1850	Allocated and occupied South Perth Loc 9
6 July 1855	Died of fever

Service and Personal Details:		
Place of Birth:	St Annes Cork	
Age on Attestation:	13 years ?7 months	
Period of Service:	1822 — 1846	
Age on Discharge:	38 years	
Length of Service:	19 years 3 days	
Foreign Service:	West Indies 4 years	7 months
Mauritius	2 years 6 months	
East Indies	about 10 years	
Reason for Discharge:	Chronic Dysentery	
Character:	Partly Good for the last three years	
Trade or Occupation:	None	
Can Sign Name:	Yes	
Height:	5' 7"	
Hair Colour:	Dark Brown	
Eyes:	Grey	
Complexion:	Sallow	
Intends to Reside:	Salford Lancashire	

CLARKE	John, Serjeant 78th Foot
Previous Regiment	72nd Foot
9 July 1850	Discharged the Service Chatham Pension paid 2nd Edinburgh Pension District 8d. per diem
28 June 1851	Arrived per *'Pyrenees'* [1]
1852	Application for land grant Albany
1854	"Pension not to be paid — he having quitted Australia without leave."
5 Mar 1854	Died while serving onboard the *'Sydney* [sic] *of London'*

Service and Personal Details:		
Place of Birth:	Paisley Renfrewshire	
Age on Attestation:	18 years	
Period of Service:	1839 — 1850	
Age on Discharge:	29 years 6 months	
Length of Service:	10 years 134 days	
Foreign Service:	East Indies	7 years 2 months
Reason for Discharge:	General debility and emaciation from repeated attacks of fever	
Character:	Good	
Trade or Occupation:	Baker	
Can Sign Name:	Yes	

Height:	5' 7½"
Hair Colour:	Fair
Eyes:	Hazel
Complexion:	Sallow
Intends to Reside:	Portobello

CLARKE	Thomas, private	
	48th Foot	
28 Feb 1865	Discharged the Service Cork Barracks	
	Pension paid Northampton	
	1/- per diem	
22 Dec 1866	Arrived per *'Corona'*	
1869	Pension paid England	
1870	Northampton England	
Service and Personal Details:		
Place of Birth:	Daventry Northamptonshire	
Age on Attestation:	17 years	
Period of Service:	1843 — 1865	
Age on Discharge:	39 years 2 months	
Length of Service:	21 years 16 days	
Foreign Service:	Ionian Isles	2 years 1 month
	Crimea	1 year 2 months
	Malta	1 year 2 months
	Gibraltar	1 year 2 months
	East Indies	2 years 1 month
Medal Entitlement:	Long Service with gratuity; Crimea with clasp; Turkish Crimean	
Reason for Discharge:	Own Request on completion of 21 years service	
Character:	Very Good	
Trade or Occupation:	Tailor	
Can Sign Name:	Yes	
Height:	5' 8¾"	
Hair Colour:	Dark Brown	
Eyes:	Blue	
Complexion:	Fair	
Intends to Reside:	Northampton	

CLAYTON	John, Corporal
	80th Foot
22 Jan 1847	Discharged the Service
29 June 1847	Admitted to Out-Pension
	Pension paid 2nd Manchester Pension District
	1/3d. per diem
8 June 1858	Arrived per *'Lord Raglan'*
1861	Purchased Swan Loc 330
1864	Appointed Assistant Warder
1879	a Serjeant Clayton in charge of the Government Mulberry Plantation and Menagerie
1881	Pension increased to 1/8½d. per diem
21 Nov 1884	Assigned Albany Lot 21
30 May 1885	a John Clayton 80th Foot granted Fee Simple Albany Lot P21

1891	At the Fremantle Court, John Clayton pensioner, charged by wife with desertion
1891	Died
Service and Personal Details:	
Place of Birth:	Macclesfield Cheshire
Age on Attestation:	18 years
Period of Service:	1842 — 1847
Age on Discharge:	23 years
Length of Service:	3 years 292 days [reckoned]
Foreign Service:	New South Wales 1 year 1 month
	India 1 year 10 months
Reason for Discharge:	Gunshot wound to upper part of left foot
Character:	Very Good
Trade or Occupation:	Silk Weaver
Height:	6' 0½"
Hair Colour:	Fair
Eyes:	Hazel
Complexion:	Sallow
Intends to Reside:	Hardsfield Cheshire

CLAYTON	Joseph, private
	39th Foot
30 Mar 1857	Discharged the Service
7 Apr 1857	Admitted to Out-Pension
	Pension paid Sheffield
	10d. per diem
19 Aug 1859	Arrived per *'Sultana'*
1880	In Almanac
1883	In Almanac
May 1885	a pensioner named Joseph Clayton was charged by Constable McGann with lying drunk on the footpath in Wellington Street
1885	Superintendent Poor Houses recommends admission to Mt Eliza Poor House of Pensioner Joseph Clayton
1889	Died
Service and Personal Details:	
Place of Birth:	Wakefield Yorkshire
Age on Attestation:	24 years
Period of Service:	1842 — 1857
Age on Discharge:	41 years
Length of Service:	16 years 262 days
Foreign Service:	East Indies 6 years 5 months
	Crimea 1 year 6 months
Medal Entitlement:	Crimea with clasp
Reason for Discharge:	Chronic Disease of the Spleen
Character:	Latterly Good
Trade or Occupation:	Hairdresser
Can Sign Name:	X his mark on discharge
Height:	5' 5½"

Hair Colour:	Dark Brown
Eyes:	Grey
Complexion:	Fair
Intends to Reside:	Sheffield Yorkshire

CLEWS Thomas, private
80th Foot

Surname Variant	CLEWES	
12 Dec 1848	Discharged the Service Chatham	
	Pension paid 2nd Manchester Pension District	
	1/- per diem	
6 Apr 1854	Arrived per *'Sea Park'*	
1858	Pension paid Sydney New South Wales	
	£30 stopped from pension for passage money	
1881	Pension paid Tasmania	
1881	W.O. Correspondence — Tasmania	
Service and Personal Details:		
Place of Birth:	Stockport Cheshire	
Age on Attestation:	15 years	
Period of Service:	1824 — 1848	
Age on Discharge:	39 years 8 months	
Length of Service:	20 years 297 days	
Foreign Service:	Mediterranean	4 years
	New South Wales	8 years
Reason for Discharge:	Chronic Rheumatism	
Character:	Very good	
Trade or Occupation:	Weaver	
Can Sign Name:	Yes	
Height:	5' 11"	
Hair Colour:	Brown	
Eyes:	Grey	
Complexion:	Fresh	
Intends to Reside:	Congleton Cheshire	

CLINTON James, private
27th Foot

25 Sept 1858	Discharged the Service Buttevant
19 Oct 1858	Admitted to Out-Pension
	11d. per diem
1858	Pension paid Monaghan
1859	Drogheda
1860	Armagh
27 May 1863	Arrived per *'Clyde'*
1873	Pension increased to 1/3d. per diem for 10 years and 2 months service in the Enrolled Force of Western Australia
1873	Employed as Assistant Warder Guildford
1875	Died
Jan 1876	Ann Clinton assigned West Guildford Town Lots
P118;	P119; P120 and P121 each of 2 acres
June 1876	Application for Title to West Guildford Town Lots P118; P119; P120 and P121

Service and Personal Details:

Place of Birth:	?Clooncare Co. Leitrim
Age on Attestation:	18 years
Period of Service:	1837 — 1858
Age on Discharge:	39 years
Length of Service:	21 years 147 days
Foreign Service:	Cape of Good Hope 7 years 91 days
Reason for Discharge:	Own request for purpose of enabling him to join the recruiting staff of the East India Forces
Character:	Good
Trade or Occupation:	Labourer
Can Sign Name:	Yes
Height:	5' 6¼"
Hair Colour:	Black
Eyes:	Brown
Complexion:	Fair
Intends to Reside:	Belfast

COATES

	George, private Rifle Brigade [1st Battalion]
28 June 1853	Discharged the Service Chatham Pension paid South London 1/- per diem
14 Aug 1854	Arrived per *'Ramillies'* "Wife of pensioner dismissed at Tilbury Fort and not to receive any part of husband's pension"
1856	To South Australia from Western Australia
1857	Pension paid Melbourne
17 Nov 1859	Died

Service and Personal Details:

Place of Birth:	St Giles Camberwell Surrey
Age on Attestation:	21 years 8 months
Period of Service:	1831 — 1853
Age on Discharge:	43 years
Length of Service:	21 years 160 days
Foreign Service:	North America 4 years 1 month
Reason for Discharge:	Worn out
Character:	Very good
Trade or Occupation:	Shoemaker
Can Sign Name:	Yes
Height:	5' 6½"
Hair Colour:	Dark Brown
Eyes:	Hazel
Complexion:	Fresh
Intends to Reside:	Kings Row Chelsea London or 16 Paradise Buildings Lambeth

CODY

	John, Corporal 36th Foot
Surname Variant	COADY
7 Sept 1858	Discharged the Service Pension paid Kilkenny

	1/2½d. per diem
19 Aug 1859	Arrived per *'Sultana'*
1878	Pension increased to 1/3d. per diem for 8 years service in the Enrolled Force
Apr 1875	Charged with being drunk and incapable in Hay Street and fined 5/- [shillings]
23 Aug 1881	Assigned and occupied North Fremantle Lots P41 and P46
5 Aug 1884	Granted Fee Simple North Fremantle Lots P41 and P 46
May 1885	Resident Magistrate Fremantle — requests admission to Mt Eliza Depot for Pensioner John Coady
1886	Correspondence to WO from S.O. Perth W.A
Jan 1887	Died from the effects of senile decay

Service and Personal Details:

Place of Birth:	Johnstown Kilkenny	
Age on Attestation:	19 years	
Period of Service:	1831 — 1858	
Age on Discharge:	45 years	
Length of Service:	26 years 146 days	
Foreign Service:	North America	3 years 19 days
	Ionian Isles	4 years 72 days
Reason for Discharge:	Worn out due to length of service	
Character:	Very Good	
Trade or Occupation:	Labourer	
Can Sign Name:	X his mark on discharge	
Height:	5' 7"	
Hair Colour:	Brown	
Eyes:	Grey	
Complexion:	Sallow	
Intends to Reside:	Jersey	

COFFIN	William, Serjeant
	59th Foot
Surname Variant	COFFEN
29 Nov 1865	Discharged the Service Glasgow
12 Dec 1865	Pension paid Glasgow
	2/- per diem
1 June 1865	Pension paid Southampton
13 July 1867	Arrived per *'Norwood'* [2]
1868	Employed as Assistant Warder
Dec 1874	Died aged 54 of Enteric Fever
1876	Application for relief by Theresa Coffin, widow of William Coffin [died 2 years ago], and her four children.

Service and Personal Details:

Place of Birth:	Bishops Waltham Hampshire
Age on Attestation:	18 years
Period of Service:	1844 — 1865
Age on Discharge:	39 years
Length of Service:	21 years 7 days

Foreign Service:	China	4 years 27 days
	East Indies	116 days
	Cape of Good Hope	3 years 332 days
Medal Entitlement:	Good Conduct with gratuity; China medal with clasp	
Reason for Discharge:	Own Request 'free' after 21 years service	
Character:	Very Good	
Trade or Occupation:	Labourer	
Can Sign Name:	Yes	
Height:	5' 11"	
Hair Colour:	Brown	
Eyes:	Grey	
Complexion:	Fair	
Intends to Reside:	Northampton [England]	

COGHLAN	Michael, Corporal 75th Foot	
Surname Variant	COGLAN	
5 Feb 1867	Discharged the Service Chatham	
1867	Pension paid 2nd West London Pension District	
1867	Pension paid Athlone 1/- per diem	
9 Jan 1868	Arrived per *'Hougoumont'*	
1868	Appointed Assistant Warder	
1869	To New South Wales from Freemantle [sic]	
1870	Pension paid Melbourne	
1874	Hobart Town	
1896	Pension paid Athlone	
1900	Athlone	
1900	Correspondence with W.O. recommending increase in pension to 18d. [1/6d.] per diem on account of increased disability	
1907	W.O. correspondence to sanction increase of pension to 24d. [2/-] per diem	
Service and Personal Details:		
Place of Birth:	Ballinasloe Roscommon	
Age on Attestation:	19 years 6 months	
Period of Service:	1847 — 1867	
Age on Discharge:	39 years 1 month	
Length of Service:	19 years 215 days	
Foreign Service:	At Sea	227 days
	East Indies	12 years 195 days
Medal Entitlement:	Good Conduct with gratuity; Indian Mutiny with clasp for Delhi	
Reason for Discharge:	Chronic Rheumatism and Hernia	
Character:	Very Good	
Trade or Occupation:	Labourer	
Can Sign Name:	Yes	
Height:	5' 8"	
Hair Colour:	Dark Brown	
Eyes:	Grey	

Complexion:	Sallow
Intends to Reside:	Ballinsloe Galway

COLDWELL	James, Corporal 57th Foot	
Surname Variant	CALDWELL	
10 Jan 1847	Discharged the Service Chatham	
12 Aug 1847	Pension paid Stockport 1/3½d. per diem	
1849	Pension paid 2nd Manchester Pension District	
1 June 1850	Arrived per *'Scindian'*	
1850	?Police Constable stationed Perth	
1851	Appointed Night Warder	
1855	Pension paid Western Australia	
Jan 1857	Contributed 3/- to the Florence Nightingale Fund	
1863	Stationed Perth District	
1864	Serjeant J Caldwell serving in the Pensioner Force at Perth contributed to the Greenough Fire Relief Fund	
1865	To Melbourne from Perth Western Australia	
1866	Pension paid Victoria	
1871	India	
1874	West London	
1874	Stafford	
1875	Melbourne	
Service and Personal Details:		
Place of Birth:	Manchester Lancashire	
Age on Attestation:	16 years	
Period of Service:	1824 — 1847	
Age on Discharge:	39 years	
Length of Service:	20 years 7 months	
Foreign Service:	New South Wales	5 years 3 months
	East Indies	15 years 4 months
Reason for Discharge:	Worn out	
Character:	Excellent	
Trade or Occupation:	Silk Weaver	
Can Sign Name:	Yes	
Height:	5' *"	
Hair Colour:	Light Brown	
Eyes:	Blue	
Complexion:	Fair	
Intends to Reside:	Manchester	

COLEMAN	Thomas, private 41st Foot
12 Oct 1831	Discharged the Service Pension paid Kilkenny 6d. per diem
7 Feb 1853	Arrived per *'Dudbrook'*
1854	Witness at Military Court
1855	At Fremantle — signed protest against high cost of provisions
1854	'Deserted from the Enrolled Force in August'

1858	Pension paid Melbourne
Service and Personal Details:	
Place of Birth:	Ballinkillen Co. Carlow
Age on Attestation:	17 years
Period of Service:	1825 — 1830
Age on Discharge:	23 years [or 25 years depending on record]
Length of Service:	4 years 4 days [reckoned] [5 years 4 months with 1 year served underage]
Foreign Service:	East Indies 4 years 1 day
Reason for Discharge:	Chronic Liver Disease
Character:	Good efficient soldier, trustworthy and sober
Trade or Occupation:	Labourer
Height:	5' 5½"
Hair Colour:	Light Brown
Eyes:	Grey
Complexion:	Fair

COLGAN	John, Corporal 67th Foot
Surname Variant	COGLAN; COGHLAN
10 Jan 1860	Discharged the Service Pension paid Enniskillen 9d. per diem
31 Dec 1862	Arrived per *'York'*
1876	Residing Albany
8 June 1881	Assigned Albany Lot P1
Feb 1885	Application for Title Albany Lot P1
Service and Personal Details:	
Place of Birth:	Enniskillen Fermanagh
Age on Attestation:	19 years
Period of Service:	1837 — 1860
Age on Discharge:	41 years
Length of Service:	21 years 156 days
Foreign Service:	Gibraltar 3 years 165 days West Indies 5 years 271 days
Reason for Discharge:	Own Request having served 21 years service
Character:	Good
Trade or Occupation:	Servant
Can Sign Name:	Yes
Height:	5' 10½"
Hair Colour:	Dark Brown
Eyes:	Grey
Complexion:	Fresh
Intends to Reside:	Brookborough Co. Fermanagh

COLLEGE	James, private 2nd/12th Foot
30 July 1861	Discharged the Service Plymouth Pension paid Bristol 9d. per diem

1862	Pension paid Bermuda	
15 Feb 1863	Arrived per *'Merchantman'* [1]	
1864	Appointed Assistant Warder	
1871	Died	
Service and Personal Details:		
Place of Birth:	Birmingham Warwickshire	
Age on Attestation:	18 years	
Period of Service:	1840 — 1861	
Age on Discharge:	39 years 4 months	
Length of Service:	21 years 9 days	
Foreign Service:	Cape of Good Hope	7 years 3 months
	Mauritius	8 years 2 months
Reason for Discharge:	Own Request after 21 years service	
Character:	Good	
Trade or Occupation:	Labourer	
Can Sign Name:	X his mark on discharge	
Height:	5' 8"	
Hair Colour:	Grey	
Eyes:	Dark	
Complexion:	Sallow	
Intends to Reside:	Bristol	

COLLINS	Daniel, private EIC 2nd European Light Infantry Out Pension No 576
Oct 1861	Admitted to Out-Pension Pension paid 2nd East London Pension District 1/- per diem
27 May 1863	Arrived per *'Clyde'*
Mar 1869	Died
July 1872	Jean Collins — widow of Pensioner Collins is destitute
Service and Personal Details:	
Where Born:	St Mary's Co. Cork
Trade or Occupation:	Labourer
Date Attested:	1840
Where Enlisted	London
Embarked India:	per *'Lord William Bentinck'*
Presidency:	Bombay
Length of Service:	20 years 4 months
Age on Discharge:	42 years
Reason for Discharge:	Time expired
Character:	none given
Height:	5' 5¼"
Complexion:	Fresh
Eye Colour:	Hazel
Hair Colour:	Dark Brown
Remarks:	Survived a shipwreck
Intends to Reside:	Cork
COLTON	William, gunner and driver [3772] RA 5th battalion

Surname Variant	COTTON
21 May 1856	Discharged approved
10 June 1856	Discharged the Service Woolwich
Pension paid 2nd Dublin Pension District	
8d. per diem	
9 Jan 1868	Arrived per *'Hougoumont'*
1869	To Adelaide from Fremantle [WO22/252]
1870	?Pension paid Fremantle [depending on WO record source]
1876	To Melbourne from Perth West. Australia

Service and Personal Details:

Place of Birth:	Drumhairn Co. Fermanagh	
Age on Attestation:	18 years 6 months	
Period of Service:	1853 — 1856	
Age on Discharge:	21 years	
Length of Service:	2 years 178 days	
Foreign Service:	"the Crimea"	9 months
Medal Entitlement:	Crimea Medal with clasp	
Reason for Discharge:	Wound of the left thigh	
Character:	Very Good	
Trade or Occupation:	Labourer	
Can Sign Name:	Yes	
Height:	5' 10¼"	
Hair Colour:	Sandy	
Eyes:	Hazel	
Complexion:	Fresh	

COLWELL	Owen, private
	84th Foot
Previous Regiment	88th Foot
Dec 1858	Discharged the Service Chatham
4 Jan 1859	Admitted to Out-Pension
	Pension paid Bolton
	1/- per diem
1859	Pension paid Liverpool
28 Dec 1863	Arrived per *'Lord Dalhousie'* as a Convict Guard
1866	To South Australia from Perth West Australia
1866	To Victoria from South Australia
1869	W.O. correspondence re. - address

Service and Personal Details:

Place of Birth:	St Peters Athlone Roscommon	
Age on Attestation:	19 years 6 months	
Period of Service:	1837— 1858	
Age on Discharge:	40 years 11 months	
Length of Service:	21 years 164 days	
Foreign Service:	Malta	3 years
	East Indies	10 years 6 months
Reason for Discharge:	Own Request on completing 21 years service	
Character:	Very Good	
Trade or Occupation:	Labourer	
Can Sign Name:	X his mark on discharge	

Height:	5' 9"
Hair Colour:	Brown
Eyes:	Light Brown
Complexion:	Fair
Intends to Reside:	Bolton Lancashire

COMER Matthew, private
76th Foot

Surname Variants	[some] COMMER; COMAR; COOMER; COOMAN; CONNER
28 Nov 1854	Discharged the Service Chatham Pension paid Athlone 1/- per diem
1855	Pension paid Clonmel
4 June 1856	Onboard '*Runnymede*' and gave evidence in the trial of William Nevin
10 July 1857	Arrived per '*Clara*' [1]
1864	To South Australia from Fremantle per '*Sea Ripple*'
1867	Died South Australia

Service and Personal Details:

Place of Birth:	Killtoom Athlone Roscommon	
Age on Attestation:	19 years	
Period of Service:	1833 — 1854	
Age on Discharge:	40 years or 39 years	
Length of Service:	21 years 11 month	
Foreign Service:	West Indies &	
	Bermuda	7 years 8 months
	Mediterranean	5 years
	North America	2 years 4 months
Medal Entitlement:	Good Conduct with gratuity	
Reason for Discharge:	Chronic Catarrh and worn out	
Character:	Very Good	
Trade or Occupation:	Labourer	
Can Sign Name:	X his mark on discharge	
Height:	5' 9¼"	
Hair Colour:	Brown	
Eye Colour:	Hazel	
Complexion:	Fresh	
Intends to Reside:	Athlone Co. Roscommon	

COMERFORD Martin, private
33rd Foot

Surname Variants	COMMERFORD; CUMMERFORD
3 July 1855	Discharged the Service Chatham Pension paid Kilkenny 8d. per diem
1855	Serving in the Kilkenny Militia
1856	Pension paid Birr
1858	Pension paid 1st Dublin Pension District
8 June 1858	Arrived per '*Lord Raglan*'
1858	To Champion Bay to take charge of the Govt. Bonded Store
1859	Employed as Tide waiter
1864	Appointed Postmaster Geraldton

	Quarter Master Sergeant of the Geraldton Volunteer Rifle Corps
1877	Serving as Postmaster and Clerk of Customs
Dec 1889	Died
Service and Personal Details:	
Place of Birth:	Killmanaugh Co. Kilkenny
Age on Attestation:	17 years
Period of Service:	1847 — 1855
Age on Discharge:	23 years 3 months
Length of Service:	6 years 337 days [reckoned]
Foreign Service:	Crimea [no time period given]
Medal Entitlement:	Crimea with clasps
Reason for Discharge:	Loss of left thumb from gunshot wound received in the trenches at Sebastopol
Character:	Good
Trade or Occupation:	Labourer
Can Sign Name:	Yes
Height:	5' 9½"
Hair Colour:	Dark Brown
Eyes:	Grey
Complexion:	Fresh

COMMERFORD	James, Serjeant 88th Foot
21 May 1850	Discharged the Service Castlebar
1 July 1850	Admitted to Out-Pension Pension paid 2nd Edinburgh Pension District 1/4½d. per diem
2 June 1853	Embarked per *'Phoebe Dunbar'* "Dismissed from Local Force for insubordinative [sic] conduct and landed at Dublin"

CONDON	Jeremiah, private EIC 1st Bombay Fusiliers Out Pension No 607
6 Jan 1861	Admitted to Out-Pension Pension paid 2nd Cork Pension District 9d. per diem
1862	Pension paid 2nd East London Pension District
22 Dec 1865	Arrived per *'Vimiera'*
1866	Pension paid Fremantle Pension District
1873	Residing Fremantle
22 Sept 1883	Assigned Lot P76 North Fremantle named as James Condon
27 Oct 1882	On the 1st October at Fremantle Jeremiah Condon did feloniously and carnally know and abuse Elizabeth Hearns, aged eleven years and ten months,
1883	Due to a legal technicality the charge was dismissed — Discharged at Supreme Court
30 Aug 1884	Granted Fee Simple North Fremantle Lot P76
1888	Residing Fremantle
June 1897	Residing Fremantle

Service and Personal Details:	
Where Born:	St Pauls Cork
Trade or Occupation:	Carpenter
Date Attested:	1846
Embarked India:	per *'Mount Stewart Elphinstone'*
Presidency:	Bombay
Length of Service:	16 years 5 months
Age on Discharge:	36 years
Reason for Discharge:	Unfit for further service
Character:	Good
Medal Entitlement:	Punjaub; Indian Mutiny
Complexion:	Fresh
Height:	5' 7" or 5' 5¾"
Eye Colour:	Grey
Hair Colour:	Brown
Intends to Reside:	Cork

CONGDON	William, private Army Staff Corps — Staff of Depots
Previous Regiment	65th Foot
12 Apr 1837	Discharged the Service Pension paid 2nd West London Pension District 7d. per diem
6 Apr 1854	Arrived per *'Sea Park'*
1856	Appointed Assistant Warder
1856	Compounder of Medicine Convict Establishment
1865	Discharged because of ill health
1865	Died
Feb 1865	Funeral Fremantle aged 64

Service and Personal Details:	
Place of Birth:	St Andrews Plymouth Devon
Age on Attestation:	18 years
Period of Service:	1820 — 1837
Age on Discharge:	34 years
Length of Service:	16 years 198 days
Reason for Discharge:	Unfit for further service
Character:	Very Good, but as Sergeant at the Invalid Depot his character has been bad
Trade or Occupation:	Shoemaker
Can Sign Name:	Yes
Height:	5' 5½"
Hair Colour:	Light Brown
Eyes:	Grey
Complexion:	Fresh
Married:	*c*1822 Sarah Ann Scott Hampshire
Children:	Sarah b. *c*1831 Ireland John James b. *c*1835 Hampshire Daniel b. *c*1837 Kent [became a JP and member of Parliament] m. *c*1861 Jane Fairbairn Pinjarra William b. *c*1839 England

	Edward b. *c*1841 Essex
	James b. *c*1843 England
CONLAN	Michael, Serjeant
	77th Foot
Surname Variant	CONLON
23 Aug 1859	Discharged to Pension Chatham
	Pension paid
	1/8d. per diem
	Possibly arrived per *'Palmeston'*
1861	Pension paid Western Australia
1863	Stationed Perth District
1864	Serjeant M Conlon serving in the Pensioner Force at Perth contributed to the Greenough Fire Relief Fund

Service and Personal Details:		
Place of Birth:	Rathfarham Dublin	
Age on Attestation:	18 years	
Period of Service:	1837 — 1859	
Age on Discharge:	40 years 1 month	
Length of Service:	22 years 2 days	
Foreign Service:	Mediterranean &	
	Turkey & Crimea	5 years 1 month
	West Indies &	
	North America	5 years 5 months
	Australia & East Indies	2 years 1 month
Medal Entitlement:	Crimea	
Reason for Discharge:	Chronic Dysentery and failing health	
Character:	Good	
Trade or Occupation:	Tailor	
Can Sign Name:	Yes	
Height:	5' 9"	
Hair Colour:	Brown	
Eyes:	Grey	
Complexion:	Sallow	
Intends to Reside:	Glasgow	

CONLEY	Martin [William], private
	71st Foot
Surname Variant	CONLAN
30 July 1861	Discharged the Service Stirling Castle
	Pension paid 2nd Glasgow Pension District
	9½d. per diem
15 Apr 1864	Arrived per *'Clara'* [2]
1866	To South Australia from Perth West. Australia
1867	Pension paid Melbourne
Service and Personal Details:	
Place of Birth:	Barony Glasgow
Age on Attestation:	19 years
Period of Service:	1838 — 1861
Age on Discharge:	41 years 11 months

Length of Service:	22 years 8 days	
Foreign Service:	Canada	4 years 4 months
	West Indies	3 years 2 months
	Corfu	1 year 10 months
	Crimea	1 year 4 months
	Malta	1 year 7 months
	East Indies	3 years 3 months
Medal Entitlement:	Crimea; Indian Mutiny	
Reason for Discharge:	Own Request having served over 21 years	
Character:	Good	
Trade or Occupation:	Potter	
Can Sign Name:	Yes	
Height:	5' 6¼"	
Hair Colour:	Red	
Eyes:	Grey	
Complexion:	Fair	
Intends to Reside:	Glasgow	

CONNEALLY Timothy, private
9th Foot

9 Oct 1855 Discharged the Service Chatham
Pension paid Galway
9d. per diem
June 1857 Pension paid Chester
27 May 1863 Arrived per *'Clyde'*
1866 Pension paid South Australia [12/WA/252]

Service and Personal Details:

Place of Birth:	St Nicholas Galway	
Age on Attestation:	19 years	
Period of Service:	1854 — 1855	
Age on Discharge:	21 years	
Length of Service:	1 year 100 days	
Foreign Service:	Crimea	6 months
Medal Entitlement:	Crimean with clasp	
Reason for Discharge:	Wounded lower part of right arm by musket ball	
Character:	Good	
Trade or Occupation:	Tobacco Spinner	
Height:	5' 6½"	
Hair Colour:	Light Brown	
Eyes:	Hazel	
Complexion:	Fresh	
Distinguishing Marks:	Small pock on face	
Intends to Reside:	Galway	

CONNELLY John, private
29th Foot

Previous Regiment 88th Foot
Surname Variants CONNALLY; CONNOLLY
23 June 1868 Discharged the Service Chatham
Pension paid Newcastle
1/1d. per diem
1873 Pension paid Greenwich

19 Feb 1874	Arrived per *'Naval Brigade'*
circa June 1875	Transferred from Fremantle to Perth Pension District
1876	Stationed Perth with rank of private
June 1878	At this date "Unable to pay Fee Simple for his assigned land"
1881	Assigned Cockburn Loc P6 at Koogee [sic] — Request for an occupation certificate for John Connally [Pensioner] who has been assigned 20 acres Lot 6 at Lake Munster
1881	Pension increased to 1/3½d. per diem for service in the Enrolled Force
1884	Granted Fee Simple Cockburn Loc P6
21 Mar 1887	Superintendent Fremantle Prison That Pensioner J. Connolly be temporarily employed as Prison Guard
June 1897	Residing Fremantle
Feb 1900	Attended fete at Fremantle Oval

Service and Personal Details:

Place of Birth:	Clifden Galway	
Age on Attestation:	17 years	
Period of Service:	1846 — 1868	
Age on Discharge:	39 years 3 months	
Length of Service:	21 years 7 days	
Foreign Service:	East Indies	10 years
	Malta	2 years
	Canada	11 months
Medal Entitlement:	Indian Mutiny with clasp for Central India	
Reason for Discharge:	Own Request after 21 years service	
Character:	Good	
Trade or Occupation:	Labourer	
Can Sign Name:	X his mark on discharge	
Height:	5' 6½"	
Hair Colour:	Brown	
Eyes:	Grey	
Complexion:	Fresh	
Distinguishing Marks:	Vaccination on right arm; scar on right thigh and shin	
Intends to Reside:	Newcastle on Tyne	

CONNER — see — COMER Mathew, private
76th Foot

CONNOLLY — John, private, private
63rd Foot

Surname Variants	[some] CONNOLY; CONNELLY; CONNELLEY
8 June 1829	Arrived per *'HMS Sulphur'*
1834	Discharged at own request in Colony
	Applied for Perth Lot No. 20 Sec. T
Mar 1852	Died aged 52 — cause of death, thrown from his horse

Service and Personal Details:

Place of Birth:	Armatris Parish Cootehill, Co. Monaghan	
Age on Enlistment:	19 years	
Period of Service:	1819 — 1834	
Length of Service:	14 years	
Foreign Service:	Portugal about	18 months
	Western Australia	5 years
Character:	Good and efficient soldier, well conducted	
Trade or Occupation:	Labourer	
Height:	5' 7"	
Hair Colour:	Brown	
Eyes:	Brown	
Complexion:	Fresh	

CONNOLLY James, private
26th Foot

Surname Variant	CONNELLY
29 Apr 1856	Discharged the Service Chatham 6d. per diem
1856	Pension paid Sligo
1856	Liverpool
1858	Manchester
1862	Bermuda
15 Feb 1863	Arrived per *'Merchantman'* [1]
16 Sept 1868	Purchased Geraldton Town Lot 365
1874	Pension increased to 11d. per diem for service in the Enrolled Force
1878	To Adelaide from Perth Western Australia

Service and Personal Details:

Place of Birth:	Aberdeen Aberdeenshire	
Age on Attestation:	18 years	
Period of Service:	1840 — 1856	
Age on Discharge:	33 years 6 months	
Length of Service:	15 years 137 days	
Foreign Service:	China	8 months
	East Indies	6 months
	Gibraltar	3 years 2 months
	Canada	1 year 6 months
	Bermuda	1 year 2 months
Reason for Discharge:	Chronic Hepatitis	
Character:	Good	
Trade or Occupation:	Labourer	
Can Sign Name:	Yes	
Height:	5' 9"	
Hair Colour:	Fair	
Eyes:	Grey	
Complexion:	Fair	
Intends to Reside:	Chatham	

CONNOLLY Michael, private
19th Foot

27 Feb 1855	Discharged the Service Chatham

Pension paid Deptford
1/- per diem
29 Jan 1862 — Arrived per *'Lincelles'*
1863 — Pension paid Deptford

Service and Personal Details:
Place of Birth: Oranmore Galway
Age on Attestation: 18 years
Period of Service: 1839 — 1855
Age on Discharge: 33 years 6 months
Length of Service: 15 years 172 days
Foreign Service: Mediterranean 5 years 9 months
West Indies 2 years 4 months
North America 3 years 2 months
Medal Entitlement: Crimean clasp for Alma
Reason for Discharge: Wounded in the left hand by a musket ball at the battle of Alma

Character: Latterly good
Trade or Occupation: Servant
Can Sign Name: Yes

Height: 5' 7½"
Hair Colour: Dark
Eyes: Hazel
Complexion: Dark
Intends to Reside: Galway

CONNOLLY Richard, private
73rd Foot
Surname Variant [some] CONNELLY; CONNOLLEY; CONOLLY
8 Jan 1840 — Discharged the Service Chatham
Pension paid Jersey
6d. per diem
28 June 1851 — Arrived per *'Pyrenees'* [1]
1852 — Assigned York Lot P1
Jan 1857 — Contributed 1/- to the Florence Nightingale Fund
1860 — Application for Title to York Lot P1
1861 — Residing York
1864 — private R Connolley [sic] serving in the Pensioner Force at York contributed to the Greenough Fire Relief Fund
1865 — Pension paid Western Australia
1881 — Died

Service and Personal Details:
Place of Birth: St Marys Athlone Westmeath
Age on Attestation: 21 years
Period of Service: 1824 — 1839
Age on Discharge: 36 years 7 months
Length of Service: 15 years 237 days [reckoned]
Foreign Service: Gibraltar 2 years 7 months
Malta 4 years 3 months
Ionian Isles 3 year 10 months
North America 1 year 3 months
Reason for Discharge: Unfit for further service

Character:	Very Good
Trade or Occupation:	Labourer
Can Sign Name:	Yes
Height:	5' 8¼"
Hair Colour:	Dark
Eyes:	Blue
Complexion:	Dark
Married:	Elizabeth Barrett
Children:	Richard b. *c*1844 Jersey m. *c*1871 Bridget Connor York

CONNOR — Jeremiah, private
22nd Foot
On the 14th Aug 1875 at his residence York after a long and painful illness Jeremiah Connor from HM 22 Foot and prior to his demise a resident in Newcastle WA for a period of 22 years; deeply lamented by his sorrowing family and all who knew him aged 74
according to the Index of "Soldiers Documents" held at TNA Kew no Jeremiah Conner, Connor, Connors or O'Conner, O'Connor, or O'Connors 22nd Foot can be found in the "Discharged to Pension" Records prior to 1854

CONNOR — Owen, private
99th Foot

Surname Variants	CONNER; CONNERS; CONNORS
4 Sept 1841	Discharged the Service Dublin Pension paid Birr 6d. per diem
1847	Pension paid Galway
1849	Liverpool
21 May 1851	Arrived per *'Mermaid'*
1851	Assigned and occupied Fremantle Lot P1
1858	Title application for North Fremantle Lot P1
Aug 1863	Owen Conner, Pensioner, application for pauper relief for himself and family as 'Wife and children are starving." Residents Office — Reply: he is residing on his own 'fee simple' and as both used to good provision by military pay, both are able bodied — application refused
1863	To Adelaide from Perth Western Australia
1865	Pension paid South Australia
1872	South Australia
1875	South Australia

Service and Personal Details:

Place of Birth:	Annadown Co. Galway
Age on Attestation:	16 years
Period of Service:	1824 — 1841
Age on Discharge:	31 years
Length of Service:	15 years 112 days — reckoned

Foreign Service:	Mauritius	11 years 160 days
Reason for Discharge:	Fistula of the Urethra	
Character:	Good Efficient Trustworthy and Sober	
Trade or Occupation:	Labourer	
Can Sign Name:	X his mark on discharge	
Height:	5' 7"	
Hair Colour:	Fair	
Eyes:	Grey	
Complexion:	Fresh	

CONNOR	Peter, private	
	73rd Foot	
Surname Variants	CONNORS; CONOR	
18 Nov 1846	Discharged the Service Clare Castle	
9 Mar 1847	Admitted to Out-Pension	
	Pension paid Athlone	
	1/- per diem	
1859	Pension paid 2nd Dublin Pension District	
2 Apr 1856	Arrived per *'William Hammond'*	
1858	Assigned and occupied North Fremantle Lot 15 formerly assigned to Tansey	
1873	Pension increased to 1/3d. for 10¾ years service in the Enrolled Force	
1874	Correspondence with W.O. from S.O.P. Fremantle	
Nov 1881	a Peter Connor died aged 74 at Singapore	
Service and Personal Details:		
Place of Birth:	? Ferbane Offaly	
Age on Attestation:	18 years	
Period of Service:	1825 — 1846	
Age on Discharge:	39 years 5 months	
Length of Service:	21 years 153 days	
Foreign Service:	Gibraltar	2 years 7 months
	Malta	4 years 3 months
	Ionian Isles	3 years 10 months
	North America	3 years 2 months
Reason for Discharge:	Chronic Hepatitis	
Character:	Good	
Trade or Occupation:	Weaver	
Can Sign Name:	Yes	
Height:	5' 10"	
Hair Colour:	Brown	
Eyes:	Blue	
Complexion:	Fresh	

CONNOR	Thomas, private
	28th Foot
Previous Regiment	99th Foot
Surname Variant	CONNORS; CONNER
29 Jan 1856	Discharged the Service Chatham
	Pension paid 1st East London Pension District
	8d. per diem
15 Apr 1864	Arrived per *'Clara'* [2]

Oct 1864	To South Australia per *'Sea Ripple'*	
1865	Pension paid Adelaide from Fremantle	
1870	South Australia	
1871	Melbourne	
1872	South Australia	
Service and Personal Details:		
Place of Birth:	Killarney Co. Clare	
Age on Attestation:	18 years	
Period of Service:	1853 — 1856	
Age on Discharge:	21 years	
Length of Service:	2 years ?5 days	
Foreign Service:	Malta & Turkey & Crimea	1 year 9 months
Medal Entitlement:	Crimea with clasps	
Reason for Discharge:	Wounded in left hand by musket ball	
Character:	Good	
Trade or Occupation:	Labourer	
Height:	5' 6¾"	
Hair Colour:	Dark Brown	
Eyes:	Grey	
Complexion:	Fresh	
Intends to Reside:	Limerick	

CONNOR	William, private [drummer] 69th Foot	
Surname Variant	CONNER	
8 Aug 1871	Discharged the Service Chichester Pension paid Tullamore 1/- per diem	
19 Feb 1874	Arrived per *'Naval Brigade'*	
8 Aug 1871	To Adelaide from Perth West Australia	
1875	Pension paid South Australia	
Service and Personal Details:		
Place of Birth:	Forfar Dundee	
Age on Attestation:	17 years	
Period of Service:	1849 — 1871	
Age on Discharge:	39 years 1 month	
Length of Service:	21 years 26 days	
Foreign Service:	Gibraltar	3 years 2 months
	Bermuda	4 years 8 months
	Canada	5 years 4 months
Medal Entitlement:	Long Service and Good Conduct with £5 gratuity	
Reason for Discharge:	Served over 21 years	
Character:	Very Good	
Trade or Occupation:	Weaver	
Can Sign Name:	Yes	
Height:	5' 10"	
Hair Colour:	Fair	
Eyes:	Grey	
Complexion:	Fair	
Intends to Reside:	Claran Kings County	

CONNORS	Darby, private
	22nd Foot
Surname Variant	CONNOR
9 June 1837	Discharged the Service Buttervant
18 July 1837	Appeared before Medical Board Dublin
9 Aug 1837	Discharged to pension
1837	Pension paid Carlow
	6d. per diem
1846	Pension paid 1st Dublin Pension District
7 Feb 1853	Arrived per *'Dudbrook'*
Jan 1861	Assigned Newcastle Lot S11
Jan 1861	Title Application for Newcastle Lot S11 Deed No 1796
1873	Pension increased to 1/1d. per diem for 14½ years service in the Enrolled Force
Service and Personal Details:	
Place of Birth:	? Clenigen Carlow
Age on Attestation:	18 years
Period of Service:	1825 — 1837
Age on Discharge:	30 years
Length of Service:	12 years 12 days
Foreign Service:	Jamaica 10 years
Reason for Discharge:	Chronic Bronchitis; Worn Out and Large Rupture on right side
Character:	Indifferent
Trade or Occupation:	Labourer
Can Sign Name:	Yes
Height:	5' 6¼"
Hair Colour:	Brown
Eyes:	Grey
Complexion:	Fair

CONNORS	James, private EIC
	Bengal European Infantry
Surname Variant	CONNOR
	Out Pension No 350
9 June 1847	Discharged the Service
1847	Embarked UK per *'Prince of Wales'*
1848	Pension paid Kilkenny
	1/- per diem
25 Oct 1850	Arrived per *'Hashemy'*
18 Nov 1858	Assigned Bunbury Pensioner Lot P8
4 Dec 1858	Application for Title to Bunbury Lot P8
1875	Pension paid Western Australia
1886	Died aged 76
Service and Personal Details:	
Where Born:	Kilkenny
Trade or Occupation:	Labourer
Age on Enlistment:	20 years
Date Enlisted:	15th June 1830
Where Enlisted:	Kilkenny

Embarked India:	per *'Lady Melville'* 19th Jan 1831
Presidency:	Bengal
Length of Service:	16 years 1 month
Age on Discharge:	36 years
Reason for Discharge:	Wound received on left knee at Sobraon
Medal Entitlement:	Sutlej
Character:	Good
Height:	5' 6½"
Complexion:	Fresh
Visage:	Long
Eye Colour:	Grey
Hair Colour:	Brown

CONNORS

	John, private [drummer 304]
	45th Foot
Previous Regiment	46th Foot
Surname Variant	CONROY
23 Sept 1851	Discharged the Service Chatham
	Pension paid 2nd West London Pension District
	1/- per diem
19 Aug 1853	Guard on board *'Robert Small'*
	Died on voyage out

COOK

	Henry, Lance Serjeant
	35th Foot
5 Nov 1846	Discharged the Service Charles Fort Kinsale
1848	Pension paid Woolwich
	Assistant Warder on Prison Hulk at Woolwich
	4d. per diem
1854	Possibly arrived per *'Esmeralda'*
12 Dec 1873	Aged 60 years
20 June 1883	Assigned North Fremantle Lot P74
29 Aug 1884	Granted Fee Simple North Fremantle Lot P74
1885	Pension increased to 5½d. per diem

Service and Personal Details:

Place of Birth:	St Georges London Middlesex
Age on Attestation:	17 years 10 months
Period of Service:	1831 — 1846
Age on Discharge:	32 years 10 months
Length of Service:	14 years 332 days
Reason for Discharge:	Own Request with right of Registry for Deferred Pension of 4d. per diem on attaining 60 years
Character:	Very Good and deserving soldier
Trade or Occupation:	Groom
Can Sign Name:	Yes
Height:	5' 8"
Hair Colour:	Red
Eyes:	Hazel
Complexion:	Fresh

COOK

	James, private
	12th Foot
22 June 1852	Discharged the Service Chatham

	Pension paid Northampton
	8d. per diem
24 Nov 1858	Arrived per *'Edwin Fox'*
1867	Pension paid New Zealand
1871	Died
Service and Personal Details:	
Place of Birth:	Chard Somerset
Age on Attestation:	19 years
Period of Service:	1836 — 1852
Age on Discharge:	36 years
Length of Service:	16 years 84 days
Foreign Service:	Mauritius 10 years
Reason for Discharge:	Unfit for further service caused by constitutional infirmity
Character:	Very good
Trade or Occupation:	Labourer
Can Sign Name:	Yes
Height:	5' 8¼"
Hair Colour:	Dark Brown
Eyes:	Blue
Complexion:	Fair
Intends to Reside:	Woodford nr. Weedon Northamptonshire

COOPER	George, Colour Serjeant
	59th Foot
Previous Regiment	62nd Foot
Surname Variant	COPPER
15 Oct 1850	Discharged the Service Tralee
3 Dec 1850	Admitted to Out-Pension
	Pension paid Nottingham
	1/3d. per diem
1851	Residing Tythby Cum Cropwell with wife Margaret
18 July 1855	Arrived per Convict Ship *'Adelaide'*
Jan 1857	Contributed 3/6 to the Florence Nightingale Fund
2 Nov1874	Died of Pleurisy Fremantle aged 63
Service and Personal Details:	
Place of Birth:	Cropwell Butler Nottinghamshire
Age on Attestation:	18 years
Period of Service:	1834 — 1850
Age on Discharge:	34 years 2 months
Length of Service:	16 years 55 days
Foreign Service:	Mediterranean 3 years 95 days
	West Indies 3 years 6 days
Reason for Discharge:	Abscess and unfit for further service
Character:	Very Good
Trade or Occupation:	Labourer
Can Sign Name:	Yes
Height:	5' 10¼"
Hair Colour:	Light Brown
Eyes:	Grey

Complexion:	Fresh
Intends to Reside:	Cropwell Butler

COOTE	Thomas, private 82nd Foot
Surname Variant	COOK
22 Nov 1853	Discharged the Service Chatham Pension paid Perth Scotland 6d. per diem for 18 months
24 May 1855	Arrived per *'Stag'*
1861	Died

Service and Personal Details:

Place of Birth:	Mullingar Westmeath
Age on Attestation:	22 years
Period of Service:	1843 — 1853
Age on Discharge:	33 years
Length of Service:	10 years 234 days
Foreign Service:	Canada 2 years 1 day
Reason for Discharge:	Extensive Varicose Veins of both extremities
Character:	Indifferent
Trade or Occupation:	Labourer
Can Sign Name:	X his mark on discharge
Height:	5' 8½"
Hair Colour:	Red
Eyes:	Grey
Complexion:	Fresh
Intends to Reside:	Perth Scotland

COPE	James, Corporal 67th Foot [father John — mother Elizabeth and brother of Thomas Cope EIC]
15 Apr 1850	Discharged the Service Gibraltar Granted a Deferred Pension of 4d. per diem on attaining the age of 60 years
17 July 1867	Arrived per *'Norwood'* as a Warder
19 Aug 1872	Aged 50
1872	Stationed at Canning Bridge
1872	Ordered to dispose of his pigs
1874	Stationed Fremantle Prison
1878	Evicted from quarters
31 Mar 1881	In receipt of Deferred Pension
20 July 1882	W.O. correspondence — Forms to Fremantle "A44" to A.G. that Discharge Document may be retained
1887	Discharge Document returned
May 1900	Died Jarrahdale

Service and Personal Details:

Place of Birth:	Mortlam [sic] Surrey [Richmond on death information]
Age on Attestation:	17 years
Period of Service:	1839 — 1850

Age on Discharge:	26 years 7 months
Length of Service:	9 years 207 days
Foreign Service:	Gibraltar 2 years
Reason for Discharge:	A reduction in the regiment and him paying his own passage to England in accordance with Horse Guards Circular dated Feb. 1850 and authority date Gibraltar March 1850
Character:	Good
Trade or Occupation:	Baker
Can Sign Name:	Yes
Height:	5' 8"
Hair Colour:	Brown
Eyes:	Brown
Complexion:	Sallow
Intends to Reside:	Richmond

COPE

	Thomas, private EIC Madras European Regiment Out Pension No 628
10 Sept 1861	Discharged to Out-pension Pension paid South London Pension District 1/- per diem
1862	"Selected as Convict Guard on *'York'* — left sick at Weymouth"
1862	Pension paid Salisbury District
1863	Pension paid East London Pension District
12 Sept 1864	Arrived per *'Merchantman'* [2]
1868	Residing Fremantle
1868	Gave notice that he would not be responsible for debts contracted by his wife Ellen.
1870	Pension paid South Australia [12/WA/397]
Mar 1870	a Thomas and Ellen Cope departed the Colony per *'Emily Smith'*
1879	Pension paid South Australia
Nov 1897	a Thomas Cope died at his brother James's residence at Jarrahdale aged 77

Service and Personal Details:

Where Born:	Mortlake Richmond Surrey
Date of Birth:	circa 1820
Trade or Occupation:	Baker
Presidency:	Madras
Length of Service:	22 years 9 months
Age on Discharge:	39 years
Reason for Discharge:	Time expired
Character:	Unexceptional
Height:	5' 5"
Complexion:	Dark
Eye Colour:	Black
Hair Colour:	Black
Intends to Reside:	Mortlake Surrey

CORBOY Michael, private

	19th Foot	
4 May 1858	Discharged the Service Chatham	
	Pension paid Preston	
	11d. per diem	
1858	Pension paid Liverpool	
19 Aug 1859	Arrived per *'Sultana'*	
1863	To Adelaide from Perth Western Australia "Pension subject to stoppage of 2/3d for support of wife and family in Western Australia"	
1864	Pension paid Melbourne	
1879	Half pension stopped for support of wife	
1884	Correspondence with W.O.	
Service and Personal Details:		
Place of Birth:	Nenagh Tipperary	
Age on Attestation:	19 years	
Period of Service:	1837 — 1858	
Age on Discharge:	40 years 2 months	
Length of Service:	21 years 50 days	
Foreign Service:	Mediterranean	5 years 3 months
	West Indies	2 years 4 months
	North America	3 years 2 months
Reason for Discharge:	Chronic Rheumatism	
Character:	Good	
Trade or Occupation:	Mason	
Can Sign Name:	Yes	
Height:	5' 9"	
Hair Colour:	Brown	
Eyes:	Grey	
Complexion:	Fresh	
Intends to Reside:	Blackburn Lancaster	
CORCORAN	John, private	
	3rd Foot	
16 Nov 1848	Discharged the Service Limerick	
9 Jan 1849	Admitted to Out-Pension	
	Pension paid Tullamore	
	1/- per diem	
10 Sept 1856	Arrived per *'Runnymede'*	
9 Aug 1863	Died aged 54	
22 Nov 1864	Application for Title to Perth Lot 35/Y by a Catherine Corcoran	
Service and Personal Details:		
Place of Birth:	Durrane Kings County	
Age on Attestation:	20 years	
Period of Service:	1826 — 1848	
Age on Discharge:	42 years	
Length of Service:	21 years 98 days	
Foreign Service:	East Indies	13 years 7 months
Reason for Discharge:	Rheumatism and Liver Complaint	
Character:	Habitual drunk	
Trade or Occupation:	Servant	
Can Sign Name:	X his mark on discharge	

Height:	5' 6½"
Hair Colour:	Dark Brown
Eyes:	Grey
Complexion:	Fresh

CORNELLY	Farrell, private 65th Foot
Surname Variants	CORNALLY; CONNELLY; CONELLY
28 July 1846	Discharged the Service Chatham Pension paid Falmouth 1/- per diem
1851	Residing Prestow [sic] Budock, Cornwall
2 Aug 1852	Arrived per *'William Jardine'*
11 Feb 1853	Employed as Night Warder
26 Oct 1856	Died buried at Lynton

Service and Personal Details:

Place of Birth:	Melan Kings County
Age on Attestation:	17 years
Period of Service:	1825 — 1846
Age on Discharge:	41 years or 38 years 1 month
Length of Service:	20 years 9 days [reckoned]
Foreign Service:	West Indies 8 years North America 3 years 6 months
Reason for Discharge:	Chronic Cough and General Debility
Character:	Good
Trade or Occupation:	Servant
Can Sign Name:	Yes
Height:	5' 7"
Hair Colour:	Dark
Eyes:	Grey
Complexion:	Fresh
Intends to Reside:	Falmouth the following family information is from the 1851 UK Census
Married:	Elizabeth
Children:	Edward b. 1844 Rochdale Lancs. James b. 1845 Ireland Thomas b. 1846 Sheerness Kent Ellen b. 1848 Falmouth Farrall b. 1850 Budock Cornwall
	the following information is from the '*William Hammond*'s' passenger list and W.A. parish records
Married:	Bridget O'Loughlin
Children:	Elizabeth b. *c*1853 Fremantle Farrell b. *c*1856 Port Gregory

CORNICK	George, private 59th Foot
Surname Variant	CORMICK

28 June 1864	Discharged the Service Preston Pension paid Dorchester 11d. per diem
9 Jan 1868	Arrived per *'Hougoumont'*
1872	Pension paid Western Australia
circa Dec 1875	Transferred from Fremantle to 1st Perth District
1878	Pension increased to 1/1d. per diem for service in the Enrolled Force
1881	Pension increased to 1/1½d. per diem for service in the Enrolled Force
7 Mar 1883	Received Fee Simple Fremantle Lot P73
1890	Died at his house behind Fremantle prison

Service and Personal Details:

Place of Birth:	Great Toll Dorchester	
Age on Attestation:	21 years	
Period of Service:	1842 — 1864	
Age on Discharge:	41 years 9 months	
Length of Service:	21 years 47 days	
Foreign Service:	Hong Kong	5 years 284 days
	Cape of Good Hope	49 days
Reason for Discharge:	Own Request having served over 21 years	
Character:	Good	
Trade or Occupation:	Labourer	
Can Sign Name:	Yes	
Height:	5' 9¼"	
Hair Colour:	Dark Brown	
Eyes:	Brown	
Complexion:	Swarthy	
Intends to Reside:	Dorchester	

COSS

	John, private 24th Foot
Previous Regiment	21st Foot
22 June 1852	Discharged the Service Chatham Pension paid Halifax 1/2d. per diem
24 May 1855	Arrived per *'Stag'*
Jan 1857	Contributed 1/- to the Florence Nightingale Fund
1857	Pension paid Hobart Town
1875	Hobart Town

Service and Personal Details:

Place of Birth:	Maryborough Queens County	
Age on Attestation:	18 years	
Period of Service:	1827 — 1852	
Age on Discharge:	44 years	
Length of Service:	24 years 96 days	
Foreign Service:	Van Dieman's Land	6 years 6 months
	East Indies	12 years 5 months
Reason for Discharge:	Worn out from long service	
Character:	Very Good	
Trade or Occupation:	Weaver	
Can Sign Name:	Yes	

Height:	5' 8"
Hair Colour:	Fair
Eyes:	Blue
Complexion:	Fair
Intends to Reside:	Queens County

COSTELLO	John, private 40th Foot
Surname Variants	COSTELLOE; COSTELLOS
9 July 1845	Medical Examination
15 Aug 1845	Discharged the Service Chatham Pension paid Kilkenny 9d. per diem
25 Oct 1850	Arrived per *'Hashemy'*
20 Nov 1858	Assigned Bunbury Pensioner Lot P7
Dec 1858	Application for Title to Bunbury Lot P7
23 Apr 1884	The Resident Magistrate Bunbury — Landing Waiter at Bunbury, re. payment to John Costello as substitute during illness of ?***** Employed as Lighthouse keeper, tidewaiter, and Customs Officer Member of the first Bunbury Municipal Council and member of the Town Trust
July 1902	Died aged 84 at his residence in White Road Bunbury
1902	Grant of Probate

Service and Personal Details:

Place of Birth:	Freshford Kilkenny	
Age on Attestation:	18 years	
Period of Service:	1836 — 1845	
Age on Discharge:	28 years	
Length of Service:	8 years 256 days	
Foreign Service:	East Indies	8 years 2 months
Medal Entitlement:	Bronze Star Maharajpore; Afghan medal inscribed with Candahar and Ghuzni	
Reason for Discharge:	Impaired Vision	
Character:	Very Good	
Trade or Occupation:	Labourer	
Can Sign Name:	X his mark on discharge	
Height:	5' 6¾"	
Hair Colour:	Dark Brown	
Eyes:	Grey	
Complexion:	Fresh	
Intends to Reside:	Freshford Co. Kilkenny	

COSTELLO	William, private Royal Canadian Rifles
Previous Regiment	31st Foot
Surname Variant	COSTOLO
10 July 1860	Discharged the Service Chatham Pension paid Enniskillen 1/- per diem
1861	Pension paid 1st East London Pension District
1864	Disembarked the *'Merchantman'* at Portland

15 Aug 1865	Arrived per *'Racehorse'*
1874	Pension increased to 1/3d. per diem for service in the Enrolled Force
June 1881	Assigned Perth Town Lot 85/E at Claisebrook
May 1884	Granted Fee Simple Perth Town Lot 85/E
1892	Died
Service and Personal Details:	
Place of Birth:	Galway Co. Galway
Age on Attestation:	20 years
Period of Service:	1839 — 1860
Age on Discharge:	41 years 1 month
Length of Service:	20 years 342 days
Foreign Service:	India 6 years 11 months
	Canada 1 year 10 months
Medal Entitlement:	Long Service and Good Conduct
Reason for Discharge:	Unfit for further service
Character:	Very Good
Trade or Occupation:	Labourer
Can Sign Name:	X his mark on discharge
Height:	5' 6"
Hair Colour:	Dark Brown
Eyes:	Hazel
Complexion:	Fresh
Intends to Reside:	Enniskillin Fermanagh

COSTIGAN	George, Drummer 11th Foot
18 Aug 1863	Discharged the Service Fermoy Pension paid 1st Cork Pension District 1/- per diem
22 Dec 1865	Arrived per *'Vimiera'*
23 Aug 1881	Assigned North Fremantle Lots P40 and P47
1881	Pension increased to 1/6d. per diem for 13 years service in the Enrolled Force
Aug 1884	Granted Fee Simple North Fremantle Lots P40 and P47
1885	Died
1885	Resident Magistrate Fremantle — recommends relief to Ann Costigan
Service and Personal Details:	
Place of Birth:	Shandon Co. Cork
Age on Attestation:	14 years
Period of Service:	1836 — 1863
Age on Discharge:	41 years 5 months
Length of Service:	23 years 136 days
Foreign Service:	Australian Colonies 5 years 6 months
Reason for Discharge:	Having completed 21 actual years service
Character:	Latterly good
Trade or Occupation:	None
Can Sign Name:	Yes

Height:	5' 8½"
Hair Colour:	Dark Brown
Eyes:	Hazel
Complexion:	Sallow
Intends to Reside:	Cork

COUGHLAN Patrick, private
43rd Foot

Previous Regiments	5th Fusiliers; 23rd Foot
20 July 1858	Discharged the Service Chatham Pension paid 1st Cork Pension District 1/- per diem
19 Aug 1859	Arrived per *'Sultana'*
11 Oct 1862	Died

Service and Personal Details:

Place of Birth:	Ballincollig Co. Cork	
Age on Attestation:	19 years	
Period of Service:	1837 — 1858	
Age on Discharge:	40 years	
Length of Service:	20 years 154 days	
Foreign Service:	East Indies	15 years 3 months
Reason for Discharge:	Worn out and Chronic Rheumatism and lame from injury to hip from falling from the ramparts of the fort	
Character:	Very Good	
Trade or Occupation:	Labourer	
Can Sign Name:	Yes	
Height:	5' 8"	
Hair Colour:	Brown	
Eyes:	Hazel	
Complexion:	Fresh	
Intends to Reside:	Cork Co. Cork	

COULSON John Wood
see — John Calson, private
RM

COURTNEY Nicholas, private
22nd Foot

27 Feb 1861	Discharged the Service Parkhurst I.O.W.
12 Mar 1861	Admitted to Out-Pension Pension paid 1st Dublin Pension District 9d. per diem
29 Jan 1862	Arrived per *'Lincelles'*
1863	Pension paid Sydney New South Wales

Service and Personal Details:

Place of Birth:	St Pauls Dublin	
Period of Service:	1839 — 1861	
Age on Discharge:	39 years 6 months	
Length of Service:	21 years 63 days	
Foreign Service:	East Indies	13 years 11 months

Medal Entitlement:	Campaign in Scinde 1842 and the Campaign in the Southern Mahratta Country 1844 and the taking and destruction on the ? Borre Valley Peshawar 1853
Reason for Discharge:	Own Request having served over 21 years
Character:	Latterly Good — previously indifferent
Trade or Occupation:	Labourer
Can Sign Name:	X his mark on discharge
Height:	5' 5½"
Hair Colour:	Dark Brown
Eyes:	Grey
Complexion:	Fresh
Intends to Reside:	No. 20 Boot Lane Dublin

COWEN	Henry, private 52nd Foot
16 Sept 1856	Discharged the Service Chatham Pension paid Longford 6d. per diem
1859	Pension paid 1st West London Pension District Given Leave of Absence from the Commissioners of Chelsea Hospital to reside in South America for 2 years
1862	Pension paid South London
1862	Longford
28 Dec 1863	Arrived per *'Lord Dalhousie'* as a Convict Guard
1865	Pension paid Perth Western Australia
1865	On Nominal List to proceed to Camden Harbour per *'Tien Tsin'*
1866	a Henry Cowan departed colony per *'Fitzroy'*
1866	Pension paid 2nd West London Pension District "Stoppage of £1-13-9 to Mrs Bartlett"
1866	Pension increased to 9d. per diem
1866	Pension paid Longford
1 Aug 1866	Paisley
1 Apr 1873	Longford
1 May 1873	1st Glasgow Pension District
1874	2nd Glasgow Pension District

Service and Personal Details:

Place of Birth:	Templemichael Longford	
Age on Attestation:	18 years	
Period of Service:	1842 — 1855	
Age on Discharge:	32 years	
Length of Service:	12 years 326 days	
Foreign Service:	North America	3 years 4 months
	East Indies	2 years
Reason for Discharge:	Ophthalmia	
Character:	Good	
Trade or Occupation:	Servant [1842] — Shoemaker [1856]	
Can Sign Name:	Yes	
Height:	5' 6¾"	

Hair Colour:	Light Brown
Eyes:	Hazel
Complexion:	Fresh
Intends to Reside:	Longford

COYLE	Charles, private
	84th Foot
4 Oct 1864	Discharged the Service Dublin
	Pension paid Sheffield
	8d. per diem
22 Dec 1865	Arrived per *'Vimiera'*
1870	Refused to support wife and child and sentenced to one month hard labour
Dec 1871	Charged with being drunk
1872	In prison for seven days for drunkenness, and pension suspended
31 Dec 1875	To South Australia from Fremantle
1876	Pension paid South Australia
1877	To Melbourne
1882	Pension paid Melbourne

Service and Personal Details:

Place of Birth:	Templemichael Longford	
Age on Attestation:	19 years	
Period of Service:	1844 — 1864	
Age on Discharge:	40 years 8 months	
Length of Service:	21 years 7 days	
Foreign Service:	East Indies	14 years 10 months
Reason for Discharge:	Having completed 21 years service	
Character:	Bad	
Trade or Occupation:	Labourer	
Can Sign Name:	X his mark on discharge	
Height:	5' 9½"	
Hair Colour:	Brown	
Eyes:	Grey	
Complexion:	Fresh	
Intends to Reside:	Sheffield Yorkshire	

COYLE	John, Serjeant
	27th Foot
Previous Regiment	Cape Mounted Rifles
6 June 1848	Discharged the Service Chatham
	Pension paid Londonderry
	1/10d. per diem
1849	Pension paid London
1849	Paisley
1 June 1850	Arrived per *'Scindian'*
June 1850	Employed Gate Keeper Convict service
1851	Resigned Convict service and 'struck off' Enrolled Pensioner Force
1852	Pension paid New South Wales
1853	Pension paid 1st East London Pension District
1854	Pension paid Paisley
1865	Londonderry

29 Oct 1866	Died
Service and Personal Details:	
Place of Birth:	Raphoe Donegal
Age on Attestation:	20 years
Period of Service:	1827 — 1848
Age on Discharge:	40 years 11 months
Length of Service:	20 years 330 days
Foreign Service:	Cape of Good Hope 12 years 230 days
Reason for Discharge:	Chronic Rheumatism
Character:	Good
Trade or Occupation:	Labourer
Can Sign Name:	Yes
Height:	5' 11"
Hair Colour:	Grey
Eyes:	Brown
Complexion:	Fresh
Intends to Reside:	Londonderry

CRAGGS Benjamin, private
7th Dragoon Guards

Surname Variant	CRAIG
25 Apr 1843	Discharged the Service Gosport
1843	Pension paid Tullamore
6 Apr 1854	Arrived per *'Sea Park'* 7d. per diem
1854	Employed as Night Warder
1866	Correspondence to W.O. from S.O. Perth Western Australia
1873	Pension increased to 1/- per diem for service in the Enrolled Force
1874	Correspondence with War Office
1875	Admitted to Mt Eliza Depot
1876	Pensioner Benjamin Craggs at 1/- per day from the 7th Dragoons, an inmate of Mt. Eliza Poor House since 3rd April 1875 [paying 9d per day.] 'I would point out that this Pensioner has an old and infirm wife, unable to work, and without the means of subsistence. Her son to whom she might have looked for support, has left the Colony and I understand her stepson who is married is unable to assist beyond giving her a room in his home'
1876	Left Depot
1877	Immigration Office: — Applicant B. Craggs is a Pensioner in receipt of 1/- per diem, he is in receipt of 5/- per week from the Govt. Outdoor Relief, I beg respectfully to state I could not recommend him for an increased allowance
1879	a Benjamin Craig died aged 75
Service and Personal Details:	
Place of Birth:	? Cloneneagh Queens County
Age on Attestation:	20 years

Period of Service:	1825 — 1843
Age on Discharge:	37 years 9 months
Length of Service:	17 years 285 days
Reason for Discharge:	Total loss of motion of right ankle joint due to a kick from horse
Character:	Good
Trade or Occupation:	Blacksmith
Can Sign Name:	Yes
Height:	5' 10"
Hair Colour:	Light Brown
Eyes:	Blue
Complexion:	Fresh
Intends to Reside:	Portlarkington Queens

CRAIG	William James, Corporal EIC [L/MIL/9/78]
	2nd European Regiment
Previous Regiments	2nd Bengal Fusiliers; Bengal Sappers and Miners
	Out Pension No 461
1855	Invalided to Europe
17 June 1856	Admitted to Out-Pension
	Pension paid Drogheda District
1858	1st Dublin Pension District
	2nd Cork Pension District
	9d. per diem
9 Aug 1859	Arrived per *'Sultana'*
4 Sept 1864	Died at Albany
1867	"Wife Margaret in receipt of Lord Clive Pension of 4½d. being half her late husband's pension rate per diem"

Service and Personal Details:

Where Born:	St Marys Shandon Cork
Trade or Occupation:	Medical Student
Date Enlisted:	15th Feb 1841
Embarked India:	Feb 1842 per *'Henry'*
Age on Departure:	25 years
Presidency:	Bengal
Period of Service:	Unlimited
Length of Service:	14 years 6 months [reckoned]
Age on Discharge:	38 years
Reason for Discharge:	Dislocation of Humerus
Character:	Good
Height:	5' 5" or 5' 6"
Complexion:	Fresh
Eye Colour:	Brown
Hair Colour:	Brown
Intends to Reside:	Cork
Married:	Margaret prior to embarking for India

CRAIG	Margaret
1865	on death of her husband in receipt of Lord Clive Pension of 4½d. per diem

CRAWFORD	James, private [298]
	21st Hussars
Previous Regiments	54th Foot; 87th Foot
25 July 1865	Discharged the Service Netley
	Pension paid 2nd Liverpool Pension District
	9d. per diem
1865	Pension paid Newry
1865	Ballymena
1866	Liverpool
22 Dec 1866	Arrived per *'Corona'*
1870	Pension paid Perth Western Australia
circa Dec 1875	Transferred from 1st Perth to 1st East London Pension District

Service and Personal Details:	
Place of Birth:	Birkenhead Cheshire
Age on Attestation:	17 years 11 months
Period of Service:	1845 — 1865
Age on Discharge:	37 years 6 months
Length of Service:	17 years 252 days - revised to 18 years 261 days [reckoned]
Foreign Service:	India 10 years 248 days
Reason for Discharge:	Debility; Unfit for further service
Character:	Very Good
Trade or Occupation:	Groom
Can Sign Name:	X his mark on discharge
Height:	5' 6¾"
Hair Colour:	Dark Brown
Eyes:	Grey
Complexion:	Fresh
Intends to Reside:	Birkenhead Cheshire

CRITCH	Henry, Corporal
	35th Foot
Previous Regiment	16th Foot
19 Sep 1863	Discharged the Service Chatham
6 Oct 1863	Admitted to Out-Pension
	Pension paid Chatham
	1/-d. per diem
13 July 1867	Arrived per *'Norwood'* [2]
July 1881	Assigned North Fremantle Lot P69
1881	Pension increased to 1/6d. per diem for service in the Enrolled Force
1884	Granted Fremantle Lot P69
Oct 1888	Charged with being drunk — dismissed with a caution
Nov 1890	Fell and broke his thigh near Mr Albert's store
1890	Died

Service and Personal Details:	
Place of Birth:	Dover Kent
Age on Attestation:	19 years
Period of Service:	1842 — 1863
Age on Discharge:	40 years
Length of Service:	21 years 8 days

Foreign Service:	Mauritius	2 years 4 months
	East Indies	4 years 3 months
Medal Entitlement:	Good Conduct with gratuity	
Reason for Discharge:	Own Request after 21 years service	
Character:	Good	
Trade or Occupation:	Labourer	
Can Sign Name:	Yes	
Height:	5' 8"	
Hair Colour:	Light Brown	
Eyes:	Grey	
Complexion:	Fresh	
Intends to Reside:	Chatham	

CRONAN	Patrick, private	
	83rd Foot	
Surname Variant	CRONIN	
Previous Regiment	88th Foot	
20 May 1844	Discharged the Service	
11 June 1844	Admitted to Out-Pension	
	Pension paid Kilkenny	
	10d. per diem	
1846	Pension paid 1st East London Pension District	
1851	Pension paid South London Pension District	
2 Aug 1852	Arrived per *'William Jardine'*	
1853	possibly employed as Night Warder	
1853	Left colony without leave	
1854	"Pension suspended"	
1858	Pension paid East London Pension District	
1858	Tralee	
Service and Personal Details:		
Place of Birth:	Ahadoe Co. Kerry	
Age on Attestation:	18 years	
Period of Service:	1821 — 1844	
Age on Discharge:	41 years 2 months	
Length of Service:	23 years 61 days	
Foreign Service:	Ionian Isles	10 years 10 months
	Canada	5 years
Reason for Discharge:	Own Request	
Character:	Good	
Trade or Occupation:	Labourer	
Can Sign Name:	X his mark on discharge	
Height:	5' 7"	
Hair Colour:	Fair	
Eyes:	Grey	
Complexion:	Fair	
Intends to Reside:	Killarney Ireland	

CRONIN	Owen, Corporal
	RA 6th Battalion 18th Brigade
Previous Regiments	EIC — Bombay Fusiliers or 1st European Regiment of Fusiliers; Bombay Artillery
Surname Variant	CRONAN

July 1863	Embarked for England per *'Morayshire'*
1863	Discharged the Service Netley
1864	Pension paid 1st Cork Pension District 1/- per diem
1867	W.O. correspondence to Military Secretary Dublin
9 Jan 1868	Arrived per *'Hougoumont'*
1869	Died

Service and Personal Details:	
Place of Birth:	Grenville Co. Cork
Date of Attestation:	April 1845
Age on Attestation:	20 years
To India:	per *'Mary Anne'*
Period of Service:	1845 — 1868
Age on Discharge:	39 years 4 months
Length of Service:	19 years 355 days [including 2 years boon]
Foreign Service:	India 19 years 96 days
Medal Entitlement:	Central India with clasp and Punjaub with two clasps
Reason for Discharge:	Scurvy
Character:	Very Good
Trade or Occupation:	Labourer
Can Sign Name:	Yes
Height:	5' 9"
Hair Colour:	Light Brown
Eyes:	Blue
Complexion:	Fresh
Remarks:	Claims his share of Prize Money for Dhar and Central India
Intends to Reside:	Cork Ireland

CROOKS James, private
3rd Foot Guards

11 June 1850	Discharged the Service London
	Pension paid 1st West London Pension District 1/1d. per diem
1850	Pension paid Liverpool
1 Oct 1850	Pension paid 1st North London Pension District
1 Nov 1850	1st Edinburgh Pension District
1851	Liverpool
14 Aug 1854	Arrived per *'Ramillies'*
1856	On Rottnest EPG provision account
Jan 1857	Contributed 2/- to the Florence Nightingale Fund
1857	To South Australia from Western Australia
1872	Pension paid Victoria
April 1872	"Off Roll Absent — Pension stopped"

Service and Personal Details:	
Place of Birth:	South Leith Midlothian Scotland
Age on Attestation:	19 years
Period of Service:	1827 — 1850
Age on Discharge:	42 years 9 months
Length of Service:	23 years 65 days
Reason for Discharge:	Chronic cough

Character:	Very Good trustworthy and efficient
Trade or Occupation:	Bookbinder
Can Sign Name:	Yes
Height:	5' 11¼"
Hair Colour:	Light
Eyes:	Blue
Complexion:	Fresh
Intends to Reside:	London

CROSS John Henry, private

	9th Lancers
Previous Regiment	10th Hussars
22 July 1856	Discharged the Service Chatham Pension paid 2nd Plymouth Pension District 1/- per diem
10 July 1857	Arrived per *'Clara'* [1]
1864	Pension paid Western Australia
20 Apr 1864	Died Fremantle

Service and Personal Details:

Place of Birth:	Lincoln Lincolnshire
Age on Attestation:	15 years 7 months
Period of Service:	1830 — 1855
Age on Discharge:	42 years
Length of Service:	23 years 106 days
Foreign Service:	Bengal East Indies 13 years
Medal Entitlement:	Gwalior Campaign; Sutlej Campaign with clasp for Sobroan; Punjab Campaign; Battle of Chillianwalla and Goojrat
Reason for Discharge:	General Debility
Character:	Very good
Trade or Occupation:	Labourer
Can Sign Name:	Yes
Height:	5' 8"
Hair Colour:	Light Brown
Eyes:	Grey
Complexion:	Fair
Intends to Reside:	Hartland nr Bideford Devon

CROSSLEY see — CROWLEY William EIC

CROWDY Thomas, Serjeant

	RM
6 Aug 1855	On Pension Roll £32/-/- per annum
1861	Requests compensation for heifer that was killed and eaten by convicts at Freshwater Bay
1864	Pension paid Perth
1867	Residing North Fremantle
July 1867	Corporal Crowdy had the guard on Monday
1868	Employed as Temp. Assistant Warder Fremantle
1875	Pension to be paid South Australia

Sept 1875	Drowned at sea in the wreck of the *'Mary Herbert'* on her voyage between Albany and Fremantle

the following entry may not necessarily refer to Thomas Crowdy RM

12 Nov 1866	J. J. HARWOOD & CO. Have been instructed by Mr. T. CROWDY, [who is about to proceed to England], to Sell by Public Auction at their Rooms, in Henry Street, a Valuable Property in Essex Street, consisting of a front Cottage with 6 rooms and 4 cottages with two rooms each in rear. The whole bringing in an Annual Rent of £52, The property is presently occupied by C. Marshall. Also Grant No. 31, at North Fremantle now in possession of T. Crowdy. Considered the best Cottage and containing one acre more or less, partly under kitchen garden, vines, and fig trees, with a commodious stockyard, with stalls for 15 head of cattle [Trove]

Service and Personal Details:

Place of Birth:	Thame Oxfordshire
Age on Attestation:	19 years
Marine Division:	Portsmouth
Period of Service:	1830 — 1852
Length of Service:	21 years 8 months 28 days
Reason for Discharge:	Own Request having served 21 years
Trade or Occupation:	Footman
Can Sign Name:	Yes
Remarks:	Serving onboard the "*Stromboli*" during the Syrian Campaign and as present at the capture of Sidon and Acre
Height:	5' 9"
Hair Colour:	Brown
Eyes:	Grey
Complexion:	Fresh

CROWE	James, Corporal [1872] 97th Foot
Previous Regiment	38th
Surname Variant	CROW
27 July 1861	Discharged the Service Colchester
13 Aug 1861	Admitted to Out-Pension Pension paid Limerick 1/3d. per diem
27 May 1863	Arrived per *'Clyde'*
1867	Serving as Corporal of Pensioners at North Fremantle
1867	Witness at the trial of James Alcock
1867	To South Australia from Fremantle
1868	Pension paid South Australia "To report himself every two years"
1898	Attended Memorial Day Adelaide
1908	Died

Service and Personal Details:

Place of Birth:	Cappaghwhite Tipperary	
Age on Attestation:	19 years	
Period of Service	1840 — 1861	
Age on Discharge:	40 years	
Length of Service:	21 years	
Foreign Service:	Ionian Isles & Malta	5 years 2 months
	Jamaica	3 years 3 months
	America	1 year 10 months
	Greece & Crimea	2 years 1 month
	India	2 years 3 months
Medal Entitlement:	Crimea with clasp; Turkish Crimean; Indian Mutiny with clasp for Lucknow	
Reason for Discharge:	Having completed 21 years service and at Own Request	
Character:	Very Good	
Trade or Occupation:	Labourer	
Can Sign Name:	Yes	
Height:	5' 9"	
Hair Colour:	Dark Brown	
Eyes:	Hazel	
Complexion:	Fresh	
Remarks:	From Pension Register — to report himself every two years	
Married:	*c*1852 Ann Nova Scotia	

CROWE	Samuel, private
	50th Foot
Previous Regiments	62nd Foot; 44th Foot
24 Dec 1850	Discharged the Service Chatham
	Pension paid 2nd West London Pension District
	8d. per diem
14 Aug 1854	Arrived per *'Ramillies'*
1856	£15/0/0 misappropriated by Captain Foss
1865	Pension paid 2nd West London Pension District
1868	Pension paid Jersey
1869	Taunton Exeter
19 Mar 1870	Died

Service and Personal Details:

Place of Birth:	St Andrews Dublin
Age on Attestation:	19 years 10 months
Period of Service:	1834 — 1850
Age on Discharge:	36 years 10 months
Length of Service:	16 years 268 days
Reason for Discharge:	Unfit for further service
Character:	Very Good
Trade or Occupation:	Servant
Can Sign Name:	Yes
Height:	5' 6"
Hair Colour:	Dark Brown
Eyes:	Grey

Complexion:	Sallow
Intends to Reside:	Edgeware Road London

CROWLEY William, private EIC
1st European Regiment

Out Pension No 568	
10 Sept 1861	Admitted to Out-pension Pension paid 1st Dublin Pension District 1/- per diem
1861	Pension paid 2nd Dublin Pension District
1862	1st Dublin Pension District
1863	Pension paid 1st East London Pension District
31 Dec 1862	Arrived per *'York'*
1864	To Sydney from Western Australia
1865	Pension paid Sydney New South Wales

Service and Personal Details:

Where Born:	St Catherines London Middlesex
Trade or Occupation:	Shoemaker
Where Enlisted:	London
Date of Attestation:	Oct 1840
Embarked India:	per *'Lady East'*
Presidency:	Madras
Length of Service:	19 years 7 months
Age on Discharge:	39 years
Reason for Discharge:	Time Expired
Character:	none given
Height:	5' 5"
Complexion:	Fresh
Eye Colour:	Hazel
Hair Colour:	Dark Brown
Intends to Reside:	Dublin

CUNNINGHAM James, private
31st Foot

23 Mar 1847	Discharged the Service Chatham Pension paid Chatham 1/- per diem
2 Aug 1852	Arrived per *'William Jardine'*
1854	Employed as a Warder
1858	Contributed to the Indian relief Fund
1860	Pension paid Cambridge
1862	Kings Lynn
1868	Died

Service and Personal Details:

Place of Birth:	St Annes Dublin
Age on Attestation:	17 years
Period of Service:	1825 — 1847
Age on Discharge:	39 years
Length of Service:	21 years 67 days
Foreign Service:	East Indies 21 years
Medal Entitlement:	Afghanistan in 1840; and Sutlej with clasps for Moodkee, Ferozashah, Aliwal and Sobroan
Reason for Discharge:	Chronic pains and uncoordinated action of the heart

Character: Indifferent
Trade or Occupation: Labourer
Can Sign Name: Yes

Height: 5' 11"
Hair Colour: Dark
Eyes: Dark
Complexion: Swarthy
Intends to Reside: Chatham

CUNNINGHAM James, private [Military Pensioner]
51st Foot

21 Oct 1840 Arrived with detachment of the 51st from V.D.L.
24 Aug 1847 Discharged the Service Perth West. Australia
Pension paid Perth Western Australia
1/- per diem
1851 "Pension paid by Commissariat until transferred to Staff Officer Pensions — Capt Bruce"
1853 Made complaint against Capt. Bruce
18 May 1871 Died

Service and Personal Details:
Place of Birth: Peahoon Galway
Age on Attestation: 18 years
Period of Service: 1825 — 1847
Age on Discharge: 40 years 5 months
Length of Service: 21 years 125 days
Foreign Service: Ionian Isles 6 years 52 days
Australian Colonies 7 years
Reason for Discharge: Chronic Rheumatism and quite worn out

Character: Good
Trade or Occupation: Labourer
Can Sign Name: Yes

Height: 5' 7½"
Hair Colour: Brown
Eyes: Hazel
Complexion: Fair

CUNNINGHAM James, Serjeant
60th Foot

21 June 1859 Discharged the Service Chatham
Pension paid Birr
1/6d. per diem
1863 Pension paid Edinburgh
12 Sept 1864 Arrived per *'Merchantman'* [2]
1881 Pension increased to 2/2d. per diem for service in the Enrolled Force
10 Apr 1881 Assigned Canning Pensioner Allotment 135; 'held by him until Aug 1882 but relinquished'
1885 a James Cunningham applied for £15 building grant for Koogee [sic] Lot P14
1885 Died aged 53

Service and Personal Details:	
Place of Birth:	Ballingarry Co Tipperary
Age on Attestation:	18 years
Period of Service:	1847 — 1858
Age on Discharge:	29 years 7 months
Length of Service:	9 years 361 days
Foreign Service:	East Indies 8 years 348 days
Medal Entitlement:	Indian Mutiny with clasp
Reason for Discharge:	Was wounded at Delhi 14th Sept 1857 by a bullet through the right buttock
Character:	Exemplary
Trade or Occupation:	Labourer
Can Sign Name:	Yes
Height:	5' 9"
Hair Colour:	Dark Brown
Eyes:	Grey
Complexion:	Fresh
Intends to Reside:	Ballingarry

CUNNINGHAM	James, gunner & driver RA 11th Battalion
9 Sept 1856	Discharged the Service Woolwich Pension paid Armagh 1/- per diem
1858	Pension paid Tullamore
1859	Athlone Galway
1860	Monaghan
1861	Armagh
1861	Belfast
1862	Armagh
9 June 1862	Arrived per *'Norwood'* [1]
1878	Pension paid Melbourne
1879	Sydney
1880	Sydney

Service and Personal Details:	
Place of Birth:	Armagh Co. Armagh
Age on Attestation:	17 years 4 months
Period of Service:	1835 — 1856
Age on Discharge:	38 years 5 months
Length of Service:	20 years 122 days
Foreign Service:	Cape of Good Hope 10 years 6 months
Expedition to the East	2 years 1 month
Medal Entitlement:	Kaffir War; Crimea with 3 clasps; Turkish Crimean
Reason for Discharge:	Chronic Rheumatism and Fatigue
Character:	Very Good
Trade or Occupation:	Labourer
Can Sign Name:	Yes
Height:	5' 11¾"
Hair Colour:	Grey
Eyes:	Grey
Complexion:	Fresh

CUNNINGHAM	John, private [796]	
	83rd Foot	
25 May 1852	Discharged the Service Chatham	
	Pension paid 2nd Glasgow Pension District	
	1/- per diem	
6 Apr 1854	Arrived per *'Sea Park'*	
Jan 1857	a private J Cunningham contributed 1/- to the Florence Nightingale Fund	
1875	Pension paid Western Australia	
8 Mar 1883	Assigned North Fremantle Lot P81	
28 Sept 1883	Applied for North Fremantle Lot P81	
1884	Granted Fee Simple North Fremantle Lot P81	
1885	Died	
Service and Personal Details:		
Place of Birth:	Enniskillen Fermanagh	
Age on Attestation:	17 years 9 months	
Period of Service:	1831 — 1852	
Age on Discharge:	39 years	
Length of Service:	20 years 168 days	
Foreign Service:	North America	9 years
	East Indies	2 years 5 months
Reason for Discharge:	Unfit for service	
Character:	Very Good	
Trade or Occupation:	Labourer	
Can Sign Name:	X his mark on discharge	
Height:	5' 10"	
Hair Colour:	Dark	
Eyes:	Grey	
Complexion:	Dark	
Intends to Reside:	Enniskillen	

CURLEY	Michael, private
	60th Foot
Previous Regiments	45th; Royal Canadian Rifles; 69th
Surname Variant	CUSLEY
30 Apr 1872	Discharged the Service Chichester
	Pension paid Athlone
	10½d per diem
19 Feb 1874	Arrived per *'Naval Brigade'*
June 1881	Assigned Perth Town Lot 135/V
24 Aug 1881	Allocated Perth Railway Block Lot 143/V
	Pension increased to 1/1d. per diem
25 Sept 1883	Granted Fee Simple Perth Railway Block Lot 143/V
May 1886	Private Michael Cusley [sic] — Resignation of his position as private on the Enrolled Guard
Aug 1886	Died - buried East Perth Pioneer Cemetery
Service and Personal Details:	
Place of Birth:	? Noore Dublin
Age on Attestation:	17 years 10 months
Period of Service:	1853 — 1872

Age on Discharge:	36 years 6 months
Length of Service:	18 years 206 days [reckoned]
Foreign Service:	Malta 1 month
	Turkey & Crimea 2 years 4 months
	Mauritius 6 months
	East Indies 4 years 3 months
	Canada 8 years 6 months
Medal Entitlement:	Crimea with 3 clasps; Crimean Turkish
Reason for Discharge:	His own request
Character:	Very Good
Trade or Occupation:	Labourer
Can Sign Name:	Yes
Height:	5' 5¾"
Hair Colour:	Dark Brown
Eyes:	Hazel
Complexion:	Fresh
Intends to Reside:	? Bali***** Ireland

CURTIN	John
	18th Foot
Surname Variant	CURTAIN
12 Aug 1856	Discharged the Service Fermoy
1858	Pension paid Clonmel
1859	Pension paid 1st Cork Pension District
	8d. per diem
31 Dec 1862	Arrived per *'York'*
1863	a John Curtin employed as Assistant Warder
14 Sept 1864	Died

CURTIS	Francis, private
	14th Light Dragoons
Surname Variant	CURTISS
21 Aug 1860	Discharged the Service Dublin
	Pension paid 1st North London Pension District
	8d. per diem
1861	Pension paid Birmingham Coventry
9 June 1862	Arrived per *'Norwood'* [1]
1871	Pension suspended during imprisonment [Six months] for breaking into a dwelling house and stealing 2 pairs of boots
1873	Convicted at Freemantle [sic] W.A. one pair lasts and 2 pairs of slippers — was sentenced to six months imprisonment. Pension to be suspended during imprisonment and on release pension amount to be reduced to 7d per diem
1875	Pension paid Western Australia
1878	Refused increase of pension
1881	Convicted for stealing 2 rugs and sentenced to 6 months imprisonment
1882	Struck off Pension List
1883	Refused restoration of pension
5 Apr 1889	at Perth, charged with vagrancy by Sergt. Claffey
1890	Restoration of Pension
Sept 1894	Died - buried East Perth Pioneer Cemetery

Service and Personal Details:

Place of Birth:	Falmouth Cornwall	
Age on Attestation:	22 years 6 months	
Period of Service:	1841 — 1860	
Age on Discharge:	41 years	
Length of Service:	19 years 7 days	
Foreign Service:	East Indies	18 years 5 months
Medal Entitlement:	Punjaub Campaign with bars for Battle of Chillianwallah and Goojerat; medal for Persia and Central India	
Reason for Discharge:	Rheumatism	
Character:	Good	
Trade or Occupation:	Shoemaker	
Can Sign Name:	Yes	
Height:	5' 7½"	
Hair Colour:	Dark Brown	
Eyes:	Blue	
Complexion:	Fair	
Intends to Reside:	26 Sussex Place Regents Park London	

CUTHBERT William, private
97th Foot

10 Aug 1847	Discharged the Service Chatham Pension paid 2nd Edinburgh Pension District 1/- per diem
2 Aug 1852	Arrived per *'William Jardine'*
1854	"Deserted the Force"
1854	Departed colony

Service and Personal Details:

Place of Birth:	Golspie Sutherland Scotland	
Age on Attestation:	17 years	
Period of Service:	1824 — 1847	
Age on Discharge:	40 years	
Length of Service:	21 years 52 days	
Foreign Service:	East Indies	11 years 24 days
	Mediterranean	6 years 39 days
Reason for Discharge:	Worn out	
Character:	Since 1845 - Very Good	
Trade or Occupation:	Tailor	
Can Sign Name:	Yes	
Height:	5' 6"	
Hair Colour:	Fair	
Eyes:	Grey	
Complexion:	Fair	
Intends to Reside:	Edinburgh	

DAIN James, private
47th Foot

Surname Variant	DEAN
21 Oct 1853	Discharged the Service Birr
13 Dec 1853	Admitted to Out-Pension

	Pension paid Stockport	
	1/- per diem	
1862	Pension paid Manchester pension District	
9 June 1862	Arrived per *'Norwood'* [1]	
1872	Died	
Service and Personal Details:		
Place of Birth:	Macclesfield Cheshire	
Age on Attestation:	18 years	
Period of Service:	1832 — 1853	
Age on Discharge:	39 years 6 months	
Length of Service:	21 years	
Foreign Service:	Mediterranean	6 years 5 months
	West Indies	2 years 9 months
Reason for Discharge:	Chronic Rheumatism	
Character:	Irregular soldier but of late improved	
Trade or Occupation:	Weaver	
Can Sign Name:	Yes	
Height:	5' 7½"	
Hair Colour:	Fair	
Eyes:	Grey	
Complexion:	Fresh	
Intends to Reside:	Macclesfield	

DALEY	Richard, gunner EIC
	Bombay Artillery 1st Battalion
Surname Variant	DALY
	Out Pension No 344
3 Sept 1860	Admitted to Out-pension
	Pension paid Limerick pension District
	1/- per diem
15 Apr 1864	Arrived per *'Clara'* [2]
1865	On Nominal List to proceed to Camden Harbour per *'Tien Tsin'*
Mar 1866	Purchased Fremantle Lot 395 for £6/-/-
Aug 1871	Fremantle Town Lot Y46 purchased by Jane, wife of pensioner Richard Daley
1872	a Richard Daly residing at Fremantle
1875	Pension paid Western Australia
circa Dec 1875	Transferred from Fremantle to 1st Perth District
1876	Applied to bring together Fremantle Town Lots 745 and 746 respectively under the Transfer of Land Act 1874
1880	Charged with drunkenness
Aug 1881	Allocated Perth Pensioner Lot 135/V [originally assigned to M Curley]
Nov 1881	Assigned Perth Pension Lot 135 of 1 acre [Title Deed No 6/39]
Dec 1883	Granted Fee Simple Perth Pensioner Lot 135/V
1885	"Charged with assaulting Emily Timewell" 1886 a Richard Daley was a assaulted and left seriously wounded by Morris Carroll and Alfred Caporn
1894	Died

Service and Personal Details:	
Where Born:	Newport Tipperary
Trade or Occupation:	Labourer
Presidency:	Bombay
Length of Service:	19 years 3 months
Age on Discharge:	38 years
Reason for Discharge:	To be pensioned
Character:	Good
Height:	5' 9"
Complexion:	Fresh
Eye Colour:	Blue
Hair Colour:	Light Brown
Intends to Reside:	Limerick

DALTON	John, private 87th Foot
12 July 1870	Discharged the Service Netley Pension paid Waterford 7d. per diem for 18 months
1870	Pension paid Clonmel
1871	Preston
19 Feb 1874	Arrived per *'Naval Brigade'*

Service and Personal Details:		
Place of Birth:	Cahir Co. Tipperary	
Age on Attestation:	19 years	
Period of Service:	1861 — 1870	
Age on Discharge:	28 years 6 months	
Length of Service:	6 years 148 days	
Foreign Service:	Gibraltar	1 year 8 months
	Malta	2 years 3 months
Reason for Discharge:	Fracture of left forearm at Malta	
Character:	Good	
Trade or Occupation:	Labourer	
Can Sign Name:	Yes	
Height:	5' 10¾"	
Hair Colour:	Light Brown	
Eyes:	Grey	
Complexion:	Sallow	
Distinguishing Marks:	Letter "D" on left side	
Intends to Reside:	Waterford	

DALTON	Timothy, Corporal 84th Foot
Surname Variant	D'ALTON
11 June 1850	Discharged the Service Chatham Pension paid Chatham 1/4d. per diem
28 June 1851	Arrived per *'Pyrenees'* [1]
1851	Employed as Night Warder
1873	Pension increased to 1/5d. per diem for one year and 9 months service in the Enrolled Force
Apr 1875	Died - buried East Perth Pioneer Cemetery

Service and Personal Details:		
Place of Birth:	Walshestown Westmeath	
Age on Attestation:	18 years	
Period of Service:	1828 — 1850	
Age on Discharge:	40 years 2 months	
Length of Service:	22 years 74 days [reckoned]	
Foreign Service:	Jamaica	5 years 29 days
	East Indies	5 years 312 days
Reason for Discharge:	Chronic Rheumatism and Varicose Veins in both legs	
Character:	Good	
Trade or Occupation:	Labourer	
Can Sign Name:	Yes	
Height:	5' 9"	
Hair Colour:	Grey	
Eyes:	Hazel	
Complexion:	Sallow	

DALY James, gunner and driver
RA 6th Battalion

Surname Variant	DAILEY	
11 July 1848	Discharged the Service Woolwich Pension paid 1st Belfast Pension District 1/-½d. per diem	
7 Feb 1853	Arrived per '*Dudbrook*'	
1873	Pension increased to 1/3d. per diem for 16 years 5 months service in the Enrolled Guard	
23 Oct 1876	Died	
Service and Personal Details:		
Place of Birth:	St Peters Roscommon Co. Tyrone	
Age on Attestation:	18 years	
Period of Service:	1826 — 1848	
Age on Discharge:	40 years 2 months	
Length of Service:	22 years 102 days	
Foreign Service:	Nova Scotia	11 years 3 months
	Cape of Good Hope	1 year 2 months
Medal Entitlement:	Good Conduct and Long Service	
Reason for Discharge:	Chronic Rheumatism	
Character:	Exemplary	
Trade or Occupation:	Sawyer	
Can Sign Name:	Yes	
Height:	5' 8"	
Hair Colour:	Brown	
Eyes:	Grey	
Complexion:	Fresh	

DALY Michael, private
10th Foot

Surname Variant	DALEY; DAILLY
20 Mar 1860	Discharged the Service Devonport Pension paid Limerick 1/- per diem

31 Dec 1862	Arrived per *'York'*
1863	Stationed Perth District
1864	a private M Daly serving in the Pensioner Force at Fremantle District contributed to the Greenough Fire Relief Fund
1872	Correspondence with War Office
1875	Pension paid Western Australia
1879	Pension increased to 1/6d. per diem for 17 years service in the Enrolled Force
11 Nov 1880	Joined Enrolled Guard — stationed at Perth
June 1881	Assigned Perth Town Lot 75/E
June 1881	Perth Town Lot 75/E cancelled
July 1881	Assigned Perth Town Lot 112/V in lieu
Dec 1883	Granted Fee Simple Perth Town Lot 112/V
1897	Stationed at Perth
1901	Died

Service and Personal Details:

Place of Birth:	St Marys Limerick Co. Limerick
Age on Attestation:	19 years
Period of Service:	1838 — 1860
Age on Discharge:	40 years 2 months
Length of Service:	21 years 66 days
Foreign Service:	East Indies 15 years
Medal Entitlement:	Good Conduct with gratuity; Punjaub with two clasps; Indian Mutiny with clasp
Reason for Discharge:	Own Request
Character:	Very Good
Trade or Occupation:	Labourer
Can Sign Name:	Yes
Height:	5' 8¼"
Hair Colour:	Light
Eyes:	Blue
Complexion:	Fresh
Intends to Reside:	City of Limerick

DALY Thaddeus [Thady], Corporal
25th Foot

27 Sept 1853	Discharged the Service Chatham Pension paid 1st Dublin Pension District 9d. per diem
1855	Serving in Dublin Militia
1856	Pension paid 2nd West London Pension District
19 Aug 1859	Arrived per *'Sultana'*
1865	To Adelaide from Perth Western Australia
1866	Pension paid South Australia
1875	South Australia

Service and Personal Details:

Place of Birth:	St Johns Limerick
Age on Attestation:	18 years
Period of Service:	1838 — 1853
Age on Discharge:	34 years or 33 years 3 months
Length of Service:	15 years 223 days

Foreign Service:	Cape of Good Hope	2 years 5 months
	East Indies	1 year 3 months
Reason for Discharge:	Scrofula	
Character:	Good	
Trade or Occupation:	Labourer	
Can Sign Name:	Yes	
Height:	5' 6"	
Hair Colour:	Dark Brown	
Eyes:	Black	
Complexion:	Dark	
Intends to Reside:	Limerick	

DALY	William, Serjeant
	4th Foot
8 July 1851	Discharged the Service Chatham
	Pension paid 1st Dublin Pension District
	2/- per diem
4 Apr 1854	Arrived per *'Sea Park'*
1863	Stationed Fremantle Pension District
1876	Pension paid Sydney
1880	Sydney

Service and Personal Details:

Place of Birth:	Batterstown Dublin	
Age on Attestation:	18 years	
Period of Service:	1827 — 1851	
Age on Discharge:	42 years 6 months	
Length of Service:	24 years 21 days	
Foreign Service:	New South Wales	5 years 3 months
	East Indies	10 years 6 months
Reason for Discharge:	Chronic Rheumatism and General Debility	
Character:	Very Good	
Trade or Occupation:	Tailor	
Can Sign Name:	Yes	
Height:	5' 8½"	
Hair Colour:	Brown	
Eyes:	Grey	
Complexion:	Fair	
Intends to Reside:	Dublin	

DALZIELL	John, 2nd Corporal [Military Pensioner]
	Royal Engineers
15 June 1860	Discharged the Service Fremantle West. Aust.
11 Aug 1860	Discharged approved
1864	a John Dalziel purchased Perth Town Lot H52 for £12/-/-
1882	Pension to be granted at 60 which he can reckon for himself notwithstanding the clerical error in the Cert. [sic] of Registry Pension rate not given
1884	Correspondence with W.O.
1885	Applied to be registered as the proprietor in fee simple to Perth Building Lot Q8

June 1897	Attended banquet at Perth
July 1900	Died at his residence 16, Nash Street Perth

Service and Personal Details:

Place of Birth:	West Church Edinburgh	
Age on Enlistment:	17 years	
Period of Service:	1841 — 1860	
Age on Discharge:	34 years 342 days	
Length of Service:	17 years 342 days	
Foreign Service:	Gibraltar	6 years 126 days
	West Australia	8 years 178 days
Reason for Discharge:	Discharge with pay for 12 months. Deferred pension to commence at 60 years of age	
Character:	Exemplary	
Trade or Occupation:	Plumber [Painter]	
Can Sign Name:	Yes	
Height:	5' 7¾"	
Hair Colour:	Dark Brown	
Eyes:	Blue	
Complexion:	Dark	
Intends to Reside:	Perth Western Australia	

DANFORD	Peter, gunner
	RHA
9 Apr 1850	Discharged the Service Woolwich
	Pension paid Woolwich
	1/- per diem
1850	Pension paid 1st East London Pension District
1851	Residing Mile End Old Town London
7 Feb 1853	Arrived per *'Dudbrook'*
11 Apr 1853	Died

Service and Personal Details:

Place of Birth:	Selbridge Co. Kildare
Age on Attestation:	20 years
Period of Service:	1828 — 1850
Age on Discharge:	41 years 13 days
Length of Service:	21 years 191 days
Reason for Discharge:	Chronic Rheumatism and injury of left fore arm
Character:	Exemplary
Trade or Occupation:	Labourer
Can Sign Name:	Yes
Height:	5' 11¼"
Hair Colour:	Black
Eyes:	Brown
Complexion:	Swarthy

DANIEL	Richard, private
	35th Foot
Previous Regiments	16th; 61st; 98th
Surname Variant	DANIELS
6 Mar 1862	Discharged the Service Chatham
	Pension paid Clonmel

	1/- per diem	
31 Dec 1862	Arrived per *'York'*	
1864	Pension paid Madras	
1875	Madras	
Service and Personal Details:		
Place of Birth:	St Marys Clonmel Tipperary	
Age on Attestation:	18 years 1 month	
Period of Service:	1841 — 1862	
Age on Discharge:	39 years 1 month	
Length of Service:	21 years 10 days	
Foreign Service:	China	2 years 10 months
	East Indies	14 years 7 months
Medal Entitlement:	Punjaub Campaign	
Reason for Discharge:	Own Request after 21 years service	
Character:	Very Good	
Trade or Occupation:	Labourer	
Can Sign Name:	X his mark on discharge	
Height:	5' 8"	
Hair Colour:	Black	
Eyes:	Hazel	
Complexion:	Fresh	
Intends to Reside:	Clonmel Ireland	

DANIELS	Hugh, private
	98th Foot
Previous Regiment	61st Foot
Surname variant	DANIEL
Apr 1860	Discharged the Service Canterbury
1 May 1860	Admitted to Out-Pension
	Pension paid Clonmel
	8d. per diem
31 Dec 1862	Arrived per *'York'*
1865	Pension paid Western Australia
1869	Western Australia
Jan 1876	Convicted at Fremantle and sentenced to 84 days imprisonment and fine of 20/- for being found drunk on duty on the Barrack Guard of the Enrolled Force Half pay to be suspended and the other half paid to wife during imprisonment
Nov 1876	Having continuously served in the Duty Force for three years is now granted permission to occupy P13 [of 20 acres] in the township of Clarence in the District of Cockburn Sound
June 1878	Pension increased to 1/2½d. per diem for service in the Enrolled Force
3 Jan 1879	Inquest on Hugh Daniels, Army Pensioner, who died suddenly on the 2nd inst. Verdict — 'Death from accidentally falling on his head and fracturing his skull, while in a state of intoxication'
1881	Letter — re issue of free grant of land to Bridget Daniel, widow of Hugh Daniel (Pensioner) [SROWA B005]
1884	Widow [Bridget] awarded Coogee Loc P13

Service and Personal Details:
Place of Birth: St Peters and Pauls Clonmel Co. Tipperary
Age on Attestation: 18 years
Period of Service: 1838 — 1860
Age on Discharge: 39 years 4 months
Length of Service: 21 years 11 days [reckoned]
Foreign Service: China 2 years 10 months
India 8 years 4 months
Medal Entitlement: Punjaub 1848/9
Reason for Discharge: Own Request having served 21 years

Character: Indifferent
Trade or Occupation: Labourer
Can Sign Name: X his mark on discharge

Height: 5' 10"
Hair Colour: Dark Brown
Eyes: Hazel
Complexion: Fresh
Intends to Reside: ? Bucket Street Clonmel

DARLEY John [Charles], gunner EIC
2nd Troop 1st Brigade Horse Artillery
Out Pension No 293

7 June 1856	Admitted to Out-pension Pension paid Tower Hill London
1856	1st East London Pension District
1856	Birmingham
1858	2nd Plymouth Pension District 1/- per diem [or 9d depending on record]
27 May 1863	Arrived per *'Clyde'*
1864	private J Darley serving in the Pensioner Force at Fremantle District contributed to the Greenough Fire Relief Fund
1875	Third of pension suspended and the other portion paid to wife and child during his imprisonment"
Apr 1879	Pensioner John Darley discharged from prison at Gordon River
Apr 1881	Application for Title to Perth Lot 121/Y
15 May 1881	Granted Title to Perth Pensioner Lot 121/Y
Sept 1885	Died buried East Perth Pioneer Cemetery
1916	a Charles and Emma Darley residing at Darley Street South Perth

Service and Personal Details:
Where Born: Stoke Warwickshire
Trade or Occupation: Labourer
Where Enlisted: Tower Hill London
Presidency: Bengal
Length of Service: 15 years 8 months
Age on Discharge: 35 or 37 [depending on record]
Reason for Discharge: Chronic Hepatitis, Varicose Veins and broken constitution from effects of climate
Character: Good

Height:	5' 8"
Complexion:	Fair
Eye Colour:	Blue
Hair Colour:	Brown
Intends to Reside:	Tower Hill

DAVENPORT	Thomas, private RM
Surname Variant	DEVONPORT
6 Jan 1846	Admitted to Out-Pension Plymouth £18/4/- per annum
1851	Residing at 14 Lower Hill St Leicester
Oct 1852	To WA as Convict Guard
7 Feb 1853	Arrived per *'Dudbrook'*
1855	Residing in North Fremantle with wife and four children
Jan 1857	Contributed 2/- to the Florence Nightingale Fund
1865	To South Australia from Perth West. Australia
Feb 1875	Died

Service Details and Personal:	
Place of Birth:	Ashby de la Zouche Leicestershire
Age on Attestation:	20 years
Period of Service:	1824 — 1846
Age on Discharge:	42 years
Amount of Service:	21 years 2 months 27 days
Reason for Discharge:	Length of Service
Trade or Occupation:	Labourer
Medal Entitlement:	Good Service
Character & Conduct:	Good
Married:	Mary Wolner
Children:	Thomas b. *c*1840 East Stonehouse Devon Robert b. *c*1844 East Stonehouse Devon d. *c*1859 aged 16 Western Australia Mary b. *c*1846 East Stonehouse Plymouth Eliza b. *c*1848 Ashby de la Zouche Sarah Jane b. *c*1850 Leicestershire Sarah b. *c*1852

DAVEY	Henry, private RM
Surname Variant	DARCY
Mar 1850	Pension paid Taunton £4/12/- per diem
1 June 1850	Arrived per *'Scindian'*
Nov 1852	Assigned Pensioner Lot P2 at York
Jan 1857	Contributed 2/- to the Florence Nightingale Fund
1859	Application for Title P2 at York
1864	ptve H Davey serving in the Pensioner Force at York contributed to Greenough Fire Relief Fund
1881	Residing York
1892	Died

Service and Personal Details:	
Place of Birth:	North Petherton Somerset
Marine Division:	Plymouth

Trade or Occupation:	Mason
Height:	5' 7"
Hair Colour:	Brown
Eyes:	Grey
Complexion:	Fresh

DAVEY	William private 50th Foot
12 Mar 1857	Discharged the Service Belfast
21 Apr 1857	Admitted to Out-Pension Pension paid 2nd East London Pension District 8d. per diem
1867	Pension paid 1st East London Pension District
13 July 1867	Arrived per *'Norwood'* [2]
1868	Pension paid Melbourne
19 Mar 1870	Died

Service and Personal Details:

Place of Birth:	Cullompton Devon	
Age on Attestation:	19 years	
Period of Service:	1841 — 1857	
Age on Discharge:	34 years 8 months	
Length of Service:	15 years 257 days	
Foreign Service:	East Indies	6 years 8 months
	Malta	1 month
	Turkey & Crimea	2 years 3 months
Medal Entitlement:	Sutlej with clasps for Moodkee Ferozeshur; Aliwal and Sobroan; Crimea with clasps	
Reason for Discharge:	Chronic Rheumatism.	
Character & Conduct:	Very Good	
Trade or Occupation:	Labourer	
Can Sign Name:	X his mark on discharge	
Height:	5' 8½"	
Hair Colour:	Brown	
Eyes:	Hazel	
Complexion:	Fresh	
Remarks:	Admitted to hospital at Scutari	
Intends to Reside:	? Englis Town Essex	

DAVIDSON	Archibald, private 25th Foot
31 June 1841	Discharged the Service Chatham
12 July 1841	Admitted to Out-Pension 1/1d. per diem
10 July 1857	Arrived per *'Clara'* [1]
1873	Pension increased to 1/3d. per diem for 13 years 11 months service in the Enrolled Force
1872	an A. Davidson residing at Fremantle
1874	Correspondence from S.O. Fremantle to W.O.
circa Dec 1874	Transferred from Fremantle to 1st Perth District Originally allocated North Fremantle Lot P52 [This Pensioner Allotment was re-assigned to William Ralph George]

21 Aug 1878	Died - buried East Perth Pioneer Cemetery	
Service and Personal Details:		
Place of Birth:	?Ferryburn Fife	
Age on Attestation:	16 years	
Period of Service:	1825 — 1841	
Age on Discharge:	32 years	
Length of Service:	13 years 309 days	
Foreign Service:	West Indies	10 years 94 days
Reason for Discharge:	Unfit for further service	
Character:	Good	
Trade or Occupation:	Weaver	
Can Sign Name:	X his mark on discharge	
Height:	5' 5"	
Hair Colour:	Brown	
Eyes:	Blue	
Complexion:	Fair	
Intends to Reside:	Banff	

DAVIDSON James, private [2066]

82nd Foot

Previous Regiments	1st Foot; 2nd/1st Foot	
28 Sept 1852	Discharged the Service Chatham Pension paid Wales East Pension District 1/- per diem	
14 Aug 1854	Arrived per *'Ramillies'*	
1857	To South Australia from Western Australia	
1883	Address given to W.O. as Adelaide South Australia	
Service and Personal Details:		
Place of Birth:	Wick Caithness Scotland	
Age on Attestation:	21 years 2 months	
Period of Service:	1831 — 1852	
Age on Discharge:	42 years [41 years 10 months]	
Length of Service:	20 years 265 days	
Foreign Service:	West Indies	5 years 253 days
	Canada	10 years 20 days
Reason for Discharge:	Chronic Rheumatism, worn out and unfit for further military duty	
Character:	Good	
Trade or Occupation:	Baker	
Can Sign Name:	Yes	
Height:	5' 6½"	
Hair Colour:	Brown	
Eyes:	Hazel	
Complexion:	Dark	
Intends to Reside:	Cardiff but decided on Inverness Scotland	

DAVIES Daniel, private

Rifle Brigade

2 Dec 1856	Discharged the Service Chatham Pension paid 1st East London Pension District 9d. per diem

15 Aug 1865	Arrived per *'Racehorse'*
July 1866	Pension paid 1st East London Pension District

Service and Personal Details:

Place of Birth:	Hackney London
Age on Attestation:	17 years 6 months
Period of Service:	1852 — 1856
Age on Discharge:	23 years
Length of Service:	3 years 346 days
Foreign Service:	Crimea
Medal Entitlement:	Crimea with clasps
Reason for Discharge:	Delicacy of Chest and Break-up of Back due to a wound received at Inkerman
Character:	Good
Trade or Occupation:	Labourer
Can Sign Name:	Yes
Height:	5' 9½"
Hair Colour:	Brown
Eyes:	Hazel
Complexion:	Fresh
Intends to Reside:	Charles St., Bethnal Green London

DAVIES Daniel, private [see also 1172]
23rd Foot; ?40th

Surname Variant	DAVIS
14 Apr 1857	Discharged the Service Chatham Pension paid Bristol 8d. per diem
9 June 1862	Arrived per *'Norwood'* [1]
1865	Pension paid Adelaide from Perth WA
1870	Died South Australia

Service and Personal Details:

Place of Birth:	Monmouth Wales
Age on Attestation:	34 years [excluding service in India]
Period of Service:	1854 — 1857 [excluding service in India]
Age on Discharge:	36 years 3 months
Length of Service:	2 years 96 days excluding service in India
Foreign Service:	India 8 years Turkey & Crimea 1 year 6 months
Medal Entitlement:	Candahar; Ghuznee Cabool; Bronze Star for Maharajpore; Crimea with clasp
Reason for Discharge:	Severely wounded in India and Dyspnoea
Character:	Good
Trade or Occupation:	Paper maker
Can Sign Name:	Yes
Height:	5' 9"
Hair Colour:	Light Brown
Eyes:	Hazel
Complexion:	Fresh
Intends to Reside:	Christ's Parish Bristol

DAVIES	William, private
	51st Foot
Surname Variant	DAVIS
12 Nov 1850	Discharged the Service Chatham
	Pension paid 2nd North London Pension District
	9d. per diem
1852	Pension paid 1st East London Pension District
19 Aug 1853	Arrived per *'Robert Small'*
1855	Residing North Fremantle Lot P12 with wife ?Julia

Service and Personal Details:		
Place of Birth:	St Georges London	
Age on Enlistment:	19 years	
Period of Service:	1833 — 1850	
Age on Discharge:	37 years or 35 years 9 months	
Length of Service:	16 years 217 days	
Foreign Service:	Australian Colonies	8 years 6 months
	East Indies	2 years 8 months
Reason for Discharge:	Rheumatism, Dysentery and Disease of the Chest	
Character:	Prior to 1845 his character was indifferent, but since then it has been good	
Trade or Occupation:	Confectioner	
Can Sign Name:	Yes	
Height:	5' 6¾"	
Hair Colour:	Brown	
Eyes:	Blue	
Complexion:	Fair	
Remarks:	Embarked for New South Wales & Van Diemans	
Land — 1838		
Intends to Reside:	St George Hanover Square London	

DAVIS	Isaac, private
	69th Foot
Surname Variant	DAVIES
25 Oct 1858	Discharged the Service Dublin
2 Nov 1858	Admitted to Out-Pension
	Pension paid 2nd Portsmouth Pension District
	8d. per diem
29 Jan 1862	Arrived per *'Lincelles'*
1864	private I Davis serving in the Pensioner Force at Perth contributed to the Greenough Fire Relief Fund
1867	"Perished onboard the *'Emma'*"

Service and Personal Details:		
Place of Birth:	Petersfield Hampshire	
Age on Attestation:	18 years	
Period of Service:	1837 — 1858	
Age on Discharge:	39 years 6 months	
Length of Service:	21 years 197 days	
Foreign Service:	West Indies	1 year
	North America	3 years 7 months
	Mediterranean	3 years 3 months
Reason for Discharge:	Chronic Ophthalmia and chronic rheumatism	

Character:	Good
Trade or Occupation:	Labourer
Can Sign Name:	X his mark on discharge
Height:	5' 6"
Hair Colour:	Light Brown
Eyes:	Blue
Complexion:	Fresh
Intends to Reside:	Southwick Hampshire

DAVIS	John, private EIC known as John Law Davis in Western Australia [Title Deeds data SRO Cons 5000/477 – DAVIES] 2nd Madras European Light Infantry Out Pension No 235
17 Apr 1850	Admitted to Out-pension Pension paid 2nd East London Pension District 9d. per diem
7 Feb 1853	Arrived per *'Dudbrook'*
1857	Occupying West Guildford Lot P114
10 Oct 1864	Applied for Title to West Guildford Lot P114
1870	Died

Service and Personal Details:

Where Born:	Newry Co. Down
Trade or Occupation:	Labourer
Age on Enlistment:	24 years
Presidency:	Madras
Service Period:	Unlimited
Length of Service:	2 years 4 months or 2 years
Age on Discharge:	26 years
Reason for Discharge:	Injury on head from accident on duty
Character:	Good
Height:	5' 6½"
Complexion:	Fair
Visage:	Round
Eye Colour:	Hazel
Hair Colour:	Dark Brown
Intends to Reside:	c/o Mrs Murray Star Alley Radcliffe Highway

DAVIS	John, gunner EIC
also known as	Matthias I **TWOHILL** Bengal Artillery 2nd Brigade Out Pension No 239
12 June 1850	Admitted to Out-pension Pension paid Tralee Pension District 1/3 per diem
19 Aug 1859	Arrived per *'Sultana'*
1856	To South Australia from Western Australia
1857	Pension paid Victoria
1875	Victoria
10 Aug 1976	Died

Service and Personal Details:

Where Born:	Lower Canada

Trade or Occupation:	Clerk
Age on Enlistment:	20 years
Where Enlisted:	Liverpool
Service Period:	Unlimited
Presidency:	Bengal
Length of Service:	8 years 2 months
Age on Discharge:	28 years
Reason for Discharge:	Both shoulders useless from a wound caused by a round shot while in action at Soodalapor
Character:	Good
Height:	5' 9¼"
Complexion:	Swarthy
Visage:	Oval
Eye Colour:	Hazel
Hair Colour:	Brown
Intends to Reside:	Killarney Tralee Co Kerry Ireland

DAVIS William, private
80th Foot

Previous Regiment	13th Foot
23 Dec 1851	Discharged the Service Chatham Pension paid South London Pension District 1/- per diem
19 Aug 1853	Arrived per *'Robert Small'*
1857	a William Davis assigned Albany Lot P3
Jan 1857	Contributed 2/- to the Florence Nightingale Fund
?1858	a William Davis died [aged 40] at King George's Sound
Aug 1860	Application for Title to Albany Lot P3 by Elizabeth Davis

Service and Personal Details:

Place of Birth:	Dartford Kent
Age on Attestation:	14 years
Period of Service:	1825 — 1851
Age on Discharge:	40 years
Length of Service:	21 years 4 days
Foreign Service:	East Indies 21 years
Medal Entitlement:	Afghan; Jellahabad
Reason for Discharge:	Accident in Barracks — Bombay 1845
Character:	Tolerably good
Trade or Occupation:	Labourer
Can Sign Name:	Yes
Height:	5' 11"
Hair Colour:	Black
Eyes:	Hazel
Complexion:	Sallow
Intends to Reside:	Chatham

DAY John, private
31st Foot

23 Feb 1847	Discharged the Service Pension paid Clonmel

	6d. per diem
1849	Pension paid Cardiff [Wales East Pension District]
1 June 1850	Arrived per *'Scindian'*
Aug 1850	Assigned Military Pensioner Allotment P16 at South Perth
Dec 1851	Assigned and occupied North Fremantle Lot P5
1851	Employed as Night Warder
Sept 1852	Died drowned when the boat he was in was swamped

Service and Personal Details:

Place of Birth:	Clanulty Tipperary	
Age on Attestation:	23 years 1 month	
Period of Service:	1840 — 1847	
Age on Discharge:	29 years	
Length of Service:	6 years 249 days	
Foreign Service:	East Indies	6 years
Medal Entitlement:	Afghan; Sikh with clasps for Moodkee and Ferozeshar	
Reason for Discharge:	Gunshot wound to right hand	
Character:	Extremely Good [or Good depending on record]	
Trade or Occupation:	Labourer	
Can Sign Name:	Yes	
Height:	5' 8"	
Hair Colour:	Brown	
Eyes:	Grey	
Complexion:	Sallow	
Intends to Reside:	Clonmel	

DEDMAN	John William, private
	2nd Foot
Previous Regiment	69th Foot
Surname Variant	DEADMAN
11 June 1844	Discharged the Service Chatham
	Pension paid Portsmouth
	11d. per diem
21 May 1851	Arrived per *'Mermaid'*
Nov 1852	Assigned Bunbury Lot P9
Dec 1858	Advised that he would not be responsible for any debts contracted by his wife Harriet
17 Oct 1859	Assigned Bunbury Lot P10
May 1859	Application for Title to Bunbury Lot P9
Dec 1859	Application for Title Bunbury Lot P10
Oct 1959	Departed colony
1860	Pension paid Portsmouth England

Service and Personal Details:

Place of Birth:	Chawton Hampshire	
Age on Attestation:	17 years	
Period of Service:	1823 — 1844	
Age on Discharge:	39 years	
Length of Service:	19 years 32 days	
Foreign Service:	East Indies	18 years 4 months
Reason for Discharge:	Chronic Debility and Rheumatism	

Character:	Very Good, efficient and trustworthy	
Trade or Occupation:	Labourer	
Can Sign Name:	Yes	
Height:	5' 10"	
Hair Colour:	Dark Brown	
Eyes:	Hazel	
Complexion:	Swarthy	
Remarks:	Landed at Gravesend from Bombay May 1844	
Intends to Reside:	Chawton nr. Alton Hampshire	

DELANEY	Edward, private	
	97th Foot	
Previous Regiment	82nd Foot	
Surname Variant	DELANY	
2 Oct 1860	Discharged the Service Colchester	
	Pension paid Chatham	
	9d. per diem	
9 Jan 1868	Arrived per *'Hougoumont'*	
1878	Employed as Assistant Warder at Fremantle	
	Pension increased to 1/1d. per diem	
circa 1881	Fremantle — an Edward Delaney was seriously injured when run over by the wheel of John Forrest's carriage	
1884	Granted Fremantle Lot P70	
1889	Mrs Harper proprietor of Fremantle Lot P70	
June 1897	Residing Fremantle	
1898	Died	
Service and Personal Details:		
Place of Birth:	Abbyleix Queens County Ireland	
Age on Attestation:	18 years	
Period of Service:	1839 — 1860	
Age on Discharge:	39 years	
Length of Service:	21 years 16 days	
Foreign Service:	Jamaica	2 years 4 months
	Canada	5 years 2 months
	Crimea	10 months
	East Indies	2 years 5 months
Medal Entitlement:	Crimea; Indian Mutiny	
Reason for Discharge:	Having completed 21 years service and at own request	
Character:	Good	
Trade or Occupation:	Labourer	
Can Sign Name:	X his mark on discharge	
Height:	5' 6"	
Hair Colour:	Light Brown	
Eyes:	Hazel	
Complexion:	Fresh	
Intends to Reside:	Plymouth	

DELANEY	Michael, private
	89th Foot

31 July 1855	Discharged the Service Chatham Pension paid Clonmel 8d. per diem
9 June 1862	Arrived per *'Norwood'* [1]
1866	Growing bananas below Mt Eliza
10 Sept 1874	Died
1876	Fremantle — Ellen Delaney in receipt of outdoor relief money

Service and Personal Details:

Place of Birth:	Piltown Kilkenny
Age on Attestation:	18 years
Period of Service:	1852 — 1855
Age on Discharge:	21 years 11 months or 22 years 8 months
Length of Service:	3 years 114 days [reckoned]
Foreign Service:	Crimea
Medal Entitlement:	Crimea with clasp, Turkish Crimea
Reason for Discharge:	Loss of toes of the right foot in the trenches before Sebastopol
Character:	none annotated
Trade or Occupation:	Labourer
Height:	5' 9"
Hair Colour:	Brown
Eyes:	Grey
Complexion:	Fair
Distinguishing Marks:	Pock pitted
Intends to Reside:	Piltown Kilkenny

DELANEY William, private

	4th Foot
17 July 1866	Discharged the Service Pension paid 1st North London Pension District 9d. per diem
13 July 1867	Arrived per *'Norwood'* [2]
1868	Stationed Bunbury
30 Sept 1869	Pension paid Madras
12 Apr 1872	Died

Service and Personal Details:

Place of Birth:	St Pauls Dublin	
Age on Attestation:	14 years	
Period of Service:	1840 — 1866	
Age on Discharge:	none given	
Length of Service:	20 years 253 days	
Foreign Service:	Malta & Turkey	1 year
	Crimea	1 year 4 months
	Mauritius	1 year 5 months
	India	13 years 11 months
Medal Entitlement:	Crimea with clasp for Sebastopol and Turkish Crimean	
Reason for Discharge:	At his own request free with pension after 21 years service	
Character:	Indifferent	

Trade or Occupation:	Labourer
Can Sign Name:	Yes
Height:	5' 8"
Hair Colour:	Dark Brown
Eyes:	Grey
Complexion:	Fair
Intends to Reside:	Tottenham Court Road London

DENMAN	John, private RM
Feb 1853	Discharged the Service
24 May 1855	Arrived per *'Stag'*
1856	£8. 0. 0 misappropriated by Capt Foss
1856	Claim of £8 against Capt Foss
Jan 1857	Contributed 2/- to the Florence Nightingale Fund
1859	Died - buried East Perth Pioneer Cemetery

Service and Personal Details:

Place of Birth:	Sherbourne Dorset
Age on Attestation:	18 years 10 months
Marine Division:	Chatham
Period of Service:	1831 — 1853
Length of Service:	21 years 4 months 4 days [reckoned]
Reason for Discharge:	Length of Service
Trade or Occupation:	Tailor
Can Sign Name:	Yes
Height:	5' 8"
Hair Colour:	Brown
Eyes:	Grey
Complexion:	Fresh

DEVANY	Edward, private 27th Foot
Surname Variants	DEVANEY; DELANEY; DEVARNEY
16 Dec 1856	Discharged the Service Chatham Pension paid 1st Belfast Pension District 1/2d. per diem
28 Dec 1863	Arrived per *'Lord Dalhousie'*
Oct 1864	From Fremantle to South Australia with wife and four children per *'Sea Ripple'*
1865	Pension paid Adelaide

Service and Personal Details:

Place of Birth:	Drumahaire Sligo
Age on Attestation:	18 years
Period of Service:	1833 — 1856
Age on Discharge:	41 years 4 months
Length of Service:	23 years 74 days
Foreign Service:	Cape of Good Hope 12 years 8 months
Medal Entitlement:	Kaffir Campaign; Long Service and Good Conduct with gratuity
Reason for Discharge:	Varicose Veins in both legs
Character:	Very Good
Trade or Occupation:	Tailor

Can Sign Name:	X his mark on discharge
Height:	5' 7¼"
Hair Colour:	Brown
Eyes:	Blue
Complexion:	Fresh
Intends to Reside:	Belfast

DEVITT

	Hugh, private 9th Foot
18 Oct 1864	Discharged the Service Limerick 9d. per diem Pension paid 1st Dublin Pension District
22 Dec 1866	Arrived per *'Corona'*
1873	Residing Fremantle
1881	Pension increased to 1/- per diem for 9 years service in the Enrolled Force
31 Jan 1884	Title Application to Fremantle Lot P62
1897	Stationed at Perth
19 Mar 1906	Died at his residence Thompson Rd., North Fremantle aged 83

Service and Personal Details:

Place of Birth:	Rathcoole Dublin	
Age on Attestation:	20 years	
Period of Service:	1843 — 1864	
Age on Discharge:	41 years 4 months	
Length of Service:	21 years 150 days	
Foreign Service:	East Indies	2 years 5 months
	Malta	9 months
	Crimea	1 year 5 months
	Canada	1 year 4 months
	Ionian Isles	4 years 3 months
	Malta	16 days
	Gibraltar	69 days
Medal Entitlement:	Good Conduct with gratuity; Sutlej with 2 clasps; Crimea; with clasp; Turkish Crimean	
Reason for Discharge:	Own Request having completed 21 years service	
Character:	Latterly somewhat irregular	
Trade or Occupation:	Labourer	
Can Sign Name:	Yes	
Height:	5' 6"	
Hair Colour:	Brown	
Eyes:	Grey	
Complexion:	Fresh	
Intends to Reside:	Dublin	

DEVLIN

	Felix, private 86th Foot
Surname Variants	DEVELIN; DEVLYN
12 June 1860	Discharged the Service Chatham Pension paid Chatham 9d. per diem

31 Dec 1862	Arrived per *'York'*
1865	Employed as Assistant Warder
circa 1868	Assigned Victoria Loc G35 [deed No 2221]
1874	Pension increased to 1/2½d. per diem
1877	Title Application to Loc X6 and X7 totalling 34.2 acres Victoria District Bootenal
1894	Died

Service and Personal Details:

Place of Birth:	Newtown Wicklow	
Age on Attestation:	18 years	
Period of Service:	1842 — 1860	
Age on Discharge:	36 years 2 months	
Length of Service:	18 years 20 months	
Foreign Service:	East Indies	14 years 6 months
Medal Entitlement:	Central India	
Reason for Discharge:	Worn out constitution and unfit for further service	
Character:	Good	
Trade or Occupation:	Labourer	
Can Sign Name:	Yes	
Height:	5' 7½"	
Hair Colour:	Sandy	
Eyes:	Grey	
Complexion:	Sallow	
Intends to Reside:	Chatham	

DICKENSON

	James, gunner EIC Madras Artillery
Surname Variant	DICKINSON
	Out Pension No 94 Embarked UK per '*Wellington*'
4 July 1832	Admitted to Out-pension Pension paid North London Pension District 9d per diem
2 Aug 1852	Arrived per *'William Jardine'*
1864	private J Dickinson [sic] serving in the Pensioner Force at York contributed to the Greenough Fire Relief Fund
1866	Police Constable York
1875	Pension paid Perth Western Australia
1885	Died

Service and Personal Details:

Where Born:	Manchester Lancashire
Trade or Occupation:	Farmer
Age on Enlistment:	22 years
Where Enlisted:	Manchester
Presidency:	Madras
Service Period:	Unlimited
Age on Discharge:	28 years
Length of Service:	5 years 3 months
Reason for Discharge:	Unfit for any duty from an injury received in the back
Character:	Good

Height:	5' 6"
Complexion:	Fair
Visage:	Bony/ long
Eye Colour:	Hazel
Hair Colour:	Brown

DIGNAN	John, private 17th Lancers
Previous Regiment	4th Light Dragoons
Surname Variants	DIGNAM; DIGNUM; DIGNUN; DIGMAN
31 Jan 1845	Discharged the Service Chatham Pension paid 1st Dublin Pension District 11d. per diem
28 June 1851	Arrived per *'Pyrenees'* [1]
Oct 1851	a police constable Dignum gave evidence regarding a bag of tools
1852	Applied to be assigned land at Albany
1878	at Albany — suffering from Chronic Rheumatism and is a permanent invalid
Apr 1880	Died - buried East Perth Cemetery

Service and Personal Details:

Place of Birth:	St Marys Dublin
Age on Attestation:	18 years
Period of Service:	1825 — 1845
Age on Discharge:	39 years or 37 years 5 months
Length of Service:	19 years 165 days
Foreign Service:	East Indies 14 years
Reason for Discharge:	Chronic Rheumatism, disease of the spleen and general debility
Character:	Good
Trade or Occupation:	Carpenter
Can Sign Name:	Yes
Height:	5' 7"
Hair Colour:	Brown
Eyes:	Grey
Complexion:	Dark
Intends to Reside:	Dublin

DILLEY	William, private 96th Foot
Mar 1847	Arrived with detachment at Swan River per *'Java'*
1849	Left at Swan River attached to the 99th Foot awaiting instruction re. pension discharge
31 May 1849	Discharged the Service Swan River
1891	Died aged 73
Length of Service:	9 years 130 days after the age of 18
Remarks:	Discharge Compensation of £4.00

DINEEN	Edward, gunner RA Depot Brigade
Surname Variant	DENEEN
20 Dec 1859	Discharged the Service Woolwich

	Pension paid Woolwich
	10d. per diem
1860	Pension paid South London Pension District
29 Jan 1862	Arrived per *'Lincelles'*
1863	Stationed Fremantle District
1863	In prison Freemantle [sic]
1864	private E. Dineen serving in the Pensioner Force at Fremantle District contributed to the Greenough Fire Relief Fund
1865	Pension paid Freemantle [sic]
1865	South Australia
Apr 1865	Edward Deneen [sic] was charged at Adelaide Police Courts as a pauper lunatic and remanded for medical examination
1905	Pension paid Melbourne
1906	Pension increased to 1/6d. per diem
1906	Residing Melbourne
May 1906	On his way home on Good Friday he walked over the cliffs of the Glenelg River and was severely injured

Service and Personal Details:		
Place of Birth:	Mount Mellick Queens County	
Age on Attestation:	25 years	
Period of Service:	1855 — 1859	
Age on Discharge:	29 years	
Length of Service:	4 years 87 days	
Foreign Service:	Hong Kong	1 month
	India	1 year 9 months
Medal Entitlement:	Indian Mutiny with clasps	
Reason for Discharge:	Wounded on head lower jaw and right leg received at the Relief of Lucknow	
Character:	Very Good	
Trade or Occupation:	None annotated	
Can Sign Name:	Yes	
Height:	5' 9¾"	
Hair Colour:	Dark Brown	
Eyes:	Grey	
Complexion:	Fresh	

DINNING	James, private [Bugler]
	Rifle Brigade
Surname Variant	DENNING
26 Oct 1847	Discharged the Service Chatham
	Pension paid Chatham
	1/- per diem
1848	Pension paid South London
1849	Salisbury
1850	South London
30 Apr 1853	Arrived per *'Pyrenees'* [2]
1853	Employed as Assistant Warder
1857	Departed for Melbourne
1865	Pension paid Melbourne

Service and Personal Details:		
Place of Birth:	Caledon Armagh	
Age on Attestation:	17 years	
Period of Service:	1825 — 1847	
Age on Discharge:	39 years 2 months	
Length of Service:	21 years 68 days	
Foreign Service:	North America	11 years
Reason for Discharge:	Unfit for further service being worn out	
Character:	Good	
Trade or Occupation:	Labourer	
Can Sign Name:	Yes	
Height:	5' 5½	
Hair Colour:	Black	
Eyes:	Black	
Complexion:	Blackish	
Intends to Reside:	Chatham	

DITCH

	David, Serjeant
	56th Foot
9 Apr 1850	Discharged the Service Chatham
	Pension paid Deptford
	9d. per diem for 3 years
2 Aug 1852	Arrived per *'William Jardine'*
1853	Serving as police constable
1853	Employed as Night Warder
1855	Employed in Convict Service
1871	Dismissed from Convict Service
1880	Correspondence with W.O.
1881	Residing Lewishan Kent

Service and Personal Details:		
Place of Birth:	Rye Sussex	
Age on Attestation:	18 years 8 months	
Period of Service:	1839 — 1850	
Age on Discharge:	29 years 9 months	
Length of Service:	10 years 300 days	
Foreign Service:	North America	2 years ?52 days
	Gibraltar	2 years 324 days
Reason for Discharge:	Ophthalmia	
Character:	Good and efficient	
Trade or Occupation:	Carpenter	
Can Sign Name:	Yes	
Height:	5' 6¾"	
Hair Colour:	Brown	
Eyes:	Grey	
Complexion:	Fair	
Intends to Reside:	Lewisham Kent	

DOIL

	William, private
	RM
Surname Variant	DOYLE
1855	Admitted to Out-Pension

	Pension paid Chatham
	£20/4/- per annum
1862	Pension paid Chatham
31 Dec 1862	Arrived per *'York'*
1863	Employed as Assistant Warder
1865	On Nominal List to proceed to Camden Harbour per *'Tien Tsin'*
1866	To South Australia from Perth West Australia
1875	Pension paid London

Service and Personal Details:

Place of Birth:	Barony Lanarkshire Scotland
Age on Attestation:	18 years
Marine Division:	Chatham
Period of Service:	1832 — 1855
Length of Service:	21 years 1 month 3 days
Reason for Discharge:	Length of Service
Trade or Occupation:	Labourer
Can Sign Name:	X his mark on discharge
Height:	5' 7¾"
Hair Colour:	Brown
Eyes:	Blue
Complexion:	Fresh

DOLAN Patrick, private

	47th Foot
19 May 1854	Discharged the Service Templemore
27 June 1854	Admitted to Out-Pension
	Pension paid Clonmel
	1/- per diem
1855	Pension paid Jersey
10 Sept 1856	Arrived per *'Runnymede'*
1864	Corporal P Dolan serving in the Pensioner Force at Fremantle District contributed to the Greenough Fire Relief Fund
24 Sept 1870	Died

Service and Personal Details:

Place of Birth:	St Peters Athlone Roscommon	
Age on Attestation:	18 years	
Period of Service:	1833 — 1854	
Age on Discharge:	39 years 3 months	
Length of Service:	21 years 92 days	
Foreign Service:	Mediterranean	6 years 5 months
	West Indies	2 years 9 months
Reason for Discharge:	Chronic Catarrh originated in Malta in 1840	
Character:	That of a Good Soldier	
Trade or Occupation:	Hatter	
Can Sign Name:	Yes	
Height:	5' 7½"	
Hair Colour:	Dark Brown	
Eyes:	Grey	
Complexion:	Fair	
Intends to Reside:	Liverpool Lancaster	

DONEGAN	John, private [297]	
	21st Foot	
Surname Variants	[some] DRONECAN; DOONECAN; ONNEGAN; DOANEGAN; DOONOCAN; DONOVAN; DONEGAIN	
28 July 1846	Discharged the Service Chatham	
	Pension paid 2nd Edinburgh Pension District	
	1/- per diem	
1848	Pension paid 1st Edinburgh Pension District	
18 July 1855	Arrived per *'Adelaide'*	
Jan 1857	a private J Dronecan contributed 2/- to the Florence Nightingale Fund	
1863	Widow of ptve Doonecan [sic] of the 21st Foot applies for Newcastle Town Lot S3 of 4 acres	
1876	Son's wedding announcement	
Service and Personal Details:		
Place of Birth:	Castle Connor Sligo Westmeath	
Where Enlisted;	Westmeath	
Age on Enlistment:	18 years	
Period of Service:	1823 — 1845	
Age on Discharge:	42 years	
Length of Service:	21 years 277 days	
Foreign Service:	West Indies	2 years 20 days
	Van Dieman's Land	9 years
	East Indies	6 years 157 days
Reason for Discharge:	Chronic Rheumatism and general debility contracted at Dinapore in Bengal, attended with severe pains in the back and limbs; loss of appetite and strength attributable to climate and service. Not aggravated by vice, misconduct or intemperance. Disqualified from service in India by chronic rheumatism and impaired constitution	
Character:	Very Good	
Trade or Occupation:	Labourer	
Can Sign Name:	X his mark on discharge	
Height:	5' 10"	
Hair Colour:	Dark	
Eyes:	Hazel	
Complexion:	Dark	
Intends to Reside:	Galasheels Roxburgh	
Married:	*c*1831 Margaret Watson	
Children:	Jane b. *c*1827 aged 66 in 1892 [from Mother's obit]	
	William b. 1836 [107th Foot] Scotland	
	m. *c*1876 Jane Stevens Toodyay	
	James b. 1841 ? India	
	m. *c*1866 Ellen Cockman Perth	
	Agnes b. *c*1844 ? India	
	m. *c*1866 John Henry Monger York	
	George b. *c*1849 Scotland	
	Thomas b. *c*1851 Scotland	

	m. *c*1872 Charlotte Herbert Newcastle
DONEGAN	William, private 107th Foot
Previous Regiment	79th Foot
24 Mar 1874	Discharged the Service Pension paid Perth West. Aust. Pension District 1/1d. per diem
1880	Died aged 44 Toodyay
Service and Personal Details:	
Place of Birth:	Melrose Roxburgh
Age on Enlistment:	18 years
Period of Service:	1853 — 1874
Age on Discharge:	39 years 2 months
Length of Service:	21 years 43 days
Foreign Service:	Turkey & Crimea 2 years 43 days India 16 years 181 days
Medal Entitlement:	Long Service and Good Conduct with gratuity; Crimea with 4 clasps; Turkish Crimean; Indian Mutiny with clasp
Reason for Discharge:	his having claimed it on completion of his second period of 'Limited Service'
Character:	Very Good
Trade or Occupation:	Tailor
Can Sign Name:	Yes
Height:	6' 1½"
Hair Colour:	Brown
Eyes:	Black
Complexion:	Dark
Intends to Reside:	Perth Western Australia
Married:	*c*1876 Jane Stevens Toodyay
Tuesday 11 April 1876	At Newcastle Church William Donegain, [sic] pensioner, 107 Foot., second son of late John Donegain, pensioner of 21st [R. N. B. F]., to Jane Stevens, second daughter of A. Stevens, gardener, at Back Flats, Newcastle
DONNELLAN	William, private 31st Foot
Surname Variant	DONLON
15 Aug 1845	Discharged the Service Chatham Pension paid Ennis 1/- per diem
1846	Pension paid Kilkenny
1846	Ennis
1852	Canterbury
31 Aug 1853	Arrived per *'Phoebe Dunbar'*
1856	To South Australia from Western Australia
1879	Pension paid Adelaide South Australia
Service and Personal Details:	
Place of Birth:	? Loughrea Galway

Age on Attestation:	18 years
Period of Service:	1825 — 1845
Age on Discharge:	42 years
Length of Service:	19 years 266 days
Foreign Service:	East Indies 19 years
Medal Entitlement:	Afghan Campaign of 1842
Reason for Discharge:	General Debility
Character:	Tolerable
Trade or Occupation:	Labourer
Can Sign Name:	X his mark on discharge
Height:	5' 8¼"
Hair Colour:	Dark Brown
Eyes:	Hazel
Complexion:	Fresh
Intends to Reside:	Loughrea Galway

DONNELLY	John, private - drummer [2213] 51st Foot
Previous Regiment	4th Foot
20 Jan 1857	Discharged the Service Chatham Pension paid 2nd Dublin Pension District 6d per diem
15 Aug 1865	Arrived per *'Racehorse'*
circa June 1874	Transferred from 2nd Perth Pension District to 1st Perth Pension District
Jan 1878	Died - buried East Perth Pioneer Cemetery

Service and Personal Details:

Place of Birth:	Clandalkins Dublin
Age on Attestation:	15 years
Period of Service:	1838 — 1857
Age on Discharge:	33 years
Length of Service:	15 years 17 days
Foreign Service:	Malta 10 months East Indies 14 years [from Obituary — present with General Godwin's forces at the capture of Rangoon, Prome and Pegu]
Reason for Discharge:	Chronic Ophthalmia and impaired vision
Character:	Good
Trade or Occupation:	Trunk maker
Can Sign Name:	Yes
Height:	5' 7"
Hair Colour:	Brown
Eyes:	Grey
Complexion:	Fresh
Intends to Reside:	Dublin

DONNELLY	Patrick [Thomas Patrick], Corporal [drummer] 46th Foot
7 May 1867	Discharged the Service Netley Pension paid 2nd Manchester Pension District 1/1½d. per diem
9 Jan 1868	Arrived per *'Hougoumont'*

Apr 1881	Application for Title to Perth Lot 122/Y
1881	Pension increased to 1/7d. per diem for service in the Enrolled Force
22 Aug 1887	Applies for Relief or employment
1890	Died - buried East Perth Pioneer Cemetery
1890	Probate granted for a Patrick Donnelly

Service and Personal Details:

Place of Birth:	St Nicholas Dublin	
Age on Attestation:	15 years	
Period of Service:	1842 — 1867	
Age on Discharge:	40 years 2 months	
Length of Service:	21 years 160 days	
Foreign Service:	Turkey	2 years 7 months
	Corfu	2 years 5 months
	East Indies	8 years 1 month
Medal Entitlement:	Crimea with clasp; Turkish Crimea	
Reason for Discharge:	Asthma	
Character:	Very Good	
Trade or Occupation:	Labourer	
Can Sign Name:	Yes	
Height:	5' 5½"	
Hair Colour:	Brown	
Eyes:	Grey	
Complexion:	Fair	
Intends to Reside:	Manchester	

DONOHUE	Roderick, private 68th Foot
Surname Variants	DONAHUE; DONOHOE
3 Oct 1856	Discharged the service Fermoy
3 Nov 1856	Admitted to Out-Pension Pension paid Birr 8d. per diem
1857	Pension paid Fermoy
1858	Pension paid 1st Cork Pension District
31 Dec 1862	Arrived per *'York'*
1880	Magazine Guard duty at Fremantle
1881	Pension increased to 1/4d. per diem for service in the Enrolled Force [served for 19 years in the Enrolled Duty Force at Fremantle]
July 1881	Assigned Perth Town Lot 82/E of 2 roods 16 perches at Claisebrook
?Aug 1882	Died at the Colonial Hospital aged 48 years
Sept 1883	Application for Title to Perth Lot 82/E
July 1884	Fee Simple for Perth Town Lot 82/E granted to widow

Service and Personal Details:

Place of Birth:	Lorrha Tipperary
Age on Attestation:	18 years
Period of Service:	1852 — 1856
Age on Discharge:	22 years 8 months
Length of Service:	4 years 267 days

Foreign Service:	Malta 10 months
	Crimea 1 year 5 months
Medal Entitlement:	French War Medal for meritorious conduct on the battlefield — Crimea [not verified]; Crimea with clasps; Turkish Crimean
Reason for Discharge:	Wounded in the right arm by a piece of shell whilst in the trenches in the Crimea
Character:	Good
Trade or Occupation:	Labourer
Can Sign Name:	Yes
Height:	5' 7½"
Hair Colour:	Dark Brown
Eyes:	Hazel
Complexion:	Fair
Intends to Reside:	Birr Kings County

DONOGHUE Timothy, private
101st Foot

Previous Regiment	1st Bengal European Fusiliers
	Out Pension No 391
1 June 1862	Embarked UK per *"Lady Jocelyn'*
20 May 1862	Discharged the Service
11 June 1862	Pension to commence
	Pension paid Tralee Pension District
	1/- per diem
4 July 1866	Arrived per *'Belgravia'*
July 1870	Died aged 47

Service and Personal Details:

Place of Birth:	Caherciveen Co Kerry
Presidency:	Bengal
Period Served:	22 years
Age on Discharge:	40 years
Reason for Discharge:	Time expired
Character:	Good
Trade or Occupation:	Labourer
Height:	5' 8"
Hair Colour:	Light Brown
Eye Colour:	Grey
Complexion:	Fresh
Intends to Reside:	Caherciveen Co Kerry

DONOVAN John, private
39th Foot

16 Aug 1844	Discharged the Service Chatham
	Pension paid 1st Cork Pension District
	1/1d. per diem
1854	Pension increased to 1/2d. per diem
2 Apr 1856	Arrived per *'William Hammond'*
July 1856	£9/0/0 balance of pay due on landing at colony but money misappropriated by Capt Foss
Jan 1857	a Corporal J Donovan contributed 1/6d. to the Florence Nightingale Fund

1859	Pension paid Dublin	
1860	Jersey	
1861	Pension paid 2nd West London Pension District	
Service and Personal Details:		
Place of Birth:	St Johns Limerick	
Age on Attestation:	19 years	
Period of Service:	1824 — 1844	
Age on Discharge:	40 years	
Length of Service:	19 years 282 days	
Foreign Service:	New South Wales	6 years
	India	11 years
Medal Entitlement:	Maharajpoor 1843	
Reason for Discharge:	Compound fracture of the right clavicle by a grape shot in action at Maharajpoor 1843	
Character:	Was for many years a well conducted soldier but latterly his general conduct... very indifferent	
Trade or Occupation:	Shoemaker	
Can Sign Name:	X his mark on discharge	
Height:	5' 8½"	
Hair Colour:	Brown	
Eyes:	Grey	
Complexion:	Fair	
Intends to Reside:	Limerick	

DOODY John, private
95th Foot

10 Sept 1867	Discharged the Service Pembroke Dock Pension paid 2nd West London Pension District 1/- per diem	
9 Jan 1868	Arrived per *'Hougoumont'*	
15 July 1881	Assigned North Fremantle Lot 66	
1881	Pension increased to 1/5½d. per diem for service in the Enrolled Force	
1882	Employed as an Assistant Light House Keeper	
1883	Harbour Master — Leave of absence to assist Lightkeeper J Doody. Papers enclosed:	
1884	The Pilot Rottnest — Consideration for Assistant Keeper J. Doody for his Services in extinguishing the fire at Rottnest Light House	
1885	Lightkeeper Rottnest — Sickness of Assistant Lightkeeper Doody	
5 Aug 1884	Granted Fee Simple North Fremantle Lot P66	
1886	Superintendent of Rottnest Island — Alleged assault on Mrs. Rickers by assistant Light Keeper Doody	
Service and Personal Details:		
Place of Birth:	Killarney Co. Kerry	
Age on Attestation:	18 years	
Period of Service:	1841 — 1867	
Age on Discharge:	39 years	
Length of Service:	21 years 16 days	
Foreign Service:	Hong Kong	2 years 1 month

	Crimea	1 year 5 months
	India	9 years 8 months
Medal Entitlement:	Good Conduct and Long Service; Crimean; Crimean Turkish; Central India	
Reason for Discharge:	Own request after 21 years service	
Character:	Very Good	
Trade or Occupation:	Labourer	
Can Sign Name:	Yes	
Height:	5' 10"	
Hair Colour:	Light Brown	
Eyes:	Grey	
Complexion:	Fresh	
Distinguishing Marks:	Pocked marked	
Intends to Reside:	London	

DORAN Bryan, private
49th Foot

Previous Regiment	3rd Foot
10 July 1855	Discharged the Service Chatham Pension paid Birr 9d. per diem
12 Sept 1864	Arrived per *'Merchantman'* [2]
1867	Pension paid Melbourne from 2nd Perth W.A.
1870	Pension paid Eastern Colonies

Service and Personal Details:

Place of Birth:	Kildalky Meath	
Age on Attestation:	18 years	
Period of Service:	1847 — 1855	
Age on Discharge:	30 [sic] years	
Length of Service:	7 years 318 days	
Foreign Service:	Malta and Crimea	[no time period given]
Medal Entitlement:	Crimea with clasps	
Reason for Discharge:	Left arm partially disabled by gunshot wound received at Inkerman	
Character:	Good	
Trade or Occupation:	Labourer	
Can Sign Name:	Yes	
Height:	5' 8"	
Hair Colour:	Sandy	
Eyes:	Hazel	
Complexion:	Fair	
Married:	Sarah Dunne	
Children:	Stephen b. *c*1867 South Australia Richard b. *c*1869 South Australia	

DORAN James, Corporal
26th Foot

Surname Variant	DORNAN
9 Oct 1849	Discharged the Service Cork
11 Dec 1849	Admitted to Out-Pension Pension paid Stirling

	1/1d. per diem	
14 Aug 1854	Arrived per *'Ramillies'*	
1855	Employed by Commissariat [WO61/56]	
1858	Employed as a Gaoler Geraldton	
1863	On November 30, about 10 o'clock, a.m., a fire broke out in a stubble-field near Messrs. Cook & Haley's mill, belonging to Pensioner Doran.	
1868	Granted Greenough Loc G1 and G2	
1875	Pension paid Western Australia	
Service and Personal Details:		
Place of Birth:	St Cuthberts Edinburgh	
Age on Attestation:	17 years	
Period of Service:	1827 — 1849	
Age on Discharge:	38 years 10 months	
Length of Service:	20 years 318 days	
Foreign Service:	East Indies	12 years 4 months
	China	2 years 7 months
Medal Entitlement:	China	
Reason for Discharge:	Chronic Rheumatism and impaired bodily activity	
Character:	Latterly very good	
Trade or Occupation:	Labourer	
Can Sign Name:	Yes	
Height:	6' 0½"	
Hair Colour:	Grey	
Eyes:	Blue	
Complexion:	Fair	
Intends to Reside:	Kirkgate Alloa Stirlingshire	

DORAN	Joseph, private	
	83rd Foot	
Surname Variant	DOREN	
14 Nov 1854	Discharged the Service Chatham	
	Pension paid Newry	
	8d. per diem	
1855	Serving in the Antrim Militia	
1856	Pension paid 2nd Dublin Pension District	
12 Sept 1864	Arrived per *'Merchantman'* as a Convict Guard	
1873	A J Doran pensioner, residing Fremantle	
1874	Pension paid Western Australia	
1874	Pension increased to 1/- per diem	
1869	Departed Colony per *'Sea Ripple'*	
30 Sept 1875	Pension paid South Australia from Fremantle	
19 Oct 1880	Died	
Service and Personal Details:		
Place of Birth:	Glasgow Lanarkshire	
Age on Attestation:	19 years 10 months	
Period of Service:	1833 — 1854	
Age on Discharge:	41 years or 40 years 10 months	
Length of Service:	20 years 357 days	
Foreign Service:	East Indies	4 years 336 days
North America		9 years 23 days
Reason for Discharge:	Chronic pains and Dyspnoea	

Character:	Good
Trade or Occupation:	Labourer
Can Sign Name:	Yes
Height:	5' 6"
Hair Colour:	Fair
Eyes:	Grey
Complexion:	Fair
Intends to Reside:	Newry
DOTSON	James, Corporal
	2nd Dragoon Guards
Previous Regiment	7th Dragoon Guards
Surname Variant	DALSON
26 Oct 1854	Discharged the Service Dundalk
12 Dec 1854	Admitted to pension
	Pension paid 1st Manchester Pension District
	9d. per diem
1855	Pension paid Liverpool
1856	W.O. Correspondence - "Refused increase — Not entitled to reckon Corporal's Service for addition to pension — not having completed a 3rd period"
10 Sept 1856	Arrived per *'Runnymede'*
1857	To South Australia from Western Australia
Apr 1876	Pension paid at Melbourne
Service and Personal Details:	
Place of Birth:	Gouran Kilkenny
Age on Attestation:	21 years
Period of Service:	1836 — 1854
Age on Discharge:	39 years
Length of Service:	18 years 188 days
Reason for Discharge:	Extensive Varicose veins of right leg and thigh
Character:	Good
Trade or Occupation:	Servant
Can Sign Name:	Yes
Height:	5' 11"
Hair Colour:	Brown
Eyes:	Grey
Complexion:	Swarthy
Distinguishing Marks:	Mole on right breast
Intends to Reside:	London
DOUGHERTY	Peter, private
	8th Foot
14 May 1861	Discharged the Service
	Pension paid Longford
	8d. per diem
9 June 1862	Arrived per *'Norwood'* [1]
1864	ptve P Dougherty serving in the Pensioner Force Perth contributed to the Greenough Fire Relief Fund
1866	To South Australia from Perth West Australia

Service and Personal Details:

Place of Birth:	Dundee Forfarshire	
Age on Attestation:	18 years	
Period of Service:	1839 — 1861	
Age on Discharge:	39 years	
Length of Service:	21 years 126 days	
Foreign Service:	North America	6 months
	East Indies	12 years 6 months
Medal Entitlement:	Indian Mutiny with clasp;	
Reason for Discharge:	Own request having completed 21 years service	
Character:	Good	
Trade or Occupation:	Flax Dresser	
Can Sign Name:	Yes	
Height:	5' 7¾"	
Hair Colour:	Dark Brown	
Eyes:	Grey	
Complexion:	Fair	
Distinguishing Marks:	Pitted with small pock marks	
Intends to Reside:	Longford	

DOWN

	William Carpenter, private 14th Light Dragoons
26 Nov 1860	Discharged the Service Dublin
4 Dec 1860	Admitted to Out-Pension Pension paid Cork 10d. per diem
22 Dec 1865	Arrived per *'Vimiera'*
30 July 1877	Assigned and occupied Perth Pensioner Lot 150/Y
1878	Pension increased to 1/3d. per diem for service in the Enrolled Force
Jan 1881	Application for Title to Perth Lot 150, Perth for William C. Down [Pensioner].
25 Feb 1881	Granted Fee Simple Perth Pensioner Lot 150/Y
1889	Librarian of the Mechanic's Institute
1895	Correspondence with W.O.
1934	according to the Secretary of the Western Australian Police Department "Lance Corporal Down served in the Punjaub Campaign 1848 — 1849, and was present at Rammoggur [sic] where his horse was shot from under him. passage of the Chenab [sic]; was present at the battles of Chillianwallah and Goojenat [sic]; pursuit of the enemy over the Jhelum and of the Khyber Pass (medal with two clasps). Was present in the Persian Campaign of 1857 (medal with clasp); Indian Campaign of 1857—1858 which included the suppression of the mutiny at Arungabad [sic]; the siege and capture of Dhar; in action at Mundescore [sic]; relief of Nemuch [sic]; the siege and capture of Chandersee [sic]; the battle of Betwa where he was wounded;

	the siege and capture of Jhansi; in action at Koonah [sic] and Golowlie; the capture of Calpee [sic] and Morar [sic]; Present at the recapture of Gwalior and in action at Ranode [sic] and pursuit of Feroze Shah [sic] (medal with clasp). He landed in Western Australia in 1865 and served in the Enrolled Pensioner Force for 11 years. He then became the librarian for the Swan River Mechanics' Institute and office keeper in the main office of the Commissioner of Police for seven years
Service and Personal Details:	
Place of Birth:	St Peters Cork
Age on Attestation:	20 years 2 months
Period of Service:	1841 — 1860
Age on Discharge:	39 years 6 months
Length of Service:	19 years 43 days
Foreign Service:	East Indies 17 years 3 months
Medal Entitlement:	Persia; Central India with clasp
Reason for Discharge:	Compound fracture of the lower third right leg caused by falling from ladder during fatigue duty at Meerut
Character:	Good
Trade or Occupation:	Letter Press Printer
Can Sign Name:	Yes
Height:	5' 7"
Hair Colour:	Brown
Eyes:	Blue
Complexion:	Fair
Remarks:	Entitled to 'batta' for Persian Expedition 1857 and prize money for Central India 1857/1858
Intends to Reside:	No. 74 Sunday's Well Cork
DOYLE	James, private [Military Pensioner] 96th Foot
Previous Regiment	95th Foot
22 July 1847	Arrived per *'Java'* with regiment
15 May 1849	Discharged the Service Perth West. Australia Pension paid Perth Western Australia 1/- per diem
1857	To South Australia from Western Australia
circa 1872	W.O. correspondence-."Nephew for address"
1872	"with information [Adelaide South. Australia]"
1872	"Nephew - William Doyle"
Service and Personal Details:	
Place of Birth:	Coachford Co. Cork
Age on Attestation:	18 years
Period of Service:	1823 — 1849
Age on Discharge:	43 years
Length of Service:	22 years 280 days

Foreign Service:	Bermuda & North America	12 years
	Australia	8 years
Reason for Discharge:	Worn out and unfit for further service	
Character:	Very indifferent	
Trade or Occupation:	Labourer	
Can Sign Name:	Yes	
Height:	5' 6½"	
Hair Colour:	Light Brown	
Eyes:	Blue	
Complexion:	Fair	

DOYLE

	John, private
	55th Foot
Previous Regiment	13th Foot
8 Apr 1856	Discharged the Service Chatham Pension paid 2nd Dublin Pension District 9d. per diem
15 Aug 1865	Arrived per *'Racehorse'*
Mar 1874	Assigned Perth Military Pensioner Lot 144/Y
1881	Pension increased to 1/3d per diem for service in the Enrolled Force of Western Australia
Apr 1881	Application for Title to Perth Lot 144/Y
1884	Perth Town Lot 144/Y grant confirmed
June 1897	Residing Fremantle
Feb 1900	Attended fete at Oval
Oct 1904	Died "On the 6th October 1904 the funeral of Mr John Doyle took place at Fremantle."

Service and Personal Details:

Place of Birth:	Lucan Dublin	
Age on Attestation:	18 years	
Period of Service:	1849 — 1856	
Age on Discharge:	25 years	
Length of Service:	6 years 6 days	
Foreign Service:	Gibraltar	2 years 11 months
	Turkey	1 year 3 months
Medal Entitlement:	Crimean with clasps	
Reason for Discharge:	Gunshot fracture of both bones in right forearm	
Character:	Good	
Trade or Occupation:	Labourer	
Can Sign Name:	X his mark on discharge	
Height:	5' 7½"	
Hair Colour:	Dark Brown	
Eyes:	Dark Grey	
Complexion:	Fresh	
Intends to Reside:	Dublin	

DOYLE

	Patrick, private [Military Pensioner]
	51st Foot
25 July 1848	Discharged the Service Chatham Pension paid Chatham

	1/- per diem	
1849	Pension paid Swan River	
16 Aug 1851	a Patrick Doyle appointed Police Force Perth	
15 Dec 1851	a Patrick Doyle dismissed from Perth Police Force	
8 Aug 1855	Pension paid Swan River	
Service and Personal Details:		
Place of Birth:	Augerlos Co. Tyrone	
Age on Enlistment:	18 years	
Period of Service:	1827 — 1848	
Age on Discharge:	41 years 342 days	
Length of Service:	20 years 342 days	
Foreign Service:	Australian Colonies	8 years 6 months
	East Indies	9 months
Reason for Discharge:	Knee joint severely injured by being jammed between heavy boxes or baggage onboard ship	
Character:	Very Good	
Trade or Occupation:	Labourer	
Can Sign Name:	X his mark on discharge	
Height:	5' 7¼"	
Hair Colour:	Brown	
Eyes:	Grey	
Complexion:	Fresh	
Remarks:	Arrived Calcutta April 1847	
Intends to Reside:	Chatham	

DRONOGHAN — see — DONEGAN John, private 21st Foot

DUEHAM — Jeremiah, private 34th Foot

Surname Variants	DURHAM; DUCKHAM; DUEHAN	
29 Nov 1859	Discharged the Service	
	Pension paid 1st Dublin Pension District	
	9d. per diem	
27 May 1863	Arrived per *'Clyde'*	
1866	Pension paid Adelaide South Australia	
1867	Calcutta	
1867	East London	
1867	Dublin	
Service and Personal Details:		
Place of Birth:	Holy Cross Thurles Tipperary	
Age on Enlistment:	18 years	
Period of Service:	1838 — 1859	
Age on Discharge:	39 years 4 months	
Length of Service:	21 years 10 days	
Foreign Service:	North America	1 year 2 months
	Mediterranean	4 years 8 months
	West Indies	3 years 1 month
	Crimea	1 year 4 months
Medal Entitlement:	Crimea with clasps; Turkish Crimean	
Reason for Discharge:	Having completed 21 years actual service	
Character:	Good	

Trade or Occupation:	Servant
Can Sign Name:	X his mark on discharge
Height:	5' 7"
Hair Colour:	Dark Brown
Eyes:	Hazel
Complexion:	Fresh
Intends to Reside:	Dublin

DULLART Nicholas [Michael], private
57th Foot

Surname Variant	DULLARD
7 May 1857	Discharged the Service Fermoy
2 June 1857	Admitted to Out-Pension Pension paid Kilkenny 6d. per diem
28 Dec 1863	Arrived per *'Lord Dalhousie'*
1865	On Nominal List to proceed to Camden Harbour per '*Tien Tsin*'
1870	Purchased Perth Town Lot 226/Y
Sept 1870	Appears on Perth District Electoral List
1874	Allegedly was maliciously wounded by Henry Feast [sic]
1874	Granted Perth Town Lot 118/Y
1879	Application by Vincent King to be certified as owner of Perth Building Lot Y226 which was originally granted to Nicholas Dullart
1883	Pension paid Clonmel

Service and Personal Details:

Place of Birth:	Grange Co. Kilkenny
Age on Enlistment:	21 years
Period of Service:	1852 — 1857
Age on Discharge:	26 years 4 months
Length of Service:	5 years 114 days
Foreign Service:	Crimea 1 year 4 months
Medal Entitlement:	Crimea with clasp
Reason for Discharge:	Wounded in the back by piece of shell whilst on sentry in the trenches before Sebastopol
Character:	Very Good
Trade or Occupation:	Labourer
Can Sign Name:	X his mark on discharge
Height:	5' 10¾"
Hair Colour:	Dark Brown
Eyes:	Light Blue
Complexion:	Sallow
Intends to Reside:	Kilkenny

DULSTON John, private
80th Foot

Surname Variants	DUNSON; DULSON; DUNSON
25 July 1843	Discharged the Service Chatham Pension paid Wolverhampton 11d. per diem

1 June 1850	Arrived per *'Scindian'*	
1854	To South Australia from Western Australia	
Oct 1871	Died aged about 68 at his residence on North-Eastern Rd., South Australia	
Service and Personal Details:		
Place of Birth:	Shifnall Shropshire	
Age on Enlistment:	17 years	
Period of Service:	1823 — 1843	
Age on Discharge:	36 years	
Length of Service:	18 years 186 days	
Foreign Service:	Mediterranean	7 years
	New South Wales	6 years 2 months
Reason for Discharge:	General Debility	
Character:	Very Good	
Trade or Occupation:	Labourer	
Can Sign Name:	X his mark on discharge	
Height:	5' 5¾"	
Hair Colour:	Dark Brown	
Eyes:	Hazel	
Complexion:	Dark	
Intends to Reside:	Birmingham	
Married:	Ann	

DUNBAR	George, Orderly Room Clerk [Serjeant] 92nd Foot	
Previous Regiment	78th Foot from 1844 — 1857	
24 June 1862	Discharged the Service Chatham Pension paid Inverness 1/- per diem	
12 Sept 1864	Arrived per *'Merchantman'* [2]	
1872	"Off Pension List for offence" To be struck off the Pension List for frivolous and groundless charges against the Staff Officer — Perth West. Aust.	
1873	Pension restored	
1889	a George Dunbar assaulted and beat a little girl	
Oct 1895	Died – buried East Perth Pioneer Cemetery	
Service and Personal Details:		
Place of Birth:	Dingwall Rosshire	
Age on Enlistment:	32 years 6 months	
Period of Service:	1857 — 1862	
Age on Discharge:	37 years 4 months	
Length of Service:	17 years 82 days	
Foreign Service:	East Indies	11 years 304 days
Reason for Discharge:	Paralysis from disease of nervous system caused by the sun while on march from Calcutta to Umballa [sic]	
Character:	Good	
Trade or Occupation:	Printer	
Can Sign Name:	Yes	

Height:	5' 7"	
Hair Colour:	Black	
Eyes:	Dark Blue	
Complexion:	Dark	
Intends to Reside:	Dingwall	
DUNCAN	Henry, private	
	73rd Food	
19 Feb 1849	Discharged the Service Fermoy	
27 Mar 1849	Admitted to Out-Pension	
	Pension paid Carlisle	
	1/- per diem	
10 July 1857	Arrived per *'Clara'* [1]	
1865	Pension paid Western Australia	
1866	Assigned Pensioner Lot P27 North Fremantle	
circa 1868	To South Australia from Fremantle	
Service and Personal Details:		
Place of Birth:	South Leith Mid Lothian	
Age on Enlistment:	19 years	
Period of Service:	1827 — 1849	
Age on Discharge:	40 years 8 months	
Length of Service:	21 years 241 days	
Foreign Service:	Gibraltar	2 years 7 months
	Malta	4 years 3 months
	Ionian Isles	3 years 10 months
	North America	3 years 1 month
Reason for Discharge:	Worn out in the service	
Character:	Good	
Trade or Occupation:	Shoemaker	
Can Sign Name:	X his mark on discharge	
Height:	5' 8"	
Hair Colour:	Black	
Eyes:	Dark	
Complexion:	Fresh	
Intends to Reside:	Cockermouth Cumberland	
DUNLOP	Robert, Company Serjeant	
	RA 10th Battalion	
Surname Variant	DUNLAP	
11 July 1848	Discharged the Service Woolwich	
13 July 1848	Admitted to Out-Pension	
	Pension paid 2nd Dublin Pension District	
	1/7d per diem	
1849	Pension paid Enniskillen	
1858	Belfast	
24 Nov 1858	Arrived per *'Edwin Fox'*	
1861	Dismissed as warder from prison for drunkenness	
1862	Pension paid Singapore	
1866	Admitted an In Pensioner Kilmainham	
1874	Reverted to Out Pension	
1875	Admitted Royal Hospital Kilmainham	
1876	Reverted to Out Pension	
Service and Personal Details:		

Place of Birth:	Aughalougher Co. Fermanagh	
Age on Enlistment:	18 years	
Period of Service:	1826 — 1848	
Age on Discharge:	40 years 3 months	
Length of Service:	22 years 99 days	
Foreign Service:	Malta	11 years 11 months
	Cape of Good Hope	6 years 5 months
Reason for Discharge:	Fell on right hip onboard '*Tigris*' due to ship lurching heavily	
Character:	Exemplary	
Trade or Occupation:	Labourer	
Can Sign Name:	Yes	
Height:	5' 11"	
Hair Colour:	Brown	
Eyes:	Grey	
Complexion:	Fair	

DUNLOP	William, private 1st Foot
28 July 1857	Discharged the Service Chatham Pension paid Ballymena 6d. per diem
1861	Pension increased to 8d. per diem
1862	Pension paid Bermuda
15 Feb 1863	Arrived per '*Merchantman*' [1]
1864	ptve W Dunlop serving in the Pensioner Force at Perth contributed to Greenough Fire Relief Fund
1865	On Nominal List to proceed to Camden Harbour per '*Tien Tsin*'
1866	South Australia from Perth per' *Emily Smith*'
1866	Pension paid Adelaide South Australia
1867	Ballymena Ireland

Service and Personal Details:

Place of Birth:	Ahoghill Co. Antrim	
Age on Enlistment:	20 years	
Period of Service:	1841 — 1857	
Age on Discharge:	35 years 6 months	
Length of Service:	15 years 179 days	
Foreign Service:	Gibraltar	3 years 1 month
	West Indies	2 years
	North America	1 year 8 months
Reason for Discharge:	Varicose Veins in right leg and foot	
Character:	Good	
Trade or Occupation:	Labourer	
Can Sign Name:	Yes	
Height:	5' 8½"	
Hair Colour:	Dark Brown	
Eyes:	Light Blue	
Complexion:	Fresh	
Intends to Reside:	Ballymena Co. Antrim	

DUNN	George, private
	13th Foot
Previous Regiment	47th Foot
Surname Variant	DUNNE
16 Apr 1860	Discharged the Service Fermoy
1 May 1860	Admitted to Out-Pension Pension paid 1st Dublin Pension District 8d. per diem
12 Sept 1864	Arrived per *'Merchantman'* [2] as a Convict Guard
Jan 1871	Assigned North Fremantle Lot P21
1880	Grant of £15 [pounds] sanctioned
1881	Pension increased to 1/2d. per diem for 16 years service in the Enrolled Force
Mar 1882	Granted Fee Simple North Fremantle Lot P21
26 Mar 1887	Pensioner George Dunne — petitioning for Employment
Feb 1888	Applies for quarters in Fremantle Barracks
1889	W.O. Correspondence — Convicted at Perth Western Australia of beating and assaulting Anne Bayley and sentenced to 6 months hard labour. Pension suspended during imprisonment
Apr 1889	A military pensioner named George Dunne [sic] pleaded guilty to have unlawfully assaulted and beaten a little girl aged nine years. Sentenced to 6 months imprisonment with hard labor.
1891	Inmate of the Depot aged 69
1895	Died – ? buried East Perth Cemetery

Service and Personal Details:		
Place of Birth:	Lakenham Norfolk	
Age on Enlistment:	18 years 1 month	
Period of Service:	1838 — 1860	
Age on Discharge:	40 years 1 month	
Length of Service:	21 years 164 days	
Foreign Service:	Malta	2 years 1 month
	West Indies	2 years 8 months
	Turkey	5 months
	Crimea	1 year 8 months
	Gibraltar	2 months
Medal Entitlement:	Crimean with 3 clasps and Turkish Crimean	
Reason for Discharge:	Having completed 21 years service	
Character:	Good	
Trade or Occupation:	Woolcomber	
Can Sign Name:	Yes	
Height:	5' 10"	
Hair Colour:	Light	
Eyes:	Grey	
Complexion:	Fresh	
Intends to Reside:	Dublin	

DUNN	John, private
	84th Foot
14 Sept 1852	Discharged the Service Chatham Pension paid Maryborough

	1/- per diem
4 Apr 1854	Arrived per *'Sea Park'*
1854	Employed as Night Warder
1857	To South Australia from Western Australia
1858	Pension paid Victoria
1875	Victoria

Service and Personal Details:		
Place of Birth:	Portarlington Queens County	
Age on Enlistment:	20 years	
Period of Service:	1831 —- 1852	
Age on Discharge:	41 years	
Length of Service:	20 years 94 days	
Foreign Service:	West Indies	3 years 154 days
	East Indies	9 years 89 days
Reason for Discharge:	Unfit for further service	
Character:	Good — after arriving in India	
Trade or Occupation:	Labourer	
Can Sign Name:	Yes	
Height:	5" 7¾"	
Hair Colour:	Dark Brown	
Eyes:	Hazel	
Complexion:	Sallow	
Remarks:	Aug 1838 Sentenced to 100 lashes	
Feb 1839 Sentenced to 100 lashes		
Intends to Reside:	Portarlington but decided on Maryborough	

DUNN	Patrick, private
	4th Dragoons
Surname Variant	DUNNE
2 Nov 1848	Discharged the Service Athlone
9 Jan 1849	Admitted to Out-Pension
	Pension paid Clonmel
	1/- per diem
6 Apr 1854	Arrived per *'Sea Park'* with family
1864	Fremantle Resident: He is wholly unable to earn his living owing to disease. He pays a portion of his pension in maintenance of his wife, an incorrigible drunkard and lately an inmate of the Lunatic Asylum.
17 July 1870	Died

Service and Personal Details:		
Place of Birth:	Newtown Co. Wicklow	
Age on Attestation:	19 years	
Period of Service:	1824 — 1848	
Age on Discharge:	43 years	
Length of Service:	24 years 41 days	
Foreign Service:	East Indies	16 years
Medal Entitlement:	Served in campaign in Afghanistan and Scinde in 1839	
Reason for Discharge:	Fever, Dysentery, Chronic Rheumatism	

Character:	Good
Trade or Occupation:	Servant
Can Sign Name:	Yes
Height:	5' 9"
Hair Colour:	Brown
Eyes:	Blue
Complexion:	Fresh

DUNNE	Edward, private
	4th Foot
23 Nov 1852	Discharged the Service Chatham
	Pension paid Maryborough
	10d. per diem
	1/-d. per diem
1854	Pension paid Kilkenny
14 Aug 1854	Arrived per *'Ramilles'*
1855	Employed by Convict Establishment as a Warder
1873	Died

Service and Personal Details:		
Place of Birth:	Lea Queens County	
Age on Attestation:	18 years	
Period of Service:	1830 — 1852	
Age on Discharge:	40 years 2 months	
Length of Service:	20 years 299 days	
Foreign Service:	New South Wales	5 years 6 months
	East Indies	10 years 6 months
Reason for Discharge:	Affected by Lumbago and is worn out	
Character:	Good	
Trade or Occupation:	Labourer	
Can Sign Name:	Yes	
Height:	5' 10"	
Hair Colour:	Light Brown	
Eyes:	Grey	
Complexion:	Sallow	
Intends to Reside:	Dublin	

DUNNE	William, private
	3rd Foot
Previous Regiment	41st Foot
Surname Variant	DUNN
22 Jan 1856	Discharged the Service
	Pension paid Tullamore
	6d. per diem
	Employed Bermuda
1861	Pension increased to 8d. per diem
1862	Pension paid Bermuda
15 Feb 1863	Arrived per *'Merchantman'* [1]
	"Stoppage of part pension for child in Tullamore"
30 June 1864	To South Australia from Perth West Australia

Service and Personal Details:	
Place of Birth:	Tullamore Kings County
Age on Enlistment:	18 years

Period of Service:	1854 — 1855	
Age on Discharge:	20 years	
Length of Service:	1 year 291 days	
Foreign Service:	Malta	6 months
	Crimea	8 months
Medal Entitlement:	Crimea	
Reason for Discharge:	Loss of middle finger of left hand at the Redan	
Character:	Good	
Trade or Occupation:	Labourer	
Height:	5' 6¼"	
Hair Colour:	Brown	
Eyes:	Hazel	
Complexion:	Fresh	
Intends to Reside:	Tullamore	

DURNIN	James, private 38th Foot
Surname Variants	DURNAN; DURNAM
22 Nov 1853	Discharged the Service Chatham Pension paid Enniskillen 6d. per diem
1854	Pension paid Turkey
1854	Enniskillen
1856	Monaghan
1857	Enniskillen
1859	Armagh
1859	Drogheda
1860	Cavan
1860	Newry
1860	Monaghan
11 Feb 1861	Arrived per *'Palmeston'*
1865	Gaol Keeper Toodyay
1875	Pension paid Western Australia
1875	Residing Fremantle
1876	Assigned Cockburn Sound Loc P7 [Kogee [sic] or Lake Munster] of 20 acres
1879	Pension increased to 1/- per diem for 17 years service in the Enrolled Force
Dec 1879	Died
1884	Title Application to Cockburn Loc P7 granted to Widow
7 Oct 1899	Letters of Administration for James Durnin, a Military Pensioner, late of Fremantle to James Durnin [son]

Service and Personal Details:		
Place of Birth:	Lisnarrick Co. Fermanagh	
Age on Enlistment:	20 years	
Period of Service:	1839 — 1853	
Age on Discharge:	33 years 3 months	
Length of Service:	14 years 277 days	
Foreign Service:	Mediterranean	2 years 6 months
Gibraltar		2 years 8 months
Jamaica		2 years

Reason for Discharge:	Varicose Veins left leg
Character:	Very Good
Trade or Occupation:	Labourer
Can Sign Name:	Yes
Height:	5' 9½"
Hair Colour:	Dark Brown
Eyes:	Grey
Complexion:	Sallow
Intends to Reside:	Kent St., Borough London

DUTHIE	John, private 95th Foot
11 June 1867	Discharged the Service Netley Pension paid 2nd West London Pension District 1/- per diem
9 Jan 1868	Arrived per *'Hougoumont'*
June 1875	Died — Accidentally drowned W.O. Correspondence — "this man was drowned on 14/6/75 by falling overboard when crossing the River Swan in a boat"

Service and Personal Details:

Place of Birth:	All Saints Newcastle-upon-Tyne	
Age on Enlistment:	17 years 2 months	
Period of Service:	1845 — 1867	
Age on Discharge:	39 years 1 month	
Length of Service:	20 years 169 days	
Foreign Service:	China	3 years 8 months
	Crimea	2 years 3 months
	India	9 years 4 months
Medal Entitlement:	Good Conduct and Long Service with gratuity; Crimea with clasps; Indian Mutiny with clasp for Central India	
Reason for Discharge:	Chronic Rheumatism	
Character:	Very Good	
Trade or Occupation:	Brush maker	
Can Sign Name:	Yes	
Height:	5' 5¾"	
Hair Colour:	Dark Brown	
Eyes:	Hazel	
Complexion:	Fair	
Intends to Reside:	Westminster London	

DUTTON	Joseph, Corporal RA — 3rd Brigade
27 Dec 1864	Discharged the Service Woolwich Pension paid Liverpool 1/3½d. per diem
9 Jan 1868	Arrived per *'Hougoumont'*
1875	Pension paid Perth Western Australia

1875	Convicted at Perth Western Australia of being drunk and insubordinate [he being an Enrolled Pensioner] Sent to prison for 84 days during which half pension is suspended and half paid to child	
circa June 1875	Transferred from Fremantle to Perth District	
1878	Died drowned	
Sept/Oct 1885	Mrs Mary Dutton — applies for Pensioners' Grant of land	
May 1923	Mary Dutton a pensioner's wife was charged with using very bad language toward Major Finnerty	
Service and Personal Details:		
Place of Birth:	Farndon Chester	
Age on Enlistment:	18 years	
Period of Service:	1843 — 1864	
Age on Discharge:	40 years	
Length of Service:	22 years 118 days	
Foreign Service:	St Helena	8 years 3 months
	Turkey	10 months
	Malta	3 years 2 months
Medal Entitlement:	Crimean with clasp for Sebastopol; Turkish Crimean	
Reason for Discharge:	Having completed 21 years service	
Character:	Good	
Trade or Occupation:	Shoemaker	
Can Sign Name:	Yes	
Height:	5' 11½"	
Hair Colour:	Brown	
Eyes:	Hazel	
Complexion:	Fresh	
Intends to Reside:	20 Red Lion St., Woolwich	

DYSART	Hugh, private 21st Foot	
Surname Variant	DYSSART	
8 July 1851	Discharged the Service Pension paid 1st Edinburgh Pension District 9d. per diem	
1851	Pension paid 1st Glasgow Pension District	
1851	Pension paid Paisley	
1852	Ayr	
1852	Edinburgh	
10 Sept 1856	Arrived per *'Runnymede'*	
1868	"Off Enrolled Pensioner Guard Roll for felony"	
1873	Restored to pension	
Mar 1883	Died at the Mt Eliza Depot	
Service and Personal Details:		
Place of Birth:	Tarbolton Ayrshire Scotland	
Age on Enlistment:	18 years 11 months	
Period of Service:	1830 — 1851	
Age on Discharge:	39 years	
Length of Service:	20 years 190 days	
Foreign Service:	Australian Colonies	upwards 6 years

	India	upwards 7 years
Reason for Discharge:	Chronic ophthalmia; Unfit for further service	
Conduct:	Bad	
Trade or Occupation:	Collier	
Can Sign Name:	X his mark on discharge	
Height:	5' 7" or 5' 11"	
Hair Colour:	Brown	
Eye Colour:	Black	
Complexion:	Dark	
Intends to Reside:	Glasgow	

EARL Henry, private [593]
64th Foot

Surname Variants	ERRILL; EARLE
10 July 1849	Discharged the Service Chatham 1/- per diem
1849	Pension paid Birr
6 Apr 1854	Arrived per *'Sea Park'*
1855	Assigned North Fremantle Lot P18
Jan 1857	Contributed 1/- to the Florence Nightingale Fund
1863	Application for Title to North Fremantle Lot P 18
23 July 1879	Remanded at Fremantle on 7th inst for maliciously maiming and wounding, Andrew Burns, whereby the said Andrew Burns has suffered the loss of one of his eyes, also injury to one of his ears, and did otherwise assault the said Andrew Burns, by kicking him about the body.
Oct 1879	Charged with the assault on fellow pensioner Andrew Burns — found not guilty and discharged
Sept 1889	Died - buried East Perth Pioneer Cemetery

Service and Personal Details:

Place of Birth:	Castlecomer Kilkenny	
Age on Enlistment:	16 years	
Period of Service:	1826 — 1849	
Age on Discharge:	39 years 6 months	
Length of Service:	21 years 124 days	
Foreign Service:	Jamaica	6 years 6 months
	North America	2 years 10 months
Reason for Discharge:	Failing Efficiency and activity after long tropical service	
Character:	Good	
Trade or Occupation:	Labourer	
Can Sign Name:	Yes	
Height:	5' 7½"	
Hair Colour:	Brown	
Eye Colour:	Blue	
Complexion:	Fair	
Intends to Reside:	Parsons Town	

ECCLESTON William, private
67th Foot

Surname Variants	ECCLESTONE; EGGLESTON; ENTERTON
23 Apr 1850	Discharged the Service Chatham
	Pension paid Coventry
	1/- per diem
31 Aug 1853	Arrived per *'Phoebe Dunbar'*
1859	Employed as Assistant Warder
1865	To Bunbury from Fremantle
1874	Retired as Warder
1895	Died at Boyanup

Service and Personal Details:

Place of Birth:	St Marys Warwick Warwickshire	
Age on Enlistment:	18 years	
Period of Service:	1828 — 1850	
Age on Discharge:	39 years	
Length of Service:	21 years 234 days	
Foreign Service:	Gibraltar	3 years [total]
	West Indies	7 years
	North America	2 years
Reason for Discharge:	Worn out from long service	
Character:	Good	
Trade or Occupation:	Coachsmith	
Can Sign Name:	Yes	
Height:	5' 9"	
Hair Colour:	Brown	
Eyes:	Hazel	
Complexion:	Fresh	
Remarks:	Reverted to private at own request	
Intends to Reside:	Warwick	

EDGAR	Archibald, Corporal
	RHA — 9th Battalion
11 July 1848	Discharged the Service Woolwich
1848	Employed as Assistant Warder '*Warrior*' Hulk Woolwich
Mar 1851	Embarked *'Pyrenees'* [1]
1851	Disembarked to marry
Apr 1851	Married Brixham Devon
19 Oct 1851	Arrived per *'Morning Star'*
1854	Acting Barrack Serjeant Fremantle
1855	Commissariat Storekeeper
1867	Described as Auctioneer
1874	Described as Farmer
1874	"Was 50 on the 3rd Aug 1874"
1875	Described as Blacksmith
1879	Described Harness maker
1881	Awarded Deferred pension of 4d. per diem
1882	Correspondence with W.O. regarding Deferred Pension
1884	Residing Perth Western Australia
1888	Correspondence with W.O. Payment of Pension Perth Western Australia.
1891	Died aged 67

Service and Personal Details:

Place of Birth:	Langholm Dumfriesshire
Age on Enlistment:	16 years 9 months
Period of Service:	1841 — 1848
Age on Discharge:	23 years 344 days
Length of Service:	5 years 344 days
Reason for Discharge:	Incipient disease of the lungs and weakness of his lower limbs
Character:	Exemplary
Trade or Occupation:	None
Can Sign Name:	Yes
Height:	5' 8¾"
Hair Colour:	Fair
Eyes:	Blue
Complexion:	Fresh
Married:	Jemimah Adams Brixham Devon [June qtr 1851]

EFFORD	Samuel, gunner RA 5th Brigade
10 June 1863	Discharged the Service Plymouth
23 June 1863	Admitted to Out-Pension Pension paid 2nd Plymouth Pension District 1/2d. per diem
28 Dec 1863	Arrived per *'Lord Dalhousie'* as a Convict Guard
1878	Pension increased to 1/8d. per diem for service in the Enrolled Force
1881	Assigned Freshwater Bay Loc P251
1883	Application for Title Freshwater Bay Loc P251
Mar 1884	Title Deed for land at Freshwater Bay Loc 226 for pensioner S. Efford
May 1894	Died – buried East Perth Pioneer Cemetery

Service and Personal Details:

Place of Birth:	Rothwell Northamptonshire
Age on Enlistment:	18 years 10 months
Period of Service:	1839 — 1863
Age on Discharge:	42 years 6 months
Length of Service:	23 years 242 days
Foreign Service:	Gibraltar 11 years 8 months
Medal Entitlement:	Long Service and Good Conduct with gratuity
Reason for Discharge:	Completed 21 years and upwards
Character:	Exemplary
Trade or Occupation:	Woolcomber
Can Sign Name:	Yes
Height:	5' 7½"
Hair Colour:	Grey
Eyes:	Grey
Complexion:	Sallow
Intends to Reside:	Plymouth
Married:	Eliza
Children:	William b. 1846 Gibraltar m. *c*1885 Elizabeth Dinsdale Fremantle

	Elizabeth Anne b. 1848 Gibraltar
	m. *c*1875 Robert Thompson Fremantle
	Margaret b. 1850 Gibraltar
	m. *c*1867 John McMullen Perth
	Samuel b. 1859 Gibraltar
	m. *c*1899 Eliza Cunden Victoria Park

EGAN

	John, private
	49th Foot
Surname Variant	EAGAN
27 Jan 1857	Discharged the Service Chatham
	Pension paid Halifax
	6d. per diem
15 Aug 1865	Arrived per *'Racehorse'*
1866	Pension paid Adelaide from Perth West. Australia

Service and Personal Details:

Place of Birth:	Athlone Westmeath
Age on Enlistment:	27 years
Period of Service:	1854 — 1856
Age on Discharge:	29 years 6 months
Length of Service:	2 years 163 days
Foreign Service:	Crimea 4 months
Medal Entitlement:	Crimea with clasp
Reason for Discharge:	Suffers from the effects of a gunshot wound on the left hip received in the trenches at Sevastopol
Character:	Good
Trade or Occupation:	Labourer
Can Sign Name:	X his mark on discharge
Height:	5' 7"
Hair Colour:	Brown
Eyes:	Grey
Complexion:	Dark
Remarks:	Received payment from Patriotic Fund

EGGAR

	Arthur, Corporal
	RHA — 4th Battalion
Surname Variant	EGGER
10 July 1849	Discharged the Service Woolwich
	Pension paid 2nd Portsmouth Pension District
	9d. per diem
21 May 1851	Arrived per *'Mermaid'*
18 Aug 1853	Died [WO correspondence]

Service and Personal Details:

Place of Birth:	Alton Hampshire
Age on Enlistment:	18 years
Period of Service:	1834 — 1849
Age on Discharge:	33 years 4 days
Length of Service:	15 years 4 days
Reason for Discharge:	Chronic Bowel Complaint
Character:	Exemplary
Trade or Occupation:	Labourer
Can Sign Name:	Yes

Height:	5' 11½"
Hair Colour:	Dark Brown
Eyes:	Hazel
Complexion:	Dark

ELDER

	Andrew, private
	25th Foot
14 July 1841	Discharged the Service Chatham
28 July 1841	Admitted to Out-pension
	Pension paid Dundee
	6d. per diem
1846	Pension paid Perth Scotland
14 Aug 1854	Arrived per *'Ramillies'*
1869	Died aged 61

Service and Personal Details:

Place of Birth:	Inverkeithing Fife Scotland	
Age on Enlistment:	17 years	
Period of Service:	1826 — 1841	
Age on Discharge:	32 years	
Length of Service:	14 years 52 days [reckoned]	
Foreign Service:	West Indies	7 years 4 months
Reason for Discharge:	Pulmonic Disease and general bad health	
Character:	Indifferent	
Trade or Occupation:	Weaver	
Can Sign Name:	Yes	
Height:	5' 7"	
Hair Colour:	Brown	
Eyes:	Grey	
Complexion:	Fair	
Intends to Reside:	Dundee	

ELLARD

	John, private
	25th Foot
Previous Regiment	4th Foot
Surname Variant	ELLAND
10 Aug 1852	Discharged the Service Chatham
	Pension paid Tralee
	1/- per diem
1854	Pension paid Turkey
6 Apr 1854	Arrived per *'Sea Park'*

Service and Personal Details:

Place of Birth:	Banagher Offaly Kings County	
Age on Enlistment:	19 years	
Period of Service:	1831 — 1852	
Age on Discharge:	40 years	
Length of Service:	20 years 133 days	
Foreign Service:	New South Wales	5 years 1 month
	East Indies	14 years 86 days
Reason for Discharge:	Chronic Rheumatism and worn out	
Character:	Latterly Good	
Trade or Occupation:	Labourer	

Can Sign Name:	Yes	
Height:	5' 8"	
Hair Colour:	Dark Brown	
Eyes:	Grey	
Complexion:	Swarthy	
Intends to Reside:	Tralee	

ELLIS	John, Serjeant	
	78th Foot	
28 Oct 1845	Discharged the Service Chatham	
	Pension paid Chatham	
	1/7d. per diem	
1846	To Jamaica as Barrack Serjeant	
1854	Pension paid Woolwich	
1854	Canterbury	
2 Apr 1856	Arrived per *'William Hammond'*	
1857	Employed in Commissariat [WO61/56]	
1864	Pension paid Calcutta	
Service and Personal Details:		
Place of Birth:	Presteign Hertfordshire	
Age on Enlistment:	18 years	
Period of Service:	1824 — 1845	
Age on Discharge:	40 years	
Length of Service:	21 years	
Foreign Service:	Ceylon	12 years 7 months
	East Indies	2 years 7 months
Reason for Discharge:	Unfit for further service	
Character:	Good	
Trade or Occupation:	Servant	
Can Sign Name:	Yes	
Height:	5' 6½"	
Hair Colour:	Dark Brown	
Eyes:	Grey	
Complexion:	Sallow	
Intends to Reside:	Chatham	

ELLIS	Thomas, private
	2nd Foot
14 Aug 1855	Discharged the Service Chatham
	Pension paid 1st Manchester Pension District
	7d per diem
24 Nov 1858	Arrived per *'Edwin Fox'*
1865	Fremantle — Pensioner Ellis 2nd Foot, unable to follow any employment and perhaps never will be able to do so. Memorandum for Capt. Finnerty. Ref. Thomas Ellis, 2nd Foot 'His career since arriving per *'Edwin Fox'* in 1859 has been that of a drunken worthless man'
1871	Died aged 50
Service and Personal Details:	
Place of Birth:	Blackburn Lancashire

Age on Enlistment:	18 years	
Period of Service:	1839 — 1855	
Age on Discharge:	34 years	
Length of Service:	15 years 146 days	
Foreign Service:	Cape of Good Hope	3 years 5 months
	East Indies	5 years 10 months
Medal Entitlement:	[No Thomas Ellis 2nd Foot can be found on the Indian Mutiny Medal Rolls]	
Reason for Discharge:	Unfit for further service	
Character:	Generally Tolerable and Good for the last 2 years	
Trade or Occupation:	Fustian Scourer	
Can Sign Name:	Yes	
Height:	5' 7½"	
Hair Colour:	Dark Brown	
Eyes:	Blue	
Complexion:	Fresh	
Intends to Reside:	Manchester	

ENGLISH

	Peter, private [Bugler]	
	2nd/60th Foot	
11 June 1853	Discharged the Service Birr	
9 Aug 1853	Admitted to Out-Pension	
	Pension paid Carlow	
	1/- per diem	
1856	Pension paid 2nd Dublin Pension District	
19 Aug 1859	Arrived per *'Sultana'*	
1863	To South Australia from Fremantle West Australia	
1875	Pension paid South Australia	
17 Dec 1880	Died South Australia	
Service and Personal Details:		
Place of Birth:	Ipswich Suffolk	
Age on Enlistment:	14 years	
Period of Service:	1828 — 1853	
Age on Discharge:	39 years 5 months	
Length of Service:	21 years 51 days	
Foreign Service:	Gibraltar	5 years 5 months
	Jamaica	2 years 11 months
	Quebec	3 years 1 month
Reason for Discharge:	Chronic Rheumatism and is worn out	
Character:	Bad	
Trade or Occupation:	Shoemaker	
Can Sign Name:	Yes	
Height:	5' 5¾"	
Hair Colour:	Dark Brown	
Eyes:	Blue	
Complexion:	Fresh	
Intends to Reside:	Plymouth Devon	

EVANS

	Thomas, gunner
	RHA
12 Jan 1847	Discharged the Service
	Pension paid Birmingham

	1/- per diem
1848	Pension paid Worcester
25 Oct 1850	Arrived per *'Hashemy'*
Dec 1855	a Thomas Evans died aged 47 years – buried East Perth Pioneer Cemetery

the following entry may not necessarily refer to Thomas Evans RHA

1853	a Thomas Evans gave evidence as to the accidental fatal shooting of George Phillips

Service and Personal Details:

Place of Birth:	Kidderminster Worcestershire
Age on Enlistment:	19 years
Period of Service:	1826 — 1847
Age on Discharge:	40 years 12 days
Length of Service:	21 years
Reason for Discharge:	Chronic Rheumatism
Character:	Indifferent
Trade or Occupation:	Carpet Weaver
Can Sign Name:	Yes
Height:	5' 11"
Hair Colour:	Dark Brown
Eyes:	Dark Brown
Complexion:	Fresh

EVANS	Thomas, Corporal
	43rd Foot
Previous Regiments	1st; 25th
15 July 1862	Discharged the Service Chatham
	Pension paid Chatham
	1/1½d. per diem
4 July 1866	Arrived per *'Belgravia'*
6 July 1871	Died aged 48 Fremantle

Service and Personal Details:

Place of Birth:	St Peter Hereford Herefordshire	
Age on Enlistment:	18 years 7 months	
Period of Service:	1841 — 1861	
Age on Discharge:	39 years 11 months	
Length of Service:	20 years 257 days	
Foreign Service:	East Indies	19 years 2 months
Medal Entitlement:	Central India;	
Reason for Discharge:	Unfit for further service — suffering from Malaria and Rheumatic pains	
Character:	Good	
Trade or Occupation:	Shoemaker	
Can Sign Name:	Yes	
Height:	5' 6¾"	
Hair Colour:	Dark Brown	
Eyes:	Hazel	
Complexion:	Sallow	
Intends to Reside:	Hereford in the County of Hereford	

Married:	1855 Ann McCloskey Madras India
Children:	Sophia Maria b. 1853 Madras India
	m. *c*1868 Timothy Flynn Fremantle
	Amelia Elizabeth b. 1857 Madras India
	m. *c*1882 John Allpike
	Helena; b. *c*1861

EVANS	Thomas, Corporal
	44th Foot
Previous Regiments	1st; 2nd/60th
30 May 1865	Discharged the Service
	Pension paid Canterbury
	1/1d. per diem
1866	Pension paid Worcester
1868	Birmingham
1873	Greenwich
19 Feb 1874	Arrived per *'Naval Brigade'*
1876	Stationed Perth
1883	Granted Coogee Loc 1 at Cockburn Sound
1884	Pension increased to 1/3½d. per diem for service in the Enrolled Pensioner Force
June 1897	Stationed at Perth
1907	Died aged 81 - ? buried East Perth Cemetery

Service and Personal Details:

Place of Birth:	Ledbury Hereford
Age on Enlistment:	17 years 8 months
Period of Service:	1843 — 1865
Age on Discharge:	41 years
Length of Service:	21 years 235 days
Foreign Service:	East Indies 17 years 9 months
Medal Entitlement:	Punjab with clasps; Indian Mutiny with clasp
Reason for Discharge:	Own Request on completion of 21 years service
Character:	Very Good
Trade or Occupation:	Labourer
Can Sign Name:	Yes
Height:	5' 6¼"
Hair Colour:	Brown [Bald]
Eyes:	Grey
Complexion:	Fresh
Intends to Reside:	Canterbury Kent

FAHEY	Darby, [Darbey; James] gunner EIC
	Invalid Battalion Bengal Artillery
Surname Variants	FARLEY; FARHEY; FABEY
	Out Pension No 291
1 July 1863	Admitted to Out-pension
	Pension paid Galway
	1/- per diem
22 Dec 1865	Arrived per *'Vimiera'*
1875	Residing Western Australia
8 Feb 1880	Died Fremantle aged 58 [committed suicide]

Service and Personal Details:

Where Born:	Galway

Trade or Occupation:	Labourer
Date Enlisted:	1st May 1843
Presidency:	Bengal
Length of Service:	21 years 5 months
Age on Discharge:	40 years 8 months or 40 years
Character:	Good
Reason for Discharge:	Time expired and worn out
Medal Entitlement:	Indian Mutiny
Height:	5' 7¾"
Complexion:	Sallow
Eye Colour:	Blue
Hair Colour:	Black
Intends to Reside:	Galway
Married:	Mary McNamara
Children:	James b. *c*1866 d. *c*1869 aged 3 Margaret Mary [Fahey] b. *c*1868 Rottnest m. *c*1888 Ned Edvin Aresen Fremantle [also known as Edvard Aresem; Areson; or Edward Harrison;]
1934	Darbey Fahey's [sic] Indian Mutiny Medal which had been languishing in the Perth Police Head quarters was handed over to his daughter Mrs Harrison Mary [Fahey] b. *c*1871 m. *c*1894 George Seabert Fremantle

FAHEY	James, private 9th Foot
13 Nov 1846	Discharged the Service Chatham Pension paid Clonmel 9d. per diem
1855	Pension paid Preston
1855	Dublin
24 Nov 1858	Arrived per *'Edwin Fox'*
1859	a James Fahey employed as Assistant Warder
1860	To South Australia from Perth West Australia
1860	Pension paid Adelaide South Australia
1876	Sydney New South Wales
11 Jan 1878	Died

Service and Personal Details:

Place of Birth:	Clonmel Tipperary
Age on Enlistment:	17 years 3 months
Period of Service:	1831 — 1846
Age on Discharge:	32 years
Length of Service:	13 years 244 days
Foreign Service:	East Indies 11 years
Medal Entitlement:	Sutlej with clasp
Reason for Discharge:	Lost part of the fingers of right hand caused by a gunshot wound received at Sobroan
Character:	Very Good
Trade or Occupation:	Labourer
Height:	5' 9"

Hair Colour:	Dark
Eyes:	Hazel
Complexion:	Sallow
Intends to Reside:	Clonmel

FAHEY	Patrick, private	
	71st Foot	
Previous Regiment	78th Foot	
4 Aug 1863	Discharged the Service Netley	
	Pension paid Kilkenny	
	9d. per diem	
4 July 1866	Arrived per *'Belgravia'*	
1874	Assigned Perth Military Pensioner Lot 142/Y	
1874	Applied for £15 Improvement Grant re: Perth Town Lot 142/Y	
July 1880	Died – buried East Perth Pioneer Cemetery	
1881	Title Application for Perth Town Lot 142/Y by his widow Mary	
Service and Personal Details:		
Place of Birth:	Callan Kilkenny	
Age on Enlistment:	19 years	
Period of Service:	1845 — 1863	
Age on Discharge:	36 years 6 months	
Length of Service:	17 years 185 days	
Foreign Service:	Crimea	1 year 6 months
	Malta	1 year 8 months
	East Indies	4 years
Medal Entitlement:	Crimea; Turkish Crimea	
Reason for Discharge:	Hepatitis	
Character:	Good	
Trade or Occupation:	Labourer	
Can Sign Name:	Yes	
Height:	5' 6¾"	
Hair Colour:	Dark and Grey	
Eyes:	Grey	
Complexion:	Fresh	
Intends to Reside:	Callan Co. Kilkenny	

FAIRBROTHER	Samuel, private
	29th Foot
Previous Regiments	38th; 31st
25 July 1848	Discharged the Service Chatham
	Pension paid Wolverhampton
	1/- per diem
1 June 1850	Arrived per *'Scindian'*
Sept 1850	Assigned South Perth Military Pensioner Loc P1
1853	Charged with selling a quantity of firewood and obtaining payment by fraudulent means. Case dismissed — "not found"
Jan 1857	Contributed 1/- to the Florence Nightingale Fund
Service and Personal Details:	
Place of Birth:	West Bromage [sic] Staffordshire

Age on Enlistment:	17 years	
Period of Service:	1825 — 1848	
Age on Discharge:	39 years 5 months	
Length of Service:	20 years 203 days	
Foreign Service:	East Indies	21 years 1 month
Reason for Discharge:	General Infirmity and loss of health	
Character:	Indifferent	
Trade or Occupation:	Key Filer	
Can Sign Name:	X his mark on discharge	
Height:	5' 5½"	
Hair Colour:	Light Brown	
Eyes:	Hazel	
Complexion:	Fresh	
Distinguishing Marks:	SFB tattooed on left fore arm	
Intends to Reside:	West Bromage [sic] Stafford	

FAIRGRIEVE Richard, private [bugler]
71st Foot

Surname Variant	FAIRGROVE
8 July 1862	Discharged the Service Stirling Castle Pension paid 2nd Glasgow Pension District 10d. per diem
15 Apr 1864	Arrived per *'Clara'* [2]
1864	Employed as Assistant Warder
1865	Pension paid Madras
1866	Hull
1874	Glasgow

Service and Personal Details:

Place of Birth:	Cannongate Edinburgh	
Age on Enlistment:	20 years	
Period of Service:	1840 — 1862	
Age on Discharge:	41 years 1 month	
Length of Service:	21 years 7 days	
Foreign Service:	Canada	2 years 5 months
	West Indies	3 years 2 months
	Corfu	1 year 9 months
	Crimea	1 year 4 months
	Malta	1 year 7 months
	East Indies	1 year 4 months
Medal Entitlement:	Crimea	
Reason for Discharge:	Own Request having served 21 years	
Character:	Good	
Trade or Occupation:	Japanner [sic]	
Can Sign Name:	Yes	
Height:	5' 8¾	
Hair Colour:	Dark Brown	
Eyes:	Black	
Complexion:	Dark	
Intends to Reside:	Glasgow	

FALLASSEY Peter, private
2nd Foot

Surname Variants	[some] FALLESSEY; FALLASEY; FALLADAY; FARRADAY; FALLACY; FARRACY; FALLASY; FALLASSY
15 May 1852	Discharged the Service Kinsale
29 June 1852	Admitted to Out-Pension Pension paid 1st Dublin Pension District 7d. per diem for 3 years
30 Apr 1853	Arrived per *'Pyrenees'* [2]
1855	Correspondence with W.O. — "Refused further pension"

Service and Personal Details:

Place of Birth:	Bandon Co. Cork
Age on Enlistment:	23 years
Period of Service:	1839 — 1852
Age on Discharge:	35 years 11 months
Length of Service:	12 years 336 days
Foreign Service:	East Indies 5 years 11 months
Reason for Discharge:	Affection of the Heart attended with difficulty of breathing
Character:	Good
Trade or Occupation:	Labourer
Can Sign Name:	X his mark on discharge
Height:	5' 5¾"
Hair Colour:	Dark Brown
Eyes:	Grey
Complexion:	Fresh

FALLON James, Serjeant
54th Foot

Previous Regiments	95th; 20th
Surname Variants	FALLEN; FOLON
4 Nov 1844	Discharged the Service Mullingar
11 Mar 1845	Admitted to Out-Pension Pension paid 2nd Dublin Pension District 1/7½d. per diem
10 July 1857	Arrived per *'Clara'* [1]
1863	Stationed Perth District
1864	Serjeant J Fallon serving in the Pensioner Force at Perth contributed to the Greenough Fire Relief Fund
Sept 1870	Appears on Perth District Electoral List
1873	Pension increased to 2/- per diem for service in the Enrolled Force
12 Oct 1873	Died - buried East Perth Cemetery
8 Oct 1884	Perth Town Lot 120/Y [James Street] granted to his widow Catherine
1893	Patrick and Bridget Fallon apply for transfer of Fee Simple of Perth Town Lot Y120

Service and Personal Details:

Place of Birth:	Kilcolman Co. Mayo
Age on Enlistment:	20 years
Period of Service:	1823 — 1843

Age on Discharge:	40 years 10 months
Length of Service:	20 years 280 days
Foreign Service:	New South Wales
	East Indies [Bombay & Madras] 13 years
Reason for Discharge:	Chronic Rheumatism
Character:	Very Good
Trade or Occupation:	Labourer
Can Sign Name:	Yes
Height:	5' 7"
Hair Colour:	Brown
Eyes:	Grey
Complexion:	Fresh
Remarks;	Wrecked on the *'Royal Charlotte'* transport in the Torres Strait 20 June 1824 and was 42 days on a rock on his passage from New South Wales to India

FANNON	Patrick, private
	99th Foot
Previous Regiment	67th Foot
Surname Variants	FANNOW; FANNER
30 Sept 1862	Discharged the Service Cork
	Pension paid Athlone
	11d. per diem
22 Dec 1865	Arrived per *'Vimiera'*
1881	Pension increased to 1/4d. per diem for service in the Enrolled Force
8 Oct 1883	Assigned North Fremantle Lot P68
30 Aug 1884	Granted Fee Simple North Fremantle Lot 68
1886	Resident Magistrate Newcastle — Pensioner P. Fanner [sic] for Mt. Eliza Depot, 12 May 1886
1893	Died aged 69

Service and Personal Details:

Place of Birth:	Drum Athlone Co. Roscommon	
Age on Enlistment:	17 years	
Period of Service:	1840 — 1862	
Age on Discharge:	39 years	
Length of Service:	21 years 41 days [reckoned]	
Foreign Service:	North America	2 years 3 months
	Gibraltar	3 years 1 month
	West Indies	2 years 1 month
Reason for Discharge:	Own Request on completion of 21 year service	
Character:	Good	
Trade or Occupation:	Labourer	
Can Sign Name:	X his mark on discharge	
Height:	6' 1"	
Hair Colour:	Dark Brown	
Eyes:	Grey	
Complexion:	Fair	
Intends to Reside:	Athlone	

FARLEY	Edward, private EIC Bengal Infantry
Surname Variant	FAHEY W.O. Out-Pension No 157
9 June 1847	Discharged the Service
June 1847	Embarked UK per *'Prince of Wales'* Pension paid 2nd Dublin Pension District 9d. per diem
28 June 1851	Arrived per *'Pyrenees'* [1]
1852	Employed as Assistant Warder [CSR 238]
1853	Serving as Police Constable Fremantle
1857	pension paid Western Australia
1858	"Left Colony without transfer" Pension paid Melbourne
1875	Melbourne
Service and Personal Details:	
Where Born:	Dublin
Trade or Occupation:	Labourer
Where Enlisted:	Dublin
Presidency:	Bengal
Length of Service:	3 years 11 months
Age on Discharge:	26 years
Reason for Discharge:	Wound received on the right hand at Ferozeshah
Character:	Good
Height:	5' 6"
Complexion:	Fresh
Visage:	Oval
Eye Colour:	Grey
Hair Colour:	Black
FARMER	John, private 74th Foot
27 Aug 1861	Discharged the Service Pension paid Chatham 1/- per diem
15 Aug 1865	Arrived per *'Racehorse'*
1866	Died "found in the bush" about 12 miles from Fremantle
28 Jan 1866	Fremantle — Destitute condition of Mrs Elizabeth Farmer, widow of Pensioner who was found dead in the bush a few days since. Up to time of death was receiving from the Enrolled Pay at the rate of 1/3 per day. Leaves wife and 2 children. [CSR 578]
Mar 1866	Last week it was reported to the Fremantle Police that a pensioner named Farmer believed to be of unsound mind, had been missing from his home since 16th inst. After a 3 day search by the police and natives, the body of Farmer was found in the bush about 10 to 12 miles from Fremantle. It is said the body to have been injured about the legs by a bush fire, but whether before or after death is not certain

Aug 1867	In need of relief: Mrs Hamilton was the widow of Pensioner Farmer who died [mad] in the bush. She lately married Hamilton, mate of the "Emma" and who is missing crew on that vessel.

Service and Personal Details:

Place of Birth:	Rossleay Co. Monaghan	
Age on Enlistment:	18 years 2 months	
Period of Service:	1840 — 1861	
Age on Discharge:	39 years 7 months	
Length of Service:	21 years 175 days	
Foreign Service:	North America	3 years 9 months
Reason for Discharge:	Own Request having completed 21 years service	
Character:	Very Good	
Trade or Occupation:	Labourer	
Can Sign Name:	X his mark on discharge	
Height:	5' 8½"	
Hair Colour:	Fair	
Eyes:	Blue	
Complexion:	Fresh	
Intends to Reside:	Chatham	

FARMER	Peter, private
	98th Foot
Previous Regiment	9th Foot
12 May 1863	Discharged the Service
	Pension paid 2nd West London Pension District 9d. per diem
1866	Pension paid Woolwich
22 Dec 1866	Arrived per *'Corona'*
1868	Employed as Temporary Assistant Warder
1876	Joined Police Force
1877	Constable Peter Farmer, an inoffensive and mild looking man was assaulted by George Johnson, George Cook and George Barker
1877	Died aged 54

Service and Personal Details:

Place of Birth:	St Andrews Dublin	
Age on Enlistment:	18 years 1 month	
Period of Service:	1841 — 1865	
Age on Discharge:	39 years 7 months	
Length of Service:	21 years 6 days	
Foreign Service:	East Indies	15 years 3 months
Medal Entitlement:	Sutlej Campaign; and Punjaub 1849	
Reason for Discharge:	Own Request on completing 21 years service	
Character:	Good	
Trade or Occupation:	Labourer	
Can Sign Name:	Yes	
Height:	5' 6½"	
Hair Colour:	Black	
Eyes:	Dark Brown	

Complexion:	Dark
Can Sign Name:	Yes
Intends to Reside:	5 Pulford St., Pimlico London

FARRELL	James, private [700]
	40th Foot
Previous Regiment	87th
9 Jan 1866	Discharged the Service Netley
	Pension paid Carlow
	9d. per diem
1866	Pension paid 1st Dublin Pension District
1866	Pension increased to 1/- per diem
22 Dec 1866	Arrived per *'Corona'*
1874	Pension paid New Zealand
1875	Tasmania
1875	W.O. Correspondence regarding Enrolled Force Western Australia

Service and Personal Details:		
Place of Birth:	Wicklow Co. Wicklow	
Age on Enlistment:	29 years [in the 40th Foot]	
[enlisted Melbourne Victoria]		
Period of Service:	1860 — 1866 [period from restoration]	
Age on Discharge:	33 years 7 months	
Length of Service:	15 years 143 days	
Foreign Service:	Australia & New Zealand	5 years
	India	no time given
Reason for Discharge:	Unfit for further service can only partially raise right arm and injury to leg on the line of march with his regiment [87th] in India 1853	
Character:	Very Good	
Trade or Occupation:	Labourer	
Signed Name:	X his mark on discharge	
Height:	6'	
Hair Colour:	Dark Brown	
Eyes:	Grey	
Complexion:	Fresh	
Remarks;	Attested the Service at Melbourne Victoria	
Intends to Reside:	Wicklow	

FARRELL	John, private
	21st Foot
3 July 1855	Discharged the Service Chatham
	Pension paid 1st Dublin Pension District
	8d. per diem
1858	Pension paid 1st Liverpool Pension District
1860	Pension withheld while in prison
22 Dec 1866	Arrived per *'Corona'*
1871	Died

Service and Personal Details:	
Place of Birth:	Carlow Carlow
Age on Enlistment:	17 years 10 months
Period of Service:	1854 — 1855

Age on Discharge:	18 years 7 months	
Length of Service:	235 days	
Foreign Service:	Expeditionary Army in the East	5 months
Medal Entitlement:	Crimea with clasps	
Reason for Discharge:	Gunshot wound received in the trenches	
Character:	Good	
Trade or Occupation:	Baker	
Height:	5' 5"	
Hair Colour:	Dark	
Eyes:	Brown	
Complexion:	Fresh	

FARRELL	John, private 43rd Foot
Previous Regiments	28th; 22nd
15 July 1862	Discharged the Service Chatham Pension paid 1st Dublin Pension District 9d. per diem
12 Sept 1864	Arrived per *'Merchantman'* [2] as a "Convict Guard to Western Australia"
1867	"Perished onboard the *'Emma'*" "Pension arrears to Jane Bridget"

Service and Personal Details:

Place of Birth:	St Bridgets Dublin	
Age on Enlistment:	22 years	
Period of Service:	1841 — 1861	
Age on Discharge:	43 years 1 month	
Length of Service:	20 years 140 days	
Foreign Service:	Australia	3 months
	East Indies	19 years 4 months
Medal Entitlement:	Central India	
Reason for Discharge:	Chronic Rheumatism and Dysentery	
Character:	Good	
Trade or Occupation:	Labourer	
Can Sign Name:	X his mark on discharge	
Height:	5' 5½"	
Hair Colour:	Light Brown	
Eyes:	Grey	
Complexion:	Fresh	
Intends to Reside:	Goran Co. Kilkenny or Dublin	

FARRELL	Lawrence, Corporal EIC Madras Invalid Battalion Out Pension No 256
3 Sept 1860	Admitted to Out-pension Pension paid 2nd Dublin Pension District 1/- per diem
12 Sept 1864	Arrived per *'Merchantman'* [2]
1865	To Adelaide from Perth Western Australia
1875	Died South Australia

Service and Personal Details:

Where Born:	Dublin
Trade or Occupation:	House painter
Length of Service:	20 years 11 months
Age on Discharge:	40 years
Character:	Good
Reason for Discharge:	Admitted to pension
Height:	5' 5¼"
Complexion:	Fresh
Eye Colour:	Grey
Hair Colour:	Brown
Intends to Reside:	Dublin

FARRELL see — FENNELL Michael, private 59th Foot

FARRELL Michael, private 77th Foot

Previous Regiment	99th Foot
22 Jan 1856	Discharged the Service Chatham Pension paid Fermoy 8d. per diem
1857	Pension paid Clonmel
24 Nov 1858	Arrived per *'Edwin Fox'*
1862	Employed as Temporary Gaoler
1868	Granted Greenough Locs 36 and 37 of 20 acres each Title Deed no's 1/26 and 2222
May 1874	Pension increased to 9d. per diem
Nov 1874	"Exchange of old Pension Certificate for new one"
1889	Pension paid Perth Western Australia
1893	Perth Western Australia
1898	Perth Western Australia
1902	W.O. Correspondence regarding Medal
1902	Medically examined Sydney
Mar 1903	Pension increased to 1/6d. per diem
May 1903	Pension paid New South Wales

Service and Personal Details:

Place of Birth:	Castlemartyr Co. Cork
Age on Enlistment:	17 years 9 months
Period of Service:	1852 — 1856
Age on Discharge:	23 years
Length of Service:	2 years 319 days
Foreign Service:	Mediterranean, & Turkey & Crimea 9 months
Medal Entitlement:	Crimea with clasps
Reason for Discharge:	Wounded by fragment of shell
Character:	Good
Trade or Occupation:	Labourer
Can sign name:	blank; X his mark on Attestation
Height:	5' 6"
Hair Colour:	Brown
Eyes:	Grey
Complexion:	Fresh
Intends to Reside:	Castlemartyr Cork

FARRELL	Patrick, private
	88th Foot
Previous Regiment	26th Foot
26 Jan 1857	Discharged the Service Dublin
3 Feb 1857	Admitted to Out-Pension
	Pension paid Ipswich
	10d. per diem
1858	Pension paid Jersey
31 Dec 1862	Arrived per *'York'*
1863	Stationed Perth District
1864	private P Farrell serving in the Pensioner Force at Perth contributed to the Greenough Fire Relief Fund
1871	Assigned North Fremantle Lot P25
July 1878	"Finished walls etc of Cottage" — applies for £15 improvement grant Pension increased to 1/3½d. per diem for service in the Enrolled Guard
1891	For authority to employ I. Hodges, R. Quinn and P. Farrell as temporary Wardens. [SRO]
1893	Died
Service and Personal Details:	
Place of Birth:	Ardagh Co. Longford
Age on Enlistment:	18 years
Period of Service:	1846 — 1856
Age on Discharge:	27 years 9 months
Length of Service:	9 years 265 days
Foreign Service:	Service in the 'East' 1 year 9 months
Medal Entitlement:	Crimea with clasp
Reason for Discharge:	Wounded by gunshot wound to the chest at Alma and slight wound to outer right ankle
Character:	Latterly Good
Trade or Occupation:	Labourer
Can Sign Name:	X his mark on discharge
Height:	5' 6½"
Hair Colour:	Brown
Eyes:	Blue
Complexion:	Fair
Intends to Reside:	Colchester Essex

FARRINGDON	Frederick James, private [drummer]
	2nd Foot
Surname Variant	FARRINGTON
16 Jan 1872	Discharged the Service Chichester
	Pension paid 1st Portsmouth Pension District
	1/-½d. per diem
1872	Pension paid Cardiff
19 Feb 1874	Arrived per *'Naval Brigade'*
1881	Occupying Lot 14 Swan St North Fremantle
1881	Pension increased to 1/3d. per diem for 6 years service in the Enrolled Force
23 June 1881	Assigned Perth Town Lot 86/E at Claisebrook
20 Dec 1883	Granted Fee Simple Perth Town Lot 86/E

Aug 1887 y	Died aged 54 — buried Fremantle Cemeter	
Apr 1889	Mrs Farrington applied for Quarters in the Fremantle Barracks	
Service and Personal Details:		
Place of Birth:	Subdeanery Chichester Sussex	
Age on Enlistment:	14 years 6 months	
Period of Service:	1846 — 1871	
Age on Discharge:	39 years	
Length of Service:	21 years 311 days	
Foreign Service:	Cape of Good Hope	8 years 1 month
	China	7 months
	East Indies	5 years 3 months
Medal Entitlement:	Kaffir; China with 2 claps	
Reason for Discharge:	Own Request having completed 21 years service	
Character:	Very Good	
Trade or Occupation:	Labourer	
Can Sign Name:	Yes	
Height:	5' 9"	
Hair Colour:	Red	
Eyes:	Grey	
Complexion:	Fresh	
Remarks:	Not in possession of a certificate of education	
Intends to Reside:	Chichester Surrey	
Married:	*c*1859 Frances Chitty b. *c*1841 South Africa	

FARROW	Thomas, private 45th Foot	
Sept 1860	Discharged the Service Aldershot Pension paid Preston 11d per diem	
31 Dec 1862	Arrived per *'York'*	
Nov 1863	Died aged 44	
Service and Personal Details:		
Place of Birth:	Bury St Edmund's Suffolk	
Age on Enlistment:	21 years	
Period of Service:	1839 — 1860	
Age on Discharge:	42 years	
Length of Service:	21 years 13 days [reckoned]	
Foreign Service:	Gibraltar	1 year 9 months
	Monte Video	10 months
Cape of Good Hope	12 years 10 months	
Medal Entitlement:	Kaffir Campaign	
Reason for Discharge:	Own Request on completing 21 years service	
Character:	Very good	
Trade or Occupation:	Labourer	
Can Sign Name:	Yes	
Height:	5' 7"	
Hair Colour:	Dark Brown	
Eyes:	Hazel	

Complexion:	Fresh
Can Sign Name:	Yes
Distinguishing Marks:	Pock pitted
Intends to Reside:	London

FAWL

	Andrew, private	
	12th Foot	
Surname Variants	FAULL; FALL	
29 May 1860	Discharged the Service Chatham	
	Pension paid Chatham	
	9d. per diem	
11 Feb 1861	Arrived per *'Palmeston'*	
1862	Pension paid Sydney	
8 Dec 1863	Died New South Wales	
Service and Personal Details:		
Place of Birth:	St Peter St Pierre Island of Guernsey	
Age on Enlistment:	15 years	
Period of Service:	1837 — 1859	
Age on Discharge:	38 years 2 months	
Length of Service:	19 years 303 days	
Foreign Service:	Mauritius	9 years 11 months
	Australia	3 years 3 months
Reason for Discharge:	Chronic Rheumatism	
Character:	Good	
Trade or Occupation:	Labourer	
Can Sign Name:	Yes	
Height:	6' 0¾"	
Hair Colour:	Brown	
Eyes:	Grey	
Complexion:	Fair	
Intends to Reside:	Chatham	

FAY

	Henry, private	
	6th Foot	
Previous Regiment	45th Foot	
10 Aug 1852	Discharged the Service Chatham	
	1/2d. per diem	
1852	Pension paid Preston	
19 Aug 1853	Arrived per *'Robert Small'*	
30 June 1860	Died Rottnest	
Service and Personal Details:		
Place of Birth:	St Michaels and St Johns Dublin	
Age on Enlistment:	17 years	
Period of Service:	1825 — 1852	
Age on Discharge:	44 years 4 months	
Length of Service:	25 years 270 days [reckoned]	
Foreign Service:	East Indies	15 years 6 months
	Cape of Good Hope	5 years 3 months
Medal Entitlement:	Good Conduct with gratuity	
Reason for Discharge:	Subject to palpitations of the heart	
Character:	Very Good	
Trade or Occupation:	Labourer	

Can Sign Name:	Yes
Height:	5' 5"
Hair Colour:	none annotated
Eyes:	Grey
Complexion:	Sallow
Intends to Reside:	Dublin but decided on Preston Lancashire
Married:	Ann McElliott
Children:	Henry Patrick [Patrick Henry]
	[Fremantle Infantry bandmaster for 27 years]
	m. *c*1870 Ann Childerhouse Perth
	Laurence b. c1849 South Africa
	m. *c*1874 Elizabeth McCann Fremantle

FEGAN	Michael, Serjeant EIC [L/MIL/12/111]
	1st Bombay European Fusiliers
	Out Pension No 282
17 Feb 1862	Admitted to Out-pension
	Pension paid Athlone
	1/- per diem
9 Jan 1868	Arrived per *'Hougoumont'*
1871	Pension paid Manchester Pension District
1871	Dublin Pension District
1874	Died

Service and Personal Details:

Where Born:	Athlone Westmeath Ireland
Trade or Occupation:	Labourer
Date Attested:	27th Sept 1840
Where Enlisted:	Athlone
Embarked India:	per *'Lady East'*
Presidency:	Bombay
Length of Service:	21 years 2 months
Age on Discharge:	39 years
Reason for Discharge:	Time expired
Medal Entitlement:	Indian Mutiny
Character:	Good
Height:	5' 8¼"
Complexion:	Swarthy
Eye Colour:	Grey
Hair Colour:	Brown
Intends to Reside:	Manchester
Married:	April 1854 Anastasia Rooney Bombay India

FELTHAM	James Frederick, Serjeant
	65th Foot
8 Jan 1867	Discharged the Service Aldershot
	Pension paid 2nd Plymouth Pension District
	1/5d per diem
13 July 1867	Arrived per *'Norwood'* [2]
1868	Employed as Assistant Warder
June 1897	Residing Fremantle
Feb 1900	Attended fete at Oval

30 Oct 1905	Died his funeral to leave his residence 116 Attfield St., South Fremantle
1905	Probate granted [James Frederick Feltham late of Fremantle, military pensioner]
Service and Personal Details:	
Place of Birth:	Meer Wiltshire
Age on Enlistment:	19 years
Period of Service:	1845 — 1867
Age on Discharge:	40 years
Length of Service:	21 years 13 days
Foreign Service:	Australia Colonies 19 years 6 months
Reason for Discharge:	Own Request having completed 21 years service
Character:	Exemplary
Trade or Occupation:	Labourer
Can Sign Name:	Yes
Height:	5' 8"
Hair Colour:	Fair
Eyes:	Hazel
Complexion:	Fresh
Intends to Reside:	Devonport Devon
FENNELL	Michael, private 59th Foot
Surname Variants	FINNELL; FARRELL
17 Jan 1871	Discharged the Service Chichester Pension paid 1st Glasgow Pension District 1/1d. per diem
1871	Pension paid Perth Scotland
1872	Stirling Scotland
1872	Perth Scotland
1873	Greenwich
19 Feb 1874	Arrived per *'Naval Brigade'*
11 Nov 1880	Joined Enrolled Guard — stationed Perth
1881	Pension increased to 1/3½d. per diem for service in the Enrolled Force
1881	Assigned Canning Pensioner Lot 137 [3C]
1881	S.O.P — Applications for land for pensioners M. Fennell and S. Efford. [SROWA]
Feb 1882	Relinquished Canning Pensioner Lot 137 [3C]
14 Jan 1885	Application for Title to Albany Lot P14
1885	Temporary appointment of private Fennell to be gardener and caretaker of the Government House Domain
June 1897	Stationed at Perth Employed as caretaker of the Perth Town Hall
Aug 1907	Died buried in the Roman Catholic section of East Perth Pioneer Cemetery
Service and Personal Details:	
Place of Birth:	Chelsea London Middlesex
Age on Enlistment:	17 years 6 months
Period of Service:	1848 — 1870
Age on Discharge:	39 years 6 months

Length of Service:	21 years 102 days	
Foreign Service:	China	4 years 330 days
	Ceylon	1 year 197 days
	Cape of Good Hope	2 years 331 days
	India	1 year 212 days
Reason for Discharge:	His [sic] having claimed it on termination of his second period of 'Limited Service'	
Character:	Very Good	
Trade or Occupation:	Labourer	
Can Sign Name:	X his mark on discharge	
Height:	5 7"	
Hair Colour:	Brown	
Eyes:	Hazel	
Complexion:	Fresh	
Intends to Reside:	Glasgow Scotland	

FENNESSY

	John, private	
	94th Foot	
Previous Regiments	96th; 53rd	
Surname Variant	FENNESSEY	
29 Oct 1861	Discharged the Service Chatham	
	Pension paid Clonmel	
	9d. per diem	
1862	Pension paid Bermuda	
15 Feb 1863	Arrived per *'Merchantman'* [1]	
1865	To South Australia from Perth West Australia	
1875	Pension paid South Australia	
1890	Correspondence with W.O. Adelaide	
1892	Correspondence with W.O.	
Service and Personal Details:		
Place of Birth:	Cashel Co. Tipperary	
Age on Enlistment:	19 years	
Period of Service:	1847 — 1861	
Age on Discharge:	33 years 6 months	
Length of Service:	14 years 176 days	
Foreign Service:	Van Dieman's Land	1 year 3 months
	East Indies	12 years 3 months
Medal Entitlement:	Indian Mutiny with clasp	
Reason for Discharge:	Unfit for further service	
Character:	Good	
Trade or Occupation:	Labourer	
Can Sign Name:	X his mark on discharge	
Height:	5' 8"	
Hair Colour:	Light Brown	
Eyes:	Blue	
Complexion:	Fresh	
Intends to Reside:	Clonmel Co. Tipperary	

FENTON

	Joseph, private
	28th Foot
14 July 1846	Discharged the Service Chatham
Pension paid Woolwich	

1/- per diem		
1849	Pension paid Deptford	
31 Aug 1853	Arrived per *'Phoebe Dunbar'*	
Jan 1857	Contributed 1/- to the Florence Nightingale Fund	
1864	Pension paid Liverpool	
15 Jan 1868	Died	
Service and Personal Details:		
Place of Birth:	St Pauls Dublin	
Age on Enlistment:	13 years	
Period of Service:	1821 — 1846	
Age on Discharge:	37 years 5 months 6 days	
Length of Service:	19 years 89 days [after the age of 18]	
Foreign Service:	Corfu	8 years
	New South Wales	6 years 5 months
	Mediterranean	3 years 2 months
Reason for Discharge:	Worn out by length of service	
Character:	Good	
Trade or Occupation:	Labourer	
Can Sign Name:	Yes	
Height:	5' 6"	
Hair Colour:	Red	
Eyes:	Grey	
Complexion:	Fresh	
Remarks:	Shortness of breath especially when playing his instrument	
Intends to Reside:	Deptford Kent	

FERGUSON	James, Corporal	
	84th Foot	
9 Oct 1855	Discharged the Service Chatham	
	Pension paid Monaghan	
	8d. per diem for 3 years	
10 Sept 1856	Arrived per *'Runnymede'*	
1857	Pension paid Melbourne	
Service and Personal Details:		
Place of Birth:	Monaghan Co. Monaghan	
Age on Enlistment:	18 years	
Period of Service:	1843 — 1855	
Age on Discharge:	30 years	
Length of Service:	11 years 23 days	
Foreign Service:	East Indies	10 years 74 days
Reason for Discharge:	Chronic Dysentery and Disease of the Liver	
Character:	Very Good	
Trade or Occupation:	Labourer	
Can Sign Name:	Yes	
Height:	5' 7½"	
Hair Colour:	Dark Brown	
Eyes:	Grey	
Complexion:	Fresh	
Distinguishing Marks:	Slight Burn on left cheek	
Intends to Reside:	Monaghan	

FIELD	James, private 13th Light Dragoons
25 Oct 1853	Discharged the Service Chatham Pension paid Leeds 7d. per diem
1854	Pension paid Hull
1855	York [UK]
1857	Toronto
1858	Leeds
8 June 1858	Arrived per *'Lord Raglan'*
1861	Pension paid Sydney
1875	Sydney
Service and Personal Details:	
Place of Birth:	Wakefield Yorkshire
Age on Enlistment:	19 years
Period of Service:	1835 — 1853
Age on Discharge:	37 years
Length of Service:	17 years 313 days
Foreign Service:	East Indies 3 years 6 months
Reason for Discharge:	Varicose Veins of right leg
Character:	Very Good
Trade or Occupation:	Bricklayer
Can Sign Name:	X his mark on discharge
Height:	5' 7"
Hair Colour:	Dark Brown
Eyes:	Grey
Complexion:	Fair
FINLAY	William, private 97th Foot
Previous Regiment	78th Foot
Surname Variants	[some] FINDLAY; FINALY; FINLEY
10 Aug 1847	Discharged Chatham
1847	Pension paid Stockport 1/- per diem
1 June 1850	Arrived per *'Scindian'*
1850	Assigned Freshwater Bay Loc 238
Oct 1851	Employed as Assistant Overseer
1851	Employed at York Convict Depot
Feb 1852	Resigned from Convict Service
1854	Pension paid Western Australia
Jan 1857	Contributed 2/- to the Florence Nightingale Fund
1858	Application for Title Freshwater Bay Loc 238 and 260
1859	a William Finlay charged with drunkenness
1861	William Finlay 97th Foot — pension paid South Australia
1877	Pension paid South Australia
c1885	Pension paid Western Australia
Feb 1886	William Finlay — a Pensioner 1/-. diem for admission to Mt. Eliza Poor House
3 Mar 1886	Admitted to Mt Eliza Invalid Depot
11 June 1890	Died aged 80 of 'age and decay'

Service and Personal Details:		
Place of Birth:	Dundee Forfarshire	
Age on Enlistment:	15 years	
Period of Service:	1822 — 1847	
Age on Discharge:	40 years	
Length of Service:	21 years 218 day [service under 18 years not reckoned]	
Foreign Service:	East Indies	10 years 28 days
	Mediterranean	4 years 39 days
Reason for Discharge:	Worn out from long service in various climates	
Character:	Generally Good	
Trade or Occupation:	Cotton spinner	
Can Sign Name:	Yes	
Height:	5' 9"	
Hair Colour:	Brown	
Eyes:	Grey	
Complexion:	Fair	
Intends to Reside:	Stockport Cheshire	

FINNEGAN	James, private 9th Foot
4 Nov 1856	Discharged the Service Dublin Pension paid 1st Dublin Pension District 7d. per diem pending enquiry
1857	Pension increased to 8d. per diem
22 Dec 1866	Arrived per *'Corona'*
Dec 1873	Died – buried East Perth Pioneer Cemetery
1876	Wife [C Finnegan] of Pensioner James Finnegan of the Enrolled Force who died 23rd December 1873, leaving her destitute with two children [aged 4 years and 1½ years] present ages requiring relief
1876	Mrs C Finnegan in receipt of outdoor relief money — Perth

Service and Personal Details:		
Place of Birth:	St Nicholas Dublin	
Age on Enlistment:	17 years 10 months	
Period of Service:	1848 — 1856	
Age on Discharge:	25 years 6 months	
Length of Service:	8 years	
Foreign Service:	Malta	8 months
	Crimea	1 month
Medal Entitlement:	Crimea with clasp	
Reason for Discharge:	Severely hurt by being struck in the back during explosion of the magazine or a mine at the Redan in the Crimea 1855	
Character:	Harness maker	
Trade or Occupation:	Good	
Can Sign Name:	X his mark on discharge	
Height:	5' 6¼"	
Hair Colour:	Brown	

Eyes:	Brown
Complexion:	Fair
Intends to Reside:	Dublin

FINNEGAN

	Thomas, Serjeant
	Army Medical Corps — [Army Hospital Corps]
Previous Regiment	68th
Surname Variant	FINNIGAN
6 Aug 1861	Discharged the Service
	Pension paid 1st Cork Pension District
	1/11d. per diem
1862	Pension paid 2nd Portsmouth Pension District
1862	Pension paid 1st Cork Pension District
28 Dec 1863	Arrived per *'Lord Dalhousie'*
Sept 1869	a Thomas Finnigan forfeited Perth Town Lot H51 due to the non payment of the balance of the purchase money
11 Nov 1880	Joined Enrolled Guard — stationed Perth
1881	Pension increased to 2/5d. per diem for service in the Enrolled Pensioner Force
Feb 1883	Assigned North Fremantle Lot P98
26 June 1884	Granted Fee Simple North Fremantle Lot P98
1893	Correspondence with W.O.
1901	Residing 45 Tuckfield Street Fremantle
Oct 1907	Died

Service and Personal Details:

Place of Birth:	Belfast Co. Antrim	
Age on Enlistment:	18 years 2 months	
Period of Service:	1840 — 1861	
Age on Discharge:	39 years 2 months	
Length of Service:	21 years 10 days	
Foreign Service:	Quebec	9 years 9 months
	Malta	3 years 181 days
	Balaklava [sic]	306 days
	East Indies	306 days
Medal Entitlement:	Crimea; Indian Mutiny with clasp	
Reason for Discharge:	Own Request having served 21 years	
Character:	Good	
Trade or Occupation:	Labourer	
Can Sign Name:	Yes	
Height:	5' 10½"	
Hair Colour:	Brown	
Eyes:	Blue	
Complexion:	Fresh	
Intends to Reside:	Fermoy Co. Cork	

FISHER

	John, private
	74th Foot
19 June 1860	Discharged the Service Aberdeen
	Pension paid 2nd Glasgow Pension District
	11d. per diem
12 Sept 1864	Arrived per *'Merchantman'* [2]
1875	Pension paid Western Australia

1878	Pension increased to 1/4½d. per diem for service in the Enrolled Force	
4 May 1880	Died aged 60 On the 5th May at Mr. P. Taafe's, Fremantle, before J. G. Slade, RM and Coroner, Inquest on the body of John Fisher, pensioner, who died on the 4th inst. Verdict — "Death from Suffocation while in a state of Drunkenness	
Service and Personal Details:		
Place of Birth:	Glasgow Lanarkshire	
Age on Enlistment:	20 years	
Period of Service:	1839 — 1860	
Age on Discharge:	none given	
Length of Service:	21 years 11 days	
Foreign Service:	North America	3 years 9 months
	Cape of Good Hope	2 years 8 months
	East Indies	5 years 9 months
Medal Entitlement:	For service in South Africa and recommended for the Indian Mutiny medal	
Reason for Discharge:	Own Request having completed 21 years service	
Character:	Good	
Trade or Occupation:	Comb maker	
Can Sign Name:	Yes	
Height:	5' 6"	
Hair Colour:	Fair	
Eyes:	Grey	
Complexion:	Fair	
Intends to Reside:	Glasgow	

FITZCHARLES	Charles, private 74th Foot	
10 Apr 1849	Discharged the Service Limerick Pension paid 2nd Glasgow Pension District 6d. per diem for 3 years	
25 Oct 1850	Arrived per *'Hashemy'*	
18 Oct 1851	Died	
Service and Personal Details:		
Place of Birth:	Barony Lanarkshire	
Age on Enlistment:	19 years	
Period of Service:	1838 — 1849	
Age on Discharge:	29 years 7 months	
Length of Service:	10 years 225 days	
Foreign Service:	West Indies	2 years 4 months
	North America	3 years 10 months
Reason for Discharge:	Chronic Chest Disease	
Character:	Good	
Trade or Occupation:	Cotton Spinner	
Can Sign Name:	X his mark on discharge	
Height:	5' 9"	
Hair Colour:	Black	

Eyes:	Blue
Complexion:	Fair
Intends to Reside:	Barony parish Glasgow

FITZGERALD James, private

	2nd/12th Foot
26 Dec 1865	Discharged the Service Chatham
	Pension paid Bristol
	11d per diem
13 July 1867	Arrived per *'Norwood'* [2]
1884	Was admitted into the Mt. Eliza Poor House due to him suffering from cancer in lips and neck,
April 1885	Died – buried East Perth Pioneer Cemetery

Service and Personal Details:

Place of Birth:	Rathkeale Limerick	
Age on Enlistment:	17 years 5 months	
Period of Service:	1842 — 1865	
Age on Discharge:	40 years 8 months	
Length of Service:	21 years 22 days	
Foreign Service:	Cape of Good Hope	7 years 4 months
	Mauritius	8 years 2 months
Medal Entitlement:	Kaffir War 1851 - 1853	
Reason for Discharge:	Having served over 21 years	
Character:	Good	
Trade or Occupation:	Labourer	
Can Sign Name:	Yes	
Height:	5' 10¼"	
Hair Colour:	Brown	
Eyes:	Hazel	
Complexion:	Fresh	
Distinguishing Marks:	Letter 'D' and marks of cupping	
Intends to Reside:	Bristol	

FITZGERALD Michael, private

	40th Foot
16 Aug 1844	Discharged the Service Chatham
	Pension paid Carlow
	9d. per diem
1845	Pension paid Dublin
28 June 1851	Arrived per *'Pyrenees'* [1]
1852	Assigned Albany Lot P4
Jan 1857	Contributed 2/- to the Florence Nightingale Fund
May 1859	Application for Land Title Albany P4
3 Nov 1861	Died

Service and Personal Details:

Place of Birth:	Carlow Co. Carlow	
Age on Enlistment:	19 years	
Period of Service:	1835 — 1844	
Age on Discharge:	29 years	
Length of Service:	8 years 38 days	
Foreign Service:	East Indies	7 years 1 month
Medal Entitlement:	Afghan campaign — medal inscribed Candahar; Ghuznee; Kabul; Maharajpore 1843	

Reason for Discharge:	Wounded in action by grape shot in upper and inner part of left thigh
Character:	Good
Trade or Occupation:	Labourer
Can Sign Name:	X his mark on discharge
Height:	5' 9"
Hair Colour:	Light Brown
Eyes:	Grey
Complexion:	Fair
Intends to Reside:	Carlow

FITZMAURICE	Lewis [Dennis], private 1st Dragoons
Surname Variant	FITZMORRIS
11 Sept 1855	Discharged the Service Chatham Pension paid 1st North London Pension District 6d. per diem
1856	Pension increased to 9d. per diem permanent
13 July 1867	Arrived per *'Norwood'* [2]
8 Aug 1871	Residents Office Fremantle Dennis Fitzmorris, [sic] Pensioner. This man is in receipt of 6d per diem which he is willing to forfeit should he be admitted to the House.
17 Aug 1873	Died aged 45 - buried East Perth Cemetery

Service and Personal Details:

Place of Birth:	Fermoy Co. Cork	
Age on Enlistment:	19 years	
Period of Service:	1846 — 1855	
Age on Discharge:	28 years	
Length of Service:	8 years 338 days	
Foreign Service:	Turkey & Crimea	10 months
Medal Entitlement:	Crimea	
Reason for Discharge:	Disabled by frostbite of both feet	
Character:	Good	
Trade or Occupation:	Tailor	
Can Sign Name:	Yes	
Height:	5' 9¼"	
Hair Colour:	Auburn	
Eyes:	Light Blue	
Complexion:	Fair	
Intends to Reside:	Preston	

FITZPATRICK	Bernard, private 6th Dragoons
4 Feb 1850	Discharged the Service Dublin
12 Mar 1850	Admitted to Out-Pension Pension paid Bristol 7d. per diem
18 Oct 1851	Arrived per *'Minden'*
1854	Employed as Night Warder without permission of Staff Office Pensions

1858	Pension paid New South Wales
21 Jan 1875	Died New South Wales

Service and Personal Details:

Place of Birth:	Edgworthston Longford
Age on Enlistment:	17 years 10 months
Period of Service:	1832 — 1850
Age on Discharge:	35 years 10 months
Length of Service:	17 years 225 days
Reason for Discharge:	Chronic Chest Disease
Character:	Very Good
Trade or Occupation:	Blacksmith
Can Sign Name:	X his mark on discharge
Height:	5' 9¾"
Hair Colour:	Sandy
Eyes:	Grey
Complexion:	Fresh
Intends to Reside:	Bristol

FITZPATRICK Michael, private
103rd Foot

Previous Regiment	1st Bombay Fusiliers
22 May 1866	Discharged the Service Camp Colchester Pension paid 2nd Manchester Pension District 1/- per diem
13 July 1867	Arrived per *'Norwood'* [2]
1877	Enrolled Pensioner Private Michael Fitzpatrick of the Fremantle Enrolled Force. This man named in the margin has been committed to prison for 3 months by sentence of District Court Martial on the 30th
1877	Assigned Cockburn Sound Loc 2 at Coogee, [Lake Munster]
1881	Pension increased to 1/5½d. per diem for service in the Enrolled Force
Dec 1882	Applied for Title to Cockburn Sound Loc 2 at Coogee[sic], [Lake Munster]
26 Nov 1883	Granted Cockburn Sound Loc 2 at Coogee [sic]
1884	Fremantle — Dr Barnett complaint to Superintendent of Police re: refusal of Pensioner Fitzpatrick [Rottnest] to pay for attention to his son
June 1897	Residing Fremantle
Feb 1900	Attended fete at Fremantle Oval
1912 Died	

Service and Personal Details:

Place of Birth:	Kilmacow Kilkenny	
Age on Enlistment:	18 years 6 months	
Period of Service:	1847 — 1867	
Length of Service:	21 years 11 days	
Age on Discharge:	37 years 6 months	
Foreign Service:	India	17 years 113days

Medal Entitlement:	Punjaub Campaign; Persia with clasp
Reason for Discharge:	Own Request on completion of 21 years service
Character:	Very Good
Trade or Occupation:	Labourer
Can Sign Name:	X his mark on discharge
Height:	5' 6½"
Hair Colour:	Brown
Eyes:	Blue
Complexion:	Sallow
Remarks:	Entitled to 2 years Boon
Intends to Reside:	General Post Office Manchester
Married:	1859 Ann Mary Rosa [O'Neill] Bombay
Children:	John b. 1860 Belgaum India Elizabeth b. 1863 India Mary Ann b. *c*1867 Fremantle m. *c*1894 George Beswick Fremantle Teresa b. *c*1869 m. *c*1894 Arthur Woollams Fremantle Joseph b. *c*1871 Perth m. *c*1888 Catherine Goodbody Fremantle Margaret b. *c*1873 d. *c*1874 Clara b. *c*1874 d. *c*1874 Fremantle Bridget b. *c*1874 d. *c*1874 Fremantle Francis [Frank] b. *c*1875 Fremantle m. *c*1894 May Canavan Fremantle Helen or Ellen b. *c*1877 d. *c*1877
Married:	*c*1878 Elizabeth Farmer Fremantle
Children:	Helen Maud b. *c*1879 m. *c*1895 George Barron Fremantle
Marriage Details:	Bombay Ecclesiastical Returns N3/33/258 5th September 1859 At the Fort Chapel Ahmedabad
Name:	Michael Fitzpatrick Bachelor
Age:	27 years
Rank:	private 1st Bombay Fusiliers
Place:	Kurrachi on leave from Bombay
Father:	Michael
By:	One Proclamation of Banns — to —
Name:	Ann Mary Rosa Spinster
Age:	15 years
Father:	John
Baptismal Details:	Bombay Ecclesiastical Returns N3/35/31 Roman Catholic Persuasion
Date of Birth:	21 December 1860
Date of Baptism:	2nd January 1861
Name:	John
Sex:	Male
Father:	Michael Fitzpatrick
Rank:	private HM 1st Bombay Fusiliers
Mother:	Ann Mary

Place:	Begaum

FITZPATRICK

	Thomas, private	
	2nd/12th Foot	
Previous Regiment	59th Foot	
27 May 1862	Discharged the Service	
	Pension paid Bristol	
	9d. per diem	
1862	Pension paid Bermuda	
15 Feb 1963	Arrived per *'Merchantman'* [1]	
1864	private T Fitzpatrick serving in the Pensioner Force at Perth contributed to the Greenough Fire Relief Fund	
1867	Died aged 39	
Service and Personal Details:		
Place of Birth:	Anna Co. Cavan	
Age on Enlistment:	18 years 2 months	
Period of Service:	1840 — 1862	
Age on Discharge:	40 years	
Length of Service:	21 years 148 days	
Foreign Service:	Mauritius	8 years 11 months
	Cape of Good Hope	7 years 2 months
Medal Entitlement:	Kaffir War of 1852/3	
Reason for Discharge:	Own Request having completed 21 years	
Character:	Very Good	
Trade or Occupation:	Tailor	
Can Sign Name:	X his mark on discharge	
Height:	5' 8¾"	
Hair Colour:	Light Brown	
Eyes:	Grey	
Complexion:	Fresh	
Intends to Reside:	Bristol	

FITZSIMMONS

	John, Serjeant	
	RA 2nd Battalion	
Surname Variant	FITZSIMONS	
9 July 1850	Discharged the Service	
	Pension paid Woolwich	
	9d. per diem	
25 Oct 1850	Arrived per *'Hashemy'* as a Warder	
1851	Pension paid Swan River	
1854	To Eastern Colonies from Perth	
1865	Pension increased to 1/3d. per diem	
Service and Personal Details:		
Place of Birth:	Omagh Co. Tyrone	
Age on Enlistment:	18 years	
Period of Service:	1835 — 1850	
Age on Discharge:	33 years 4 months	
Length of Service:	15 years 113 days	
Foreign Service:	Canada	7 years 2 months
Reason for Discharge:	Fistula	
Character:	Exemplary	

Trade or Occupation:	Shoemaker
Can Sign Name:	Yes
Height:	5' 9¾"
Hair Colour:	Fair
Eyes:	Brown
Complexion:	Fresh
Remarks:	Subsisted until 29th July 1850
Intends to Reside:	Woolwich

FLAHERTY Matthew, private
40th Foot

Previous Regiment	41st Foot
Surname Variant	FLAGHARTY
1 May 1840	Discharged the Service Pension paid Tullamore 9d. per diem
6 Apr 1854	Arrived per *'Sea Park'*
1855	To South Australia from Fremantle West. Aust.
1856	Pension paid Victoria

Service and Personal Details:

Place of Birth:	Ballachmachy Co. Tipperary	
Age on Enlistment:	17 years	
Period of Service:	1821 — 1839	
Age on Discharge:	36 years	
Length of Service:	17 years 239 days	
Foreign Service:	Australian Colonies	4 years 1 month
	East Indies	10 years 10 months
Reason for Discharge:	Unfit for further service	
Character:	Latterly Good	
Trade or Occupation:	Labourer	
Can Sign Name:	Yes	
Height:	5' 6"	
Hair Colour:	Brown	
Eyes:	Grey	
Complexion:	Fair	
Remarks:	London at Gravesend April 1840	

FLANAGAN Patrick, Corporal
25th Foot

Previous Regiment	69th Foot
10 Sept 1850	Discharged the Service Chatham Pension paid Tullamore 1/3½d. per diem
2 Aug 1852	Arrived per *'William Jardine'*
1854	Turnkey at Champion Bay Gaol
1864	a Corporal P Flanagan serving in the Pensioner Force at Perth contributed 2/- to the Greenough Fire Relief Fund
1865	Died aged 60

Service and Personal Details:

Place of Birth:	Westmeath Ireland

Age on Enlistment:	22 years
Period of Service:	1828 — 1850
Age on Discharge:	44 years 6 months
Length of Service:	21 years 32 days
Foreign Service:	? West Indies 7 years
	? North America 3 years 7 months
Reason for Discharge:	Chronic Rheumatism, Dyspnoea and palpitations of the heart
Character:	Good
Trade or Occupation:	Labourer
Can Sign Name:	Yes
Height:	5' 9½"
Hair Colour:	Dark Brown
Eyes:	Grey
Complexion:	Dark

FLANAGHAN	Richard, private
	87th Foot
Surname Variant	FLANAGAN
24 Aug 1852	Discharged the Service Chatham
	Pension paid Manchester
1856	Pension 2nd Plymouth Pension District
1856	Serving as a prison guard Dartmoor
	1/- per diem
2 Apr 1856	Arrived per *'William Hammond'*
1856	In Western Australia
1856	Off EPG Roll for military offence
1856	Restored to EPG Roll
1873	Pension increased to 1/3d. per diem for 7½ years service in the Enrolled Force
circa Mar 1874	Transferred from 2nd Perth Pension District to 1st Perth Pension District
Dec 1881	Died – buried East Perth Pioneer Cemetery

Service and Personal Details:

Place of Birth:	Killoughart Co. Leitrim
Age on Enlistment:	18 years
Period of Service:	1831 — 1852
Age on Discharge:	39 years
Length of Service:	20 years 109 days [reckoned]
Foreign Service:	Mauritius 4 years 9 months
	East Indies 2 years 3 months
Reason for Discharge:	Disease of the Lungs
Character:	Good and efficient soldier
Trade or Occupation:	Labourer
Can Sign Name:	Yes
Height:	5' 7"
Hair Colour:	Light Brown
Eyes:	Grey
Complexion:	Fair
Intends to Reside:	Manchester
Married:	Ellen

Children:	John m. *c*1875 Margaret Campbell Albany Richard Charles b. *c*1853 Manchester m. *c*1875 Mary Anne Thomas Perth William Joseph b. *c*1855 Princetown Devon m. *c*1873 Ellen Moran Perth James Michael [youngest son]

FLEMING Douglas, private

	91st Foot
Surname Variant	FLEMMING
13 Aug 1844	Discharged the Service Chatham Pension paid 2nd Glasgow Pension District
1851	"In prison" 6d. per diem
30 Apr 1853	Arrived per *'Pyrenees'* [1]
1854	Pension paid Perth Western Australia
Dec 1861	"Convicted of theft" — potatoes and onions. Sentenced to 6 months imprisonment and struck off the Pension List
1873	Recommended for restoration of pension
1879	Convicted at Geraldton of arson of a hayrick. Sentenced to 5 years penal servitude and struck off the Pension List
May 1883	Died drowned — committed suicide

Service and Personal Details:

Place of Birth:	Douglas Lanarkshire	
Age on Enlistment:	18 years	
Period of Service:	1831 — 1844	
Age on Discharge:	32 years	
Length of Service:	12 years 293 days	
Foreign Service:	St Helena	3 years 4 months
	Cape of Good Hope	4 years 7 months
Reason for Discharge:	Chronic Ophthalmia	
Character:	Very Good	
Trade or Occupation:	Labourer	
Can Sign Name:	Yes	
Height:	5' 8"	
Hair Colour:	Fair	
Eyes:	Grey	
Complexion:	Fair	
Intends to Reside:	Douglas Lanarkshire	

FLEMING John, Corporal [2940]

	22nd Foot
9 Dec 1862	Discharged the Service Chatham Pension paid Southampton 1/- per diem
1863	Pension paid Portsmouth
1863	North London
1863	Deptford
1867	Gloucester
9 Jan 1868	Arrived per *'Hougoumont'*
1871	Pension paid Sydney

Service and Personal Details:		
Place of Birth:	Kilfinane Co. Limerick	
Age on Enlistment:	19 years	
Period of Service:	1846 — 1862	
Age on Discharge:	35 years 3 months	
Length of Service:	16 years 33 days	
Foreign Service:	East Indies	7 years 2 months
Reason for Discharge:	Chronic Bronchitis	
Character:	Good	
Trade or Occupation:	Labourer	
Can Sign Name:	Yes	
Height:	5' 8"	
Hair Colour:	Dark Brown	
Eyes:	Blue	
Complexion:	Fresh	
Intends to Reside:	Portsmouth Hampshire	
Married:	*c*1869 Martha Giltman or Giltinan Perth	
1864	a Martha Giltinan purchased Perth Town Lot W16 for £6	

FLEMING	William, Corporal	
	27th Foot	
Previous Regiment	91st Foot	
Surname Variant	FLEMMING	
19 Sept 1871	Discharged the Service Aldershot	
	Pension paid Glasgow	
	1/2½d. per diem	
1873	Pension paid Greenwich	
19 Feb 1874	Arrived per *'Naval Brigade'*	
Sept 1875	Wife on remand for stabbing her husband	
1881	Pension increased to 1/5d. per diem for service in the Enrolled Guard	
July 1881	Assigned North Fremantle Lot P71	
2 Mar 1884	Granted Fee Simple North Fremantle Lot P71	
Service and Personal Details:		
Place of Birth:	Omagh Co. Derry	
Age on Enlistment:	17 years 11 months	
Period of Service:	1852 — 1871	
Age on Discharge:	none given	
Length of Service:	19 years 138 days [reckoned]	
Foreign Service:	East Indies	13 years 3 months
Medal Entitlement:	Indian Mutiny	
Reason for Discharge:	Unfit for further service from an attack of Erysipilas [sic] in 1870	
Character:	Good	
Trade or Occupation:	Labourer	
Can Sign Name:	Yes	
Height:	5' 9"	
Hair Colour:	Fair	
Eyes:	Grey	

Complexion:	Fair
Remarks:	No school certificate
Intends to Reside:	Glasgow Scotland
Married:	1861 Isabella Mitchell [Porter] India
Children:	Isabella b.1863 Gonda India
	m. *c*1880 Sylvestor [sic] F Schryver Fremantle
	Jane b. 1866 Bengal India
	m. *c*1887 Edward E Lawson Fremantle

FLOOD	William, private
	84th Foot
Previous Regiment	69th Foot
25 Mar 1862	Discharged the Service
	Pension paid Halifax
	1/- per diem
1862	Pension paid 2nd Manchester Pension District
1862	Pension paid Birr
15 Aug 1865	Arrived per *'Racehorse'*
1868	Employed as Assistant Warder
Mar 1872	Died — committed suicide "shot himself in a fit of temporary insanity"

Service and Personal Details:

Place of Birth:	Roskrea Kings County
Age on Enlistment:	18 years
Period of Service:	1841 — 1862
Age on Discharge:	38 years 5 months
Length of Service:	21 years 143 days
Foreign Service:	East Indies 17 years 83 days
Medal Entitlement:	Indian Mutiny with clasp for Lucknow
Reason for Discharge:	Own Request having completed 21 years service
Character:	Very Good
Trade or Occupation:	Labourer
Can Sign Name:	X his mark on discharge
Height:	5' 11"
Hair Colour:	Light
Eyes:	Grey
Complexion:	Fresh
Intends to Reside:	Halifax Yorkshire

FLYNN	Denis, private
	53rd Foot
Previous Regiment	12th Foot
12 Aug 1851	Discharged the Service Chatham
	Pension paid Tralee
	7d. per diem for 2 years
2 Aug 1852	Arrived per *'William Jardine'*
1853	Employed as Night Warder

Service and Personal Details:

Place of Birth:	Kilkenny
Age on Enlistment:	20 years 9 months
Period of Service:	1843 — 1851
Age on Discharge:	31 years

Length of Service:	7 years 208 days
Foreign Service:	East Indies — 5 years 9 months
Reason for Discharge:	Chronic Rheumatism
Character:	Very Good
Trade or Occupation:	Labourer
Can Sign Name:	X his mark on discharge
Height:	5' 8"
Hair Colour:	Sandy
Eyes:	Hazel
Complexion:	Fresh
Intends to Reside:	Tralee Co. Kerry

FLYNN

	James, private
	40th Foot
Previous Regiment	99th Foot
11 Apr 1862	Discharged the Service Birr
29 Apr 1862	Admitted to Out-Pension
	Pension paid Carlow
	1/- per diem
	pension paid 1st Dublin pension District
12 Sept 1864	Arrived per *'Merchantman'* [2] as a "Convict Guard to Western Australia"
1866	Pension paid South Australia
1867	Melbourne

Service and Personal Details:

Place of Birth:	Carlow Co. Carlow
Age on Enlistment:	18 years
Period of Service:	1841 — 1862
Age on Discharge:	39 years
Length of Service:	21 years 25 days
Foreign Service:	Australian Colonies — 16 years
Medal Entitlement:	New Zealand
Reason for Discharge:	Own Request on completion of 21 years
Character:	Very Good
Trade or Occupation:	Labourer
Can Sign Name:	Yes
Height:	5' 9"
Hair Colour:	Brown
Eyes:	Blue
Complexion:	Fresh
Intends to Reside:	Carlow

FLYNN

	John, Colour Serjeant
	39th Foot
12 Sept 1848	Discharged the Service Chatham
	Pension paid Tralee
	2/- per diem
6 Apr 1854	Arrived per *'Sea Park'*
1855	Pension paid New Zealand
4 May 1864	Died

Service and Personal Details:

Place of Birth:	St Johns Limerick
Age on Enlistment:	16 years
Period of Service:	1825 — 1848
Age on Discharge:	40 years
Length of Service:	20 years 361 days
Foreign Service:	New South Wales about 5 years East Indies 11 years 5 months
Reason for Discharge:	Worn Out and suffers from Rheumatic Pains
Character:	Good
Trade or Occupation:	Marble polisher
Can Sign Name:	Yes
Height:	5' 11"
Hair Colour:	Fair
Eyes:	Grey
Complexion:	Fresh
Intends to Reside:	Bristol

FLYNN	John, Corporal 49th Foot
Previous Regiment	3rd Foot
17 Mar 1857	Discharged the Service Chatham Pension paid Clonmel 6d. per diem
1859	Pension paid Cork
9 June 1862	Arrived per *'Norwood'* [1]
1864	private J Flynn serving in the Pensioner Force at Perth contributed to the Greenough Fire Relief Fund
circa 1873	Assigned Perth Lot 119/Y
1876	Pension increased to 1/1d. per diem due to ceasing to draw pay in the Enrolled Pensioner Force of Western Australia Proprietor of land in Murray Street
Jan 1877	Died – buried East Perth Pioneer Cemetery
1889	Samuel Henry John Flynn Deposed: "I am a shoemaker and have lived at Pensioner's Village for the last eighteen years. I have a brother named John"
1889	Robert George Flynn deposed; "I am a bootmaker living in Perth. I believe I was twenty one last April. My father John Flynn was a military pensioner and to the best of my knowledge has been dead these ten or twelve years. My father had property at the Pensioner's Village Perth"
	Robert George b. *c*1867 Perth m. *c*1894 Alice Emily Read Guildford

Service and Personal Details:	
Place of Birth:	Cahir Co. Tipperary
Age on Enlistment:	20 years
Period of Service:	1845 — 1857

Age on Discharge:	32 years 1 month	
Length of Service:	11 years 350 days	
Foreign Service:	Malta	3 years
	Turkey	5 months
	Crimea	7 months
Medal Entitlement:	Crimea with 3 clasps; Turkish Crimea	
Reason for Discharge:	Defective sight, and gunshot wound in right thigh	
Character:	Good	
Trade or Occupation:	Labourer [on discharge Painter and Glazier]	
Can Sign Name:	Yes	
Height:	5' 9¼"	
Hair Colour:	Fair	
Eyes:	Grey	
Complexion:	Fair	
Intends to Reside:	Co. Tipperary	

FLYNN

FLYNN	John, gunner St Helena Corps [Captain Thomas M Hunter's Company of St Helena Artillery]
14 Apr 1836	Discharged the service
June 1836	Admitted to Out-Pension Pension paid Cork 9d. per diem
19 Aug 1853	Arrived per *'Robert Small'*
1854	Employed in Convict Service without seeking permission of Staff Officer Pension
21 Feb 1859	Died

Service and Personal Details:

Place of Birth:	Cork
Age on Enlistment:	not given
Period of Service:	**** — 1836
Age on Discharge:	27 years
Length of Service:	'Hath served the Honorable the United Company of Merchants of England trading to the East Indies for the space of 5 years 334 days'
Reason for Discharge:	Disbandment of the Corps
Character:	Good
Trade or Occupation:	Tailor
Can Sign Name:	Yes
Height:	5' 7¼"
Hair Colour:	Sandy
Eyes:	Grey
Complexion:	Fresh

FLYNN	Patrick, private 64th Foot
10 Sept 1850	Discharged the Service Chatham Pension paid Galway 6d. per diem for a year
1850	Pension paid 2nd Dublin Pension District
28 June 1851	Arrived per *'Pyrenees'* [1]

1852	Pension ceased

Service and Personal Details:

Place of Birth:	Clarn Co. Galway
Age on Enlistment:	18 years
Period of Service:	1847 — 1850
Age on Discharge:	21 years
Length of Service:	2 years 122 days
Foreign Service:	East Indies 6 months
Reason for Discharge:	Fever, Dysentery and Catarrhal symptoms
Character:	Very Good
Trade or Occupation:	Labourer
Can Sign Name:	Yes
Height:	5' 7"
Hair Colour:	Brown
Eyes:	Brown
Complexion:	Sallow
Intends to Reside:	Headford Galway

FOGARTE Patrick, private
58th Foot

Surname Variants	FOGARTEY; FOGATEY; FOGARTY
28 Mar 1863	Discharged the Service Dublin
14 Apr 1863	Admitted to Out-Pension Pension paid 2nd Dublin Pension District 10d. per diem
15 Aug 1865	Arrived per *'Racehorse'*
1889	a Patrick Fogarty died

Service and Personal Details:

Place of Birth:	Milltown Dublin
Age on Enlistment:	18 years
Period of Service:	1841 — 1863
Age on Discharge:	40 years 4 months
Length of Service:	21 years 22 days
Foreign Service:	Australian Colonies 14 years
Reason for Discharge:	Having completed 21 years service
Character:	Good
Trade or Occupation:	Labourer
Can Sign Name:	X his mark on discharge
Height:	5' 6¾"
Hair Colour:	Dark Brown
Eyes:	Hazel
Complexion:	Swarthy
Intends to Reside:	Dublin

FOLEY John, Serjeant
88th Foot

22 July 1851	Discharged the Service Chatham Pension paid Cork 9d. per diem
2 Aug 1852	Arrived per *'William Jardine'*
1852	Pension paid Western Australia

circa 1852	Departed Colony without permission	
1857	Pension paid Victoria	
Service and Personal Details:		
Place of Birth:	Ballincollig Co. Cork	
Age on Enlistment:	18 years	
Period of Service:	1836 — 1851	
Age on Discharge:	34 years	
Length of Service:	15 years 154 days	
Foreign Service:	Malta	6 years 6 months
	West Indies	3 years 6 months
	Nova Scotia	6 months
Reason for Discharge:	Impaired Vision and general bad health	
Character:	Latterly Good	
Trade or Occupation:	Miller	
Can Sign Name:	Yes	
Height:	5' 9"	
Hair Colour:	Fair	
Eyes:	Grey	
Complexion:	Fair	
Intends to Reside:	Cork	

FOOT

	Joseph, private	
	76th Foot	
Surname Variant	FOOTE	
27 Sept 1837	Discharged the Service	
	Pension paid 2nd West London Pension District	
	1/- per diem	
1 June 1850	Arrived per *'Scindian'*	
1850	Assigned Freshwater Bay Lots 8 and 14	
Nov 1852	Died - ? buried East Perth Pioneer Cemetery	
Service and Personal Details:		
Place of Birth:	Quidhampton Wiltshire	
Age on Enlistment:	16 years	
Period of Service:	1815 — 1836	
Length of Service:	19 years 334 days	
Foreign Service:	British North America &	2 years
	West Indies	
Reason for Discharge:	Chronic Dysentery and Dyspnoea	
Character:	Good	
Trade or Occupation:	Labourer	
Can Sign Name:	Yes	
Height:	5' 10"	
Hair Colour:	Brown	
Eyes:	Hazel	
Complexion:	Fair	
Remarks:	Landed at Gravesend Aug 1837	
Married:	Catherine	
Children:	Robert b. 1840 England	
	Joseph b. 1843 England	
	John b. 1844 England	

	Scindian Gibson b. 1850 born at sea
1877	the Foote brother were shipwrecked when the ship they were on — the 'Bunyip" floundered on the south east coast. They then walked from Culver Cliffs to Israelite Bay where they arrived in a very distressed condition

FORAN John, gunner EIC
Bombay Artillery

Surname Variant	FOREN
Pension No 71	
9 May 1832	Discharged the Service Pension paid 1st East London Pension District 9d. per diem
18 Oct 1851	Arrived per *'Minden'*
1852	Employed as Night Warder
1868	Title Application for Victoria [Bootenal] Locs G15 and G16
1877	Died

Service and Personal Details:

Where Born:	Dublin
Trade or Occupation:	Labourer
Where Enlisted:	Dublin
Embarked India:	per *'Lady Raffles'*
Presidency:	Bombay
Length of Service:	9 years 6 months
Character:	Good
Reason for Discharge:	Injury to left hand
Height:	5' 7"
Complexion:	Dark
Visage:	Round
Eye Colour:	Blue
Hair Colour:	Brown

FORBES James, private
77th Foot

10 Apr 1849	Discharged the Service Chatham Pension paid Southampton 6d. per diem for 2½ years
28 June 1851	Arrived per *'Pyrenees'* [1]
1851	Pension ceased
1852	Employed as Night Warder

Service and Personal Details:

Place of Birth:	Ballinarule Co. Mayo	
Age on Enlistment:	20 years	
Period of Service:	1839 — 1849	
Age on Discharge:	30 years 1 month	
Length of Service:	10 years 34 days	
Foreign Service:	Mediterranean	1 year 3 months
	Jamaica	3 years
	North America	2 years 2 months
Reason for Discharge:	Pulmonary Disease	

Character:	Good
Trade or Occupation:	Labourer
Can Sign Name:	X his mark on discharge
Height:	5' 6½"
Hair Colour:	Dark Brown
Eyes:	Hazel
Complexion:	Fresh
Intends to Reside:	Chatham but decided on Neil Co. Mayo

FORD

	Michael, Serjeant
	96th Foot
Previous Regiment	23rd Foot
13 May 1849	Discharged the Service Perth West Australia
9 Oct 1849	Admitted to Out-Pension
	Pension paid Perth Western Australia
	1/4d per diem
	Arrived per *'Java'* with regiment
1852	To Port Philip — Victoria
1865	Pension paid Victoria
1875	Port Philip

Service and Personal Details:

Place of Birth:	Kilfinnan Co. Limerick	
Age on Enlistment:	18 years	
Period of Service:	1828 — 1849	
Age on Discharge:	43 years	
Length of Service:	21 years 93 days	
Foreign Service:	North America	3 years
	Australia	7 years 6 months
Reason for Discharge:	Worn out and unfit for further service	
Character:	Very Good	
Trade or Occupation:	Labourer	
Can Sign Name:	Yes	
Height:	5' 6"	
Hair Colour:	Light Brown	
Eyes:	Hazel	
Complexion:	Fair	

FORDE

	John, private
	28th Foot
Surname Variant	FORD
22 June 1852	Discharged the Service Chatham
	Pension paid Londonderry
	10d. per diem
1853	Pension paid Turkey
	Pension increased to 1/- per diem
1855	Pension paid Donegal
1856	Omagh
11 Feb 1861	Arrived per *'Palmeston'*
1864	Serving Fremantle District
Nov 1870	Died - buried East Perth Pioneer Cemetery

Service and Personal Details:

Place of Birth:	St Pauls Dublin

Age on Enlistment:	18 years 3 months	
Period of Service:	1830 — 1852	
Age on Discharge:	40 years	
Length of Service:	20 years 334 days	
Foreign Service:	New South Wales	6 years 9 months
	East Indies	5 years 5 months
Reason for Discharge:	Chronic Rheumatism and Chest Affection [sic]	
Character:	Bad	
Trade or Occupation:	Labourer	
Can Sign Name:	Yes	
Height:	5' 9"	
Hair Colour:	Black	
Eyes:	Black	
Complexion:	Fresh	
Intends to Reside:	Tyrone	

FORDHAM Charles, private
80th Foot

13 July 1847	Discharged the Service Chatham Pension paid 2nd West London Pension District 11d. per diem
6 Apr 1854	Arrived per *'Sea Park'*
Jan 1857	Contributed 2/- to the Florence Nightingale Fund
1867	a Charles Fardham [sic], house and land owner signed a memorial to Governor Hampton Land proprietor Preston Point
*c*1874	Died

Service and Personal Details:

Place of Birth:	Newington London Surrey	
Age on Enlistment:	18 years 2 months	
Period of Service:	1841 — 1847	
Age on Discharge:	24 years 4 months	
Length of Service:	5 years 137 days	
Foreign Service:	New South Wales	2 years 9 months
	East Indies	1 year 10 months
Medal Entitlement:	Sutlej with clasps	
Reason for Discharge:	Having been blown up by a mine and of receiving a gunshot wound	
Character:	Very Good	
Trade or Occupation:	Milkman	
Height:	5' 6"	
Hair Colour:	Brown	
Eyes:	Grey	
Complexion:	Sallow	
Intends to Reside:	London	
Married:	*c*1851 Mary Burman St Pancras London	
Children:	a Charles Fordham b. *c*1853 London m. *c*1871 Elizabeth Conway Fremantle	

FORSYTHE Ambrose, private

	81st Foot	
17 Dec 1847	Discharged the Service Chatham	
	Pension paid Longford	
	1/- per diem	
1849	Pension paid Cavan	
28 June 1851	Arrived per *'Pyrenees'* [1]	
1854	Received sum of £15 towards cost of dwelling	
Jan 1857	Contributed 2/- to the Florence Nightingale Fund	
Nov 1862	Assigned Kojonup Lot P5 of 10 acres	
Nov 1862	Application of Title for Kojonup Lot P5	
1864	ptve Forsythe Pensioner Force at Kojonup contributed to the Greenough Fire Relief Fund	
1873	Pension increased to 1/3d. per diem for 20 years and 1 month service in the Enrolled Force	
1874	Died aged 75	
Service and Personal Details:		
Place of Birth:	Old Castle Co. Meath	
Age on Enlistment:	21 years	
Period of Service:	1826 — 1847	
Age on Discharge:	43 years 11 months	
Length of Service:	19 years 307 days	
Foreign Service:	Gibraltar	3 years 6 months
	West Indies	3 years 6 months
	Canada	4 years 1 month
Reason for Discharge:	Chronic Rheumatism	
Character:	Bad and drunken	
Trade or Occupation:	Weaver	
Can Sign Name:	X his mark on discharge	
Height:	5' 8"	
Hair Colour:	Brown	
Eyes:	Grey	
Complexion:	Dark	
Intends to Reside:	Old Castle Co. Meath	

FORTESCUE	William, private [WO 97/647/34]	
	54th Foot	
Surname Variant	FORTESQUE	
13 Jan 1841	Admitted to Out-pension	
	6d. per diem	
18 Oct 1851	Arrived per *'Minden'*	
9 Apr 1859	Died - buried East Perth Cemetery	
Service and Personal Details:		
Place of Birth:	Shoreditch Middlesex	
Period of Service:	1826 — 1840	
Age on Discharge:	34 years	
Length of Service:	14 years 6 months	
Foreign Service:	India	13 years 3 months
Reason for Discharge:	Disponea and Palpitation for many years	
Character:	Very Good, Trustworthy and Efficient	
Trade or Occupation:	Tailor	
Can Sign Name:	Yes	

Height: 5' 5¾"
Hair Colour: Brown
Eyes: Hazel
Complexion: Fair

FOSTER James, private
73rd Foot
10 Aug 1853 Discharged the Service Chatham
Pension paid 1st Dublin Pension District
7d. per diem for 18 months
19 Aug 1853 Arrived per *'Robert Small'*
1853 Employed as Night Warder
May 1854 Pension ceased

Service and Personal Details:
Place of Birth: Dunboyne Meath
Age on Enlistment: 21 years
Period of Service: 1845 — 1852
Age on Discharge: 28 years
Length of Service: 7 years 26 days
Foreign Service: Cape of Good Hope 5 years 6 months
Medal Entitlement: Kaffir War 1851
Reason for Discharge: Constitution impaired by Cardiac Disease

Character: Good
Trade or Occupation: Labourer
Can Sign Name: X his mark on discharge

Height: 5' 8"
Hair Colour: Brown
Eyes: Grey
Complexion: Fair
Intends to Reside: Dunboyne Meath

FOSTER John, private
15th Foot
26 Dec 1854 Discharged the Service Chatham
Pension paid Cavan
8d. per diem for 3 years
2 Apr 1856 Arrived per *'William Hammond'*
Wife refused to accompany him to Australia
1857 To Adelaide from Perth Western Australia
1882 W.O. correspondence to the Treasury Melbourne regarding Deferred Pension

Service and Personal Details:
Place of Birth: Newtown Butler Co. Fermanagh
Age on Enlistment: 20 years
Period of Service: 1842 — 1854
Age on Discharge: 33 years or 31 years 3 months
Length of Service: 11 years 106 days
Foreign Service: Ceylon 8 years 4 months
Reason for Discharge: Disease of the Lungs

Character: Good
Trade or Occupation: Labourer

Can Sign Name:	Yes	
Height:	5' 7¼"	
Hair Colour:	Dark Brown	
Eyes:	Hazel	
Complexion:	Fresh	
Intends to Reside:	Redhill Cavan	
FOWLER	Edward, Corporal	
	RM	
1851	Discharged the Service	
	£19/16/- per annum	
1855	Allocated land North Fremantle Lot P7	
1868	Departed colony for Eastern States	
Service and Personal Details:		
Place of Birth:	Worfield nr. Bridgnorth [sic] Shropshire	
Age on Attestation:	19 years	
Marine Division:	Portsmouth	
Period of Service:	1830 — 1851	
Length of Service:	21 years 5 days	
Reason for Discharge:	Length of service	
Trade or Occupation:	Labourer	
Can Sign Name:	No	
Height:	5' 8½"	
Hair Colour:	Light Brown	
Eyes:	Hazel	
Complexion:	Fair	
FOX	David, private	
	12th Foot	
1857	While serving in Western Australia a private D Fox of the 12th Foot contributed to the Florence Nightingale Fund	
15 June 1858	Discharged the Service Chatham	
	Pension paid Ipswich	
	9½d. per diem	
19 Aug 1859	Arrived per *'Sultana'*	
Aug 1863	Died - buried East Perth Pioneer Cemetery	
Service and Personal Details:		
Place of Birth:	Stowmarket Suffolk	
Age on Enlistment:	18 years 2 months	
Period of Service:	1836 — 1857	
Age on Discharge:	40 years 4 months	
Length of Service:	21 years 260 days	
Foreign Service:	Mauritius	10 years
	Australian Colonies	3 years 2 months
Reason for Discharge:	Chronic Rheumatism	
Character:	Very Good	
Trade or Occupation:	Shoemaker	
Can Sign Name:	Yes	
Height:	5' 10"	
Hair Colour:	Brown	

Eyes: Blue
Intends to Reside: Mendlesham Suffolk

FRANCIS George, private
53rd Foot
Discharged the Service Chatham
Pension paid Coventry
1/- per diem
24 May 1855 Arrived per *'Stag'*
1855 Serving as Warder on Rottnest Island
1857 Pension paid South Australia

Service and Personal Details:
Place of Birth: Hinkley Leicester
Age on Enlistment: 18 years
Period of Service: 1823 — 1844
Age on Discharge: 39 years
Length of Service: 20 years 225 days
Foreign Service: Gibraltar & Malta & Ionian Isles 10 years 6 months
Reason for Discharge: Chronic Rheumatism

Character: Good
Trade or Occupation: Stocking Weaver
Can Sign Name: Yes

Height: 5' 9"
Hair Colour: Brown
Eyes: Grey
Complexion: Fresh
Intends to Reside: Hinkley Leicestershire

FRASER Henry John, private
98th Foot
Surname Variant FRAZER
12 Sept 1848 Discharged the Service Chatham
Pension paid 2nd Glasgow Pension District
1/- per diem
1856 Pension paid Dartmoor
"Convict Guard at Dartmoor and has been deserted by his wife who is not to receive any portion of his pension"
1856 In military hospital Plymouth
1856 Embarked per *'William Hammond"*
1856 Died onboard *'William Hammond'*
1856 £10/15/0 being the amount of the effects and credits of the above named late pensioner misappropriated by Capt Foss

FRASER John, private
92nd Foot
Surname Variant FRAZER
23 Nov 1848 Discharged the Service Limerick
9 Jan 1849 Pension paid 2nd Dublin Pension District
1/- per diem
18 Oct 1851 Arrived per *'Minden'*

Oct 1851	Employed as Night Warder	
Jan 1852	Resigned or dismissed from Convict Service	
Service and Personal Details:		
Place of Birth:	Nairn Scotland	
Age on Enlistment:	18 years	
Period of Service:	1827 — 1848	
Age on Discharge:	39 years 4 months	
Length of Service:	21 years 61 days [reckoned]	
Foreign Service:	Gibraltar	1 year 11 months
	Malta	5 years 2 months
	West Indies	2 years 11 months
Reason for Discharge:	Worn out from length of service	
Character:	Good	
Trade or Occupation:	Labourer	
Can Sign Name:	Yes	
Height:	5' 7"	
Hair Colour:	Fair	
Eyes:	Grey	
Complexion:	Fair	

FREEMAN

	John, private 85th Foot	
7 Nov 1846	Discharged the Service Limerick	
9 Feb 1847	Admitted to Out-Pension Pension paid Ennis	
Apr 1847	6d. per diem for 2 years to be reviewed	
1851	6d. per diem made permanent	
7 Feb 1853	Arrived per *'Dudbrook'*	
Jan 1857	Contributed 1/- to the Florence Nightingale Fund	
1857	To South Australia from Western Australia per 'Frances' " £18/15/3 stopped for passage"	
5 Feb 1857	Died Adelaide	
Service and Personal Details:		
Place of Birth:	Ennistimon Co. Clare	
Age on Enlistment:	20 years	
Period of Service:	1842 — 1846	
Age on Discharge:	24 years 4 months	
Length of Service:	4 years 89 days	
Foreign Service:	West Indies	2 years 5 months
Reason for Discharge:	Ophthalmia and Impaired Vision in Both Eyes	
Character:	Indifferent	
Trade or Occupation:	Labourer	
Can Sign Name:	X his mark on discharge	
Height:	5' 8¾"	
Hair Colour:	Brown	
Eyes:	Blue	
Complexion:	Fresh	

FREEMAN

Joseph, private
59th Foot

6 Apr 1852	Discharged the Service Fermoy	
11 May 1852	Admitted to Out-Pension	
	Pension paid Leicester	
	1/- per diem	
2 Apr 1856	Arrived per *'William Hammond'*	
1857	Employed as Assistant Warder	
1858	Pension paid Madras	
1877	Leicester	
1883	Correspondence with W.O.	
Service and Personal Details:		
Place of Birth:	Sheepshead Loughbourgh Leicestershire	
Age on Enlistment:	18 years	
Period of Service:	1831 — 1852	
Age on Discharge:	39 years 3 months	
Length of Service:	21 years 39 days	
Foreign Service:	Mediterranean	6 years 154 days
	West Indies	3 years 6 days
Reason for Discharge:	General Debility	
Character:	Indifferent	
Trade or Occupation:	Framework Knitter	
Can Sign Name:	Yes	
Height:	6' 1½"	
Hair Colour:	Light	
Eyes:	Grey	
Complexion:	Fair	
Intends to Reside:	Sheepshead Leicestershire	

FULLER	William, private	
	37th Foot	
14 Nov 1848	Discharged the Service Chatham	
	Pension paid 1st North London Pension District	
	1/- per diem	
18 Oct 1851	Arrived per *'Minden'*	
1851	Allocated land at Albany	
1854	To South Australia from Western Australia	
Service and Personal Details:		
Place of Birth:	Monksman Hertfordshire	
Age on Enlistment:	15 years	
Period of Service:	1824 — 1848	
Age on Discharge:	39 years	
Length of Service:	21 years 26 days	
Foreign Service:	West Indies	8 years 4 months
Reason for Discharge:	Chronic Rheumatism	
Character:	Very Good	
Trade or Occupation:	Labourer	
Can Sign Name:	X his mark on discharge	
Height:	5' 9"	
Hair Colour:	Dark Brown	
Eyes:	Hazel	
Complexion:	Fresh	
Intends to Reside:	St Albans Hertfordshire	

GAFNEY	George, private	
	13th Light Dragoons	
Surname Variants	GAFFNEY; GAFFEY; GAFFNY; GARTNEY	
27 May 1841	Discharged the Service Canterbury	
9 June 1841	Admitted to Out-Pension	
	Pension paid Tullamore	
	9d. per diem	
21 May 1851	Arrived per *'Mermaid'*	
1851	Assigned and occupied North Fremantle Lot P7	
	Pension increased to 1/4d. per diem	
Service and Personal Details:		
Place of Birth:	Newtown ?Kilbeggan Westmeath	
Age on Enlistment:	18 years	
Period of Service:	1823 — 1841	
Age on Discharge:	35 years	
Length of Service:	17 years 309 days	
Foreign Service:	East Indies	15 years 356 days
Reason for Discharge:	Pectoral Complaints of severe character	
Character:	Good and Efficient Soldier	
Trade or Occupation:	Labourer	
Can Sign Name:	Yes	
Height:	5' 6¾"	
Hair Colour:	Dark Brown	
Eyes:	Grey	
Complexion:	Fair	
Intends to Reside:	Killibeggin Westmeath	

GAILY	David, private	
	18th Foot	
Surname Variants	GAILLY; GAILEY	
11 Sept 1846	Discharged the Service Chatham	
	1/- per diem	
1846	Pension paid Waterford	
30 Apr 1853	Arrived per *'Pyrenees'* [2]	
Jan 1857	Contributed 2/- to the Florence Nightingale Fund	
1860	Purchased Newcastle Lot S17	
1866	Assigned Newcastle Lot S7	
1873	Pension increased to 1/3d. per diem for 16 years and 11 months service in the Enrolled Force	
1881	Died	
1886	Grant of Probate for a David Gaily	
Service and Personal Details:		
Place of Birth:	Old Ross Co. Wexford	
Age on Enlistment:	18 years	
Period of Service:	1825 — 1845	
Age on Discharge:	39 years	
Length of Service:	20 years 18 days	
Foreign Service:	Mediterranean	3 years 94 days
	Ceylon	3 years 76 days
	China	5 years 180 days
Reason for Discharge:	Debility as result of Severe Fever	

Character:	Extremely Good
Trade or Occupation:	Labourer
Can Sign Name:	X his mark on discharge
Height:	5' 8½"
Hair Colour:	Dark
Eyes:	Grey
Complexion:	Fair
Intends to Reside:	Ross Co. Wexford

GALBRAITH	William, Corporal 89th Foot
Surname Variants	GALBRAITHE; GALBRATH; GALBREATH
16 Sept 1861	Discharged the Service Fermoy Barracks
5 Nov 1861	Admitted to Out-Pension Pension paid 2nd Belfast Pension District 1/- per diem
1862	Pension paid Bermuda
15 Feb 1863	Arrived per *'Merchantman'* [1]
1863	Employed as Assistant Warder
1878	Pension increased to 1/3d. per diem for service in the Enrolled Force
Jan 1880	Died - ? buried East Perth Pioneer Cemetery
Jan 1880	Inquest on the body of William Galbraith, who fell dead in the Street, on 3rd inst. Verdict — Death from heart disease and heat apoplexy.
1880	Pensioner Galbraith's wife and children asking for Poor Relief

the following entry may not necessarily refer to a child of William Galbraith 89th Foot

Aug 1884	Very Rev. Dean Gregg — re: Selina Galbraith five and a half years old asking that she maybe placed on the Govt. list of children in the Perth Protestant Orphanage
Jan 1893	James Galbraith, Serjeant [89th Foot] residing at 28 Hudson street Belfast, asking for information regarding his brother William
1893	According to a newspaper article "it was about Christmas time some 12 years previous William Galbraith was found dead at South Perth"

Service and Personal Details:

Place of Birth:	?Magherafelt Co. Derry	
Age on Enlistment:	17 years 9 months	
Period of Service:	1844 — 1861	
Age on Discharge:	34 years 9 months	
Length of Service:	16 years 281 days	
Foreign Service:	Gibraltar	[total] 8 months
	Crimea	5 months
	Malta	4 months
	Cape of Good Hope	1 year
	East Indies	1 year 5 months
Medal Entitlement:	Crimea with clasp; Crimean Turkish	
Reason for Discharge:	Rheumatism and Insanity	

Character:	Very Good
Trade or Occupation:	Labourer
Can Sign Name:	Yes
Height:	5' 7½"
Hair Colour:	Brown
Eyes:	Blue
Complexion:	Fresh
Intends to Reside:	Belfast

GALE Thomas, private
11th Foot

Surname Variant	GATE
25 July 1854	Discharged the Service Chatham
	Pension paid Oxford
	1/- per diem
24 Nov 1858	Arrived per *'Edwin Fox'*
1875	Pension paid Western Australia
1876	a Thomas Gale died aged 74

Service and Personal Details:

Place of Birth:	Childrey Wantage Berkshire	
Age on Enlistment:	20 years 2 months	
Period of Service:	1831 — 1854	
Age on Discharge:	43 years	
Length of Service:	22 years 355 days	
Foreign Service:	Ionian Isles	7 months
	North America	2 years 1 month
	Australian Colonies	9 years 1 month
Reason for Discharge:	Worn out and Chronic Rheumatism	
Character:	Good	
Trade or Occupation:	Labourer	
Can Sign Name:	X his mark on discharge	
Height:	5' 6"	
Hair Colour:	Brown	
Eyes:	Hazel	
Complexion:	Fresh	
Intends to Reside:	London but decided on Wantage Berkshire	

GALE William, private
22nd Foot

11 Sept 1849	Discharged the Service
	Pension paid Waterford Ireland
	1/- per diem
18 July 1855	Arrived per *'Adelaide'*
Jan 1857	Contributed 1/- to the Florence Nightingale Fund
1859	Pension paid Waterford
1862	Jersey
1862	Waterford

Service and Personal Details:

Place of Birth:	St Patricks Waterford
Age on Enlistment:	18 years
Period of Service:	1828 — 1849
Age on Discharge:	38 years 129 days

Length of Service:	20 years 178 days	
Foreign Service:	East Indies	7 years 133 days
	West Indies	8 years 88 days
Reason for Discharge:	Failing Efficiency	
Conduct:	Good	
Trade or Occupation:	Shoemaker	
Can Sign Name:	Yes	
Height:	5' 6"	
Hair Colour:	Grey	
Eye Colour:	Grey	
Complexion:	Sallow	
Intends to Reside:	Waterford Ireland	

GALLAGHER John, private
31st Foot

13 Jan 1863	Discharged the Service Chatham Pension paid Sligo 6d. per diem
12 Sept 1864	Arrived per *'Merchantman'* [2]
1875	Pension paid Western Australia
1877	Tried and convicted at Fremantle for being drunk when on guard duty. Sentenced to 112 days imprisonment and pension to be suspended to one half — the other half to be paid to his wife
1878	Pension increased to 1/- per diem for service in the Enrolled Force
1881	Pension increased further to 1/1d. per diem
1883	Died
1883	Widow of John Gallagher was granted Cockburn Loc P19
1884	the Master of schooner 'Ivy' reported that a passenger named Richard Gallagher jumped overboard at Jurien Bay and drowned despite efforts to save him
Feb 1884	Mark Gallagher — brother of drowned man stated that no steps were taken to recover body

Service and Personal Details:

Place of Birth:	Street Westmeath	
Age on Enlistment:	22 years	
Period of Service:	1843 — 1862	
Age on Discharge:	41 years 1 month	
Length of Service:	18 years 193 days	
Foreign Service:	Mediterranean	4 years 161 days
	Crimea	1 year ?24 days
	Cape of Good Hope	138 days
	East Indies	3 years 186 days
	China	2 years 166 days
Medal Entitlement:	Sutlej with three clasps; Crimea with clasps; Turkish Crimean	
Reason for Discharge:	Chronic Rheumatism	
Character:	Indifferent	

Trade or Occupation:	Labourer
Can Sign Name:	Yes
Height:	5' 8"
Hair Colour:	Brown
Eyes:	Grey
Complexion:	Fresh
Distinguishing Marks:	Marked with small pox
Intends to Reside:	Sligo

GALLAGHER	John, private 41st Foot
29 Dec 1843	Discharged the Service Chatham
9 Jan 1844	Admitted to Out-Pension Pension paid Ballaghadreen Boyle 8d. per diem
1847	Pension paid Coventry
1848	Liverpool
31 Aug 1853	Arrived per *'Phoebe Dunbar'*
1857	Pension paid South Australia
1859	Melbourne
1875	Melbourne

Service and Personal Details:

Place of Birth:	Castlemore Co. Mayo	
Age on Enlistment:	19 years	
Period of Service:	1835 — 1843	
Age on Discharge:	28 years	
Length of Service:	8 years 72 days	
Foreign Service:	East Indies	7 years
Medal Entitlement:	Afghanistan 1842	
Reason for Discharge:	Wounded on both hands by sabre cut to both hands and two wounds to head — Scinde March 1842	
Character:	Very Good	
Trade or Occupation:	Labourer	
Can Sign Name:	Yes	
Height:	5' 8"	
Hair Colour:	Brown	
Eyes:	Grey	
Complexion:	Sallow	
Intends to Reside:	Co. Mayo	

GALLAGHER	John, private 92nd Foot
Surname Variant	GALLACHER
12 May 1849	Discharged the Service Clonmel
10 July 1849	Admitted to Out-Pension Pension paid Dundee 1/- per diem
7 Feb 1853	Arrived per *'Dudbrook'*
30 May 1866	Died

Service and Personal Details:

Place of Birth:	Barony Lanarkshire

Age on Enlistment:	17 years	
Period of Service:	1826 — 1849	
Age on Discharge:	40 years	
Length of Service:	21 years 145 days	
Foreign Service:	Gibraltar	1 year 9 months
	Malta	5 years 4 months
	West Indies	1 year 4 months
Reason for Discharge:	Worn out from length of service	
Character:	Very Indifferent	
Trade or Occupation:	Labourer	
Can Sign Name:	Yes	
Height:	5' 6½"	
Hair Colour:	Dark Brown	
Eyes:	Light Blue	
Complexion:	Dark	
Intends to Reside:	Dundee	

GALLAGHER Patrick, Corporal
80th Foot

Previous Regiments	1st; 13th
Surname Variant	GALLAGHAR
10 July 1849	Discharged the Service Chatham Pension paid Liverpool 1/3d. per diem
1849	Pension paid Castlebar
14 Aug 1854	Arrived per *'Ramillies'*
Jan 1857	contributed 2/- to the Florence Nightingale Fund
1864	Serjeant P Gallagher serving in the Pensioner Force at Fremantle District contributed to the Greenough Fire Relief Fund
24 Sept 1864	Died

Service and Personal Details:

Place of Birth:	Crossmalina Co. Mayo	
Age on Enlistment:	22 years	
Period of Service:	1827 — 1848	
Age on Discharge:	42 years 4 months	
Length of Service:	21 years 109 days	
Foreign Service:	East Indies	21 years 109 days
Medal Entitlement:	Medals for Ghuznee; Jellahabad; Cabool	
Reason for Discharge:	Worn out from service	
Character:	Good	
Trade or Occupation:	Labourer	
Can Sign Name:	Yes	
Height:	5' 8"	
Hair Colour:	Brown	
Eyes:	Brown	
Complexion:	Sallow	
Intends to Reside:	Glasgow	

GALLAGHER Patrick, gunner
RA 7th Battalion

10 Oct 1848	Discharged the Service Woolwich

	Pension paid Woolwich	
	1/- per diem	
1848	Pension paid South London Pension District	
1 June 1850	Arrived per *'Scindian'*	
1855	Pension paid Melbourne	
1859	Londonderry	
1859	Omagh	
1859	Londonderry	
Service and Personal Details:		
Place of Birth:	Arstrow Co. Tyrone	
Age on Enlistment:	17 years	
Period of Service:	1826 — 1848	
Age on Discharge:	39 years 3 months	
Length of Service:	21 years 68 days	
Foreign Service:	Corfu	1 year
	West Indies	2 years 3 months
Reason for Discharge:	Chronic Rheumatism	
Character:	Exemplary	
Trade or Occupation:	Labourer	
Can Sign Name:	X his mark on discharge	
Height:	5' 9¾"	
Hair Colour:	Black	
Eyes:	Brown	
Complexion:	Fresh	
Place of Birth:	Arstrow [sic] Tyrone	

GALLAGHER	Peter, Corporal	
	3rd Foot	
15 Jan 1856	Discharged the Service Chatham	
	Pension paid Halifax	
	1/- per diem	
1857	Pension paid Ennis	
24 Nov 1858	Arrived per *'Edwin Fox'*	
1861	Allocated and occupied land Cockburn Sound District Loc 127	
1863	Stationed Fremantle District	
1871	a Peter Gallagher died aged 37 [AVRI]	
Service and Personal Details:		
Place of Birth:	Ardrahan Galway	
Age on Enlistment:	17 years 8 months	
Period of Service:	1851 — 1855	
Age on Discharge:	24 years or 21 years 11 months	
Length of Service:	3 years 349 days	
Foreign Service:	Malta	6 months
	Greece	6 months
	Crimea	6 months
Medal Entitlement:	Crimea	
Reason for Discharge:	Amputation of whole of ring finger and part of last phalanx of little finger of left hand	
Character:	Very Good	
Trade or Occupation:	Labourer	
Can Sign Name:	Yes	

Height:	5' 6½"
Hair Colour:	Dark Brown
Eyes:	Blue
Complexion:	Sallow
Intends to Reside:	Bradford Yorkshire

GANDELL Henry, private
36th Foot

Surname Variants	GANDLE; CANDLE
23 Nov 1859	Discharged the Service Athlone
13 Dec 1859	Admitted to Out-Pension
	Pension paid Salisbury
	1/- per diem
1861	Pension paid South London Pension District
31 Dec 1862	Arrived per *'York'*
July 1867	'Corporal Gandell had the Guard on Saturday'
1867	Witness at the trial of James Alcock
24 Mar 1872	Died cause of death — "a Cold"

Service and Personal Details:

Place of Birth:	Islington London Middlesex	
Age on Enlistment:	20 years	
Period of Service:	1838 — 1859	
Age on Discharge:	41 years	
Length of Service:	21 years 17 days	
Foreign Service:	North America	1 year 346 days
	Ionian Isles	4 years 78 days
Medal Entitlement:	Good Conduct and Long Service with gratuity	
Reason for Discharge:	Own Request on completing 21 years service	
Character:	Good	
Trade or Occupation:	Grocer	
Can Sign Name:	Yes	
Height:	5' 6"	
Hair Colour:	Light Brown	
Eyes:	Grey	
Complexion:	Fresh	
Distinguishing Marks:	Scar on left corner of upper lip	
Intends to Reside:	Weymouth Dorset	

GANE Charles, private
17th Foot

Surname Variant	GAME
Previous Service	18th Comp. Portsmouth Division Royal Marines
1827	Attested aged 18 years
	[ADM157/346/96 folios 96 — 97]
1831	Bought himself out of the Royal Marines for £20
10 Apr 1849	Discharged the Service [Army] Chatham
	Pension paid 2nd North London Pension District
	8d. per diem
1849	Pension paid Halifax
1850	Leicester
7 Feb 1853	Arrived per *'Dudbrook'* with family
Jan 1857	Contributed 2/- to the Florence Nightingale Fund
1857	Employed as Assistant Warder

1861	Died — found drowned at Guildford. [presumed he committed suicide]	
13 Apr 1864	Residents Office Fremantle: Mrs. Game [sic] is well worthy of outdoor relief. Husband was a Warder known in Guildford, Pensioner Game [sic] whilst employed as a Warder, was found drowned near Guildford in March 1861. She has been a hardworking woman since her husband's death, earning a living for herself and two children by casual needlework, and children always attending Sunday School	
Service and Personal Details:		
Place of Birth:	Hitchin Hertfordshire	
Age on Enlistment:	23 years 4 months	
Period of Service:	1833 — 1849	
Age on Discharge:	37 years	
Length of Service:	15 years 275 days	
Foreign Service:	New South Wales	3 years
	East Indies	10 years 5 months
Medal Entitlement:	Afghan Campaign of 1839	
Reason for Discharge:	Chronic Hepatic Disease	
Character:	Good	
Trade or Occupation:	Wool comber	
Can Sign Name:	Yes	
Height:	5' 7½"	
Hair Colour:	Light Brown	
Eyes:	Grey	
Complexion:	Fresh	
Intends to Reside:	Hitchin Hertfordshire	
Married:	1850 Elizabeth Davenport Leicester	
Children:	Charles b. 1852 Leicester	

GANLEY	John, private 68th Foot	
28 June 1859	Discharged the Service Fermoy Pension paid Roscommon 11d. per diem	
11 Feb 1861	Arrived per *'Palmeston'*	
1878	Died aged 58 in the bush near Cape Riche	
Service and Personal Details:		
Place of Birth:	Clune Co. Leitrim	
Age on Enlistment:	18 years	
Period of Service:	1838 — 1859	
Age on Discharge:	39 years 9 months	
Length of Service:	21 years 62 days	
Foreign Service:	West Indies	2 years 4 months
	North America	2 years 10 months
	Malta	3 years **months
	Turkey & Crimea	1 year 4 months
Medal Entitlement:	Crimea	

Reason for Discharge:	Having completed 21 years service	
Character:	Good	
Trade or Occupation:	Labourer	
Can Sign Name:	X his mark on discharge	
Height:	5' 7"	
Hair Colour:	Brown	
Eyes:	Grey	
Complexion:	Fair	
Intends to Reside:	Clune Co. Leitrim	

GARDINER John, private
64th Foot

26 Apr 1859	Discharged the Service Chatham Pension paid 2nd Glasgow Pension District 8½d. per diem	
27 May 1863	Arrived per *'Clyde'*	
1865	To South Australia from Fremantle West Aust [12/WA/208]	

Service and Personal Details:

Place of Birth:	Barony Glasgow Lanarkshire	
Age on Enlistment:	19 years	
Period of Service:	1836 — 1858	
Age on Discharge:	41 years 11 months	
Length of Service:	21 years 220 days	
Foreign Service:	West Indies	2 years 10 months
	North America	2 years 9 months
	India	9 years 4 months
Medal Entitlement:	Persia with clasp; Indian Mutiny	
Reason for Discharge:	Old and Worn out	
Character:	Indifferent	
Trade or Occupation:	Labourer	
Can Sign Name:	X his mark on discharge	
Height:	5' 9½"	
Hair Colour:	Fair	
Eyes:	Hazel	
Complexion:	Fair	
Intends to Reside:	Glasgow	

GARDNER Thomas, private
48th Foot

Surname Variants	GARDINER; GARDENER
18 Dec 1855	Discharged the Service Chatham 1/- per diem
1856	Pension paid Newcastle
19 Aug 1859	Arrived per *'Sultana'*
1864	private T Gardner serving in the Pensioner Force Fremantle District contributed to the Greenough Fire Relief Fund
1865	Pension paid Western Australia
1872	a Thomas Gardener residing at Fremantle
1876	Granted North Fremantle Lot P29

1878	Pension increased to 1/6d. per diem for service in the Enrolled Force
1877	Pension paid South Australia from Fremantle

the following entry may not necessarily refer to the death of Thomas Gardiner 48th Foot

1881	a Thomas Gardiner died South Australia

Service and Personal Details:

Place of Birth:	Goldaming Surrey	
Age on Enlistment:	19 years	
Period of Service:	1833 — 1855	
Age on Discharge:	41 years	
Length of Service:	21 years 244 days	
Foreign Service:	Gibraltar	4 years
	West Indies	3 years 1 month
Reason for Discharge:	Chronic Rheumatism	
Character:	Very Good	
Trade or Occupation:	Servant	
Can Sign Name:	X his mark on discharge	
Height:	5' 6"	
Hair Colour:	Light Brown	
Eyes:	Grey	
Complexion:	Fair	
Remarks:	Deserted from Fermoy on the 8th April 1839. Rejoined 22 May 1839. Tried by District Court Martial and sentenced for 3 Lunar Months	
Intends to Reside:	Tynemonth Northumberland	

GARDINER Thomas, private [drummer]

	79th Foot
Previous Regiment	91st Foot
4 Oct 1864	Discharged the Service Netley Pension paid 2nd Glasgow Pension District 1/- per diem
4 July 1866	Arrived per *'Belgravia'*
1881	Pension increased to 1/6d. per diem for service in the Enrolled Force
5 Mar 1883	Assigned North Fremantle Lot P95
13 Dec 1883	Granted Fee Simple North Fremantle Lot P95
1884	Stationed Perth serving on Guard Duty at Government House
June 1884	Died at the Colonial Hospital

Service and Personal Details:

Place of Birth:	Lanark Lanarkshire	
Age on Enlistment:	15 years 9 months	
Period of Service:	1841 — 1864	
Age on Discharge:	39 years 4 months	
Length of Service:	20 years 146 days	
Foreign Service:	Cape Good Hope	6 years 7 months
	Turkey & Crimea	1 year 9 months

	India	6 years 4 months
Medal Entitlement:	Kaffir War; Crimean with 2 clasps; Turkish Crimean; Indian Mutiny with clasp ; and according to Newspaper — Good Conduct	
Reason for Discharge:	Rheumatism and worn out	
Character:	Good	
Trade or Occupation:	Cotton Spinner	
Can Sign Name:	Yes	
Height:	5' 6"	
Hair Colour:	Dark Brown	
Eyes:	Grey	
Complexion:	Fresh	
Distinguishing Marks:	Flat Footed	
Intends to Reside:	Glasgow	

GARDINER	Thomas, Corporal RA 10th Battalion	
13 July 1847	Discharged the Service Woolwich Pension paid Woolwich 1/2d. per diem	
1851	Residing Woolwich Assistant Warder on '*Warrior*' — Convict Hulk, Woolwich Dockyard Greenwich	
30 Jan 1852	Arrived possibly per *'Marion'*	
1852	Pension paid Western Australia from Woolwich	
	The following entry may not necessarily refer to Thomas Gardiner Royal Artillery	
Feb 1871	a Thomas Gardiner died aged 62 from an Abscess on Head	
Service and Personal Details:		
Place of Birth:	Kilmore Armagh	
Age on Enlistment:	18 years	
Period of Service:	1826 — 1847	
Age on Discharge:	39 years	
Length of Service:	21 years 10 days	
Foreign Service:	Corfu	6 years 11 months
	West Indies	6 years
Reason for Discharge:	Chronic Cough and Defective Sight	
Character:	Very Good	
Trade or Occupation:	Weaver	
Can Sign Name:	Yes	
Height:	5' 8½"	
Hair Colour:	Fair	
Eyes:	Grey	
Complexion:	Fair	

GARDINER	John, private EIC 3rd Bengal European Regiment
Surname Variant	GARDNER; GARDINIER

	W.O. Pension No 245
20 Jan 1860	Admitted to Out-pension Pension paid 1st Glasgow Pension District 9d. per diem
28 Dec 1863	Arrived per *'Lord Dalhousie'*
1864	a John Gardner [sic] employed as Assistant Warder
1872	a John Gardiner serving as Armourer to the Metropolitan Volunteer Rifle Corps
Feb 1883	Assigned Canning Pensioner Loc 136 [2C] of 20 acres
Jan 1884	Application for Crown Grant for Canning Loc P136
Dec 1885	For Sale — Canning Loc P136 of 20 acres with frontage to public road and river.
June 1897	Residing Perth
May 1909	Died Buried East Perth Pioneer Cemetery

Service and Personal Details:

Where Born:	Glasgow Scotland
Trade or Occupation:	Labourer
Age on Enlistment:	20 years 7 months [or 21 years]
Presidency:	Bengal
Length of Service:	1 year 7 months
Age on Discharge:	21 years
Character:	Good
Reason for Discharge:	Gunshot wound of left knee and thigh
Medal Entitlement:	Indian Mutiny
Height:	5' 6½"
Complexion:	Fresh
Eye Colour:	Blue
Hair Colour:	Brown
Remarks:	Native of Glasgow in County of Glasgow
Kingdom of Scotland	

GARISH

	Henry, private 4th Foot
Surname Variant	GARRISH
28 Mar 1865	Discharged the Service Manchester Pension paid Manchester 6d. per diem
13 July 1867	Arrived per *'Norwood'* [2]
1868	Employed as Assistant Warder
1870	Residing Rottnest Island
28 Feb 1871	Died aged 38 of Rapid Consumption

Service and Personal Details:

Place of Birth:	Wilton Wiltshire	
Age on Enlistment:	17 years 11 months	
Period of Service:	1850 — 1865	
Age on Discharge:	33 years 3 months	
Length of Service:	15 years 90 days	
Foreign Service:	India	6 years 243 days
Medal Entitlement:	Indian Mutiny with clasps	
Reason for Discharge:	Chronic Hepatitis	
Character:	Good	

Trade or Occupation:	Labourer
Can Sign Name:	Yes
Height:	5' 7"
Hair Colour:	Dark
Eyes:	Grey
Complexion:	Florid
Intends to Reside:	Sheffield

GARNER	George, private
	98th Foot
24 July 1866	Discharged the Service Netley
	Pension paid 2nd Manchester Pension District
	1/- per diem
1867	Pension paid 1st East London Pension District
13 July 1867	Arrived per *'Norwood'* [2]

Service and Personal Details:

Place of Birth:	St Georges Manchester	
Age on Enlistment:	18 years 2 months	
Period of Service:	1845 — 1866	
Age on Discharge:	38 years 7 months	
Length of Service:	20 years 110 days	
Foreign Service:	East Indies	16 years 60 days
Medal Entitlement:	Punjaub Campaign	
Reason for Discharge:	Chronic Rheumatism and worn out	
Character:	Very Good	
Trade or Occupation:	Labourer	
Can Sign Name:	Yes	
Height:	5' 10"	
Hair Colour:	Brown	
Eyes:	Grey	
Complexion:	Fresh	
Distinguishing Marks:	Cupping marks on left side	
Intends to Reside:	Manchester	

GAUNT	William, private
	31st Foot
Surname Variants	GAUNS; GHENT
23 Mar 1847	Discharged the Service Chatham
1847	Pension paid Huntingdon
	1/- per diem
1849	Serving as a Police Constable — Huntingdon
1851	Stationed at Dartmoor
18 Oct 1851	Arrived per *'Minden'*
1855	Residing North Fremantle with wife and 4 children
Jan 1857	Contributed 2/6 to the Florence Nightingale Fund
1959	Occupying North Fremantle Lot ?P20 with wife and 4 children
1859	Applied for Land Title North Fremantle
1864	ptve W Gaunt Pensioner Force at Perth contributed to the Greenough Fire Relief Fund

1864	Mrs Gaunt recommended as Colonial [Govt] midwife
1865	One of the original member of the Pensioners Benevolent Society
Sept 1870	On Perth District Electoral List
1873	Pension increased to 1/3d. per diem for 14½ years service in the Enrolled Force
1873	Residing Claisebrook
30 May 1887	Died aged 79. buried in Methodist Section of the East Perth Pioneer Cemetery

Service and Personal Details:

Obtained from family [please note that the family holds copyright on the descendency information as some information is only held by certain family members]

Place of Birth:	Warrington Huntingdonshire
Age on Enlistment:	18 years
Period of Service:	1826 — 1847
Age on Discharge:	39 years
Length of Service:	21 years 3 months
Foreign Service:	India 20 years
Medal Entitlement:	Afghan with clasps for Mazeen and Tazeen
Reason for Discharge:	Impaired constitution by long service in a tropical climate. His disabilities have not been occasioned by vice or intemperance
Character:	Very Good
Trade or Occupation:	Labourer
Can Sign Name:	X his mark on Attestation
Height:	5' 8"
Hair Colour:	Brown
Eyes:	Hazel
Complexion:	Sallow
Intends to Reside:	Warrington nr Huntingdon
Married:	1834 Lucinda Yeald India
Children	John born and died India
Ann born and died India	
Married:	1846 Ann Barthorn neé Denby India
Children:	Mary Joyce [daughter of Ann] b. 1834 India m. 1853 Walter Ludlow Fremantle John Joyce [son of Ann] b. 1836 India to South Australia per 'Swallow' Frederick b. 1847 Broughton Huntingdon Jane b. 1849 Huntingdon m. 1868 Francis Dunn Fremantle Sophia b. 1855 Fremantle William b. 1856 Fremantle William b. 1858 Fremantle d. 1875 Perth
Married:	1886 Theresa Bogue Perth

GEDDES William, private

	72nd Foot
25 Nov 1856	Discharged the Service Pension paid 2nd Glasgow Pension District 8d. per diem
1858	Pension paid Paisley
19 Aug 1859	Arrived per *'Sultana'*
1866	Pension paid South Australia from Perth
1875	South Australia
1877	Residing Wellington District
Feb 1886	Superintendent Minorgan — requests admission for Pensioner William Geddes into Mt. Eliza Poor
House	
15 Sept 1888	Assigned Loc 1076 at Butlers Swamp [not verified]
Jan 1889	From Staff Sergeant of Pensioners — Application for admittance for William Geddes to Mt Eliza Depot
May 1889	Found destitute and when complained of being ill in Court, the attendant medical officer stated there was nothing wrong with the old man That afternoon a after pensioner Geddes had staggered out of Court he was found later lying on the new jetty complaining of pains in his right side. Water Constable Delaney came to his aid and when his condition didn't improve he was taken in a bus to the police station by Constable Harrington, where he [Geddes] died shortly after 5 o'clock
1889	Died from heart disease

Service and Personal Details:		
Place of Birth:	Denny Stirlingshire	
Age on Enlistment:	19 years 3 months	
Period of Service:	1835 — 1856	
Age on Discharge:	39 years 6 months	
Length of Service:	20 years 175 days	
Foreign Service:	Cape of Good Hope	1 year 2 months
	Gibraltar	3 years 2 months
	West Indies	3 years 4 months
	North America	3 years 3 months
	Malta	6 months
Reason for Discharge:	Chronic Dyspnoea	
Character:	Good	
Trade or Occupation:	Calico Printer	
Can Sign Name:	X his mark on discharge	
Height:	5' 6"	
Hair Colour:	Fair	
Eyes:	Blue	
Complexion:	Fair	
Intends to Reside:	Stirling but decided on Glasgow	

GEDDINGS	George, private [10]
61st Foot	
Previous Regiment	28th Foot
Surname Variants	GIDDINGS; GIDINGS
28 Oct 1860	Discharged the Service Plymouth

	Pension paid Trowbridge	
	11d. per diem	
1860	Pension paid 2nd Portsmouth Pension District	
9 Jan 1862	Arrived per *'Norwood'* [1]	
1878	Pension increased to 1/3d. per diem for service in the Enrolled Guard	
1879	S.O. Perth West. Aust. — reporting that man's old certificate is not forthcoming it having been burnt in the bush	
Oct 1881	Died - buried East Perth Pioneer Cemetery	
Service and Personal Details:		
Place of Birth:	Devizes Wiltshire	
Age on Enlistment:	18 years	
Period of Service:	1839 — 1860	
Age on Discharge:	39 years 3½ months	
Length of Service:	21 years 106 days	
Foreign Service:	New South Wales	1 year 163 days
	East Indies	7 years 208 days
	Turkey	6 months
	Crimea	1 year 8 months
	Mauritius	1 year 24 days
Medal Entitlement:	Crimea with clasp	
Reason for Discharge:	Own Request on completing 21 years service	
Character:	Very Good	
Trade or Occupation:	Labourer	
Can Sign Name:	X his mark on discharge	
Height:	5' 7"	
Hair Colour:	Brown	
Eyes:	Blue	
Complexion:	Sallow	
Intends to Reside:	Devizes Wiltshire	

GEORGE	William Ralph, Corporal EIC
	Bengal Artillery
	Pension No 168
1847	Embarked UK per *'Prince of Wales'*
28 June 1848	Admitted to Out-pension
	Pension paid Salisbury
	9d. per diem
1851	Police Officer London Middlesex
1855	Pension paid Salisbury Pension District
1861	Prison Officer Portland Prison [Dorset Census]
1864	Pension paid Western Australia
1870	Warder transferred to Guildford
1872	a W. R. George residing at Fremantle [a sister Mrs Carrick]
15 July 1881	Assigned North Fremantle Lot P52
6 Oct 1883	Granted Fee Simple North Fremantle Lot P5
1886	Supervisor for the Fremantle Municipal Council
1890	a W.R. George caretaker of Town Hall
13 Sept 1899	Died
Oct 1899	Grant of Probate

Service and Personal Details:	
Where Born:	St Pancras Middlesex London
Trade or Occupation:	Carpenter
Presidency:	Bengal
Length of Service:	6 years 1 month
Age on Discharge:	27 years
Reason for Discharge:	Left hand disabled by musket shot
Character:	Very Good
Medal Entitlement:	Sutlej campaign
Height:	5' 7½"
Complexion:	Dark
Visage:	Long
Eye Colour:	Grey
Hair Colour:	Brown

GERAGHTY	Daniel, private
	86th Foot
8 Nov 1859	Discharged the Service Chatham
	Pension paid Tullamore
	8d. per diem
22 Dec 1865	Arrived per *'Vimiera'*
1881	Died
Service and Personal Details:	
Place of Birth:	Portarlington Co. Queens
Age on Enlistment:	18 years
Period of Service:	1852 — 1859
Age on Discharge:	25 years or 24 years 10 months
Length of Service:	6 years 319 days
Foreign Service:	East Indies 5 years 9 months
Medal Entitlement:	Indian Mutiny
Reason for Discharge:	Left hand chopped off by a sword at Jhansi
Character:	Very Good
Trade or Occupation:	Labourer
Can Sign Name:	X his mark on discharge
Height:	5' 11¾"
Hair Colour:	Dark Brown
Eyes:	Hazel
Complexion:	Sallow
Intends to Reside:	Monastereven Co. Kildare

GIBBS	Alfred, gunner
	RHA
16 July 1861	Discharged the Service
	Pension paid Bath
	8d. per diem for 3 years
1864	8d. per diem for a further year
1865	Pension paid Woolwich
Sept 1865	Pension made permanent
4 July 1866	Arrived per *'Belgravia'*
1869	To South Australia from Fremantle or [depending in the record source]
1869	To Adelaide from Perth Western Australia

Service and Personal Details:		
Place of Birth:	Bath Somerset	
Age on Enlistment:	21 years 10 months	
Period of Service:	1848 — 1861	
Age on Discharge:	34 years	
Length of Service:	12 years 326 years	
Foreign Service:	'Expedition to the East'	6 months
	India	3 years 6 months
Reason for Discharge:	Double Rupture on right side	
Character:	Exemplary	
Trade or Occupation:	Labourer	
Can Sign Name:	Yes	
Height:	5' 9¼"	
Hair Colour:	Dark Brown	
Eyes:	Hazel	
Complexion:	Fresh	

GIBSON	George, gunner
RA — 1st Battalion	
10 Apr 1849	Discharged the Service Woolwich
	Pension paid South London
	1/- per diem
20 May 1854	Embarked per *'Ramillies'*
Died on voyage out	

GIFFNEY	Michael, private
	19th Foot
Surname Variant	GIFFENEY
9 Feb 1859	Discharged the Service Chatham
22 Feb 1859	Admitted to Out-Pension
	Pension paid Wicklow
	11d. per diem
1859	Pension paid Liverpool
19 Aug 1859	Arrived per *'Sultana'*
Dec 1884	The Resident Magistrate at Williams to Mount Eliza Poor House — re Michael Giffney, a Pensioner Destitute recommend admission
1884	Was found destitute at Williams and admitted to Mt Eliza Invalid Depot
1891	Died - buried East Perth Cemetery

Service and Personal Details:		
Place of Birth:	Killbride Co. Wicklow	
Age on Enlistment:	21 years	
Period of Service:	1838 — 1859	
Age on Discharge:	42 years 1 month	
Length of Service:	21 years 17 days	
Foreign Service:	Mediterranean	5 years 3 months
	West Indies	2 years 4 months
	North America	3 years 2 months
	Turkey & Crimea	2 years 8 months
Medal Entitlement:	Good Conduct and Long Service with gratuity; Crimea with clasp	
Reason for Discharge:	Own request having completed 21 years service	

Character:	Very Good
Trade or Occupation:	Labourer
Can Sign Name:	X his mark on discharge
Height:	5' 7½"
Hair Colour:	Light Brown
Eyes:	Hazel
Complexion:	Sallow
Intends to Reside:	Wicklow Co. Wicklow

GILBERSON	William, private 62nd Foot
Surname Variants	GILBERTSON; GILBERTON
19 Feb 1856	Discharged the Service Chatham Pension paid Woolwich 9d. per diem
4 July 1866	Arrived per *'Belgravia'*
circa June 1874	Transferred from 2nd Perth Pension District to 1st Perth Pension District
1881	Pension increased to 1/3d. per diem for service in the Enrolled Force
1885	Granted Cockburn Sound Loc 233 Willagee Swamp
June 1886	Employed as Orderly Mt Eliza Depot
Dec 1887	Orderly Gilbertson unfit for duty on the 24th and 25th inst. due to drink
June 1897	Stationed at Perth
1909	Discharge pension increased to 12d. to a Total Rate of 18d. which included 6d. per day for service in Enrolled Guard of Western Australia
1907	Invited to a Veteran's dinner at Esplanade Hotel
1909	Attended Veteran's Dinner
1915	Residing Alfred Street, Leederville
Dec 1916	Died

Service and Personal Details:

Place of Birth:	Skibbereen Co. Cork
Age on Enlistment:	17 years 7 months
Period of Service:	1854 — 1856
Age on Discharge:	21 years or 19 years 2 months
Length of Service:	1 year 63 days
Foreign Service:	Malta & Crimea 1 year 2 months
Medal Entitlement:	Crimea with clasp; Turkish Crimea
Reason for Discharge:	Grape shot wound to arm
Character:	Good
Trade or Occupation:	Labourer
Can Sign Name:	Yes
Height:	5' 6½"
Hair Colour:	Dark Brown
Eyes:	Hazel
Complexion:	Sallow
Intends to Reside:	Skibbereen Co. Cork

GILBRIDE	John, private

	88th Foot
Surname Variant	GUILBRIDE
10 July 1855	Discharged the Service Chatham Pension paid Sligo 1/- per diem
15 Aug 1865	Arrived per *'Racehorse'*
1876	Assigned Loc P11 at Lake Munster
Dec 1877	Enrolled pensioner convicted by a District Court Martial at Fremantle of insubordination and absence and sentenced to 112 days imprisonment during which half pension is to be suspended, the other half to wife
1878	Case reconsidered and whole of suspended pension ordered to be paid to wife
1879	Payment of £15 [pounds] sanctioned
1881	Pension increased to 1/5d. per diem for service in the Enrolled Force
1885	Title Application Loc ?P11 at Lake Munster
1888	Appeared as plaintiff at Fremantle Police Court for having been allegedly assaulted by Stephen Lucas. The case was dismissed with Costs as it was proved the defendant never assaulted the plaintiff
1888	Residing Coojee [sic]
June 1897	Residing Fremantle
1903	Died aged 82

Service and Personal Details:		
Place of Birth:	Barnadarig Co. Sligo	
Age on Enlistment:	18 years	
Period of Service:	1845 — 1855	
Age on Discharge:	27 years	
Length of Service:	9 years 174 days [reckoned]	
Foreign Service:	West Indies	1 year 4 months
	North America	1 year 1 month
	Crimea	
Medal Entitlement:	Crimea with clasps	
Reason for Discharge:	Permanent lameness of the left leg from a wound received at Inkerman	
Character:	Good	
Trade or Occupation:	Labourer	
Can Sign Name:	X his mark on discharge	
Height:	5' 8¾"	
Hair Colour:	Brown	
Eyes:	Hazel	
Complexion:	Fresh	
Remarks:	Embarked with the service company on the 4th	
April 1854		

GILL	James, private EIC
	1st Bengal European Fusiliers
	Out Pension No 242
13 July 1859	Admitted to Out-pension
	Pension paid 1st Dublin Pension District
	9d. per diem
22 Dec 1866	Arrived per *'Corona'*
Aug 1868	To Melbourne from Fremantle
1881	Pension increased to 1/3d.

Service and Personal Details:

Where Born:	Galway
Trade or Occupation:	Labourer
Age on Discharge:	30 years
Length of Service:	3 years 4 months
Reason for Discharge:	Wounds received before Delhi
Character:	Good
Medal Entitlement:	Indian Mutiny
Height:	5' 7¾"
Complexion:	Sallow
Eye Colour:	Hazel
Hair Colour:	Brown
Intends to Reside:	Dublin

GILMORE	Joseph, private
	8th Foot
Surname Variant	GILMOR
11 May 1852	Discharged the Service Chatham
	Pension paid 1st Belfast Pension District
	1/- per diem
1852	Pension paid 1st Manchester Pension District
10 July 1857	Arrived per *'Clara'* [1]
1864	Stationed Perth District
1864	private J Gilmore serving in the Pensioner Force at Perth contributed to the Greenough Fire Relief Fund
15 Feb 1871	Died aged 58

Service and Personal Details:

Place of Birth:	Belfast Co. Antrim	
Age on Enlistment:	18 years	
Period of Service:	1830 — 1852	
Age on Discharge:	40 years	
Length of Service:	21 years 65 days	
Foreign Service:	North America	5 years 149 days
	West Indies	5 years 329 days
	East Indies	3 years 283 days
Reason for Discharge:	Chronic Rheumatism and worn out	
Character:	Good	
Trade or Occupation:	Weaver	
Can Sign Name:	X his mark on discharge	
Height:	5' 11"	
Hair Colour:	Brown	
Eyes:	Hazel	

Complexion:	Fresh
Intends to Reside:	Salford

GILMORE	William, private 96th Foot
Previous Regiment	94th Foot
Surname Variant	GILLMORE
14 Mar 1848	Discharged the Service Chatham Pension paid 2nd Belfast Pension District 1/- per diem
21 May 1851	Arrived per *'Mermaid'*
1851	Assigned and occupied North Fremantle P13 [this land was allocated to Robert Holliwell [sic] on the death of William Gilmore]
July 1856	Died

Service and Personal Details:		
Place of Birth:	Ballymairrett Co. Down	
Age on Enlistment:	17 years	
Period of Service:	1823 — 1848	
Age on Discharge:	41 years	
Length of Service:	22 years 132 days	
Foreign Service:	Bermuda	3 years
	Nova Scotia	8 years
	Australia	7 years
Reason for Discharge:	Age and Infirmity	
Character:	Good	
Trade or Occupation:	Weaver	
Can Sign Name:	X his mark on discharge	
Height:	5' 5¾"	
Hair Colour:	Black	
Eyes:	Black	
Complexion:	Fresh	
Intends to Reside:	Belfast	

GLADSTONE	Robert, private 1st Foot Guards
27 Dec 1849	Discharged the Service London
8 Jan 1850	Admitted to Out-Pension Pension paid 1st East London Pension District 10d. per diem
1853	Assigned Pensioner grant at Pt Gregory [?possibly arrived per *'Pyrenees'*]
1857	To South Australia from Perth West Australia Pension subject to stoppages of £22/10/0 for repayment of passage. Transfer Certificate dated 28 May 1858
1858	Pension paid South Australia
1863	Died South Australia

Service and Personal Details:	
Place of Birth:	Derby Derbyshire
Age on Enlistment:	19 years
Period of Service:	1828 — 1849
Age on Discharge:	40 years 10 months

Length of Service:	21 years 326 days	
Foreign Service:	Canada	2 years 7 months
Reason for Discharge:	Own Request having completed 21 years	
Character:	Irregular but during the last 3 years has much improved	
Trade or Occupation:	Millwright and Engineer	
Can Sign Name:	Yes	
Height:	5' 10"	
Hair Colour:	Light Brown	
Eyes:	Light Blue	
Complexion:	Fair	

GLANVILLE	William, Serjeant
	47th Foot
Previous Service	85th
1849	Discharged at own request with gratuity
1849	Warder *'Warrior'* hulk
28 June 1851	Arrived per *'Pyrenees'* [1]
1851	Employed as Warder — Convict Establishment
1853	Accused of stealing 29 bottles of wine and sundrous [sic] other items – found not guilty
1854	possibly residing Cape Town [not verified]
Service and Personal Details:	
Place of Birth:	?St Andrew's Devon
Period of Service:	1831 – 1849
Length of Service:	18 years
Foreign Service:	Gibraltar - 1835; Malta – 1842; Barbados – 1842; St Kitt's - 1844
Reason for Discharge:	Own request
Trade or Occupation:	Brushmaker
Can Sign Name:	Yes

GLASGOW	William, gunner
	RA 6th Battalion
1 June 1852	Discharged the Service
1854	Pension paid Charlemont
	7d. per diem
18 July 1855	Arrived per *'Adelaide'*
1860	Pension paid Ballymena

GLASSON	Cornelius, private
	58th Foot
25 Nov 1851	Discharged the Service Chatham
	Pension paid Chatham
	9d. per diem
2 Aug 1852	Arrived per *'William Jardine'*
1853	Employed as Night Warder without sanction from Staff Officer Pensions
1873	Tried by District Court Martial for being drunk on guard. Sentenced to 56 days imprisonment during which his pension to be suspended
1875	an attempt was made to pick the pockets of a pensioner named Glasson

1879	a Cornelius Glasson employed as foreman in Mr Monger's sandalwood yard
July 1881	Assigned Perth Town Lot 83/E Claisebrook
May 1884	Application for Title to Perth Lot 83/E
Oct 1884	Granted Fee Simple Perth Town Lot 83/E Claisebrook
Dec 1886	Died - buried East Perth Pioneer Cemetery
Dec 1886	Police Magistrate Perth — Minutes taken at the Inquest on body of Cornelius Glasson, found dead on his grant near the Old Recreation Ground [East] Perth

Service and Personal Details:

Place of Birth:	Buttervant Co. Cork	
Age on Enlistment:	17 years	
Period of Service:	1833 — 1851	
Age on Discharge:	34 years 7 months or 36 years	
Length of Service:	16 years 211 days	
Foreign Service:	East Indies	2 years 4 months
Australian Colonies	5 years 10 months	
Reason for Discharge:	Violent Palpitations of the Heart	
Character:	Good	
Trade or Occupation:	Labourer	
Can Sign Name:	X his mark on discharge	
Height:	5' 11¼"	
Hair Colour:	Fair	
Eyes:	Grey	
Complexion:	Fair	
Intends to Reside:	Chatham	

GLEESON David, private
37th Foot

Surname Variant	GLEESHEN
11 Nov 1851	Discharged the Service Chatham Pension paid Limerick 1/- per diem
18 July 1855	Arrived per *'Adelaide'*
1863	Stationed Perth District
1864	a Serjeant E. Gleeshen [sic] serving in the Pensioner Force at Perth contributed to the Greenough Fire Relief Fund
Mar 1863	To Eastern Colonies from Fremantle
1875	Pension paid New South Wales
1877	Victoria

Service and Personal Details:

Place of Birth:	Adair Co. Limerick	
Age on Enlistment:	20 years	
Period of Service:	1827 — 1851	
Age on Discharge:	42 years 5 months or 44 years or 45 years	
Length of Service:	22 years 243 days	
Foreign Service:	West Indies	8 years 4 months
	Bermuda	2 years
Reason for Discharge:	Chronic Rheumatism	

Character:	Good
Trade or Occupation:	Labourer
Can Sign Name:	Yes
Height:	6' 0½"
Hair Colour:	Light Brown
Eyes:	Grey
Complexion:	Fresh
Intends to Reside:	Limerick

GLOVER Edward, private

	RM
6 July 1854	Discharged the Service Pension paid 2nd East London Pension District £9/4/- per annum
9 June 1862	possibly arrived per *'Norwood'* [1]
1864	a private E Glover serving in the Pensioner Force at Perth contributed to the Greenough Fire Relief Fund
1867	Employed as temporary Assistant Warder at Guildford
circa June 1874	Transferred from 2nd Perth Pension District to 1st Perth Pension District
1893	Died South Australia aged 70

Service and Personal Details:	
Place of Birth:	Kent
Age on Attestation:	19 years
Marine Division:	Chatham
Period of Service:	1840 — 1854
Length of Service:	14 years
Reason for Discharge:	as an Invalid
Trade or Occupation:	Shoemaker
Can Sign Name:	Yes
Remarks:	Served one year under age
Height:	5' 7"
Hair Colour:	Dark Brown
Eyes:	Grey
Complexion:	Fair

GLUSHON Edward, Corporal

	62nd Foot
Surname Variants	GLUSHEN; GLASHEN; GLUSTON
26 Aug 1856	Discharged the Service Mullingar Pension paid Carlow 8½d per diem
11 Feb 1861	Arrived per *'Palmeston'*
1865	Pension paid Western Australia
Sept 1887	Died - ? buried East Perth Pioneer Cemetery

Service and Personal Details:	
Place of Birth:	St Nicholas Dublin
Age on Enlistment:	18 years
Period of Service:	1834 — 1856

Age on Discharge:	39 years 7 months	
Length of Service:	21 years 116 days	
Foreign Service:	East Indies	11 years 9 months
Medal Entitlement:	Sutlej Campaign	
Reason for Discharge:	Partial loss of power in lower extremities	
Character:	Latterly Very Good	
Trade or Occupation:	Labourer	
Can Sign Name:	Yes	
Height:	5' 7¼"	
Hair Colour:	Black	
Eyes:	Blue	
Complexion:	Dark	
Distinguishing Marks:	Slight gunshot wound of left thigh	
Intends to Reside:	Carlow	

GOGGINS Thomas, private
47th Foot

Surname Variant	COGGINS	
28 May 1852	Discharged the Service Templemore	
13 July 1852	Admitted to Out-Pension	
	Pension paid 1st Dublin Pension District	
	1/- per diem	
30 Apr 1853	Arrived per *'Pyrenees'* [2]	
Jan 1857	Contributed 1/- to the Florence Nightingale Fund	
1861	Assigned Newcastle Lot S9	
1861	Application for Title to Newcastle Lot S9	
circa 1865	Departed colony	
1875	Pension paid Victoria	
16 June 1875	Died	

Service and Personal Details:

Place of Birth:	Killochert Co. Leitrim	
Age on Enlistment:	18 years	
Period of Service:	1830 — 1853	
Age on Discharge:	39 years 5 months	
Length of Service:	21 years 165 days	
Foreign Service:	Mediterranean	6 years
	West Indies	9 months
Reason for Discharge:	Impaired Health and Chronic Rheumatism	
Character:	Good	
Trade or Occupation:	Labourer	
Can Sign Name:	Yes	
Height:	5' 7¼"	
Hair Colour:	Sandy	
Eyes:	Grey	
Complexion:	Fair	
Intends to Reside:	Dublin	

GOINA Valentine, private
46th Foot

Surname Variants	GUINAN; GUYNAM; GOYNAN; GOYNA
27 Sept 1858	Discharged the Service
5 Oct 1858	Admitted to Out-Pension

	Pension paid 1st Dublin Pension District
	1/- per diem
1860	Pension paid Kilkenny
12 Sept 1864	Arrived per *'Merchantman'* [2] as a Convict Guard
circa 1867	Died

Service and Personal Details:

Place of Birth:	Kells Co. Meath	
Age on Enlistment:	20 years	
Period of Service:	1837 — 1858	
Age on Discharge:	41 years 11 months	
Length of Service:	20 years 346 days	
Foreign Service:	Gibraltar	2 years
	West Indies	3 years
	North America	3 years 2 months
Medal Entitlement:	Good Conduct and Long Service with gratuity	
Reason for Discharge:	Chronic disease of Chest and Liver	
Character:	Exemplary	
Trade or Occupation:	Labourer	
Can Sign Name:	X his mark on discharge	
Height:	5' 6½"	
Hair Colour:	Light Brown	
Eyes:	Hazel	
Complexion:	Fresh	
Intends to Reside:	Liverpool	

GOLDING William, driver and trumpeter RHA

16 July 1861	Discharged the Service Woolwich
	Pension paid Woolwich
	1/1d. per diem
22 Dec 1866	Arrived per *'Corona'*
Sept 1870	On Perth District Electoral List
1874	Pension paid Woolwich

Service and Personal Details:

Place of Birth:	Dartford Kent	
Age on Enlistment:	18 years 2 months	
Period of Service:	1840 — 1861	
Age on Discharge:	39 years 8 months	
Length of Service:	21 years 174 days	
Foreign Service:	Expedition to the East	5 months
	India	3 years 6 months
Medal Entitlement:	Long Service and Good Conduct with gratuity; Indian Mutiny	
Reason for Discharge:	Rupture	
Character:	Exemplary	
Trade or Occupation:	Labourer	
Can Sign Name:	Yes	
Height:	5' 4¾"	
Hair Colour:	Light Brown	
Eyes:	Grey	
Complexion:	Fresh	

GOOCH	Frederick, private
	53rd Foot
Previous Regiments	94th; 97th
24 Mar 1863	Discharged the Service Chichester
	Pension paid Ipswich
	1/1d. per diem
13 July 1867	Arrived per *'Norwood'* [2]
1880	Pension increased to 1/7d. per diem for 13 years service in the Enrolled Force
Feb 1881	Died aged 60
1881	March On the 23rd ult., In quest at Fremantle Police Court, before J. G. Slade, R.M. and Coroner, on the body of Frederick Gooch, pensioner, who died at the Freemasons Hotel, Fremantle, on the 21st inst. Verdict— "Death from Natural Causes."

Service and Personal Details:		
Place of Birth:	Ipswich Suffolk	
Age on Enlistment:	18 years 3 months	
Period of Service:	1841 — 1863	
Age on Discharge:	39 years 4 months	
Length of Service:	21 years 174 days	
Foreign Service:	East Indies	15 years 4 months
Medal Entitlement:	Indian Mutiny with clasp	
Reason for Discharge:	Own Request having completed 21 years service	
Character:	Very Good	
Trade or Occupation:	Labourer	
Can Sign Name:	X his mark on discharge	
Height:	5' 8"	
Hair Colour:	Light Brown	
Eyes:	Blue	
Complexion:	none annotated	
Intends to Reside:	Whitton Ipswich	

GOOD	William, private
	Falkland Island Corps
Previous Regiments	18th; 94th
25 May 1864	Discharged the Service
	Pension paid Jersey
	1/2 per diem
1 July 1864	Pension paid 2nd Plymouth Pension District
1 Aug 1864	2nd Dublin Pension District
1 Sept 1864	Carlow
1 May 1865	Preston
1 Aug	Halifax
13 July 1867	Arrived per *'Norwood'* [2]

Service and Personal Details:	
Place of Birth:	Whitesea Peterborough Cambridgeshire
Age on Enlistment:	18 years 4 months
Period of Service:	1840 — 1864
Age on Discharge:	42 years 1 month

Length of Service:	23 years 287 days	
Foreign Service:	India	13 years 123 days
	Crimea	1 year 201 days
	Falkland Islands	6 years 169 days
Medal Entitlement:	Long Service and Good Conduct; Crimean with clasp; Turkish Crimean	
Reason for Discharge:	Disbandment of Corps	
Character:	Exemplary	
Trade or Occupation:	Labourer	
Can Sign Name:	Yes	
Height:	5' 7"	
Hair Colour:	Light Brown	
Eyes:	Brown	
Complexion:	Fresh	
Remarks:	Accepted compensation on his rations for one daughter from May 1860 — Jan 1863; and one son from Feb 1863 — Jan 1864	
Intends to Reside:	Newry Co. Down	

GOODALL

	Edmond, private	
	80th Foot	
Surname Variant	GOODHALL	
2 Dec 1856	Discharged the Service Chatham	
	Pension paid Stockport	
	1/- per diem	
1858	Pension paid Nottingham	
1858	Stockport	
29 Jan 1862	Arrived per *'Lincelles'*	
1867	Lost onboard the *'Emma'*	

Service and Personal Details:

Place of Birth:	Macclesfield Cheshire	
Age on Enlistment:	18 years	
Period of Service:	1832 — 1856	
Age on Discharge:	42 years 9 months	
Length of Service:	21 years 148 days	
Foreign Service:	New South Wales	3 years 10 months
	India	9 years 6 months
Medal Entitlement:	1st Sikh; ?Pegu	
Reason for Discharge:	Unfit for further service	
Character:	Indifferent	
Trade or Occupation:	Labourer	
Can Sign Name:	Yes	
Height:	5' 7"	
Hair Colour:	Brown	
Eyes:	Grey	
Complexion:	Fresh	
Intends to Reside:	Macclesfield	

GOODBODY

	Matthew, Serjeant
	29th Foot
Previous Regiment	43rd Foot
11 Sept 1855	Discharged the Service

	Pension paid Jersey
	1/6d. per diem
12 Sept 1864	Arrived per *'Merchantman'* [2]
1865	Purchased Fremantle Town Lot 706 for £6
Oct 1866	a M Goodbody forfeited Perth Town Lot X35 due to non payment of the balance of purchase money
1867	Employed as Assistant Warder
1875	Applies for £15 improvement grant for Perth Town Lot 140/V
1876	Stationed Perth with rank of Serjeant
1878	Pension increased to 2/1d per diem
1879	Night Warder Perth Goal
Feb 1879	Residing Perth
Apr 1881	Application for Title to Perth Lot 140/Y
18 Dec 1882	Joined Enrolled Guard at Fremantle
1884	Granted Fee Simple Perth Town Lot 140/V
1905	Died age 85 years
1909	[newspaper article] Living with his daughter and her husband Mr W. Pollett for the past 16 years Resided in the State for 45 years and served with the Guards in Fremantle for over 20 years

Service and Personal Details:	
Place of Birth:	Castlebrook Mount Mellick Queens County
Age on Attestation:	circa 19 years [Newspaper gives Attestation as "early age"]
Period of Service:	1839 — 1855
Age on Discharge:	32 years
Length of Service:	15 years 6 months [or 15 years 1 month]
Foreign Service:	East Indies 12 years 3 months
Medal Entitlement:	Punjaub with Clasps; Sutlej Campaign
Reason for Discharge:	Impaired health; Premature Age; Emaciation; Hepatic Disease aggravated by Haemorrhoids
Character:	Very Good
Trade or Occupation:	Weaver
Can Sign Name:	Yes
Height:	5' 8"
Hair Colour:	Brown
Eyes:	Hazel
Complexion:	Fair [or Sallow depending on record source]
Married:	1850 Bridget Sheridan
Children:	May b. 1853 Ireland Peter b. 1855 England Winifred b. 1859 St Helier d. *c*1864 Perth Anne b. 1860 St Helier Jersey m. *c*1879 John Nugent Fremantle Mary Jane b. *c*1865 Fremantle m. *c*1886 William T Pollett Roebourne

GOODMAN	John. private
	1st Foot
12 Aug 1862	Discharged the Service Camp Colchester
	1/- per diem

	Pension paid 1st East London Pension District
1862	Pension paid 1st Glasgow Pension District
1865	1st East London Pension District
15 Aug 1865	Arrived per *'Racehorse'*
1867	Employed as Assistant Warder
19 Feb 1874	Granted Northam Loc P5
Apr 1878	Pension increased to 1/5½d. per diem for service in the Enrolled Force
1878	To South Australia from Perth West Australia

Service and Personal Details:

Place of Birth:	Newry Co. Down	
Age on Enlistment:	17 years	
Period of Service:	1839 — 1862	
Age on Discharge:	41 years	
Length of Service:	21 years 58 days	
Foreign Service:	Gibraltar	6 years 3 months
	West Indies	2 years 1 month
	North America	3 years 4 months
	Turkey & Crimea	2 years 2 months
	India	2 years 7 months
Medal Entitlement:	Crimea	
Reason for Discharge:	Own request having completed 21 years service	
Character:	Good	
Trade or Occupation:	Flax Dresser	
Can Sign Name:	Yes	
Height:	5' 8"	
Hair Colour:	Fair	
Eyes:	Hazel	
Complexion:	Fresh	
Intends to Reside:	Glasgow Scotland	
Married:	Margaret Comerford; Comaford or Coverford	
Children:	John Thomas	
1896	"at 1.30 am the remains of his late mother Margaret Goodman will be removed from his residence for internment in the West Terrace Cemetery South Australia Thomas Joseph b. *c*1853 Newport Wales m. *c*1876 Ellen Minden Gorman Perth	

GORDON	Andrew, Corporal 40th Foot
Surname Variant	GORMAN
6 Nov 1849	Discharged the Service Dublin
11 Dec 1849	Admitted to Out-Pension Pension paid Wolverhampton 10d per diem
1 June 1850	Arrived per *'Scindian'*
1850	Assigned and occupied land Lot 1 at Butler's Swamp/Freshwater Bay
1851	a Pensioner Gordon was employed as a Schoolmaster. [this employment could apply to either Andrew or James Gordon]

1855	Pension paid Sydney
1857	"Part pension stopped for wife and children remaining in Colony"
Service and Personal Details:	
Place of Birth:	Roscommon Ireland
Age on Enlistment:	19 years
Period of Service:	1834 — 1849
Age on Discharge:	34 years 9 months
Length of Service:	15 years
Foreign Service:	East Indies 10 years 1 month
Medal Entitlement:	2nd Afghan Campaign medal inscribed
Candahar, Ghuznee and Cabool 1842	
Reason for Discharge:	Chronic Rheumatism
Character:	Good
Trade or Occupation:	Labourer
Can Sign Name:	Yes
Height:	5' 9¾"
Hair Colour:	Light Brown
Eyes:	Blue
Complexion:	Fresh
Intends to Reside:	Dudley Worcestershire

GORDON

	James, gunner RA 10th Battalion
13 Oct 1846	Discharged the Service Woolwich Pension paid 2nd Edinburgh Pension District 1/- per diem
18 Oct 1851	Arrived per *'Minden'*
1852	Employed as Night Warder
Jan 1857	Contributed 2/- to the Florence Nightingale Fund
Nov 1869	"an old man named James Gordon, a pensioner had gone into the bush on the morning of the 13th inst to collect blackboy for fuel, and had not returned by morning, was considered lost, and a search party was sent out. When he was found, it was suggested he go into Invalid Depot, leaving pension for his wife."
Service and Personal Details:	
Place of Birth:	West Kirk Midlothian
Age on Enlistment:	22 years
Period of Service:	1825 — 1846
Age on Discharge:	43 years 4 months
Length of Service:	21 years 196 days
Foreign Service:	Corfu 10 years 3 months
Reason for Discharge:	Chronic Rheumatism
Character:	Exemplary
Trade or Occupation:	Clerk
Can Sign Name:	Yes
Height:	5' 8"

Hair Colour:	Light Brown
Eyes:	Blue
Complexion:	Fair
Remarks:	Married — 7th Oct 1838

GORMAN	James, Corporal 13th Foot
10 Feb 1852	Discharged the Service Chatham Pension paid 1st Dublin Pension District 8d. per diem for 3 years
1853	Pension paid 1st Belfast Pension District
7 Feb 1853	Arrived per *'Dudbrook'*
1853	Employed by Convict Establishment without sanction of Staff Officer Pensions
Feb 1855	Correspondence with W.O. — Refused further pension
2 Mar 1855	Letter to man from W.O.
4 Mar 1855	Pension ceased Employed as Special Constable Albany Awarded Deferred Pension of 4d. per diem on attaining 60 years of age
1880	Identification Forms sent to S.O. Fremantle and to the man
1882	Died Albany [age given as 63]
1883	Correspondence with W.O. — widow asking for assistance — reply "No funds"

Service and Personal Details:

Place of Birth:	St Thomas Dublin	
Age on Enlistment:	20 years	
Period of Service:	1838 — 1852	
Age on Discharge:	33 years 3 months	
Length of Service:	12 years 327 days	
Foreign Service:	East Indies	4 years 9 months
	Gibraltar	6 months
Medal Entitlement:	Afghan campaign	
Reason for Discharge:	Varicose Veins in both legs which first appeared on the Retreat from Cabul [sic] 1842	
Character:	Very Good	
Trade or Occupation:	Hairdresser	
Can Sign Name:	Yes	
Height:	5' 5¾"	
Hair Colour:	Brown	
Eyes:	Grey	
Complexion:	Fresh	
Intends to Reside:	Dublin	

GORMAN	John, private 50th Foot
13 July 1847	Discharged the Service Chatham Pension paid 2nd North London Pension District 8d. per diem

18 Oct 1851	Arrived per *'Minden'*
Jan 1857	Contributed 6/- to the Florence Nightingale Fund
1863	Stationed Perth District
Feb 1864	a Serj Major J Gorman serving in the Pensioner Force at Perth contributed to the Greenough Fire Relief Fund
1865	Purportedly founded the Vincent de Paul Society
Sept 1870	On Perth District Electoral List
13 Apr 1872	Died - buried East Perth Pioneer Cemetery
Service and Personal Details:	
Place of Birth:	Chelsea Middlesex
Age on Enlistment:	18 years
Period of Service:	1841 — 1847
Age on Discharge:	25 years
Length of Service:	5 years 102 days
Foreign Service:	East Indies 4 years 220 days
Medal Entitlement:	Action at Punniar — 1843; Army of the Sutlej and was present at the battles of Moodkee, Ferozashah, Aliwal and Sobroan
Reason for Discharge:	Wounded at Sobraoan
Character:	Good
Trade or Occupation:	Clerk
Can Sign Name:	Yes
Height:	5' 5"
Hair Colour:	Light Brown
Eyes:	Grey
Complexion:	Swarthy
Intends to Reside:	London

GRADY	Thomas, private 4th Foot 2nd Brigade, 4th Division
Previous Regiment	99th Foot
Surname Variant	O'GRADY
28 Oct 1856	Discharged the Service Chatham Pension paid Galway 8d. per diem
1856	Pension paid Liverpool
26 June 1857	Serjeant T Grady was decorated with the Victoria Cross by Her Majesty Queen Victoria at the 1st Investiture of that award in Hyde Park — London [London Gazette]
1857	WO - Refused increase in pension
1859	Pension paid 1st Liverpool Pension District
1859	Galway
9 June 1862	Arrived per *'Norwood'* [1]
1864	private T Grady serving in the Pensioner Force at Perth contributed to the Greenough Fire Relief Fund
23 Nov 1866	Melbourne per *'Gem'*
1867	Pension paid Melbourne
1867	Refused increase in pension - Melbourne
Mar 1891	"Extract from Melbourne Herald, calling attention to absence of pension

19 May 1891	Died aged 59 Melbourne Victoria
Service and Personal Details:	
Place of Birth:	Cleddagh Galway
Age on Enlistment:	17 years 9 months
Period of Service:	1853 — 1856
Age on Discharge:	21 years or 20 years 3 months
Length of Service:	3 years 4 days after deductions
Foreign Service:	'Army in the East' 1 year
Medal Entitlement:	Victoria Cross; Distinguished Conduct Medal Crimea with clasp; Crimean Turkish
Reason for Discharge:	Unfit for further service From Regimental Surgeons Report: 23/11/54 When on duty in the trenches before Sebastopol received a gunshot wound of the left arm. The ball passing through deltoid muscle and grazing the bone resulting in numbness and lost of power in the left arm
Character:	Very Good — [Not in possession of a Good
Conduct Badge]	
Trade or Occupation:	Labourer
Can Sign Name:	X his mark on discharge
Height:	5' 5¼"
Hair Colour:	Dark Brown
Eyes:	Blue
Complexion:	Fresh
Remarks:	In receipt of further annuity of £10 per annum for his Victoria Cross
Married:	Catherine
Children:	Mary Ellen John Martin b. 1869
Memorials:	Melbourne General Cemetery Victoria The Priory Lancaster United Kingdom
1995	A spokesman from the King's Regimental Museum commented that in 1986 the Victoria Cross medal awarded to Thomas Grady was given by a relative to the Australian War Memorial

WO98/1 6th June 1856

"... I am directed by Lord Panure to transmit for the consideration of His Royal Highness The General Commander in Chief a copy of a letter [with its endorsements] in original from Thomas Grady out pensioner, stating the grounds upon which he considers himself entitled to the Victoria Cross ..."

Private T Grady
1. [on] 18th Oct 1854
For having volunteered to repair the embrasures of the Sailor's Battery on the left attack, and effected the same with assistance of the other volunteers under a very heavy fire from the line of batteries

2. [on] Nov 22nd 1854
For gallant conduct on Nov 22nd 1854 in the repulse of the Russian attach on the advanced trench of the left attack when on being severely wounded he refused to give the front, encouraged by such determined bearing the weak force engaged with the enemy to maintain its position ..."

Thomas Grady
4th King's [Royal Lancaster] Regiment

"This brave Irishman on Oct 18th 1854 volunteered to repair the embrasures of the battery on the Left Attack, assisted by another [unknown] This act was accomplished successfully in clear daylight under a heavy fire from a whole line of batteries. Again on Nov 22nd during the repulse of the attack on the most advanced trenches, although severely wounded he refused to quit his post among his comrades, but kept encouraging them "to hold on" and was the means of saving the position and preventing the guns being spiked"

"On the 18th Oct 1854 in the Crimea private Grady volunteered to repair the embrasure of the Sailors' Battery on the Left Attack and carried out this attack under very heavy fire from a line of batteries. On the 22nd Nov during a
repulse of a Russian attack, although severely wounded private Grady
refused to leave the front and his example encouraged the weak force which was engaging the enemy to maintain their positions"

GRAHAM	Edward, private	
	98th Foot	
10 Sept 1850	Discharged the Service Chatham	
	Pension paid Liverpool	
	7d. per diem for 18 months	
21 May 1851	Arrived per *'Mermaid'*	
Service and Personal Details:		
Place of Birth:	Bray Wicklow	
Age on Enlistment:	21 years	
Period of Service:	1843 — 1850	
Age on Discharge:	27 years	
Length of Service:	5 years 352 days	
Foreign Service:	China	1 year 340 days
East Indies	2 years 309 days	
Reason for Discharge:	Unfit for further service	
Character:	Very Good	
Trade or Occupation:	Labourer	
Can Sign Name:	Yes	
Height:	5' 6"	
Hair Colour:	Brown	
Eyes:	Blue	
Complexion:	Fresh	
Intends to Reside:	Liverpool	

GRAHAM	James, Serjeant
	7th Foot
5 Feb 1856	Discharged the Service Chatham
	Pension paid Newry
	1/6d. per diem

1862	Pension paid 1st Liverpool Pension District
9 June 1862	Arrived per *'Norwood'* [1]
1864	Serjeant J Graham Pensioner Force at Perth contributed to the Greenough Fire Relief Fund
1865	Employed as police constable
1866	Employed as Assistant Warder
1875	Pension paid Western Australia
10 June 1883	Assigned North Fremantle Lot P94
14 Dec 1883	Granted Fee Simple North Fremantle Lot P94
17 Aug 1894	Died aged 65

Service and Personal Details:

Place of Birth:	Drumgrath Rathfriland Co. Down
Age on Enlistment:	17 years 9 months
Period of Service:	1847 — 1855
Age on Discharge:	26 years 8 months
Length of Service:	8 years 245 days
Foreign Service:	Crimea [no time given]
Medal Entitlement:	Crimean with clasps
Reason for Discharge:	Severely wounded by gunshot wound to the face during the final attack on the Redan Sept 1855
Character:	Good
Trade or Occupation:	Weaver
Can Sign Name:	Yes
Height:	5' 6"
Hair Colour:	Light Brown
Eyes:	Blue
Complexion:	Fair
Intends to Reside:	Rathfriland

GRANT

	George, gunner EIC Madras Artillery Out Pension No 122
19 May 1841	Discharged the Service
May 1841	Embarked UK per *'Wellington'*
	Pension paid 1st North London Pension District 9d. per diem
18 Oct 1851	Arrived per *'Minden'*
1871	Resident's Office Fremantle: - George Grant, Pensioner, requires relief. 9d per diem. Willing to forfeit pension should he be admitted to the Poor House
Mar 1876	Died - buried East Perth Pioneer Cemetery

Service and Personal Details:

Where Born:	Middlesex
Trade or Occupation:	Printer
Where Enlisted:	London
Presidency:	Madras
Service Period:	Unlimited
Age on Discharge:	34 years
Length of Service:	14 years 122 days
Reason for Discharge:	Being emaciated of unhealthy appearance and chronic dysentery of long standing

Character:	Good
Height:	5' 6½"
Complexion:	Fair
Visage:	Oval
Eye Colour:	Brown
Hair Colour:	Brown

GRANT

	James, private
	89th Foot
26 Oct 1852	Discharged the Service Templemore
14 Dec 1852	Admitted to Out-Pension
	Pension paid 2nd West London Pension District
	6d. per diem
14 Aug 1854	Arrived per *'Ramillies'*
1856	To South Australia from Fremantle W.A.
1871	"Off Roll — Not Appeared"

Service and Personal Details:

Place of Birth:	Hampton Gloucestershire	
Age on Enlistment:	20 years 6 months	
Period of Service:	1838 — 1852	
Age on Discharge:	34 years 9 months	
Length of Service:	14 years 92 days	
Foreign Service:	West Indies	2 years 2 months
	North America	5 years 10 months
Reason for Discharge:	Health completely broken down	
Character:	Very Good	
Trade or Occupation:	Groom	
Can Sign Name:	Yes	
Height:	5' 6"	
Hair Colour:	Brown	
Eyes:	Blue	
Complexion:	Sallow	
Distinguishing Marks:	Scar on the right side of upper lip	
Intends to Reside:	Pimlico London	

GRATTEN

	John, private
	49th Foot
Surname Variants	GRATTAN; GRATTON
3 June 1856	Discharged the Service Chatham
	Pension paid Dublin
	8d. per diem
1862	Pension paid Tullamore
9 June 1862	Arrived per *'Norwood'* [1]
Feb 1866	a John Grattan forfeited Perth Town Lot N111 due to the non payment of the balance of purchase money
1868	Allocated Greenough Locs G40, G41 and G42
1881	Pension increased to 1/2d. per diem for service in the Enrolled Force
1882	Stationed Vasse
May 1884	Died - ? buried East Perth Pioneer Cemetery

Service and Personal Details:		
Place of Birth:	Edinderry Kings County	
Age on Enlistment:	18 years	
Period of Service:	1848 — 1856	
Age on Discharge:	27 years or 26 years	
Length of Service:	6 years 219 days	
Foreign Service:	Ionian Isles	2 years
	Crimea	1 year 6 months
Medal Entitlement:	Crimea with clasp	
Reason for Discharge:	Amputation of right ring finger due to shell wound	
Character:	Latterly Good	
Trade or Occupation:	Labourer	
Can Sign Name:	Yes	
Height:	5' 6¾"	
Hair Colour:	Brown	
Eyes:	Hazel	
Complexion:	Fair	
Intends to Reside:	Dublin	

GRAY	John Richard, private
	4th Light Dragoons
Previous Regiment	57th Foot [Drummer]
20 Oct 1855	a John Richard Gray sick at Scuteri
11 Aug 1856	a John Richard Gray returned to regiment
May 1861	Discharged the Regiment Dublin
1861	Pension paid Ipswich
	8d. per diem for 3 years
1863	Pension paid Chatham
7 June 1864	Pension ceased
4 July 1866	Arrived per *'Belgravia'*
1877	Refused increase in pension
1886	John R. Gray — claim for increase of Pension
1880	Awarded Deferred Pension of 5d. per diem
	Residing Adelaide Str, Perth Western Australia
1887	Correspondence with W.O.
1887	Newspaper article informing that — He was a warder for many years but has been obliged to resign his post in the Government service owing to having lost the use of both legs
June 1891	Died aged 60

Service and Personal Details:		
Place of Birth:	Chatham Kent	
Age on Enlistment:	15 years	
Period of Service:	1845 — 1861 [includes period before age of 18]	
Age on Discharge:	30 years 4 months	
Length of Service:	12 years 145 days	
Foreign Service:	Turkey & Crimea	1 year 10 months
Medal Entitlement:	Crimea with clasps; Turkish Crimean	
Reason for Discharge:	Varicose veins in both legs	
Character:	Good	
Trade or Occupation:	none	
Can Sign Name:	Yes	

Height:	5' 8"
Hair Colour:	Dark Brown
Eyes:	Hazel
Complexion:	Fresh
Intends to Reside:	27 Norwich Rd., Ipswich

GRAY	Simon [Simeon], private [306] 4th Dragoon Guards
28 Dec 1847	Discharged the Service Chatham Pension paid Hull 7d. per diem
1848	Pension paid Newcastle
7 Feb 1853	Arrived per *'Dudbrook'*
1854	Pension paid Western Australia
1855	To New South Wales from Western Australia
1865	Pension paid Sydney
1869	Correspondence with W.O. for assistance to return home [to the United Kingdom]
1871	Died New South Wales

Service and Personal Details:

Place of Birth:	Osbaldwick Yorkshire
Age on Enlistment:	20 years
Period of Service:	1829 — 1847
Age on Discharge:	39 years
Length of Service:	18 years 130 days — [Home Service only]
Reason for Discharge:	Rheumatic pains and Varicose Veins in both legs
Character:	Very Good
Trade or Occupation:	Butcher
Can Sign Name:	Yes
Height:	5' 9¾"
Hair Colour:	Brown
Eyes:	Grey
Complexion:	Fresh
Remarks:	Orderly in the Station Hospital at Nottingham
Intends to Reside:	York [United Kingdom]

GREEN	Edmund, private 15th Foot
1858	Employed as Assistant Warder in UK
1861	an Edmund Green residing Gillingham Kent and employed as an Assistant Warder at the Convict Prison Chatham [1861 Census]
1863	Serving Chatham Prison
12 Sept 1864	an Edmund Green arrived per *'Merchantman'* [2] aged 37 years and 7 months with wife aged 34
24 Oct 1866	Assaulted by prisoner

GREEN	Edward, private 18th Foot
6 July 1855	Sent home "Invalided"
2 Oct 1855	Discharged the Service Chatham Pension paid Enniskillen 8d. per diem

22 Dec 1865	Arrived per *'Vimiera'*
Jan 1868	an Edward Green forfeited Perth Town Lot 156 due to the non payment of the balance of purchase money
1873	Assigned Fremantle Lot P36 at Lime Kilns
June 1874	Applies for £15 improvement grant
1876	Stationed Fremantle
1882	Edward Green [Pensioner] - Application for Fee Simple to Fremantle Lot P36 Fremantle
1881	Pension increased to 1/2d. per diem for service in the Enrolled Force
1882	Granted Fee Simple for Fremantle Lot P36
Dec 1887	Applies for employment
June 1897	Residing Fremantle
1899	Correspondence with W.O.
Feb 1900	Attended fete at Oval
1900	Died 66

Service and Personal Details:	
Place of Birth:	Drumholm Co. Donegal
Age on Enlistment:	20 years 6 months [or 20 years]
Period of Service:	1854 — 1855
Age on Discharge:	21 years 4 months
Length of Service:	285 days [or 10 months depending on record]
Foreign Service:	Crimea [no time period given]
Medal Entitlement:	Crimea
Reason for Discharge:	Amputation of Ring and Little Finger of left hand after wound from shell in the trenches before Sebastopol – 20/6/1855
Character:	"No entry in the Defaulter's Book" — 1855
Trade or Occupation:	Labourer
Can Sign Name:	blank; X his mark on Attestation
Height:	5' 4¾"
Hair Colour:	Brown
Eyes:	Grey
Complexion:	Fresh

GREEN	Walter, private 3rd Foot Guards
11 June 1850	Discharged the Service London Pension paid 1st Manchester Pension District 1/1d. per diem
1851	Living with brother Samuel
18 Oct 1851	Arrived per *'Minden'*
1851	Employed by Convict Establishment
1852	Pension paid Melbourne
1852	New South Wales
1858	Melbourne
1879	Victoria

Service and Personal Details:	
Place of Birth:	Barnsley Yorkshire
Age on Enlistment:	21 years
Period of Service:	1826 — 1850

Age on Discharge:	45 years
Length of Service:	23 years 88 days
Reason for Discharge:	Impaired vision
Character:	Generally Good and latterly Extremely So
Trade or Occupation:	Fustian Cutter
Can Sign Name:	Yes
Height:	5' 10"
Hair Colour:	Brown
Eyes:	Grey
Complexion:	Fresh
Intends to Reside:	Manchester

GREENHILL

	Samuel, private
	45th Foot
Surname Variant	GREENFIELD
15 Jan 1861	Admitted to Out-pension
	Pension paid Sheffield
	11d. per diem
1861	Pension paid Preston
1861	Sheffield
9 June 1862	Arrived per *'Norwood'* [1]
1866	Pension paid Adelaide South Australia
11 Nov 1875	Died

Service and Personal Details:

Place of Birth:	Sheffield Yorkshire	
Age on Enlistment:	19 years	
Period of Service:	1839 — 1860	
Age on Discharge:	40 years 1 month	
Length of Service:	21 years 3 days [reckoned]	
Foreign Service:	Capetown	16 years 1 month
Reason for Discharge:	Completed service. At his own request	
Character:	Very Good	
Trade or Occupation:	Table Knife Cutter	
Can Sign name:	X his mark on discharge	
Height:	5' 7"	
Hair Colour:	Brown Grey	
Eyes:	Grey	
Complexion:	Sallow	
Distinguishing Marks:	Marks of burn on breast, neck and left arm	
Intends to Reside:	Sheffield	

GREER

	John, private
	77th Foot
Previous Regiment	57th Foot
Surname Variants	GREEN; GREAR
15 July 1856	Discharged the Service Chatham
	Pension paid Liverpool
	1/- per diem
1857	Refused pension increase
1858	Pension paid Bristol
1858	Liverpool
27 May 1863	Arrived per *'Clyde'*

Oct 1864	To South Australia from Fremantle per '*Sea Ripple*' with wife and 4 children
Service and Personal Details:	
Place of Birth:	Belfast Co. Antrim
Age on Enlistment:	19 years 3 months
Period of Service:	1843 — 1856
Age on Discharge:	32 years
Length of Service:	12 years 222 days
Foreign Service:	Mediterranean and
	Turkey & Crimea 2 years 2 months
	Medal Entitlement: Crimea with clasps
Reason for Discharge:	Wounded by musket bullet
Character:	Good
Trade or Occupation:	Labourer
Can Sign Name:	Yes
Height:	5' 9"
Hair Colour:	Dark Brown
Eyes:	Light grey
Complexion:	Fresh

GREGORY	John, private
	27th Foot
6 June 1848	Discharged the Service Chatham
	Pension paid Cavan
	9d. per diem
10 Sept 1856	Arrived per '*Runnymede*'
1857	To South Australia from Western Australia
Feb 1859	Arrived Adelaide per '*Francis*'
1859	Pension paid Melbourne
1875	Victoria
Service and Personal Details:	
Place of Birth:	Tonreagan Cavan
Age on Enlistment:	20 years
Period of Service:	1830 — 1848
Age on Discharge:	37 years 4 months or 39 years
Length of Service:	17 years 137 days
Foreign Service:	Cape of Good Hope 12 years 230 days
Reason for Discharge:	Impaired Vision
Character:	Good
Trade or Occupation:	Labourer
Can Sign Name:	Yes
Height:	5' *"
Hair Colour:	Black
Eyes:	Black
Complexion:	Dark
Intends to Reside:	Ballyconnell Cavan

GREGORY	Kilner, private
also known as	Gregory KILNER
	78th Foot
Previous Regiment	39th Foot

11 Aug 1846	Discharged the Service Chatham	
	Pension paid Liverpool	
	10d. per diem	
1846	Pension paid Cork	
1847	Liverpool	
1848	Manchester	
1848	Liverpool	
1849	Dublin	
28 June 1851	Arrived per *'Pyrenees'* [1]	
?1852	Allocated land at Albany [not verified]	
1857	Pension paid South Australia	
	"£15 to be deducted from pension for the cottage"	
1883	Correspondence with Pension Office Adelaide	
Oct 1887	Died at Riverton South Australia	
Service and Personal Details:		
Place of Birth:	Kiltomy [sic] Co. Kerry	
Age on Enlistment:	17 years	
Period of Service:	1827 — 1846	
Age on Discharge:	37 years	
Length of Service:	17 years 190 days	
Foreign Service:	Ceylon	9 years 4 months
	East Indies	3 years 3 months
Reason for Discharge:	Remittent and intermittent Fever	
Character:	Good	
Trade or Occupation:	Labourer	
Can Sign Name:	Yes	
Height:	5' 8½"	
Hair Colour:	Dark Brown	
Eyes:	Grey	
Complexion:	Sallow	
Intends to Reside:	Liverpool	

GREY	David, gunner	
	RA 6th Brigade	
Surname Variant	GRAY	
20 May 1862	Discharged the Service	
3 June 1862	Admitted to Out-Pension	
	Pension paid Londonderry	
	8d. per diem	
22 Dec 1865	Arrived per *'Vimiera'*	
1867	Pension paid Adelaide	
1872	Melbourne	
Service and Personal Details:		
Place of Birth:	Glendernmoth Co. Londonderry	
Age on Attestation:	19 years	
Period of Service:	1840— 1862	
Age on Discharge:	41 years 3 months	
Length of Service:	21 years 201 days	
Foreign Service:	Jamaica	5 years 2 months
	Gibraltar	2 years 9 months
	Malta	6 years 1 month
Reason for Discharge:	none given	

Character:	Bad
Trade or Occupation:	Weaver
Can Sign Name:	Yes
Height:	5' 8"
Hair Colour:	Brown
Eyes:	Hazel
Complexion:	Fair
Intends to Reside:	Londonderry

GRICE	Joseph, private
	14th Light Dragoons
Previous Regiment	78th Foot
13 May 1861	Discharged the Service
21 May 1861	Admitted to Out-Pension
	Pension paid Leicester
	8d. per diem
1862	Pension paid Bermuda
1862	Pension increased to 9d. per diem
15 Feb 1863	Arrived per *'Merchantman'* [1]
1864	To New South Wales from Perth West. Australia
1866	Pension paid Sydney
1869	Pension paid New Zealand
1874	New South Wales
1879	New South Wales
1880	`New South Wales

Service and Personal Details:

Place of Birth:	Broughton Nottinghamshire	
Age on Enlistment:	18 years	
Period of Service:	1845 — 1861	
Age on Discharge:	34 years	
Length of Service:	16 years 3 days	
Foreign Service:	East Indies	14 years 2 months
Medal Entitlement:	Punjaub campaign with bar Goojerat with bar; Central India with clasp Siege of Jhansi	
Reason for Discharge:	Varicose Ulcers and Veins on left leg	
Character:	Very Good	
Trade or Occupation:	Baker	
Can Sign Name:	Yes	
Height:	5' 6½"	
Hair Colour:	Brown	
Eyes:	Grey	
Complexion:	Fresh	
Remarks:	Entitled to Prize Money for Central India 1857/58	
Intends to Reside:	Nether Broughton Melton Mowbray Leicester	

GRIFFIN	David, private EIC [L/AG/23/2/66]
	Bengal European Regiment
	Out Pension No 131 or 134
9 June 1847	Admitted to Out-pension
	Pension paid Cork
	9d. per diem
7 Feb 1853	Arrived per *'Dudbrook'*

Service and Personal Details:	
Where Born:	Wexford
Trade or Occupation:	Labourer
Presidency:	Bengal
Length of Service:	15 years 5 months
Age on Discharge:	34 years
Reason for Discharge:	Dyspnea [sic] and irritability of stomach
Character:	Good
Height:	5' 5"
Complexion:	Fresh
Visage:	Oval
Eye Colour:	Grey
Hair Colour:	Brown

GRIFFIN	James, private 33rd Foot
10 July 1855	Discharged the Service Pension paid Clonmel 10d. per diem
1856	Pension paid Dartmoor
10 July 1857	Arrived per *'Clara'* [1]
circa Dec 1874	Transferred from Fremantle to 2nd Perth
1875	Pension paid Western Australia
1878	Pension increased to 1/4d. per diem for service in the Enrolled Force
1878	Temporary Hospital Warder
1879	Residing at Newcastle
1889	Died aged 62 Toodyay

Service and Personal Details:		
Place of Birth:	Clonmel Co. Waterford	
Age on Enlistment:	17 years	
Period of Service:	1845 — 1855	
Age on Discharge:	26 years 4 months	
Length of Service:	8 years 118 days	
Foreign Service:	Crimea	[no time period given]
Medal Entitlement:	Crimea	
Reason for Discharge:	Left hand disabled by gunshot wound through the wrist received at Alma	
Character:	Very Good	
Trade or Occupation:	Labourer	
Can Sign Name:	X his mark on discharge	
Height:	5' 9½"	
Hair Colour:	Dark	
Eyes:	Hazel	
Complexion:	Sallow	

GRIFFIN	James, private [drummer] 59th Foot
13 Oct 1848	Discharged the Service Templemore
12 Dec 1848	Admitted to Out-Pension Pension paid Preston 1/- per diem
18 Oct 1851	Arrived per *'Minden'*

Feb 1852	Employed as Night Warder Convict Service	
1853	Pension paid Port Phillip Victoria	
	"Repaid passage money for wife"	
1864	Pension paid Victoria	
Service and Personal Details:		
Place of Birth:	Westbourne Sussex	
Age on Enlistment:	15 years	
Period of Service:	1824 — 1848	
Age on Discharge:	39 years 4 months	
Length of Service:	21 years 39 days	
Foreign Service:	East Indies	3 years 262 days
	Mediterranean	6 years 174 days
	West Indies	2 years 352 days
Reason for Discharge:	Habitual Breathing Difficulties	
Character:	Bad	
Trade or Occupation:	Labourer	
Can Sign Name:	Yes	
Height:	5' 8"	
Hair Colour:	Fair	
Eyes:	Blue	
Complexion:	Fair	

GRIFFIN	Owen, private	
	9th Foot	
Surname Variant	GRIFFEN	
28 May 1847	Discharged the Service Chatham	
	Pension paid 1st Dublin Pension District	
	9d. per diem	
7 Feb 1853	Arrived per *'Dudbrook'*	
1856	Employed as Warder Camp at North Fremantle	
1863	residing Fremantle area	
1869	Employed as Warder at North Fremantle	
1872	an Owen Griffen residing at Fremantle	
1875	Pension paid Perth Pension District West Aust	
June 1897	Residing Fremantle	
Feb 1900	Attended fete at Oval	
21 Jan 1910	Died at his residence Attfield St., Fremantle	
Service and Personal Details:		
Place of Birth:	Dunlavin Wicklow	
Age on Enlistment:	18 years	
Period of Service:	1843 — 1847	
Age on Discharge:	22 years	
Length of Service:	3 years 23 days	
Foreign Service:	East Indies	1 year 328 days
Medal Entitlement:	Sutlej	
Reason for Discharge:	Injured by gunshot while in action at Ferozeshar	
Character:	Good	
Trade or Occupation:	Labourer	
Can Sign Name:	X his mark on discharge	
Height:	5' 8"	
Hair Colour:	Brown	

Eyes:	Grey
Complexion:	Fresh
Intends to Reside:	Pound Town nr Dublin

GRIFFIN

	Patrick, private
	41st Foot
Surname Variant	GRIFFEN
28 Apr 1841	Discharged the Service Chatham
12 May 1841	Admitted to Out-Pension
	Pension paid Tullamore
	6d. per diem
21 May 1851	Arrived per *'Mermaid'*
1854	Pension paid Western Australia
1857	To South Australia from Perth Western Australia

Service and Personal Details:

Place of Birth:	Rahan Kings County	
Age on Enlistment:	18 years	
Period of Service:	1822 — 1841	
Age on Discharge:	36 years 9 months	
Length of Service:	21 years 147 days	
Foreign Service:	East Indies	16 years 11 months
Reason for Discharge:	Chronic Rheumatism due to constant exposure to heavy dews in India	
Character:	Indifferent	
Trade or Occupation:	Labourer	
Can Sign Name:	X his mark on discharge	
Height:	5' 5½"	
Hair Colour:	Dark	
Eyes:	Grey	
Complexion:	Brown	
Intends to Reside:	Clara Kings County	

GRIFFIN

	Thomas, private
	95th Foot
Previous Regiment	50th Foot
Surname Variant	GRIFFINS
14 Sept 1852	Discharged the Service Chatham
	Pension paid Carlow
	1/- per diem
19 Aug 1853	Arrived per *'Robert Small'*
1854	Employed in Convict Establishment without sanction of Staff Office Pensions
1856	Pension paid South Australia
1856	Van Dieman's Land
1875	Van Dieman's Land

Service and Personal Details:

Place of Birth:	Evera Neddeen Co. Kerry	
Age on Enlistment:	18 years	
Period of Service:	1831 — 1852	
Age on Discharge:	39 years 8 months	
Length of Service:	21 years 211 days	
Foreign Service:	Ceylon	8 years
	Hong Kong	3 years 5 months

Medal Entitlement:	Long Service and Good Conduct
Reason for Discharge:	Worn out from length of service
Character:	Good
Trade or Occupation:	Labourer
Can Sign Name:	X his mark on discharge
Height:	5' 9¾"
Hair Colour:	Grey
Eyes:	Hazel
Complexion:	Fair
Intends to Reside:	Newbridge Kildare

GUERIN	Henry, private EIC
	Bengal European Infantry
Surname Variant	GUEARIN
	Out Pension No 157
9 June 1847	Discharged the Service
1847	Embarked UK per *'Prince of Wales'*
	Pension paid Cork
9d. per diem	
1852	? Pension paid 1st East London District
7 Feb 1853	Arrived per *'Dudbrook'*
11 May 1853	Committed military offence
1853	"Struck off Enrolled Pensioner Force Roll"
1866	Pension paid 2nd East London Pension District

Service and Personal Details:

Where Born:	Limerick
Trade or Occupation:	Clerk
Where Enlisted:	Dublin
Age on Attestation:	23 years
Presidency:	Bengal
Length of Service:	5 years 2 months
Reason for Discharge:	Wounded in both legs
Character:	Good
Height:	5' 8¾"
Complexion:	Fair
Visage:	Long
Eye Colour:	Hazel
Hair Colour:	Brown

GUERIN	Roger, Serjeant
	21st Foot
Surname Variant	GUERIEN
Sept 1833	Arrived per *'Jane'* with detachment
16 July 1840	Discharged the Service at own request
25 June 1841	Discharge approved
14 July 1841	Examination of Invalid Soldiers
	Remission on amount to be paid for land grant
	Pigeon Grove near Busselton]
11 Aug 1866	Aged 60
17 June 1871	Deferred Pension of 4d. per diem ratified
1878	Died

Service and Personal Details:

Place of Birth:	Fenlow Co. Clare
Age on Enlistment:	17 years
Period of Service:	1823 — 1840
Age on Discharge:	34 years
Length of Service:	15 years 356 days [after age of 18 years]
Foreign Service:	West Indies — upwards of 3 years
	Western Australia — 6 years 321 days
Reason for Discharge:	His own request, a free discharge with 12 months pay; and to have his name registered at Chelsea Hospital and after his obtaining 60 years of age shall be entitled to a pension of 4d. per diem
Character:	That of a Good and Zealous soldier
Trade or Occupation:	Labourer
Can Sign Name:	Yes
Height:	5' 8"
Hair:	Light Brown
Eyes:	Grey
Complexion:	Fresh

GURNEY	Patrick, private
	17th Foot
Previous Regiments	65th; 74th; 52nd; 23rd
19 July 1859	Discharged the Service Chatham
	Pension paid Woolwich
	8½d. per diem
11 Feb 1861	Arrived per *'Palmeston'*
1865	Pension paid Western Australia
1868	Died aged 49
Service and Personal Details:	
Place of Birth:	Newbridge Co. Kildare
Age on Enlistment:	19 years
Period of Service:	1838— 1859
Age on Discharge:	40 years 5 months
Length of Service:	22 years 109 days
Foreign Service:	North America — 20 years 5 months
Reason for Discharge:	Unfit for further service and own request on completing 21 years service
Character:	Good
Trade or Occupation:	Labourer
Can Sign Name:	X his mark on discharge
Height:	5' 6½"
Hair Colour:	Dark Brown
Eyes:	Brown
Complexion:	Fresh
Remarks:	1841 Volunteered to serve permanently in North
America — Canada	
Intends to Reside:	Woolwich

GUY	Henry, private
	15th Hussars
Previous Regiment	14th Hussars

8 Aug 1848	Discharged the Service Chatham
1849	Warder onboard '*Warrior*' Prison Hulk Woolwich
6 Mar 1851	Left Woolwich to embark on '*Pyrenees*' [1]
1853	To Eastern colonies per '*Caroline*'
1861	Pension paid New South Wales
Mar 1879	Melbourne

Service and Personal Details:

Place of Birth:	Wargrave Kingston-upon-Thames	
Age on Enlistment:	20 years 2 months	
Period of Service:	1833— 1847	
Age on Discharge:	34 years 6 months	
Length of Service:	14 years 138 days	
Foreign Service:	East Indies	8 years 316 days
Reason for Discharge:	Own Request with the Right of Registry for a Deferred pension of 4d. per diem	
Character:	Good and Efficient soldier, Trustworthy and Sober	
Trade or Occupation:	Carpenter	
Can Sign Name:	Yes	
Height:	5' 11¼"	
Hair Colour:	Brown	
Eyes:	Hazel	
Complexion:	Fresh	

HACKETT	Owen, Serjeant
	47th Foot [Depot]
Surname Variants	HACKET; HACKELL
26 May 1851	Discharged the Service Waterford
5 Aug 1851	Admitted to out-Pension
	Pension paid 1st Dublin Pension District
	1/4½d. per diem
19 Aug 1853	Arrived per '*Robert Small*'
1856	Stationed Toodyay
Jan 1857	Contributed 1/- to the Florence Nightingale Fund
1866	Granted Newcastle Pensioner Lot S10 [pensioner Hackett's cottage located at 80 Stirling Terrace Toodyay is registered on the Heritage Council's database]
1862	Died aged 51

Service and Personal Details:

Place of Birth:	St James's Dublin	
Age on Enlistment:	21 years	
Period of Service:	1830 — 1851	
Age on Discharge:	42 years 5 months	
Length of Service:	21 years 116 days	
Foreign Service:	Mediterranean	6 years 5 months
	West Indies & British Guyana	2 years 9 months
Reason for Discharge:	Chronic Rheumatism	
Character:	Good and Trustworthy	
Trade or Occupation:	Woollen Spinner	
Can Sign Name:	Yes	

Height:	5' 7"
Hair Colour:	Brown
Eyes:	Grey
Complexion:	Fair
Intends to Reside:	Dublin

HAGAN	Denis, private	
	97th Foot	
10 Mar 1856	Discharged the Service Chatham	
	Pension paid 1st Liverpool Pension District	
	1/- per diem	
22 Dec 1866	Arrived per *'Corona'*	
1874	"Off Enrolled Force" for receiving stolen property	
1875	Pension paid Western Australia	
1881	Pension increased to 1/6d. per diem for service in Enrolled Force	
22 June 1881	Granted Northam Lot P35	
July 1889	Died [residence Murray Street West]	
Service and Personal Details:		
Place of Birth:	Newry Co. Down	
Age on Enlistment:	22 years	
Period of Service:	1845 — 1856	
Age on Discharge:	33 years 9 months	
Length of Service:	10 years 228 days	
Foreign Service:	Malta	1 year 259 days
	North America	4 years 253 days
	Greece	168 days
	Crimea	204 days
Medal Entitlement:	Crimea	
Reason for Discharge:	Gunshot wound to forearm	
Character:	Very Good	
Trade or Occupation:	Labourer	
Can Sign Name:	X his mark on discharge	
Height:	5' 7"	
Hair Colour:	Fair	
Eyes:	Grey	
Complexion:	Fresh	
Intends to Reside:	Liverpool	

HAGARTY	John, private
	17th Foot
Previous Regiment	20th Light Dragoons
Surname Variants	HAGGARTY; HAGARTY; HAGERTY
13 May 1840	Discharged the Service Chatham
	Pension paid Rochester
	1/1d. per diem plus 2d. per diem for service in India
1851	Pension paid Australia
7 July 1851	Employed as Night Warder Fremantle
	previous occupation given as "Pensioner"
Sept 1851	Resigned or dismissed from Convict Service

Service and Personal Details:

Place of Birth:	Fermoy Cork	
Age on Enlistment:	about 20	
Period of Service:	1816 — 1840	
Age on Discharge:	43 years 11 months	
Length of Service:	23 years 6 months	
	[26 years 127 days reckoned total service]	
Foreign Service:	New South Wales	6 years
	East Indies	6 years
Reason for Discharge:	Chronic Rheumatism	
Character:	Good	
Trade or Occupation:	Labourer	
Can Sign Name:	Yes	
Height:	5' 9"	
Hair Colour:	Light Brown rather grey	
Eyes:	Grey	
Complexion:	Fair	
Intends to Reside:	Fermoy	

HAGGARTY John, Corporal
21st Foot

Surname Variant	HAGARTY
14 Sept 1833	Arrived per *'Jane'* with detachment
Apr 1839	Mrs Haggerty publicly apologised to Mrs Anne Heffron wife of Patrick Heffron late of the 63rd Regiment
16 July 1840	Discharged at own request
25 June 1841	Discharged approved
Nov 1842	Issued a public apology to his wife Margaret
1845	Applied for land
1850	Employed as Surveyor's assistant
Apr 1857	a Margaret Haggerty advertised that she would not be liable for any debt contracted by her daughter Margaret or her husband John Haggerty, as "I have given him money to carry him from the colony"
1857	To South Australia per *'Swan'*
21 July 1865	Aged 60
20 Oct 1868	Deferred pension ratified

Service and Personal Details:

Place of Birth:	Clune Abbey Co. Clare	
Age on Enlistment:	18 years	
Period of Service:	1823 — 1840	
Age on Discharge:	35 years	
Length of Service:	17 years 15 days	
Foreign Service:	West Indies	3 years
	Western Australia	6 years 321 days
Reason for Discharge:	His own request, a free discharge with 12 months pay and to have his name registered at Chelsea Hospital and after his obtaining 60 years of age shall be entitled to a pension of 6d. [sixpence] per diem	
Character:	a Good and Efficient soldier	
Trade or Occupation:	Blacksmith	
Can Sign Name:	Yes	

Height:	5' 9"
Hair:	Black
Eyes:	Grey
Complexion:	Fair
HAINES	John, private
	87th Foot
26 July 1864	Discharged the Service Aldershot
	9d. per diem
	Pension paid Trowbridge
13 July 1867	Arrived per *'Norwood'* [2]
1881	Pension increased to 1/3d per diem for service in the Enrolled Force of Western Australia
1883	Assigned Perth Town Lot 32/H
April 1885	Died from an attack of paralysis aged 58
Service and Personal Details:	
Place of Birth:	Heytsbury [sic] Wiltshire
Age on Enlistment:	21 years
Period of Service:	1848 — 1864
Age on Discharge:	36 years 9 months
Length of Service:	15 years 265 days
Foreign Service:	East Indies 10 years 8 months
	China 1 year 1 month
Reason for Discharge:	Having been found unfit for further service cause, Varicose Veins
Character:	On the whole Good
Trade or Occupation:	Labourer
Can Sign Name:	X his mark on discharge
Height:	5' 9¼"
Hair Colour:	Dark Brown
Eyes:	Brown
Complexion:	Dark
Intends to Reside:	Warminster Wiltshire
HALEY	Patrick, private
	20th Foot
Surname Variants	HEALY; HEALEY
31 July 1855	Discharged the Service Chatham
	Pension paid 1st Cork pension District
	9d. per diem
1862	Pension paid Cork
27 May 1863	Arrived per *'Clyde'*
1875	Pension paid Western Australia
Aug 1876	Assigned Perth Town Lot 35/H
1881	Recommended for £15 Pensioner's Grant
1881	Pension increased to 1/3d. per diem for service in the Enrolled Force
31 Jan 1882	Granted Fee Simple Perth Town Lot 35/H
1897	Residing Murray St Perth
June 1897	Residing Perth
11 Oct 1898	Died

Service and Personal Details:

Place of Birth:	St Anns Cork	
Age on Enlistment:	17 years	
Period of Service:	1851 — 1855	
Age on Discharge:	22 years or 20 years 8 months	
Length of Service:	2 years 259 days	
Foreign Service:	North America	1 year 43 days
	Crimea	232 days
Medal Entitlement:	Crimea with clasps [according to Obituary awarded Turkish Crimea medal and clasps for Sebastopol, Balaclava, Inkerman' Alma]	
Reason for Discharge:	Disabled for service by gunshot wound	
Character:	Very Good	
Trade or Occupation:	Labourer	
Can Sign Name:	Yes	
Height:	5' 8"	
Hair Colour:	Dark Brown	
Eyes:	Grey	
Complexion:	Fresh	
Remarks:	Wounded at Inkerman	
Intends to Reside:	Cork	

HALL — Charles, private EIC
Bengal European Infantry
Out Pension No 280

1 July 1846	Discharged the Service
1846	Embarked UK per *'Queen'*
	Pension paid 1st East London Pension District 9d. per diem
7 Feb 1853	Arrived per *'Dudbrook'*
1853	Employed by Convict Establishment
22 Aug 1853	Died

Service and Personal Details:

Where Born:	Hampshire
Trade or Occupation:	Labourer
Where Enlisted:	London
Presidency:	Bengal
Length of Service:	6 years 1 month
Age on Discharge:	30 years
Reason for Discharge:	Nearly blind from ophthalmia
Character:	Indifferent
Height:	5' 6¾"
Complexion:	Fresh
Visage:	Long
Eye Colour:	Grey
Hair Colour:	Brown

HALL — John, private
3rd Light Dragoons

Previous Regiments	10th Foot; 16th Lancers
9 Aug 1849	Medical Board's assessment accepted
20 Aug 1849	Discharge approved
28 Aug 1849	Discharged the Service Chatham

	Pension paid Sheffield District
	10d. per diem
18 Oct 1851	Arrived per *'Minden'*
1854	Pension paid Western Australia
Jan 1857	Contributed 2/6 to the Florence Nightingale Fund
1858	Pension paid Calcutta District
1868	Sheffield
1870	Melbourne
1874	Victoria

Service and Personal Details:

Place of Birth:	Lincoln
Age on Enlistment:	18 years
Period of Service:	1823 — 1849
Age on Discharge:	45 years
Length of Service:	21 years 201 days
Foreign Service:	East Indies & Afghanistan 19 years 4 months
Medal Entitlement:	Campaign in Afghanistan 1838/1839; the assault and capture of Ghuznee at Maharajpore 1843; Sutlej 1846 with clasps
Reason for Discharge:	Broken constitution from long Indian service; [possibly wounded by a spear in the left hip at Aliwal]
Conduct:	Very Good
Trade or Occupation:	Weaver
Can Sign name:	Yes
Height:	5' 8"
Hair Colour:	Grey
Eye Colour:	Grey
Complexion:	Sallow
Remarks:	22nd June 1872 — W.O. correspondence the "A31" - to man "no record of wounds"
Intends to Reside:	Lincoln in the County of Lincoln but decided on Barnsley Yorkshire
Marriage Details:	Bengal Ecclesiastical Returns At Meerut 9 Oct 1845 John Hall aged 39 bachelor HM 16th Lancers married by banns Charlotte Wilson neé Collier aged 34 widow, an Indo-British born 14th April 1810, daughter of William Collier, Corporal HM 24th Light Dragoons and a native woman

HALL	William, private
	78th Foot
22 Dec 1860	Discharged the Service Chatham
	Pension paid Jersey
	8d. per diem
1860	Pension paid East London
1862	Pension paid Bermuda
15 Feb 1863	Arrived per *'Merchantman'* [1]
Oct 1864	To South Australia from Fremantle per *'Sea Ripple'*

1869	Pension paid Victoria
1881	W.O. correspondence — "A31" with comment "cannot entertain such application after lapse of so many years"

Service and Personal Details:		
Place of Birth:	Barony Glasgow Lanarkshire	
Age on Enlistment:	24 years	
Period of Service:	1845 — 1860	
Age on Discharge:	39 years 9 months	
Length of Service:	15 years 226 days	
Foreign Service:	East Indies	13 years 9 months
Medal Entitlement:	Persian Campaign of 1857; Indian Mutiny	
Reason for Discharge:	Constitutional debility the result of long service in a tropical climate	
Character:	Good	
Trade or Occupation:	Shoemaker	
Can Sign Name:	Yes	
Height:	5' 8¼"	
Hair Colour:	Black	
Eyes:	Hazel	
Complexion:	Dark	
Intends to Reside:	14 Shuttle Street Glasgow	

HALL	Wilson, private
	77th Foot
3 July 1855	Discharged the Service Chatham
	Pension paid Ballymena
	8d. per diem
1860	Pension paid Edinburgh
1860	Ballymena
15 Apr 1864	Arrived per *'Clara'* [2]
	[according to son Robert's reminiscences his father joined the police force and posted to Northampton then some years later to Geraldton]
1873	Pension increased to 1/- per diem for 7 years service in the Enrolled Force
Apr 1876	Charged with assaulting his wife
Mar 1878	Sold freehold property, [possibly situated near Russell Square where he ran a dairy business] also 3 milch cows, 2 horses and a cart
25 Oct 1879	Died suddenly of apoplexy

Service and Personal Details:		
Place of Birth:	Ballymena Co. Antrim	
Age on Enlistment:	17 years 6 months	
Period of Service:	1853 — 1855	
Age on Discharge:	19 years 1 month	
Length of Service:	1 year 79 days	
Foreign Service:	Turkey & Crimea	10 months
Medal Entitlement:	Crimea with clasps	
Reason for Discharge:	Wound to elbow received at Inkerman	
Character:	Good	

Trade or Occupation:	Weaver
Can Sign Name:	Yes
Height:	5' 5"
Hair Colour:	Fair
Eyes:	Grey
Complexion:	Fresh

HAMILTON

	George, gunner and driver RA 6th Battalion
13 Apr 1852	Discharged the Service Woolwich Pension paid Woolwich 1/- per diem
18 July 1855	Arrived per *'Adelaide'* [see newspaper 6 Feb 1932]
1855	Employed as Warder at Pinjarra, Harvey, Sawyer's Valley and Mahogany Creek [see newspaper 6 Feb 1932]
23 Jan 1864	The undersigned begs to inform the public of Fremantle and Perth, that he will not be answerable for any debts contracted by persons in his name after this date. signed George Hamilton Harvey Bridge
1865	Pension paid Western Australia
May 1890	Died aged 78 buried East Perth Pioneer Cemetery

Service and Personal Details:

Place of Birth:	West Church Edinburgh	
Age on Enlistment:	18 years	
Period of Service:	1830 — 1852	
Age on Discharge:	39 years 7 months	
Length of Service:	21 years 197 days	
Foreign Service:	Gibraltar	9 years 5 months
	Jamaica	4 years 11 months
Reason for Discharge:	Chronic Rheumatism	
Character:	Very Good	
Trade or Occupation:	Labourer	
Can Sign Name:	Yes	
Height:	5' 11"	
Hair Colour:	Dark Brown	
Eyes:	Blue	
Complexion:	Dark	
Married:	Eliza Delaney 1834 Gibraltar	
Children:	William George bp. 1835 Gibraltar James Alexander bp. 1836 Gibraltar Charlotte Elizabeth bp. 1839 Gibraltar Thomas Wilson b. *c*1843 England m. *c*1872 Rachel Corrigan Perth Archibald b. 1845 England	

the following marriage entry may not necessarily refer to George Hamilton RA

Married:	Tabitha wife of a George Hamilton d. *c*1867 aged 39

Married:	*c*1868 Christina Pearse Fremantle [wife of John Persse [sic] arrived per '*Lincelles*']
HAMILTON	James, Corporal 65th Foot
3 June 1844	Discharged the Service Mullingar
6 Aug 1844	Admitted to Out-Pension Pension paid Glasgow 1/4d. per diem
1847	Pension paid Drogheda
1847	Longford
1849	Cavan
28 June 1851	Arrived per *'Pyrenees'* [1]
1852	Stationed Kojonup
1854	Longford
1856	2nd Glasgow Pension District
1856	1st Glasgow Pension District
1857	Enniskillen
1857	Sligo
1861	Londonderry
Service and Personal Details:	
Place of Birth:	Bothwell Hamilton Lanarkshire
Age on Enlistment:	17 years
Period of Service:	1822 — 1844
Age on Discharge:	39 years 5 months
Length of Service:	21 years 152 days
Foreign Service:	West Indies 8 years North America 3 years 6 months
Reason for Discharge:	Unfit for further service
Character:	Good, Trustworthy and Obedient
Trade or Occupation:	Weaver
Can Sign Name:	Yes
Height:	5' 6"
Hair Colour:	Fair
Eyes:	Blue
Complexion:	Fresh
HAMILTON	John, private 97th Foot
22 July 1856	Discharged the Service Chatham Pension paid Armagh 8d. per diem
1861	Pension paid Belfast
1861	Liverpool
27 Aug 1861	Pension increased to 10d. per diem
1862	Pension paid Armagh
1862	Bermuda
15 Feb 1863	Arrived per *'Merchantman'* [1]
1865	To Adelaide from Western Australia
1867	Pension paid Melbourne
1868	Pension paid 1st East London Pension District
1868	2nd North London Pension District

Service and Personal Details:	
Place of Birth:	Armagh Co. Armagh
Age on Enlistment:	17 years 6 months
Period of Service:	1853 — 1856
Age on Discharge:	20 years 6 months
Length of Service:	2 years 135 days
Foreign Service:	Greece 5 months
	Crimea 1 year 1 month
Medal Entitlement:	Crimea with clasp
Reason for Discharge:	Gunshot wound to the right forearm
Character:	Good
Trade or Occupation:	Labourer
Can Sign Name:	Yes
Height:	5' 6"
Hair Colour:	Light Brown
Eyes:	Hazel
Complexion:	Fresh
Intends to Reside:	Caledon [sic] Co. Armagh

HAMMOND	John, private [Military Pensioner]
	96th Foot
22 Feb 1847	Arrived per *'Java'* with regiment
?1847	Pensioner John Hammond - Grant of Land as Pensioner, [SRO]
15 May 1849	Discharged the Service Perth Western Australia
13 Nov 1849	Discharge approved
	7d. per diem for 18 months
9 Aug 1852	a John Hamond [sic] appointed Constable Police Force Perth
	Pension paid Perth Western Australia
circa 1863	Residing in the Pinjarrah area
29 May 1875	aged 50
1882	Employed as a teamster for Mr Dearden
18 June 1884	Deferred Pension forms sent to S.O. Perth W.A.
Sept 1892	Died at Northam in his 67th years. Cause of death a fall of earth

Service and Personal Details:	
Place of Birth:	Tibbenham Norfolk
Age on Enlistment:	18 years
Period of Service:	1843 — 1847
Age on Discharge:	24 years
Length of Service:	6 years 3 days
Foreign Service:	Australia 5 years 6 months
Reason for Discharge:	Subject to Epileptic Fits
Character:	Good
Trade or Occupation:	Labourer
Can Sign Name:	Yes
Height:	5' 8"
Hair Colour:	Brown
Eyes:	Brown
Complexion:	Dark
Intends to Reside:	Western Australia

HAMMOND	Thomas, private
	80th Foot
Surname Variant	HAMMONDS
12 Oct 1847	Discharged the Service Chatham
	Pension paid Wolverhampton
	1/- per diem
1 June 1850	Arrived per *'Scindian'*
Jan 1857	Contributed 2/- to the Florence Nightingale Fund
4 July 1875	Died
Service and Personal Details:	
Place of Birth:	Wolverhampton Staffordshire
Age on Enlistment:	17 years
Period of Service:	1825 — 1847
Age on Discharge:	39 years
Length of Service:	20 years 344 days
Foreign Service:	New South Wales 4 years 2 months
	Mediterranean 3 years 11 months
Reason for Discharge:	Chronic Rheumatism; Chronic Dyspnoea and Chronic Catarrh
Character:	Good
Trade or Occupation:	Locksmith
Can Sign Name:	Yes
Height:	5' 7¾"
Hair Colour:	Brown
Eyes:	Grey
Complexion:	Sallow
Intends to Reside:	Wolverhampton

HANCOCK	David, private
	45th Foot
Sept 1850	Discharged the Service
	Pension paid 2nd West London
	7d. per diem for 3 years to 1/10/1853
7 Feb 1853	Arrived per *'Dudbrook'*
1 Oct 1853	Pension ceased
1859	Conductor of Commissariat stores at Fremantle
1889	Retired
Mar 1900	Died of senile decay at his residence at Attwell Street Fremantle
Service and Personal Details:	
Place of Birth:	Kensington London Middlesex
Period of Service:	1839 — 1850
Age on Discharge:	29 years
Foreign Service:	South Africa 7 years

HANLEY	Edward, private
	65th Foot
Surname Variants	HANDLEY; HANLY
3 June 1844	Discharged the Service Mullingar
29 July 1844	Discharge approved
6 Aug 1844	Admitted to Out-Pension

	Pension paid Tullamore	
	8d. per diem	
6 Apr 1854	Arrived per *'Sea Park'*	
1855	Charged with military offence	
Service and Personal Details:		
Place of Birth:	Hartleagh Roscommon	
Age on Enlistment:	16 years	
Period of Service:	1825 — 1844	
Age on Discharge:	34 years 6 months	
Length of Service:	16 years 148 days	
Foreign Service:	West Indies	5 years 11 months
	North America	3 years 6 months
Reason for Discharge:	Recurrent and Intermittent Fever	
Character:	Good	
Trade or Occupation:	Labourer	
Can Sign Name:	Yes	
Height:	5' 5"	
Hair Colour:	Light Brown	
Eyes:	Blue	
Complexion:	Fresh	

HANLEY	William, Corporal	
	55th Foot	
Surname Variant	HANDLEY	
27 Jan 1857	Discharged the Service Chatham	
	Pension paid Kilkenny	
	6d. per diem	
12 Sept 1864	Arrived per *'Merchantman'* [2]	
1866	Pension paid Adelaide from Fremantle	
Service and Personal Details:		
Place of Birth:	Borrisoleigh Co. Tipperary	
Age on Enlistment:	17 years 6 months	
Period of Service:	1854 — 1856	
Age on Discharge:	20 years 2 months	
Length of Service:	2 years 85 days	
Foreign Service:	Turkey & Crimea	2 years
	Mediterranean	4 months
Medal Entitlement:	Crimea with clasps	
Reason for Discharge:	Wounded in trenches before Sebastopol	
Character:	Good	
Trade or Occupation:	Baker	
Can Sign Name:	Yes	
Height:	5' 5½"	
Hair Colour:	Light Brown	
Eyes:	Grey	
Complexion:	Sallow	

HANNEY	James, private [Military Pensioner]
	Royal Sappers and Miners
Surname Variants	HANNAY; HANNY; HENNEY
8 Oct 1857	Discharged Fremantle Western Australia

Dec 1857	Discharge approved
June 1868	Granted Deferred Pension of 6d per diem
18 Apr 1880	A James Hanney formerly of Albany died in Poor House aged 65

Service and Personal Details:

Place of Birth:	Oakhampton [sic]	
Age on Enlistment:	23 years 4 months	
Period of Service:	1841 — 1857	
Age on Discharge:	39 years 4 months	
Length of Service:	15 years 333 days	
Foreign Service:	Nova Scotia	6 years 9 months
	Western Australia	6 years
Reason for Discharge:	His having been granted a free discharge with Right of Registry for Deferred Pension of 6d per day upon attaining 50 years of age	
Character:	Latterly Very Good	
Trade or Occupation:	Miner	
Can Sign Name:	Yes	
Height:	5' 10"	
Hair Colour:	Brown	
Eyes:	Grey	
Complexion:	Florid	
Intends to Reside:	Albany King George Sound Western Australia	

HANNON Patrick, private

	95th Foot
Previous Regiment	99th Foot
Surname Variant	HANNAN
6 Nov 1846	Discharged the Service Tralee
28 Dec 1846	Discharge approved
12 Jan 1847	Admitted to Out-Pension
	Pension paid 2nd Dublin Pension District
	1/- per diem
2 Feb 1853	Embarked per *'Pyrenees'* as a Convict Guard
	"Died on voyage out"
	Cause of Death — Typhus fever

Service and Personal Details:

Place of Birth:	St Michaels Limerick
Age on Enlistment:	18 years
Period of Service:	1825 — 1846
Age on Discharge:	39 years 2 months
Length of Service:	21 years 66 days
Reason for Discharge:	Rheumatism
Character:	Most Exemplary
Trade or Occupation:	Tailor
Can Sign Name:	X his mark on discharge
Height:	5' 6"
Hair Colour:	Light Brown
Eyes:	Blue
Complexion:	Fresh

HARDY	John, private	
	77th Foot	
24 Dec 1863	Discharged the Service Chatham	
12 Jan 1864	Admitted to Out-Pension	
	Pension paid Ballymena	
	10d. per diem	
4 July 1866	Arrived per *'Belgravia'*	
no date	Assigned Freshwater Bay Loc 1059	
June 1901	Died aged 78	
1901	Grant of Probate	
Service and Personal Details:		
Place of Birth:	?Waterclony Co. Antrim	
Age on Enlistment:	18 years	
Period of Service:	1842 — 1863	
Age on Discharge:	39 years 6 months	
Length of Service:	21 years 9 days [reckoned]	
Foreign Service:	Mediterranean &	
	Crimea	2 years 4 months
	New South Wales &	
	East Indies	4 years 7 months
Medal Entitlement:	Crimea with clasps; Turkish War medal	
Reason for Discharge:	Own request having served 21 years	
Character:	Good	
Trade or Occupation:	Labourer	
Can Sign Name:	Yes	
Height:	5' 6"	
Hair Colour:	Black	
Eyes:	Brown	
Complexion:	Dark	
Intends to Reside:	?Ahogill nr. Ballymena	
HARRICKS	Samuel, private	
	21st Foot	
Surname Variants	HARROCKS; HAWACKS; ERRICK	
21 Aug 1856	Discharged the Service Birr Barracks	
13 Oct 1856	Discharge approved	
21 Oct 1856	Admitted to Out-Pension	
	Pension paid Ipswich	
	6d. per diem	
24 Nov 1858	Arrived per *'Edwin Fox'*	
Service and Personal Details:		
Place of Birth:	St Peters Maldon Essex	
Age on Enlistment:	20 years 1 month	
Period of Service:	1838 — 1856	
Age on Discharge:	37 years 8 months	
Length of Service:	17 years 34 days	
Foreign Service:	East Indies	9 years
	"Army in the East"	8 months
Medal Entitlement:	Crimea with clasps	
Reason for Discharge:	Unfit for further service	
Character:	Indifferent but latterly improved	
Trade or Occupation:	Labourer	

Can Sign Name:	X his mark on discharge	
Height:	5' 7¼"	
Hair Colour:	Brown	
Eyes:	Blue	
Complexion:	Fair	
Intends to Reside:	Ipswich Suffolk	

HARRIS	John, private	
	5th Foot	
26 May 1845	Discharged the Service Belfast	
9 Sept 1845	Admitted to Out-Pension	
	Pension paid 1st Manchester Pension District	
	6d. per diem	
21 May 1851	Arrived per *'Mermaid'*	
1851	Assigned Fremantle Lot P19	
9 July 1870	Medical Board — ref Pensioner John Harris, late of the 5th Regiment, consider him to be of unsound mind.	
1870	Died aged 58	
Service and Personal Details:		
Place of Birth:	Manchester Lancaster	
Age on Enlistment:	19 years	
Period of Service:	1831 — 1845	
Age on Discharge:	33 years 1 month	
Length of Service:	13 years 283 days	
Foreign Service:	Gibraltar	3 years 11 months
	Malta	2 years 5 months
	Ionian Isles	5 years
Reason for Discharge:	Chronic Catarrh	
Character:	Good	
Trade or Occupation:	Cooper	
Can Sign Name:	Yes	
Height:	5' 10"	
Hair Colour:	Fair	
Eyes:	Blue	
Complexion:	Fresh	

HARRIS	John, private	
	97th Foot	
8 Aug 1848	Discharged the Service Chatham	
	Pension paid Trowbridge	
	1/- per diem	
1 June 1850	Arrived per *'Scindian'*	
Aug 1850	Assigned South Perth Pensioner Loc P14	
Feb 1869	Died	
Service and Personal Details:		
Place of Birth:	Pewsey Wiltshire	
Age on Enlistment:	18 years	
Period of Service:	1824 — 1848	
Age on Discharge:	none given	
Length of Service:	23 years 334 days	
Foreign Service:	East Indies	11 years 32 days

	Mediterranean 7 years
Reason for Discharge:	Worn out from age and long military service
Character:	Good
Trade or Occupation:	Labourer
Can Sign Name:	Yes
Height:	5' 5½"
Hair Colour:	Sandy
Eyes:	Grey
Complexion:	Fair
Remarks:	Right thumb partially disabled by whitlow

HARRIS

	Thomas, private
	40th Foot
6 June 1857	Discharged the Service Belfast
27 July 1857	Discharge approved
4 Aug 1857	Admitted to Out-Pension
	Pension paid Oxford
	11d. per diem
19 Aug 1859	Arrived per *'Sultana'*
14 Dec 1864	Died aged 48
	"£36/18/5½ for Silver Medal Clasp due to this man paid to Mr Rawlins"

Service and Personal Details:

Place of Birth:	St Thomas Oxford
Age on Enlistment:	18 years 6 months
Period of Service:	1834 — 1857
Age on Discharge:	41 years 2 months
Length of Service:	22 years 330 days
Foreign Service:	East Indies 10 years 6 months
Medal Entitlement:	Afghanistan and Star for Maharajpore
Reason for Discharge:	Chronic Hepatitis
Character:	Good
Trade or Occupation:	Labourer
Can Sign Name:	Yes
Height:	5' 11"
Hair Colour:	Light Brown
Eyes:	Grey
Complexion:	Fresh
Intends to Reside:	St Thomas Oxford

HARRIS

	William, Corporal
	53rd Foot
Previous Regiment	39th Foot
22 July 1851	Discharged the Service Chatham
	Pension paid 1st East London Pension District
	6d. per diem
14 Aug 1854	Arrived per *'Ramillies'*
1863	To South Australia from Perth West Australia
1864	Pension paid South Australia
18 June 1875	Died

Service and Personal Details:

Place of Birth:	Whitechapel London	
Age on Enlistment:	20 years 3 months	
Period of Service:	1839 — 1851	
Age on Discharge:	33 years	
Length of Service:	11 years 216 days	
Foreign Service:	East Indies	11 years 1 month
Reason for Discharge:	Epileptic disorder	
Character:	Very Good	
Trade or Occupation:	Tailor	
Can Sign Name:	Yes	
Height:	5' 6"	
Hair Colour:	Black	
Eyes:	Hazel	
Complexion:	Fresh	
Intends to Reside:	New Street, White Chapel London	

HARRIS	William, private
	RM
24 Nov 1858	Pension paid 1st Plymouth Pension District
30 June 1859	Departed Plymouth for Western Australia
19 Aug 1859	Arrived per *'Sultana'*
	£15/4/- per annum
1871	Pension paid South Australia
Service and Personal Details:	
Place of Birth:	North Tawton nr. Okehamptom
Age on Attestation:	20 years
Marine Division:	Plymouth [Stonehouse] Division
Period of Service:	1852 — 1857
Length of Service:	5 years 233 days
Reason for Discharge:	Bronchitis and Phthsis [sic] contracted during service
Trade or Occupation:	Farm labourer
Can Sign Name:	Yes
Character:	Good
Remarks:	On discharge was patient in the RN Hospital
Height:	5' 8½"
Hair Colour:	Brown
Eyes:	Grey
Complexion:	Fresh

HART	Patrick, private [430]
	51st Foot
25 Jan 1848	Discharged the Service Chatham
	Pension paid Tullamore
	1/- per diem
21 May 1851	Arrived per *'Mermaid'*
Sept 1851	Assigned and occupied North Fremantle Lot P4
Mar 1853	Employed by Convict establishment
1853	Left colony without permission
	Pension suspended. "Pension not drawn from 1/6/53. Left colony without leave"
1858	Pension paid Melbourne

Service and Personal Details:

Place of Birth:	Killeigh Offaly Kings Country
Age on Enlistment:	18 years
Period of Service:	1825 — 1848
Age on Discharge:	40 years or 39 years
Length of Service:	21 years 44 days
Foreign Service:	Ionian Islands 7 years
	New South Wales 10 years
	[or Van Dieman's Land depending on record source]
Reason for Discharge:	Chronic Rheumatism and Shortness of Breath
Character:	Latterly Good
Trade or Occupation:	Labourer
Height:	5' 6"
Hair Colour:	Brown
Eyes:	Grey
Complexion:	Fair
Remarks:	Embarked for New South Wales Sept. 1838

HATFIELD George, private

	RM
Nov 1839	Discharged the Service
	? £4/12/- per annum
21 May 1851	Arrived per *'Mermaid'*
1853	Employed as Night Warder
1855	Pension paid South Australia
1858	Pension paid Victoria
1888	Died at Gildan Kew Victoria

Service and Personal Details:

Place of Birth:	Dewsbury West Yorkshire
Age on Attestation:	22 years
Marine Division:	Woolwich
Period of Service:	1828 — 1839
Length of Service:	9 years ?nine months 5 days
Reason for Discharge:	Invalided

HAWKINS John, gunner and driver

	RA 2nd Battalion
22 June 1852	Discharge approved
13 July 1852	Discharged the Service Woolwich
	Pension paid Omagh
	1/- per diem
10 Sept 1856	Arrived per *'Runnymede'*
1859	To South Australia from Western Australia
1885	Died

Service and Personal Details:

Place of Birth:	Omagh Co Tyrone
Age on Enlistment:	18 years 3 months
Period of Service:	1831 — 1852
Age on Discharge:	39 years 7 months
Length of Service:	21 years 113 days
Foreign Service:	Gibraltar 1 year 11 months
Reason for Discharge:	Chronic Rheumatism

Character:	Exemplary
Trade or Occupation:	Labourer
Can Sign Name:	Yes
Height:	5' 9½"
Hair Colour:	Dark Brown
Eyes:	Dark Brown
Complexion:	Fair

HAY James, Corporal

	12th Foot
Previous Regiments	88th Foot; Madras Horse Artillery
18 Dec 1866	Discharged the Service Gosport
	Pension paid 1st Glasgow Pension District
	11d. per diem
1866	Pension paid Woolwich
13 July 1867	Arrived per *'Norwood'* [2]
1867	Died aged 40 [AVRI]

Service and Personal Details:

Place of Birth:	Barony Glasgow	
Age on Enlistment:	18 years [EIC]	
Period of Service:	1860 — 1866 [in Imperial British Army]	
Age on Discharge:	36 years	
Length of Service:	18 years 10 days	
Foreign Service:	East Indies	12 years
Reason for Discharge:	Rheumatism	
Character:	Very Good	
Trade or Occupation:	Engineer	
Can Sign Name:	Yes	
Height:	5' 6¾"	
Hair Colour:	Brown	
Eyes:	Grey	
Complexion:	Dark	
Intends to Reside:	Glasgow	

HAYDEN James, Serjeant

	10th Foot
Surname Variants	HAYDON; HEYDEN
9 Oct 1849	Discharged the Service Chatham
1849	Pension paid Clonmel
	1/1½d. per diem
25 Oct 1850	Arrived per *'Hashemy'*
1850	Employed as gaoler York
Nov 1852	Assigned Pensioner Lot P9 at York
Jan 1857	Contributed 3/- to the Florence Nightingale Fund
May 1859	Application for Title to P9 at York
1864	Serjeant J Hayden Pensioner Force at York contributed to the Greenough Fire Relief Fund
1866	To Perth to be treated for facial cancer
1880	Died York Western Australia

Service and Personal Details:

Place of Birth:	City of Dublin Dublin
Age on Enlistment:	16 years

Period of Service:	1825 — 1849	
Age on Discharge:	40 years 3 months	
Length of Service:	22 years 120 days	
Foreign Service:	Portugal	1 year 3 months
	Ionian Isles	10 years
Reason for Discharge:	Chronic Rheumatism and Dyspnoea	
Conduct:	Very Good	
Trade or Occupation:	Labourer	
Can Sign Name:	Yes	
Height:	5' 5½"	
Hair Colour:	Grey	
Eye Colour:	Grey	
Complexion:	Fresh	
Intends to Reside:	Tipperary	

HAYES Edward, private
60th Foot

Surname Variant	HAYS	
17 Oct 1845	Discharged the Service Chatham	
11 Nov 1845	Admitted to Out-Pension	
	Pension paid 1st Manchester Pension District	
	1/- per diem	
2 Apr 1856	Arrived per *'William Hammond'*	
Jan 1857	a private E Hays contributed 2/- to the Florence Nightingale Fund	
1857	Pension paid Sydney	

Service and Personal Details:

Place of Birth:	St Johns Limerick	
Age on Enlistment:	18 years	
Period of Service:	1824 — 1845	
Age on Discharge:	39 years	
Length of Service:	20 years 309 days	
Foreign Service:	Portugal	1 year 4 months
	Gibraltar &	
	Malta &	
	Ionian Isles	9 years 9 months
Reason for Discharge:	Chronic Rheumatism	
Character:	Very Good	
Trade or Occupation:	Labourer	
Can Sign Name:	Yes	
Height:	5' 7"	
Hair Colour:	Dark	
Eyes:	Grey	
Complexion:	Swarthy	
Intends to Reside:	?Killaloo Co. Clare	

HAYES John, gunner EIC
3rd Troop, 2nd Brigade Artillery

Surname Variant	HAYS
Out Pension No 347	
2 Aug 1854	Admitted to Out-pension
	Pension paid 2nd North London Pension District

	9d. per diem
29 Jan 1862	Arrived per *'Lincelles'*
1863	Pension paid Sydney New South Wales

Service and Personal Details:

Place of Birth:	London
Trade or Occupation:	Labourer
Length of Service:	7 years 1 month
Age on Discharge:	29 years
Reason for Discharge:	Pleuropneumonia the result of an injury received on duty
Character:	Good or Fair
Height:	5' 9" or 5' 6"
Complexion:	Sallow or Fresh
Visage:	Oval
Eye Colour:	Hazel
Hair Colour:	Light Brown
Intends to Reside:	Bloomsbury London

HAYES Joseph, private EIC
2nd Bombay European Light Infantry

Surname Variant	HAYS
Out Pension No 305	
29 Aug 1849	Admitted to Out-pension Pension paid 1st East London Pension District 9d. per diem
7 Dec 1853	Arrived per *'Dudbrook'*
22 June 1854	Died of epilepsy at Port Gregory

Service and Personal Details:

Place of Birth:	St Cuthberts Somerset
Trade or Occupation:	Labourer
Presidency:	Bombay
Length of Service:	9 years 3 months
Age on Discharge:	27 years
Reason for Discharge:	Chronic hepatitis and Bronchitis and wound in right arm from matchlock ball
Character:	Good
Height:	5' 9½" or 5' 8½"
Complexion:	Fresh
Visage:	Oval
Eye Colour:	Grey
Hair Colour:	Light Brown
Intends to Reside:	St Marys Axe London
Married:	Elizabeth
Children:	Phoebe b. 1849
Joseph b. 1851 England	

HAYES Patrick, private
10th Foot

Surname Variants	HAYS; HAYNES
9 July 1850	Discharged the Service Chatham 10d. per diem
1854	Pension increased to 1/- per diem

1854	Pension paid Fermoy
1850	Tralee
1855	Cork
1855	Fermoy
1857	Liverpool
1857	Limerick
1857	Clonmel
1858	Kilkenny
1861	Galway
1861	Athlone
1861	Kilkenny
27 May 1863	Arrived per *'Clyde'*
1863	Pension paid Western Australia
1881	Allocated Perth Lot 275/Y [Wanneroo Road] Pension increased to 1/6d. per diem for 16 years service in the Enrolled Force
25 Sept 1883	Assigned for North Fremantle Lot P84 in lieu of Perth Lot 275/Y [Wanneroo Road]
1884	Granted Title to North Fremantle Lot P84
1886	Died

Service and Personal Details:

Place of Birth:	Castletown Roche Co. Cork
Age on Enlistment:	18 years
Period of Service:	1839 — 1850
Age on Discharge:	29 years
Length of Service:	9 years 296 days
Foreign Service:	East Indies 7 years
Medal Entitlement:	Sutlej 1846; Mooltan 1848
Reason for Discharge:	a Tawar [native sabre] cut to left wrist
Character:	Indifferent
Trade or Occupation:	Labourer
Can Sign Name:	X his mark on discharge
Height:	5' 10"
Hair Colour:	Fair
Eyes:	Blue
Complexion:	Fresh
Remarks:	Severely wounded at Sobroan by gunshot to left leg. Severely wounded by sabre cut to left wrist at Mooltan
Intends to Reside:	Fermoy

HAYNES	Samuel, private 17th Foot
14 July 1846	Discharged the Service Chatham Pension paid Leicester 1/- per diem
18 Oct 1851	Arrived per *'Minden'*
28 June 1853	Died

Service and Personal Details:

Place of Birth:	Knighton Leicestershire
Age on Enlistment:	18 years
Period of Service:	1824 — 1846
Age on Discharge:	40 years
Length of Service:	21 years 95 days

Foreign Service:	New South Wales	5 years 4 months
	East Indies	9 years 5 months
Medal Entitlement:	Afghanistan; Ghuznee	
Reason for Discharge:	Chronic Rheumatism — unable to march	
Character:	Very Good	
Trade or Occupation:	Frame work knitter	
Can Sign Name:	Yes	
Height:	5' 6¾"	
Hair Colour:	Fair	
Eyes:	Grey	
Complexion:	Sallow	
Intends to Reside:	Leicester	

HAYTER Thomas, private
RM

Mar 1852	Discharged the Service Haslar Hospital
1858	a Thomas Hayter RM contributed to the Indian Relief Fund
1874	Died

Service and Personal Details:

Place of Birth:	Tisbury [sic] nr. Shaftsbury Wiltshire
Age on Attestation:	23 years 11 months
Marine Division:	Portsmouth
Period of Service:	1838 — 1852
Length of Service:	13 years 2 months 18 days
Reason for Discharge:	Phthisis and palpitations contracted during Service
Trade or Occupation:	Labourer
Can Sign Name:	Yes
Height:	5' 11"
Hair Colour:	Brown
Eyes:	Grey
Complexion:	Fair

HAYWARD Thomas, private
RM

Surname Variant	HAYWOOD
	£16/16/- per annum
2 Apr 1856	Possibly arrived per *'William Hammond'*
1856	"Charged with military offence"
1858	To South Australia from Western Australia

Service and Personal Details:

Place of Birth:	Worcestershire
Age on Attestation:	22 years
Marine Division:	Plymouth
Period of Service:	1828 — 1850
Length of Service:	21 years 4 months 4 days
Reason for Discharge:	Length of service
Trade or Occupation:	Servant
Can Sign Name:	Yes
Height:	5' 7¾"
Hair Colour:	Light Brown

Eyes:	Grey
Complexion:	Fresh

HEALY Thomas, private
11th Foot

Surname Variants	HEALEY; HALEY
23 Feb 1847	Discharged the Service Chatham Pension paid Chatham 1/- per diem
1847	Pension paid Tralee
31 Aug 1853	Arrived per *'Phoebe Dunbar'*
2 Nov 1853	Died [not verified]

Service and Personal Details:

Place of Birth:	Tralee Kerry
Age on Enlistment:	18 years
Period of Service:	1825 — 1847
Age on Discharge:	40 years or 39 years
Length of Service:	21 years 45days
Foreign Service:	Portugal & Corfu & North America 13 years 5 months
Reason for Discharge:	Chronic Catarrh, and Rheumatism
Character:	Very Good
Trade or Occupation:	Shoemaker
Can Sign Name:	Yes
Height:	5' 7"
Hair Colour:	Brown
Eyes:	Grey
Complexion:	Fresh
Intends to Reside:	Chatham

HEAPNY John, gunner EIC
Bengal Artillery

Surname Variants	HEAPLY; HEAPHY; HEARLY; HEALY; HEAPHY
Out Pension No 299	
1 Feb 1848	Admitted to Out-pension Pension paid 1st East London Pension District 9d. per diem
1852	Pension paid 2nd East London Pension District
7 Feb 1853	Arrived per *'Dudbrook'*
June 1853	Charged with military offence
1853	Employed in Convict Establishment without sanction of Staff Office Pension
Aug 1854	"Deserted — pension suspended"
1858	Pension paid Melbourne
26 Sept 1870	Died

Service and Personal Details:

Where Born:	Cork
Trade or Occupation:	Labourer
Where Enlisted:	Cork
Presidency:	Madras
Service Period:	Unlimited

Length of Service:	12 years 2 months
Age on Discharge:	32 years
Reason for Discharge:	Insanity
Character:	Good
Height:	5' 10"
Complexion:	Fresh
Visage:	Oval
Eye Colour:	Brown
Hair Colour:	Brown

HEARNS Patrick, Serjeant
77th Foot

Surname Variants	HEARN; HERN; HEARNES
3 May 1859	Discharged the Service Parkhurst IOW Pension paid Carlow 1/3½d. per diem
1861	Pension paid 2nd Dublin Pension District
31 Dec 1862	Arrived per *'York'*
1863	Employed in Convict Establishment
Feb 1874	Sister asking for his address
1875	Sister asking for information
1878	Died aged 61

Service and Personal Details:

Place of Birth:	Naas Co. Kildare	
Age on Enlistment:	22 years	
Period of Service:	1838 — 1859	
Age on Discharge:	43 years	
Length of Service:	21 years 12 days	
Foreign Service:	West Indies & North America	5 years 2 months
	Mediterranean	2 years 7 months
Eastern Expedition	11 months	
Medal Entitlement:	Crimea	
Reason for Discharge:	Own Request having served 21 years	
Character:	Good	
Trade or Occupation:	Shoemaker	
Can Sign Name:	Yes	
Height:	5' 8"	
Hair Colour:	Grey	
Eyes:	Hazel	
Complexion:	Sallow	
Intends to Reside:	Naas Kildare	

HEARNS see — KEARNS William, private
74th Foot

HEATHCOTE Isaac, private
Rifle Brigade 2nd Battalion

Previous Regiment	Rifle Brigade
26 Mar 1850	Discharged the Service Chatham Pension paid Sheffield 7d. per diem for 2 years
1851	Serving as Police Constable Stretford Chapelry

1851	Pension paid Manchester
18 Oct 1851	Arrived per *'Minden'*
1851	Employed as Night Warder
Dec 1852	Nearly killed by a wild bullock
1855	Unclaimed letter for him lying at the General Post Office Perth

Service and Personal Details:

Place of Birth:	Bakewell Derbyshire
Age on Enlistment:	22 years
Period of Service:	1841 — 1849
Age on Discharge:	30 years
Length of Service:	7 years 249 days
Foreign Service:	North America 6 years 10 month
Reason for Discharge:	Unfit for further service
Character:	Very Good
Trade or Occupation:	Bricklayer
Can Sign Name:	Yes
Height:	5' 7½"
Hair Colour:	Brown
Eyes:	Blue
Complexion:	Fresh
Distinguishing Marks:	Scar of a boil on left shoulder blade
Remarks:	Stationed Toronto

HENDERSON Richard, Serjeant EIC
Bombay Artillery
Out Pension No 423

15 Mar 1860	Admitted to Out-pension Pension paid 2nd Dublin Pension District 2/- per diem
1860	Pension paid Limerick Pension District
1862	Pension paid Woolwich
1862	Wales
1862	Sligo
1865	Liverpool
22 Dec 1865	Arrived per *'Vimiera'*
1867	Employed as Assistant Warder
13 Apr 1876	Died aged 55
21 Apr 1876	Mrs Margaret Henderson is the widow of Corporal Richard Henderson of the Enrolled Force, who died on the 13th Instant, and has 4 children, the eldest aged 13 years
13 June 1876	Margaret Henderson -widow. Required to sign a document agreeing to pay 10/- monthly from her wages for the upkeep of her children in the Protestant Orphanage. She declines to state any specific sum that she will pay towards the support of her children but states she would be willing to pay what she could afford as she doesn't know what she will earn

Service and Personal Details:

Where Born:	St Nicholas Dublin

Trade or Occupation:	Shoemaker
Age on Enlistment:	19 years
Date Enlisted:	6th Dec 1837
Embarked India:	per *'Sir Edward Paget'*
Presidency:	Bombay
Service Period:	Unlimited
Age on Discharge:	41 years
Length of Service:	21 years 10 months or 22 years
Period Served:	1837 — 1859
Reason for Discharge:	Time served admitted to pension
Character:	none annotated
Height:	5' 7¼"
Complexion:	Brown
Eye Colour:	Brown
Hair Colour:	Fair
Intends to Reside:	Dublin

HENNESSY

	Timothy, private [Military Pensioner]
	97th Foot
Surname Variant	HENNESSEY
6 May 1856	Discharged the Service Chatham
	Pension paid Falmouth
	9d. per diem
1859	Pension paid Jersey
1862	2nd Plymouth Pension District
1871	1st East London Pension District
1873	Freemantle [sic]
1874	Brisbane
June 1809	W.O. correspondence to Brisbane

Service and Personal Details:

Place of Birth:	Calstock Cornwall	
Age on Enlistment:	18 years	
Period of Service:	1853 — 1856	
Age on Discharge:	21 years 8 months or 20 years 10 months	
Length of Service:	2 years 229 days	
Foreign Service:	Greece	168 days
	Crimea	11 months
Medal Entitlement:	Crimea with clasp	
Reason for Discharge:	Wounded by musket ball at the Redan	
Character:	Good	
Trade or Occupation:	Labourer	
Can Sign Name:	X his mark on discharge	
Height:	5' 6"	
Hair Colour:	Brown	
Eyes:	Grey	
Complexion:	Sallow	
Intends to Reside:	Falmouth Cornwall	

HENNESSY

	Richard, private
	37th Foot
26 Jan 1847	Discharged the Service Chatham
	Pension paid Wales West Pension District
	7d. per diem

1847	Pension paid 2nd Manchester Pension District
1850	Pension paid Clonmel
1854	Correspondence with War Office
10 Sept 1856	Arrived per *'Runnymede'*
3 July 1862	Died aged 49

Service and Personal Details:

Place of Birth:	Clonmel Co. Tipperary	
Age on Enlistment:	18 years 8 months	
Period of Service:	1831 — 1847	
Age on Discharge:	34 years 7 months	
Length of Service:	15 years 342 days	
Foreign Service:	Nova Scotia	7 months
Reason for Discharge:	Varicose Veins	
Character:	Good	
Trade or Occupation:	Groom	
Can Sign Name:	X his mark on Attestation	
Height:	5' 8"	
Hair Colour:	Brown	
Eyes:	Blue	
Complexion:	Fresh	
Intends to Reside:	Caremarthen [sic]	

HEPBURN David, private
42nd Foot

Surname Variant	HEBURN
26 Mar 1850	Discharged the Service Pension paid 1st Glasgow Pension District 1/- per diem
10 Sept 1856	Arrived per *'Runnymede'*
Oct 1864	To South Australia per *'Sea Ripple'*
1865	Pension paid South Australia

Service and Personal Details:

Place of Birth:	Maybole Ayrshire	
Age on Enlistment:	19 years	
Period of Service:	1825 — 1850	
Age on Discharge:	44 years	
Length of Service:	24 years 44 days	
Foreign Service:	Malta	4 years 20 days
	Ionian isles	2 years 92 days
	Bermuda	5 years 29 days
Reason for Discharge:	Chronic Rheumatism and impaired vision	
Character:	Good	
Trade or Occupation:	Weaver	
Can Sign Name:	Yes	
Height:	5' 7"	
Hair Colour:	Grey	
Eyes:	Grey	
Complexion:	Fair	
Intends to Reside:	Perth Scotland	

HERBERT Henry, private

	Royal African Colonial Corps
	Royal Newfoundland Veteran Company
Oct 1824	Serving in Royal African Colonial Corps
17 Jan 1827	Discharged from Royal Africa Colonial Corps
14 Dec 1847	Discharged the Service Chatham
	Pension paid Cambridge
	1/- per diem
1 June 1850	Arrived per *'Scindian'*
1850	Assigned Lot 5 Butler Swamp/Freshwater Bay
Jan 1857	Contributed 2/- to the Florence Nightingale Fund
1858	Application for Title Freshwater Bay Locs P225 & P245
1875	Pension paid Western Australia
Apr 1885	Died [aged 78 according to newspaper report]

Service and Personal Details:

Place of Birth:	Ocenbury [sic] Huntingdon	
Age on Enlistment:	18 years	
Period of Service:	1824 — 1847	
Age on Discharge:	42 years	
Length of Service:	20 years 164 days	
Foreign Service:	East Indies	2 years
	Newfoundland	2 years
Reason for Discharge:	Chronic Rheumatism	
Character:	Good	
Trade or Occupation:	Labourer	
Can Sign Name:	X his mark on discharge	
Height:	5' 6½"	
Hair Colour:	Brown	
Eyes:	Grey	
Complexion:	Pale	
Intends to Reside:	Huntingdon	
Married:	*c*1833 Ann Blake Rochester Kent	
Children:	Henry [possibly] b. *c*1845	
	m. *c*1866 Leah Hunt Greenough	
	Joseph	
	m. *c*1876 Elizabeth Parnham Upper Swan	

the following entry may not necessarily refer to a child of Henry Herbert RNVC

1841 UK census	at Fort Pitt Hospital Chatham Kent a William Herbert aged 5 who was born in the County

HERDMAN	William, gunner and driver
	RA Invalid Detachment
Surname Variant	HARDMAN
23 June 1848	Discharge approved
11 July 1848	Discharged the Service Plymouth
1 Aug 1848	Admitted to Out-Pension
	Pension paid 2nd Plymouth Pension District
	1/-½d. per diem
1851	Residing Octagon St Plymouth
18 Oct 1851	Arrived per *'Minden'*

1851	Employed in Convict Establishment
1862	William Hardman and George Curedale lessees of the Trust to Quarry limestone from the north side of the Swan River
Jan 1857	Contributed 2/6 to the Florence Nightingale Fund
1873	Pension increased to 1/3d. per diem for 5 years and 4 months service in the Enrolled Force of Western Australia
circa Dec 1875	Transferred from 1st Perth District to Fremantle Pension District
Jan 1877	Assigned North Fremantle Lot P 53
27 Sept 1878	Died

Service and Personal Details:		
Place of Birth:	Bolton Lancaster	
Age on Enlistment:	18 years	
Period of Service:	1826 — 1848	
Age on Discharge:	39 years 11 months	
Length of Service:	22 years 11 days	
Foreign Service:	Canada	1 year 11 months
Reason for Discharge:	Chronic Rheumatism	
Character:	Exemplary	
Trade or Occupation:	Engineer	
Can Sign Name:	Yes	
Height:	5' 10"	
Hair Colour:	Black	
Eyes:	Grey	
Complexion:	Dark	
Intends to Reside:	Stonehouse Devon	
Married:	1830 Ellen ?Dewren Woolwich Kent	
Children:	Margaret b. *c*1831 Woolwich Kent William b. *c*1834 d. c1842 East Stonehouse Thomas bp. 1833 Stoke Damerel Plymouth Ellen bp. 1837 Stoke Damerel Plymouth m. *c*1855 John Jackson Perth Joseph bp. 1839 Stoke Damerel Plymouth Julia b. 1840 Stoke Damerel Plymouth m. *c*1855 John Bridge Perth Mary Ann b. 1844 East Stonehouse Devon m. *c*1863 George Curedale Perth Elizabeth b. 1845 East Stonehouse Devon	
Married:	1848 Elizabeth Spry Tavistock Devon [b. *c*1816 Calstock Cornwall]	
Children:	Richard b. 1849 Plymouth Devon m. *c*1871 Maria Elsegood Guildford	

HERLIHY	Thomas, private 84th Foot
Surname Variants	HERLEHEY; HERLICHY; HERLIHEY
31 Jan 1860	Discharged the Service Chatham Pension paid 1st Cork Pension District 8d. per diem

1860	Pension paid 1st East London Pension District
1860	Pension paid Deptford
31 Dec 1862	Arrived per *'York'*
1864	To South Australia from Perth West Australia

Service and Personal Details:

Place of Birth:	Shandon Co. Cork	
Age on Enlistment:	19 years	
Period of Service:	1849 — 1859	
Age on Discharge:	29 years 1 month	
Length of Service:	10 years 21 days	
Foreign Service:	India	7 years 7 days
Medal Entitlement:	Indian Mutiny	
Reason for Discharge:	Gunshot wound to left shoulder received whilst on duty at the Relief of Lucknow	
Character:	Good	
Trade or Occupation:	Labourer	
Can Sign Name:	Yes	
Height:	5' 9"	
Hair Colour:	Black	
Eyes:	Hazel	
Complexion:	Fresh	
Intends to Reside:	No 60 ? Ever Green Cork	

HERRICK Patrick, private
81st Foot

Previous Regiment	73rd Foot
Surname Variants	HERRICKS; HARRICK; HARRICKS
6 Apr 1869	Discharged the Service Buttervant Pension paid Birr 1/1d. per diem
19 Feb 1874	Arrived per *'Naval Brigade'*
13 Apr 1881	General Orders: Pensioner Joseph Jarvis to be Private vice ptve P Harricks [sic] dismissed
Jan 1881	Pension increased to 1/3½d. per diem for service in the Enrolled Force
10 Mar 1883	Assigned North Fremantle Lot P92
19 Nov 1883	Occupying No. 1 Barracks Fremantle
29 Aug 1884	Granted Fee Simple North Fremantle Lot P92
1885	Cautioned for being drunk
18 Sept 1886	Joined Enrolled Guard at Fremantle
1892	Cautioned for being drunk
June 1897	Residing Fremantle
Feb 1900	a private P Herricks 73rd Foot attended fete at Fremantle Oval
1906	a Patrick Herricks died

Service and Personal Details:

Place of Birth:	Birr Kings County	
Age on Enlistment:	17 years 9 months	
Period of Service:	1848 — 1869	
Age on Discharge:	40 years	
Length of Service:	21 years 2 days	
Foreign Service:	Cape of Good Hope	6 years 229 days
East Indies	7 years 92 days	

Medal Entitlement:	Kaffir War and Indian Mutiny
Reason for Discharge:	His having claimed it on termination of 2nd period of "Limited Engagement"
Character:	Very Good
Trade or Occupation:	Labourer
Can Sign Name:	X his mark on discharge
Height:	5' 7"
Hair Colour:	Sandy going grey
Eyes:	Grey
Complexion:	Fresh
Intends to Reside:	Birr Co. Kings
Married:	1860 Eliza Sculthorpe nee Saunders India
Children:	Catherine b. 1862 Dinapore India

HERTNAN James, private [Military pensioner]
21st Foot

Surname Variants	HERMAN; HERTMAN
30 Mar 1836	Joined Detachment at Swan River
28 July 1841	Discharged to pension in West. Australia 6d per diem
1845	Pension paid Bunbury
1877	Died

Service and Personal Details:

Place of Birth:	Clerefort Galway
Period of Service:	1826 —1840
Age on Enlistment:	20 years [stated to be]
Age on Discharge:	34 years
Length of Service:	14 years 155 days
Foreign Service:	Van Dieman's Land & Swan River 6 years
Reason for Discharge:	Varicose Veins in the Legs
Character and Conduct:	A Good and Trustworthy soldier
Trade or Occupation:	Labourer
Can Sign Name:	Yes
Height:	5' 6"
Hair Colour:	Dark Brown
Eyes:	Grey
Complexion:	Fair

HEVERAN John, Corporal [1196]
80th Foot

Surname Variants	HAVERHAM; HAVERAM; HAVERAN; HAVERN
6 Apr 1858	Discharged the Service Chatham Pension paid 2nd Belfast Pension District 1/1½d. per diem
1858	Pension paid Armagh
9 June 1862	Arrived per *'Norwood'* [1]
1864	To South Australia from Perth West Australia
no date	W.O. correspondence - Deceased — "widow applies for Pegu Prize from South Australia

Service and Personal Details:	
Place of Birth:	St Marys Athlone Westmeath
Age on Enlistment:	18 years 6 months
Period of Service:	1835 —1858
Age on Discharge:	41 years 3 months
Length of Service:	21 years 149 days
Foreign Service:	New South Wales 7 years 6 months
	East Indies 9 years 5 months
Reason for Discharge:	Worn out from long service at home and abroad
Character:	Latterly Good
Trade or Occupation:	Labourer
Can Sign Name:	Yes
Height:	5' 6½"
Hair Colour:	Light Brown
Eyes:	Grey
Complexion:	Swarthy
Distinguishing Marks:	Scar on leg
Intends to Reside:	Belfast Co. Antrim

HEVRON	Denis, private
	15th Regiment
31 Jan 1851	Discharged the Service Kandy Ceylon
	Arrived per — ship not found
1854	Employed at Convict Establishment
Sept 1865	Attained age of 50 years
29 May 1866	Deferred pension ratified
1873	Pension increased to 7d. per diem for 2 years 4 months service in the Enrolled Force
1880	Died

Service and Personal Details:	
Place of Birth:	Newtown Lamavady Co. Derry
Age on Enlistment:	18 years
Period of Service:	1833 — 1851
Age on Discharge:	35 years 4 months
Length of Service:	17 years 124 days
Foreign Service:	Canada 2 years
	Ceylon 5 years
Reason for Discharge:	Claiming Free with a gratuity of £18/0/0 on settling at the Cape with the Right of Registry for a Deferred Pension of 6d. per day upon attaining 50 years of age after a period of 17 years served and in receipt of 3d. per diem
	Good Conduct pay and badges
Character:	Good
Trade or Occupation:	Shoemaker
Can Sign Name:	X his mark on discharge
Height:	6' 1½"
Hair Colour:	Dark Brown
Eyes:	Hazel
Complexion:	Swarthy

HEWARD	Clayton, private
	15th Hussars
12 Aug 1851	Discharged the Service Chatham
18 Aug 1851	Discharge approved
	Pension paid 1st West London Pension District
	6d. per diem paid until 2/9/1952
1 Jan 1852	Pension paid St Georges Sound.
	WO Letter No 12/1st West London/26
2 Sept 1852	Pension ceased
1872	Died aged 47 - ?buried East Perth Cemetery
Service and Personal Details:	
Place of Birth:	Long Melford Suffolk
Age on Enlistment:	21 years
Period of Service:	1847 — 1851
Age on Discharge:	24 years
Length of Service:	2 years 249 days
Foreign Service:	East Indies 1 year 312 days
Reason for Discharge:	Unfit for further service secondary syphilis and cardiac disease
Character:	Good, Trustworthy and Sober
Trade or Occupation:	Draper
Can Sign Name:	Yes
Height:	5' 5¾"
Hair Colour:	Dark Brown
Eyes:	Grey
Complexion:	Fresh
Intends to Reside:	Notting Hill Kensington London

HEXTALL	William, Serjeant
	2nd/24th Foot
Previous Regiments	46th; 45th
13 Mar 1861	Discharged the Service Cork
2 Apr 1861	Admitted to Out-Pension
	Pension paid Coventry
	1/2½d. per diem
1862	Pension paid Sheffield
15 Apr 1864	Arrived per *'Clara'* [2]
1866	To Adelaide from Perth Western Australia
Jan 1867	Gave evidence to support Charles Stretch
1870	Pension paid Bengal
Service and Personal Details:	
Place of Birth:	Hinkley Leicestershire
Age on Enlistment:	17 years 9 months
Period of Service:	1839 — 1861
Age on Discharge:	39 years
Length of Service:	21 years
Foreign Service:	Cape of Good Hope 11 years 1 month
Medal Entitlement:	Long Service and Good Conduct with gratuity
Reason for Discharge:	Having completed 21 years and being on the permanent Staff of Warwick Regiment of Militia
Character:	Good
Trade or Occupation:	Labourer

Can Sign Name:	Yes
Height:	5' 9"
Hair Colour:	Grey
Eyes:	Blue
Complexion:	Fresh
Intends to Reside:	Warwick

HEYLAND	John [Francis], Serjeant 87th Foot
Surname Variant	HYLAND
5 July 1870	Discharged the Service Pension paid Halifax 1/9d. per diem
1871	Militia Staff Officer Yorkshire
1873	Pension paid Greenwich
19 Feb 1874	Arrived per *'Naval Brigade'*
1876	Stationed Fremantle
c1875	Charged with maliciously wounding his wife through jealousy and sentenced to 3 months imprisonment. Pension suspended. Pension was consequently distributed to only a third suspended and the rest paid to wife otherwise wife and children would have starved
Aug 1877	Assigned Pensioner Loc 17 at Lake Munster
May 1881	Granted title to Pensioner Loc 17 at Lake Munster
1881	Recommended for £15 Pensioner's Grant
1881	Pension increased to 1/11½d. for service in the Enrolled Force of Western Australia
1884	John Hyland — applied for employment as Night Warder Rottnest Island
June 1897	Residing Fremantle
June 1905	The body of a John Francis Hyland was found lying in a hut at Robbs Jetty
1905	Died aged 73 buried in the Anglican section of Fremantle Cemetery

Service and Personal Details:		
Place of Birth:	Drumcliffe Cavan	
Age on Enlistment:	17 years	
Period of Service:	1848 — 1870	
Age on Discharge:	none given	
Length of Service:	21 years 10 days	
Foreign Service:	East Indies	10 years 8 months
	China	1 year 1 month
	Gibraltar	1 year 5 months
Medal Entitlement:	Indian Mutiny; ?China	
Reason for Discharge:	Completing a service qualifying for pension, while serving as a supernumerary with Militia	
Character:	Good	
Trade or Occupation:	Labourer	
Can Sign Name:	Yes	
Height:	5' 8¾"	
Hair Colour:	Dark Brown	

Eyes:	Hazel
Complexion:	Freckled
Intends to Reside:	Pontefract Yorkshire
Married:	Mary Anne Caffrey; McCaffrey or Snade
Children:	Rose Margaret b. *c*1868 Gibraltar m. *c*1884 George Riley Fremantle Lillian Jane b. 1871 Pontefract

HICKEY Patrick, private

	86th Foot
Previous Regiment	28th Foot
Surname Variant	HICKY
8 Aug 1865	Discharged the Service Templemore Pension paid Kilkenny 10d. per diem
4 July 1866	Arrived per *'Belgravia'*
1872	Pension to be suspended for 2 months for drunkenness and disorderly conduct
1873	"In prison" Convicted of drunkenness at Perth and sentenced to one month's imprisonment
1874	Pension suspended during imprisonment
25 Dec 1874	Found dead in a field close to his home

Service and Personal Details:

Place of Birth:	?Bansha Tipperary	
Age on Enlistment:	23 years	
Period of Service:	1843 — 1865	
Age on Discharge:	44 years 6 months	
Length of Service:	21 years 205 days	
Foreign Service:	India	14 years 9 months
Medal Entitlement:	Indian Mutiny with clasp	
Reason for Discharge:	Own Request having served 21 years	
Character:	Very Good	
Trade or Occupation:	Labourer	
Can Sign Name:	Yes	
Height:	5' 5½"	
Hair Colour:	Fair	
Eyes:	Blue	
Complexion:	Fair	
Intends to Reside:	Templemore Co. Tipperary	

HIGGINS Hugh, gunner

	RA Depot Brigade
19 July 1859	Discharged the Service Woolwich
8 Aug 1858	Discharge approved
16 Aug 1859	Admitted to Out-Pension
Pension paid Ballymena	
	8d. per diem
31 Dec 1862	Arrived per *'York'*
1864	ptve H Higgins Pensioner Force at Perth contributed to the Greenough Fire Relief Fund
1866	South Australia from Perth per' *Emily Smith'*
1866	Pension paid South Australia
1872	Applied to "Control Office" Adelaide

1873	Pension increased to 1/- per diem
1873	Pension paid Adelaide
1875	Convicted at Police Court Adelaide for an assault on Caroline [sic] Higgins. Sentenced to three months imprisonment and pension to be suspended to one half, the other half to wife
Feb 1875	Hugh Higgins was charged on the information of his wife Catherine with assaulting her. Sentenced to 3 months imprisonment with hard labour
1879	Hugh Higgins was charged with beating and attempting to take the life of his wife Catherine. Sentenced to one month imprisonment with hard labor
1883	Found drowned in the Torrens Lake

Service and Personal Details:

Place of Birth:	Ballymena Co. Antrim	
Age on Enlistment:	18 years	
Period of Service:	1855 — 1859	
Age on Discharge:	22 years	
Length of Service:	4 years 42 days	
Foreign Service:	Cape of Good Hope	5 months
	East Indies	1 year 7 months
Medal Entitlement:	Indian Mutiny	
Reason for Discharge:	When on duty at Lucknow on the March 1858 a bullet struck him in the face and neck.	
Character:	Very Good	
Trade or Occupation:	Weaver	
Can Sign Name:	Yes	
Height:	5' 6¾"	
Hair Colour:	Dark Brown	
Eyes:	Brown	
Complexion:	Fresh	
Remarks:	Severely wounded at the capture of Lucknow	

HIGGINS	William, private 38th Foot
12 Nov 1861	Discharged the Service Camp Colchester Pension paid 2nd Belfast Pension District 9d. per diem
9 Jan 1868	Arrived per *'Hougoumont'*
1869	Pension paid Calcutta
1870	Pension paid 2nd Belfast Pension District
1884	Correspondence with S.O. Armagh

Service and Personal Details:

Place of Birth:	Shankill Lurgan Armagh	
Age on Enlistment:	17 years	
Period of Service:	1839 — 1861	
Age on Discharge:	38 years 2 months	
Length of Service:	21 years 11 days	
Foreign Service:	Mediterranean	5 years 4 months
	Jamaica	2 years

	North America	3 years 3 months
	Turkey	4 months
	Crimea	1 year 2 months
	East Indies	2 years
Medal Entitlement:	Crimea with clasps; Turkish Crimea; Indian Mutiny with clasp	
Reason for Discharge:	Own request having served 21 years	
Character:	Good	
Trade or Occupation:	Weaver	
Can Sign Name:	Yes	
Height:	5' 8½"	
Hair Colour:	Brown	
Eyes:	Blue	
Complexion:	Fresh	
Intends to Reside:	Co. Armagh	

HILL	Robert, private 80th Foot	
Previous Regiments	30th; 9th; 24th	
5 Oct 1858	Discharged the Service Pension paid Bristol 8½d. per diem	
1859	Pension paid West Wales	
1859	Bristol	
11 Feb 1861	Arrived per *'Palmeston'*	
1865	Pension paid Western Australia	
1869	Madras	
1870	2nd West London Pension District	
1873	Bristol	
1873	Carlisle	
1873	2nd North London Pension District	
30 June 1876	Died	
Service and Personal Details:		
Place of Birth:	St Cuthberts Carlisle Cumberland	
Age on Enlistment:	17 years	
Period of Service:	1835 — 1858	
Age on Discharge:	40 years 4 months	
Length of Service:	21 years 354 days	
Foreign Service:	East Indies	16 years 3 months
Medal Entitlement:	Afghanistan; Sutlej Campaign with clasps; Central India with clasps	
Reason for Discharge:	Chronic Rheumatism	
Character:	Good	
Trade or Occupation:	Weaver	
Can Sign Name:	Yes	
Height:	5' 7"	
Hair Colour:	Brown	
Eyes:	Grey	
Complexion:	Fresh	

HILL	William, private 63rd Foot

4 June 1852	Discharged the Service Dublin
28 June 1852	Discharge approved
13 July 1852	Admitted to Out-Pension
	Pension paid 2nd Dublin Pension District
	1/- per diem
30 Apr 1853	Arrived per *'Pyrenees'* [2]
Jan 1857	Contributed 2/- to the Florence Nightingale Fund
1855	Applied [without permission from Col. Bruce] for position of Light House Keeper at Breaksea Island
1864	Disappeared from Breaksea Island
23 Mar 1864	"Found drowned in West Aust about this time"
18 Sept 1871	Albany Lot P13 purchased by widow Margaret Ann Learny [sic] – [Trove]
1872	Granted Title to Albany Suburban Lot P13 [Cons 5713]

Service and Personal Details:		
Place of Birth:	St Margarets Leicester	
Age on Enlistment:	18 years 9 months	
Period of Service:	1831 — 1852	
Age on Discharge:	39 years 6 months	
Length of Service:	20 years 312 days	
Foreign Service:	East Indies	13 years 6 months
	Van Dieman's Land	1 year 9 months
Reason for Discharge:	Chronic Rheumatism	
Conduct:	Good	
Trade or Occupation:	Shoemaker	
Can Sign name:	Yes	
Height:	5' 9½"	
Hair:	Black	
Eyes:	Brown	
Complexion:	Sallow	

HILLIEAR	James, private
	48th Foot
Surname Variants	HILLIER; HILLEEAR; HILLYAR; HELLYARD
19 Feb 1849	Discharged the Service Dublin
26 Mar 1848	Discharge approved
10 Apr 1849	Admitted to Out-Pension
	Pension paid Trowbridge
	7d. per diem for 3 years
18 Oct 1851	Arrived per *'Minden'*
1852	Pension ceased
*c*1854	a James Hillier found dead near Herdsman's Lake - ? buried East Perth Cemetery

Service and Personal Details:		
Place of Birth:	Marlborough Wiltshire	
Age on Enlistment:	18 years 1 months	
Period of Service:	1835 — 1849	
Age on Discharge:	32 years 8 months	
Length of Service:	13 years 269days	
Foreign Service:	Gibraltar	5 years 4 months
	West Indies	3 years 1 month
Reason for Discharge:	Chronic Cough and difficulty breathing	

Character:	Very Good
Trade or Occupation:	Labourer
Can Sign Name:	X his mark on discharge
Height:	5' 6½"
Hair Colour:	Dark
Eyes:	Light Grey
Complexion:	Fresh
Intends to Reside:	Burbridge Wiltshire
HINTHORNE	John, private 81st Foot
Surname Variants	HENTHORN; HEWTHORN; HINTON
26 Dec 1848	Discharged the Service Chatham Pension paid Liverpool 1/- per diem
1849	Pension paid Cavan
1849	Dublin
1849	Tullamore
2 Aug 1852	Arrived per *'William Jardine'*
1853	Employed in Convict Establishment
1854	Pension paid Western Australia
1856	Claim of £10 against Capt Foss
1857	Pension paid South Australia from Fremantle
1859	Victoria
circa 1860	Admitted as In-Pensioner Kilmainham
1870	Reverted to Out-Pension
1872	Admitted to In-Pension Chelsea Hospital
1873	"Died there-in"
Service and Personal Details:	
Place of Birth:	Larahe [sic] Co. Cavan
Age on Enlistment:	20 years
Period of Service:	1826 — 1848
Age on Discharge:	42 years 6 months
Length of Service:	22 years
Reason for Discharge:	Chronic Rheumatism of right thigh and Hernia
Character:	Good
Trade or Occupation:	Labourer
Can Sign Name:	X his mark on Attestation
Height:	5' 8"
Hair Colour:	Brown
Eyes:	Grey
Complexion:	Fresh
Intends to Reside:	Liverpool
Married:	Margaret
Oct 1853	sister Ellen Cowvan [sic] of Augtllif [sic] Carvan is requested to write and send her address to her sister Margaret Cowvan [sic] who with her husband John Hinthorne of the corps of Enrolled Pensioners is now at Fremantle West. Australia

HITCHCOCK	John, private
	25th Foot
12 Nov 1861	Discharged the Service
	Pension paid 1st East London Pension District
	8d. per diem
28 Dec 1863	Arrived per *'Lord Dalhousie'*
1866	Pension paid Adelaide from Perth West. Aust.
1876	"Probably died in the far bush"

Service and Personal Details:

Place of Birth:	Skibbereen Co. Cork	
Age on Enlistment:	20 years	
Period of Service:	1840 — 1861	
Age on Discharge:	none given	
Length of Service:	21 years 15 days	
Foreign Service:	Gibraltar	3 years 8 months
	East Indies	10 years 8 months
Reason for Discharge:	Own request having completed 21 years	
Character:	Good	
Trade or Occupation:	Tailor	
Can Sign Name:	Yes	
Height:	5' 8½"	
Hair Colour:	Dark Brown	
Eyes:	Grey	
Complexion:	Sallow	
Intends to Reside:	Woolwich Kent	

HOBBS	Abraham, Corporal
	76th Foot
6 Mar 1860	Discharged the Service
	Pension paid 1st Cork Pension District
	10d. per diem
1860	Pension paid 2nd Dublin Pension District
31 Dec 1862	Arrived per *'York'*
1863	Stationed Perth District
1864	a Serjeant A Hobbs Pensioner Force at Perth contributed to the Greenough Fire Relief Fund
1873	Pension paid Melbourne
1875	Perth Western Australia
1876	Pensioner A. Hobbs having returned to the Colony and being employed upon the Night Duty Force is, I submit in a position to maintain the whole of his children viz One. In the Poor House Two. In the Orphanages. 'These 3 are his own children and maintained at the expense of the Government.'
1878	Pension increased to 1/2d. per diem for service in the Enrolled Force
1893	Admitted In - Pensioner Kilmainham Hospital
1904	Died

Service and Personal Details:

Place of Birth:	Millstreet Co. Cork
Age on Enlistment:	18 years
Period of Service:	1843 — 1860

Age on Discharge:	35 years	
Length of Service:	16 years 338 days	
Foreign Service:	Mediterranean	5 years
	North America	4 years 6 months
Reason for Discharge:	Defective Vision in both eyes	
Character:	Good	
Trade or Occupation:	Labourer	
Can Sign Name:	Yes	
Height:	5' 7¾"	
Hair Colour:	Light Brown	
Eyes:	Grey	
Complexion:	Fresh	
Remarks:	1856 — Stationed Nova Scotia	
Intends to Reside:	Cork	

HODGES Joseph, Corporal
12th Lancers

Previous Regiment	3rd Light Dragoons
Surname Variant	HODGE
Oct 1856	Discharged the Service Maidstone
1861	Pension paid Chatham
1864	Arrived per *'Clara'* [2]
Oct 1871	Awarded Deferred pension of 4d. per diem
1871	W.O. correspondence with Captain Finnerty
1872	a Joseph Hodges residing at Fremantle
1881	W.O. correspondence with Lt Col Angelo
1891	For authority to employ I. Hodges, R. Quinn and P. Farrell as temporary Warders
1899	W.O. correspondence with Treasury Perth
Feb 1900	Attended fete at Fremantle Oval
1907	Invited to Veteran's dinner at Esplanade Hotel

Service and Personal Details:

Place of Birth:	Hintsridge Stalbridge Somerset	
Age on Enlistment:	about 21 years	
Period of Service:	1841 — 1856	
Age on Discharge:	35 years	
Length of Service:	14 years 219 days	
Foreign Service:	East Indies	9 years 9 months
	the Crimea	1 year
Medal Entitlement:	Sutlej; Punjab with clasp; Crimean medals	
Reason for Discharge:	Own request for a Free Discharge with Right of Registry for Deferred Pension of 4d. per day upon attaining 50 years of age	
Character:	Good	
Trade or Occupation:	Labourer	
Can Sign Name:	Yes	
Height:	5' 7½"	
Hair Colour:	Brown	
Eyes:	Grey	
Complexion:	Fresh	

Remarks:	Tried by District Court Martial 13th March 1854 for disgraceful conduct in having made fraudulent alterations in receipts for oats
Intends to Reside:	Poole Dorsetshire
Remarks:	see Battye Library Acc3779A to view medals

HODGSON	James, private 94th Foot
8 Oct 1861	Discharged the Service Chatham Pension paid Chatham 1/- per diem
31 Dec 1862	Arrived per *'York'*
5 Dec 1882	Assigned Perth Town Lot 33/H
1878	Pension increased to 1/6d. per diem for service in the Enrolled Force
Aug 1884	Granted Fee Simple for Perth Town Lot 33/H

Service and Personal Details:		
Place of Birth:	Preston Lancaster	
Age on Enlistment:	19 years 10 months	
Period of Service:	1840 — 1861	
Age on Discharge:	40 years 10 months	
Length of Service:	21 years 8 days	
Foreign Service:	Gibraltar	9 months
	East Indies	12 years 8 months
Reason for Discharge:	Own Request having completed 21 years service	
Character:	Very Good	
Trade or Occupation:	Weaver	
Can Sign Name:	X his mark on discharge	
Height:	5' 6½"	
Hair Colour:	Dark Brown	
Eyes:	Hazel	
Complexion:	Dark	
Intends to Reside:	Chatham	

HOGAN	Patrick, private 33rd Foot [Depot]
Previous Regiments	30th; 47th
12 Feb 1856	Discharged the Service Chatham Pension paid Limerick 9d. per diem
29 Jan 1862	Arrived per *'Lincelles'*
1864	ptve P Hogan Pensioner Force Perth contributed to the Greenough Fire Relief Fund
1868	Granted Pensioner Lot H33 — Perth
1875	Pension paid Western Australia
1880	Died

Service and Personal Details:	
Place of Birth:	Knockhay Co. Limerick
Age on Enlistment:	17 years
Period of Service:	1853 — 1856
Age on Discharge:	19 years
Length of Service:	2 years 4 days

Foreign Service:	Crimea [no time period given]
Medal Entitlement:	Crimea with clasp; Turkish Crimean
Reason for Discharge:	Gunshot fracture of the femur received in action at the Crimea
Character:	Good
Trade or Occupation:	Labourer
Can Sign Name:	X his mark on discharge
Height:	5' 6"
Hair Colour:	Dark Brown
Eyes:	Grey
Complexion:	Sallow
Distinguishing Marks:	Scar on the forehead and on side of neck
Intends to Reside:	Rathkeale

HOGAN	Stephen, private
	17th Foot
17 July 1846	Discharged the Service Chatham
	Pension paid Chatham
	10d. per diem
1846	Pension paid Ennis
1847	Liverpool
1852	Athlone
2 Apr 1856	Arrived per *'William Hammond'*
July 1856	£3 15 10 balance due on landing at colony but misappropriated by Capt Foss
Jan 1857	Contributed 2/- to the Florence Nightingale Fund
Dec 1857	Assigned Pensioner Lot P13 at York
26 Apr 1860	Purchased York Lot 267
1864	ptve S Hogan Pensioner Force York contributed to the Greenough Fire Relief Fund
Mar 1867	Application for Title to P13 at York
1873	Pension increased to 1/3d per diem for having served 15 years 8 months in the Enrolled Force and from ceasing to draw pay said Force
Aug 1886	Mrs Stephen Hogan applying for relief to support her and five children [SROWA]
Aug 1886	Superintendent at Rottnest — Suggests that a competent man [Stephen Hogan] be appointed as groom for stallion [SROWA — 1886/3312]
Apr 1888	Died

Service and Personal Details:

Place of Birth:	Ballinakill Galway	
Age on Enlistment:	19 years	
Period of Service:	1827 — 1846	
Age on Discharge:	39 years	
Length of Service:	18 years 208 days	
Foreign Service:	New South Wales	5 years 5 months
	East Indies	9 years 6 months
Medal Entitlement:	Campaign of Afghanistan and the capture of Ghuznee	
Reason for Discharge:	Chronic Hepatitis	
Character:	Very Good	

Trade or Occupation:	Labourer
Can Sign Name:	X his mark on discharge
Height:	5' 11¾"
Hair Colour:	Dark Brown
Eyes:	Grey
Complexion:	Sallow
Intends to Reside:	Ballinakill nr Woodfords Galway

HOGAN	Thomas, private
	14th Foot
15 June 1861	Discharged the Service Fermoy
9 July 1861	Admitted to Out-Pension
	Pension paid Limerick
	10d. per diem
27 May 1863	Arrived per *'Clyde'*
1863	Employed by Convict Establishment
1864	In prison — Perth
	"deduction made from next issue of pension on account of imprisonment at Perth West. Australia
Nov 1864	To South Australia from Fremantle
1865	Pension paid South Australia

Service and Personal Details:

Place of Birth:	St Johns Limerick	
Age on Enlistment:	19 years	
Period of Service:	1838 — 1861	
Age on Discharge:	none given	
Length of Service:	23 years 34 days	
Foreign Service:	West Indies	2 years 3 months
	North America	6 years 2 months
Reason for Discharge:	Own Request having completed 21 years service	
Character:	Good	
Trade or Occupation:	Labourer	
Can Sign Name:	Yes	
Height:	5' 10"	
Hair Colour:	Brown	
Eyes:	Grey	
Complexion:	Fresh	
Intends to Reside:	Limerick	

HOLGATE	Robert, gunner and driver
	RA 2nd Battalion
Surname Variant	ALGATE
27 Dec 1847	Discharge approved
11 Jan 1848	Discharged the Service Jersey
	[Subsisted to 31st Jan 1848]
	Pension paid Jersey
	1/-½d. per diem
1851	Residing Breton Yard St Helier
10 Sept 1856	Arrived per *'Runnymede*
7 Jan 1868	Died Fremantle committed suicide

Service and Personal Details:

Place of Birth:	Coln Lancashire

Age on Enlistment:	19 years	
Period of Service:	1826 — 1848	
Age on Discharge:	40 years	
Length of Service:	21 years 361 days	
Foreign Service:	Mauritius	3 years 3 months
	West Indies	5 years 4 months
Reason for Discharge:	Chronic Rheumatism	
Character:	Exemplary	
Trade or Occupation:	Weaver	
Can Sign Name:	Yes	
Height:	5' 9"	
Hair Colour:	Black	
Eyes:	Brown	
Complexion:	Fresh	
Intends to Reside:	Jersey	
Married:	Mary	
Children:	Mary b. 1841 Barbados	
	m. *c*1857 Thomas Randal Fremantle	
	John b. 1845 England	
	m. *c*1865 Sarah Harwood Fremantle	
	Harriet b. 1850 St Helier Jersey	
	m. *c*1869 William Atkins Bunbury	

HOLLIDAY William, private
63rd Foot

Surname Variant	HOLIDAY	
11 Apr 1848	Discharged the Service Chatham	
	Pension paid Lynn	
	9d. per diem	
24 May 1855	Arrived per *'Stag'*	
Jan 1857	Contributed 1/- to the Florence Nightingale Fund	
1859	To South Australia from Western Australia	

Service and Personal Details:

Place of Birth:	Titteshall Norfolk	
Age on Enlistment:	20 years 5 months	
Period of Service:	1831 — 1848	
Age on Discharge:	38 years	
Length of Service:	17 years 33 days	
Foreign Service:	East Indies	13 years
	Van Diemans Land	2 years 1 month
Reason for Discharge:	Unfit for further service	
Character:	Good	
Trade or Occupation:	Labourer	
Can Sign Name:	X his mark on discharge	
Height:	5' 7"	
Hair Colour:	Brown	
Eyes:	Grey	
Complexion:	Sallow	
Intends to Reside:	Titteshall nr East Denham Norfolk	

HOLLOWAY John, private
62nd Foot

4 Aug 1858	Discharged the Service Belfast	
7 Sept 1858	Admitted to Out-Pension Pension paid Carlow 1/- per diem	
1859	Pension paid 2nd Dublin Pension District	
29 Jan 1862	Arrived per *'Lincelles'*	
6 Aug 1868	Allocated North Fremantle Lot P28	
1869	W.O. correspondence to brother	
1878	Pension increased to 1/5½d per diem for service in the Enrolled Force	
1878	Employed as Assistant Warder	
21 Jan 1979	Granted Fremantle Lot P28	
Service and Personal Details:		
Place of Birth:	Carlow Ireland	
Age on Enlistment:	20 years	
Period of Service:	1837 — 1858	
Age on Discharge:	41 years 3 months	
Length of Service:	20 years 359 days	
Foreign Service:	East Indies	9 years 9 months
	Cape of Good Hope	9 months
	Malta	10 months
Reason for Discharge:	Chronic Rheumatism	
Character:	Good	
Trade or Occupation:	Servant	
Can Sign Name:	Yes	
Height:	5' 9¼"	
Hair Colour:	Brown	
Eyes:	Blue	
Complexion:	Fresh	
Intends to Reside:	Carlow	

HOLLYWELL	Robert, gunner EIC Bengal Artillery 5th Brigade
Surname Variants	[some] HELLIWELL; HELLEWELL; HALLIWELL; HOLLIWELL; HOLLIWEL; HALLWELL
Out Pension No 338	
1853	Embarked [with wife] for UK per *'Prince of Wales'*
10 Aug 1853	Admitted to Out-pension Pension paid Halifax Pension District 9d. per diem
2 Apr 1856	Arrived per *'William Hammond'*
1856	Assigned North Fremantle Pensioner Lot P13 at Swan St North Fremantle
1856	Claim of £15 against Capt Foss
July 1856	£5. 10. 0 balance due on landing at colony but misappropriated by Capt. Foss
July 1856	£50 which was deposited with for safe custody was misappropriated by the Captain
1863	Granted Fee Simple for Pensioner Lot P13 North Fremantle
1869	Pension paid London
1874	Halifax Lancashire

Feb 1875	a John Holliwel [sic] of North Fremantle witnessed the handwritten Will of Thomas Crowdy
1886	Died
1889	Mrs Hellewell [sic] proprietor of Fremantle Lot P13
1834	Put up for auction North Fremantle Lot P13 and a portion of North Fremantle Lot P12

Service and Personal Details:	
Where Born:	Hebdon Bridge Heptonstall Yorkshire
Trade or Occupation:	Labourer
Age on Enlistment:	24 years
Date Enlisted:	27th Jan 1842
Where Enlisted:	Westminster London
Embarked India:	8th June 1842 — per '*Madagascar*'
Presidency:	Bengal
Length of Service:	10 years 6 months
Age on Discharge:	35 years
Character:	Good
Reason for Discharge:	An injury received on the left foot by the trail of a gun at exercise
Height:	5' 10¼"
Complexion:	Fresh
Visage:	Oval
Eye Colour:	Blue
Hair Colour:	Brown
Marital Status:	Married prior to embarkation
Remarks:	Wife Hannah [from Embarkation Returns]
Intends to Reside:	Todworden Halifax
Married:	Hannah/Ann
Children:	William b. 1844 d. 1844 Benares India
	William b. 1845 d. 1849 Cawnpore India
	Robert b. 1847 d. 1847 Lahore India
	Joshua b. 1848 d. 1848 Lahore India
	Thomas b. 1850 d. 1850 Lahore India
	Isaac b. 1852 Umballa India
	m. *c*1885 Rosina Goodwin
	Hannah b 1855
	Roden b. *c*1862 Fremantle
	m. *c*1879 Mary Elizabeth Shaw Liverpool

HOLLYWOOD	Thomas, private
	28th Foot
Previous Regiment	69th Foot
Surname Variant	HOLLIWOOD
7 Aug 1855	Discharged the Service Chatham
	Pension paid 1st Liverpool Pension District
	8d. per diem for 3 years
1856	Pension paid 1st Dublin Pension District
10 July 1857	Arrived per '*Clara*' [1]
1858	Pension made permanent at 6d. per diem
1863	Pension paid Perth Western Australia
1866	South Australia from Perth per' *Emily Smith'*
1867	Adelaide

6 Feb 1876	Died South Australia	
Service and Personal Details:		
Place of Birth:	Dublin Ireland	
Age on Enlistment:	18 years	
Period of Service:	1843 — 1855	
Age on Discharge:	31 years or 30 years 6 months	
Length of Service:	11 years 346 days	
Foreign Service:	Mediterranean	3 years 4 months
	Malta &	
	Turkey & Crimea	1 year 2 months
Medal Entitlement:	Crimea	
Reason for Discharge:	Unfit for further service	
Character:	Good	
Trade or Occupation:	Labourer	
Can Sign Name:	X his mark on Attestation	
Height:	5' 6"	
Hair Colour:	Dark Brown	
Eyes:	Light Brown	
Complexion:	Fresh	
Remarks:	Attacks of fever at Scutari	
Intends to Reside:	Liverpool	

HOLMAN William, Corporal

	81st Foot	
16 Apr 1852	Discharged the Service Dublin	
11 May 1852	Admitted to Out-Pension	
	Pension paid Falmouth	
	8d. per diem for 3 years	
30 Apr 1853	To Tilbury Fort	
31 Aug 1853	Arrived per *'Phoebe Dunbar'*	
Service and Personal Details:		
Place of Birth:	St Michaels London	
Age on Enlistment:	20 years 10 months	
Period of Service:	1840 — 1852	
Age on Discharge:	32 years 11 months	
Length of Service:	12 years 33 days	
Foreign Service:	West Indies	1 year 5 months
	Canada	4 years 3 months
Reason for Discharge:	Ruptured left side	
Character:	Very Good	
Trade or Occupation:	Blacksmith	
Can Sign Name:	Yes	
Height:	5' 7"	
Hair Colour:	Auburn	
Eyes:	Hazel	
Complexion:	Pale	
Intends to Reside:	Camborne Cornwall	

HOLT Charles, private

	51st Foot
Surname Variant	BOLT

25 June 1840	Arrived per *'Runnymede'* with regiment
Oct 1841	a Charles Hold serving as constable Perth
11 Mar 1847	Discharged the Service Perth West. Aust.
24 Aug 1847	Discharge approved
	Pension paid Perth Western Australia
	1/- per diem
Mar 1849	Pension paid South Australia
Dec 1849	To transfer to Van Diemans Land
Dec 1849	Died

Service and Personal Details:

Place of Birth:	Rochdale Lancashire
Age on Enlistment:	18 years
Period of Service:	1825 — 1847
Age on Discharge:	39 years 7 months
Length of Service:	21 years 239 days
Foreign Service:	Australian Colonies 7 years 10 months
Reason for Discharge:	Affected with Rheumatism; Worn out and unfit for service in India
Character:	Good
Trade or Occupation:	Woollen Weaver
Can Sign Name:	Yes
Height:	5' 8¼"
Hair Colour:	Brown
Eyes:	Grey
Complexion:	Sallow

HOOPER

	Thomas, private
	89th Foot
11 Oct 1853	Discharged the Service Cork Barracks
8 Nov 1853	Admitted to Out-Pension
	Pension paid Kilkenny
	6d. per diem for 3 years
18 July 1855	Arrived per *'Adelaide'*
1857	Appointed Assistant Warder
1859	Dismissed from Convict Service

Service and Personal Details:

Place of Birth:	Clapham Surrey
Age on Enlistment:	19 years 11 months
Period of Service:	1839 — 1853
Age on Discharge:	34 years 3 months
Length of Service:	14 years 141 days
Reason for Discharge:	Disease of both lungs
Character:	Indifferent
Trade or Occupation:	Hairdresser
Can Sign Name:	Yes
Height:	5' 6¾"
Hair Colour:	Brown
Eyes:	Hazel
Complexion:	Sallow
Intends to Reside:	Templemore

HOPE	William, private
	Rifle Brigade - 2nd Battalion
15 Oct 1866	Discharged the Service Winchester
30 Oct 1866	Admitted to Out-Pension
	Pension paid 2nd North London Pension District
	8d. per diem
1871	Residing as a lodger aged 44 at 16 Ruddocks Buildings St Leonards Moorfields London
1873	Pension paid Greenwich
19 Feb 1874	Arrived per *'Naval Brigade'*
1875	Convicted of having been drunk on guard and sentenced to 112 day in prison during which pension is to be suspended
1875	In prison — pension suspended
1878	Pension increased to 9½d. per diem for service in the Enrolled Force
1880	a William Hope died aged 53

Service and Personal Details:		
Place of Birth:	Marylebone Middlesex	
Age on Enlistment:	18 years 8 months	
Period of Service:	1845 — 1866	
Age on Discharge:	39 years 9 months	
Length of Service:	21 years 5 days	
Foreign Service:	North America	6 years 1 month
	Crimea	1 year 3 months
	India	2 years 4 months
Medal Entitlement:	Crimea with clasps; Turkish Crimea; Indian Mutiny with clasp	
Reason for Discharge:	Own Request having served 21 years	
Character:	Latterly Good	
Trade or Occupation:	Tailor	
Can Sign Name:	Yes	
Height:	5' 7¼"	
Hair Colour:	Brown	
Eyes:	Hazel	
Complexion:	Fair	
Intends to Reside:	PO Vere Str., Cavendish Square London	

HOPPER	Martin, private
	86th Foot
Previous Regiment	28th Foot
14 July 1863	Discharged the Service Dublin
	Pension paid Clonmel
	9d. per diem
22 Dec 1865	Arrived per *'Vimiera'*
10 Sept 1868	Died aged 41
1880	"Pensioner Hopper's son crippled in an explosion"

Service and Personal Details:	
Place of Birth:	Mullingar Westmeath
Age on Enlistment:	19 years
Period of Service:	1844 — 1863
Age on Discharge:	37 years 11 months

Length of Service:	18 years 286 days
Foreign Service:	East Indies 14 years 7 months
Medal Entitlement:	Indian Mutiny with clasp
Reason for Discharge:	Chronic Hepatitis and Worn Out
Character:	Good
Trade or Occupation:	Labourer
Can Sign Name:	Yes
Height:	5' 7"
Hair Colour:	Grey
Eyes:	Blue
Complexion:	Sallow
Intends to Reside:	Clonmel Ireland

HORGAN Cornelius, gunner
RA Depot Brigade

20 Sept 1859	Discharged the Service Woolwich Pension paid Woolwich 8d. per diem
31 Dec 1862	Arrived per *'York'*
1866	To South Australia from Fremantle
1876	Pension paid South Australia
1878	South Australia
1880	Residing at Morgan South Australia
1888	Pension paid Adelaide

Service and Personal Details:

Place of Birth:	St Marys Co. Cork	
Age on Enlistment:	18 years 8 months	
Period of Service:	1838 — 1859	
Age on Discharge:	40 years	
Length of Service:	21 years 102 days	
Foreign Service:	West Indies	5 years
	Crimea	10 months
Medal Entitlement:	Crimea with clasp	
Reason for Discharge:	Having competed 21 years service	
Character:	Indifferent	
Trade or Occupation:	Tailor	
Can Sign Name:	Yes	
Height:	5' 7¼"	
Hair Colour:	Brown	
Eyes:	Grey	
Complexion:	Fair	
Distinguishing Marks:	Scars of small pox on face	

HORNBY Michael [Military Pensioner]
96th Foot

Previous Regiment	51st Foot
Surname Variant	HORNSBY
25 June 1840	Arrived per *'Runnymede'* with regiment
10 mar 1847	Transferred to the 96th Foot
21 Nov 1848	Requested to be discharged
31 Apr 1849	Discharged the Service Perth Western Australia
28 Feb 1851	Discharge Approved

11 Mar 1851	Pension ratified
1882	Died

Service and Personal Details:

Place of Birth:	Leytham Lancashire	
Age on Enlistment:	22 years	
Period of Service:	1827 — 1848	
Age on Discharge:	43 years 11 months	
Length of Service:	19 years 305 days [reckoned]	
Foreign Service:	Australasia	9 years
Reason for Discharge:	His having applied for a modified pension of 10 pence per diem in consequence of having served upwards of 21 years in accordance with the Warrant dated May 1839 for the purpose of settling in Western Australia	
Character:	Very Good	
Trade or Occupation:	Labourer	
Can Sign Name:	No	
Height:	5' 6"	
Hair Colour:	Dark Brown	
Eyes:	Blue	
Complexion:	Fresh	

HORRIGAN Jeremiah, private [1012]
5th Foot

8 May 1866	Discharged the Service Athlone Pension paid 1st North London Pension District 1/- per diem
9 Jan 1868	Arrived per *'Hougoumont'*
Jan 1876	Convicted of indecently exposing his person to 2 children. Sent to prison for 3 months and to be struck off the Pension List
Apr 1876	Died aged 48 found dead in his bed — cause of death — fatty degeneration of the heart

Service and Personal Details:

Place of Birth:	Cork Ireland	
Age on Enlistment:	18 years	
Period of Service:	1845 — 1866	
Age on Discharge:	39 years	
Length of Service:	21 years 19 days	
Foreign Service:	Gibraltar	4 years 1 month
	West Indies	3 years 5 months
	Canada	3 years 4 months
	East Indies	3 years 6 months
Reason for Discharge:	Own Request having completed 21 years	
Character:	Latterly Very Good	
Trade or Occupation:	Shoemaker	
Can Sign Name:	Yes	
Height:	5' 6"	
Hair Colour:	Dark Brown	
Eyes:	Grey	

Complexion:	Fresh
Intends to Reside:	No. 47 Euston Rd., London

HOURIGAN	Richard, Serjeant 4th Light Dragoons
Previous Regiment	3rd Light Dragoons
Surname Variant	HOURRIGAN
10 June 1862	Discharged the Service Pension paid Limerick 2/- per diem
1864	Transferred from Limerick to South Australia
1867	Pension paid Adelaide
1874	Perth Western Australia
1881	Pension increased to 2/2½d. per diem for 6 years service in the Enrolled Guard
1881	"Special Constable taking charge of deserters"
1881	Pension paid Adelaide South Australia

Service and Personal Details:

Place of Birth:	?Lathron Tipperary	
Age on Enlistment:	16 years 5 months	
Period of Service:	1836 — 1862	
Age on Discharge:	42 years	
Length of Service:	24 years 10 days	
Foreign Service:	East Indies	13 years 6 months
	"Army in the East" & Turkey & Crimea	10 months
Medal Entitlement:	Sutlej with clasps; Punjaub with clasps; Crimea with clasp and Turkish Crimea	
Reason for Discharge:	Own request having served over 21 years	
Character:	Good	
Trade or Occupation:	Labourer	
Can Sign Name:	Yes	
Height:	5' 9½"	
Hair Colour:	Light Brown	
Eyes:	Blue	
Complexion:	Fresh	
Intends to Reside:	Wood House Farm. Cahir-conlish Limerick	

HOUSTON	William Russell, private 89th Foot [Depot]
Surname Variant	HOWSTON
16 Apr 1860	Discharged the Service Fermoy Barracks Pension paid Fermoy 1/-½d. per diem
29 Jan 1862	Arrived per *'Lincelles'*
1863	Stationed Perth District
1864	a Serjeant W Houston Pensioner Force Perth contributed to the Greenough Fire Relief Fund
1864	Appointed Warder at Geraldton
1878	Increased to 1/6½d. per diem for service in the Enrolled Force Served as Sergeant in the Enrolled Guard until the Force was disbanded Member of the MRV Band

24 July 1892	Died aged 75 - buried East Perth Cemetery	
Service and Personal Details:		
Place of Birth:	Carnmony Belfast Co. Antrim	
Age on Enlistment:	18 years	
Period of Service:	1838 — 1860	
Age on Discharge:	40 years 2 months	
Length of Service:	22 years 43 days	
Foreign Service:	West Indies	2 years 4 months
	North America	5 years 10 months
	Gibraltar	9 months
Reason for Discharge:	Own request having served 21 years	
Character:	Very Good	
Trade or Occupation:	Labourer	
Can Sign Name:	Yes	
Height:	5' 7½"	
Hair Colour:	Sandy	
Eyes:	Grey	
Complexion:	Fresh	
Intends to Reside:	Belfast Co. Antrim	
Comments:	according to son's obituary his father was a sergeant in the 33rd — Duke of Wellington's Regiment of Foot and the family arrived per '*Vymera*' [sic] in 1865	

HOWARD	Michael, private 10th Foot
25 Oct 1859	Discharged the Service Pension paid Clonmel 8d. per diem
11 Feb 1861	Arrived per *'Palmeston'*
no date	Held Title to Freshwater Bay Loc 1074
1864	Catherine Howard unable to locate husband, Pensioner Michael Howard following her discharge from hospital where she has been for 6 months
Mar 1865	Family of Pensioner Howard [who went to Champion Bay, promising to send money and did not], requiring poor relief.
1875	Pension paid Western Australia
1877	Convicted for drunk and incapable in a public street. Sentenced to 21 days imprisonment during which his pension to be suspended
1877	Convicted for 2nd time for being drunk and incapable. Sentenced to 21 days imprisonment with pension suspended
23 Dec 1889	Admitted to Mt Eliza Depot
1890	Died aged 72 "of natural decay"

Service and Personal Details:	
Place of Birth:	Lismore Co. Waterford
Age on Enlistment:	18 years
Period of Service:	1838 — 1859

Age on Discharge:	? 39 years	
Length of Service:	21 years 257 days	
Foreign Service:	East Indies	10 years 10 months [or 16 years 10 months depending on record source]
Medal Entitlement:	Good Conduct; 2 medals and clasps for service in the field	
Reason for Discharge:	Having served upwards of 21 years	
Character:	Good	
Trade or Occupation:	Labourer	
Can Sign Name:	X his mark on discharge	
Height:	5' 6"	
Hair Colour:	Dark Brown	
Eyes:	Grey	
Complexion:	Fresh	

HOWARD	William, Corporal and drummer 89th Foot	
Previous Regiments	96th; 18th; 86th	
29 Aug 1865	Discharged the Service Cork Pension paid Chatham 1/2d. per diem	
9 Jan 1868	Arrived per *'Hougoumont'* with wife and son	
1868	Pension paid Western Australia	
1868	Employed in Convict Establishment	
1873	Pension to be paid Calcutta	
29 Dec 1873	Died	
Service and Personal Details:		
Place of Birth:	Chatham Kent	
Age on Enlistment:	14 years 3 months	
Period of Service:	1842 — 1865	
Age on Discharge:	37 years	
Length of Service:	19 years 25 days	
Foreign Service:	Van Diemans Land	5 years 5 months
	East Indies	5 years 3 months
	Crimea	4 months
	Turkey 4 months	
	East Indies	5 years 1 month
Medal Entitlement:	Crimea with clasp and Turkish Crimean	
Reason for Discharge:	Chronic Hepatitis	
Character:	Very Good	
Trade or Occupation:	Labourer	
Can Sign Name:	Yes	
Height:	6'	
Hair Colour:	Fair	
Eyes:	Blue	
Complexion:	Fresh	
Intends to Reside:	Chatham	

HOWE	Robert, private 18th Foot
Previous Regiment	51st Foot

May 1855	Invalided to England
7 Aug 1855	Discharged the Service Chatham Pension paid Ayr [12/Ayr/8] 6d. for 2 years
1855	Pension increased to 8d. per diem for the rest of the period
1856	Pension paid West Australia from Ayr [12/Ayr/8]
1857	Western Australia

Service and Personal Details:

Place of Birth:	Enniskillen Co. Fermanagh
Age on Enlistment:	18 years
Period of Service:	1846 — 1855
Length of Service:	9 years 140 days
Foreign Service:	Crimea
Medal Entitlement:	Crimea with clasp
Reason for Discharge:	Unfit for further service from Phthisis
Character:	Good
Trade or Occupation:	Labourer
Can Sign Name:	X his mark on Attestation
Height:	5' 5½"
Hair Colour:	Fair
Eyes:	Grey
Complexion:	Fresh

HOWES William, private
54th Foot [Depot]

7 Apr 1857	Discharged the Service Chatham Pension paid Norwich 7d. per diem
24 Nov 1858	Arrived per *'Edwin Fox'*
July 1877	a William Howes sentenced at York Police Court as a 'rogue and a vagabond'

Service and Personal Details:

Place of Birth:	Crooks Place Norwich Norfolk	
Age on Enlistment:	18 years	
Period of Service:	1841 — 1857	
Age on Discharge:	33 years 8 months	
Length of Service:	15 years 254 days	
Foreign Service:	Gibraltar	[total] 2 years 41 days
	Malta	1 year 73 days
	West Indies	3 years 136 days
	North America	3 years 80 days
Reason for Discharge:	Weak and worn out and reduction of Army	
Character:	Very Good	
Trade or Occupation:	Labourer	
Can Sign Name:	Yes	
Height:	5' 7"	
Hair Colour:	Dark Brown	
Eyes:	Dark Brown	
Complexion:	Fresh	
Intends to Reside:	Norfolk	

HUBBLE	John, private 32nd Foot
9 Dec 1840	Discharged the Service Pension paid Greenwich 6d. per diem
1849	Pension paid Deptford
1 June 1850	Arrived per *'Scindian'*
Aug 1850	Assigned Military Pensioner Plot P4 South Perth
1862	York. Residents Office — refers Pensioner Hubble for loss of sight, and inability to provide for himself and Jane Hunt
1862	John Hubble seeks relief from public funds
1891	Admitted to Depot 11 [sic] years ago and is now quite blind
July 1894	Died – buried East Perth Pioneer Cemetery
Service and Personal Details:	
Place of Birth:	Trosly Kent
Age on Enlistment:	19 years
Period of Service:	1835 — 1840
Age on Discharge:	24 years
Length of Service:	4 years 317 days
Foreign Service:	Canada 4 years 3 months
Reason for Discharge:	Fracture of left thigh due to falling through a wooden bridge
Character:	A man of generally sober habits
Trade or Occupation:	Labourer
Can Sign Name:	X his mark on discharge
Height:	5' 7"
Hair Colour:	Light Brown
Eyes:	Grey
Complexion:	Fair
HUBBLE	William, private 32nd Foot
Surname Variant	HUBLE
9 Jan 1839	Discharged the Service Pension paid Greenwich 6d. per diem
1849	Pension paid Deptford
1 June 1850	Arrived per *'Scindian'*
Sept 1850	Assigned a Military Location at South Perth
1864	private W Hubble Pensioner Force Kojonup contributed to the Greenough Fire Relief Fund
Feb 1879	Died – buried East Perth Pioneer Cemetery
Service and Personal Details:	
Place of Birth:	Wrotham Kent
Age on Enlistment:	18 years
Period of Service:	1836 — 1839
Age on Discharge:	19 years [or 20 years depending on record]
Length of Service:	1 year 249 days [or 2 years 2 months depending on record]
Foreign Service:	Canada 1 year

Reason for Discharge:	Wounded by gunshot in the right leg in action against the rebels at Point au Pelee Island
Character:	Indifferent
Trade or Occupation:	Groom [or Labourer depending on record]
Can Sign Name:	X his mark on discharge
Height:	5' 7¼"
Hair Colour:	Brown
Eyes:	Grey
Complexion:	Fresh

HUDSON Patrick, private

	28th Foot
1 May 1866	Discharged the Service Pension paid Halifax 1/- per diem
13 July 1867	Arrived per *'Norwood'* [2] Residents Office Fremantle Request sanction of His Excellency, the Governor for the admission of Patrick Hudson, Pensioner to Perth Colonial Hospital. He is willing to forfeit pension of 1/- per diem if admitted to Hospital. He will need conveyance as is not able to walk.
1871	Died

Service and Personal Details:

Place of Birth:	St Johns Sligo	
Age on Enlistment:	21 years	
Period of Service:	1844 — 1866	
Age on Discharge:	43 years	
Length of Service:	21 years 5 days	
Foreign Service:	Malta &	
	Crimea	3 years 91 days
	East Indies	9 years 70 days
Medal Entitlement:	Crimea with clasp; and Turkish Crimean	
Reason for Discharge:	Having completed 21 actual years service	
Character:	Good	
Trade or Occupation:	a Nailor	
Can Sign Name:	Yes	
Height:	5' 8"	
Hair Colour:	Brown	
Eyes:	Grey	
Complexion:	Sallow	
Distinguishing Marks:	Letter 'D'	
Intends to Reside:	62 Clifford Street.. Bradford Yorkshire	

HUDSON Samuel, private

	Royal Canadian Rifles
Previous Regiment	17th Foot
5 July 1859	Discharged the Service Chatham Pension paid South London Pension District 8d. per diem
1861	Pension paid Nottingham

1862	South London
27 May 1863	Arrived per *'Clyde'*
Feb 1867	Samuel Hudson pensioner — gave notice that he would not be answerable for any debts his wife contracted in Colony
circa Dec 1875	Transferred from Fremantle to 1st Perth District
Apr 1881	Died aged 62 – buried East Perth Cemetery

Service and Personal Details:

Place of Birth:	Loughborough Leicestershire	
Age on Enlistment:	20 years	
Period of Service:	1838 — 1859	
Age on Discharge:	21 years 54 days	
Length of Service:	41 years 4 months	
Foreign Service:	Mediterranean	7 months
	East Indies	8 years 6 years
	Crimea	1 year 2 months
	North America	2 years 9 months
Medal Entitlement:	Crimea	
Reason for Discharge:	Own Request having completed 21 years	
Character:	Good	
Trade or Occupation:	Framework knitter	
Can Sign Name:	X his mark on discharge	
Height:	5' 6"	
Hair Colour:	Brown	
Eyes:	Grey	
Complexion:	Fair	
Intends to Reside:	No. 18 West Square St George's Road	
Southwark London		

HUGHES	Edward, private [3611]
	74th Foot
5 Aug 1858	Discharged the Service Chatham
	Pension paid 2nd Belfast Pension District
	10d. per diem
1858	Serving in the Antrim Militia
27 May 1863	Arrived per *'Clyde'*
Nov 1886	Pensioner E Hughes petitions for the release of his son Edward from prison.
1891	Correspondence from W.O. to Colonial Treasurer Perth Western Australia
Sept 1895	an Edward Hughes died aged 83 [51 on arrival] Buried East Perth Pioneer Cemetery

Service and Personal Details:

Place of Birth:	Armagh Co. Armagh	
Age on Enlistment:	17 years 6 months	
Period of Service:	1836 — 1857	
Age on Discharge:	39 years 2 months	
Length of Service:	20 years 154 days	
Foreign Service:	Van Diemans Land	9 years 1 month
	East Indies	10 years 8 months
Medal Entitlement:	Medal for services in Burmah 1852/53	
Reason for Discharge:	Worn out by service	

Character:	Good	
Trade or Occupation:	Labourer	
Can Sign Name:	Yes	
Height:	5' 6½"	
Hair Colour:	Light Brown	
Eyes:	Blue	
Complexion:	Fair	
Distinguishing Marks:	A speck in the left eye	
Intends to Reside:	Belfast Co. Antrim	

HUGHES	Evan, gunner and driver Royal Artillery 2nd Battalion	
13 Apr 1852	Discharged the Service Woolwich 1/- per diem	
14 Aug 1854	Arrived per *'Ramillies'*	
1877	Pensioner Evan Hughes at 1/- per diem for admission to the Invalid Depot	
June 1880	Died – buried East Perth Pioneer Cemetery	
Service and Personal Details:		
Place of Birth:	Llangennniew [sic] Montgomeryshire	
Age on Enlistment:	20 years 11 months	
Period of Service:	1831 — 1852	
Age on Discharge:	42 years	
Length of Service:	21 years 36 days	
Foreign Service:	Bermuda	4 years 2 months
	Canada	2 years 4 months
	Nova Scotia	1 year 6 months
Reason for Discharge:	Chronic Rheumatism	
Character:	Exemplary	
Trade or Occupation:	Labourer	
Can Sign Name:	Yes	
Height:	5' 11"	
Hair Colour:	Black	
Eyes:	Blue	
Complexion:	Dark	

HUGHES	James, private 28th Foot	
13 Jan 1852	Discharged the Service Chatham Pension paid 2nd Plymouth Pension District	
1/- per diem		
24 Nov 1858	Arrived per *'Edwin Fox'*	
6 Nov 1860	Died	
Service and Personal Details:		
Place of Birth:	Armagh Co. Armagh	
Age on Enlistment:	18 years	
Period of Service:	1830 — 1852	
Age on Discharge:	39 years	
Length of Service:	20 years 295 days	
Foreign Service:	New South Wales	6 years 8 months
	East Indies	10 years 7 months
Reason for Discharge:	Oppression of the chest	

Character:	Good	
Trade or Occupation:	Servant	
Can Sign Name:	Yes	
Height:	5' 6¾"	
Hair Colour:	Brown	
Eyes:	Blue	
Complexion:	Fresh	
Intends to Reside:	Plymouth	

HUGHES Patrick, private
2nd/60th Foot

Previous Regiment	84th	
21 Aug 1861	Discharged the Service ?Winchester	
3 Sept 1861	Admitted to Out Pension	
	Pension paid Kilkenny	
	11d. per diem	
28 Dec 1863	Arrived per *'Lord Dalhousie'*	
June 1878	Pension increased to 1/5d for service in the Enrolled Force of Western Australia	
no date	Assigned Freshwater Bay Loc 1067	
Feb 1885	Application for Title Freshwater Bay Loc 1067	
1885	Colonial Surgeon requests relief to Pensioner Patrick Hughes	
*c*1886	Died	

Service and Personal Details:

Place of Birth:	Callen Kilkenny	
Age on Enlistment:	17 years	
Period of Service:	1839 — 1861	
Age on Discharge:	39 years	
Length of Service:	21 years 6 days	
Foreign Service:	Corfu	5 months
	Jamaica	2 years 11 months
	Canada	3 years
	Cape of Good Hope	7 years 1 month
	East Indies	1 year 6 months
Medal Entitlement:	Kaffir War — 1851 - 1853	
Reason for Discharge:	Own request after 21 years service	
Character:	Very Good	
Trade or Occupation:	Labourer	
Can Sign Name:	Yes	
Height:	5' 8"	
Hair Colour:	Brown	
Eyes:	Hazel	
Complexion:	Dark	
Intends to Reside:	Callan Kilkenny	

HUGHES Thomas, Sub Conductor EIC
Ordnance Department

Pervious Regiment	1st Bombay European Regiment	
Surname Variant	HUGHS	
	Out Pension No 514	
Sept 1864	Admitted to Out-pension	

	Pension paid 2nd Dublin Pension District
	2/6d. per diem
22 Dec 1866	Arrived per *'Corona'*
1867	Purchased Fremantle Lot S46
1876	Assigned Cockburn Sound Loc P177 grant at Willagee Swamp
8 Apr 1880	Died
Mar 1894	Cockburn Sound Loc P177 grant at Willagee Swamp to son Edward James or Thomas

Service and Personal Details:	
Where Born:	Dublin
Trade or Occupation:	Coachman
Length of Service:	22 years
Age on Discharge:	38 years
Reason for Discharge:	Time expired
Character:	Very Good
Height:	5' 10½"
Complexion:	Fair
Eye Colour:	Blue
Hair Colour:	Brown
Intends to Reside:	Dublin
Married:	Catherine McEvoy
Children:	Thomas b. 1866 at sea
	Rose b. *c*1871
	William b. *c*1873
1887	William Hughes a brother of the notorious Thomas Hughes was charged with carrying an unlicensed gun [Trove]
	Edward James b. *c*1876 Fremantle

HULLIHAN	John, private
	30th Foot
Surname Variants	HOULAHAN; HOULLAHAN; HOUGLAHAN
9 Aug 1853	Discharged the Service Fermoy
	Pension paid Leeds
	1/- per diem
1854	Pension paid 1st Manchester Pension District
2 Apr 1856	Arrived per *'William Hammond'*
1875	Pension paid Western Australia
Oct 1891	Died aged 90 at Bunbury
1898	Grant of Probate

Service and Personal Details:		
Place of Birth:	Killallerton Ballinasloa Co. Galway	
Age on Enlistment:	18 years	
Period of Service:	1831 — 1853	
Age on Discharge:	40 years 4 months	
Length of Service:	21 years 40 days	
Foreign Service:	Bermuda	2 years 11 months
	North America	1 year 11 months
Reason for Discharge:	Chronic Catarrh and Worn Out	
Character:	Good	
Trade or Occupation:	Labourer	

Can Sign Name:	X his mark on discharge
Height:	5' 7¾"
Hair Colour:	Dark Brown
Eyes:	Grey
Complexion:	Fresh
Intends to Reside:	Leeds

HULME	Robert, Corporal
	9th Foot
25 July 1848	Discharged the Service Liverpool
10 Oct 1848	Admitted to Out-Pension
	Pension paid Liverpool
	1/2½d per diem
1848	Pension paid Manchester
21 May 1851	Arrived per *'Mermaid'*
1873	Pension increased to 1/3d. per diem for 14 years and 5 months service with the Enrolled Force
1876	Died aged 67

Service and Personal Details:

Place of Birth:	Eccles Manchester	
Age on Enlistment:	17 years	
Period of Service:	1826 — 1848	
Age on Discharge:	39 years	
Length of Service:	21 years 67 days	
Foreign Service:	Mauritius	2 years 195 days
	East Indies	11 years 134 days
Medal Entitlement:	Afghanistan; Sutlej with clasps	
Reason for Discharge:	Chronic Rheumatism	
Character:	Good	
Trade or Occupation:	Cotton Spinner	
Can Sign Name:	Yes	
Height:	5' 6½"	
Hair Colour:	Light Brown	
Eyes:	Grey	
Complexion:	Fair	
Remarks:	Gunshot wound to right foot at the Khyber Pass and on the left cheek at Ferozashar	

HUMMERSTON	George, private [Military Pensioner]
	12th Foot
Previous Regiment	99th Foot
Surname Variant	HUMMERSTONE; HAMMERSTONE
1835	Transferred to 12th Foot
5 May 1849	Arrived per *'Ratcliffe'* with regiment
Nov 1849	Tried and sentenced to 7 days imprisonment at Swan River
circa 1860	Departed for Eastern States
12 Dec 1864	Proceeding of Regimental Board at Sydney
20 June 1865	Discharge approved
	1/-½d. per diem
Apr 1893	Died

Service and Personal Details:

Place of Birth:	St Margarets London Middlesex	
Age on Enlistment:	19 years	
Period of Service:	1842 — 1864	
Age on Discharge:	not given	
Length of Service:	22 years 27 days	
Foreign Service:	Australian Colonies	21 years 47 days
Reason for Discharge:	Chronic Rheumatism	
Character:	Very Good	
Trade or Occupation:	Labourer	
Can Sign Name:	Yes	
Height:	5' 5¼"	
Hair Colour:	Brown	
Eyes:	Grey	
Complexion:	Dark	
Intended Residence:	Brisbane Queensland	

HUNT James, private
10th Foot

12 Mar 1850	Discharged to pension Pension paid 1st Liverpool Pension District 9d. per diem
1855	Pension paid Liverpool
1855	Jersey
1856	Newcastle
1858	York
19 Aug 1859	Arrived per *'Sultana'*
16 Nov 1861	To Adelaide from Perth Western Australia

Service and Personal Details:

Place of Birth:	Askeaton Co. Limerick	
Age on Enlistment:	18 years	
Period of Service:	1838 — 1849	
Age on Discharge:	none given	
Length of Service:	4 years 189 days	
Foreign Service:	East Indies	4 years
Medal Entitlement:	Mooltan 1848	
Reason for Discharge:	Wounded through chest by musket ball	
Character:	Good	
Trade or Occupation:	Labourer	
Can Sign Name:	X his mark on discharge	
Distinguishing Mark:	Marked with the letter 'D'	

HUNT James, private
RM

Dec 1849	Discharged the Service £15/4/- per diem
1850	Pension paid Wolverhampton
1 June 1850	Arrived per *'Scindian'*
1850/1851	Assigned and occupied South Perth Loc P8
1851	From this date — Not liable of any debts his wife Jane may incur
1878	Died

Service and Personal Details:

Place of Birth:	Corsley Wiltshire
Age on Attestation:	19 years
Marine Division:	Portsmouth
Period Of Service:	1828 — 1849
Length of Service:	21 years 13 days
Reason for Discharge:	Length of service
Medal Entitlement:	China Campaign
Trade or Occupation:	Labourer
Can Sign Name:	No
Height:	5' 7"
Hair Colour:	Light Brown
Eyes:	Hazel
Complexion:	Fresh

HUNTER Michael, private
61st Foot

22 Sept 1857	Discharged the Service Chatham Pension paid Halifax 1/- per diem
24 Nov 1858	Arrived per *'Edwin Fox'*
1865	Pension paid Perth Western Australia
circa Dec 1874	Transferred from Fremantle to 1st Perth
12 Sept 1883	Assigned Perth Pensioner Lot 24/H [these were located left rear of Mt Eliza Barracks]
May 1884	Granted Fee Simple Perth Town Lot 24/H
Feb 1884	Authority for admission of Pensioner M. Hunter into Mt. Eliza Poor House
1886	Died

Service and Personal Details:

Place of Birth:	Paisley Renfrewshire
Age on Enlistment:	17 years
Period of Service:	1833 — 1857
Age on Discharge:	40 years 9 months
Length of Service:	21 years 16 days
Foreign Service:	East Indies 7 years 11 months
Medal Entitlement:	Medal and claps for the Punjaub
Reason for Discharge:	Chronic Pains and Varicose Veins in both legs
Character:	Good
Trade or Occupation:	Weaver
Can Sign Name:	X his mark on discharge
Height:	5' 6"
Hair Colour:	Red
Eyes:	Grey
Complexion:	Fair
Intends to Reside:	Bradford Yorkshire

HURLEY John, private
87th Foot

Previous Regiment	54th Foot
Surname Variants	HURDLEY; HEARDLY
8 Apr 1862	Discharged the Service Pension paid Clonmel

	6d. per diem	
28 Dec 1863	Arrived per *'Lord Dalhousie'*	
1880	Granted Cockburn Sound Loc 232 Willagee Swamp	
1881	Pension increased to 1/- per diem for service in the Enrolled Force. Served 16 years 10 months in the Enrolled Pensioner Force	
Apr 1883	Died at Jarrahdale from injuries	
Service and Personal Details:		
Place of Birth:	Dungarven Co. Waterford	
Age on Enlistment:	23 years	
Period of Service:	1847 — 1862	
Age on Discharge:	38 years 1 month	
Length of Service:	15 years 12 days	
Foreign Service:	East Indies	10 years 8 months
	China	1 year 1 month
Reason for Discharge:	Chronic Bronchitis	
Character:	Indifferent	
Trade or Occupation:	Labourer	
Can Sign Name:	X his mark on discharge	
Height:	5' 8¼"	
Hair Colour:	Fair	
Eyes:	Hazel	
Complexion:	Fresh	
Intends to Reside:	Glasgow	

HUSSEY	Edward, private	
	36th Foot	
24 July 1849	Discharged the Service Chatham	
	Pension paid Chatham	
	10d. per diem	
1853	Pension paid Tralee	
6 Apr 1854	Arrived per *'Sea Park'*	
1856	Employed as clerk Orderly Office	
Jan 1857	Contributed 3/- to the Florence Nightingale Fund	
1865	Pension paid Western Australia	
Sept 1869	Died	
Service and Personal Details:		
Place of Birth:	Bandon Co. Cork	
Age on Enlistment:	22 years	
Period of Service:	1830 — 1849	
Age on Discharge:	42 years	
Length of Service:	18 years 133 days	
Foreign Service:	West Indies	6 years 293 days
	North America	3 years 168 days
	Ionian Isles	2 years 52 days
Reason for Discharge:	Visceral Disease and Chronic Ophthalmia	
Character:	Good	
Trade or Occupation:	Card Maker	
Can Sign Name:	Yes	
Height:	5' 10¾"	

Hair Colour:	Sandy
Eyes:	Grey
Complexion:	Fresh
Intends to Reside:	Cork

HUSTON Arthur, gunner and driver
RA Invalid Battalion

Surname Variant	HOUSTON
12 Apr 1853	Discharged the Service Tilbury Fort Pension paid 3rd London Pension District 1/- per diem
6 Apr 1854	Arrived per *'Sea Park'*
Sept 1854	Appointed Night Warder without sanction from Commanding Officer [CSO 303]
1854	Pension paid Western Australia
1854	Acting Overseer Convict Establishment at Bunbury
1857	Resigned as Warder Signed over Bunbury Lot 227
1857	To South Australia from Western Australia
20 Mar 1880	Died

Service and Personal Details:

Place of Birth:	Drumglass Tyrone	
Age on Enlistment:	19 years 9 months	
Period of Service:	1832 — 1853	
Age on Discharge:	39 years 11 months	
Length of Service:	21 years 13 days	
Foreign Service:	Barbados	3 months
	Jamaica	1 year 10 months
	Nova Scotia	6 years
Reason for Discharge:	Chronic Rheumatism	
Character:	Indifferent	
Trade or Occupation:	Miner	
Can Sign Name:	Yes	
Height:	5' 8½"	
Hair Colour:	Sandy	
Eyes:	Grey	
Complexion:	Fair	

HUTCHINSON Richard, private
93rd Foot

Surname Variants	HUTCHISON; HUTCHESON
28 July 1863	Discharged the Service Netley Pension paid Edinburgh 1/- per diem
1863	Pension paid 2nd Glasgow Pension District
4 July 1866	Arrived per *'Belgravia'*
1868	Pension paid Melbourne
1873	South Australia
1874	Glasgow

Service and Personal Details:

Place of Birth:	Glasgow Lanarkshire
Age on Enlistment:	18 years

Period of Service:	1848 — 1862	
Age on Discharge:	33 years 4 months	
Length of Service:	14 years 246 days	
Foreign Service:	Crimea	2 years 4 months
	East Indies	5 years 1 month
Medal Entitlement:	Crimea with 4 clasps; Turkish Crimea; Indian Mutiny with clasps	
Reason for Discharge:	Arthritic Rheumatism	
Character:	Good	
Trade or Occupation:	Shoemaker	
Can Sign Name:	Yes	
Height:	5' 8"	
Hair Colour:	Black	
Eyes:	Dark	
Complexion:	Dark	
Intends to Reside:	Edinburgh	

HYLAND John, private
37th Foot

29 Apr 1862	Discharged the Service Pension paid 1st Liverpool Pension District 1/1d. per diem
1862	Pension paid 2nd Manchester Pension District
1863	Pension paid Glasgow
28 Dec 1863	Arrived per *'Lord Dalhousie'*
1864	Occupied West Guildford Lots 122 and 125
1873	Pension increased to 1/3d. per diem for 9 years service in the Enrolled Force
20 Nov 1874	Died
28 Jan 1876	Grant of West Guildford Lots to widow Eliza
June 1876	R. Furlong Sergeant Police: Mrs. Hyland whose late husband was a Pensioner — she is living in a cottage in West Guildford, which was granted to her late husband. She was recommended for outdoor relief during winter months. Now found that Mrs. Hyland and children are starving and in 'immediate want'

Service and Personal Details:

Place of Birth:	Naas Co. Kildare	
Age on Enlistment:	19 years	
Period of Service:	1841 — 1862	
Age on Discharge:	40 years 3 months	
Length of Service:	21 years 52 days	
Foreign Service:	Ceylon	10 years 2 months
	Bengal	3 years 9 months
Medal Entitlement:	Good Conduct with gratuity and Indian Mutiny	
Reason for Discharge:	Own Request on completing 21 years service	
Character:	Very Good	
Trade or Occupation:	Labourer	
Can Sign Name:	X his mark on discharge	
Height:	5' 8½"	

Hair Colour:	Brown
Eyes:	Dark
Complexion:	Fresh
Intends to Reside:	Back of the 'Welsh Harp' Cooper Street
Runcorn Cheshire	

IMPEY Matthew, private
3rd Dragoon Guards

Previous Regiment	15th Hussars
2 June 1863	Discharged the Service Canterbury
	Pension paid 1st North London Pension District
	1/1d. per diem
15 Aug 1865	Arrived per *'Racehorse'*
1866	Pension paid Melbourne
1867	New Zealand

Service and Personal Details:

Place of Birth:	Dunstable Bedfordshire	
Age on Enlistment:	18 years 1 month	
Period of Service:	1831 — 1862	
Age on Discharge:	42 years 1 month	
Length of Service:	24 years 16 days	
Foreign Service:	East Indies	17 years 8 months
Medal Entitlement:	Long Service and Good Conduct with gratuity	
Reason for Discharge:	Own request on completing 24 years service	
Character:	Very Good	
Trade or Occupation:	Groom	
Can Sign Name:	Yes	
Height:	5' 7"	
Hair Colour:	Brown	
Eyes:	Hazel	
Complexion:	Fresh	
Intends to Reside:	Hasting Street, Luton Bedfordshire	

INSKIP William Henry, Colour Serjeant
94th Foot

13 Jan 1852	Discharged the Service Chatham
	Pension paid Woolwich
	1/10d per diem
1852	Pension increased to 2/- per diem
6 Apr 1854	Arrived per *'Sea Park'*
1854	Serving as Sergeant Major Fremantle District
	Enrolled Force Duty Force
1855	Pension paid Sydney

Service and Personal Details:

Place of Birth:	Ingliston Essex	
Age on Enlistment:	18 years 11 months	
Period of Service:	1831 — 1852	
Age on Discharge:	39 years 11 months	
Length of Service:	20 years 51 days	
Foreign Service:	Malta	8 months
	Ceylon	2 months
	East Indies	11 years 11 months

Reason for Discharge:	Epileptic Attacks induced by serving long period in tropical climates
Character:	Very Good
Trade or Occupation:	Labourer
Can Sign Name:	Yes
Height:	5' 7½"
Hair Colour:	Dark Brown
Eyes:	Grey
Complexion:	Sallow
Intends to Reside:	West Tilbury Essex

INSLEY	Charles, Serjeant
	62nd Foot
31 Mar 1857	Discharged the Service Birr Barracks
5 May 1857	Admitted to Out-Pension
	Pension paid Sheffield
	1/5d. per diem
Dec 1857	Pension paid North Stafford
1858	Leicester
24 Nov 1858	Arrived per *'Edwin Fox'*
1865	Pension paid Perth Western Australia

Service and Personal Details:	
Place of Birth:	Loughborough Leicestershire
Age on Enlistment:	18 years 7 months
Period of Service:	1834 — 1857
Age on Discharge:	41 years
Length of Service:	22 years 102 days
Foreign Service:	East Indies 11 years 8 months
Medal Entitlement:	Medal and clasp for the Sutlej Campaign
Reason for Discharge:	Chronic Rheumatism
Character:	Good
Trade or Occupation:	Lace Maker
Can Sign Name:	Yes
Height:	5' 9"
Hair Colour:	Dark Brown
Eyes:	Hazel
Complexion:	Fresh
Intends to Reside:	Loughborough

IRELAND	Richard, Corporal
	63rd Foot
14 Aug 1860	Discharged the Service Chatham
	Pension paid Bristol
	1/1½d. per diem
1860	Pension paid 2nd Manchester Pension District
27 May 1863	Arrived per *'Clyde'*
1868	Employed Assistant Warder
circa June 1874	Transferred from 2nd Perth Pension District to 1st Perth Pension District
1878	Pension increased to 1/6d. per diem for service in the Enrolled Force

12 Sept 1883	Assigned Perth Pensioner Lot 27/H [located left rear of Mt Eliza Barracks]	
24 Sept 1888	Died - buried East Perth Cemetery	
Service and Personal Details:		
Place of Birth:	Painswick Gloucestershire	
Age on Enlistment:	19 years 3 months	
Period of Service:	1839—1860	
Age on Discharge:	40 years 8 months	
Length of Service:	20 years 294 days	
Foreign Service:	East Indies	7 years 7 months
	Crimea	1 year 10 months
	Nova Scotia	3 years 11 months
Medal Entitlement:	Crimea	
Reason for Discharge:	Chronic Rheumatism	
Character:	Very Good	
Trade or Occupation:	Labourer	
Can Sign Name:	Yes	
Height:	5' 6"	
Hair Colour:	Dark Brown	
Eyes:	Hazel	
Complexion:	Dark	
Intends to Reside:	Bristol England	

IRELAND	Robert, private	
	RA Depot Brigade	
15 Nov 1859	Discharged the Service Woolwich	
	Pension paid Woolwich	
	1/- per diem	
1860	Pension paid 1st Belfast Pension District	
27 May 1863	Arrived per *'Clyde'*	
Oct 1864	To South Australia per *'Sea Ripple'*	
1865	Pension paid Adelaide South Australia	
10 Oct 1872	Died Adelaide South Australia	
Service and Personal Details:		
Place of Birth:	Whitewell Cummoney Co Antrim	
Age on Enlistment:	21 years	
Period of Service:	1838 — 1859	
Age on Discharge:	42 years	
Length of Service:	21 years 240 days	
Foreign Service:	Gibraltar	15 years 8 months
Reason for Discharge:	His having completed 21 years service	
Character:	Exemplary	
Trade or Occupation:	Butcher	
Can Sign Name:	Yes	
Height:	5' 8½"	
Hair Colour:	Light	
Eyes:	Blue	
Complexion:	Fair	
Religion:	Swedenborgian	

ISLAND	John, private
	2nd Foot
11 May 1850	Discharged the Service Newry
9 July 1850	Admitted to Out-Pension
	8d. per diem
	Pension paid Manchester
18 Oct 1851	Arrived per *'Minden'*
Jan 1857	Contributed 2/- to the Florence Nightingale Fund
1860	Died aged 38 - buried East Perth Cemetery

Service and Personal Details:

Place of Birth:	St Helens Liverpool	
Age on Enlistment:	19 years	
Period of Service:	1839 — 1850	
Age on Discharge:	29 years 11 months	
Length of Service:	10 years 264 days	
Foreign Service:	East Indies	5 years 10 months
Reason for Discharge:	Wounded in left ankle in India before the enemy	
Character:	Good	
Trade or Occupation:	Labourer	
Can Sign Name:	X his mark on discharge	
Height:	5' 10"	
Hair Colour:	Brown	
Eyes:	Hazel	
Complexion:	Fresh	
Intends to Reside:	St Helens Liverpool	

IVE	John James, Corporal
	2nd Foot
25 Oct 1852	Discharged the Service Kinsale
9 Nov 1852	Admitted to Out-Pension
	10d. per diem
	Pension paid Leeds
1855	Serving with West Yorkshire Militia
1856	Pension paid Leeds York
	Leeds
8 June 1858	Arrived per *'Lord Raglan'*
1861	To South Australia from Western Australia
1875	Pension paid South Australia
2 May 1876	Died South Australia

Service and Personal Details:

Place of Birth:	Clerkenwell London	
Age on Enlistment:	18 years 3 months	
Period of Service:	1836 — 1852	
Age on Discharge:	34 years 10 months	
Length of Service:	16 years 224 days	
Foreign Service:	East Indies	9 years 42 days
Reason for Discharge:	Disease of the Heart	
Character:	Good	
Trade or Occupation:	Draper	
Can Sign Name:	Yes	
Height:	5' 8"	

Hair Colour:	Brown
Eyes:	Grey
Complexion:	Fresh

JACKSON	James, private	
	48th Foot	
12 Dec 1849	Discharged the Service Dublin	
	Pension paid 1st Dublin Pension District	
	6d. per diem for 5 years	
1850	Pension paid 1st East London Pension District	
2 Aug 1852	Arrived per *'William Jardine'*	
1875	Pension paid Western Australia	
1875	W.O. correspondence with S.O. Perth West. Aust.	
Service and Personal Details:		
Place of Birth:	Dublin	
Age on Enlistment:	18 years	
Period of Service:	1835 — 1850	
Age on Discharge:	32 years 2 months	
Length of Service:	14 years 34 days	
Foreign Service:	Gibraltar	5 years 4 months
	West Indies	3 years 1 month
Reason for Discharge:	Rupture of right side	
Character:	Bad though Latterly Improving	
Trade or Occupation:	Labourer	
Can Sign Name:	Yes	
Height:	5' 7"	
Hair Colour:	Dark Brown	
Eyes:	Hazel	
Complexion:	Sallow	
Intends to Reside:	Dublin	

JACKSON	John, gunner EIC
	Bombay Artillery
	War Office Pension No 136
24 June 1861	Admitted to Out-pension
	Pension paid 2nd Dublin Pension District
	1/- per diem
9 Jan 1868	Arrived per *'Hougoumont'*
1870	To Melbourne from Perth Western Australia
1871	Pension paid Melbourne
1875	Tasmania
1878	Victoria
Service and Personal Details:	
Where Born:	Dublin
Trade or Occupation:	Labourer
Service Period:	Unlimited
Presidency:	Bombay
Age on Discharge:	40 years
Length of Service:	24 years 8 months
Reason for Discharge:	Time expired
Character:	Good

Height:	5' 8¾"
Complexion:	Fair
Eye Colour:	Grey
Hair Colour:	Brown
Intends to Reside:	Dublin

JACKSON William, private
108th Foot

Previous Regiments	42nd; 74th
24 Apr 1866	Discharged the Service Netley Pension paid Edinburgh 10d. per diem "Was to travel on the *'Hougoumont'* but disappeared in Edinburgh"
1874	Pension paid 2nd Glasgow Pension District
14 Apr 1874	Died

JAFFREY James, private
44th Foot

Previous Regiment	92nd Foot
Surname Variants	JAFFERY; JEFFERY; JEFFREY
6 Nov 1855	Discharged the Service
13 Nov 1855	Admitted to Out-pension Pension paid Paisley 11d. per diem
12 Sept 1864	Arrived per *'Merchantman'* [2]
1866	Employed Convict Establishment Perth
1881	Pension increased to 1/5d. per diem
Aug 1881	Assigned and occupied North Fremantle Lot P65
Aug 1884	Granted Fee Simple North Fremantle Lot P65
Dec 1885	For Sale — North Fremantle Town Lot P65 of 2 acres facing Thompson's Rd., and Rocky Bay

Service and Personal Details:

Place of Birth:	Abbey Paisley Renfrewshire	
Age on Enlistment:	17 years 6 months	
Period of Service:	1845 — 1855	
Age on Discharge:	28 years [or 30 years depending on record]	
Length of Service:	7 years 311	
Foreign Service:	Ionian Isles	2 years 1 month
	Gibraltar	1 year 11 months
	Malta	1 month
	Turkey	4 months
	Crimea	1 year 3 months
Medal Entitlement:	Crimea	
Reason for Discharge:	Shell wound to fore arm received at Sebastopol	
Character:	Good	
Trade or Occupation:	Labourer	
Can Sign Name:	Yes	
Height:	5' 5¾"	
Hair Colour:	Brown	
Eyes:	Blue	
Complexion:	Fresh	
Intends to Reside:	Paisley	

JAMES	Edward, Regimental Serjeant Major 21st Hussars
Previous Regiments European Cavalry	6th Dragoons; Bengal Artillery; 3rd Bengal
26 Apr 1870	Discharged the Service Netley Pension paid Deptford 2/-½d. per diem
1870	Pension paid 1st North London Pension District
1871	1st East London Pension District
19 Feb 1874	Arrived per *'Naval Brigade'*
1881	Assigned Perth Pensioner Lot 30/H
1881	Perth Pensioner Lot 30/H cancelled
July 1881	Received in lieu Perth Lot 76/E Claisebrook
Jan 1882	Application for Title to Perth Lot 76/E
17 Sept 1883	Pensioner Sergeant E James to be granted Fee Simple Perth Lot 76/E Perth
1883	Late Lance Corporal of Police — Application to be allowed to retain appointment of Drill Instructor to the Police
1886	Drill Instructor to City Police
Jan 1887	Died – buried East Perth Pioneer Cemetery

Service and Personal Details:

Place of Birth:	Deptford Kent	
Age on Enlistment:	27 years 6 months	
Period of Service:	1858 — 1870	
Age on Discharge:	39 years ? 1 month	
Length of Service:	14 years 82 days [reckoned - over 21 years total]	
Foreign Service:	India	11 years 127 days
	Crimea	2 years 40 days
Medal Entitlement:	Long and Meritorious Service with gratuity; Crimea with 3 clasps; Turkish Crimean; Mutiny	
Reason for Discharge:	Hernia right side and Impaired Vision	
Character:	Very Good	
Trade or Occupation:	Servant	
Can Sign Name:	Yes	
Height:	6'	
Hair Colour:	Light Brown	
Eyes:	Blue	
Complexion:	Fresh	
Intends to Reside:	Trinity Close, Black Heath Hill Greenwich Kent	
Married:	1863 Emily Dowling nee Smith Bengal India	
Children [some] :	Albert Edward b. 1864 Umballa Bengal India Florence Ellen b. *c*1865 Umballa Bengal India m. *c*1886 Jacob van Buskirk Bingay Perth Madeline Clara b. 1866 Umballa India Edith Amelia b. 1867 Umballa India Octavius Percy b. 1870 Bombay India m. 1.] *c*1896 Alice McManus Perth m. 2.] *c*1903 Alice Langden Guildford Blanche Gertrude b. 1873 England	

JAMES	William, private

also known as	William **JAMIS**
	99th Foot
5 Apr 1849	Arrived per *'Radcliffe'* with regiment
8 Mar 1853	Discharge approved
	Pension paid Perth Western Australia
	7½d. per diem for 2½ years
1856	Died
Service and Personal Details:	
Place of Birth:	Maidstone Kent
Age on Enlistment:	23 years
Period of Service:	1842 — 1853
Age on Discharge:	33 years
Length of Service:	10 years 170 days
Foreign Service:	Australian Colonies 8 years
Reason for Discharge:	Deafness and loss of part of right fore finger
Character:	Good
Trade or Occupation:	Groom
Can Sign Name:	X his mark on discharge
Height:	5' 7"
Hair Colour:	Dark Brown
Eyes:	Brown
Complexion:	Sallow
Intended Residence:	Perth Western Australia
JANES	Robert, private
	RM
Surname Variant	JAMES
	Discharged the Service
	£16/14/- per annum
1867	Pension paid Trowbridge
9 Jan 1868	Arrived per *'Hougoumont'*
1873	Died aged 40 Fremantle
JARVIS	Henry, Serjeant
	Sappers and Miners
17 Dec 1851	Arrived per *'Anna Robinson'*
22 July 1863	Discharged the Service Pembroke
28 July 1863	Discharge approved
14 Nov 1877	Aged 50
Nov 1877	Deferred Pension paid Adelaide South Australia
20 Aug 1878	Deferred Pension ratified
1906	Died
Service and Personal Details:	
Place of Birth:	Warbleton Lewes Sussex
Age on Enlistment:	21 years 6 months
Period of Service:	1849 — 1863
Service to 1855:	5 years 7 months
Age at 1855:	27 years 1 month
Age on Discharge:	35 years 8 months
Length of Service:	14 years 69 days
Foreign Service:	Western Australia 8 years

Reason for Discharge:	His having been granted a Free Discharge with Right of Registry of 4d. per diem on attaining 50 years of age and appointed Foreman of Works in the Western Australian Convict Establishment
Character:	Exemplary
Trade or Occupation:	Carpenter
Can Sign Name:	Yes
Height:	5' 9"
Hair Colour:	Dark Brown
Eye Colour:	Hazel
Complexion:	Dark
Intended Residence:	Fremantle Western Australia

JARVIS	Joseph, drummer
	2nd/5th Foot
Previous Regiment	85th Foot
17 Nov 1868	Discharged the Service
	Pension paid Leicester
	1/1d. per diem
1873	Pension paid Greenwich
19 Feb 1874	Arrived per *'Naval Brigade'*
	Assigned Cockburn Sound Loc P227 at Willagee Swamp
1881	Pension increased to 1/3½d. per diem for 6 years service in Enrolled Force
1884	Granted Cockburn Sound Loc P227 at Willagee Swamp
June 1897	Residing Fremantle
1899	W.O. Correspondence — Mr Brown for address
Feb 1900	a Joseph Jarvis 2nd Fusiliers attended fete at Fremantle Oval
1908	Died aged 79 buried Fremantle Cemetery

Service and Personal Details:

Place of Birth:	Sheffield Yorkshire	
Age on Enlistment:	14 years	
Period of Service:	1843 — 1868	
Age on Discharge:	39 years 3 months	
Length of Service:	21 years 71 days [reckoned]	
Foreign Service:	West Indies	1 year 5 months
	Mauritius	3 years
	Cape of Good Hope	8 years 11 months
Medal Entitlement:	Long Service and Good Conduct with gratuity	
Reason for Discharge:	Own request having served 21 years	
Character:	Very Good	
Trade or Occupation:	Labourer	
Can Sign Name:	Yes	
Height:	5' 3"	
Hair Colour:	Brown	
Eyes:	Hazel	
Complexion:	Fresh	
Intends to Reside:	Leicester	

JEFFERS	Charles, private
	89th Foot
5 May 1862	Discharged the Service Fermoy
27 May 1862	Admitted to Out-Pension
	Pension paid 2nd Dublin Pension District
	8d. per diem
9 Jan 1868	Arrived per *'Hougoumont'*
1869	Pension paid Calcutta

Service and Personal Details:

Place of Birth:	St Georges Dublin	
Age on Enlistment:	16 years	
Period of Service:	1839 — 1862	
Age on Discharge:	39 years	
Length of Service:	21 years 11 days [reckomed]	
Foreign Service:	North America	10 months
	Gibraltar	8 months
	Crimea	4 months
Medal Entitlement:	Crimean with clasp; Turkish Crimean	
Reason for Discharge:	Own Request having completed 21 years	
Character:	Good	
Trade or Occupation:	Labourer	
Can Sign Name:	Yes	
Height:	5' 5¾"	
Hair Colour:	Brown	
Eyes:	Grey	
Complexion:	Fresh	
Intends to Reside:	Dublin	

JENNINGS	Daniel [David], private
	60th Foot
10 June 1853	Discharged the Service Birr
9 Aug 1853	Admitted to Out-Pension
	Pension paid Southampton
	1/- per diem
18 July 1855	Arrived per *'Adelaide'* "as a Convict Guard
Jan 1857	Contributed 1/- to the Florence Nightingale Fund
1863	Stationed Perth District
1864	ptve D Jennings Pensioner Force at Perth contributed to the Greenough Fire Relief Fund
Jan 1865	Application for Title to Perth Lot116/Y
1873	Pension increased to 1/3d. per diem for 17 years 7 months service in the Enrolled Force
1892	Residing Hardinge Street, Perth
May 1893	Died — buried East Perth Pioneer Cemetery

Service and Personal Details:

Place of Birth:	Sherbourne Hampshire	
Age on Enlistment:	18 years 5 months	
Period of Service:	1831 — 1853	
Age on Discharge:	40 years 1 month	
Length of Service:	21 years 239 days	
Foreign Service:	Gibraltar	5 years 5 months
	Jamaica	2 years 11 months
	Quebec	3 years 1 month

Reason for Discharge:	Chronic Rheumatism and worn out
Character:	Very Good
Trade or Occupation:	Labourer
Can Sign Name:	X his mark on discharge
Height:	5' 9"
Hair Colour:	Dark Brown
Eyes:	Grey
Complexion:	Sallow
Intends to Reside:	Reading Berkshire

JENNINGS	Thomas, Serjeant
	61st Foot
9 Mar 1852	Discharged the Service
	Pension paid Galway
	1/6d. per diem
14 Aug 1854	Arrived per *'Ramillies'*
Jan 1857	Contributed 2/6 to the Florence Nightingale Fund
1858	Pension paid Melbourne

Service and Personal Details:

Place of Birth:	Holymount Co. Mayo	
Period of Service:	circa 1831 — 1852	
Age on Discharge:	40 years	
Length of Service:	21 years 2 months	
Foreign Service:	India	5 years 7 months
Reason for Discharge:	Chronic Rheumatism, Dyspnoea and declining activity	
Character:	Very Good	
Trade or Occupation:	Labourer	
Can Sign Name:	Yes	
Height:	5' 10¾"	
Hair Colour:	Brown	
Eyes:	Grey	
Complexion:	Fresh	

JERROLD	Charles, private
	43rd Foot
11 Oct 1853	Discharged the Service Chatham
	Pension paid Ipswich
	8d. per diem
24 May 1855	Arrived per *'Stag'*
27 Jan 1859	Died

Service and Personal Details:

Place of Birth:	St Marys Bury St Edmunds Suffolk	
Age on Enlistment:	18 years	
Period of Service:	1837 — 1853	
Age on Discharge:	34 years 3 months	
Length of Service:	16 years 70 days	
Foreign Service:	North America	5 years 10 months
Reason for Discharge:	Unfit for further service	
Character:	Good	

Trade or Occupation:	Labourer
Can Sign Name:	X his mark on discharge
Height:	5' 6"
Hair Colour:	Brown
Eyes:	Hazel
Complexion:	Fresh
Intends to Reside:	Bury St Edmunds

JOHNSON Benjamin, private
Rifle Brigade

Surname Variant	JOHNSTON
22 Nov 1853	Discharged the Service Chatham Pension paid 2nd West London Pension District 1/- per diem
24 May 1855	Arrived per *'Stag'*
1856	To South Australia from Western Australia
1858	Pension paid Victoria
1875	Sydney

Service and Personal Details:

Place of Birth:	All Saints Hereford
Age on Enlistment:	18 years 6 months
Period of Service:	1832 — 1853
Age on Discharge:	40 years or 39 years 5 months
Length of Service:	20 years 309 days
Foreign Service:	Malta & Ionian Isles 5 years 7 months Cape of Good Hope 3 years
Medal Entitlement:	Kaffir War
Reason for Discharge:	Rheumatism
Character:	Good
Trade or Occupation:	Bricklayer
Can Sign Name:	Yes
Height:	5' 7¼"
Hair Colour:	Brown
Eyes:	Hazel
Complexion:	Fresh
Intends to Reside:	Pimlico London

JOHNSON Robert, Corporal
62nd Foot

6 June 1862	Discharged the Service Belfast
24 June 1862	Admitted to Out-Pension Pension paid 2nd Belfast Pension District 9½d. per diem
1864	Pension paid 2nd Glasgow Pension District
1865	Pension paid 1st East London Pension District
15 Aug 1865	Arrived per *'Racehorse'*
1869	Pension paid Melbourne

Service and Personal Details:

Place of Birth:	Drumbow Dublin Co. Down
Age on Enlistment:	20 years
Period of Service:	1841 — 1862

Age on Discharge:	41 years 1 month	
Length of Service:	21 years 8 days	
Foreign Service:	East Indies	5 years 4 months
	Cape of Good Hope	7 months
Reason for Discharge:	Own request having completed 21 years service	
Character:	Good	
Trade or Occupation:	Tailor	
Can Sign Name:	Yes	
Height:	5' 5"	
Hair Colour:	Dark Brown	
Eyes:	Grey	
Complexion:	Sallow	
Intends to Reside:	Belfast	

JOHNSON	William Robert, private	
	53rd Foot	
25 Nov 1856	Discharged the Service Chatham	
	Pension paid 2nd Manchester Pension District	
	1/- per diem	
8 June 1858	Arrived per *'Lord Raglan'*	
1861	Pension paid Melbourne	
Service and Personal Details:		
Place of Birth:	Limerick Ireland	
Age on Enlistment:	14 years [from Royal Military Asylum]	
Period of Service:	1832 — 1856	
Age on Discharge:	39 years 2 months	
Length of Service:	20 years 33 days	
Foreign Service:	Gibraltar &	
	Malta &	
	Ionian Isles	7 years 4 months
	East Indies	8 years 7 months
Medal Entitlement:	Medal and clasp for Sutlej; Punjaub Campaign	
Reason for Discharge:	Impaired general health	
Character:	Good	
Trade or Occupation:	Labourer	
Can Sign Name:	Yes	
Height:	5' 8"	
Hair Colour:	Light Brown	
Eyes:	Grey	
Complexion:	Fresh	
Distinguishing Marks:	An extensive scar on the left arm	

JOHNSON	William, private
	74th Foot
10 Dec 1861	Discharged the Service Chatham
	Pension paid Chatham
	9d. per diem
13 July 1867	Arrived per *'Norwood'* [2]
1869	Pension paid Melbourne
Service and Personal Details:	
Place of Birth:	St Ninians Stirling Scotland

Age on Enlistment:	20 years	
Period of Service:	1840 — 1861	
Age on Discharge:	41 years	
Length of Service:	17 years 296 days [reckoned]	
Foreign Service:	North America	3 years 9 months
	Cape of Good Hope	2 years 8 months
	East Indies	7 years 3 months
Medal Entitlement:	South Africa 1851/1853; medal and prize money for the capture of Shoolapore [sic]	
Reason for Discharge:	Chronic Rheumatism and quite worn out	
Character:	Latterly Good	
Trade or Occupation:	Labourer	
Can Sign Name:	Yes	
Height:	5' 9"	
Hair Colour:	Dark Brown	
Eyes:	Grey	
Complexion:	Dark	
Distinguishing Marks:	Marked with letter 'D'	
Intends to Reside:	Glasgow but decided on Chatham	

JOHNSON	William, Corporal 2nd Dragoons Assistant Warder
1865	Warder at Portland Prison
Rate of salary	£51/-/- per annum
4 July 1866	Arrived per *'Belgravia'*
1879	Died

Service and Personal Details:

Place of Birth:	Old Macher Aberdeen Scotland
Age on Attestation:	20 years
Period of Service:	1855 — 1863
Length of Service:	8 years 86 days
Reason for Discharge:	Own Request having bought himself out
Character:	Very Good
Trade or Occupation:	Labourer

JOHNSTON	William, Corporal EIC Bengal Artillery
Surname Variant	JOHNSON; JOHNSTONE Out Pension No 121
Aug 1858	Admitted to Out-pension Pension paid 1st Glasgow Pension District
1/3d. per diem	
1859	Pension paid Belfast
1861	Pension paid 2nd Glasgow Pension District
1862	Bermuda
15 Feb 1863	Arrived per *'Merchantman'* [1]
1869	a William Johnston employed by Convict Establishment at York Western Australia

the following two entries could refer to either William Johnson/Johnstone

July 1872	Assigned Pensioner Lot P5 at York
Nov 1872	Application for Title to P5 at York

Service and Personal Details:	
Where Born:	Glasgow
Trade or Occupation:	Sawyer
Length of Service:	6 years 4 months
Age on Discharge:	32 years
Reason for Discharge:	Right arm rendered useless by accidence from a gun carriage wheel
Height:	5' 9¾"
Complexion:	Fresh
Eye Colour:	Grey
Hair Colour:	Dark Brown
Intends to Reside:	Glasgow
Married:	? Jane
Children:	Martha
	m. *c*1868 Thomas Giblett York
	William J
	a Mary Johnston
	m. *c*1913 Frederick Bussell Vines Wellington

JOHNSTON	James, private
	84th Foot
Previous Regiment	46th Foot
Surname Variant	JOHNSTONE
10 June 1862	Discharged the Service Aldershot
	Pension paid Gloucester
	1/- per diem
1862	Pension paid 2nd Manchester Pension District
31 Dec 1862	Arrived per *'York'*
1865	To Eastern Colonies from Perth West Australia
1873	Pension paid Adelaide South Australia
1879	Correspondence with W.O.
Service and Personal Details:	
Place of Birth:	St Peters Manchester Lancashire
Age on Enlistment:	19 years 8 months
Period of Service:	1842 — 1862
Age on Discharge:	39 years 10 months
Length of Service:	21 years 73 days
Foreign Service:	East Indies 17 years 17 days
Medal Entitlement:	Indian Mutiny with two clasps
Reason for Discharge:	Own Request having served 21 years
Character:	Very Good
Trade or Occupation:	Silk Weaver
Can Sign Name:	Yes
Height:	5' 9½"
Hair Colour:	Brown
Eyes:	Hazel
Complexion:	Fresh
Distinguishing Marks:	Pock Pitted
Intends to Reside:	Manchester

JOHNSTONE	William, private
	28th Foot

Surname Variant	JOHNSTON
19 Mar 1855	Discharged the Service
27 Mar 1855	Admitted to Out-Pension
	Pension paid Aberdeen
	1/- per diem
1856	Pension paid 2nd Plymouth Pension District
19 Aug 1858	Arrived per *'Sultana'*
1867	Residing North Fremantle
1867	"Off Roll for manslaughter" convicted of killing James Alcock
4 July 1867	William Johnson, was charged with the murder of Andrew Alcock at Fremantle on the 7th May 1867 Edward Ball corporal of Pensioners at North Fremantle stated he knew the pensioner living at North Fremantle also knew the deceased [also a pensioner] but not on the Force. Verdict of not guilty of murder but guilty of manslaughter and sentenced to 6 years penal servitude

Service and Personal Details:		
Place of Birth:	Stokenchurch Oxfordshire	
Age on Enlistment:	18 years 2 months	
Period of Service:	1833 — 1855	
Age on Discharge:	40 years	
Length of Service:	21 years 105 days	
Foreign Service:	New South Wales	6 years
	East Indies	6 years
Reason for Discharge:	Having completed 21 years service	
Character:	Very Good	
Trade or Occupation:	Labourer	
Can Sign Name:	X his mark on discharge	
Height:	5' 8"	
Hair Colour:	Dark Brown	
Eyes:	Hazel	
Complexion:	Fresh	
Distinguishing Marks:	Pock pitted	
Intends to Reside:	Aberdeen	

JONES	James, private [702]
	38th Foot
27 Aug 1844	Discharged the Service Chatham
	Pension paid Wolverhampton
	9d. per diem
1844	Pension paid Chatham
1849	Stafford
1849	Wolverhampton
1 June 1850	Arrived per *'Scindian'*
Aug 1850	Assigned and occupied Pensioner Allotment P13 at South Perth

Service and Personal Details:	
Place of Birth:	West Bromage [sic] Staffordshire
Age on Enlistment:	18 years
Period of Service:	1826 — 1844

Age on Discharge:	36 years 3 months	
Length of Service:	17 years 203 months	
Foreign Service:	East Indies	2 years 352 days
Reason for Discharge:	Fever	
Character:	Very Good	
Trade or Occupation:	Miner	
Can Sign Name:	X his mark on discharge	
Height:	6'	
Hair Colour:	Brown	
Eyes:	Grey	
Complexion:	Sallow	

JONES

	John, private
	RM
	£13/12/- per annum
28 June 1851	Arrived per *'Pyrenees'* [1]
1852	Employed as Gaoler Toodyay
1858	Occupied Toodyay Lot P3
3 Jan 1871	Died of dysentery and weakness aged 57
4 Jan 1871	Buried Fremantle

JONES

	Robert, private
	Rifle Brigade
8 Aug 1848	Discharged the Service Chatham
	Pension paid Bolton
	6p per diem
2 Aug 1852	Arrived per *'William Jardine'*

Service and Personal Details:

Place of Birth:	Wigan Lancashire	
Age on Enlistment:	19 years	
Period of Service:	1826 — 1848	
Age on Discharge:	41 years	
Length of Service:	20 years 172 days	
Foreign Service:	Malta	5 years
	Ionian Isles	5 years 3 months
	Bermuda	11 months
	North America	5 years 9 months
Reason for Discharge:	Chronic Catarrh and old tumour on the right outer hamstring	
Character:	Bad	
Trade or Occupation:	Stonemason	
Can Sign Name:	Yes	
Height:	5' 8½"	
Hair Colour:	Light Brown	
Eyes:	Grey	
Complexion:	Fresh	
Intends to Reside:	Wigan Lancashire	

JONES

	Samuel, private
	12th Foot
12 Nov 1861	Discharged the Service Cork
	9d. per diem
	Pension paid 1st Manchester Pension District

13 July 1867	Arrived per *'Norwood'* [2]	
1868	Pension paid Melbourne	
1869	"Coming home" — Pension to be paid Manchester	

Service and Personal Details:

Place of Birth:	Chester Cheshire	
Age on Enlistment:	17 years	
Period of Service:	1839 — 1861	
Age on Discharge:	39 years	
Length of Service:	21 years 14 days [1 year 2 months under age]	
Foreign Service:	Mauritius	8 years 2 months
	Cape of Good Hope	7 years 5 months
Reason for Discharge:	Own request having completed 21 years service	
Character:	Good	
Trade or Occupation:	Shoemaker	
Can Sign Name:	Yes	
Height:	5' 7"	
Hair Colour:	Dark Brown	
Eyes:	Dark Brown	
Complexion:	Sallow	
Intends to Reside:	Manchester	

JONES	Thomas, private	
	59th Foot	
Previous Regiment	6th Foot	
24 Feb 1849	Discharged the Service Birr	
24 Apr 1849	Admitted to Out-Pension	
	Pension paid Shropshire	
	1/- per diem	
1850	Pension paid Nottingham	
14 Aug 1854	Arrived per *'Ramillies'*	
1855	Pension paid Adelaide South Australia	
1871	Died	

Service and Personal Details:

Place of Birth:	Whittington Shropshire	
Age on Enlistment:	20 years	
Period of Service:	1828 — 1849	
Age on Discharge:	40 years 10 months	
Length of Service:	20 years 301 days	
Foreign Service:	Mediterranean	6 years 70 days
Reason for Discharge:	Unfit for further service	
Character:	Very Good	
Trade or Occupation:	Iron Monger	
Can Sign Name:	Yes on Attestation	
Height:	5' 8½"	
Hair Colour:	Black	
Eyes:	Black	
Complexion:	Fair	
Intends to Reside:	Wittington [sic]	

JONES	Thomas, gunner EIC
	Madras Horse Artillery "B" Troop

	Out Pension No 108
28 Feb 1855	Admitted to Out-pension
	Pension paid South London Pension District
	1/- per diem
10 Sept 1856	Arrived per *'Runnymede'*
1858	Pension paid Western Australia
1861	Melbourne
1875	Pension paid Melbourne

Service and Personal Details:

Where Born:	St Saviours Southwark London
Trade or Occupation:	Harness Maker
Age on Enlistment:	21 years
Service Period:	Unlimited
Presidency:	Madras
Age on Discharge:	43 years
Length of Service:	21 years 2 months
Reason for Discharge:	Own request
Character:	Good
Height:	5' 7" or 5'7½"
Complexion:	Fresh
Eye Colour:	Blue
Hair Colour:	Brown or Light Brown
Intends to Reside:	Kennington Surrey

JONES	William, Serjeant
	6th Foot
13 May 1840	Discharged the Service
	Pension paid Leicester
	9d. per diem for 2 years conditional
10 Sept 1856	Arrived per *'Runnymede'*
1858	To South Australia from Fremantle
1860	Died

Service and Personal Details:

Place of Birth:	Morley Yorkshire
Age on Enlistment:	18 years
Period of Service:	1834 — 1840
Age on Discharge:	23 years 1 month
Length of Service:	5 years 36 days
Foreign Service:	East Indies 4 years 1 month
Reason for Discharge:	Remittent Fever caused by an attack of Cholera
Character:	Very Good
Trade or Occupation:	Clothier
Can Sign Name:	Yes
Height:	5' 8½"
Hair Colour:	Brown
Eyes:	Grey
Complexion:	Fair
Remarks:	Landed Gravesend 13th April 1840
Intends to Reside:	Leeds

JONES	William, Serjeant
	77th Foot

26 Nov 1850	Discharged the Service Chatham Pension paid Brighton 2/- per diem	
1852	Pension paid Woolwich	
30 Apr 1853	Arrived per *'Pyrenees'* [2]	
1854	Pension paid Adelaide South Australia	
4 Jan 1855	Died Adelaide	

Service and Personal Details:

Place of Birth:	Edenbridge Kent	
Age on Enlistment:	20 years	
Period of Service:	1829 — 1850	
Age on Discharge:	41 years	
Length of Service:	20 years 354 days	
Foreign Service:	West Indies	3 years 4 months
	Mediterranean	5 years 4 months
Reason for Discharge:	Chronic Pulmonary Disease	
Character:	Good	
Trade or Occupation:	Labourer	
Can Sign Name:	Yes	
Height:	5' 8½"	
Hair Colour:	Brown	
Eyes:	Grey	
Complexion:	Fresh	
Intends to Reside:	Tunbridge Kent	

JONES	William, private Rifle Brigade — Depot 1st Battalion	
2 Dec 1856	Discharged the Service Chatham Pension paid 2nd Belfast Pension District 6d. per diem	
4 July 1866	Arrived per *'Belgravia'*	
12 Feb 1880	Assigned North Fremantle Lots P43 and P44	
Jan 1881	Pension increased to 1/- per diem for service in the Enrolled Force of Western Australia	
1881	Recommended for £15 Pensioner's Grant	
Oct 1883	Granted Fee Simple North Fremantle Lots P43 and P44	
Nov 1897	Died - residing Fremantle	

Service and Personal Details:

Place of Birth:	Guilford [sic] Devon [sic]	
Age on Enlistment:	24 years	
Period of Service:	1854 — 1856	
Age on Discharge:	26 years 3 months	
Length of Service:	341 days	
Foreign Service:	Crimea	8 months
Medal Entitlement:	Crimea with clasp; ?Turkish Crimean Landed in Crimea 1st Dec 1854; Served at the siege of Sevastopol 5th May 1855	
Reason for Discharge:	Frost bite on right hand and arm resulting in the amputation of right forefinger	

Character:	Bad
Trade or Occupation:	Labourer
Can Sign Name:	X his mark on discharge
Height:	5' 6½"
Hair Colour:	Auburn
Eyes:	Grey
Complexion:	Fresh
Intends to Reside:	Dover but decided on 24 John Street Belfast Ireland

JOSE	William Serjeant [Military Pensioner]
	Royal Sapper and Miners
Feb 1861	Discharged the Service Fremantle West Aust
1874	Residing Norfolk St. Fremantle
1879	Awarded Deferred Pension of 6d. per diem

Service and Personal Details:

Place of Birth:	Kenwyn Truro Cornwall	
Age on Enlistment:	22 years 8 months	
Period of Service:	1841 — 1861	
Age on Discharge:	42 years	
Length of Service:	19 years 88 days	
Foreign Service:	Halifax	7 years 9 months
	West Aust	9 years 47 days
Reason for Discharge:	Granted a Free Discharge to settle in Colony with 12 months pay and Right of Registry for a Deferred Pension on him attaining 60 years	
Character:	Very Good	
Trade or Occupation:	Sawyer	
Can Sign Name:	Yes	
Height:	5' 7"	
Hair Colour:	Dark Brown	
Eyes:	Dark Brown	
Complexion:	Ruddy	
Intends to Reside:	Freemantle [sic] West Australia	

JOSLIN	David, private
	2nd Foot
Surname Variant	JOSKIN
4 Apr 1867	Discharged the Service Chatham
23 Apr 1867	Admitted to Out-Pension
	10d. per diem
	Pension paid 2nd North London Pension District
1867	Pension paid 1st North London Pension District
9 Jan 1868	Arrived per *'Hougoumont'* [aged 39 on arrival]
	In stepson's obituary described as Warder on board the *Hougomont* [sic]
May 1881	Applied for an adjoining block of land
1881	Pension increased to 1/3d. per diem for 11 years service in the Enrolled Force
1882	Assigned North Fremantle Lot 789 located at Lime Kilns
1891	Died

1899	Grant of Probate	
Service and Personal Details:		
Place of Birth:	Thaxted Essex	
Age on Enlistment:	20 years	
Period of Service:	1845 — 1867	
Age on Discharge:	41 years 5 months	
Length of Service:	21 years 136 days	
Foreign Service:	Cape of Good Hope	8 years 7 months
	China	7 months
Medal Entitlement:	Kaffir; China with 2 clasps	
Reason for Discharge:	Own Request having served 21 years	
Character:	Good	
Trade or Occupation:	Labourer	
Can Sign Name:	Yes	
Height:	5' 9"	
Hair Colour:	Brown	
Eyes:	Black	
Complexion:	Fair	
Intends to Reside:	No. 1 Vine Str. Higher Pond Street London	
Married:	m. 1867 Sarah Bush Middlesex	
Children:	Thomas Bush [stepson] b. *c*1857 England [father killed in the Crimea] m. *c*1880 Sarah Ann Smirk Rockingham	
	William b. *c*1868 d. *c*1868 Fremantle	
	William Joslin b. *c*1870	

JOYCE	John, private	
	37th Foot	
Surname Variant	JOICE	
25 Jan 1848	Discharged the Service Chatham	
	Pension paid Cork	
	1/- per diem	
19 Aug 1853	Arrived per *'Robert Small'*	
Jan 1857	Contributed 2/- to the Florence Nightingale Fund	
1857	Assigned Pensioner Lot P7 at York	
1863	Application for Title to P7 at York	
1864	ptve J Joyce Pensioner Force York contributed to the Greenough Fire Relief Fund	
Aug 1871	Pensioner John Joyce 37th Regt of Foot, pension rate of a shilling per diem applies for relief	
1872	Died	
Service and Personal Details:		
Place of Birth:	Ballinamond Co. Cork	
Age on Enlistment:	20 years	
Period of Service:	1827 — 1848	
Age on Discharge:	41 years	
Length of Service:	20 years 355 days	
Foreign Service:	Bermuda	2 years
	Jamaica	6 years 5 months
	Nova Scotia	2 years 9 months
Reason for Discharge:	Chronic Rheumatism	
Character:	Very Good	

Trade or Occupation:	Labourer
Can Sign Name:	X his mark on discharge
Height:	5' 9"
Hair Colour:	Dark Brown
Eyes:	Grey
Complexion:	Fresh
Intends to Reside:	Cork

JOYCE

	Martin, Corporal EIC
	Bengal Artillery 1st Battalion 3rd Company
	Out Pension No 107
1854	Embarked for UK per *'Adelaide'*
1 Nov 1854	Admitted to Out-pension
	Pension paid Galway
	1/- per diem
8 June 1858	Arrived per *'Lord Raglan'*
4 Nov 1868	Purchased Fremantle Town Lots 834 and 835
7 Oct 1874	Applied for Cottage Improvement Grant
22 May 1875	Granted £15 Cottage Improvement Grant
7 Dec 1875	Died

Service and Personal Details:

Where Born:	Moria Galway
Trade or Occupation:	Clerk
Presidency:	Bengal
Length of Service:	14 years 4 months
Age on Discharge:	39 or 43 [depending on record source]
Reason for Discharge:	Contusion of the knee
Character:	Good
Height:	5' 11"
Complexion:	Fresh
Eye Colour:	Brown
Hair Colour:	Brown
Intends to Reside:	Clifden [sic] Galway

JUDGE

	James, private
	10th Foot
Previous Regiment	16th Foot
8 June 1847	Discharged the Service Chatham
	Pension paid Chatham
	9d. per diem
2 Aug 1852	Arrived per *'William Jardine'*
Jan 1857	Contributed 1/- to the Florence Nightingale Fund
1860	Off Pension List — "Not Appeared"

Service and Personal Details:

Place of Birth:	Maidstone Kent	
Age on Enlistment:	17 years 9 months	
Period of Service:	1840 — 1847	
Age on Discharge:	27 years	
Length of Service:	5 years 49 days	
Foreign Service:	India	4 years
Medal Entitlement:	Present at the Battle of Sobroan	
Reason for Discharge:	Unfit for further service	

Character: Good
Trade or Occupation: Baker
Can Sign Name: X his mark on discharge

Height: 5' 5"
Hair Colour: Dark
Eyes: Grey
Complexion: Fair
Intends to Reside: Maidstone

KAIN Bernard, private
29th Foot

Surname Variants: KEAN; KEANE; CAIN
11 Jan 1853: Discharged the Service Chatham
Pension paid Chatham
1/- per diem
18 July 1855: Arrived per *'Adelaide'*
1856: Employed by Convict Establishment
Jan 1857: Contributed 1/- to the Florence Nightingale Fund
1867: Assigned Freshwater Bay Loc P234and P248
1877: at Fremantle, on or about the 28th September. Bernard Kain, free; is charged on warrant issued at Fremantle, on the 9th inst., with unlawfully burying or assist to bury the body of a male child in a private garden or enclosure, for the purpose of concealing the birth
1879: Charged along with his son Fredrick with cattle stealing at Fremantle
1879: Sub-District Officers will cause enquiries to be made and report to Detective Office, whether Frederick Kain, son of Bernard Kain, Pensioner, of Fremantle, is residing in their districts or not. The officer in whose district Frederick Kain does reside will ascertain whether he is the reputed owner of any cattle, and, if so, the description of such cattle, and whether his brother, Benjamin Kain, has recently been seen driving any cattle in any part of the Colony.
1881: Application for Title to Butler Swamp Loc 234 & P248
1885: Bernard Kain of Fremantle, military pensioner applying to be registered as in Fee Simple to Avon Loc 135 of 10 acres
1894: Died at Henry Str., Fremantle, the residence of his son-in-law William Lovegrove

Service and Personal Details:
Place of Birth: Killown Londonderry
Age on Enlistment: 19 years
Period of Service: 1831 — 1852
Age on Discharge: 40 years
Length of Service: 21 years 16 days
Foreign Service: East Indies 9 years 5 months
Medal Entitlement: Sutlej with clasp for Sobraon; Punjab with clasps for Chillianwallah, and Goojerat
Reason for Discharge: Chronic Rheumatism

Character:	Good
Trade or Occupation:	Labourer
Can Sign Name:	Yes
Height:	5' 6"
Hair Colour:	Grey
Eyes:	Grey
Complexion:	Fair
Intends to Reside:	Richmond Middlesex
*c*1877	a description of Bernard Kain
Age:	about 60
Build:	Slight
Height:	5' 5"
Hair Colour:	Grey
Eye Colour:	Grey
Visage:	Long
Complexion:	Fair
Married:	Catherine McSweeney; MacSweeney
Children:	Catherine b. 1842 Ghazeepore India
	a Catherine b. 1847 Kussowlee India
	m. *c*1865 Frederick Platt Perth
	Susannah Jane b. *c*1853 England
	m. *c*1887 William Lovegrove Fremantle
	Frederick
	m. *c*1871 Emma Amelia Briggs Perth
	Benjamin
	Mary Ann b. *c*1856 Fremantle

KAIREY	John, private
	84th Foot
Previous Regiment	33rd Foot
Surname Variants	KAIRY; GAIREY
28 June 1841	Discharged the Service Dublin
7 July 1841	Pension paid 2nd Manchester Pension District
	7d. per diem
18 Oct 1851	Arrived per *'Minden'*
Nov 1852	Assigned Pensioner Lot P10 at York
Jan 1857	Contributed 2/- to the Florence Nightingale Fund
1859	Application to Title of P10 at York
1860	"Cancelled his application for York Lot 268 and his deposit was refunded"
1864	Pension paid Australia
19 Sept 1867	Died — a Pensioner named John I. Gairey [sic] died in the Lunatic Asylum on the 19th Sept 1869

Service and Personal Details:		
Place of Birth:	Baries Co Down	
Age on Enlistment:	18 years	
Period of Service:	1826 — 1841	
Age on Discharge:	33 years 4 months	
Length of Service:	15 years 54 days	
Foreign Service:	West Indies	10 years 4 months
Reason for Discharge:	Inflammation of the Spleen	

Character:	Good
Trade or Occupation:	Weaver
Can Sign Name:	Yes
Height:	5' 7"
Hair Colour:	Brown
Eyes:	Blue
Complexion:	Sallow
Intends to Reside:	Mountrath Queens County

KAVANAGH	Edward, private [2285]
	85th Foot
Surname Variant	CAVANAGH
12 May 1868	Discharged the Service Shorncliffe
	Pension paid 2nd Dublin Pension District
	1/- per diem
1868	Pension paid Kilkenny
1869	Athlone
1871	Dublin
1871	Newcastle
1872	Leeds
19 Feb 1874	Arrived per *'Naval Brigade'*

Service and Personal Details:

Place of Birth:	Abbeyleix Queens County	
Age on Enlistment:	17 years	
Period of Service:	1844 — 1868	
Age on Discharge:	41 years	
Length of Service:	21 years 7 days	
Foreign Service:	Mauritius	3 years 1 month
	Cape of Good Hope	7 years 1 month
Reason for Discharge:	His having served 21 years	
Character:	Good	
Trade or Occupation:	Labourer	
Can Sign Name:	Yes	
Height:	5' 11"	
Hair Colour:	Fair	
Eyes:	Grey	
Complexion:	Fair	
Intends to Reside:	Maryborough Queens County	

KEAN	William, private
	88th Foot
Previous Regiment	16th Foot
Surname Variants	[some] KANE; KAIN; KEANE; KEEN; CAIN; CAINE; CRANE
9 Dec 1856	Discharged the Service Chatham
	Pension paid Birr
	9d. per diem
24 Nov 1858	Arrived per *'Edwin Fox'*
1881	Assigned Fremantle Pensioner Allotment
1881	Pension increased to 1/- per diem for service in the Enrolled Force
1883	Improvements to No. 43 Coburn Sound grant
1884	Granted Fremantle Lot S43

15 Oct 1887	Serj. McCarthy reports the death of the wife of Pensioner Kean	
Service and Personal Details:		
Place of Birth:	Nenagh Co. Tipperary	
Age on Enlistment:	20 years	
Period of Service:	1839 — 1856	
Age on Discharge:	37 years	
Length of Service:	16 years 346 days	
Foreign Service:	Turkey & Crimea	2 years ** months
	India	1 year 1 month
	Gibraltar	1 year
	Corfu	4 years 1 month
	West Indies	2 years
Medal Entitlement:	Crimea with clasps	
Reason for Discharge:	Bladder Disease	
Character:	Very Good	
Trade or Occupation:	Labourer	
Can Sign Name:	X his mark on discharge	
Height:	5' 7"	
Hair Colour:	Light Brown	
Eyes:	Dark Blue	
Complexion:	Fresh	
Remarks:	Invalided to Scutari for treatment	

KEARNON	Michael, gunner RA	
Previous Regiments	EIC European Infantry; Bombay Artillery; G Battery Coastal Brigade	
Surname Variants	KEERNON; KEIRNAN; KIERNAN	
24 Sept 1872	Discharged the Service Aldershot	
5 Oct 1872	Discharge Approved	
	Pension paid Carlow	
	1/- per diem	
1873	Pension paid 1st Liverpool Pension District	
19 Feb 1874	Arrived per *'Naval Brigade'*	
1881	Assigned Bunbury Loc P405	
1886	Application for Title to Bunbury Loc P405	
1 May 1887	Granted Bunbury Loc 405 at Turkey Point	
Service and Personal Details:		
Place of Birth:	Eddistown Naas Co. Kildare	
Age on Enlistment:	20 years	
Period of Service:	1853 — 1872	
Age on Discharge:	39 years ? 2 months	
Length of Service:	20 years 350 days	
Foreign Service:	India	17 years 4 months
Medal Entitlement:	Indian Mutiny with clasp for Central India	
Reason for Discharge:	His having claimed it on termination of his second period of limited engagement	
Character:	Good	
Trade or Occupation:	Labourer	
Can Sign Name:	Yes	

Height:	5' 8"	
Hair Colour:	Fair	
Eyes:	Blue	
Complexion:	Fresh	
Remarks:	Elected for Indian Pension Rules	
Intends to Reside:	Naas Co. Kildare	

KEARNS William, private
74th Foot

Surname Variants	KEARNES; HEARNS	
26 Mar 1861	Discharged the Service Aberdeen Pension paid Monaghan 8d. per diem	
1862	Pension paid Paisley	
1863	Glasgow	
15 Apr 1864	Arrived per *'Clara'* [2]	
6 Aug 1864	Died aged 42	

Service and Personal Details:

Place of Birth:	Clones Co. Monaghan	
Age on Enlistment:	19 years 11 months	
Period of Service:	1840 — 1861	
Age on Discharge:	41 years	
Length of Service:	21 years 6 days	
Foreign Service:	North America	3 years 9 months
	Cape of Good Hope	2 years 9 months
	East Indies	4 years 5 months
Medal Entitlement:	In possession of a medal for service in South Africa 1851 — 1853	
Reason for Discharge:	Own Request on completion of 21 years service	
Character:	Indifferent	
Trade or Occupation:	Labourer	
Can Sign Name:	Yes	
Height:	5' 7½"	
Hair Colour:	Brown	
Eyes:	Blue	
Complexion:	Fresh	
Intends to Reside:	Clones Co. Monaghan	

KEARNY John, private
63rd Foot

Surname Variant	KEARNEY
27 Aug 1847	Discharged the Service Chatham Pension paid Castlebar 1/- per diem
25 Oct 1850	Arrived per *'Hashemy'*
1873	Pension increased to 1/1½d. per diem for 2 years 11 months service in the Enrolled Force
Aug 1881	Assigned Perth Railway Block Lot 145/V
16 Dec 1883	Granted Fee Simple Perth Railway Block Lot 145/V
29 May 1883	Died
1883	Land grant to widow Joanna left destitute with three children — the oldest aged 7 years

Service and Personal Details:
Place of Birth: Mountmellick Queens County
Age on Enlistment: 17 years
Period of Service: 1825 — 1847 [1846 depending on record]
Age on Discharge: 40 years
Length of Service: 21 years 126 days
Foreign Service: Van Diemans Land 6 years
East Indies 12 years 199 days
Reason for Discharge: Unfit for further service

Character: Good and efficient soldier
Trade or Occupation: Shoemaker
Can Sign Name: X his mark on discharge

Height: 5' 8"
Hair Colour: Grey
Eyes: Hazel
Complexion: Fresh
Intends to Reside: Castlebar Ireland

KEAUGHRAN Edward, gunner and driver
RA 2nd Battalion
Surname Variants KEAUGHRANE; KEUGHRAN; KEOGHAN
9 Jan 1849 Discharged the Service Woolwich
Pension paid Athlone
1/1d. per diem
21 May 1851 Arrived per *'Mermaid'*
1851 Assigned and occupied North Fremantle Lot P8
Jan 1857 Contributed 2/- to the Florence Nightingale Fund
1861 Pension paid Madras from Fremantle
1862 Mauritius

Service and Personal Details:
Place of Birth: Athlone Westmeath
Age on Enlistment: 18 years
Period of Service: 1826 — 1849
Age on Discharge: 40 years 11 months
Length of Service: 22 years 359 days
Foreign Service: Portugal 1 year 3 months
Malta 9 years 10 months
Reason for Discharge: Suffering from Chronic Rheumatism

Character: Exemplary
Trade or Occupation: Labourer
Can Sign Name: Yes

Height: 5' 9½"
Hair Colour: Black
Eyes: Dark Blue
Complexion: Fresh
Remarks: Subsisted to 29th Jan 1849
Intends to Reside: Athlone

KEEFE John, private [1163]
7th Foot
16 July 1861 Discharged the Service Chatham
Pension paid 1st Dublin Pension District

	11d. per diem	
15 Aug 1865	Arrived per *'Racehorse'*	
1869	Pension paid Wellington New Zealand	

KEELY	Michael, private	
	17th Foot	
Surname Variant	KELLY	
13 June 1854	Discharged the Service	
1854	Pension paid South London Pension District	
	7d. per diem for 18 months	
18 July 1855	Arrived per *'Adelaide'*	
Aug 1855	Pension paid Adelaide South Australia	
23 Dec 1855	Pension ceased	
		Service and Personal Details:
Place of Birth:	Allen Co. Kildare	
Age on Enlistment:	18 years	
Period of Service:	1838 — 1854	
Age on Discharge:	about 38 years	
Length of Service:	20 years 150 days	
Foreign Service:	Gibraltar	5 years
	West Indies	3 years 3 months
	North America	2 years 2 months
	Turkey & Crimea	2 years 2 months
	East Indies	2 years 10 months
Medal Entitlement:	Crimea	
Character:	Good	
Trade or Occupation:	Labourer	
Intends to Reside:	Dublin	

KEENAN	James, private	
	1st Foot	
30 Sept 1856	Discharged the Service Chatham	
	8d. per diem	
	Pension paid Longford	
1859	Liverpool	
1860	Longford	
1861	Athlone	
1862	Longford	
27 May 1863	Arrived per *'Clyde'*	
1864	ptve J Keenan in the Pensioner Force Perth contributed to the Greenough Fire Fund	
1865	Pension paid South Australia	
1876	"Probably died in the far bush" [7/Australia/19]	
		Service and Personal Details:
Place of Birth:	Temple Michael Co. Longford	
Age on Enlistment:	18 years	
Period of Service:	1835 — 1856	
Age on Discharge:	39 years 2 months	
Length of Service:	21 years 78 days	
Foreign Service:	Canada	7 years 2 months
	West Indies	2 years 4 months
	Cephalonia	2 years 2 months
	Crimea	1 year 2 months
Medal Entitlement:	Crimea with clasp	

Reason for Discharge:	Worn out from length of service and exposure whilst on duty
Character:	Good
Trade or Occupation:	Groom
Can Sign Name:	X his mark on discharge
Height:	5' 8"
Hair Colour:	Dark Brown
Eyes:	Grey
Complexion:	Fresh
Intends to Reside:	Longford

KEESHON Michael, private [2787]
49th Foot

Surname Variants	KEESHAN; KEESHAM
22 Feb 1870	Discharged the Service Colchester Pension paid Halifax 1/- per diem
1873	Pension paid Greenwich
19 Feb 1874	Arrived per *'Naval Brigade'*
Jan 1876	Acquitted of the charge of larceny
1881	Pension increased to 1/2½d per diem for service in the Enrolled Force
1889	a Michael Keeshon died aged 58
18 Dec 1889	An old pensioner, named Michael Keeshan, who was living in Fremantle, was found dead yesterday morning in Manning's Paddock. The deceased had been gathering blackboy, and he was found by his wife and son lying in the paddock, his horse and cart being near. Dr. Hope visited the body and found that death had resulted from apoplexy, probably accelerated by the excessive heat of the previous day. The deceased was an old soldier, and took part in the Crimean war. [Trove]

Service and Personal Details:

Place of Birth:	Barna Kings County	
Age on Enlistment:	19 years	
Period of Service:	1848 — 1870	
Age on Discharge:	40 years 2 months	
Length of Service:	12 years 7 months	
Foreign Service:	Ionian Isles	2 years 1 month
	Turkey	5 months
	Malta	1 year
	Crimea	1 year 10 months
	West Indies	3 years 2 months
	East Indies	4 years 1 month
Medal Entitlement:	Good Conduct with gratuity; Crimea with clasps; Turkish Crimean	
Reason for Discharge:	Termination of 2nd period of 'Limited Service'	
Character:	Very Good	
Trade or Occupation:	Labourer	
Can Sign Name:	Yes	

Height:	5' 9"
Hair Colour:	Brown
Eyes:	Grey
Complexion:	Fair
Remarks:	Wounded in the right leg by mine exploding
Intends to Reside:	Co. Tipperary

KEHOE John, Corporal
48th Foot [Depot]

21 May 1857	Discharged the Service Fermoy
7 July 1857	Admitted to Out-Pension
	Pension paid 1st Dublin Pension District
	1/- per diem
1859	Pension paid 2nd Dublin Pension District
1859	Kilkenny
27 May 1863	Arrived per *'Clyde'*
1865	Pension paid Kilkenny
5 Aug 1869	Died

Service and Personal Details:

Place of Birth:	Ballinaklill Queens County	
Age on Enlistment:	21 years	
Period of Service:	1836 — 1857	
Age on Discharge:	42 years 2 months	
Length of Service:	21 years 66 days	
Foreign Service:	Gibraltar	5 years 4 months
	West Indies	3 years 1 month
Reason for Discharge:	Chronic Rheumatism	
Character:	Good	
Trade or Occupation:	Labourer	
Can Sign Name:	Yes	
Height:	5' 6½"	
Hair Colour:	Dark Brown	
Eyes:	Hazel	
Complexion:	Fresh	
Intends to Reside:	Isle of Wight at the "Ro** of Newport"	

KELLINGTON Edward, Corporal
87th Foot

Previous Regiments	96th; 43rd
14 June 1864	Discharged the Service Aldershot
	Pension paid 1st Portsmouth Pension District
	1/1½d per diem
1867	Pension paid Chatham
1870	Pension paid 2nd West London Pension District
19 Feb 1974	Arrived per *'Naval Brigade'*
1875	Convicted by District Court Martial at Perth of being drunk on duty and striking Corporal Martin of the Enrolled Force. Sentenced to 168 days imprisonment during which half pension suspended the other half paid to wife
1876	Pension increased to 1/4d. per diem for service in the Enrolled Pensioner Force

Aug 1880	Assigned North Fremantle Lot P68
25 Feb 1883	Died
	North Fremantle Lot P68 Pensioner Allotment was re-assigned to Patrick Fannon

Service and Personal Details:

Place of Birth:	Mary-le-bone London	
Age on Enlistment:	19 years 2 months	
Period of Service:	1842 — 1864	
Age on Discharge:	40 years 7 months	
Length of Service:	21 years 116 days	
Foreign Service:	New South Wales	5 years 3 months
	East Indies	11 years
	Crimea	1 year 2 months
Medal Entitlement:	Indian Mutiny and recommended for a medal for Long Service and Good Conduct	
Reason for Discharge:	Own Request having served 21 years	
Character:	Very Good	
Trade or Occupation:	Labourer	
Can Sign Name:	Yes	
Height:	5' 9½"	
Hair Colour:	Light	
Eyes:	Blue	
Complexion:	Fresh	
Intends to Reside:	Portsmouth	

KELLY	Bernard, Lance Corporal
	2nd/25th Foot
Previous Regiment	34th Foot
18 June 1863	Discharged the Service Edinburgh
	Pension paid Cavan
	9d. per diem
4 July 1866	Arrived per *'Belgravia'*
Oct 1874	Assigned Perth Pensioner Lot 57/E
	[located Bennett and Wellington Streets]
1874	Applies for £15 Improvement Grant Perth Lot 57/E
1881	Pension increased to 1/3d. per diem for service in the Enrolled Force
Apr 1881	Application for Title to Perth Lot E57
16 June 1881	Granted Fee Simple Perth Pensioner Lot 55/E
June 1897	Stationed at Perth
Sept 1900	Died buried East Perth Cemetery

Service and Personal Details:

Place of Birth:	Castleblaney Co. Monaghan
Age on Enlistment:	none given
Period of Service:	1847 — 1863
Age on Discharge:	35 years 9 months
Length of Service:	16 years 178 days
Foreign Service:	Corfu 5 months
East Indies	2 years 6 months
Medal Entitlement:	Indian Mutiny with clasp for Lucknow
Reason for Discharge:	Varicose Veins in both legs

Character:	Very Good
Trade or Occupation:	Labourer
Can Sign Name:	Yes
Height:	5' 7"
Hair Colour:	Black, Grey in parts
Eyes:	Grey
Complexion:	Fresh
Distinguishing Marks:	Scar of ulcer on outer right leg
Intends to Reside:	Cavan

KELLY	Edward, private	
	4th Foot	
7 Aug 1860	Discharged the Service	
	Pension paid 1st Dublin Pension District	
	9d. per diem	
27 May 1863	Arrived per *'Clyde'*	
1864	Pension paid Madras	
1875	Madras	
Service and Personal Details:		
Place of Birth:	St Marys Dublin	
Age on Enlistment:	20 years	
Period of Service:	1838 — 1860	
Age on Discharge:	41 years 9 months	
Length of Service:	21 years 225 days	
Foreign Service:	East Indies	11 years 4 months
	Malta &	
	Turkey & Crimea	2 years 4 months
	Mauritius	1 month
Medal Entitlement:	Claims Indian Medal; ?Crimea	
Reason for Discharge:	Own Request having served over 21 years	
Character:	Good	
Trade or Occupation:	Shoemaker	
Can Sign Name:	X his mark on discharge	
Height:	5' 6½"	
Hair Colour:	Brown	
Eyes:	Grey	
Complexion:	Fair	
Distinguishing Marks:	Scar above left outer ankle; Spermatic Chord slightly tortuous	

KELLY	Henry, private
	70th Foot
Previous Regiment	13th foot
4 Sept 1860	Discharged the Service
	Pension paid Enniskillin
	9d. per diem
27 May 1863	Arrived per *'Clyde'*
1875	Pension paid Western Australia
1876	Pension increased to 1/1d per diem for service in the Enrolled Force
24 Aug 1881	Assigned Perth Railway Block Lot 148/V
15 Dec 1883	Granted Fee Simple Perth Railway Block Lot 148/V

June 1885	Pensioner Henry Kelly and Wife for Relief
1886	Died

Service and Personal Details:

Place of Birth:	?Dekky Wollin Co. Fermanagh
Age on Enlistment:	21 years
Period of Service:	1839 — 1860
Age on Discharge:	42 years 1 month
Length of Service:	21 years 27 days
Foreign Service:	East Indies 20 years 5 months
Medal Entitlement:	Jellalabad; Kabul; Burmah
Reason for Discharge:	Own request having served 21 years
Character:	Good
Trade or Occupation:	Shoemaker
Can Sign Name:	Yes
Height:	5' 5¼"
Hair Colour:	Black
Eyes:	Grey
Complexion:	Dark
Intends to Reside:	Lowtherstown Co. Fermanagh

KELLY James, private
58th Foot

12 Oct 1852	Discharged the Service Pension paid Maryborough 7d. per diem for 2 years
6 Apr 1854	Arrived per *'Sea Park'*
4 Nov 1854	Died

Service and Personal Details:

Place of Birth:	Rosenalis Queens County
Age on Enlistment:	17 years 10 months
Period of Service:	1842 — 1852
Age on Discharge:	28 years or 27 years 3 months
Length of Service:	9 years 146 days
Foreign Service:	Australian Colonies 7 years ? month
Reason for Discharge:	Disease of the Lungs which first appeared when stationed at Auckland New Zealand
Character:	Latterly Good
Trade or Occupation:	Labourer
Can Sign Name:	Yes
Height:	5' 7"
Hair Colour:	Brown
Eyes:	Grey
Complexion:	Fresh
Intends to Reside:	Dublin

KELLY Jeremiah, Corporal
86th Foot

14 July 1857	Discharged the Service Chatham Pension paid Clonmel 1/3½d. per diem
29 Jan 1862	Arrived per *'Lincelles'*

1864	private J Kelly Pensioner Force at Perth contributed to the Greenough Fire Relief Fund
1865	On Nominal List to proceed to Camden Harbour per *'Tien Tsin'*
1866	Pension paid Adelaide South Australia

Service and Personal Details:

Place of Birth:	Cashel Co. Tipperary
Age on Enlistment:	21 years
Period of Service:	1836 — 1857
Age on Discharge:	41 years
Length of Service:	21 years 5 days
Foreign Service:	East Indies 11 years 11 months
Reason for Discharge:	Own Request and to serve on the Permanent Staff of the Tipperary Militia
Character:	Very Good
Trade or Occupation:	Carpenter
Can Sign Name:	blank; Yes on Attestation
Height:	6'
Hair Colour:	Dark Brown
Eyes:	Blue
Complexion:	Fresh

KELLY John, private
41st Foot

9 Dec 1856	Discharged the Service Chatham Pension paid Athlone 9d. per diem
1860	Pension increased to 1/- per diem
29 Jan 1862	Arrived per *'Lincelles'*
1868	Assigned Victoria Loc 48 and 49
1874	Pension increased to 1/3d. per diem
1888	Granted Fee Simple Victoria Loc 48 and 49 [a pensioner Kelly's cottage located at Scott Rd., is registered on the Heritage Council's database]
1908	Died

Service and Personal Details:

Place of Birth:	Templepatrick Westmeath
Age on Enlistment:	18 years 6 months
Period of Service:	1854 — 1856
Age on Discharge:	21 years 3 months
Length of Service:	2 years 193 days
Foreign Service:	Crimea [not time period given
Medal Entitlement:	Crimea
Reason for Discharge:	Received a gunshot wound to the right shoulder
Character:	Good
Trade or Occupation:	Labourer
Can Sign Name:	Yes
Height:	5' 6"
Hair Colour:	Brown
Eyes:	Blue
Complexion:	Fresh

Intends to Reside:	Westmeath
KELLY	John [information from Trove — possibly same man as previous entry] 71st Foot the Welsh Fusiliers; [however the Welsh Fusiliers Regimental Number is the 41st. The 71st Foot's regimental name is the Highland Light Infantry — the City of Glasgow Regiment]
1862	Arrived in the State Resided in the Geraldton area for 42 years
Apr 1908	Died aged 78 at Geraldton
Service and Personal Details:	
Place of Birth:	County Longford Ireland
Medal Entitlement:	Crimean with clasps
Obituary:	Leaves a widow, 3 sons, and 4 daughters Among his descendants being Mr John and Michael Kelly; Mrs F.H.Criech [sic] and Miss Kelly of Geraldton. Mrs Martin of Kelmscott; Mr Francis Kelly and Mrs Houlahan of Kalgoolie

KELLY	Joseph Plunket, private 12th Foot
13 May 1850	Discharged the Service Chatham Pension paid 1st Glasgow Pension District 1/- per diem
1850	Pension paid Aberdeen
1851	Pension paid Edinburgh
1851	Dundee
1852	1st Edinburgh Pension District
1852	Newcastle
1852	Edinburgh
1854	Turkey
1854	Edinburgh
1855	Pension paid Edinburgh
2 Apr 1856	Arrived per *'William Hammond'*
1856	"Charged with Military Offence"
1859	Pension paid Cape Town South Africa
1865	Residing at the Cape of Good Hope
1866	Admitted to In-Pension
1866	Reverted to Out-Pension to join his friends
1867	Admitted to In-Pension
Service and Personal Details:	
Place of Birth:	Kilkavan Roscommon
Age on Enlistment:	19 years
Period of Service:	1829 — 1850
Age on Discharge:	40 years or 38 years ** months
Length of Service:	20 years 262 days
Foreign Service:	Mauritius 5 years 8 months
Reason for Discharge:	Totally unfit from Chronic Rheumatism
Character:	Indifferent
Trade or Occupation:	a Yeoman
Can Sign Name:	Yes

Height:	5' 8"	
Hair Colour:	Light Brown	
Eyes:	Blue	
Complexion:	Tan	
Intends to Reside:	Glasgow	

KELLY	Patrick, private	
	33rd Foot	
25 Aug 1858	Discharged the Service Fermoy	
2 Nov 1858	Admitted to Out-Pension	
	Pension paid 1st Dublin Pension District	
	1/- per diem	
1859	Pension paid 1st Cork Pension District	
1862	1st Dublin Pension District	
27 May 1863	Arrived per *'Clyde'*	
circa June 1874	Transferred from 2nd Perth Pension District to 1st Perth Pension District	
1875	Pension paid Western Australia	
22 Jan 1878	Died aged 60 at the Military Hospital Perth	

Service and Personal Details:		
Place of Birth:	Rathfarnham Dublin	
Age on Enlistment:	17 years	
Period of Service:	1836 — 1858	
Age on Discharge:	38 years	
Length of Service:	20 years 360 days	
Foreign Service:	Gibraltar	1 year
	West Indies	2 years ? months
	North America	4 years 5 months
	Crimea	1 year 9 months
Medal Entitlement:	Crimea	
Reason for Discharge:	Chronic Rheumatism	
Character:	Very Good	
Trade or Occupation:	Labourer	
Can Sign Name:	Yes	
Height:	5' 7"	
Hair Colour:	Brown	
Eyes:	Blue	
Complexion:	Fair	
Intends to Reside:	Dublin	

KELLY	Thomas, Serjeant	
	10th Foot	
Previous Regiment	53rd Foot	
10 July 1860	Discharged the Service Chatham	
	Pension paid Carlow	
	1/3d. per diem	
29 Jan 1862	Arrived per *'Lincelles'*	
1863	Stationed Perth District	
1863	Assigned South Perth Loc P9 of 5 acres	
1864	a Serjeant Kelly stationed at Perth contributed 2/6d into the Greenough Fire Relief Fund Prior to his death he was residing at Bindoon	
Jan 1888	Died at Guildford Hospital	

1889	W.O. correspondence with S.O. Perth West. Aust.
Service and Personal Details:	
Place of Birth:	Dunlaven Co. Wicklow
Age on Enlistment:	21 years
Period of Service:	1839 — 1860
Age on Discharge:	42 years 5 months
Length of Service:	18 years 292 days
Foreign Service:	East Indies 17 years 1 month
Medal Entitlement:	Punjab with 2 clasps; Sutlej; Indian Mutiny with one clasp for Lucknow
Reason for Discharge:	Unfit for further service
Character:	Good
Trade or Occupation:	Labourer
Can Sign Name:	X his mark on discharge
Height:	5' 8½"
Hair Colour:	Brown
Eyes:	Dark
Complexion:	Fresh
Intends to Reside:	Dunlaven Co. Wicklow
Married:	Catherine Ann Farrell
Children:	Mary Ann b. 1849 India m. *c*1863 William Boxhall Perth William Henry b. 1851 Wuzeerabad India m. *c*1874 Mary Ellen Thompson New Norcia Bernard b. 1854 Lahore India m. *c*1882 Mary Ann Butler New Norcia

KELLY	Thomas, private [1999] 83rd Foot
10 May 1864	Discharged the Service Pension paid 2nd West London Pension District 10d. per diem
1864	Pension paid 1st West London Pension District
1864	Pension paid 2nd West London Pension District
22 Dec 1866	Arrived per *'Corona'*
1869	Pension paid Bombay
Service and Personal Details:	
Place of Birth:	Killimer Loughrea Co. Galway
Age on Enlistment:	19 years
Period of Service:	1842 — 1864
Age on Discharge:	40 years
Length of Service:	21 years 5 days
Foreign Service:	East Indies 10 years 9 months
Medal Entitlement:	Indian Mutiny with clasp
Reason for Discharge:	Own Request having served 21 years
Character:	Latterly Very Good
Trade or Occupation:	Tailor
Can Sign Name:	Yes
Height:	5' 9"
Hair Colour:	Black

Eyes:	Grey
Complexion:	Fresh
Distinguishing Marks:	Scar on right thigh
Intends to Reside:	Pimlico London

KELLY	Thomas, gunner EIC 2nd Battalion Bombay Artillery Out Pension No 144
1851	Embarked UK per *'Earl Hardwicke'*
18 June 1851	Admitted to Out-pension 9d. per diem
1858	Serving with the Lancashire Militia
1860	Pension paid Carlow
1860	Liverpool
1861	Wales
1861	Trowbridge
1861	Bristol
9 June 1862	Arrived per *'Norwood'* [1]
circa June 1874	Transferred from 1st Perth District to Fremantle
Feb 1883	Assigned North Fremantle Lot P90

Service and Personal Details:	
Where Born:	Wicklow
Trade or Occupation:	Cabinet maker
Where Enlisted:	Liverpool
Length of Service:	2 years 5 months
Age on Discharge:	22 years
Reason for Discharge:	Injury of right foot on the line of march by a gun accidentally going over it; or injury of left foot
Character:	Good
Height:	5' 8"
Complexion:	Fresh
Eye Colour:	Blue
Hair Colour:	Fair
Intends to Reside:	Wicklow

KENNEDY	James, private 87th Foot
12 May 1860	Discharged the Service Loughal Ireland
29 May 1860	Discharge approved Pension paid 2nd Glasgow Pension District 8d. per diem
27 May 1863	Arrived per *'Clyde'*
1867	Charged with wounding William Clarke Verdict —"not guilty"
14 Sept 1867	Died "of natural causes"

Service and Personal Details:		
Place of Birth:	Ballyraget Co. Kilkenny	
Age on Enlistment:	18 years	
Period of Service:	1839 — 1860	
Age on Discharge:	39 years	
Length of Service:	21 years 12 days	
Foreign Service:	Mauritius	3 years 3 months
	East Indies	9 years 10 months
Medal Entitlement:	Long Service and Good Conduct	

Reason for Discharge:	Having completed 21 years service
Character:	Very Good
Trade or Occupation:	Labourer
Can Sign Name:	X his mark on discharge
Height:	5' 7"
Hair Colour:	Dark Brown
Eyes:	Grey
Complexion:	Sallow
Intends to Reside:	Glasgow Scotland

KENNEDY Michael John, Serjeant
48th Foot

29 Jan 1856	Discharged the Service Chatham Pension paid Kilkenny 1/8d. per diem
15 Apr 1864	Arrived per *'Clara'* [2]
1864	Serving as Assistant Warder [served for many years as Warder at the Lunatic Asylum at Fremantle Residing Finnerty Street Fremantle
1884	Claimed damages from J.C Campbell for seduction of his daughter Lillian
Apr 1892	Died aged 71 — cause of death was heart disease
1896	a Michael John Kennedy printer heir-in-law to Michael Kennedy late of Fremantle — warder, applied for transfer of Title of Fremantle Town Lot 867 and Cottesloe Suburban Lot 83
1903	Correspondence with W.O.

Service and Personal Details:

Place of Birth:	Dunean Co. Antrim	
Age on Enlistment:	18 years	
Period of Service:	1839 — 1855	
Age on Discharge:	35 years 7 months	
Length of Service:	16 years 77 days	
Foreign Service:	Gibraltar	3 years 5 months
	West Indies	3 years 1 month
	Ionian Isles	2 years 1 month
	Crimea	7 months
Medal Entitlement:	Crimea with clasp	
Reason for Discharge:	Loss of sight in right eye in the trenches before Sebastopol	
Character:	Good	
Trade or Occupation:	Weaver	
Can Sign Name:	Yes	
Height:	5' 11½"	
Hair Colour:	Brown	
Eyes:	Grey	
Complexion:	Fair	
Intends to Reside:	Antrim	

KENNEDY Timothy, private

	54th Foot
26 Aug 1856	Discharged the Service Chatham
	Pension paid 2nd Plymouth Pension District
	1/-½d. per diem
10 July 1857	Arrived per *'Clara'*
1878	Pension increased to 1/6½d. per diem for service in the Enrolled Force
	Pension reverted to former rate on re-entering the Force
1881	Pension again increased to 1/6½d. per diem
1886	Appointed to the Enrolled Guard — stationed at Fremantle
1894	Died

Service and Personal Details:		
Place of Birth:	? Drumerlagher Co. Limerick	
Age on Enlistment:	18 years	
Period of Service:	1834 — 1856	
Age on Discharge:	40 years 5 months	
Length of Service:	22 years 53 days	
Foreign Service:	East Indies	4 years 289 days
Reason for Discharge:	Chronic Rheumatism	
Character:	Very Good	
Trade or Occupation:	Labourer	
Can Sign Name:	X his mark on discharge	
Height:	5' 7"	
Hair Colour:	Sandy	
Eyes:	Grey	
Complexion:	Fresh	
Intends to Reside:	Plymouth	

KENNY	James, private [715]
	75th Foot
Previous Regiments	10th ; 64th
29 Apr 1862	Discharged the Service Chatham
May 1862	Admitted to Out Pension [43697]
	Pension paid Kilkenny
	7d. per diem
22 Dec 1865	Arrived per *'Vimiera'*
1876	Died age 50 – ?buried East Perth Cemetery

Service and Personal Details:		
Place of Birth:	Ballinakill Woodford Galway	
Age on Enlistment:	19 years	
Period of Service:	1844 — 1861	
Age on Discharge:	?37 years 1 month	
Length of Service:	17 years 221 days	
Foreign Service:	East Indies	16 years 263 days
Medal Entitlement:	Punjaub with 2 clasps; Indian Mutiny with clasp	
Reason for Discharge:	Chronic Disease of the Liver	
Character:	Latterly Good	
Trade or Occupation:	Labourer	

Can Sign Name:	X his mark on discharge and on the WO22/226
Height:	5' 10"
Hair Colour:	Dark Brown
Eyes:	Grey
Complexion:	Dark Brown
Intends to Reside:	Lough*** Galway

KENNY

	John, private
	90th Foot
Surname Variant	KENNEY
26 May 1852	Discharged the Service Cork
13 July 1852	Admitted to Out-Pension
	Pension paid 2nd Manchester Pension District
	10d. per diem
24 May 1855	Arrived per *'Stag'*
Dec 1867	Application for Title Greenough Locs G11 and G12 — located Bootenal, Victoria District
17 Aug 1864	Died Greenough aged 49
1868	Greenough Locs G11 and G12 awarded to son John

Service and Personal Details:

Place of Birth:	Enniscorthy Co. Wexford	
Age on Enlistment:	18 years 4 months	
Period of Service:	1833 — 1852	
Age on Discharge:	37 years	
Length of Service:	18 years 253 days	
Foreign Service:	Ceylon	6 years 1 month
	Mauritius	2 months
Cape of Good Hope	1 year 10 months	
Reason for Discharge:	Unfit for further service	
Character:	Very Good	
Trade or Occupation:	Labourer	
Can Sign Name:	Yes	
Height:	5' 8"	
Hair Colour:	Light Brown	
Eyes:	Grey	
Complexion:	Sallow	
Intends to Reside:	Manchester	

KENNY

	John, Sapper
	Royal Sapper and Miners
Dec 1861	Discharged the Service Fremantle West. Aust.
1885	Awarded Deferred Pension of 4d. per diem

Service and Personal Details:

Place of Birth:	St Mary's Athlone Westmeath	
Age on Enlistment:	22 years	
Period of Service:	1847 — 1861	
Age on Discharge:	36 years 7 months	
Length of Service:	14 years 210 days	
Foreign Service:	West Aust	10 years

Reason for Discharge:	Granted a Free Discharge to settle in Colony with 12 months pay and Right of Registry for a Deferred Pension on him attaining 60 years
Character:	Very Good
Trade or Occupation:	Carpenter
Can Sign Name:	Yes
Height:	5' 7"
Hair Colour:	Brown
Eyes:	Grey
Complexion:	Sallow and Pockmarked
Intends to Reside:	Perth Western Australia

KENNEY	Michael, private [1996] 24th Foot
Surname Variant	KENNY
22 May 1862	Discharged the Service Pension paid Newry 1/1d per diem
12 Sept 1864	Arrived per *'Merchantman'* [2]
1881	Pension increased to 1/7d. per diem for service in the Enrolled Force
June 1883	Assigned Fremantle Lot P88
30 Aug 1884	Granted Fee Simple Fremantle Lot P88
1892	Died aged 70
Service and Personal Details:	
Place of Birth:	Killarey Co. Armagh
Age on Enlistment:	18 years
Period of Service:	1841 — 1862
Age on Discharge:	39 years 1 month
Length of Service:	21 years 30 days
Foreign Service:	East Indies 14 years 10 months
Medal Entitlement:	Punjaub medal with 2 clasps. [Recommended for a silver medal with a gratuity for Long Service and Good Conduct]
Reason for Discharge:	Own request having completed 21 years
Character:	Exemplary
Trade or Occupation:	Labourer
Can Sign Name:	X his mark on discharge
Height:	5' 7¾"
Hair Colour:	Dark Brown
Eyes:	Blue
Complexion:	Fresh
Intends to Reside:	Newry Co. Armagh

KERR	John, private 84th Foot
Previous Regiment	33rd Foot
25 Nov 1839	Discharged the Service
11 Dec 1839	Admitted to Out-Pension Pension paid Ayr 6d per diem

1842	Granted permanent pension
1853	Pension paid 2nd Glasgow Pension District
1856	Pension paid Manchester
1856	Ayr
10 July 1857	Arrived per *'Clara'* [1]
1863	Stationed Perth District
1864	ptve J Kerr Pensioner Force Perth contributed to the Greenough Fire Relief Fund
1865	Pension paid Western Australia

Service and Personal Details:

Place of Birth:	Monaghan Ireland
Age on Enlistment:	17 years
Period of Service:	1825 — 1839
Age on Discharge:	30 years
Length of Service:	12 years 300 days
Foreign Service:	West Indies 11 years 64 days
Reason for Discharge:	Chronic Hepatitis and Chronic Catarrh
Character:	Good
Trade or Occupation:	Weaver
Can Sign Name:	X his mark on discharge
Height:	5' 5"
Hair Colour:	Brown
Eyes:	Grey
Complexion:	Sallow
Intends to Reside:	Portlong Co. Derry

KERR William A, private [drummer]
7th Foot

Previous Regiment	26th Foot
3 July 1855	Discharged the Service Chatham Pension paid 1st Liverpool Pension District 9d. per diem
1857	Pension paid Leeds
1858	Liverpool
19 Aug 1859	Arrived per *'Sultana'*
1860	a William Archibald Kerr employed as Assistant Warder
1861	To South Australia from Western Australia
1862	Pension paid South Australia
1863	Melbourne
21 Aug 1863	Died Victoria

Service and Personal Details:

Place of Birth:	St Marys Chatham Kent
Age on Enlistment:	15 years
Period of Service:	1850 — 1855
Age on Discharge:	20 years
Length of Service:	1 year 358 days [after the age of 18]
Foreign Service:	Crimea [Varna] [no time period given]
Medal Entitlement:	Crimea with clasp
Reason for Discharge:	Injury of right shoulder caused by gunshot wound received at Alma
Character:	Good

Trade or Occupation:	None
Can Sign Name:	Yes
Height:	5' 3¼"
Hair Colour:	Dark Brown
Eyes:	Hazel
Complexion:	Fresh
Intends to Reside:	Manchester

KILGALLON Michael, private
12th Foot [Depot]

Surname Variants	[some] KILLGALLON; KILGALLEN; KILLGON
29 Aug 1859	Discharged the Service Walmer
13 Sept 1859	Admitted to Out-Pension
	Pension paid Sligo
	9d. per diem
15 Aug 1865	Arrived per *'Racehorse'*
8 Apr 1875	Granted Northam Loc 3
1875	Pension increased to 1/2d. per diem for service in the Enrolled Force
1884	Perth cheque for delivery to Private Kilgallon
June 1897	Residing Northam
1907	Died

Service and Personal Details:

Place of Birth:	St Johns Sligo	
Age on Enlistment:	18 years	
Period of Service:	1838 — 1859	
Age on Discharge:	39 years	
Length of Service:	21 years 13 days	
Foreign Service:	Mauritius	7 years 6 months
	Australian colonies	4 years 4 months
Reason for Discharge:	Own Request having completed 21 years	
Character:	Good	
Trade or Occupation:	Labourer	
Can Sign Name:	X his mark on discharge	
Height:	5' 10"	
Hair Colour:	Light Brown	
Eyes:	Grey	
Complexion:	Fresh	
Intends to Reside:	Sligo Ireland	

KILLIN William, private
103rd Foot

Previous Regiment	1st Bombay Fusiliers
Surname Variants	[some] KELLIN; KILLEN; KILEEN; KILLEEN
26 May 1863	Discharged the Service
	Pension paid 2nd Glasgow Pension District
	1/- per diem
9 Jan 1868	Arrived per *'Hougoumont'*
1876	Stationed Fremantle

1879	Pension increased to 1/4½d. per diem for ten years service as a private in the Enrolled Force of Western Australia
Aug 1879	Pensioner Killen to Poor Relief Pensioner Killen to Asylum
Nov 1879	Died at Fremantle Lunatic Asylum "of natural causes"
Oct 1880	"Mrs Killen wife of Pensioner Killen requesting Poor Relief"

Service and Personal Details:

Place of Birth:	Cork Co. Cork
Age on Enlistment:	20 years
Period of Service:	1843 — 1863
Age on Discharge:	39 years 278 days
Length of Service:	21 years 278 days
[Granted a Boon of two years]	
Foreign Service:	East Indies 19 years 8 months
Medal Entitlement:	Punjaub Medal with clasps for Mooltan and Goojerat; Indian Mutiny
Reason for Discharge:	Having completed upwards of 21 years service
Character:	Very Good
Trade or Occupation:	Labourer
Can Sign Name:	Yes
Height:	5' 6"
Hair Colour:	Brown
Eyes:	Grey
Complexion:	Fresh
Remarks:	Elected for Indian Pension Rules
Intends to Reside:	163 Cowcaden Street, Glasgow Scotland

KILMURRY	Patrick, private
	3rd Foot
Previous regiment	59th Foot
Surname Variant	KILMURRAY
9 Jan 1841	Discharged the Service
23 June 1841	Admitted to Out-Pension
	Pension paid Chatham
	6d. per diem
1852	Pension paid Tullamore
2 Aug 1852	Arrived per *'William Jardine'*
1854	Residing Albany
1856	Claim of £15 against Capt Foss
1857	To South Australia from Western Australia per *'Robert Clive'*
7 Oct 1861	Died Adelaide aged 58

Service and Personal Details:

Place of Birth:	Kilbeggan Westmeath
Age on Enlistment:	17 years
Period of Service:	1825 — 1841
Age on Discharge:	32 years
Length of Service:	13 years 329 days

Foreign Service:	East Indies	upwards of 14 years
Reason for Discharge:	Unfit for further service	
Character:	Good	
Trade or Occupation:	Servant	
Can Sign Name:	Yes	
Height:	5' 11¾"	
Hair Colour:	Brown	
Eyes:	Blue	
Complexion:	Flesh	

KILNER	James, Serjeant	
	RA 25th Brigade	
Previous Regiment	Bengal Artillery	
Mar 1865	Embarked for the UK per ship *'Malabar'*	
19 Sept 1865	Discharged to pension Sheerness	
	Pension paid Brighton	
	2/- per diem	
1866	Pension paid Deptford	
1871	Residing 16 Railway Grove St Pauls Deptford	
1873	Pension paid Greenwich	
19 Feb 1874	Arrived per *'Naval Brigade'*	
30 Apr 1874	Died	
Service and Personal Details:		
Place of Birth:	East Grinstead Sussex	
Age on Enlistment:	21 years 8 months	
Period of Service:	1845 — 1865	
Age on Discharge:	42 years	
Length of Service:	22 years 175 day	
	[corrected from 21 years 307 days]	
Foreign Service:	East Indies	20 years 353 days
Reason for Discharge:	Own Request having served over 22 years	
Character:	Very Good corrected to Exemplary	
Trade or Occupation:	Groom	
Can Sign Name:	Yes	
Height:	5' 11½"	
Hair Colour:	Dark	
Eyes:	Blue	
Complexion:	Sallow	
Distinguishing Marks:	Scar on forefinger of left hand	
Remarks:	Elected for Indian Pension Rules	
Intends to Reside:	East Grinstead Surrey	
Married:	1850 Mary Ann Norbury Bengal India	

KILNER	Mary Ann, widow
	Husband — Serjeant 25 Brigade RA E Battalion
25 Aug 1874	Pension of 4½d. per diem [Lord Clive Fund] paid Perth Western Australia
1876	Mrs Kilner in receipt of outdoor relief money Perth
1889	Died aged 65 – buried East Perth Cemetery

KILPATRICK	Daniel, private
	92nd Foot
23 July 1861	Discharged the Service
	Pension paid 2nd Glasgow Pension District
	1/-½d. per diem
12 Sept 1864	Arrived per *'Merchantman'* [2]
1865	Advertising Notice - Mr D Kilpatrick is opening a business in High Street Fremantle and states that he has long experience as a master tailor in the Army and as a civilian [Trove] [by the logo at top of notice would indicated that Daniel Kilpatrick is possibly a Freemason]
1873	possibly residing near Roebourne
1878	Pension increased to 1/5½d. per diem for service in the Enrolled Force
24 Aug 1881	Assigned Perth Railway Block Lot 152/V
19 Aug 1883	Granted Fee Simple Perth Railway Block Lot 152/V
Dec 1883	Died aged 64 at his son's residence Bally Bally

Service and Personal Details:

Place of Birth:	Whitekirk Haddington Scotland	
Age on Enlistment:	18 years 5 months	
Period of Service:	1839 — 1861	
Age on Discharge:	40 years 6 months	
Length of Service:	22 years 43 days	
Foreign Service:	West Indies	2 years 1 month
	Mediterranean	3 years 2 months
Reason for Discharge:	Having completed 22 years service	
Character:	Good	
Trade or Occupation:	Tailor	
Can Sign Name:	Yes	
Height:	5' 8"	
Hair Colour:	Black	
Eyes:	Black	
Complexion:	Dark	
Intends to Reside:	Glasgow	

KINCH	John, private
	1st Foot Guards [Grenadier Guards]
24 July 1855	Discharged the Service London
	Pension paid Oxford
	7d. per diem for 18 months
1856	Pension paid 1st West London Pension District
1862	Pension paid Bath
1863	Pension paid 1st West London Pension District
1863	1st East London Pension District
1864	Pension made permanent
15 Aug 1865	Arrived per *'Racehorse'*
1866	Pension paid Adelaide South Australia To South Australia per *'Letty'*
1875	"Part of pension stopped for wife residing in Fremantle"
1879	Pension paid Victoria - " 2/3 stoppage for wife"

1880	W.O. correspondence with Under Treasurer Melbourne
1890	W.O. Correspondence - "A31"

Service and Personal Details:

Place of Birth:	Langford Berkshire	
Age on Enlistment:	17 years 10 months	
Period of Service:	1847 — 1855	
Age on Discharge:	25 years 10 months	
Length of Service:	7 years 267 days	
Foreign Service:	Army in the East	10 months
Reason for Discharge:	Chronic Hepatitis [did not serve in the Crimea]	
Character:	Very Good	
Trade or Occupation:	Labourer	
Can Sign Name:	Yes	
Height:	5' 7¾"	
Hair Colour:	Light Brown	
Eyes:	Blue	
Complexion:	Fresh	

KING William, gunner and driver
RA 7th Battalion

13 Jan 1852	Discharged the Service Woolwich Pension paid Nottingham 1/- per diem
2 Apr 1856	Arrived per *'William Hammond'*
Jan 1857	Contributed 2/- to the Florence Nightingale Fund
1857	Land North Fremantle originally assigned to Patrick Shea
1861	Pension paid Queensland

Service and Personal Details:

Place of Birth:	St Marys Nottingham	
Age on Enlistment:	17 years	
Period of Service:	1829 — 1852	
Age on Discharge:	39 years 11 months	
Length of Service:	21 years 150 days	
Foreign Service:	Corfu	8 years 11 months
Reason for Discharge:	Chronic Rheumatism	
Character:	Very Good	
Trade or Occupation:	Labourer	
Can Sign Name:	Yes	
Height:	5' 7"	
Hair Colour:	Brown	
Eyes:	Hazel	
Complexion:	Dark	

KINGDOM John, private
43rd Foot

Surname Variant	KINGDON
8 Aug 1843	Discharged the Service Chatham Pension paid 2nd West London Pension District 1/- per diem

1 June 1850	Arrived per *'Scindian'*
1850	Assigned land Freshwater Bay
1 Oct 1851	Died

Service and Personal Details:

Place of Birth:	Linkinhorne Cornwall	
Age on Enlistment:	18 years	
Period of Service:	1820 — 1843	
Age on Discharge:	41 years	
Length of Service:	23 years 42 days	
Foreign Service:	Gibraltar	7 years
	Portugal	1 year 3 months
	North America	7 years 10 months
Reason for Discharge:	Impaired Constitution from age and service	
Character:	Good and efficient	
Trade or Occupation:	Labourer	
Can Sign Name:	X his mark on discharge	
Height:	5' 7½"	
Hair Colour:	Brown	
Eyes:	Grey	
Complexion:	Fresh	
Intends to Reside:	Mary-le-Bone London	

KINNAIRD James Robert, private

	50th Foot
Previous Regiments	45th; 39th
Surname Variants	KINNEARD; KENNARD
12 July 1853	Discharged the Service Chatham
	Pension paid Preston
	9d. per diem
1854	Pension paid Woolwich
1856	Pension paid 1st East London Pension District
1856	Deptford
19 Aug 1859	Arrived per *'Sultana'*
1866	To Adelaide from Perth Western Australia
1874	Died

Service and Personal Details:

Place of Birth:	Drummore Co Down	
Age on Enlistment:	19 years 3 months	
Period of Service:	1835 — 1853	
Age on Discharge:	37 years or 36 years 9 months	
Length of Service:	17 years 189 days	
Foreign Service:	East Indies	8 years 29 days
Reason for Discharge:	Chronic Dysentery and Liver Disease	
Character:	Good	
Trade or Occupation:	Labourer	
Can Sign Name:	Yes	
Height:	5' 7"	
Hair Colour:	Brown	
Eyes:	Grey	
Complexion:	Fresh	
Intends to Reside:	Preston Lane	

KIRK	Francis, gunner and driver
	RA 8th Battalion
13 Oct 1846	Discharged the Service Woolwich
	Pension paid Woolwich
	1/-½d. per diem
1849	Pension paid Athlone
21 May 1851	Arrived per *'Mermaid'*
1852	Employed as Warder at Toodyay
1866	Allocated Newcastle Pensioner Lot S12 [pensioner Kirk's cottage located at 68 Stirling Terrace Toodyay is registered on the Western Australian Heritage Council's database]
1866	Employed as Police Constable Toodyay
1869	Died

Service and Personal Details:		
Place of Birth:	Achalive Co. Tyrone	
Age on Enlistment:	16 years 11 months	
Period of Service:	1823 — 1846	
Age on Discharge:	39 years 10 months	
Length of Service:	22 years 13 days	
Foreign Service:	Corfu	8 years 3 months
Reason for Discharge:	Chronic Rheumatism	
Character:	Exemplary	
Trade or Occupation:	Labourer	
Can Sign Name:	X his mark on discharge	
Height:	5' 7½"	
Hair Colour:	Fair	
Eyes:	Blue	
Complexion:	Fair	

KIRBY	Richard, private
	84th Foot
14 Apr 1863	Discharged the Service Pembroke Dock
	Pension paid Limerick
	1/- per diem
22 Dec 1865	Arrived per *'Vimiera'*
1866	Pension paid Adelaide
1867	Auckland
1869	Sydney

Service and Personal Details:		
Place of Birth:	Galbally Limerick	
Age on Enlistment:	18 years	
Period of Service:	1842 — 1863	
Age on Discharge:	39 years	
Length of Service:	21 years 6 days	
Foreign Service:	East Indies	17 years
Medal Entitlement:	Indian Mutiny with Clasps	
Reason for Discharge:	Own Request after 21 years service	
Character:	Very Good	
Trade or Occupation:	Labourer	
Can Sign Name:	Yes	

Height:	5' 7"
Hair Colour:	Brown
Eyes:	Grey
Complexion:	Fresh
Remarks:	Claims Prize Money for Lucknow
Intends to Reside:	Limerick

KIRKBY

	Arthur Robert, private 17th Lancers
Surname Variant	KIRBY
6 Aug 1867	Discharged the Service Aldershot Pension paid Leeds 6d. per diem for 6 months
1 Oct 1867	Pension paid Perth Western Australia
1869	Correspondence from W.O. to Perth West. Aust.
1892	Died aged 53 — committed suicide
15 Sept 1892	Report that Robert Kirby of Bullens Yard' Wellington St, — hung himself

Service and Personal Details:

Place of Birth:	Leeds Yorkshire
Age on Enlistment:	19 years
Period of Service:	1866 — 1867
Age on Discharge:	20 years 5 months
Length of Service:	1 year 124 days
Reason for Discharge:	Fractured Fibular from a kick from a horse
Character:	Good
Trade or Occupation:	Clerk
Can Sign Name:	Yes
Height:	5' 8"
Hair Colour:	Light Brown
Eyes:	Grey
Complexion:	Fresh
Intends to Reside:	No. 1 Montpellier Terrace Woodhouse
Cliff nr. Leeds	
Children:	Jesse [son from newspaper article — Trove]

KIRWAN

	John, Serjeant [322] 30th Foot
Previous Regiment	63rd
Surname Variant	KIRWIN
21 June 1847	Discharged the Service Newcastle-on-Tyne
13 July 1847	Admitted to Out-Pension Pension paid Northampton 1/1d. per diem
1 June 1850	Arrived per *'Scindian'*
June 1850	Employed as Steward Convict Establishment
1851	Assigned land Freshwater Bay Lot 17 [see "Reference to ½ Acre Lots" — Pensioner Lots Freshwater Bay ; Topographical Return to 30th June 1851] — source Claremont Museum
Sept 1851	Described as Serjeant Major in the [Fremantle] Local Force

7 Oct 1851	a Serjeant John Kirwan appointed to Police Force Perth	
1854	"Absconded with clothing"	
	Struck off Enrolled Force	
1857	To South Australia from Western Australia	
	Arrived South Australia per *'Anna Dixon'*	
1873	"Shot himself dead." — Adelaide	

Service and Personal Details:		
Place of Birth:	Kilmain Co. Mayo	
Age on Enlistment:	18 years	
Period of Service:	1825 — 1847	
Age on Discharge:	39 years 8 months	
Length of Service:	21 years 201 days	
Foreign Service:	Bermuda	5 years 4 months
Reason for Discharge:	Own Request, receiving the Modified Rate of Pension under conditions prescribed	
Character:	For the first five years good then he became an habitual drunkard	
Trade or Occupation:	Labourer	
Can Sign Name:	Yes	
Height:	5' 11½"	
Hair Colour:	Dark Brown	
Eyes:	Hazel	
Complexion:	Fresh	
Intends to Reside:	Stoke ?Bruerne Towcester	

KNOCKTON George, private

	50th Foot	
21 May 1861	Discharged the Service Parkhurst IOW	
	Pension paid Limerick	
	1/1d. per diem	
1861	Pension paid 1st Dublin Pension District	
15 Feb 1863	Arrived per *'Merchantman'* [1]	
Oct 1864	Departed colony per *'Sea Ripple*	
1864	Pension paid South Australia	

Service and Personal Details:		
Place of Birth:	Kilcolman Co. Limerick	
Age on Enlistment:	20 years	
Period of Service:	1840 — 1861	
Age on Discharge:	41 years	
Length of Service:	21 years 9 days	
Foreign Service:	India	5 years
	Crimea	2 years 2 months
Medal Entitlement:	Good Conduct and Long Service; Crimea with 3 clasps; Turkish Crimean	
Reason for Discharge:	Own Request having served 21 years	
Character:	Very Good	
Trade or Occupation:	Labourer	
Can Sign Name:	X his mark on discharge	
Height:	5' 5"	

Hair Colour:	Dark Brown
Eyes:	Grey
Complexion:	Fresh
Intends to Reside:	No 6 Henry Street, Limerick Ireland

KNOX	James, Quartermaster Serjeant
	21st Foot
22 June 1852	Discharged the Service Chatham
	Pension paid Aberdeen
	2/- per diem
19 Aug 1853	Arrived per *'Robert Small'*
1854	Pension paid Hobart Town

Service and Personal Details:		
Place of Birth:	Old Macher Scotland	
Age on Enlistment:	18 years	
Period of Service:	1831 — 1852	
Age on Discharge:	39 years 6 months	
Length of Service:	21 years 6 days	
Foreign Service:	Van Diemans Land	5 years
	East Indies	5 years
Medal Entitlement:	Long Service and Good Conduct with gratuity	
Reason for Discharge:	Unfit for further service	
Character:	Most exemplary	
Trade or Occupation:	Labourer	
Can Sign Name:	Yes	
Height:	5' 8"	
Hair Colour:	Brown	
Eyes:	Blue	
Complexion:	Fresh	
Intends to Reside:	Aberdeen	

LAMBE	Patrick, private
	98th Foot
Previous Regiment	21st Foot
Surname Variant	LAMB
1845	In hospital India
10 July 1849	Discharged the Service Chatham
11 July 1849	Admitted as an Out–Pensioner Royal Hospital Chelsea
Pension paid Kilkenny	
	1/- per diem
18 July 1855	Arrived per *'Adelaide'*
no date	Assigned Perth Town Lot 27/Y
Jan 1865	Application for Title to Perth Lot 27/Y
Nov 1865	Advertised to sell a 2 roomed cottage Lot 27/Y located in the Perth Pensioner Village [Trove]
1866	Pension paid Adelaide South Australia To South Australia per *'Harriet Hope"*
1872	Pension paid South Australia
Jan 1872	Patrick Lamb [sic] a pensioner was fined 10/- for drunkenness

Service and Personal Details:

Place of Birth:	Clonaslee Queens County
Age on Enlistment:	18 years
Period of Service:	1827 — 1849
Age on Discharge:	? 41 years
Length of Service:	21 years 212 days [23 years 3 days reckoned]
Foreign Service:	New South Wales [period not given]
	East Indies 9 years 5 months
Reason for Discharge:	Worn out and unfit for further service
Character:	Very Good
Trade or Occupation:	Weaver
Can Sign Name:	X His mark on Discharge; Yes on Attestation
Height:	5' 6¾"
Hair Colour:	Fair
Eyes:	Blue
Complexion:	Fresh
Information from Pension Certificate	
Height:	5' 9½"
Hair Colour:	Fair
Eyes:	Grey
Intends to Reside:	Clonaslee Queens County

LAMBE Thomas, Serjeant EIC

	Bombay 1st European Fusiliers
Surname Variant	LAMB
	Out Pension No 178
5 June 1856	Admitted to Out-pension
	Pension paid Edinburgh
	1/- per diem
1864	Pension paid Newcastle United Kingdom
15 Apr 1864	Arrived per *'Clara'* [2]
1866	To South Australia from Perth West Australia
1867	Pension paid Singapore
1867	Bengal
1897	Entertained at banquet commemorating Queen Victoria's Jubilee
June 1897	Residing Perth
April 1905	Died Fremantle aged 83

Service and Personal Details:

Where Born:	Lander Berwick
Trade or Occupation:	Labourer
Presidency:	Bombay
Age on Discharge:	36 years
Length of Service:	15 years 3 months
Reason for Discharge:	Rheumatism
Character:	Good
Height:	5' 7"
Complexion:	Dark
Eye Colour:	Hazel
Hair Colour:	Dark
Intends to Reside:	Newcastle

LATHAM	John, private	
	42nd Foot	
Surname Variant	LATHERM	
31 May 1845	Discharged the Service Malta	
8 July 1845	Admitted to Out-Pension	
	Pension paid Edinburgh from Malta	
	10d. per diem	
31 Aug 1853	Arrived per *'Phoebe Dunbar*	
1854	Employed in Convict Establishment without sanction of Staff Office Pensions	
1864	Allocated Newcastle Pensioner land at Newcastle	
1875	Pension paid Perth Western Australia	
1882	Died aged 81	
Service and Personal Details:		
Place of Birth:	Glasgow Lanarkshire	
Age on Enlistment:	18 years	
Period of Service:	1823 — 1845	
Age on Discharge:	40 years 1 month	
Length of Service:	21 years 252 days	
Foreign Service:	Gibraltar	6 years 9 days
	Ionian Isles	3 years 309 days
	Malta	5 years 52 days
Reason for Discharge:	Own Request having served 21 years	
Character:	Good	
Trade or Occupation:	Labourer	
Can Sign Name:	Yes on Discharge; No on Attestation X his mark	
Height:	5' 10½"	
Hair Colour:	Brown	
Eyes:	Brown	
Complexion:	Swarthy	
Intends to Reside:	ptve John Latham intends to reside in Malta and receive his pension in Malta	

LATIMER	William, Serjeant
	7th Foot
Previous Regiment	24th Foot
21 Apr 1857	Discharged the Service Chatham
	1/3d. per diem
1857	Pension paid Cavan
	Serving in Cavan Militia
12 Sept 1864	Arrived per *'Merchantman'* [2]
1879	Assigned North Fremantle Lot P20
1879	Payment of £15 sanctioned
1881	Allocated North Fremantle Lot P37
31 Jan 1882	Granted Fee Simple North Fremantle Lot P37
1881	Pension increased to 1/11d. per diem for 16 years service as Serjeant in the Enrolled Force
30 Aug 1886	Died aged 59 at the Barracks
Service and Personal Details:	
Place of Birth:	Drung Ballyhais Co. Cavan
Age on Enlistment:	18 years 6 months
Period of Service:	1846 — 1857
Age on Discharge:	29 years 2 months

Length of Service:	10 years 240 days	
Foreign Service:	Turkey & Crimea	9 months
Medal Entitlement:	Crimea	
Reason for Discharge:	Injury of left side and lumber region from a gunshot wound received in the Crimea	
Character:	Good	
Trade or Occupation:	Labourer	
Can Sign Name:	Yes	
Height:	5' 9"	
Hair Colour:	Dark Brown	
Eyes:	Grey	
Complexion:	Swarthy	
Intends to Reside:	Castlehill Cavan Co. Cavan	

LAUGHLAN	William, private 83rd
Previous Regiment	96th Foot
Surname Variants	[some] McLAUGHLIN; LAUGHLIN; UGHTON; LOUGHLIN
17 June 1862	Discharged the Service Chatham Pension paid Derby 1/- per diem
1863	Pension paid Preston
28 Dec 1863	Arrived per *'Lord Dalhousie'* as a Convict Guard
circa June 1874	Transferred from 2nd Perth Pension District to 1st Perth Pension District
1878	Pension increased to 1/6d. per diem for service in the Enrolled Force
22 Sept 1883	Granted North Fremantle Lot 75
1884	Died – buried East Perth Cemetery

Service and Personal Details:

Place of Birth:	Ballymahon Longford	
Age on Enlistment:	17 years	
Period of Service:	1839 — 1861	
Age on Discharge:	39 years 10 months	
Length of Service:	19 years 148 days	
Foreign Service:	New South Wales	5 years 245 days
	East Indies	12 years 160 days
Medal Entitlement:	Indian Medal with clasp	
Reason for Discharge:	Long service and general debility	
Character:	Latterly Good	
Trade or Occupation:	Labourer	
Can Sign Name:	Yes	
Height:	5' 7½"	
Hair Colour:	Brown	
Eyes:	Grey	
Complexion:	Fresh	
Intends to Reside:	Tamworth Staffordshire	
Married:	*c*1866 a William Laughlin married Theresa Bogue at Perth	

LAVERY	John, private	
	48th Foot	
21 May 1857	Discharged the Service	
7 July 1857	Admitted to Out-Pension	
	Pension paid Newcastle	
	1/- per diem	
24 Nov 1858	Arrived per *'Edwin Fox'*	
1865	Pension paid Western Australia	
26 Mar 1867	Died	
Service and Personal Details:		
Place of Birth:	Ballinmore Banbrigge Co. Armagh	
Age on Attestation:	23 years	
Period of Service:	1836 — 1857	
Age on Discharge:	44 years 2 months	
Length of Service:	21 years 63 days	
Foreign Service:	Gibraltar	5 years 4 months
	West Indies	3 years 1 month
Reason for Discharge:	General weakness and palpitations	
Character:	Very Good	
Trade or Occupation:	Labourer	
Can Sign Name:	Yes	
Height:	5' 6¾"	
Hair Colour:	Light Brown	
Eyes:	Blue	
Complexion:	Fresh	
Distinguishing Marks:	Nose inclined to the right side, slightly pitted with small pox; has mark of an issue [sic] on the right knee	
Intends to Reside:	Manchester	

LAWRIE	John, private	
	27th Foot	
Previous Regiment	45th Foot	
22 Aug 1848	Discharged the Service Chatham	
	Pension paid Newcastle	
	8d. per diem	
8 June 1858	Arrived per *'Lord Raglan'*	
1865	Pension paid Perth Western Australia	
Service and Personal Details:		
Place of Birth:	Innerwick Dunbar East Lothian	
Age on Enlistment:	18 years 3 months	
Period of Service:	1834 — 1848	
Age on Discharge:	32 years 3 months	
Length of Service:	13 years 52 days	
Foreign Service:	East Indies	1 year 173 days
	Gibraltar	1 year 274 days
	Cape of Good Hope	1 year 272 days
	Monte Video	298 days
Reason for Discharge:	Impaired Vision and Broken Constitution	
Character:	Generally Good	
Trade or Occupation:	Baker	
Can Sign Name:	blank; Yes on attestation	

Height:	5' 7"
Hair Colour:	Light Brown
Eyes:	Blue
Complexion:	Fresh
Intends to Reside:	Dunbar [sic] Haddington

LEAHY	Redmond, private [1888] 37th Foot
Surname Variants	LEAHEY; LEIHY; LAKEY; LEALY
8 Mar 1864	Discharged the Service Pembroke Dock Pension paid 1st Cork Pension District 11d. per diem
9 Jan 1868	Arrived per *'Hougoumont'*
circa Sept 1874	Transferred from 2nd Perth Pension District to Fremantle
1881	Pension increased to 1/4d. per diem for service in the Enrolled Force
5 Aug 1884	Granted North Fremantle Lot P67
Dec 1885	Resident Magistrate Fremantle — for Mt. Eliza Depot, Pensioner Redmond Leihy [sic]
1889	Died

Service and Personal Details:

Place of Birth:	St Finbar Cork Co. Cork	
Age on Enlistment:	19 years	
Period of Service:	1842 — 1864	
Age on Discharge:	40 years 5 months	
Length of Service:	21 years 141 days	
Foreign Service:	Ceylon	10 years 4 months
	Bengal	3 years
Medal Entitlement:	Indian Mutiny	
Reason for Discharge:	Own Request after 21 years service	
Character:	Latterly Good	
Trade or Occupation:	Labourer	
Can Sign Name:	X his mark on discharge	
Height:	5' 9½"	
Hair Colour:	Brown	
Eyes:	Grey	
Complexion:	Fresh	
Intends to Reside:	Cork	

LEARY	Daniel, private [3165] 57th Foot
Previous Regiment	48th Foot
31 July 1855	Discharged the Service Chatham Pension paid Sheffield 9d. per diem
31 Dec 1862	Arrived per *'York'*
1864	pvte D Leary Pensioner Force at Perth contributed to the Greenough Fire Relief Fund
1865	a D Leary to South Australia per *'Harriet Hope'*
1871	a D Leary arrived from Adelaide per "*Emily Smith'*
Aug 1876	Allocated Perth Town Lot 31/H

1880	His 2 years 175 days service in the Enrolled Force can't be allowed to reckon as man was not re-enrolled within 12 months of discharge from the Force on 2/7/1865	
1881	Pension increased to 1/1½d. per diem for service in the Enrolled Force	
Jan 1882	Assigned Perth Town Lot 31/H	
Sept 1883	Application for Title Perth Town Lot 31/H	
12 Oct 1883	Granted Fee Simple Perth Town Lot 31/H	
Service and Personal Details:		
Place of Birth:	St Barrys Cork Co. Cork	
Age on Enlistment:	19 years	
Period of Service:	1837 — 1855	
Age on Discharge:	36 years 8 months	
Length of Service:	18 years 2 months [13 years 8 months forfeited by conviction of felony — total service 4 years 4 months]	
Foreign Service:	Gibraltar	upwards 5 years
	Corfu	1 year 7 months
	West Indies	upwards 3 years
	Army in the East	7 months
Medal Entitlement:	Crimea	
Reason for Discharge:	Left hand disabled by gunshot wound to the left arm received at Inkermann	
Character:	Good	
Trade or Occupation:	Weaver	
Can Sign Name:	Yes	
Height:	5' 8"	
Hair Colour:	Light Brown	
Eyes:	Grey	
Complexion:	Fresh	

LEARY	Patrick, private 46th Foot	
Previous Regiment	95th Foot	
24 Nov 1846	Discharged the Service Chatham Pension paid Jersey 1/- per diem	
7 Feb 1853	Arrived per *'Dudbrook'*	
1854	Employed by Convict Establishment	
10 Jan 1871	Died aged 63	
Service and Personal Details:		
Place of Birth:	?Clorough Co. Cork	
Age on Enlistment:	18 years	
Period of Service:	1823 — 1846	
Age on Discharge:	42 years	
Length of Service:	22 years 195 days	
Foreign Service:	Mediterranean	10 years 7 months
	Gibraltar	1 year 5 months
	West Indies	3 years
	North America	1 year 4 months
Reason for Discharge:	Unfit for further service	

Character:	Good	
Trade or Occupation:	Labourer	
Can Sign Name:	Yes	
Height:	5' 6¾"	
Hair Colour:	Brown	
Eyes:	Hazel	
Complexion:	Fresh	
Intends to Reside:	Jersey	
LEE	George, Serjeant	
	77th Foot	
11 Oct 1859	Discharged the Service Chatham	
	Pension paid 2nd Dublin Pension District	
	1/5d. per diem	
1861	Pension paid Edinburgh	
31 Dec 1862	Arrived per *'York'*	
1864	Pension paid 1st East London Pension District	
1864	Preston	
1871	Pension increased to 1/9d. per diem	
Service and Personal Details:		
Place of Birth:	Naas Co. Kildare	
Age on Enlistment:	20 years	
Period of Service:	1837 — 1859	
Age on Discharge:	42 years	
Length of Service:	22 years 33 days	
Foreign Service:	Mediterranean &	
	Turkey & Crimea	3 years 6 months
	West Indies &	
	North America	5 years 2 months
	Australia	1 year 4 months
Medal Entitlement:	Distinguished Conduct with gratuity; Good Conduct with gratuity; Crimea with clasps;	
Turkish Crimea		
Reason for Discharge:	Own Request having served 22 years	
Character:	Very Good	
Trade or Occupation:	Comb maker	
Can Sign Name:	Yes	
Height:	5' 7"	
Hair Colour:	Brown	
Eyes:	Blue	
Complexion:	Fair	
Intends to Reside:	Dublin	
LEE	Patrick, private	
	41st Foot	
9 Jan 1844	Discharged the Service Chatham	
12 Jan 1844	Admitted to Out-Pension	
	Pension paid Bagnallstown Kilkenny	
	11d. per diem	
25 Oct 1850	Arrived per *'Hashemy'*	
20 Dec 1852	Assigned Bunbury Pensioner Lot P5	
4 Dec 1858	Application Title Bunbury Pensioner Lot P5	

1870	Died
22 Aug 1899	Removal of Old Buildings — Only about three of the pensioner buildings which were erected in the district over 40 years ago, are now standing. The last to be razed to the ground was that owned by Pensioner Patrick Lee in Stephen Street. All the buildings were of one design and easily distinguished by the porch in front

Service and Personal Details:

Place of Birth:	Donleckney Carlow	
Age on Enlistment:	18 years	
Period of Service:	1824 — 1844	
Age on Discharge:	42 years	
Length of Service:	19 years 13 days	
Foreign Service:	East Indies	17 years 8 months
Medal Entitlement:	Afghan and Burmese	
Reason for Discharge:	Unfit for further service	
Character:	Good	
Trade or Occupation:	Labourer	
Can Sign Name:	X his mark on discharge	
Height:	5' 7¾"	
Hair Colour:	Brown	
Eyes:	Grey	
Complexion:	Sallow	
Intends to Reside:	Bagnellstown	

LEIGHTON

	John, private 6th Dragoons
9 Aug 1853	Discharged the Service Pension paid 1st Edinburgh Pension District 8d. per diem for 3 years
10 Sept 1856	Arrived per *'Runnymede'*
1857	Employed as Assistant Warder
1870	Granted a Deferred Pension of 5d. per diem
1875	Pension paid Fremantle
1898	Died aged 78

Service and Personal Details:

Place of Birth:	Leagan Longford
Age on Enlistment:	20 years
Period of Service:	1840 — 1853
Age on Discharge:	33 years 4 months
Length of Service:	13 years 139 days
Reason for Discharge:	Unfit for further service
Character:	Very Good
Trade or Occupation:	Boot and Shoemaker
Can Sign Name:	Yes
Height:	5' 10"
Hair Colour:	Fair
Eyes:	Grey

Complexion:	Fresh
Intends to Reside:	Edinburgh
LENNOX	William, private
	77th Foot
15 Jan 1856	Discharged the Service Chatham
	Pension paid Ballymena
	8d. per diem
8 June 1858	Arrived per *'Lord Raglan'*
1858	Possibly serving as police constable
1864	Pension paid Ballymena
1898	Died Kilmainham Hospital
Service and Personal Details:	
Place of Birth:	Castle Dawson Derry
Age on Enlistment:	17 years 9 months
Period of Service:	1846 — 1855
Age on Discharge:	26 years 10 months
Length of Service:	8 years 296 days
Foreign Service:	Mediterranean &
	Turkey & Crimea 1 year 8 months
Medal Entitlement:	Crimea with clasps; Turkish Crimean
Reason for Discharge:	Disabled by loss of last two phalanges of right hand after musket ball wound
Character:	Good
Trade or Occupation:	Weaver
Can Sign Name:	Yes
Height:	5' 5¼"
Hair Colour:	Dark Brown
Eyes:	Hazel
Complexion:	Fresh
Intends to Reside:	Antrim
LILLIS	John, private
	69th Foot
Surname Variant	LELLIS
23 Jan 1855	Discharged the Service Chatham
	Pension paid Limerick
	1/- per diem
1859	Pension paid Deptford
31 Dec 1862	Arrived per *'York'*
1864	ptve J Lellis [sic] Pensioner Force at Perth contributed to the Greenough Fire Relief Fund
1864	Owned grocery business Murray St., Perth
1874	Pension increased to 1/3d. per diem
8 May 1878	Assigned Perth Military Pensioner Lot 138/Y
1880	Grant of £15 [pounds] sanctioned
Apr 1881	Application for Title to Perth Lot 138
14 June 1881	Granted Fee Simple Perth Pensioner Lot 138/Y
30 Dec 1896	Died — Buried East Perth Pioneer Cemetery
Service and Personal Details:	
Place of Birth:	St Johns Co. Limerick
Age on Enlistment:	15 years 8 months
Period of Service:	1830 — 1855

Age on Discharge:	40 year or 39 years 8 months	
Length of Service:	20 years 291 days	
Foreign Service:	West Indies	7 years 1 month
	North America	3 years 6 months
	Mediterranean	3 years 4 months
Reason for Discharge:	Chronic Rheumatism caused by exposure	
Character:	Indifferent	
Trade or Occupation:	Labourer	
Can Sign Name:	Yes	
Height:	5' 7"	
Hair Colour:	Light Brown	
Eyes:	Light Blue	
Complexion:	Fresh	
Distinguishing Marks:	A little freckled	
Intends to Reside:	Limerick	

LILLIS

	Stephen, private 69th Foot
Previous Regiment	25th Foot
Surname Variants	LELLIS; LILLAS
10 Dec 1861	Discharged the Service Pension paid Deptford 10½d. per diem
31 Dec 1862	Arrived per *'York'*
1864	ptve Stephen Lellis [sic] Pensioner Force at Perth contributed to the Greenough Fire Relief Fund
1872	Summons to hearing for claim of £1/19/6½
1874	Pension increased to 1/3d. per diem
31 July 1875	Perth Poor House — To Hon Acting Col. Sec. Correspondence re Pensioner Stephen Lillas [sic] application for his 2 young daughters [aged 10 and 8] to be placed in the Catholic Orphanage as Government inmates, his wife has left him for some years and he is now living with another man in the bush and is unable to work from the effects of an old wound and is also suffering from a Fistula; his pension is 1/3 per day but is barely sufficient to maintain him and a little boy [Trove]
1877	Pensioner Stephen Lillis at 1/3 a day from the 69th Foot is recommended for admission to Mount Eliza Depot.
1878	Died
14 Oct 1885	Edward Lillis — enquiring, Is he entitled to Late Pensioner Lillis's Grant of Land

Service and Personal Details:

Place of Birth:	St Marys Co. Limerick	
Age on Enlistment:	18 years	
Period of Service:	1837 — 1861	
Age on Discharge:	42 years	
Length of Service:	22 years 270 days	
Foreign Service:	North America	3 years 7 months
	Mediterranean	3 years 6 months
	West Indies	5 years 11 months

	East Indies	2 years 2 months
Reason for Discharge:	Own Request having served 22 years	
Character:	Latterly Good	
Trade or Occupation:	Weaver	
Can Sign Name:	Yes	
Height:	5' 9"	
Hair Colour:	Light Brown	
Eyes:	Blue	
Complexion:	Fair	
Intends to Reside:	London	

LINDSAY	George Francis William, private	
	47th Foot	
12 Jan 1864	Discharged the Service Netley	
29 Mar 1864	Admitted to Out-Pension	
	Pension paid Athlone	
	[6d. per diem conditional for 18 months]	
	Pension increased to 1/-½d. per diem	
1865	Pension paid 2nd Manchester Pension District	
1865	Liverpool	
13 July 1867	Arrived per *'Norwood'* [2]	
circa June 1874	Transferred from 2nd Perth Pension District to 1st Perth Pension District	
29 Nov 1874	Died aged 49	
Service and Personal Details:		
Place of Birth:	St Peters Jersey	
Age on Enlistment:	14 years	
Period of Service:	1852 — 1863	
Age on Discharge:	25 years	
Length of Service:	6 years 390 days [or 11 years 4 months depending on record source]	
Foreign Service:	Malta	1 year 4 months
	Turkey	6 months
	Crimea	9 months
	Gibraltar	5 months
	Canada	2 years 3 months
Medal Entitlement:	Crimea with clasps; Turkish Crimean	
Reason for Discharge:	Secondary Syphilis	
Character:	Good	
Trade or Occupation:	Soldier's Son	
Can Sign Name:	Yes	
Height:	5' 7½"	
Hair Colour:	Light Brown	
Eyes:	Hazel	
Complexion:	Fresh	
Intends to Reside:	Dulverton Somerset	

LINDSAY	Robert, private
	2nd Foot
Previous Regiment	69th Foot
19 Oct 1847	Discharged the Service Athlone
11 Jan 1848	Admitted to Out-Pension

	Pension paid Longford
	1/- per diem
1849	Pension paid Birmingham
1849	Chatham
1 June 1850	Arrived per *'Scindian'*
1850	Assigned Land Freshwater Bay
1854	On duty Freshwater Bay
Jan 1857	Contributed 2/- to the Florence Nightingale Fund
Feb 1858	Application for Title Freshwater Bay Loc P223 and P243
1864	Bitten by a black snake Freshwater Bay
June 1877	Fremantle Pensioner Force: Referring to Pensioner Robert Lindsay at 1/- per day from the 2nd Foot — receiving his pension in advance and spending it on 'drink' leaving his wife destitute. While drinking he broke through his wife's window and took the only palliasse she had to lay on, sold it and drank the money. [Trove]
July 1877	Request for Major Finnerty to make arrangements for Mrs. Lindsay to receive half of her husband's pension as was done on a former occasion when Pensioner Lindsay was in the Poor House
1881	Fremantle — Pensioner Robert Lindsay charged with being drunk
1883	Pension to be increased to 1/6d. per diem
1883	Died

Service and Personal Details:

Place of Birth:	Locha Co. Tipperary	
Age on Enlistment:	18 years	
Period of Service:	1824 — 1847	
Age on Discharge:	40 years 8 months	
Length of Service:	22 years 260 days	
Foreign Service:	East Indies	18 years 11 months
Reason for Discharge:	General debility	
Character:	Good	
Trade or Occupation:	Labourer	
Can Sign Name:	Yes	
Height:	5' 9½"	
Hair Colour:	Light Brown	
Eyes:	Blue	
Complexion:	Fair	

LING John [Joseph], Colour Serjeant

	8th Foot
Previous Regiment	Coldstream Guards
24 Aug 1852	Discharged the Service Chatham
	1/11d. per diem
1852	Pension paid 1st North London Pension District
1852	Oxford
1853	1st North London Pension District
1858	Southampton
19 Aug 1859	Arrived per *'Sultana'*
31 Dec 1862	Pension paid Madras

1865	Pension paid 1st West London Pension District	
1865	Pension paid Exeter	
1870	Cardiff	
1874	Jersey	

Service and Personal Details:

Place of Birth:	Alicante Spain	
Age on Enlistment:	16 years 205 days	
Period of Service:	1830 — 1851	
Age on Discharge:	none given	
Length of Service:	20 years 71 days	
Foreign Service:	North America	3 years 236 days
	East Indies	5 years 64 days
Reason for Discharge:	Hepatic Disease	
Character:	Very Good	
Trade or Occupation:	Drummer	
Can Sign Name:	Yes	
Height:	5' 7"	
Hair Colour:	Light Brown	
Eyes:	Grey	
Complexion:	Fresh	
Intends to Reside:	Poona India	

LISLE James, private

	66th Foot	
Surname Variant	LISE	
29 Sept 1863	Discharged the Service Colchester	
	Pension paid Bristol	
	1/- per diem	
15 Aug 1865	Arrived per *'Racehorse'*	
1866	Pension paid New Zealand	
1875	New Zealand	

Service and Personal Details:

Place of Birth:	St Nicholas Bristol Gloucestershire	
Age on Enlistment:	19 years	
Period of Service:	1842 — 1863	
Age on Discharge:	40 years	
Length of Service:	21 years 11 days	
Foreign Service:	Gibraltar	4 years 36 days
	West Indies	3 years 151 days
	Canada	3 years 123 days
	East Indies	5 years 15 days
Reason for Discharge:	Own Request having served 21 years	
Character:	Good	
Trade or Occupation:	Cutler	
Can Sign Name:	Yes	
Height:	5' 8"	
Hair Colour:	Brown	
Eyes:	Hazel	
Complexion:	Dark	
Intends to Reside:	Bristol	

LITTON	John, Serjeant 38th Foot
26 Feb 1861	Awarded a Conditional Pension of 8d. per diem for 2 years
27 Aug 1861	Admitted to Out-Pension Pension paid Woolwich
1864	Pension commuted to Permanent status
Feb 1864	Pension increased to 10d. per diem
4 July 1866	Arrived per *'Belgravia'*
circa June 1874	Transferred from 2nd Perth Pension District to Freemantle [sic] Pension District
1877	Correspondence with W.O. regarding Lloyds Patriotic Fund
11 Nov 1880	Joined Enrolled Guard at Fremantle
1881	Pension increased to 1/5½d per diem for service in the Enrolled Force
1885	Cockburn Loc P9
1887	Correspondence from W.O. to S.O. Perth and Colonial Treasurer
1897	Died

Service and Personal Details:

Place of Birth:	Shoreditch London Middlesex	
Age on Enlistment:	18 years 4 months	
Period of Service:	1850 — 1860	
Age on Discharge:	none given	
Length of Service:	9 years 313 days	
Foreign Service:	Turkey	4 months
	Crimea	5 months
	East Indies	2 years 5 months
Medal Entitlement:	Crimea with clasps; Turkish Crimean; Indian Mutiny with clasp	
Reason for Discharge:	Own Request after limited service	
Character:	Very Good	
Trade or Occupation:	Labourer	
Can Sign Name:	Yes	
Height:	5' 7¼"	
Hair Colour:	Brown	
Eyes:	Hazel	
Complexion:	Dark	

LLOYD	Thomas, private 99th Foot
3 July 1855	Discharged the Service Chatham Pension paid Longford 7d. per diem for 3 years
10 Sept 1856	Arrived per *'Runnymede'*
1857	To South Australia from Western Australia per *'C.W. Bradley'*
26 July 1858	Pension ceased

Service and Personal Details:

Place of Birth:	Carrigallen Co. Leitrim
Age on Enlistment:	18 years

Period of Service:	1839 — 1855
Age on Discharge:	34 years
Length of Service:	14 years 64 days
Foreign Service:	Australian Colonies 12 years
Reason for Discharge:	Impaired vision in both eyes from ophthalmia
Character:	Indifferent, but good for the last two years
Trade or Occupation:	Labourer
Can Sign Name:	X his mark on discharge
Height:	5' 8"
Hair Colour:	Bark Brown
Eyes:	Blue
Complexion:	Sallow
Distinguishing Marks:	Pock pitted
Intended Residence:	? Granard Longford

LOCKE William Reuben, Serjeant

	57th Foot
Previous Regiment	6th Foot
Surname Variant	LOCK
3 Mar 1857	Discharged the Service Fermoy Barracks
7 Apr 1857	Admitted to Out-Pension
	Pension paid 2nd Dublin Pension District
	1/3d. per diem
1857	Pension paid Athlone
1857	Clonmel
1858	Athlone
1861	2nd Portsmouth Pension District
1863	Athlone
15 Aug 1865	Arrived per *'Racehorse'*
July 1874	Died aged 50 of Dropsy of the Heart

Service and Personal Details:

Place of Birth:	Enniscorthy Co. Wexford	
Age on Enlistment:	19 years 6 months	
Period of Service:	1845 — 1857	
Age on Discharge:	31 years 4 months	
Length of Service:	11 years 229 days	
Foreign Service:	North America	2 years 1 month
	Ionian Isles	1 year 6 months
	Crimea	1 year 8 months
	Malta	1 month
Medal Entitlement:	Crimea	
Reason for Discharge:	Unfit for service due to Pulmonary Consumption, as the result of wounds and exposure whilst on active service in the Crimea and while a prisoner in Russian captivity. Received violent blows on the chest with the butt of a musket on the 22nd of March 1855 during a sortie made by the enemy at Sebastopol. Subsequently suffered from acute pneumonia which terminated in tubecular [sic] in the lungs	
Character:	Good	
Trade or Occupation:	Labourer	

Can Sign Name:	Yes	
Height:	5' 8½"	
Hair Colour:	Light Brown	
Eyes:	Hazel	
Complexion:	Fair	
Intends to Reside:	Wexford	

LOGG

	Daniel, private	
	42nd Foot	
23 Mar 1860	Discharged the Service Stirling Castle	
10 Apr 1860	Admitted to Out-Pension	
	Pension paid 1st Glasgow pension District	
	1/- per diem	
27 May 1863	Arrived per *'Clyde'*	
1867	Pension paid South Australia from Perth W.A.	
1869	Western Australia	
1875	Western Australia	
Service and Personal Details:		
Place of Birth:	Kilpatrick Lanarkshire	
Age on Enlistment:	18 years	
Period of Service:	1836 — 1860	
Age on Discharge:	none given	
Length of Service:	21 years 26 days	
Foreign Service:	Corfu	about 3 years
	Malta	about 3 years
	Bermuda &	
	Nova Scotia	none given
	Turkey	about 4 months
	Crimea	1 year 5 months
Medal Entitlement:	Distinguished Conduct with gratuity; Crimea with clasps	
Reason for Discharge:	Own Request having completed 21 years service	
Character:	Good	
Trade or Occupation:	Printer	
Can Sign Name:	Yes	
Height:	5' 8¾"	
Hair Colour:	Brown	
Eyes:	Dark	
Complexion:	Fair	
Intends to Reside:	Glasgow	

LOTON

	Robert, Serjeant
	58th Foot
13 Apr 1842	Discharged the Service Dublin
	Pension paid Liverpool
	9d. per diem
1849	Pension paid Glasgow
1851	Dublin
19 Aug 1853	Arrived per *'Robert Small'*
1853	Employed as Night Warder without sanction of Staff Officer Pensions
1864	Serjeant Loton Pensioner Force at Kojonup contributed to the Greenough Fire Relief Fund

1864	Appointed Postmaster Kojonup
1873	Pension increased to 1/3d. per diem for 11½ years service in the Enrolled Force
1877	Residing Kojonup
June 1897	Residing Fremantle
1897	Died

Service and Personal Details:

Place of Birth:	Naas Co. Kildare	
Age on Enlistment:	18 years	
Period of Service:	1827 — 1842	
Age on Discharge:	32 years 2 months	
Length of Service:	15 years 66 days	
Foreign Service:	Ceylon	10 years 6 months
Reason for Discharge:	Chronic Rheumatism	
Character:	Good	
Trade or Occupation:	Labourer	
Can Sign Name:	Yes	
Height:	5' 6½"	
Hair Colour:	Brown	
Eyes:	Grey	
Complexion:	Fair	

LUCAS	Stephen, private 98th Foot
20 Sept 1864	Discharged the Service Colchester Pension paid Southampton 9d. per diem
19 Feb 1874	Arrived per *'Naval Brigade'*
1881	Pension increased to 11½d. per diem for service in the Enrolled Force
1880	Assigned Land at Lake Munster Loc P15
1881	Recommended for £15 Pensioner's Grant
1882	Fremantle — Stephen Lucas reported to be cutting wood on Coogee Town site
1888	Summons to appear at Fremantle Police Court for allegedly assaulting John Gilbridge The case was dismissed with Costs as it was proved the defendant never assaulted the plaintiff
1888	Residing Coojee [sic]
June 1897	Residing Fremantle
1903	Residing Southampton
1909	Correspondence with W.O.

Service and Personal Details:

Place of Birth:	Salisbury Wiltshire	
Age on Enlistment:	20 years	
Period of Service:	1850 — 1864	
Age on Discharge:	34 years	
Length of Service:	14 years 52 days	
Foreign Service:	India	10 years 5 months
Medal Entitlement:	India medal with clasp "North West Frontier"	
Reason for Discharge:	Unfit for further service - Secondary syphilis	

Character:	Very Good
Trade or Occupation:	Blacksmith
Can Sign Name:	X his mark on discharge
Height:	5' 7"
Hair Colour:	Brown
Eyes:	Brown
Complexion:	Fresh
Intends to Reside:	c/o Major Lacey Staff Officer of Pensioners
Portsmouth	

LUDLAM Thomas, private [3249]
24th Foot

Surname Variant	LUDLUM
1 Sept 1863	Discharged the Service Aldershot Pension paid Leicester 1/1d. per diem
22 Dec 1866	Arrived per *'Corona'* "Part pension stoppage for wife"
1867	Wife of Thomas Ludlam [EPG] arrived per *'Norwood'* [2]
Nov 1870	Died age 45

Service and Personal Details:

Place of Birth:	St Marys Leicester Leicestershire	
Age on Enlistment:	18 years 4 months	
Period of Service:	1842 — 1863	
Age on Discharge:	39 years 9 months	
Length of Service:	21 years 65 days	
Foreign Service:	East Indies	14 years 8 months
Medal Entitlement:	Punjaub with 2 clasps	
Reason for Discharge:	Own Request having served 21 years	
Character:	Very Good	
Trade or Occupation:	Labourer	
Can Sign Name:	X his mark on discharge	
Height:	5' 9"	
Hair Colour:	Brown	
Eyes:	Grey	
Complexion:	Sallow	
Remarks:	Name registered for a Good Conduct Medal	
Intends to Reside:	No 5 Green Lane Leicester	

LYNCH James, private
81st Foot

9 Sept 1856	Discharged the Service Chatham Pension paid 2nd Dublin Pension District 8d. per diem
19 Aug 1859	Arrived per *'Sultana'*
1861	Pension paid Sydney New South Wales

Service and Personal Details:

Place of Birth:	Lucan Dublin
Age on Enlistment:	18 years
Period of Service:	1835 — 1855
Age on Discharge:	40 years

Length of Service: 20 years 58 days
Foreign Service: Gibraltar 1 year
West Indies 3 years 6 months
Canada 4 years 1 month
East Indies 11 months
Reason for Discharge: Repeated and severe attacks of Dysentery

Character: Indifferent
Trade or Occupation: Labourer
Can Sign Name: Yes

Height: 5' 8"
Hair Colour: Light Brown
Eyes: Blue
Complexion: Fresh
Intends to Reside: Lucan Dublin

LYNCH Patrick, private
10th Foot
12 Aug 1845 Discharged the Service Chatham
Pension paid Limerick
1/- per diem
7 Feb 1853 Arrived per *'Dudbrook'*
31 Jan 1860 Died

Service and Personal Details:
Place of Birth: Rathkeal Co. Limerick
Age on Enlistment: 17 years
Period of Service: 1824 — 1845
Age on Discharge: 40 years or 39 years
Length of Service: 20 years 24 days
Foreign Service: Portugal 1 year 3 months
Ionian Isles 10 years
Reason for Discharge: Chronic Rheumatism

Character: Very Good
Trade or Occupation: Labourer
Can Sign Name: X his mark on discharge

Height: 5' 7"
Hair Colour: Brown
Eyes: Grey
Complexion: Sallow
Intends to Reside: Cappagh [sic] Co. Limerick

LYNCH Peter, private
77th Foot
26 Jan 1860 Discharged the Service Chatham
14 Feb 1860 Pension paid Ennis
9d. per diem
1861 Pension paid Liverpool
9 June 1862 Arrived per *'Norwood'* [1]
1864 ptve P Lynch Pensioner Force at Perth contributed to the Greenough Fire Relief Fund
1881 Pension increased to 1/3d. per diem for service in the Enrolled Force
1881 Assigned North Fremantle Lot P93

7 Mar 1883	Received Fee Simple North Fremantle Lot P93	
1885	Winifred Lynch charged with disorderly behaviour and her husband charged with inciting her to resist arrest	
1886	Died	
Service and Personal Details:		
Place of Birth:	Castle Blakeney Galway	
Age on Enlistment:	19 years	
Period of Service:	1838 — 1860	
Age on Discharge:	40 years	
Length of Service:	21 years 26 days	
Foreign Service:	Mediterranean & Turkey & Crimea	4 years 4 months
	West Indies & North America	5 years 2 months
	Australia & East Indies	1 year 8 months
Medal Entitlement:	Good Conduct with gratuity of £ 5; Crimea with clasps; Turkish Crimean	
Reason for Discharge:	Own Request having served 21 years	
Character:	Good	
Trade or Occupation:	Labourer	
Can Sign Name:	X his mark on discharge	
Height:	5' 10¼"	
Hair Colour:	Brown	
Eyes:	Brown	
Complexion:	Fresh	
Intends to Reside:	? Gorle Galway	

LYONS	James, private 68th Foot
Previous Regiment	59th Foot
3 July 1855	Discharged the Service Pension paid 2nd Belfast Pension District 8d. per diem
31 Dec 1862	Arrived per *'York'*
1864	ptve J Lyons Pensioner Force at Fremantle District contributed to the Greenough Fire Relief Fund
1864	To New South Wales from Fremantle
Service and Personal Details:	
Place of Birth:	Ballinahinch Co. Down
Age on Enlistment:	20 years
Period of Service:	1851 — 1855
Period of Service:	3 years 364 days
Age on Discharge:	24 years
Length of Service:	4 years 3 months
Foreign Service:	Served with Expeditionary Army in the East
Medal Entitlement:	Crimea with clasps
Reason for Discharge:	Impaired use of left hand and forearm. Injury is above wrist caused by a large fragment of stone in the trenches 12 Dec 1854

Character:	Good
Trade or Occupation:	Miner
Can sign Name:	Yes
Height:	5' 8½"
Hair Colour:	Brown
Eyes:	Blue
Complexion:	Fresh

LYONS	Michael, private
	49th Foot
Previous Regiment	68th Foot
3 July 1855	Discharged the Service Chatham
	Pension paid Tralee
	1/- per diem
1860	Pension paid Galway
1860	Tralee
29 Jan 1862	Arrived per *'Lincelles'*
1864	ptve M Lyons Pensioner Force at Fremantle contributed to the Greenough Fire Relief Fund
22 June 1872	Died — inquest found death by suicide

Service and Personal Details:

Place of Birth:	Killorglin Co. Kerry
Age on Enlistment:	19 years
Period of Service:	1839 — 1855
Age on Discharge:	34 years
Length of Service:	15 years 62 days
Foreign Service:	none given
Medal Entitlement:	?Crimea
Reason for Discharge:	Disabled by gunshot wound to shoulder
Character:	Indifferent
Trade or Occupation:	Labourer
Can Sign Name:	Yes
Height:	5' 8"
Hair Colour:	Brown
Eyes:	Grey
Complexion:	Fair

LYONS	Patrick, gunner EIC
	3rd Battalion Artillery
	Out Pension No 189
22 July 1857	Admitted to Out-pension
	Pension paid Clonmel
	9d. per diem
9 June 1862	Arrived per '*Norwood*' [1]
1864	ptve P Lyons Pensioner Force at Perth contributed to the Greenough Fire Relief Fund
1 Oct 1867	Pension paid Adelaide from Fremantle
1876	Pension paid South Australia

Service and Personal Details:

Where Born:	Tipperary
Trade or Occupation:	Labourer
Presidency:	Bengal

Age on Discharge:	38 years
Length of Service:	9 years 154 days
Reason for Discharge:	Amputation of the thumb
Character:	Good
Height:	5' 7"
Complexion:	Fresh
Eye Colour:	Grey
Hair Colour:	Brown
Intends to Reside:	?Emly Clonmel District

McALISTER Donald, private
78th Foot

14 Jan 1862	Discharged the Service Aldershot
	Pension paid 2nd Glasgow Pension District
	9½d. per diem
1862	Pension paid Bermuda
15 Feb 1863	Arrived per *'Merchantman'* [1]
5 Feb 1864	Died

Service and Personal Details:

Place of Birth:	Falkirk Stirlingshire
Age on Enlistment:	16 years 3 months
Period of Service:	1839 — 1861
Age on Discharge:	39 years 1 month
Length of Service:	22 years 27 days
Foreign Service:	East Indies 17 years 6 months
Medal Entitlement:	Persia; Indian Campaign with 2 clasps
Reason for Discharge:	Own Request having completed 22 years
Character:	Very Good
Trade or Occupation:	Cotton Spinner
Can Sign Name:	Yes
Height:	5' 8½"
Hair Colour:	Brown
Eyes:	Blue
Complexion:	Fair
Intends to Reside:	c/o Paymaster of Pensions Glasgow

McALLISTER Peter, private EIC
1st Madras European Infantry Regiment

Surname Variants	McALISTER; McALESTER
	Out Pension No 649
24 Dec 1856	Admitted to Out-pension
	Pension paid 1st Dublin Pension District
	9d. per diem
19 Aug 1859	Arrived per *'Sultana'*
1859	Departed colony per *'Champion'*
1861	Pension paid Madras
1866	Madras

Service and Personal Details:

Where Born:	Dublin
Trade or Occupation:	Shoemaker
Presidency:	Madras
Age on Discharge:	36 years

Length of Service: 16 years 2 months
Reason for Discharge: Unfit for service because of loss of teeth
Character: Good
Intends to Reside: Dublin

Height: 5' 6"
Complexion: Fair
Eye Colour: Hazel
Hair Colour: Brown
Intends to Reside: Dublin

McARDLE see — McCARDLE Michael
Royal Canadian Rifles

McAULEY James, private
48th Foot [Depot]
13 Sept 1853 Discharged the Service Chatham
Pension paid 2nd Manchester Pension District
1/- per diem
10 July 1857 Arrived per *'Clara'* [1]
1866 Pension paid South Australia from Perth W. A.

Service and Personal Details:
Place of Birth: Drumlane Co. Cavan
Age on Enlistment: 18 years
Period of Service: 1835 — 1853
Age on Discharge: 36 years
Length of Service: 18 years 1 day [reckoned]
Foreign Service: Gibraltar 5 years 4 months
West Indies 3 years 1 month
Reason for Discharge: Tumour of thigh and stiffness of knee joint

Character: Good
Trade or Occupation: Labourer
Can Sign Name: Yes

Height: 5' 6½"
Hair Colour: Dark Brown
Eyes: Blue
Complexion: Fresh
Intends to Reside: Burnley Lancashire

McCAFFRY Bernard, private
50th Foot
Surname Variants [some] McCAFFREY; McCAFFERY;
McCAFFRAY
McCAFFEY
22 June 1847 Discharged the Service Chatham
Pension paid Enniskillen
7d. per diem
2 Apr 1856 Arrived per *'William Hammond'*
1861 Charged with drunkenness
10 Nov 1863 Off Roll for Felony — Larceny; pension withheld while in prison
1866 Employed as a shoemaker in Perth
1874 Died

1884	Perth — Ann McCaffrey charged with being drunk
July 1884	Superintendent of Poor Houses — Mrs. McCaffery for outdoor relief [wife of EPG]
Service and Personal Details:	
Place of Birth:	Durravellon Co. Fermanagh
Age on Enlistment:	18 years
Period of Service:	1831 — 1846
Age on Discharge:	34 years
Length of Service:	14 years 176 days
Foreign Service:	New South Wales 7 years 64 days East Indies 5 years 146 days
Medal Entitlement:	Punniar 1843 and Sutlej
Reason for Discharge:	Shot wound to the finger of right hand
Character:	Good
Trade or Occupation:	Labourer
Can Sign Name:	blank; Yes on Attestation
Height:	6'
Hair Colour:	Dark
Eyes:	Grey
Complexion:	Dark
Remarks:	Tried by Garrison Court Martial for disgraceful behaviour in aiding in a robbery and habitual drunkenness
Intends to Reside:	Manchester

McCALL	John, private 68th Foot
Surname Variants	McCAULL; McCOLE
8 Jan 1861	Discharged the Service Fermoy Pension paid 2nd Belfast Pension District 7d. per diem
22 Dec 1866	Arrived per *'Corona'*
Dec 1876	Died
1878	Mrs. McCall, widow of Pensioner McCall of the Enrolled Force who died in December 1876 begs me to apply for a continuance of the Outdoor relief which has been afforded her up to the 9th instant. I believe Mrs. McCall to be a thoroughly respectable woman and further that her circumstances have in no respect altered for the better since the time that relief was granted: You are aware that she has three young children, the youngest only a year old. I write this letter because the poor woman us suffering from a severe attack of Ophthalmia which prevents her moving out of the house.
Service and Personal Details:	
Place of Birth:	Lurgan Armagh Ireland
Age on Enlistment:	26 years
Period of Service:	1855 — 1860
Age on Discharge:	32 years
Length of Service:	5 years 21 days [reckoned]

Foreign Service:	Malta	2 months
	Ionian islands	1 year 2 months
	Turkey & Crimea	2 months
Reason for Discharge:	Chronic Ophthalmia	
Character:	Good	
Trade or Occupation:	Groom	
Can Sign Name:	X his mark on discharge	
Height:	5' 5"	
Hair Colour:	Brown	
Eyes:	Grey	
Complexion:	Fresh	
Intends to Reside:	Belfast	

McCALL	John, gunner	
	RHA	
16 Oct 1860	Discharged the Service Woolwich	
	Pension paid Carlisle	
	10d. per diem	
1865	Pension paid Edinburgh	
4 July 1866	Arrived per *'Belgravia'*	
1866	Pension paid Madras	
1872	Correspondence with W.O.	
11 Jan 1873	Died	
Service and Personal Details:		
Place of Birth:	Minnihire Dumfries	
Age on Enlistment:	18 years	
Period of Service:	1839 — 1860	
Age on Discharge:	39 years 7 months	
Length of Service:	21 years 26 days	
Foreign Service:	Bengal	2 years 7 months
Reason for Discharge:	Own Request having completed 21 years	
Character:	Very Good	
Trade or Occupation:	Groom	
Can Sign Name:	Yes	
Height:	5' 8"	
Hair Colour:	Light	
Eyes:	Blue	
Complexion:	Fair	

McCANN	Arthur, gunner and driver
	RA 6th Battalion
11 July 1854	Discharged the Service Woolwich
	7d. per diem for 18 months
18 July 1855	Arrived per *'Adelaide'*
31 Jan 1856	In receipt of a Temporary Pension which expired on this date
21 Jan 1876	Awarded Deferred Pension of 4d. per diem
11 Feb 1876	Aged 50
Aug 1877	W.O. Correspondence with S.O.P. Perth W.A.
Service and Personal Details:	
Place of Birth:	Shankhill Lurgan Co. Armagh
Age on Enlistment:	21 years

Period of Service:	1847 — 1854
Age on Discharge:	28 years 5 months
Length of Service:	7 years 170 days
Foreign Service:	Corfu 1 year 3 months
Reason for Discharge:	Varicose Veins of the left leg
Character:	Good
Trade or Occupation:	Weaver
Can Sign Name:	Yes
Height:	5' 9"
Hair Colour:	Brown
Eyes:	Grey
Complexion:	Fair

McCANN Garrett, private

98th Foot

Surname Variants	McCARNE; McCAN
15 Nov 1841	Discharged the Service
21 Nov 1841	Admitted to Out-Pension
	Pension paid Cranmore Galway
	7d. per diem
1851	Pension paid Athlone
21 May 1851	Arrived per *'Mermaid'*
1851	Assigned and occupied North Fremantle Lot P11
1865	Pension paid Australia
1873	Pension increased to 1/1d. per diem for 12 years service in the Enrolled Force
1875	Pension paid Athlone from Fremantle

Service and Personal Details:

Place of Birth:	Colrey Westmeath
Age on Enlistment:	18 years
Period of Service:	1824 — 1841
Age on Discharge:	35 years 7 months
Length of Service:	17 years 232 days
Foreign Service:	Cape of Good Hope 13 years
Reason for Discharge:	Chronic Catarrh and Asthma
Character:	Latterly Indifferent
Trade or Occupation:	Labourer
Can Sign Name:	X his mark on discharge
Height:	5' 6"
Hair Colour:	Dark
Eyes:	Hazel
Complexion:	Dark

McCANN Hugh, Corporal

86th Foot

Previous Regiment	67th Foot
24 July 1839	Discharged the Service Salford
	Pension paid Maryborough
	6d. per diem for 3 years
18 Oct 1842	Pension made permanent
1852	Correspondence with W.O.
6 Apr 1854	Arrived per *'Sea Park'*

1856	Employed as Assistant Warder
1856	Claim of £9 against Capt Foss [£9/0/0 misappropriated by Capt Foss]
Jan 1857	Contributed 1/- to the Florence Nightingale Fund
29 Apr 1873	Died

Service and Personal Details:

Place of Birth:	In Army [67th Regiment]
Age on Enlistment:	15 years
Period of Service:	1824 — 1839
Age on Discharge:	30 years
Length of Service:	12 years 14 days — reckoned
Reason for Discharge:	Chronic cough with impeded respiration
Character:	That of a Good soldier, efficient trustworthy and sober
Trade or Occupation:	Labourer
Can Sign Name:	Yes
Height:	5' 8¾"
Hair Colour:	Brown
Eyes:	Grey
Complexion:	Fresh

McCANN Patrick, private
10th Foot

Previous Regiment	31st Foot
21 July 1860	Discharged the Service Devonport Pension paid 2nd Plymouth Pension District 1/- per diem
27 May 1863	Arrived per *'Clyde'*
1866	Pension paid Queensland from Perth W.A. to Eastern States per *'Kestrel'*'

Service and Personal Details:

Place of Birth:	Ballas Co. Wicklow
Age on Enlistment:	22 years
Period of Service:	1839 — 1860
Age on Discharge:	43 years
Length of Service:	21 years 3 days
Foreign Service:	East Indies 13 years
Medal Entitlement:	Kabul and Sutlej with 3 clasps
Reason for Discharge:	Own Request having completed 21 years service
Character:	Very Good
Trade or Occupation:	Labourer
Can Sign Name:	Yes
Height:	5' 7"
Hair Colour:	Brown
Eyes:	Grey
Complexion:	Fresh

McCARDLE Michael, Serjeant
Royal Canadian Rifles

Previous Regiment	41st Foot
Surname Variants	McARDLE; M'CARDLE

10 July 1860	Discharged the Service Chatham
14 Aug 1860	Admitted to Out-Pension Pension paid Enniskillen 1/6d. per diem
27 May 1863	Arrived per '*Clyde*'
1874	Ann McCardle charged with assaulting her husband and "putting him in bodily fear"
Feb 1876	Charged with grossly insulting language towards Mr F Graven pawnbroker
Mar 1876	'The gallant son of Mars had been dismissed the previous day from the Enrolled Force because of his proclivity for non-templar activities.'
28 Mar 1876	Sentenced 42 days imprisonment for destruction of a quantity of household effects and with assaulting his wife and daughters
1876	Convicted at Perth Western Australia of an assault on his wife and sent to prison for 42 days Half pension to be suspended the other half paid to wife during imprisonment
1878	Pension increased to 2/- per diem for service in the Enrolled Force
Jan 1882	Assigned Perth Town Lot 34/H
Aug 1882	Application for Title Perth Town Lot 34/H
1883	Granted Fee Simple Perth Town Lot 34/H
1883	W.O. Correspondence with S.O. Omagh

Service and Personal Details:

Place of Birth:	Churchill Co. Fermanagh	
Age on Enlistment:	18 years	
Period of Service:	1839 — 1860	
Age on Discharge:	39 years or 38 years 11 months	
Length of Service:	20 years 294 days	
Foreign Service:	India	2 years 11 months
Canada	1 year 10 months	
Reason for Discharge:	Chronic Catarrh	
Character:	Very Good	
Trade or Occupation:	Labourer	
Can Sign Name:	Yes	
Height:	5' 5½"	
Hair Colour:	Dark Brown	
Eyes:	Hazel	
Complexion:	Fresh	
Intends to Reside:	Derrygormelly Co. Fermanagh	
Married:	Ann	
Children:	Francis b. *c*1856 d. *c*1881	
Mary Ann b. *c*1864		
March 1889	Robert M'Ardle [sic] deposed: I am a livery stable keeper. My father left Perth between four and five years ago and has been dead these three years [Trove] brother Michael printer sister Susan spinster b. *c*1865 England sister Mary Jane spinster	

	sister Anne [Annie] spinster b. *c*1867 Perth
McCARTHY	Cathage, Corporal 84th Foot
Previous Regiment	40th; St Helena Corps
Surname Variant	McCARTY
16 July 1867	Discharged the Service Camp Colchester Pension paid 1st East London Pension District 11d. per diem
1867	Pension increased to 1/1d. per diem
9 Jan 1868	Arrived per *'Hougoumont'*
14 Jan 1870	Fremantle Pensioner Carthage McCarthy though not insane is mentally and physically incapable of taking proper care of himself. Pensioner Carthage McCarthy admitted to Poor House
30 June 1870	Fremantle Asylum — Thomas Bishop and Carty [sic] Mcarthy at present time both men are of sound mind.
circa June 1874	Transferred from Fremantle to 2nd Perth District
1875	Pension increased to 1/1½d. per diem for service in the Australian Enrolled Force
1886	Died
April 1886	On the 5th inst., at Fremantle Police Court before Godfrey Knight, Acting R.M. and Coroner, the inquest on the body of Cartney [sic] McCarthy [pensioner], who was found drowned at Point Walter on the previous day. Verdict — Found drowned.
Service and Personal Details:	
Place of Birth:	Kilverhan Co. Kerry
Age on Enlistment:	31 years 3 months
Period of Service:	1858 — 1867
Age on Discharge:	40 years 4 months
Length of Service:	21 years 241 days
Foreign Service:	St Helena 7 years 7 months
Reason for Discharge:	Own Request having completed 21 years service
Character:	Good
Trade or Occupation:	Clerk
Can Sign Name:	Yes
Height:	5' 7¾"
Hair Colour:	Brown
Eyes:	Blue
Complexion:	Fresh
Intends to Reside:	Bethnal Place Hackney London
McCARTHY	Timothy, Serjeant
also known as	**GOGGIN** or **GOGGINS** 18th Foot
Previous Regiments	50th; 94th
15 Jan 1856	Discharged the Service Chatham Pension paid 1st Cork Pension District 1/6d. per diem

8 June 1858	Arrived per *'Lord Raglan'*
no date	Acted as Assistant storekeeper at Guildford, Bunbury and Fremantle
1865	Pension paid Western Australia
1876	Stationed Perth with rank of Serjeant Major
11 Nov 1880	Joined Enrolled Guard at Fremantle
Jan 1881	Pension increased to 2/-d. per diem for service in the Enrolled Force
no date	In charge of the Explosives Department at Fremantle
1 June 1881	Assigned Perth Town Lot 111/V
1883	Granted Fee Simple Perth Town Lot 111/V
1885	Proprietor Perth Building Lot O/10
1887	Income of 2/6d. per diem on disbandment of the Enrolled Guard
Dec 1888	a Mrs McCarthy was assaulted by Pensioner McMeekham
1888	Increase of salary for Serj. Major T McCarthy caretaker Fremantle Magazine
June 1897	Residing Fremantle
Feb 1900	Attended fete at Oval
3 Jan 1908	Died aged 85 — funeral cortege moved from his late residence 204 Wellington Street Perth

Service and Personal Details:

Place of Birth:	Mallon Co. Cork
Age on Enlistment:	18 years 2 months
Period of Service:	1841 — 1855
Age on Discharge:	32 years 7 months
Length of Service:	14 years 145 days
Foreign Service:	Crimea [no time period given]
Medal Entitlement:	Crimean with clasp; Turkish Crimean
Reason for Discharge:	Wounded by musket shot in the thigh received at the Redan
Character:	Good
Trade or Occupation:	Labourer
Can Sign Name:	Yes
Height:	5' 5½"
Hair Colour:	Dark Brown
Eyes:	Grey
Complexion:	Fresh
Intends to Reside:	Cork

McCAUGHRAN William, gunner EIC

Bombay Artillery 2nd Battalion

Surname Variants	McCOUGHRAN; McCAUGHAN
	Out Pension No 519
1850	Embarked UK per *'Aboukir'*
26 June 1850	Admitted to Out-pension
	Pension paid Liverpool
	1/- per diem
1850	Pension paid Ballymena
19 Aug 1853	Arrived per *'Robert Small'*
Jan 1857	Contributed 2/- to the Florence Nightingale Fund

Sept 1863	Died aged 54 Albany

Service and Personal Details:

Where Born:	Bellehanger Antrim
Trade or Occupation:	White smith
Where Enlisted:	Manchester
Presidency:	Bombay
Length of Service:	21 years 7 months
Age on Discharge:	43 years
Reason for Discharge:	Own Request and time expired
Character:	Good
Intends to Reside:	Liverpool
Height:	5' 7"
Complexion:	Sallow
Visage:	Oval
Eye Colour:	Brown
Hair Colour:	Brown
Intends to Reside:	Liverpool

McCAULEY James, private

	52nd Foot
Previous Regiment	18th Foot
Surname Variant	MACAULEY
26 Feb 1861	Discharged the Service Chatham Pension paid Chatham 8d. per diem
1861	Pension paid West London
31 Dec 1862	Arrived per *'York'*
1866	Pension paid South Australia from Perth W. A.
1869	Calcutta
1874	W.O. correspondence with Commander in Chief Ootacamund

Service and Personal Details:

Place of Birth:	Sleaforth Sligo	
Age on Attestation:	17 years 1 month	
Period of Service:	1839 — 1861	
Age on Discharge:	39 years	
Length of Service:	21 years 19 days	
Foreign Service:	China	7 years 5 months
	East Indies	9 years 5 months
Medal Entitlement:	China Medal and Burmah with clasp	
Reason for Discharge:	Own Request having completed 21 years	
Character:	Good	
Trade or Occupation:	Labourer	
Can Sign Name:	X his mark on discharge	
Height:	5' 7"	
Hair Colour:	Brown	
Eyes:	Grey	
Complexion:	Fair	
Remarks:	Wounded in right shoulder at Canton	
Intends to Reside:	Chatham	

McCLUSKEY William, private

	71st Foot
Surname Variant	McCLUSKY
20 Feb 1872	Discharged the Service Fort George [Canada] Pension paid 2nd Dublin Pension District 11d. per diem
19 Feb 1874	Arrived per *'Naval Brigade'*
1881	Pension increased to 1/1½d. per diem for service in the Enrolled Force
Aug 1881	"Orderly at Poor Home"
25 Nov 1882	"Pensioner McCluskey recommended as Hospital Orderly to Charles Bompas — Vasse"
30 Nov 1882	Appointed Orderly Vasse Hospital
Sept 1883	Assigned North Fremantle Lot P80
26 Aug 1884	Granted Fee Simple North Fremantle Lot P80
1891	Died

Service and Personal Details:

Place of Birth:	Cahir Co. Tipperary	
Age on Enlistment:	17 years	
Period of Service:	1849 — 1872	
Age on Discharge:	39 years 3 months	
Length of Service:	21 years 44 day	
Foreign Service:	Canada	4 years 4 months
	Crimea	1 year 6 months
	Malta	1 year 7 months
	East Indies	6 years 2 months
Medal Entitlement:	Crimea with clasp; Turkish Crimean; Central India; North West Frontier Medal with clasp	
Reason for Discharge:	Own Request having completed 21 years	
Character:	Good	
Trade or Occupation:	Shoemaker	
Can Sign Name:	Yes	
Height:	5' 8½"	
Hair Colour:	Brown	
Eyes:	Grey	
Complexion:	Sallow	
Intends to Reside:	Dublin	

McCORMICK	Martin, private and drummer 99th Foot
Surname Variant	McCORMACK
25 Sept 1846	Discharged the Service Chatham Pension paid Athlone 8d. per diem
1850	Pension paid Tullamore
21 May 1851	Arrived per *'Mermaid'*
Sept 1851	Assigned and occupied North Fremantle Lot P3
1852	Employed by Convict Establishment
10 May 1869	Died

Service and Personal Details:

Place of Birth:	Kilmanagh Westmeath
Age on Enlistment:	11 years 5 months
Period of Service:	1825 — 1846

Age on Discharge:	36 years
Length of Service:	14 years 164 days
Foreign Service:	Mauritius 11 years
	New South Wales 2 years
Reason for Discharge:	General break up of Constitution
Character:	Good Trustworthy and Sober
Trade or Occupation:	Labourer
Can Sign Name:	Yes
Height:	5' 8"
Hair Colour:	Sandy
Eyes:	Grey
Complexion:	Sallow
Intends to Reside:	Moate Westmeath

McCORMICK

	Patrick, private
	5th Foot [Depot]
7 May 1867	Discharged the Service
	Pension paid Athlone
	1/- per diem
9 Jan 1868	Arrived per *'Hougoumont'*
1876	Died — aged 47

Service and Personal Details:

Place of Birth:	St Marys Athlone Westmeath
Age on Enlistment:	17 years 3 months
Period of Service:	1846 — 1867
Age on Discharge:	38 years 2 months
Length of Service:	21 years 17 days
Foreign Service:	Mauritius 9 years 8 months
	East Indies 4 years
Medal Entitlement:	Indian Mutiny with 2 clasps
Reason for Discharge:	Own Request having completed 21 years
Character:	Very Good
Trade or Occupation:	Labourer
Can Sign Name:	Yes
Height:	5' 5"
Hair Colour:	Dark Brown
Eyes:	Grey
Complexion:	Fair
Intends to Reside:	Athlone

McCORRY

	Richard, private
	38th Foot
Surname Variant	McCORREY; McCARRY
20 Oct 1862	Discharged the Service Camp Colchester
4 Nov 1862	Admitted to Out-Pension
	Pension paid Ballymena
	1/1d. per diem
4 July 1866	Arrived per *'Belgravia'*
11 Dec 1888	Died at Northam aged 69

Service and Personal Details:

Place of Birth:	Lurgan Co. Antrim

Age on Enlistment:	18 years	
Period of Service:	1840 — 1862	
Age on Discharge:	41 years 3 months	
Length of Service:	21 years 187 days	
Foreign Service:	Ionian Islands	2 years 7 months
	Gibraltar	2 years 7 months
	West India	2 years 3 months
	Nova Scotia	3 years 4 months
	Crimea	1 year 9 months
	Turkey	5 months
[2nd period of service]	East Indies	3 years 9 months
Medal Entitlement:	Crimea with 3 clasps; Turkish Crimean; and medal for distinguished conduct in the field	
Reason for Discharge:	Having completed 21 years service [in total]	
Character:	Very Good	
Trade or Occupation:	Labourer	
Can Sign Name:	Yes	
Height:	5' 6"	
Hair Colour:	Brown	
Eyes:	Hazel	
Complexion:	Fresh	

McCOURT	James, private
	18th Foot
29 July 1856	Discharged the Service Chatham
	Pension paid 1st Dublin Pension District
	9d. per diem
1856	Pension paid Newry
1857	Dublin
1862	Bermuda
15 Feb 1863	Arrived per *'Merchantman'* [1]
1864	In Band
1873	Pension increased to 1/1½d. for ceasing to draw pay in and having served 9 years in the Enrolled Pensioner Force
Apr 1875	Assigned Pensioner Allotment 20 at Bootenal
1881	Granted Pensioner Allotment 20 at Bootenal

Service and Personal Details:

Place of Birth:	Bundoran Co. Donegal	
Age on Enlistment:	18 years	
Period of Service:	1835 — 1856	
Age on Discharge:	39 years	
Length of Service:	21 years 15 days	
Foreign Service:	Ceylon	3 years 2 months
	China	7 years 6 months
	India	6 years
Reason for Discharge:	Chronic Rheumatism	
Character:	Good	
Trade or Occupation:	Labourer	
Can Sign Name:	Yes	
Height:	5' 6¾"	
Hair Colour:	Black	

Eyes:	Hazel
Complexion:	Sallow
Intends to Reside:	Harburgh [sic] Parish Dublin
Married:	Esther Reddin or Redden
Children:	Hugh Timothy b. *c*1862 Daniel b.1863 at sea Mary Anne or Marian Houston b. *c*1867 married Charles N Kidman — [the actress Nicol Kidman is possibly a descendant] William Reddin b. *c*1869 m. *c*1896 Maria Manning John b. *c*1871 James brother [from obituary — Trove]

McCREERY	Thomas, private 6th Foot
Surname Variants	McCREARY; McCREECY; McCLEERY; McCREEDY
6 Nov 1849	Discharged the Service Fermoy
15 Jan 1850	Admitted to Out-Pension Pension paid Dundee 6d. per diem for 6 months conditional
20 May 1851	Pension made permanent
10 Sept 1856	Arrived per *'Runnymede'*
1872	a Thomas McCreary residing at Fremantle

The following two paragraphs may not refer to Thomas McCreery

Sept 1873	A pensioner named McCreery living at North Fremantle has been committed on a Coroner's warrant to take his trial for manslaughter. An inquest, several times adjourned, terminated on Monday. It was held upon the body of Mrs. McCreery who was suspected to have met her death through ill-treatment received at the hands of her husband. The alleged ill-usage took place on the 1st inst., the woman, who was six months advanced in gestation, dying on the 17th. The evidence advanced was sufficient to prove that the woman had been maltreated, and a Coroner's jury of six found a verdict of against McCreery of manslaughter
Sept 1873	a T McCreary [sic] writes to newspaper stating that the doctor's evidence proved his wife had died from natural causes and the Attorney General "at once threw out the indictment"
1875	Pension paid Western Australia
22 Dec 1876	Assigned North Fremantle Lot P56
1879	Payment of £15 [pounds] sanctioned
1881	Pension increased to 1/- per diem for 24 years service in the Enrolled Force
1882	Pension increased to 1/2d. per diem
Apr 1882	Granted Fee Simple North Fremantle Lot P56
June 1897	Residing Fremantle

June 1908	Died Northam and his remains brought to Fremantle for internment in the old Fremantle Cemetery
Service and Personal Details:	
Place of Birth:	Enniskillen Co. Fermanagh
Age on Enlistment:	17 years 6 months
Period of Service:	1846 — 1849
Age on Discharge:	20 years
Length of Service:	2 years 170 days
Reason for Discharge:	Ophthalmia right eye and impaired vision in the left
Character:	Good
Trade or Occupation:	Weaver
Can Sign Name:	X his mark on discharge
Height:	5' 6"
Hair Colour:	Light Brown
Eyes:	Grey
Complexion:	Fresh

McCUE	William, private 6th Dragoon Guards
15 May 1848	Discharged the Service Dundalk
11 July 1848	Admitted to Out-Pension Pension paid Liverpool 10d. per diem
1851	Pension paid Falmouth
30 Apr 1853	To Tilbury Fort
31 Aug 1853	Arrived per *'Phoebe Dunbar'*
Jan 1857	Contributed 1/- to the Florence Nightingale Fund
1865	Died aged 59 Albany
Service and Personal Details:	
Place of Birth:	Orney Co. Tyrone
Age on Enlistment:	19 years
Period of Service:	1827 — 1848
Age on Discharge:	39 years 7 months
Length of Service:	20 years 182 days
Reason for Discharge:	Chronic Rheumatism
Character:	Good and Efficient soldier
Trade or Occupation:	Tailor
Can Sign Name:	Yes
Height:	5' 9½"
Hair Colour:	Light Brown
Eyes:	Hazel
Complexion:	Fresh

McCULLEN	Henry, private 5th Foot
25 Jan 1848	Discharged the Service Chatham Pension paid 2nd Plymouth Pension District

	6d. per diem
30 Apr 1853	To Tilbury Fort
31 Aug 1853	Arrived per *'Phoebe Dunbar'*
Jan 1857	Contributed 2/- to the Florence Nightingale Fund
1864	Pension paid Western Australia
1875	Died aged 70

Service and Personal Details:

Place of Birth:	Loughbrickland Co. Down	
Age on Enlistment:	19 years	
Period of Service:	1827 — 1848	
Age on Discharge:	39 years	
Length of Service:	19 years 331 days	
Foreign Service:	Gibraltar	4 years
	Malta	2 years 5 months
	Ionian Isles	5 years
Reason for Discharge:	Varicose Veins	
Character:	Very Bad	
Trade or Occupation:	Labourer	
Can Sign Name:	X his mark on discharge	
Height:	5' 6¾"	
Hair Colour:	Light Brown	
Eyes:	Grey	
Complexion:	Fresh	
Intends to Reside:	Devonport	

McCULLOCK Charles, private

	79th Foot
Previous Regiment	72nd Foot
26 Aug 1856	Discharged the Service Chatham
	Pension paid 2nd Glasgow Pension District
	8d. per diem
1862	Pension paid Bermuda
15 Feb 1863	Arrived per *'Merchantman'* [1]
1863	Absence without leave and drunkenness
1864	Pension paid 1st East London Pension District
1864	Northampton
1865	Liverpool

Service and Personal Details:

Place of Birth:	Paisley Renfrewshire	
Age on Enlistment:	17 years 9 months	
Period of Service:	1853 — 1856	
Age on Discharge:	20 years 9 months or 20 years 8 months	
Length of Service:	2 years 245 days	
Foreign Service:	Turkey	1 year 5 months
Medal Entitlement:	Crimea with clasp	
Reason for Discharge:	Loss of forefinger of left hand caused by explosion of shell sustained in the trenches	
Character:	Good	
Trade or Occupation:	Labourer	
Can Sign Name:	Yes	
Height:	5' 5½"	

Hair Colour:	Dark Brown
Eyes:	Hazel
Complexion:	Fresh
Intends to Reside:	Glasgow

McCULLUM David, private
99th Foot

Surname Variants	McCULLAM; McCALLUM	
5 Apr 1849	Arrived per *'Radcliffe'* with regiment	
1855	Transferred to 1st/12th Foot	
10 Dec 1857	Examined by Regimental Board West. Australia	
1 June 1858	Admitted to Out-Pension Perth West. Australia 1/1½d. per diem	
1881	Granted Land Albany Lot P28	
1901	Died aged 82	
Service and Personal Details:		
Place of Birth:	Rye Co. Donegal	
Age on Attestation:	14 years 5 months	
Period of Service:	1830 — 1857	
Age on Discharge:	41 years 7 months	
Length of Service:	23 years 239 days	
Foreign Service:	Australia	15 years 3 months
Reason for Discharge:	Pains in the chest and spitting blood	
Character:	Good	
Trade or Occupation:	Labourer	
Can Sign Name:	Yes	
Height:	5' 9"	
Hair Colour:	Brown	
Eyes:	Hazel	
Complexion:	Fair	
Intends to Reside:	Perth Western Australia	

McDANIEL James, private
86th Foot

14 June 1853	Discharged the Service Chatham Pension paid Carlow 1/- per diem	
24 May 1855	Arrived per *'Stag'*	
1859	To South Australia from Western Australia	
1866	Pension paid Adelaide South Australia	
25 Jan 1872	Died	
Service and Personal Details:		
Place of Birth:	Arles Carlow Queens County	
Age on Enlistment:	19 years	
Period of Service:	1831 — 1852	
Age on Discharge:	41 years or 40 years 11 months	
Length of Service:	21 years 245 days	
Foreign Service:	West Indies	4 years
	East Indies	10 years 3 months
Reason for Discharge:	Long Service and Rheumatism	
Character:	Good	
Trade or Occupation:	Tailor	

Can Sign Name:	X his mark on discharge
Height:	5' 8¾"
Hair Colour:	Brown
Eyes:	Blue
Complexion:	Sallow
Intends to Reside:	Carlow

McDERMOTT	William, private 67th Foot	
3 Apr 1866	Discharged the Service Belfast Pension paid 2nd Belfast Pension District 1/- per diem	
9 Jan 1868	Arrived per *'Hougoumont'*	
Apr 1874	Requests payment of £15 improvement grant for Lot 149/Y	
circa June 1874	Transferred from 2nd Perth Pension District to 1st Perth Pension District	
1878	Granted title to Perth Town Lot 149/Y	
1879	Pension increased to 1/5d. per diem for 11 years service as a private in the Enrolled Force of W. A.	
Oct 1902	Admitted as an In-Pensioner Kilmainham	
July 1903	Reverted to Out-Pension	
Service and Personal Details:		
Place of Birth:	Rathcool Co. Kildare	
Age on Enlistment:	18 years	
Period of Service:	1845 — 1866	
Age on Discharge:	39 years	
Length of Service:	21 years 12 days	
Foreign Service:	Gibraltar	3 years 6 months
	West Indies	5 years 10 months
	East Indies	4 months
	China	5 years 8 months
Medal Entitlement:	Long Service and Good Conduct with gratuity; China medal with clasps for Pekin and Taku Forts	
Reason for Discharge:	Own Request having served 21 years	
Character:	Very Good	
Trade or Occupation:	Labourer	
Can Sign Name:	X his mark on discharge	
Height:	5' 7¼"	
Hair Colour:	Sandy	
Eyes:	Grey	
Complexion:	Fair	
Intends to Reside:	Belfast	

McDONALD	Finlay, private 42nd Foot
Previous Regiment	? 74th Foot during the period 1825 — 1833
13 Jan 1852	Discharged the Service Chatham Pension paid 1st Edinburgh Pension District 6d. per diem
30 Apr 1853	Arrived per *'Pyrenees'* [2]
1853	Employed By Convict Establishment
1855	To South Australia from Fremantle West. Aust.

1856	Pension paid Melbourne	
Service and Personal Details:		
Place of Birth:	Dalkeith Edinburgh	
Age on Attestation:	21 years	
Period of Service:	1837 — 1852	
Age on Discharge:	43 years 9 months	
Length of Service:	14 years 203 days	
Foreign Service:	Mediterranean	6 years 3 months
	Bermuda	4 years 3 months
Reason for Discharge:	Unfit for further service	
Character:	Good	
Trade or Occupation:	Weaver	
Can Sign Name:	Yes	
Height:	5' 9"	
Hair Colour:	Fair	
Eyes:	Blue	
Complexion:	Fair	
Intends to Reside:	Edinburgh	

McDONALD

	James, private	
	30th Foot	
Previous Regiment	72nd Foot	
12 Dec 1848	Discharged the Service Chatham	
	9d. per diem	
1848	Pension paid 1st Edinburgh Pension District	
1849	Falkland Isles	
1852	1st Edinburgh Pension District	
31 Aug 1853	Arrived per *'Phoebe Dunbar'*	
1856	To South Australia from Western Australia	
1875	Pension paid Adelaide South Australia	
Service and Personal Details:		
Place of Birth:	West Church Edinburgh	
Age on Attestation:	18 years	
Period of Service:	1827 — 1848	
Age on Discharge:	40 years or 38 years 10 months	
Length of Service:	20 years 154 days	
Foreign Service:	Bermuda	7 years 2 months
	North America	2 years 1 month
Reason for Discharge:	Hernia	
Character:	Bad	
Trade or Occupation:	Mason	
Can Sign Name:	Yes	
Height:	5' 8"	
Hair Colour:	Brown	
Eyes:	Hazel	
Complexion:	Dark	
Intends to Reside:	Edinburgh	

McDONALD

	Peter, Shoeing Smith
	RHA
10 July 1849	Discharged the Service Woolwich

	Pension paid 1st East London Pension District
	1/- per diem
7 Feb 1853	Arrived per *'Dudbrook'*
1853	Employed by Convict Establishment without sanction of Staff Officer Pensions
1854	Pension paid Western Australia
1859	Madras from Fremantle
24 June 1864	Died

Service and Personal Details:

Place of Birth:	St Pauls Dublin
Age on Attestation:	18 years
Period of Service:	1828 — 1849
Age on Discharge:	39 years 101 days
Length of Service:	21 years 88 days
Reason for Discharge:	Chronic Cough and Rheumatism
Character:	Very Good
Trade or Occupation:	Shoeing Smith
Can Sign Name:	Yes
Height:	5' 8"
Hair Colour:	Dark Brown
Eyes:	Hazel
Complexion:	Fresh

McDONALD	William, private
	50th Foot
Surname Variant	MacDONALD
25 June 1861	Discharged the Service
	Pension paid Preston
	11d. per diem
1862	Pension paid Bermuda
15 Feb 1863	Arrived per *'Merchantman'* [1]
June 1863	Died shot himself Pensioner William McDonald of the Enrolled Force shot himself on the night of the 11th, He has left a wife and 5 young children totally unprovided for. McDonald did not subscribe to the Pensioners Benevolent Fund and has no claim on it.

Service and Personal Details:

Place of Birth:	Mary-le-bone London Middlesex	
Age on Attestation:	19 years	
Period of Service:	1840 — 1861	
Age on Discharge:	40 years 6 months	
Length of Service:	21 years 48 days	
Foreign Service:	India	6 years 11 months
	Ceylon	3 years 7 months
	Crimea	1 year 2 months
Medal Entitlement:	Bronze Star of India; Sutlej; Crimea with three clasps and the Turkish Crimean	
Reason for Discharge:	Own Request having completed 21 years service	
Character:	Good	
Trade or Occupation:	Labourer	

Can Sign Name:	Yes
Height:	5' 4¾"
Hair Colour:	Brown
Eyes:	Blue
Complexion:	Fresh
Intends to Reside:	No. 89 High Street, Preston Lancashire

McDONALD	William, private 88th Foot
Surname Variants	McDONNALL; McDONNELL
11 Mar 1840	Discharged the Service Dublin Pension paid 2nd Dublin Pension District 6d. per diem
28 June 1851	Arrived per *'Pyrenees'* [1]
Nov 1852	Assigned Kojonup Sub Lot P2
1854	Pension paid Western Australia
1854	Received sum of £15 towards cost of dwelling
Jan 1857	Contributed 2/- to the Florence Nightingale Fund
1858	Applied for Land Title Kojonup
1864	ptve McDonnell Pensioner Force at Kojonup contributed to the Greenough Fire Relief Fund
Oct 1862	Granted Title Kojonup Lot P2
Dec 1879	Died
1879	Cottage was sold to Henry Larsen the local innkeeper

Service and Personal Details:	
Place of Birth:	Doneybrook Dublin
Age on Attestation:	18 years
Period of Service:	1825 — 1840
Age on Discharge:	33 years
Length of Service:	14 years 307 days
Foreign Service:	Ionian Isles 10 years 10 months
Reason for Discharge:	Pulmonic Disease from repeated Chronic Catarrh from Prurient Remittent Fever
Character:	Good
Trade or Occupation:	Servant
Can Sign Name:	Yes
Height:	5' 7"
Hair Colour:	Brown
Eyes:	Black
Complexion:	Sallow

McDONOUGH	Thomas, private 50th Foot
3 July 1855	Discharged the Service Chathan Pension paid Preston 9d. per diem
1862	Pension paid Bermuda
15 Feb 1863	Arrived per *'Merchantman'* [1]
1864	ptve T McDonough Pensioner Force at Perth contributed to the Greenough Fire Relief Fund
1870	Died

Service and Personal Details:	
Place of Birth:	Ballyfannon Co. Sligo
Age on Attestation:	17 years 6 months
Period of Service:	1848 — 1855
Age on Discharge:	24 years
Length of Service:	6 years 207 days
Foreign Service:	Crimea [35 days only in Crimea]
Reason for Discharge:	Wounded
Character:	Good
Trade or Occupation:	Labourer
Can Sign Name:	X his mark on discharge
Height:	5' 6¼"
Hair Colour:	Brown
Eyes:	Grey
Complexion:	Fresh

McELROY	James, gunner EIC Bengal Artillery Out Pension No 712
? July 1859	Admitted to Out-pension Pension paid Newry 9d. per diem
19 Feb 1874	Arrived per *'Naval Brigade'*
Nov 1881	Assigned Perth Military Pensioner Lot 268/Y
Oct 1883	Application for Title to Perth Lot 268/Y located on Wanneroo Rd
1891	Died
Service and Personal Details:	
Where Born:	?Dunnmara Co Down
Trade or Occupation:	Labourer
Presidency:	Bengal
Length of Service:	2 years 2 months
Age on Discharge:	22 years
Reason for Discharge:	Partial paralysis of lower extremities
Character:	Good
Height:	5' 8"
Complexion:	Fair
Eye Colour:	Blue
Hair Colour:	Brown or Light Brown
Intends to Reside:	?Dromara Co. Dowm

McENTEE	James, private 49th Foot
Surname Variant	McINTEE
10 July 1855	Discharged the Service Chatham Pension paid Monaghan 9d. per diem
1862	Pension paid Armagh
1862	Pensioned increased to 1/- per diem
1862	Applied for Royal Bounty of 6d. in addition to his pension
9 June 1862	Arrived per *'Norwood'* [1]

1864	ptve J McEntee Pensioner Force at Perth contributed to the Greenough Fire Relief Fund
1866	To South Australia from Perth West. Australia

Service and Personal Details:

Place of Birth:	Tydavent Co. Monaghan
Age on Attestation:	19 years
Period of Service:	1843 — 1855
Age on Discharge:	30 years
Length of Service:	11 years 73 days
Foreign Service:	Crimea
Medal Entitlement:	Crimea
Reason for Discharge:	Lameness due to gunshot wound to the thigh received at Inkerman
Character:	Good
Trade or Occupation:	Farmer
Can Sign Name:	Yes
Height:	5' 8"
Hair Colour:	Sandy
Eyes:	Hazel
Complexion:	Fair

McFALL — see — McGALL John
RA 9th Battalion

McFARREN — William, private
17th Foot

14 Aug 1846	Discharged the Service Chatham Pension paid Omagh 1/- per diem
24 May 1855	Arrived per *'Stag'*
Jan 1857	Contributed 1/- to Florence Nightingale Fund
1857	To Adelaide from Western Australia

Service and Personal Details:

Place of Birth:	Drumcliff Co. Sligo	
Age on Attestation:	19 years	
Period of Service:	1826 — 1846	
Age on Discharge:	39 years 6 months	
Length of Service:	20 years 279 days	
Foreign Service:	New South Wales	5 years 215 days
	India	9 years 130months
Reason for Discharge:	Disease of the Lungs, Infirm from length of service	
Character:	Very Good	
Trade or Occupation:	Labourer	
Can Sign Name:	X his mark on discharge	
Height:	5' 7"	
Hair Colour:	Brown	
Eyes:	Blue	
Complexion:	Dark	

McGALL — John, Serjeant

	RA 9th Battalion
Surname Variants	McGALE; McGAUL; McFALL
9 July 1850	Discharged the Service Woolwich
	Pension paid 2nd Edinburgh Pension District
	9d. per diem [6d on discharge document]
21 May 1851	Arrived per *'Mermaid'*
1851	Employed by Convict Establishment
1858	Pension paid Melbourne [12/WA/39]

Service and Personal Details:		
Place of Birth:	Cranston Dalkeith Midlothian	
Age on Enlistment:	18 years 2 months	
Period of Service:	1830 — 1850	
Age on Discharge:	37 years 9 months	
Length of Service:	19 years 182 days	
Foreign Service:	Mauritius	8 years 7 months
	West Indies	5 years 6 months
Reason for Discharge:	Dullness of Hearing and Nervous Tremors	
Character and Conduct:	Very Good	
Trade or Occupation:	Labourer	
Can Sign Name:	Yes	
Height:	5' 9½"	
Hair Colour:	Light Brown	
Eyes:	Blue	
Complexion:	Sallow	

McGANN	Thomas, private
	3rd Foot
12 Jan 1856	Discharged the Service Chatham
	Pension paid Tullamore
	8d. per diem
4 July 1866	Arrived per '*Belgravia*
1874	Pension increased to 11½d per diem
1874	Discharged from Enrolled Force due to failing eyesight
1875	Died aged 44 – buried East Perth Cemetery
1876	Catherine McGann In receipt of outdoor relief money — Perth

Service and Personal Details:		
Place of Birth:	Kildare Co. Kildare	
Age on Enlistment:	24 years	
Period of Service:	1854 — 1856	
Age on Discharge:	26 years 1 month	
Length of Service:	1 years 84 days	
Foreign Service:	Crimea	8 months
Medal Entitlement:	Crimea; Turkish Crimean	
Reason for Discharge:	Partial loss of power in left arm caused by piece of shell	
Character:	Indifferent	
Trade or Occupation:	Labourer	
Can Sign Name:	blank; X his mark on Attestation	

Height:	5' 6½"
Hair Colour:	Dark Brown
Eyes:	Blue
Complexion:	Fresh
Intends to Reside:	Naas Co. Kildare

McGARVEY	Bernard, private 28th Foot
Surname Variant	McGARVIE
22 June 1852	Discharged the Service Chatham Pension paid 1st Manchester Pension District 1/- per diem
6 Apr 1854	Arrived per *'Sea Park'*
1855	"Off EP Roll for gross misconduct"
1857	To South Australia from Western Australia
1865	Pension paid Adelaide
1872	"Not Appeared"

Service and Personal Details:		
Place of Birth:	Muckeny Castleblaney Co. Monaghan	
Age on Enlistment:	18 years	
Period of Service:	1830 — 1852	
Age on Discharge:	40 years	
Length of Service:	20 years 329 days	
Foreign Service:	New South Wales	6 years 10 months
	East Indies	5 years 3 months
Reason for Discharge:	Chronic Rheumatism and debility	
Character:	Bad	
Trade or Occupation:	Groom	
Can Sign Name:	Yes	
Height:	5' 7"	
Hair Colour:	Brown	
Eyes:	Dark Blue	
Complexion:	Fresh	
Intends to Reside:	Manchester	

McGEE	James, private 89th Foot
5 May 1857	Discharged the Service Chatham Pension paid 2nd West London Pension District 9d. per diem
8 June 1858	Arrived per *'Lord Raglan'*
1863	Stationed Perth District
1864	ptve J McGee Pensioner Force at Perth contributed to the Greenough Fire Relief Fund
23 Jan 1867	Perth — Pensioner James McGee is in receipt of a pension of 9d. per diem. He is not employed on the Enrolled Duty Force.
12 June 1876	Roebourne Police reported that James McGee of the Fremantle Enrolled Force was accidentally drowned at the Flying Foam Passage

Service and Personal Details:	
Place of Birth:	St Marys Limerick

Age on Enlistment:	18 years	
Period of Service:	1837 — 1857	
Age on Discharge:	37 years 11 months	
Length of Service:	18 years 154 days	
Foreign Service:	West Indies	2 years 4 months
	North America	5 years 10 months
	Gibraltar	7 months
	Crimea	3 months
Medal Entitlement:	Crimea	
Reason for Discharge:	Delicate Constitution and Chronic Diarrhoea	
Character:	Very Good	
Trade or Occupation:	Labourer	
Can Sign Name:	X his mark on discharge	
Height:	5'7½"	
Hair Colour:	Light Brown	
Eyes:	Blue	
Complexion:	Fresh	
Intends to Reside:	Bayswater Paddington London	

McGEE	Joseph [James], private
	Rifle Brigade
10 July 1855	Discharged the Service
	Pension paid Newry
	8d. per diem
15 Apr 1864	Arrived per *'Clara'* [2]
1865	To Adelaide from Western Australia
13 Mar 1879	Died South Australia

Service and Personal Details:

Place of Birth:	Newry Co. Down	
Age on Enlistment:	16 years	
Period of Service:	1850 — 1855	
Age on Discharge:	none given	
Length of Service:	2 years 227 days [after age of 18]	
Foreign Service:	Cape of Good Hope	1 year 10 months
	"East of Europe"	1 year
Medal Entitlement:	Kaffir War; Crimea with clasp	
Reason for Discharge:	Disabled by gunshot wound of left hand	
Character:	Good	
Trade or Occupation:	Labourer	
Can Sign Name:	X his mark on discharge	
Height:	5' 6¼"	
Hair Colour:	Brown	
Eyes:	Hazel	
Complexion:	Sallow	

McGENNISS	Patrick, private
	46th Foot
Surname Variants	[some] MEGINESS; McGENNIS; McGUENNIS; McGUINESS; McGUINNES; McGUINNESS
4 Aug 1857	Discharged the Service Dublin

	Pension paid 1st Liverpool Pension District
	11d. per diem
24 Nov 1858	Arrived per *'Edwin Fox'*
	Allocated Greenough Locs G23 and G24
1874	Pension increased to 1/3d. per diem
Aug 1875	Died aged 56 [surname Meginess]

Service and Personal Details:		
Place of Birth:	Banbridge Co. Down	
Age on Enlistment:	18 years	
Period of Service:	1836 — 1857	
Age on Discharge:	39 years 4 months	
Length of Service:	21 years 144 days	
Foreign Service:	Gibraltar	4 years 4 months
	West Indies	3 years
	North America	3 years 2 months
	Crimea	7 months
Medal Entitlement:	Crimea with clasps for Alma and Inkerman, [Recommended for a Good Conduct and Long Service medal]	
Reason for Discharge:	Renal Disease and Rheumatism	
Character:	Good	
Trade or Occupation:	Weaver	
Height:	5' 7"	
Hair Colour:	Dark Brown	
Eyes:	Grey	
Complexion:	Sallow	
Intends to Reside:	No. 73 Albert St., Liverpool	

McGILL	Thomas, private
	83rd Foot
24 Sept 1861	Discharge approved
	Pension paid Chatham
	8d. per diem
1861	Pension increased to 10d. per diem
1861	Pension paid Londonderry
1862	Newcastle
1862	Londonderry
1863	Sligo
15 Aug 1865	Arrived per *'Racehorse'*
circa March 1874	Transferred from Fremantle to Athlone
1874	Pension paid Sligo

Service and Personal Details:		
Place of Birth:	Coleraine Co. Derry	
Age on Enlistment:	17 years 9 months	
Period of Service:	1839 — 1861	
Age on Discharge:	39 years 10 months	
Length of Service:	21 years 12 days	
Foreign Service:	East Indies	11 years
Medal Entitlement:	Indian Mutiny with clasp for Central India	
Reason for Discharge:	Own Request having served for 21 years	
Character:	Good	
Trade or Occupation:	Labourer	

Can Sign Name:	X his mark on discharge
Height:	5'5¾"
Hair Colour:	Dark Brown
Eyes:	Grey
Complexion:	Fresh
Intends to Reside:	Coleraine Ireland

McGINN	Owen, private
	94th Foot
Previous Regiment	63rd Foot
25 July 1848	Discharged the Service
	Pension paid 1st East London Pension District
	1/- per diem
1850	Pension paid 1st Cork Pension District
1850	Fermoy
1853	1st Cork Pension District
1854	Fermoy
2 Apr 1856	Arrived per *'William Hammond'*
1876	Approval to admit to Mt. Eliza Depot and to pay three quarters of this man's pension into the Colonial Treasury towards his maintenance.
June 1888	Died – buried East Perth Cemetery

Service and Personal Details:		
Place of Birth:	Carrickmacross Monaghan	
Age on Enlistment:	18 years	
Period of Service:	1827 — 1848	
Age on Discharge:	39 years	
Length of Service:	20 years 225 days	
Foreign Service:	Van Dieman's Land	6 years 9 months
	East Indies	12 years 9 months
Reason for Discharge:	Worn out from length of service and climate	
Character:	Very Good	
Trade or Occupation:	Labourer	
Can Sign Name:	X his mark on discharge	
Height:	5' 9"	
Hair Colour:	Brown	
Eyes:	Grey	
Complexion:	Fresh	
Intends to Reside:	Leytonstone Essex	

McGINNESS	George, private
	99th Foot
Surname Variants	[some] McGUINESS; McGINNIS; McGUINNESS
21 Sept 1863	Discharged the Service Cork
13 Oct 1863	Admitted to Out-Pension
	Pension paid Newry
	11d. per diem
22 Dec 1865	Arrived per *'Vimiera'*
1871	Granted Perth Town Lot 52/H
Apr 1872	Died — Buried East Perth Pioneer Cemetery

Service and Personal Details:		
Place of Birth:	Nobbar Co. Meath	
Age on Enlistment:	18 years	
Period of Service:	1840 — 1863	
Age on Discharge:	40 years 8 months	
Length of Service:	21 years 137 days	
Foreign Service:	Australian Colonies	13 years 2 months
Reason for Discharge:	Own Request having completed 21 years	
Character:	Good	
Trade or Occupation:	Labourer	
Can Sign Name:	X his mark on discharge	
Height:	5' 7¼"	
Hair Colour:	Brown	
Eyes:	Grey	
Complexion:	Fresh	
Intends to Reside:	Navan Co. Meath	

McGINNIS	John, private
	45th Foot
Previous Regiment	89th Foot
	[some] McGUINNIS; McGINNES; McGUINNESS
25 Oct 1864	Discharged the Service Parkhurst I.O.W. Pension paid 1st Belfast Pension District 10d. per diem
22 Dec 1865	Arrived per *'Vimiera'*
no date	Assigned Freshwater Bay Loc 1072
circa March 1876	Transferred from Fremantle to 1st Perth District
Aug 1885	Application for Title to Freshwater Bay Loc 1072
1873	Pension paid Western Australia
1886	a John McGuinness died

Service and Personal Details:		
Place of Birth:	Belfast Co. Down	
Age on Attestation:	17 years	
Period of Service:	1842 — 1864	
Age on Discharge:	39 years 7 months	
Length of Service:	21 years 16 days	
Foreign Service:	Gibraltar	1 year 9 months
	Monte Video	10 months
	Cape of Good Hope	12 years 10 months
Medal Entitlement:	Kaffir War 1851/53	
Reason for Discharge:	Own Request having completed 21 years service	
Character:	Good	
Trade or Occupation:	Labourer	
Can Sign Name:	X his mark on discharge	
Height:	5' 10½"	
Hair Colour:	Brown	
Eyes:	Dark Brown	
Complexion:	Fresh	
Intends to Reside:	Belfast Co. Down	

McGLADE	Peter, private [Military Pensioner]

	51st Foot
Surname Variant	McLAID
25 June 1840	Arrived per *'Runnymede'* with regiment
11 Mar 1847	Discharged the Service Perth Western Australia
24 Aug 1847	Discharge Approved
	Pension paid Perth Western Australia
	1/- per diem
1851	Pension paid by Commissariat until transferred to Capt Bruce, Staff Officer Pensions
1853	Employed as Night Warder
Sept 1860	Died

Service and Personal Details:

Place of Birth:	Killiavey Armagh
Age on Enlistment:	18 years
Period of Service:	1826 — 1847
Age on Discharge:	39 years
Length of Service:	21 years 54 days
Foreign Service:	Ionian Isles &
	Australian Colonies 7 years
Reason for Discharge:	Chronic Rheumatism, Rupture on left side and being worn out and unfit for service in India
Character:	Always been a Good Character
Trade or Occupation:	Labourer
Can Sign Name:	Yes
Height:	5' 4¾"
Hair Colour:	Dark
Eyes:	Hazel
Complexion:	Dark
Remarks:	Embarked Van D. Land [sic] 22 June 1839
Intends to Reside:	Western Australia

McGLOUGHLIN	Thomas, private
	29th Foot
Surname Variants	McGLAUGHLIN; McLOUGHLIN
3 Apr 1866	Discharged the Service Chatham
	Pension paid Newcastle upon Tyne
	1/- per diem
9 Jan 1868	Arrived per *'Hougoumont'*
14 July 1879	Assigned North Fremantle Lot P57
1879	Payment of £15 [pounds] sanctioned
1881	Pension increased to 1/5½d. per diem for service in the Enrolled Force
27 Apr 1882	Granted Fee Simple North Fremantle Lot P57
Aug 1884	Died aged 57

Service and Personal Details:

Place of Birth:	Birr Kings County
Age on Attestation:	18 years 5 months
Period of Service:	1845 — 1866
Age on Discharge:	39 years 5 months
Length of Service:	21 years 8 days [reckoned]
Foreign Service:	East Indies 14 years

Medal Entitlement:	Good Conduct and Long Service with gratuity; Punjaub with 2 clasps
Reason for Discharge:	Own Request having completed 21 years service
Character:	Very Good
Trade or Occupation:	Tailor
Can Sign Name:	X his mark on discharge
Height:	5' 6"
Hair Colour:	Brown
Eyes:	Blue
Complexion:	Sallow
Intends to Reside:	Newcastle on Tyne

McGOVERN	Patrick, private 64th Foot
Surname Variants	McGOVARN; McGOWAN
1 June 1858	Discharged the Service Chatham Pension paid Sligo 1/-½d. per diem
4 July 1866	Arrived per *'Belgravia'*
1870	Purchased Fremantle Town Lot 638
1878	Pension increased to 1/5½d. per diem for service in the Enrolled Force
no date	W.O. correspondence stating that man had re-entered the Enrolled Force and that the pension increase granted by the Chelsea Board had been suspended
1881	Pension increased to 1/6½d. per diem for further service in the Enrolled Force
1883	Granted Cockburn Sound Loc P12 Lake Munster
May 1891	Died

Service and Personal Details:

Place of Birth:	Enniskillen Cavan	
Age on Attestation:	20 years ?4 months	
Period of Service:	1835 — 1858	
Age on Discharge:	43 years or 42 years 3 months	
Length of Service:	22 years 8 days [reckoned]	
Foreign Service:	Jamaica	2 years 10 months
	North America	2 years 9 months
	India	8 years 6 months
Reason for Discharge:	Chronic Rheumatism, Cough, Dyspnoea	
Character:	Very Good	
Trade or Occupation:	Labourer	
Can Sign Name:	Yes	
Height:	5' 6½"	
Hair Colour:	Brown	
Eyes:	Grey	
Complexion:	Fair	
Intends to Reside:	Sligo Co. Sligo but decided on Glasgow	

McGRATH	Bernard, private 106th Foot

Previous Regiment	2nd Bombay European Light Infantry
26 May 1863	Discharged the Service Netley Pension paid 2nd Dublin Pension District 9d. per diem
15 Aug 1865	Arrived per *'Racehorse'* Request for the allocation of Cockburn Sound Lot P3 to B.N. McGrath
1871	Charged with violently assaulting his wife
1881	Pension increased to 1/-½d. per diem for service in the Enrolled Force
21 Sept 1883	Cockburn Sound Loc 3 Grant at Coogee confirmed Application for lots at Lake Munster on behalf of B. McGrath
no date	Allocated Canning Pensioner Lot 137 [3C] which had been relinquished by Michael Fennell in Feb 1882
June 1897	Residing Fremantle
Feb 1900	Attended fete at Oval
1908	Died aged 79

Service and Personal Details:

Place of Birth:	Bowers Court Co. Wicklow	
Age on Attestation:	20 years 7 months	
Period of Service:	1849 — 1863	
Age on Discharge:	34 years 7 months	
Length of Service:	15 years 170 days	
Foreign Service:	East Indies	13 years ?6 months
Medal Entitlement:	Persia with clasp 1856/7	
Reason for Discharge:	Varicose Veins both legs and Broken Constitution	
Character:	Good	
Trade or Occupation:	Labourer	
Can Sign Name:	Yes	
Height:	5' 8"	
Hair Colour:	Brown	
Eyes:	Grey	
Complexion:	Fresh	
Remarks:	Elected for Indian Pension Rules	
Intends to Reside:	Bowerscourt Enniskillen Co. Wicklow	

McGRATH	Denis, private 57th Foot
Previous Regiment	47th Foot
25 June 1872	Discharged the Service Kinsale Pension paid Liverpool 1/-½d per diem
1873	Pension paid Greenwich
19 Feb 1874	Arrived per *'Naval Brigade'*
1881	Transferred to New Zealand

Service and Personal Details:

Place of Birth:	Cork Co. Cork
Age on Enlistment:	17 years
Period of Service:	1849 — 1872

Age on Discharge:	40 years	
Length of Service:	22 years 15 days	
Foreign Service:	Corfu	1 year 6 months
	Crimea	9 months
	Malta	3 years 1 month
	East Indies	2 years 7 months
	New Zealand	6 years 7 months
Medal Entitlement:	Crimea; Turkish Crimean; New Zealand	
Reason for Discharge:	Own Request on termination of his 2nd period of Limited Engagement	
Character:	Very Good	
Trade or Occupation:	Labourer	
Can Sign Name:	X his mark on discharge	
Height:	5' 9¾"	
Hair Colour:	Brown	
Eyes:	Grey	
Complexion:	Fresh	
Intends to Reside:	Liverpool	

McGRATH	John, private
	87th Foot
26 June 1849	Discharged the Service Chatham
	Pension paid Dundee
	1/- per diem
24 May 1855	Arrived per *'Stag'*
	Application for Title Greenough Loc G9 and G10 — Bootenal Victoria District
1873	Pension increased to 1/3d. per diem for 11 years 5 months service in the Enrolled Force
1878	Died

Service and Personal Details:

Place of Birth:	Middleton Co. Cork	
Age on Attestation:	20 years	
Period of Service:	1827 — 1849	
Age on Discharge:	42 years 3 months	
Length of Service:	22 years 2 days	
Foreign Service:	Mauritius	12 years 100 days
Reason for Discharge:	Diminishing Efficiency and Rheumatism	
Character:	Very Good	
Trade or Occupation:	Labourer	
Can Sign Name:	X his mark on discharge	
Height:	5' 7¾"	
Hair Colour:	Brown	
Eyes:	Blue	
Complexion:	Dark	
Intends to Reside:	Dundee	

McGRATH	John Peter, private
	22nd Foot
12 Sept 1854	Discharged the Service Chatham
	Pension paid Birr

	9d. per diem	
10 July 1857	Arrived per *'Clara'* [1]	
1858	Pension paid Melbourne [12/WA/35]	
Service and Personal Details:		
Place of Birth:	Portmanna Galway	
Age on Attestation:	19 years	
Period of Service:	1833 — 1854	
Age on Discharge:	40 years	
Length of Service:	20 years 17 days	
Foreign Service:	East Indies	12 years 133 days
Reason for Discharge:	Suffers from Rheumatic Pains	
Character:	Latterly Good	
Trade or Occupation:	Labourer	
Can Sign Name:	Yes	
Height:	5' 8"	
Hair Colour:	Sandy	
Eyes:	Grey	
Complexion:	Fresh	
Intends to Reside:	Birr	

McGREGOR	George, private	
	European Veterans Service Corps	
Previous Regiments	1st Madras Fusiliers; 102nd Foot	
13 Jan 1866	Discharged the Service Vizapipatam	
23 Oct 1866	Admitted to Out-Pension	
	Pension paid Edinburgh	
	1/- per diem	
1866	Pension paid 2nd Glasgow Pension District	
9 Jan 1868	Arrived per *'Hougoumont'*	
Service and Personal Details:		
Place of Birth:	Cathcart Glasgow Renfrewshire	
Age on Enlistment:	18 years	
Period of Service:	1846— 1866	
Age on Discharge:	39 years 303 days	
Length of Service:	22 years 203 days [including 2 years Boon]	
Foreign Service:	Burmah	5 years 6 months
	Bengal	2 years 6 months
	Madras	13 years 303 days
Medal Entitlement:	"Three War medals with clasps"	
Reason for Discharge:	Having completed 21 years service	
Character:	Good	
Trade or Occupation:	Currier	
Can Sign Name:	X his mark on discharge	
Height:	5' 6½"	
Hair Colour:	Brown	
Eyes:	Blue	
Complexion:	Fair	
Intends to Reside:	Glasgow	

McGUINNESS	James, private
	18th Foot

15 Jan 1856	Discharged the Service Pension paid Armagh 8d. per diem
11 Feb 1861	Arrived per *'Palmeston'*
31 Mar 1864	Pension paid South Australia from Fremantle

Service and Personal Details:

Place of Birth:	Armagh Co. Armagh	
Age on Discharge:	30 years	
Length of Service:	11 years 8 months	
Foreign Service:	Crimea	8 months
Medal Entitlement:	Crimea	
Reason for Discharge:	Stiffness of the fingers of the right hand from Grape Shot wound received at the Redan	
Character:	Indifferent	
Trade or Occupation:	Labourer	
Height:	5' 6"	
Hair Colour:	Brown	
Eyes:	Grey	
Complexion:	Fresh	

McGUIRE Owen, private
5th Foot

25 Jan 1848	Discharged the Service Chatham Pension paid Plymouth 1/- per diem
1851	Residing 4 Mount Street Stoke Dameral St Stephen's Parish Devonport [Plymouth]
2 Apr 1856	Arrived per *'William Hammond'*
1878	possibly residing at Geraldton

Service and Personal Details:

Place of Birth:	Aughnamullen Co. Monaghan	
Age on Enlistment:	21 years	
Period of Service:	1826 — 1848	
Age on Discharge:	42 years or 41 years	
Length of Service:	20 years 288 days	
Foreign Service:	Gibraltar	4 years
	Malta	2 years 5 months
	Ionian Isles	5 years
Reason for Discharge:	Chronic Pulmonic Disease	
Character:	Indifferent to 1845, but since that date Good	
Trade or Occupation:	Labourer	
Can Sign Name:	X his mark on discharge	
Height:	5' 8"	
Hair Colour:	Light Brown	
Eyes:	Grey	
Complexion:	Fresh	
Intends to Reside:	Devonport	

McGUIRE Philip, private
57th Foot

16 June 1843	Discharged the Service Fort Pitt Pension paid Enniskillen 1/- per diem
1843	Pension paid Londonderry
1849	Pension paid 1st Edinburgh Pension District
31 Aug 1853	Arrived per *'Phoebe Dunbar'*
1854	Appointed without sanction as Assistant Warder to the Convict establishment
Jan 1857	Contributed 2/- to the Florence Nightingale Fund
1857	To South Australia from Western Australia [possibly with wife] "£13/4/5 due for payment of passage"

Service and Personal Details:		
Place of Birth:	Sligo Sligo	
Age on Attestation:	18 years	
Period of Service:	1822 — 1843	
Age on Discharge:	40 years	
Length of Service:	20 years 75 days	
Foreign Service:	New South Wales	3 years 7 months
	East Indies	11 years 3 months
Reason for Discharge:	Chronic Catarrh and General Debility	
Trade or Occupation:	Labourer	
Can Sign Name:	Yes	
Height:	5' 9¼"	
Hair Colour:	Brown	
Eyes:	Blue	
Complexion:	Swarthy	
Intends to Reside:	Dublin	

McGUIRE	Philip, private RM
May 1848	Discharged the Service Chatham
Sept 1848	Pension paid Enniskillen £4/12/- per annum
Mar 1852	Allocated land Albany
1853	Granted land at Albany subject to improvement conditions
1855	a Philip McGuire serving as Mounted Police stationed at Beaufort Hills 23 miles north of Kojonup
1864	possibly employed as a police constable Albany
1905	Died

Service and Personal Details:	
Place of Birth:	Enniskillen Co. Fermanagh Ireland
Age on Attestation:	21 years
Marine Division:	Chatham
Period of Service:	1847 — 1848
Length of Service:	6 months 18 days [reckoned]
Reason for Discharge:	Cataract of the right eye caused by a bone shaken from a table cloth hitting eye
Trade or Occupation:	Labourer

McILWAINE	Henry, Company Serjeant Major
5 May 1896	Discharged the Service Petershead Royal Artillery possibly 2/8d per diem
Feb 1900	Attended fete at Fremantle Oval
Service and Personal Details:	
Place of Birth:	Killea Drummore Co. Donegal
Age on Enlistment:	20 years 11 months
Period of Service:	?1873 — 1896
Age on Discharge:	46 years
Length of Service:	23 years 30 days [reckoned]
Medal Entitlement:	Good Conduct
Reason for Discharge:	Debility clearly the effects of long tropical service
Character:	Exemplary
Trade or Occupation:	Woollen Draper
Can Sign Name:	Yes
Height:	5' 7¾"
Hair Colour:	Light Brown
Eyes:	Blue
Complexion:	Fresh
Intends to Reside:	Western Australia

McINTOSH	William, Serjeant [WO 97/1247/167] RA 8th Battalion
9 July 1850	Discharged the Service Woolwich Pension paid Woolwich 1/9½d. per diem
21 May	1851 Arrived per *'Mermaid'*
1851	Employed by Convict Establishment
1862	Pension paid 1st East London Pension District
1863	Pension paid Inverness Liverpool
15 Apr 1864	Returned to Western Australia per *'Clara'* [2]
1865	Pension paid Perth Western Australia
1866	East London
1866	Edinburgh
1866	W.O. Correspondence — Applied for the In-Pension but did not appear
1869	Pension paid Melbourne
1870	Edinburgh
Service and Personal Details:	
Place of Birth:	St Cuthberts Edinburgh Midlothian
Age on Enlistment:	20 years
Period of Service:	1828 — 1850
Age on Discharge:	42 years
Length of Service:	22 years 9 days
Foreign Service:	Mauritius 10 years 9 months
Reason for Discharge:	Chronic Rheumatism
Character:	Exemplary
Trade or Occupation:	Bookbinder
Can Sign Name:	Yes
Height:	5' 8¼"
Hair Colour:	Brown

Eyes:	Hazel
Complexion:	Fair

McINTYRE	Daniel, private
	13th Foot
Surname Variant	McINTIRE
20 May 1847	Discharged the Service Dublin
13 July 1847	Admitted to Out-Pension
	Pension paid 1st Glasgow Pension District
	1/- per diem
1847	Pension paid Paisley
1847	Birr
1848	Athlone
21 May 1851	Arrived per *'Mermaid'*
Aug 1851	Appointed Assistant Warder Convict Service
Sept 1851	Dismissed or resigned from Convict Department
1856	Dismissed from Enrolled Force
1856	Forfeited pension — Gross misconduct
1856	Re-instated into Enrolled Force
Jan 1857	Contributed 2/- to the Florence Nightingale Fund
1857	Pension paid Van Dieman's Land
1858	Athlone
1859	Tullamore
1861	? Quebec
1862	Tullamore
1864	Athlone
1874	Died Tullamore Ireland

Service and Personal Details:

Place of Birth:	Gillen Kings County
Age on Attestation:	17 years
Period of Service:	1825 — 1847
Age on Discharge:	39 years 4 months
Length of Service:	21 years 113 days [reckoned]
Foreign Service:	East Indies 18 years 8 months
Medal Entitlement:	Jellalabad [entitled to two]; Cabool [sic]
Reason for Discharge:	Infirm from age and length of service
Character:	Very Good
Trade or Occupation:	Labourer
Can Sign Name:	Yes
Height:	5' 7"
Hair Colour:	Dark
Eyes:	Hazel
Complexion:	Grey
Married:	*c*1831 Jane White Dinapore India
Children:	Patrick b. *c*1834 Agra India
	John b. *c*1837 Kurnaul India
	Daniel d. 1840 Bengal India
	James b. *c*1847 Ireland

McKAY	Angus, Serjeant
	RA
1 Feb 1870	Discharged the Service Leith Fort

	Pension paid Woolwich 2/- per diem
Apr 1895	Correspondence with W.O.
Service and Personal Details:	
Place of Birth:	Tolbooth Edinburgh
Age on Attestation:	20 years
Period of Service:	1849 — 1870
Age on Discharge:	41 years
Length of Service:	21 years 10 days
Foreign Service:	Turkey & Crimea 2 years New Zealand 7 years
Medal Entitlement:	Long Service and Good Conduct; Crimean with 3 clasps; Turkish Crimean; New Zealand; Awarded Meritorious Service Annuity Medal [the issue of this medal is very limited — to qualify the holder must already be in possession of a Long Service and Good Conduct Medal]
Reason for Discharge:	Time Served
Character:	Very Good
Trade or Occupation:	Farmer's Servant
Can Sign Name:	Yes
Height:	5' 10¾"
Hair Colour:	Dark Brown
Eyes:	Grey
Complexion:	Fresh
Intends to Reside:	No. 9 Bankside Str., Tolbooth Edinburgh
Remarks:	[see Trove] Enlisted Edinburgh in the RA on the 23rd Jan 1849 and was Discharged the Service 1st Feb 1870 at Woolwich having served 21 years and ten days. Serving 16 years as a non-commissioned officer and 13 years as a Sergeant Between 1849 and April 1854, he served in England and Ireland and in Turkey and the Crimea from May 1854 to July 1856, and was present at the battles of Alma and Inkerman; [sortie of the 28th October], as well as the various sieges of Sebastapol. He served in the Maori War from Dec. 1860 to March 1868, being present at the Te-el-pah, Waitara, Taranaki [1861], Tateranail 1863, Waikato [1863 — 1866] and at the actions at Koheroa, Meri-Meri, Rangariri, Ngaruawahia, Paterangi, Rangia-wahia and Orakau. He was mentioned in dispatches for services to the regiment at Rangariri for throwing by hand a live 5 ½ in. mortar shell over the works into the Pah.

In April 1864, he was also mentioned in General Carey's dispatches for clearing the enemy out of their rifle pits with hand grenades. He was in charge of the Central Magazine at Auckland from 1864 to 1868 then employed as artillery instructor to the Dunedin District Artillery and Naval Volunteers. He was employed in a similar capacity in Otago from 1873 to 1891. He was awarded the Crimean medal, with clasps for Alma, Inkerman and Sebastopol; the Turkish Crimean the New Zealand War medal as well as the Long Service and Good Conduct medal, with a gratuity of £15

McKAY	George, private [1297]	
	25th Foot	
3 Mar 1861	Discharged the Service	
	Pension paid Edinburgh	
	10d. per diem	
15 Aug 1865	Arrived per *'Racehorse'*	
3 Jan 1876	Died	
Service and Personal Details:		
Place of Birth:	St Marys Edinburgh	
Age on Attestation:	17 years 3 months	
Period of Service:	1839 — 1861	
Age on Discharge:	none given	
Length of Service:	21 years 13 days	
Foreign Service:	Cape of Good Hope	2 years 4 months
	East Indies	12 years 10 months
	Gibraltar	3 years
Reason for Discharge:	Own Request having served 21 years	
Character:	Good	
Trade or Occupation:	Labourer	
Can Sign Name:	Yes	
Height:	5' 7"	
Hair Colour:	Dark Brown	
Eyes:	Grey	
Complexion:	Dark	
Intends to Reside:	Edinburgh Scotland	

McKAY	John, private
	26th Foot
9 Oct 1849	Discharged the Service Cork
11 Dec 1849	Admitted to Out-Pension
	Pension paid Cork
	1/- per diem
1849	Pension paid 1st Manchester Pension District
1850	Pension paid Edinburgh
31 Aug 1853	Arrived per *'Phoebe Dunbar'*
Jan 1857	Contributed 2/- to the Florence Nightingale Fund
1873	Pension increased to 1/3d. per diem for 15 years 2 months service in the Enrolled Force
1872	a J McKay residing at Fremantle
1874	Stationed Fremantle

	[Was assigned the land vacated by Tranailles]
1883	Died
Service and Personal Details:	
Place of Birth:	Edinburgh Scotland
Age on Attestation:	17 years
Period of Service:	1827 — 1849
Age on Discharge:	39 years 3 months
Length of Service:	21 years 12 days
Foreign Service:	East Indies 13 years 5 months
	China 1 year 6 months
Medal Entitlement:	China
Reason for Discharge:	Chronic Pulmonary Disease
Character:	Pretty [sic] Good
Trade or Occupation:	Cooper
Can Sign Name:	Yes
Height:	5' 11"
Hair Colour:	Brown
Eyes:	Dark
Complexion:	Dark
Intends to Reside:	Edinburgh
Married:	? 1837 Margaret Raleigh or Railie India
Children:	John b. 1846
	m. *c*1866 Matilda Bicknell Perth
	Emily b. 1847
	m. *c*1867 William Flood Fremantle
	Annie Rita
	[daughter of John and Margaret]
	m. *c*1879 Jesse Hammond Fremantle
	[author of "Western Pioneers"]
	William James McKay
	m. *c*1887 Emma Miles York
	Ronald b. *c*1860 North Fremantle
	[son of John and Margaret]
	m. *c*1891 Lily Davies York
	Phoebe b. *c*1863
	m. *c*1887 John Dickson Fremantle
	Catherine b. *c*1865
	m. *c*1891 John Wood Fremantle
1909	daughters from obituary — Mrs John Dickson; Mrs J Hammond; Mrs John Woods [Trove]
McKAY	John, private [1337]
	92nd Foot
2 Oct 1860	Discharged the Service
	Pension paid Dundee
	1/- per diem
15 Aug 1865	Arrived per *'Racehorse'*
1867	Pension paid New Zealand from Perth West. Aust.
Service and Personal Details:	
Place of Birth:	Tongue Sunderland
Age on Attestation:	18 years

Period of Service:	1839 — 1860	
Age on Discharge:	39 years	
Length of Service:	21 years 7 days	
Foreign Service:	Malta	7 months
	West Indies	2 years 10 months
Reason for Discharge:	Own Request having completed upwards of 21 years service	
Character:	Good	
Trade or Occupation:	Labourer	
Can Sign Name:	Yes	
Height:	5'6"	
Hair Colour:	Brown	
Eyes:	Grey	
Complexion:	Fair	
Intends to Reside:	Dundee	

McKAY	John, Corporal	
	96th Foot	
2 Apr 1861	Discharged the Service	
	Pension paid 2nd Glasgow Pension District	
	1/3d. per diem	
15 Feb 1863	Arrived per *'Merchantman'* [1]	
1865	Pension paid Western Australia	
31 Aug 1871	Died	
Service and Personal Details:		
Place of Birth:	North Leith Midlothian	
Age on Enlistment:	15 years	
Period of Service:	1836 — 1861	
Age on Discharge:	40 years	
Length of Service:	21 years 19 days	
Foreign Service:	Australia	7 years 10 months
	East Indies	6 years 1 month
	Gibraltar	10 months
Reason for Discharge:	Being unfit for further service	
Character:	Latterly Good	
Trade or Occupation:	Labourer	
Can Sign Name:	Yes	
Height:	5' 6"	
Hair Colour:	Dark Brown	
Eyes:	Hazel	
Complexion:	Fresh	

McKEARNAN	John, private [99]
	99th Foot
Surname Variants	[some] McKEENAN; McKEERNAN; McKIERNAN, McKERNAN; McKERNON
17 May 1841	Discharged the Service Dublin
9 June 1841	Admitted to Out-Pension
	Pension paid Kilkenny
	6d. per diem
24 Oct 1850	Arrived per *'Hashemy'*
1865	Pension paid Van Dieman's Land [sic]

Service and Personal Details:

Place of Birth:	Leeds Yorkshire
Age on Enlistment:	17 years
Period of Service:	1824 — 1841
Age on Discharge:	34 years
Length of Service:	16 years 5 days [reckoned]
Foreign Service:	Mauritius 11 years 157 days
Reason for Discharge:	Chronic Liver Complaint, Severe Cough, Severe Emaciation of Body and Rheumatic Pains
Character:	Indifferent but sober
Trade or Occupation:	Labourer
Can Sign Name:	X his mark on discharge
Height:	5' 6"
Hair Colour:	Black
Eyes:	Brown
Complexion:	Fresh

McKEE	John, gunner
	RA 3rd Brigade
21 May 1861	Discharged the Service
	Pension paid Woolwich
	11d. per diem
31 Dec 1862	Arrived per *'York'*
1864	Pension paid Perth Western Australia
1865	To Adelaide from Perth Western Australia
1907	W.O. correspondence with Under Treasury Adelaide
June 1907	Pension increased to 1/- per diem
1912	Died Adelaide South Australia

Service and Personal Details:

Place of Birth:	Woolwich Kent
Age on Enlistment:	14 years 9 months
Period of Service:	1837 — 1861
Age on Discharge:	39 years
Length of Service:	21 years 10 days [reckoned]
Foreign Service:	Mauritius 8 years 7 months Crimea 1 year
Medal Entitlement:	Long Service and Good Conduct with gratuity; Crimea
Reason for Discharge:	Own Request having completed 21 years service
Character:	Very Good
Trade or Occupation:	Shoemaker
Can Sign Name:	Yes
Height:	5' 7"
Hair Colour:	Brown
Eyes:	Grey
Complexion:	Fresh
Intends to Reside:	Woolwich

McKELLAR	Duncan, gunner
	RA 7th Battalion

Surname Variant	McKELLER
8 Oct 1850	Discharged the Service Woolwich 1/-½d. per diem
19 Aug 1853	Arrived per *'Robert Small'*
1853	Employed in Convict Establishment without sanction of Staff Officer Pensions
1854	Pension paid Western Australia
Jan 1857	contributed 2/- to the Florence Nightingale Fund
1860	To South Australia from Western Australia
1876	Pension paid Melbourne
1877	Pension paid New South Wales
1880	New South Wales

Service and Personal Details:		
Place of Birth:	?Killarchan Renfrewshire	
Age on Enlistment:	18 years	
Period of Service:	1828 — 1850	
Age on Discharge:	40 years	
Length of Service:	22 years 8 days [reckoned]	
Foreign Service:	Corfu	5 years 4 months
	Canada	5 years 11 months
Medal Entitlement:	Long Service and Good Conduct	
Reason for Discharge:	Chronic Rheumatism	
Character:	Exemplary	
Trade or Occupation:	Labourer	
Can Sign Name:	Yes	
Height:	5' 9"	
Hair Colour:	Dark	
Eyes:	Brown	
Complexion:	Fresh	

McKENZIE	Donald, private [2728]
also known as	Donald **MUNRO**
	Rifle Brigade
Previous Regiments	72nd, 52nd, 79th
Surname Variant	McKENSIE
July 1872	Discharged the Service 10d. per diem Pension paid Inverness
1873	Greenwich
19 Feb 1874	Arrived per *'Naval Brigade'*
Jan 1884	Assigned Bunbury Loc P403 at Turkey Point
[no date]	Free grant of land to Donald McKenzie [Pensioner], being ten acres, Lot P403 Turkey Point, Bunbury. S.O.P.
June 1884	Granted Bunbury Loc 403 at Turkey Point
1887	Pension increased to 1/-½d per diem
1887	Died aged 51
Aug 1887	Sarah the widow of Donald McKenzie made application to be registered as the proprietor of Cockburn Sound Loc P 15 of 20 acres

Service and Personal Details:	
Place of Birth:	Inverness Scotland
Age on Discharge:	36 years 6 months

Period of Service:	1853 — 1872	
Length of Service:	17 years 2 months	
Foreign Service:	Malta	5 months
	Crimea	1 year 1 month
	India	13 years 6 months
Medal Entitlement:	Crimea with clasp; Turkish Crimean; Indian Mutiny with clasp	
Reason for Discharge:	Total disorganisation of right eye from injury due to cricket ball in India in 1867. Sight in other eye impaired.	
Character:	Very Good	
Trade or Occupation:	Labourer	
Can Sign Name:	Yes	
Height:	5' 7½"	
Hair Colour:	Brown	
Eyes:	Hazel	
Complexion:	Fresh	

McKENZIE — Roderick, private
40th Foot

Previous Regiment	45th Foot
Surname Variant	McKENSIE
13 Feb 1844	Discharged the Service Chatham Pension paid Aberdeen 10d. per diem
25 Oct 1850	Arrived per *'Hashemy'*
1852	Pension paid Glasgow
1855	Aberdeen

Service and Personal Details:

Place of Birth:	Elgin Morayshire	
Age on Enlistment:	20 years	
Period of Service:	1825 — 1844	
Age on Discharge:	39 years 2 months	
Length of Service:	17 years 246 days	
Foreign Service:	East Indies	17 years 246 days
Medal Entitlement:	Medal for service in Afghanistan	
Reason for Discharge:	Unfit for further service	
Character:	Indifferent	
Trade or Occupation:	Weaver	
Can Sign Name:	X his mark on discharge	
Height:	5' 5¾"	
Hair Colour:	Black	
Eyes:	Grey	
Complexion:	Fair	
Intends to Reside:	Aberdeen	
Married:	Agnes b. *c*1815 Premay Aberdeenshire	

McKINNON — John, private
42nd Foot

21 July 1863	Discharged the Service Victoria Hospital Netley

	Pension paid Chatham	
	1/1d. per diem	
15 Aug 1865	Arrived per *'Racehorse'*	
1867 - 1871	Employed as a Temporary Assistant Warder	
30 June 1874	Died	
Service and Personal Details:		
Place of Birth:	Tobermory Argyllshire	
Age on Enlistment:	20 years	
Period of Service:	1842 — 1862	
Age on Discharge:	41 years 1 month	
Length of Service:	20 years 145 days	
Foreign Service:	Malta	4 years 3 months
	Bermuda	4 years 2 months
	Nova Scotia	1 year
	Turkey & Crimea	2 years
	East Indies	4 years 11 months
Medal Entitlement:	Good Conduct and Long Service with gratuity; Crimea with clasps; Turkish Crimean; Indian Mutiny with clasp	
Reason for Discharge:	Sunstroke	
Character:	Exemplary	
Trade or Occupation:	Labourer	
Can Sign Name:	Yes	
Height:	5' 9¾"	
Hair Colour:	Brown	
Eyes:	Grey	
Complexion:	Fresh	
Intends to Reside:	Maidstone Kent	

McLAUGHLIN	Robert, private EIC
	Bengal Infantry
Surname Variant	McLOUGHLIN
Out Pension No 404	
10 July 1844	Discharged the Service
July 1844	Embarked UK per *'Prince of Wales'*
	Pension paid 1st East London Pension District
	9d. per diem
18 Oct 1851	Arrived per *'Minden'*
Jan 1857	Contributed 1/- to the Florence Nightingale Fund
22 Oct 1857	"Quitted Australia without leave"
1858	Pension paid Fort William Bengal India
	[family remained in Victoria]
Service and Personal Details:	
Where Born:	Amboyna
Trade or Occupation:	None given
Where Enlisted:	Calcutta
Presidency:	Bengal
Length of Service:	7 years 8 months
Age on Discharge:	37 years
Reason for Discharge:	Injury to one of his testicles in Afghanistan
Character:	Bad
Medal Entitlement:	Afghanistan

Height:	5' 11"
Complexion:	Fair
Visage:	Oval
Eye Colour:	Grey
Hair Colour:	Light Brown

McLAURIN — William, gunner
Coastal Brigade Royal Artillery

Previous Regiment	72nd Foot
5 Jan 1864	Discharged the Service Jersey Pension paid Newcastle 1/- per diem
9 Jan 1868	Arrived per *'Hougoumont'*
June 1878	Pension increased to 1/5d. per diem for service in the Enrolled Force
Dec 1878	Pension paid South Australia from Fremantle
1899	Admitted to In-Pension Chelsea Hospital
21 Feb 1903	Died

Service and Personal Details:

Place of Birth:	Berwick Northumberland	
Age on Enlistment:	18 years	
Period of Service:	1842 — 1863	
Age on Discharge:	39 years	
Length of Service:	21 years 12 days [reckoned]	
Foreign Service:	Gibraltar	3 years 3 months
	West Indies	10 months
	Malta	3 years 9 months
Medal Entitlement:	Long Service and Good Conduct with gratuity	
Reason for Discharge:	His having completed 21 years service	
Character:	Exemplary	
Trade or Occupation:	Brush Maker	
Can Sign Name:	Yes	
Height:	5' 7¾"	
Hair Colour:	Dark Brown	
Eyes:	Blue	
Complexion:	Fresh	
Intends to Reside:	Newcastle on Tyne	

McLOUGHLIN — see — McGOUGHLIN Thomas, private
29th Foot

McLOUGHLIN — see — O'LOUGHLIN Michael, private
88th Foot

McMAHON — James, private
21st Foot

12 June 1849	Discharged the Service Chatham Pension paid Tullamore 1/- per diem
10 Sept 1856	Arrived per *'Runnymede'*
1857	Employed as Assistant Warder
1869	Retired as Assistant Warder due to ill health
1873	Pension increased to 1/1½d. per diem for 3 years 4 months service in the Enrolled Force

1874	Residing Fremantle
1 Apr 1875	Died aged 65
Service and Personal Details:	
Place of Birth:	?Portumna Co. Galway
Age on Enlistment:	18 years
Period of Service:	1828 — 1849
Age on Discharge:	39 years or 38 years 8 months
Length of Service:	20 years 234 days
Foreign Service:	Van Diemans Land 6 years
	East Indies 7 years
Reason for Discharge:	Chronic Rheumatism, Chronic Catarrh and Extreme Emaciation
Character:	Good
Trade or Occupation:	Labourer
Can Sign Name:	X his mark on discharge
Height:	5' 11¾"
Hair Colour:	Fresh
Eyes:	Hazel
Complexion:	Brown
Intends to Reside:	Waterford

McMAHON	James, private
	38th Foot
12 Dec 1855	Discharged the Service
	Pension paid Limerick
	9d. per diem
10 July 1857	Arrived per *'Clara'* [1]
1859	Employed as Assistant Warder
1874	Pension paid Western Australia
Service and Personal Details:	Medical Examination - 22nd Dec 1855
Place of Birth:	Killburn Broadford Co. Clare
Period of Service:	1849 — 1855
Age on Discharge:	25 years
Length of Service:	5 years 6 months
Foreign Service:	Turkey 4 months
	Crimea 1 year 1 month
Medal Entitlement:	Crimea with 2 clasps
Reason for Discharge:	Stiffness and weakness of right thigh and leg after gunshot wound to thigh 18/6/1855 at the Cemetery. Ball entered posterior surface of the thigh and emerged on the anterior surface 1½ inches lower down. It does not appear to have injured the femur
Character:	Good
Trade or Occupation:	Labourer
Height:	5' 8¾"
Hair Colour:	Brown
Eyes:	Blue
Complexion:	Fresh

McMAHON	John, private

	41st Foot	
18 Nov 1856	Discharged the Service Chatham	
	8d. per diem	
1857	Pension paid Ennis	
9 June 1862	Arrived per *'Norwood'* [1]	
1864	a John McMahon died	
Service and Personal Details:		
Place of Birth:	Newmarket Co. Clare	
Age on Enlistment:	21 years	
Period of Service:	1848 — 1856	
Age on Discharge:	29 years 6 months	
Length of Service:	8 years 136 days	
Foreign Service:	Ionian Isles	1 year 11 months
	Malta	1 year 1 month
	Turkey	5 months
	Crimea	1 year 2 months
Medal Entitlement:	Crimea with three clasps	
Reason for Discharge:	Grape shot wound to the left arm	
Character:	Good	
Trade or Occupation:	Labourer	
Can Sign Name:	Yes	
Height:	5' 8¾"	
Hair Colour:	Sandy	
Eyes:	Blue	
Complexion:	Fresh	
Intends to Reside:	Newmarket on Fergus Co. Clare	

McMAHON	John, private
	47th Foot
Surname Variant	MAHON
29 Jan 1856	Discharged the Service Chatham
	Pension paid Limerick
	9d. per diem
19 Aug 1859	Arrived per *'Sultana'*
1863	a J McMahon residing Fremantle area
1865	Pension paid Western Australia
1866	Residing Northam
1875	Pension increased to 1/3d. per diem for service in the Enrolled Force
June 1897	Residing Northam
1892	Correspondence with W.O. [the "A31"]
Feb 1900	Attended fete at Fremantle Oval
1909	Attended Veteran's Dinner
May 1915	a John Mahon's [47th Foot] address care of Police Station Northam
1923	Died aged 87
Service and Personal Details:	
Place of Birth:	Grain Tipperary Co. Limerick
Age on Enlistment:	19 years
Period of Service:	1852 — 1855
Age on Discharge:	22 years

Length of Service:	3 years 12 days
Foreign Service:	Malta &
	Turkey & Crimea 1 year
Medal Entitlement:	Crimea with three clasps
Reason for Discharge:	Deep Ulcer on left calf and gun shot wound to right shoulder received at Inkerman
Character:	Good
Trade or Occupation:	Labourer
Can Sign Name:	Yes
Height:	5' 6¾"
Hair Colour:	Red
Eyes:	Hazel
Complexion:	Fresh
Intends to Reside:	Limerick

McMAHON Patrick, gunner

	RA 18th Brigade
Previous Regiment	HEIC Artillery
22 Dec 1868	Discharged the Service Woolwich
	Pension paid Ennis
	1/- per diem
19 Feb 1874	Arrived per *'Naval Brigade'*
1878	Pension increased to 1/2d. per diem for service in the Enrolled Force

Service and Personal Details:

Place of Birth:	Ennis Co. Clare
Age on Enlistment:	21 years
Period of Service:	1849 — 1868
Age on Discharge:	40 years 8 months
Length of Service:	21 years 248 days
Foreign Service:	India 19 years 59 days
Reason for Discharge:	Own Request having completed 21 yeas
Character:	Very Good
Trade or Occupation:	Labourer
Can Sign Name:	X his mark on discharge
Height:	5' 8¾"
Hair Colour:	Sandy
Eyes:	Blue
Complexion:	Fresh
Remarks:	Elected English [British Army] Pension Rules
Intends to Reside:	nr. Ennis Ireland

McMAHON Timothy, private

	16th Foot
1 June 1853	Discharged the Service Castlebar
12 July 1853	Admitted to Out-Pension
	Pension paid Leeds
	6d. per diem
24 May 1855	Arrived per *'Stag'*
Jan 1857	Contributed 1/- to the Florence Nightingale Fund
21 June 1861	Died aged 41 Geraldton

Service and Personal Details:		
Place of Birth:	Kilrush Co. Clare	
Age on Enlistment:	21 years	
Period of Service:	1839 — 1853	
Age on Discharge:	35 years 3 months	
Length of Service:	14 years 96 days	
Foreign Service:	East Indies	1 year 176 days
Reason for Discharge:	Varicose Veins	
Character:	Very Good	
Trade or Occupation:	Labourer	
Can Sign Name:	X his mark on discharge	
Height:	5' 8¼"	
Hair Colour:	Black	
Eyes:	Grey	
Complexion:	Fresh	
Intends to Reside:	Leeds Yorkshire	

McMEEKUM	Alexander, private [2742] 77th Foot
Surname Variants	McMEEKIN; McMEEKAN; McMEEKLUM; McMECHIN
30 Oct 1864	Discharged the Service Pension paid Ballymena 8d. per diem
28 Dec 1863	Arrived per *'Lord Dalhousie'* Pension increased to 1/2d per diem
Aug 1881	Assigned North Fremantle Lot P55 which was originally allocated to Robert Hulme
12 Oct 1883	Granted Fee Simple North Fremantle Lot P55
Dec 1888	Assaulted his wife with a broom, and was "bound to keep the peace for three months"
June 1897	Stationed at Perth
1907	Died — buried in the Presbyterian section of Karrakatta Cemetery

Service and Personal Details:	
Place of Birth:	Connor Ballymena Co. Antrim
Age on Enlistment:	17 years 11 months
Period of Service:	1853 — 1855
Age on Discharge:	19 years
Length of Service:	1 year 232 days
Foreign Service:	none annotated
Medal Entitlement:	Crimea with three clasps; Turkish Crimean [from Crimean Medal Rolls]
Reason for Discharge:	Unfit for further service
Character:	Good
Trade or Occupation:	Weaver
Can Sign Name:	X his mark on Attestation
Height:	5' 6¾"
Hair Colour:	Brown
Eyes:	Grey
Complexion:	Fresh

Distinguishing Marks:	Scar on left cheek
Intends to Reside:	Ballymena Co. Antrim

McMILLEN	John, private 51st Foot
Surname Variant	McMILLAN
13 Jan 1857	Discharged the Service Chatham Pension paid 1st Belfast Pension District 8d. per diem
15 Aug 1865	Arrived per *'Racehorse'* Assigned Northam Loc P1
1876	Applied for £15 improvement grant
1878	Pension increased to 11½d. per diem for service in the Enrolled Force
6 June 1879	Granted Northam Loc P1
Sept 1882	Sold his land [Northam Suburban Lot P1] and household furniture by public auction
1891	Died found drowned near Pensioner Depot
Service and Personal Details:	
Place of Birth:	Greyabbey Co. Down
Age on Enlistment:	18 years
Period of Service:	1836 — 1857
Age on Discharge:	38 years
Length of Service:	20 years 135 days
Foreign Service:	Van Deiman's Land 7 years 7 months East Indies 7 years 5 months
Reason for Discharge:	Worn out from long service
Character:	Good
Trade or Occupation:	Labourer
Can Sign Name:	Yes
Height:	5' 7"
Hair Colour:	Brown
Eyes:	Grey
Complexion:	Fresh
Intends to Reside:	Newtown Co. Down

McMULLEN	David, gunner RA — Coastal Brigade
Surname Variant	McMULLAN; McMULLIN
12 June 1861	Discharged the Service Irish Fort
16 July 1861	Admitted to Out-Pension Pension paid Londonderry 1/2d. per diem
22 Dec 1865	Arrived per *'Vimiera'*
no date	Assigned Perth Military Pensioner Lot 125
1874	Applied for £15 Improvement Grant
1878	Pension increased to 1/7½d. per diem for service in the Enrolled Force
Apr 1881	Application for Title to Perth Lot 125/Y
1891	Died buried East Perth Pioneer Cemetery
Service and Personal Details:	
Place of Birth:	Belfast Co. Antrim
Age on Enlistment:	18 years

Period of Service:	1838 — 1861
Age on Discharge:	41 years 2 months
Length of Service:	23 years ?62 days
Foreign Service:	Newfoundland 6 years 1 month
Medal Entitlement:	Long Service and Good Conduct with gratuity
Reason for Discharge:	Having completed service for pension
Character:	Exemplary
Trade or Occupation:	Labourer
Can Sign Name:	Yes
Height:	5' 10"
Hair Colour:	Dark Brown
Eyes:	Blue
Complexion:	Swarthy
Intends to Reside:	City of Londonderry

McMULLIN Thomas, gunner and driver
RA 4th Battalion

Surname Variants	McMULLAN; McMULLEN
11 Apr 1848	Discharged the Service Woolwich Pension paid Woolwich 1/- per diem
1 June 1850	Arrived per *'Scindian'* Allocated land at Freshwater Bay
Jan 1857	Contributed 2/- to the Florence Nightingale Fund
Feb 1858	Application for Title Freshwater Bay Loc P229 and P252 [Swan Location 252] Also held Title to Freshwater Bay Locs P228 and P230 [Title Deed Nos 1111; 1293; 133]
1859	On purchase Crown Grant for P230 issued to Thomas McMullen
1865	Pension paid Perth Western Australia
1886	prior to this date a Thomas McMullen was the holder of the Crown Grant Swan Location P260. In 1886 he contracted to sell this Grant to a James Glyde [Swan Loc P60 was originally granted to William Finlay — Feb 1858]
Apr 1891	Died aged 83 Buried East Perth Cemetery

Service and Personal Details:

Place of Birth:	Portsmouth Hampshire	
Age on Enlistment:	18 years	
Period of Service:	1826 — 1848	
Age on Discharge:	39 years 9 months	
Length of Service:	21 years 263 days	
Foreign Service:	Corfu	6 years 11 months
	Canada	6 years 1 month
Reason for Discharge:	Chronic Rheumatism	
Character:	Exemplary	
Trade or Occupation:	Weaver	
Can Sign Name:	Yes	
Height:	5' 9½"	
Hair Colour:	Light Brown	

Eyes:	Grey
Complexion:	Brown

McNAMARA	James, private 84th Foot
11 Aug 1846	Discharged the Service Chatham Pension paid Limerick 11d. per diem
1853	Pension paid Ennis
6 Apr 1854	Arrived per *'Sea Park'*
1875	Pension paid Western Australia
1883	Died Will dated 1872 – bequeaths No 19 Grant and buildings in the military Village North Fremantle obtained by me from Her Majesty's Government for past good and faithful service to my dear wife

Service and Personal Details:		
Place of Birth:	St Johns Waterford	
Age on Enlistment:	17 years	
Period of Service:	1825 — 1846	
Age on Discharge:	40 years	
Length of Service:	19 years 36 days [reckoned]	
Foreign Service:	West Indies	10 years 54 days
	East Indies	3 years 124 days
Reason for Discharge:	Chronic Rheumatism and General Debility	
Character:	Very Good	
Trade or Occupation:	Labourer	
Can Sign Name:	X his mark on discharge	
Height:	5' 5½"	
Hair Colour:	Grey	
Eyes:	Grey	
Complexion:	Fair	
Intends to Reside:	Limerick Co. Limerick	

McNAMARA	James, private EIC 1st Madras Fusiliers Out Pension No 798
14 Dec 1860	Admitted to Out-pension 1/- per diem
22 Dec 1866	Arrived per *'Corona'*
1875	Pension paid New Zealand

Service and Personal Details:	
Place of Birth:	Limerick
Trade or Occupation:	Labourer
Where Enlisted:	London
Age on Discharge:	37 years
Length of Service:	21 years
Reason for Discharge:	Own request; time expired
Character:	Good
Height:	5' 7" or 5' 5½"
Complexion:	Fair or Fresh

Eye Colour:	Grey
Hair Colour:	Light Brown or Brown
Intends to Reside:	Limerick

McNAMARA

	John, private 66th Foot
11 Feb 1862	Discharged the Service Colchester Pension paid Ennis 1/- per diem
22 Dec 1865	Arrived per *'Vimiera'*
1878	Pension increased to 1/5d. per diem for service in the Enrolled Force
9 Aug 1883	Assigned Perth Pensioner Lot 271/Y
1884	Granted Fee Simple Pensioner Lot 271/Y
1889	Charged with assaulting his wife with a wooden lath [sic]
1893	Died

Service and Personal Details:

Place of Birth:	Quin Co. Clare	
Age on Enlistment:	19 years	
Period of Service:	1840 — 1862	
Age on Discharge:	40 years 1 month	
Length of Service:	21 years 32 days	
Foreign Service:	Gibraltar	4 years 1 month
	West Indies	3 years 5 months
	Canada	3 years 4 months
	East Indies	2 years 9 months
Reason for Discharge:	Own Request having completed 21 years service	
Character:	Very Good	
Trade or Occupation:	Labourer	
Can Sign Name:	Yes	
Height:	5' 8½"	
Hair Colour:	Fair	
Eyes:	Grey	
Complexion:	Fresh	
Distinguishing Marks:	Slight mark on corner of left eyebrow	
Intends to Reside:	Ennis Co. Clare	

McNEE

	Malcolm, Serjeant EIC Bengal Horse Artillery Out Pension No 612
15 Aug 1855	Admitted to Out-pension Pension paid Dundee "2/- per diem of which a 1/- is paid from the Lord Clive Pension Fund"
1861	Pension paid Edinburgh
1862	Woolwich
31 Dec 1862	Arrived per *'York'*
Feb 1864	ptve M McNee Pensioner Force at Fremantle contributed to the Greenough Fire Relief Fund
1864	Purchased Perth Town Lot W14 for £6
1878	Residing Perth

1884	McNee, Malcolm. Pensioner — Application for a Free Grant of land
Oct 1884	Assigned Albany Sub 20X
Nov 1884	Application for Title to Albany Sub 20X
1897	Residing Perth
Aug 1897	Died aged 83
	Buried East Perth Pioneer Cemetery

Service and Personal Details:

Where Born:	Greenock Scotland or Renfrew North Britain
Trade or Occupation:	Wood Turner
Where Enlisted:	Westminster
Presidency:	Bengal
Length of Service:	21 years 7 months
Age on Discharge:	41 or 42 [depending on record source]
Reason for Discharge:	Own Request — time expired
Medal Entitlement:	Afghan — Clasp for Cabool [sic]
Character:	Good
Remarks:	Wounded in Afghanistan 1841 — 1842
Height:	5' 11"
Complexion:	Fresh
Eye Colour:	Grey
Hair Colour:	Brown
Intends to Reside:	2nd Glasgow Division

McNIECE	John, private
	8th Foot
Previous Regiment	15th Foot
Surname Variants	McNEECE; McNEICE
31 Aug 1858	Discharged the Service
	Pension paid Sligo
	1/-½d. per diem
1862	Pension paid Bermuda
15 Feb 1863	Arrived per *'Merchantman'* [1]
	Assigned land Greenough
1874	Pension increased to 1/3d. per diem
1874	Title to Greenough Locs G31 and G32 confirmed
12 July 1892	Died

Service and Personal Details:

Place of Birth:	St Johns Sligo	
Age on Enlistment:	18 years	
Period of Service:	1836 — 1858	
Age on Discharge:	40 years [or 41 years depending on record]	
Length of Service:	21 years 280 days [or 22 years 6 months]	
Foreign Service:	North America	4 years 153 days
	East Indies	9 years 86 days
Medal Entitlement:	Indian Mutiny	
Reason for Discharge:	Quite worn out and useless	
Character:	Very Good	
Trade or Occupation:	Shoemaker	
Can Sign Name:	X his mark on discharge	
Height:	5' 8"	
Hair Colour:	Brown	

Eyes:	Blue	
Complexion:	Fresh	
McPHERSON	Alexander, private	
	71st Foot	
Previous Regiment	93rd Foot	
2 Dec 1856	Discharged the Service Chatham	
	Pension paid Inverness	
	7d. per diem	
1857	Pension paid 1st East London Pension District	
1857	Pension paid Woolwich	
29 Jan 1862	Arrived per *'Lincelles'*	
Oct 1864	To South Australia from Fremantle per '*Sea Ripple*' with wife	
1875	Pension paid Adelaide South Australia	
Service and Personal Details:		
Place of Birth:	Inverness Inverness-shire	
Age on Enlistment:	16 years 6 months	
Period of Service:	1841 — 1856	
Age on Discharge:	32 years 2 months	
Length of Service:	14 years 19 days	
Foreign Service:	East Indies	11 years 11 months
	Crimea	1 year 6 months
	Malta	1 month
Medal Entitlement:	Crimea	
Reason for Discharge:	Unfit for further service	
Character:	Very Good	
Trade or Occupation:	Labourer	
Can Sign Name:	Yes	
Height:	5' 6"	
Hair Colour:	Dark Brown	
Eyes:	Dark Grey	
Complexion:	Fresh	
McPHIE	John, private	
	75th Foot	
Surname Variant	McPHEE	
13 Aug 1845	Discharged the Service Chatham	
	Pension paid Stirling	
	1/- per diem	
1846	Pension paid Perth Scotland	
1849	Dundee	
2 Aug 1852	Arrived per *'William Jardine'*	
1853	Employed in Convict Service	
1854	Pension paid Melbourne	
14 Aug 1858	Died	
Service and Personal Details:		
Place of Birth:	Kilmela Argyllshire	
Age on Enlistment:	20 years	
Period of Service:	1824 — 1845	
Age on Discharge:	41 years	
Length of Service:	21 years 171 days	
Foreign Service:	Cape of Good Hope	13 years

Reason for Discharge:	Unfit for further service due to Rheumatism
Character:	Good
Trade or Occupation:	Labourer
Can Sign Name:	X his mark on discharge
Height:	5' 7¼"
Hair Colour:	Dark
Eyes:	Dark
Complexion:	Pale
Intends to Reside:	Stirling

McQUADE	Peter, Serjeant 72nd Foot
28 Aug 1849	Discharged the Service Chatham Pension paid 1st Portsmouth Pension District 1/4d. per diem
19 Aug 1853	Arrived per *'Robert Small'*
1854	Employed by Commissariat at York for taking charge of Public Buildings. Paid 1/- per diem but still on of the Roll of the Enrolled Pensioner
Guard Force	
Jan 1857	Contributed 6/- to the Florence Nightingale Fund
Dec 1857	Assigned York Lot P17
May 1863	Application for Title for York Lot P17
1864	Serjeant P McQuade Pensioner Force at York contributed to the Greenough Fire Relief Fund
1873	Pension increased to 2/- per diem for 18 years service and from the date of ceasing to draw pay in the Enrolled Force
1879	Correspondence with W.O.
Oct 1886	Died

Service and Personal Details:	
Place of Birth:	St Cuthberts Edinburgh Midlothian
Age on Enlistment:	17 years
Period of Service:	1826 — 1849
Age on Discharge:	40 years 6 months
Length of Service:	22 years 47 days [reckoned]
Foreign Service:	Cape of Good Hope 11 years 11 months
Reason for Discharge:	Rheumatic Pains of the back and shoulders
Character:	Good
Trade or Occupation:	Mason
Can Sign Name:	Yes
Height:	5' 8"
Hair Colour:	Dark
Eyes:	Hazel
Complexion:	Fresh
Remarks:	Stationed Fermoy 1844
Intends to Reside:	Portsmouth

McSHERRY	Edward, private 50th Foot
Surname Variant	McCHERRY

14 Sept 1847	Discharged the Service Chatham
	Pension paid 1st Belfast Pension District
	8d. per diem
1855	Pension paid 1st Glasgow Pension District
1856	1st Belfast Pension District
29 July 1862	Arrived per *'Lincelles'*
1864	Pension paid South Australia from Fremantle
1873	W.O. correspondence

Service and Personal Details:

Place of Birth:	? Tentona Co. Tyrone
Age on Enlistment:	18 years 2 months
Period of Service:	1841 — 1846
Age on Discharge:	27 years
Length of Service:	4 years 361 days
Foreign Service:	East Indies 4 years 147 days
Medal Entitlement:	Punniar; Sutlej with 3 clasps
Reason for Discharge:	Wounded in action at Ferozeshar 1845
Character:	Bad
Trade or Occupation:	Joiner
Can Sign Name:	X his mark on discharge
Height:	5' 7¼"
Hair Colour:	Dark
Eyes:	Grey
Complexion:	Dark
Intends to Reside:	London

MACK Michael, private
19th Foot

11 Nov 1856	Discharged the Service Chatham
	Pension paid Kilkenny
	8d. per diem
22 Dec 1866	Arrived per *'Corona'*
1874	Assigned Perth Military Pensioner Lot 146
1877	Applied for £15 improvement grant for his cottage on Perth Town Lot 146/Y
1878	Pension increased to 1/1½d. for service in the Enrolled Force
no date	W.O. Correspondence stating that man had re-entered the Enrolled Force and that the increase granted by the Chelsea Commissioners had been suspended.
Apr 1881	Application for Title to Perth Lot 146/Y
1881	Pension increased to 1/2d. per diem for further service in the Enrolled Force
July 1885	On duty at the Magazine rear of the Barracks
1894	Died – buried East Perth Cemetery

Service and Personal Details:

Place of Birth:	Kells Co. Kilkenny
Age on Enlistment:	20 years
Period of Service:	1854 — 1856
Age on Discharge:	30 years or 21 years 10 months
Length of Service:	1 year 316 days

Foreign Service:	Crimea	1 year 49 days
Medal Entitlement:	Crimea	
Reason for Discharge:	Musket ball wound to the left shoulder	
Character:	Good	
Trade or Occupation:	Labourer	
Can Sign Name:	Yes	
Height:	5' 6½"	
Hair Colour:	Dark Brown	
Eyes:	Grey	
Complexion:	Fresh	
Intends to Reside:	Kilkenny	

MACKEY	Patrick, private	
	77th Foot	
Surname Variants	MACKAY; McKAY; McKEY; MACKIE	
24 Dec 1850	Discharged the Service Chatham	
	Pension paid Londonderry	
	1/- per diem	
30 Apr 1853	Arrived per *'Pyrenees'* [2]	
Service and Personal Details:		
Place of Birth:	Ballymurphy Co. Antrim	
Age on Enlistment:	16 years	
Period of Service:	1827 — 1850	
Age on Discharge:	39 years or 31 years	
Length of Service:	20 years 299 days	
Foreign Service:	Jamaica	9 years 5 months
	Mediterranean	5 years 4 months
	North America	2 years 2 months
Reason for Discharge:	Chronic Rheumatism	
Character:	Good	
Trade or Occupation:	Labourer	
Can Sign Name:	Yes	
Height:	5' 8"	
Hair Colour:	Brown	
Eyes:	Brown	
Complexion:	Fair	
Intends to Reside:	Newport Monmouthshire but decided on Port Stewart Co. Derry	

MAGEE	Robert, Serjeant
	RA 18th Brigade
Previous Regiment	HEIC Artillery
Surname Variant	MACGEE
29 Aug 1865	Discharged the Service Sheerness
	Pension paid 2nd Glasgow Pension District
	2/- per diem
1865	Pension paid 1st Belfast Pension District
4 July 1866	Arrived per *'Belgravia'*
1867	To South Australia from Perth West Australia
1868	Pension paid South Australia
1870	Auckland New Zealand

Service and Personal Details:	
Place of Birth:	Hillsborough Co. Down
Age on Attestation:	20 years
Period of Service:	1845 — 1865
Age on Discharge:	40 years
Length of Service:	22 years 7 days or 21 years 61 days
Foreign Service:	India 20 years 216 days
Medal Entitlement:	Persia; and Indian Mutiny with clasp
Reason for Discharge:	Own Request having served 21 years
Character:	Very Good
Trade or Occupation:	Labourer
Can Sign Name:	Yes
Height:	5' 9"
Hair Colour:	Brown
Eyes:	Grey
Complexion:	Bronzed
Remarks:	Elected Indian Pension Rules
Intends to Reside:	Glasgow

MAGUIRE	Edward, private
	27th Foot
Surname Variant	McGUIRE
13 Mar 1852	Discharged the Service Dublin
6 Apr 1852	Admitted to Out-Pension
	Pension paid Omagh
	1/- per diem
2 Apr 1856	Arrived per *'William Hammond'*
Jan 1857	Contributed 1/- to the Florence Nightingale Fund
1859	'Not appeared for several months'
1865	Pension paid Perth Western Australia

Service and Personal Details:	
Place of Birth:	Ana [sic] Co. Cavan
Age on Attestation:	18 years 6 months
Period of Service:	1830 — 1852
Age on Discharge:	39 years
Length of Service:	21 years 86 days
Foreign Service:	Cape of Good Hope 12 years 229 days
Medal Entitlement:	Good Conduct and Long Service; Kaffir War 1846/47
Reason for Discharge:	Chronic Catarrh and Worn Out
Character:	Good
Trade or Occupation:	Labourer
Can Sign Name:	Yes
Height:	5' 6¾"
Hair Colour:	Grey
Eyes:	Grey
Complexion:	Fresh
Intends to Reside:	New Town Stewart Co. Tyrone

MAGUIRE	Patrick, private
	8th Foot
Surname Variants	MACGUIRE; McGUIRE

15 Nov 1859	Discharged the Service Chatham
1861	Pension paid 2nd West London Pension District 1/- per diem
1863	Pension paid 2nd West London Pension District
28 Dec 1863	Arrived per *'Lord Dalhousie'*

Service and Personal Details:

Place of Birth:	Enniskeen Cavan	
Age on Attestation:	18 years	
Period of Service:	1842 — 1859	
Age on Discharge:	35 years 5 months	
Length of Service:	17 years 134 days	
Foreign Service:	East Indies	12 years 259 days
Medal Entitlement:	Indian Mutiny	
Reason for Discharge:	Wounded left hip at the storming of Delhi	
Character:	Good	
Trade or Occupation:	Labourer	
Can Sign Name:	Yes	
Height:	5' 8½"	
Hair Colour:	Fair	
Eyes:	Grey	
Complexion:	Fresh	
Intends to Reside:	Chatham	

MAHER Dennis [Danniel], Corporal
16th Foot

15 May 1844	Discharged the Service Dublin
16 July 1844	Admitted to Out-Pension Pension paid 1st Liverpool Pension District 11d. per diem
1847	Pension paid 1st Portsmouth Pension District
1848	Pension paid Tullamore
1851	Tilbury
21 May 1851	To arrive per *'Mermaid'*
1855	Pension paid Tullamore

Service and Personal Details:

Place of Birth:	St Marys Co. Kilkenny	
Age on Attestation:	18 years	
Period of Service:	1825 — 1844	
Age on Discharge:	36 years 9 months	
Length of Service:	18 years 274 days	
Foreign Service:	East Indies	12 years 5 months
Reason for Discharge:	Chronic Rheumatism and Varicose Veins	
Character:	Good	
Trade or Occupation:	Labourer	
Can Sign Name:	Yes	
Height:	5' 9"	
Hair Colour:	Brown	
Eyes:	Grey	
Complexion:	Fresh	
Remarks:	Stationed Chinsurah 1833	
Intends to Reside:	Liverpool	

MAHER	Thomas, private
	35th Foot
12 Oct 1849	Discharged the Service Mullingar
11 Dec 1849	Admitted to Out-Pension
	Pension paid Birr
	6d. per diem
1851	Pension paid Kilkenny
1853	On EPG draft for W.A. from Kilkenny
31 Aug 1853	Arrived per *'Phoebe Dunbar'*
1853	Charged with military offence
1856	On Rottnest detachment
Jan 1857	Contributed 2/- to the Florence Nightingale Fund
1857	To South Australia from Western Australia
1858	Pension paid Victoria
1876	Victoria
1879	Correspondence with W.O. [the "A31"]
Mar 1886	Will drawn up
23 Mar 1886	Died
1887	Grant of Probate

Service and Personal Details:

Place of Birth:	Loughmo Co. Tipperary	
Age on Enlistment:	18 years	
Period of Service:	1835—1849	
Age on Discharge:	32 years 8 months	
Length of Service:	14 years 249 days	
Foreign Service:	Mauritius	9 years 97 days
Reason for Discharge:	Chronic Catarrh	
Character:	Good	
Trade or Occupation:	Labourer	
Can Sign Name:	X his mark on discharge	
Height:	5' 7"	
Hair Colour:	Light Brown	
Eyes:	Grey	
Complexion:	Fresh	
Intends to Reside:	Church Str., Templemore Co. Tipperary	

MAHER	Thomas, Serjeant
	94th Foot
Previous Regiment	10th Foot [enlisted as Boy then Drummer]
Surname Variant	MAGHER
12 May 1868	Discharged the Service Dover
	Pension paid 1st West London Pension District
	1/4½d. per diem
23 Apr 1873	Discharged after serving 5 years with the Royal Westminster Light Infantry Regiment of Militia occupation given as Musician
19 Feb 1874	Arrived per *'Naval Brigade'*
1881	Pension increased to 1/7d. per diem for service in the Enrolled Force
Mar 1881	Perth Lot 33/H relinquished by permission
Aug 1881	Assigned Perth Railway Block 124/V in lieu

Oct 1884	Granted Fee Simple for Perth Railway Block 124/V
1902	Died aged 72

Service and Personal Details:

Place of Birth:	Zante Ionian Isles
Age on Attestation:	13 years
Period of Service:	1842 — 1868
Age on Discharge:	39 years
Length of Service:	21 years 19 days
Foreign Service:	East Indies 22 years 43 days
Medal Entitlement:	Good Conduct and Long Service with gratuity; Sutlej; Punjaub with 2 clasps; Indian Mutiny with 2 clasps
Reason for Discharge:	Own Request having served over 21 years
Character:	Very Good
Trade or Occupation:	Labourer
Can Sign Name:	Yes
Height:	5' 8¾"
Hair Colour:	Dark Brown
Eyes:	Grey
Complexion:	Dark
Intends to Reside:	Hammersmith Middlesex

MAHONY	Anthony, private EIC 1st European Regiment of Fusiliers
Surname Variant	MAHONEY
Feb 1854	Discharged the Service
Mar 1861	A discharged soldier from the East India Company's service sentenced to 6 months imprisonment
1861	Anthony Mahony, a discharged soldier from the East India Company's Service was brought up before the Magistrate for the 6th time, and charged with being drunk and using obscene language in Hay Street. As Mahoney had no apparent means of obtaining an honest living, and it being also proven on the evidence of several policeman that he was leading an idle and disorderly life, he was sentenced to three months' imprisonment as a vagrant.
1875	Was charged by PC Earle of being drunk and incapable in Murray Street Anthony Mahoney was dismissed with a caution
1880	Charged with throwing a stone through a church window during the divine worship

Service and Personal Details:

Place of Birth:	Killarney Co. Kerry
Trade or Occupation:	Slater and plasterer
Presidency:	Bombay
Age on Discharge:	24 years
Length of Service:	7 years
Reason for Discharge:	Chronic Rheumatism

Character:	Good	
Height:	5' 6"	
Complexion:	Fresh	
Eye Colour:	Grey	
Hair Colour:	Dark Brown	
MAHONY	James, private EIC	
	1st European Fusiliers	
Surname Variant	MALONEY	
	Out Pension No 769	
17 Oct 1860	Admitted to Out-pension	
	Pension paid Tralee	
	1/- per diem	
28 Dec 1863	Arrived per *'Lord Dalhousie'* as a Convict Guard	
1865	To Adelaide from Perth Western Australia	
Service and Personal Details:		
Place of Birth:	Milltown Co. Kerry	
Trade or Occupation:	Servant	
Age on Discharge:	37 years	
Length of Service:	19 years 5 months	
Reason for Discharge:	Time expired	
Height:	5' 4½"	
Complexion:	Fresh	
Eye Colour:	Blue	
Hair Colour:	Dark Brown	
Intends to Reside:	Tralee	
MAINS	John, private	
	98th Foot	
Previous Regiment	9th Foot	
26 Aug 1851	Discharged the Service Chatham	
	Pension paid 2nd Glasgow Pension District	
	1/- per diem	
24 May 1855	Arrived per *'Stag'*	
1856	Pension paid Adelaide	
1868	Pension to be paid Victoria	
1869	Move cancelled	
1969	Pension paid 2nd Glasgow Pension District	
1872	Admitted as an In-Pensioner at Chelsea Hospital	
1 Mar 1875	Died	
Service and Personal Details:		
Place of Birth:	Renfrewshire Scotland	
Age on Attestation:	20 years 9 months	
Period of Service:	1829 — 1851	
Age on Discharge:	42 years 5 months	
Length of Service:	20 years 275 days	
Foreign Service:	Mauritius	2 years 195 days
	East Indies	14 years 305 days
Medal Entitlement:	Sutlej with 3 clasps	
Reason for Discharge:	Chronic Rheumatism and worn out	
Character:	Good	
Trade or Occupation:	Bookbinder	

Can Sign Name:	Yes
Height:	5' 10"
Hair Colour:	Grey
Eyes:	Grey
Complexion:	Pale
Intends to Reside:	Greenock Renfrew

MALLET	Richard, gunner RA 11th Battalion
Surname Variant	MALLETT
10 July 1855	Discharged the Service Woolwich Pension paid 2nd Plymouth Pension District 8d. per diem
10 Sept 1856	Arrived per *'Runnymede'*
1857	Pension paid Adelaide
1857	Melbourne

Service and Personal Details:

Place of Birth:	Liskeard Cornwall
Age on Attestation:	21 years 6 months
Period of Service:	1848 — 1855
Age on Discharge:	28 years 5 months
Length of Service:	6 years 308 days
Foreign Service:	Turkey & Crimea 11 months
Medal Entitlement:	Crimea with clasp
Reason for Discharge:	Wound to right wrist
Character:	Very Good
Trade or Occupation:	Miner
Can Sign Name:	X his mark on discharge
Height:	5' 8½"
Hair Colour:	Brown
Eyes:	Grey
Complexion:	Sallow

MALLEY	Thomas, private 15th Foot
1858	Transferred to Army Hospital Corps
8 Sept 1868	Discharged the Service Pension paid Galway 9d. per diem
1873	Pension paid Greenwich
19 Feb 1874	Arrived per *'Naval Brigade'*
1875	"In prison" Enrolled Pensioner convicted by District Court Martial at Perth W.A. of being drunk on duty and sent to prison for 168 days during which half pension suspended the other half to wife
1881	Assigned Fremantle Pensioner Allotment
1881	Pension increased to 11d. per diem for 4 years served in Western Australia
1884	Granted Fremantle Lot 775

Service and Personal Details:

Place of Birth:	Galway Co. Galway	
Age on Attestation:	17 years 10 months	
Period of Service:	1846 — 1868	
Age on Discharge:	39 years 5 months	
Length of Service:	21 years 45 days	
Foreign Service:	Ceylon	5 years 1 month
	Gibraltar	11 months
	North America	6 years 3 months
	Bermuda	3 months
Reason for Discharge:	Own Request having served 21 years	
Character:	Good	
Trade or Occupation:	Labourer	
Can Sign Name:	Yes	
Height:	5' 6½"	
Hair Colour:	Light Brown	
Eyes:	Blue	
Complexion:	Fresh	
Intends to Reside:	Galway Ireland	

MALLOY see — MULLOY Patrick. private
64th Foot

MALONE Edmond [Edward], private
88th Foot

11 Dec 1855	Discharged the Service Chatham	
	Pension paid Sligo	
	8d. per diem	
1857	Pension paid Liverpool	
8 June 1858	Arrived per *'Lord Raglan'*	
1860	To South Australia from Fremantle W.A.	
1883	W.O. correspondence re. "Examination forms to Adelaide"	
1884	Pension increased to 1/- per diem	

Service and Personal Details:

Place of Birth:	Kilkevin Nock Co. Clare	
Age on Attestation:	17 years	
Period of Service:	1844 — 1855	
Age on Discharge:	34 years [sic]	
Length of Service:	10 years 139 days	
Foreign Service:	West Indies	8 years 11 months
	North America	? 8 years 1 month
	Turkey & Crimea	[no time given]
Medal Entitlement:	Crimea	
Reason for Discharge:	Disabled by wounds to hand and fingers whilst on duty in the trenches	
Character:	Good	
Trade or Occupation:	Labourer	
Can Sign Name:	X his mark on Attestation	
Height:	5' 8"	
Hair Colour:	Light Brown	

Eyes: Grey
Complexion: Fresh
Intends to Reside: Sligo

MANGAN Andrew, Serjeant EIC
Bengal European Infantry
Out Pension No 407
10 July 1847 Admitted to Out-pension
Pension paid 1st East London Pension District
1/- per diem
18 Oct 1851 Arrived per *'Minden'*
1852 "Pension not drawn since 1st Nov 1852"
Left Colony without transfer
1858 Pension paid Melbourne
1875 Off Roll — "Not Appeared"

Service and Personal Details:
Where Born: Kildare
Trade or Occupation: Labourer
Age on Enlistment: 19 years
Date Enlisted: 30th June 1829
Where Enlisted: Dublin
Service Period: Unlimited
Embarked India: per *'William Fairlee'* 1st Jan 1830
Presidency: Bengal
Age on Discharge: 33 years
Length of Service: 14 years 1 month
Reason for Discharge: Affection of the liver
Character: Good

Height: 5' 5"
Complexion: Fresh
Visage: Oval
Eye Colour: Grey
Hair Colour: Brown
Remarks: Scar on forehead

Married: 1834 Jane Tyrell Dinapore India
Children: Catherine b. *c*1834 India
Ellen bp. 1836 Agra

Marriage Details: Bengal Ecclesiastical Returns N1/39/21
24th Jan 1834 Dinapore
Andrew Mangan, bachelor private HC Eur. Regiment and Jane Tyrell, widow, of Dinapore were married by banns by me and with the consent of the Commanding Officer.
Duly signed and attested — Thomas W Stevens

MANNING John, Corporal
39th Foot
26 June 1846 Discharged the Service Chatham
Pension paid Brighton
1/1½d. per diem
1847 Pension paid Cork
31 Aug 1853 Arrived per *'Phoebe Dunbar'*
1863 Pension paid Melbourne

Service and Personal Details:	
Place of Birth:	St Anne Shandon Cork
Age on Attestation:	18 years
Period of Service:	1825 — 1845
Age on Discharge:	39 years
Length of Service:	20 years 101 days
Foreign Service:	New South Wales 5 years
	East Indies ?11 years
Reason for Discharge:	Rheumatism and Worn out from long service
Character:	Generally Good
Trade or Occupation:	Shoemaker
Can Sign Name:	Yes
Height:	5' 7½"
Hair Colour:	Dark Brown
Eyes:	Grey
Complexion:	Dark
Intends to Reside:	Cork but decided on East Grinstead Surrey

MANNING

	Michael, gunner EIC
	Bengal Artillery
	Out Pension No 454
1847	Embarked UK per *'Alfred'*
25 May 1847	Admitted to Out-pension
	1/- per diem
1847	Pension paid 2nd North London Pension District
18 Oct 1851	Arrived per *'Minden'*
1852	Employed by Convict Establishment
1856	On military charge after 3 years duty at Champion Bay
1856	Dismissed from Enrolled Pensioner Force for misconduct
1856	To South Australia from Western Australia
1857	Pension paid Victoria
1866	Victoria

Service and Personal Details:	
Where Born:	Surrey
Trade or Occupation:	Bricklayer
Where Enlisted:	London
Presidency:	Bengal
Length of Service:	21 years 8 months
Age on Discharge:	40 years
Reason for Discharge:	Old and worn out from length of service
Character:	Indifferent in consequence of drinking
Height:	5' 5¼"
Complexion:	Fresh
Visage:	Oval
Eye Colour:	Grey
Hair Colour:	Dark Brown

MANNING

	Thomas, private
	68th Foot
24 May 1851	Discharged the Service Birr

2 Sept 1851	Admitted to Out-Pension Pension paid 1st Cork Pension District 6d. per diem
19 Aug 1853	Arrived per *'Robert Small'*
1855	Employed by Convict Establishment
23 Dec 1856	Died

Service and Personal Details:

Place of Birth:	Upper Shannon Co. Cork
Age on Attestation:	18 years
Period of Service:	1837 — 1851
Age on Discharge:	31 years 9 months
Length of Service:	13 years 270 days
Foreign Service:	Jamaica 2 years 5 months Canada 2 years 10 months
Reason for Discharge:	Scrofulous Abscess situated on left side of neck
Character:	Good
Trade or Occupation:	Tailor
Can Sign Name:	X his mark on discharge
Height:	5' 8¾"
Hair Colour:	Brown
Eyes:	Blue
Complexion:	Fair
Intends to Reside:	Cork

MANSBRIDGE	William Henry, Serjeant 3rd Madras European Regiment for the period of 2 years 8 months
65th Foot	
13 Aug 1860	Transferred to the 2nd/14th Foot
9 Apr 1860	Enlistment finally approved at Birr for the 65th Foot
1860	Admitted to hospital
1865	Discharged
1868	Re-engaged Hobart Town for 13 years 84 days
July 1874	Deserted Aldershot
Dec 1874	Re-joined
1875/76	In prison
1878	Embarked for India per *'HMS Crocodile'*
21 Mar 1885	Discharged Bombay East Indies Pension increased to 2/3d. per diem
24 July 1885	Joined Enrolled Guard — stationed Perth
no date	Caretaker of the Magazine at Fremantle
1897	Stationed at Perth
no date	Caretaker and Chief Messenger in the Colonial Secretary's Department
1913	Residing at Leederville—[4 Leeder Street]
1914	Died

Service and Personal Details:

Place of Birth:	Mary-le-bone London Middlesex
Age on Attestation:	25 years
Period of Service:	1860 — 1885 [excluding HEIC Service]
Age on Discharge:	none given
Length of Service:	22 years 235 days [excluding HEIC Service]

	Continued in Service after 21 years 27th June 1885	
Foreign Service:	New Zealand	5 years 319 days
	Australia	3 years 251 days
	East Indies	6 years 141 days
	[excluding HEIC Service]	
Medal Entitlement:	Indian Mutiny 1857/1859; New Zealand War Medal 1861/1866; Afghan 1879/80	
Reason for Discharge:	In consequence of the termination of his second period of limited engagement	
Character:	Good and habits temperate until a few months ago when he was admitted to hospital from effect of drink	
Trade or Occupation:	Shoemaker	
Can Sign Name:	Yes	
Certificate of Education:	2nd Class obtained 19 April 1877	
Height:	5' 6¼"	
Chest measurement:	36"	
When Vaccinated:	As a Child	
Hair Colour:	Light Brown	
Eyes:	Blue	
Complexion:	Fresh	
Pulse [Regular]:	81 beats	
Respiration:	69 inhalations	
Muscular Development:	Very Good	
Remarks:	Slight scalp wound	
Next of Kin:	Wife Margaret	

MARKEY	Christopher, private 44th Foot [Reserve Battalion]
Surname Variant	MARKEE
26 Mar 1850	Discharged the Service Chatham
1850	Pension paid Drogheda 6d. per diem for 1 year
25 Oct 1850	Arrived per *'Hashemy'*
1851	Pension ceased

due to the difference in the birth date the following four entries may not necessarily refer to Christopher Markey 44th Foot

1853	Enlisted in Police Force and dismissed within a month for drunkenness
1855	At Baylup — charged with stealing a horse being the property of William McKnoe — verdict outcome "Not Guilty"
1860	Convicted at Perth of stealing a mare property unknown Found guilty and sentenced to 6 years imprisonment
1862	Expiration of sentence
1875	Died

Service and Personal Details:

Place of Birth:	Kells Meath
Age on Attestation:	17 years 10 months
Period of Service:	1846 — 1850

Age on Discharge:	20 years 10 months	
Length of Service:	3 years 78 days	
Foreign Service:	Malta	1 year 6 months
Reason for Discharge:	Fractured left forearm from a kick from a horse while employed as a groom to Colonel Williams	
Character:	Indifferent	
Trade or Occupation:	Servant	
Can Sign Name:	X his mark on discharge	
Height:	5' 6"	
Hair Colour:	Light Brown	
Eyes:	Grey	
Complexion:	Fair	
Intends to Reside:	Cavan Meath	

MARRISON John, private
77th Foot

Surname Variant	MORRISON
27 Feb 1855	Discharged the Service Chatham Pension paid 2nd Plymouth Pension District 1/- per diem
24 Nov 1858	Arrived per *'Edwin Fox'*
1861	Pension paid Melbourne
1875	Melbourne

Service and Personal Details:

Place of Birth:	Reepham Norfolk	
Age on Attestation:	18 years	
Period of Service:	1833 — 1855	
Age on Discharge:	39 years 7 months	
Length of Service:	21 years 202 days	
Foreign Service:	Mediterranean	5 years 4 months
	Jamaica	3 years
	North America	2 years 2 months
	Turkey	10 months
Medal Entitlement:	Good Conduct and Long Service with gratuity	
Reason for Discharge:	Chronic Rheumatism and General Debility	
Character:	Good	
Trade or Occupation:	Labourer	
Can Sign Name:	X his mark on discharge	
Height:	5' 7"	
Hair Colour:	Light Brown	
Eyes:	Grey	
Complexion:	Light	
Intends to Reside:	Norwich	

MARS James, private [2923]
13th Foot

Previous Regiment	36th Foot
9 June 1868	Discharged the Service Pension paid Newcastle 1/- per diem
1873	Pension paid Greenwich
19 Feb 1874	Arrived per *'Naval Brigade'*

8 June 1881	Assigned Lake Munster Loc P 5 of 20 acres
1881	Pension increased to 1/2d. per diem for 4 years service in the Enrolled Force
12 Jan 1885	Title Application for Lake Munster Lot P5
29 Apr 1885	Died
6 June 1885	Cockburn Sound Grant Loc P5 at Coogee to widow Ellen
1898	For Sale — Loc P5 of 20 acres with 10 chain frontage to lake at Lake Coogee

Service and Personal Details:

Place of Birth:	Garvagh Co. Londonderry	
Age on Attestation:	17 years 6 months	
Period of Service:	1846 — 1868	
Age on Discharge:	39 years 1 month	
Foreign Service:	Ionian Isles	4 years 2 months
	Gibraltar	7 months
	Crimea	1 year
	Cape of Good Hope	1 year 4 months
	East Indies	6 years 3 months
Medal Entitlement:	Crimea; Turkish Crimea; Central India with clasp; Indian Mutiny	
Reason for Discharge:	Own Request having served over 21 years	
Character:	Good	
Trade or Occupation:	Labourer	
Can Sign Name:	X his mark on discharge	
Height:	5' 6½"	
Hair Colour:	Light Brown	
Eyes:	Grey	
Complexion:	Fresh	
Intends to Reside:	North Shields Northumberland	

MARSHALL	Alexander, private
	92nd Foot
7 Sept 1858	Discharged the Service Chatham
	Pension paid 2nd Glasgow Pension District
	8d. per diem
19 Aug 1859	Arrived per *'Sultana'*
1861	To South Australia from Perth Western Australia
1878	Pension paid South Australia
1879	W.O. correspondence — "A31"
1898	Attended Memorial Day Adelaide

Service and Personal Details:

Place of Birth:	Neilston Renfrewshire	
Age on Attestation:	18 years 2 months	
Period of Service:	1837 — 1858	
Age on Discharge:	39 years 7 months	
Length of Service:	21 years 98 days	
Foreign Service:	Malta	3 years 4 months
	West Indies	2 years 10 months
	Ionian Isles	2 years 1 month
	Gibraltar	4 years
	Crimea	9 months

Reason for Discharge:	Chronic Rheumatism and Catarrh
Character:	Good
Trade or Occupation:	Plumber
Can Sign Name:	Yes
Height:	5' 7"
Hair Colour:	Light Brown
Eyes:	Grey
Complexion:	Fresh

MARTIN	Daniel, private 80th Foot
Previous Regiment	39th Foot
26 June 1849	Discharged the Service Chatham Pension paid Tralee 1/- per diem
31 Aug 1853	Arrived per *'Phoebe Dunbar'*
Sept 1854	Appointed Convict establishment without sanction
1863	Stationed Perth District
1864	ptve D Martin Pensioner Force at Perth contributed to the Greenough Fire Relief Fund
1873	Pension increased to 1/3d. per diem for 13 years 10 months service with the Enrolled Force
1876	In receipt of outdoor relief money — Perth
Apr 1878	Office Poor House Pensioner D. Martin, married with three children at home, who has been in receipt of 1/- per diem outdoor relief since July 11th 1875 is not deserving of it, he is constantly drinking and his wife does the same, further she has a mangle and earns by that — as in my opinion they are neither worthy or in need of it
1881	Died

Service and Personal Details:		
Place of Birth:	Anna Tralee Co. Kerry	
Age on Attestation:	17 years	
Period of Service:	1827 — 1848	
Age on Discharge:	39 years	
Length of Service:	20 years 36 days	
Foreign Service:	New South Wales	4 years 2 months
	East Indies	15 years 11 months
Medal Entitlement:	Campaign against Rajah of Coorg 1834, action at Maharajpore 1843	
Reason for Discharge:	Worn out from service	
Character:	Very Good	
Trade or Occupation:	Labourer	
Can Sign Name:	X his mark on discharge	
Height:	5' 8¾"	
Hair Colour:	Fair	
Eyes:	Grey	
Complexion:	Fair	
Intends to Reside:	Tralee	

MARTIN	Edward, private
	RM
June 1844	Discharged the Service
	Pension paid
	£18/4/- per annum
1863	Pension paid Falmouth
28 Dec 1863	Arrived per *'Lord Dalhousie'*
Service and Personal Details:	
Place of Birth:	Darlaston, Stafford
Age on Attestation:	22 years
Marine Division:	Plymouth
Period of Service:	1828 — 1844
Length of Service:	15 years 11 months 4 days
Reason for Discharge:	Invalided for Phthisis and Palpations
Trade or Occupation:	Brickmaker
Can Sign Name:	Yes
Height:	5' 8½"
Hair Colour:	Dark Brown
Eyes:	Hazel
Complexion:	Fair

MARTIN	James, private
	15th Foot
22 Aug 1838	Discharged the Service and admitted as an Out-Pensioner of Her Majesty's Royal Hospital at Chelsea
1838	Pension paid Mullingar
	6d. per diem
1838	Pension paid Carrick on Suir
1838	Clonmel
1850	Pension paid 1st Manchester Pension District
6 Apr 1854	Arrived per *'Sea Park'* with family
Jan 1857	Contributed 2/- to the Florence Nightingale Fund
Dec 1857	Assigned Pensioner Lot P14 at York
1864	private J Martin serving in the Pensioner Force at York contributed to Greenough Fire Relief Fund
May 1863	Application for Title to P14 at York
	[three roomed cottage with slabbed barn]
1873	Pension increased to 1/1½d. for 15 years and 9 months service in the Enrolled Force
1877	Died at York
Service and Personal Details:	
Place of Birth:	St Johns Co. Waterford
Age on Attestation:	17 years
Period of Service:	1824 — 1838
Age on Discharge:	31 years
Length of Service:	13 years 80 days [after age of 18 years]
Foreign Service:	Canada [not time period given]
Reason for Discharge:	Lameness of left leg caused by facture of both bones above left ankle caused by falling off No. 2 Tower when attempting to close the shutters on a window
Character:	Very Good

Trade or Occupation:	Labourer
Can Sign Name:	X his mark on discharge; but states can read and write on the West. Aust. 1859 Census declaration
Height:	5' 5"
Hair Colour:	Light
Eyes:	Blue
Complexion:	Fresh
Intends to Reside:	Waterford

MARTIN	John, private 74th Foot
11 June 1861	Discharged the Service Pension paid Stirling 1/- per diem
15 Apr 1864	Arrived per *'Clara'* [2]
1865	To South Australia from Perth West Australia

Service and Personal Details:		
Place of Birth:	Dunfermline Fifeshire Scotland	
Age on Attestation:	16 years 2 months	
Period of Service:	1838 — 1861	
Age on Discharge:	39 years	
Length of Service:	21 years 10 days	
Foreign Service:	Cape of Good Hope	2 years 8 months
	East Indies	5 years 11 months
	North America	3 years 9 months
Medal Entitlement:	Medal for service in South Africa	
Reason for Discharge:	Own Request having completed 21 years service	
Character:	Very Good	
Trade or Occupation:	Weaver	
Can Sign Name:	Yes	
Height:	5' 8¼"	
Hair Colour:	Dark Brown	
Eyes:	Grey	
Complexion:	Fair	
Distinguishing Marks:	Scar of boil on right side of small of back	
Intends to Reside:	Dunfermline	

MARTIN	Thomas, Corporal 99th Foot
19 Dec 1862	Discharged the Service Cork
6 Jan 1863	Admitted to Out-Pension 1/- per diem Pension paid 2nd Dublin Pension District
9 Jan 1868	Arrived per *'Hougoumont'*
1881	Pension increased to 1/5½d. per diem for service in the Enrolled Force
Apr 1881	Assigned North Fremantle Lot P72
1881	Recommended for £15 Pensioner's Grant
13 Oct 1883	Granted Fee Simple North Fremantle Lot P72
1886	Died

Service and Personal Details:	
Place of Birth:	Oldcastle Co. Meath

Age on Attestation:	18 years	
Period of Service:	1841 — 1862	
Age on Discharge:	39 years 9 months	
Length of Service:	21 years 20 days	
Foreign Service:	Australia	13 years
	East India	1 year 1 month
	China	2 years 4 months
Reason for Discharge:	Own Request having completed 21 years service	
Character:	Good	
Trade or Occupation:	Shoemaker	
Can Sign Name:	Yes	
Height:	5' 7"	
Hair Colour:	Dark Brown	
Eyes:	Grey	
Complexion:	Fresh	
Intends to Reside:	Black Rock Dublin	

MASH John, private
4th Foot

Surname Variants	MUSH; NASH	
24 Aug 1847	Discharged the Service Chatham	
	Pension paid Cambridge	
	1/- per diem	
24 May 1855	Arrived per *'Stag'*	
June 1856	At Fremantle	
1856	To South Australia from Western Australia	
	"£12/17/2 to be stopped for cost of wife's passage"	
1863	Pension paid South Australia	
1875	Adelaide South Australia	

Service and Personal Details:

Place of Birth:	Sheedy Camp Cambridgeshire	
Age on Attestation:	18 years	
Period of Service:	1826 — 1847	
Age on Discharge:	39 years 3 months or 38 years 4 months	
Length of Service:	20 years 129 days	
Foreign Service:	Portugal	1 year 3 months
	New South Wales	6 years 5 months
	East Indies	8 years 6 months
Reason for Discharge:	Impaired Constitution and General Debility	
Character:	Very Good	
Trade or Occupation:	Labourer	
Can Sign Name:	X his mark on discharge	
Height:	5' 9½"	
Hair Colour:	Grey	
Eyes:	Grey	
Complexion:	Swarthy	
Intends to Reside:	Luton Cambridgeshire	

MATHEWS Patrick, Serjeant
86th Foot

Surname Variant	MATTHEWS
1 June 1858	Discharged the Service Chatham

	Pension paid 2nd Manchester Pension District
	2/- per diem
19 Aug 1859	Arrived per *'Sultana'*
1864	Serjeant Major P Matthews Pensioner Force at Fremantle District contributed to the Greenough Fire Relief Fund
1866	Pension paid Madras from Fremantle
1867	Madras
1868	Died Madras

Service and Personal Details:	
Place of Birth:	St Nicholas Dublin
Age on Attestation:	22 years
Period of Service:	1837 — 1858
Age on Discharge:	43 years 2 months or 42 years 8 months
Length of Service:	20 years 253 days
Foreign Service:	East Indies 15 years 2 months
Medal Entitlement:	Good Conduct and Long Service with gratuity
Reason for Discharge:	Chronic Dyspnoea
Character:	Excellent
Trade or Occupation:	Harness maker
Can Sign Name:	Yes
Height:	5' 9"
Hair Colour:	Grey
Eyes:	Grey
Complexion:	Dark
Intends to Reside:	In the County of Kent England but decided on Salford nr. Manchester Lancashire

MAY	Alfred, private
	25th Foot
13 Nov 1860	Discharged the Service
	Pension paid South London
	8d. per diem
1861	Pension paid Woolwich
29 Jan 1862	Arrived per *'Lincelles'*
1863	To Eastern Colonies from Fremantle
1865	Pension paid South Australia
1867	"Not heard of since 1867"

Service and Personal Details:		
Place of Birth:	London Middlesex	
Age on Attestation:	18 years	
Period of Service:	1839 — 1860	
Age on Discharge:	39 years	
Length of Service:	21 years 15 days	
Foreign Service:	Cape of Good Hope	2 years 9 months
	East Indies	12 years 8 months
	Gibraltar	2 years 8 months
Reason for Discharge:	Own Request having served 21 years	
Character:	Good	
Trade or Occupation:	Groom	
Can Sign Name:	Yes	

Height:	5' 7"
Hair Colour:	Brown
Eyes:	Hazel
Complexion:	Fresh
Intends to Reside:	London

MAYBERRY	Thomas, private 35th Foot
8 Nov 1853	Discharged the Service Chatham Pension paid 1st East London Pension District 6d. per diem
1856	Pension paid Fermoy
1857	Pension paid 1st Cork Pension District
1858	1st Cork Pension District
1862	Bermuda
15 Feb 1863	Arrived per *'Merchantman'* [1]
June 1867	Died aged 36 Albany District

Service and Personal Details:

Place of Birth:	St Marys Cork
Age on Attestation:	16 years 6 months
Period of Service:	1847 — 1853
Age on Discharge:	23 years 7 months
Length of Service:	5 years 48 days reckoned – [18 months served Underage]
Reason for Discharge:	Unfit for further service due to accident at Chobham Camp resulting in loss of forefinger of right hand
Character:	Good
Trade or Occupation:	Hairdresser
Can Sign Name:	X his mark on discharge
Height:	5' 8½"
Hair Colour:	Fair
Eyes:	Grey
Complexion:	Fresh
Intends to Reside:	Old Road Stepney London

MEADE	Thomas, private 7th Foot
Surname Variants	MEAD; MEEDE
21 Aug 1855	Discharged the Service Chatham Pension paid Clonmel 9d. per diem
9 June 1862	Arrived per *'Norwood'* [1]
1875	Pension paid Western Australia
1878	Pension increased to 1/3d per diem for service in the Enrolled Force
Dec 1882	Convicted before two Justices at Perth Western Australia of assaulting his wife and sentenced to 3 months imprisonment with hard labour. Half pension suspended and half paid to wife for time in prison
23 Aug 1883	Assigned Perth Military Pensioner Lot 28/H [located left rear of Mt Eliza Barracks]
Apr 1884	Application for Title Perth Lot ?38/H

30 Aug 1884	Granted Fee Simple Perth Pensioner Lot 28/H
Service and Personal Details:	
Place of Birth:	Fethard Co. Tipperary
Age on Attestation:	20 years
Period of Service:	1852 — 1855
Age on Discharge:	25 years or 23 years
Length of Service:	3 years 46 days
Foreign Service:	Turkey and Crimea approx 1 year
Medal Entitlement:	Crimea [not verified]
Reason for Discharge:	Loss of middle finger of right hand at Alma
Character:	Good
Trade or Occupation:	Shoemaker
Can Sign Name:	Yes
Height:	5' 7"
Hair Colour:	Black
Eyes:	Grey
Complexion:	Sallow
Intends to Reside:	Clonmel

MEALIA	Michael, private 99th Foot
Surname Variants	MELIA; MEALEN
29 Oct 1860	Discharged the Service
13 Nov 1860	Admitted to Out-Pension Pension paid Kilkenny 8d. per diem
31 Dec 1862	Arrived per *'York'*
no date	Assigned Freshwater Bay Loc 1058
1874	Pension increased to 11½d. per diem for service in the Enrolled Force
July 1878	Convicted before Police Magistrate Perth Western Australia of holding intercourse with prisoners without permission. Sent to prison for one month during which time pension to be suspended [Note: on Form 41/1 sent to S.O.P. Perth W.A. on 31/12/1878 — enquiry is made whether man is still in Enrolled Force as the nature of his offence seems to point to this and he has already been increased for service in this Force]
1877	Staff Officer Pensions: Ann Melia [Mealia] wife of Pensioner, but has not lived with him for 10 years seeks help for admission of son [aged 8 years 4 months], to Protestant Orphanage
Nov 1885	Admitted to Mt Eliza Poor House
1891	Inmate of the Depot aged 69
June 1897	Residing Perth
1900	Died
Service and Personal Details:	
Place of Birth:	St Peters Athlone Roscommon
Age on Attestation:	18 years
Period of Service:	1839 — 1860
Age on Discharge:	39 years 3 days

Length of Service:	21 years 90 days
Foreign Service:	Australian Colonies 13 years 2 months
Reason for Discharge:	Own Request having served 21 years
Character:	Good
Trade or Occupation:	Labourer
Can Sign Name:	Yes
Height:	5' 7"
Hair Colour:	Light Brown
Eyes:	Hazel
Complexion:	Fair
Intends to Reside:	Kilkenny

MEEHAN	Patrick, private EIC
	2nd Bengal European Infantry
	Out Pension No 745
3 Sept 1860	Admitted to Out-pension
	Pension paid Limerick
	1/- per diem
1861	Pension paid 2nd Liverpool Pension District
1862	Bermuda
15 Feb 1863	Arrived per *'Merchantman'* [1]
1864	To Adelaide from Fremantle pension District
30 Jan 1871	Died

Service and Personal Details:

Place of Birth:	Limerick
Trade or Occupation:	Tailor
Where Enlisted:	Cork
Presidency:	Bengal
Length of Service:	20 years 11 months
Age on Discharge:	40 years
Reason for Discharge:	Time expired
Character:	Good
Medal Entitlement:	Indian Mutiny
Height:	5' 5¼"
Complexion:	Fresh
Eye Colour:	Grey
Hair Colour:	Brown or Black
Intends to Reside:	Limerick

MEEKHUMS	James, private
	61st Foot
Previous Regiment:	96th Foot
16 July 1861	Pension paid Chatham
	8d. per diem
1864	Pension paid Deptford
15 Aug 1865	Arrived per *'Racehorse'*
1878	Pension increased to 1/1½d. per diem
1878	Wife bedridden
1878	Died aged 49

Service and Personal Details:

Place of Birth:	Sevenoaks Kent
Age on Discharge:	33 years

Length of Service:	15 years 7 months	
Foreign Service:	Australia	3 years
	East Indies	9 years 9 months
	Mauritius	1 year 2 months
Reason for Discharge:	Chronic Bronchitis, Heart Disease, often Buboes in groin, Chest infection from service. Buboes from syphilis. Varia left leg	
Character:	Good	
Trade or Occupation:	Bricklayer	
Height:	5' 9"	
Hair Colour:	Brown	
Eyes:	Hazel	
Complexion:	Fresh	

MEER	Patrick, private	
	89th Foot [Depot]	
Surname Variants	MEERE; MEIR; MEARS	
18 July 1860	Discharged the Service	
	Pension paid Ennis	
	8½d. per diem	
28 Dec 1863	Arrived per *'Lord Dalhousie'* as a Convict Guard	
1866	On Duty Rottnest Island	
1867	Pension paid Western Australia	
1876	Assigned Perth Town Lot 123/Y	
Apr 1881	Application for Title to Perth Lot 123/Y	
1881	Pension increased to 1/1½d. per diem for service in the Enrolled Force	
1889	Residing John Street Perth	
June 1890	Died – buried East Perth Cemetery	
Service and Personal Details:		
Place of Birth:	Kilnaboy ?Coraphin Co. Clare	
Age on Attestation:	19 years	
Period of Service:	1837 — 1860	
Age on Discharge:	42 years 1 month	
Length of Service:	22 years 254 days	
Foreign Service:	West Indies	2 years 2 months
	North America	5 years 10 months
	Gibraltar	8 months
	Crimea	1 year 5 months
	Gibraltar	3 months
	Cape of Good Hope	1 year
	East Indies	2 years 4 months
Medal Entitlement:	Crimea with clasp; Turkish Crimean	
Reason for Discharge:	Own Request having completed 21 years service	
Character:	Good	
Trade or Occupation:	Labourer	
Can Sign Name:	Yes	
Height:	5' 7¼"	
Hair Colour:	Grey	
Eyes:	Hazel	
Complexion:	Swarthy	
Intends to Reside:	Corofin [sic] nr. Ennis Co. Clare	

MEIKLAM	Roger, private 2nd Foot
Surname Variants	MIEKLAM; MEIKHAM
18 July 1865	Discharged the Service Cork Pension paid Paisley 1/- per diem
13 July 1867	Arrived per *'Norwood'* [2]
1868	Employed by Convict Establishment
1871	Pension paid Melbourne
1872	Returned to Colony
circa June 1874	Transferred from Fremantle to 2nd Perth District
1877	Died Western Australia aged 52
Service and Personal Details:	
Place of Birth:	Renfrew Renfrewshire
Age on Attestation:	20 years
Period of Service:	1844 — 1965
Age on Discharge:	41 years
Length of Service:	21 years 17 days
Foreign Service:	Cape of Good Hope 6 years 10 months
Medal Entitlement:	Long and Meritorious Service with gratuity; Kaffir War
Reason for Discharge:	Own Request after 21 years service
Character:	Most Exemplary
Trade or Occupation:	Sawyer
Can Sign Name:	Yes
Height:	5' 10"
Hair Colour:	Dark
Eyes:	Hazel
Complexion:	Fresh
Intends to Reside:	James Street Paisley Scotland

MELLOWS	Joseph, private 64th Foot
Previous Regiment	8th Foot
Surname Variants	MALLEWS; MALLOWS
30 Aug 1864	Discharged the Service Chatham 1/- per diem
1865	Pension paid Nottingham
4 July 1866	Arrived per *'Belgravia'*
1879	Payment of £15 [pounds] sanctioned
18 Oct 1879	Granted North Fremantle Lot P23
1881	Pension increased to 1/6d. per diem for service in the Enrolled Force
1 Jan 1881	Joined Enrolled Guard — stationed Perth
4 Aug 1887	Registrar Supreme Court -. Temporary Employment of J. Mellows vice Regan [ill] as Caretaker Supreme Court
1888	Died – buried East Perth Cemetery
1888	Grant of Probate
1888	Mrs Joseph Mellows proprietor of Fremantle Lot P23

Service and Personal Details:

Place of Birth:	Woodbury Nottingham
Age on Attestation:	18 years 6 months
Period of Service:	1843 — 1864
Age on Discharge:	39 years
Length of Service:	21 years 17 days
Foreign Service:	India 15 years
Medal Entitlement:	Good Conduct and Long Service with gratuity
Reason for Discharge:	Own Request having served 21 years
Character:	Very Good
Trade or Occupation:	Labourer
Can Sign Name:	Yes
Height:	5' 9¼"
Hair Colour:	Brown
Eyes:	Hazel
Complexion:	Dark
Distinguishing Marks:	Pocked Marked
Intends to Reside:	Woodbury Nottingham

MELLUISH William, [Military Pensioner]
Royal Sappers and Miners

Surname Variants	MELLHUISH; MELLHUISH; MELLISH
17 Dec 1851	Arrived per *'Anna Robinson'* with regiment
21 Dec 1861	Discharged the Service at Fremantle Western Australia with compensation and the Right of a Deferred Pension
6 Apr 1878	Attained age of 60 6d. per diem Deferred pension ratified
1889	W.O. Correspondence — Deferred Pension Forms sent to Western Australia. [Perth]
1894	Died Albany

Service and Personal Details:

Place of Birth:	Broadclyst Exeter Devon
Age on Attestation:	23 years
Period of Service:	1841 — 1861
Service to 1855:	13 years 10 months
Age at 1855:	36 years 10 months
Age on Discharge:	43 years 8 months
Length of Service:	20 years 252 days
Foreign Service:	Bermuda 5 years 4 months Western Australia 9 years 11 months
Reason for Discharge:	He having been granted a Free Discharge to settle in the Colony with 12 months pay; and Right of Registry to Deferred Pension of 6d. per diem on attaining 60 years of age
Character:	Good
Trade or Occupation:	Carpenter
Can Sign Name:	Yes
Height:	5' 7½"
Hair Colour:	Brown
Eyes:	Grey
Complexion:	Fair

Distinguishing Marks:	Scar on right cheek
Intends to Reside:	Albany Western Australia
MELVILLE	Robert, private RM
Surname Variant	MELVILL
1 May 1856	Discharged the Service Devonport Pension paid 2nd Plymouth Pension District £16/16/0 per annum
Oct 1856	At Dartmoor Prison
10 Sept 1856	Arrived per *'Runnymede'*
1859	Employed as Assistant Warder
1869	Died
1881	Robert Melville's widow and son's request for a Pensioner Land Grant was refused as Grant not applied for during his domicile in West. Aust.
Service and Personal Details:	
Place of Birth:	Dumfriesshire Scotland.
Age on Attestation:	18 years 8 months
Marine Division:	Plymouth
Period of Service:	1833 — 1856
Reason for Discharge:	Length of Service
Length of Service:	22 years 5 months 5 days
Trade or Occupation:	Labourer
Can Sign Name:	Yes
Height:	5' 7½"
Hair Colour:	Brown
Eyes:	Hazel
Complexion:	Fresh
MEREDITH	John, Corporal 10th Foot
22 July 1851	Discharged the Service Chatham Pension paid 1st Dublin Pension District 1/- per diem
1851	Pension paid 1st Galway Pension District
2 Aug 1852	Arrived per *'William Jardine'*
1854	Pension paid Western Australia
1855	London
1855	Dublin
1866	W.O. correspondence with S.O.P. Dublin
Service and Personal Details:	
Place of Birth:	Higginstown Co. Meath
Age on Attestation:	21 years
Period of Service:	1840 — 1851
Age on Discharge:	32 years
Length of Service:	10 years 168 days
Foreign Service:	East Indies 8 years
Medal Entitlement:	Sutlej with clasp; Mooltan Sept 1848
Reason for Discharge:	Wounded left hip at Battle of Mooltan 1848
Character:	Very Good
Trade or Occupation:	Labourer
Can Sign Name:	Yes

Height:	5' 8"
Hair Colour:	Sandy
Eyes:	Grey
Complexion:	Sallow
Intends to Reside:	Dublin

MILLER	Samuel, gunner and driver
	RA 5th Battalion
8 Oct 1850	Discharged the Service Woolwich
	Pension paid Woolwich
	7d. per diem for 2½ years
21 May 1851	Arrived per *'Mermaid'*
16 Aug 1851	Appointed Constable Police Force Perth
1857	Serving Rottnest
1868	a Samuel Millar died aged 46

Service and Personal Details:

Place of Birth:	Glasgow Lanarkshire	
Age on Attestation:	18 years	
Period of Service:	1840 — 1850	
Age on Discharge:	28 years 9 months	
Length of Service:	10 years 242 days	
Foreign Service:	Malta	4 years
Reason for Discharge:	Rupture in left groin and spitting blood	
Character:	Good	
Trade or Occupation:	Labourer	
Can Sign Name:	X his mark on discharge	
Height:	5' 7"	
Hair Colour:	Brown	
Eyes:	Grey	
Complexion:	Fair	

MILLER	William, private
	74th Foot
Surname Variant	MILLAR
19 Oct 1850	Discharged the Service Clonmel
3 Dec 1850	Admitted to Out-Pension
	Pension paid Ballymena
	6d. per diem
1852	Pension paid 1st Belfast Pension District
1852	Ballymena
1859	Pension paid 2nd Belfast Pension District
1860	2nd Glasgow Pension District
27 May 1863	Arrived per *'Clyde'*
1864	To South Australia from Fremantle West. Aust.

Service and Personal Details:

Place of Birth:	Ballynare Co. Antrim	
Age on Attestation:	21 years	
Period of Service:	1836 — 1850	
Age on Discharge:	35 years 8 months	
Length of Service:	14 years 37 days	
Foreign Service:	West Indies	3 years 5 months
	North America	3 years 9 months

Reason for Discharge:	Unfit for further service	
Character:	Good	
Trade or Occupation:	Labourer	
Can Sign Name:	Yes	
Height:	5' 6¾"	
Hair Colour:	Brown	
Eyes:	Grey	
Complexion:	Fair	
Distinguishing Marks:	Marked with letter "D"	
Intends to Reside:	Belfast Co. Antrim	
MILLER	William Henry, gunner	
	RA 14th Brigade	
Surname Variant	MILLAR	
12 Sept 1865	Discharged the Service Netley	
	Pension paid Falmouth	
	10d. per diem	
4 July 1866	Arrived per *'Belgravia'*	
1883	Granted Land Victoria Loc 18 at Bootenal	
Oct 1892	Died Geraldton	
1899	Widow awarded Land Grant	
Service and Personal Details:		
Place of Birth:	Falmouth Cornwall	
Age on Attestation:	21 years 3 months	
Period of Service:	1843 — 1865	
Age on Discharge:	43 years 8 months	
Length of Service:	20 years 244 days	
Foreign Service:	St Helena	8 years 3 months
	Turkey Expedition	10 months
	East Indies	6 years 5 months
Medal Entitlement:	Crimean with clasp; Turkish Crimean	
Reason for Discharge:	Worn out; Chronic Rheumatism	
Character:	Very Good	
Trade or Occupation:	Shoemaker	
Can Sign Name:	Yes	
Height:	5' 8¾"	
Hair Colour:	Dark Brown	
Eyes:	Grey	
Complexion:	Fresh	
Intends to Reside:	Penryn Cornwall	
MILLS	Thomas, private	
	26th Foot	
20 June 1865	Discharged the Service Portsmouth	
25 July 1865	Admitted to Out-Pension	
	Pension paid Paisley	
	7d. per diem	
13 July 1867	Arrived per *'Norwood'* [2]	
1868	Pension paid Melbourne	
1886	Correspondence from W.O. to S.O.P. Stirling	
Service and Personal Details:		

Place of Birth:	Abbey Paisley Renfrewshire
Age on Attestation:	18 years
Period of Service:	1847 — 1865
Age on Discharge:	36 years 4 months
Length of Service:	18 years 34 days
Foreign Service:	Gibraltar 3 years 2 months
	Canada East 1 year 6 months
	Bermuda 4 years 11 months
Reason for Discharge:	Asthma and Extremely Feeble
Character:	Good
Trade or Occupation:	Weaver
Can Sign Name:	Yes
Height:	5' 7¾"
Hair Colour:	Brown
Eyes:	Grey
Complexion:	Fresh
Intends to Reside:	No. 38 Storey Street Paisley

MILLWARD	Samuel J.W., private
	10th Royal Hussars
Previous Regiment	4th Light Dragoons
Surname Variant	MILWARD
4 Apr 1852	Discharged the Service Chatham
	Pension paid 1st West London Pension District
	6d. per diem
1861	Residing 9 Hemlock [sic] Close London
15 Apr 1864	Arrived per *'Clara'* [2]
1868	Secretary of the Temperance Society
1875	Pension paid Western Australia
1886	Died aged 69

Service and Personal Details:

Place of Birth:	Stoke Damerall [sic] Devon
	[Samuel Millward was baptised at the Morrice Street Wesleyan Chapel Devonport - May 1817]
Age on Attestation:	? years
Period of Service:	1836 — 1851
Age on Discharge:	35 years or 34 years 8 months
Length of Service:	13 years 111 days [reckoned]
Foreign Service:	East Indies 9 years 222 days
Reason for Discharge:	Own request
Can Sign Name:	Yes
Character:	Very Good
Trade or Occupation:	Brazier
Can Sign Name:	Yes
Height:	5' 9¾"
Hair Colour:	Auburn
Eyes:	Blue
Complexion:	Fresh
Intends to Reside:	London
Marriage:	1854 Ann Welsford b. 1812 Plymouth

Children:	Samuel b. 1856 Bristol Florence Welsford b. 1859 Middlesex m. *c*1887 Charles Connolly Greenough	
MILTON	Stephen, private 70th Foot	
31 Jan 1860	Discharged the Service Pension paid 2nd Glasgow Pension District 11d. per diem	
15 Feb 1863	Arrived per *'Merchantman'* [1]	
1875	Pension paid Western Australia	
1879	Pension increased to 1/2½ per diem for 8 years service in the Enrolled Force	
1884	Granted Perth Town Lot 30/H	
1886	Charged with disorderly conduct	
Dec 1888	Resident Medical Officer Newcastle	
1888	Resident Medical Officer Newcastle — Stephen Milton, Military Pensioner 1/2½. per diem. For admission to Mt. Eliza Poor House	
1890	Died	
Service and Personal Details:		
Place of Birth:	Carlow Co. Carlow	
Age on Attestation:	18 years	
Period of Service:	1838 — 1860	
Age on Discharge:	39 years 7 months	
Length of Service:	21 years 20 days	
Foreign Service:	West Indies	2 years 4 months
	Canada	2 years
	East Indies	8 years 11 months
Medal Entitlement:	Indian Mutiny	
Reason for Discharge:	Own Request having completed 21 years service	
Character:	Good	
Trade or Occupation:	Shoemaker	
Can Sign Name:	Yes	
Height:	5' 7"	
Hair Colour:	Brown	
Eyes:	Hazel	
Complexion:	Sallow	
Intends to Reside:	Glasgow Lanarkshire	
Married:	Christina the relict of the late Stephen Milton died August 1898 at the residence of her son-in-law W Golden	
Children:	Janet	
MINORGAN	Thomas, Colour Serjeant 24th Foot	
Previous Regiments	10th; 4th	
17 Dec 1867	Discharged the Service Sheffield Pension paid Dublin 1/6d. per diem	

1873	Discharged Dublin City Militia at own request and by purchase as he being about to emigrate to Australia and to fill a Government situation
1873	Pension paid Greenwich
19 Feb 1874	Arrived per *'Naval Brigade'*
1880	Re-located to Fremantle having served as Drill Instructor Metropolitan Volunteer Rifles for some 6 years
Jan 1881	Pension increased to 1/8½d. per diem for service in the Enrolled Force
6 Apr 1881	Title Application for Perth Military Pensioner Lot 126/Y [located John St. West Perth]
1881	Grant of £15 [pounds] recommended
1881	Serjeant Minorgan applies for Pensioner Grant of land at Albany
May 1881	Correspondence with W.O. enquiring as to whether the whole of man's service in the Militia and Enrolled Force should be reckoned for increase in pension
1881	Pension increased to 2/- per diem [former service of 5½ years as Serjeant on Permanent Staffing of Dublin City Militia being specially allowed to reckon]
June 1885	Police Occurrence Books — Mr T. Minorgan re. Abraham Bew, a Pensioner for Relief
Feb 1886	Superintendent Minorgan — Pensioner William Geddes for admission into Mt. Eliza Poor House
1887	Secretary of State. - Application by Staff Sergeant T. Minorgan for Annuity and Medal
1889	Staff Sergeant Minorgan — Civil Service, application for employment
June 1897	Stationed at Perth
1899	Presented with the Meritorious Service Medal with Annuity
1903	Discharge Document retuned to W.O.
1907	Correspondence with W.O.
1909	Attended Veteran's Dinner
1911	Died aged 79
1912	Grant of Probate

Service and Personal Details:		
Place of Birth:	St James Dublin	
Age on Attestation:	19 years	
Period of Service:	1851 — 1867	
Age on Discharge:	35 years	
Length of Service:	16 years	
Foreign Service:	Malta	7 months
	Crimea	2 years 4 months
Medal Entitlement:	Crimea with 3 clasps; Long Service with Good	
Conduct; Meritorious Service		
Reason for Discharge:	Chronic Rheumatism	
Character:	Very Good	
Trade or Occupation:	Labourer	
Can Sign Name:	Yes	

Height:	5' 7¼"
Hair Colour:	Brown
Eyes:	Hazel
Complexion:	Fresh
Intends to Reside:	No. 28 Henrietta Street Dublin

MITCHELL Frederick George John, Corporal
Coldstream Guards

Foreign Service	Egypt: Abu Klea and Nile 1884 — 1885
1887	Joined Western Australian Police Force Resided 49 years in Western Australia Served 39 years with the Police. At time of retirement was stationed at Narrogin as Inspector of Southern/South Western Region
1936	Residing 37 Ventnor Ave., West Perth
Dec 1936	Died

MITCHELL Matthew, private
65th Foot

Surname Variant	MICHELL
10 June 1842	Discharged the Service Fort Pitt Pension paid 2nd Dublin Pension District 1/- per diem
1850	At Tilbury prior to embarkation
25 Oct 1850	Arrived per *'Hashemy'* "The pensioner's wife refused to accompany him"
1852	Departed Colony

Service and Personal Details:

Place of Birth:	Castle Ellis Co. Wexford	
Age on Attestation:	18 years	
Period of Service:	1821 — 1842	
Age on Discharge:	39 years	
Length of Service:	21 years	
Foreign Service:	West Indies	8 years
	North America	3 years 6 months
Reason for Discharge:	Catarrh caused by fever caught whilst serving in the West Indies	
Character:	That of a Trustworthy and Faithful Soldier	
Trade or Occupation:	Labourer	
Can Sign Name:	X his mark on discharge	
Height:	5' 6¾"	
Hair Colour:	Grey	
Eyes:	Grey	
Complexion:	Sallow	
Intends to Reside:	Dublin	

MITCHELL John, drummer
63rd Foot

8 June 1829	Arrived per *'HMS Sulphur'*
Dec 1831	Court-martial and imprisoned until 10 Jan 1832 due to deserting his post on sentry
Aug 1833	Granted Perth Town Lots 5/V; & 20/V
26 June 1839	Admitted to pension

1846	Pension paid Western Australia 1/- per diem
1853	Employed as Night Warder Convict Service
29 Oct 1868	Died aged 72

Service and Personal Details: WO97/768/4

Place of Birth:	Baileborough Co. Cavan	
Age on Enlistment:	18 years	
Period of Service:	1818 — 1838	
Age on Discharge:	38 years	
Length of Service:	20 years 129 days	
Foreign Service:	Portugal	18 months
	Western Australia	5 years 3 months
	India	4 years 6 months
Reason for Discharge:	Chronic Rheumatism and Varicose state of the veins of the left Spermatic Chord caused by being severely strained while assisting in moving a ship from the sand on which she was wrecked.	
Character:	Irregular	
Trade or Occupation:	Weaver	
Can Sign Name:	Yes	
Height:	5' 6½"	
Hair Colour:	Brown	
Eyes:	Grey	
Complexion:	Ruddy	
Remarks:	Landed at Gravesend — 18th May 1839	
Married:	Jane	
Children:	Joseph [said to have been born on board the '*HMS Sulphur*']	
	Robert William b. ?1831 Perth	

MOFFATT	Thomas, gunner EIC Artillery
Surname Variant	MORPHETT Out Pension No 696
20 July 1859	Admitted to Out-pension Pension paid 2nd East London Pension District 9d. per diem
22 Dec 1866	Arrived per '*Corona*'
12 Oct 1872	Drowned

Service and Personal Details:

Place of Birth:	Poplar Middlesex
Trade or Occupation:	Labourer
Age on Discharge:	30 years
Length of Service:	2 years 6 months
Reason for Discharge:	Injury to knee joint on field service
Character:	Good
Height:	5' 7½"
Complexion:	Fresh
Eye Colour:	Grey
Hair Colour:	Brown

Intends to Reside:	St Georges in the East
MOLLOY	John, private 23rd Foot
Surname Variant	MALLOY
8 Jan 1861	Discharged the Service Chatham Pension paid Athlone 1/-½d. per diem
9 June 1862	Arrived per *'Norwood'* [1]
1863	Stationed Perth District
1864	a Corporal J Molloy contributed 2/- to the Greenough Fire Relief Fund
circa June 1874	Transferred from 2nd Perth Pension District to 1st Perth Pension District
Oct 1876	Convicted before District Court Martial at Perth Western Australia of being drunk when on duty as Gaol Guard — when serving in the Enrolled Force. Sentence on 25/7/1876 to pay fine a fine of a Pound and to be imprisoned for 84 days during which time his pension is suspended
Mar 1877	Application from wife for half of pension during imprisonment
? June 1878	Pension increased to 1/6½d. for diem for service in the Enrolled Force
Apr-Sept 1878	Paid 6d per diem by Colonial Secretary
1878	Pension paid Sth. Australia from 1st Perth District
31 Mar 1880	Perth from South Australia
July 1881	Assigned Perth Lot 78/E
Apr 1882	Died
Sept 1883	Application for Title to Perth Lot 78/E
Dec 1883	Fee Simple issued for Perth Town Lot 78/E
1884	Wife advising of change of Title to Perth Town Lot 78/E

Service and Personal Details:

Place of Birth:	Gibraltar Andalusia	
Age on Attestation:	18 years 6 months	
Period of Service:	1838 — 1861	
Age on Discharge:	41 years 3 months	
Length of Service:	21 years 18 days	
Foreign Service:	Canada	11 years 1 month
	Turkey & Crimea	1 year 1 month
	East Indies	1 year 1 month
Medal Entitlement:	Crimean with clasp and Turkish Crimean	
Reason for Discharge:	Own Request after 21 years service	
Character:	Good	
Trade or Occupation:	Labourer	
Can Sign Name:	Yes	
Height:	5' 6½"	
Hair Colour:	Dark Brown	
Eyes:	Blue	
Complexion:	Fresh	
Intends to Reside:	Athlone	

MOLONEY	Patrick, gunner EIC
	Bengal Artillery 2nd Company 5th Battalion
	Out Pension No 585
July 1854	Embarked UK per *'Alfred'*
24 Nov 1854	Admitted to Out-pension
	Pension paid 2nd West London Pension District
	9d. per diem
1860	Pension paid East London
28 Dec 1863	Arrived per *'Lord Dalhousie'* as a Convict Guard
1865	Pension paid Adelaide
1873	Pension not paid — "Not Appeared"
Service and Personal Details:	
Where Born:	Tipperary Ireland
Trade or Occupation:	Shoemaker
Where Enlisted:	Liverpool
Presidency:	Bengal
Length of Service:	2 years 8 months
Age on Discharge:	26 years
Reason for Discharge:	Dislocation of the clavicle received in action at Rangoon
Character:	Good
Medal Entitlement:	Burmah
Height:	5' 9"
Complexion:	Florid
Eye Colour:	Hazel
Hair Colour:	Black
Intends to Reside:	Clonmel Ireland
MONAGHAN	Bernard, private
	3rd Foot
Surname Variant	MONOGHAN
3 Dec 1847	Discharged the Service Dublin
11 Jan 1848	Admitted to Our-Pension
	Pension paid 1st Dublin Pension District
	1/- per diem
1848	Pension paid Jersey
1848	Portsmouth
1852	Cambridge
1853	Pension paid 2nd West London Pension District
14 Aug 1854	Arrived per *'Ramillies'*
Jan 1857	Contributed 2/- to the Florence Nightingale Fund
1864	Pension paid South Australia " The £6-10-0 advanced to his wife to be recovered from his pension."
	" Wife remained in Western Australia"
1875	Pension paid Victoria
Service and Personal Details:	
Place of Birth:	St Marys Enniscorthy Co. Wexford
Age on Attestation:	20 years
Period of Service:	1826 — 1847
Age on Discharge:	41 years 3 months
Length of Service:	21 years 116 days
Foreign Service:	East Indies 18 years

Medal Entitlement:	Campaign against Gwalior and in action at Punniar for which he has received a Bronze Star
Reason for Discharge:	Chronic Hepatitis and Varicose Veins
Character:	Good
Trade or Occupation:	Labourer
Can Sign Name:	Yes
Height:	5' 9"
Hair Colour:	Dark Brown
Eyes:	Grey
Complexion:	Dark

MONAGHAN

	Michael, private 9th Foot
Surname Variant	MINAGHAN
4 Dec 1855	Discharged the Service Chatham Pension paid Galway 1/- per diem
31 Dec 1862	Arrived per *'York'*
1863	Stationed Rottnest
1863	"Indicted for rape" whilst stationed at Rottnest
10 July 1863	Fremantle Mary Monaghan and child applied for relief. Wife of Pensioner Monaghan destitute owing to conviction of husband.
1864	a Michael Monaghan contributed to the Greenough Fire Relief Fund
1864	Keeper Fremantle police lock-up
1867	Residing at York
1868	Pension paid South Australia from Perth WA [£6-10-0 advanced to this man to be recovered from his pension]
1872	Pension paid South Australia
1873	Fined – Indecent Language
1874	Fined – Fighting and attempted burglary
1875	Pension suspended during 1 month term of imprisonment for neglecting to enter service at Adelaide South Australia
June 1876	Convicted at the Criminal Sittings of the Supreme Court of Adelaide on the 14th March 1876 of burglary and sent to prison for 2 years during which time his pension to be suspended
Nov 1876	Case reconsidered whereby half pension to be suspended and the other half paid to wife during imprisonment
1880	Removed from pension list
1886	To be restored to Pension List of 12d. per day provided a reference to Police at Adelaide South Australia as to his character prove satisfactory [Other information papered over in document]
1906	Pension to be resorted to 12d per day subject to the convenience of the Secretary of State
1898	Attended Memorial Day
Aug 1906	To have addition 6d. per day for "Gallant Conduct" — French War Medal

1910	Corporal Michael Monaghan of Rose Street [off West Terrace Adelaide] celebrated his 86th birthday
1914	Died Adelaide South Australia
Service and Personal Details:	
Place of Birth:	Taum Co. Galway
Age on Attestation:	19 years
Period of Service:	1854 — 1855
Age on Discharge:	21 years or 20 years 8 months
Length of Service:	1 year 361 days
Foreign Service:	Crimea 8 months
Medal Entitlement:	Crimean; Turkish Crimean; French Military Medal 'For Valour'
Reason for Discharge:	Disabled by loss of 2 phalanges of right hand
Character:	Good
Trade or Occupation:	Labourer
Can Sign Name:	blank; [Corporal on discharge] No on Attestation
Height:	5' 7¼"
Hair Colour:	Dark Brown
Eyes:	Grey
Complexion:	Fresh
Intends to Reside:	Tuam Co. Galway
Remarks:	Presented with a silk pocket handkerchief embroidered by Queen Victoria. This handkerchief went missing after Corporal Monaghan loaned it to the then Governor of South Australia.
1914	Corporal Monaghan received a replacement handkerchief from Queen Mary [unverified information sourced from newspaper- 'Trove']

MONAGHAN	Peter, private and drummer 35th Foot
8 May 1860	Discharged the Service Chatham Pension paid Tullamore 9d. per diem
1861	Pension paid Birr
1862	Bermuda
15 Feb 1863	Arrived per *'Merchantman'* [1]
Nov 1866	Assistant Warder
July 1870 - Feb 1871	In Guildford Road Party
17 Oct 1870	Had a valuable dog and government property wheelbarrow stolen by un-identified prisoners at Upper Swan Bridge
1874	Residing Albany and was appointed as Chief Clerk to the Albany Council
1878	Pension increased to 12d. West. Aust District
June 1881	Assigned Albany Lot P2
Feb 1885	Application for Title Albany Lot P2
1885	Appointed Drill Instructor to the Albany Defence Rifles Bandmaster of the first brass band in Albany

Mar 1906	Died aged 83 at Albany	
Service and Personal Details:		
Place of Birth:	Island of St Christopher West Indies	
Age on Attestation:	14 years 3 months	
Period of Service:	1835 — 1859	
Age on Discharge:	39 years 4 months or 38 years 3 months	
Length of Service:	20 years 190 days	
Foreign Service:	Mauritius	10 years 328 days
	East Indies	4 years 328 days
Medal Entitlement:	India Mutiny	
Reason for Discharge:	Chronic Rheumatism affecting shoulder, hips and loins	
Character:	Latterly Good	
Trade or Occupation:	Labourer	
Can Sign Name:	Yes	
Height:	5' 9"	
Hair Colour:	Red	
Eyes:	Grey	
Complexion:	Fresh	
Intends to Reside:	Tullamore Kings County Ireland	

MONEY	William Whalan, Serjeant [Bugler] 56th Foot	
Previous Regiment	85th Foot	
11 Oct 1844	Discharged the Service Dublin	
	Pension paid Oxford England	
	10d. per diem	
1847	possibly to New Zealand per '*Minerva*' as a Royal New Zealand Fencible	
1847	Pension paid Howick New Zealand	
1854	Arrived Albany from Auckland New Zealand	
1854	Pension paid Albany from New Zealand	
1859	Departed Albany for Eastern States	
1871	W.O. Correspondence recorded	
1876	Warder at Young Gaol New South Wales	
1877	W.O. Correspondence with Treasury Sydney	
1883	Wife charged with bigamy at Gouldburn NSW	
Service and Personal Details:		
Place of Birth:	New South Wales	
Age on Attestation:	14 years	
Period of Service:	1825 — 1844	
Age on Discharge:	33 years 5 months	
Length of Service:	15 years 174 days	
Foreign Service:	Mediterranean	5 years 11 months
	North America	6 years 1 month
Reason for Discharge:	Chronic Rheumatism	
Character:	Good Trustworthy and sober soldier, but Latterly	
Indifferent		
Trade or Occupation:	Knitter	
Can Sign Name:	Yes	
Height:	6'	

Hair Colour:	Dark Brown
Eyes:	Hazel
Complexion:	Sallow
Distinguishing Marks:	Marks of Blistering and Cupping

MOODY	Thomas, Serjeant
	3rd Dragoon Guards
Previous Regiments	3rd Light Dragoons; 13th Light Dragoons
1 June 1858	Discharged the Service Chatham
	Pension paid 1st North London Pension District
	1/- per diem
1858	Pension paid Salisbury
1859	1st North London Pension District
1860	Perth Scotland
1860	1st North London Pension District
29 Jan 1862	Arrived per *'Lincelles'*
1863	To New South Wales from Fremantle
1863	Pension paid New South Wales
1875	1st East London Pension District

Service and Personal Details:		
Place of Birth:	St Marys Liverpool Lancashire	
Age on Attestation:	18 years	
Period of Service:	1842 — 1858	
Age on Discharge:	33 years 5 months or 34 years 4 months	
Length of Service:	15 years 136 days	
Foreign Service:	East Indies	10 years
	Turkey & Crimea	2 years
Medal Entitlement:	Sutlej Medal with 2 clasps; Punjab with 2 clasps; Crimean Medal with 4 clasps	
Reason for Discharge:	Tibia and Fibula of right leg fractured from kick from horse	

Character:	Good
Trade or Occupation:	Whitesmith
Can Sign Name:	Yes

Height:	5' 6"
Hair Colour:	Dark Brown
Eyes:	Hazel
Complexion:	Dark
Intends to Reside:	35 Henrietta Street Covent Garden London

MOORE	Michael, private
	99th Foot
7 Mar 1855	Discharged the Service Western Australia
Sept 1855	Discharge approved
18 Sept 1855	Pension ratified
	1/- per diem
1855	Pension paid South Australia

MOORE	Peter, private
	22nd Foot
Previous Regiment	28th Foot
6 May 1862	Discharged the Service Chatham
	Pension paid Manchester
	10d. per diem

28 Dec 1863	Arrived per *'Lord Dalhousie'*	
1878	Pension increased to 1/2d. per diem for service in the Enrolled Force	
1882	Gave evidence at the Supreme Court	
5 Apr 1884	Assigned North Fremantle Lot P78	
1 Oct 1884	Granted Fee Simple for North Fremantle Lot P78	
1887	Died	
Service and Personal Details:		
Place of Birth:	Newtown Co. Wicklow	
Age on Attestation:	18 years	
Period of Service:	1843 — 1862	
Age on Discharge:	36 years	
Length of Service:	17 years 301 days	
Foreign Service:	East Indies	approx 11 years
	Malta	3 months
Reason for Discharge:	Chronic Inflammation of the Liver	
Character:	Good	
Trade or Occupation:	Labourer	
Can Sign Name:	Yes	
Height:	5' 7½"	
Hair Colour:	Dark Brown	
Eyes:	Blue	
Complexion:	Fresh	
Intends to Reside:	Manchester Lancashire	

MOORE	Robert, private 54th Foot	
4 Mar 1862	Discharged the Service Pension paid 1st Belfast Pension District 1/- per diem	
1863	Pension paid 2nd Manchester Pension District	
15 Aug 1865	Arrived per *'Racehorse'*	
1866	Pension paid Madras	
Service and Personal Details:		
Place of Birth:	Ahoghill Co. Antrim	
Age on Attestation:	18 years	
Period of Service:	1840 — 1862	
Age on Discharge:	39 years 5 months	
Length of Service:	21 years 166 days	
Foreign Service:	Gibraltar	2 years 8 months
	Malta	1 year 2 months
	West Indies	3 years 4 months
	North America	3 years 3 months
	Mauritius	1 month
	East Indies	3 years 3 months
Medal Entitlement:	Good Conduct and Long Service without gratuity; Indian Mutiny	
Reason for Discharge:	Own Request having completed 21 years service	
Character:	Very Good	
Trade or Occupation:	Weaver	
Can Sign Name:	Yes	

Height:	5' 9½"
Hair Colour:	Dark Brown
Eyes:	Blue
Complexion:	Fresh
Intends to Reside:	North Street Belfast Co. Antrim
MORAN	Michael, private 12th Foot
23 Sept 1836	Discharged the Service Pension paid Athlone 9d. per diem
21 May 1851	Arrived per *'Mermaid'*
Sept 1851	Assigned and occupied North Fremantle Lot P9
Jan 1857	Contributed 2/- to the Florence Nightingale Fund
1858	Applied for Land Title at North Fremantle
1858	Confirmation of grant for North Fremantle Lot P9
1864	ptve M Moran Pensioner Force Fremantle District contributed to the Greenough Fire Relief Fund
1869	In March 1869 Police Constable Michael Moran consented to allow the sum of £1 per month to be deducted from his pay and given to his father, on the first of the succeeding month. This was done and the money forwarded
21 July 1871	Residents Office Fremantle — Michael Moran, Pensioner in receipt of 9d per diem, has been bedridden for 14 years, has applied for Govt. Relief. Accompanying report by Sergeant Furlong, it will be seen that Moran and his family are living in the utmost misery and distress.
1874	Died
Service and Personal Details:	
Place of Birth:	Lifford Co. Donegal
Age on Attestation:	15 years 7 months
Period of Service:	1823 — 1836
Age on Discharge:	28 years
Length of Service:	11 years 100 days
Foreign Service:	Gibraltar 10 years 5 months
Reason for Discharge:	Vision considerably impaired
Character:	Very Good
Trade or Occupation:	Tailor
Can Sign Name:	X his mark on discharge
Height:	5' 11"
Hair Colour:	Brown
Eyes:	Blue
Complexion:	Fair
Remarks:	Granted a Permanent Pension of 9d. per diem by Board — W.O. Letter dated 16/1/39
MORAN	Terence, private [2503] 15th Foot
Surname Variant	MOREN
1 Jan 1867	Discharged the Service

	Pension paid Jersey
	10d. per diem
13 July 1867	Arrived per *'Norwood'* [2]
1868	Employed by Convict Establishment
circa June 1874	Transferred from Fremantle to 1st Perth District
1877	Died - buried East Perth Cemetery

Service and Personal Details:		
Place of Birth:	Michaelstown Co. Cork	
Age on Attestation:	19 years	
Period of Service:	1845 — 1866	
Age on Discharge:	40 years 5 months	
Length of Service:	21 years 49 days	
Foreign Service:	Ceylon	9 years 9 months
	Gibraltar	11 months
	North America	4 years 10 months
Reason for Discharge:	Own Request having completed 21 years service	
Character:	Good	
Trade or Occupation:	Labourer	
Can Sign Name:	Yes	
Height:	5' 10"	
Hair Colour:	Grey	
Eyes:	Black	
Complexion:	Sallow	
Intends to Reside:	Jersey Channel Islands	

MORAN	Timothy, private
	50th Foot
16 Aug 1844	Discharged the Service Chatham
	Pension paid 2nd Manchester Pension District
	6d. per diem
8 June 1858	Arrived per *'Lord Raglan'*
1857	Outdoor Paupers in the Colonial Hospital — This man is a Pensioner, his pension is at present given to his wife and children who live at Fremantle; he is suffering from diseased lungs and dropsy from enlarged liver and is incurable.
	He is aged 40 and married
19 Mar 1863	Died

Service and Personal Details:		
Place of Birth:	Roscrea Templemore Co. Tipperary	
Age on Attestation:	17 years	
Period of Service:	1831 — 1844	
Age on Discharge:	30 years	
Length of Service:	11 years 287 days	
Foreign Service:	New South Wales	6 years 96 days
	East Indies	2 years 209 days
Medal Entitlement:	Punniar	
Reason for Discharge:	Wounded right foot in action at Punniar 1843	
Character:	Indifferent	
Trade or Occupation:	Shoemaker	
Can Sign Name:	Yes	

Height:	5' 8½"
Hair Colour:	Black
Eyes:	Hazel
Complexion:	Sallow
Intends to Reside:	Cork
Religion:	Catholic

MORGAN	Henry, gunner and driver RA 10th Battalion
13 Apr 1847	Discharged the Service Woolwich Pension paid 2nd Manchester Pension District 1/- per diem
1848	Pension paid Sheffield
1850	Pension paid 2nd Manchester Pension District
1 June 1850	Arrived per *'Scindian'*
1850	Assigned Freshwater Bay Loc 8
13 Sept 1850	Died

Service and Personal Details:

Place of Birth:	Manchester Lancashire
Age on Attestation:	21 years
Period of Service:	1825 — 1847
Age on Discharge:	42 years 4 months
Length of Service:	21 years 53 days
Foreign Service:	Corfu 8 years 3 months
Reason for Discharge:	Chronic Cough and Chronic Rheumatism
Character:	Very Good
Trade or Occupation:	Carder
Can Sign Name:	X his mark on discharge
Height:	5' 10½"
Hair Colour:	Dark Brown
Eyes:	Grey
Complexion:	Fair

MORGAN	Henry, private EIC 1st Madras European Fusiliers Out Pension No 487
27 June 1849	Admitted to Out-pension Pension paid Gloucester Pension District 9d. per diem
1850	Pension paid Wales East Pension District
14 Aug 1854	Arrived per *'Ramillies'*
1856	To South Australia from Western Australia
1858	Henry Morgan — tailor of Franklin Street., Adelaide; charged with being a dangerous lunatic
1866	Pension paid Adelaide South Australia
26 Dec 1880	Died aged 73 at his residence at French Street Adelaide South Australia

Service and Personal Details:

Where Born:	Berkley [sic] Gloucester
from Obituary:	born on the 15th Aug 1808 in the vicinity of Clifton Bristol [Trove]

Trade or Occupation:	Servant
Age on Enlistment:	19 years
Date Enlisted:	27th Feb 1827
Where Enlisted:	London
Embarked India:	19th May 1828 per *'Hercules'* [L/MIL/9/42]
Presidency:	Madras
Length of Service:	19 years 1 month or 19 years
Age on Discharge:	39 years or 41 years depending on record source
Reason for Discharge:	Liver complaint
Character:	Not Good
Intends to Reside:	Gloucester
Height:	5' 5¾" or 5' 8" depending on record source
Complexion:	Fair
Visage:	Round
Eye Colour:	Blue
Hair Colour:	Fair or light [depending on record source]
Marriage Details:	Madras Ecclesiastical Returns N2/20/179 11th Jan 1841 Secunderabad Henry Morgan, private 1st M.E. Regiment Batchelor, and Mary Conlin, a native Christian Widow, were married by banns at St John's Church Secunderabad

MORGAN Robert, gunner and driver
Coastal Brigade [RA] No. 6 Division

20 Mar 1866	Discharged the Service Tilbury Fort Pension paid 1st East London Pension District 1/2½d. per diem
4 July 1866	Arrived per *'Belgravia'*
1876	Died buried East Perth Pioneer Cemetery

Service and Personal Details:

Place of Birth:	Moy Co. Tyrone
Age on Attestation:	17 years 9 months
Period of Service:	1841 — 1866
Age on Discharge:	42 years 9 months
Length of Service:	24 years 272 days
Foreign Service:	Jamaica 4 years 11 months
Reason for Discharge:	Completed service entitling him to pension
Character:	Exemplary
Trade or Occupation:	Shoemaker
Can Sign Name:	Yes
Height:	5' 7½"
Hair Colour:	Brown
Eyes:	Grey
Complexion:	Fair
Intends to Reside:	Western Australia

MORIATY Bartholomew, Corporal EIC
1st Madras Fusiliers

Surname Variant	MORIARTY Out Pension No 787
14 Dec 1860	Admitted to Out-pension

	Pension paid Tralee
	1/- per diem
1862	Pension paid 2nd East London Pension District
27 May 1863	Arrived per *'Clyde'*
1864	a Bartholomew Moriarty to South Australia per *'Europa'* with wife
1865	Pension paid Adelaide from Fremantle
1867	Pension paid Calcutta

Service and Personal Details:	
Where Born:	Kerry
Trade or Occupation:	none given
Presidency:	Madras
Age on Discharge:	39 years
Length of Service:	21 years
Reason for Discharge:	Time expired
Medal Entitlement:	Indian Mutiny with clasps
Character:	Good
Height:	5' 5½"
Complexion:	Sallow
Eye Colour:	Grey
Hair Colour:	Brown
Intends to Reside:	?Cahirciveen

MORRISSEY	Patrick, private
	10th Foot
Surname Variants	MORRISEY; MORRISSY; MORRISAY
9 Sept 1851	Discharged the Service Chatham
	Pension paid Waterford
	7d. per diem for 2 years
2 Aug 1852	Arrived per *'William Jardine'*
1852	Employed as Night Warder
1853	Pension ceased

Service and Personal Details:	
Place of Birth:	St Patricks Waterford Co. Waterford
Age on Attestation:	18 years
Period of Service:	1843 — 1850
Age on Discharge:	26 years
Length of Service:	7 years 15 days
Foreign Service:	India five years 6 months
Medal Entitlement:	Served in Campaigns of Mooltan 1848 and Goojerat 1849
Reason for Discharge:	Chronic Dysentery
Character:	Good
Trade or Occupation:	Labourer
Can Sign Name:	X his mark on discharge
Height:	5' 7¼"
Hair Colour:	Brown
Eyes:	Grey
Complexion:	Swarthy
Intends to Reside:	Waterford
Married:	Anastasia d. *c*1857

MORTIMER	Arthur, gunner and driver
	RA 2nd Battalion
8 July 1845	Discharged the Service Woolwich
	Pension paid Aberdeen
	1/- per diem
25 Oct 1850	Arrived per *'Hashemy'*
1851	Employed in Convict Establishment
Service and Personal Details:	
Place of Birth:	St Nicholas Aberdeen Aberdeenshire
Age on Attestation:	17 years
Period of Service:	1823 — 1845
Age on Discharge:	39 years 53 days
Length of Service:	21 years 16 days
Foreign Service:	North America 6 years 3 months
Reason for Discharge:	Chronic Rheumatism
Character:	Good
Trade or Occupation:	Weaver
Can Sign Name:	Yes
Height:	5' 7½"
Hair Colour:	Light
Eyes:	Blue
Complexion:	Fair
MORTON	Samuel, private
	95th Foot
Previous Regiment	80th Foot
13 Aug 1847	Discharged the Service Chatham
	Pension paid Birr
	1/- per diem
1851	Pension paid Kilkenny
7 Feb 1853	Arrived per *'Dudbrook'*
Jan 1857	Contributed 2/- to the Florence Nightingale Fund
1861	Pension paid Sydney
1975	New South Wales
1881	Died
Service and Personal Details:	
Place of Birth:	Burnall Derbyshire
Age on Attestation:	18 years
Period of Service:	1824 — 1847
Age on Discharge:	41 years 7 months
Length of Service:	23 years 33 days
Foreign Service:	Mediterranean 10 years 9 months
	Ceylon 7 years 10 months
Reason for Discharge:	Worn out from length of service
Trade or Occupation:	Labourer
Can Sign Name:	Yes
Height:	5' 7½"
Hair Colour:	Brown
Eyes:	Brown
Complexion:	Fair
Intends to Reside:	Templemore

MOTTRAM	Samuel, private [Military Pensioner]
	51st Foot
Previous Regiment	90th Foot
Surname Variant	MORTTRAM; MORTON
25 June 1840	Arrived per *'Runnymede'* with regiment
11 Mar 1847	Discharged the Service Perth Western Australia
24 Aug 1847	Discharge approved
	1/- per diem
1861	Pension paid Melbourne from Fremantle
	"Drunken wife to join husband."
	£7-16-8 Stoppage from pension
*c*1882	Died Victoria aged 82

Service and Personal Details:		
Place of Birth:	Stone Staffordshire	
Age on Attestation:	23 years	
Period of Service:	1826 — 1847	
Age on Discharge:	43 years 8 months	
Length of Service:	20 years 265 days	
Foreign Service:	Australian Colonies	about 9 years
	Ionian Isles	5 years 6 months
Reason for Discharge:	Rheumatic Affection and unfit for further service	
Character:	That of a Good Soldier	
Trade or Occupation:	Labourer	
Can Sign Name:	Yes	
Height:	5' 10¼"	
Hair Colour:	Brown	
Eyes:	Hazel	
Complexion:	Fair	
Intends to Reside:	Western Australia	
Married:	Catherine Magnor or Pope d. *c*1868	
Children:	Margaret Mary b. *c*1837 Ireland	
	m. *c*1851 William Branson Perth	
	John b. *c*1839 Tasmania	
	m. *c*1860 Sarah Coote Bunbury	
	Jane b. *c*1842 Rottnest island	
	m. 1] *c*1858 William Brom Perth	
	m. 2] *c*1867 Nehemiah Fisher Albany	
	Samuel b. *c*1847 Garden Island	
	Ann b. *c*1849 Perth	
	James b. *c*1852 Perth	

MUIR	William, private EIC
	1st Bombay European Infantry
	Out Pension No 771
1860	Embarked UK per *'Cossipore'*
17 Oct 1860	Admitted to Out-pension
	Pension paid 2nd East London Pension District
	1/- per diem
31 Dec 1862	Arrived per *'York'*
1879	an H Kingston was a passenger on the *'Rosette'* when she went missing off the Fortescue River
24 Aug 1881	Assigned Perth Railway Block Lot 132/V

15 Dec 1883	Granted Fee Simple Perth Railway Block Lot 132/V
1886	Taken to hospital suffering from injuries received when knocked down by a train at the Occidental Hotel crossing [Trove]
1886	Died

Service and Personal Details:

Place of Birth:	Lismore Waterford
Trade or Occupation:	Shoemaker
Where Enlisted:	Liverpool
Presidency:	Bombay
Length of Service:	19 years 7 months
Age on Discharge:	37 years
Reason for Discharge:	To be pensioned
Character:	Good
Medal Entitlement:	Indian Mutiny
Height:	5' 5½" or 5' 6½"
Complexion:	Fresh
Eye Colour:	Grey
Hair Colour:	Brown
Intends to Reside:	Wapping
Married:	1861 Catherine Ferguson England
Children:	Mary Kingston b.1840 [stepdaughter] Thomas Kingston b.1845 [stepson] m. *c*1874 Elizabeth May Toodyay Charles Kingston b. *c*1846 [stepson] James Kingston b.1848 [stepson] Charles Kingston b.1852 ?d. *c*1861 [stepson] Henry Kingston b.1855 d. *c*1879 [stepson] Francis Kingston b.1857 [stepson] m. *c*1885 Bridget O'Neil Perth Catherine b. *c*1862 Kent m. *c*1883 William Seymour Perth
Nov 1872	Charles Kingston disposed— "I am a free man, stepson of a pensioner" [Trove]
June 1872	Charles Kingdom disposed — "I know Annie Claffey and have been in her company" [Trove]

MUIRHEAD	Archibald, gunner and driver RA 1st Battalion
26 May 1857	Discharged the Service Woolwich
9 June 1857	Admitted to Out-Pension Pension paid 1st Portsmouth Pension District 10d. per diem
27 May 1863	Arrived per *'Clyde'*
1869	Charged with being drunk and fighting at the Shamrock Hotel Perth.

Service and Personal Details:

Place of Birth:	Glasgow Lanarkshire
Age on Attestation:	18 years 4 months
Period of Service:	1835 — 1857

Age on Discharge:	39 years 9 months	
Length of Service:	21 years 182 days	
Foreign Service:	West Indies	5 years 10 months
	Gibraltar	8 years 10 months
Reason for Discharge:	Chronic Rheumatism	
Character:	Very Good	
Trade or Occupation:	Printer of Calico	
Can Sign Name:	Yes	
Height:	5' 8¾"	
Hair Colour:	Fair	
Eyes:	Grey	
Complexion:	Fair	

MULDOON Owen, private EIC
2nd Bengal European Regiment
Out Pension No 536

6 Aug 1851	Admitted to Out-pension Pension paid Drogheda Pension District 9d. per diem
2 Apr 1856	Arrived per *'William Hammond'*
1857	To South Australia from Western Australia "Pension subject to stoppage of £20/2/0 "for repayment of passage money
1865	Residing Tea Tree Gully South Australia
1866	Pension paid Adelaide South Australia
1892	Died aged 75 at Gilbert Street West of senile decay

Service and Personal Details:

Where Born:	Enniskean Co Meath
Trade or Occupation:	Labourer
Where Enlisted:	Dublin
Presidency:	Bengal
Length of Service:	9 years 4 months
Age on Discharge:	27 or 28 [depending on record]
Reason for Discharge:	Wasted right leg and lameness from wound received at Goojerat. Wounded in the right leg in action
Character:	Good
Medal Entitlement:	Punjaub with clasp
Height:	5' 5"
Complexion:	Fresh
Eye Colour:	Grey
Hair Colour:	Fair
Intends to Reside:	Enniskean nr Nobber Co Meath

MULLIGAN Christopher, private
86th Foot

11 May 1852	Discharged the Service Chatham Pension paid 1st Dublin Pension District 7d. per diem for 2 years
19 Aug 1853	Arrived per *'Robert Small'*
1867	Died aged 50

Service and Personal Details:

Place of Birth:	? Donnymure Co. Meath
Age on Attestation:	22 years
Period of Service:	1839 — 1852
Age on Discharge:	34 years 10 months
Length of Service:	8 years 164 days
Foreign Service:	East Indies 7 years
Reason for Discharge:	Unfit for further service
Character:	Good
Trade or Occupation:	Labourer
Can Sign Name:	X his mark on discharge
Height:	5' 7¼"
Hair Colour:	Brown
Eyes:	Grey
Complexion:	Fresh
Remarks:	Marked with letter "D"
Intends to Reside:	Dunboyne Co. Meath

MULLOY Patrick, private
64th Foot

Previous Regiment	22nd Foot
Surname Variants	MALLOY; MOLLOY
27 Mar 1860	Discharged the Service Pension paid 2nd Belfast Pension District 1/- per diem
27 May 1863	Arrived per *'Clyde'*
1881	Pension paid Tasmania

Service and Personal Details:

Place of Birth:	Belfast Co. Antrim
Age on Attestation:	20 years
Period of Service:	1839 — 1860
Age on Discharge:	41 years
Length of Service:	21 years 34 days
Foreign Service:	East Indies 18 years 5 months
Medal Entitlement:	Medal for Meanee; Persia with clasp ; Indian Service Medal 1857 - 1858
Reason for Discharge:	Own Request having served 21 years
Character:	Very Good
Trade or Occupation:	Labourer
Can Sign Name:	X his mark on discharge
Height:	5' 6½"
Hair Colour:	Brown
Eyes:	Grey
Complexion:	Fresh
Intends to Reside:	Belfast

MUNDAY William, private
1st Foot

Surname Variant	MUNDY
15 Nov 1859	Discharged the Service Pension paid Hull 1/- per diem

11 Feb 1861	Arrived per *'Palmeston'*	
circa Dec 1873	Transferred from 1st Perth District to Fremantle	
1878	Pension increased to 1/2½d. per diem for 5 years service in the Enrolled Force	
Service and Personal Details:		
Place of Birth:	Mary-le-bone London Middlesex	
Age on Attestation:	20 years 7 months	
Period of Service:	1838 — 1859	
Age on Discharge:	42 years 5 months	
Length of Service:	21 years 288 days	
Foreign Service:	Canada &	
	Nova Scotia &	
	West Indies	8 years 3 months
	Cephalonia &	
	Crimea	3 years 4 months
	Malta &	
	Gibraltar	2 years 2 months
Medal Entitlement:	Crimea	
Reason for Discharge:	Own Request having completed 21 years service	
Character:	Very Good	
Trade or Occupation:	Cordwainer	
Can Sign Name:	Yes	
Height:	5' 7"	
Hair Colour:	Dark Brown	
Eyes:	Brown	
Complexion:	Fresh	
Intends to Reside:	Hull	

MUNRO	Archibald, private	
	Royal Sappers and Miners 20th Company	
Dec 1861	Discharged with gratuity at Fremantle	
Service and Personal Details:		
Place of Birth:	Oban Argyle	
Age on Discharge:	44 years	
Length of Service:	19 years 10 months	
Foreign Service:	Gibraltar	6 years 4 months
	Australia	10 years 4 months
Reason for Discharge:	Granted a Free Discharge to settle in Colony with gratuity and Right of Registry for a Deferred Pension on him attaining 60 years	
Character:	Good	
Trade or Occupation:	Carpenter	
Height:	5' 8"	
Hair Colour:	Brown	
Eyes:	Hazel	
Complexion:	Dark	

MURPHY	Cornelius, private
	84th Foot
Previous Regiment	63rd Foot
5 Aug 1856	Discharged the Service Chatham

	Pension paid 1st Cork Pension District
	8d. per diem
8 June 1858	Arrived per *'Lord Raglan'*
1864	To New South Wales from Perth West Australia
1875	Pension paid Sydney

Service and Personal Details:

Place of Birth:	St Nicholas Cork Co. Cork
Age on Attestation:	19 years 9 months
Period of Service:	1835 — 1855
Age on Discharge:	41 year or 40 years 7 months
Length of Service:	20 years 329 days
Foreign Service:	East Indies 20 years 88 days
Reason for Discharge:	Declining health and Impaired vision
Character:	Indifferent
Trade or Occupation:	Labourer
Can Sign Name:	Yes
Height:	5' 11"
Hair Colour:	Brown
Eyes:	Blue
Complexion:	Fresh
Intends to Reside:	Cork Ireland

MURPHY James, private

	19th Foot
16 Dec 1825	Discharged the Service
	Pension paid 1st East London Pension District
	9d. per diem
1 June 1850	Arrived per *'Scindian'*
1850	Assigned land Freshwater Bay
1854	Pension paid Western Australia
Jan 1857	Contributed 2/- to the Florence Nightingale Fund
Sept 1858	Application for Title Freshwater Bay Loc P237
12 May 1860	Pension paid Melbourne from Perth West. Aust.

Service and Personal Details:

Place of Birth:	Carlow Co. Carlow
Age on Attestation:	20 years
Period of Service:	1822 — 1825
Age on Discharge:	22 years
Length of Service:	2 years 352 days
Reason for Discharge:	Disease of the ligaments and bones of the left ankle joint
Character:	Very Good
Trade or Occupation:	Labourer
Can Sign Name:	X his mark on discharge
Height:	5' 10¼"
Hair Colour:	Brown
Eyes:	Hazel
Complexion:	Sallow

MURPHY Jeremiah, Corporal

29th Foot

22 Dec 1846	Discharged the Service Pension paid 2nd North London Pension District 1/3d. per diem
14 Aug 1854	Arrived per *'Ramillies'*

Service and Personal Details:

Place of Birth:	Tralee Co. Kerry	
Age on Attestation:	17 years [underage 1 year]	
Period of Service:	1827 — 1846	
Age on Discharge:	36 years [or 35 years depending on record]	
Length of Service:	18 years 58 days [or 18 years 10 months]	
Foreign Service:	Mauritius	8 years 4 months
	East Indies	3 years 8months
Reason for Discharge:	Wounded in the left thigh by a round shot in action	
Character:	Good for the last 7 years	
Trade or Occupation:	Labourer	
Can Sign Name:	X his mark on discharge	
Height:	5' 7"	
Hair Colour:	Light Brown	
Eyes:	Blue	
Complexion:	Fresh	
Intends to Reside:	London	

MURPHY	Jeremiah, private 40th Foot
18 June 1861	Discharged the Service Chatham Pension paid 1st East London Pension District 8d. per diem
4 July 1866	Arrived per *'Belgravia'*
1867	Assistant Warder
1873	"Pension suspended"
1873	W.O. correspondence — Convicted of desertion from Force of Enrolled Pensioners in Western Australia. Pension suspended during imprisonment of 84 days
1903	Died

Service and Personal Details:

Place of Birth:	Middleton Co. Cork	
Age on Attestation:	18 years	
Period of Service:	1852 — 1860	
Age on Discharge:	27 years 3 months	
Length of Service:	8 years 271 days	
Foreign Service:	Australia [sic]	8 years 7 months
Reason for Discharge:	Gunshot wound left arm	
Character:	Indifferent	
Trade or Occupation:	Labourer	
Can Sign Name:	Yes	
Height:	5' 8½"	
Hair Colour:	Brown	
Eyes:	Hazel	
Complexion:	Fresh	

Remarks:	At Waitara [New Zealand] on 27th June 1860
Intends to Reside:	Middleton Co. Cork

MURPHY

	John, private
	22nd Foot
22 June 1852	Discharged the Service Chatham
	Pension paid Jersey
	10d. per diem
1854	Pension paid 2nd Plymouth Pension District
24 May 1855	Arrived per *'Stag'*
1856	Claim of £17 against Capt Foss
1857	Pension paid Adelaide South Australia
2 Oct 1858	Died

Service and Personal Details:

Place of Birth:	Gillion Kings County	
Age on Attestation:	18 years	
Period of Service:	1832 — 1851	
Age on Discharge:	37 years	
Length of Service:	18 years 275 days	
Foreign Service:	East Indies	8 years 343 days
Reason for Discharge:	Chronic Hepatitis	
Character:	Good	
Trade or Occupation:	Labourer	
Can Sign Name:	X his mark on discharge	
Height:	5' 8"	
Hair Colour:	Dark Brown	
Eyes:	Grey	
Complexion:	Sallow	
Intends to Reside:	Liverpool	

MURPHY

	John [William], private
	95th Foot
Previous Regiments	83rd; 21st
20 Dec 1869	Discharged the Service Pembroke Dock
4 Jan 1870	Admitted to Pension
	1/1d. per diem
1865	Jersey
1865	Plymouth
1866	Carlow
1866	Bristol
1873	Bristol
1874	Arrived per *'Naval Brigade'*
11 Nov 1880	Joined Enrolled Guard — stationed Perth
Jan 1881	Pension increased to 1/3½d. per diem for service in the Enrolled Force of Western Australia
July 1881	Assigned Perth Pensioner Lot 75/E
Nov 1883	Application for Title to Perth Lot 75/E
2 Mar 1884	Granted Perth Town Lot 75/E
July 1887	Commandant Volunteers — recommending J. Murphy [late of Enrolled Guard] for Employment,
June 1897	Stationed at Perth
May 1909	Died buried Roman Catholic Section of East Perth Cemetery
Sept 1909	Grant of Probate to Mary Dorothy Murphy

Service and Personal Details:	
Place of Birth:	Tulla Co. Clare
Age on Attestation:	21 years
Period of Service:	1848 — 1869
Age on Discharge:	42 years
Length of Service:	20 years 5 months [reckoned]
Foreign Service:	India 20 years 5 months
Medal Entitlement:	Indian Mutiny with clasp for Central India; Long Service and Good Conduct with gratuity of £5/-/-
Reason for Discharge:	Claimed it on termination of his second period of limited engagement
Character:	Very Good
Trade or Occupation:	Labourer
Can Sign Name:	Yes
Height:	5' 9"
Hair Colour:	Black
Eyes:	Hazel
Complexion:	Fresh
Intends to Reside:	Limerick Co. Limerick

MURPHY	Michael Joseph, Serjeant Major [Imperial soldier]
Campaigns Served	India
	Africa
	Afghanistan
Medal Entitlement	Robert's Kandahar Star; Afghanistan
1920	Died aged 67
Married:	Elizabeth McCarthy
Children:	Charles
	m. *c*1898 Sarah Walsh Perth
	Arthur b. *c*1896 Fremantle
	Mrs M Bramwell
	Eileen

MURPHY	Patrick, private EIC
	2nd Madras Light Infantry
	Out Pension No 641
6 Aug 1856	Admitted to Out-pension
	Pension paid Clonmel
	9d per diem
1866	Pension paid Carlow
22 Dec 1866	Arrived per *'Corona'*
8 June 1873	Died
Service and Personal Details:	
Where Born:	Clonmel Ireland
Trade or Occupation:	Labourer
Presidency:	Madras
Age on Discharge:	32 years
Length of Service:	14 years 4 months
Reason for Discharge:	Severe strain of left ankle
Character:	Very Good

Height:	5' 5"
Complexion:	Fresh
Eye Colour:	Grey
Hair Colour:	Brown
Intends to Reside:	Clonmel Ireland

MURPHY	Peter, private
	31st Foot
12 Sept 1838	Discharged the Service
	Pension paid Roscommon
	6d. per diem
1847	Pension paid Liverpool
1847	Roscommon
1849	Manchester
1 June 1850	Arrived per *'Scindian'*
1850	Assigned Freshwater Bay Loc P231
1858	Application for Title Freshwater Bay Loc P231 and P247
1859	Pension paid Melbourne Victoria
1871	2nd West London Pension District
1873	Athlone

Service and Personal Details:	
Place of Birth:	Ballinasloe Co. Galway
Age on Attestation:	18 years
Period of Service:	1824 — 1837
Age on Discharge:	30 years
Length of Service:	12 years 324 days
Foreign Service:	East Indies [no time period given]
Reason for Discharge:	"Anchylosis of two fingers of left hand"
Character:	Very Good
Trade or Occupation:	Labourer
Can Sign Name:	Yes
Height:	5' 6½"
Hair Colour:	Brown
Eyes:	Grey
Complexion:	Fair
Remarks:	Landed at Gravesend 18th July 1838

MURRAY	James Albert
	18th Foot — [the Royal Irish Regiment]
1881	Arrived Australia and resided in Adelaide
circa 1883	Arrived Western Australia
1915	Residing 13 Howard Str. Leederville
1915	Died aged 66

Service and Personal Details:	
Place of Birth:	Co. Armagh Ireland
Period of Service:	1869 — circa 1881
Length of Service:	circa 12 years
Foreign Service:	India
Medal Entitlement:	Afghan 1878/1880
Trade or Occupation:	Engineer and Boilermaker
Married:	widow of private Daniel Gleeson

MURRAY	John, Serjeant EIC
	1st Bombay European Fusiliers
	Out Pension No 505
1849	Embarked UK per *'Meeanee'*
8 Aug 1849	Admitted to Out-pension
	Pension paid 1st East London Pension District
	1/9d. per diem
13 July 1867	Arrived per *'Norwood'* [2]
1870	To Melbourne from Fremantle
1871	Pension paid Melbourne
Service and Personal Details:	
Where Born:	Fort Barry Cork
Trade or Occupation:	Chemist
Where Enlisted:	London
Presidency:	Bombay
Length of Service:	1 year 7 months
Age on Discharge:	29 years
Reason for Discharge:	Loss of middle finger and power of remaining fingers of left hand from wounds received at Moultan [sic]
Character:	Good
Remarks:	6d extra on pension for gallant conduct while in action at Moultan [sic]
Height:	6' 1½"
Complexion:	Fresh
Visage:	Oval
Eye Colour:	Hazel
Hair Colour:	Dark Brown
Intends to Reside:	2 Ellen Place, Ellen Street, St George in the East

MURRIN	Lewis, private
	52nd Foot
Surname Variant	MURREN
31 Aug 1858	Discharged the Service Chatham
	Pension paid Tullamore
	9d. per diem
1860	Pension paid 2nd Dublin Pension District
1861	Pension paid 1st East London Pension District
1861	Pension paid 1st Portsmouth Pension District
1861	Assistant Warder in United Kingdom
31 Dec 1862	Arrived per *'York'* as a Convict Guard
1862	Employed by Convict Establishment
1863	To Eastern Colonies from Perth West Aust
1890	W.O. correspondence to — c/o Officer paying Imperial Pensioners Sydney New South Wales
1891	W.O. correspondence to Treasury Sydney — pension commuted
Service and Personal Details:	
Place of Birth:	Tullamore Kings County
Age on Attestation:	17 years
Period of Service:	1853 — 1858
Age on Discharge:	22 years 7 months

Length of Service: 3 years 325 days [after age of 18 years]
Foreign Service: India 4 years 2 months
Medal Entitlement: Indian Mutiny
Reason for Discharge: Wounded in leg by musket ball

Character: Good
Trade or Occupation: Labourer
Can Sign Name: Yes

Height: 5' 7"
Hair Colour: Light Brown
Eyes: Blue
Complexion: Fresh

NASH John, private
77th Foot
22 Nov 1853 Discharged the Service Chatham
Pension paid 2nd West London Pension District
1/- per diem
2 Apr 1856 Arrived per *'William Hammond'*
July 1856 £4/13/2 balance due on landing at colony but misappropriated by Capt Foss
29 Aug 1856 Died

Service and Personal Details:
Place of Birth: Edmonton Middlesex
Age on Attestation: 20 years 6 months
Period of Service: 1832 — 1853
Age on Discharge: 41 years 8 months
Length of Service: 21 years 43 days
Foreign Service: Malta &
Corfu &
Mediterranean 5 years 4 months
Jamaica 2 years 11 months
North America 2 years 4 months
Reason for Discharge: Chronic Rheumatism

Character: Very Good
Trade or Occupation: Plumber
Can Sign Name: Yes

Height: 5' 6¼"
Hair Colour: Brown
Eyes: Brown
Complexion: Fresh
Intends to Reside: Fulham Road Chelsea

NAUGHTON Joseph, private EIC
Previous Regiments Bengal Fusiliers 2nd European Battalion
Invalid Battalion
Surname Variants [some] McNAUGHTON; NAGHTEN; NORTON; NAWTON; LAUGHTON
Out Pension No 89
Mar 1860 Admitted to Out-pension
1860 Embarked UK per *'Lady Melville'*
Pension paid Kilkenny
1/- per diem

15 Aug 1865	Arrived per *'Racehorse'*
Feb 1866	Guard at North Fremantle Quarry
Dec 1869	a J Naughton forfeited Fremantle Town Locs 676 and 677 due to the non payment of the balance of purchase money
1874	Applies for £15 improvement grant
4 Apr 1870	Fremantle Pensioner Joseph Naughton — now quite sane and capable of taking care of himself. the following entry may not necessarily refer to private Joseph Naughton EIC
14 May 1879	'To Newcastle to replace Pensioner James Griffin who is unfit'
Apr 1881	Application for Title to Perth Lot 148/Y
28 June 1881	Died buried East Perth Pioneer Cemetery

Service and Personal Details:

Place of Birth:	Kilkenny Co Kilkenny
Trade or Occupation:	Coachman
Where Enlisted:	Waterford
Presidency:	Bengal
Length of Service:	20 years 7 months
Age on Discharge:	38 years
Reason for Discharge:	Admitted to Out-Pension
Character:	Good
Height:	5' 6¼"
Complexion:	Fresh
Eye Colour:	Grey
Hair Colour:	Brown
Intends to Reside:	Kilkenny

NAYLOR	Henry Dyson, private 13th [Light] Dragoons
Surname Variant	MAYLOR
23 Oct 1855	Discharged the Service Chatham Pension paid South London 1/- per diem
1855	Pension paid Deptford
1856	Pension paid Perth Scotland due to him serving as one of the Queen's Bodyguards to Maharajah Mandeep Singh
1858	Pension paid South London
9 June 1862	Arrived per *'Norwood'* [1]
1863	Stationed Perth District Western Australia
1864	ptve H D Naylor Pensioner Force at Perth contributed to the Greenough Fire Relief Fund
1865	On Nominal List to proceed to Camden Harbour per *'Tien Tsin'* Night Warder at Fremantle Prison
Nov 1876	Assigned Koojee Loc P8 of 20 acres
1876	Stationed Fremantle
1876	Granted Koojee Loc P8
1877	Pension increased to 1/6d. per diem for 15 years service in the Enrolled Force
1880	Selected for Enrolled Guard
1884	Application for Title to Koojee Loc P8

Dec 1887	H. Naylor - Application for employment
1894	Died aged 59
Service and Personal Details:	
Place of Birth:	Mildenhall Suffolk
Age on Attestation:	16 years 5 months
Period of Service:	1851 — 1855
Age on Discharge:	20 years 4 months
Length of Service:	2 years 60 days [after age of 18 years]
Foreign Service:	Crimea [no time period given]
Medal Entitlement:	Crimea with clasps; Turkish Crimean
Reason for Discharge:	Unfit for further service from disfigurement of the face by fracture of lower jaw at Balaclava. Also being seriously wounded, one of the wounds being caused by a cannon rammer which struck him in the loins — also a gun-shot wound to the shoulder
Character:	Very Good
Trade or Occupation:	Servant
Can Sign Name:	blank; X his mark on Attestation
Height:	5' 7"
Hair Colour:	Dark Red
Eyes:	Brown
Complexion:	Sallow
Distinguishing Marks:	Anchor on left arm

NEAL	James, 2nd Class Serjeant Instructor Musketry 8th Hussars	
Surname Variant	NEIL	
4 Nov 1873	Discharged the Service Longford ? 2/7 per diem	
1875	Residing Perth Western Australia	
Service and Personal Details:		
Place of Birth:	St Lukes London	
Age on Attestation:	18 years	
Period of Service:	1851 — 1873	
Age on Discharge:	38 years 1 month	
Length of Service:	22 years 67 days	
Foreign Service:	Turkey & Crimea	2 years
	East Indies	6 years 1 month
Medal Entitlement:	Crimea with 4 clasps; Turkish Crimean Indian Mutiny with clasp; Good Conduct Medal with gratuity for distinguished service in the field	
Reason for Discharge:	Own request having served 21 years	
Character:	Very Good	
Trade or Occupation:	Hatter	
Can Sign Name:	Yes	
Height:	5' 10½" or 5' 9¾" [depending on record]	
Hair Colour:	Brown	
Eyes:	Brown or Blue [depending on record]	
Complexion:	Pale	
Remarks:	Wife Eliza schoolmistress at Regimental School	
Intends to Reside:	Culpar Fife	

NEESON	Patrick, private
	88th Foot
22 Nov 1853	Discharged the Service Chatham
	Pension paid 2nd Manchester Pension District
	6d. per diem
11 Feb 1861	Arrived per *'Palmeston'*
1874	Pension increased to 1/-½d. per diem
1881	Died
1890	Administrator Land as to the occupation of land under Mt Eliza let to late pensioner Neeson
Service and Personal Details:	
Place of Birth:	Mohill Co. Leitrim
Age on Attestation:	18 years
Period of Service:	1838 — 1853
Age on Discharge:	33 years or 32 years 8 months
Length of Service:	14 years 299 days
Foreign Service:	Malta 6 years 1 month
	West Indies 3 years 4 months
	North America 1 year 1 month
Reason for Discharge:	Large Varicose Veins in both legs
Character:	Good
Trade or Occupation:	Labourer
Can Sign Name:	Yes
Height:	5' 7"
Hair Colour:	Brown
Eyes:	Brown
Complexion:	Fresh
Intends to Reside:	Manchester

NEILL	Timothy, bombardier EIC
	Bombay Artillery
Previous Regiment	HEIC 1st European Regiment
Surname Variant	NEIL
	Out Pension No 106
10 Aug 1861	Admitted to Out-pension
1861	Embarked UK per *'Assaye'*
	Pension paid 2nd Dublin Pension District
	1/- per diem
27 May 1863	Arrived per *'Clyde'*
1864	Pension paid Adelaide from Perth West Australia
1871	Pension paid Bombay
1873	Dublin
Service and Personal Details:	
Place of Birth:	Enniskerry Ireland or Dublin
Trade or Occupation:	Labourer
Date Enlisted:	29th Nov 1839
Where Enlisted:	Dublin
Embarked India:	per *'Euxine*
Presidency:	Bombay
Length of Service:	20 years 2 months or 21 years 5 months
Age on Discharge:	38 years or 39 years
Reason for Discharge:	Time expired or pensioned
Character:	Good

Medal Entitlement:	Indian Mutiny
Height:	5' 5"
Complexion:	Fresh
Eye Colour:	Hazel
Hair Colour:	Sandy
Intends to Reside:	Dublin

NELSON Joseph, Sergeant
Royal Sappers and Miners 20th Company

1851	Residing St Mary's Alley Woolwich
17 Dec 1851	Arrived per *'Anna Robinson'* with regiment
1857	Contributed to the Florence Nightingale Fund
1858	Serving as Assistant. Lighthouse Keeper at Breaksea Island
19 Oct 1860	Discharged the Service Fremantle
22 Dec 1860	Discharge approved
June 1867	Storekeeper Albany, premises located on corner of York Street and Stirling Terrace
26 Dec 1879	In receipt of Deferred Pension
1881	Deferred Pension Forms to Staff Officer Fremantle Western Australia
Nov 1907	Died aged 88

Service and Personal Details:

Place of Birth	Welton Hull Yorkshire
Age on Attestation:	22 years 10 months
Period of Service:	1842 — 1861
Service to 5th Feb 1855:	12 years 4 months
Age at 5th Feb 1855:	35 years 1 month
Age on Discharge:	40 years 10 months
Length of Service:	17 years 357 days
Foreign Service:	Gibraltar 4 years 186 days Western Australia 8 years 304 days
Reason for Discharge:	Granted a Free Discharge with 12 months pay, with the Right of Registry for a Deferred Pension of 6d. per day on him attaining 60 years of age
Character:	Exemplary
Trade or Occupation:	Blacksmith
Can Sign Name:	Yes
Height:	5' 8¾"
Hair Colour:	Brown
Eye Colour:	Hazel
Complexion:	Fair
Distinguishing Marks:	Small scar under Right Eye
Intended Residence:	Albany King George Sound Western Australia

NELSON Samuel, private
69th Foot

28 July 1863	Discharged the Service Netley Pension paid Omagh 10d. per diem
22 Dec 1865	Arrived per *'Vimiera'*

1872	"To be struck off the Pension List for bringing frivolous and groundless charges against the Staff Officer Pensions — Perth Western Australia	
1873	Restored to Pension List	
3 June 1874	Died aged 49	
Service and Personal Details:		
Place of Birth:	Cloughee [sic] Co Tyrone	
Age on Attestation:	19 years	
Period of Service:	1843 — 1863	
Age on Discharge:	38 years 8 months	
Length of Service:	18 years 354 days	
Foreign Service:	Mediterranean	5 years 5 months
	West Indies	5 years 11 months
	East Indies	4 years 9 months
Reason for Discharge:	Constitution broken down from long service and Paralysis of left arm	
Character:	Good	
Trade or Occupation:	Labourer	
Can Sign Name:	X his mark on discharge	
Height:	5' 7¼"	
Hair Colour:	Brown	
Eyes:	Grey	
Complexion:	Fair	
Distinguishing Marks:	Pock pitted	
Intends to Reside:	Clougher [sic] Co. Tyrone	

NEVILLS

NEVILLS	James, private	
	59th Foot	
Surname Variants	NEVILS; NEVILLE; NEVILLES	
6 Apr 1852	Discharged the Service Fermoy	
11 May 1852	Admitted to Out-Pension	
	Pension paid Athlone	
	1/- per diem	
18 July 1855	Arrived per *'Adelaide'*	
1856	To South Australia from Western Australia	
Service and Personal Details:		
Place of Birth:	Kilbeggan Co. Westmeath	
Age on Attestation:	18 years 2 months	
Period of Service:	1831 — 1852	
Age on Discharge:	39 years 3 months	
Length of Service:	21 years 24 days	
Foreign Service:	Mediterranean	6 years 154 days
	West Indies	2 years 271 days
Reason for Discharge:	General Debility	
Character:	Good	
Trade or Occupation:	Labourer	
Can Sign Name:	Yes	
Height:	5' 8¼"	
Hair Colour:	Fair	
Eyes:	Hazel	
Complexion:	Fresh	

Intends to Reside:	Jersey
NEVIN	William, Corporal EIC
	Pension paid 2nd Plymouth Pension District
1855	Serving at Dartmoor Prison 3rd Plymouth District
June 1856	Embarked per *'Runnymede'*
	Murdered Serjeant Robinson prior to departure –
	"Struck off Pension Roll for murder — hung"
NEWSTEAD	Nathaniel, private [Military Pensioner]
	96th Foot
22 Feb 1847	Arrived per *'Java'* with regiment
15 May 1849	Discharged the Service Perth West Australia
	Pension paid Western Australia
	6d. per diem for 2 years
1852	Pension made permanent
1855	Mail Carrier between Albany and Kojonup
1864	ptve Newstead Pensioner Force at Kojonup
	contributed to the Greenough Fire Relief Fund
1873	Residing Kojonup
1874	Pension increased to 1/2½d. per diem
1897	Died
Service and Personal Details:	
Place of Birth:	Thorpe Norfolk
Age on Attestation:	18 years
Period of Service:	1840 — 1849
Age on Discharge:	26 years 6 months
Length of Service:	8 years 236 days
Foreign Service:	Australia
Reason for Discharge:	Extreme Deafness
Character:	Very Good
Trade or Occupation:	Labourer
Can Sign Name:	Yes
Height:	5' 5"
Hair Colour:	Brown
Eyes:	Brown
Complexion:	Dark
Distinguishing Marks:	? *** under left ear
Married:	*c*1860 Mary Robinson Perth
	[wife of the late Sergeant Robinson]
NICOL	John, private
	72nd Foot
14 Nov 1848	Discharged the Service Chatham
	Pension paid Birmingham
	1/- per diem
1850	Pension paid Maryborough
6 Apr 1854	Arrived per *'Sea Park'*
1854	To South Australia from Perth West. Australia
	"£19/15/- passage money to be paid"
1856	Pension paid Adelaide South Australia
1857	Pension paid Melbourne
1875	Melbourne

Service and Personal Details:	
Place of Birth:	Balteagh Co. Derry
Age on Attestation:	20 years 1 month
Period of Service:	1826 — 1848
Age on Discharge:	42 years
Length of Service:	21 years 330 days
Foreign Service:	Cape of Good Hope 12 years
Reason for Discharge:	Lumbago and Chronic Cough
Character:	Very Good
Trade or Occupation:	Labourer
Can Sign Name:	X his mark on discharge
Height:	5' 11¾"
Hair Colour:	Brown
Eyes:	Blue
Complexion:	Fresh
Distinguishing Marks:	Little finger of left hand contracted
Intends to Reside:	Birmingham

NICHOLLS	John, private
	51st Foot [Depot]
Surname Variant	NICHOLS
20 Jan 1857	Discharged the Service Chatham Pension paid Cambridge 10d. per diem
29 Jan 1862	Arrived per *'Lincelles'*
1864	ptve J Nichols Pensioner Force at Perth contributed to the Greenough Fire Relief Fund
1878	Pension increased to 1/4d. per diem for service in the Enrolled Force
12 Jan 1882	Assigned Perth Railway Block Lot 156/V
May 1882	Granted Fee Simple Perth Railway Block Lot 156/V
1892	Died

Service and Personal Details:	
Place of Birth:	Great Evesden Cambridge
Age on Attestation:	20 years
Period of Service:	1837 — 1857
Age on Discharge:	39 years
Length of Service:	19 years 125 days
Foreign Service:	Van Diemans Land 7 years East Indies 8 years 3 months
Reason for Discharge:	Impaired Health and hernia
Character:	Very Good
Trade or Occupation:	Labourer
Can Sign Name:	X his mark on discharge
Height:	5' 10"
Hair Colour:	Fair
Eyes:	Hazel
Complexion:	Fresh
Intends to Reside:	***** Warwick

NICHOLLS	Joseph, private	
	76th Foot	
Surname Variant	NICHOLS	
25 Nov 1840	Discharged the Service Fort Pitt Chatham	
	Pension paid Cambridge	
	10d. per diem	
1 June 1850	Arrived per *'Scindian'*	
17 Feb 1856	Died	
Service and Personal Details:		
Place of Birth:	Ulsthorpe Leicestershire	
Age on Attestation:	17 years	
Period of Service:	1821 — 1840	
Age on Discharge:	36 years 6 months or 38 years	
Length of Service:	18 years 209 days	
Foreign Service:	Canada	6 years 4 months
	West Indies	6 years 5 months
Reason for Discharge:	Chronic Rheumatism	
Character:	Good	
Trade or Occupation:	Stocking Weaver	
Can Sign Name:	X his mark on discharge	
Height:	5' 6¾"	
Hair Colour:	Brown	
Eyes:	Hazel	
Complexion:	Fresh	
Remarks:	Landed at Gravesend 28th October 1840	
Intends to Reside:	Cambridge	

NICHOLSON	John, private	
	1st Foot	
Surname Variant	NICOLSON	
6 Nov 1848	Discharged the Service Dublin	
9 Jan 1849	Admitted to Out-Pension	
	Pension paid Halifax England	
	6d. per diem	
1 June 1850	Arrived per *'Scindian'*	
1851	Deserted and Struck Off Roll	
1853	"Deserted Enrolled Pensioner Force and left the Colony"	
Service and Personal Details:		
Place of Birth:	Herewood Leeds Yorkshire	
Age on Attestation:	18 years 7 months	
Period of Service:	1832 — 1848	
Age on Discharge:	35 years 4 months	
Length of Service:	16 years 274 days	
Foreign Service:	Canada	7 years 9 months
	Nova Scotia	5 months
	West Indies	1 year 4 months
Reason for Discharge:	Consumption	
Character:	Latterly Good	
Trade or Occupation:	Labourer	
Can Sign Name:	Yes	

Height:	5' 10½"
Hair Colour:	Brown
Eyes:	Grey
Complexion:	Sallow

NICHOLSON	Thomas, private
	7th Foot
22 Jan 1856	Discharged the Service Chatham
	Pension paid 1st Manchester Pension District
	10d. per diem
11 Feb 1861	Arrived per *'Palmeston'*
1863	To Sydney from Fremantle
1865	Transferred to Manchester Pension District

Service and Personal Details:

Place of Birth:	London Middlesex
Age on Attestation:	18 years 8 months
Period of Service:	1853 — 1855
Age on Discharge:	22 years or 20 years 11 months
Length of Service:	2 years 88 days
Foreign Service:	Turkey [no time period given]
Medal Entitlement:	Crimea with clasp
Reason for Discharge:	Gunshot wound to left arm
Character:	Good
Trade or Occupation:	Tailor
Can Sign Name:	X his mark on discharge
Height:	5' 9"
Hair Colour:	Light Brown
Eyes:	Grey
Complexion:	Fresh
Intends to Reside:	Manchester Lancashire

NICHOLSON	William, private
	31st Foot
23 Feb 1847	Discharged the Service
23 Mar 1847	Admitted to Out-pension
	Pension paid 2nd North London Pension District
	1/- per diem
1847	Pension paid Southampton
1848	Athlone
21 May 1851	Arrived per *'Mermaid'*
Sept 1851	Assigned and occupied North Fremantle Lot P2
1858	Applied for Title to land North Fremantle
1860	To South Australia from Western Australia
22 Feb 1875	Died Adelaide South Australia

Service and Personal Details:

Place of Birth:	Caltra Co. Galway
Age on Attestation:	17 years
Period of Service:	1825 — 1847
Age on Discharge:	39 years
Length of Service:	21 years 248 days
Foreign Service:	East Indies 18 years 5 months
Medal Entitlement:	Afghan; present at the battles of Mazeen and Tezeen

Reason for Discharge:	Repeated attacks of Hepatitis; Fever & Dysentery
Character:	Very Good
Trade or Occupation:	Labourer
Can Sign Name:	X his mark on discharge
Height:	5' 7"
Hair Colour:	Fair [or Red depending on record source]
Eyes:	Grey [or Hazel depending on record]
Complexion:	Fair

NOLAN Michael, private
20th Foot

22 Nov 1853	Discharged the Service Chatham Pension paid Limerick 6d. per diem for 2½ years
14 Aug 1854	Arrived per *'Ramillies'* "Transfer to Eastern Colonies withheld" "Absent without leave"

Service and Personal Details:

Place of Birth:	St John's Limerick	
Age on Attestation:	17 years	
Period of Service:	1842 — 1853	
Age on Discharge:	28 years	
Length of Service:	10 years 196 days	
Foreign Service:	Bermuda	4 years 291 days
	North America	6 years 54 days
Reason for Discharge:	Suffers from very considerable shortness of breath on exertion attended with cough	
Character:	Good	
Trade or Occupation:	Labourer	
Can Sign Name:	Yes	
Height:	5' 7"	
Hair Colour:	Fair	
Eyes:	Blue	
Complexion:	Fair	
Distinguishing Marks:	Slightly pock marked	
Intends to Reside:	Limerick	

NOLAN Patrick, private
28th Foot

3 Jan 1865	Discharged the Service Fermoy Pension paid Waterford 8d. per diem
1865	Pension paid 2nd Liverpool Pension District
22 Dec 1866	Arrived per *'Corona'*
1872	a P Nolan residing at Fremantle
1881	Pension increased to 1/2½d. for service in the Enrolled Force
15 Sept 1884	Cockburn Sound Lot P18 granted to widow
1884	Died

Apr 1884	An inquest held at Fremantle on the remains of a military pensioner named Patrick Nolan, formerly of the 28th Foot. Nolan, known as "Old Brags" came into Fremantle from Coogee to draw his pension and due to imbibing too freely afterwards, that on the way home he fell from his cart and injured his spine. Verdict — "Death while under the influence of liquor"	
Service and Personal Details:		
Place of Birth:	Crookestown Co. Kildare	
Age on Attestation:	18 years	
Period of Service:	1843 — 1864	
Age on Discharge:	39 years 5 months	
Length of Service:	21 years 111 days	
Foreign Service:	East Indies	4 years 1 month
	Turkey & Crimea	2 years 1 month
	Malta	2 years 6 months
Medal Entitlement:	Crimea with clasps	
Reason for Discharge:	His having completed 21 years service	
Character:	Good	
Trade or Occupation:	Labourer	
Can Sign Name:	X his mark on discharge	
Height:	5' 8"	
Hair Colour:	Brown	
Eyes:	Grey	
Complexion:	Fair	
Intends to Reside:	Waterford Ireland	

NOONAN William, private

54th Foot

26 Sept 1848	Discharged the Service Chatham Pension paid 2nd North London Pension District 1/- per diem	
2 Aug 1852	Arrived per *'William Jardine'*	
Oct 1852	"Off Roll" pension suspended for one month	
Jan 1857	Contributed 2/- to the Florence Nightingale Fund	
Dec 1861	Assigned Kojonup Lot P4	
Sept 1862	Application for Title to Kojonup Lot P4	
29 Apr 1862	Died aged 54 at Kojonup	
Service and Personal Details:		
Place of Birth:	Kilmallock Co. Limerick	
Age on Attestation:	20 years	
Period of Service:	1826 — 1848	
Age on Discharge:	42 years or 41 years 7 months	
Length of Service:	20 years 344 days	
Foreign Service:	East Indies	13 years 88 days
Reason for Discharge:	Chronic Rheumatism	
Character:	Bad to 1845 — since that date improved though still indifferent	
Trade or Occupation:	Labourer	
Can Sign Name:	Yes	

Height:	5' 7½"
Hair Colour:	Brown
Eyes:	Grey
Complexion:	Fresh
Intends to Reside:	London

NORRIE

NORRIE	George, private
	92nd Foot
Surname Variants	NORRICE; NORICE, NORIE
15 May 1848	Discharged the Service Limerick
11 July 1848	Admitted to Out-Pension
	Pension paid Aberdeen
	1/- per diem
30 Apr 1853	Arrived per *'Pyrenees'* [2]
1855	Shown as living at North Fremantle with wife
1856	Wished to hand over his North Fremantle Lot to Henry Earl of the 64th Foot
1858	To Eastern Colonies from West. Australia
	" £8/12/- passage money to be repaid"
1875	Pension paid South Australia

Service and Personal Details:

Place of Birth:	Tyrie Aberdeenshire	
Age on Attestation:	22 years	
Period of Service:	1826 — 1848	
Age on Discharge:	42 years 9 months	
Length of Service:	21 years 295 days	
Foreign Service:	Gibraltar	1 year 11 months
	Malta	5 years 2 months
	West Indies	5 years 10 months
Reason for Discharge:	Worn out from length of service	
Character:	Good	
Trade or Occupation:	Weaver	
Can Sign Name:	X his mark on discharge	
Height:	5' 7¾"	
Hair Colour:	Black	
Eyes:	Grey	
Complexion:	Dark	

NORTON

NORTON	Joseph, gunner
	RA — Coastal Brigade
19 May 1863	Discharged the Service Woolwich
	Pension paid 2nd Dublin Pension District
	11½d. per diem
15 Aug 1865	Arrived per *'Racehorse'*
1871	Pension paid Calcutta
1872	Pension paid 1st East London Pension District
1872	Pension paid Dublin
1873	Toronto
1873	Dublin
2 Feb 1874	Died

Service and Personal Details:

Place of Birth:	Rish Island of Lambay Dublin

Age on Attestation:	19 years	
Period of Service:	1841 — 1863	
Age on Discharge:	41 years 4 months	
Length of Service:	22 years 20 days	
Foreign Service:	Canada	6 years
	Crimea	1 year 8 months
Medal Entitlement:	Crimea with clasp; Turkish Crimea	
Reason for Discharge:	Having completed service for pension	
Character:	Very Good	
Trade or Occupation:	Labourer	
Can Sign Name:	X his mark on discharge	
Height:	5' 8"	
Hair Colour:	Brown	
Eyes:	Grey	
Complexion:	Fresh	
Intends to Reside:	Dublin	

NUGENT Robert, private
60th Foot

10 June 1853	Discharged the Service Birr
9 Aug 1853	Admitted to Out-Pension Pension paid 2nd Dublin Pension District 1/- per diem
19 Aug 1859	Arrived per *'Sultana'*
1862	Pension paid Sydney New South Wales
1869	Died

Service and Personal Details:

Place of Birth:	Newtown Co. Kildare	
Age on Attestation:	18 years	
Period of Service:	1832 — 1853	
Age on Discharge:	39 years	
Length of Service:	20 years 354 days	
Foreign Service:	Gibraltar	5 years 5 months
	Jamaica	2 years 11 months
	Quebec	3 years 1 month
Reason for Discharge:	Ulcer on cornea of left eye	
Character:	Very Good	
Trade or Occupation:	Labourer	
Can Sign Name:	X his mark on discharge	
Height:	5' 9¼"	
Hair Colour:	Sandy	
Eyes:	Blue	
Complexion:	Fair	
Intends to Reside:	Dublin	

NUGENT Samuel, private
58th Foot

23 Jan 1849	Discharged the Service Chatham Pension paid 2nd Dublin Pension District 1/- per diem
28 June 1851	Arrived per *'Pyrenees'* [1]
Oct 1851	Employed as Night Warder

Feb 1852	Resigned or dismissed
no date	Assigned Freshwater Bay Loc 1071
1853	Employed as Warder in Convict Service
1873	Pension increased to 1/1½d. per diem for 3 years service in the Enrolled Force
Feb 1885	Application for Title to Freshwater Bay Loc 1071
1886	Died

Service and Personal Details:

Place of Birth:	Clones Co. Monaghan	
Age on Attestation:	18 years	
Period of Service:	1825 — 1849	
Age on Discharge:	42 years 6 months or 41 years	
Length of Service:	23 years 47 days	
Foreign Service:	Ceylon	10 years 7 months
	Australian Colonies	3 years 11 months
Reason for Discharge:	Chronic Rheumatism	
Character:	Very Good	
Trade or Occupation:	Labourer	
Can Sign Name:	X his mark on discharge	
Height:	5' 5½"	
Hair Colour:	Light Brown	
Eyes:	Blue	
Complexion:	Fresh	
Intends to Reside:	Oldham Lancashire	

NUGENT

William, Corporal EIC
Bengal Artillery
Out Pension No 43

1847	Embarked UK per *'Alfred'*
25 May 1847	Admitted to Out-pension
	Pension paid Clonmel
	9d. per diem
28 June 1851	Arrived per *'Pyrenees'* [1]
3 Dec 1851	Charged with military offence — "Off List"
1855	"Restored to Enrolled Force"
1872	Died aged 58 Fremantle

Service and Personal Details:

Where Born:	Waterford
Trade or Occupation:	Farrier
Where Enlisted:	Waterford
Presidency:	Bengal
Length of Service:	10 years 4 months
Age on Discharge:	34 years
Reason for Discharge:	Gunshot wound received at battle of Ferozeshar
Character:	Fair
Medal Entitlement:	Sutlej
Height:	5' 8¼"
Complexion:	Fresh
Visage:	Oval
Eye Colour:	Blue
Hair Colour:	Brown

OAK	William, private	
	46th Foot	
Surname Variant	OAKS	
13 Mar 1849	Discharged the Service	
	Pension paid Trowbridge	
	7d. per diem	
1 June 1850	Arrived per *'Scindian'*	
28 May 1871	Died	
Service and Personal Details:		
Place of Birth:	Corton Wiltshire	
Age on Attestation:	19 years	
Period of Service:	1833 — 1849	
Age on Discharge:	34 years 10 months	
Length of Service:	15 years 99 days	
Foreign Service:	Gibraltar	4 years 130 days
	West Indies	3 years
	North America	3 years 76 days
Reason for Discharge:	Chronic Catarrh	
Character:	Excellent	
Trade or Occupation:	Labourer	
Can Sign Name:	X his mark on discharge	
Height:	5' 10¼"	
Hair Colour:	Brown	
Eyes:	Hazel	
Complexion:	Fresh	
Intends to Reside:	Heytesbury	

OAKLEY	Charles, private
	Royal Marine Light Infantry
Aug 1860	Discharged the Service
1865	Pension paid Derby
	£16/16/- per annum
15 Aug 1865	Arrived per *'Racehorse'*
1868	Pension paid South Australia from Fremantle "Stoppages from pension for family in Western Australia " [this information given in Melbourne Pension District WO22/257 - page 80]
Dec 1869	Pension paid Victoria
Dec 1871	" £1/8/- stoppage from pension for wife in Western Australia now ceased and not to be deducted from his pension"
1875	Pension paid Victoria
Service and Personal Details:	
Place of Birth:	Stoughton Chichester Sussex
Age on Attestation:	21 years 6 months
Marine Division:	Portsmouth
Period of Service:	1839 — 1860
Length of Service:	21 years 16 days
Reason for Discharge:	Length of Service and at own request
Medal Entitlement:	Syrian Campaign. 2 medals and clasp
Trade or Occupation:	Labourer

Can Sign Name:	X his mark on discharge
Height:	5' 7"
Hair Colour:	Dark Brown
Eyes:	Hazel
Complexion:	Dark
Married:	*c*1866 Harriet Miriam Burton Fremantle
Children:	Charles Thomas b. *c*1867 Fremantle m. *c*1888 Ellen Wright Perth

OATEN	Samuel, private 13th Foot
Surname Variant	OATES
10 Aug 1858	Discharged the Service Chatham Pension paid Taunton 7d. per diem for 3 years conditional
1861	Pension increased to 9d. per diem conditional for a year
1864	Pension made permanent
1865	Pension paid Bristol
19 Feb 1874	Arrived per *'Naval Brigade'*
1874	Pension paid Perth Western Australia
1881	Assigned Fremantle Sub Lot 32 located at Lime Kilns
1881	Allocation of Fremantle Lot 32 [31] to Pensioner S. Oaten. S.O.P. [CONS541/B274]
1881	Pension increased to 11½d. per diem for having served 6 years and from date of ceasing service in the Enrolled Force
1884	Granted Title to Fremantle Sub Lot 32
June 1897	Residing Fremantle
1890	Fremantle Sub Lot 32 with 2 room cottage and lime kiln and various other buildings to be sold [newspaper]
1891	W.O. Correspondence with Treasury Perth W.A. -"A31"
1898	Died

Service and Personal Details:		
Place of Birth:	Pitminster nr. Taunton Somerset	
Age on Attestation:	17 years	
Period of Service:	1846 — 1858	
Age on Discharge:	29 years	
Length of Service:	10 years 351 days	
Foreign Service:	Gibraltar	4 years 3 months
	Turkey & Crimea	1 year
	Cape of Good Hope	1 year 4 months
Medal Entitlement:	Crimea with clasps	
Reason for Discharge:	Impaired Vision from Ophthalmia	
Character:	Good	
Trade or Occupation:	Labourer	
Can Sign Name:	X his mark on discharge	
Height:	5' 7"	
Hair Colour:	Light Brown	

Eyes:	Hazel	
Complexion:	Fair	
Intends to Reside:	Taunton Somerset	
Married: [Sept Qtr 5c 569]	1860 Eliza Gibbons Taunton Somerset	
Children:	Elizabeth Ann b. *c*1864 Somerset m. *c*1883 Frederick Beswick Fremantle John b. *c*1865 Bristol m. *c*1886 Mary Theresa Aguilar Guildford William b. *c*1868 m. *c*1892 Ellen Curedale Fremantle	

O'BRIEN see also — BRIEN Daniel, private 65th Foot

O'BRIEN

	John, private 59th Foot	
7 July 1841	Discharged the Service Pension paid Kilkenny 6d. per diem	
24 May 1855	Arrived per *'Stag'*	
1856	Pension paid Van Dieman's Land	
Service and Personal Details:		
Place of Birth:	Mountmellick Queens County	
Age on Attestation:	19 years	
Period of Service:	1824 — 1841	
Age on Discharge:	35 years 7 months	
Length of Service:	16 years 202 days	
Foreign Service:	Gibraltar	1 year 253 days
	Malta	307 days
Reason for Discharge:	Chronic Rheumatism	
Character:	That of a good soldier	
Trade or Occupation:	Butcher	
Can Sign Name:	Yes	
Height:	5' 8"	
Hair Colour:	Black	
Eyes:	Brown	
Complexion:	Fresh	

O'BRIEN

	Kennedy, gunner EIC Bengal Artillery
Surname Variant	O'BRIAN Out Pension No 76
16 June 1847	Discharged the Service 9d. per diem
1847	Embarked UK per *'Bombay'*
1860	Pension paid 2nd East London Pension District
11 Feb 1861	Arrived per *'Palmeston'*
1863	Stationed Perth District
1864	ptve K O'Brien Pensioner Force at Perth contributed to the Greenough Fire Relief Fund

July 1877	Northam — a Serjeant O'Brien in charge of the Pensioner Force was killed when his horse ran away with him resulting in him dashing his brains out against a tree
Dec 1882	'in consideration of Application of Title Northam Loc 30' [CONS 5000 — SROWA]
1882	Northam Loc 30 Grant to married daughter Mary Ann Timewell

Service and Personal Details:

Place of Birth:	Dublin
Trade or Occupation:	Tailor
Where Enlisted:	London
Length of Service:	17 years 5 months
Age on Discharge:	36 years
Reason for Discharge:	Hepatitis
Height:	5' 7"
Complexion:	Dark
Visage:	Oval
Eye Colour:	Blue
Hair Colour:	Brown
Remarks:	a Mary Ann O'Brian m. *c*1868 James Whelan Perth a Mary Anne O'Brien or Whalen ?m. *c*1875 Frank B Timewell Fremantle [or according the daughter, her mother's name was Mary Whaylen and that her mother had lived with Timewell for 16 years but never married him]

O'BRIEN Timothy, private

87th Foot

Previous Regiments	89th; 2nd/5th
16 Apr 1872	Discharged the Service Chichester Pension paid Chatham 1/- per diem
19 Feb 1874	Arrived per *'Naval Brigade'*
20 May 1874	Died

Service and Personal Details:

Place of Birth:	Corofin Co. Clare	
Age on Enlistment:	24 years	
Period of Service:	1851 — 1872	
Age on Discharge:	45 years	
Length of Service:	21 years 9 days	
Foreign Service:	East Indies	8 years 5 months
	China	1 year 2 months
	Gibraltar	1 year 8 months
	Malta	4 years 1 month
Medal Entitlement:	Indian Mutiny	
Reason for Discharge:	Own Request having completed 21 years service	
Character:	Very Good	
Trade or Occupation:	Tailor	
Can Sign Name:	Yes	

Height:	5' 6¾"
Hair Colour:	Sandy
Eyes:	Grey
Complexion:	Fresh
Intends to Reside:	Chatham

O'BEIRNE	James, private	
	51st Foot	
Surname Variants	[some] O'BYRNE; O'BURN; O'BOURNE; O'BURNES; BURNS	
28 Aug 1846	Discharged the Service Chatham	
	Pension paid Roscommon	
	1/- per diem	
1847	Pension paid Jersey	
2 Aug 1852	Arrived per *'William Jardine'*	
1871	Died	
****	N. O'Byrne — Relict of J. O'Byrne, Pensioner; Application for free grant of Perth Town Lot [reply: she is not entitled to any]	
Service and Personal Details:		
Place of Birth:	Kilcoleman Mayo	
Age on Attestation:	18 years	
Period of Service:	1824 — 1846	
Age on Discharge:	39 years 10 months	
Length of Service:	21 years 314 days	
Foreign Service:	Ionian Isles	10 years
	Van Dieman's Land	7 years
Reason for Discharge:	Unfit for further service and Chronic Cough	
Character:	Very Good	
Trade or Occupation:	Blacksmith	
Can Sign Name:	Yes	
Height:	5' 8"	
Hair Colour:	Light Brown	
Eyes:	Grey	
Complexion:	Fair	
Remarks:	1839 — Embarked New South Wales	
Intends to Reside:	Claremorris Co. Mayo	
Married:	1829 Nicoletta Salustri Ionian Isles	
Children:	Mary Ann b. *c*1833	
	m. *c*1860 Richard Buck Perth	
	John b. 1837	
	Ellen b. 1839	
	m. *c*1856 Alfred Bath Fremantle	
	George b. *c*1843 Van Dieman's Land	
	Ann b. *c*1846 Van Dieman's Land	
	Clara b. *c*1850 Channel Isles	
	m. *c*1871 Robert Owen Fremantle	
	James b. *c*1854 Fremantle	
	m. *c*1883 Mary Jane Enright Fremantle	
	Bridget b. *c*1857 Fremantle	
	m. *c*1890 John Robert Freeman Fremantle	

O'BRYAN	Michael, Serjeant 60th Foot
Surname Variants	O'BYRNE; O'BRIEN
10 June 1853	Discharged the Service Birr
25 July 1853	Discharge approved
9 Aug 1853	Pension paid Tullamore 1/10½d. per diem
2 Apr 1856	Arrived per *'William Hammond'*
July 1856	£15/16/5 balance due on landing at colony but misappropriated by Capt Foss
1860	Pension paid Sydney New South Wales
Service and Personal Details:	
Place of Birth:	Philipstown Offaly Kings County
Age on Enlistment:	19 years 8 months
Period of Service:	1832 — 1853
Age on Discharge:	40 years 9 months
Length of Service:	20 years 346 days
Foreign Service:	Gibraltar 5 years 5 months Jamaica 2 years 11 months Quebec Canada 3 years 1 month Cape of Good Hope ?1 year 4 months
Reason for Discharge:	Chronic affection of the chest; Rheumatism and worn out
Character:	Very Good
Trade or Occupation:	Labourer
Can Sign Name:	Yes
Height:	5' 6½" [5' 7" on Attestation]
Hair Colour:	Dark Brown
Eyes:	Grey
Complexion:	Dark
Intends to Reside:	Philipstown

O'BYRNE	Patrick, private 12th Foot
Previous Regiments	86th; 32nd
Surname Variant	O'BRYNE
21 May 1853	Discharged the Service Belfast
12 July 1853	Admitted to Out-Pension Pension paid Northampton 1/- per diem
1854	Pension paid Ipswich
1854	London
1854	Ipswich
18 July 1855	Arrived per *'Adelaide'*
1866	Assigned North Fremantle Lot P4
1868	Pension increased to 1/3d. per diem for service in the Enrolled Force of Western Australia
1883	Died aged 71
Service and Personal Details:	
Place of Birth:	Carrick on Shannon Co. Leitrim
Age on Enlistment:	20 years
Period of Service:	1832 — 1853
Age on Discharge:	40 years 5 months

Length of Service:	20 years 111 days	
Foreign Service:	Mauritius	4 years 6 months
	Canada	3 years 3 months
	Cape of Good Hope	3 months
Reason for Discharge:	Asthma and Impaired Vision	
Character:	Very Good	
Trade or Occupation:	Labourer	
Can Sign Name:	X his mark on discharge	
Height:	5' 6¾"	
Hair Colour:	Black	
Eyes:	Grey	
Complexion:	Sallow	
Intends to Reside:	Daventry Northamptonshire	

O'CONNELL

	Daniel, trumpeter
	6th Dragoon Guards
Previous Regiment	2nd Dragoon Guards
7 Sept 1858	Discharged the Service Chatham
	Pension paid 1st Dublin Pension District
	8d. per diem
1858	Pension paid Sheffield
11 Feb 1861	Arrived per *'Palmeston'*
1863	Stationed Albany
1865	Joined the Police Force
July 1886	Assigned Albany Lot P6 of three acres
1887	Application for Title to Albany Lot P6
1990's	Serving in police force
1903	W.O. correspondence to the Under Treasurer
	Western Australia
1909	Attended Veteran's Dinner
1915	Residing Cavendish Street Perth
Nov 1922	Died

Service and Personal Details:

Place of Birth:	Jock's Lodge Edinburgh	
Age on Attestation:	14 years 10 months & 14 days	
Period of Service:	1847 — 1858	
Age on Discharge:	25 years 1 month	
Length of Service:	7 years 119 days [reckoned after age of 18]	
Foreign Service:	Turkey & Crimea	11 months
	East Indies	13 months
Medal Entitlement:	Crimea; Turkish Crimea; Indian Mutiny & clasp	
Reason for Discharge:	Gun shot wound to the thigh of left leg	
Character:	Good	
Trade or Occupation:	Musician	
Can Sign Name:	Yes	
Height:	5' 6"	
Hair Colour:	Brown	
Eyes:	Black	
Complexion:	Fresh	

O'CONNER

John, gunner EIC
Bengal Artillery

Surname Variant	O'CONNOR	
	Out Pension No 61	
10 July 1844	Admitted to Out-pension	
	Pension paid Wolverhampton District	
	9d. per diem	
1 June 1850	Arrived per *'Scindian'*	
Aug 1850	Assigned land P15 at South Perth	
1851	Resigned his land allocation at South Perth	
1851	Assigned and occupied North Fremantle Lot P17	
1854	Left Colony without transfer	
1858	Pension paid Melbourne	
1866	Melbourne	
Service and Personal Details:		
Place of Birth:	Limerick	
Trade or Occupation:	Stave Cutter	
Where Enlisted:	Limerick	
Presidency:	Bengal	
Length of Service:	3 years 4 months	
Age on Discharge:	24 years	
Reason for Discharge:	Hernia	
Character:	Fair	
Height:	5' 7"	
Complexion:	Fresh	
Visage:	Oval	
Eye Colour:	Blue	
Hair Colour:	Brown	
O'CONNOR	see —- Jeremiah CONNOR	
	22nd Foot	
O'CONNOR	John, private	
	21st Foot	
Previous Regiment	22nd Foot	
28 June 1853	Discharged the Service Chatham	
	Pension paid Limerick	
	1/- per diem	
18 July 1855	Arrived per *'Adelaide'*	
1856	Pension paid Van Dieman's Land	
Service and Personal Details:		
Place of Birth:	Askeaton Co. Limerick	
Age on Enlistment:	18 years	
Period of Service:	1832 — 1853	
Age on Discharge:	39 years	
Length of Service:	21 years 22 days	
Foreign Service:	Australian Colonies	upwards of 5 years
	India	upwards of 7 years
Reason for Discharge:	Chronic Rheumatism	
Character:	Good	
Trade or Occupation:	Labourer	
Can Sign Name:	Yes	
Height:	6'	
Hair Colour:	Brown	

Eyes:	Blue
Complexion:	Fair
Intends to Reside:	Paddington London

O'CONNOR	John [James], private 4th Dragoons Guards
Surname Variant	O'CONNER
6 Jan 1857	Discharged the Service Chatham 8d. per diem for 3 years
8 June 1858	Arrived per *'Lord Raglan'*
1860	Died aged 38

Service and Personal Details:	
Place of Birth:	St Finbars Cork Co. Cork
Age on Attestation:	24 years
Period of Service:	1846 — 1856
Age on Discharge:	34 years 7 months
Length of Service:	10 years 211 days
Foreign Service:	Turkey & Crimea 2 years 1 month
Medal Entitlement:	Crimean with clasps
Reason for Discharge:	Ruptured on right side, occurred when on mounted duty in the Crimea
Character:	Good
Trade or Occupation:	Labourer
Can Sign Name:	Yes
Height:	5' 9¼"
Hair Colour:	Light Brown
Eyes:	Blue
Complexion:	Fresh

O'CONNOR	Patrick, Corporal EIC 1st Bombay European Fusiliers Out Pension No 85
19 Sept 1849	Admitted to Out-pension Pension paid Cork 9d. per diem
1850	Pension paid Leeds
6 Apr 1854	Arrived per *'Sea Park'*
8 Apr 1854	"Charged with military offence"
1854	Deserted Enrolled Pensioner Force
1854	" Not appeared since Oct 1854"
1858	Pension paid Melbourne
1866	Melbourne

Service and Personal Details:	
Where Born:	Kilturbet Co. Leitrim
Trade or Occupation:	Labourer
Presidency:	Bombay
Length of Service:	3 years 10 months
Age on Discharge:	25 years
Character:	Good
Reason for Discharge:	Loss of use of 4th and 5th fingers of left hand from a gunshot wound received whilst in action at Mooltan [sic]

Height:	5' 6"
Complexion:	Sallow
Eye Colour:	Hazel
Hair Colour:	Black
Intends to Reside:	Boyle Roscommon

O'DEA

	Martin, Corporal 41st Foot
Surname variant	O'DAY
18 Mar 1856	Discharged the Service Pension paid Ennis 1/- per diem
1865	Pension paid Ennis
22 Dec 1865	Arrived per *'Vimiera'*
1866	Employed as Assistant Warder
1874	Assigned Perth Military Pensioner Lot 145/Y
1874	"In prison — half pension to wife"
1875	Submitted for consideration whether a small daily pecuniary allowance can be made to the wife of Enrolled Pensioner Private Martin O'Dea of the Perth Force under the following Circumstances. Viz. Her husband, hitherto a very well conducted man, has recently been tried by Court Martial and is now undergoing his sentence of imprisonment in the Fremantle Prison during which his pay will be stopped I have permitted her to remain in Barracks and have [pending approval of Secretary of State of War] directed her husband's pension of 1/- a day to be paid to her until his return to duty on the 9th of June, but this is insufficient to support herself and three children, and her present condition precludes her from doing anything towards earning a livelihood.
26 May 1875	To Hon Col. Sec. Informing that he has been compelled to remove the woman named from the Barracks. She has received outdoor relief until the 31st May after which it will cease. Her husband will be released on or about the 9th of June
circa Sept 1875	Transferred from Fremantle to 1st Perth District
1880	Grant of £15 [pounds] sanctioned
Apr 1881	Application for Title to Perth Lot 145
1885	Served in the Enrolled Guard Pension increased to 1/4d. per diem
1891	Residing off Murray Street Armourer for the Metropolitan Volunteer Rifles
26 Apr 1893	Died – buried East Perth Pioneer Cemetery

Service and Personal Details:

Place of Birth:	?Drunclift Ennis Co. Clare	
Age on Attestation:	18 years	
Period of Service:	1848 — 1856	
Age on Discharge:	none annotated	
Length of Service:	7 years 149 days	
Foreign Service:	Ionian Isles	1 year 4 months

	Malta & Turkey	1 year 1 month
	Crimea	1 year 7 months
Medal Entitlement:	Crimea with clasps; Turkish Crimea medal	
Reason for Discharge:	Medically unfit for further service	
Character:	Very Good	
Trade or Occupation:	Labourer	
Can Sign Name:	Yes	
Height:	5' 8"	
Hair Colour:	Black	
Eyes:	Dark Blue	
Complexion:	Fresh	
Intends to Reside:	Ennis Co. Clare	

ODGERS John, Corporal
85th Foot

Surname Variants	ODGES; ODJERS	
24 Oct 1854	Discharged the Service Chatham	
	Pension paid Bristol	
	9d. per diem for 3 years conditional	
1857	Pension made permanent	
10 July 1857	Arrived per *'Clara'* [1]	
1866	Granted North Fremantle Lot P26	
1872	a John Odges [sic] residing at Fremantle	
1873	Residing Fremantle	
1874	Pension increased to 1/3d. per diem	
1875	Pension paid Western Australia	

Service and Personal Details:

Place of Birth:	St Clements Truro Cornwall	
Age on Attestation:	17 years 8 months	
Period of Service:	1839 — 1854	
Age on Discharge:	33 years	
Length of Service:	14 years 246 days	
Foreign Service:	North America	3 years 5 months
	West Indies	2 years 5 months
Reason for Discharge:	Suffers from Rupture	
Character:	Very Good	
Trade or Occupation:	Labourer	
Can Sign Name:	blank; Yes on Attestation	
Height:	5' 6½"	
Hair Colour:	Brown	
Eyes:	Hazel	
Complexion:	Pale	
Intends to Reside:	Bristol	

Personal Details from South Australian Advertiser July 1997

Regiment:	19th Regiment of Light Infantry	
Place of Birth:	Truro Cornwall	
Date of Birth:	2nd Dec 1820	
Age on Attestation:	17 years	
Length of Service:	20 years 2 months	
Foreign Service:	Crimea	1 year 5 months

Medal Entitlement:	Crimea with clasps for Alma and Inkerman; Turkish Crimean
Reason for Discharge:	Received flesh wound right arm
1897	Died aged 77 Prior to death was employed as Town Hall porter at Hindmarsh for the past 6 years
Remarks:	On discharge went to Western Australia and was employed as a prison guard at Fremantle Arrived South Australia 1881

O'HANLON — Hugh, private
57th Foot

Surname Variant	HANLON
30 May 1866	Discharged the Service Cork Pension paid 1st Cork Pension District 1/-½d. per diem
22 Dec 1866	Arrived per *'Corona'* Pension increased to 1/6½d. per diem for service in the Enrolled Force
1 Oct 1881	Joined Enrolled Guard — stationed Perth
16 Feb 1883	Assigned North Fremantle Lot P87
12 Oct 1883	Granted Fee Simple North Fremantle Lot P87
1887	Died

Service and Personal Details:

Place of Birth:	Clonallen Warrenspoint Co. Down	
Age on Attestation:	18 years 6 months	
Period of Service:	1841 — 1866	
Age on Discharge:	42 years 1 month	
Length of Service:	22 years 268 days	
Foreign Service:	East Indies	3 years 9 months
	Corfu	1 year 6 months
	Crimea	8 months
Medal Entitlement:	Crimea with clasps; Turkish Crimea	
Reason for Discharge:	Own Request having completed over 21 years	
Character:	Good	
Trade or Occupation:	Labourer	
Can Sign Name:	Yes	
Height:	5' 7"	
Hair Colour:	Light Brown	
Eyes:	Grey	
Complexion:	Fresh	
Remarks:	Lost his Turkish Crimean medal	
Intends to Reside:	Cork	

O'HARA — Luke, private
89th Foot

14 Sept1847	Discharged the Service Chatham Pension paid Hull 1/- per diem
2 Aug 1851	Arrived per *'William Jardine'*

Service and Personal Details:

Place of Birth:	Clonguish Co. Longford

Age on Attestation:	18 years	
Period of Service:	1825 — 1847	
Age on Discharge:	41 years or 39 years 7 months	
Length of Service:	21 years 192 days	
Foreign Service:	East Indies	4 years 10 months
	West Indies	2 years 6 months
Reason for Discharge:	Worn out constitution	
Character:	Good	
Trade or Occupation:	Labourer	
Can Sign Name:	X his mark on discharge	
Height:	5' 6"	
Hair Colour:	Fair	
Eyes:	Grey	
Complexion:	Fair	
Intends to Reside:	Hull	

O'KEEFE

	Michael, private
	37th Foot
Surname Variant	O'KEAFF
17 Nov 1857	Discharged the Service Chatham
	Pension paid Limerick
	1/- per diem
19 Aug 1859	Arrived per *'Sultana'*
1864	ptve M O'Keefe Pensioner Force at Perth contributed to the Greenough Fire Relief Fund
1865	Pension paid Western Australia
16 July 1871	Died

Service and Personal Details:

Place of Birth:	St Johns Limerick Co. Limerick	
Age on Attestation:	18 years	
Period of Service:	1836 — 1857	
Age on Discharge:	38 years 11 months	
Length of Service:	20 years 64 days	
Foreign Service:	Jamaica	1 year 2 months
	Nova Scotia	2 years 10 months
	Ceylon	9 years 10 months
Medal Entitlement:	Long Service and Good Conduct with gratuity	
Reason for Discharge:	Chronic Rheumatism	
Character:	Very Good	
Trade or Occupation:	Tailor	
Can Sign Name:	Yes	
Height:	5' 6¾"	
Hair Colour:	Dark Brown	
Eyes:	Hazel	
Complexion:	Fair	
Intends to Reside:	Limerick	

O'KEEFE

	Moses, private
	44th Foot
Surname Variant	O'KEEFF
18 June 1840	Admitted to Out-pension
	Pension paid Fermoy

	6d. per diem
1846	Pension paid 2nd West London Pension District
1 June 1850	Arrived per *'Scindian'*
1850	Assigned land Freshwater Bay
1858	Application for Title Freshwater Bay Loc P224
1864	Employed as Police Constable at Albany
1870 — 1872	Assistant Lighthouse Keeper art Breaksea Island
28 Oct 1873	Pension increased to 11d. per diem for service in the Enrolled Force
1873	Employed at the P & O coaling wharf at Albany
1879	Died aged 77 Albany
1894	Swan Loc P224 of 9 and a half acres advertised for sale by D. O'Keefe — Albany

Service and Personal Details:

Place of Birth:	Fermoy Cork
Period of Service:	1825 — 1840
Age on Discharge:	37 years [or 35 years depending on record]

OLIVER	Stephen, Serjeant
	6th Dragoons
12 Apr 1841	Discharged the Service
	Pension paid Wolverhampton
	9d. per diem
7 Feb 1853	Arrived per *'Dudbrook'*
1853	Appointed without sanction as Night Warder Convict establishment
1855	Serving as Warder Convict Dept.
1856	Employed as Police Constable
1856	Pension paid Van Dieman's Land [sic]

Service and Personal Details:

Place of Birth:	?Disertenagh Co. Tyrone
Age on Attestation:	19 years
Period of Service:	1825 — 1841
Age on Discharge:	34 years
Length of Service:	15 years 173 days
Reason for Discharge:	Unfit for further service
Character:	Very Good
Trade or Occupation:	Cabinetmaker
Can Sign Name:	Yes
Height:	5' 10¾"
Hair Colour:	Black
Eyes:	Dark
Complexion:	Fresh

OLIVER	William, private [WO97/501/20]
	31st Foot
28 Dec 1847	Discharged the Service Chatham
	Pension paid Chatham
	11d. per diem
1847	Pension paid 1st Manchester Pension District
1849	Pension paid Cambridge Pension District
1851	Residing 26 Old Crown Yard Huntingdon

30 Aug 1853	Arrived per *'Phoebe Dunbar'*
Apr 1853	Night Warder Convict Establishment
	Allocated West Guildford Lot P117 of 2 acres
1873	Pension increased to 1/1½d. per diem for 5½ years service in the Enrolled Force
circa June 1875	Transferred from 1st Perth to Fremantle District
1881	Died
22 Sept 1881	Inquest at the Police Court, Fremantle before James Manning, J.P., and Acting Coroner, on the body of William Oliver [pensioner], who died suddenly at No. 1 barracks, on 22nd Sept. Verdict — "Death from natural causes."

Service and Personal Details:

Place of Birth:	Manchester Lancashire	
Age on Attestation:	16 years	
Period of Service:	1826 — 1847	
Age on Discharge:	38 years	
Length of Service:	19 years 307 days [after age of 18]	
Foreign Service:	East Indies	18 years 6 months
Medal Entitlement:	Afghanistan with clasps for Mezeen and Tazeen	
Reason for Discharge:	Chronic Rheumatism and worn out	
Character:	Good	
Trade or Occupation:	Labourer	
Can Sign Name:	X his mark on discharge	
Height:	5' 7"	
Hair Colour:	Dark	
Eyes:	Hazel	
Complexion:	Dark	
Intends to Reside:	Ashton under Lyne	
Married:	1847 Mary Ann Church Huntingdon	
Children:	Elizabeth Ann b.1850 d. *c*1865	

O'LOUGHLIN	Michael, private
	88th Foot
Surname Variants	[some] McLAUGHEN; McLAUGHLAN; McLAUGHLIN
25 June 1861	Discharged the Service Colchester
	Pension paid Ennis
	11d. per diem
12 Sept 1864	Arrived per *'Merchantman'* [2]
April 1876	Died suddenly at H.M. Lefroy's vineyard on the 9th from heart disease

Service and Personal Details:

Place of Birth:	Kilmanahan Co. Clare	
Age on Attestation:	18 years	
Period of Service:	1839 — 1861	
Age on Discharge:	39 years 5 months	
Length of Service:	21 years 277 days	
Foreign Service:	Malta	6 years 1 month
	West Indies	2 years 4 months
	East Indies	2 years 10 months

Medal Entitlement:	India medal
Reason for Discharge:	Own Request having served over 21 years
Character:	Good
Trade or Occupation:	Labourer
Can Sign Name:	X his mark on discharge
Height:	5' 6"
Hair Colour:	Brown
Eyes:	Blue
Complexion:	Fresh
Intends to Reside:	Ennistymon Co. Clare

OPRAY Robert, private
20th Foot

Surname Variants	O'PRAY; OPREY; OXPRAY; O''PREY
18 July 1861	From Chatham to Invalid Depot
20 Aug 1861	Discharged the Service
	Pension paid 1st Belfast Pension District
	9d. per diem
1862	Pension paid 1st Glasgow Pension District
1862	1st Belfast Pension District
15 Aug 1865	Arrived per *'Racehorse'*
1867	To Melbourne from Fremantle
1905	Pension increased to 18d. per diem

Service and Personal Details: Medical Board Examination
Tuesday 20th Aug 1861

Place of Birth:	Newtonards Co. Down
Age on Discharge:	23 years
Length of Service:	6 years 3 months [under age for 6 months]
Foreign Service:	India 1 year 4 months
Medal Entitlement:	Indian Medal Clasp for Lucknow
Reason for Discharge:	Wounded in back and left shoulder at Lucknow
Character:	Very Good
Trade or Occupation:	Shoemaker
Height:	5' 4½"
Hair Colour:	Dark
Eyes:	Hazel
Complexion:	Fresh

O'REILLY Philip, private
80th Foot

Surname Variants	O'RIELLY; O'REILY; REILLY
28 Nov 1854	Discharged the Service Fort George
	Pension paid Chatham
	10d. per diem
1855	Pension paid Portsmouth
1855	Chatham
1856	Kilkenny
24 Nov 1858	Arrived per *'Edwin Fox'*
1873	Pension increased to 11d. per diem for 2 years service in the Enrolled Force
circa Mar 1874	Transferred from 2nd Perth Pension District to 1st Perth Pension District

1875	Assigned Bunbury Loc 401
1880	Grant of £15 [pounds] sanctioned
20 Oct 1880	Granted Bunbury Loc 401 [P62] Turkey Point
1882	Convicted before the Police Magistrate Perth W.A. of feloniously stealing 16/4d from another pensioner. Sentenced to 6 months imprisonment with hard labour. Pension to be suspended while imprisoned
1886	W.O. correspondence with S.O. Perth W.A.
1890	Died – buried East Perth Cemetery

Service and Personal Details:

Place of Birth:	Ballyhall Co. Kilkenny
Age on Attestation:	18 years
Period of Service:	1831 — 1854
Age on Discharge:	39 years
Length of Service:	22 years 83 days
Foreign Service:	New South Wales 7 years 6 months
East Indies	9 years 5 months
Medal Entitlement:	Sutlej and 2nd Burma Campaign
Reason for Discharge:	Own Request having served over 21 years
Character:	Indifferent
Trade or Occupation:	Shoemaker
Can Sign Name:	Yes
Height:	5' 6½"
Hair Colour:	Dark Brown
Eyes:	Blue
Complexion:	Sallow
Intends to Reside:	Chatham

OSMOND Edward [Samuel], private
RM

Surname Variants	OSBORNE; OSBOURNE
20 Apr 1848	Discharged the Service Pension paid 2nd Plymouth Pension District £15/4/- per annum
1851	Residing St Budeaux Plymouth
24 Nov 1858	Arrived per *'Edwin Fox'*
no date	Held title to Freshwater Bay Locs P233; P241 and P242 with Title Deed No 2/277
1864	Pension paid Western Australia
1874	Died aged 67
1876	His Freshwater Bay land granted to son

Service and Personal Details:

Place of Birth: [Hemyock [sic] Devon on discharge]	Wellington Somerset
Age on Attestation:	20 years
Period of Service:	1827 — 1848
Length of Service:	21 years
Reason for Discharge:	Time served
Trade or Occupation:	Labourer

Character:	Good	
Can Sign Name:	X his mark on discharge	
Height:	5' 7¾"	
Hair Colour:	Brown	
Eyes:	Blue	
Complexion:	Fair	

OSTERMAYNER

	Frederick, private	
	20th Foot	
Surname Variant	OSTERMAYNOR	
14 Sept 1847	Discharged the Service Chatham	
	Pension paid 1st Manchester District	
	1/- per diem	
6 Apr 1854	Arrived per *'Sea Park'*	
Jan 1857	Contributed 2/- to the Florence Nightingale Fund	
1 Mar 1857	Died Western Australia	
Service and Personal Details:		
Place of Birth:	Tullamore Offaly	
Age on Attestation:	13 years	
Period of Service:	1822 — 1847	
Age on Discharge:	38 years 6 months	
Length of Service:	20 years 102 days	
Foreign Service:	Bermuda	5 years 184 days
	East Indies	10 years 77 days
	Nova Scotia	26 days
Reason for Discharge:	Chronic Rheumatism	
Character:	Good	
Trade or Occupation:	Shoemaker	
Can Sign Name:	Yes	
Height:	5' 8"	
Hair Colour:	Fair	
Eyes:	Grey	
Complexion:	Fresh	
Remarks:	In the Band	
Intends to Reside:	Manchester	

OWENS

	Patrick, private
	12th Foot
28 Dec 1847	Discharged the Service Chatham
	Pension paid Liverpool
	1/- per diem
1848	Pension paid Sligo
1848	Wales
1849	Jersey
1851	Bristol
1852	Sailed as a convict Guard on the *'Robert Small'*
30 Apr 1853	Died in Queenstown Harbour

PAIN

	John, private
	40th Foot
Surname Variants	PAINE; PAYNE
14 Apr 1846	Discharged the Service
	Pension paid Taunton

	10d. per diem	
1 June 1850	Arrived per *'Scindian'*	
1854	Pension paid Perth Western Australia	
1868	Died aged 66	
Service and Personal Details:		
Place of Birth:	Edington or [Erdington] Somerset	
Age on Attestation:	22 years	
Period of Service:	1827 — 1846 or	
	1824 — 1846 [depending on record source]	
Age on Discharge:	40 years	
Length of Service:	18 years 111 days	
Foreign Service:	New South Wales &	
	Van Dieman's Land	2 years
	India	15 years 10 months
Reason for Discharge:	Chronic Rheumatism and Impaired Constitution	
Character:	Very Good	
Trade or Occupation:	Labourer	
Height:	5' 7¼"	
Hair Colour:	Grey/Brown	
Eyes:	Grey	
Complexion:	Dark	

PALMER	Charles Henry, Corporal	
	70th Foot	
14 Sept 1852	Discharged the Service Chatham	
	1/4d. per diem	
1855	Pension paid Chatham	
18 July 1855	Arrived per *'Adelaide'*	
Jan 1857	Contributed 2/6 to the Florence Nightingale Fund	
Oct 1864	Assigned Newcastle Lot S13 Deed No 2054	
Mar 1865	Title Application to Newcastle Pensioner Lot S13	
16 July 1865	Died	
Service and Personal Details:		
Place of Birth:	Whitechurch Ramsgate Kent	
Age on Attestation:	17 years 10 months	
Period of Service:	1831 — 1852	
Age on Discharge:	39 years 2 months	
Length of Service:	21 years 125 days	
Foreign Service:	Gibraltar	2 years 73 days
	Malta	1 year 266 days
	West Indies	3 years
	Canada	2 years 24 days
	East Indies	2 years 194 days
Medal Entitlement:	Recommended for the Good Conduct medal	
Reason for Discharge:	Chronic Pains	
Character:	Good	
Trade or Occupation:	Labourer	
Can Sign Name:	Yes	
Height:	5' 8¼"	
Hair Colour:	Light Brown	
Eyes:	Blue	

Complexion:	Fair
Intends to Reside:	Chatham
Married:	Anastasia
Children:	Letitia
	m. *c*1859 John Robertson Toodyay

PALMER	George, private
	99th Foot
25 Oct 1856	Discharged the Service Cork
3 Mar 1857	Admitted to Out-Pension
	Pension paid Manchester
	8d. per diem
1857	Pension paid Dundee
1857	Manchester
1857	Glasgow
19 Aug 1859	Arrived per *'Sultana'*
1860	To South Australia from Perth West. Aust.
1861	Pension paid Tasmania
1875	W.O. correspondence "A31" with S.O.P. 1st Cork Pension District

Service and Personal Details:

Place of Birth:	Glasgow Lanarkshire
Age on Attestation:	18 years
Period of Service:	1842 — 1856
Age on Discharge:	31 years 10 months
Length of Service:	13 years 321 days
Foreign Service:	Australian Colonies 12 years 2 months
Reason for Discharge:	Accident received at Gun Drill
Character:	Good
Trade or Occupation:	Flax dresser
Can Sign Name:	Yes
Height:	5' 8"
Hair Colour:	Black
Eyes:	Hazel
Complexion:	Fresh
Intends to Reside:	Glasgow Scotland

PALMER	George, private
	RM
	Discharged the Service Portsmouth
	Pension paid
	£13/12/- per annum
13 Dec 1857	From Southampton to Western Australia

Service and Personal Details:

Place of Birth:	Henley-in-Arden Warwickshire
Age on Attestation:	20 years 4 months
Period of Service:	1830 — 1849
Length of Service:	19 years 1 month 7 days
Reason for Discharge:	Invalided with Phthisis contracted during service
Trade or Occupation:	Labourer
Can Sign Name:	Yes

PARKE	James, Corporal
	7th Foot
9 Feb 1842	Admitted to Out-pension
	Pension paid Carlow
	11½d. per diem
1848	Pension paid 1st Manchester
1848	Drogheda
28 Jun 1851	Arrived per *'Pyrenees'* [1]
1853	Off Roll for military offence
1856	Restored to Enrolled Force
7 Nov 1873	Died

Examination of Invalid Soldiers: Wednesday 9th February 1842 [WO117/4]

Place of Birth:	Mohill Co Leitrim
Period of Service:	1819 — 1842
Age on Discharge:	40 years
Length of Service:	22 years 5 months
Foreign Service:	10 years 6 months
Reason for Discharge:	At his own request
Character:	Very Good
Trade or Occupation:	Cordwainer
Can Sign Name:	Yes
Height:	5' 9¾"
Hair Colour:	Grey
Eyes:	Hazel
Complexion:	Sallow

PARKER	George, gunner EIC
	Bombay Horse Artillery
	Out Pension No 115
1849	Embarked UK per *'HMS Meeanee'*
8 Aug 1849	Admitted to Out-pension
	Pension paid Galway
	1/3d. per diem
8 June 1858	Arrived per *'Lord Raglan'*
1861	Employed by Convict establishment
1866	Pension paid Western Australia
24 Oct 1877	Died aged 49

Service and Personal Details:

Where Born:	St Nicholas Galway
Trade or Occupation:	Labourer
Where Enlisted:	Galway
Presidency:	Bombay
Length of Service:	2 years 11 months
Age on Discharge:	22 years
Character:	Good
Reason for Discharge:	Left leg useless from wounds received at Moultan
Intends to Reside:	Galway
Height:	5' 6" or 5' 7"
Complexion:	Fresh
Eye Colour:	Grey
Hair Colour:	Brown
Intends to Reside:	Galway

PARKER		Ninian, private
		78th Foot
	6 Dec 1859	Discharged the Service
		Pension paid Paisley
		11½d. per diem
	11 Feb 1861	Arrived per *'Palmeston'*
	26 Mar 1861	Died

Service and Personal Details:	
Place of Birth:	Paisley Renfrewshire
Age on Attestation:	18 years 4 months
Period of Service:	1836 — 1859
Age on Discharge:	41 years
Length of Service:	22 years 281 days
Foreign Service:	East Indies 17 years 3 months
Medal Entitlement:	Persian Campaign
Reason for Discharge:	Own Request having served 21 years
Character:	Very Good
Trade or Occupation:	Labourer
Can Sign Name:	Yes
Height:	5' 6¼"
Hair Colour:	Fair
Eyes:	Blue
Complexion:	Fair
Intends to Reside:	4, High St Johnstone Renfrewshire

PARKINSON		Nathaniel, private
		89th Foot [Depot]
	4 Sept 1855	Discharged the Service Chatham
		Pension paid Cambridge
		8d. per diem for 1 [one] year conditional
	1859	Pension made permanent
	1862	Pension paid 1st East London District
	9 June 1862	Arrived per *'Norwood'* [1]
	1864	Pension paid Sydney New South Wales
	1878	Died New South Wales

Service and Personal Details:	
Place of Birth:	Ramsey Huntingdonshire
Age on Attestation:	18 years
Period of Service:	1851 — 1855
Age on Discharge:	23 years or 22 years * months
Length of Service:	4 years 37 days
Foreign Service:	Crimea [no time period given]
Medal Entitlement:	Crimea with clasp; Turkish Crimean
Reason for Discharge:	Disabled from frost bite at Sebastopol
Character:	Good
Trade or Occupation:	Labourer
Can Sign Name:	Yes
Height:	5' 6¾"
Hair Colour:	Fair
Eyes:	Grey

Complexion:	Fresh
Distinguishing Marks:	Scar on left cheek and right hand
Intends to Reside:	Ramsey Huntingdonshire

PASSMORE	Henry, Petty Officer Royal Navy
1863	Serving at Dartmoor Prison
15 Aug 1865	Arrived per *'Racehorse'* as a Warder
1865 - 1872	Serving as Assistant Warder in various locations in Western Australia
1873 - 1879	Serving onboard government dredge
1907	Invited to Veteran's dinner at Esplanade Hotel
1915	Residing Raleigh Street North Fremantle
1920	Died

Service and Personal Details:	
Place of Birth:	Barnstable Devon
Campaign Service:	Baltic [Crimean Campaign]
Height:	5' 6"
Hair Colour:	Light
Eyes:	Blue
Complexion:	Fair

PARSONS	Richard, Serjeant 4th Foot
28 July 1846	Discharged the Service Chatham Pension paid Wolverhampton 9d. per diem
7 Feb 1853	Arrived per *'Dudbrook'*
30 Jan 1855	Died Fremantle

Service and Personal Details:		
Place of Birth:	Dudley Worcestershire	
Age on Attestation:	18 years 6 months	
Period of Service:	1831 — 1846	
Age on Discharge:	33 years 1 month	
Length of Service:	14 years 214 days	
Foreign Service:	New South Wales	5 years 11 months
	East Indies	6 years 3 months
Reason for Discharge:	General Debility and Chronic Liver Disease	
Character:	Very Good	
Trade or Occupation:	a Nailer	
Can Sign Name:	Yes	
Height:	5' 7½"	
Hair Colour:	Brown	
Eyes:	Blue	
Complexion:	Fresh	
Intends to Reside:	Dudley Worcestershire	
Married:	Ann Bracken	
Children:	Phoebe b. *c*1839 Poonamallee India Isaac b. 1843 d. 1845 Secunderabad India Asenath b. 1845 Secunderabad India Richard b. 1849 England Jessimina b. 1853 England	

Marriage Details:	At Poonamallee 3rd April 1839 Serjeant Richard Parson of HM 4th or King's Own Regiment Bachelor and Ann Bracken Indo-British Spinster were married by banns In the presence of Simon and Margaret Dring

PATERSON

	John, gunner and driver Royal Artillery 2nd Battalion
11 Jan 1853	Discharged the Service Woolwich 1/- per diem Pension paid 2nd Edinburgh Pension District
1856	2nd Edinburgh Pension District
1857	2nd Edinburgh Pension District
19 Aug 1859	Arrived per *'Sultana'*
1861	Pension paid Woolwich
1862	Edinburgh

Service and Personal Details:

Place of Birth:	Cannongate Edinburgh	
Age on Attestation:	17 years 5 months	
Period of Service:	1831 — 1853	
Age on Discharge:	39 years 4 months	
Length of Service:	21 years 71 days	
Foreign Service:	West Indies	6 years 7 months
Reason for Discharge:	Chronic Rheumatism	
Character:	Good for the last 2½ years	
Trade or Occupation:	Labourer	
Can Sign Name:	Yes	
Height:	5' 7"	
Hair Colour:	Brown	
Eyes:	Hazel	
Complexion:	Fresh	

PEACOCK

	Gough, private 40th Foot
24 May 1859	Discharged the Service Chatham Pension paid Limerick 1/2d. per diem
11 Feb 1861	Arrived per *'Palmeston'*
1864	ptve G Peacock Pensioner Force at Perth contributed to the Greenough Fire Relief Fund
1867	Died

Service and Personal Details:

Place of Birth:	St Johns Limerick Co. Limerick	
Age on Attestation:	20 years	
Period of Service:	1839 — 1858	
Age on Discharge:	40 years 4 months	
Length of Service:	19 years 194 days	
Foreign Service:	Afghanistan	3 years 4 months
	India	1 year 3 months
	Australia 6 years 1 month	

Medal Entitlement:	2nd Afghan Campaign with 3 inscriptions; Bronze Star for Maharajpore
Reason for Discharge:	Wounded in right shoulder by grape shot
Character:	Good
Trade or Occupation:	Chandler
Can Sign Name:	Yes
Height:	5' 8"
Hair Colour:	Light Brown
Eyes:	Grey
Complexion:	Fresh
Intends to Reside:	Limerick

PEDIE

	James, private	
	71st Foot	
Surname Variant	PEDDIE	
14 Oct 1861	Discharged the Service Stirling Castle	
29 Oct 1861	Admitted to Out-Pension	
	Pension paid Edinburgh	
	1/- per diem	
15 Feb 1863	Arrived per *'Merchantman'* [1]	
Service and Personal Details:		
Place of Birth:	Monedie Perth Scotland	
Age on Attestation:	17 years 11 months	
Period of Service:	1839 — 1861	
Age on Discharge:	39 years 11 months	
Length of Service:	21 years 328 days	
Foreign Service:	Canada	2 years 5 months
	West Indies	3 years 2 months
	Corfu	1 year 10 months
	Crimea	1 year 4 months
	Malta	1 month
Medal Entitlement:	Long Service and Good Conduct without gratuity; Crimea	
Reason for Discharge:	Own Request having served over 21 years	
Character:	Very Good	
Trade or Occupation:	Tailor	
Can Sign Name:	Yes	
Height:	5' 6"	
Hair Colour:	Brown	
Eyes:	Grey	
Complexion:	Fair	
Intends to Reside:	Edinburgh	

PELCHER

	William, Serjeant
	50th Foot
Surname Variant	PILCHER; POACHER
27 Mar 1849	Discharged the Service Chatham
	1/3d. per diem
1860	Pension paid Canterbury
1861	Dublin
1862	Pension paid 2nd West London Pension District
31 Dec 1862	Arrived per *'York'*

Feb 1864	ptve W Pilcher Pensioner Force Fremantle District contributed to the Greenough Fire Relief Fund
1864	To South Australia from Fremantle West. Aust.
1881	W.O. correspondence to Office of Payments of Imperial Pensions South Australia – [the "A31"] - full amount under regulations in force at discharge

Service and Personal Details:

Place of Birth:	St Mary's Dover Kent	
Age on Attestation:	19 years 2 months	
Period of Service:	1838 — 1849	
Age on Discharge:	29 years 6 months	
Length of Service:	10 years 82 days	
Foreign Service:	New South Wales	1 year 103 days
	East Indies	7 years 26 days
Medal Entitlement:	Bronze Star for action at Punniar 1843; Sutlej with clasps	
Reason for Discharge:	Gunshot wound to right hand received at Ferozeshar 1845	
Character:	Good	
Trade or Occupation:	Shoemaker	
Can Sign Name:	Yes	
Height:	5' 7¼"	
Hair Colour:	Light Brown	
Eyes:	Hazel	
Complexion:	Fresh	
Intends to Reside:	Manchester	

PENDERGRAST John, private
87th Foot

Surname Variants	[some] PRENDERGERST; PRENDERGAST; PENDERGAST
4 Oct 1859	Discharged the Service 1/- per diem
1864	Pension paid Clomnel
15 Apr 1864	Arrived per *'Clara'* [2]
1868	Assigned Greenough Loc 12 at Bootenal
1874	Pension increased to 1/3d. per diem for service in the Enrolled Force
1884	Grant of Greenough Loc 12 at Bootenal confirmed
1891	Died aged 71

Service and Personal Details:

Place of Birth:	Castlebar Co. Mayo	
Age on Attestation:	18 years	
Period of Service:	1838 — 1859	
Age on Discharge:	39 years	
Length of Service:	21 years 31 days	
Foreign Service:	East Indies	7 years 10 months
Medal Entitlement:	Good Conduct medal	
Reason for Discharge:	Own Request having completed over 21 years	
Character:	Extremely Good	
Trade or Occupation:	Labourer	

Can Sign Name:	X his mark on discharge
Hair Colour:	Light Brown
Eyes:	Blue
Complexion:	Fresh

PERKINS Job, private

	25th Foot
Previous Regiment	5th Foot
29 July 1856	Discharged the Service Chatham
	Pension paid 1st Manchester Pension District
	1/- per diem
1856	Pension paid Sheffield
19 Aug 1859	Arrived per *'Sultana'*
1863	To Sydney from Western Australia
1875	Pension paid Sydney New South Wales
1888	W.O. Correspondence — the "A31"
1893	Discharge Document sent to W.O.

Service and Personal Details:

Place of Birth:	Loughborough Leicestershire
Age on Attestation:	18 years
Period of Service:	1834 — 1856
Age on Discharge:	39 years 8 months
Length of Service:	21 years 254 days
Foreign Service:	East Indies 13 years
Reason for Discharge:	Chronic Rheumatism and worn out
Character:	Exemplary
Trade or Occupation:	Framework Knitter
Can Sign Name:	Yes
Height:	5' 10"
Hair Colour:	Brown
Eyes:	Grey
Complexion:	Fair
Intends to Reside:	Sheffield but decided on Manchester

PERSSE John, Corporal

	74th Foot
Previous Regiment	5th; 25th
Surname Variants	PERSE; PIESSE; PEARCE
4 Sept 1860	Discharged the Service
	Pension paid Dundee
	1/2½d. per diem
1860	Pension paid Aberdeen
1861	Salisbury
28 Jan 1862	Arrived per *'Lincelles'*
1862	Pension paid Freemantle [sic]
1863	Residing Fremantle
1863	Pension paid Western Australia
3 Nov 1864	Died

Service and Personal Details:

Place of Birth:	Athenry Co. Galway
Age on Attestation:	18 years
Period of Service:	1839 — 1860

Age on Discharge:	39 years
Length of Service:	21 years 128 days
Foreign Service:	East Indies 13 years 1 month
Reason for Discharge:	Own Request having completed 21 years service
Character:	Good
Trade or Occupation:	Labourer
Can Sign Name:	Yes
Height:	5' 7¼"
Hair Colour:	Fair
Eyes:	Blue
Complexion:	Fair
Intends to Reside:	Dundee

PHIBBS

	William, private EIC
	1st Bombay European Infantry
	Out Pension No 179
1860	Embarked United Kingdom per *'Cossipore'*
17 Oct 1860	Admitted to Out-pension
	Pension paid 1st Dublin Pension District
	1/- per diem
27 May 1863	Arrived per *'Clyde'*
1866	To New South Wales from Fremantle
1874	Pension paid Dublin

Service and Personal Details:

Place of Birth:	Kill Co. Kildare
Trade or Occupation:	Labourer
Where Enlisted:	Dublin
Presidency:	Bombay
Length of Service:	19 years 5 months
Age on Discharge:	37 years
Character:	Very Good
Reason for Discharge:	To be pensioned
Medal Entitlement:	Indian Mutiny
Height:	5' 4¾"
Complexion:	Fresh
Eye Colour:	Grey
Hair Colour:	Brown
Intends to Reside:	Dublin

PHILLIPS

	Henry, private
	Rifle Brigade
Previous Regiment	77th Foot
22 Nov 1853	Discharged the Service Chatham
	Pension paid Cambridge
	1/- per diem
18 July 1855	Arrived per *'Adelaide'*
Jan 1857	contributed 2/- to the Florence Nightingale Fund
1861	Employed as Assistant Warder Rottnest Island
1 Nov 1862	Died

Service and Personal Details:

Place of Birth:	Trinity Exeter Devon

Age on Attestation:	20 years 8 months	
Period of Service:	1832 — 1853	
Age on Discharge:	42 years or 41 years 2 months	
Length of Service:	21 years 19 days [reckoned]	
Foreign Service:	Malta &	
	Ionian Isles	8 years 7 months
	Cape of Good Hope	3 years 7 months
Reason for Discharge:	Rheumatism	
Character:	Very Good	
Trade or Occupation:	Blacksmith	
Can Sign Name:	Yes	
Height:	5' 7"	
Hair Colour:	Brown	
Eyes:	Grey	
Complexion:	Dark	
Intends to Reside:	Huntingdon	

PICKERING	Joseph
	Rifle Brigade
17 Nov 1863	Discharged the Service
	Pension paid Leicester
	10d. per diem
1866	Pension paid Liverpool
4 July 1866	Arrived per *'Belgravia'*
2 Oct 1866	Assigned 40 acres at Wellington near Collie
1881	Pension increased to 1/4d. per diem for service in the Enrolled Force
24 Feb 1883	Applied for North Fremantle Lot P89
1884	Granted North Fremantle Town Lot P89
June 1897	Residing Fremantle
1897	Died at Fremantle — described as late of Fremantle pensioner and dairyman

Service and Personal Details:

Place of Birth:	St Martins Leicester	
Age on Attestation:	17 years 6 months	
Period of Service:	1842 — 1863	
Age on Discharge:	39 years	
Length of Service:	20 years 337 months	
Foreign Service:	Ionian Isles	1 year 8 months
	Cape of Good Hope	5 years 5 months
	Crimea	1 year 10 months
	North America	1 year 10 months
Medal Entitlement:	Kaffir War 1846/7; South Africa against the insurgent Boers 1848; Crimea with 4 clasps; Turkish Crimean	
Reason for Discharge:	Own Request after 21 years of "allowed to reckon" service	
Character:	Very Good	
Trade or Occupation:	Woolcomber	
Can Sign Name:	Yes	
Height:	5' 8"	

Hair Colour:	Brown
Eyes:	Hazel
Complexion:	Fresh

PIDGEON	George, private
	62nd Foot
Surname Variant	PIGEON
4 May 1855	Discharged the Service Mullingar Ireland
5 June 1855	Admitted to Out-Pension
	Pension paid Leicester
	9d. per diem
10 Sept 1856	Arrived per *'Runnymede'*
Dec 1857	Assigned Pensioner Lot P12 at York
Mar 1865	Application for Title to P12 York
1864	ptve G Pidgeon Pensioner Force at York contributed to the Greenough Fire Relief Fund
1866	Stationed Rottnest Island
1869	Mrs Pidgeon and two children requesting to be admitted to Poor House
1870	Remains of what was believed to be George Pidgeon found in bush near York

Service and Personal Details:		
Place of Birth:	St Margarets Leicestershire	
Age on Attestation:	18 years 6 months	
Period of Service:	1834 — 1855	
Age on Discharge:	39 years 8 months	
Length of Service:	21 years 38 days	
Foreign Service:	East Indies	12 years 9 months
Reason for Discharge:	Worn out from long service in the tropics	
Character:	Good	
Trade or Occupation:	Trimmer and Dyer	
Can Sign Name:	Yes	
Height:	5' 10"	
Hair Colour:	Brown	
Eyes:	Grey	
Complexion:	Sallow	
Intends to Reside:	Leicester England	

PIGGOTT	Samuel, private
	51st Foot
Previous Regiments	96th; 99th
Surname Variant	PIGGETT
25 June 1840	Arrived per *'Runnymede'*
1847	Transferred to 96th Foot
1848	Serving as a Police Constable Albany
1849	Transferred to 99th Foot
31 Aug 1854	Discharged the Service Perth West. Aust.
19 Feb 1855	Discharge approved
	Serving as Serjeant of Police Albany
1864	Purchased pastoral lease at Hay River — known as 'Moolicup or Mulikup'
Aug 1881	Deferred Pension forms sent to S. O. P. Fremantle
1884	Died Albany

Service and Personal Details:	
Place of Birth:	Potton Bedfordshire
Age on Attestation:	18 years
Period of Service:	1838 — 1854
Age on Discharge:	34 years 5 months
Length of Service:	16 years 33 days
Foreign Service:	Australian Colonies
Reason for Discharge:	Receiving a Free Discharge and gratuity of 12 months pay with Right of Registry for a Deferred Pension of 6d. per diem on attaining 60 years
Character:	Very Good
Trade or Occupation:	Labourer
Can Sign Name:	Yes
Height:	5' 8"
Hair Colour:	Dark Brown
Eye Colour:	Hazel
Complexion:	Fair
Intended Residence:	Albany King George Sound West Aust
PIKE	Thomas, private 53rd Foot
Previous Regiment	62nd Foot
Surname Variant	FIKE
12 Feb 1856	Discharged the Service Chatham Pension paid Bristol 1/- per diem
19 Aug 1859	Arrived per *'Sultana'*
1864	ptve T Fike [sic] Pensioner Force at Fremantle contributed to the Greenough Fire Relief Fund
Aug 1864	Died
Service and Personal Details:	
Place of Birth:	Portsmouth Hampshire
Age on Attestation:	19 years 2 months
Period of Service:	1835 — 1855
Age on Discharge:	40 years
Length of Service:	20 years 312 days
Foreign Service:	East Indies 19 years 8 months
Medal Entitlement:	Good Conduct; 2 medals for service in the field
Reason for Discharge:	Chronic Rheumatism
Character:	Very Good
Trade or Occupation:	Drover
Can Sign Name:	X his mark on discharge
Height:	5' 8"
Hair Colour:	Red
Eyes:	Grey
Complexion:	Fair
Distinguishing Marks:	Wound of gunshot on forefinger of left hand
Intends to Reside:	Bristol
PIMLOTT	William, Corporal Royal Artillery 7th Battalion

10 Mar 1857	Discharged the Service Woolwich Pension paid Inverness 8d. per diem for 2 years	
1 July 1857	Pension to be paid Perth Western Australia from Inverness Scotland [12/Inverness/35]	
1858	To South Australia from West Aust [12/WA/17]	
1858	Pension paid Victoria	
Mar 1859	Pension ceased	
1863	Died aged 33 at the Police Barracks Sydney	
Service and Personal Details:		
Place of Birth:	Island of Corfu	
Age on Attestation:	12 years 10 months	
Period of Service:	1845 — 1857	
Age on Discharge:	24 years 11 months	
Length of Service:	6 years 354 days	
Foreign Service:	Gibraltar	7 years 5 months
	Malta	2 months
Reason for Discharge:	Disease of the Lungs	
Character:	Very Good	
Trade or Occupation:	Labourer	
Can Sign Name:	Yes	
Height:	5' 8½"	
Hair Colour:	Dark Brown	
Eyes:	Hazel	
Complexion:	Fresh	

PINDAR	Enoch, private 20th Foot	
Surname Variants	PINDER; PENDER	
23 Nov 1858	Discharged the Service Chatham Pension paid Halifax 1/2d. per diem	
15 Feb 1863	Arrived per *'Merchantman'* [1]	
Jan 1865	Departed for UK per *'Daylight'*	
1865	Pension paid Halifax United Kingdom	
1895	W.O. Correspondence — insufficient grounds to increase pension	
1898	W.O. Correspondence	
Service and Personal Details:		
Place of Birth:	Halifax Yorkshire	
Age on Attestation:	18 years 8 months	
Period of Service:	1854 — 1858	
Age on Discharge:	23 years 6 months	
Length of Service:	4 years 274 days	
Foreign Service:	Crimea	1 year 308 days
	India	311 days
Medal Entitlement:	Crimea with clasps	
Reason for Discharge:	Wounded by round shot to the left side of the lower jaw — Feb 1858.	
Character:	Good	
Trade or Occupation:	Labourer	
Can Sign Name:	Yes	

Height:	5' 7½"
Hair Colour:	Light
Eyes:	Grey
Complexion:	Fresh
Distinguishing Marks:	Pock pitted
Intends to Reside:	Halifax Yorkshire
Married:	*c*1862 Elizabeth Greenwood Huddersfield
Children:	Emma Sarah b. *c*1863 Fremantle
	Annie b. 1867 Halifax Yorkshire
	Charles b. 1871 Sowerby Bridge Yorkshire
	Major Harry b. 1873 Sowerby Bridge
	Marina b. 1875 Sowerby Bridge

PINKER — Isaac [Military Pensioner]

	50th Foot
Previous Regiment	21st Foot
1865	Re-engaged at Wanganui New Zealand for 11 years 176 days
1867	Residing Brisbane
5 Apr 1877	Discharged the Service Kinsale
1881	an Isaac Pinker employed as a Freestone Sawyer
1883	Arrived per *'Arafura'* from London [Isaac Pinker nominated by Philip Mack]
1890	the charge of cattle trespass against an Isaac Pinker [possibly son] was with-drawn
July 1910	Died aged 85

Service and Personal Details:

Place of Birth:	Box Corsham Wiltshire	
Age on Attestation:	18 years	
Period of Service:	1856 — 1877	
Age on Discharge:	39 years 3 months	
Length of Service:	21 years 73 days	
Foreign Service:	Ceylon	6 years 1 month
	New Zealand	5 years * months
Medal Entitlement:	Long Service and Good Conduct New Zealand War	
Reason for Discharge:	On termination of 2nd period of "Limited Service"	
Character:	Good — habits temperate	
Trade or Occupation:	Labourer	
Can Sign Name:	Yes	
Height:	5' 6½"	
Chest Measurement:	33"	
Weight:	140 lbs	
Small Pox Scars:	None	
Vaccination marks:	On left arm	
When Vaccinated:	In Infirmary	
Hair Colour:	Light Brown	
Pulse:	72 beats	
Respiration:	20 inspirations	
Muscular Development:	Medium	
Eyes:	Grey	

Complexion:	Fresh
Remarks:	Doesn't have any Education Certificate
Intends to Reside:	Bristol but decided on Ireland
Married:	*c*1868 Norah Walsh New South Wales
Children:	John b. *c*1868 New South Wales
	James Patrick b *c*1871 Gloucestershire
	m. *c*1900 Martha Louisa Newman Guildford
	Mary Elizabeth b. *c*1873 Hampshire
	William b. *c*1875 Colchester
	Norah b. *c*1877 Ireland
	[died *c*1899 aged 24 born Kinsale Ireland]
	Isaac b. *c*1878 Bristol
	Kate b. *c*1885 Swan District
	m. *c*1904 Charles Newman Guildford

PLACKETT Samuel, private
8th Foot [Depot]

Surname Variant	PLASKETH
22 May 1866	Discharged the Service Newry
	Pension paid Northampton
	1/1d. per diem
9 Jan 1868	Arrived per *'Hougoumont'*
1873	Pension increased to 1/3d per diem for service in the Enrolled Force Stationed Fremantle
15 Sept 1873	Died

Service and Personal Details:

Place of Birth:	Newport Pagnell Buckinghamshire
Age on Attestation:	20 years
Period of Service:	1845 — 1866
Age on Discharge:	41 years
Length of Service:	21 years 20 days
Foreign Service:	East Indies 14 years 1 month
Medal Entitlement:	Long Service and Good Conduct with gratuity; Indian Mutiny
Reason for Discharge:	Own Request having completed 21 years service
Character:	Very Good
Trade or Occupation:	Labourer
Can Sign Name:	Yes
Height:	5' 7½"
Hair Colour:	Brown
Eyes:	Grey
Complexion:	Fresh
Intends to Reside: Northamptonshire	No. 2 Cosford Yard Abner Street

POLKINGHORNE Humphrey, private
6th Dragoons

18 July 1855	Invalided and sent home from Crimea
23 Dec 1856	Discharged the Service Chatham
	Pension paid Falmouth
	7d. per diem
24 Nov 1858	Arrived per *'Edwin Fox'*
31 Dec 1862	Pension paid South Australia

1874	South Australia
Service and Personal Details:	
Place of Birth:	Perranarworthal Truro Cornwall
Age on Attestation:	21 years 11 months
Period of Service:	1838 — 1856
Age on Discharge:	40 years 9 months
Length of Service:	18 years 36 days
Foreign Service:	"The East" 1 year 1 month
Medal Entitlement:	Crimea with clasp
Reason for Discharge:	General breakdown of his constitution and health owing to the effects of fever contracted during service in the Crimea
Character:	Good
Trade or Occupation:	Cooper
Can Sign Name:	Yes
Height:	5' 11"
Hair Colour:	Dark Brown
Eyes:	Brown
Complexion:	Fair
Intends to Reside:	Cornwall

POLLITT	Thomas, private [1517] 50th Foot
Surname Variants	POLLETT; PALLETT; PELLITT; POLLIT
12 Sept 1848	Discharged the Service Chatham Pension paid Leeds 8d. per diem
1857	Pension paid Newcastle
8 June 1858	Arrived per *'Lord Raglan'*
1861	Stationed Geraldton area and employed as Assistant Warder
18 Feb 1862	Died — Committed suicide. [WO letter 7596/336]
Service and Personal Details:	
Place of Birth:	Astley Lancashire
Age on Attestation:	19 years
Period of Service:	1840 — 1848
Age on Discharge:	27 years
Length of Service:	7 years 252 days
Foreign Service:	New South Wales 120 days East Indies 6 years 191 days
Medal Entitlement:	In action Punniar 1843; Sutlej with 2 clasps
Reason for Discharge:	Wounded left thigh by round shot at Ferozeshar 1845
Character:	Good
Trade or Occupation:	Collier
Can Sign Name:	X his mark on discharge
Height:	5' 5¾"
Hair Colour:	Brown
Eyes:	Grey

Complexion:	Sallow
Intends to Reside:	Bolton Lancashire

PORTER	Henry, private
	107th Foot
Previous Regiment	10th; 81st
25 July 1865	Discharged the Service Netley
	Pension paid Woolwich
	10d. per diem
1866	Pension paid Deptford
1866	Pension paid 1st East London Pension District
1867	Pension paid Chatham
1867	Kilkenny
1867	Southampton
1867	Dorchester
1867	Portsmouth
9 Aug 1868	Arrived per *'Hougoumont'*
19 Jan 1876	Died aged 49

Service and Personal Details:	
Place of Birth:	Abbyleix Queens County
Age on Attestation:	18 years
Period of Service:	1844 — 1865
Age on Discharge:	39 years 3 months or 38 years 198 days
Length of Service:	20 years 198 days
Foreign Service:	India 19 years 50 days
Medal Entitlement:	Long Service and Good Conduct with gratuity; Punjaub Campaign with 2 clasps; Indian Mutiny with clasp for Lucknow
Reason for Discharge:	Lumbago and Rheumatic Pains
Character:	Very Good
Trade or Occupation:	Labourer
Can Sign Name:	Yes
Height:	5' 9½"
Hair Colour:	Fair
Eyes:	Grey
Complexion:	Fair
Distinguishing Marks:	Bullet wound at back of right shoulder
Remarks:	Elected for British Pension Rules
Intends to Reside:	Abbyleix Queens but decided on Woolwich

PORTLOCK	Henry, private
also known as	Henry **JONES**
	1st Foot
20 May 1854	Discharged the Service Castlebar
11 July 1854	Admitted to Out-Pension
	Pension paid Birmingham
	1/- per diem
2 Apr 1856	Arrived per *'William Hammond'* as a Convict Guard
July 1856	£4/16/10 balance due on landing at colony but misappropriated by Capt Foss
Jan 1857	Contributed 1/- to the Florence Nightingale Fund
Jan 1861	Departed colony per *'Lord Raglan'*

1861	Pension paid 1st East London Pension District	
1861	Pension paid Worcester	
1883	Admitted to In-Pension Chelsea	
1890	Died	
Service and Personal Details:		
Place of Birth:	Birmingham Warwickshire	
Age on Attestation:	18 years 4 months	
Period of Service:	1832 — 1854	
Age on Discharge:	40 years 4 months	
Length of Service:	21 years 56 days	
Foreign Service:	Canada	7 years 2 months
	West Indies	2 years 5 months
Reason for Discharge:	Chronic Rheumatism	
Character:	Good	
Trade or Occupation:	Gardner [sic]	
Can Sign Name:	Yes	
Height:	5' 7½"	
Hair Colour:	Dark	
Eyes:	Hazel	
Complexion:	Dark	
Distinguishing Marks:	Scar on right cheek	

POWER	John, Garrison Serjeant Major [3449]	
	Corps of Armourer Serjeants	
Previous Regiment	96th Foot	
2 June 1863	Discharged the Service Plymouth	
	Pension paid 2nd Plymouth Pension District 2/6d. per diem	
28 Dec 1863	Arrived per *'Lord Dalhousie'*	
no date	Assigned Perth Military Pensioner Lot 143/Y	
1876	Applies for £15 improvement grant for Perth Town Lot 143/Y	
1881	Pension increased to 3/- per diem for service in the Enrolled Force	
Apr 1881	Application for Title to Perth Lot 143/Y	
1882	Enquiring about issue of Fee Simple for Pensioner's Grant No. 143	
1882	To Eastern Colonies	
Service and Personal Details:		
Place of Birth:	Roscommon	
Age on Attestation:	15 years 11 months	
Period of Service:	1840 — 1863	
Age on Discharge:	39 years 1 month	
Length of Service:	21 years 28 days	
Foreign Service:	Australia	7 years 9 months
	India	5 years 6 months
	Gibraltar	10 months
Medal Entitlement:	Good Conduct medal with gratuity	
Reason for Discharge:	Own Request having completed 21 years service	
Character:	Exemplary	

Trade or Occupation:	none
Can Sign Name:	Yes
Height:	5' 6½"
Hair Colour:	Light Brown
Eyes:	Grey
Complexion:	Fresh
Intends to Reside:	Millbay Barracks Plymouth

POWER

	John, private EIC 2nd Bombay European Infantry Out Pension No. 198
10 Aug 1861	Admitted to Out-pension Pension paid Ennis 1/- per diem
1862	Pension paid Bermuda
15 Feb 1863	Arrived per *'Merchantman'* [1]
1864	ptve J Power Pensioner Force at Perth contributed to the Greenough Fire Relief Fund Assigned Perth Town Lot 124/Y
Apr 1881	Application for Title to Perth Lot 124/Y

Service and Personal Details:

Place of Birth:	Ennistyna [sic] Ireland
Trade or Occupation:	Labourer
Length of Service:	21 years
Age on Discharge:	40 years
Reason for Discharge:	Time expired
Character:	Good
Height:	5' 6¼"
Complexion:	Fresh
Eye Colour:	Grey
Hair Colour:	Brown
Intends to Reside:	Ennis Ireland

POWER

	Michael, private 3rd Foot
9 Oct 1866	Discharged the Service Pension paid Birmingham 8d. per diem for 27 months conditional
1867	Pension paid Portsmouth
1869	Kilkenny
1871	Pension made permanent at 6d. per diem
1872	Pension paid Birmingham
19 Feb 1874	Arrived per *'Naval Brigade'*
1877	Stationed Perth — charged with unlawful possession
April 1877	Assigned Pensioner Allotment at Bootenal
1881	Recommended for £15 Pensioner's Grant
1883	Granted Fee Simple Victoria Loc 21 Bootenal
1894	Pension increased to 8d. per diem on account of his Good Conduct Badges

Service and Personal Details:

Place of Birth:	Thurles Co. Tipperary
Age on Attestation:	24 years

Period of Service:	1857 — 1866	
Age on Discharge:	32 years 11 months	
Length of Service:	8 years 330 days	
Foreign Service:	Malta	4 years 2 months
	Gibraltar	2 years
	West Indies	2 years
Reason for Discharge:	Pulmonary Consumption	
Character:	Good	
Trade or Occupation:	Labourer	
Can Sign Name:	Yes	
Height:	5' 6½"	
Hair Colour:	Light Brown	
Eyes:	Grey	
Complexion:	Fair	
Intends to Reside:	Birmingham	

PRATT John, private
24th Foot

Previous Regiment	98th Foot	
10 Oct 1845	Discharged the Service Limerick	
	Pension paid Limerick	
	1/- per diem	
25 Oct 1850	Arrived per *'Hashemy'*	
20 Nov 1852	Assigned Bunbury Pension Lot P4	
4 Dec 1858	Application for Title to Bunbury Pensioner Lot P4	

Service and Personal Details:

Place of Birth:	Rathdowen Co. Queens Ireland	
Age on Attestation:	17 years 7 months	
Period of Service:	1824 — 1845	
Age on Discharge:	39 years	
Length of Service:	20 years 302 days	
Foreign Service:	Cape of Good Hope	12 years 6 months
	Canada	3 years 2 months
Reason for Discharge:	Worn out and suffers from fixed pain in back caused from loading baggage	
Character:	Good	
Trade or Occupation:	Weaver	
Can Sign Name:	X his mark on discharge	
Height:	5' 4½"	
Hair Colour:	Dark	
Eyes:	Hazel	
Complexion:	Sallow	

PRATT Richard, Corporal
24th Foot

27 Feb 1863	Discharged the Service Cork
17 Mar 1863	Admitted to Out-Pension
	Pension paid Waterford
	1/1½d. per diem
22 Dec 1865	Arrived per *'Vimiera'*
1878	Employed by Convict Establishment

1878	Pension increased to 1/7d. per diem for service in the Enrolled Force
Sept 1883	Granted Title to Perth Lot 131/V
1884	Died

Service and Personal Details:

Place of Birth:	Cheltenham Gloucestershire	
Age on Attestation:	35 years 4 months	
Period of Service:	? — 1863	
Age on Discharge:	44 years 2 months	
Length of Service:	22 years 14 days	
Foreign Service:	China	1 year 6 months
	East Indies	14 years 4 months
Medal Entitlement:	Long Service and Good Conduct with gratuity; China 1842; Punjaub with clasps	
Reason for Discharge:	Own Request having completed 21 years	
Character:	Very Good	
Trade or Occupation:	Butcher	
Can Sign Name:	Yes	
Height:	6' 0½"	
Hair Colour:	Dark Brown	
Eyes:	Hazel	
Complexion:	Sallow	
Remarks:	Wounded in right hand at Chillianwallah on	
13 January 1849		
Intends to Reside:	Oxford Oxfordshire	

PRENDAVILLE Thomas, private [398]
51st Foot

Surname Variants	PRENDERVILLE; PRENDIVILLE
25 June 1840	Arrived per *'Runnymede'*
11 Mar 1847	Discharged the Service
24 Aug 1847	Pension approved and ratified
Aug 1847	Drowned

Service and Personal Details:

Place of Birth:	?Ballymaston Kings County	
Age on Attestation:	22 years	
Period of Service:	1825 — 1847	
Age on Discharge:	44 years	
Length of Service:	22 years 56 days	
Foreign Service:	Ionian Isles	5 years 7 months
	Australia	8 years 1 month
Reason for Discharge:	Worn out and not fit for service in India	
Character:	Very Good	
Trade or Occupation:	Labourer	
Can Sign Name:	Yes	
Height:	5' 7¾"	
Hair Colour:	Black	
Eye Colour:	Grey	
Complexion:	Dark	

PRESS Daniel, private

	41st Foot
Surname Variant	PIESS; PRESSE
25 Apr 1827	Discharged the Service Chatham
	Pension paid Taunton
	9d. per diem
1850	"Pension to be paid Western Australia from Taunton" — [12/Taunton/5]
1865	Pension paid Western Australia
1865	to Sydney New South Wales
1868	Died in the quarter ending 30/6/1868

Service and Personal Details:

Place of Birth:	Wiltscombe Somerset	
Age on Attestation:	16 years	
Period of Service:	1811 — 1827	
Age on Discharge:	about 31 years	
Length of Service:	14 years 217 days [after age of 18 years]	
Foreign Service:	India	4 years 2 years
Reason for Discharge:	Chronic Dysentery	
Character:	Very Good	
Trade or Occupation:	Labourer	
Can Sign Name:	X his mark on discharge	
Height:	5' 8"	
Hair Colour:	Brown	
Eyes:	Grey	
Complexion:	Fair	
Distinguishing Marks:	Extensive scar on abdomen	
Intends to Reside:	Somerset	

PRESTON	John, private
	17th Foot
23 May 1848	Discharged the Service Chatham
	Pension paid Leicester
	8d. per diem
1850	Pension paid East London Pension District
1850	Leicester
18 Oct 1851	Arrived per *'Minden'*
1854	"Struck off Enrolled Pensioner Guard Roll for absenting himself from Colony without leave and to refund the cost of passage out."
1855	Pension paid 1st East London Pension District
1878	Admitted to In-Pension Chelsea
1879	To refund passage money from Australia, this to be stopped from his pension

Service and Personal Details:

Place of Birth:	Stony Stainton Leicestershire	
Age on Attestation:	17 years 5 months	
Period of Service:	1832 — 1848	
Age on Discharge:	34 years	
Length of Service:	15 years 200 days	
Foreign Service:	New South Wales	2 years 112 days
	East Indies	11 years 85 days
Reason for Discharge:	Chronic Rheumatism	

Character:	Good
Trade or Occupation:	Frame work knitter
Can Sign Name:	Yes
Height:	5' 10"
Hair Colour:	Dark Brown
Eyes:	Blue
Complexion:	Fresh
Intends to Reside:	Leicester

PRIME

	John, gunner and driver
	Royal Artillery 11th Battalion
14 Oct 1851	Discharged the Service Edinburgh
4 Nov 1851	Admitted to Out-Pension
	Pension paid 2nd Edinburgh Pension District
	1/- per diem
2 Aug 1852	Arrived per *'William Jardine'*
1853	a John Prime police constable Fremantle
1854	Pension paid Perth Western Australia
1855	Melbourne
11 Apr 1860	Died

Service and Personal Details:

Place of Birth:	Earsham Norfolk	
Age on Attestation:	18 years	
Period of Service:	1830 — 1851	
Age on Discharge:	39 years 6 months	
Length of Service:	21 years 177 days	
Foreign Service:	Newfoundland	9 years 4 months
Reason for Discharge:	Chronic Rheumatism	
Character:	Exemplary	
Trade or Occupation:	Printer	
Can Sign Name:	Yes	
Height:	6' 0½"	
Hair Colour:	Brown	
Eyes:	Grey	
Complexion:	Fair	
Remarks:	Subsisted from 14th October to 3rd November	
1851 inclusive		
Intends to Reside:	Edinburgh	

PTOLEMY

	Andrew, private
	79th Foot
Previous Regiments	9th; 80th
Surname Variant	PTOLOMY; PTOLEMEY
4 Aug 1863	Discharged the Service Netley
	Pension paid 2nd Dublin Pension District
	1/- per diem
15 Aug 1865	Arrived per *'Racehorse'*
24 Aug 1881	Assigned Perth Railway Block 130/V
1881	Pension increased to 1/6d. per diem for service in the Enrolled Force

Jan 1882	Andrew Ptolomey, a pensioner, aged 60, 5ft. 6 or 7in. tall, sallow complexion long visage; lately resided in Murray Street Perth, is inquired for as last heard of on the 4th Jan. Present whereabouts, if known to police, to be reported to Detective Office, Perth.
18 Dec 1883	Granted Fee Simple for Perth Railway Block 130/V
1887	Convicted of stealing a pair of trousers. Sentenced to 2 calendar months to hard labor and struck off the Pension List
1888	Pension restored
1889	Convicted of stealing a Razor valued at 10/-. Sentenced to 3 calendar months hard labor and struck off the Pension List
1890	W.O. correspondence to Colonial Treasurer regarding restoration of pension
1893	Died aged 67 killed in Howick St. Cause of death — dangerous riding by a William Taylor

Service and Personal Details:

Place of Birth:	St Catherines Dublin
Age on Attestation:	18 years
Period of Service:	1842 — 1863
Age on Discharge:	38 years 4 months
Length of Service:	20 years 33 days
Foreign Service:	Burmah & India 18 years 2 months
Medal Entitlement:	Good Conduct with gratuity; Burmah with clasp; India Mutiny with clasp for Lucknow
Reason for Discharge:	Chronic Rheumatism and broken constitution
Character:	Very Good
Trade or Occupation:	Weaver
Can Sign Name:	X his mark on discharge
Height:	5' 6¼
Hair Colour:	Brown
Eyes:	Grey
Complexion:	Fresh
Intends to Reside:	Dublin

PURCELL	William, private 47th Foot
28 May 1852	Discharged the Service Templemore
28 June 1852	Discharge approved
13 July 1852	Pension paid 1st Dublin Pension District 1/- per diem
6 Apr 1854	Arrived per *'Sea Park'*
Jan 1857	Contributed 2/- to the Florence Nightingale Fund
1 Dec 1860	Purchased Newcastle Lot S15
10 Mar 1864	Died aged 52

2 Jan 1867	Two young children belonging to Mrs[Jiley, Isley or Foley], late Mrs. Purcell, the widow of a pensioner — left destitute in this town,, the mother having been committed to prison Johanna Foley was arrested on charge of Bigamy	
1867	Children of Johanna Foley left destitute and being sent down to Poor House in Perth	
1886	Newcastle Sub Lot 4 granted to son William	
1887	[William Purcell residing at Dongarra and heir at law of the late William Purcell military pensioner applied to be registered as the proprietor of Suburban Lot S22]	
Service and Personal Details:		
Place of Birth:	St Peters Dublin	
Age on Attestation:	20 years	
Period of Service:	1831 — 1852	
Age on Discharge:	41 years 4 months	
Length of Service:	21 years 20 days	
Foreign Service:	Mediterranean	6 years 5 months
	West Indies & British Guyana	2 years 9 months
Reason for Discharge:	Chronic Rheumatism	
Character:	That of a rather indifferent soldier	
Trade or Occupation:	Painter	
Can Sign Name:	Yes	
Height:	5' 7"	
Hair Colour:	Sandy	
Eyes:	Grey	
Complexion:	Fair	
Intends to Reside:	Dublin	

PURTILL	William, private	
	32nd Foot	
Previous Regiment	78th; 21st	
Surname Variants	PURTELL; PARTILL; PURTIL; PURTEIN	
22 July 1851	Discharged the Service Chatham	
	Pension paid Limerick	
	10d. per diem	
1852	Serving with Turkish Contingent [possibly in Army Ambulance Corps]	
1855	Pension paid Limerick	
19 Aug 1859	Arrived per *'Sultana'*	
1862	Assistant Warder at various locations in W. A.	
1865	Pension paid Western Australia	
Mar 1874	Died aged 47 years	
Service and Personal Details:		
Place of Birth:	Limerick Co. Clare	
Age on Attestation:	18 years 6 months	
Period of Service:	1845 — 1850	
Age on Discharge:	25 [sic] years	
Length of Service:	5 years 184 days	
Foreign Service:	East Indies	3 years 10 months

Medal Entitlement:	India
Reason for Discharge:	Wounded in the right arm by a ball Dec 1848
Character:	Good
Trade or Occupation:	Labourer
Can Sign Name:	Yes
Height:	5' 8"
Hair Colour:	Light Brown
Eyes:	Grey
Complexion:	Pale
Intends to Reside:	Limerick
Married:	Mary Carroll
Children:	Catherine b. *c*1856 Ireland m. *c*1875 James Feltham Fremantle Mary Sultana b. 1859 [murdered by John Duffy] m. *c*1884 Michael McGann Fremantle Ellen [?Nellie] b. *c*1861 Guildford *c*1892 at St John's Church Fremantle Nellie, the third daughter of the late William Purtill married Charles E Slee Bridget b. *c*1862 d. *c*1863 Guildford Helen b. *c*1864 d. *c*1864 York Bridget b. *c*1864 d. *c*1864 York Sarah Ann b. *c*1865 York m. *c*1894 Jeremiah Conway Fremantle William Patrick b. *c*1866 Fremantle Charlotte b. *c*1868 Busselton m. *c*1893 James William Willis Fremantle Frederick b. *c*1871 Vasse
circa 1875	To His Excellency the Governor — 'May it please your Excellency The widow of William Purtil [sic] late Warder Imperial Convict Service for 15 years, 18 months in the Ambulance Corps during the Russian War, served 7 years in the 32nd Regiment and was discharged through wounds received in action during the attack on Moltan [sic] with a pension 10d per diem which ceased with the death of my husband
1884	Fremantle — Report on murder of Mary Sultana McGann, John Duffy committed for trial on charge of murder — SROWA 1884/2023

DUFFY

	John
Sources	Bombay Judicial Proceedings: Z/P/3189 City of London — Guildhall Library Lloyds Newspaper List of Vessels — Microfilm Western Australian State Record Office
1884/2233	Perth — Service of subpoenas re John Duffy
1885/0107	Sheriff — 1. John Duffy Sentenced to Death
1885/0294	His Excellency the Administrator — John Duffy Sentenced to Death — Regarding Petition for Reprieve of John Duffy

	Bombay Judicial Proceedings	
Date of Birth:	1817	
Where Born:	Not given	
Married:	Yes	
Children:	One	
Literate:	Yes	
Religion:	Protestant	
Trade or Profession:	Blacksmith	
Where Convicted:	Bombay	
Date of Conviction:	1851	
Crime:	Wounding with intent	
Sentence:	Life	
Remarks:	John DUFFY tried by Supreme Court and sentenced to Van Dieman's Land Tried at 3rd Criminal Sessions of September last — [ie September 1852]	
Arrived per:	*'General Godwin'* 1854	
Age on arrival:	37	
Height:	5' 8 ¾"	
Hair Colour:	Grey	
Eye Colour:	Dark Blue	
Visage:	Long and large	
Complexion:	Swarthy	
Build:	Stout	
Distinguishing Marks:	Biles [sic] on both eyes	

PURVIS

	William. private	
	2nd/60th Foot	
17 Jan 1861	Discharged the Service Winchester	
5 Feb 1861	Admitted to Out-Pension	
	Pension paid 1st Glasgow Pension District [Argyle]	
	9d. per diem	
1862	Pension paid Paisley	
15 Feb 1863	Arrived per *'Merchantman'* [1]	
1867	Died — Lost onboard the *'Emma'*	

Service and Personal Details:

Place of Birth:	Pollock Paisley Renfrewshire	
Age on Attestation:	18 years	
Period of Service:	1839 — 1861	
Age on Discharge:	39 years 7 months	
Length of Service:	21 years 10 days	
Foreign Service:	Jamaica	2 years 3 months
	Canada	3 years
	Cape of Good Hope	7 years 7 months
Reason for Discharge:	Own Request having completed 21 years service	
Character:	Latterly Good	
Trade or Occupation:	Gardiner [sic]	
Can Sign Name:	Yes	
Height:	5' 9"	
Hair Colour:	Dark	
Eyes:	Grey	
Complexion:	Dark	
Intends to Reside:	Dunoon Argyle	

QUIN	Robert, Serjeant
	Royal Engineers [Royal Sappers and Miners]
20 July 1863	Probably arrived per *'Eena'*
3 July 1866	Discharged the Service Western Australia
23 June 1866	Discharge approved
	2/- per diem
	Employed as Government Surveyor at Gingin
1886	Died
Service and Personal Details:	
Place of Birth:	Ballina Co. Mayo
Age on Attestation:	18 years 8 months
Period of Service:	1845 — 1866
Age on Discharge:	39 years 8 months
Length of Service:	21 years
Foreign Service:	Western Australia 2 years 8 months
Medal Entitlement:	Good Conduct & Long Service with gratuity
Reason for Discharge:	Having completed 21 years service
Character:	Exemplary
Trade or Occupation:	Surveyor
Can Sign Name:	Yes
Height:	5' 10¾"
Hair Colour:	Dark Brown
Eye Colour:	Grey
Complexion:	Fresh
Intended Residence:	Western Australia

QUINN	Alexander, private
	95th Foot
Surname Variant	QUIN
Previous Regiments	50th; 78th; 31st
19 July 1864	Discharged the Service Netley
	Pension paid Armagh
	1/1d per diem
22 Dec 1865	Arrived per *'Vimiera'*
1856	Employed as Assistant Warder
1868	an Alex Quinn granted Greenough Locs G51; G52 and G53
1872	an Alexander Quin residing at Fremantle
1875	Employed as Warder at Fremantle
Sept 1890	Charged with deserting his wife Annie who was better known as Mrs Cadden
Jan 1891	Gave notice that he was not responsible for his wife's debts and that he had provided for her under a Deed of Separation
July 1891	Charged with committing wilful and corrupt perjury against Hyman Wiess
1893	Residing Hampton Rd., Fremantle
Apr 1894	Died
Service and Personal Details:	
Place of Birth:	Armagh Co. Armagh
Age on Attestation:	18 years

Period of Service:	1841 — 1863	
Age on Discharge:	40 years 6 months	
Length of Service:	21 years 328 days	
Foreign Service:	New South Wales	2 years 3 months
	East Indies	18 years 8 months
	China	1 year 11 months
Medal Entitlement:	Sutlej with clasp; Burmah with clasp; Indian Mutiny with 2 clasps; Persia with clasp; China with clasp	
Reason for Discharge:	Chronic Rheumatism and wounded on numerous occasions	
Character:	Good	
Trade or Occupation:	Labourer	
Can Sign Name:	Yes	
Height:	5' 9¼"	
Hair Colour:	Fair	
Eyes:	Blue	
Complexion:	Fair	
Intends to Reside:	Armagh Co. Armagh	

QUINN	Edward, private [WO117/19]	
	35th Foot	
Surname Variant	QUIN	
28 Mar 1871	Discharged the Service	
	Pension paid Halifax	
	1/3d. per diem	
1873	Pension paid Greenwich	
19 Feb 1974	Arrived per *'Naval Brigade'*	
1879	Died aged 51	
Service and Personal Details:		
Place of Birth:	Co. Tipperary	
Age on Attestation:	17 years 8 months	
Period of Service:	1845 — 1871	
Age on Discharge:	43 years	
Foreign Service:	East Indies	13 years 2 months
	Crimea [Sebastopol]	
Length of Service:	25 years 9 months [reckoned]	
Medal Entitlement:	Long Service and Good Conduct with gratuity	
Reason for Discharge:	Own request having served over 21 years	
Character:	Very good	
Trade or Occupation:	Labourer	
Can sign Name:	X his mark on discharge	
Height:	5' 6"	
Hair Colour:	Brown	
Eyes:	Grey	
Complexion:	Fresh	

QUINN	James, Colour Serjeant
	55th Foot
Previous Regiment	4th Floot
22 Nov 1852	Discharged the Service Tralee

14 Dec 1842	Discharge approved Pension paid 2nd Dublin Pension District 2/- per diem	
1856	Pension Paid 2nd Dublin Pension District	
1856	2nd West London Pension District	
1856	1st Portsmouth Pension District	
1856	Woolwich	
1857	1st East London Pension District	
1858	2nd Dublin Pension District	
1859	1st Glasgow Pension District	
1862	2nd West London Pension District	
1863	South London	
1863	2nd West London Pension District	
1864	1st East London Pension District	
15 Aug 1865	Arrived per *'Racehorse'*	
1866	Pension paid Adelaide from Fremantle	
1867	Melbourne	
1867	Adelaide	
1872	Due to insubordinate behaviour toward the Colonial Treasurer Adelaide James Quinn was deprived of pension for 18 months	
1872	Half pension to be paid to Colonial Authorities for support of child	
Service and Personal Details:		
Place of Birth:	Nenagh Tipperary	
Age on Attestation:	17 years 6 months	
Period of Service:	1831 — 1852	
Age on Discharge:	39 years	
Length of Service:	21 years	
Foreign Service:	New South Wales	4 years 11 months
	East Indies	3 years 9 months
	China	3 years 2 months
Medal Entitlement:	Received silver medal for services in China	
Reason for Discharge:	Being appointed onto the permanent Staff of the Royal Denbighshire Militia	
Character:	Very good and efficient	
Trade or Occupation:	Labourer	
Can Sign Name:	Yes	
Height:	5' 9"	
Hair Colour:	Brown	
Eyes:	Hazel	
Complexion:	Fair	
Intends to Reside:	Wrexham Denbighshire North Wales	
Children:	'Daughter of Serjeant Major Quinn for passage per "*Racehorse*"'	

QUINN	James, private 88th Foot
25 June 1861	Discharged the Service Colchester Pension paid Ennis 9d. per diem
12 Sept 1864	Arrived per *'Merchantman'* [2]

Service and Personal Details:		
Place of Birth:	Kilmanhan Co Clare	
Age on Attestation:	19 years	
Period of Service:	1839 — 1861	
Age on Discharge:	40 years 8 months	
Length of Service:	21 years 149 days	
Foreign Service:	Malta	6 years 1 month
	West Indies	3 years 4 months
	North America	1 year 1 month
	Turkey & Crimea	2 years 4 months
	East Indies	2 years *** days
Medal Entitlement:	Own request after 21 years service	
Reason for Discharge:	Crimea; Crimean Turkish; Indian Mutiny	
Character:	Latterly Good	
Trade or Occupation:	Labourer	
Can Sign Name:	Yes	
Height:	5' 7¼"	
Hair Colour:	Black	
Eyes:	Blue	
Complexion:	Fresh	
Intends to Reside:	Ennistymon Co. Clare	

QUINN	Patrick, Serjeant Major Royal Artillery 25th Brigade
Surname Variant	QUIN
26 May 1868	Discharged the Service Netley
26 July 1868	Admitted to Out-Pension Pension paid Ipswich 2/6d. per diem
1 Apr 1869	Pension paid Woolwich Arrived possibly per '*Strathmore*'
1 Apr 1871	Pension paid Perth Western Australia
1873	Residing Fremantle
1881	Pension increased to 2/11d. per diem for service in the Enrolled Force
Sept 1885	Remanded by Sergeant Peacocke for carnally knowing and abusing Eva Maud Jones, a girl under the age of 12 years Sentenced to 2 years hard labour.
Oct 1885	'Charged with Criminal Assault" and sentenced to 2 years hard labor' Half pension suspended, the other half to be paid to wife for time in prison
no date	Assigned Freshwater Bay Loc 1070
circa 1885	Held Title to Freshwater Bay Loc 1070
1886	Loss or otherwise of Pensioner Quinn's pension through imprisonment
June 1897	Residing Fremantle
Feb 1900	a T [sic] Quinn Royal Artillery attended fete at Fremantle Oval
1903	Died

Service and Personal Details:	
Place of Birth:	?Gorth Lebreth Co. Donegal

Age on Attestation:	18 years
Period of Service:	1846 — 1868
Age on Discharge:	39 years 6 months
Length of Service:	21 years 31 days
Foreign Service:	Cape of Good Hope 6 years 202 days
	East Indies 6 years 146 days
Medal Entitlement:	Long Service and Good Conduct with gratuity
Reason for Discharge:	Asthemia [sic]
Character:	Exemplary
Trade or Occupation:	Labourer
Can Sign Name:	Yes
Height:	5' 7"
Hair Colour:	Light Brown
Eyes:	Grey
Complexion:	Fair
Intends to Reside:	Ipswich

QUIRK

	David, private
	RM
	Discharged the Service Portsmouth
	£18/4/- per annum
1851	Residing 66 Longbrook Street St Sidwell's Exeter
1858	Pay cost of cottage

Service and Personal Details:

Place of Birth:	Fermoy Cork Ireland
Age on Attestation:	18 years
Marine Division:	Portsmouth
Period of Service:	1828 — 1849
Age on Discharge:	39 years
Length of Service:	21 years 10 months 24 days to 17th Dec 1849
Medal Entitlement:	Medal for services on the coast off Syria and medal for Good Conduct and Long Service
Reason for Discharge:	Own Request — Length of Service
Character:	Good
Trade or Occupation:	Labourer
Can Sign Name:	X his mark on discharge
Height:	5' 7¾"
Hair Colour:	Brown
Eyes:	Hazel
Complexion:	Fair
Remarks:	Wife on Book

QUIRK

	James, private
	54th Foot
Previous Regiment	20th Foot
24 Feb 1841	Discharged the Service Chatham
10 Mar 1841	Admitted to Out-Pension
	Pension paid Kilkenny
	6d. per diem
25 Oct 1850	Arrived per *'Hashemy'*
6 Sept 1851	Appointed Constable Police Force at Perth
21 Mar 1852	Dismissed from Perth Police Force
Jan 1857	Contributed 1/- to the Florence Nightingale Fund

1861	Pension paid Melbourne
Service and Personal Details:	
Place of Birth:	Castlecomer Co. Kilkenny
Age on Attestation:	17 years
Period of Service:	1826 — 1841
Age on Discharge:	32 years
Length of Service:	13 years 336 days
Foreign Service:	East Indies about 13 years
Reason for Discharge:	Varicose Veins in left leg and worn out
Character:	Indifferent
Trade or Occupation:	a Nailor
Can Sign Name:	Yes
Height:	5' 9"
Hair Colour:	Brown
Eyes:	Hazel
Complexion:	Sallow

RADFORD	Edward, private 104th Foot
Previous Regiment	2nd Bombay Fusiliers
Surname Variant	RADCLIFFE
2 June 1863	Discharged the Service Pension paid Bristol 11d. per diem
15 Aug 1865	Arrived per *'Racehorse'*
1867	Died Lost on the *'Emma'*, arrears of Enrolled "Pay of £19/17/6 issued to sister"
Service and Personal Details:	
Place of Birth:	Redcliff Somerset
Age on Attestation:	29 years 11 months
Period of Service:	1852 — 1863
Age on Discharge:	43 [sic] years
Length of Service:	Entitled to reckon 21 years & 109 days
Foreign Service:	East Indies 10 years 8 months
Reason for Discharge:	Admitted to pension
Character:	Good
Trade or Occupation:	Coachsmith
Can Sign Name:	Yes
Height:	5' 6½"
Hair Colour:	Brown
Eyes:	Brown
Complexion:	Fresh
Intends to Reside:	Bristol

RAMSEY	Robert, Serjeant RA 9th Battalion
Surname Variant	RAMSAY
13 July 1847	Discharged the Service Woolwich
Aug 1847	Initial Pension payment Pension paid Woolwich 1/10d. per diem

18 Oct 1851	Arrived per *'Minden'*	
1851	Employed in Convict Establishment	
1855	Promoted to Principle Warder Fremantle	
1887	Died aged 80 years	

Service and Personal Details:		
Place of Birth:	Kiltown Roscommon	
Age on Enlistment:	18 years	
Period of Service:	1825 — 1847	
Age on Discharge:	40 years 5 months	
Length of Service:	22 years 194 days	
Foreign Service:	West Indies	4 years 1 month
	Gibraltar	7 years 11 months
Reason for Discharge:	Deafness in right ear and Rheumatism	
Character:	Exemplary	
Trade or Occupation:	Labourer	
Can Sign Name:	Yes	
Height:	5' 8½"	
Hair Colour:	Dark	
Eyes:	Black	
Complexion:	Brown	
Remarks:	Subsisted to the 2nd August 1847 and to reside at Deptford	

RANDAL	Thomas, private	
	Rifle Brigade 2nd battalion	
Surname Variants	RANDALL; RANDELL	
12 June 1855	Discharged the Service Chatham	
	Pension paid 2nd West London Pension District 8d. per diem	
10 July 1857	Arrived per *'Clara'* [1]	
1859	Employed as Assistant Warder	
1875	Pension paid Western Australia	
1881	Pension increased to 1/2d. per diem for service in the Enrolled Force	

Service and Personal Details:		
Place of Birth:	St Lukes Chelsea Middlesex	
Age on Attestation:	18 years	
Period of Service:	1847 — 1855	
Age on Discharge:	25 years 9 months	
Length of Service:	7 years 294 days	
Foreign Service:	North America	3 years
	"In the East"	1 year
Medal Entitlement:	Crimea	
Reason for Discharge:	Wounded by shell fragment	
Character:	Good	
Trade or Occupation:	Labourer	
Can Sign Name:	Yes	
Height:	5' 7"	
Hair Colour:	Brown	
Eyes:	Hazel	
Complexion:	Fresh	

Intends to Reside:	Symonds Place Chelsea
RANDALL	Walter, private 17th Lancers [ex 11th Hussars [1830]
Surname Variant	RANDELL
Apr 1872	Discharged the Service Longford Pension paid Brighton
May 1877	Possibly arrived per *'Hastings'* Serving as police constable
14 Dec 1886	Deferred pension of 4d per diem
10 Mar 1887	W.O. Correspondence re Deferred Pension Forms to S.O. Perth Western Australia
1897	a William Randall residing Perth District
8 Mar 1898	Deferred pension increased to 1/-
Service and Personal Details:	
Place of Birth:	Sweaversea Cambridge
Age on Attestation:	18 years
Period of Service:	1854 — 1872
Age on Discharge:	35 years 4 months
Length of Service:	17 years 33/38 days [reckoned]
Foreign Service:	Crimea 1 year India 7 years 3 months
Medal Entitlement:	Crimea with clasps Turkish Crimean and Indian Mutiny recorded on parchment certificate of discharge
Reason for Discharge:	His own request free after 17 years service
Character:	Good
Trade or Occupation:	Labourer
Can Sign Name:	Yes
Height:	5' 9"
Hair Colour:	Brown
Eyes:	Hazel
Complexion:	Dark
Intends to Reside:	3 ****Street off Trafalgar Street Brighton
RAWSON	William, private 19th Foot
24 Mar 1857	Discharged the Service Chatham Pension paid Derby 8d. per diem
1862	Pension paid Bermuda
15 Feb 1863	Arrived per *'Merchantman'* [1]
1864	ptve W Rawson Pensioner Force at Perth contributed to the Greenough Fire Relief Fund
1868	To South Australia from Perth West Australia
1872	W.O. correspondence with Adelaide Pension District the "A31"
1876	Pension paid South Australia
Service and Personal Details:	
Place of Birth:	South Winfield Alpeton Derby
Age on Attestation:	20 years

Period of Service:	1846 — 1857	
Age on Discharge:	31 years 4 months	
Length of Service:	10 years 126 days	
Foreign Service:	North America	2 years
	Turkey	4 months
	Crimea & Turkey	4 months
Medal Entitlement:	Crimea with clasp	
Reason for Discharge:	Chronic enlargement of scrotum and weakness in left leg	
Character:	Very Good	
Trade or Occupation:	Labourer	
Can Sign Name:	X his mark on discharge	
Height:	5' 10"	
Hair Colour:	Brown	
Eyes:	Dark	
Complexion:	Fair	
Remarks:	80 days at Scutari	
Intends to Reside:	Wingfield North Derby	

RAY

	Thomas, private
	50th Foot
26 Sept 1848	Discharged the Service Chatham
	Pension paid 1st East London pension District
	6d. per diem for 2 years conditional
1851	Granted Permanent Pension of 8d. per diem
14 Aug 1854	Arrived per '*Ramillies*'
1854	Pension paid Western Australia
1857	Pension paid Melbourne [12/WA/7]
Feb 1861	Died — 'killed at a railway station in Melbourne'

Service and Personal Details:

Place of Birth:	St Pancras London Middlesex	
Age on Attestation:	18 years 6 months	
Period of Service:	1841 — 1847	
Age on Discharge:	25 years	
Length of Service:	6 years 67 days	
Foreign Service:	East Indies	5 years 286 days
Medal Entitlement:	Punniar 1843; Sutlej with 4 clasps	
Reason for Discharge:	Impaired Vision with total loss in right eye	
Character:	Good	
Trade or Occupation:	Labourer	
Can Sign Name:	X his mark on discharge	
Height:	5' 7"	
Hair Colour:	Fair	
Eyes:	Grey	
Complexion:	Sallow	
Intends to Reside:	Bethnal Green London	

REANEY

	Patrick, Corporal
	95th Foot
Surname Variant	REANY
11 Dec 1855	Discharged the Service Chatham
	Pension paid Deptford

	1/- per diem
1855	Pension paid Galway
1857	Pension paid 2nd Plymouth Pension District
1860	2nd West London Pension District
1864	Pension paid Liverpool
15 Aug 1865	Arrived per *'Racehorse'*
1866	Employed as Assistant Warder
1881	Pension increased to 1/3½d. per diem for service in the Enrolled Force
July 1881	Assigned Perth Town Lot 81/E Claisebrook
July 1883	Application for Title to Perth Lot 81/E at Claisebrook
1889	Died – buried East Perth Cemetery

Service and Personal Details:

Place of Birth:	Claremorris Co. Mayo
Age on Attestation:	21 years 5 months
Period of Service:	1851 — 1855
Age on Discharge:	27 years or 26 years
Length of Service:	4 years 199 days
Foreign Service:	Turkey & Crimea 1 year 6 months
Medal Entitlement:	Crimea with clasps; Turkish Crimea
Reason for Discharge:	Wounded in trenches before Sebastopol
Character:	Good
Trade or Occupation:	Sawyer
Can Sign Name:	Yes
Height:	5' 7"
Hair Colour:	Dark Brown
Eyes:	Grey
Complexion:	Fresh
Intends to Reside:	Tooley Street London Bridge

REARDON	Jeremiah, private [Military Pensioner]
	65th Foot
Previous Regiment	99th Foot
Surname Variant	READON; RIORDEN
19 Apr 1864	Discharged the Service Netley
	7d. per diem for 2 years conditional
	Pension paid 1st Cork Pension District
1864	Pension paid 1st East London Pension District
1866	Pension made permanent
1 Apr 1865	Pension paid New Zealand
1865	Pension paid Perth Western Australia
1875	Perth Western Australia
1876	Pension paid East London from West Australia
1 Nov 1876	Pension paid Cork
1894	Admitted to Kilmainham as In-Pensioner
1915	Died

Service and Personal Details:

Place of Birth:	Cork Co. Cork
Age on Attestation:	22 years
Period of Service:	1857 — 1864
Age on Discharge:	29 years 3 months
Length of Service:	6 years 243 days

Foreign Service:	New Zealand	4 years 4 months
Reason for Discharge:	Weak eyes	
Character:	Good	
Trade or Occupation:	Servant	
Can Sign Name:	X his mark on discharge	
Height:	5' 10"	
Hair Colour:	Red	
Eyes:	Grey	
Complexion:	Fresh	
Intends to Reside:	Cork	

REARDON	Michael, Corporal [3287]	
	1st Foot	
Previous Regiment	67th	
Surname Variant	REANON	
10 Oct 1865	Discharged the Service Camp Colchester	
	1/1½d. per diem	
1867	Pension paid Newcastle-upon-Tyne	
9 Jan 1868	Arrived per *'Hougoumont'*	
10 Aug 1869	Died aged 45	
Service and Personal Details:		
Place of Birth:	St Marys Co. Cork	
Age on Attestation:	22 years	
Period of Service:	1844 — 1865	
Age on Discharge:	43 years	
Length of Service:	21 years 12 days [entitled to reckon]]	
Foreign Service:	Gibraltar	3 years 55 days
	Turkey &	
	Crimea	2 years 61 days
	East Indies	6 years 350 days
Medal Entitlement:	Crimea with clasps; Turkish Crimean	
Reason for Discharge:	His own request free with pension after 21 years	
Character:	Good	
Trade or Occupation:	Labourer	
Can Sign Name:	Yes	
Height:	5' 11¾"	
Hair Colour:	Brown	
Eyes:	Grey	
Complexion:	Fresh	
Intends to Reside:	London	

REDDAWAY	Henry Blackmore, private
	RM
Surname Variants	[some] REDAWAY; RIDDAWAY; RUDAWAY
Nov 1849	Discharged the Service
1851	Pension paid Plymouth Pension District
	£18/4/- per annum
1851	Residing No 1 Portland Place St Leonard' Exeter
1853	Pension paid Exeter Pension District
31 Aug 1853	Arrived per *'Phoebe Dunbar'*

1854	Employed by Convict Establishment without sanction of Staff Office Pensions Allocated North Fremantle Lot P51 which was subsequently re-assigned to George Rutley
1863	an H Rudaway residing Fremantle District
1864	an H.B. Reddaway purchased Fremantle Town Lot 355 for £7/15/-
1868	Employed as Principle Warder at Bunbury
1872	an H Reddaway residing at Fremantle
Mar 1885	Died aged 77

Service and Personal Details:

Place of Birth:	Okehampton Devon
Age on Attestation:	20 years
Marine Division:	Plymouth
Period of Service:	1828 — 1849
Length of Service:	21 years and 23 days
Reason for Discharge:	Time Served — Length of Service
Trade or Occupation:	Whitesmith
Can Sign Name:	Yes
Height:	5' 9¼"
Hair Colour:	Brown
Eyes:	Grey
Complexion:	Fair
Married:	1834 Elizabeth Clynick Plymouth
Children:	Margaret b. 1835 Pembrokeshire Mary Elizabeth b.1835 Devon m. *c*1857 George Campbell Fremantle William b. 1838 Okehampton Emily Rebecca b. 1844 Stonehouse m. *c*1873 John Frederick Thomas Fremantle George Clynick b. 1846 East Stonehouse Louisa b. 1851 Devon m. *c*1893 George Smith Shuffrey Fremantle Ellen Margaret b. *c*1854 Fremantle Henry Alfred b. *c*1858 d. *c*1864 Fremantle

REDDIN

	John, private 21st Foot
11 Oct 1853	Discharged the Service Dublin
8 Nov 1853	Admitted to Out-Pension Pension paid Limerick 6d. per diem for 18 months
18 July 1855	Arrived per *'Adelaide'*
1855	Pension paid Adelaide South Australia

Service and Personal Details:

Place of Birth:	St Johns Limerick Co. Limerick	
Age on Attestation:	19 years	
Period of Service:	1846 — 1853	
Age on Discharge:	26 years 6 months	
Length of Service:	7 years 187 days	
Foreign Service:	East Indies	upwards of 1 year
Reason for Discharge:	Pulmonary Consumption	

Character:	Indifferent, but Latterly Good
Trade or Occupation:	Labourer
Can Sign Name:	X his mark on discharge
Height:	5' 8"
Hair Colour:	Brown
Eyes:	Blue
Complexion:	Fresh
Intends to Reside:	Limerick

REDDIN Michael, Corporal
61st Foot

Surname Variant	REDDEN
11 May 1847	Discharged the Service Chatham
	Pension paid Newcastle
	1/2½d. per diem
1 June 1850	Arrived per *'Scindian'*
1850	Assigned land Freshwater Bay
6 July 1854	Died

Service and Personal Details:

Place of Birth:	Johns Gate Limerick	
Age on Attestation:	20 years	
Period of Service:	1825 — 1847	
Age on Discharge:	42 years 4 months	
Length of Service:	22 years 99 days	
Foreign Service:	Ceylon	11 years 4 months
Reason for Discharge:	Varicose Veins of the left leg	
Character:	Good	
Trade or Occupation:	Tobacconist	
Can Sign Name:	Yes	
Height:	5' 7½"	
Hair Colour:	Dark	
Eyes:	Grey	
Complexion:	Sallow	
Intends to Reside:	North Shields Northumberland	
1877	a Michael Reddin [serving on the Harbour Master's boat] was drowned on the 7th Jan near Point Calver on the Eucla Telegraph Line [from Police Gazette]	

REDFORD Joseph, private
47th Foot

11 Mar 1856	Discharged the Service Chatham
	1/- per diem
1856	Pension paid Bolton
24 Nov 1858	Arrived per *'Edwin Fox'*
1860	Pension paid London
1861	Manchester
1864	Pension paid Toronto

Service and Personal Details:

Place of Birth:	Bolton Lancaster

Age on Attestation:	17 years 10 months
Period of Service:	1842 — 1856
Age on Discharge:	31 years 10 months
Length of Service:	13 years 259 days
Foreign Service:	Corfu &
	Malta &
	Turkey & Crimea 4 years 8 months
Medal Entitlement:	Crimea with clasps
Reason for Discharge:	Wounded by piece of shell to left shoulder
Character:	Good
Trade or Occupation:	Steam Loom Weaver
Can Sign Name:	Yes
Height:	5' 6"
Hair Colour:	Brown
Eyes:	Hazel
Complexion:	Fresh
Intends to Reside:	Manchester

REDMOND	Felix, private EIC
	Bengal Artillery
	Out Pension No 116
26 Feb 1840	Admitted to Out-pension
	Pension paid 2nd Dublin Pension District
	6d. per diem
28 June 1851	Arrived per *'Pyrenees'* [1]
1852	Pension paid South Australia
1854	Melbourne
1866	South Australia
1866	2nd Dublin Pension District
1867	Cork
9 Nov 1871	Died

Service and Personal Details:

Place of Birth:	Dublin
Trade or Occupation:	Labourer or Printer
Where Enlisted:	Manchester
Presidency:	Bengal
Length of Service:	2 years 9 months
Age on Discharge:	34 years
Character:	Good
Reason for Discharge:	Insane
Height:	5' 10"
Complexion:	Pale
Visage:	Square
Eye Colour:	Grey
Hair Colour:	Black

REDMOND	Michael, gunner
	Royal Artillery 6th Battery
Previous Service	HEIC — 2nd European Light Infantry
8 May 1866	Discharged the Service
	Pension paid 2nd Dublin Pension District
	1/1d. per diem
9 Jan 1868	Arrived per *'Hougoumont'*

Aug 1881	Assigned Cockburn Sound Loc 234 Pension increased to 1/5d. per diem for service in the Enrolled Force
1885	Granted Cockburn Sound Loc 234 Willagee Swamp
June 1897	Stationed at Perth
1898	Died – buried East Perth Cemetery
Service and Personal Details:	
Place of Birth:	Coolfoney Co. Wicklow
Age on Attestation:	23 Years
Period of Service:	1846 — 1866
Age on Discharge:	42 years 6 months
Length of Service:	20 years 358 days - recalculated to 21 years 19 days
Foreign Service:	India 18 years 303 days
Reason for Discharge:	Own Request having served over 21 years
Character:	Very Good
Trade or Occupation:	Labourer
Can Sign Name:	X his mark on discharge
Height:	5' 6"
Hair Colour:	Dark Brown
Eyes:	Blue
Complexion:	Florid
Remarks:	Elected Indian Pension Rules
Intends to Reside:	Carlow Ireland

REDMOND	Patrick, gunner EIC Bengal Horse Artillery Out Pension No 254
10 June 1857	Admitted to Out-pension Pension paid Birr 9d. per diem
1858	Pension paid Dublin
1858	Pension paid 2nd Cork Pension District
19 Aug 1859	Arrived per *'Sultana'*
1866	Pension paid Western Australia "£6 to be stopped from pension"
17 Sept 1883	Assigned North Fremantle Lot P82
30 Aug 1884	Granted Fee Simple North Fremantle Lot P82
Oct 1885	Colonial Surgeon Fremantle — Pensioner Patrick Redmond for Mt. Eliza Depot, Resident Magistrate Fremantle — Pensioner P. Redmond for Mt. Eliza
Jan 1889	Superintendent of Poor Houses — Relief for Pensioner P. Redmond and wife
1891	Inmate of the Depot
14 Sept 1893	By Proclamation, dated the 12th instant, certain land included in North Fremantle Lot P82 granted to P. Redmond, military pensioner, was resumed for the purposes of a railway.
1894	a Patrick Redmond died
Service and Personal Details:	
Place of Birth:	Birr Kings Co.

Trade or Occupation:	Servant or labourer depending on record	
Where Enlisted:	Athlone	
Length of Service:	15 years 8 months	
Age on Discharge:	37 years	
Character:	Very good	
Reason for Discharge:	Broken down constitution and liver disease	
Height:	5' 6" or 5'7½"	
Complexion:	Swarthy	
Eye Colour:	Grey	
Hair Colour:	Sandy	
Intends to Reside:	Roscrea Birr District	

REED

	Samuel, private	
	73rd Foot	
8 Jan 1840	Discharged the Service	
	Pension paid 1st East London Pension District	
	9d. per diem	
7 Feb 1853	Arrived per *'Dudbrook'*	
1860	To South Australia from Fremantle West. Aust.	
1861	Pension paid Sydney New South Wales	
1875	Sydney	

Service and Personal Details:

Place of Birth:	Epping Essex	
Age on Attestation:	18 years	
Period of Service:	1821 — 1839	
Age on Discharge:	35 years 8 months	
Length of Service:	17 years 248 days	
Foreign Service:	Gibraltar	2 years 7 months
	Malta	4 years 10 months
	Ionian Isles	3 years 10 months
	North America	1 year 3 months
Reason for Discharge:	Injury to the knee joint received at Montreal	
Character:	Good Soldier	
Trade or Occupation:	Labourer	
Can Sign Name:	Yes	
Height:	5' 11½"	
Hair Colour:	Brown	
Eyes:	Grey	
Complexion:	Fair	

REEVES

	Josiah, private	
	RM	
13 Apr 1860	Discharged the Service	
	£15/4/- per annum	
1865	Pension paid Trowbridge	
15 Aug 1865	Arrived per *'Racehorse'*	
1868	Pension paid South Australia from Fremantle	

Service and Personal Details:

Place of Birth:	Chippenham	
Age on Attestation:	18 years 8 months	
Marine Division:	Chatham	
Period of Service:	1837 — 1860	

Length of Service:	22 years 132 days
Reason for Discharge:	Length of Service
Trade or Occupation:	Labourer
Can Sign Name:	Yes
Height:	5' 6¾"
Hair Colour:	Light
Eyes:	Grey
Complexion:	Fresh

REID	John, private
	98th Foot
15 July 1840	Discharged the Service
	Pension paid Stirling
	7d. per diem
14 Aug 1854	Arrived per *'Ramillies'*
Jan 1857	Contributed 1/- to the Florence Nightingale Fund
1864	To South Australia from Fremantle
1865	Pension paid Adelaide South Australia

Service and Personal Details:

Place of Birth:	Stirling Stirlingshire Scotland
Age on Attestation:	20 years
Period of Service:	1824 — 1840
Age on Discharge:	35 years
Length of Service:	15 years 192 days
Foreign Service:	Mauritius 11 years 219 days
Reason for Discharge:	Hepatic Disease, Debility of Constitution and Emaciation
Character:	Good and efficient soldier
Trade or Occupation:	Weaver
Can Sign Name:	Yes
Height:	5' 6"
Hair Colour:	Sandy
Eyes:	Hazel
Complexion:	Fresh

REILLY	John, Corporal
	57th Foot
Surname Variants	RIELLY; RIELY; RILEY
10 Oct 1856	Discharged the Service Birr Barracks
18 Nov 1856	Admitted to Out-Pension
	Pension paid Birr
	9d. per diem
1857	Pension paid 2nd Dublin Pension District
19 Aug 1859	Arrived per *'Sultana'*
1871	Serving as Assistant Warder Guildford
1872	Granted Lot 83 Guildford township
1874	Pension increased to 1/3½d.
1874	Stationed Perth Pension District
June 1883	The resignation of a Corporal John Reilly of the Rottnest Guard
June 1897	Residing Guildford
1902	Died aged 82

Service and Personal Details:

Place of Birth:	St Marys Dublin	
Age on Attestation:	20 years	
Period of Service:	1838 — 1856	
Age on Discharge:	38 years	
Length of Service:	18 years 262 days	
Foreign Service:	Malta	10 months
	East Indies	8 years
Reason for Discharge:	General Debility	
Character:	Good	
Trade or Occupation:	Tailor	
Can Sign Name:	Yes	
Height:	5' 7½"	
Hair Colour:	Brown	
Eyes:	Grey	
Complexion:	Fresh	
Intends to Reside:	Dublin	

the following entry may not necessarily refer to a a child of John Reilly 57th Foot

Nov 1872	John Riley disposed "I am a herdsman at Guildford and the son of a pensioner"

REILLY Joseph [John], Colour Serjeant 46th Foot

Surname Variants	RIELLY; REILLEY
28 Sept 1847	Discharged the Service Fort George Guernsey Pension paid 1st Dublin Pension District 1/8d. per diem
1848	Pension paid Jersey
1850	Pension increased to 1/9d. per diem
1850	Pension paid Southampton
1850	Tilbury
1850	Woolwich
28 June 1851	Arrived per *'Pyrenees'* [1]
3 Dec 1863	Died aged 59

Service and Personal Details:

Place of Birth:	Branickstown Co. Meath	
Age on Attestation:	21 years	
Period of Service:	1826 — 1847	
Age on Discharge:	42 years 5 months	
Length of Service:	21 years 9 months	
Foreign Service:	India	5 years 10 months
Reason for Discharge:	At his own request	
Character:	Good	
Trade or Occupation:	Labourer or Coach Builder [depending on record source]	
Can Sign Name:	Yes	
Height:	5'7"	
Hair Colour:	Grey	
Eyes:	Grey	
Complexion:	Fresh	
Intends to Reside:	Spalding Lincolnshire	

Married:	Catherine Regan
Children:	Joseph Thomas b. *c*1836 Richmond Barracks Dublin [founder of the "Northam Advertiser"]
	m. *c*1855 Mary Lucille Burrows Perth
	Philip
	m. *c*1876 Ellen Mary Butler Perth
	? a Catherine Reilly
	m. *c*1863 William Brown Perth
	Jane Mary
	m. *c*1866 Joseph Lucas Fremantle

REILLY	Michael, Serjeant EIC
	Bombay European Light Infantry
	Out Pension No 250
3 June 1857	Admitted to Out-pension
	Pension paid 1st Dublin Pension District
	9d. per diem [1/- per diem depending on record]
1857	Pension paid 2nd Dublin Pension District
24 Nov 1858	Arrived per *'Edwin Fox'*
Nov 1863	Purchased Kojonup Lot P13
1864	Serjeant Reilly Pensioner Force at Kojonup contributed to the Greenough Fire Relief Fund
1866	Granted Title to Kojonup Lot P3
1873	Serving as Serjeant of Pensioners at Kojonup
1884	Residing Kojonup
Aug 1884	Died

Service and Personal Details:

Where Born:	Leixlip Dublin
Trade or Occupation:	Labourer
Age on Enlistment:	21 years
Date Enlisted:	3rd Feb 1840
Where Enlisted:	Dublin
Service Period:	Unlimited
Embarked India:	per "*Northumberland*" 11th April 1840
Length of Service:	16 years 11 months
Age on Discharge:	40 years
Reason for Discharge:	Incontinence of urine and Rheumatism
Height:	5' 5¾"
Complexion:	Pale
Eye Colour:	Blue or pale depending on record
Hair Colour:	Brown
Intends to Reside:	Leixlip Dublin

REILLY	see — RILEY Patrick, private 16th Foot

REILLY	Patrick, private
	32nd Foot
Previous Regiment	75th Foot
10 July 1860	Discharged the Service Chatham
	Pension paid Kilkenny
	8d. per diem

28 Dec 1863	Arrived per *'Lord Dalhousie'*
1866	To Adelaide from Western Australia
1875	Pension paid Adelaide South Australia
1876	"Probably died in the far bush" 7/Australia/19

Service and Personal Details:

Place of Birth:	Callan Co. Kilkenny	
Age on Attestation:	18 years	
Period of Service:	1848 — 1860	
Age on Discharge:	30 years 9 months	
Length of Service:	12 years 226 days	
Foreign Service:	East Indies	9 years
Medal Entitlement:	Indian Mutiny and clasp for Lucknow	
Reason for Discharge:	Wounded by sabre at Lucknow	
Character:	Bad	
Trade or Occupation:	Labourer	
Can Sign Name:	X his mark on discharge	
Height:	5' 10¼"	
Hair Colour:	Light Brown	
Eyes:	Grey	
Complexion:	Fresh	
Intends to Reside:	Callan Kilkenny	

REILLY Patrick, private
64th Foot

23 Sept 1856	Discharged the Service Chatham
	Pension paid Enniskillen
	1/- per diem
1856	Pension paid 2nd West London Pension District
1857	Pension paid Salisbury
1857	Plymouth
1857	Jersey
1858	Portsmouth
24 Nov 1858	Arrived per *'Edwin Fox'*
1874	Pension paid Victoria

Service and Personal Details:

Place of Birth:	Enniskillen Co. Fermanagh	
Age on Attestation:	18 years	
Period of Service:	1835 — 1855	
Age on Discharge:	39 years or 38 years 1 month	
Length of Service:	20 years 41 days	
Foreign Service:	Jamaica	1 year 7 months
	North America	2 years 9 months
	India	6 years 5 months
Medal Entitlement:	Indian Mutiny	
Reason for Discharge:	Chronic Hepatitis	
Character:	Exemplary	
Trade or Occupation:	Labourer	
Can Sign Name:	Yes	
Height:	5' 9¼"	
Hair Colour:	Black	
Eyes:	Brown	

Complexion:	Dark
Intends to Reside:	Enniskillen Co. Fermanagh

REUBERY	Michael, private
	Cape Mounted Rifles
Previous Regiments	82nd; 91st
Surname Variants	RUBERY; RUBRY; RUBERRY
10 Dec 1861	Discharged the Service Chatham
	Pension paid 2nd Manchester Pension District
	11d. per diem
22 Dec 1866	Arrived per *'Corona'*
1868	Employed in Convict Establishment
1881	Pension increased to 1/5d. per diem for service in the Enrolled Force
7 Sept 1883	Applied for North Fremantle Lot P97
1884	Granted North Fremantle Town Lot P97
1887	Applies for quarters in Fremantle Barracks
June 1897	Residing Fremantle
Feb 1900	Attended fete at Fremantle Oval
1901	Died aged 84

Service and Personal Details:

Place of Birth:	Gort Co. Galway
Age on Attestation:	19 years
Period of Service:	1842 — 1861
Age on Discharge:	38 years 9 months
Length of Service:	19 years 275 days
Foreign Service:	Cape of Good Hope 18 years 8 months
Medal Entitlement:	Good Conduct; Kaffir War 1851/53
Reason for Discharge:	Affected by a Rupture
Character:	Good
Trade or Occupation:	Shoemaker
Can Sign Name:	Yes
Height:	5' 8"
Hair Colour:	Dark Brown
Eyes:	Grey
Complexion:	Fresh
Intends to Reside:	No. 1 ? Thirbet Street Manchester

REYNOLDS	Joseph, private
	43rd Foot
16 July 1861	Discharged the Service Chatham
	Pension paid 2nd North London Pension District
	1/- per diem
1863	Pension paid Woolwich
27 May 1863	Arrived per *'Clyde'*
1864	Pension paid South Australia
1868	Madras
1875	Madras

Service and Personal Details:

Place of Birth:	Crayford Kent
Age on Attestation:	22 years
Period of Service:	1840 — 1861
Age on Discharge:	43 years ? months

Length of Service:	20 years 293 days	
Foreign Service:	Cape of Good Hope	1 year 11 months
	East Indies	7 years
Medal Entitlement:	Indian Mutiny	
Reason for Discharge:	Rheumatic pains and weakness of strength	
Character:	Good	
Trade or Occupation:	Labourer	
Can Sign Name:	Yes	
Height:	5' 7¼"	
Hair Colour:	Dark Brown	
Eyes:	Grey	
Complexion:	Dark	
Intends to Reside:	Crayford Kent but decided on Charing Cross London	

REYNOLDS	Patrick, Corporal	
	84th Foot	
31 Dec 1861	Discharged the Service	
	Pension paid Kilkenny	
	10d. per diem	
1862	Pension paid East London Pension District	
1862	Bermuda	
15 Feb 1863	Arrived per *'Merchantman'* [1]	
1864	ptve P Reynolds Pensioner Force Fremantle contributed to the Greenough Fire Relief Fund	
1865	Pension paid Western Australia	
1865	To South Australia from Perth West Australia	
1866	Pension paid South Australia	
Service and Personal Details:		
Place of Birth:	Johnstown Kilkenny	
Age on Attestation:	16 years 2 months	
Period of Service:	1839 — 1861	
Age on Discharge:	38 years 9 months	
Length of Service:	21 years 82 days	
Foreign Service:	East Indies	17 years 16 days
Medal Entitlement:	Indian Mutiny with clasps	
Reason for Discharge:	On completion of 21 years service	
Character:	Good	
Trade or Occupation:	Labourer	
Can Sign Name:	Yes	
Height:	5' 6½"	
Hair Colour:	Dark Brown	
Eyes:	Grey	
Complexion:	Fresh	
Remarks:	Wounded at Lucknow	
Intends to Reside:	Castlecomer Co. Kilkenny	

RICE	Matthew, Corporal	
	Rifle Brigade	
Previous Regiment	74th Foot	
13 Nov 1855	Discharged the Service	

	Pension paid Staffordshire
	1/- per diem
1863	Pension paid Birmingham
27 May 1863	Arrived per *'Clyde'*
4 Sept 1868	Purchased York Lot 276
1875	Pension paid Western Australia
1878	Pension increased to 1/6d. per diem for service in the Enrolled Force
1883	Died – buried East Perth Cemetery

Service and Personal Details:

Place of Birth:	Loughan Island Co. Down
Age on Attestation:	18 years
Period of Service:	1834 — 1855
Age on Discharge:	39 years
Length of Service:	21 years 9 days
Foreign Service:	Malta &
	Ionian Isles 5 years 7 months
	Cape of Good Hope 3 years 7 months
Medal Entitlement:	Kaffir War 1846 and 1853
Reason for Discharge:	Appointed to the permanent staff of the 3rd King's Own Stafford Rifle Regiment of Militia
Character:	Good
Trade or Occupation:	Labourer
Can Sign Name:	Yes
Height:	5' 9¼"
Hair Colour:	Light Brown
Eyes:	Grey
Complexion:	Fresh
Remarks:	Transferred to the Rifle Brigade for the purpose of serving with and elder brother

RICE	Samuel, Corporal EIC [L/MIL/10/302/114]
	1st Bombay European Fusiliers
	[a Samuel Rice 101st Foot]
	Out Pension No 301
1860	a Samuel Rice embarked UK per *'Cossipore'*
17 Oct 1860	Admitted to Out-pension
	Pension paid 2nd East London Pension District
	1/- per diem
31 Dec 1862	Arrived per *'York'*

Service and Personal Details:

Place of Birth:	Bethnal Green Middlesex
Trade or Occupation:	Weaver
Where Enlisted:	London
Presidency:	Bombay
Length of Service:	19 years 7 months
Age on Discharge:	39 years
Reason for Discharge:	To be pensioned
Character:	Good
Medal Entitlement:	Indian Mutiny
Height:	5' 5"
Complexion:	Fresh

Eye Colour:	Grey
Hair Colour:	Brown
Intends to Reside:	Bethnal Green

RICHARDSON	John, Corporal
	60th Foot [Depot]
13 May 1862	Discharged the Service Chatham
	Pension paid Newry
	1/2d. per diem
1862	Pension paid 2nd Belfast Pension District
22 Dec 1865	Arrived per *'Vimiera'*
July 1866	Died Fremantle

Service and Personal Details:

Place of Birth:	Louth Drogheda Louth
Age on Attestation:	18 years
Period of Service:	1841 — 1862
Age on Discharge:	38 years 7 months
Length of Service:	20 years 188 days
Foreign Service:	East Indies 14 years 172 days
Medal Entitlement:	Long Service and Good Conduct; Punjaub with 2 clasps; Indian Mutiny with clasp
Reason for Discharge:	Bullet wound to right leg received at Delhi
Character:	Very Good
Trade or Occupation:	Brazier
Can Sign Name:	Yes
Height:	5' 8"
Hair Colour:	Dark Brown
Eyes:	Blue
Complexion:	Fresh
Intends to Reside:	Drogheda

RICHARDSON	Robert, private
	10th Foot
Previous Regiment	13th Foot
13 May 1855	Discharged the Service Chatham
	Pension paid Limerick
	1/- per diem
10 Sept 1856	Arrived per *'Runnymede'*
1862	Pension paid Sydney New South Wales
1866	Died

Service and Personal Details:

Place of Birth:	Donoughmore Co. Limerick
Age on Attestation:	19 years
Period of Service:	1834 — 1855
Age on Discharge:	40 years 1 month
Length of Service:	21 years 17 days
Foreign Service:	East Indies 19 years
Medal Entitlement:	Afghanistan with clasps; Cabool; Sutlej with clasp; Punjaub with clasps for Mooltan and Goojerat
Reason for Discharge:	Chronic pains
Character:	Very Good
Trade or Occupation:	Labourer

Can Sign Name:	Yes
Height:	5' 7"
Hair Colour:	Dark Brown
Eyes:	Brown
Complexion:	Fresh
Remarks:	Wounded left shoulder at Sobroan
Intends to Reside:	Limerick
RICHARDSON	William, private Royal Canadian Rifles
Previous Regiments	97th; 85th
9 Sept 1851	Discharged the Service Chatham Pension paid Coventry 1/2d. per diem
19 Aug 1853	Arrived per *'Robert Small'*
1854	Pension paid Western Australia
1856	To South Australia from Western Australia
June 1870	Died
Service and Personal Details:	
Place of Birth:	Shenton Leicestershire
Age on Attestation:	16 years
Period of Service:	1824 — 1851
Age on Discharge:	44 years or 42 years 11 months
Length of Service:	24 years 336 days
Foreign Service:	Ceylon 11 years 1 month North America 12 years 8 months
Reason for Discharge:	Service reckoning as upward of 25 years
Character:	Tolerably Good
Trade or Occupation:	Weaver
Can Sign Name:	Yes
Height:	5' 6¾"
Hair Colour:	Light
Eyes:	Grey
Complexion:	Fresh
Intends to Reside:	Hinckley Leicester
RICKEY	Walter, private 63rd Foot
8 Aug 1848	Discharged the Service Chatham Pension paid Cavan 1/- per diem
19 Aug 1853	Arrived per *'Robert Small'*
Jan 1857	Contributed 2/- to the Florence Nightingale Fund
1857	Assigned Pensioner Loc P8 at York
1862	Application for Title to P8 at York
Sept 1869	Medical Officer York: 'I certify that Pensioner Walter Rickey, who is not in the force, and is now suffering severe illness, is much in want of wine and I recommend him to the Resident Magistrate for a temporary supply of wine.'
1875	Died York Western Australia aged 67
Service and Personal Details:	

Place of Birth:	Knockbride Cootehill Co. Cavan	
Age on Attestation:	18 years	
Period of Service:	1827 — 1848	
Age on Discharge:	40 years	
Length of Service:	20 years 279 days	
Foreign Service:	New South Wales	5 years
	East Indies	13 years
Reason for Discharge:	Health broken down due to length of service and climate	
Character:	Good	
Trade or Occupation:	Labourer	
Can Sign Name:	Yes	
Height:	5' 8½"	
Hair Colour:	Brown	
Eyes:	Grey	
Complexion:	Sallow	
Intends to Reside:	Cootehill	

RILEY Patrick, private
2nd/16th Foot

Surname Variant	REILLY
7 May 1861	Discharged the Service Pension paid Tullamore 9d. per diem
22 Dec 1866	Arrived per *'Corona'* Pension increased to 1/2d. per diem for service in the Enrolled Force
Mar 1876	a Patrick Reilly applied to be certified as owner in Fee Simple of Perth building Lot L48
7 Aug 1882	Application for Title to York Lot 275

Service and Personal Details:

Place of Birth:	Killoughy Kings County	
Age on Attestation:	19 years 9 months	
Period of Service:	1846 — 1861	
Age on Discharge:	33 years 6 months	
Length of Service:	14 years 252 days	
Foreign Service:	West Indies	1 year 239 days
	Canada	1 year 207 days
Reason for Discharge:	Chronic Bronchitis	
Character:	Very Good	
Trade or Occupation:	Labourer	
Can Sign Name:	X his mark on discharge	
Height:	5' 6¾"	
Hair Colour:	Black	
Eyes:	Grey	
Complexion:	Sallow	
Intends to Reside:	London Middlesex	

RING Mark, private
28th Foot

Previous Regiment	40th Foot

11 Dec 1846	Discharged the Service Chatham Pension paid Kilkenny 6d. per diem
1849	Pension paid Falkland Isles
19 Aug 1859	Arrived per *'Sultana'*
July 1867	Application for Title to Lot 115
1864	A little girl, between two and three years old, the child of Corporal Ring, of the Pensioner Force, living at the back of Perth, was drowned in a well on Tuesday afternoon. Immediately after the child was missed a search was made but when found life was extinct. [Trove]
1864	Corporal Mark Ring Pensioner Force at Perth contributed 2/- to the Greenough Fire Relief Fund
13 Apr 1869	Died aged 45 – buried East Perth Cemetery

Service and Personal Details:

Place of Birth:	Danes Fort Kilkenny	
Age on Attestation:	22 years	
Period of Service:	1833 — 1846	
Age on Discharge:	35 years	
Length of Service:	11 years 340 days	
Foreign Service:	East Indies	11 years
Reason for Discharge:	Chronic Rheumatism and Hernia	
Character:	Good	
Trade or Occupation:	Labourer	
Can Sign Name:	X his mark on discharge	
Height:	5' 9"	
Hair Colour:	Light Brown	
Eyes:	Grey	
Complexion:	Fresh	
Intends to Reside:	Kilkenny	

RINGWOOD	Jeffery, private 58th Foot
Previous Regiment	13th Foot
9 Nov 1842	Discharged the Service Dublin
10 Jan 1843	Admitted to Out-Pension Pension paid 2nd Dublin Pension District 1/- per diem
28 June 1851	Arrived per *'Pyrenees'* [1]
1877	Died

Service and Personal Details:

Place of Birth:	Castledermott Co. Kildare	
Age on Attestation:	21 years	
Period of Service:	1821 — 1842	
Age on Discharge:	42 years	
Length of Service:	21 years 100 days [reckoned]	
Foreign Service:	Ceylon	10 years 248 days
Reason for Discharge:	Chronic Rheumatism	
Character:	Good	
Trade or Occupation:	Baker	

Can Sign Name:	Yes
Height:	5' 11"
Hair Colour:	Dark
Eyes:	Blue
Complexion:	Dark

RISEAM	William, private
	RM
	Discharged the Service
	Pension paid Limerick
	£15/4/- per annum
24 May 1855	Arrived per *'Stag'*
Service and Personal Details:	
Place of Birth:	St Leonards Shoreditch Middlesex
Age on Attestation:	19 years
Period of Service:	1826 — 1847
Length of Service:	21 years 14 days
Reason for Discharge:	Length of Service
Trade or Occupation:	Labourer
Can Sign Name:	Yes
Intends to Reside:	32 Richard Street., Limehouse Field nr Stepney Church London
Height:	5' 6¾"
Hair Colour:	Light Brown
Eyes:	Hazel
Complexion:	Fair

RITCHEY	Matthew, private
	41st Foot
Surname Variants	RITCHIE; RICHIE
29 July 1856	Discharged the Service Chatham
	Pension paid Newry
	8d. per diem
1860	Pension paid 2nd Belfast Pension District
1861	1st Belfast Pension District
27 May 1863	Arrived per *'Clyde'*
1865	Pension paid Western Australia
	Pension increased to 10d. per diem for service in the Enrolled Force
no date	Assigned Pensioner Loc G25 at Bootenal
1881	Recommended for £15 Pensioner's Grant for G25
1882	Title Application for Pensioner G26 at Bootenal
1882	Granted Title to Victoria Lot G26
1886	Alice Richie was found sleeping in the open air because her patents couldn't keep her at home. She stated that she couldn't read or write
Apr 1888	Applies for quarters in Barracks
1892	Died
Service and Personal Details:	
Place of Birth:	Killieagh Co. Down
Age on Attestation:	17 years 6 months
Period of Service:	1849 — 1856
Age on Discharge:	24 years 7 months

Length of Service:	6 years 197 days	
Foreign Service:	Ionian Isles	1 year 11 months
	Malta	1 year 1 month
	Turkey & Crimea	2 years
Medal Entitlement:	Crimea with clasps; Turkish Crimean	
Reason for Discharge:	Wounded by musket shot to right foot	
Character:	Indifferent	
Trade or Occupation:	Labourer	
Can Sign Name:	Yes	
Height:	5' 7½"	
Hair Colour:	Light	
Eyes:	Grey	
Complexion:	Fresh	
Remarks:	Drunk returning from Scutari Souk	

ROACH Michael, private
86th Foot

Previous Regiment	83rd Foot
29 Mar 1870	Discharged the Service Pension paid Newry 1/1d. per diem
1870	Pension paid Dublin
1871	Newcastle
19 Feb 1874	Arrived per *'Naval Brigade'*
1876	Stationed Perth
1881	Pension increased to 1/3½d. for 6 years service in the Enrolled Force

Service and Personal Details:

Place of Birth:	Kells Co. Kilkenny	
Age on Attestation:	18 years 10 months	
Period of Service:	1848 — 1870	
Age on Discharge:	40 years 1 month	
Length of Service:	21 years 118 days	
Foreign Service:	Gibraltar	2 years 6 months
	East Indies	10 years 2 months
	Mauritius	8 months
	Cape of Good Hope	1 year 9 months
Reason for Discharge:	Having completed 21 years service	
Character:	Very Good	
Trade or Occupation:	Mason	
Can Sign Name:	Yes	
Height:	5' 8"	
Hair Colour:	Brown	
Eyes:	Grey	
Complexion:	Fresh	
Remarks:	At Poona for 11 years	
Intends to Reside:	Waterford	

ROBARTS Richard, private
24th Foot

Previous Regiment	50th Foot
Surname Variant	ROBERTS

26 Feb 1861	Discharged the Service Chatham	
1861	Pension paid 2nd Plymouth Pension District 11d. per diem	
1862	Pension paid Bermuda	
15 Feb 1863	Arrived per *'Merchantman'* [1]	
1865	To Melbourne from Fremantle	
Service and Personal Details:		
Place of Birth:	St Columb Cornwall	
Age on Attestation:	18 years 2 months	
Period of Service:	1840— 1861	
Age on Discharge:	39 years 2 months	
Length of Service:	21 years 14 days	
Foreign Service:	East Indies	19 years 3 months
Medal Entitlement:	Bronze Star for Gwalior; Sutlej Campaign with 2 clasps; Punjaub with clasp	
Reason for Discharge:	Own Request on completing 21 years service	
Character:	Very Good	
Trade or Occupation:	Labourer	
Can Sign Name:	X his mark on discharge	
Height:	5' 11"	
Hair Colour:	Brown	
Eyes:	Light Blue	
Complexion:	Fair	
Remarks:	Wounded on the left cheek at Chillinwallah	
Intends to Reside:	St Columb Cornwall	
ROBB	William, private Royal Canadian Rifles	
Previous Regiments	92nd; 42nd	
30 July 1861	Discharged the Service Chatham Pension paid 2nd Glasgow Pension District 1/- per diem	
15 Apr 1864	Arrived per *'Clara'* [2]	
1865	Pension paid Madras	
1869	Cape	
Service and Personal Details:		
Place of Birth:	Tyrie [sic] Aberdeenshire	
Age on Attestation:	19 years	
Period of Service:	1840 — 1861	
Age on Discharge:	40 years or 39 years 10 months	
Length of Service:	20 years 312 days	
Foreign Service:	Malta	4 years ?
	Bermuda	3 years ? months
	Crimea	2 years 1 month
	Canada	2 years 10 months
Medal Entitlement:	Crimea	
Reason for Discharge:	Own Request having completed 21 years service	
Character:	Very Good	
Trade or Occupation:	Labourer	
Can Sign Name:	Yes	
Height:	5' 7"	

Hair Colour:	Fair	
Eyes:	Hazel	
Complexion:	Fresh	
Distinguishing Marks:	WR and ship's anchor on left arm and W Robb on right arm	
Intends to Reside:	England but decided on Glasgow	
ROBERTS	Jacob, gunner and driver Royal Artillery 2nd Battalion	
Surname Variant	ROBARTS	
9 June 1857	Discharged the Service Woolwich Pension paid Canterbury 8d. per diem	
1857	Pension paid Leicester	
24 Nov 1858	Arrived per *'Edwin Fox'*	
1867	To Sydney from Perth Western Australia	
1876	Pension paid Sydney	
1880	Sydney	
Service and Personal Details:		
Place of Birth:	Uppingham Rutland	
Age on Attestation:	18 years 8 months	
Period of Service:	1835 — 1857	
Age on Discharge:	40 years 1 month	
Length of Service:	21 years 79 days	
Foreign Service:	Canada	5 years 2 months
	Fort Garry	2 years 2 months
	Corfu	5 years 8 months
Reason for Discharge:	Chronic Rheumatism	
Character:	Good	
Trade or Occupation:	Ostler	
Can Sign Name:	Yes	
Height:	5' 9"	
Hair Colour:	Light Brown	
Eyes:	Light Blue	
Complexion:	Fair	
ROBERTS	James, private 16th Lancers	
Surname Variant	ROBARTS	
21 Apr 1857	Discharged the Service Pension paid Norwich 7d. per diem	
1857	Pension paid South London	
1862	Pension paid 1st West London District	
31 Dec 1862	Arrived per *'York'* as a Convict Guard	
1864	prve J Roberts Pensioner Force at Perth contributed Greenough Fire Relief Fund	
1865	On Nominal List to proceed to Camden Harbour per *'Tien Tsin'*	
1866	Pension paid Melbourne	
1867	Auckland	
1875	Sydney	
1897	W.O. correspondence	

Service and Personal Details:	
Place of Birth:	Marlow Buckinghamshire
Age on Attestation:	18 years 6 months
Period of Service:	1839 — 1857
Age on Discharge:	36 years
Length of Service:	17 years 140 days
Foreign Service:	India upwards of 6 years
Medal Entitlement:	Maharajpore 1843 [Star] ; Aliwal 1846 [Medal] and Sobraon 1846 [Clasp]
Reason for Discharge:	Very bad fracture of leg from kick of horse
Character:	Good soldier seldom in hospital, Trustworthy and Sober
Trade or Occupation:	Groom
Can Sign Name:	Yes
Height:	5' 7"
Hair Colour:	Light Brown
Eyes:	Grey
Complexion:	Fresh
Intends to Reside:	Norwich

ROBERTS	John, private 31st Foot
Surname Variant	ROBARTS
8 Apr 1856	Discharged the Service Chatham Pension paid 1st Dublin Pension District 9d. per diem
1858	Pension paid Athlone
1859	1st Dublin Pension District
1862	Bermuda
15 Feb 1863	Arrived per *'Merchantman'* [1]
1866	To Adelaide from Fremantle
16 Mar 1866	Residents Office Fremantle. — Submission of care for Mrs. Ann Roberts for temporary relief. Her husband, a Pensioner has been seeking passage for himself and family to Adelaide.
1875	Pension paid Adelaide South Australia
1886	W.O. correspondence the "A31" Adelaide
1898	Attended Memorial Day Adelaide
1899	Sentenced to 3 months imprisonment for Larceny and confined in Adelaide Goal. Pension suspended for the time in prison

Service and Personal Details:	
Place of Birth:	St Catherines Dublin
Age on Attestation:	17 years
Period of Service:	1846 — 1856
Age on Discharge:	27 years or 26 years 5 months
Length of Service:	8 years 122 days [after age of 18]
Foreign Service:	Ionian Isles 2 years 4 months Crimea 8 months
Medal Entitlement:	Crimea
Reason for Discharge:	Left shoulder wounded by shell fragment
Character:	Good

Trade or Occupation:	Labourer
Can Sign Name:	X his mark on discharge
Height:	5' 5¾"
Hair Colour:	Brown
Eyes:	Grey
Complexion:	Fresh
Intends to Reside:	Dublin

ROBERTSON Robert, private
12th Foot

Previous Regiment	99th Foot
15 June 1858	Discharged the Service Chatham Pension paid Perth Scotland 10d. per diem
1858	Allowed to join Perth Militia [Scotland]
1860	Pension paid Jersey
1861	Pension paid Perth Scotland
12 Sept 1864	Arrived per *'Merchantman'* [2] "Reported for fraud"
1869	Pension paid Mauritius

Service and Personal Details:

Place of Birth:	Blairgowrie Perth Scotland
Age on Attestation:	18 years 6 months
Period of Service:	1836 — 1858
Age on Discharge:	40 years 5 months
Length of Service:	21 years 8 days
Foreign Service:	Australian Colonies 14 years 2 months
Reason for Discharge:	Chronic Rheumatism
Character:	Very Good
Trade or Occupation:	Writer
Can Sign Name:	Yes
Height:	5' 8½"
Hair Colour:	Fair
Eyes:	Grey
Complexion:	Fresh
Intends to Reside:	Blairgowrie Scotland

ROBINSON Benjamin, Serjeant
74th Foot

19 Feb 1849	Discharged the Service Limerick
10 Apr 1849	Admitted to Out-Pension Pension paid Charlmont 1/3d. per diem
1849	Pension paid 2nd Dublin Pension District
1855	2nd Plymouth Pension District
1855	Pension increased to 1/6d. per diem
1856	Employed as Warder Dartmoor Prison
10 Sept 1856	Embarked per *'Runnymede'* "Shot dead while employed as Sergeant Major in Command of the Convict Guard on the ship *'Runnymede'*" "Murdered by Corporal Nevin of the Pensioner Guard" [see Plymouth newspapers of that date]

ROBINSON	John, Corporal	
	9th Foot	
18 May 1852	Discharged the Service Galway	
13 July 1852	Admitted to Out-Pension	
	Pension paid 1st Dublin Pension District	
	1/1d. per diem	
30 Apr 1853	Arrived per *'Pyrenees'* [2]	
Jan 1857	Contributed 2/6 to the Florence Nightingale Fund	
*c*1859	Died	
Service and Personal Details:		
Place of Birth:	Longford Longford	
Age on Attestation:	19 years 9 months	
Period of Service:	1831 — 1852	
Age on Discharge:	40 years 10 months	
Length of Service:	20 years 360 days	
Foreign Service:	Mauritius	2 years 195 days
	East Indies	11 years 124 days
Medal Entitlement:	Afghanistan 1842; Sutlej with 2 clasps	
Reason for Discharge:	Chest Complaint and Impaired Efficiency	
Character:	Latterly Good	
Trade or Occupation:	Labourer	
Can Sign Name:	Yes	
Height:	5' 10"	
Hair Colour:	Black	
Eyes:	Hazel	
Complexion:	Dark	
Intends to Reside:	Dublin	

ROBINSON	Thomas, gunner	
	RA Depot Brigade	
Previous Regiment	RA 6th Battalion 8th Brigade	
19 Aug 1862	Discharged the Service Woolwich	
	Pension paid Woolwich	
	9d. per diem	
27 May 1863	Arrived per *'Clyde'*	
1864	Pension paid Ceylon	
1867	Kilkenny	
19 Nov 1871	Died	
Service and Personal Details:		
Place of Birth:	Armagh Co. Armagh	
Age on Attestation:	22 years	
Period of Service:	1849 — 1862	
Age on Discharge:	35 years 5 months	
Length of Service:	15 years 54 days	
Foreign Service:	India	13 years 9 months
Reason for Discharge:	Chronic Rheumatism	
Character:	Very Good	
Trade or Occupation:	Labourer	
Can Sign Name:	Yes	
Height:	6'	

Hair Colour:	Light Brown
Eyes:	Brown
Complexion:	Dark

ROCHE	Edward, private
	34th Foot
Previous Regiment	6th Foot
Surname Variant	ROACH
1 Jan 1856	Discharged the Service Chatham
	Pension paid Co. Mayo
	8d. per diem
15 Aug 1865	Arrived per *'Racehorse'*
1876	Applied for £15 improvement grant for Perth Town Lot 141/Y
1878	"Discharged from Enrolled Pensioner Force"
4 June 1878	Pension increased to 1/-½d. for service in the Enrolled Force of Western Australia
Apr 1881	Application for Title to Perth Lot 141/Y
1893	Died

Service and Personal Details:

Place of Birth:	Belmullett Co. Mayo
Age on Attestation:	17 years 6 months
Period of Service:	1846 — 1855
Age on Discharge:	28 years or 27 years
Length of Service:	8 years 360 days
Foreign Service:	In the "East"
Medal Entitlement:	Crimea
Reason for Discharge:	Disabled by loss by amputation of middle and ring finger of right hand after wounded by musket ball on the 7th June at the attack on the Quarrie [sic]
Character:	Good
Trade or Occupation:	Farm Servant
Can Sign Name:	X his mark on Attestation
Height:	5' 5½"
Hair Colour:	Brown
Eyes:	Blue
Complexion:	Fresh
Intends to Reside:	Belmullett Co. Mayo

ROCK	James, private [Military Pensioner]
	96th Foot
	[subsequently employed in the Enrolled Force]
22 Feb 1847	Arrived per *'Java'* with regiment
15 May 1849	Discharged the Service Perth West. Aust.
9 Oct 1849	Admitted to Out-Pension
	Pension paid Perth Western Australia
	1/- per diem
1864	ptve Rock Pensioner Force at Kojonup contributed to the Greenough Fire Relief Fund
Feb 1879	Pensioner James Rock to Poor House
1878	Died

Service and Personal Details:

Place of Birth:	Clones Monaghan	
Age on Attestation:	18 years	
Period of Service:	1824 — 1849	
Age on Discharge:	43 years	
Length of Service:	24 years 68 days	
Foreign Service:	Bermuda &	
	North America	12 years
	Australia	7 years
Reason for Discharge:	Worn out and unfit for further service	
Character:	Indifferent	
Trade or Occupation:	Labourer	
Can Sign Name:	X his mark on discharge	
Height:	5' 7"	
Hair Colour:	Brown	
Eyes:	Grey	
Complexion:	Fresh	
Distinguishing Marks:	Pock pitted	

ROFFEY	Richard, private
	59th Foot
Previous Regiment	40th Foot
24 Feb 1849	Discharged the Service Birr
24 Apr 1849	Admitted to Out-Pension
	1/- per diem
	Pension paid South London
1 June 1850	Arrived per *'Scindian'*
Aug 1850	Allocated Pensioner Loc P12 at South Perth
1851	Employed as a Schoolmaster
1857	Pension paid East London

Service and Personal Details:

Place of Birth:	Lambeth Surrey	
Age on Attestation:	20 years	
Period of Service:	1827 — 1849	
Age on Discharge:	41 years 4 months	
Length of Service:	20 years 303 days	
Foreign Service:	Mediterranean	2 years 157 days
	West Indies	1 year 117 days
Reason for Discharge:	Wasting bodily strength and activity	
Character:	Indifferent	
Trade or Occupation:	Baker	
Can Sign Name:	Yes	
Height:	5' 6½"	
Hair Colour:	Light Brown	
Eyes:	Hazel	
Complexion:	Fair	
Intends to Reside:	Lambeth	

ROGERS	Mark Dore, private
	83rd Foot
22 Sept 1857	Discharged the Service Chatham
22 Sept 1857	Discharge approved
	Pension paid Jersey

	1/- per diem
1858	Pension paid Stockport
1858	Cork
19 Aug 1859	Arrived per *'Sultana'*
1862	Wife of Pensioner Rogers was struck by lightning
1864	ptve M D Rogers Pensioner Force at Perth contributed to the Greenough Fire Relief Fund
1872	Died aged 54 – buried East Perth Cemetery

Service and Personal Details:		
Place of Birth:	Kingston Hampshire	
Age on Attestation:	20 years	
Period of Service:	1836 — 1857	
Age on Discharge:	41 years	
Length of Service:	21 years 3 days	
Foreign Service:	East Indies	7 years
Medal Entitlement:	Good Conduct with gratuity	
Reason for Discharge:	Chronic Pains and Dyspnoea	
Character:	Very Good	
Trade or Occupation:	Labourer	
Can Sign Name:	X his mark on discharge	
Height:	5' 7½"	
Hair Colour:	Brown	
Eyes:	Hazel	
Complexion:	Fresh	
Intends to Reside:	Jersey	

ROLSTON	James, Corporal
	8th Foot
Surname Variant	RALSTON
31 Jan 1860	Discharged the Service Chatham
	Pension paid 2nd West London Pension District
	1/5½d. per diem
27 May 1863	Arrived per *'Clyde'*
1864	ptve J Rolson Pensioner Force at Fremantle District contributed to the Greenough Fire Relief Fund
1867	To New South Wales from Fremantle
31 Sept 1868	Died

Service and Personal Details:		
Place of Birth:	Armagh Co. Armagh	
Age on Attestation:	19 years 8 months	
Period of Service:	1839 — 1860	
Age on Discharge:	40 years 8 months	
Length of Service:	21 years 6 days	
Foreign Service:	North America	1 year 201 days
	East Indies	12 years 186 days
Medal Entitlement:	Long Service and Good Conduct with gratuity; Indian Mutiny	
Reason for Discharge:	Being employed as Company Serjeant at the Royal Military Asylum Chelsea	
Character:	Very Good	

Trade or Occupation:	Labourer
Can Sign Name:	Yes
Height:	5' 8"
Hair Colour:	Black
Eyes:	Grey
Complexion:	Fresh
Intends to Reside:	Royal Military Asylum Chelsea

RONAN

	Thomas, private
	58th Foot
22 July 1840	Discharged the Service Fort Pitt Chatham
	Pension paid Ennis
	6d. per diem
24 May 1855	Arrived per *'Stag'*
16 Aug 1861	Died aged 49

Service and Personal Details:

Place of Birth:	St Marys Limerick	
Age on Attestation:	17 years	
Period of Service:	1825 — 1840	
Age on Discharge:	31 years	
Length of Service:	13 years 307 days	
Foreign Service:	Ceylon	10 years 6 months
Reason for Discharge:	Chronic Catarrh	
Character:	Good	
Trade or Occupation:	Servant	
Can Sign Name:	X his mark on Attestation	
Height:	5' 5½"	
Hair Colour:	Fair	
Eyes:	Blue	
Complexion:	Fair	
Intends to Reside:	Ennis Co. Clare	

ROONEY

	Henry, private
	15th Foot
Surname Variant	ROMEY
25 Nov 1856	Discharged the Service Chatham
1856	Pension paid Jersey
1857	Exeter
	1/- per diem
25 Oct 1858	Arrived per *'Edwin Fox'*
1863	Stationed Perth District
1864	ptve H Rooney Pensioner Force at Perth contributed to the Greenough Fire Relief Fund
1874	Pension increased to 1/3d. per diem
circa March 1874	Transferred from 1st Perth District to Fremantle
1875	Correspondence with W.O.
Jan 1878	Perth — stolen from him whilst he was asleep, a red handkerchief containing his parchment discharge and pension papers
April 1878	Died of sunstroke near South Dandalup Brook [4 miles from Pinjarra]

Service and Personal Details:		
Place of Birth:	Navan Co. Meath	
Age on Attestation:	19 years	
Period of Service:	1835 — 1856	
Age on Discharge:	40 years 1 month	
Length of Service:	21 years 45 days	
Foreign Service:	Canada	2 years
	Ceylon	9 years 8 months
Reason for Discharge:	Unfit for further service	
Character:	Good	
Trade or Occupation:	Shoemaker	
Can Sign Name:	Yes	
Height:	5' 11"	
Hair Colour:	Brown	
Eyes:	Grey	
Complexion:	Fresh	
Intends to Reside:	Jersey	

ROONEY	John, private	
	81st Foot	
Previous Regiments	29th; 47th	
14 Oct 1842	Discharged the Service Fort Pitt	
	7d per diem	
	Pension paid 2nd Dublin Pension District	
1846	Ballymena	
7 Feb 1853	Arrived per *'Dudbrook'*	
1855	Pension paid Van Diemans Land [sic]	
Service and Personal Details:		
Place of Birth:	Kildare Co. Kildare	
Age on Attestation:	18 years	
Period of Service:	1826 — 1842	
Age on Discharge:	33 years 8 months	
Length of Service:	15 years 140 days [reckoned]	
Foreign Service:	Gibraltar	3 years 10 months
	West Indies	2 years 5 months
Reason for Discharge:	Chronic Catarrh and Defective Vision	
Character:	Tolerably Good	
Trade or Occupation:	Labourer	
Can Sign Name:	Yes	
Height:	5' 7"	
Hair Colour:	Black	
Eyes:	Brown	
Complexion:	Sallow	
Intends to Reside:	Athy Co. Kildare	

ROURKE	James, private
	27th Foot
6 June 1848	Discharged the Service Chatham
	Pension paid 1st Manchester Pension District
	1/- per diem
1848	Pension paid 2nd West London Pension District
1 June 1850	Arrived per *'Scindian'*

1850	a James Rourke assigned land at Freshwater Bay	
1851	Employed as Assistant Warder	
1852	Convicted of stealing	
1853	Convicted of Felony — pension suspended	
1854	Refused Restoration by War Office	
Service and Personal Details:		
Place of Birth:	Drumlane Co. Cavan	
Age on Attestation:	16 years	
Period of Service:	1826 — 1848	
Age on Discharge:	40 years or 38 years 11 months	
Length of Service:	20 years 359 days	
Foreign Service:	West Indies	4 years 335 days
	Cape of Good Hope	12 years 230 days
Medal Entitlement:	Kaffir Campaign	
Reason for Discharge:	Chromic Rheumatism	
Character:	Good	
Trade or Occupation:	Labourer	
Can Sign Name:	Yes	
Height:	5' 5"	
Hair Colour:	Grey	
Eyes:	Grey	
Complexion:	Fresh	
Intends to Reside:	Ashton under Lyne	

ROWE	William, private	
	16th Foot	
20 Aug 1841	Discharged the Service	
8 Sept 1841	Admitted to Out-Pension	
	Pension paid Framlington Ipswich	
	6d. per diem	
1848	Pension paid South London	
1849	Pension paid 1st West London Pension District	
1851	Woolwich	
19 Aug 1853	Arrived per *'Robert Small'*	
Aug 1854	"Deserted Enrolled Force"	
1858	Pension paid Melbourne	
Service and Personal Details:		
Place of Birth:	Framagam [sic] Suffolk	
Age on Attestation:	17 years	
Period of Service:	1825 — 1841	
Age on Discharge:	32 years 8 months	
Length of Service:	14 years 189 days	
Foreign Service:	East Indies	10 years 168 days
Reason for Discharge:	Enfeebled and Enervated by climate and service	
Character:	Very Good	
Trade or Occupation:	Labourer	
Can Sign Name:	X his mark on discharge	
Height:	5' 5¾"	
Hair Colour:	Brown	
Eyes:	Blue	
Complexion:	Fresh	

Intends to Reside:	Framlingham
RUDD	John, private 57th Foot
26 July 1859	Discharged the Service Cork Barracks
7 Aug 1859	Admitted to Out–Pension Pension paid Chatham 1/- per diem
29 Jan 1862	Arrived per *'Lincelles'*
1864	ptve J Rudd Pensioner Force at Fremantle District contributed to the Greenough Fire Relief Fund
18 Dec 1870	Died
Service and Personal Details:	
Place of Birth:	Grantham Lincolnshire
Age on Attestation:	20 years
Period of Service:	1837 — 1859
Age on Discharge:	41 years
Length of Service:	21 years 287 days
Foreign Service:	East Indies 7 years 9 months
Medal Entitlement:	Long Service and Good Conduct with gratuity
Reason for Discharge:	Own Request having completed 21 years service
Character:	Very Good
Trade or Occupation:	Tailor
Can Sign Name:	Yes
Height:	5' 7½"
Hair Colour:	Dark Brown
Eyes:	Hazel
Complexion:	Dark
Distinguishing Marks:	Scar on left leg
Intends to Reside:	Rochester
RUDDOCK	George, private 2nd Foot Guards [Coldstream Guards]
Surname Variant	RUDDUCK,
27 June 1848	Discharged the Service London Pension paid Norwich 1/-½d. per diem
1849	Pension paid Lynn
25 Oct 1850	Arrived per *'Hashemy'* as a Convict Guard
1855	Dismissed from Enrolled Pensioner Guard Force for drunkenness "To refund expense of passage"
1862	Attempted suicide
30 May 1868	Died
Service and Personal Details:	
Place of Birth:	Feltwell Norfolk
Age on Attestation:	20 years
Period of Service:	1825 — 1848
Age on Discharge:	42 years
Length of Service:	22 years 185 days
Foreign Service:	Quebec 4 years 6 month
Reason for Discharge:	Impaired breathing and double rupture

Character:	Good and efficient soldier, Trustworthy and Sober
Trade or Occupation:	Labourer
Can Sign Name:	X his mark on discharge
Height:	5' 9½"
Hair Colour:	Light Brown
Eyes:	Grey
Complexion:	Fair
Remarks:	Serving in Lieut. Colonel Forbes's Company

RUSH	James, Corporal 88th Foot
30 Oct 1855	Discharged the Service Chatham Pension paid Galway 1/- per diem
19 Feb 1874	Arrived per *'Naval Brigade'*
1878- 1887	cleaned, repaired, issued and shipped arms to the new Volunteer corps and outlying stations
8 June 1881	Assigned Perth Pensioner Lot 118/V
Jan 1881	Pension increased to 1/2½d. per diem for service in the Enrolled Force
May 1881	Pension increased further to 1/8d. per diem which includes the former service of 15½ years as Colour Serjeant on the Permanent Staff of the South Mayo Rifle Militia to be specially allowed toward pension
1881	Application for Perth Town Lot V118 for J. Rush [Pensioner] [SROWA]
July 1885	Granted Fee Simple Perth Pensioner Lot 118/V

Service and Personal Details:

Place of Birth:	Westport Co. Mayo	
Age on Attestation:	21 years	
Period of Service:	1850 — 1855	
Age on Discharge:	26 years	
Length of Service:	5 years 89 years	
Foreign Service:	Crimea	[no time period given]
Medal Entitlement:	Crimea with clasp	
Reason for Discharge:	Wounded in the trenches before Sebastopol	
Character:	Very Good	
Trade or Occupation:	Tailor	
Can Sign Name:	Yes	
Height:	5' 9*"	
Hair Colour:	Brown	
Eyes:	Hazel	
Complexion:	Fresh	
Intends to Reside:	Westport	

RUSSELL	William, private 4th Foot
24 Sept 1861	Discharged the Service Chatham Pension paid Chatham 7d. per diem
1861	Pension paid Manchester

1862	Birr
22 Dec 1865	Arrived per *'Vimiera'*
1876	Pension increased to 10d. per diem for 6 years service in the Enrolled Force
1 May 1876	Died aged 48

Service and Personal Details:

Place of Birth:	Birr Kings County
Age on Discharge:	35 years 1 month
Length of Service:	Restored to 16 years 358 days
Foreign Service:	India 15 years
	[the man's statement and information from pocket ledger]
Reason for Discharge:	Pulmonary Consumption and enlargement of liver. Cicatrix of gunshot wound to left arm stated to have been received in action at Gwalior in 1857 [this claim has not been certified]
Character:	Good
Trade or Occupation:	Labourer
Can Sign Name:	X his mark on discharge
Height:	5' 11"
Hair Colour:	Brown
Eyes:	Brown
Complexion:	Fresh
Remarks:	Documents referring to previous 16 years service now not available
Intends to Reside:	Birr Kings County

RUTLEY

	George, Corporal
	RA 14th Brigade
3 May 1870	Discharged the Service Woolwich
	Pension paid Woolwich
	1/5½d. per diem
1871	Pension paid East London Pension District
1873	Greenwich
19 Feb 1874	Arrived per *'Naval Brigade'*
1881	Pension increased to 1/8½d. per diem for service in the Enrolled Force
22 Aug 1881	Assigned Lot P51 North Fremantle which was relinquished by Reddaway [18 Aug 1881]
29 Aug 1884	Granted Fee Simple North Fremantle Lot P51
June 1897	Residing Fremantle
1898	Died aged 66

Service and Personal Details:

Place of Birth:	Cullompton Devon	
Age on Attestation:	17 years 6 months	
Period of Service:	1846 — 1870	
Age on Discharge:	41 years 8 months	
Length of Service:	23 years 199 days	
Foreign Service:	Gibraltar	5 years 6 months
	India	10 years 4 months
	China	11 months
Medal Entitlement:	China with clasp	

Reason for Discharge:	Own Request having served 23 years
Character:	Good
Trade or Occupation:	Labourer
Can Sign Name:	Yes
Height:	5' 9"
Hair Colour:	Fair
Eyes:	Blue
Complexion:	Fresh
Intends to Reside:	Post Office Exeter

RYAN	James, private
	16th Lancers
22 June 1847	Discharged the Service Chatham
	Pension paid Halifax
	10d. per diem
1848	Pension paid South London
1849	Halifax
31 Aug 1853	Arrived per *'Phoebe Dunbar'*
1855	Employed as Assistant Warder
1855	Pension paid Western Australia
1867	To South Australia from Perth
1867	Pension paid South London
1868	Halifax
1869	Hull
1869	Jersey
1869	Halifax
1870	Admitted to In-Pension
1874	Wife for allowance from man's Civil Pension
Feb 1884	Died
1884	Widow for balance of pension

Service and Personal Details:

Place of Birth:	St Olaves Surrey	
Age on Attestation:	18 years 2 months	
Period of Service:	1840 — 1847	
Age on Discharge:	25 years	
Length of Service:	7 years 102 days	
Foreign Service:	East Indies	upwards of 6 years
Medal Entitlement:	Maharajapor 1843; Aliwal 1846	
Reason for Discharge:	Gun shot wound to heel of right foot	
Character:	Good and efficient soldier	
Trade or Occupation:	Labourer	
Can Sign Name:	X his mark on Attestation	
Height:	5' 10"	
Hair Colour:	Sandy	
Eyes:	Hazel	
Complexion:	Fair	
Intends to Reside:	Bradford Yorkshire	

RYAN	Michael, private
	27th Foot
11 Jan 1837	Discharged the Service
	Pension paid Galway

	6d. per diem for 3 years	
1842	Pension made permanent	
1867	W.O. correspondence with Deputy Assistant Commissary General Ryland	
1875	Pension paid Perth Western Australia	
Service and Personal Details:		
Place of Birth:	St Nicholas Co. Galway	
Age on Attestation:	24 years	
Period of Service:	1828 — 1836	
Age on Discharge:	32 years	
Length of Service:	9 years 1 day	
Foreign Service:	West Indies	1 year 29 days
Reason for Discharge:	Varicose Veins of the right thigh	
Character:	Good and efficient soldier	
Trade or Occupation:	Dealer	
Can Sign Name:	X his mark on discharge	
Height:	5' 7½"	
Hair Colour:	Dark Brown	
Eyes:	Blue	
Complexion:	Fresh	
Intends to Reside:	Galway	

RYAN	Patrick, private	
	46th Foot	
25 May 1864	Discharged the Service Netley	
	Pension paid Kilkenny	
	10d. per diem	
22 Dec 1866	Arrived per *'Corona'*	
1870	Pension paid Melbourne	
1871	Kilkenny	
1874	Clonmel	
1875	Limerick	
1876	Cork	
1882	Admitted to Kilmainham Hospital	
10 May 1894	Died	
Service and Personal Details:		
Place of Birth:	Thurles Co. Tipperary	
Age on Attestation:	17 years 6 months	
Period of Service:	1842— 1863	
Age on Discharge:	39 years 2 months	
Length of Service:	20 years 248 days	
Foreign Service:	Crimea	1 year 7 months
	Corfu	2 years 4 months
	India	5 years 1 month
Medal Entitlement:	Crimea with clasp; Turkish Crimea	
Reason for Discharge:	Worn out	
Character:	Good	
Trade or Occupation:	Groom	
Can Sign Name:	Yes	
Height:	5' 4¾"	
Hair Colour:	Sandy	

Eyes:	Hazel
Complexion:	Fresh
Intends to Reside:	Liverpool

RYAN	Stephen, private	
	2nd Foot	
22 Apr 1869	Discharged the Service	
	Pension paid 1st Cork Pension District	
	1/1d per diem	
19 Feb 1874	Arrived per *'Naval Brigade'*	
27 Aug 1881	Assigned Fremantle Lots P 38 and P 39	
	Pension increased to 1/5½d. per diem for 6 years service in the Enrolled Force	
21 June 1884	Granted Fee Simple Fremantle Lots P38 and P39	
June 1897	Residing Fremantle	
1889	Charged with being drunk in Fremantle, but as this was the prisoner's first appearance his case was dismissed with a caution	
Feb 1900	Attended fete at Fremantle Oval	
Service and Personal Details:		
Place of Birth:	Frankford Kings County	
Age on Attestation:	20 years	
Period of Service:	1847 — 1869	
Age on Discharge:	41 years 6 months	
Length of Service:	21 years 166 days	
Foreign Service:	Cape of Good Hope	8 years 7 months
	China	7 months
Medal Entitlement:	Long Service and Good Conduct without gratuity; Kaffir War 1851/1853	
Reason for Discharge:	Own Request after serving two periods of "Limited Service"	
Character:	Very Good	
Trade or Occupation:	Labourer	
Can Sign Name:	X his mark on discharge	
Height:	5' 9¼"	
Hair Colour:	Red	
Eyes:	Grey	
Complexion:	Fresh	
Intends to Reside:	Cork Hill Cork	

RYAN	Thomas, private
	60th Foot
22 June 1852	Discharged the Service Chatham
	Pension paid 1st Cork Pension District
	1/- per diem
1852	Pension paid Clonmel
30 Apr 1853	Arrived per *'Pyrenees'* [2]
1856	Pension paid Adelaide South Australia
	"Only to be paid half pension until passage for wife is re-imbursed"
1859	Pension paid Cape of Good Hope to West London
1861	Pension paid Jersey
1861	2nd Plymouth Pension District

1862	Pension paid 2nd West London Pension District
1872	Admitted to Kilmainham Hospital
1873	Died 'there-in'

Service and Personal Details:

Place of Birth:	Clonmel Co. Tipperary	
Age on Attestation:	18 years	
Period of Service:	1831 — 1851	
Age on Discharge:	39 years 5 months or 38 years 9 months	
Length of Service:	20 years 236 days	
Foreign Service:	East Indies	6 years 17 days
Medal Entitlement:	Punjaub 1849 with bars; ? Afghanistan	
Reason for Discharge:	Rheumatic pains and worn out	
Character:	Very Good	
Trade or Occupation:	Clerk	
Can Sign Name:	Yes	
Height:	5' 4¾"	
Hair Colour:	Black	
Eyes:	Grey	
Complexion:	Fresh	
Remarks:	Appointed Bugler 1839	
Intends to Reside:	Cork	

RYAN William, Corporal
61st Foot

15 Oct 1872	Discharged the Service Enniskillen Pension paid Jersey 1/5½d. per diem
1872	Pension paid 2nd Dublin Pension District
1873	Waterford
19 Feb 1874	Arrived per *'Naval Brigade'*
1881	Assigned North Fremantle Lot P63
1881	Permit to occupy North Fremantle Lot P63
29 Aug 1884	Granted Fee Simple North Fremantle Lot P64
1887	53 years of age

Service and Personal Details:

Place of Birth:	St Johns Waterford Co. Waterford	
Age on Attestation:	19 years	
Period of Service:	1851 — 1872	
Age on Discharge:	40 years	
Length of Service:	21 years 10 days	
Foreign Service:	India	6 years 9 months
	Mauritius	1 year 1 month
	Canada & Bermuda	2 year 9 months
Medal Entitlement:	Indian Mutiny with clasp	
Reason for Discharge:	Claimed on second period of 'Limited Engagement"	
Character:	Very Good	
Trade or Occupation:	Labourer	
Can Sign Name:	Yes	
Height:	5' 10"	

Hair Colour:	Brown	
Eyes:	Grey	
Complexion:	Fresh	
Intends to Reside:	St Helier Jersey Channel Islands	

RYDER Thomas, private [3449]
RM

Surname Variant	RIDER	
2 July 1845	Admitted to Pension Pension paid 1st Plymouth Pension District £9/4/- per annum	
18 Oct 1851	Arrived per *'Minden'*	
1851	Serving in Police Force	
1853	To Victoria from Western Australia	

Service and Personal Details:

Place of Birth:	Stokenham Kingsbridge Devon	

SALMON John, private
Royal Canadian Rifles

Previous Regiment	63rd Foot	
15 Nov 1864	Discharged the Service Pension paid Birmingham 9d. per diem	
9 Jan 1868	Arrived per *'Hougoumont'*	
1869	Pension paid Calcutta	
1870	Mauritius	
1884	Admitted to In-Pension Chelsea	
14 Feb 1891	Died	

Service and Personal Details:

Place of Birth:	Eccleshall Staffordshire	
Age on Attestation:	18 years	
Period of Service:	1843 — 1864	
Age on Discharge:	39 years 4 months	
Length of Service:	21 years	
Foreign Service:	East Indies	3 years 9 months
	Crimea	7 months
	North America	8 years 2 months
Medal Entitlement:	Crimea	
Reason for Discharge:	Own Request having served 21 years service	
Character:	Good	
Trade or Occupation:	Brush maker	
Can Sign Name:	Yes	
Height:	5' 7"	
Hair Colour:	Dark Brown	
Eyes:	Hazel	
Complexion:	Fresh	
Intends to Reside:	Wolverhampton Staffordshire	

SAMPY Michael, private
56th Foot

Surname Variants	SAMPHY; SAMPEY; SAMFRY; SAMPFREY	
27 Apr 1863	Discharged the Service Colchester	
19 May 1863	Admitted to Out-Pension	

	9d. per diem	
	Pension paid 2nd West London Pension District	
1863	Pension paid Woolwich	
1863	1st East London Pension District	
15 Aug 1865	Arrived per *'Racehorse'*	
1870	Pension paid Perth Western Australia	
1871	To Victoria from 2nd Perth [WA] District	
1875	Pension paid Melbourne	
Service and Personal Details:		
Place of Birth:	Chelsea Middlesex	
Age on Attestation:	17 years 6 months	
Period of Service:	1840 — 1862	
Age on Discharge:	40 years 5 months	
Length of Service:	21 years 4 days	
Foreign Service:	Gibraltar	4 years 7 months
	Bermuda	3 years 7 months
	Crimea	1 year
	East Indies	4 years 11 months
Medal Entitlement:	Crimea with clasp; Turkish Crimean	
Reason for Discharge:	Own Request on completing 21 years service	
Character:	Amended to Latterly Good	
Trade or Occupation:	Labourer	
Can Sign Name:	Yes	
Height:	5' 9½"	
Hair Colour:	Brown	
Eyes:	Grey	
Complexion:	Sallow	
Intends to Reside:	Chelsea Middlesex	

SARGENT	William, private
	17th Lancers
Surname Variant	SARGEANT
11 Apr 1850	Discharged the Service Dublin
14 May 1850	Admitted to Out-Pension
	Pension paid Brighton
	10d. per diem
1850	Pension paid Northampton
24 May 1855	Arrived per *'Stag'*
1856	Employed as Assistant Warder
1863	To New South Wales from Fremantle
1875	Pension paid Sydney
1876	New South Wales
1879	Pension paid Brighton
1880	Admitted as In-Pensioner Chelsea Hospital
Service and Personal Details:	
Place of Birth:	Wartling Sussex
Age on Attestation:	18 years
Period of Service:	1827 — 1850
Age on Discharge:	40 years 4 months
Length of Service:	21 years 258 days
Reason for Discharge:	Varicose Veins
Character:	Good

Trade or Occupation:	Gardener
Can Sign Name:	Yes
Height:	5' 8"
Hair Colour:	Dark Brown
Eyes:	Hazel
Complexion:	Dark
Intends to Reside:	Brighton

SAVAGE	William, private 29th Foot
17 Sept 1847	Discharged the Service Chatham Pension paid Londonderry 8d. per diem
31 Aug 1853	Arrived per *'Phoebe Dunbar'*
1854	Employed by Convict Establishment
1866	Died

Service and Personal Details:

Place of Birth:	Coleraine Londonderry	
Age on Attestation:	21 years	
Period of Service:	1839 — 1847	
Age on Discharge:	29 years or 28 years 5 months	
Length of Service:	7 years 158 days	
Foreign Service:	East Indies	4 years 1 month
Medal Entitlement:	Sutlej	
Reason for Discharge:	Worn out and Dysentery	
Character:	Indifferent	
Trade or Occupation:	Labourer	
Can Sign Name:	Yes	
Height:	5' 8½"	
Hair Colour:	Dark Brown	
Eyes:	Grey	
Complexion:	Dark	
Distinguishing Marks:	Scar of gunshot wound Achilles tendon left leg and scar in left ?groin	
Remarks:	Wounded at Ferozeshar	
Intends to Reside:	Coleraine Londonderry	

SAVILLE	William, private 95th Foot
Surname Variant	SAVILE
12 Aug 1845	Discharged the Service Chatham Pension paid 2nd West London Pension District 1/- per diem
2 Aug 1852	Arrived per *'William Jardine'*
1852	Employed Convict Establishment without sanction of Staff Officer Pensions
1854	"Left colony without transfer"
29 Dec 1856	Died Van Dieman's Land

Service and Personal Details:

Place of Birth:	Roxton Bedfordshire
Age on Attestation:	18 years
Period of Service:	1823 — 1845

Age on Discharge:	40 years	
Length of Service:	21 years 83 days	
Foreign Service:	Malta &	
	Ionian Isles	10 years 9 months
	Ceylon	5 years 11 months
Reason for Discharge:	Ophthalmia — all but blind	
Character:	Bad	
Trade or Occupation:	Miller	
Can Sign Name:	X his mark on discharge	
Height:	5' 5½"	
Hair Colour:	Brown	
Eyes:	Hazel	
Complexion:	Fresh	
Intends to Reside:	Fulham Middlesex	

SCANLAN Frederick, gunner and driver
RA 11th Battalion

Surname Variant	SCANLON
12 Aug 1856	Discharged the Service Woolwich 1/1d. per diem
1857	Pension paid 2nd West London Pension District
1857	2nd Plymouth Pension District
1861	2nd West London Pension District
15 Apr 1864	Arrived per *'Clara'* [2]
1881	Pension increased to 1/9d. per diem for service in the Enrolled Force
26 Apr 1881	Assigned Perth Town Lot 26
June 1881	Resigned it and received in lieu Perth Town Lot 77/E
15 Sept 1882	Charged with administering an overdose of opium to William Barr pensioner Verdict " Manslaughter against Frederick Scanlan."
Oct 1883	Application for Title to Perth Lot 77/E
1892	Died

Service and Personal Details:

Place of Birth:	St Georges Dublin	
Age on Attestation:	18 years 3 months	
Period of Service:	1832 — 1856	
Age on Discharge:	41 years 11 months	
Length of Service:	23 years 168 days	
Foreign Service:	Gibraltar	10 years
Reason for Discharge:	Chronic Rheumatism	
Character:	Very Good	
Trade or Occupation:	Clerk	
Can Sign Name:	Yes	
Height:	5' 8"	
Hair Colour:	Grey	
Eyes:	Blue	
Complexion:	Fresh	

SCANLON Stephen, private

	87th Foot
Previous Regiment	49th Foot
Surname Variant	SCANLAN
12 May 1857	Discharged the Service Chatham
	Pension paid Limerick
	1/- per diem
1857	Pension paid Jersey
29 Jan 1862	Arrived per *'Lincelles'*
1863	To Eastern Colonies from Perth West Australia
1875	W.O. correspondence with S.O.P. Limerick
1883	W.O. correspondence with S.O.P. Tralee

Service and Personal Details:

Place of Birth:	Limerick Co. Limerick	
Age on Attestation:	18 years	
Period of Service:	1835 — 1857	
Age on Discharge:	40 years 4 months	
Length of Service:	21 years 245 days	
Foreign Service:	Mauritius	6 years 11 months
East Indies	4 years 5 months	
Reason for Discharge:	Chronic Cough and Varicose Veins in left leg	
Character:	Very Good	
Trade or Occupation:	Labourer	
Can Sign Name:	X his mark on discharge	
Height:	5' 7¼"	
Hair Colour:	Dark Brown	
Eyes:	Grey	
Complexion:	Fresh	
Intends to Reside:	Limerick	

SCANNELL	John, private
	27th Foot
25 May 1852	Discharged the Service Dublin
29 June 1852	Admitted to Out–Pension
	Pension paid Paisley
	1/- per diem
10 Sept 1856	Arrived per *'Runnymede'*
1859	To South Australia from Western Australia
1860	Pension paid Adelaide
1975	South Australia

Service and Personal Details:

Place of Birth:	Newtown Co. Cork	
Age on Attestation:	20 years	
Period of Service:	1831 — 1852	
Age on Discharge:	41 years	
Length of Service:	21 years 72 days	
Foreign Service:	Cape of Good Hope	12 years 229 days
Reason for Discharge:	Chronic Catarrh and Worn Out	
Character:	Good	
Trade or Occupation:	Labourer	
Can Sign Name:	X his mark on discharge	
Height:	5' 10¼"	

Hair Colour:	Dark Brown
Eyes:	Grey
Complexion:	Fresh
Intends to Reside:	Paisley

SCOTT James, private

	16th Foot
14 Nov 1857	Discharged the Service Netley
5 Jan 1858	Admitted to Out-Pension
	Pension paid 1st Liverpool Pension District
	6d. per diem for 3 years
1862	Pension made permanent
1865	Pension paid 1st Dublin Pension District
22 Dec 1866	Arrived per *'Corona'*
1880	Died

Service and Personal Details:

Place of Birth:	? Sisbellow Co. Fermanagh	
Age on Attestation:	21 years 9 months	
Period of Service:	1844 — 1857	
Age on Discharge:	34 years 10 months	
Length of Service:	13 years 20 days	
Foreign Service:	Gibraltar	1 year 1 month
	Ionian Isles	4 years 4 months
	West Indies	3 years 4 months
	Canada	2 years 8 months
Reason for Discharge:	Extreme Varicose Veins in left leg	
Character:	Good	
Trade or Occupation:	Labourer	
Can Sign Name:	Yes	
Height:	5' 10¼"	
Hair Colour:	Dark	
Eyes:	Hazel	
Complexion:	Dark	
Intends to Reside:	Enniskillen Co. Fermanagh	

SCOTT John M, private

	Land Transport Corps
Campaign Served	Crimea
1876	Found — a Silver English Crimean Medal with clasp for Sebastopol with J.M. Scott No 1356 12 Battalion L.T.C incised on rim, also Turkish Crimean Medal [see 'page' 6613 and 6616 on Crimean Medal Roll CD ROM]
8 Apr 1862	Medal sent to him
1910	Attended Veteran's Dinner

SCULL James, gunner EIC [L/MIL/5/67]

	Madras Artillery
	Out Pension No 266
1847	Embarked UK per *'Wellesley'*
5 May 1847	Admitted to Out-pension
	Pension paid Bristol
	9d. per diem
19 Aug 1853	Arrived per *'Robert Small'*

27 Sept 1854	Appointed to Convict Establishment without sanction from Staff Officer Pensions
1856	Left colony per *'William Hammond'*
1856	Pension paid Madras

Service and Personal Details:

Where Born:	Lancashire
Trade or Occupation:	Servant
Where Enlisted:	London
Presidency:	Madras
Age on Discharge:	29 years
Length of Service:	6 years 9 months
Character:	Good
Reason for Discharge:	Unfit for further service. [Disabled in China]
Medal Entitlement:	China Campaign
Height:	5' 10"
Complexion:	Fair
Visage:	Long
Eye Colour:	Grey
Hair Colour:	Light

SEERY	John, private
	2nd/10th Foot
Previous Regiments	6th; 43th
31 Dec 1867	Discharged the Service Netley
	Pension paid Athlone Pension District
	10d. per diem
1868	Pension paid Longford
1873	Greenwich
19 Feb 1874	Arrived per *'Naval Brigade'*
1881	Pension increased to 1/-½d. per diem for 6 years service in the Enrolled Force
Aug 1881	Assigned Perth Railway Block Lot 150/V
29 Aug 1884	Granted Fee Simple Perth Railway Block Lot 150/V
1897	Stationed at Perth
29 Sept 1898	Died aged 69 — buried in Roman Catholic section of East Perth Pioneer Cemetery

Service and Personal Details:

Place of Birth:	Granard Co. Longford	
Age on Attestation:	17 years	
Period of Service:	1845 — 1867	
Age on Discharge:	39 years	
Length of Service:	20 years 191 days	
Foreign Service:	Cape of Good Hope	2 years 1 month
	East Indies	11 years 5 months
	New Zealand	2 years 6 months
Medal Entitlement:	Kaffir; Indian Mutiny	
Reason for Discharge:	Asthemia [sic] and worn out	
Character:	Very Good	
Trade or Occupation:	Labourer	
Can Sign Name:	Yes	

Height:	5' 10"	
Hair Colour:	Dark Brown	
Eyes:	Grey	
Complexion:	Sallow	
Intends to Reside:	Tashenny, 3 miles from Ballmahon Longford	
Married:	1861 Ellen Shaw Madras India	
Children:	John b. 1863 m. *c*1891 Alice Johnston Perth Thomas b. 1866 Bangalore India m. *c*1891 Mary Fennell Perth Mary b. 1868 m. *c*1900 Henry Edwards Perth Rose Mary b. *c*11872 m. *c*1903 Hugh Wilson Morton Boulder William Richard b. 1873 m. *c*1905 Cecilia Sweeney Perth Frances b. *c*1877 Perth m. *c*1897 Albert Duncuff Perth Joseph b. *c*1879 Perth Margaret b. *c*1881 Perth m. *c*1902 William Dillon Kalgoolie Ellen Mary b. *c*1884 Perth James Patrick b. *c*1886 Perth	
5th Feb 1861	At Madras Fort St George [N/2/42] John Seery aged 33 Bachelor, private HM 43rd Foot married by banns to Ellen Shaw aged 16 Spinster, daughter of Patrick Shaw	

SELFF

	William, private 52nd Foot	
22 Dec 1860	Discharged the Service Pension paid Gloucester 1/- per diem	
1863	Pension paid Bristol	
27 May 1863	Arrived per *'Clyde'*	
1876	Died aged 56	

Service and Personal Details:

Place of Birth:	Trowbridge Wiltshire	
Age on Attestation:	20 years	
Period of Service:	1839 — 1860	
Age on Discharge:	41 years	
Length of Service:	21 years 19 days	
Foreign Service:	West Indies	1 year 3 months
	North America	5 years 11 months
	East Indies	6 years 11 months
Medal Entitlement:	Indian Mutiny with clasp for Delhi	
Reason for Discharge:	Own Request having completed 21 years service	
Character:	Very Good	
Trade or Occupation:	Cordwainer	
Can Sign Name:	X his mark on discharge	

Height:	5' 6"
Hair Colour:	Light Brown
Eyes:	Grey
Complexion:	Fresh
Remarks:	Wounded by a bullet to the right cheek in the assault on Delhi
Intends to Reside:	Newport Monmouthshire

SEWARD

	Charles, private
	4th Foot
Surname Variant	SEAWARD
8 Aug 1848	Discharged the Service Chatham
	Pension paid Exeter
	1/- per diem
1849	Pension paid Salisbury
1850	Exeter
31 Aug 1853	Arrived per *'Phoebe Dunbar'*
Dec 1854	Pension paid South Australia
Jan 1855	Victoria
1875	Victoria
1875	Died Victoria

Service and Personal Details:

Place of Birth:	Withycombe Devon	
Age on Attestation:	21 years	
Period of Service:	1827 — 1848	
Age on Discharge:	42 years	
Length of Service:	21 years 24 days	
Foreign Service:	Portugal	1 year 3 months
	New South Wales	4 years 6 months
	East Indies	10 years 5 months
Reason for Discharge:	Worn out from long service in the East	
Character:	Very Good	
Trade or Occupation:	Wheelwright	
Can Sign Name:	Yes	
Height:	5' 7½	
Hair Colour:	Light Brown	
Eyes:	Grey	
Complexion:	Sallow	
Intends to Reside:	Exmouth Devon	

SHAPTER

	Thomas, private
	60th Foot
Surname Variant	SHAFTER; SHAPSTER
16 Feb 1864	Discharged the Service Winchester
	Pension paid 2nd North London Pension District
	1/- per diem
13 July 1867	Arrived per *'Norwood'* [2]
1869	To Adelaide from Perth West Australia

Service and Personal Details:

Place of Birth:	Mortlake Surrey
Age on Attestation:	20 years 7 months
Period of Service:	1842 — 1864

Age on Discharge:	41 years 10 months	
Length of Service:	21 years 95 days	
Foreign Service:	East Indies	11 years 141 days
Reason for Discharge:	Own Request having completed 21 years service	
Character:	Very Good	
Trade or Occupation:	Carpenter	
Can Sign Name:	Yes	
Height:	5' 7"	
Hair Colour:	Light	
Eyes:	Grey	
Complexion:	Fresh	
Intends to Reside:	Orchard Street Balls Pond Islington	

SHARKEY see — STARKEY Peter
41st Foot

SHAUGHNESSY Thomas, private
82nd Foot

Previous regiment	88th Foot	
24 Nov 1863	Discharged the Service Camp Colchester	
	Pension paid Athlone	
	1/- per diem	
1865	Pension paid 2nd Belfast Pension District	
1865	Pension paid Southampton	
13 July 1867	Arrived per *'Norwood'* [2]	
23 Dec 1872	Died	
Service and Personal Details:		
Place of Birth:	Shannon Bridge Roscommon	
Age on Attestation:	17 years 9 months	
Period of Service:	1842 — 1863	
Age on Discharge:	38 years 1 month	
Length of Service:	21 years 14 days	
Foreign Service:	Malta	1 year 1 month
	West Indies	3 years 4 months
	North America	1 year 1 month
	Crimea	2 years 3 months
	East Indies	5 years 7 months
Medal Entitlement:	Good Conduct with gratuity; Crimea with clasps; Turkish Crimea; Indian Mutiny	
Reason for Discharge:	Own Request having completed 21 years service	
Character:	Very Good	
Trade or Occupation:	Labourer	
Can Sign Name:	X his mark on discharge	
Height:	5' 7"	
Hair Colour:	Light Brown	
Eyes:	Blue	
Complexion:	Fair	
Intends to Reside:	Post Office Athlone Co. Roscommon	

SHAW William, private
2nd Foot Guards [Coldstream]

Surname Variant	STRAW

8 Mar 1853	Discharged the Service London	
	Pension paid Newcastle	
	7d. per diem	
11 Feb 1861	Arrived per *'Palmeston'*	
31 Mar 1864	Transferred to South Australia from Perth W.A.	
1874	Pension paid Adelaide South Australia	
April 1877	Admitted as In-Pensioner Chelsea	
9 Oct 1877	Died	
Service and Personal Details:		
Place of Birth:	Brancepeth Durham	
Age on Attestation:	18 years 10 months	
Period of Service:	1838 — 1853	
Age on Discharge:	33 years 10 months	
Length of Service:	14 years 353 days	
Foreign Service:	Canada	1 year 8 months
Reason for Discharge:	Fractured shoulder joint	
Character:	Good and efficient soldier	
Trade or Occupation:	Labourer	
Can Sign Name:	Yes	
Height:	5' 9½"	
Hair Colour:	Dark Brown	
Eyes:	Hazel	
Complexion:	Fresh	
Intends to Reside:	Durham	

SHAW	William, private [Trumpeter]	
	RA Depot Brigade	
15 Oct 1861	Discharged the Service Woolwich	
	Pension paid Brighton	
	8d. per diem	
15 Aug 1865	Arrived per *'Racehorse'*	
1867	Pension paid Melbourne	
Service and Personal Details:		
Place of Birth:	Woolwich Kent	
Age on Attestation:	13 years	
Period of Service:	1835 — 1861	
Age on Discharge:	39 years 8 months	
Length of Service:	21 years 199 days [after age of 18]	
Foreign Service:	New South Wales	4 years 9 months
	Canada	5 years 10 months
Reason for Discharge:	His having completed 21 years service	
Character:	Indifferent	
Trade or Occupation:	none annotated	
Can Sign Name:	Yes	
Height:	5' 8"	
Hair Colour:	Light Brown	
Eyes:	Grey	
Complexion:	Fair	

SHEA	Patrick, private [drummer]
	77th Foot

14 May 1850	Discharged the Service Chatham	
1850	Pension paid Jersey	
	1/- per diem	
1851	Residing 6 Poonah Rd St Helier Jersey	
7 Feb 1853	Arrived per *'Dudbrook'*	
	Assigned land North Fremantle	
1855	Charged with military offence	
Dec 1862	Patrick Shea is suffering from disease of the heart and unable to pursue any laborious occupation.	
1873	Died	
Service and Personal Details:		
Place of Birth:	Ennis Co. Clare	
Age on Attestation:	14 years	
Period of Service:	1823 — 1850	
Age on Discharge:	40 years 3 months	
Length of Service:	21 years 47 days	
Foreign Service:	West Indies	10 years 3 months
	Mediterranean	2 months
Reason for Discharge:	Chronic Rheumatism	
Character:	Very Bad	
Trade or Occupation:	Labourer	
Can Sign Name:	Yes	
Height:	5' 5"	
Hair Colour:	Brown	
Eyes:	Grey	
Complexion:	Sallow	
Distinguishing Marks:	Marks of Corporal Punishment	
Intends to Reside:	Hull Yorkshire but decided on Jersey	

SHEA	Timothy, private	
	37th Foot	
Surname Variants	SHEE; SHAY	
12 Sept 1854	Discharged the Service Chatham	
	Pension paid Tralee	
	6d. per diem for 3 years	
1856	Refused further pension	
10 July 1857	Arrived per *'Clara'* [1]	
Dec 1857	W.O. correspondence with S.O.P Freemantle [sic] regarding pension	
1875	Request for Deferred Pension refused	
Apr 1878	W.O. Correspondence to Colonial Secretary Western Australia	
1881	a Timothy Shea died aged 60	
Service and Personal Details:		
Place of Birth:	Cahirciveen Co. Kerry	
Age on Attestation:	17 years 8 months	
Period of Service:	1842 — 1854	
Age on Discharge:	30 years	
Length of Service:	11 years 124 days - 12 years 3 months reckoned [underage service of 6 months]	
Foreign Service:	Ceylon	6 years 10 months

Reason for Discharge:	Tumour of the upper jawbone of several years standing causing great enlargement of the bones of the face
Character:	Latterly Indifferent amended to Good
Trade or Occupation:	Labourer
Can Sign Name:	X his mark on discharge
Height:	5' 6½"
Hair Colour:	Dark Brown
Eyes:	Hazel
Complexion:	Fresh
Intends to Reside:	Chatham

SHEEHAN

	Patrick, private
	53rd Foot
Surname Variant	SHEENAN
17 May 1870	Discharged the Service
	Pension paid Chatham
	1/- per diem
1870	Pension paid Shrewsbury
1871	Cork
1871	Limerick
1873	Greenwich
19 Feb 1874	Arrived per *'Naval Brigade'*
1881	Pension increased to 1/2½d. per diem for service in the Enrolled Force
1881	Pension paid New Zealand

Service and Personal Details:

Place of Birth:	Ardagh Newcastle Co. Limerick	
Age on Attestation:	19 years	
Period of Service:	1849 — 1870	
Age on Discharge:	40 years	
Length of Service:	upwards of 21 years	
Foreign Service:	East Indies	2 years 5 months
	North America	3 years 2 months
	West Indies	5 months
Medal Entitlement:	Indian Mutiny with clasp for Lucknow	
Reason for Discharge:	Claimed on the termination of second period of 'Limited Engagement'	
Character:	Very Good	
Trade or Occupation:	Labourer	
Can Sign Name:	Yes	
Height:	5' 8"	
Hair Colour:	Dark Brown	
Eyes:	Grey	
Complexion:	Fresh	
Intends to Reside:	Shrewsbury	

SHEIL

	Michael, private
	61st Foot
Surname Variants	SHIEL; SHIELS; SHEILES; SHIRT
10 Oct 1848	Discharged the Service Chatham

	Pension paid Chatham
	1/- per diem
1849	Pension paid Limerick
31 Aug 1853	Arrived per *'Phoebe Dunbar'*
19 Feb 1854	Died

Service and Personal Details:

Place of Birth:	Kiltown Roscommon	
Age on Attestation:	20 years	
Period of Service:	1827 — 1848	
Age on Discharge:	41 years 8 months	
Length of Service:	21 years 242 days	
Foreign Service:	Ceylon	11 years 4 months
Reason for Discharge:	Chronic Rheumatism and Dyspnoea	
Character:	Good	
Trade or Occupation:	Servant	
Can Sign Name:	X his mark on discharge	
Height:	5' 10½	
Hair Colour:	Brown	
Eyes:	Grey	
Complexion:	Fresh	

SHEMELS Benjamin, Corporal [drummer]
73rd Foot

Surname Variants	SHEMEL; SHEMELD; SHEMELDS; SEMELDS
29 Aug 1871	Discharged the Service
	Pension paid Sheffield
	1/-½d. per diem
1873	Pension paid Greenwich
19 Feb 1874	Arrived per *'Naval Brigade'*
1878	Residing Fremantle area
1881	Assigned Cockburn Sound Loc 229
1881	Pension increased to 1/3d. per diem for service in the Enrolled Force
1884	Granted Cockburn Sound Loc 229 Willagee Swamp
June 1897	Residing Fremantle
Feb 1900	Attended fete at Oval
1907	Invited to Veteran's dinner at Esplanade Hotel
1909	Died

Service and Personal Details:

Place of Birth:	Enniskillen Co. Fermanagh	
Age on Attestation:	14 years	
Period of Service:	1846 — 1870	
Age on Discharge:	39 years 3 months	
Length of Service:	21 years 14 days	
Foreign Service:	Cape of Good Hope	4 years 10 months
	East Indies	3 years 5 months
	China	10 months
Medal Entitlement:	Indian Mutiny; ?Long Service and Good Conduct	
Reason for Discharge:	Own Request after 21 years service	
Character:	Very Good for the last 9 years	

Trade or Occupation: None
Can Sign Name: Yes

Height: 6'
Hair Colour: Brown
Eyes: Grey
Complexion: Fair
Distinguishing Marks: Slightly pockmarked
Intends to Reside: Sheffield

Married: *c*1870 Maria Creamer nee Gilthorpe
Children: Elizabeth Creamer b. *c*1863 Canada [stepdaughter]
m. *c*1885 Godfrey Dixon Fremantle
Mary Creamer b. *c*1865 [stepdaughter]
m. *c*1885 John McNeece Fremantle

SHEPPARD Henry, private
35th Foot

Surname Variants SHEPARD; SHEPERD; SHEPPERD; SHIPARD
20 Apr 1852 Discharged the Service Dublin
8 June 1852 Admitted to Our-Pension
Pension paid 1st Manchester Pension District
1/- per diem
1852 Pension paid Dublin
2 Apr 1856 Arrived per *'William Hammond'*
1863 Stationed Perth District
1864 ptve H Sheppard Pensioner Force at Perth contributed to the Greenough Fire Relief Fund
no date Assigned Perth Military Pensioner Lot 113
Jan 1865 Application for Title to Perth Lot 113
11 Jan 1870 Died

Service and Personal Details:
Place of Birth: St Johns London Middlesex
Age on Attestation: 18 years 11 months
Period of Service: 1831 — 1852
Age on Discharge: 40 years 1 month
Length of Service: 21 years 64 days
Foreign Service: Mauritius 10 years 328 days
Reason for Discharge: Chronic Catarrh and Asthma

Character: Good
Trade or Occupation: Labourer
Can Sign Name: Yes

Height: 5' 9½"
Hair Colour: Light Brown
Eyes: Grey
Complexion: Fair

SHEPPARD William, gunner and driver
RA 12th Battalion

Surname Variant SHIPHARD
12 Feb 1856 Discharged the Service Woolwich
Pension paid Woolwich

	8d. per diem
10 Sept 1856	Arrived per *'Runnymede'*
1857	To South Australia from Western Australia
1857	Pension paid Victoria
1888	Correspondence with W.O.

Service and Personal Details:

Place of Birth:	Coventry Warwickshire
Age on Attestation:	18 years
Period of Service:	1852 — 1856
Age on Discharge:	20 years 11 months
Length of Service:	3 years 320 days
Foreign Service:	'Expedition to the East' 1 year 2 months
Medal Entitlement:	Crimea with clasp
Reason for Discharge:	Wounded in right leg by shell fragment
Character:	Very Good
Trade or Occupation:	Labourer
Can Sign Name:	X his mark on discharge
Height:	5' 8"
Hair Colour:	Dark
Eyes:	Grey
Complexion:	Fresh

SHERIDAN Bernard, private

	47th Foot
Previous Regiment	34th Foot
Surname Variants	SHEIRDAN; SHERDIN; SHERIDION
17 May 1853	Discharged the Service Limerick
12 July 1853	Admitted to Out-Pension
	Pension paid Ireland
	1/- per diem
10 July 1857	Arrived per *'Clara'* [1]
1866	Stationed Rottnest
1866	Advertised for information regarding his 13 year old son Bernard
8 May 1871	Resident Office Fremantle - Request for admission to Poor Relief, Bernard Sheridan, an old soldier at 1/- per diem.
1878	Pensioner Sheridan admitted to Poor House
1883	Died aged 75

Service and Personal Details:

Place of Birth:	Balinrobe Co. Mayo
Age on Attestation:	18 years
Period of Service:	1831 — 1853
Age on Discharge:	39 years 7 months
Length of Service:	21 years 207 days
Foreign Service:	Mediterranean 6 years 5 months
	West Indies 5 months
Reason for Discharge:	Chronic Rheumatism and impaired health
Character:	Good and Efficient soldier
Trade or Occupation:	Labourer
Can Sign Name:	X his mark on discharge

Height:	5' 6¼"
Hair Colour:	Sandy
Eyes:	Hazel
Complexion:	Fresh
Intends to Reside:	Ballinrobe

SHIELDS	Lesley, Colour Serjeant RA 7th Battalion
11 Jan 1848	Discharged the Service Woolwich Pension paid Ballymena 1/10d. per diem
Oct 1848	Pension increased to 2/- per diem
1854	Pension paid Turkey
1855	Chatham
1855	2nd West London
10 Sept 1856	Arrived per *'Runnymede'*
1863	Pension paid Sydney New South Wales

Service and Personal Details:

Place of Birth:	Drumrose Londonderry	
Age on Attestation:	19 years	
Period of Service:	1826 — 1848	
Age on Discharge:	40 years 5 months	
Length of Service:	21 years 195 days	
Foreign Service:	Corfu	6 years 11 months
	Newfoundland	3 years 3 months
Reason for Discharge:	Chronic Rheumatism and Stricture of Urethra	
Character:	Exemplary	
Trade or Occupation:	Labourer	
Can Sign Name:	Yes	
Height:	5' 10"	
Hair Colour:	Light Brown	
Eyes:	Blue	
Complexion:	Fair	

SHINNERS	Daniel, private EIC 1st Bengal European Fusiliers
also known as	**GLEESON**
Surname Variants	SHINNARS; SKINNERS; SKINNER Pension No 358
Aug 1854	Admitted to Out-pension Pension paid Kilkenny 9d. per diem
1856	Pension paid Birr
8 June 1858	Arrived per *'Lord Raglan'*
1864	ptve Shinners Pensioner Force at Kojonup contributed to the Greenough Fire Relief Fund
21 Aug 1875	Grant Application Kojonup Lot P10
Aug 1877	Died suddenly in hospital aged 58
1877	Enrolled Pensioner, Private Daniel Shinners at 9d per day from the EIC, died at Perth of liver complaint leaving a family of 6 children, who are presently living in the Mt. Eliza Barracks.

His wife, whom he left at Kojonup, while he came to serve at Perth for a time on the Enrolled Force with the view of raising a little money, ran off 2 or 3 years go with a low ticket
of leave man, named Ford, with whom she is now living in Albany — previously she had always been a good and respectable character. Shinners Cottage and land at Kojonup are made over to Mr. H. I. Parker in payment of debts. Pensioner David Shinners was of good character and has served about 16 years in the Enrolled Force. The eldest daughter will probably obtain service in some family.
The second son — for the oldest of the family [named Michael] is employed shepherding up country and is apprenticed to Mr. Randall — I would recommend that the third son, John Thomas, be employed in the Telegraph Office.
I enclose a specimen of his hand-writing - he has been two years at the Roman Catholic School in Perth and was previously for 3 years at school in Kojonup.
The youngest boy and 2 youngest girls I would earnestly recommend for admission into the Roman Catholic Orphanage. They have been attending the Roman Catholic School for some time past.

Service and Personal Details:	
Date of Birth:	1819
Place of Birth:	Mullingar Ireland
Trade or Occupation:	Tailor
Presidency:	Bengal
Age on Discharge:	36 years
Length of Service:	15 years 8 months
Character:	Good
Reason for Discharge:	Hepatitis and enlarged liver
Height:	5' 6"
Complexion:	Fresh
Eye Colour:	Blue
Hair Colour:	Brown
Intends to Reside:	Templemore Ireland

SHIRT see — SHIELS Michael
1st Foot

SHORE William Henry, private
2nd Dragoons

Surname Variant	SHONE
8 May 1848	Discharged the Service Athlone
11 July 1848	Admitted to Our-Pension
	Pension paid Wales East Pension District
	6d. per diem for ?3years [to 30/9/1851]
25 Oct 1850	Arrived per *'Hashemy'*

1853	a William Shore charged with assaulting Ephrim Due [sic]
Service and Personal Details:	
Place of Birth:	Mid Calder Midlothian
Age on Attestation:	21 years
Period of Service:	1838 — 1848
Age on Discharge:	31 years
Length of Service:	10 years 40 days
Reason for Discharge:	Chronic difficulty breathing
Character:	Good
Trade or Occupation:	Farrier
Can Sign Name:	Yes
Height:	6' 3½"
Hair Colour:	Brown
Eyes:	Blue
Complexion:	Dark

SIBBALD

	William, private 72nd Foot
3 Dec 1861	Discharged the Service Chatham Pension paid 2nd Glasgow Pension District 10d. per diem
1862	Pension paid Liverpool
1862	2nd Glasgow Pension District
31 Dec 1862	Arrived per *'York'*
1864	Pension paid Sydney
1879	Victoria
Service and Personal Details:	
Place of Birth:	Blantyre Hamilton Lanarkshire
Age on Attestation:	18 years
Period of Service:	1843 — 1861
Age on Discharge:	35 years 6 months
Length of Service:	17 years 238 days — former service of 16 years 77 days in the 72nd Highlanders allowed to reckon
Foreign Service:	Gibraltar 3 years 2 months West Indies 4 months Crimea 1 year East Indies 2 years
Medal Entitlement:	Crimea; India Mutiny
Reason for Discharge:	Chronic Bronchitis and worn out
Character:	Very Good
Trade or Occupation:	Labourer
Can Sign Name:	Yes
Height:	5' 6½"
Hair Colour:	Black
Eyes:	Blue
Complexion:	Swarthy
Remarks:	Wounded in the back of the head by shell
fragment in Crimea	
Intends to Reside:	Blantyre nr. Glasgow

SIGSTON	Charles Vere [Vear], private 16th Lancers
Surname Variants	STIGSONS; SIGATON; LEGSTON; SIGSTAN
1 June 1854	Discharged the Service Dublin
12 June 1854	Discharge approved
27 June 1854	Admitted to Out-Pension Pension paid 1st Portsmouth Pension District 9d. per diem for 3 years conditional
1855	Pension paid North London pension District
1859	Pension made permanent
29 Jan 1862	Arrived per *'Lincelles'*
1864	ptve C V Legston [sic] Pensioner Force at Fremantle District contributed to the Greenough Fire Relief Fund
1874	Pension paid Western Australia
1874	Pension increased to 11d. per diem
1881	Assigned North Fremantle Lot P51 initially allocated to Reddin
9 Sept 1883	Died aged 72
Service and Personal Details:	
Place of Birth:	Clewer Windsor Berkshire
Age on Attestation:	21 years 11 months
Period of Service:	1838 — 1854
Age on Discharge:	38 years 3 months
Length of Service:	16 years 150 days
Foreign Service:	East Indies 7 years 9 months
Medal Entitlement:	Sutlej; In action at Aliwal and Sobroan
Reason for Discharge:	Unfit for further service
Character:	Good and efficient soldier
Trade or Occupation:	Groom
Can Sign Name:	Yes
Height:	5' 7¾"
Hair Colour:	Dark Brown
Eyes:	Hazel
Complexion:	Dark
Intends to Reside:	London
Married: London, England	*c*1833 Elizabeth Hanwell Saint Mary le bone,
Children:	William Henry b. *c*1835 Mary-le-bone Middlesex m. *c*1868 Mary Goodgame Hindmarsh [All Saints Church — South Australia] John Thomas b. *c*1837 d. *c*1839
SIMCROX	Philip, private 90th Foot
Surname Variants	SIMCROIX; SIMCOX; SINCOX; St CROIX; LENCROIX
5 Feb 1856	Discharged the Service Chatham Pension paid Jersey 9d. per diem

1862	Pension paid Bermuda	
15 Feb 1863	Arrived per *'Merchantman'* [1]	
1864	To Adelaide from Perth Western Australia	
1864	Pension paid Melbourne	
1879	Victoria	
1909	W.O. correspondence regarding 'Patriot Fund'	
Service and Personal Details:		
Place of Birth:	St Peter's St Helier Jersey	
Age on Attestation:	24 years	
Period of Service:	1854 — 1855	
Age on Discharge:	25 years 3 months	
Length of Service:	1 year 96 days	
Foreign Service:	Malta	3 months
	Crimea	6 months
Medal Entitlement:	Crimea with clasp	
Reason for Discharge:	Gunshot wound to the back	
Character:	Good	
Trade or Occupation:	Carpenter	
Can Sign Name:	Yes	
Height:	5' 6"	
Hair Colour:	Dark Brown	
Eyes:	Hazel	
Complexion:	Dark	
Intends to Reside:	Jersey	

SIMS	John, private 76th Foot	
Surname Variant	SIMMS	
12 May 1860	Discharged the Service Belfast	
28 May 1860	Admitted to Out-Pension Pension paid Trowbridge 1/- per diem	
1861	Residing Ogbourne St Andrews	
1862	Pension paid Bermuda	
15 Feb 1863	Arrived per *'Merchantman'* [1]	
1864	ptve J Sims Pensioner Force at Fremantle District contributed to the Greenough Fire Relief Fund	
1864	To South Australia from Fremantle	
1883	Died South Australia	
1885	W.O. correspondence — nephew asking for information	
Service and Personal Details:		
Place of Birth:	Ogbourne St Andrew Malborough Wiltshire	
Age on Attestation:	17 years	
Period of Service:	1838 — 1860	
Age on Discharge:	39 years 11 months	
Length of Service:	21 years 55 days	
Foreign Service:	West Indies	3 months
	Bermuda	4 months
	North America	5 years 4 months
	Ionian isles	2 years 11 months

	Malta 2 years 1 months
Medal Entitlement:	Good Conduct with gratuity
Reason for Discharge:	Own Request having completed 21 years service
Character:	Very Good
Trade or Occupation:	Labourer
Can Sign Name:	X his mark on discharge
Height:	5' 6¼"
Hair Colour:	Light Brown
Eyes:	Hazel
Complexion:	Fresh
Intends to Reside:	Marlborough Wiltshire
Married:	Charlotte b. circa 1834 Washington America [see 1861 Census]

SIMMS	George, private
	73rd Foot
8 June 1863	Discharged to Pension Aldershot
23 June 1863	Admitted to Out-Pension
	1/- per diem
Feb 1900	Attended fete at Fremantle Oval [from the newspaper article[Trove] it is unclear as to whether George Simms served in a Naval Brigade or arrived per the '*Naval Brigade*']

SIMPSON	James, private
	13th Foot
20 May 1847	Discharged the Service Dublin
13 July 1847	Admitted to Out–Pension Pension paid South London
1/- per diem	
1848	Pension paid Portsmouth
	"Bandsman onboard the 'Prince Regent'"
14 Aug 1854	Arrived per *'Ramillies'*
1854	Pension paid Western Australia
1855	To Adelaide from Perth Western Australia
1856	Pension paid Victoria
1860	London
1875	Admitted to In-Pension
7 Nov 1877	Died

Service and Personal Details:	
Place of Birth:	Battersea London
Age on Attestation:	18 years
Period of Service:	1826 — 1847
Age on Discharge:	39 years 4 months
Length of Service:	21 years 119 days
Foreign Service:	East Indies 17 years
Medal Entitlement:	3 medals Storming of Ghuznee, General Action of Jellalabad and recapture of Cabool
Reason for Discharge:	Constitution completely broken down from age and Repeated Fevers
Character:	Very Good

Trade or Occupation:	Labourer
Can Sign Name:	X his mark on discharge
Height:	5' 6"
Hair Colour:	Light Brown
Eyes:	Grey
Complexion:	Dark

SIMPSON William, private
92nd Foot

12 May 1848	Discharged the Service Limerick
11 July 1848	Admitted to Out-Pension
	Pension paid 2nd Edinburgh Pension District
	1/- per diem
31 Aug 1853	Arrived per *'Phoebe Dunbar'*
1856	To South Australia from Western Australia
	" £13/17/10 passage money to be paid"
3 Nov 1858	Died

Service and Personal Details:

Place of Birth:	Dunfermline Fife	
Age on Attestation:	17 years	
Period of Service:	1826 — 1848	
Age on Discharge:	39 years 2 months	
Length of Service:	21 years 56 days	
Foreign Service:	Gibraltar	1 year 11 months
	Malta	5 years 2 months
	West Indies	2 years 10 months
Reason for Discharge:	Worn out from length of service	
Character:	Good	
Trade or Occupation:	Weaver	
Can Sign Name:	Yes on Discharge	
Height:	5' 9"	
Hair Colour:	Brown	
Eyes:	Hazel	
Complexion:	Dark	

SINCLAIR David, private [ADM157/19/475 Folios 475-476]
RM

Discharged the Service 1851	Pension paid Edinburgh
	£15/4/- per annum
18 Oct 1851	Arrived per *'Minden'*
1856	To South Australia from Western Australia

Service and Personal Details:

Place of Birth:	Old Greyfriars Edinburgh
Age on Attestation:	18years
Marine Division:	Chatham
Period of Service:	1827 — 1848
Length of Service:	21 years 12 days
Reason for Discharge:	Length of Service
Can Sign Name:	Yes
Trade or Occupation:	Blacksmith

Height:	5' 6"
Hair Colour:	Brown
Eyes:	Grey
Complexion:	Fair

SKILLEN John, private
5th Foot

Surname Variants	SKILLIN; SKILLING	
12 Feb 1847	Discharged the Service Chatham Pension paid 1st Manchester Pension District 1/- per diem	
1847	Pension paid Armagh	
1848	Belfast	
1850	Pension paid 1st Manchester Pension District	
1 June 1850	Arrived per *'Scindian'*	
1850	Appointed to Convict establishment	
1851	Employed as Night Warder Fremantle	
1851	According to newspaper report [Trove] — Discharged the Service for alleged drunkenness and ill-usage of wife	
Feb 1851	Died committed suicide	
Service and Personal Details:		
Place of Birth:	Newry Co Down	
Age on Attestation:	18 years	
Period of Service:	1824 — 1846	
Age on Discharge:	41 years or 40 years 2 months	
Length of Service:	21 years 249 days	
Foreign Service:	West Indies	1 year 2 months
	Gibraltar	3 years 11 months
	Malta	2 years 5 months
	Ionian Isles	5 years
Reason for Discharge:	Unfit for further service	
Character:	Good	
Trade or Occupation:	Labourer	
Can Sign Name:	Yes	
Height:	5' 10"	
Hair Colour:	Black	
Eyes:	Blue	
Complexion:	Dark	
Intends to Reside:	Armagh	

SLATTERY John, private
48th Foot

Surname Variant	SLATER
7 Oct 1861	Discharged the Service Cork
29 Oct 1861	Admitted to Out-Pension Pension paid 1st Belfast Pension District 11½d per diem
1862	Pension paid Bermuda
15 Feb 1863	Arrived per *'Merchantman'* [1]
1864	ptve J Slattery Pensioner Force at Fremantle contributed to the Greenough Fire Relief Fund

1865	Pension paid South Australia from Fremantle	
Service and Personal Details:		
Place of Birth:	Roscea Co. Tipperary	
Age on Attestation:	18 years	
Period of Service:	1839 — 1861	
Age on Discharge:	40 years	
Length of Service:	21 years 342 days	
Foreign Service:	Gibraltar	4 years 7 months
	West Indies	3 years 1 month
	Ionian Isles	3 years 4 months
	Crimea	1 year 2 months
	East Indies	2 years 7 months
Medal Entitlement:	Crimea with clasp; Turkish Crimean	
Reason for Discharge:	Own Request having completed 21 years service	
Character:	Good	
Trade or Occupation:	Labourer	
Can Sign Name:	X his mark on discharge	
Height:	5' 7½"	
Hair Colour:	Grey	
Eyes:	Blue	
Complexion:	Sallow	
Remarks:	Slightly wounded in the trenches	
Intends to Reside:	Belfast	

SLAVERY	see — LAVERY John 48th Foot

SLAVIN	James, private 34th Foot	
Previous Regiment	25th Foot	
Surname Variant	SLAVEN	
29 July 1856	Discharged the Service Chatham Pension paid Omagh 8d. per diem	
1857	Pension paid Birr	
1862	Bermuda	
15 Feb 1863	Arrived per *'Merchantman'* [1]	
May 1874	Pension increased to 1/1d. per diem	
by 1874	Granted Greenough Locs 29 and 30 According to Obituary — served in Police Force	
Dec 1916	Died	
Service and Personal Details:		
Place of Birth:	Dromore Co. Tyrone	
Age on Attestation:	17 years	
Period of Service:	1853 — 1856	
Age on Discharge:	20 years 1 month	
Length of Service:	2 years 125 days	
Foreign Service:	Crimea	1 year 3 months
Medal Entitlement:	Crimea	
Reason for Discharge:	Wounded severely in the right hand by shell at the storming of the Redan	
Character:	Good	

Trade or Occupation:	Labourer
Can Sign Name:	Yes
Height:	5' 5½"
Hair Colour:	Light Brown
Eyes:	Grey
Complexion:	Fair
Intends to Reside:	Dromore Co. Tyrone

SLY

	Robert, private
	14th Foot
19 Oct 1853	Discharged the Service Dublin
13 Nov 1853	Admitted to Out-Pension
	Pension paid Carlow
	1/- per diem
2 Apr 1856	Arrived per *'William Hammond'*
July 1856	£8/14/6 balance due on landing at colony which was misappropriated by Capt Foss
Jan 1857	Contributed 1/- to the Florence Nightingale Fund
Dec 1857	Assigned York Pensioner Lot P16
1860	Applied for Title York Lot 265 at £1/0/0 per acre
1864	ptve R Sly Pensioner Force at York contributed to the Greenough Fire Relief Fund
Dec 1865	Purchased York Lot 123 for £5/0/0
Mar 1867	Application for Title to P16 at York
1873	Pension increased to 1/3d. per diem for 15 years 11 months service in the Western Australian Enrolled Force
1875	a Robert Sly died

Service and Personal Details:

Place of Birth:	Old Laughlin Carlow	
Age on Attestation:	20 years	
Period of Service:	1832 — 1853	
Age on Discharge:	40 years 11 months	
Length of Service:	20 years 344 days	
Foreign Service:	West Indies	5 years 1 month
	North America	6 years 2 months
Reason for Discharge:	Impaired Constitution from service and climate	
Character:	Indifferent	
Trade or Occupation:	Labourer	
Can Sign Name:	X his mark on discharge	
Height:	5' 8"	
Hair Colour:	Auburn	
Eyes:	Hazel	
Complexion:	Freckled	
Intends to Reside:	Carlow Co. Carlow	

SMALL

	Hugh, private
	61st Foot
Previous Regiment	81st Foot
10 May 1862	Discharged the Service Chatham
10 June 1862	Admitted to Out-Pension
	Pension paid Liverpool

	1/- per diem	
15 Apr 1864	Arrived per *'Clara'* [2]	
1867	To Adelaide from Fremantle	
Service and Personal Details:		
Place of Birth:	Drumlane Co. Cavan	
Age on Attestation:	18 years	
Period of Service:	1842— 1862	
Age on Discharge:	37 years 10 or 11 months	
Length of Service:	19 years 289 days	
Foreign Service:	East Indies	13 years 9 months
	Mauritius	1 year 2 months
Medal Entitlement:	Punjaub with 2 clasps; Indian Mutiny with clasp	
Reason for Discharge:	Chronic Rheumatism; pains around old wound; Tapeworm and congestion of liver and spleen	
Character:	Very Good	
Trade or Occupation:	Butcher	
Can Sign Name:	Yes	
Height:	5' 6"	
Hair Colour:	Dark Brown	
Eyes:	Grey	
Complexion:	Sallow	
Remarks:	Gazetted to share of Delhi prize money	
Intends to Reside:	Plymouth Devon	

SMITH	Charles, private	
	103rd Foot	
Previous Regiment	1st Bombay Fusiliers	
29 Aug 1865	Discharged the Service	
	Pension paid Falmouth	
	1/- per diem	
4 July 1866	Arrived per *'Belgravia'*	
1867	Appointed Schoolmaster at Rottnest	
1869	Pension paid East London	
1869	Ipswich	
1870	North London	
1870	Falmouth	
1873	Manchester	
Service and Personal Details:		
Place of Birth:	Falmouth Cornwall	
Age on Attestation:	20 years 1 month	
Period of Service:	1845 — 1865	
Age on Discharge:	none given	
Length of Service:	21 years 186 days [reckoned]	
Foreign Service:	India	20 years 323 days
Medal Entitlement:	Punjaub medal with 2 clasps	
Reason for Discharge:	Own Request after 21 years service	
Character:	Good	
Trade or Occupation:	Labourer	
Can Sign Name:	Yes	
Height:	5' 10½"	
Hair Colour:	Dark Brown	

Eyes:	Hazel
Complexion:	Fresh
Intends to Reside:	Falmouth Cornwall

SMITH	Hugh, private	
	6th Foot	
Previous Regiment	45th Foot	
27 Sept 1853	Discharged the Service Chatham	
	Pension paid Sheffield	
	7d. per diem	
24 May 1855	Arrived per *'Stag'*	
Jan 1857	Contributed 1/- to the Florence Nightingale Fund	
1857	Pension paid South Australia	
June 1857	Pension paid Melbourne Victoria	
1877	"Probably died in the far bush"	
Service and Personal Details:		
Place of Birth:	Leith Midlothian Scotland	
Age on Attestation:	18 years 6 months	
Period of Service:	1836 — 1853	
Age on Discharge:	36 years 3 months	
Length of Service:	17 years 75 days	
Foreign Service:	East Indies	5 years 11 months
	Cape of Good Hope	6 years 4 months
Medal Entitlement:	Served in Kaffir War 1846/47 and in 1850/53	
Reason for Discharge:	Varicose Veins left thigh	
Character:	Middling	
Trade or Occupation:	Labourer	
Can Sign Name:	Yes	
Height:	5' 7½"	
Hair Colour:	Brown	
Eyes:	Blue	
Complexion:	Fresh	
Intends to Reside:	Sheffield Yorkshire	

SMITH	Isaac, private
	12th Foot
15 June 1858	Discharged the Service Chatham
	Pension paid 1st Belfast Pension District
	1/-½d. per diem
1862	Pension paid 2nd Liverpool Pension District
15 Apr 1864	Arrived per *'Clara'* [2]
	Originally allocated Perth Town Lot 32/H, but resigned it by permission and received in lieu Perth Town Lot 80/E Claisebrook
1878	Pension increased to 1/6d. per diem for service in the Enrolled Force
July 1881	Assigned Perth Town Lot 80/E Claisebrook
July 1883	Application for Title to Perth Town Lot 80/E
10 Feb 1884	Granted Fee Simple for Perth Pensioner Lot 80/E at Claisebrook

1892	Died aged 81 – buried East Perth Cemetery Enquiry by Ellen Smith re right to claim grant of land due to her late husband Isaac Smith, late 12th Foot and Pensioner Guard.

Service and Personal Details:

Place of Birth:	Wickham Market Suffolk
Age on Attestation:	19 years
Period of Service:	1836 — 1858
Age on Discharge:	41 years 4 months
Length of Service:	21 years 333 days
Foreign Service:	Mauritius 10 years Australian Colonies 3 years 2 months
Medal Entitlement:	Good Conduct with gratuity
Reason for Discharge:	Chronic Rheumatism
Character:	Exemplary
Trade or Occupation:	Labourer
Can Sign Name:	X his mark on discharge
Height:	5' 6¼"
Hair Colour:	Brown
Eyes:	Brown
Intends to Reside:	Chatham Kent

SMITH

	James, private 4th Light Dragoons
15 Apr 1851	Discharged the Service Dublin
28 Apr 1851	Discharge approved
13 May 1851	Admitted to Out-Pension Pension paid South London 1/- per diem
2 Aug 1851	Arrived per *'William Jardine'*
1854	Pension paid Western Australia
1855	Melbourne
1860	Pension paid London
10 May 1867	Died London

Service and Personal Details:

Place of Birth:	Musselborough Midlothian
Age on Attestation:	20 years
Period of Service:	1826 — 1851
Age on Discharge:	44 years 3 months
Length of Service:	24 years 90 days
Foreign Service:	East Indies 14 years 9 months
Medal Entitlement:	Medal for service in Afghanistan and Scinde
Reason for Discharge:	Chronic Rheumatism and worn out
Character:	Good
Trade or Occupation:	Carpenter
Can Sign Name:	X his mark on discharge
Height:	5' 8¼"
Hair Colour:	Brown
Eyes:	Hazel
Complexion:	Fresh
Intends to Reside:	Bow London

SMITH	see — SMYTHE James 99th Foot
SMITH	James, private Royal Newfoundland Company
Previous Regiments	34th; 8th; 30th
27 Nov 1849	Discharged the Service Chatham Pension paid Preston 7d. per diem
19 Aug 1853	Arrived per '*Robert Small*'
1854	Pension paid Western Australia
Jan 1861	Assigned Pensioner Loc S8 at Newcastle
1861	Application for Title to Newcastle Loc S8 [pensioner James Smith's cottage located at 92 Stirling Terrace Toodyay is registered on the Heritage Council's database]
1864	To South Australia from Perth West Australia

the following entry may not necessarily refer to James Smith Newfoundland Company. [But as the pension amount quoted in the article is the same as that which James Smith is receiving per diem then it is possible that they are the same person]

25 July 1865	Fremantle Pensioner John Smith from *** at 7d a day, sold his allotment at Newcastle to Mr. Monger in August 1862 for £2 [pounds]. Didn't get on with his wife and requested transfer to Adelaide. [*note. He then went to England.]
1865	Pension paid Adelaide South Australia
1865	Pension paid London
1865	Preston
1868	Admitted to In-Pension
1873	Died Chelsea Hospital

Service and Personal Details:

Place of Birth:	Blackburn Lancashire	
Age on Attestation:	18 years 1 month	
Period of Service:	1835 — 1849	
Age on Discharge:	33 years	
Length of Service:	15 years 74 days	
Foreign Service:	Newfoundland	5 years 8 months
	British North America	7 years 4 months
Reason for Discharge:	Lost all front teeth in upper jaw	
Character:	Good	
Trade or Occupation:	Cotton Weaver	
Can Sign Name:	Yes	
Height:	5' 8"	
Hair Colour:	Brown	
Eyes:	Grey	
Complexion:	Sallow	
Intends to Reside:	Blackburn Lancashire	

SMITH	John, Corporal [drummer] 21st Foot
18 July 1856	Discharged the Service Birr Barracks

19 Aug 1856	Admitted to Out-Pension Pension paid Carlow 1/4d. per diem
1858	Pension paid Liverpool
19 Aug 1859	Arrived per *'Sultana'*
1863	Stationed Perth District
1864	a Corporal J Smith Pensioner Force at Perth contributed to the Greenough Fire Relief Fund
1866	Transferred to Adelaide from Perth West. Aust.
6 Nov 1870	Died

Service and Personal Details:

Place of Birth:	Yarmouth Norfolk	
Age on Attestation:	14 years	
Period of Service:	1831 — 1856	
Age on Discharge:	39 years	
Length of Service:	21 years and 1 day	
Foreign Service:	Van Diemans Land	7 years
	East Indies	8 years
Medal Entitlement:	Long Service and Good Conduct	
Reason for Discharge:	Having completed 21 years service and being appointed to the Permanent Staff of the Kildare Militia	
Character:	Very Good	
Trade or Occupation:	Labourer	
Can Sign Name:	blank [served as Corporal for 8+ years]	
Height:	5' 4"	
Hair Colour:	Brown	
Eyes:	Hazel	
Complexion:	Fresh	
Intends to Reside:	With the Kildare Militia	

SMITH John, Colour Serjeant
21st Foot

Sept 1833	Arrived per *'Jane'* with regiment 2/1¼d. per diem
14 July 1841	Discharged to pension Pension paid Western Australia
1842	Granted land near Hyde Park
1833	Employed by Commissariat as Barrack Serjeant
27 Feb 1862	Died aged 67 years

Service and Personal Details:

Place of Birth:	Cavan	
Age on Attestation:	17 years [appeared to be]	
Period of Service:	1812 — 1840	
Age on Discharge:	45 years	
Length of Service:	27 years 212 days	
Foreign Service:	Australia	6 years
Reason for Discharge:	At his Own Request for length of service and being considered worn out	
Character:	Most exemplary	

Trade or Occupation:	Labourer	
Can Sign Name:	Yes	
Height:	5' 6"	
Hair Colour:	Brown	
Eyes:	Grey	
Complexion:	Fair	
Remarks:	Stationed Fremantle Western Australia	
SMITH	John, private	
	Royal Canadian Rifles	
Previous Regiment	19th Foot	
16 July 1861	Discharged the Service Chatham	
	Pension paid Carlow	
	1/3d. per diem	
27 May 1863	Arrived per *'Clyde'*	
1867	Pension paid Carlow	
1868	Jersey	
1874	Pension paid 1st East London Pension District	
1875	Pension paid Auckland New Zealand	
Service and Personal Details:		
Place of Birth:	Clonaslee Mountmellick Queens County	
Age on Attestation:	18 years	
Period of Service:	1836 — 1861	
Age on Discharge:	43 years 5 months	
Length of Service:	25 years 82 days	
Foreign Service:	Mediterranean	5 years 3 months
	West Indies	2 years 4 months
	North America	13 years
Reason for Discharge:	Having completed 25 years service	
Character:	Very Good	
Trade or Occupation:	Labourer	
Can Sign Name:	X his mark on discharge	
Height:	5' 8"	
Hair Colour:	Light Brown	
Eyes:	Blue	
Complexion:	Fresh	
Intends to Reside:	England but decided on Carlow	
SMITH	Joseph, Serjeant	
	RA 17th Brigade	
Previous Regiment	HEIC Madras Artillery	
20 Nov 1866	Discharged the Service Woolwich	
	Pension paid 1st Portsmouth Pension District	
	1/9½d. per diem	
1867	Pension paid Jersey	
1867	Pension paid 1st East London Pension District	
1868	Pension paid Woolwich	
9 Jan 1868	Arrived per *'Hougoumont'*	
1869	Pension to be paid Wellington New Zealand	
1871	Pension paid New South Wales	
1876	Sydney	
1880	Sydney	

Service and Personal Details:	
Place of Birth:	St Barnabas Manchester Lancashire
Age on Attestation:	18 years 6 months
Period of Service:	1846 — 1866
Age on Discharge:	39 years
Length of Service:	22 years 167 days [including Boon]
Foreign Service:	East Indies 19 years 62 days
Medal Entitlement:	Long Service and Good Conduct; Burmah; Indian Mutiny
Reason for Discharge:	Having completed 21 years service
Character:	Exemplary
Trade or Occupation:	Carder
Can Sign Name:	Yes
Height:	5' 8"
Hair Colour:	Black
Eyes:	Hazel
Complexion:	Sallow
Distinguishing Marks:	Scar on left of sternum and scar behind left ear
Remarks:	Elected H.M. Pension Rules
Intends to Reside:	Woolwich

SMITH	Thomas, Serjeant 41st Foot
26 Feb 1861	Discharged the Service Aldershot
1861	Pension paid Jersey 2/- per diem
1862	Pension paid Bermuda
15 Feb 1863	Arrived per *'Merchantman'* [1]
1869	Application for Title Geraldton Sub Locs 40 and 41 at £1/0/0 per acre [also purchased Geraldton Locs 38 and 39]
11 Apr 1872	Died
1884	Mr. William Smith — Pensioners Grant of Land, which was not claimed by Sergeant Thomas Smith, is asked for by the son

Service and Personal Details:	
Place of Birth:	Lutterworth Leicestershire
Age on Attestation:	22 years
Period of Service:	1840 — 1861
Age on Discharge:	43 years 1 month
Length of Service:	21 years 31 days
Foreign Service:	India 3 years 2 months Jamaica & West Indies 3 years
Medal Entitlement:	Afghan
Reason for Discharge:	Own Request having served 21 years
Character:	Very Good
Trade or Occupation:	Stocking Weaver
Can Sign Name:	Yes
Height:	5' 5¼"

Hair Colour:	Brown
Eyes:	Dark
Complexion:	Sallow

SMITH	William, private
	50th Foot
22 June 1847	Discharged the Service Chatham
	Pension paid South London
1858	Deptford
	8d. per diem
19 Aug 1859	Arrived per *'Sultana'*
1866	Pension paid Melbourne
1873	In prison Melbourne
	"Pension to be suspended during imprisonment and on release reduced to 6d. per diem. The Staff Officer of the Western Australia District reported that this man was convicted of Bigamy at Perth W. A on 6/9/72 and was sentenced to six months hard labor [sic]" [WO letter G82093]
1874	Pension paid Calcutta

Service and Personal Details:

Place of Birth:	Merton Surrey	
Age on Enlistment:	19 years	
Period of Service:	1843 — 1847	
Age on Discharge:	25 [sic] years	
Length of Service:	3 years 131 days [reckoned]	
Foreign Service:	India	2 years 8 months
Medal Entitlement:	Sutlej with clasp	
Reason for Discharge:	Disability caused by sabre wound to the upper third of the right leg at Moodkee	
Character:	Good	
Trade or Occupation:	Labourer	
Can Sign Name:	X his mark on discharge	
Height:	5' 7½"	
Hair Colour:	Brown	
Eyes:	Grey/Brown	
Complexion:	Fair	
Married:	Elizabeth	
Children:	Elizabeth b. 1850 Maidstone Kent	

SMITH	William Pugh, Serjeant
	12th Foot
Sept 1863	Proceeding Regimental board
12 Jan 1864	Discharged the Service Western Australia
	1/6d per diem
Oct 1864	Purchased Perth Town Lot W15 for £6/-/-
	Pension paid Australia
1878	Employed by Convict Establishment
4 June 1878	Pension increased to 2/1d per diem for service in the Enrolled Force
24 Aug 1881	Assigned Perth Railway Block Lot 149/V

14 Dec 1883	Granted Fee Simple Perth Railway Block Lot 148/V
1883	Residing Beaufort Street
	According to Obituary — employed as Warder
Feb 1884	Died – buried East Perth Cemetery

Service and Personal Details:

Place of Birth:	Lambeth London Surrey
Age on Attestation:	16 years 11 months
Period of Service:	1843 — 1863
Age on Discharge:	37 years 1 month
Length of Service:	19 years 38 days
Foreign Service:	Australian Colonies 8 years 239 days
Reason for Discharge:	Discharged the Service due to disease of the Lumber Vertebrae, a severe contusion of the back from a fall from a cliff while engaging with the enemy at the Kaffir War in 1852. Was also speared through the left leg by the Kaffirs in 1852 He suffers much from pain and tenderness and it will always incapacitate him from earning
Character:	Very Good
Trade or Occupation:	Labourer
Can Sign Name:	Yes
Height:	5' 5½"
Hair Colour:	Brown
Eye Colour:	Hazel
Complexion:	Fresh
Intends to Reside:	Western Australia

SMYTHE James, private
99th Foot

Surname Variants	SYMTH; SMITH
10 Jan 1862	Discharged the Service Cork
4 Feb 1862	Admitted to Out-Pension
	Pension paid Athlone
	1/1d. per diem
27 May 1863	Arrived per *'Clyde'*
25 May 1874	Died aged 54

Service and Personal Details:

Place of Birth:	St John Athlone Roscommon
Age on Attestation:	19 years
Period of Service:	1838 — 1862
Age on Discharge:	42 years
Length of Service:	23 years 7 days
Foreign Service:	Australian Colonies 13 years 4 months
Reason for Discharge:	Own Request having completed 21 years service
Character:	Good
Trade or Occupation:	Labourer
Can Sign Name:	Yes
Height:	5' 8"
Hair Colour:	Dark Brown [turning Grey]

Eyes:	Grey	
Complexion:	Sallow	
Intends to Reside:	Athlone	
SNADEN	John Allen, Warrant Officer	
	Royal Engineers	
	Discharged the Service Dublin	
1886	Pension paid Western Australia	
May 1896	Died suddenly at Pingelly — Mr J Snaden	
	Public Works Supervisor at Beverley	
11 June 1896	Eastern District. York Sub-district. Beverley Station. Death and Estate of Snaden, Military Pensioner. died 1896 born Alla Scotland	
	Biography of John Allen Snaden located in Battye Library — MN1428; ACC450A	
Service and Personal Details:		
Place of Birth:	Alloa Clackmannan	
Age on Attestation:	18 years 9 months	
Period of Service:	1861 — 1886	
Age on Discharge:	43 years	
Length of Service:	25 years 60 days	
Foreign Service:	Malta	10 years 16 days
	Corfu	83 days
Medal Entitlement:	Long Service and Good Conduct with gratuity of £5	
Reason for Discharge:	Length of Service	
Character:	Very Good	
Trade or Occupation:	Miner	
Can Sign Name:	Yes	
Education:	Architectural School — 1866;	
	First Class Diploma in Civil Engineering from Royal College of Science Dublin and Gold medal in Applied Mechanic from Science and Arts Dept.	
Height:	5' 11"	
Hair Colour:	Dark Brown	
Eyes:	Hazel	
Complexion:	Fresh	
Distinguishing Marks:	Two scars near middle of back	
Intends to Reside:	The Cottage Erskine Place Alloa Scotland	
SNOWELL	Michael, private	
	62nd Foot	
4 May 1855	Discharged the Service Mullingar	
5 June 1855	Admitted to Out-Pension	
	Pension paid Carlow	
	7d. per diem	
10 Sept 1856	Arrived per *'Runnymede'*	
1857	To South Australia from Western Australia	
1858	Pension paid Victoria	
Service and Personal Details:		
Place of Birth:	Hacketstown Co. Carlow	
Age on Attestation:	19 years	

Period of Service:	1845 — 1855
Age on Discharge:	29 years 3 months
Length of Service:	10 years 73 days
Reason for Discharge:	Chronic Disease of the Lungs
Character:	Very Good
Trade or Occupation:	Servant
Can Sign Name:	Yes
Height:	5' 6¾"
Hair Colour:	Dark Brown
Eyes:	Grey
Complexion:	Fresh
Intends to Reside:	Carlow

SOUTHRON Thomas, private
7th Hussars

Previous Regiment	3rd Light Dragoons
Surname Variant	SOUTHERON; SOTHERON
14 July 1857	Discharged the Service Chatham Pension paid Newcastle 8d. per diem
8 June 1858	Arrived per *'Lord Raglan'*
1886	Admitted to Mt Eliza Invalid Depot
Feb 1887	Died of senile decay aged 70

Service and Personal Details:

Place of Birth:	St Nicholas Durham
Age on Attestation:	22 years
Period of Service:	1838 — 1857
Age on Discharge:	41 years 1 month
Length of Service:	19 years 31 days
Foreign Service:	East Indies 12 years 11 months
Medal Entitlement:	Cabool [sic]; Punjaub with clasps for Goojerat and Chillianwallah
Reason for Discharge:	Chronic Rheumatism
Character:	Good
Trade or Occupation:	Tailor
Can Sign Name:	Yes
Height:	5' 7½"
Hair Colour:	Light Brown
Eyes:	Grey
Complexion:	Light
Intends to Reside:	Durham

SPENCER John, Serjeant
Royal Sappers and Miners

17 Dec 1851	Arrived per *'Anna Robinson'*
14 Aug 1855	Discharged to pension Fremantle Pension paid Fremantle 1/7½d. per diem
1856	Pension paid Victoria
1857	Died Victoria

Service and Personal Details:

Place of Birth:	Cheltenham Gloucestershire	
Period of Service:	1833 — 1855	
Service to 5th Feb 1855:	22 years 1 month	
Age at 5th Feb 1855:	46 years 2 months	
Age on Discharge:	46 years 3 months	
Length of Service:	24 years 2 months	
Foreign Service:	Halifax N.S.	7 years 2 months
	Mauritius	2 years 1 month
	Western Australia	3 years 2 months
Reason for Discharge:	Disease of the Chest; Bronchitis and Emphysema	
Character:	Apart from the three incidences whilst he was serving as private, his conduct has been exemplary	
Trade or Occupation:	Carpenter	
Can Sign Name:	Yes	
Height:	5' 9"	
Hair Colour:	Dark Brown	
Eye Colour:	Blue	
Complexion:	Pale	
Remarks:	4 children by 1855	
Intended Residence:	To reside at Fremantle Western Australia	

SPRANKLIN G

	James, private	
	91st Foot	
Previous Regiment	90th Foot	
Surname Variant	SPRANKLIN	
23 Oct 1852	Discharged the Service Enniskillen	
29 Nov 1852	Discharge approved	
14 Dec 1852	Admitted to Out-Pension	
	Pension paid Chatham	
	1/- per diem	
1852	Pension paid Salisbury	
1853	Portsmouth	
14 Aug 1854	Arrived per *'Ramillies'*	
1856	Pension paid Chatham	
1856	Pension increased to 1/2d. per diem	
1856	Pension paid Tralee	
1857	Pension increased to 1/6d. per diem	
1861	Pension paid Salisbury	
1867	a James Spranklin died aged 57	

Service and Personal Details:

Place of Birth:	Wareham Dorset	
Age on Attestation:	18 years 6 months	
Period of Service:	1831 — 1852	
Age on Discharge:	39 years 7 months	
Length of Service:	21 years 27 days	
Foreign Service:	Ceylon	2 years
Reason for Discharge:	Chronic Rheumatism	
Character:	Good	
Trade or Occupation:	Servant	
Can Sign Name:	Yes	
Height:	5' 8½"	
Hair Colour:	Light Brown	

Eyes:	Grey
Complexion:	Fresh
Remarks:	While employed on military duty as a Guard on board ship proceeding from this country to Western Australia with Convicts he became affected by a disorder of the eyes which resulted in a total loss of loss of vision shortly after his arrival in the Colony
Intends to Reside:	Dublin

STANFIELD	Charles, Bombardier EIC Bombay Artillery
Surname Variant	STANSFIELD; STARFIELD Out Pension No 438
7 Sept 1859	Admitted to Out-pension Pension paid Woolwich 1/- per diem
1859	Pension paid 2nd East London Pension District
1861	Residing Wapping Tower Hamlets
29 Jan 1862	Arrived per *'Lincelles'*
1864	ptve C Stanfield Pensioner Force at Perth contributed to the Greenough Fire Relief Fund
25 Aug 1865	Died
Service and Personal Details:	
Place of Birth:	London
Trade or Occupation:	Carpenter
Where Enlisted:	London
Presidency:	Bombay
Length of Service:	20 years 5 months or 20 years 4 months
Age on Discharge:	41 years
Character:	Good
Reason for Discharge:	General debility and Chronic Rheumatism
Height:	5' 8½"
Complexion:	Sallow
Eye Colour:	Hazel
Hair Colour:	Light Brown
Intends to Reside:	Gravesend

STANDFORD	James, private 96th Foot
Surname Variants	STANFORD; SANFORD
23 Oct 1849	Discharged the Service Chatham Pension paid Liverpool 1/2d. per diem
21 May 1851	Arrived per *'Mermaid'*
1851	Employed as Assistant Warder
1852	Transferred to Port Philip Victoria
17 Jan 1867	Died New Zealand
Service and Personal Details:	
Place of Birth:	Athlone Roscommon
Age on Attestation:	21 years
Period of Service:	1824 — 1849
Age on Discharge:	46 years

Length of Service:	20 years 115 days	
Foreign Service:	Bermuda	3 years
	Nova Scotia	8 years
	Australia	8 years
Reason for Discharge:	Rheumatism	
Character:	Good	
Trade or Occupation:	Shoemaker	
Can Sign Name:	Yes	
Height:	5' 6"	
Hair Colour:	Dark	
Eyes:	Hazel	
Complexion:	Fresh	
Intends to Reside:	Liverpool	

STANLEY

	Thomas, private
	6th Foot [Depot]
7 May 1861	Discharged the Service
	Pension paid Coventry
	1/1d. per diem
1862	Pension paid Birmingham
15 Apr 1864	Arrived per *'Clara'* [2]
1865	Pension paid Adelaide from [12/WA/240]
Aug 1865	a T Stanley to South Australia per *'Harriet Hope'*
1866	Victoria
1875	Queensland

Service and Personal Details:

Place of Birth:	St Michaels Coventry Warwickshire	
Age on Attestation:	19 years 4 months	
Period of Service:	1839 — 1861	
Age on Discharge:	41 years	
Length of Service:	21 years 183 days	
Foreign Service:	North America	2 years 1 month
	East Indies	2 years 9 months
Medal Entitlement:	Long Service and Good Conduct with gratuity	
Reason for Discharge:	Having completed 21 years service	
Character:	Very Good	
Trade or Occupation:	Watchmaker	
Can Sign Name:	Yes	
Height:	5' 5"	
Hair Colour:	Black	
Eyes:	Dark	
Complexion:	Dark	
Intends to Reside:	Coventry Warwickshire	

STANMER

	Robert, gunner
	RA No. 2 Division Coastal Brigade
Surname Variants	STANNER; STAMMER; STAMMERS
15 Mar 1870	Discharged the Service Shoreham
	Pension paid Belfast
	1/1d. per diem
1873	Pension paid Greenwich
19 Feb 1874	Arrived per *'Naval Brigade'*

June 1877	Pension paid Perth Western Australia
1877	a Robert Stammers to South Australia per *'Amur'* with wife and three children
1879	Pension paid South Australia

Service and Personal Details:		
Place of Birth:	Steyning Sussex	
Age on Attestation:	20 years 7 months	
Period of Service:	1848 — 1870	
Age on Discharge:	42 years	
Length of Service:	21 years 8 days	
Foreign Service:	Corfu	6 years 5 months
	Crimea	11 months
	Malta	2 years 7 months
Medal Entitlement:	Crimea with clasp; Turkish Crimean	
Reason for Discharge:	Claimed on second period of 'Limited Service'	
Character:	Very Good	
Trade or Occupation:	Labourer	
Can Sign Name:	Yes	
Height:	5' 10"	
Hair Colour:	Dark Brown	
Eyes:	Hazel	
Complexion:	Dark	
Intends to Reside:	Charlton Street Steyning Sussex	

STANTON	Edward, private 33rd Foot
23 July 1855	Discharged the Service Chatham Pension paid North Stafford 1/2d. per diem
1862	Pension paid Newcastle under Lyne
9 June 1862	Arrived per *'Norwood'* [1]
1864	ptve E Stanton contributed to the Greenough Fire Relief Fund
28 May 1869	Residents Office Fremantle Re — Eliza Stanton and her 3 children, whose husband and father [Edward Stanton Pensioner] has deserted them
circa Sept 1874	Transferred from 1st Perth to Fremantle District
July 1880	Died Inquest on body of Edward Stanton, pensioner, who died suddenly in High Street Fremantle, on the 1st inst. returned a verdict of Death caused by rupture of a blood vessel, caused by violent coughing."
1881	Widow of Pensioner Stanton applies for land Grant

Service and Personal Details:		
Place of Birth:	Market Drayton Shropshire	
Age on Attestation:	20 years	
Period of Service:	1853 — 1855	
Age on Discharge:	21 years 9 months	
Length of Service:	2 years 10 days total service	
Foreign Service:	Crimea	[no time period given]
Medal Entitlement:	Crimea with clasp; Turkish Crimean	

Reason for Discharge:	Gunshot wound to left kidney and back
Character:	Good
Trade or Occupation:	Labourer
Can Sign Name:	X his mark on discharge
Height:	5' 7½"
Hair Colour:	Dark Brown
Eyes:	Grey
Complexion:	Sallow
Remarks:	"….. with the exception of compensation for loss of ?**** in the Crimea"

STAPLES	William, gunner
	RA Invalid Detachment
1855	possibly served in Anglo-Turkish Contingent
15 Mar 1859	Discharged the Service Woolwich
	Pension paid Leicester
	1/- per diem
1859	Pension paid Woolwich
11 Feb 1861	Arrived per *'Palmeston'*
1863	To South Australia from Fremantle
1863	Pension paid Adelaide from Fremantle

Service and Personal Details:

Place of Birth:	St Martins Leicester Leicestershire	
Age on Attestation:	18 years 1 month	
Period of Service:	1838 — 1859	
Age on Discharge:	39 years 3 months	
Length of Service:	21 years 58 days	
Foreign Service:	Malta	6 years 3 months
	Crimea	[no time given]
Medal Entitlement:	Good Conduct and Long Service with gratuity and Crimea	
Reason for Discharge:	Having completed 21 years service	
Character:	Exemplary	
Trade or Occupation:	Framework Knitter	
Can Sign Name:	Yes	
Height:	5' 8"	
Hair Colour:	Brown	
Eyes:	Grey	
Complexion:	Fair	

STARK	James, private
	9th Foot
Surname Variant	STARKE
25 May 1847	Discharged the Service Chatham
	Pension paid 1st North London Pension District
	6d. per diem
1847	Pension paid Hull
1 June 1850	Arrived per *'Scindian'*
1884	W.O. correspondence with S.O. Perth W.A.
28 July 1888	Died Geraldton

1888	Northern District, Geraldton Sub-district Police Station. Re — finding of dead man near Geraldton by David Warren. Possibly the remains of James Stark
Service and Personal Details:	
Place of Birth:	South Leith Roxburghshire
Age on Attestation:	19 years
Period of Service:	1840 — 1846
Age on Discharge:	27 years
Length of Service:	6 years 6 days [reckoned]
Foreign Service:	East Indies 4 years 260 days
Medal Entitlement:	Sutlej with clasp
Reason for Discharge:	Wounded in action at Moodkee
Character:	Very Good
Trade or Occupation:	Joiner
Can Sign Name:	Yes
Height:	5' 6"
Hair Colour:	Dark
Eyes:	Grey
Complexion:	Dark
Intends to Reside:	North Shields

STARKEY	Peter, private 41st Foot
Surname Variant	STARKIE; SHARKEY
16 Mar 1859	Discharged the Service Chatham
30 Aug 1859	Admitted to Out-Pension Pension paid Galway 8d. per diem
11 Feb 1861	Arrived per *'Palmeston'*
1864	ptve P Starkey Pensioner Force at Perth contributed to the Greenough Fire Relief Fund
1865	On Nominal List to proceed to Camden Harbour per '*Tien Tsin*'
1868	Employed as Temp. Assistant. Warder Fremantle
1912	Died
Service and Personal Details:	
Place of Birth:	Galway Co. Galway
Age on Attestation:	17 years 10 months
Period of Service:	1848 — 1858
Age on Discharge:	28 years 7 months
Length of Service:	10 years 95 days
Foreign Service:	Ionian Isles & Malta 3 years Turkey and Crimea 2 years 3 months West Indies 1 year 7 months
Medal Entitlement:	Crimea with 3 clasps; ? French Legion of Honour
Reason for Discharge:	Own Request after 10 years 'Limited Service'
Character:	Good
Trade or Occupation:	Smith
Can Sign Name:	Yes

Height:	5' 7"	
Hair Colour:	Light Brown	
Eyes:	Blue	
Complexion:	Fresh	

STEEL	James, gunner and driver	
	RA 4th Battalion	
11 Aug 1857	Discharged the Service Woolwich	
	Pension paid Woolwich	
	8d. per diem	
19 Aug 1859	Arrived per *'Sultana'*	
1861	To South Australia from Western Australia	
1863	Pension paid Auckland New Zealand	

Service and Personal Details:		
Place of Birth:	Woolwich Kent	
Age on Attestation:	17 years 9 months	
Period of Service:	1835 — 1857	
Age on Discharge:	39 years 6 months	
Length of Service:	21 years 218 days	
Foreign Service:	Mauritius	4 years 215 days
Reason for Discharge:	Chronic Rheumatism	
Character:	Good	
Trade or Occupation:	Bookbinder	
Can Sign Name:	Yes	
Height:	5' 8"	
Hair Colour:	Dark Brown	
Eyes:	Hazel	
Complexion:	Fair	

STEELE	James Henry, private [drummer]	
	89th Foot	
28 July 1863	Discharged the Service Netley	
	Pension paid 2nd Belfast Pension District	
	6d. per diem	
22 Dec 1865	Arrived per *'Vimiera'*	
1867	Employed as Assistant Warder	
1868	Pension paid Adelaide South Australia	
1897	Correspondence with W.O.	
1898	Attended Memorial Day Adelaide	
May 1901	Died at Frewville South Australia aged 68 years	

Service and Personal Details:		
Place of Birth:	Glenavey Co. Antrim	
Age on Attestation:	14 years 9 months	
Period of Service:	1845 — 1863	
Age on Discharge:	32 years 8 months or 31 years 10 months	
Length of Service:	13 years 216 days	
Foreign Service:	Gibraltar	11 months
	Crimea	1 year 5 months
	Cape of Good Hope	1 year
	East Indies	5 years 2 months
Medal Entitlement:	Crimea with clasp; Turkish Crimean	
Reason for Discharge:	Varicose Veins of both legs	

Character:	Indifferent
Trade or Occupation:	None
Can Sign Name:	Yes
Height:	6' 3¼"
Hair Colour:	Light Brown
Eyes:	Blue
Complexion:	Fresh
Intends to Reside:	Antrim

STEIN	James, Serjeant Royal Sappers and Miners
Surname Variant	STEEN
17 Dec 1851	Arrived per *'Anna Robinson'* with regiment
1857	Contributed to the Florence Nightingale Fund
31 Dec 1861	Discharged the Service Fremantle West Aust
20 Mar 1862	Discharge approved
1864	a James John Stein purchased Fremantle Suburban Lot No 16 at auction for £6/5/-
27 Nov 1877	Deferred Pension forms to Fremantle
23 Nov 1878	Deferred Pension ratified 6d. per diem
1879	Applying for Fee Simple Fremantle Lot 167
Dec 1880	a John James Stein died aged 70 a resident of Fremantle and Geraldton

Service and Personal Details:

Place of Birth:	St Luke's London Middlesex
Age on Attestation:	24 years 3 months
Period of Service:	1842 — 1861
Service to 5th Feb 1855:	12 years 10 months
Age at 5th Feb 1855:	37 years 1 month
Age on Discharge:	44 years
Length of Service:	19 years 293 days
Foreign Service:	Nova Scotia 7 years 4 months Western Australia 10 years 8 months
Reason for Discharge:	His having been granted a Free Discharge at his own request to settle in the Australian Colonies with a gratuity of 12 months pay and the Right of Registry to a Deferred pension of 6d. per diem on attaining the age of 60 years
Character:	Exemplary
Trade or Occupation:	Painter
Can Sign Name:	Yes
Height:	5' 9"
Hair Colour:	Dark Brown with grey
Eye Colour:	Hazel
Complexion:	Tanned
Remarks:	widower by Feb 1855 with 1 child in 1855
Intended Residence:	Fremantle Western Australia

STEMP	James, Serjeant RA 4th Division Depot [Coastal Brigade]

Surname Variant	STAMP
30 June 1863	Discharged the Service Woolwich
	Pension paid South London Pension District
	10d. per diem 2 years conditional
1863	Employed as a Warder at Millbank Prison
1865	Arrived per *'Vimiera"*
1865	Pension paid Western Australia
11 Feb 1866	Died
Service and Personal Details:	
Place of Birth:	Camberwell Surrey
Age on Attestation:	18 years
Period of Service:	1854 — 1863
Age on Discharge:	27 years
Length of Service:	8 years 177 days
Foreign Service:	China Expedition 3 years 8 months
Medal Entitlement:	China
Reason for Discharge:	Consumption and Fistula
Character:	Exemplary
Trade or Occupation:	Gardiner [sic]
Can Sign Name:	Yes
Height:	5' 9½"
Hair Colour:	Dark Brown
Eyes:	Hazel
Complexion:	Sallow
Intends to Reside:	East Dulwich Lane Dulwich Surrey

STENNETT	John, private
	41st Foot
27 Oct 1863	Discharged the Service Ayr
	Pension paid Chatham
	1/- per diem
1864	Pension paid Chatham
1865	Pension paid West. Australia from Chatham
1865	Arrived per *'Racehorse'* as Assistant Warder
1 July 1865	Pension paid Western Australia
31 Dec 1876	Pension paid South Australia from Fremantle
Jan 1884	Admitted to In-Pension Chelsea
28 Aug 1910	Died

STEVENS	James, gunner EIC
	Bengal Artillery
	Out Pension No 271
1847	Embarked UK per *'Alfred'*
25 May 1847	Admitted to Out-pension
	Pension paid 2nd North London Pension District
	1/- per diem
1 June 1850	Arrived per *'Scindian'*
Sept 1850	Assigned South Perth Pensioner Loc P7
24 Feb 1854	"Dismissed from Enrolled Force"
1865	Pension paid Western Australia
29 Jan 1867	Died
Service and Personal Details:	
Place of Birth:	Middlesex

Trade or Occupation:	Labourer or Tailor
Where Enlisted:	London
Length of Service:	21 years
Age on Discharge:	41 years
Character:	Indifferent
Reason for Discharge:	Disease of Liver and Length of Service
Height:	5' 5½"
Complexion:	Dark
Visage:	Oval
Eye Colour:	Dark
Hair Colour:	Brown

STEWART Daniel, Corporal
76th Foot

Surname Variant	STUART
27 May 1857	Discharged the Service Birr
4 Aug 1857	Admitted to Out-Pension Pension paid Enniskillen 8d. per diem
15 Feb 1863	Arrived per *'Merchantman'* [1]
circa June 1874	Transferred from 2nd Perth Pension District to 1st Perth Pension District
1875	Pension increased to 1/1½d. for 11 years service in the Enrolled Force

the following entry may not necessarily refer to Daniel Stewart 76th Foot

20 Nov 1879	Newcastle. 'A Pensioner Orderly Stuart [sic] compelled to leave due to ill health. Invalided whilst on Force.'
Jan 1882	Assigned Perth Lot 273/Y
1882	Died
1883	Application of Title to Perth Lot 273/Y by Elizabeth widow of Daniel Stewart 76th Foot

Service and Personal Details:

Place of Birth:	Perth Perthshire Scotland	
Age on Attestation:	16 years 6 months	
Period of Service:	1839 — 1857	
Age on Discharge:	33 years 9 months	
Length of Service:	15 years 284 days	
Foreign Service:	Bermuda	10 months
	North America	4 years 1 month
	Ionian Isles	3 years
	Malta	2 years
Reason for Discharge:	Palpitations and Disease of heart	
Character:	Good	
Trade or Occupation:	Labourer	
Can Sign Name:	Yes	
Height:	5' 6"	
Hair Colour:	Brown	
Eyes:	Blue	
Complexion:	Fresh	
Intends to Reside:	Fivemiletown Co. Tyrone	

STEWART	Thomas, Corporal [730]	
	87th Foot	
Previous Regiments	91st; 53rd	
30 May 1865	Discharged the Service Portsmouth	
	Pension paid Paisley	
	1/1½d. per diem	
1865	Pension paid 2nd Glasgow Pension District	
13 July 1867	Arrived per *'Norwood'* [2]	
1881	Pension increased to 1/7d. per diem for service in the Enrolled Force	
Jan 1884	Application for Title to Lot P 404 Turkey Point, nr. Bunbury on behalf of Thomas Stewart Pensioner]	
31 July 1888	Superintendent Fremantle Prison — That Pensioner T. Stewart may be employed as Temporary Extra Guard	
June 1897	Residing Fremantle	
1898	Died	
Service and Personal Details:		
Place of Birth:	Perth Scotland	
Age on Attestation:	17 years 2 months	
Period of Service:	1844 — 1865	
Age on Discharge:	39 years 1 month 7 days	
Length of Service:	21 years 242 days	
Foreign Service:	East Indies	15 years 4 months
	China	1 year 2 months
Medal Entitlement:	Sutlej;with clasp for Sobroan; Punjaub; North West Frontier with clasps for Goojerat; Indian Mutiny with clasps for Delhi and Relief of Lucknow	
Reason for Discharge:	Own Request having completed 21 years service	
Character:	Very Good	
Trade or Occupation:	Blacksmith	
Can Sign Name:	Yes	
Height:	5' 7¼"	
Hair Colour:	Dark	
Eyes:	Blue	
Complexion:	Fresh	
Intends to Reside:	Greenock	

STOKES	John, private
	63rd Foot
3 July 1855	Discharged the Service
	Pension paid 2nd Dublin Pension District
	1/- per diem
15 Aug 1865	Arrived per *'Racehorse'*
1867	Application for Title to Fremantle Town Lot S40 located at Lime Kilns at a £1/0/0 per acre
Nov 1876	a Lake Munster Lot assigned to a Jno. Stokes and was cancelled on the 16th Sept 1991
1881	Pension increased to 1/6d. per diem for service in the Enrolled Force
Jan 1882	Allocated Fremantle Sub Loc 41

1885	Application for Title Fremantle Sub Lot 41
1888	Pay Master of Pensioners — Grant of £15 to Pensioner John Stokes, as to 2nd Nov 1888
June 1897	Residing Fremantle
Mar 1900	Died aged 65 at his residence at Hampton Rd Fremantle
1900	Grant of Probate

Service and Personal Details:	
Place of Birth:	Baldoyle Dublin
Age on Attestation:	17 years 6 months
Period of Service:	1852 — 1855
Age on Discharge:	20 years 1 month
Length of Service:	2 years 30 days
Foreign Service:	"with the Expeditionary Army in the East" for 9 months
Medal Entitlement:	Crimea with clasp; Turkish Crimean
Reason for Discharge:	Disabled by gunshot wound to chest
Character:	Good
Trade or Occupation:	Labourer
Can Sign Name:	Yes
Height:	5' 6½"
Hair Colour:	Dark Brown
Eyes:	Hazel
Complexion:	Fresh
Intends to Reside:	Dublin

STOKES Michael, gunner EIC
Bengal Artillery
Out Pension No 255

13 May 1846	Discharged the Service
1846	Embarked UK per '*Walmer Castle*'
	Pension paid 2nd North London Pension District 1/- per diem
1 June 1850	Arrived per *'Scindian'*
July 1850	Assigned and occupies land Freshwater Bay
Jan 1857	Contributed 2/- to the Florence Nightingale Fund
Feb 1858	Application for Title Freshwater Bay Loc P222 and P242
1858	Died

Service and Personal Details:	
Where Born:	Limerick
Trade or Occupation:	Labourer
Where Enlisted:	Limerick
Presidency:	Bengal
Length of Service:	21 years 1 month
Age on Discharge:	42 years
Character:	Indifferent
Reason for Discharge:	Impaired Constitution and general debility
Height:	5' 9"
Complexion:	Dark
Visage:	Long
Eye Colour:	Blue

Hair Colour:	Brown
STOKES	William, private
	30th Foot
Previous Regiment	88th Foot — transfer cancelled
28 Nov 1848	Discharged the Service Chatham
1849	Pension paid Birmingham
	1/- per diem
1849	Pension paid Falkland Isles
1857	Birmingham
1857	Liverpool
1857	Londonderry
11 Feb 1861	Arrived per *'Palmeston'*
1873	Pension increased to 1/3d. per diem for 8½ years service in the Enrolled Force
1878	Application for Title to Greenough Locs G3 & G4
1881	Died
Service and Personal Details:	
Place of Birth:	Lewisham Kent
Age on Attestation:	15 years
Period of Service:	1824 — 1848
Age on Discharge:	39 years
Length of Service:	21 years 6 days [reckoned]
Foreign Service:	East Indies 1 year 8 months
Reason for Discharge:	Chronic Rheumatism
Character:	Good
Trade or Occupation:	Labourer
Can Sign Name:	Yes
Height:	5' 8"
Hair Colour:	Brown
Eyes:	Blue
Complexion:	Fresh
Intends to Reside:	Jersey
Married:	Ellen O'Neill
Children:	John b. *c*1843 Ireland d. *c*1871 Geraldton
	Louisa b. *c*1847 Sunderland England
	m. *c*1864 Frederick Gibson Geraldton
	Henry b. *c*1850 Falkland Isles
	m. *c*1874 Mary Fletcher Perth
	James b. *c*1852 Falkland Isles
	m. *c*1877 Mary Ann McMullen
	Elizabeth b. *c*1856 Falkland Islands
	m. *c*1896 Edmund Beringer Geraldton
	Mary b. *c*1859 Ireland
	m. *c*1881 Edward Arundel Geraldton
	? Thomas b. *c*1865
	m. *c*1888 Jane Baker Geraldton
	William [brother from obituary]
STONE	Frederick, private
	46th Foot
11 Jan 1848	Discharged the Service Chatham
	Pension paid Norwich

	6d. per diem
1849	Pension paid Kings Lynn Norfolk
21 May 1851	Arrived per *'Mermaid'*
1863	Stationed Perth District
	Assigned Perth Town Lot 28/Y
1864	ptve F Stone Pensioner Force at Perth contributed to the Greenough Fire Relief Fund
Jan 1865	Application for Title to Perth Lot 28/Y
1868	Application for Title to Perth Lots 153; 154; 184 and 185 at £6/0/0 per Lot
Aug 1874	Pension increased to 1/1½d. for 15 years 5 months service and from date of discharge from Enrolled Force
Feb 1877	Convicted at the Police Court Perth W. A. of assaulting his wife and was sent to prison for one month during which half pension was to be suspended, the other half paid to wife
1886	Residing Hardinge Street Perth
July 1886	Died buried in Wesleyan Section of East Perth Pioneer Cemetery

Service and Personal Details:		
Place of Birth:	West Basham nr Fakenham Norfolk	
Age on Attestation:	18 years	
Period of Service:	1833 — 1848	
Age on Discharge:	32 years	
Length of Service:	13 years 352 days [reckoned]	
Foreign Service:	Gibraltar	4 years 130 days
	West Indies	3 years
	North America	2 years 249 days
Reason for Discharge:	Chronic Dysentery	
Character:	Good	
Trade or Occupation:	Labourer	
Can Sign Name:	X his mark on discharge	
Height:	5' 7"	
Hair Colour:	Brown	
Eyes:	Hazel	
Complexion:	Fresh	
Distinguishing Marks:	Scar on right side	
Intends to Reside:	West Basham nr. Fakenham Norfolk	

STONE	James, private
	40th Foot
26 Dec 1845	Discharged the Service Chatham
	Pension paid Londonderry Ireland
	6d. per diem
1855	Pension paid Dartmoor Devon
1855	Refused pension increase
2 Apr 1856	Arrived per *'William Hammond'*
1868	Assigned Greenough Locs G27 and G28
1874	Pension increased to 1/3d. per diem for service in the Enrolled Force
1878	Application for Title to Greenough Locs G27 and G28

Jan 1887	Died aged 73 Greenough	
1896	Bridget Baker and Mrs Stone Senior — proprietors of Geraldton Town Lot 265	
Service and Personal Details:		
Place of Birth:	St Patricks Dublin	
Age on Attestation:	21 years	
Period of Service:	1836 — 1845	
Age on Discharge:	31 years	
Length of Service:	8 years 68 days	
Foreign Service:	East Indies	3 years 3 months
	Scinde & Baloochistan & Afghanistan	3 years 11 months
Medal Entitlement:	2nd Afghan Campaign with 3 inscriptions [sic]; Bronze Star for Maharajpore	
Reason for Discharge:	Wounded left thigh at the Battle of Maharajpore	
Character:	Very Good	
Trade or Occupation:	Labourer	
Can Sign Name:	Yes	
Height:	5' 8"	
Hair Colour:	Dark Brown	
Eyes:	Grey	
Complexion:	Sallow	
Intends to Reside:	Buncrana Co. Donegal	

STONE	William, private 60th Foot	
8 July 1856	Discharged the Service Chatham Pension paid 2nd Dublin Pension District 7d. per diem	
19 Aug 1859	Arrived per *'Sultana'*	
1864	a William Stone residing Cantonment Fremantle	
1878	Application for Title North Fremantle Lot P22	
1878	Died	
Service and Personal Details:		
Place of Birth:	St Marys Limerick	
Age on Attestation:	18 years	
Period of Service:	1839 — 1855	
Age on Discharge:	35 years	
Length of Service:	16 years 162 days	
Foreign Service:	East Indies & Scinde	9 years 345 days
Reason for Discharge:	Rheumatism and Disease of the Liver	
Character:	Latterly Good	
Trade or Occupation:	Plaisterer [sic]	
Can Sign Name:	Yes	
Height:	5' 9½"	
Hair Colour:	Brown	
Eyes:	Blue	
Complexion:	Fresh	
Intends to Reside:	Dublin	

STRATTON	George, private
	RA Coastal Brigade
Surname Variant	STRETTON
9 Oct 1860	Discharge approved
16 Oct 1860	Discharged the Service Woolwich
	Pension paid 2nd Edinburgh Pension District
	1/- per diem
13 July 1867	Arrived per *'Norwood'* [2]
1874	Died
Service and Personal Details:	
Place of Birth:	West Church Edinburgh
Age on Attestation:	21 years
Period of Service:	1839 — 1860
Age on Discharge:	42 years 1 month
Length of Service:	21 years 42 days
Foreign Service:	Gibraltar 7 years
Medal Entitlement:	Long Service and Good Conduct with gratuity
Reason for Discharge:	Having completed 21 years service
Character:	Latterly Exemplary
Trade or Occupation:	Skinner
Can Sign Name:	Yes
Height:	5' 8"
Hair Colour:	Brown
Eyes:	Grey
Complexion:	Fair

STRETCH	Charles, private
	45th Foot
Surname Variant	STRITCH
19 Mar 1861	Discharged the Service Chatham
	9d. per diem
1861	Pension paid Trowbridge
1864	Pension paid Dorchester
15 Apr 1864	Arrived per *'Clara'* [2]
1865	Pension paid South Australia from Perth WA
Aug 1865	a C Stritch, [sic] Henry Stritch [sic] and an Elizabeth Stretch departed for South Australia per *'Harriet Hope'*
1866	Port Adelaide — Charles Stretch who stated that he had recently arrived from the Swan River was charge with having no visible means of support. He was found in the living forecastle of the *'Charlotte Gladstone'*
1867	Adelaide — brought up on remanded charge of stealing a watch at Gawler on Oct 1865 William Hextall gave evidence stating that the prisoner did not leave Fremantle until sometime after the robbery
1868	Pension paid Bengal
1869	Trowbridge
1870	Bath
6 Dec 1874	Died

Service and Personal Details:

Place of Birth:	St Johns Devizes Wiltshire	
Age on Attestation:	17 years 2 months	
Period of Service:	1846 — 1860	
Age on Discharge:	31 years 11 months	
Length of Service:	13 years 196 days	
Foreign Service:	Cape of Good Hope	11 years 7 months
Medal Entitlement:	Kaffir War 1850/53	
Reason for Discharge:	Lameness caused by amputation of the greater part of the second toe of right foot	
Character:	Very Good	
Trade or Occupation:	Labourer	
Can Sign Name:	X his mark on discharge	
Height:	5' 11"	
Hair Colour:	Light Brown	
Eyes:	Hazel	
Complexion:	Fresh	
Intends to Reside:	Devizes Wiltshire	

STRETTON James, private [drummer]
99th Foot

10 June 1857	Discharged the Service Cork
27 July 1857	Discharge approved
4 Aug 1857	Admitted to Out-Pension
	Pension paid 2nd Dublin Pension District
	1/- per diem
19 Aug 1859	Arrived per *'Sultana'*
1861	Employed by Convict Establishment
1871	Pension paid Melbourne Victoria
1874	"Off Pension not appeared"

Service and Personal Details:

Place of Birth:	Chichester Sussex	
Age on Attestation:	14 years 3 months	
Period of Service:	1832 — 1857	
Age on Discharge:	39 years 3 months	
Length of Service:	21 years 93 years	
Foreign Service:	Mauritius	4 years 29 days
	Australian Colonies	12 years 325 days
Reason for Discharge:	Chronic Rheumatism	
Character:	Good	
Trade or Occupation:	none	
Can Sign Name:	Yes	
Height:	5' 6"	
Hair Colour:	Fair	
Eyes:	Blue	
Complexion:	Fair	
Intends to Reside:	Dublin	

STRONGMAN John, private
3rd Light Dragoons

Previous Regiment 16th Lancers

9 Aug 1853	Discharged the Service Chatham Pension paid Falmouth 9d. per diem
24 May 1855	Arrived per *'Stag'*
23 Apr 1871	Died
Service and Personal Details:	
Place of Birth:	Halstone [sic] Cornwall
Age on Attestation:	20 years 3 months
Period of Service:	1834 — 1853
Age on Discharge:	39 years 5 months
Length of Service:	19 years 81 days
Foreign Service:	East Indies 18 years ?1 month
Medal Entitlement:	Afghanistan 1838/9; Sutlej with clasp; Punjaub Cheniah and Sadoolapor 1848; Punjaub with clasps for Chillianwalla and Goojerat 1849
Reason for Discharge:	Long service in tropical climate and worn out
Character:	Good
Trade or Occupation:	Stone Mason
Can Sign Name:	Yes
Height:	5' 10"
Hair Colour:	Dark Brown
Eyes:	Brown
Complexion:	Sallow
Intends to Reside:	Halstone [sic] Cornwall

STURMAN	George see — Joseph WRIGHT

SULLIVAN	Daniel, private 82nd Foot
9 Jan 1855	Discharged the Service Chatham Pension paid Tralee 6d. per diem for 2 years
Dec 1855	Pension paid Dartmoor Devon
1856	Dartmoor
4 June 1856	Onboard *'Runnymede'* and gave evidence in trial of William Nevin
1856	Pension payments extended for a further nine months
10 July 1857	Arrived per *'Clara'* [1]
1857	Pension ceased
1857	Died
Service and Personal Details:	
Place of Birth:	Cahirciveen Co. Kerry
Age on Attestation:	18 years 6 months
Period of Service:	1845 — 1855
Age on Discharge:	30 years or 28 years
Length of Service:	9 years 195 days
Reason for Discharge:	Disease of the Lungs
Character:	Good
Trade or Occupation:	Labourer

Can Sign Name:	X his mark on discharge
Height:	5' 11"
Hair Colour:	Brown
Eyes:	Hazel
Complexion:	Fresh
Intends to Reside:	Tralee

SULLIVAN John, Corporal

	6th Dragoon Guards
10 Nov 1865	Discharged the Service Hounslow
1865	Serving Chatham Prison
1866	aged 34 years
24 Dec 1866	Arrived per *'Corona'*
	Employed as Assistant Warder

Service and Personal Details:

Place of Birth:	St Finbars Cork	
Age on Attestation:	19 years 8 months	
Period of Service:	1851 — 1865	
Age on Discharge:	33 years 11 months	
Length of Service:	14 years 85 days	
Foreign Service:	Crimea and Turkey	10 months
	East Indies	4 years 2 months
Medal Entitlement:	Indian Mutiny	
Reason for Discharge:	Own Request Free, and with Right of Registry for a Deferred Pension of 4d. per diem when attaining 50 years of age	
Character:	Very Good	
Trade or Occupation:	Seedsman	
Can Sign Name:	Yes	
Height:	5' 8"	
Hair Colour:	Sandy	
Eyes:	Hazel	
Complexion:	Fresh	
Intends to Reside:	Hooper's Post Office, Great Russell Street,	
Covent Garden London		

SULLIVAN John, private

	10th Foot
Previous Regiment	39th Foot
13 Aug 1850	Discharged the Service
	Pension paid Tralee
	9d. per diem
6 Apr 1854	Arrived per *'Sea Park'*
1874	Pension increased to 1/3d. per diem
19 Apr 1875	Assigned North Fremantle Lot P54
29 Han 1883	Application for Title North Fremantle Lot P54
20 Apr 1883	Granted Fee Simple North Fremantle Lot P54
Mar 1897	John Sullivan of Fremantle — pensioner made application to be registered as proprietor in Fee Simple of North Fremantle Lot P1
June 1897	Residing North Fremantle
Oct 1897	Died at his residence Swan St., Fremantle

Service and Personal Details:		
Place of Birth:	Tralee Co. Kerry	
Period of Service:	1840 — 1850	
Age on Discharge:	30 years	
Length of Service:	9 years 11 months [reckoned]	
Foreign Service:	India	8 years 2 months
Medal Entitlement:	Sutlej; Punjaub	
Reason for Discharge:	Wounded left side of neck	
Character:	Good	
Trade or Occupation:	Labourer	
Height:	5' 8"	
Hair Colour:	Dark	
Eyes:	Blue	
Complexion:	Dark	

SULLIVAN	John, private	
	15th Foot	
Previous Regiments	45th; 33rd	
17 July 1866	Discharged the Service Netley	
	Pension paid 2nd Cork Pension District	
	10d. per diem	
1866	Pension paid 2nd West London Pension District	
1867	2nd North London Pension District	
13 July 1867	Arrived per *'Norwood'* [2]	
1868	Pension paid Adelaide from Fremantle	
Service and Personal Details:		
Place of Birth:	Buttervant Co. Cork	
Age on Attestation:	24 years	
Period of Service:	1850 — 1866	
Age on Discharge:	40 years 6 months	
Length of Service:	15 years 357 days [reckoned]	
Foreign Service:	Malta	1 month
	Constantinople	5 months
	North America	4 years 4 months
	Crimea	1 year 10 months
	East Indies	4 years 11 months
	Mauritius	3 months
Medal Entitlement:	Crimean with clasps and Turkish Crimean	
Reason for Discharge:	Loss of portion of little finger of right hand	
Character:	Very Good	
Trade or Occupation:	Labourer	
Can Sign Name:	X his mark on discharge	
Height:	5' 7"	
Hair Colour:	Brown	
Eyes:	Grey	
Complexion:	Fresh	
Intends to Reside:	?Mallow Co. Cork	

SULLIVAN	Joseph, private
	19th Foot
5 Apr 1859	Discharged the Service Chatham

	Pension paid 1st East London Pension District
	10d. per diem
31 Dec 1862	Arrived per *'York'*
1865	Pension paid South Australia
1869	New South Wales

Service and Personal Details:

Place of Birth:	Grogan Rathdowney Queens County	
Age on Attestation:	18 years 3 months	
Period of Service:	1838 — 1859	
Age on Discharge:	39 years 5 months	
Length of Service:	21 years 67 days	
Foreign Service:	Mediterranean	5 years 3 months
	West Indies	2 years 4 months
	North America	3 years 2 months
Reason for Discharge:	Having completed 21 years service	
Character:	Good	
Trade or Occupation:	Shoemaker	
Can Sign Name:	X his mark on discharge	
Height:	5' 6½"	
Hair Colour:	Brown	
Eyes:	Blue	
Complexion:	Fresh	
Intends to Reside:	Rathdowney Queens County	

SULLIVAN	Joseph, private EIC
	Bombay European Infantry
	Out Pension No 223
15 May 1844	Discharged the Service
1844	Embarked UK per *'Thomas Coutts'*
	Pension paid Cork
	9d. per diem
4 June 1856	Onboard *'Runnymede'* and gave evidence in the trial of William Nevin
10 July 1857	Arrived per *'Clara'* [1]
1865	Pension paid Perth Western Australia
May 1880	Joseph Sullivan EIC to Mt Eliza Poor House
1884	Died aged 75 widower with no children

Service and personal Details:

Place of Birth:	Cork
Trade or Occupation:	Labourer
Where Enlisted:	Cork
Presidency:	Bombay
Length of Service:	15 years 5 months
Age on Discharge:	34 years
Character:	Very Good
Reason for Discharge:	Chronic Rheumatism
Height:	5' 6"
Complexion:	Sallow
Visage:	Oval
Eye Colour:	Grey

Hair Colour:	Brown
SULLIVAN	Patrick, private 95th Foot
3 July 1855	Discharged the Service Chatham Pension paid Tralee 1/- per diem
1862	Pension paid Bermuda
15 Feb 1863	Arrived per *'Merchantman'* [1]
1873	Residing Fremantle
1875	Pension paid Western Australia
11 Nov 1880	Joined the Enrolled Guard — stationed Perth
1881	Pension increased to 1/2d. per diem for service in the Enrolled Force
4 July 1881	Assigned Perth Town Lot 86/E Claisebrook
9 Feb 1885	Granted fee Simple Perth Town Lot 86/E
June 1897	Stationed at Perth
Dec 1900	Died buried Roman Catholic section of East Perth Pioneer Cemetery
Service and Personal Details:	
Place of Birth:	Killarney Co. Kerry
Age on Attestation:	17 years 9 months
Period of Service:	1846 — 1855
Age on Discharge:	27 years 3 months
Length of Service:	8 years 6 months
Foreign Service:	Hong Kong China 1 year 8 months Turkey & Crimea 10 months
Medal Entitlement:	Crimea with clasps
Reason for Discharge:	Loss of index finger of left hand after gunshot wound
Character:	Good
Trade or Occupation:	Labourer
Can Sign Name:	X his mark on discharge
Height:	5' 6½"
Hair Colour:	Dark Brown
Eyes:	Grey
Complexion:	Fresh
Intends to Reside:	Killarney Co. Kerry
SULLIVAN	Timothy, private 48th Foot
12 June 1847	Discharged the Service Belfast
19 July 1847	Discharge approved
27 July 1847	Admitted to Out-Pension Pension paid 1st Dublin Pension District 1/- per diem
28 June 1851	Arrived per *'Pyrenees'* [1]
1853	Reference to a Timothy Sullivan being efficient in handling arms [CSO 303]
1854	Received sum of £15 towards cost of dwelling
Jan 1857	Contributed 2/- to the Florence Nightingale Fund
1858	Applied for Title to land at Kojonup
1862	Occupying Kojonup Lot P1

1864	ptve Sullivan Pensioner Force at Kojonup contributed to the Greenough Fire Relief Fund
1885	Died

Service and Personal Details:

Place of Birth:	Killarney Co. Kerry	
Age on Attestation:	17 years	
Period of Service:	1825 — 1847	
Age on Discharge:	39 years	
Length of Service:	20 years 335 days	
Foreign Service:	Gibraltar	5 years
	East Indies	8 years
	West Indies	3 years
Reason for Discharge:	Chronic Rheumatism and defective hearing	
Character:	Rather Irregular	
Trade or Occupation:	Labourer	
Can Sign Name:	Yes	
Height:	5' 7¾"	
Hair Colour:	Sandy	
Eyes:	Grey	
Complexion:	Sallow	

SULLIVAN Timothy, private
48th Foot

26 Mar 1861	Discharged the Service Pension paid 1st Cork Pension District 1/- per diem
31 Dec 1862	Arrived per *'York'* [aged 55]
1864	Pension paid Perth Western Australia
1865	Mauritius
1875	Pension paid Hamilton Scotland

SUTCLIFFE Richard, private
50th Foot

Surname Variant	SUTLIFFE
Mar 1857	Discharged the Service Dublin
21 Apr 1857	Admitted to Out-pension Pension paid Halifax 8d per diem
1859	Arrived per *'Sultana'*
1873	W.O. Correspondence "the A31"
1887	W.O. Correspondence
1888	Duplicate Pension Certificate to Adelaide

Service and Personal Details:

Place of Birth:	Halifax Yorkshire	
Age on Attestation:	18 years 8 months	
Period of Service:	1841— 1857	
Age on Discharge:	33 years 11 months	
Length of Service:	15 years 85 days	
Foreign Service:	East Indies	5 years 8 months
	Turkey & Crimea	2 years 3 months
Medal Entitlement:	Bronze Star for action at Punniar, Sutlej with 3 clasps; Crimea with 2 clasps	
Reason for Discharge:	Varicose Veins and ulcers on both legs	

Character:	Very Good
Trade or Occupation:	Woolcomber
Can Sign Name:	Yes
Height:	none given
Hair Colour:	Light Brown
Eyes:	Grey
Complexion:	Fair
Distinguishing Marks:	Small scar on right side of upper lip
Remarks:	Wounded at Ferozeshar by bayonet thrust to right thigh
Intends to Reside:	Gibbert Lane Halifax

SUTHERLAND	Alexander, private 24th Foot
11 Oct 1864	Discharged the Service Cork Pension paid Waterford 1/- per diem
1864	Pension paid 1st Cork Pension District
13 July 1867	Arrived per *'Norwood'* [2]
1873	Charged with violently assaulting F. B. Timewell
1875	Applied for £15 dwelling improvement grant
1881	Pension increased to 1/6d. per diem for service in the Enrolled Force
Apr 1881	Application for Title to Perth Lot 128/Y
15 May 1881	Confirmation of Grant Perth Lot 128/Y
1884	Died

Service and Personal Details:

Place of Birth:	St Leilys Limerick Co. Limerick	
Age on Attestation:	18 years 7 months	
Period of Service:	1841 — 1864	
Age on Discharge:	41 years 11 months	
Length of Service:	22 years 337 days	
Foreign Service:	East Indies	17 years 10 months
Medal Entitlement:	Punjaub with clasp; Indian Mutiny	
Reason for Discharge:	Own Request having served over 21 years	
Character:	Good	
Trade or Occupation:	Servant	
Can Sign Name:	Yes	
Height:	5' 8¼"	
Hair Colour:	Dark Brown	
Eyes:	Grey	
Complexion:	Sallow	
Remarks:	Wounded in left arm by grape shot at Chillianwallah 1849	
Intends to Reside:	Ballybricken Co. Waterford	

SUTTON	Samuel, private RM
Oct 1847	Discharged the Service Chatham Pension paid Leicestershire £13/12/- per annum
1 June 1850	Arrived per *'Scindian'*

July 1850	Assigned Freshwater Bay Loc P232
1850	Assigned and occupied Freshwater Bay Locs P253 and 255
Jan 1857	Contributed 2/- to the Florence Nightingale Fund
Feb 1858	Application for Title Freshwater Bay Loc P232
1863	Stationed Perth District
1864	ptve S Sutton Pensioner Force at Perth contributed to the Greenough Fire Relief Fund
1871	Application for Title to Freshwater Bay Lots 253; 254; 255 ;256
1876	"That gallant marine, Samuel Sutton, of Fresh Water Bay, was touchingly dealt with last Saturday in a fine of £5 and costs 27s. for unsoldier like conduct in storming the stronghold of his neighbours the Herberts armed with a carving knife and rattan [sic], and cowardly assaulting the old lady and her husband, as well as inflicting a few weak blows on their daughter who was protecting her aged parents." [Trove]
1891	Died aged 81 — buried Anglican section of East Perth Pioneer Cemetery

Service and Personal Details:

Place of Birth:	Loughborough Leicestershire
Age on Attestation:	19 years 11 months
Marine Division:	Chatham and Woolwich
Period of Service:	1830 — 1847
Length of Service:	17 years 21 days
Trade or Occupation:	Stocking Weaver
Reason for Discharge:	Invalided for Hernia [right side] contracted in and by service — 'unserviceable'

SUTTON William, Schoolmaster Serjeant 24th Foot

31 Aug 1858	Discharged the Service Chatham Pension paid 1st East London Pension District 1/7d. per diem
1862	Pension paid Plymouth
9 June 1862	Arrived per *'Norwood'* [1]
1864	Serjeant W Sutton Fremantle Pensioner Force contributed to the Greenough Fire Relief Fund
May 1864	Died — the body of a William Sutton was found decomposing in Mrs Brown's paddock

Service and Personal Details:

Place of Birth:	St James London	
Age on Attestation:	18 years 4 months	
Period of Service:	1836 — 1858	
Age on Discharge:	40 years 3 months	
Length of Service:	21 years 17 days	
Foreign Service:	Canada	3 years 2 months
	East Indies	11 years 6 months
Medal Entitlement:	Punjaub with 2 clasps	
Reason for Discharge:	Chronic Rheumatism; ill health and long service	
Character:	Good	

Trade or Occupation: Engineer
Can Sign Name: Yes

Height: 5' 7"
Hair Colour: Light Brown
Eyes: Grey
Complexion: Sallow

SWEENEY Alexander, gunner
RA Invalids Artillery
Surname Variant SWEENY
21 Sept 1859 Discharged the Service Woolwich
1/- per diem
11 Feb 1861 Arrived per *'Palmeston'*
1862 Employed as Assistant Warder
1865 Pension paid Western Australia
1884 Perth — Pensioner A Sweeney appointed as private on the Rottnest Guard
Nov 1891 Died. On the 5th November 1891 the remains of Mr Alex Sweeney a pensioner of the Royal Artillery were interred in Fremantle Cemetery

Service and Personal Details:
Place of Birth: All Saints Newtown Cuningham Donegal
Age on Attestation: 19 years 5 months
Period of Service: 1838 — 1859
Age on Discharge: 40 years 11 months
Length of Service: 21 years 10 days
Foreign Service: St Helena 8 years 3 months
Crimea 6 months
Medal Entitlement: Crimea with clasp; Turkish Crimea
Reason for Discharge: Having completed 21 years service

Character: Very Good
Trade or Occupation: Labourer
Can Sign Name: Yes

Height: 5' 10½"
Hair Colour: Light Brown
Eyes: Blue
Complexion: Fair
Intends to Reside: Woolwich

SWEENEY Hugh, private
11th Foot
Surname Variant SWEENY
12 Feb 1840 Discharged the Service
Pension paid Maidstone Kent
6d. per diem
1851 In prison — Maidstone
2 Aug 1852 Arrived per *'William Jardine'*
11 Jan 1868 Died

Service and Personal Details:
Place of Birth: Aragill Co. Monaghan
Age on Attestation: 17 years
Period of Service: 1823 — 1840

Age on Discharge:	33 years 3 months	
Length of Service:	15 years 153 days	
Foreign Service:	Portugal	1 year 3 months
	Ionian Isles	10 years
Reason for Discharge:	Stiffness and swelling of the right thigh	
Character:	Good	
Trade or Occupation:	Labourer	
Can Sign Name:	X his mark on discharge	
Height:	6'	
Hair Colour:	Dark Brown	
Eyes:	Grey	
Complexion:	Dark	
Intends to Reside:	Maidstone	

SWEENEY	John, private	
	19th Foot	
Previous Regiment	67th Foot	
Surname Variant	SWEENY	
27 Feb 1855	Discharged the Service Chatham	
	Pension paid Fermoy	
	9d. per diem	
1858	Pension paid Cork	
11 Feb 1861	Arrived per *'Palmeston'*	
1868	Assigned Greenough Locs G7 of approx 15 acres and G8 of approx 16 acres ?961/1922	
1874	Pension increased to 1/2d. per diem	
May 1874	Application for Title Greenough Locs G7; G8	
1889	Died aged 66 Greenough	
Service and Personal Details:		
Place of Birth:	Coolclough Co. Cork	
Age on Attestation:	17 years 9 months	
Period of Service:	1846 — 1855	
Age on Discharge:	28 years 6 months	
Length of Service:	8 years 192 days	
Foreign Service:	Gibraltar	3 years 34 days
	Crimea	[no time given]
Medal Entitlement:	Crimea with clasp	
Reason for Discharge:	Loss of left index finger from a gunshot wound received at the battle of Alma	
Character:	Very Good	
Trade or Occupation: Discharge	Labourer on Attestation, Shoemaker on	
Can Sign Name:	Yes	
Height:	5' 6"	
Hair Colour:	Brown	
Eyes:	Grey	
Complexion:	Dark	
Intends to Reside:	Kantwik [sic] Co. Cork	

SWEENEY	Terrence [sic], private
	98th Foot
Previous Regiment:	86th Foot

Surname Variant	SWEENY
14 Apr 1857	Discharged the Service
	Pension paid Exeter
	11d. per diem
1858	Pension paid Clonmel
1858	Plymouth
1859	Deptford
1860	Woolwich
27 May 1863	Arrived per *'Clyde'*
	Part of pension to be paid to wife in Woolwich
1865	To Adelaide from Western Australia
1865	"No more pension to wife"
1868	Pension paid Chatham
1868	Woolwich

Service and Personal Details:

Place of Birth:	Clogheen Co Tipperary	
Age on Discharge:	38 years	
Length of Service:	20 years 3 months	
Foreign Service:	China	2 years 9 months
	India	7 years 4 months
Reason for Discharge:	Rheumatism and Impaired Constitution	
Character:	Very Good	
Trade or Occupation:	Weaver	
Height:	5' 9½"	
Hair Colour:	Light Brown	
Eyes:	Grey	
Complexion:	Fresh	

SWIFT	George, private [977]
	88th Foot
8 Sept 1846	Discharged the Service Chatham
	Pension paid Liverpool
	1/- per diem
1848	Pension paid 2nd Dublin Pension District
28 June 1851	Arrived per *'Pyrenees'* [1]
Oct 1851	Appointed Night Warder
Jan 1852	Resigned or dismissed
1854	"Discharged from Local Force for insubordination and to refund passage money"
1856	Replaced on Enrolled Force Roll
1858	Subscribed 1/8d. to Indian Relief Fund
24 Oct 1869	Died Fremantle District aged 61
12 Apr 1884	W.O. correspondence — Query to the Secretary of State for the Colonies — " Was Pensioner George Swift entitled to a grant of land?"

Service and Personal Details:

Place of Birth:	Dublin	
Age on Attestation:	19 years	
Period of Service:	1824 — 1846	
Age on Discharge:	41 years 6 months or 39 years 6 months	
Length of Service:	21 years 308 days	
Foreign Service:	Malta	5 years 7 months
	Ionian Isles	10 years 10 months

Reason for Discharge:	Rheumatic pains in the loins
Character:	Good
Trade or Occupation:	Labourer
Can Sign Name:	Yes
Height:	5' 8½"
Hair Colour:	Dark
Eyes:	Grey
Complexion:	Sallow
Intends to Reside:	Liverpool

SWIFT James, Corporal
88th Foot

11 Dec 1849	Discharged the Service Chatham Pension paid Dublin Pension District 7d. per diem for 2 years
24 Oct 1850	Arrived possibly per *'Hashemy'*
1853	Signed petition

Service and Personal Details:

Place of Birth:	St George Dublin	
Age on Attestation:	15 years 6 months	
Period of Service:	1840 — 1849	
Age on Discharge:	24 years 6 months or 25 years	
Length of Service:	6 years 193 days [reckoned]	
Foreign Service:	Malta	6 years
	West Indies	2 years 5 months
Reason for Discharge:	Chronic Chest Disease	
Character:	Good	
Trade or Occupation:	Labourer	
Can Sign Name:	Yes	
Height:	5' 9"	
Hair Colour:	Brown	
Eyes:	Hazel	
Complexion:	Swarthy	
Intends to Reside:	Dublin	

SWIFT William, private
84th Foot

25 Oct 1853	Discharged the Service Chatham Pension paid 1st Liverpool Pension District 1/- per diem
1855	Pension paid 2nd Glasgow Pension District
1856	Pension paid Liverpool Serving in the 2nd Lancashire Militia
8 June 1858	Arrived per *'Lord Raglan'*
Jan 1865	On Nominal List to proceed to Camden Harbour per *'Tien Tsin'* [from Trove]
1873	Pension increased to 1/3d. for 11 years 8 months service in the Enrolled Force
1875	Pension paid Western Australia
1879	a William Swift died

Service and Personal Details:

Place of Birth:	Liverpool Lancashire
Age on Attestation:	19 years
Period of Service:	1831 — 1853
Age on Discharge:	41 years 6 months or 40 years 9 months
Length of Service:	21 years 243 days
Foreign Service:	East Indies 10 years 109 days
Reason for Discharge:	Declining health and activity
Character:	Good
Trade or Occupation:	White smith
Can Sign Name:	Yes
Height:	5' 11"
Hair Colour:	Black
Eyes:	Grey
Complexion:	Dark
Intends to Reside:	Liverpool Lancashire

SYFAS Daniel, private

also known as	David **PIGEON**
	14th Foot
Surname Variant	SYLAS
19 Oct 1853	Discharged the Service Dublin
28 Nov 1852	Discharge approved
13 Dec 1853	Admitted to Out-Pension
	Pension paid Preston
	1/- per diem
1854	Pension paid 1st Liverpool Pension District
10 July 1857	Arrived per *'Clara'* [1]
	Pension paid Plymouth
1857	Liverpool
1896	W.O. Correspondence

Service and Personal Details:

Place of Birth:	Barton Woodstock Oxfordshire
Age on Attestation:	18 years 1 month
Period of Service:	1832 — 1853
Age on Discharge:	39 years 10 months
Length of Service:	21 years 49 days
Foreign Service:	West Indies 1 year 6 months
Reason for Discharge:	General Debility
Character:	Good
Trade or Occupation:	Labourer
Can Sign Name:	Yes
Height:	5' 7"
Hair Colour:	Light Brown
Eyes:	Hazel
Complexion:	Sallow
Intends to Reside:	Preston Lancashire

TAAFFE Francis, private

	22nd Foot
Surname Variant	TAAFE; TAAFA; TAIFFE
13 Feb 1861	Discharged the Service Parkhurst IOW
26 Feb 1861	Discharge approved

	Pension paid Parkhurst Isle of Wight
	10d. per diem
1861	Pension paid 1st Liverpool Pension District
15 Aug 1865	Arrived per *'Racehorse'*
	Assigned Freshwater Bay Loc 1062
Apr 1874	Charged with manslaughter of James Regan
Apr 1874	Acquitted and allegation dismissed
1875	Pension paid Western Australia
1876	Stationed Fremantle
July 1879	Mrs Taaffe selling mangle [Trove]
Jan 1886	Francis Taaffe charges his wife Bridget with using insulting language towards him and asked the Bench to protect him against the tongue of his wife
1888	Residing Dandaragan
June 1897	Residing Fremantle
1898	Died

Service and Personal Details:

Place of Birth:	Swords Dublin
Age on Attestation:	18 years
Period of Service:	1839 — 1861
Age on Discharge:	39 years 4 months
Length of Service:	21 years 135 days
Foreign Service:	East Indies 13 years 9 months
Medal Entitlement:	Long Service and Good Conduct with gratuity; Scinde — medal for Battle of Meeanee and Hyderabad
Reason for Discharge:	Own Request having served over 21 years
Character:	Good
Trade or Occupation:	Labourer
Can Sign Name:	Yes
Height:	5' 9½"
Hair Colour:	Dark Brown
Eyes:	Hazel
Complexion:	Fresh
Distinguishing Marks:	Crossed cupped over loins
Intends to Reside:	Liverpool

TAGETT	John, Corporal EIC
	Bombay Artillery
Surname Variants	TAGGETT; TAYETT; TARGETT;
Out Pension No 178	
13 May 1861	Admitted to Out-pension
	Pension paid 2nd West London Pension District
	9d. per diem
1862	Pension paid Chatham
1862	Pension paid 2nd West London Pension District
15 Apr 1864	Arrived per *'Clara'* [2]
1865	To Adelaide from Western Australia [12/WA 240]
July 1865	a John Targett to Adelaide per *'Mary Cummings'*
1878	Pension paid South Australia

Service and Personal Detail:

Place of Birth:	Hammersmith London
Trade or Occupation:	Servant
Where Enlisted:	London
Presidency:	Bombay
Length of Service:	15 years 6 months
Age on Discharge:	39 years
Character:	Good
Reason for Discharge:	Unfit for further service
Height:	5' 7½
Complexion:	Fresh
Eye Colour:	Hazel
Hair Colour:	Brown
Intends to Reside:	Hammersmith

TALBORT Robert, private
99th Foot

Surname Variant	TALBOT
25 Oct 1856	Discharged the Service Cork
23 Feb 1857	Discharge approved
3 Mar 1857	Admitted to Out-Pension Pension paid 2nd Belfast Pension District 6d. per diem
1859	Refused increase
19 Feb 1874	Arrived per *'Naval Brigade'*
28 Feb 1877	To Eastern Colonies from 2nd Perth District
1883	W.O. correspondence with a Reverend. T H Armstrong

Service and Personal Details:

Place of Birth:	Lisburn Co. Antrim
Age on Attestation:	18 years
Period of Service:	1842 — 1856
Age on Discharge:	32 years
Length of Service:	14 years 24 days
Foreign Service:	Australian Colonies 12 years 4 months
Reason for Discharge:	Varicose Veins in both legs
Character:	Good
Trade or Occupation:	Labourer
Can Sign Name:	X his mark on discharge
Height:	5' 6¼"
Hair Colour:	Fair
Eyes:	Grey
Complexion:	Hazel
Intends to Reside:	Banbridge Co. Antrim

TALBOT Robert, private
51st Foot — King's Own

Campaigns Served	Afghanistan 1878 — 1880
no date	After leaving the army emigrated to Queensland where he joined the police force with late Police Inspector Walsh.
no date	Lived for a number of years in the Kimberleys
no date	Managed hotel in Perth
no date	Residing Church Street Perth

June 1933	Died aged 84 years	
TANSEY	Patrick, private	
	73rd Foot	
26 Aug 1842	Discharged the Service Fort Pitt	
	Pension paid Athlone	
	9d. per diem	
21 May 1851	Arrived per *'Mermaid'*	
1851	Assigned and occupied North Fremantle Lot P15 from which he was evicted	
1855	Pension paid Australia	
1856	"Charged with Military Offence"	
3 Jan 1871	Died	
Service and Personal Details:		
Place of Birth:	Schrule Longford	
Age on Attestation:	19 years	
Period of Service:	1826 — 1842	
Age on Discharge:	36 years 9 months	
Length of Service:	15 years 164 days	
Foreign Service:	Mediterranean	9 years 4 months
	Canada	3 years 1 months
Reason for Discharge:	Loss of sight in right eye and Impaired Vision in left and completely worn out	
Character:	Bad	
Trade or Occupation:	Labourer	
Can Sign Name:	Yes	
Height:	5' 8¼"	
Hair Colour:	Grey	
Eyes:	Grey	
Complexion:	Fair	
Intends to Reside:	Ballymahon Longford	
TAYLOR	James, private	
	2nd Foot	
19 Oct 1847	Discharged the Service Athlone	
8 Feb 1848	Admitted to Out-Pension	
	1/- per diem	
	Pension paid Ipswich	
1 June 1850	Arrived per *'Scindian'*	
Jan 1857	a J Taylor contributed 2/- to the Florence Nightingale Fund	
28 Mar 1862	Died	
Service and Personal Details:		
Place of Birth:	Wingfield Suffolk	
Age on Attestation:	17 years	
Period of Service:	1826 — 1847	
Age on Discharge:	38 years 8 months	
Length of Service:	20 years 263 days	
Foreign Service:	East Indies	17 years 7 months
Reason for Discharge:	General infirmity	
Character:	Very Good	

Trade or Occupation:	Labourer
Can Sign Name:	X his mark on discharge
Height:	5' 5½"
Hair Colour:	Brown
Eyes:	Brown
Complexion:	Sallow

TAYLOR	John, Serjeant
	21st Hussars
Previous Regiments	12th Lancers; 9th Lancers; 3rd B. E. Cavalry;
26 Apr 1864	Discharged the Service Netley
	1/4½d. per diem
	Pension paid Derby
22 Dec 1866	Arrived per *'Corona'*
Service and Personal Details:	
Place of Birth:	Ashy de la Zouch Leicestershire
Age on Attestation:	14 years 4 months
Period of Service:	1835 — 1864
Age on Discharge:	43 years ?1 month
Length of Service:	24 years 207 days
Foreign Service:	India 24 years
Medal Entitlement:	Good Conduct with gratuity; Sutlej; Punjaub; Indian Mutiny
Reason for Discharge:	Chronic Rheumatism and worn out
Character:	Good
Trade or Occupation:	Labourer
Can Sign Name:	Yes
Height:	5' 9½"
Hair Colour:	Brown
Eyes:	Grey
Complexion:	Fresh
Remarks:	Serving under British Pension Rules
Intends to Reside:	Ashy de la Zouch Leicestershire

TAYLOR	Joseph, private
	2nd Dragoon Guards
24 Oct 1853	Discharged the Service Royal Barracks Dublin
14 Nov 1853	Discharge approved
22 Nov 1853	Admitted to Out-Pension
	Pension paid 1st Manchester Pension District
	1/- per diem
8 June 1858	Arrived per *'Lord Raglan'*
1 May 1873	Pension increased to 1/3d. per diem for 12½ years service in the Enrolled Force
12 Apr 1874	Payment of £15 improvement grant for Cottage
1874	Stationed Fremantle
1874	"Wife in Asylum"
1878	Died aged 68
Service and Personal Details:	
Place of Birth:	Castleton Lancashire
Age on Attestation:	19 years
Period of Service:	1829 — 1853

Age on Discharge:	43 years
Length of Service:	24 years 34 days
Reason for Discharge:	Rupture in left side
Character:	Good
Trade or Occupation:	Weaver
Can Sign Name:	Yes
Height:	6' 1¼"
Hair Colour:	Light
Eyes:	Grey
Complexion:	Fresh
Intends to Reside:	Rochdale Lancashire

TAYLOR	William, private [Military pensioner]
	12th Foot
Previous Regiment	99th Foot
Dec 1864	Discharged the Service Sydney New South Wales
20 June 1865	Pension ratified
20 July 1865	Discharge approved
	As the Proceeding of the Regimental Board took place at Sydney New South Wales on the 12th December 1864 private William Taylor probably arrived in W.A. from that State shortly afterwards
1865	Pension paid Perth Western Australia
	8d. per diem
1866	Pension paid Taunton

Service and personal Details:

Place of Birth:	Hazelbury Yeovil Somerset
Age on Attestation:	18 years 8 months
Period of Service:	1842 — 1865
Age on Discharge:	40 years
Length of Service:	21 years 137 days months
Foreign Service:	Australian Station 21 years 86 days
Reason for Discharge:	Pleuritus [sic] and Chronic Rheumatism
Character & Conduct:	Indifferent
Trade or Occupation:	Servant
Can Sign Name:	Yes
Height:	5' 5¾"
Hair Colour:	Brown
Eye Colour:	Blue
Complexion:	Dark
Intends to Reside:	Perth Western Australia

TEAGUE	Thomas, private
	Royal Canadian Rifles
Previous Regiment	56th Foot
9 Nov 1852	Discharged the Service Chatham
	Pension paid Newcastle
	1/2d. per diem
24 May 1855	Arrived per *'Stag'*
1856	To South Australia from Western Australia
1860	Pension paid Victoria
1871	Adelaide South Australia

1872	Off Roll — "Not Appeared"
Service and Personal Details:	
Place of Birth:	Cadoxton Glamorganshire
Age on Attestation:	19 years
Period of Service:	1827 — 1852
Age on Discharge:	41 years
Length of Service:	24 years 177 days
Foreign Service:	West Indies 8 years 3 months North America 12 years
Reason for Discharge:	Having completed in total 25 years and Failing Efficiency and Impaired Hearing
Character:	Very Good
Trade or Occupation:	Labourer
Can Sign Name:	X his mark on discharge; Yes on Attestation
Height:	5' 9"
Hair Colour:	Brown
Eyes:	Grey
Complexion:	Fair

TEAPLER James, private
37th Foot

12 Mar 1867	Discharged the Service Preston Pension paid 2nd Manchester Pension District 10d. per diem
9 Jan 1868	Arrived per *'Hougoumont'*
1881	Pension increased to 1/3d. per diem for service in the Enrolled Force
27 Aug 1881	Assigned North Fremantle Lots P42 and P45
12 May 1882	a James Teapler aged 54 applying for a position in Public Service as Warder Champion Bay
1883	Application for Title to North Fremantle Lots P42 and P45
29 Aug 1884	Granted Fee Simple North Fremantle Lots P42 and P45
June 1897	Residing Perth
Feb 1906	W.O. correspondence to H.E. the Governor of Western Australia
1907	Died
Service and Personal Details:	
Place of Birth:	Tullamore Co. Limerick
Age on Attestation:	20 years
Period of Service:	1845 — 1867
Age on Discharge:	42 years
Length of Service:	21 years 17 days
Foreign Service:	Ceylon 9 years 11 months Bengal 3 years 10 months
Medal Entitlement:	Indian Mutiny
Reason for Discharge:	Having completed 21 years service
Character:	Good
Trade or Occupation:	Labourer
Can Sign Name:	Yes

Height: 5' 11"
Hair Colour: Brown
Eyes: Hazel
Complexion: Fresh
Distinguishing Marks: A few slight whitish spots on his breast
Intends to Reside: Manchester

TEED William, private
Rifle Brigade
12 July 1853 Discharged the Service Dover Castle
Pension paid Leicester
1/- per diem
2 Apr 1856 Arrived per *'William Hammond'*
1856 "Charged with military offence"
1859 Charged with drunkenness
1862 Died

Service and Personal Details:
Place of Birth: St Marys Leicester
Age on Attestation: 18 years 2 months
Period of Service: 1831 — 1853
Age on Discharge: 41 years or 40 years 6 months
Length of Service: 21 years 145 days
Foreign Service: North America 5 years
Malta &
Ionian Isles 5 years 7 months
Cape of Good Hope 3 years 7 months
Medal Entitlement: Kaffir War 1846/7 and against the Intransigent Boers 1848
Reason for Discharge: Worn Out from length of service

Character: Indifferent
Trade or Occupation: Labourer
Can Sign Name: Yes

Height: 5' 9½"
Hair Colour: Brown
Eyes: Grey
Complexion: Fair
Intends to Reside: St Marys Leicester

TELFORD James, gunner and driver
Royal Artillery — 1st Battalion
Surname Variant TILFORD
13 Oct 1846 Discharged the Service Woolwich
Pension paid Perth Scotland
1/- per diem
14 Aug 1854 Arrived per *'Ramilies'*
1856 Employed as Assistant warder
1863 Stationed Perth District
1864 ptve J Telford Pensioner Force at Perth contributed to the Greenough Fire Relief Fund
14 May 1865 Died aged 58 buried East Perth Cemetery

Service and Personal Details:
Place of Birth: Kilsythe Stirlingshire

Age on Attestation:	18 years	
Period of Service:	1825 — 1846	
Age on Discharge:	39 years 105 days	
Length of Service:	21 years 105 days	
Foreign Service:	Nova Scotia	6 years 3 months
	Spain	3 years 6 months
Reason for Discharge:	Rupture of right groin	
Character:	Very Good	
Trade or Occupation:	Labourer	
Can Sign Name:	Yes	
Height:	5' 10½"	
Hair Colour:	Brown	
Eyes:	Hazel	
Complexion:	Fresh	

THACKER

	James, private
	1st Foot
3 Aug 1858	Discharged the Service
	Pension paid Kings Lynn
	1/-½d. per diem
19 Aug 1859	Arrived per *'Sultana'*
1875	Pension paid Western Australia
10 Mar 1883	Assigned North Fremantle Town Lot P91
1881	Pension increased to 1/6d. per diem for 12 years service in the Enrolled Force
1884	Application for Title to North Fremantle Town Lot P91
June 1897	Residing Fremantle
Feb 1900	Attended fete at Oval
1901	Died aged 85

Service and Personal Details:

Place of Birth:	Swaffham Norfolk	
Age on Attestation:	18 years 2 months	
Period of Service:	1836 — 1858	
Age on Discharge:	41 years	
Length of Service:	21 years 343 days	
Foreign Service:	Canada	6 years
	Nova Scotia	5 months
	West Indies	1 year 4 months
	Cephalonia	2 years 3 months
Medal Entitlement:	Good Conduct and Long Service with gratuity	
Reason for Discharge:	Worn out and suffers from Phthisis Pulmonatis	
Character:	Very Good	
Trade or Occupation:	Labourer	
Can Sign Name:	X his mark on discharge	
Height:	5' 7"	
Hair Colour:	Sandy	
Eyes:	Brown	
Complexion:	Fair	
Intends to Reside:	Swaffham	

THOMPSON	James, private [Trumpeter]	
	16th Lancers	
Previous Regiment	13th Light Dragoons	
12 Nov 1860	Discharged the Service Aldershot	
	Pension paid Brighton	
	8d. per diem	
1863	was to embark per *'Clyde'*	
THOMPSON	Robert, Serjeant	
	RA Depot Brigade	
13 Sept 1867	Discharged the Service Woolwich	
3 Dec 1867	Admitted to Out-Pension	
	Pension paid Cardiff	
	1/1½d. per diem	
1868	Pension increased to 1/8d. per diem	
1873	Pension paid Greenwich	
19 Feb 1874	Arrived per *'Naval Brigade'*	
14 Mar 1876	Assigned North Fremantle Lot P48	
1881	Pension increased to 1/10½d per diem for service in the Enrolled Force	
May 1883	Application for Title North Fremantle Lot P48	
6 Sept 1883	Granted Fee Simple North Fremantle Lot P48	
1883	Died	
Service and Personal Details:		
Place of Birth:	Dromore Co. Down	
Age on Attestation:	17 years 10 months	
Period of Service:	1846 — 1867	
Age on Discharge:	39 years	
Length of Service:	21 years	
Foreign Service:	Canada	5 years 3 months
	Crimea	10 months
	Gibraltar	[no time period given]
Medal Entitlement:	Crimea	
Reason for Discharge:	Having completed 21 years service	
Character:	Very Good	
Trade or Occupation:	Labourer	
Can Sign Name:	Yes	
Height:	5' 9½"	
Hair Colour:	Light Brown	
Eyes:	Grey	
Complexion:	Fair	
Intends to Reside:	Swansea Glamorganshire South Wales	
THOMPSON	William, private	
	20th Foot	
29 July 1856	Discharged the Service Chatham	
	Pension paid Limerick	
	7d. per diem	
8 June 1859	Arrived per *'Lord Raglan'*	
1864	Pension paid Adelaide South Australia	
1864	New Zealand	
Service and Personal Details:		

Place of Birth:	St Johns Limerick Ireland	
Age on Attestation:	19 years	
Period of Service:	1842 — 1856	
Age on Discharge:	33 years	
Length of Service:	14 years 70 days	
Foreign Service:	Bermuda	4 years 291 days
	North America	6 years 56 days
	Crimea	1 year 272 days
Medal Entitlement:	Crimea	
Reason for Discharge:	Unfit for further service	
Character:	Good	
Trade or Occupation:	Labourer	
Can Sign Name:	Yes	
Height:	5' 8½"	
Hair Colour:	Dark	
Eyes:	Blue	
Complexion:	Fresh	
Intends to Reside:	Limerick	

THOMPSON	William, gunner EIC
	Bengal Artillery 2nd Battalion
	Out Pension No 119
8 Aug 1851	Discharged the Service
	Embarked UK per *'Sutlej'*
	Pension paid Sligo Pension District
	1/3d per diem or 1/4d depending on record
30 Apr 1853	Arrived per *'Pyrenees'* [2]
1853	Charged with Military Offence
1854	Charged with Military Offence
1857	Pension paid Calcutta [12/WA/111]
Service and Personal Details:	
Where Born:	Ballyshannon Co Donegal
Trade or Occupation:	Clerk
Where Enlisted:	London
Presidency:	Bengal
Length of Service:	22 years 1 month
Age on Discharge:	44 years
Character:	Good
Reason for Discharge:	Broken constitution and debility. Two fingers of his hand smashed in the Khyber Pass
Medal Entitlement:	Afghanistan
Height:	5' 9½" or 5' 10" depending on record source
Complexion:	Fresh
Eye Colour:	Blue
Hair Colour:	Sandy
Intends to Reside:	Mt Charles Sligo

THORNTON	James, private
	Royal Canadian Rifles
Previous Regiment	16th Foot
8 July 1862	Discharged the Service Chatham
	Pension paid 2nd Glasgow Pension District
	1/- per diem

12 Sept 1864	Arrived per *'Merchantman'* [2]	
11 Nov 1868	Died	

Service and Personal Details:

Place of Birth:	Bleris Co. Antrim	
Age on Attestation:	20 years	
Period of Service:	1841 — 1862	
Age on Discharge:	41 years	
Length of Service:	21 years 21 days	
Foreign Service:	West Indies	1 year
	North America	7 years 6 months
Reason for Discharge:	Having served 21 years	
Character:	Very Good	
Trade or Occupation:	Weaver	
Can Sign Name:	Yes	
Height:	5' 6½"	
Hair Colour:	Brown	
Eyes:	Blue	
Complexion:	Fresh	
Intends to Reside:	Glasgow	

THROSSELL Michael, Corporal
17th Lancers [Dragoons]

12 Oct 1836	Discharged the Service
9 Nov 1836	Admitted to Out-Pension
	Pension paid Drogheda
	6d. per diem
1845	Pension paid Cambridge
1846	Northampton
1 June 1850	Arrived per *'Scindian'*
1850	Employed by Convict Establishment
1855	Died — buried in Anglican section of East Perth Pioneer Cemetery

Service and Personal Details:

Place of Birth:	Titchmarsh Northamptonshire
Age on Attestation:	18 years
Period of Service:	1827 — 1836
Age on Discharge:	26 years 8 months
Length of Service:	8 years 249 days
Reason for Discharge:	Dislocated bones of left foot due to horse falling along with rider
Character:	Good and efficient soldier, trustworthy and sober
Trade or Occupation:	Labourer
Can Sign Name:	Yes
Height:	5' 10"
Hair Colour:	Brown
Eyes:	Grey
Complexion:	Fresh

TIERNEY Matthew, private
57th Foot

Surname Variant	TEARNEY

28 May 1860	Discharged the Service Cork	
12 June 1860	Discharge approved	
	Pension paid 1st Cork Pension District	
	1/-½d. per diem	
1861	Pension paid 2nd Manchester Pension District	
31 Dec 1862	Arrived per *'York'*	
Oct 1876	Attempted suicide at convict prison	
1876	Died aged 57	
	Inquest at Fremantle Prison Hospital on the body of Matthew Tiemey free, late a private of the Enrolled Force, returned a Verdict of — " Died from the effects of a gunshot wound in the left jaw, caused by an accident while on sentry at the prison.	
Service and Personal Details:		
Place of Birth:	St Marks Dublin	
Age on Attestation:	20 years	
Period of Service:	1837 — 1860	
Age on Discharge:	42 years 5 months	
Length of Service:	22 years 152 days	
Foreign Service:	East Indies	7 years 9 months
	Corfu	1 year 6 months
	Crimea	1 year 3 months
Medal Entitlement:	Crimea with clasps and Turkish Crimean	
Reason for Discharge:	Own Request having served over 21 years	
Character:	Very Good	
Trade or Occupation:	Labourer	
Can Sign Name:	X his mark on discharge	
Height:	5' 7½"	
Hair Colour:	Brown	
Eyes:	Brown	
Complexion:	Sallow	
Intends to Reside:	Baggot Street Dublin	

TOBIN	John, Corporal	
	29th Foot	
Previous Regiments	6th; 40th	
28 Aug 1849	Discharged the Service Chatham	
	Pension paid 1st Dublin Pension District	
	1/3d. per diem	
30 Apr 1853	Arrived per *'Pyrenees'* [2]	
1853	Employed by Convict service without sanction of Staff Officer Pensions	
Service and Personal Details:		
Place of Birth:	St Michans Dublin	
Age on Attestation:	20 years	
Period of Service:	1827 — 1849	
Age on Discharge:	42 years or 41 years 1 month	
Length of Service:	21 years 55 days	
Foreign Service:	East Indies	20 years 3 months
Reason for Discharge:	Physical debility	

Character:	Very Good
Trade or Occupation:	Servant
Can Sign Name:	Yes
Height:	5' 9"
Hair Colour:	Sandy
Eyes:	Grey
Complexion:	Fair
Intends to Reside:	Queen's Street Dublin

TONRY	William, private 19th Foot
Surname Variants	TONNY; TOMY; TOAMY
24 July 1855	Discharged the Service Pension paid Roscommon 9d. per diem
1861	Pension paid Montreal
1862	Chatham
1862	Pension paid 1st East London Pension District
9 June 1862	Arrived per *'Norwood'* [1]
1865	Pension paid Melbourne from Perth West. Aust.
1868	Victoria
1870	New South Wales
1874	Adelaide South Australia

Service and Personal Details:

Place of Birth:	Stokestown Roscommon
Age on Attestation:	24 years
Period of Service:	1848 — 1855
Age on Discharge:	30 years
Length of Service:	6 years 141 days
Foreign Service:	none annotated
Medal Entitlement:	Crimea with clasp
Reason for Discharge:	Gunshot wound to the centre of the calf and to the left knee injuring the tibia, also gunshot would to the back and ball still lodged therein. Received at Inkerman
Character:	Indifferent
Trade or Occupation:	Labourer
Can Sign Name:	Yes
Height:	6'
Hair Colour:	Light Brown
Eyes:	Grey
Complexion:	Fresh

TOOHILL	James, private 63rd Foot
Previous Regiment	69th Foot
Surname Variant	TOOTILL
24 May 1870	Discharged the Service Kinsale Pension paid Limerick 1/1d. per diem
1873	Pension paid Greenwich
19 Feb 1874	Arrived per *'Naval Brigade'*

1878	Pension increased to 1/3d. per diem for service in the Enrolled Force
1883	Application for Title Location X22 Bootenal/ Greenough
Dec 1887	Granted Pensioner Location 22 at Bootenal
June 1897	Residing Perth
1913	a James Toohill died

Service and Personal Details:

Place of Birth:	Cappa Rathkeale Co. Limerick	
Age on Attestation:	17 years	
Period of Service:	1847 — 1870	
Age on Discharge:	39 years 6 months	
Length of Service:	21 years 179 days	
Foreign Service:	West Indies	5 years 11 months
	East Indies	2 years 6 months
	British North America	1 year
Medal Entitlement:	Long Service and Good Conduct	
Reason for Discharge:	Claimed it on 2nd period of 'Limited Engagement'	
Character:	Very Good	
Trade or Occupation:	Labourer	
Can Sign Name:	Yes	
Height:	5' 8"	
Hair Colour:	Brown	
Eyes:	Grey	
Complexion:	Dark	
Intends to Reside:	Post Office Limerick	

TOOLE Felix, private
86th Foot

14 June 1859	Discharged the Service Dublin Pension paid Liverpool 1/- per diem
31 Dec 1862	Arrived per *'York'*
Feb 1864	ptve F Toole Pensioner Force at Perth contributed to the Greenough Fire Relief Fund
1864	To South Australia from Perth West Australia
1865	Pension paid Melbourne
1865	Madras
1868	Carlow

Service and Personal Details:

Place of Birth:	Hacketstown Co. Carlow	
Age on Attestation:	18 years	
Period of Service:	1837 — 1859	
Age on Discharge:	39 years 9 months	
Length of Service:	21 years 286 days	
Foreign Service:	East Indies	13 years 7 months
Medal Entitlement:	Long Service and Good Conduct with gratuity	
Reason for Discharge:	Own Request having served 21 years	
Character:	Good	
Trade or Occupation:	Labourer	
Can Sign Name:	X his mark on discharge	

Height:	5' 8"
Hair Colour:	Light Brown
Eyes:	Grey
Complexion:	Fresh
Intends to Reside:	Liverpool

TOOLE	Patrick, private
	29th Foot
Previous Regiment	62nd Foot
5 Nov 1861	Discharge approved
12 Nov 1861	Discharged the Service Chatham
	Pension paid Preston
	1/- per diem
1862	Pension paid Bermuda
15 Feb 1863	Arrived per *'Merchantman'* [1]
May 1875	"In prison" Convicted at Freemantle [sic] Court House West Australia of selling 'Porter' without a licence. Was fined £30 or on default to go to prison for 3 months and 7 days during which time his pension would be suspended
21 Jan 1874	Assigned North Fremantle Lot P50
1878	Pension increased to 1/6d. per diem for service in the Enrolled Force
Mar 1879	Reverted to former rate on being retaken into the Force
1881	Pension again increased to 1/6d. per diem
Jan 1883	Application for Title North Fremantle Lot P50
10 Apr 1883	Granted Fee Simple North Fremantle Lot P50
1884	Died

Service and Personal Details:		
Place of Birth:	Galway Ireland	
Age on Attestation:	18 years	
Period of Service:	1843 — 1861	
Age on Discharge:	36 years	
Length of Service:	18 years 13 days	
Foreign Service:	East Indies	12 years 9 months
Medal Entitlement:	Punjaub Medal with clasp for Chillianwallah	
Reason for Discharge:	Chronic Ophthalmia	
Character:	Very Good	
Trade or Occupation:	Labourer	
Can Sign Name:	Yes	
Height:	5' 5½"	
Hair Colour:	Light Brown	
Eyes:	Blue	
Complexion:	Sallow	
Intends to Reside:	Preston Lancashire	

TOOVEY	Michael, private EIC
	2nd Bengal European Regiment
Surname Variants	TOOHEY; TOOKEY; TOOEY; TOOMEY
	Out Pension No 136
17 June 1856	Admitted to Out-pension
	Pension paid Ennis

	9d. per diem
1862	Pension paid Bermuda
15 Feb 1863	Arrived per *'Merchantman'* [1]
1864	ptve M Tookey Pensioner Force Fremantle District contributed to the Greenough Fire Relief Fund
circa 1865	Serjeant Toovey, an ex-Indian regular was stationed at Round Pond, supervising the convicts who clearing and making the road from Perth to Albany [Trove]
12 Oct 1867	Died

Service and Personal Details:	
Place of Birth:	Duncliff Co. Clare
Trade or Occupation:	Labourer
Presidency:	Bengal
Length of Service:	14 years 1 month
Age on Discharge:	36 years
Character:	Good
Reason for Discharge:	Worn out
Height:	5' 10"
Complexion:	Fair
Eye Colour:	Brown
Hair Colour:	Sandy
Intends to Reside:	Ennis

TOPPING

	William, private
	37th Foot
19 Mar 1861	Discharged the Service Chatham
	Pension paid Preston
	1/-½d. per diem
31 Dec 1862	Arrived per *'York'*
1866	Pension paid South Australia from Perth W.A.
1870	"Pension to wife as man in asylum"

Service and Personal Details:		
Place of Birth:	Leeds Yorkshire	
Age on Attestation:	17 years 6 months	
Period of Service:	1839 — 1861	
Age on Discharge:	39 years or 38 years 8 months	
Length of Service:	20 years 91 days	
Foreign Service:	Nova Scotia	8 months
	Ceylon	10 years 8 months
	Bengal	2 years 3 months
Reason for Discharge:	Chronic Dysentery	
Character:	Good	
Trade or Occupation:	Labourer or Ribbon Weaver	
Can Sign Name:	Yes	
Height:	5' 7"	
Hair Colour:	Fair	
Eyes:	Blue	
Complexion:	Fair	
Intends to Reside:	Preston Lancashire	

TORNAY	Richard, private
	41st Foot
Previous Regiment	48th Foot
Surname Variants	TORNEY; TIERNEY
26 Sept 1843	Discharged the Service Fort Pitt
	Pension paid 2nd Belfast Pension District
	1/- per diem
15 Aug 1865	Arrived per *'Racehorse'*
16 Sept 1871	Died
Service and Personal Details:	
Place of Birth:	Downpatrick Co. Down
Age on Attestation:	19 years
Period of Service:	1819 — 1843
Age on Discharge:	43 years
Length of Service:	23 years 335 days
Foreign Service:	East Indies &
	Scinde &
	Afghanistan 18 years 8 months
Medal Entitlement:	Afghanistan 1842
Reason for Discharge:	Repeated attacks of Intermittent Fever
Character:	Good
Trade or Occupation:	Carpenter
Can Sign Name:	Yes
Height:	6'
Hair Colour:	Grey
Eyes:	Blue
Complexion:	Fresh
Intends to Reside:	Downpatrick Co. Down

TOWERS	Peter, private
	RM
Surname Variant	TORVIES
7 July 1836	Discharged the Service
1850	Pension paid Chatham
1 June 1850	Arrived per *'Scindian'*
22 Jan 1854	"Dismissed from Enrolled Force as unfit for further service in the Enrolled Force"
1855	Charged with drunkenness
1866	Died
Service and Personal Details:	
Place of Birth:	High Church Edinburgh, Midlothian Scotland
Age on Attestation:	19 years
Marine Division:	Chatham
Period of Service:	1828 — 1836
Length of Service:	7 years 8 months 3 days
Reason for Discharge:	as an Invalid
Trade or Occupation:	Shoemaker
Can Sign Name:	Yes
Height:	5' 6¼"
Hair Colour:	Fair
Eyes:	Blue
Complexion:	Fair

TRACEY	John, private
	18th Foot
Surname Variants	TRACY; TREACEY
1 Jan 1856	Discharged the Service Chatham
	Pension paid Fermoy
	8d. per diem
1859	Pension paid 1st Cork Pension District
9 June 1862	Arrived per *'Norwood'* [1]
1864	ptve J Tracey Pensioner
	Force at Perth contributed to the Greenough Fire Relief Fund
1865	Pension paid Western Australia
1865	Employed as Assistant Warder Champion Bay
1868	Granted Greenough Locs 44 and 45
Apr 1871	'a John Tracey - Pensioner Application for Title Geraldton Loc 2' [CONS 5000 — SROWA]
1874	Pension increased to 1/1½d. per diem for service in the Enrolled Force
1893	Died Geraldton

Service and Personal Details:		
Place of Birth:	Mallow Co. Cork	
Age on Attestation:	19 years	
Period of Service:	1854 — 1855	
Age on Discharge:	20 years 1½ months	
Length of Service:	1 year 45 days	
Foreign Service:	Crimea	6 months
Medal Entitlement:	Crimea	
Reason for Discharge:	Amputation of fore and middle finger	
Character:	Good	
Trade or Occupation:	Labourer	
Can Sign Name:	X his mark on Attestation	
Height:	5' 7½"	
Hair Colour:	Black	
Eyes:	Hazel	
Complexion:	Freckled	

TRACEY	Thomas, private
	86th Foot
Previous Regiment	27th Foot
22 May 1855	Discharged the Service Chatham
	Pension paid 1st Liverpool Pension District
	9d. per diem for 3 years
1859	Pension made permanent
29 Jan 1862	Arrived per *'Lincelles'*
31 Dec 1862	Pension paid South Australia

Service and Personal Details:	
Place of Birth:	Innis McSaint Co. Fermanagh
Age on Attestation:	20 years
Period of Service:	1839 — 1855
Age on Discharge:	38 years
Length of Service:	14 years 337 days

Foreign Service:	East Indies 12 years 1 month
Reason for Discharge:	Rheumatism and ?Cymanche Tonsillans
Character:	Good
Trade or Occupation:	Labourer
Can Sign Name:	Yes
Height:	5' 10"
Hair Colour:	Dark Brown
Eyes:	Grey
Complexion:	Dark
Intends to Reside:	Manchester

TRANAILLES	Charles, private
also known as	**TRAYNAILS**
	29th Foot
Previous Regiment	62nd Foot
Surname Variants	TRAINAILES; TRENAIL; TRAINAILE
13 Aug 1850	Discharged the Service Chatham Pension paid 2nd Plymouth Pension District 7d. per diem
7 Feb 1853	Arrived per *'Dudbrook'*
1853	"Charged with military offence"
1855	On Military Return with wife occupying land at North Fremantle
Jan 1857	Contributed 2/- to the Florence Nightingale Fund
July 1860	Application for Title Freshwater Bay Loc P235 and P257
1867	Died – buried East Perth Cemetery

Service and Personal Details:

Place of Birth:	Bradford Peverell Dorset
Age on Attestation:	21 years
Period of Service:	1835 — 1850
Age on Discharge:	36 years 4 months or 35 years 7 months
Length of Service:	14 years 216 days
Foreign Service:	East Indies 14 years 7 months
Reason for Discharge:	Labouring under Chronic Hepatitis
Character:	Very Good
Trade or Occupation:	Farmer's Servant
Can Sign Name:	X his mark on discharge
Height:	5' 6"
Hair Colour:	Fair
Eyes:	Blue
Complexion:	Fresh
Intends to Reside:	Dorchester but decided on Plymouth
Married:	Martha

TRASEY	Joseph, gunner and driver
	RA 2nd Battalion
Surname Variants	TASEY; TRACEY
21 Sept 1853	Discharge approved
11 Oct 1853	Discharged the Service Woolwich Pension paid 2nd North London Pension District

	7d. per diem
14 Aug 1854	Arrived per *'Ramillies'*
Jan 1857	contributed 2/- to the Florence Nightingale Fund
1857	Pension paid Melbourne Victoria "Found dead in the prairie, eaten by dogs, supposed to have died of thirst"

Service and Personal Details:		
Place of Birth:	St Lukes London Middlesex	
Age on Attestation:	20 years	
Period of Service:	1838 — 1853	
Age on Discharge:	35 years 7 months	
Length of Service:	15 years 195 days	
Foreign Service:	North America	12 years 4 months
Reason for Discharge:	Disease of the Heart	
Character:	Good	
Trade or Occupation:	Labourer	
Can Sign Name:	Yes	
Height:	5' 9"	
Hair Colour:	Light Brown	
Eyes:	Hazel	
Complexion:	Fresh	

TRAVERS	John, gunner
	RA 4th Brigade
27 Nov 1866	Discharged the Service Sheerness
	Pension paid Edinburgh
	11d. per diem
13 July 1867	Arrived per *'Norwood'* [2]
1871	Pension paid Calcutta
1872	Dundee
1874	Glasgow
1875	Edinburgh
1881	Admitted to In-Pension Chelsea
2 Mar 1892	Died

Service and Personal Details:		
Place of Birth:	Westkirk Scotland	
Age on Attestation:	18 years 6 months	
Period of Service:	1845 — 1866	
Age on Discharge:	39 years 8 months	
Length of Service:	20 years 342 days	
Foreign Service:	Canada	7 years 5 months
	Turkey	2 years
Medal Entitlement:	Crimea with clasps; Turkish Crimea	
Reason for Discharge:	Having completed 21 years service	
Character:	Good	
Trade or Occupation:	Shoemaker	
Can Sign Name:	Yes	
Height:	5' 9½"	
Hair Colour:	Dark Brown and Grey	
Eyes:	Blue	
Complexion:	Fresh	

Intends to Reside:	No. 55 Princes Street Edinburgh

TRAYHOURN	Richard, private [35] 96th Foot	
Surname Variants	[some] TRAYHORNE; TRAYHORN; TRAYHURN; TRAYHERN	
14 Mar 1848	Discharged the Service Chatham Pension paid Bristol 1/- per diem	
25 Oct 1850	Arrived per *'Hashemy'*	
1851	Employed by Convict Establishment as a Tailor	
16 Aug 1851	Appointed as Police Constable in the Police Force at Perth	
Jan 1853	Dismissed from police force	
no date	Assigned Perth Military Pensioner Lot 109	
1855	Pension paid VDL [sic]	
1856	Charged with military offence	
Jan 1857	Contributed 2/- to the Florence Nightingale Fund	
May 1861	Application for Title to Perth Lot 109	
1864	ptve R Trayhorne Pensioner Force at Perth contributed to the Greenough Fire Relief Fund	
1863	Stationed Perth District	
Dec 1871	Died VDL [sic] — War Office Correspondence	
15 Dec 1871	Died aged 66 at Perth.	
Service and Personal Details:		
Place of Birth:	Thornbury Bristol Gloucestershire	
Age on Attestation:	17 years	
Period of Service:	1824 — 1848	
Age on Discharge:	41 years	
Length of Service:	22 years 85 days	
Foreign Service:	Bermuda	3 years
	Nova Scotia	8 years
	Australia	5 years
Reason for Discharge:	Unfit for further service	
Character:	Good	
Trade or Occupation:	Tailor	
Can Sign Name:	Yes	
Height:	5' 5½"	
Hair Colour:	Brown	
Eyes:	Hazel	
Complexion:	Fresh	
Intends to Reside:	Thornbury nr. Bristol	

TRETS	Robert, private 96th Foot
Surname Variant	TRETT
12 July 1853	Discharged the Service Chatham Pension paid Norwich 1/- per diem
2 Apr 1856	Arrived per *'William Hammond'*
1882	Residing near Lake Sutherland
June 1897	Residing Fremantle
1909	Died

Service and Personal Details:	
Place of Birth:	Barlingham Norwich Norfolk
Age on Attestation:	18 years 2 months
Period of Service:	1830 — 1853
Age on Discharge:	40 years
Length of Service:	22 years 20 days
Foreign Service:	North America 4 years
	Australia 7 years 9 months
	India 3 years 8 months
Reason for Discharge:	Fever, Ophthalmia and Emaciation
Character:	Very Good
Trade or Occupation:	Labourer
Can Sign Name:	X his mark on discharge
Height:	5' 8¼"
Hair Colour:	Brown
Eyes:	Hazel
Complexion:	Fresh
Distinguishing Marks:	Scar against left eye
Intends to Reside:	nr. Burlingham Norfolk

TRIGWELL	Henry, Serjeant [Military Pensioner]
	Royal Sappers and Miners 20th Company
1851	Arrived per *'Anna Robinson'* with regiment
20 Mar 1861	Discharge approved
21 Dec 1861	Discharged the Service Fremantle
25 Mar 1862	Admitted to Out-Pension
	Pension paid Perth Western Australia
	1/10. per diem
1865	Pension paid Western Australia
1868	Residing Preston River with 11 children and fined for selling 'sugar beer'
1890	Died

Service and Personal Details:	
Place of Birth:	Ringmer Lewes Sussex
Age on Attestation:	21 years 4 months
Period of Service:	1836 — 1861
Age on Discharge:	46 years
Length of Service:	25 years 13 days
Foreign Service:	Gibraltar 7 years
	West Australia 10 years
Medal Entitlement:	Good Conduct and Long Service with gratuity of £10
Reason for Discharge:	Having elected to remain in the Australian Colonies
Character:	Exemplary
Trade or Occupation:	Smith
Can Sign Name:	Yes
Height:	5' 6"
Hair Colour:	Brown getting grey
Eyes:	Hazel
Complexion:	Fresh
Intends to Reside:	District of Bunbury Western Australia

Married:	Agnes Anne Garland
Children:	Henry John b. *c*1844 Gibraltar m. *c*1875 Josephine Armstrong Bunbury John b. *c*1846 England

TRUEMAN	John, Serjeant	
	64th Foot	
Previous Regiment	86th Foot	
Surname Variant	TRUMAN	
5 Feb 1861	Discharged the Service Chatham Pension paid Carlow 1/3d. per diem	
15 Apr 1864	Arrived per *'Clara'* [2]	
1866	Pension paid New Zealand from Fremantle	
1871	Died	
Service and Personal Details:		
Place of Birth:	Arklow Co. Wicklow	
Age on Attestation:	21 years	
Period of Service:	1843 — 1861	
Age on Discharge:	39 years	
Length of Service:	17 years 339 days	
Foreign Service:	East Indies	14 years 6 months
Reason for Discharge:	Chronic Rheumatism and Dysentery	
Character:	Very Good	
Trade or Occupation:	Servant	
Can Sign Name:	Yes	
Height:	5' 8½"	
Hair Colour:	Dark Brown	
Eyes:	Grey	
Complexion:	Dark	
Intends to Reside:	Invalid Depot Chatham but decided on Arklow Co. Wicklow	

TUBBS	Joseph, private	
	40th Foot	
Surname Variant	TUBB	
9 July 1845	Discharged the Service Chatham Pension paid 2nd West London Pension District 10d. per diem	
1851	Pension paid 2nd North London Pension District	
14 Aug 1854	Arrived per *'Ramillies'*	
1858	Pension paid South Australia	
18 Nov 1872	a Joseph Tubbs died South Australia	
Service and Personal Details:		
Place of Birth:	St Georges Knightsbridge London	
Age on Attestation:	21 years	
Period of Service:	1827 — 1845	
Age on Discharge:	39 years	
Length of Service:	17 years 84 days	
Foreign Service:	Van Diemans Land	5 months
	East Indies	10 years 11 months

	Scinde & Beloochistan & Afghanistan 3 years 11 months
Medal Entitlement:	2nd Afghan with 3 inscriptions; Bronze Star for Maharajpore
Reason for Discharge:	Wounded gun shot through right foot
Character:	Indifferent
Trade or Occupation:	Carpenter
Can Sign Name:	Yes
Height:	5' 7"
Hair Colour:	Dark
Eyes:	Grey
Complexion:	Sallow
Intends to Reside:	London

TUITE	Richard, private EIC Bengal European Light Infantry Out Pension No 15
8 Aug 1849	Admission to pension Pension paid 2nd Dublin Pension District 6d. per diem for one year to Aug 1850
1850	Pension paid 2nd East London Pension District
21 May 1851	Arrived per *'Mermaid'* "Dismissed from EPG for drunkenness" "Removal from Local Force as quite unfit to be trusted with arms" [WO4/289]
1852	Convicted for stealing from his employer
Feb 1853	Found drunk in the street
April 1853	Sought passage home
1853	Pension paid 2nd East London Pension District
1855	"£15 deducted from pension for passage home"
1858	Pension paid 2nd East London Pension District
1859	1st Dublin Pension District

Service and Personal Details: [L/AG/23/2/66]

Where Born:	St Thomas Dublin
Trade or Occupation:	Labourer
Where Enlisted:	Waterford
Presidency:	Bengal
Length of Service:	8 years 6 months or 9 years 6 months
Age on Discharge:	39 or 34 years [depending on record source]
Character:	Good
Reason for Discharge:	Chronic rheumatism: injury to left hip and suffering from scurvy
Height:	5' 7"
Complexion:	Fresh
Visage:	Oval
Eye Colour:	Blue
Hair Colour:	Brown
Intends to Reside:	No. 12 Spring Garden Parade Ballybough Rd., Dublin

TULLY	Bartholomew, private

	81st Foot	
16 Apr 1852	Discharged the Service Dublin	
	6d. per diem for 3 years	
6 Apr 1854	Arrived per *'Sea Park'* [WO4/290]	
Service and Personal Details:		
Place of Birth:	Kells Co. Meath	
Age on Attestation:	22 years	
Period of Service:	1839—1852	
Age on Discharge:	35 years 1 month	
Length of Service:	13 years 68 days	
Foreign Service:	West Indies	2 years 6 months
	Canada	4 years 1 month
Reason for Discharge:	Chronic Rheumatism	
Character:	Tolerably Good	
Trade or Occupation:	Labourer	
Can Sign Name:	X his mark on discharge	
Height:	5' 7½"	
Hair Colour:	Black	
Eyes:	Brown	
Complexion:	Dark	
Intends to Reside:	Kells Co. Meath	

TULLY	Bryan, private
	32nd Foot
Surname Variant	TULLEY
6 Nov 1860	Discharged the Service
	Pension paid 1st Dublin Pension District
	6d. per diem
9 June 1862	Arrived per *'Norwood'* [1]
1864	ptve Bryan Tully Pensioner Force at Perth contributed to the Greenough Fire Relief Fund
1864	Employed as Assistant Warder Held Title to Freshwater Bay Lot 1075 at Butlers Swamp
1872	Pension suspended and struck off Enrolled Force
1873	Pension suspended during 84 days imprisonment on conviction of desertion from Force of Enrolled Pensioners in Western Australia
Nov 1874	Convicted before Magistrate at Geraldton W.A. of not fulfilling engagement to cook in the Geraldine Mine. Sentenced to 3 months imprisonment during which pension suspended
Apr 1875	Convicted at the Supreme Court of Western Australia of obtaining money under false pretences. Imprisoned for 3 months during which pension suspended Further report on the above — considered and decision revised, so that pension to be paid to Colonial Govt. for wife and family during 6 months imprisonment and on final release from which his name to be struck off the Pension List
1875	Pension cancelled
1876	At Geraldton — Mary Tully in receipt of outdoor relief money

1879	Remanded Fremantle
1881	a Bryan Tully residing 51 Exeter St Plymouth
1885	Pensioner Bryan Tully — Petitions for continuation of payment of his pension which was forfeited due to desertion and imprisonment.
Feb 1886	To be restored to pension at former rate of 6d. per diem
Aug 1886	Charged with drunkenness
July 1894	Inquest held at Fremantle on the death of a Michael Bryan Tully aged about 60

Service and Personal Details:

Place of Birth:	Kilbarry Navan Co. Meath	
Age on Attestation:	18 years	
Period of Service:	1853 — 1860	
Age on Discharge:	25 years 6 months	
Length of Service:	8 years 140 days	
Foreign Service:	East Indies	6 years 10 months
Medal Entitlement:	Indian Mutiny with clasp	
Reason for Discharge:	Shot in the shoulder at Lucknow and Chronic Dysentery	
Character:	Good	
Trade or Occupation:	Labourer	
Can Sign Name:	Yes	
Height:	5' 6½"	
Hair Colour:	Dark Brown	
Eyes:	Hazel	
Complexion:	Sallow	
Intends to Reside:	Dublin	

TUNBRIDGE Peter, private
Royal Canadian Rifles

Previous Regiments	66th; 67th; 89th
9 Sept 1851	Discharged the Service Chatham Pension paid Galway 1/- per diem
6 Apr 1854	Arrived per *'Sea Park'*
Aug 1854	Died

Service and Personal Details:

Place of Birth:	Glandelagh Rathdrum Co. Wicklow	
Age on Attestation:	21 years	
Period of Service:	1831 — 1851	
Age on Discharge:	42 years	
Length of Service:	21 years 99 days	
Foreign Service:	North America	17 years 9 months
Reason for Discharge:	Chronic Rheumatism	
Character:	Very Good	
Trade or Occupation:	Carpenter	
Can Sign Name:	Yes	
Height:	5' 7"	
Hair Colour:	Fair	

Eyes:	Grey
Complexion:	Sallow
Intends to Reside:	Ballinrobe [sic] Co. Mayo

TUNNY John, Hospital Serjeant
80th Foot

Surname Variant	TUNNEY
23 July 1850	Discharged the Service Chatham Pension paid Stockport 1/9d. per diem
1851	Pension paid Maryborough
7 Feb 1853	Arrived per *'Dudbrook'*
Jan 1857	Contributed 3/- to the Florence Nightingale Fund
1873	Employed as Special Constable Albany
1873	In charge of Pensioners at Albany
1873	Pension increased to 2/- per diem for 20 years service in the Enrolled Force
1881	Application for Title Albany Sub P8 at £4/10/0 per acre
Feb 1893	Died at Gracefield near Cranbrook aged 85

Service and Personal Details:

Place of Birth:	Ballena Co. Mayo	
Age on Attestation:	17 years	
Period of Service:	1827 — 1849	
Age on Discharge:	40 years	
Length of Service:	21 years 183 days	
Foreign Service:	New South Wales	7 years 4 months
	East Indies	4 years 11 months
Medal Entitlement:	Sutlej with clasps	
Reason for Discharge:	Worn out from length of service and climate	
Character:	Very good	
Trade or Occupation:	Labourer	
Can Sign Name:	Yes	
Height:	5' 8½"	
Hair Colour:	Slightly Grey	
Eyes:	Brown	
Complexion:	Fresh	
Intends to Reside:	Stockport Cheshire	

TURNER George, private
Rifle Brigade [Depot]

29 Apr 1856	Discharged the Service Chatham Pension paid 2nd West London Pension District 9d. per diem
11 Feb 1861	Arrived per *'Palmeston'* Assigned Albany Pensioner Lot P7
1863	Stationed Perth District
1864	ptve G Turner Pensioner Force at Perth contributed to the Greenough Fire Relief Fund
1865	Pension paid Western Australia
1 Feb 1878	Application for Title Albany Pensioner Lot P7
1893	Died
1893	Albany Sub-district. Albany Station. Death of George Turner, — committed suicide.

Service and Personal Details:	
Place of Birth:	Southwark London Middlesex
Age on Attestation:	20 years
Period of Service:	1854 — 1855
Age on Discharge:	21 years
Length of Service:	354 days
Foreign Service:	Malta and Crimea 8 months
Medal Entitlement:	Crimea
Reason for Discharge:	Partial loss of right hand
Character:	Good
Trade or Occupation:	Labourer
Can Sign Name:	X his mark on discharge
Height:	5' 8½"
Hair Colour:	Dark Brown
Eyes:	Hazel
Complexion:	Fresh
Intends to Reside:	Kensington

TURNER John, private [WO97/528/117]
35th Foot

8 Aug 1848	Discharged the Service Chatham Pension paid 2nd North London Pension District 1/- per diem
1855	Pension paid Birr
1855	Cork
10 Sept 1856	Arrived per *'Runnymede'*
no date	Assigned Perth Pensioner Lot 111
1864	ptve J Turner Pensioner Force at Perth contributed to the Greenough Fire Relief Fund
Jan 1865	Application for Title to Perth Lot 111

Service and Personal Details:	
Place of Birth:	Cork Co. Cork
Age on Attestation:	18 years
Period of Service:	1827 — 1848
Age on Discharge:	40 years or 38 years 9 months
Length of Service:	20 years 226 days
Foreign Service:	West Indies 3 years 115 days Mauritius 10 years 328 days
Reason for Discharge:	Chronic Catarrh and General Debility
Character:	Very Good
Trade or Occupation:	Labourer
Can Sign Name:	X his mark on discharge
Height:	5' 8¼"
Hair Colour:	Light Brown
Eyes:	Grey
Complexion:	Sallow
Intends to Reside:	London Holborn

TURNER John, Serjeant
71st Foot

Previous Regiment	70th Foot

7 Sept 1858	Discharged the Service Chatham Pension paid 2nd Belfast Pension District 1/5½d. per diem	
15 Aug 1865	Arrived per *'Racehorse'*	
Nov 1865	a John Turner — rank given as Serjeant applied for Title Fremantle Town Lots 670; 671and 674 at £6/0/0 per lot	
1870	Died	
Service and Personal Details:		
Place of Birth:	Abbey St Albans Hertfordshire	
Age on Attestation:	19 years	
Period of Service:	1837 — 1858	
Age on Discharge:	40 years 4 months	
Length of Service:	21 years 153 days	
Foreign Service:	West Indies	2 years 5 months
	Canada	2 years 6 months
	West Indies	3 years 2 months
	Corfu	1 year 10 months
	Crimea	1 year 4 months
	Malta	1 month
Medal Entitlement:	Crimea	
Reason for Discharge:	Chronic Rheumatism	
Character:	Very Good	
Trade or Occupation:	Labourer	
Can Sign Name:	Yes	
Height:	5' 7"	
Hair Colour:	Dark	
Eyes:	Hazel	
Complexion:	Grey	

TURNER	John, private 90th Foot
18 Nov 1856	Discharged the Service Chatham Pension paid 1st East London Pension District 8d. per diem
27 May 1863	Arrived per *'Clyde'*
1874	Pension paid Adelaide South Australia
1875	Melbourne
1875	New Zealand
1876	From New Zealand to Western Australia
1878	Complains of being dismissed from Enrolled Force Western Australia and asks for Court of Enquiry
1 Apr 1881	Assigned Mt Eliza Perth Pensioner Lot 29/H
14 Apr 1881	At Fremantle, — John Turner, pensioner, stout, aged 51, 5'. 5" tall, brown hair turning grey, blue eyes, visage full, complexion fresh assaulting Sarah Turner, at Fremantle, on the 13th inst.
May 1881	W.O. correspondence
Nov 1883	Application for Title Perth Lot 29/H

17 Jan 1885	At York, — John Turner, middling stout, age 54 years; 5' 5" tall; hair and eyes grey; round visage; fresh complexion; pensioner; larceny of five £1 notes, One half sovereign, and a silver watch, the property of Joseph Watkins. Outcome — Case discharged
Service and Personal Details:	
Place of Birth:	Bethnal Green London Middlesex
Age on Attestation:	23 years
Period of Service:	1854 — 1856
Age on Discharge:	24 years
Length of Service:	1 year 296 days
Foreign Service:	Malta 1 month Crimea 11 months
Medal Entitlement:	Crimea with clasp
Reason for Discharge:	Suffers from the effects of a wound
Character:	Good
Trade or Occupation:	Tailor on Enlistment, Weaver on Discharge
Can Sign Name:	X his mark on discharge
Height:	5' 5"
Hair Colour:	Light Brown
Eyes:	Blue
Complexion:	Fresh
Intends to Reside:	Hunt Street Mile End New Town London

TURNER	William, private 78th Foot
Previous Regiment	28th Foot
13 May 1862	Discharged the Service Chatham Pension paid South London 9d. per diem
4 July 1866	Arrived per *'Belgravia'*
Mar 1879	Advertises - not answerable for his wife's debts
1881	Pension increased to 1/3d. per diem for service in the Enrolled Force
24 Aug 1881	Assigned North Fremantle Lot P59
Nov 1883	Application for Title North Fremantle Lot P59
24 Dec 1883	Granted Fee Simple North Fremantle Lot P59
June 1897	Residing Fremantle
no date	Employed as sexton of the old Fremantle cemetery
1907	Died aged 83 at Fremantle
[not verified]	Stolen on the 9th ult., from a box in owner's dwelling, Norfolk street, — Three silver [Army] medals one Persian, one Indian Mutiny, and the other a Good Conduct medal, with owner's name stamped on edge, the property of William Turner. Suspicion attaches to Mary Jane Hayes and Elizabeth Johnson, prostitutes
Service and Personal Details:	
Place of Birth:	Lambeth Surrey
Age on Attestation:	18 years 2 months

Period of Service:	1843 — 1862
Age on Discharge:	36 years 9 months
Length of Service:	18 years 220 days
Foreign Service:	East Indies 13 years 9 months
Medal Entitlement:	Good Conduct; Persia with clasp; Indian Mutiny
Reason for Discharge:	Chronic Hepatitis and Chronic Bronchitis and Palpitations of the Heart
Character:	Good
Trade or Occupation:	Labourer
Can Sign Name:	Yes
Height:	5' 5¾"
Hair Colour:	Brown
Eyes:	Hazel
Complexion:	Fresh
Distinguishing Marks:	Leech bites on both sides of Abdomen. Scar on neck
Intends to Reside:	No. 7 Bowling Green Street, Kennington Surrey

ULTIGHAN	Francis, Serjeant
	40th Foot
Previous Regiment	38th Foot
Surname Variant	UTTIGAN
22 May 1848	Discharged the Service Galway
28 Aug 1848	Discharge Approved
12 Sept 1848	Admitted to pension
	Pension paid 1st Edinburgh Pension District
	1/8d per diem
8 June 1858	Arrived per *'Lord Raglan'*
1865	Pension paid Western Australia
1875	Western Australia
1876	Died aged 68

Service and Personal Details:

Place of Birth:	Shanna Co. Tyrone	
Age on Attestation:	16 years	
Period of Service:	1825 — 1848	
Age on Discharge:	39 years	
Length of Service:	21 years 2 days	
Foreign Service:	New South Wales & Van Dieman's Land	1 year 3 months
	East Indies	12 years 7 months
	Scind & Afghanistan	3 years 11 months
Medal Entitlement:	2nd Afghan Campaign inscribed with Candahar, Ghuznee and Cabool; Bronze Star for Battle of Maharajpore	
Reason for Discharge:	Chronic Rheumatism	
Character:	Good	
Trade or Occupation:	Labourer	
Can Sign Name:	Yes	
Height:	5' 8½"	
Hair Colour:	Grey	

Eyes:	Blue
Complexion:	Dark

UNDERWOOD	William [6466]
	Grenadier Guards
Previous Regiment	Royal Artillery
1856	Invalided to UK
circa 1864	Emigrated to Victoria
	Employed with the Victorian Railways
circa 1875	Employed with the WAGR
July 1909	Died in the Perth Public Hospital

UNWIN	Emmanuel, private [Military Pensioner]
	Royal Sappers and Miners
1852	Employed as Instructing Warder Convict Dept.
14 Aug 1855	Discharged the Service Woolwich
	7d per diem for 15 months
1856	To Victoria with family
1888	Died aged 60

Service and Personal Details:

Place of Birth:	Blythe Redford Nottinghamshire	
Age on Attestation:	20 years 6 months	
Period of Service:	1849 — 1855	
Age on Discharge:	26 years 1 month	
Length of Service:	5 years 227 days	
Foreign Service:	Western Australia	3 years 6 months
Reason for Discharge:	Injury to left knee	
Character:	Very Good	
Trade or Occupation:	Stonemason	
Can Sign Name:	Yes	
Height:	5' 7½"	
Hair Colour:	Black	
Eyes:	Hazel	
Complexion:	Dark	
Remarks:	Sent to West. Australia after injury circa July 1851	

UPTON	Denis, private
	87th Foot
Previous Regiment	16th Foot
8 Jan 1861	Discharged the Service
	Pension paid Ennis
	11d. per diem
28 Dec 1863	Arrived per *'Lord Dalhousie'*
1878	Pension increased to 1/5d. per diem for service in the Enrolled Force
1878	To South Australia from Western Australia
	His land allocation re-assigned to J Connolly

Service and Personal Details:

Place of Birth:	New Castle Co. Limerick
Age on Attestation:	18 years
Period of Service:	1839 — 1860
Age on Discharge:	39 years
Length of Service:	21 years 14

Foreign Service:	East Indies	9 years 306 days
Medal Entitlement:	Indian Mutiny with clasps	
Reason for Discharge:	Own Request having completed 21 years service	
Character:	Very Good	
Trade or Occupation:	Labourer	
Can Sign Name:	Yes	
Height:	5' 8"	
Hair Colour:	Light Brown	
Eyes:	Blue	
Complexion:	Fresh	
Intends to Reside:	Limerick	

URQUHART William, Serjeant
RA 11th Battalion

11 Apr 1854	Discharged the Service Woolwich Pension paid Woolwich 1/3d. per diem
14 Aug 1854	Arrived per *'Ramillies'*
Jan 1857	Contributed 3/- to the Florence Nightingale Fund
1873	Pension increased to 1/8d. per diem for 10½ years service in the Enrolled Force
1873	Application for Title Bunbury [Wellington] Loc 402 at Turkey Pont Applies for £15 improvement grant
1877	Convicted at Fremantle Police Court of Theft and sentenced to 1 month imprisonment. Half pension to be suspended the other half paid to wife. Man to be named against another offence
June 1879	Grant of £15 sanctioned
18 Oct 1879	Granted Fee Simple Bunbury Loc 402 at Turkey Point
1885	Died

Service and Personal Details:

Place of Birth:	Fodderty Dingwall Ross	
Age on Attestation:	20 years	
Period of Service:	1834 — 1854	
Age on Discharge:	40 years 3 months	
Length of Service:	19 years 292 days	
Foreign Service:	Newfoundland	9 year 4 months
Reason for Discharge:	Fracture of left knee	
Character:	Very Good	
Trade or Occupation:	Labourer	
Can Sign Name:	Yes	
Height:	6' 0½"	
Hair Colour:	Very Good	
Eyes:	Brown	
Complexion:	Blue	
Intends to Reside:	Fair	

VAGG Edward, private
15th Hussars

29 Sept 1863	Discharged the Service Dublin Pension paid 1st West London Pension District 1/1d. per diem
13 July 1867	Arrived per *'Norwood'* [2] Pension increased to 1/6½d per diem for 12 years service in the Enrolled Force
1874	An Edward Vagg — charged with being drunk and incapable in Murray Street
1885	Application for Title Cockburn Sound Loc 230 Willagee Swamp
1896	Residing Hampton Rd., Beaconsfield
1896	Died
1897	Grant of Probate
1898	a Mrs J Vagg advertised to rent a three room house in Cottesloe

Service and Personal Details:		
Place of Birth:	Paddington London Middlesex	
Age on Attestation:	18 years 1 month	
Period of Service:	1839 — 1863	
Age on Discharge:	42 years 4 months	
Length of Service:	24 years 81 days	
Foreign Service:	Madras	14 years 4 months
Reason for Discharge:	Having completed 24 years service	
Character:	Good	
Trade or Occupation:	Sawyer	
Can Sign Name:	Yes	
Height:	5' 7"	
Hair Colour:	Light Brown	
Eyes:	Grey	
Complexion:	Fresh	
Intends to Reside:	Paddington London	

VALENTINE Joseph [John], private
Royal Canadian Rifles

Previous Regiments	48th; 71st
18 Sept 1866	Discharged the Service Pension paid Northampton 1/- per diem
13 July 1867	Arrived per *'Norwood'* [2]
24 Aug 1881	Assigned Perth Railway Block Lot 147/V
1881	Pension increased to 1/4½d. per diem for service in the Enrolled Force
1883	Application Perth Railway Block Lot 147/V
1895	a Joseph Valentine died aged 72

Service and Personal Details:		
Place of Birth:	Northampton	
Age on Attestation:	19 years 2 months	
Period of Service:	1840 — 1866	
Age on Discharge:	45 years 2 months	
Length of Service:	23 years 9 months	
Foreign Service:	Canada	23 years 9 months
Reason for Discharge:	Own Request after 25 years service	

Character:	Good
Trade or Occupation:	Labourer
Can Sign Name:	Yes
Height:	5' 8¼"
Hair Colour:	Brown
Eyes:	Blue
Complexion:	Fresh
Intends to Reside:	Northampton

VANCE	John, gunner RA — Coastal Brigade
19 Aug 1862	Discharged the Service Woolwich Pension paid 1st East London Pension District 1/- per diem Pension paid Woolwich
15 Aug 1865	Arrived per *'Racehorse'*
1867	John Vance, pensioner, charged with stealing timber. Sentenced to six month hard labour
1868	a John Vance was charged with landing on a reef of rocks adjacent to Rottnest Island with the intention to fish
1881	Pension increased to 1/2d. per diem for service in the Enrolled Force
1882	Convicted before two Justices at York W.A. of feloniously stealing 80 lbs of meal or meat, grapes, 10 lbs potatoes and 3 soup plates the property of his master. Sentenced to 4 months imprisonment with hard labor. Reference to Treasury Solicitor as to whether pension is forfeited under the provision of Act 33 & 34 Vic: Cap: 23 having regard to the fact that he was deal with under the larceny summary convictions ordained 20 Vic: No 5
1882	Reply from Treasury — pension is not to be forfeited but half pension to be suspended and half paid to man's wife for the time he is in prison
1885	Application for Title Cockburn Sound Loc 228
1891	W.O. correspondence re: Patriotic Fund
1891	Died

Service and Personal Details:	
Place of Birth:	Belfast Co. Antrim
Age on Attestation:	18 years 5 months
Period of Service:	1841 — 1862
Age on Discharge:	39 years 5 months
Length of Service:	21 years 16 days
Foreign Service:	Gibraltar 6 years 1 month Turkey & Crimea 1 year 10 months
Medal Entitlement:	Crimea with 4 clasps; Turkish Crimean; French Military War Medal
Reason for Discharge:	His having completed 21 years service
Character:	Exemplary
Trade or Occupation:	Helper to a Smith
Can Sign Name:	Yes

Height:	5' 7½"
Hair Colour:	Dark
Eyes:	Grey
Complexion:	Dark
Intends to Reside:	Woolwich

VILLIERS Arthur, gunner and driver
RA — Coastal Brigade

19 Aug 1863	Discharged the Service Pension paid Woolwich 10d. per diem
15 Aug 1865	Arrived per *'Racehorse'*
1868	W.O. correspondence with S.O.P. 1st Dublin
1868	Pension increased to 1/- per diem

Service and Personal Details:

Place of Birth:	Calverley Bradford York
Age on Attestation:	20 years 8 months
Period of Service:	1852 — 1863
Age on Discharge:	31 years 11 months
Length of Service:	11 years 54 days
Foreign Service:	Crimea 2 months
Medal Entitlement:	Crimea with 3 clasps; Turkish Crimean
Reason for Discharge:	Gunshot wound to the right arm
Character:	Exemplary
Trade or Occupation:	Labourer
Can Sign Name:	Yes
Height:	5' 8"¼"
Hair Colour:	Dark Brown
Eyes:	Dark Brown
Complexion:	Fresh
Intends to Reside:	No. 3 Bath Street Irishtown Dublin

WADE James, private
87th Foot

15 Dec 1863	Discharged the Service Buttervant Pension paid 2nd Dublin Pension District 1/2d. per diem
15 Aug 1865	Arrived per *'Racehorse'*
1867	Died

Service and Personal Details:

Place of Birth:	Balinasloe Co. Galway
Age on Attestation:	18 years
Period of Service:	1838 — 1863
Age on Discharge:	43 years 7 months
Length of Service:	25 years 160 days
Foreign Service:	Mauritius 3 years 6 months East Indies 8 years 6 months
Reason for Discharge:	Own Request having served 25 years
Character:	Good
Trade or Occupation:	Labourer
Can Sign Name:	Yes

Height:	5' 10"
Hair Colour:	Grey
Eyes:	Grey
Complexion:	Fresh
Intends to Reside:	No. 57 George Gorman Lane Dublin

WALKER	Philip, private
	89th Foot [Depot]
23 Nov 1859	Discharged the Service Fermoy
13 Dec 1859	Admitted to pension
	Pension paid Dublin
	1/- per diem
1862	Pension paid 2nd Dublin Pension District
31 Dec 1862	Arrived per *'York'*
1864	ptve P Walker Pensioner Force at Perth contributed to the Greenough Fire Relief Fund
circa June 1874	Transferred from 2nd Perth Pension District to 1st Perth Pension District
1875	Pension increased to 1/3d. per diem for service in the Enrolled Force
1865	Application for Title Perth Sub Lot 150 at £2/-/- per acre
1869	Pension paid Western Australia
1869	Charged for allowing his stock to trespass
July 1875	To Victoria from 1st Perth [WA] Pension District
1891	W.O. correspondence re. Patriotic Fund

Service and Personal Details:

Place of Birth:	Drummara Co. Down	
Age on Attestation:	18 years	
Period of Service:	1838 — 1859	
Age on Discharge:	39 years	
Length of Service:	24 years 24 days	
Foreign Service:	West Indies	2 years 3 months
	North America	5 years 10 months
	Gibraltar	8 months
	Crimea	5 months
Medal Entitlement:	Crimea	
Reason for Discharge:	Own Request having completed 24 years	
Character:	Good	
Trade or Occupation:	Labourer	
Can Sign Name:	X his mark on discharge	
Height:	5' 9"	
Hair Colour:	Light Brown	
Eyes:	Hazel	
Complexion:	Fresh	
Intends to Reside:	Dublin	

WALKER	William, private [3107]
	95th Foot
Previous Regiment	48th Foot
26 June 1855	Discharged the Service Chatham
	Pension paid Carlisle

	10d. per diem
1856	Serving in Northumberland Militia
1856	Pension paid 1st Edinburgh Pension District
1857	Pension paid Carlisle
19 Aug 1859	Arrived per *'Sultana'*
1864	ptve W. Walker Pensioner Force at Fremantle contributed to the Greenough Fire Relief Fund
1865	Pension paid Western Australia
1875	Western Australia
1896	W.O. Correspondence to Under Treasurer Adelaide for man to be medically examined
1897	W.O. Correspondence with Under Treasurer Adelaide South Australia
17 Aug 1901	Mr William Walker a Crimean Veteran died Brompton Park [Adelaide] on Thursday aged 75. Mr Walker served in the 95th Regiment in the Crimea where he was severely wounded. He was a Warder at Fremantle West Australia and has been a resident of Hindmarsh for several years [Obituary]

Service and Personal Details:	
Place of Birth:	Liverpool Lancashire
Age on Attestation:	17 years
Period of Service:	1853 — 1855
Age on Discharge:	18 years 7 months
Length of Service:	196 days
Foreign Service:	Turkey & Crimea 10 months
Medal Entitlement:	Crimea with clasps
Reason for Discharge:	Loss of power to right arm after gunshot wound
Character:	Good
Trade or Occupation:	Shoemaker
Can Sign Name:	X his mark on discharge
Height:	5' 9"
Hair Colour:	Dark Brown
Eyes:	Hazel
Complexion:	Fresh
Religion:	Protestant
Remarks:	Was wounded at Inkerman
Intends to Reside:	Carlisle

WALL	Thomas, Lance Serjeant
	2nd Foot
24 Feb 1857	Discharged the Service Colchester
	10d. per diem
	Pension paid 1st East London Pension District
29 Jan 1862	Arrived per *'Lincelles'*
no date	Assigned Freshwater Bay Loc 1068
Feb 1885	Application for Freshwater Bay Loc 1068
1886	a Thomas Wall residing Bannister St., Fremantle
1888	Died aged 72

Service and Personal Details:	
Place of Birth:	Poplar London Middlesex

Age on Attestation:	22 years 9 months
Period of Service:	1839 — 1857
Age on Discharge:	39 years 10 months
Length of Service:	17 years 57 days
Foreign Service:	East Indies 5 years 3 months
Reason for Discharge:	Chronic Bronchitis and Dyspnoea
Character:	Good
Trade or Occupation:	Porter
Can Sign Name:	Yes
Height:	5' 6"
Hair Colour:	Brown
Eyes:	Grey
Complexion:	Fresh

WALLACE Arthur, private
77th Foot

Previous Regiment	86th Foot
Surname Variant	WALLIS
18 Dec 1855	Discharged the Service Chatham Pension paid 2nd Dublin Pension District 8d. per diem
9 June 1862	Arrived per *'Norwood'* [1]
1864	ptve A Wallace Pensioner Force at Perth contributed to the Greenough Fire Relief Fund

Service and Personal Details:

Place of Birth:	Castlepollard Westmeath
Age on Attestation:	18 years
Period of Service:	1853 — 1855
Age on Discharge:	21 years or 20 years 1 month
Length of Service:	2 years 68 days
Foreign Service:	Mediterranean & Turkey & Crimea 1 year 8 months
Medal Entitlement:	Crimea with clasps
Reason for Discharge:	Wounded in action
Character:	Good
Trade or Occupation:	House Painter
Can Sign Name:	blank; X his mark on Attestation
Height:	5' 6¼"
Hair Colour:	Light Brown
Eyes:	Grey
Complexion:	Fresh
Intends to Reside:	Dublin

WALSH Daniel, private
60th Foot

Previous Regiment	17th Foot
Surname Variant	WELCH
13 July 1852	Discharged the Service Chatham Pension paid Tralee 6d. per diem for 15 months
30 Apr 1853	Arrived per *'Pyrenees'* [2]
Aug 1854	Refused further pension by W.O.

Service and Personal Details:

Place of Birth:	Knockagarhil Castle Island Co. Kerry
Age on Attestation:	19 years
Period of Service:	1847 — 1852
Age on Discharge:	24 years or 23 years 4 months
Length of Service:	4 years 202 days
Foreign Service:	Upper & Lower Scinde 135 days East Indies 1 year 213 days
Reason for Discharge:	Chronic Diarrhoea and general bad health
Character:	Good
Trade or Occupation:	Labourer
Can Sign Name:	Yes
Height:	5' 6¾"
Hair Colour:	Dark Brown
Eyes:	Grey
Complexion:	Fresh
Intends to Reside:	Dingle Co. Kerry
Married:	Ann Cullen
Children:	Daniel b. *c*1855 Fremantle

WALSH	Michael, private [1138] 10th Foot
Surname Variant	WELCH
31 Dec 1861	Discharged the Service Preston Pension paid Preston 10d. per diem
27 May 1863	Arrived per *'Clyde'*
1864	ptve M Walsh Pensioner Force at Fremantle contributed to the Greenough Fire Relief Fund Pension increased to 1/4d per diem for 16 years service in the Enrolled Force
Jan 1884	Application for Title North Fremantle Lot P79, [Alfred Road]
1 Oct 1884	Granted Fee Simple North Fremantle Lot P79
May 1886	'M. Walsh, Pensioner - Enrolled Guard, wishes to be appointed to vacant post'
1895	Died aged 73

Service and Personal Details:

Place of Birth:	St Johns Kilkenny
Age on Attestation:	17 years 6 months
Period of Service:	1839 — 1861
Age on Discharge:	38 years 10 months
Length of Service:	21 years 135 days
Foreign Service:	East Indies 16 years 9 months
Medal Entitlement:	Sutlej; Punjaub with clasps for Mooltan and Goojerat
Reason for Discharge:	Own Request having served 21 years
Character:	Very Good
Trade or Occupation:	Labourer

Can Sign Name:	X his mark on discharge
Height:	5' 7"
Hair Colour:	Light Brown
Eyes:	Hazel
Complexion:	Fair
Intends to Reside:	Preston

WALSH Michael, private
49th Foot

Surname Variant	WELCH	
20 Jan 1862	Discharged the Service Belfast	
4 Feb 1862	Discharge Approved	
	Pension paid Armagh	
	1/- per diem	
1862	Pension paid Bermuda	
15 Feb 1863	Arrived per *'Merchantman'* [1]	
1875	Pension paid Western Australia	
1878	Pension increased to 1/6d. per diem for service in the Enrolled Force	
	W.O. stated that man had re-entered the Enrolled Force and that the increase granted by Chelsea had been suspended	
20 Sept 1879	Assigned North Fremantle Lot P58	
1881	Pension increased to 1/6d. per diem	
May 1881	Application for Title North Fremantle Lot P58	
27 Apr 1882	Granted Fee Simple North Fremantle Lot P58	
1884	Died aged 42 on arrival	
Service and Personal Details:		
Place of Birth:	Mitchellstown Co. Cork	
Age on Attestation:	19 years	
Period of Service:	1840 — 1862	
Age on Discharge:	40 years 3 months	
Length of Service:	21 years 109 days	
Foreign Service:	East Indies	1 year 2 months
	China	1 year 6 months
	Ionian Isles	2 years
	Malta	1 year
	Crimea	1 year 5 months
Medal Entitlement:	China; Crimea; Turkish Crimean	
Reason for Discharge:	Own Request having completed 21 years service	
Character:	Good	
Trade or Occupation:	Labourer	
Can Sign Name:	X his mark on discharge	
Height:	5' 5¼"	
Hair Colour:	Brown	
Eyes:	Blue	
Complexion:	Fresh	
Remarks:	Slightly wounded in right arm	
Intends to Reside:	Armagh	

WALSH Michael, Bugle Major EIC
Bombay Artillery

	Out Pension No 164
5 May 1844	Discharged the Service
11 May 1844	Embarked for England per '*Thomas Coutts*"
1844	Pension paid 2nd Dublin Pension District 9d. per diem
1850	Pension paid 2nd Cork Pension District
18 Oct 1851	Arrived per '*Minden*'
1853	Pension paid Port Phillip
1856	Bombay
1857	Pension paid 2nd North London Pension District
1858	Pension paid Jersey

Service and Personal Details:	
Where Born:	Athy Kildare
Trade or Occupation:	Labourer
Age on Attestation:	19 years
Where Attested:	Kilkenny
Date Attested:	8th Sept 1828
Embarked India:	6th Jan 1829 per '*Hertfordshire*'
Presidency:	Bombay
Length of Service:	15 years 3 months
Age on Discharge:	34 years
Character:	Fair
Reason for Discharge:	Organic disease of the stomach with palpitations of the heart
Height:	5' 10" [on discharge]
Complexion:	Sallow [on discharge]
Eye Colour:	Blue
Hair Colour:	Brown

WALSH	Nicholas, private [2566] 10th Foot
Surname Variant	WELCH
17 Aug 1858	Discharged the Service Chatham Pension paid Kilkenny 8d. per diem
4 July 1866	Arrived per '*Belgravia*'
1874	Pension increased to 11½d. per diem
1874	Suffering from poor eyesight
1876	In receipt of outdoor relief money — Perth
18 June 1881	Assigned Perth Town Lot 79/E
Sept 1882	Application for Title Perth Town Lot 79/E [CONS5000 — SROWA]
1885	Pensioner N Walsh — Relief for to be discontinued
27 May 1886	Joined Enrolled Guard — stationed Perth
1886	Residing at the barracks
****	On or about the 10th June., from the Pensioners' Barracks, — pensioner's overcoat, blue cloth, lined with serge, marked NW across lining in centre of back, the property of Nicholas Walsh. Suspicion attaches to Michael Byrne, pensioner. — C.I. 270.
1889	Died aged 61 [35 on arrival]

Mar 1890	Wife Margaret applies to be registered as the proprietor of an estate in fee simple for the parcel of land, being Perth Town Lot E 79

Service and Personal Details:

Place of Birth:	St Johns Kilkenny	
Age on Attestation:	19 years	
Period of Service:	1847 — 1857	
Age on Discharge:	30 years 4 months	
Length of Service:	10 years 242 days	
Foreign Service:	East Indies	10 years
Medal Entitlement:	Punjaub with clasp for Mooltan; Indian Mutiny	
Reason for Discharge:	Gunshot wound in left arm received in action	
Character:	Very Good	
Trade or Occupation:	Labourer	
Can Sign Name:	X his mark on discharge	
Height:	5' 6"	
Hair Colour:	Brown	
Eyes:	Blue	
Complexion:	Fresh	
Intends to Reside:	Callan Co. Kilkenny	

WALSH Patrick, private
36th Foot

9 Dec 1851	Discharged the Service Chatham
24 Feb 1852	Discharge approved Pension paid Chatham 1/- per diem
14 Aug 1854	Arrived per *'Ramillies'*
Jan 1857	Contributed 2/- to the Florence Nightingale Fund
1860	Employed as Warder Rottnest
1864	Pension paid Perth Western Australia
1865	Pension paid New South Wales

Service and Personal Details:

Place of Birth:	Doneraile Mallow Co. Cork	
Age on Attestation:	18 years 3 months	
Period of Service:	1831 — 1851	
Age on Discharge:	39 years	
Length of Service:	20 years 223 days	
Foreign Service:	West Indies	6 years 293 days
	North America	3 years 168 days
	Ionian Isles	4 years 86 days
Reason for Discharge:	Chronic Disease of the Lungs and Varicose Veins in both legs	
Character:	Indifferent	
Trade or Occupation:	Labourer	
Can Sign Name:	Yes	
Height:	5' 7¾"	
Hair Colour:	Dark Brown	
Eyes:	Grey	
Complexion:	Sallow	
Intends to Reside:	North Shields	

WALSH	Thomas, Serjeant
	96th Foot
Previous Regiment	50th Foot
23 Sept 1851	Discharged the Service Chatham Pension paid 1st Cork Pension District 2/- per diem
30 Apr 1853	Arrived per *'Pyrenees'* [2]
1859	Serving as Sergeant of Police
1858	Applied for Land Title Victoria Location
1859	Applied for Land Title Geraldton
1883	Died
From Headstone:	WALSH, Thomas, born in Cork, Ireland, June 9th 1811, died at Geraldton May 2nd 1883 For 23 years he served in His Majesty's 96th and 50th Regiments of Foot, and upon receiving his discharge was awarded a good conduct medal and a pension for long service. He was for some years engaged in the government service of this colony in which he was a resident for 30 years. He has left behind him many sorrowing relatives and friends.

Service and Personal Details:

Place of Birth:	Youghall Co. Cork	
Age on Attestation:	16 years	
Period of Service:	1826 — 1851	
Age on Discharge:	41 years 3 months	
Length of Service:	22 years 74 days	
Foreign Service:	Australia	14 years 11 months
	Bengal	1 year 7 months
Reason for Discharge:	Unfit for further service	
Character:	Very Good	
Trade or Occupation:	Labourer	
Can Sign Name:	Yes	
Height:	5' 7"	
Hair Colour:	Sandy	
Eyes:	Grey	
Complexion:	Fair	
Intends to Reside:	Cork	

WARD	John, private
	23rd Foot [Depot]
5 Nov 1852	Enrolled to serve as a Volunteer with the 3rd Lancashire Regiment of Militia
9 Nov 1854	Attested with the 23rd Foot to serve for a Limited Period of 10 years
29 Apr 1856	Discharged the Service Chatham Pension paid Preston 1/- per diem
1862	Pension paid Bermuda
15 Feb 1863	Arrived per *'Merchantman'* [1]
1865	On Nominal List to proceed to Camden Harbour per *'Tien Tsin'*

1866	Pension paid Preston England	
Service and Personal Details:		
Place of Birth:	Preston Lancashire	
Age on Attestation:	28 years	
Period of Service:	1854 — 1856	
Age on Discharge:	29 years 1 month or 33 years	
Length of Service:	1 year 23 days [reckoned]	
Foreign Service:	Crimea	10 months
Medal Entitlement:	Crimea	
Reason for Discharge:	Unfit for further service due to gunshot wound of right shoulder	
Character:	Good	
Trade or Occupation:	Joiner	
Can Sign Name:	Yes	
Height:	5' 8½"	
Hair Colour:	Dark Brown	
Eyes:	Hazel	
Complexion:	Light	
Intends to Reside:	Preston	

WARD

	John, private 38th Foot	
23 Dec 1851	Discharged the Service Pension paid Cavan 6d. per diem for 3 years	
19 Aug 1853	Arrived per *'Robert Small'*	
31 Aug 1853	Died	
Service and Personal Details:		
Place of Birth:	Dring Cavan	
Period of Service:	1839 — 1851	
Age on Discharge:	32 years	
Length of Service:	12 years 10 months	
Foreign Service:	Mediterranean	2 years 6 months
	Gibraltar	2 years 10 months
	Jamaica	2 years
	North America 3 years 3 months	
Reason for Discharge:	Chronic Pleurisy of left side of Chest	
Character:	Good	
Trade or Occupation:	Labourer	
Height:	5' 10"	
Hair Colour:	Brown/Grey	
Eyes:	Grey	
Complexion:	Fresh	

WARD

	John, private 99th Foot
12 May 1841	Discharged the Service Pension paid 2nd Dublin Pension District 11d. per diem
1851	Pension paid Manchester Dublin

30 Apr 1853	Arrived per *'Pyrenees'* [2]
22 July 1862	Died aged 56

Service and Personal Details:

Place of Birth:	Garristown Dublin
Age on Attestation:	18 years
Period of Service:	1824 — 1841
Age on Discharge:	35 years
Length of Service:	17 years 5 days
Foreign Service:	Mauritius 11 years 149 days
Reason for Discharge:	Rheumatic pains in limbs great emaciation of body and extensive varicose veins of both legs
Character:	Good efficient soldier and Trustworthy
Trade or Occupation:	Cotton Weaver
Can Sign Name:	X his mark on discharge
Height:	5' 7"
Hair Colour:	Brown
Eyes:	Grey
Complexion:	Fair

WAREHAM Henry, private EIC [L/MIL/12/122]
1st Bombay European Fusiliers or 1st European Infantry

Surname Variants	WARHAM; WHARHAM; WHERHAM
	Out Pension No 339
Oct 1860	Admitted to Out-pension
	Pension paid Worcester
	1/- per diem
1860	Pension paid Derby
1861	Pension paid 1st East London Pension District
22 Dec 1865	Arrived per *'Vimiera'*
Sept 1867	Fremantle Town Lot 631 was sold at auction for £6
1878	Died aged 58

Service and Personal Details:

Where Born:	St Martius or St Martin, Worcester
Trade or Occupation:	Labourer
Age on Enlistment:	18 years
Date Enlisted:	10th Dec 1840
Embarked India:	per *'Euxine'*
Presidency:	Bombay
Length of Service:	19 years 7 months
Age on Discharge:	37 or 38 [depending on record]
Reason for Discharge:	Pensioned — time expired
Character:	[none given]
Medal Entitlement:	Jellalabad; Punjaub with clasps for Mooltan and Goojerat; Indian Mutiny
Height:	5' 4" or 5' 4½"
Complexion:	Fresh
Eye Colour:	Grey
Hair Colour:	Brown
Intends to Reside:	Shadwell

the following UK census information may not necessarily refer to Henry Wareham EIC

1861 census	a Henry Wareham residing with Elizabeth b. 1829 Bombay India
Children:	Julia b. 1860 Stepney

WARNER Charles, private

	63rd Foot
8 June 1829	arrived possibly per *'HMS Sulphur'*
Mar 1834	Discharged in Colony
	1/1d. per diem
	Storekeeper, upholsterer and thatcher
1840's	Storekeeper at Bunbury
1842	a C Warner purchased Bunbury Town Lot 46 for £25
1844	Wellington District — a C Warner applied for a Dog Licence
1847	Residing Perth

Service and Personal Details:

Place of Birth:	Milham Norfolk	
Age on Attestation:	17 years	
Period of Service:	1808 — 1829	
Age on Discharge:	About 38 years	
Length of Service:	21 years 2 months	
Foreign Service:	India	6 years 5 months
Reason for Discharge:	Being ineligible for foreign service from advanced age and constitutional rheumatism	
Character:	Good	
Trade or Occupation:	Labourer	
Can Sign Name:	X his mark on discharge	
Height:	5' 4½"	
Hair Colour:	Dark	
Eye Colour:	Hazel	
Complexion:	Fresh	

WARNER William, private

	6th Foot [Depot]
7 May 1861	Discharged the Service Colchester
	Pension paid Coventry
	8d. per diem
27 May 1863	Arrived per *'Clyde'*
1864	ptve W Warner Pensioner Force at Perth contributed to the Greenough Fire Relief Fund
1875	Pension paid Perth Western Australia
Nov 1876	Incarcerated Perth Goal and fined
1878	Convicted by Civil Power of being drunk in the streets of Perth and sentenced to 21 days imprisonment with suspension of pension during imprisonment
1879	Convicted in the Police Court of Perth Western Australia on two counts of being drunk and incapable. Sentenced on each occasion to 21 days imprisonment during which time his pension is suspended

	Served for many years in the M.R.V Band
22 July 1880	Died at his residence in Hay Street [described as bandsman and pensioner in obituary]
Service and Personal Details:	
Place of Birth:	Coventry Warwickshire
Age on Attestation:	23 years 2 months
Period of Service:	1839 — 1861
Age on Discharge:	44 years 7 months
Length of Service:	21 years 113 days
Foreign Service:	Cape of Good Hope 11 years 1 month
	East Indies 3 years 4 months
Medal Entitlement:	Kaffir War of 1846
Reason for Discharge:	Own Request after 21 years service
Character:	Good
Trade or Occupation:	Ribbon Weaver
Can Sign Name:	Yes
Height:	5' 5¼"
Hair Colour:	Dark Brown
Eyes:	Blue
Complexion:	Fresh
Intends to Reside:	Coventry Warwickshire

WARREN	John, private
	3rd Light Dragoons
Previous Regiment	16th Lancers
27 June 1848	Discharged the Service Chatham
	Pension paid Preston
	10d. per diem
1850	Pension paid Sheffield
18 Oct 1851	Arrived per *'Minden'*
1852	"Off Register — committed felony" Charged with theft
July 1854	W.O. correspondence to S.O. Perth W.A. — "refused restoration"
Service and Personal Details:	
Place of Birth:	Kirkham Lancaster
Age on Attestation:	21 years
Period of Service:	1828 — 1847
Age on Discharge:	42 years
Length of Service:	19 years 186 days [reckoned]
Foreign Service:	East Indies 18 years 3 months
Medal Entitlement:	Afghanistan 1838/1839; Maharajpore 1843; Sutlej with clasps 1846
Reason for Discharge:	Gunshot wound in the loins also contusion of the testicles whilst on mounted duty
Character:	Good
Trade or Occupation:	Weaver
Can Sign Name:	X his mark on Attestation
Height:	5' 7¼"
Hair Colour:	Brown

Eyes:	Grey
Complexion:	Sallow
Intends to Reside:	Preston Lancashire

WATERS	John, private EIC
	1st Bombay European Infantry
	Out Pension No 355
6 June 1861	Admitted to Out-pension
	Pension paid Kilkenny
	9d. per diem
28 Dec 1863	Arrived per *'Lord Dalhousie'* as a Convict Guard
Oct 1864	Departed Colony per *'Sea Ripple'*
1864	Pension paid Adelaide
1867	Sydney
1872	Off Roll — "Not Appeared"

WATKINS	John, private
	94th Foot
27 May 1841	Discharged the Service Fort Pitt
9 June 1841	Admitted to Out-Pension
	Pension paid Bury St Edmunds — [Cambridge]
	6d. per diem
1 June 1850	Arrived per *'Scindian'*
Aug 1850	Assigned a Military Pensioner's Land Grant P17 at South Perth
1854	Charged with Military Offence
1861	"Off Pension"
1865	Pension restored
1875	Pension paid Western Australia
1876	Residing Perth
Feb 1899	W.O. Correspondence
1902	Died aged 96

Service and Personal Details:	
Place of Birth:	Dalham Suffolk
Age on Attestation:	19 years 4 months
Period of Service:	1833 — 1841
Age on Discharge:	27 years
Length of Service:	Entitled to reckon 7 years 133 days
Foreign Service:	India 11 months
Reason for Discharge:	Attacked and wounded by natives on his return to barracks July 1840
Character:	Very Good
Trade or Occupation:	Servant
Can Sign Name:	Yes
Height:	5' 6½"
Hair Colour:	Dark Brown
Eyes:	Hazel
Complexion:	Fresh
Intends to Reside:	Newmarket

WATSON	James, gunner and driver
	RA 6th Battalion
14 Oct 1845	Discharged the Service Woolwich

	Pension paid Edinburgh
	7d. per diem
1851	Pension paid Manchester
1851	Pension paid 2nd Glasgow Pension District
1851	Refused increase in pension
2 Aug 1852	Arrived per *'William Jardine'*
31 Oct 1852	"Left colony without permission"
1858	Pension paid Melbourne

Service and Personal Details:

Place of Birth:	St Johns Glasgow Lanarkshire	
Age on Attestation:	19 years	
Period of Service:	1830 — 1845	
Age on Discharge:	34 years 1 month	
Length of Service:	16 years 57 days	
Foreign Service:	Gibraltar	9 years 5 months
Reason for Discharge:	Asthma and alleged defective sight in right eye.	
Character:	Very Good	
Trade or Occupation:	Framework knitter	
Can Sign Name:	Yes	
Height:	5' 8½"	
Hair Colour:	Dark Brown	
Eyes:	Grey	
Complexion:	Sallow	

WATSON

	John, Corporal
	86th Foot
10 June 1846	Discharged the Service Chatham
	Pension paid Carlow
	1/- per diem
1849	Pension paid 2nd Dublin Pension District
28 June 1851	Arrived per *'Pyrenees'* [1]
16 Aug 1851	a John Watson appointed Police Force Perth
1852	Pension paid Hobart Town

Service and Personal Details:

Place of Birth:	Ballytore Kildare	
Age on Attestation:	16 years 9 months	
Period of Service:	1825 — 1845	
Age on Discharge:	40 years or 37 years 3 months	
Length of Service:	19 years 15 days [reckoned]	
Foreign Service:	West Indies	10 years 5 months
	East Indies	3 years 2 months
Reason for Discharge:	Hepatitis and Rheumatism	
Character:	Indifferent	
Trade or Occupation:	Labourer	
Can Sign Name:	Yes	
Height:	5' 6"	
Hair Colour:	Fair	
Eyes:	Brown	
Complexion:	Fair	
Intends to Reside:	Carlow	

WATSON	John, private	
	87th Foot	
Previous Regiment	35th Foot	
19 Feb 1861	Discharged the Service	
	Pension paid 2nd Manchester Pension District	
	1/- per diem	
29 Jan 1862	Arrived per *'Lincelles'*	
1865	Pension paid Adelaide South Australia	
3 Mar 1871	Died	
Service and Personal Details:		
Place of Birth:	Dundrane Londonderry Co. Derry	
Age on Attestation:	17 years	
Period of Service:	1838 — 1861	
Age on Discharge:	40 years	
Length of Service:	21 years 10 days	
Foreign Service:	Mauritius	6 years 279 days
	East Indies	7 years 199 days
Medal Entitlement:	Indian Mutiny	
Reason for Discharge:	Own Request having served 21 years	
Character:	Very Good	
Trade or Occupation:	Labourer	
Can Sign Name:	X his mark on discharge	
Height:	5' 9"	
Hair Colour:	Light Brown	
Eyes:	Grey	
Complexion:	Fair	
Intends to Reside:	Manchester	

WATSON	Thomas, private	
	61st Foot	
Previous Regiment	49th Foot	
2 July 1861	Discharged the Service Parkhurst I.O.W	
	Pension paid 2nd London Pension District	
	1/- per diem	
1862	Pension paid Wales East Pension District	
31 Dec 1862	Arrived per *'York'*	
1878	Pension increased to 1/6d per diem for service in the Enrolled Force	
1881	Reverted to original rate, but again increased to 1/6d. per diem	
Nov 1881	Assigned North Fremantle Lot P64	
Dec 1883	Application for Title to North Fremantle Lot P64	
7 June 1884	Joined Enrolled Guard — stationed Perth	
29 Aug 1884	Granted Fee Simple North Fremantle Lot P64	
1893	Died	
Service and Personal Details:		
Place of Birth:	Weston Baldock Hertfordshire	
Age on Attestation:	23 years 9 months	
Period of Service:	1840 — 1861	
Age on Discharge:	45 years	
Length of Service:	21 years 11 days	
Foreign Service:	China	1 year ?6 months
	East Indies	13 years 8 months

Medal Entitlement:	China; Punjaub with clasps; India Mutiny
Reason for Discharge:	Own Request having served 21 years
Character:	Very Good
Trade or Occupation:	Labourer
Can Sign Name:	X his mark on discharge
Height:	5' 7"
Hair Colour:	Dark Brown
Eyes:	Grey
Complexion:	Sallow
Intends to Reside:	Wellyn Hertfordshire

WATTS	James, private
	89th Foot [Depot]
11 May 1861	Discharged the Service Fermoy Barracks
28 May 1861	Admitted to Out-Pension
	Pension paid Birr
	10d. per diem
22 Dec 1865	Arrived per *'Vimiera'*
1868	Received £15 Improvement Grant
1876	Maliciously wounded by Joseph Parkinson
6 June 1879	Application for Title Kojonup Lot P7
1882	Died aged 60
13 July 1882	Inquest at Kojonup, before J. C. Rosselloty, R.M. and Coroner, on the body of James Watts who was found dead 2 miles from Kojonup, on the 10th Jun. Verdict — " Death from inflammation of the right lung, accelerated by exposure to wet and cold and from excessive drinking."

Service and Personal Details:

Place of Birth:	Westbury Wiltshire	
Age on Attestation:	18 years	
Period of Service:	1840 — 1861	
Age on Discharge:	39 years	
Length of Service:	21 years 10 days	
Foreign Service:	North America	4 years 7 months
	Gibraltar [total]	2 years 1 month
	Crimea	1 year 5 months
	Cape of Good Hope	1 year
	East Indies	1 year 4 months
Medal Entitlement:	Crimea with clap; Turkish Crimean	
Reason for Discharge:	Own Request having served 21 years	
Character:	Good	
Trade or Occupation:	Labourer	
Can Sign Name:	X his mark on discharge [witnessed]	
Height:	5' 7"	
Hair Colour:	Dark Brown	
Eyes:	Hazel	
Complexion:	Dark	
Intends to Reside:	Parsonstown Kings County	

WATTS	William, Serjeant

	21st Foot
10 Oct 1843	Discharged the Service Chatham
	Pension paid Leicester
	2/2d. per diem
1843	Pension paid Bath
1848	Hull
1 June 1850	Arrived per *'Scindian'*
1851	Pension paid Van Diemans Land
1852	"Absent without leave"
1859	Pension paid Bath England

Service and Personal Details:

Place of Birth:	St Marys Leicester	
Age on Attestation:	18 years	
Period of Service:	1818 — 1843	
Age on Discharge:	44 years	
Length of Service:	29 years 134 days	
Foreign Service:	West Indies	7 years 10 months
Reason for Discharge:	Chronic Rheumatism and difficulty with breathing	
Character:	Very Good	
Trade or Occupation:	Labourer	
Can Sign Name:	Yes	
Height:	5' 8¾"	
Hair Colour:	Dark	
Eyes:	Hazel	
Complexion:	Dark	
Intends to Reside:	Bath	

WEBB

	Henry, Corporal
	2nd/8th Foot
Previous Regiment	96th Foot
13 Nov 1860	Discharged the Service
	Pension paid Limerick
	1/2½d. per diem
1862	Pension paid 1st East London Pension District
27 May 1863	Arrived per *'Clyde'*
29 Mar 1865	Died
1885	Ann Kelly asking about the whereabouts of Pensioner Henry Webb

Service and Personal Details:

Place of Birth:	Baldock Hertfordshire	
Age on Attestation:	17 years	
Period of Service:	1838 — 1860	
Age on Discharge:	approx 37 years	
Length of Service:	20 years 354 days	
Foreign Service:	Van Diemans land	7 years 3 months
	East Indies	6 years
	Gibraltar	2 years 10 months
Reason for Discharge:	Own Request after 21 years of [reckoned total] service	
Character:	Good	
Trade or Occupation:	Labourer	

Can Sign Name:	Yes
Height:	5' 9"
Hair Colour:	Light and Grey
Eyes:	Grey
Complexion:	Fair
Intends to Reside:	Limerick

WEDDERBURN	Peter, private	
	Royal Canadian Rifles	
Previous Regiments	54th; 30th	
9 Sept 1851	Discharged the Service Chatham	
	Pension paid 2nd Edinburgh Pension District	
	1/- per diem	
30 Apr 1853	Arrived per *'Pyrenees'* [2]	
1853	Employed by Convict establishment	
1854	Pension paid Western Australia	
1855	To South Australia from Western Australia	
1857	Pension paid Melbourne Victoria	
Dec 1867	Died	
Service and Personal Details:		
Place of Birth:	Linlithgow West Lothian	
Age on Attestation:	21 years	
Period of Service:	1828 — 1851	
Age on Discharge:	43 years 6 months or 44 years 3 months	
Length of Service:	23 years 75 days	
Foreign Service:	West Indies	7 years 3 months
	North America	9 years 6 months
Reason for Discharge:	Chronic Bronchitis and Debility	
Character:	Good	
Trade or Occupation:	Coachman	
Can Sign Name:	X his mark on discharge	
Height:	5' 8½"	
Hair Colour:	Brown	
Eyes:	Grey	
Complexion:	Fresh	
Intends to Reside:	England but decided on Edinburgh	

WEIR	see — WIER William private EIC

WEIR	James, Serjeant
	44th Foot
Surname Variants	WIER; WAR
11 Sept 1849	Discharged the Service
	Pension paid Ipswich
	2/- per diem
24 May 1855	Arrived per *'Stag'*
Jan 1857	Contributed 2/- to the Florence Nightingale Fund
1858	Pension paid Madras
15 Feb 1859	Died
Service and Personal Details:	
Place of Birth:	Minto Dunbartonshire Scotland
Age on Attestation:	17 years

Period of Service:	1826 — 1849	
Age on Discharge:	40 years	
Length of Service:	22 years 158 days	
Foreign Service:	East Indies	17 years 250 days
Medal Entitlement:	Afghan	
Reason for Discharge:	Rheumatism and wounded by a musket ball in right side of neck at Afghanistan 1842	
Character:	Very Good	
Trade or Occupation:	Weaver	
Can Sign Name:	Yes	
Height:	5' 5¼"	
Hair Colour:	Grey	
Eyes:	Grey	
Complexion:	Fresh	
Intends to Reside:	Horsham Sussex but decided on Colchester	

WELDON Robert, private
31st Foot

Surname Variant	WELDEN
17 Sept 1847	Discharged the Service Chatham Pension paid Drogheda 8d. per diem
6 Apr 1854	Arrived per *'Sea Park'*
1857	To South Australia from Western Australia
1879	Pension paid Adelaide South Australia

Service and Personal Details:

Place of Birth:	St Georges Dublin	
Age on Attestation:	18 years	
Period of Service:	1843 — 1847	
Age on Discharge:	23 years	
Length of Service:	3 years 225 days	
Foreign Service:	East Indies	2 years 3 months
Medal Entitlement:	Sutlej with clasps	
Reason for Discharge:	Gunshot wound to left leg	
Character:	Very Good	
Trade or Occupation:	Labourer	
Can Sign Name:	X his mark on discharge	
Height:	5' 7½"	
Hair Colour:	Dark Brown	
Eyes:	Grey	
Complexion:	Sallow	
Intends to Reside:	Drogheda	

WELLS Alexander, gunner and driver
RA 4th Battalion

20 Mar 1851	Discharge approved
8 Apr 1851	Discharged the Service Woolwich Pension paid Brighton 7d. per diem
1856	Pension paid Woolwich
10 July 1857	Arrived per *'Clara'* [1]
3 June 1863	Died

Service and Personal Details:	
Place of Birth:	Leigh Tonbridge Kent
Age on Attestation:	18 years
Period of Service:	1836 — 1851
Age on Discharge:	33 years 3 months
Length of Service:	15 years 83 days
Foreign Service:	Cape of Good Hope 8 years 238 days
Reason for Discharge:	Varicose Veins in both legs
Character:	Very Good
Trade or Occupation:	Labourer
Can Sign Name:	X his mark on discharge [witnessed]
Height:	5' 8¼"
Hair Colour:	Dark Brown
Eyes:	Hazel
Complexion:	Dark

WELLSTEAD	Thomas William, private RA 2nd Battalion
14 Oct 1851	Discharged the Service Woolwich Pension paid 2nd West London Pension District 6d. per diem for 3 years
1852	Pension paid 2nd North London Pension District
2 Aug 1852	Arrived per *'William Jardine'*
1852	Employed by Convict Service without sanction of Staff Officer Pensions
May 1857	Refused further pension
1865	? Principle Warder in charge of the Bake House
1874	a Thomas William Wellstead died aged 57 in Victoria

Service and Personal Details:	
Place of Birth:	Portsmouth Hampshire
Age on Attestation:	20 years
Period of Service:	1838 — 1851
Age on Discharge:	33 years 6 months
Length of Service:	13 years 163 days
Foreign Service:	West Indies 5 years 6 months
Reason for Discharge:	Injury to right knee
Character:	Good
Trade or Occupation:	Gardener
Can Sign Name:	Yes
Height:	5' 8½"
Hair Colour:	Dark Brown
Eyes:	Dark
Complexion:	Swarthy
Remarks:	Subsisted to 3rd November 1851
Intends to Reside:	London

WEST	John, private 76th Foot
25 Mar 1851	Discharged the Service Chatham Pension paid Kings Lynn 8d. per diem for 3 years

2 Aug 1852	Arrived per *'William Jardine'*
1852	Employed by Convict Establishment
15 Apr 1854	Pension ceased
1878	Deferred Pension Forms sent to Paymaster of Pensions Adelaide South Australia
1878	Granted Deferred Pension of 5d. per diem backdated to March 1877
1878	Man's address is now Box 63 General Post Office Adelaide South Australia

Service and Personal Details:		
Place of Birth:	Upwell Cambridgeshire	
Age on Attestation:	20 and a ¼ years	
Period of Service:	1839 — 1851	
Age on Discharge:	32 years	
Length of Service:	11 years 225 days	
Foreign Service:	Bermuda	10 months
	Nova Scotia	11 months
	Ionian Isles	2 years 7 months
Reason for Discharge:	Chronic Rheumatism and Catarrh	
Character:	Very Good	
Trade or Occupation:	Labourer	
Can Sign Name:	X his mark on discharge	
Height:	5' 8"	
Hair Colour:	Sandy	
Eyes:	Blue	
Complexion:	Pale	
Intends to Reside:	Upwell Cambridgeshire	

WHELAN	Thomas, private 13th Foot
24 Aug 1864	Discharged the Service Dover
20 Sept 1864	Admitted to Out-Pension Pension paid Birr 8d. per diem
1864	Pension paid 1st Liverpool Pension District
1865	Pension paid 2nd Liverpool Pension District
9 Jan 1868	Arrived per *'Hougoumont'* Assigned North Fremantle Lot P24
1876	Stationed Fremantle
12 Apr 1878	Finished walls etc of Cottage and requests payment of £15 improvement grant
1878	Pension increased to 1/- per diem for service in the Enrolled Force
1879	Application for Title to North Fremantle Lot P24
1895	Residing Swann St., Fremantle
1895	Died

Service and Personal Details:	
Place of Birth:	Castledermott Co. Kildare
Age on Attestation:	17 years 2 months
Period of Service:	1845 — 1864
Age on Discharge:	35 years
Length of Service:	18 years 197 days

Foreign Service:	Gibraltar	4 years 3 months
	Crimea	1 year
	Cape of Good Hope	1 year 4 months
	East Indies	6 years
Medal Entitlement:	Crimea with clasp; Turkish Crimean' Indian Mutiny	
Reason for Discharge:	Pulmonary Consumption	
Character:	Yes	
Trade or Occupation:	Labourer	
Can Sign Name:	Yes	
Height:	5' 9"	
Hair Colour:	Brown	
Eyes:	Grey	
Complexion:	Fresh	
Remarks:	Wounded by shell splinter in trenches before Sebastopol	
Intends to Reside:	Banaghur Kings County	

WHITE

	James, private [Military Pensioner]	
	21st Foot — [transferred to 21st Foot in 1823]	
Previous Regiment	26th Foot	
14 Sept 1833	Arrived per *'Jane'* with regiment	
31 July 1840	Discharged the Service	
25 June 1841	Discharge approved	
14 July 1841	Pension ratified	
	Pension paid Western Australia	
	1/1½d. per diem	
1841	Died	
Service and Personal Details:		
Place of Birth:	Halifax Canada	
Age on Attestation:	11 years	
Period of Service:	1811 — 1840	
Age on Discharge:	39 years	
Length of Service:	23 years 108 days	
Foreign Service:	West Indies	over 3 years
	Australian Colonies	6 years
Reason for Discharge:	Own Request for length of service and being worn out	
Conduct:	Indifferent but clean and obedient	
Trade or Occupation:	Labourer	
Can Sign Name:	Yes	
Height:	5' 8½"	
Hair Colour:	Light/ Sandy	
Eyes:	Blue	
Complexion:	Fair	

WHITE

	James, private
	84th Foot
14 Jan 1862	Discharged the Service
	Pension paid Birr

	1/- per diem
1863	Pension paid Dublin
1863	Liverpool
15 Apr 1864	Arrived per *'Clara'* [2]
Oct 1864	To Adelaide per *'Sea Ripple'*
1864	Pension paid Adelaide South Australia
1865	India
1866	1st Liverpool Pension District
4 July 1873	Died

Service and Personal Details:		
Place of Birth:	Ballybrith Birr Kings County	
Age on Attestation:	16 years	
Period of Service:	1839 — 1861	
Age on Discharge:	38 years 1 month	
Length of Service:	21 years 24 days	
Foreign Service:	East Indies	17 years 16 days
Medal Entitlement:	Indian Mutiny	
Reason for Discharge:	Own Request having served 21 years	
Character:	Very Good	
Trade or Occupation:	Labourer	
Can Sign Name:	Yes	
Height:	5' 6"	
Hair Colour:	Brown	
Eyes:	Grey	
Complexion:	Fair	
Intends to Reside:	Birr Ireland	

WHITE	Patrick, private
	3rd Foot
Previous Regiment	89th
12 May 1847	Discharged the Service Dublin
21 June 1847	Discharge approved
13 July 1847	Admitted to Out-Pension
	Pension paid Dublin Pension District
	1/- per diem
28 June 1851	Arrived per *'Pyrenees'* [1]
circa 1852	Allocated land Albany
23 Mar 1855	Died Pensioners Village 1/¼ miles from Albany having committed suicide

Service and Personal Details:		
Place of Birth:	Howth Dublin	
Age on Attestation:	18 years	
Period of Service:	1826 — 1847	
Age on Discharge:	39 years 4 months	
Length of Service:	21 years 87 days	
Foreign Service:	East Indies	18 years 8 months
Medal Entitlement:	Bronze Star for Battle of Punniar	
Reason for Discharge:	Impaired Vision and Chronic Rheumatism	
Character:	Irregular	
Trade or Occupation:	Labourer	
Can Sign Name:	Yes	

Height:	5' 8¾"
Hair Colour:	Dark Brown
Eyes:	Grey
Complexion:	Fresh

WHITE	William, private 10th Foot
13 Aug 1850	Discharged the Service Chatham Pension paid Coventry 10d. per diem
1850	Pension paid Bath
1853	Oxford
1854	Coventry
18 July 1855	Arrived per *'Adelaide'*
no date	Assigned Perth Military Pensioner Lot 114
1863	Stationed Perth District
Jan 1865	Application for Title to Perth Lot 114
1874	Pension increased to 1/3d per diem for 16 years and 7 months service in the Enrolled Force
1877	Convicted before a Justice of Peace at Perth W.A. for stealing firewood and sentenced to 2 months imprisonment [one month remitted]. No action taken on report of S.O.P.
1897	Stationed at Perth
1903	Died aged 81

Service and Personal Details:

Place of Birth:	Whitcombe nr. Bath
Age on Attestation:	18 years
Period of Service:	1839 — 1850
Age on Discharge:	30 years
Length of Service:	9 years 329 days
Foreign Service:	East Indies 7 years
Medal Entitlement:	Sutlej with clasps; Punjaub with clasps for Siege of Mooltan and Battle of Goojerat
Reason for Discharge:	Grape shot wound received in action
Character:	Good
Trade or Occupation:	Moulder
Can Sign Name:	Yes
Height:	5' 6"
Hair Colour:	Brown
Eyes:	Grey
Complexion:	Dark
Intends to Reside:	Bath

WHITE	William, Corporal 99th Foot
22 Sept 1846	Discharged the Service Chatham Pension paid Kilkenny 1/2½d. per diem
25 Oct 1850	Arrived per *'Hashemy'*
1851	Appointed Night Warder
Oct 1851	Assigned Bunbury Lot P1 of 1 acre
4 Dec 1858	Application for Title to Bunbury Lot P1

1865	a William White employed as Pound Keeper at Bunbury	
Aug 1868	Died aged 62	

Service and Personal Details:

Place of Birth:	St Nicholas Dublin	
Age on Attestation:	18 years	
Period of Service:	1824 — 1846	
Age on Discharge:	40 years 3 months	
Length of Service:	21 years 310 days	
Foreign Service:	Mauritius	11 years
	New South Wales	3 years
Reason for Discharge:	Dyspnoea and palpitations of the heart	
Character:	Good and efficient soldier trustworthy, sober and seldom in hospital	
Trade or Occupation:	Weaver	
Can Sign Name:	Yes	
Height:	5' 6½"	
Hair Colour:	Brown	
Eyes:	Grey	
Complexion:	Sallow	
Intends to Reside:	Callan Co. Kilkenny	

WHITEHOUSE William, private
36th Foot

22 Nov 1853	Discharged the Service Chatham Pension paid Bath 1/- per diem
18 July 1855	Arrived per *'Adelaide'*
1856	£15/0/0 misappropriated by Capt Foss
Jan 1857	Contributed 2/- to the Florence Nightingale Fund
1869	Pension paid Adelaide from 1st Perth West. Aust.

Service and Personal Details:

Place of Birth:	Frome Somerset	
Age on Attestation:	19 years	
Period of Service:	1832 — 1853	
Age on Discharge:	40 years 8 months	
Length of Service:	21 years and 1 day	
Foreign Service:	North America	3 years 19 days
	Ionian Isles	4 years 78 days
Reason for Discharge:	Shortness of breath and debility	
Character:	Indifferent	
Trade or Occupation:	Tailor	
Can Sign Name:	Yes	
Height:	5' 8"	
Hair Colour:	Brown	
Eyes:	Brown	
Complexion:	Fair	
Intends to Reside:	Frome Somerset	

WHITELY James, private
31st Foot

Surname Variant	WHITELEY
26 Mar 1847	Discharged the Service Chatham Pension paid Kilkenny 8d. per diem
1850	Pension paid Manchester
18 Oct 1851	Arrived per *'Minden'*
1852	Assigned Pensioner Loc P4 at York
Jan 1857	Contributed 2/- to the Florence Nightingale Fund
1859	Application for Title to P4 York
1863	Stationed York District
Nov 1864	Application for Title York Lots 229 and 230 at £1/0/0 per acre
1864	Described as Pensioner Shoemaker
1873	Pension increased to 1/-½d. per diem for 9 years and 2 months service in the Enrolled Force
1885	W.O. correspondence— the "A31"
June 1894	Died

Service and Personal Details:

Place of Birth:	Paulstown Co. Kilkenny	
Age on Attestation:	19 years ?6months	
Period of Service:	1843 — 1847	
Age on Discharge:	24 years	
Length of Service:	3 years 351 days	
Foreign Service:	East Indies	2 years 11 months
Medal Entitlement:	Sutlej	
Reason for Discharge:	Wounded in the right shoulder and right arm and the left arm at Moodkee	
Character:	Good	
Trade or Occupation:	Shoemaker	
Can Sign Name:	Yes	
Height:	5' 7½"	
Hair Colour:	Fair	
Eyes:	Grey	
Complexion:	Fair	
Intends to Reside:	Whitehall Co. Kilkenny	

WHITTLE	William, private 71st Foot
9 Feb 1858	Discharged the Service Chatham Pension paid Enniskillen 1/- per diem
12 Sept 1864	Arrived per *'Merchantman'* as a Convict Guard
12 July 1867	"Convict Guard drowned at sea onboard the '*Emma*' Arrears to representatives" [WO correspondence 1931/19 13884-13; 19]

Service and Personal Details:

Place of Birth:	Castlemacadam Rathdrum Co. Wicklow	
Age on Attestation:	18 years	
Period of Service:	1836 — 1857	
Age on Discharge:	39 years 4 months	
Length of Service:	21 years 63 days	
Foreign Service:	Canada	5 years 6 months

	West Indies	1 year 8 months
		Corfu 2 years
Reason for Discharge:	Chronic Lumbago and Varicose Veins	
Character:	Very Good	
Trade or Occupation:	Smith	
Can Sign Name:	Yes	
Height:	5' 8¾"	
Hair Colour:	Light Brown	
Eyes:	Blue	
Complexion:	Fresh	
Intends to Reside:	Brookborough Co. Fermanagh	

WHYBROW

	John, private	
	43rd Foot	
Surname Variant	WHYBROUGH	
10 Aug 1852	Examination by Regimental Medical Board	
5 July 1852	Discharged the Service Templemore	
	Pension paid Cambridgeshire	
	6d. per diem temporary for 3 years	
14 Aug 1854	Arrived per *'Ramillies'*	
1855	To South Australia from Western Australia	
Aug 1855	Pension expired	
Service and Personal Details:		
Place of Birth:	Chesterton Cambridgeshire	
Age on Attestation:	18 years	
Period of Service:	1837 — 1852	
Age on Discharge:	33 years 5 months	
Length of Service:	15 years 56 days	
Foreign Service:	North America	7 years 10 months
Reason for Discharge:	Unfit for further service	
Character:	Bad	
Trade or Occupation:	Brickmaker	
Height:	5' 6½"	
Hair Colour:	Brown	
Eyes:	Grey	
Complexion:	Dark	
Intends to Reside:	Chesterton Cambridgeshire	

WIER

	William, private EIC
	Madras European Infantry
Surname Variant	WEIR
	Out Pension No 284
7 July 1858	Admitted to Out-pension
	Pension paid 2nd Liverpool Pension District
	6d. per diem
4 July 1866	Arrived per *'Belgravia'*
15 Nov 1867	Court House Fremantle Pensioner William Weir has been dismissed from the Force and has proceeded to Champion Bay in search of work, leaving his wife and two children destitute
May 1871	Application for Title Kojonup P10 at 10/- per acre

Apr 1880	Application for Title Kojonup Lot P16
1886	Died

Service and Personal Details:

Place of Birth:	?Kilbeggan Co. Westmeath
Trade or Occupation:	Carpenter
Presidency:	Madras
Length of Service:	12 years 11 months
Age on Discharge:	35 years
Character:	Good
Reason for Discharge:	Varicose veins in right leg
Height:	5' 8"
Complexion:	Fresh
Eye Colour:	Grey
Hair Colour:	Fair
Intends to Reside:	Limehouse

WILCOX John
[son of John Wilcox — Warder]
1st Foot Guards [Grenadier Guards]

1876	Discharged the service 1/1d. per diem

Service and Personal Details:

Place of Birth:	Australia [born circa 1837]
Age on Attestation:	at 1865 29 years 7 months
Period of Service:	1855 — 1876
Age on Discharge:	40 years 8 months
Length of Service:	21 years 27 days 11 years 27 days [2nd period of service] plus 10 years previous service
Foreign Service:	"Army in the East" April 1855 — July 1856
Medal Entitlement:	Long Service and Good Conduct; Crimean with clasp; Turkish Crimean
Reason for Discharge:	Own Request after 21 [reckoned] years service
Character:	Good
Trade or Occupation:	Currier
Can Sign Name:	Yes
Height:	5' 9¾"
Hair Colour:	Dark Brown
Eyes:	Grey
Complexion:	Dark
Remarks:	Former service in the Grenadier Guards of 10 years allowed to reckon as a special case toward Good Conduct pay and Pension
Intends to Reside:	Edgeware Road London

WILCOX John, private
1st Foot Guards [Grenadier Guards]

1861	Hospital Corporal Grenadier Guards Hospital Westminster
Jan 1864	Civil Guard Chatham Prison
1864	Discharged [age 28]

1864	Arrived per *'Merchantman'* [2]
1864	Resigned as Assistant Warder
1881	Dock Constable residing 2 Davies St., Poplar

WILD

	John, private
	18th Foot
Surname Variant	WILDE
16 July 1847	Discharged the Service Chatham
	Pension paid Chatham
	1/- per diem
1848	Pension paid Clonmel
1848	Limerick
1849	Clonmel
25 Oct 1850	Arrived per *'Hashemy'*
Jan 1857	Contributed 2/- to the Florence Nightingale Fund
1862	Pension paid Western Australia
1863	Application for Title to Albany Pensioner Loc P12
1863	To Adelaide from Perth Western Australia

Service and Personal Details:

Place of Birth:	Doon Limerick	
Age on Attestation:	18 years	
Period of Service:	1826 — 1847	
Age on Discharge:	40 years	
Length of Service:	20 years 124 days	
Foreign Service:	Mediterranean	5 years
	Ceylon	3 years 34 days
	China	6 years 180 days
Reason for Discharge:	General Debility from length of service	
Character:	Bad	
Trade or Occupation:	Labourer	
Can Sign Name:	X his mark on discharge	
Height:	5' 8"	
Hair Colour:	Black	
Eyes:	Grey	
Complexion:	Dark	
Intends to Reside:	Tipperary	

WILKINSON

	John, private
	52nd Foot
Previous Regiment	18th Foot
26 Aug 1856	Discharged the Service Chatham
	Pension paid Clonmel
	9d. per diem
1857	Pension paid Kilkenny
11 Feb 1861	Arrived per *'Palmeston'*
1863	residing Fremantle area
1868	To Melbourne from Perth Western Australia
1881	W.O. correspondence

Service and Personal Details:

Place of Birth:	Tipperary Co. Tipperary
Age on Attestation:	20 years
Period of Service:	1835 — 1855
Age on Discharge:	41 years or 40 years 6 months

Length of Service:	20 years 195 days	
Foreign Service:	Ceylon	3 years 1 month
	China	7 years 6 months
	Burmah	1 year 8 months
	Bengal	6 years 1 month
Reason for Discharge:	Chronic Rheumatism	
Character:	Good	
Trade or Occupation:	Labourer	
Can Sign Name:	Yes	
Height:	5' 7¼"	
Hair Colour:	Brown	
Eyes:	Hazel	
Complexion:	Fresh	
Intends to Reside:	Tipperary	

WILLIAMS

	John, private [Military Pensioner]
	51st Foot
25 June 1840	Arrived per *'Runnymede'* with regiment
11 Mar 1847	Discharged from active service Perth WA
24 Aug 1847	Discharge approved
24 Aug 1847	Placed on Pension Roll and pension paid Perth Western Australia
31 Mar 1851	Pension paid by Commissariat Department until transferred to Capt Bruce Staff Officer Pensions Western Australia
1/- per diem	
May 1884	District Medical Officer Newcastle requesting admission of Pensioner M. Hunter into Mt. Eliza Poor House
1889	Died

Service and Personal Details:

Place of Birth:	St Peters Liverpool	
Age on Attestation:	18 years	
Period of Service:	1825 — 1847	
Age on Discharge:	39 years 8 months	
Length of Service:	21 years 63 days	
Foreign Service:	Ionian Isles	7 years 9 months
	Australian Colonies	9 years
Reason for Discharge:	Chronic Rheumatism; Deafness totally worn out and unfit for further service	
Character:	Indifferent	
Trade or Occupation:	Skinner	
Height:	5' 5½"	
Hair Colour:	Brown	
Eyes:	Hazel	
Complexion:	Fair	
Intends to Reside:	Western Australia	

WILLIAMS

Richard, private EIC
1st Bombay European Fusiliers
Out Pension No 333

17 Oct 1860	Admitted to Out-pension Pension paid 2nd East London Pension District 1/- per diem
1862	Pension paid Bermuda
15 Feb 1863	Arrived per *'Merchantman'* [1]
1 Jan 1885	Assigned Loc 1066 at Butlers Swamp
24 Mar 1885	Application for Title Freshwater Bay Loc 1066
June 1897	Residing Perth
1900	Died

Service and Personal Details:

Place of Birth:	Bethnal Green Middlesex
Trade or Occupation:	Porter
Presidency:	Bombay
Length of Service:	19 years 7 months
Age on Discharge:	39 years
Character:	none given
Reason for Discharge:	Time expired
Medal Entitlement:	Indian Mutiny
Height:	5' 5"
Complexion:	Fresh
Eye Colour:	Grey
Hair Colour:	Brown
Intends to Reside:	Bethnal Green Middlesex

WILSON Alexander, private
RM

1850	Discharged the Service
18 Oct 1851	Arrived per *'Minden'*
Jan 1857	Contributed 1/- to the Florence Nightingale Fund
1857	Died aged 52
24 Feb 1863	Fremantle Residents Office Mrs. Wilson and her daughter needing relief. Widow of a Pensioner who came out on the *'Minden'*. She is now 70 years old and daughter is also a widow,

Service and Personal Details:

Place of Birth:	St Cuthberts Edinburgh Scotland
Age on Attestation:	26 years 9 months
Marine Division:	Chatham
Period of Service:	1832 — 1850
Length of Service:	21 years 13 days
Reason for Discharge:	Length of Service
Trade or Occupation:	Brushmaker
Can Sign Name:	Yes
Remarks:	Initially discharged 1830 having paid £20,and re-attested at Chatham, in 1832.
Height:	5' 9½"
Hair Colour:	Black
Eyes:	Hazel
Complexion:	Dark

WILSON William, Corporal
Rifle Brigade Depot 2nd Battalion

9 Dec 1856	Discharged the Service Chatham 8d. per diem
1863	Stationed Perth District
1864	a ptve W Wilson Pensioner Force at Perth contributed to the Greenough Fire Relief Fund
1865	Pension paid Western Australia
Dec 1865	Application for Title Perth Town Lot N112 at £6/0/0 per Lot acre
?1887	Pension increased to 1/- per diem for service in the Enrolled Force of Western Australia

Service and Personal Details:

Place of Birth:	Rye Sussex	
Age on Attestation:	17 years 1 month	
Period of Service:	1849 — 1856	
Age on Discharge:	24 years 4 months	
Length of Service:	2 years 214 days	
Foreign Service:	"the East"	1 year 11 months
Medal Entitlement:	Crimea	
Reason for Discharge:	Gunshot wound of left shoulder at the attack on the Redan	
Character:	Good	
Trade or Occupation:	Labourer	
Can Sign Name:	Yes	
Height:	5' 6¾"	
Hair Colour:	Brown	
Eyes:	Grey	
Complexion:	Fresh	

WIMBRIDGE Thomas William, private
69th Foot

Surname Variant	WINBRIDGE
22 Dec 1846	Discharged the Service Salford Barracks Manchester 11d. per diem
1846	Pension paid 1st East London Pension District
1847	Pension paid Derby
1847	Galway
1849	Roscommon
1851	Waterford
30 Apr 1853	Arrived per *'Pyrenees'* [2]
1853	Employed by Convict Service without sanction of Staff Officer Pensions Assigned Perth Military Pensioner Lot 117/Y
Jan 1857	Contributed 1/- to the Florence Nightingale Fund
Jan 1865	Application for Title to Perth Lot 117
1871	Secretary of the Perth branch of the Pensioner's Benevolent Fund
1873	Employed by Commissariat
1875	Pensioner Lot 11/Y advertised for sale at auction
1878	Pension increased to 1/7d. per diem for service as a messenger in the Commissariat Dept
1881	Prior to death employed at the Supreme Court

1881	Died aged 74 buried in Anglican section of East Perth Pioneer Cemetery	
Service and Personal Details:		
Place of Birth:	Saint Mary-le-bone London Middlesex	
Age on Attestation:	19 years	
Period of Service:	1827 — 1846	
Age on Discharge:	39 years or 38 years 6 months	
Length of Service:	19 years 98 days	
Foreign Service:	West Indies	7 years
	North America	3 years 7 months
Reason for Discharge:	Hernia and worn out	
Character:	Good	
Trade or Occupation:	Cotton Spinner	
Can Sign Name:	Yes	
Height:	5' 8¾"	
Hair Colour:	Dark brown	
Eyes:	Blue	
Complexion:	Fresh	
Distinguishing Marks:	Freckled	
Intends to Reside:	Manchester	

WINDER	Jackson, Serjeant	
	103rd Foot	
Previous Regiment	1st [Bombay] European Fusiliers [l/MIL/12/112]	
30 May 1865	Discharged the Service Netley	
	Pension paid 2nd Manchester Pension District	
	2/- per diem	
22 Dec 1865	Arrived per *'Vimiera'*	
1867	Employed as Assistant warder	
1881	Pension increased to 2/3½d. per diem for service in the Enrolled Force of Western Australia	
June 1881	Died aged 59 Fremantle	
Service and Personal Details:		
Place of Birth:	Cleater Whitehaven Cumberland	
Age on Attestation:	19 years	
Embarked India:	per *'Forfarshire'*	
Period of Service:	1846 — 1865	
Age on Discharge:	38 years 1 month	
Length of Service:	20 years 217 days	
Foreign Service:	India	19 years 316 days
Medal Entitlement:	Punjaub Medal with two clasps; Indian Mutiny	
Reason for Discharge:	Dyspnoea	
Character:	Very Good	
Trade or Occupation:	Flax dresser	
Can Sign Name:	Yes	
Height:	5' 6"	
Hair Colour:	Fair	
Eyes:	Blue	
Complexion:	Fresh	
Remarks:	Elected for Indian Pension Rules	
Intends to Reside:	Manchester	

Married:	*c*1859 Eliza Anne Jacobs Bombay [N3/3/33]
Children:	James Jackson Winder b. 1861 Poona India
	m. *c*1885 Charlotte Cable Fremantle
	Eleanor Ada b. 1864 Bombay India
	Edmund William b. *c*1866 Fremantle
	Florence Emily b. *c*1869 Fremantle
	m. *c*1889 John Gottfried Reding [sic] Fremantle
	Robert John b. *c*1872 Canning
	Agnes Ann b. *c*1877 Fremantle
	m. *c*1896 Hugh Ferguson Fremantle

WINFIELD	John, private	
	1st Foot Guards [Grenadier]	
Surname Variant	WINGFIELD	
12 June 1849	Discharged the Service London	
	Pension paid West London Pension District	
	1/1d. per diem	
1 June 1850	Arrived per *'Scindian'*	
Jan 1857	Contributed 2/- to the Florence Nightingale Fund	
1864	Died	
Service and Personal Details:		
Place of Birth:	Castle Donnington Ashby-de-la-Zouche Leicestershire	
Age on Attestation:	19 years	
Period of Service:	1825 — 1849	
Age on Discharge:	42 years 9 months	
Length of Service:	23 years 261 days	
Foreign Service:	Portugal	1 year 4 months
	Canada	4 years 8 months
Reason for Discharge:	Chronic Rheumatism	
Conduct:	Generally Good	
Trade or Occupation:	Labourer	
Can Sign Name:	Yes	
Height:	5' 8½"	
Complexion:	Fresh	
Hair Colour:	Light Brown	
Eye Colour:	Hazel	

WOOD	Joshua, private [Military Pensioner]
	51st Foot
Previous Regiment	84th Foot
25 June 1840	Arrived per *'Runnymede'* with regiment
24 Aug 1847	Discharged the Service Western Australia
	1/2d. per diem
31 Mar 1851	Pension paid by Commissariat until transferred to Capt Bruce Staff Officer Pensions West. Australia
1854	Pension paid Western Australia
7 Nov 1854	His application for Military Pensioner land grant refused as he wasn't an EPG
1876	Died

Service and Personal Details:

Place of Birth:	Huddersfield Yorkshire	
Age on Attestation:	16 years 6 months	
Period of Service:	1820 — 1847	
Age on Discharge:	44 years	
Length of Service:	26 years 86 days	
Foreign Service:	Ionian Isles	12 years 11 months
	Australian Colonies	9 years
Reason for Discharge:	Worn Out and unfit for service in India	
Character:	Good	
Trade or Occupation:	Wheelwright	

WOODS Francis, private
16th Foot

Previous Regiment	96th Foot
4 Dec 1866	Discharged the Service Colchester
	Pension paid Limerick
	1/- per diem
1866	Pension paid North London Pension District
9 Jan 1868	Arrived per *'Hougoumont'*
31 Mar 1874	To Victoria from Fremantle

Service and Personal Details:

Place of Birth:	Charlesville Co. Cork	
Age on Attestation:	*c*18 years	
Period of Service:	1845 — 1866	
Age on Discharge:	39 years 3 months	
Length of Service:	21 years 89 days	
Foreign Service:	Canada	4 years 10 months
Medal Entitlement:	Long Service and Good Conduct with gratuity	
Reason for Discharge:	Own Request having served over 21 years	
Character:	Very Good	
Trade or Occupation:	Labourer	
Can Sign Name:	Yes	
Height:	5' 6"	
Hair Colour:	Dark Brown	
Eyes:	Blue	
Complexion:	Fresh	
Intends to Reside:	Post Office Charleville Co. Cork	

WOODS Henry, private [Military Pensioner]
96th Foot

Previous Regiment	51st
Surname Variant	WOOD
1 Apr 1847	Attached to the 96th when the 51st embarked for India
15 May 1849	Discharged the Service Perth West Australia
31 Aug 1849	Discharged approved
9 Nov 1849	Pension ratified
9 Oct 1849	Admitted to Out-Pension
	1/- per diem
	Pension paid by Commissariat until transferred to Capt Bruce Staff Officer Pensions West. Aust.
1854	Unsuccessful in application for Pensioner Land Grant as he was not an EPG

1864	Pension paid Western Australia
1865	South Australia
1871	a Henry Woods died at Up Down Rock South Australia

Service and Personal Details:

Place of Birth:	Castle Blayney Monaghan
Age on Attestation:	18 years
Period of Service:	1827 — 1849
Age on Discharge:	43 years
Length of Service:	21 years 345 days
Foreign Service:	Australasia 12 years
Reason for Discharge:	Worn out and unfit for service in the East Indies
Character:	Good
Trade or Occupation:	Labourer
Can Sign Name:	X his mark on discharge
Height:	5' 7"
Hair Colour:	Light Brown
Eyes:	Hazel
Complexion:	Fair
Remarks:	5 of the Invalids who are desirous to settle in the Colony
Intends to Reside:	Western Australia

WOODS James, Serjeant [Military Pensioner]
99th Foot

5 Apr 1849	Arrived per *'Radcliffe'* with regiment
30 June 1852	Discharged the Service Perth Western Australia
14 Dec 1852	Discharge Approved
	Pension paid Perth Western Australia
	2/- per diem
1853	Pension paid South Australia

Service and Personal Details:

Place of Birth:	Ballyshannon Co. Donegal
Age on Attestation:	20 years 1 month
Period of Service:	1832 — 1852
Age on Discharge:	44 years 7 months
Length of Service:	21 years 363 days
Foreign Service:	Australian Colonies 8 years
Reason for Discharge:	Rheumatism and fracture of right collar bone
Character:	Good
Trade or Occupation:	Weaver
Can Sign Name:	Yes
Height:	5' 6½"
Hair Colour:	Brown
Eyes:	Bluish Grey
Complexion:	Fair
Distinguishing Marks:	Mole on left cheek
Remarks:	To be filled in at Swan River. [This document was completed at Perth Western Australia the 28th day of June 1852]

WOODS	John, Corporal 5th Foot
28 June 1864	Discharged the Service Shorncliffe Pension paid 2nd West London Pension District
1/- per diem	
22 Dec 1866	Arrived per *'Corona'*
21 Jan 1873	Died
Service and Personal Details:	
Place of Birth:	Drumlane Killishandie Co. Cavan
Age on Attestation:	18 years
Period of Service:	1845 — 1864
Age on Discharge:	*c* 37 years
Length of Service:	18 years 308 days
Foreign Service:	Mauritius 9 years 8 months East Indies 4 years
Medal Entitlement:	Indian Mutiny with clasp
Reason for Discharge:	Unfit for further service aggravated by the use of spirituous liquors and Deformed Feet
Character:	Good
Trade or Occupation:	Labourer
Can Sign Name:	Yes
Height:	5' 7"
Hair Colour:	Dark Brown
Eyes:	Fresh
Complexion:	Fresh
Distinguishing Marks:	Pock pitted
Intends to Reside:	Drumlane Co. Cavan

WOODS	William, private Newfoundland Veteran Corps
Previous Regiment	30th Foot
Surname Variant	WOOD
23 Aug 1859	Discharged the Service Pension paid 2nd Manchester Pension District 1/-½d. per diem [or 1/- per diem]
1861	With family at 93 Lombard St Manchester
29 Jan 1862	Arrived per *'Lincelles'*
Mar 1863	Application for Title South Perth Loc P6 at £1/0/0 per acre
1863	Stationed Perth Pension District
1864	ptve W Woods Pensioner Force at Perth contributed to Greenough Fire Relief Fund
24 Aug 1881	Assigned Perth Railway Block Lot 144/V
28 Dec 1883	Application for Title Perth Lot 144V
May 1884	Granted Fee Simple Perth Railway Block Lot 144/V
June 1897	Residing Perth
Service and Personal Details:	
Place of Birth:	Crofts or Cross Lane Salford Manchester
Age on Discharge:	40 years
Length of Service:	22 years 2 months
Foreign Service:	West Indies 3 years 11 months

	North America	11 months
	Newfoundland	16 years 8 months
Reason for Discharge:	Subject to Rheumatism, drowsiness and headaches from service	
Character:	Good	
Trade or Occupation:	Dyer	
Height:	5' 7"	
Hair Colour:	Dark Brown	
Eyes:	Blue	
Complexion:	Fresh	
Married:	Eliza b. *c*1820 Exeter	
Children:	Samuel b. *c*1858 Newfoundland m. *c*1880 Sarah Playford Guildford William Thomas b. *c*1860 Newfoundland m. *c*1893 May Russ Perth	

WOOLHOUSE Jeremiah, private

	70th Foot
14 Sept 1852	Discharged the Service Chatham Pension paid Sheffield 1/- per diem
1852	Pension paid Hull
14 Aug 1854	Arrived per *'Ramillies'*
Jan 1857	Contributed 2/- to the Florence Nightingale Fund
Dec 1860	Application for Title Newcastle Lot S16
1 Dec 1861	Pensioner Jeremiah Woolhouse died aged 48 at Newcastle
1862	'Grant of land made out to widow Margaret and 4 daughters. Margaret married Wilson, a man of intemperate habits'

Service and Personal Details:

Place of Birth:	Aston Yorkshire	
Age on Attestation:	18 years	
Period of Service:	1831 — 1852	
Age on Discharge:	39 years 7 months	
Length of Service:	21 years 209 days	
Foreign Service:	Gibraltar	2 years 97 days
	Malta	1 year 266 days
	West Indies	3 years 70 days
	Canada	2 years 24 days
Medal Entitlement:	Good Conduct with gratuity	
Reason for Discharge:	Chronic Hepatitis and Dyspnoea	
Character:	Good	
Trade or Occupation:	Farmer's Servant	
Can Sign Name:	X his mark on discharge	
Height:	5' 7½"	
Hair Colour:	Light Brown	
Eyes:	Hazel	
Complexion:	Fresh	
Intends to Reside:	Wickesley nr. Rotherham	

WRIGHT	John, private	
	42nd Foot	
23 Apr 1850	Discharged the Service Chatham	
	Pension paid Stirling	
	6d. per diem for 3 years	
25 Oct 1850	Arrived per *'Hashemy'*	
July 1851	Assistant Warder Convict establishment	
Aug 1851	Resigned or dismissed from Convict Service	
1857	Died	
Service and Personal Details:		
Place of Birth:	Stirling Stirlingshire	
Age on Attestation:	18 years	
Period of Service:	1838 — 1850	
Age on Discharge:	29 years 8 months	
Length of Service:	11 years 119 days	
Foreign Service:	Malta	4 years 88 days
	Ionian Isles	2 years 92 days
	Bermuda	272 days
Reason for Discharge:	Chronic Hepatitis	
Character:	Good	
Trade or Occupation:	Weaver	
Can Sign Name:	Yes	
Height:	5' 8"	
Hair Colour:	Dark Brown	
Eyes:	Grey	
Complexion:	Sallow	
Intends to Reside:	Stirling	

WRIGHT	Joseph, private	
also known as	George **STURMAN**	
	45th Foot	
Previous Regiment	46th Foot	
15 Jan 1861	Admitted to Out-Pension	
	Pension paid Halifax	
	10d. per diem	
15 Aug 1865	Arrived per *'Racehorse'*	
1868	Employed by Convict Establishment	
1873	Employed as Serjeant of Pensioners	
1874	Pension increased to 1/2d. per diem	
Mar 1876	a Sergeant J Wright residing Champion Bay	
Oct 1880	Application for Title to Victoria Loc X5	
1880	Grant of £15 [pounds] sanctioned	
1888	Granted Title to Victoria Loc X5	
1902	Died [as George Sturman]	
Service and Personal Details:		
Place of Birth:	Lutterworth Leicester	
Age on Attestation:	18 years	
Period of Service:	1840 — 1861	
Age on Discharge:	39 years 1 months	
Length of Service:	21 years 34 days	
Foreign Service:	Gibraltar	1 year 9 months

	Monte Video 9 months
	Cape of Good Hope 12 years 8 months
Medal Entitlement:	Kaffir War 1850 — 1853
Reason for Discharge:	Own Request having completed 21 years service
Character:	Very Good
Trade or Occupation:	Servant
Can Sign Name:	Yes
Height:	5' 9"
Hair Colour:	Brown
Eyes:	Grey
Complexion:	Fresh
Intends to Reside:	Drewsbury Yorkshire

WRIGHTSON	John, private EIC
	1st Madras European Fusiliers
	Out Pension No 367
10 Sept 1861	Discharged to pension
	Pension paid Limerick
	1/- per diem
1863	Pension paid 2nd Cork Pension District
1864	Pension paid Galway
1864	Limerick
4 July 1866	Arrived per *'Belgravia'*
July 1874	Applied for Improvement grant of £15 for Perth Town Lot 139/Y
Apr 1881	Application for Title to Perth Lot 139/Y
1881	Granted Fee Simple for Perth Town Lot 139/Y
6 Aug 1900	Special Certificate of Title for Perth Town Lot Y139

Service and Personal Details:

Place of Birth:	Clare Ireland
Trade or Occupation:	Labourer
Presidency:	Madras
Length of Service:	16 years
Age on Discharge:	37 years
Reason for Discharge:	Wound in left thigh
Character:	Indifferent
Height:	5' 5½"
Complexion:	Fresh
Eye Colour:	Blue
Hair Colour:	Brown
Remarks:	Flesh wound to right thigh received at Lucknow
Sept 1857	
Intends to Reside:	Limerick

WYNNE	Samuel, private Military Pensioner
	51st Foot
25 June 1840	Arrived per *'Runnymede'*
11 Mar 1847	Discharged the Service
24 Aug 1847	Discharged approved
	Pension paid Western Australia
	1/-½d. per diem
22 Aug 1859	Died

Service and Personal Details:	
Place of Birth:	Warrington Lancashire
Age on Attestation:	24 years
Period of Service:	1825 — 1847
Age on Discharge:	45 years 6 months
Length of Service:	20 years 288 days
Foreign Service:	Ionian Isles 5 years 6 months
	Australian Colonies 7 years 6 months
Reason for Discharge:	Quite worn out and not fit for service in India
Character:	Indifferent
Trade or Occupation:	Labourer
Can Sign Name:	Yes
Height:	5' 8"
Hair Colour:	Brown
Eye Colour:	Grey
Complexion:	Fresh
Distinguishing Marks:	Head rather upon one side

YENDALL	William, Corporal [1083]
	51st Foot
Surname Variant	YEADELL; GENDALL; TENDALL
28 June 1859	Discharged the Service Chichester
	Pension paid 1st Liverpool Pension District
	1/1½d. per diem
11 Feb 1861	Arrived per *'Palmeston'*
1863	Stationed Perth [WA] Pension District
1868	To be sentenced to one month's hard labor for assault
Oct 1868	Auctioneers Alex Cummings received instruction from Mr Yendall who is about to leave the Colony to sell by auction the freehold property of about 4 acre corner lot — Perth Suburban Lot No 60. On it is a substantial 3 room brick cottage with a good well of water with frame complete; cow shed with 3 stalls, stockyard, pigsty, fowl houses. There are 2 acres fenced in, of that 1¼ fenced in, 47 yards of trellace [sic] of vines as well as other vines and fruit trees of various descriptions. The property is located on the commencement of the rising ground & in one of the healthiest suburbs of Perth
6 Nov 1868	Mr and Mrs Yendall and three sons to Adelaide
1866	Pension paid Adelaide from 1st Perth West. Aust.
11 Dec 1896	Increase for service as Guard of Convicts in Western Aust. Letter from Treasurer Adelaide S.A
1897	Attended Memorial Service Hindmarsh S.A.
1904	Died aged 86 years

Service and Personal Details:	
Place of Birth:	St Cuthberts Wells Somerset
Age on Attestation:	21 years
Period of Service:	1837 — 1959
Age on Discharge:	39 years 11 months

Length of Service:	21 years 318 days	
Foreign Service:	Van Dieman's Land	8 years 4 months
	East Indies	7 years 10 months
Medal Entitlement:	? Burmah with clasp for Pegu	
Reason for Discharge:	Own request having completed 21 years service	
Character:	Very Good	
Trade or Occupation:	Labourer	
Can Sign Name:	Yes	
Height:	5' 9"	
Hair Colour:	Fair	
Eyes:	Hazel	
Complexion:	Fair	
Remarks:	Served for 7 years as a Guard in the Convict Service	

YOUNG Thomas, private
39th Foot

Previous Regiment	Rifle Brigade 2nd Battalion
18 Nov 1851	Discharged the Service Dublin
13 Jan 1852	Admitted to Out-Pension Pension paid Inverness 8d. per diem
24 May 1855	Arrived per *'Stag'*
Jan 1857	Contributed 1/- to the Florence Nightingale Fund
circa 1859	Stationed at Rottnest possibly in charge of the school
1873	Pension increased to 1/3d. per diem for 16 years service in the Enrolled Force
27 Dec 1873	Died buried in the old cemetery at Guildford
28 Jan 1876	Widow granted West Guildford Loc 124 and purchased West Guildford Loc 123 for £2/-/-
1876	W Dale: 'respecting Mrs. Young's circumstances and I find that she resides at West Guildford and has a cottage and about 4 acres of land She has 2 sons the oldest is lately married and gone to reside in Perth, he will do nothing for her — the youngest is about 15 years old and employed by a Mr. Thompson of West Guildford - She has no stock only two goats – the old woman is lame, and not able to do much

Service and Personal Details:

Place of Birth:	Elgin Morayshire	
Age on Attestation:	17 years	
Period of Service:	1831 — 1851	
Age on Discharge:	37 years	
Length of Service:	18 years 252	
Foreign Service:	Ionian Isles	2 years 11 months
	Bermuda	10 months
	North America	6 years 11 months
Reason for Discharge:	Varicose Veins in both legs	
Character:	Indifferent	
Trade or Occupation:	Labourer	

Can Sign Name:	Yes
Height:	6' 0½"
Hair Colour:	Fair
Eyes:	Grey
Complexion:	Fair
Intends to Reside:	Elgin Morayshire

Unable to Locate or Verify

	1851	A pensioner choked to death — [Perth Gazette]
	1877	Widow of Pensioner who shot himself while on Guard duty some months ago [ACC36/132]
ADKINSON		
	Sept 1870	On Perth District Electoral List
	Nov 1877	Stationed at Perth
		Neglecting to salute Governor but fine and imprisonment [sentence remitted]
AINSLEE		Charles
	1882	Admitted to Mt Eliza Invalid Depot from Busselton
	1887	Died aged 70
ANDERSON		Edward
	25 Oct 1850	Arrived per *'Hashemy'*
	1851	Died aged 41 - ?buried East Perth Cemetery
ANDERSON		D
		Non military settler
ANDERSON		T
		pensioner and former soldier
	Jan 1885	Anderson fined sum of 10/- or 7 day in prison for being drunk, disorderly and causing annoyance
ANDERSON		William
		a William Anderson recorded in Fremantle burial records as being sick onboard the *'Scindian'*
	June 1850	Buried aged 51 Fremantle Cemetery
ANDERSON		William
	1850	Arrived per *'Scindian'*
	1850	possibly died 18 days after arrival
ARMENT		Thomas [HO11/17 - convict number 1137]
	1849	according to the 'Biographical Dictionary of W.A.' arrived per *'Marion'* as a Pensioner Guard
	1880	a Thomas Arment late of Albany died aged 50 at the Invalid Depot
ARMSTRONG		James, private EIC
	1880	On nominal Roll of Enrolled Pensioners at Fremantle [Broomhall]
BARDWELL		
	1915	an old Imperial soldier having served in Egypt, India and the Persian Gulf
BARROW		
	Dec 1887	A pensioner named Barrow an interpreter for the Afghans [possibly C Barron]
BASS		Robert

	according to the 'Biographical Dictionary of Western Australia' Robert Bass was an Enrolled Pensioner Guard
BENTLEY	John
	7th Foot
BISHOP	Robert
Feb 1895	an old pensioner aged about 76, living in a small log hut at Rudd's Gully found dead; shot through the head, probably suicide
BLANEY	Thomas, private
	RM
	Admitted to Out-Pension
22 Dec 1865	possibly arrived per *'Vimiera'*
BRENNAN	Denis, private
	12th Foot
Aug 1860	resigned from the Army. He became a retailer, importer, produced lime for the building industry in Perth, and bought property,
1884	died aged 59
BRIEN	Daniel, private
	65th Foot
Surname Variants	O'BRYNE; O'BRIEN
8 Nov 1837	Discharged the Service Chatham
27 Dec 1837	Admitted to Out-Pension
	5d. per diem
15 Aug 1838	Pension increased to 9d. per diem
1851	Pension paid Western Australia
1853	a Daniel O'Byrne residing in Western Australia
9 June 1858	a Daniel O'Brien 65th Foot subscribed to the Indian Famine Relief Fund
8 June 1861	a Daniel O'Brien died in West. Australia aged 58
BRITH	Francis
Surname Variant	BRITT
	said to have arrived per *'Robert Small'* not found in the War Office 'Discharged to Pension documents 1770 — 1854' at The National Archives Kew
BROWN	H
1878	Pensioner H. Brown and his children in R.C. Orphanage Also folios [SROWA 231/233/236/239]
BROWN	Patrick
1854	living at Vasse
	Not found in War Office records of 6th Foot nor in the War Office 'Discharged the Service documents 1770 -1854' at TNA Kew
BROWN	William
	RM

	prior 1851	Admitted to Out-Pension £2/2/0 per annum
	1852	arrived possibly per *'Mermaid'*
BROWN		William
	1874	a William Brown pensioner was charged with stabbing his wife [Hannah Brown described as being a woman having exceedingly loose and depraved habits]
BROWN		Hannah
	1879	wife of a pensioner died at Perth
BURROWS		Charles
	1921	Died at Redmond said to have served in India
CALLAGHAN		Michael
	28 Mar 1888	Resident Magistrate Newcastle - recommending that Michael Callaghan be admitted to Mount Eliza Invalid Depot
?CARRIGAN		William
	Nov 1850	Employed as Assistant Warder Convict service Previous occupation given as "Pensioner"
CARROL		Thomas
		11th or 18th Hussars
CARTER		
	Nov 1851	Employed as Assistant Overseer Convict Service
	Feb 1852	Dismissed from Convict Service Previous occupation given as "Pensioner"
CARTER		John
	Apr 1866	about the 30th Jan 1866 "a pensioner found dead — lost in bush near the old Sound Road [the Perth to Albany Road]
CASH		J
	Nov 1884	Superintendent Poor Houses — Pensioner James Cash [sic] in for Mt. Eliza Depot
CHAMBERLAIN		Charles, Sergeant [2981]
		1st Btn 12th Foot 2nd Detachment
	1861	Regiment Stationed at Perth
	1863	Discharged Perth
CLARK		Mary
		wife of Pensioner
	1867	died aged 48 years Albany
CLAUSEN		George
	Dec 1853	Signs memorial against high cost of living
CLIFFORD		Daniel
		Thought to be a Pensioner
	1888	House proprietor

COCKRAM	Caroline
1860	wife of Pensioner Cockram, Cookram or Cockrane
COGHLAN	John
11 Oct 1862	died aged 45 at Kojonup
COFFEE	Daniel
1865	On Nominal List to proceed to Camden Harbour per '*Tien Tsin*' as a labourer in receipt of £2.00 per annum
CONDON	Michael, Serjeant
	77th Foot
23 Aug 1859	Discharged the Service
	1/8d. per diem
COLGAN	William
	said to be a Pensioner Guard
1864	Died
CONNER	P, private
Jan 1857	Contributed 1/- to the Florence Nightingale Fund
CONNELLY	John
	Discharged the Service
1854	In Western Australia
1854	Port Gregory
COULSON	William
1874	Court House Fremantle — William Coulson has applied to have his wife admitted to the Lunatic Asylum as a Pauper patient. Coulson is a pensioner in receipt of 1 [one pound sterling] 8 shillings per month and is unable to work on account of his having only one arm. [Trove]
CRAIG	John
	Warder
CUNNINGHAM	J, private
Jan 1857	Contributed 1/- to the Florence Nightingale Fund
CUNNINGHAM	Robert, driver — ['Old Bob']
	Royal Field Artillery
19 Nov 1923	died aged 94 years at his residence at Yarloop
	Was a resident in Western Australia for 56 years
CURTIS	William
17 Oct 1881	At Fremantle, William Curtis [a pensioner], aged 60 years and employed as a shoemaker was charged with larceny of two rugs and single barrel gun.
Personal Details:	[on arrest]
Height:	5' 10"
Complexion:	Fair

	Eye Colour:	Blue
	Hair Colour:	Grey
DALY		J, private
	1864	a ptve J Daly Pensioner Force at Fremantle contributed to the Greenough Fire Relief Fund
DARCY		Henry
	1852	Assigned York Lot P2
DELANEY		John, pensioner
	1872	residing Perth
	1872	Summons to hearing for claim of £8/16/10d Debt confessed and judgement given for amount and costs
DEVONPORT		
	24 Mar 1854	Daughter Sarah died Fremantle aged 2
	1865	Departed WA to Madras [possibly Davenport]
DONEGAN		James
		Indian Army
		[son of John Donegan 21st Foot]]
	1862	Mail Service between Guildford and Toodyay
	1915	Died aged 74
DONAGHER		A, Serjeant
	1876	Stationed Fremantle
		Involved in shooting competition [Trove]
DOYLE		
	1871	possibly arrived per *'Strathmore'*
DUNBAR		Philip
	1891	a military pensioner inmate of the Depot aged 66
DUFFY		John
		49th Foot
		1/4d. per diem
DWYER		William, private
ELLIS		William, pensioner
	30 Jan 1866	Resident's Office Fremantle: William Ellis Pensioner, application for relief
ENTERTON		William
	1853	Protests against high cost of provisions
FALLER		Thomas
		Thomas Faller not found in the War Office Discharged the Service documents 1770 — 1854 at The National Archives Kew
	1852	On Duty at King George Sound applied for grant there
FARQUHAR		John,

	? Royal Sapper and Miners
13 Feb 1830	Arrived per '*Hoogley*' as a settler
FENNELL	John, Corporal [No 416]
1899	Charge of 9/- to engrave medal
FENOREFRY [sic]	J, Corporal
Feb 1864	a Corporal J Fenoredry [sic] Pensioner Force at Perth contributed 2/- to the Greenough Fire Relief Fund
FOARD	Michael, private
	99th Foot
Surname Variant	FORD
9 Sept 1840	Discharged the Service
	Pension paid Birr
	7d. per diem
1865	Refused pension increase
1865	Pension paid Athlone
22 Dec 1865	Arrived per '*Vimiera*'
FLINDELL	Francis Bassett Shenstone
	Said to have served in the Turkish Contingent
1858	arrived per '*Nile*'
FLINDELL	Francis Bassett Shenstone
	Said to have served in the Turkish Contingent
1858	arrived per '*Nile*'
FRAZER	Sergeant
FRETT	Robert
1856	Listed as sick onboard the '*William Hammond*'
FULHAM	John
	11th Foot
	6d. per diem
no date	to South Australia
GAVIN	Edward
1861	possibly arrived per '*Palmeston*'
1865	Arrived in WA [as per family history]
1865	Police Constable Toodyay and Gingin
1903	Died aged 70 [born Tipperary Ireland]
GILROY	Michael
	99th Foot
	1/- per diem
GRAINGER	Henry
7 Sept 1876	Inquest on the body of Henry Grainger a pensioner who died suddenly at his hut about 5 miles from Williams River Bridge
1876	a Henry Grainger died from apoplexy caused by excessive drinking aged 60

GRAVES		James
		possibly served in Turkish Contingent
	1852	aged 22
	31 Dec 1858	Arrived per '*Lord Raglan*'
GUDGE		Thomas/John
HALE		John, private
	Intends to Reside:	22 Healy Street Wilson Place Barnsley
HALLIWELL		a Pensioner
	7 May 1867	"shot dead North Fremantle"
HANLEY		J, private
		68th Foot
	Surname Variant	HANDLEY
	1 June 1859	Discharged the Service
		Pension paid
		11d. per diem
	circa 1881	a ptve Hanley found dead in the bush near Albany
HANNAN		
	1883	Pensioner Hannan ordered to leave the Pensioner Barracks [SROWA 33/701]
HANNON		Martin, private
	Surname Variant	HANNAN; HANSON
	1872	Granted North Fremantle Lot 20
HARRIS		Samuel
		[described as belonging to the 21st regiment]
	Sept 1859	charged by police constable Hillier with sleeping in a public street in Perth
	1859	Residing Fremantle the Charge dismissed by Thomas Newte Yule
HAYNES		John
	1885	Colonial Surgeon Fremantle —Pensioner John Haynes [sic] for admission to Mt Eliza Depot
HAWES		William
	18 Aug 1877	Discharged from Perth Goal. Offence — Vagrancy
HEALY		James,
	Surname Variants	HEALEY; HALEY
	31 Aug 1853	According to WA passenger Lists arrived per '*Phoebe Dunbar*'— described as Guard Age on arrival 45
HENSMAN		J
	1888	Mr Hensman ex soldier
HILLYARD		James
		2nd Foot
HOLMAN		John

	*c*1879	Ellen Holman daughter of John pensioner guard married David Colton at Picton
HOWELL		Henry, private
		between 1874 and 1882 said to have served in Queens regiment or Queens Guards in India
HUTCHINSON		Patrick
		43rd Foot
	1920	Died
JACKSON		James, private
		96th Foot
	1853	In Western Australia
JAMES		Arthur
	1853	recorded as 'Pensioner's child on board '*Robert Small*''
JOHNSTON		John Saunders
	27 July 1850	arrived per '*Sophia*'
	1860	Departed Colony for South Australia
	27 July 1850	John Sanders Johnston, wife Ann and six children arrived Freemantle on "*Sophia*" He was paid as a constable on the voyage out. He was a military pensioner according to his wife's death certificate He was born about 1800 at Lockerbie Scotland and married in Devon in *c*1832. Some- time 1860s, John and most of his family moved to Adelaide.
JOSE		David
	19 Aug 1859	Arrived per '*Sultana*'
K?RANAGHER		John
		84th Foot
	1859	Applied for Land Title York ACC36/432/143]
KENNY		John [pensioner]
	May 1851	employed as Gate Keeper
	Feb 1852	Resigned or dismissed from convict service
KENNY		John, Serjeant [Military Pensioner]
		63rd Foot
	1883	a John Kernney died aged 75
KENNY		John
	1876	a John Kenny reported a tin dish and a plate was stolen from the back of his house in Stirling Street — suspected was a John McCormack who came out on the '*Naval Brigade*
KENNY		John
	17 Nov 1896	Eastern District. York Police Station. Death of John Kenny, a pensioner. November 17, 1896

KEIF	Joanna Keif aged 3 months, child of guard
1850	Sick onboard convict ship *'Nile'*
KIRBY	Daniel
	Transport Dept. Varna - Turkish Contingent
1858	Arrived per *'Nile'*
KNIGHT	John
	[previous employment given as "Pensioner]
July 1851	Appointed as Assistant Warder
Aug 1851	Resigned appointment
LANE	Matthew
	Possibly served in the Turkish Contingent
LATHAM	George, private
11 Jan 1864	dismissed prior to embarkation on *'Clara'*
LINDFIELD	William
	former soldier
LISTER	Andrew or Thomas
Surname Variant	LESTER
1856	Arrived per *'William Hammond'*
1867	To New Zealand
LOWREY	John
	Pensioner
Surname Variants	LAURIE; LOWRIE; LOWREY
1868	Disobeying summons
3 Mar 1876	Inquest on his death — caused by accidentally falling from a cart
LEARY	Anne Leary, aged 3 months, child of guard
1850	Sick onboard convict ship *'Nile'*
LEE	Martin
26 Mar 1889	Recovery of £4/18/11
	Lt. Col. Rogers — asking as to the hereabouts of Pensioner Martin Lee
LEE	William George
	EIC
Colonial Pauper	
22 Mar 1864	Resident's Office, Geraldton: — "forwarded this day to Fremantle, by the *'Trois Amis'* correspondence regarding William Geo. LEE, Colonial pauper — late of the E.I.C's service, suffering from Paralysis. Lee applied to me this morning for further relief — being quite helpless, and the third instance of his applying for assistance from the Government, I thought it best to dispatch him to Head Quarters.
2 Apr 1864	The Officer Commanding the Troops: W. Lee is not a Pensioner. he is possibly one of 2 or 3 discharged soldiers of the E.I.C Service who found their way to the Colony a couple of years ago.

LEWIS		Ann
	1869	Ann Lewis pensioner's wife now living with expiree George Henfry [sic] [Trove]
MACY		John, Corporal 11th Foot a search on "MACY" restricted to reference [s]: "WO97" There are no results within The Catalogue....not found in the 11th Foot Pay and Muster Rolls [WO12/-] or WO97/- records
	25 June 1850	Discharged the Service Pension paid 1st Manchester Pension District 1/4d. per diem
	18 Oct 1851	said to have arrived per *'Minden'* [not found on *'Minden'* passenger list]
McAULLIFFE		Robert, Sergeant Major
	1884	Robert McAuliffe, Lance Corporal of Police — Petitioning His Excellency the Governor in regard to a deferred military pension.
McCARTHY		Thomas Francis, Serjeant Royal Irish Fusiliers
	1886	Arrived in Western Australia per *'Yeoman'* Landlord National Hotel Fremantle Landlord Railway Hotel Barrack Street Perth for almost 14 years
	June 1912	Died aged 64 years
	Place of Birth:	County Cork Ireland
McCARTHY		
	1909	a Mr McCarthy attended the funeral of a shipmate Mr J.W. Murphy
	Medal Entitlement:	Indian Mutiny [Trove]
McCOY		
	12 July 1867	One of the guard named M'COY [sic] had the powder, which is sometimes thrown on the ground [Trove]
McCORMICK		Edward, private
	1851	Night Warder
McCOMISH		Edward Joseph, private 12th Foot
	Surname Variants	McCORMISH; McCORMICK; McCORNISH
	1862	Serving in New Zealand
	Dec 1865	Discharged the Service
	Mar 1867	Joined the Police Force
	1879	Charged with manslaughter
	1882	Charged with shooting with intent to kill Ellen McKenna

1885	an Arthur McCormish was on remand for having set fire to the Government Paddock at the 36 mile Station. For his defence was his mother Ann Mary McCormish, father Edward McCormish and his sister Sarah McCormish were called to give evidence [Trove]
1900	an Edward McCormish died age 67
McDONALD	Finlay, private
1908	Died
McFALL	Serjeant
McHUGH	John, Pensioner
1865	Died aged 59 Albany
McKERNAN	John, private 51st Foot
Previous Regiment	? 99th Foot
Surname Variants	[some] McKEIRNAN; McKENNAN; McKERNON; McKERMAN; McLERNAN 1/- per diem
25 Oct 1850	Arrived per *'Hashemy'*
1 Dec 1851	Assigned and occupied North Fremantle Lot P10
June 1863	North Fremantle Allotment P10 sold at auction [possibly purchased by a Mr Pomeroy]
McKIVETT	John RA 6d. per diem
McLOUGHLIN	Charles
Surname Variant	McLAUGHLIN 99th Foot
1853	Employed at Perth Gaol
McLOUGHLIN	William, private 38th Foot
Surname Variant	McLAUGHLIN Discharged the Service Chatham 6d. per diem for 3 years
1859	Possibly arrived per *'Sultana"*
McLOUGHLIN	William, private 96th Foot
Surname Variant	McLAUGHLIN
28 Dec 1863	Arrived per *'Lord Dalhousie'*
MAHER	John, Serjeant 94th Foot
MATHEWS	Joseph, private 11th Foot
6 Aug 1844	Discharged the Service Pension paid Liverpool

	25 Oct 1850	possibly arrived per *'Hashemy'* as pension was paid to this man in Australia in 1851
MERRY		William
	1852	Employed as Night Guard instead of Pensioner Guard [Trove]
MILLARD		Peter said to be a pensioner
	1880	died - ?buried East Perth Cemetery
MILNE		Edward, private
		92nd Foot [Highland regiment]
	31 Aug 1852	Discharged to pension Corfu
	9 Sept 1852	Medical examination Chatham
	28 Sept 1852	Admitted to out Pension
		Pension paid 2nd North London
		7d. per diem for 2 years
	19 Oct 1854	Pension expires
MOODY		Thomas
		?RHA
	1855	Pension paid Sydney from Western Australia
MOORE		John
	1876	died from dysentery at Bunbury Hospital
MONRO		D, gunner
		RA 3rd Battalion
		10d. per diem
	30 June 1874	Pension paid Freemantle [sic]
MORIARTY		Thad
		Serjeant Ordnance Dept. ?Turkish Contingent
MURRAY		James
	18 Jan 1900	Died aged 60 — mortally injured in sawmill accident at Jarrahdale [according to obituary he served in the Crimea]
MUIR		Thomas
	Dec 1886	the body of pensioner Thomas Muir was found lying in the coach house attached to the Railway Hotel
MUIR		Peter
		[according to the "Biographical Dictionary of Western Australia" Peter Muir arrived as an Enrolled Pensioner]
McCORMACK		
	Sept 1979	Perth Prison — [ACC488]
		Pensioner McCormack as Temporary Night Watchman
		2/6d. per diem
McCORMICK		William, private

		9th Foot or 6th Foot
	Surname Variants	McCORMACK; CORMICK
	1859	possibly arrived per *'Sultana'*
	1879	Employed as Night Warder
	1879	Application to be certified as owner in Fee Simple of Fremantle building Lot W67 formerly granted to William Boyle [Warder for 14 years]
	7 Jan 1880	Died
	7 Jan 1880	Inquest on the body of on the body of William McCormick, pensioner, who died suddenly returned the Verdict of — "Death from heat apoplexy."
McCORMACK		Wilson or William
		14th Dragoons
	May 1851	Employed by Convict Department as a ?cook Pervious occupation given as "soldier"
	Dec 1851	Resigned or dismissed
McMULLEN		James., private
		RA
		1/- per diem
	1850	Land at Fresh water Bay Locs. 9 &12
	1857	Requests Fee Simple by reason of 7 years occupation
	1873	a James McMullen residing at Northam
NEWRY		Richard
		84th Foot
		1/- per diem
	1866	Pension paid New Zealand from Fremantle
	1869	Pension paid Madras
O'CONNOR		Patrick, private
		41st Foot
	18 May 1854	a Patrick O'Connor [41st Foot] died
ODGERS		John
		not found in records of the 64th Foot
PICKERING		Thomas,
		1st Foot Guards [Grenadier Guards]
	4 May 1855	Discharged the Service
	11 Feb 1861	Arrived per *'Palmeston'*
	1861	Employed as Assistant Warder
	1863	a Thomas Pickering residing Fremantle area
	1865	Resigned from Convict Establishment
PRESTON		Charles
	1852	Resumed military duties
QUIRKE		Fras [sic]
	June 1861	a Fras Quirke Application for Title to Perth Lot 108
QUINN		Henry

Mar 1880	an old soldier charged with assaulting Mr Fothergill
RANDALL	William
1863	Stationed Perth District
1864	a ptve W Gendall [sic] Perth Pensioner Force contributed to the Greenough Fire Relief Fund
1878	Died
REICHEL	R. C., private
Campaign Service	Indian Mutiny [Not found on the British Army Indian Mutiny Medal Roll]
1909	Attended Veteran's Dinner
RENSHAW	The two children of Pensioner Guard Corporal Robert Renshaw – James 11 months and new born Mary Jane died at Port Gregory
RIPLEY	Richard H., private RM Discharged the Service £9/4/- per annum From Woolwich to Perth Western Australia
ROBINSON	
22 Aug 1862	"The remains of Pensioner Robinson were found near Geraldine Mine — he had been missing for some 10 years"
RYAN	John
1850	Residing in Colony
RYAN	G, private 2nd Foot
1897	Entertained at banquet
Medal Entitlement:	Good Conduct; South Africa
RYAN	Thomas
1920	Died aged 91 – awarded Indian Mutiny medal
SAMPEY	Thomas
Apr 1887	Charged with larceny but acquitted of the charge In his defence he stated that "he had been in the army for years serving in the Cape, in the Indian Mutiny, in Egypt, in the Crimea"
SCOTT	John, Serjeant of the Pensioner Guard late of 3rd Roxburgh Rifle Volunteers [1870 date photograph at SLWA]
SCOTT	John RA — 9th Battalion From 2nd Edinburgh 6d. per diem

	30 Sept 1853	pension paid to this date
SERWARD		T. Serjeant Major
SMART		J. C. ex Imperial Army with date of 1938
SKILLING		
	18 Feb 1851	"On Tuesday last, a pensioner named Skilling, who had lately been discharged as a warder in the Convict Establishment committed suicide by hanging himself with his handkerchief from the tree near the old Fremantle Ferry. The cause of the deceased's discharge we understand to have been drunkenness and ill-usage of his wife"
SMITH		John Smith a pensioner married Mrs. Johnson
SMITH		John, private RM £6 per annum
	Mar 1864	Mrs. Smith, who died suddenly at Geraldton on Sunday last.
	22 Mar 1864	Resident's Office, Geraldton: I have also to report that I have this day paid the sum of £ 3 [pounds] 10 shillings – expenses of burial of Lucy Smith, Colonial Pauper, the wife of John Smith Pensioner late of the Royal Marines.
	2 Apr 1864	The Honorable the Officer Commanding the Troops: writes Smith and his wife were turned out of Fremantle Barracks as confirmed drunkards. He has a pension of £6 per annum from the Royal Marines. I am of the opinion that as (provision) is defined by the War Office as 'an alimentary allowance' this could be stopped to pay for a coffin
SMITH		Richard, private RM Discharged the Service £9 /4 /- per annum
SMITH		William
	Nov 1883	died aged 74 of senile gangrene. The deceased who was a soldier had remained in the institution for about 13 years
SNADDEN		John Allen No 916
	11 June 1896	Eastern District: York Sub-district. Beverley Station. Death and Estate of Snaden, Military Pensioner.
STAINES		Simon or Sydney Arrived per "*Sea Park*"
STACK		Thomas

		Land Transport Corp Crimea
STANTON		Philip aged 42, pensioner guard
	1850	Sick onboard convict ship *'Nile'* [ADM101/252]
STAPLES		William, private RM Discharged the Service £9/4/- per annum ? To South Australia from Fremantle
STINTON		Joseph, Imperial Pensioner
	Mar 1910	Died Picton
SUTCLIFFE		Walter recorded as son of Richard and Mary Sutcliffe
	13 Jan 1864	Buried Fremantle Cemetery aged 13 months
SUTCLIFFE		William recorded as Pensioner's son
	5 Apr 1862	Buried Fremantle Cemetery aged 1 year
SWEENY		private
	1864	pte Sweeny Pensioner Force at Kojonup contributed to the Greenough Fire Relief Fund
TRAY		Henry, private
	1853	Fremantle
TREW		Samuel 11th Foot
	Feb 1900	Attended fete at Oval
TIERNEY		Richard Described as Pensioner
	24 Mar 1872	Buried Fremantle Cemetery aged 72
WAGSTAFF		William [Military Pensioner] 51st Foot
	1 July 1851	Employed as Instructing Tailor Convict Service previous employment given as 'Pensioner'
	26 July 1851	Resigned from Convict establishment
	Aug 1880	a William Wagstaff, a tailor died at the Invalid Depot
WAITE		John Henry, Royal Engineers [served 12 years with the RA]
	1895	Arrived Western Australia from Victoria
	1898	Died aged 76 at his residence at Short Street, Victoria Park
	Medal Entitlement:	Crimea; Indian Mutiny [no John Waite Royal Engineers found on the Indian Mutiny Medal Rolls]

WALL		John
	7 Jan 1888	Resident Magistrate Fremantle — Mt. Eliza Depot, Pensioner John Wall for admission
WATSON		C
	Apr 1897	When charged with drunkenness, pleaded that he was an old Imperial soldier who had won the Victoria Cross for bravery
WHITE		Charles
		Said to be pensioner local force
	1857	Died
WILLIAMS		Jack — ['Ivanhoe Jack]
		Crimean Veteran
	Aug 1920	After a short illness, died aged 87 years at the Government Hospital
WOODMAN		Henry, Serjeant
		9th Lancers [see Biographical Dictionary of Western Australia]
		[no Henry Woodman 9th Lancers to be found on the Indian Mutiny Medal Roll]
		Principle Warder
	1860	Assistant Warder Millbank Prison
	1862	Applied for position in Western Australia
	27 May 1863	Arrived per *'Clyde'*
	1887	Died aged 56
	1887	Government Resident Albany — Inquest on the body of Henry Woodman
WORLEY		Edward, private
		98th Foot
		6d. per diem
	Dec 1843	Died — £1/16/6 paid to widow

Former soldiers who were discharged or arrived in pre Federation Western Australia

ABCOTT		Thomas, private 96th Foot
	22 Feb 1847	Arrived per *'Java'* with regiment
	1849	Discharged own request ? Merchant trading in Barrack St.,
ALLISON		John, private [promoted to Serjeant] 21st Foot
	Sept 1833	Arrived per *'Jane'*
	31 July 1840	Discharged own request
	1875	Died
ASHWORTH		Edmund 96th Foot
	22 Feb 1847	Arrived possibly per *'Java'*
	1849	Discharged own request Employed at the Commissariat York
	1856	Pound Keeper Guildford
	1856	Land at York
	1888	Died York
BAILEY		Thomas, Corporal 96th Foot
	22 Feb 1847	Arrived per *'Java'*
	1885	Died aged 65
	June 1885	Inquest on the body of Thomas Bailey — cause of death found to be from moving a flower pot
BAKER		Philip, Serjeant 21st Foot
	Feb 1835	Arrived Fremantle possibly per *'Caroline'* Stationed Albany
	1840	Discharged own request Remission on amount to be paid for land grant
	1843	Died Perth Western Australia
BARR		George, private 51st Foot
	Oct 1846	Convicted of breaking and entering into a dwelling and stealing a piece of calico. Was sentenced to 7 years transportation
	Nov 1846	Sentence commuted to 3 years hard labour at Fremantle Goal
BARRON		Edward, Colour Serjeant 63rd Foot
	8 June 1829	Arrived per *'HMS Sulphur'* with wife and three children
	1834	Discharged at own request
BARTLETT		George Royal Engineers
	1863	Arrived per *'Palestine'*
	1867	Died age 40 of heart disease
BEARDMAN		William, private

		51st Foot
	25 June 1840	Arrived per *'Runnymede'*
	1849	Discharged own request
	1896	Resided 17 miles from Newcastle
	May 1897	Died — committed suicide
BISHAM		Servetus, private
		Royal Sappers and Miners - 20th Company
	1851	Arrived per *'Anna Robinson'* with regiment
	1861	Discharged at own request
		Granted 20 acres Albany
	1873	Residing Albany
	1887	Died aged 61
BOOLER		Thomas, private
		Royal Sappers and Miners
	1851	Possibly arrived per *'Anna Robinson'*
	1851	Awarded prize of a case of brass instruments
	1859	Returned to UK
	1861	Residing Southwark London
		Serving as a Police constable in the Metropolitan police
	1863	Arrived per *'Palestine'*
	1863 — 1877	Assistant Warder Convict Establishment
	1877	Departed colony
BOWERS		Lawrence
		Royal Sappers and Miners
	1861	Discharged
BOWRA		John William, private
		96th Foot
BRIGGS		Thomas, private
		96th Foot
	1847	Arrived per *'Java'*
BUCK		Richard, private
		96th Foot
	1847	Arrived per *'Java'*
	Apr 1849	Discharged Perth WA
	Feb 1905	Died aged 86 at his son's residence 442 Beaufort Street Perth
BUDD		George, private
		Royal Engineers
		Licensee of the "No Place Inn"
	11 April 1882	Died aged 49
BURRELL		William, Serjeant
		51st Foot and 96th
	25 June 1840	Arrived per *'Runnymede'*
	May 1849	Discharged to compensation
BURTON		Charles
		Royal Sappers and Miners
	Surname Variant	BENTON

	1851	Arrived per *'Anna Robinson'*
	Dec 1861	Discharged with compensation
	1902	Died
CHURCH		John
	1866	Pension paid South Australia from Fremantle [part pension to be paid to wife]
COLGAN		John or James or William
		possibly 51st Foot
	1865	In charge of party of prisoners Albany
CONDRON		Michael, private
		21st Foot
		[arrived 63rd Foot per *'Sulphur'* according to Obit]
	31 July 1840	Discharged
CORP		William
		Arrived per *'Lord Dalhousie'*
CROSS		Joseph private
		1st Btn 12th Foot [East Suffolk] 2nd Detachment
	1861	Regiment Stationed at Perth
DAWSON		William, private
		Royal Sappers and Miners
	1856	Discharged
		Qualified for £10 remission on Settlers land Grant
DEARDEN		John, Corporal
		51st Foot
	25 June 1840	Arrived per *'Runnymede'* with regiment
	Dec 1840	a Serjeant Dearden of the 51st Regiment, advertised to let a property with a capacious detached kitchen, large shed and well of capital water in Hay Street
	8 Jan 1846	Discharged with compensation Perth Purchased land
	1884	Died
DOBBINS		James, private
		63rd Foot
	6 June 1829	Arrived per *'HMS Sulphur'*
	1831	his wife Jean speared by natives [Trove]
	1834	Discharged to compensation
	1845	Departed Colony — to Mauritius per *'Emma Sherratt'*
DONKERSLEY		Samuel or James private
		21st and 51st
	1847	Discharged
DONOVAN		Richard, private
		99th Foot
	5 Apr 1849	Arrived per *'Radcliff'* with regiment
	31 July 1852	Discharged

DOOLAN		Kieran, private
		21st Foot
	14 Sept 1833	Arrived per *'Jane'* with detachment
	31 July 1840	Discharged with compensation
	Oct 1846	Assigned 25 acres Wellington District
	1850	newspaper article refers to K. Doolan's Sussex Location No 14
	1885	Died aged 80
DOWNE		William H
		Assistant Warder
		Commissariat - Turkish Contingent
	1858	Arrived per *'Nile'* aged 46
DREW		Henry
		former soldier
	1852	Night Warder Convict Establishment
DREWRY		John, private
		96th Foot
	Age on Discharge	26 years
	Period of Service	1840 —1848
	22 July 1847	Arrived per *'Java'* with regiment
	1848	Discharged
DUNSKLEY		William private
		Royal Sapper and Miners
EARNSHAW		David Fothergill, private
		21st Foot
	14 Sept 1833	Arrived per *'Jane'* with regiment
	31 July 1840	Discharged
EDWARDS		William, Serjeant
		96th Foot
	1865	Died aged 73 at Beverley
ELSEGOOD		William, private
		96th Foot
	22 Feb 1847	Arrived per *'Java'* with regiment
	1849	Discharged
		Builder and contractor
	1874	Died aged 55 — buried East Perth Pioneer Cemetery
ELVERD		William Morris, private
		51st and 96th Foot
	25 June 1840	Arrived per *'Runnymede'* with regiment
	1847	Discharged
	1869	Proprietor of the "Semblance of Old England Hotel" on the Albany Perth Road at Kojonup
	1873	Died
EMERY		Thomas
		99th Foot
	5 Apr 1849	Arrived per *'Radcliffe'* with regiment

FARMANER		Joseph
		51st Foot
		One of the 2 sergeants, 31 rank and file [including 2 drummers] of the 51st remained in West. Aust. and took discharge to become settlers
	1864	Appointed postmaster at Guildford
	1866	Departed colony per *'Zephyr'*
	1899	Died
FARMER		Patrick, private
		63rd Foot
	8 June 1829	Arrived per *'HMS Sulphur'*
	25 Feb 1832	Drowned at Perth
FETTERS		John, private
		99th Foot
	1852	Discharged at own request
FLETCHER		John, private
		99th Foot
	22 Feb 1847	Arrived per *'Java'*
		Discharged at own request
	1910	Died [formerly of the Commissariat Dept.,] and buried in the family grave in East Perth Cemetery
GILL		John, private
		21st Foot
	31 July 1840	Discharged at own request
GOGAN		John, private
		Royal Engineer [Sappers and Miners]
	17 Dec 1851	Arrived per *'Anna Robinson'* with regiment
	1858	Discharged at own request and qualified for the £10 remission for Settlers Grant
GOSS		Henry, private
		96th Foot, transferred to 99th Foot
	22 Feb 1847	Arrived per *'Java'*
	1850	Employed by Harbour Master
	1871	Died aged 49
GRAINGER		David, private
		51st Foot
	26 June 1840	Arrived per *'Runnymede'* with regiment
	1848	Discharged at own request
HARRINGTON		Daniel, Serjeant
		According to Obit served in 99th for 19 years
	1858	Serving as Warder at Bermuda
	1862	Serving as Warder onboard *'Merchantman'* [1]
	circa 1865	according to obit — was transferred by the Imperial Government to the Straits Settlements as Superintendent of Singapore Gaol
HARRIS		Joseph, private

		51st foot
	25 June 1840	Arrived per *'Runnymede* 'with regiment
		Stationed Albany
	1847	Discharged with compensation Perth WA Died aged 87
HEFFRON		Patrick, private [WO97/765/11]
		63rd Foot,
	8 June 1829	Arrived per *'HMS Sulphur* 'with regiment then transferred to 21st Foot
	1840	Discharged in Western Australia
	1888	Died
HOARE		John
		12th Foot
	1883	a John Hoar died - ?buried East Perth Cemetery
HODGES		George or John, private
		63rd Foot
	8 June 1829	Arrived per *'HMS Sulphur'*
	1834	Discharged at own request
	1845	Departed colony for Mauritius per *'Emma Sherratt'*
HOGAN		Michael or Malachi, private
		21st Foot
	31 July 1840	Discharged at own request
HOLT		Henry, private
		96th Foot
	22 Feb 1847	Arrived per *'Java'*
HORNBY		Henry, private
		96th Foot transferred from 51st Foot
HORN		Charles, private
		51st Foot
	Surname Variant	HORNE
	25 June 1840	Arrived per *'Runnymede'* with regiment and posted to Albany
	circa 1848	mail carrier York and Toodyay
	1869	Died Perth
HUGHES		John
		Royal Sappers and Miners
	17 Dec 1851	Arrived per *'Anna Robinson'* with regiment
	1862	Discharged at own request
INGERSOLL		James, private
		51st Foot
	April 1847	Discharged at own request
INNES		George, private
		99th Foot
	30 June 1852	Discharged
JACKSON		Thomas, private

		96th Foot transferred to 99th Foot
JEFFERS		Edward, private 63rd Foot
	1834	Discharged in Colony
JOHNSON		John 99th Foot
	1852	Discharged
JONES		Richard 63rd Foot
JONES		Thomas 51st Foot
JONSON		John. Private 99th Foot
	30 June 1852	Discharged Western Australia
KEEN		Thomas private [2954] 1st Btn 12th Foot 2nd Detachment
	1861	Regiment Stationed at Perth
	1863	Discharged
KENNY		John Sergeant 63rd Foot
	8 June 1829	Arrived per *'HMS Sulphur'*
KENNY		John. Private Royal Sappers and Miners
	1861	Discharged
KING		William, private 96th Foot
	1847	Discharged Western Australia
LAIDLEY		Alexander, private 21st Foot
	31 July 1840	Discharged Western Australia
LOCKHART		James 41st Foot
	23 June 1863	Discharged to pension 1/- per diem To Adelaide from Western Australia [12/WA/348]
LENNAN		William Patrick, private Royal Sappers and Miners
	1858	Discharged
MAGUIRE		John, private 96th Foot
	1849	Discharged
MALEY		Kennedy, private 51st Foot

MASON		John, Serjeant 63rd Foot and 21st Foot
MATHESON	 Jan 1862	Colin, private Royal Sappers and Miners Discharged
McAULIFFE	 1884	Robert 41st Foot Robert McAuliffe, Lance Corporal of Police: Petitioning His Excellency the Governor relative to a deferred military pension.
McCORMACK		Wilson 14th Dragoons
McEVOY		James 21st Foot Purchased discharge
McGANN		Patrick, private 96th Foot
MILSOM		Charles Royal Sappers and Miners
MITCHELL	 1884	Frederick John Serving Coldstream Guards [2nd Foot Guards aged 23]
MOONEY	 July 1840	Laurence, private 21st Foot Discharged
MORIARTY		Thaddeus Former soldier - possibly served in Crimea
NASH		John, private 51st Foot
NAUGHTON	 1847	John, Corporal 96th Foot Remained when regiment left Western Australia
NEWELL		Jeremiah 12th Foot former soldier
NIGHTON	 1854	John, private 99th Foot Discharged
NORRISH	 5 July 1951	Richard, Corporal 96th Foot Discharged

O'CONNOR		John, Corporal
		21st Foot
	1840	Discharged
O'KELLY		Dennis, private
		51st Foot
PASCOE		Richard
		former soldier
	1853	Arrived per '*Sea Park*'
PEACH		Charles
		10th Hussars
		[not found in 10th Hussars pension records]
PEARCE		Edwin Theodore
		EIC
PETTY		George, private
		21st Foot
PICKERING		Thomas
		Grenadier Guards
	1861	Arrived per '*Palmeston*'
PURCELL		Michael
		former soldier
	1864	Arrived per '*Merchantman*'
PUSEY		William, private
	also known as	William **DOBSON** or William Dobson Pusey
		51st Foot
	1847	Discharged
PYE		John, gunner
		Possibly served in the Turkish Contingent
	1858	Arrived per '*Nile*'
QUIN		Michael. Drummer and Bugler
		21st Foot
	1840	Discharged
READ		John, private
		12th Foot
ROBSON		Patrick, private
		10th Foot
		1/- per diem
	1863	To Queensland from Perth Western Australia
ROSE		John, Serjeant
		Royal Sappers and Miners
	24 Feb 1852	possibly arrived per '*Will Watch*
ROUSE		Henry, Serjeant
		99th Foot

RUMMER		William Alexander, private 96th Foot
	1847	Discharged Western Australia
RYAN		Daniel Royal Sappers and Miners
	1861	Discharged
SALE		John, private 96th Foot
SAUNDERS		Joseph, private Royal Sappers and Miners
	1861	Discharged
SAUNDERS		Rice Possibly served in 'Turkish Contingent'
	1857	Assistant Warder, arrived per '*Lord Raglan*' Established drapers business in Perth [Saunders and Co]
SCOTT		Andrew, private 96th Foot
	1847	Discharged
SCOTT		James W., private 42nd Foot
	1863	Arrived per Merchantman [1]
SEATON		Richard, private 51st Foot
	Apr 1847	Discharged
SHAUGHNESSY		Thomas, Royal Artillery
SHAW		Samuel John RA
SHEPPARD		George 21st Foot
	31 July 1840	Discharged
SMITH		William, private 51st Foot
SNOWDEN		Henry former soldier
	1852	Assistant Warder arrived per '*William Jardine*'
SOMERVILLE		James, private 21st Foot
	31 July 1840	Discharged
SPROULE		James Royal Sappers and Miners
	1861	Discharged

STANTON		John, private [Serjeant on discharge]
		63rd Foot
	6 June 1829	Arrived per *'HMS Sulphur'*
STRAW		William
		1st Foot Guards
	1864	Pension paid South Australia from Perth WA
SULLIVAN		John, Corporal
		6th Dragoon Guards
	Dec 1866	Arrived per *'Corona'*
THOMPSON		John Robert, Corporal
		21st Foot
	9 Aug 1844	Discharged
THOMPSON		Alexander
		99th Foot
THOMPSON		Alexander
		Royal Sappers and Miners
TOWNSEND		William, private
		Royal Sappers and Miners
	1861	Discharged
VINCE		Henry
		96th Foot
	May 1849	Discharged
WAGSTAFF		William
		51st /99th Foot
WALLACE		George, private
		21st Foot
	1840	Discharged
WALSH		Martin
		21st Foot
	31 July 1840	Discharged
WARE		Matthew, Lance Corporal
		99th Foot
WELLSTEAD		John, private
		51st foot
	Feb 1845	Discharged
WHITE		William, private
		51st Foot
	1847	Discharged
WILMORE		George
		Possibly served in the Turkish Contingent
	1858	Arrived per *'Nile'*

LOCAL
COMPANIES

Lightning Source UK Ltd.
Milton Keynes UK
UKOW02f0808050816

280021UK00001B/120/P

9 781496 995414